Lecture Notes in Computer Science 13660

More information about this series at https://link.springer.com/bookseries/558

Jean-François Raskin · Krishnendu Chatterjee ·
Laurent Doyen · Rupak Majumdar (Eds.)

Principles
of Systems Design

Essays Dedicated to Thomas A. Henzinger
on the Occasion of His 60th Birthday

 Springer

Editors
Jean-François Raskin
Université Libre de Bruxelles
Brussels, Belgium

Krishnendu Chatterjee
Institute of Science and Technology Austria
Klosterneuburg, Austria

Laurent Doyen
École Normale Supérieure Paris-Saclay
Gif-sur-Yvette, France

Rupak Majumdar
MPI for Software Systems
Kaiserslautern, Germany

ISSN 0302-9743   ISSN 1611-3349 (electronic)
Lecture Notes in Computer Science
ISBN 978-3-031-22336-5   ISBN 978-3-031-22337-2   (eBook)
https://doi.org/10.1007/978-3-031-22337-2

This Springer imprint is published by the registered company Springer Nature Switzerland AG
The registered company address is: Gewerbestrasse 11, 6330 Cham, Switzerland

Preface

Tom Henzinger is one of the leading researchers in computer-aided verification. Fascinated by the creative power given by the developing computer hardware in the late 1970s—in particular his first encounter with programming on an Atari 400—Tom found his vocation in computer science. After getting a Master's degree from the Johannes Kepler University Linz and the University of Delaware, he worked on his PhD thesis "The Temporal Specification and Verification of Real-Time Systems" at Stanford, in the group of Zohar Manna, from 1988 to 1991. His thesis led to the foundations of the models, specification formalisms, and analysis techniques for real-time systems. It is representative of his entire research career: elegant and deep theoretical results with clear application potential.

After a postdoc at the IMAG Laboratory in Grenoble, Tom joined Cornell in 1992, then moved to UC Berkeley in 1996, and EPFL in Lausanne in 2004. In the interim, he spent a year as a Scientific Director at the Max Planck Institute for Informatics in Saarbrücken. In 2009, he was appointed as the founding President of the Institute of Science and Technology Austria, his current position.

Over the years, Tom's research has led to breakthrough insights into the foundation and application of rigorous software design. Even a summary of his work would be too long to include here. We expect the contributions in this volume will illustrate the breadth of his research areas. Here we present a personal selection of his work to highlight a few directions of Tom's major influence.

In the first decade of his career, and through a highly prolific research companionship with Rajeev Alur, he developed a series of highly influential models and tools for the design of reactive, timed, and hybrid systems, which have laid the theoretical foundation for the verification of today's multi-agent, real-time, and embedded software. This line of work extended automata, logics, and verification algorithms from finite-state reactive systems to digital systems interacting with a continuous environment in real time, also known as cyber-physical systems (CPS) in modern terminology. Of central importance is the theory of hybrid automata, which forms the foundation of CPS. In addition to delineating the expressiveness and decidability frontier for hybrid automata, Tom's research focused on practical decision procedures and tools. The HyTech tool, his model-checker for symbolic analysis of hybrid automata showed that, even if the theoretical model is undecidable, many instances of practical interest could be successfully verified. While the symbolic analysis of infinite-state models sounds commonplace today, HyTech was the first model-checker for infinite-state mixed discrete-continuous systems. Due to the interwinding between computational aspects and physical aspects of embedded software, embedded system implementations are complex and require disciplined development. To bridge the gap between mathematical models, specified as hybrid automata, and executable code, Tom proposed the notion of logical execution time (LET) as a way to reconcile and master the complexity of rigorous embedded system implementations. Tom was also one of the founding members of the steering committee of the EMSOFT conference that has since become the premier forum for cutting-edge research in the design and analysis of software that interacts with physical processes.

At the heart of Tom's work is the idea of compositionality, both in the models and in the analysis. Along with the formal models of reactive modules and interface automata, for modular design and analysis of component-based systems, Tom worked on assume-guarantee proof rules for the verification of hardware with the idea that the correctness of a component in a design is not a universal formula (all executions satisfy the specification) but requires alternation to express that for all inputs to the component satisfying some assumption, there exists an output of the component satisfying the specification, as described in the famous "You Assume, We Guarantee" paper. He further developed alternating-time temporal logics, extending temporal logics with explicit quantifiers over agents. The natural link between alternation and games connected his work with the theory of omega-regular games on graphs that he developed in an impressive variety of directions. Tom's work established the decidability and complexity frontier of several types of games, most prominently concurrent, timed, stochastic, and quantitative games, and more recently bidding games.

The use of abstraction in infinite-state model checking was already prominent in the world of hybrid systems and in assume-guarantee reasoning. In the early 2000s, inspired by predicate abstraction and counterexample-guided refinement, Tom made major advances in software model checking. His work on lazy abstraction and interpolation-based refinement allowed fully automatic analysis of source code. Under his leadership, the Blast model-checker was developed for program analysis. The work on Blast influenced several research areas such as abstract interpretation for sequential and concurrent code, SMT-based model-checking of software, interpolation as abstraction, and many others. Blast was part of a broader initiative at Berkeley to bring together programming languages, verification, and testing researchers. This initiative shaped a new generation of researchers in these areas, many of whom went on to develop their own successful research programs.

The traditional view of formal verification is to classify a model as either correct or incorrect, according to whether or not it satisfies a logical specification: the classical notion of correctness is Boolean. With the development of formal synthesis for practical applications at the beginning of the 21st century, it appeared that the Boolean setting offered too few nuances to account for the quality of synthesized systems. As part of Tom's vision, it was necessary to extend the theory of reactive systems from the classical Boolean setting to a richer quantitative setting, beyond timed and probabilistic. The extension could be obtained by lifting the fundamental notions of model refinement and pre-orders, as well as logical specifications and languages, to a quantitative setting, for instance using appropriate metrics to measure the degree to which a system satisfies a specification. Depending on the context, this quantitative notion of correctness may be interpreted as an evaluation of the fitness, reliability, or performance guarantee of a design.

We conclude this personal selection of Tom's most influential work by mentioning other areas in which Tom has had important contributions: models for executable biology, analysis of gene regulatory networks, concurrent data structures, weak memory models, the combination of formal methods and machine learning techniques, foundations for monitoring reactive systems, and many others.

Tom's contributions over the years are certainly impressive, and would not have been possible without the support of many researchers. Let us underline here one of Tom's greatest qualities: his ability to lead and inspire a research team. Indeed, at any point in time during the last thirty years, Tom has built around him a wonderful research environment and shaped the skills of a large number of students and researchers. Providing an intellectually stimulating and friendly environment to junior researchers has always been a central principle in Tom's approach. As former PhD students and postdocs of Tom, we feel it was a privilege to be part of his incredibly stimulating research group. Tom is not only a great supervisor but also, and more importantly, a mentor. Not only does Tom always suggest well-thought-out and profound research ideas but he is also able to create the sparkling atmosphere that invites his team members to express the best of themselves, beyond what they thought was possible. Since his time at Cornell, Tom has always dedicated his work to the training of junior researchers: he has supervised no fewer than 24 PhD students, and about 50 postdoc students. These figures are impressive, and the quality of his mentoring goes beyond the quantity: he has shown us how to do research and how to mentor on our own.

Tom's intellectual influence transcends the purely technical aspects of research. Working with him gave us a sense of what it means to be a good scientist, not necessarily through what he told us directly, but through his character and personality which have inspired generations of students with the humility of the smartest, the softness of the strongest, the dedication of the brightest. Tom's mentorship style is characterized by patience—he treats even beginning graduate students as colleagues and companions, not employees who are supposed to execute whatever is requested. Yet, in his gentle way and with just the right amount of words, he gets some important points across. For example, a long time ago, one of the authors of this preface complained bitterly how an idea we had dismissed as unworkable (for good reasons) had nevertheless been published by a different group. Tom listened to the rant and said he would not feel upset that we did not write a bad paper. In a different instance he would say that it is not enough to write papers, we should write papers that get read—widely. These are two examples of simple, informal comments arising out of a love for science that made us grow up as we developed our academic careers.

One aspect he holds very dearly is that of clear communication of research ideas. Every student has a memory of taking a printout to his office and getting back a marked-up copy, with more annotations than text. Over time, the annotations would get fewer as we improved. The joke among the students was that you graduate the day there is no red mark. Technical precision was necessary but not sufficient. Of the different ways of expressing an argument, he would be guided to pick the more elegant one. The elegance would be reflected also in the deliberate choice of notation, the ordering of material, and even in the choice of paper titles.

Each of us remembers the heady days working in Tom's group. We had the sense of doing great work across the group. We would have visitors from all over come and give talks and discuss problems with us. We would get "sneak previews" of breakthrough results. We would discuss technical points late into the evening. There were often last-minute, late night, work sessions before major deadlines. Each time we would decide never to do it again. There would be pizza with pineapple for group meetings, leading to a small but very vocal opposition and, eventually, two sets of pizzas—one with pineapple, one without. But at the end of the day, research remained an exciting and intellectually challenging activity. Many of us kept discussing problems with Tom many years after our degrees or contracts ended because it was always fun, always insightful, always inspiring.

Tom's rigor and vision transferred from his scientific work to his academic leadership. Tom took on the role of President of ISTA, the Institute of Science and Technology Austria, in 2009. At that point the institute had four faculty members and plans to grow up to 45. He led the institute to tremendous growth and success and in 2011 the institute was already targeting 90 faculty members. This interdisciplinary research institute attracted top faculty across disciplines like Computer Science, Life Science, Mathematics, and Physics. By 2021 the institute's plan was to grow far beyond the original intention, and to reach 160 faculty members in due course. Here again, the quality goes beyond the quantity, and his dedication and leadership has shaped a world-class research institute in Austria.

This Festschrift volume celebrates Tom's many contributions in the field of computer science. We collected 31 papers covering several directions of his work. We are very grateful to the authors and to the reviewers. Along with the papers, we also plan an in-person gathering co-located with CAV 2023 in Paris.

Thank you Tom for your intellectual and academic leadership for so many years, for the countless hours of work and friendship, and for so many beautiful results!

September 2022

Jean-François Raskin
Krishnendu Chatterjee
Laurent Doyen
Rupak Majumdar

Organization

Program Committee

Guy Avni	University of Haifa, Israel
Dirk Beyer	LMU Munich, Germany
Sergiy Bogomolov	Newcastle University, UK
Krishnendu Chatterjee	IST Austria, Austria
Luca de Alfaro	UC Santa Cruz, USA
Laurent Doyen	ENS Paris-Saclay, France
Jasmin Fisher	University College London, UK
Ranjit Jhala	University of California, San Diego, USA
Marcin Jurdzinski	University of Warwick, UK
Christoph Kirsch	University of Salzburg, Austria
Laura Kovacs	TU Wien, Austria
Jan Kretinsky	Technical University of Munich, Germany
Orna Kupferman	Hebrew University, Israel
Rupak Majumdar	MPI, Germany
Jan Otop	University of Wrocław, Poland
Nir Piterman	University of Gothenburg, Sweden
Vinayak Prabhu	MPI, Germany
Shaz Qadeer	Meta, USA
Jean-François Raskin	Université libre de Bruxelles, Belgium
Christian Schilling	Aalborg University, Denmark
Verena Wolf	Saarland University, Germany
Damien Zufferey	MPI, Germany

Additional Reviewers

Backenköhler, Michael
Bansal, Suguman
Busatto-Gaston, Damien
Ehlers, Rüdiger
Frehse, Goran
Ganty, Pierre
Giacobbe, Mirco
Guha, Shibashis
Hekal, Abdelrahman

Howell, Rowan
Lechner, Mathias
Muehlboeck, Fabian
Parys, Paweł
Potomkin, Kostiantyn
Saraç, N. Ege
Stankaitis, Paulius
Zikelic, Djordje

Contents

Probabilistic and Quantitative Verification

Software Systems Theory

Artificial Intelligence and Machine Learning

Hybrid, Timed, Cyber-Physical and Dynamical Systems

From Hybrid Automata to DAE-Based Modeling

Albert Benveniste, Benoît Caillaud$^{(\boxtimes)}$, and Mathias Malandain

Inria centre at Rennes University, Campus de Beaulieu, 35042 Rennes Cedex, France
{albert.benveniste,benoit.caillaud,mathias.malandain}@inria.fr

Abstract. Tom Henzinger was among the co-founders of the paradigm of *hybrid automata* in 1992. Hybrid automata possess different locations, holding different ODE-based dynamics; exit conditions from a location trigger transitions, resulting in starting conditions for the next location. A large research activity was developed in the formal verification of hybrid automata; this paradigm still grounds popular commercial tools such as Stateflow for Simulink.

However, modeling from first principles of physics requires a different approach: balance equations and conservation laws play a central role, and elementary physical components come with no prespecified input/output profile. All of this leads to grounding physical modeling on DAEs (Differential Algebraic Equations, of the form $f(x', x, v) = 0$) instead of ODEs. DAE-based modeling, implemented for example in the Modelica language, allows for modularity and reuse of models.

Unsurprisingly, DAE-based hybrid systems (also known as *multimode DAE systems*) emerge as the central paradigm in multiphysics modeling. Despite the growing popularity of modeling tools based on this paradigm, fundamental problems remain in the handling of multiple modes and mode changes—corresponding to multiple locations and transitions in hybrid automata. Deep symbolic analyses (grouped under the term "structural analysis" in the related community), grounded on solid foundations, are required to generate simulation code. This paper reviews the issues related to multimode DAE systems and proposes algorithms for their analysis. Computer science is instrumental in these works, with a lot to offer to the simulation scientific community.

Keywords: Hybrid automata · Multiphysics modeling · DAE · multimode DAE · Structural analysis · Index reduction

1 Tom Henzinger and Hybrid Systems in Computer Science

According to the vision of Hybrid Systems by the computer science community [1],a hybrid system possesses *control locations*, characterized by *invariants* expressed as properties on continuous states; in each location, continuous-time dynamics are specified using Ordinary Differential Equations (ODEs);

© Springer Nature Switzerland AG 2022
J.-F. Raskin and K. Chatterjee (Eds.): Principles of Systems Design, LNCS 13660, pp. 3–20, 2022.
https://doi.org/10.1007/978-3-031-22337-2_1

transitions between control locations are characterized by their *pre-* and *post-conditions* or, alternatively, by pre-conditions and a reset action. For the class of hybrid automata, a large body of knowledge, techniques and tools has been developed since the pioneering paper [1]. Tom Henzinger himself contributed extensively to this body of knowledge, with theory and tools [17]. Interestingly enough, this vision still grounds commercial modeling tools, e.g., Stateflow, which highlights the depth of the 1990's vision of hybrid automata. Still, pushed by practical considerations, alternative approaches have emerged in the 1990's in the control engineering community, with ties going back to *bond graphs* [27], a formalism that grounds the widely used industrial tool Simcenter Amesim.

2   Cyber-Physical Systems Modeling: The Need for DAEs

As a running example, we consider the idealized clutch of Fig. 1, involving two rotating shafts with no motor or brake being connected. Each shaft possesses its individual dynamics, relating rotational velocity and torque. This clutch possesses two modes: the two shafts evolve freely when the clutch is released, and are coupled by a perfect contact when the clutch is engaged. At the mode change when the clutch gets engaged, a discontinuity occurs in the rotation velocities (they are generally different before engagement, and get equal in zero time as a result of the engagement). This causes an impulse in the torques. This part of the modeling task requires particular care, as we shall see.

2.1   Modeling from First Principles of Physics Naturally Leads to Considering Acausal Models [12]

Modeling the Clutch with Hybrid State Machines: Let us first consider the model of the clutch expressed using ODE-based hybrid state machines.

$$
\begin{array}{c}
\text{released} \\
\text{location}
\end{array}
\left|
\begin{array}{l}
\omega_1' = f_1(\omega_1, \tau_1) \\
\tau_1 = 0 \\
\omega_2' = f_2(\omega_2, \tau_2) \\
\tau_2 = 0
\end{array}
\right.
\quad
\begin{array}{c}
\xrightarrow{\ \gamma:\text{F}\to\text{T}\ }_{\text{restart}_{\text{F}\to\text{T}}} \\
\xleftarrow{\ \gamma:\text{T}\to\text{F}\ }_{\text{restart}_{\text{T}\to\text{F}}}
\end{array}
\quad
\left|
\begin{array}{l}
\omega' = f_{12}(\omega, \tau) \\
\tau = 0
\end{array}
\right.
\begin{array}{c}
\text{engaged} \\
\text{location}
\end{array}
\tag{1}
$$

State machine (1) possesses two locations: released (left) and engaged (right). In the left-to-right transition, the label "$\gamma : \text{F} \to \text{T}$" sitting above the transition indicates the event that triggers the transition; the label "restart$_{\text{F}\to\text{T}}$" sitting below the transition refers to the restart action resulting from the transition—its explicit formulation is given below.

The ODE sitting in the released location is the model of two non-interacting shafts; for each one, the angular velocity ω_i and torque τ_i are related via an ODE, with the torque being zero when the clutch is released. The ODE sitting in the engaged location is clear as well: it is the model of a single shaft obtained by gluing the two shafts together; as such, the "engaged" model is global and its architecture does not reflect the physical architecture.

The two restart actions are now detailed. First, when the clutch gets released ($\text{T} \to \text{F}$), the restart values for the two velocities are equal to the velocity of the global shaft just before mode change:

$$\text{restart}_{\text{T} \to \text{F}} \ : \ \omega_1^+ = \omega_2^+ = \omega^-. \qquad (2)$$

The symmetric restart action ($\text{F} \to \text{T}$) is more involved. To derive it, we need to get closer to the physics, by specializing the two functions f_i for $i = 1, 2$:

$$f_i(\omega_i, \tau_i) = \tfrac{1}{J_i}(\tau_i - g_i(\omega_i)), \qquad (3)$$

where J_i is the moment of inertia of shaft i, and $g_i(\omega_i)$ is the friction. When the clutch gets engaged, the two shaft velocities are discontinuous, as they become equal in zero time. The resulting common value follows from the law of preservation of angular momentum, which writes: $(J_1 + J_2)\omega^+ = J_1\omega_1^- + J_2\omega_2^-$. Hence, the restart action when the clutch gets engaged is given by:

$$\text{restart}_{\text{F} \to \text{T}} \ : \ \omega^+ = \frac{J_1\omega_1^- + J_2\omega_2^-}{J_1 + J_2}. \qquad (4)$$

Formulas (1)–(4) fully specify the model of the clutch using ODE-based hybrid state machines. It can then easily be brought to the classical Alur-Henzinger hybrid automaton form [1]; this transformation has no impact on the issues discussed below.

DAE-Based Modeling: Generally, modeling in physics does not rely on hybrid automata. Let us consider electrical circuits as an illustration. First, the Kirchhoff laws are expressed as balance equations: the sum of currents at a node is zero; the sum of voltages along a loop is zero. Second, most components (e.g., resistors and capacitors) come with no prespecified input/output orientation. A similar situation actually arises in mechanics or in thermodynamics. What happens if we follow a similar approach for the clutch?

Getting the clutch model from first principles is straightforward and elegant, as shown in Fig. 1. The system and model architectures coincide: the overall model consists of a model of each individual shaft, completed with a model for the junction (the velocities coincide and the torques sum up to zero if the clutch is engaged, $\gamma = \text{T}$; the torques are zero if the clutch is released, $\gamma = \text{F}$). At an instant of mode change when the cluch gets engaged, the *a priori* different velocities of the two shafts will, in zero time, merge to a single identical velocity while the efforts on the shafts will climb up to impulses. The resulting common velocity will depend, in a determinate way, on the inertia and velocity of each shaft prior to engagement. Thus, the main characteristics of the model of Fig. 1 are the following:

1. **The model has two modes:** $\gamma = \text{F}$ and $\gamma = \text{T}$ yield different dynamics.
2. **The model is acausal:** In the released mode $\gamma = \text{F}$, the two torques are inputs and the two angular positions are outputs; in the engaged mode $\gamma = \text{T}$, both angular positions and torques are unknowns, with no input/output orientation being defined: the model is acausal in this mode.

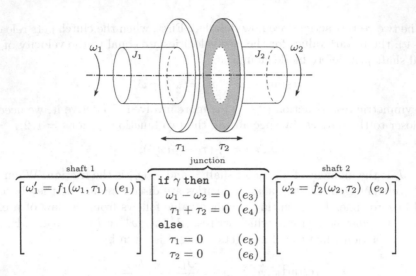

$$\left[\begin{array}{c} \underbrace{}_{\text{shaft 1}} \\ \omega_1' = f_1(\omega_1, \tau_1) \quad (e_1) \end{array}\right]\left[\begin{array}{c} \underbrace{}_{\text{junction}} \\ \texttt{if } \gamma \texttt{ then} \\ \omega_1 - \omega_2 = 0 \quad (e_3) \\ \tau_1 + \tau_2 = 0 \quad (e_4) \\ \texttt{else} \\ \tau_1 = 0 \quad (e_5) \\ \tau_2 = 0 \quad (e_6) \end{array}\right]\left[\begin{array}{c} \underbrace{}_{\text{shaft 2}} \\ \omega_2' = f_2(\omega_2, \tau_2) \quad (e_2) \end{array}\right]$$

Fig. 1. A simple clutch with two shafts and its model from first principles.

3. **The mode transition is not explicitly specified:** No equation directly addresses mode changes $\gamma : \text{T} \rightarrow \text{F}$ and $\gamma : \text{F} \rightarrow \text{T}$. Still, restart conditions can be automatically inferred from the model of Fig. 1 at compile time, as we shall see.

Modularity in Modeling: What happens if we have a chain of clutches with N shafts? The DAE-based model of Fig. 1 just extends with more replicates. In contrast, the Hybrid Automaton model (1, 2, 4) must be globally rebuilt: the number of states is 2^{N-1}; the model in each state is modified if we glue one more shaft to the chain; the restart conditions are global and we must compute the equivalent moments of inertia for each chain of shafts with engaged clutches. The conclusion is clear: *physical modeling with hybrid automata is not modular; multimode DAE-based modeling is stringently needed to achieve modularity.*

Conclusion: Acausal modeling makes the specification of large Cyber Physical Systems more modular, comfortable and elegant, and allows for better reusability. As a matter of fact, multimode DAE-based modeling is routinely used in focused areas such as electrical circuits [16], contact mechanics [24], or hydraulics. The modeling of large CPS, however, requires *physics-agnostic modeling* allowing for the combination of different physics together with the embedded control software. The Modelica language, which supports physics-agnostic multimode modeling since version 3.3 [4,13], is a *de facto* standard in this area.

2.2   A New Avenue of Paradigms, Issues, and Questions

From the observations above, we identify new paradigms, issues and questions for the computer science community:

- **How can we formally define the class of models that contains the clutch model shown in Fig. 1?**
- **Is there room for a computer scientist's way of thinking in this new area?**

Issue 1 (acausal models). *Rather than only considering ODEs (i.e., equations of the form $y' = g(y, u)$ where y is the state and u is the input), acausal modeling relies on DAEs, i.e., equations of the form $f(x', x, v) = 0$ where both x and v are unknowns, with no specification of any input/output status. What are the consequences in terms of generating simulation code?*

Issue 1 was addressed by the DAE community by introducing the notion of *index* [10,22]. An abstraction of the notion of index, in which regularity/singularity of the Jacobian is considered in a generic sense, was proposed as a way to better scale up [23,25]. This solution, known as *structural analysis* of DAE systems, is extensively used in Modelica tools.

In addition to being naturally described by an acausal model, a system may have different modes for various reasons. Mechanical impacts where the bodies may remain in contact after a collision or an active grasping/docking, idealized electrical or hydraulic switching elements, are examples of situations requiring different sets of equations for their modeling. Another reason is the control of complex scenarios like repairing a satellite with robots, or switching between start-up, normal operation and shutdown during the operation of a power plant. Models of this kind are called *multimode* models. Hence the second issue for consideration:

Issue 2 (multiple modes). *What is the consequence of considering multi-mode DAE models—in other words, DAE-based hybrid systems?*

Issue 2 was identified by authors, but is still incorrectly addressed in industrially used DAE-based modeling tools, as we shall see in the next Section. Authors have proposed dynamic approaches that perform structural analysis when needed [14, 18,19], at the cost of significant computational overheads at runtime. In addition, the compile time assistance in model debugging provided by structural analysis is lost with such approaches. On top of that, new difficulties can also arise at mode changes:

Issue 3 (synthesis of restarts at mode changes). *The designer specifies the model for each mode, but should not always be requested to specify the restart conditions resulting from a transition. How can these conditions be inferred?*

For example, restart equations for the clutch model (when entering the engaged mode) should be *synthesized* during compilation, not manually specified. For larger models, restart conditions may be very difficult to synthetize by hand, which makes Issue 3 of uttermost importance.

Last but definitely not least, we lack a reference semantics for multimode DAE systems in general:

Issue 4 (notion of solution). *No notion of solution exists for general multimode DAE systems, but only partial notions on restricted subclasses of systems.*

This came as a surprise to us when we started our study—the reader is referred to [4] for a bibliographical discussion. The work of Stephan Trenn, relying on distributions, is an important contribution to the subject. However, Trenn himself points out in [28,29] inherent difficulties to this approach, which indicates that distributions are not the ultimate answer to deal with impulsive variables in multimode DAE systems. Still, Trenn was able in [20] to define complete solutions for a class of switched DAE systems in which each mode is in *quasi-linear form*: switching conditions are time-based, not state-based. The bottom line is that, unlike for ODE-based hybrid systems or DAE-based single-mode systems, we lack reference semantics. Moreover, spurious situations can arise, leading to infinitely fast mode switching [30]. The best we can hope is to prove that our approach boils down to known approaches for certain subclasses of systems: such an equivalence result was proved in [5] for the subclass of *semi-linear DAE systems* supported by Modiamath [14].

Contribution: In [9], we addressed Issue 2 by proposing a scalable, compile-time, multimode structural analysis; in this paper, we present our approach to Issues 3 and 4. For this purpose, we need to give semantics to dynamics that combine discrete steps and continuous evolutions. This was already an issue for ODE-based hybrid systems; it becomes a steep challenge when moving to DAEs. The use of *nonstandard analysis* and *hyperreals* was already advocated in the study of ODE-based hybrid systems in the computer science community [2,3]. While it was an "alternative approach" in that case, it turned out to become instrumental for the study of DAE-based hybrid systems.

3   The Clutch Example in Existing Physical Modeling Tools

The clutch model of Fig. 1 translates as the Modelica code of Fig. 2, which is accepted by the two Modelica tools we had the opportunity to test: OpenModelica 1.17.0 [15] and Dymola 2021 [11]. However, none of these tools generates correct simulation code. Simulations fail precisely at the instant when the clutch switches from the released mode (g=false) to the engaged one (g=true), as evidenced by a division by zero exception resulting from the pivoting of a linear system of equations that becomes singular when g becomes equal to true.

We also tested the Mathematica Advanced Hybrid & DAE toolbox, a library advertised as supporting multimode DAE systems. With this toolbox, the simulation does not abort, but it returns incorrect results: the angular momentum

```
model ClutchBasic                    Real w1(start=w01, fixed=true );
parameter Real w01=1;                Real w2(start=w02, fixed=true );
parameter Real w02=1.5;              Real f1 ;   Real f2 ;
parameter Real j1=1;                 equation
parameter Real j2=2;                   g = (time>=t1) and (time<=t2 );
parameter Real k1=0.01;                j1*der(w1) = -k1*w1 + f1 ;
parameter Real k2=0.0125;              j2*der(w2) = -k2*w2 + f2 ;
parameter Real t1=5;                    0 = if g then w1-w2 else f1 ;
parameter Real t2=7;                   f1 + f2 = 0;
Boolean g(start=false );             end ClutchBasic ;
```

Fig. 2. Modelica code for the idealized clutch. This is a faithful translation in the Modelica language of the model of Fig. 1 with f_i as in (3). The input guard γ (called g) takes the value T between t_1 and t_2, and F elsewhere.

of the system is not preserved, in contradiction with the physics; also, the state jump seems to be randomly selected: a small change in the velocities before the change results in totally different values for the restart.

Takeaway. Fundamental studies are clearly needed to ensure a correct handling of events of mode change by the Modelica tools. Smoothing "`if then else`" equations could help solving the problems arising at mode changes, but requires a delicate and definitely non-modular tuning, as this tuning depends on the different time scales arising in the system. *We advocate that, as the tools reputedly support multimode DAE models, they should handle them correctly.*

Analysis of the Clutch Example. In Sect. 4, we perform the structural analysis of the model in each individual mode. This kind of symbolic analysis for acausal, DAE-based, models provided the grounds for the handling of mode changes that we propose in Sect. 5. The clutch example illustrates a major difficulty of this task, namely, the fact that restart conditions are, in general, not explicitly specified.

4 Structural Analysis of Each Individual Mode

In this section, we analyze separately the model for each mode of the clutch. In the released mode ($\gamma = $ F in the model of Fig. 1), the two shafts are independent and one obtains the following two independent ODEs for ω_1 and ω_2:

$$\begin{array}{ll} \omega_1' = f_1(\omega_1, \tau_1) & (e_1) \qquad \tau_1 = 0 \quad (e_5) \\ \omega_2' = f_2(\omega_2, \tau_2) & (e_2) \qquad \tau_2 = 0 \quad (e_6) \end{array} \tag{5}$$

In the engaged mode, however ($\gamma = $ T in the model of Fig. 1), the two velocities and torques are algebraically related:

$$\begin{array}{ll} \omega_1' = f_1(\omega_1, \tau_1) & (e_1) \qquad \omega_1 - \omega_2 = 0 \quad (e_3) \\ \omega_2' = f_2(\omega_2, \tau_2) & (e_2) \qquad \tau_1 + \tau_2 = 0 \quad (e_4) \end{array} \tag{6}$$

Equation (e_3) relates the two velocities ω_1 and ω_2 that are otherwise subject to the ODE system (e_1, e_2). This makes System (6) a DAE instead of an ODE.

In (6), torques τ_1 and τ_2 are not differentiated: they are *algebraic variables*; velocities ω_1 and ω_2 appear together with derivatives: they are *state variables*; $\omega_1', \omega_2', \tau_1, \tau_2$ are the *leading variables* of System (6): they represent the unknowns.

Suppose that the leading variables $\omega_1', \omega_2', \tau_1, \tau_2$ are determined by given *consistent* values for the state variables ω_1, ω_2, i.e., values satisfying (e_3). Then, by using an ODE solver, one could perform an integration step and update the current velocities ω_1, ω_2 using the computed values for their derivatives ω_1', ω_2'. In this case, we say that the considered DAE is an "extended ODE" [25].

It turns out that this condition does not hold for System (6) as is. To intuitively explain the issue, we move to sampled time $\mathbb{T}_\delta =_{\text{def}} \{0, \delta, 2\delta, 3\delta, \dots\}$, by applying an explicit first-order Euler scheme with constant step size $\delta > 0$:

$$\begin{array}{llll} \omega_1^\bullet = \omega_1 + \delta\, f_1(\omega_1, \tau_1) & (e_1^\delta) & \omega_1 - \omega_2 = 0 & (e_3) \\ \omega_2^\bullet = \omega_2 + \delta\, f_2(\omega_2, \tau_2) & (e_2^\delta) & \tau_1 + \tau_2 = 0 & (e_4) \end{array}, \qquad (7)$$

where, for every $t \in \mathbb{T}_\delta$,

$$\omega^\bullet(t) =_{\text{def}} \omega(t+\delta) \quad \text{and} \quad {}^\bullet\omega(t) =_{\text{def}} \omega(t-\delta) \qquad (8)$$

respectively denote the forward and backward time shift operators by an amount of δ. Suppose we are given consistent values $\omega_1 = \omega_2$ and we wish to use System (7), seen as a system of algebraic equations, to determine the value of the dependent variables (i.e., the unknowns) $\tau_1, \tau_2, \omega_1^\bullet, \omega_2^\bullet$. This attempt fails since we have only three equations e_1^δ, e_2^δ and e_4 to determine four unknowns $\tau_1, \tau_2, \omega_1^\bullet$ and $\omega_2^\bullet$; indeed, the omitted equation (e_3) does not involve any leading variable.

Since System (7) is time invariant, if the system remains in the engaged mode for at least δ seconds, then the following shifted *latent equation* also holds:

$$\omega_1^\bullet - \omega_2^\bullet = 0 \quad (e_3^\bullet) \qquad (9)$$

Replacing (e_3) with $(e_3^\bullet)$ in System (7) yields a system with four equations and four dependent variables, which is nonsingular in a generic sense. One can now use System (7) augmented with equation $(e_3^\bullet)$ to get an execution scheme for the engaged mode of the clutch. This is shown in Execution Scheme 1.

Execution Scheme 1 System (7)+System (9).

Require: consistent ω_1 and ω_2, i.e., satisfying (e_3).
1: **Solve** $\{e_1^\delta, e_2^\delta, e_3^\bullet, e_4\}$ **for** $(\omega_1^\bullet, \omega_2^\bullet, \tau_1, \tau_2)$ ▷ 4 equations, 4 unknowns
2: $(\omega_1, \omega_2) \leftarrow (\omega_1^\bullet, \omega_2^\bullet)$ ▷ update the states (ω_1, ω_2)
3: **Tick**   ▷ move to next discrete step

Since the next values of the state variables satisfy (9) by construction, the consistency condition is met at the next iteration step.

Comment 1 (structural nonsingularity [5,6]**).** The implicit assumption behind Line 1 in Execution Scheme 1 is that solving $\{e_1^\delta, e_2^\delta, e_3^\bullet, e_4\}$ always returns a unique set of values. In our example, this is true in a "generic" or "structural" sense, meaning that it holds for all but exceptional values for variables and/or parameters.[1] We refer to this as *structural nonsingularity* in the sequel.   □

Observe that the same analysis could be applied to the original continuous-time dynamics from System (6) by replacing (e_3) by the differentiated *latent equation*

$$\omega_1' - \omega_2' = 0 \ (e_3') \tag{10}$$

Since (e_3) holds at any instant, (e_3') follows as long as the solution is smooth enough for the derivatives ω_1' and ω_2' to be defined. The resulting execution scheme is given in Execution Scheme 2, which parallels Execution Scheme 1.

Execution Scheme 2 System (6)+Eq. (10).

Require: consistent ω_1 and ω_2, i.e., satisfying (e_3).
1: `Solve` $\{e_1, e_2, e_3', e_4\}$ `for` $(\omega_1', \omega_2', \tau_1, \tau_2)$ ▷ 4 equations, 4 unknowns
2: `ODESolve` (ω_1, ω_2) ▷ update the states (ω_1, ω_2)
3: `Tick`   ▷ move to next discretization step

Line 1 is identical for the two schemes and is assumed to give a unique solution, generically; it fails if one omits the latent equation (e_3'). Then, although getting the next values for ω_1 and ω_2 is easy in Execution Scheme 1, the situation changes in Execution Scheme 2: the derivatives ω_1', ω_2' are first evaluated, then an ODE solver (here denoted by `ODESolve`) is used to update the state (ω_1, ω_2) until the next time horizon.

Comparing Line 1 of Execution Scheme 1 and Line 1 of Execution Scheme 2 reveals the common principle driving the execution of dAE/DAE-based models:[2]

Principle 1 (dAE/DAE execution). *Assume an algebraic equation system solver. The key task is to massage the source model in such a way that the system of equations determining the leading variables becomes regular (i.e., possesses, locally, a unique solution).*

This transforms the original DAE system $F(X', X, Y) = 0$ into a form equivalent to an ODE $X' = G(X, Y)$; the same holds for the discrete-time counterpart.

---

[1] Numerical singularity occurs when the Jacobian matrix of the system is singular; in this specific case, this can only occur when $\partial f_1(\omega_1, \tau_1)/\partial \tau_1 + \partial f_2(\omega_2, \tau_2)/\partial \tau_2 = 0$. Unlike structural singularity, numerical singularity depends on numerical values of both coefficients and variables.

[2] dAE stands for *difference* Algebraic Equation (related to discrete time), while DAE stands for *Differential* Algebraic Equation (related to continuous time).

Differentiation Index and Structural Analysis of DAEs: The replacement of (e_3) by (e'_3), which resulted in Execution Scheme 2, is known in the literature as *index reduction* [22]. It requires adding the (smallest set of) latent equations needed for the system in Line 1 of the execution scheme to become solvable and deterministic. The number of successive time shifts or differentiations needed for obtaining all the latent equations is called the *differentiation index* [10]. Generally, for any given DAE model S, which is a system of numerical equations

$$f_i(\text{the } x_j \text{ and their derivatives}) = 0 \ , \quad i = 1, \ldots, m; \quad j = 1, \ldots, n \ , \quad (11)$$

the structural analysis consists in producing Execution Scheme 2 associated to this model. By the implicit function theorem, the existence and uniqueness of solutions of System (11) rely on the invertibility of the Jacobian matrix collecting the partial derivatives $\partial f_i / \partial u_j$, where u_j is the leading variable associated to the real variable x_j.

An approximate analysis of System (11) was developed since the 1980's that guarantees the regularity of this Jacobian matrix in a structural sense, taking only into account the occurrence/absence of a variable in an equation and its differentiation order: this data is stored into the *weighted incidence graph* $\mathcal{G}_S$ of the system, which is a labeled bipartite graph in which edge (f_i, x_j) is present with weight d_{ij} iff variable x_j occurs in f_i with degree d_{ij} [22,23,25]. In [25], the problem of finding the *offsets* of each equation f_i (i.e., the number of times it should be differentiated) was reduced to solving a certain linear program associated to the weighted incidence graph of System (11); this is known as the Σ-method. Details are found in [5,6].

5   Handling Mode Changes

Caveat: What Is the Semantics of a Multimode DAE? The semantics of ODEs (i.e., the sets of runs or trajectories they define) has been known for a long time, as existence and uniqueness theorems for their solutions are well known in mathematics. The same holds for DAEs, although the corresponding developments are much more recent [10]. In formal studies on hybrid systems, defining the semantics of a model is usually not an issue, hence, the scientific community can focus on difficult decidability issues for various classes of properties and models.

When entering the domain of multimode DAE systems, we did not expect semantics to be a problem. Many physical subdomains involve multimode DAE for their models. Electrical circuits with ideal diodes [16], contact and friction mechanics [24], and hydraulics with multiple-phase materials, are examples of this. For each of these domains, solutions of the corresponding multimode DAEs are well defined, albeit with reference to the dedicated formalism used to describe them—these formalisms differ among the various fields of physics.

In contrast, multiphysics modeling combined with the modeling of embedded digital control is beyond the scope of such dedicated modeling approaches. A notable exception stems from *bond graphs* [27], where generic notions of *effort*, *flow, junction,* and *gyrator* generalize the notions of potential, current, junction, and motor in electrical circuits. This yields a generic multiphysics formalism well suited to DAE-based modeling. However, so-called *switch bond graphs*, extending bond graphs to multimode systems, are not well developed [8]. We are therefore faced with the following demanding problem:

Problem 1 (Semantics). *Given that there is no reference semantics in mathematics for general multimode DAE systems, find a sensible subclass of multimode DAE systems:*

1. *that is rich enough for supporting complex multiphysics systems modeling,*
2. *so that checking that a given system belongs to this subclass can be checked at compile time, and*
3. *for which a semantics is well defined.*

An example of property that does not meet requirement 2 is "the class of systems whose solution trajectories are continuous with continuous derivatives". Our work [5,6] provides a systematic answer to Problem 1. We illustrate our approach on the clutch example in the next section.

5.1   Structural Analysis at Mode Changes

As discussed above, discontinuous velocities and impulsive torques are expected when the clutch gets engaged. To analyze this, we reuse the discrete-time approximation (7) with time step δ and the forward and backward shift operators introduced in (8). To capture the transition $\gamma : \text{F} \to \text{T}$, we unfold the dynamics of the clutch over two successive instants, by adding the latent equation $(e_3^\bullet)$ associated to mode $\gamma = \text{T}$:

$$
\begin{array}{l}
\begin{array}{l} \text{previous} \\ \text{instant} \\ \gamma = \text{F} \end{array}
\left\{
\begin{array}{ll}
\frac{\omega_1 - {}^\bullet\omega_1}{\delta} = f_1({}^\bullet\omega_1, {}^\bullet\tau_1) & ({}^\bullet e_1^\delta) \\[4pt]
\frac{\omega_2 - {}^\bullet\omega_2}{\delta} = f_2({}^\bullet\omega_2, {}^\bullet\tau_2) & ({}^\bullet e_2^\delta) \\[4pt]
{}^\bullet\tau_1 = 0 & \\[2pt]
{}^\bullet\tau_2 = 0 &
\end{array}
\right. \\[40pt]
\begin{array}{l} \text{current} \\ \text{instant} \\ \gamma = \text{T} \end{array}
\left\{
\begin{array}{ll}
\frac{\omega_1^\bullet - \omega_1}{\delta} = f_1(\omega_1, \tau_1) & \\[4pt]
\frac{\omega_2^\bullet - \omega_2}{\delta} = f_2(\omega_2, \tau_2) & \\[4pt]
\omega_1 - \omega_2 = 0 & (e_3) \\[2pt]
\omega_1^\bullet - \omega_2^\bullet = 0 & (e_3^\bullet) \\[2pt]
\tau_1 + \tau_2 = 0 &
\end{array}
\right.
\end{array}
\qquad
\begin{pmatrix} \text{subsystem} \\ ({}^\bullet e_1^\delta, {}^\bullet e_2^\delta, e_3) \\ \text{is conflicting} \end{pmatrix}
\qquad (12)
$$

Subsystem $({}^\bullet e_1^\delta, {}^\bullet e_2^\delta, e_3)$ possesses 3 equations, but only 2 dependent variables ω_1, ω_2 as the remaining variables are all determined at the previous time step. This subsystem is thus structurally singular (over-specified). Should the clutch model be rejected? Not quite. This problem is only an artifact of time discretization.

We will get rid of the conflict in model (12) by removing some equations from the conflicting subsystem, at the instant of mode change. To respect causality, the past will not be undone, so that equations $({}^\bullet e_1^\delta, {}^\bullet e_2^\delta)$, which were handled at the previous instant, cannot be modified. However, *we can resolve the conflict by erasing equation* (e_3) *in System* (12). Thus, at the instant of mode change, the consistency equation (e_3) from the new mode will not be satisfied. At the next instant, however, consistency equation $\omega_1 - \omega_2 = 0$ will be guaranteed by equation $(e_3^\bullet)$ of (12), and it will then remain satisfied as long as the system stays in the engaged mode. Hence, erasing (e_3) in System (12) amounts to postponing by one time step the satisfaction of this state constraint.

Acceptance/Rejection of a Model. The analysis of the released $\rightarrow$ engaged mode change succeeds for the clutch example. It might have failed if erasing contradicting equations in the present and future of the mode change had yielded a structurally under-specified system, expressing that the model would be under-specified at this mode change—see the cup-and-ball example in [5,6].

Discussion. The analysis developed here meets the requirements of Problem 1: the acceptance/rejection of the submitted model relies on a compile-time structural analysis. For an accepted model, the δ-discretized scheme defines the semantics, which is well defined in a generic sense.

Working with a fixed step size discretization of time is, however, unacceptable, even for single-mode ODEs, as stiff dynamics, whose presence cannot be checked at compile time, can always occur. In the next section, we address this difficulty by taking for our time step an "infinitesimal" number, thus getting "infinitesimal" accuracy for our discretization. This is achieved by calling nonstandard analysis to the rescue.

5.2   Nonstandard Analysis and Hyperreals to the Rescue

If DAE dynamics is approximated in discrete time, then the whole model becomes discrete-time. To avoid the problem of approximation error, our idea is to use an "infinitesimal" time step in the discrete-time approximation. This will yield an approximation that is accurate up to an infinitesimal error. This can be made rigorous by relying on *nonstandard analysis* [5,21,26], which extends the set $\mathbb{R}$ of real numbers to a superset ${}^\star\mathbb{R}$ of *hyperreals* that includes infinitely large and infinitely small numbers. For the understanding of this paper, it is enough to know the following about nonstandard analysis.

A Glimpse of Nonstandard Analysis: There exist *infinitesimals*, defined as hyperreals of ${}^\star\mathbb{R}$ that are smaller in absolute value than any nonzero real number. The usual arithmetic operations and relations are lifted to ${}^\star\mathbb{R}$. Say that $x \in {}^\star\mathbb{R}$ is *finite* if there exists a real number $y \in \mathbb{R}_+$ such that $|x| \leq y$.

> For every finite hyperreal $x \in {}^\star\mathbb{R}$, there is a unique standard real
> number $st(x) \in \mathbb{R}$ such that $st(x) - x$ is infinitesimal; $st(x)$ is called   (13)
> the *standard part* (or **standardization**) of x.

Standardizing functions or systems of equations, however, requires some care. One important issue is derivatives. For $t \mapsto x(t)$ an $\mathbb{R}$-valued signal ($t \in \mathbb{R}$),

x is differentiable at instant $t \in \mathbb{R}$ if and only if there exists $a \in \mathbb{R}$ such that, for any infinitesimal $\varepsilon \in {}^{\star}\mathbb{R}$, $\frac{x(t+\varepsilon)-x(t)}{\varepsilon} - a$ is infinitesimal; (14) then, $a = x\prime(t)$.

Nonstandard Time: For $\varepsilon > 0$ an infinitesimal time step, we consider the time index set $\mathbb{T} \subseteq {}^{\star}\mathbb{R}$:

$$\mathbb{T} = 0, \varepsilon, 2\varepsilon, 3\varepsilon, \cdots = \{n\varepsilon \mid n \in {}^{\star}\mathbb{N}\} \tag{15}$$

where ${}^{\star}\mathbb{N}$ denotes the set of *hyperintegers*, consisting of all integers augmented with additional infinite numbers called *nonstandard*. The following features of $\mathbb{T}$ are important: (1) any finite real time $t \in \mathbb{R}$ is infinitesimally close to some element of $\mathbb{T}$ (hence, $\mathbb{T}$ covers $\mathbb{R}$ and can be used to index continuous-time dynamics); and (2) $\mathbb{T}$ is "discrete": every instant $n\varepsilon$ has a predecessor $(n-1)\varepsilon$ (except for $n = 0$) and a successor $(n+1)\varepsilon$. Let x be a nonstandard signal indexed by $\mathbb{T}$. The *forward-* and *backward-shifted* signals $x^{\bullet}$ and ${}^{\bullet}x$ are defined as in (8), with ε replacing δ.

Nonstandard Semantics: Solutions of multi-mode DAE systems may be non-differentiable or even non-continuous at events of mode change. To give a meaning to x' at any instant, *we define it everywhere as*

$$x' =_{\text{def}} \frac{1}{\varepsilon}(x^{\bullet} - x), \tag{16}$$

which agrees with (14) at the instants where x is differentiable. Consider again System (12) where conflicting equation (e_3) is removed, and focus on the dynamics in the current instant, where derivatives are expanded using (16):

$$\begin{cases} \omega_1^{\bullet} = \omega_1 + \varepsilon f_1(\omega_1, \tau_1) \\ \omega_2^{\bullet} = \omega_2 + \varepsilon f_2(\omega_2, \tau_2) \\ \omega_1^{\bullet} - \omega_2^{\bullet} = 0 \text{ and } \tau_1 + \tau_2 = 0 \end{cases} \tag{17}$$

We wish to use System (17) by identifying current values for the states ω_i with the *left-limits* ω_i^- i.e., the values of the velocities just before the mode change. From these values, we would then compute the restart values for the velocities $\omega_i^+ =_{\text{def}} \omega_i^{\bullet}$, together with the torques τ_i.

5.3 From Hyperreals to Effective Code

Unfortunately, hyperreals are unknown to computers; hence, System (17) cannot be used as such, but needs to be *standardized,* by "washing out" the infinitesimal time step ε. As it is infinitesimal, it is tempting to get rid of of it in (17) by simply setting $\varepsilon = 0$. Unfortunately, doing this leaves us with a structurally singular system, since the two torques are then involved in only one equation.[3] This problem of structural singularity is in fact due to the existence of impulsive variables. To discover them in a systematic way, we perform an *impulse analysis*.

Impulse Analysis: When the clutch is released, we have $\omega_1 - \omega_2 \neq 0$, generically. Since $\omega_1^\bullet - \omega_2^\bullet = 0$ holds, $\frac{(\omega_1^\bullet - \omega_2^\bullet) - (\omega_1 - \omega_2)}{\varepsilon} = f_1(\omega_1, \tau_1) - f_2(\omega_2, \tau_2)$ cannot be finite because, if it was, then the function $\omega_1 - \omega_2$ would be continuous, contradicting the assumption that $\omega_1 - \omega_2 \neq 0$. Hence, the hyperreal $f_1(\omega_1, \tau_1) - f_2(\omega_2, \tau_2)$ is necessarily infinite. However, we assumed continuous functions f_i and finite state (ω_1, ω_2). Thus, one of the torques τ_i must be infinite at mode change, and because of equation $(e_4) : \tau_1 + \tau_2 = 0$, both torques are in fact infinite, i.e., are *impulsive*.

Eliminating Impulsive Variables: We now assume that each f_i has the form (3). Erasing (e_3) from the black part of (12) yields the following system of equations, to be solved for $\omega_1^\bullet, \omega_2^\bullet, \tau_1, \tau_2$ at the instant when γ switches from F to T:

$$\begin{cases} J_1\omega_1^\bullet = J_1\omega_1 + \varepsilon(\tau_1 - g_1(\omega_1)) & (e_1^\varepsilon) \\ J_2\omega_2^\bullet = J_2\omega_2 + \varepsilon(\tau_2 - g_2(\omega_2)) & (e_2^\varepsilon) \\ \omega_1^\bullet - \omega_2^\bullet = 0 & (e_3^\bullet) \\ \tau_1 + \tau_2 = 0 & (e_4) \end{cases} \qquad (18)$$

We eliminate the impulsive variables from System (18), namely, the two torques. Using (e_4) yields $-\tau_2 = \tau_1 =_{\text{def}} \tau$. Using $(e_3^\bullet)$ by setting $\omega^\bullet =_{\text{def}} \omega_1^\bullet = \omega_2^\bullet$ and adding the two equations (e_1^ε) and (e_2^ε) yields

$$(J_1 + J_2)\omega^\bullet = J_1\omega_1 + J_2\omega_2 - \varepsilon(g_1(\omega_1) + g_1(\omega_2)) \ .$$

It is now legitimate to set ε to 0 to standardize the right-hand side of this equation. Finally, identifying $st(\omega_i) = \omega_i^-$ and $st(\omega_i^\bullet) = \omega_i^+$ synthesizes formula (4). Alternative approaches for the computation of the reset values, which do not require the elimination of impulsive variables, are presented in [5,6].

We thus recovered the restart condition derived from conservation laws of the mechanics in Sect. 2.1, *by only using physics-agnostic symbolic reasoning*. This addresses Issue 3 of Sect. 2.2, and can be made fully automatic [5,6].

6   Discussion and Perspectives

A New Modeling Paradigm: In this paper, we advocate the use of multimode DAE systems (or DAE-based hybrid systems) for physical modeling and, thus,

---

[3] Actually, this is an example of erroneous standardization of systems of equations. In [5,6] it is proved that standardizing a system of equations by setting $\varepsilon = 0$ is correct if and only if doing so yields a structurally regular system of equations.

CPS modeling. We argued for its stringent need to bring modularity and reuse in modeling. We illustrated on a toy example the difficulties in compiling such models to derive simulation code, and proposed effective solutions. Major lessons from this study are the following:

- Since DAEs, not ODEs, are involved, we must rely on structural analysis for both all modes and mode changes of the system.
- In many cases, restart conditions at mode changes can be synthesized from a proper structural analysis.
- The compilation steps detailed above provide a compile-time analysis for accepting or rejecting models, based on over/under-specifications of it, within modes or at mode changes.
- An *impulse analysis* is also presented in [5]; this is a compile-time symbolic analysis identifying impulsive variables, which allows for the handling of models involving impulsive behaviors.
- Hyperreals and nonstandard analysis were instrumental in doing this: they allow to unify the model of time, combining continuous-time dynamics within long modes and discrete-time steps for computing restarts at mode changes.

Our Approach Gives a Semantics to Multimode DAE Systems Possessing Long Modes and Finite Cascades of Mode Switches. Note that dense infinite cascades, such as those resulting from sliding mode control [30], are not covered. Our semantics was proved to coincide with the semantics provided by the physics for the restricted class of *semilinear* systems, to which the clutch belongs [4,5]. No comparison can be stated for our method in full generality, however, due to the lack of reference semantics for multimode multiphysics systems. A full justification of the use of nonstandard analysis and standardization was provided in [5].

Making Our Approach Systematic with Algorithms that Properly Scale Up: In the grounding paper [5], we develop a comprehensive theory handling, in full generality, multimode DAE systems belonging to the class described above. The whole procedure is automatic, and effective algorithms are specified and mathematically justified.

In this paper, we did not discuss algorithmic complexity. For the clutch example, structural analyses were needed for each of the two modes (released and engaged), and each of the two transitions (released $\rightarrow$ engaged and vice-versa). Since the number of modes can grow exponentially with the number of subsystems, the *mode-centric* modeling approach associating a DAE model to each different mode cannot scale up. This can be overcome in practice by adopting the dual *equation-centric* approach, in which each equation is labeled with a predicate characterizing the set of modes in which this equation is active.[4] This dual approach, combined with an efficient encoding of the multimode Σ-method

---

[4] This equation-centric viewpoint was first used in the *clock calculus* and *conditional dependency graph* used in the compilation of the Signal synchronous language [7].

using Binary Decision Diagrams (BDD) techniques, proved to scale up nicely on significant experiments [9]. A large part of this body is implemented in our tool IsamDAE.[5] The examples coming with this tool already include thermodynamical, electrical and pneumatic models. Work is in progress toward developing *modular structural analysis* as a means to further scale up, and possibly achieve separate compilation of such models.

Grand Challenges: Let us wrap up this paper by proposing a few grand challenges for computer scientists in this area.

Correct compilation of multimode DAE systems: With the current reference tools, physically correct models need to be nontrivially twisted and massaged to get simulated, which can require assistance by tool experts. Our work addresses this challenge.

Scaling up: Large industrial models can involve up to hundreds of thousands of equations; examples are found in the energy sector. Such models are not fully supported by the existing tools. Progress is stringently needed on this issue, and should involve both high performance computing and compile-time analyses such as the ones developed above.

Modularity and separate compilation: The first step of model compilation in current tools is a flattening of the model structure. This can yield prohibitive computational costs, particularly for large systems built from many instantiations of a few component classes. As such, separate compilation of components is stringently needed.

Initialization of multimode DAE models: Specifying correct initial conditions is a widely acknowledged difficulty for designers of large DAE-based models, especially for CPS. Significant work was devoted to initialization for (single-mode) DAEs, but this remains a mostly open issue for multimode DAE models.

General concept of solutions for multimode DAEs: This is a core challenge from a mathematical viewpoint, that we partly addressed.

Acknowledgement. This work was supported by the FUI ModeliScale DOS0066450/ 00 French national grant (2018–2021) and the Inria IPL ModeliScale large scale initiative (2017–2021, https://team.inria.fr/modeliscale/).

References

1. Alur, R., Courcoubetis, C., Henzinger, T.A., Ho, P.-H.: Hybrid automata: an algorithmic approach to the specification and verification of hybrid systems. In: Grossman, R.L., Nerode, A., Ravn, A.P., Rischel, H. (eds.) HS 1991-1992. LNCS, vol. 736, pp. 209–229. Springer, Heidelberg (1993). https://doi.org/10.1007/3-540-57318-6_30

---

[5] To date, the following compilation tasks are implemented: multimode Σ-method, multimode initialization, and multimode Dulmage-Mendelsohn decomposition.

2. Benveniste, A., Bourke, T., Caillaud, B., Colaço, J., Pasteur, C., Pouzet, M.: Building a hybrid systems modeler on synchronous languages principles. Proc. IEEE **106**(9), 1568–1592 (2018)
3. Benveniste, A., Bourke, T., Caillaud, B., Pouzet, M.: Nonstandard semantics of hybrid systems modelers. J. Comput. Syst. Sci. **78**(3), 877–910 (2012)
4. Benveniste, A., Caillaud, B., Elmqvist, H., Ghorbal, K., Otter, M., Pouzet, M.: Multi-mode DAE models - challenges, theory and implementation. In: Steffen, B., Woeginger, G. (eds.) Computing and Software Science. LNCS, vol. 10000, pp. 283–310. Springer, Cham (2019). https://doi.org/10.1007/978-3-319-91908-9_16
5. Benveniste, A., Caillaud, B., Malandain, M.: The mathematical foundations of physical systems modeling languages. Ann. Rev. Control **50**, 72–118 (2020)
6. Benveniste, A., Caillaud, B., Malandain, M.: Structural analysis of multimode DAE systems: summary of results. CoRR, abs/2101.05702 (2021)
7. Benveniste, A., et al.: The synchronous languages 12 years later. Proc. IEEE **91**(1), 64–83 (2003)
8. Broenink, J., Wijbrans, K.: Describing discontinuities in bond graphs. In: Proceedings of the 1st International Conference on Bond Graph Modeling. SCS Simulation Series, vol. 25, no. 2. (1993)
9. Caillaud, B., Malandain, M., Thibault, J.: Implicit structural analysis of multimode DAE systems. In: Ames, A.D., Seshia, S.A., Deshmukh, J. (eds.) HSCC 2020: 23rd ACM International Conference on Hybrid Systems: Computation and Control, Sydney, New South Wales, Australia, 21–24 April 2020, pp. 20:1–20:11. ACM (2020)
10. Campbell, S.L., Gear, C.W.: The index of general nonlinear DAEs. Numer. Math. **72**, 173–196 (1995)
11. Dassault Systèmes AB. Dymola official webpage. https://www.3ds.com/products-services/catia/products/dymola/. Accessed 01 June 2022
12. Elmqvist, H.: A structured model language for large continuous systems, Ph.D. Lund University (1978)
13. Elmqvist, H., Mattsson, S.-E., Otter, M.: Modelica extensions for multi-mode DAE systems. In: Tummescheit, H., Arzèn, K.-E. (eds.) Proceedings of the 10th International Modelica Conference, Lund, Sweden. Modelica Association, September 2014
14. Elmqvist, H., Otter, M.: Modiamath webpage. https://modiasim.github.io/ModiaMath.jl/stable/index.html. Accessed 01 June 2022
15. Fritzson, P., et al.: The OpenModelica integrated environment for modeling, simulation, and model-based development. Model. Identif. Control **41**(4), 241–295 (2020)
16. Heemels, W., Camlibel, M., Schumacher, J.: On the dynamic analysis of piecewise-linear networks. IEEE Trans. Circuits Syst. I-Regul. Pap. **49**, 315–327 (2002)
17. Henzinger, T.A., Ho, P.-H.: HyTech: the cornell hybrid technology tool. In: Antsaklis, P., Kohn, W., Nerode, A., Sastry, S. (eds.) HS 1994. LNCS, vol. 999, pp. 265–293. Springer, Heidelberg (1995). https://doi.org/10.1007/3-540-60472-3_14
18. Höger, C.: Dynamic structural analysis for DAEs. In: Proceedings of the 2014 Summer Simulation Multiconference, SummerSim 2014, Monterey, CA, USA, 6–10 July 2014, p. 12 (2014)
19. Höger, C.: Elaborate control: variable-structure modeling from an operational perspective. In: Proceedings of the 8th International Workshop on Equation-Based Object-Oriented Modeling Languages and Tools, EOOLT 2017, Weßling, Germany, 1 December 2017, pp. 51–60 (2017)

20. Liberzon, D., Trenn, S.: Switched nonlinear differential algebraic equations: Solution theory, Lyapunov functions, and stability. Automatica **48**(5), 954–963 (2012)
21. Lindstrøm, T.: An invitation to nonstandard analysis. In: Cutland, N. (eds.) Nonstandard Analysis and its Applications, pp. 1–105. Cambridge Univ. Press, Cambridge (1988)
22. Mattsson, S.E., Söderlind, G.: Index reduction in differential-algebraic equations using dummy derivatives. Siam J. Sci. Comput. **14**(3), 677–692 (1993)
23. Pantelides, C.: The consistent initialization of differential-algebraic systems. SIAM J. Sci. Stat. Comput. **9**(2), 213–231 (1988)
24. Pfeiffer, F., Glocker, C.: Multibody Dynamics with Unilateral Contacts. Wiley, New York (2008)
25. Pryce, J.D.: A simple structural analysis method for DAEs. BIT **41**(2), 364–394 (2001)
26. Robinson, A.: Nonstandard Analysis. Princeton Landmarks in Mathematics (1996). ISBN 0-691-04490-2
27. Thoma, J.: Introduction to bond graphs and their applications. In: Pergamon International Library of Science, Technology, Engineering and Social Studies. Pergamon Press (1975)
28. Trenn, S.: Distributional differential algebraic equations. Ph.D. thesis, Technischen Universität Ilmenau (2009)
29. Trenn, S.: Regularity of distributional differential algebraic equations. MCSS **21**(3), 229–264 (2009)
30. Utkin, V.: Sliding mode control in mechanical systems. In: 20th International Conference on Industrial Electronics, Control and Instrumentation, IECON 1994, vol. 3, pp. 1429–1431, September 1994

What's Decidable About Discrete Linear Dynamical Systems?

Toghrul Karimov[1], Edon Kelmendi[1], Joël Ouaknine[1(✉)], and James Worrell[2]

[1] Max Planck Institute for Software Systems, Saarland Informatics Campus,
Saarbrücken, Germany
joel@mpi-sws.org
[2] Department of Computer Science, Oxford University, Oxford, UK

Abstract. We survey the state of the art on the algorithmic analysis of discrete linear dynamical systems, focussing in particular on reachability, model-checking, and invariant-generation questions, both unconditionally as well as relative to oracles for the Skolem Problem.

Keywords: Discrete linear dynamical systems · Model checking · Invariant generation · Orbit Problem · Linear recurrence sequences · Skolem Problem

1 Introduction

Dynamical systems are a fundamental modelling paradigm in many branches of science, and have been the subject of extensive research for many decades. A *(rational) discrete linear dynamical system (LDS)* in ambient space $\mathbb{R}^d$ is given by a square $d \times d$ matrix M with rational entries, together with a starting point $x \in \mathbb{Q}^d$.[1] The *orbit* of (M, x) is the infinite trajectory $\mathcal{O}(M, x) := \langle x, Mx, M^2x, \dots \rangle$. An example of a four-dimensional LDS is given in Fig. 1. Our main focus in the present paper is on delineating the class of assertions on the orbits of LDS that can be algorithmically decided.

$$
M \stackrel{\text{def}}{=} \begin{pmatrix} 3 & 2 & 0 & -5 \\ 0 & 1 & 0 & 3 \\ 0 & 4 & 3 & 13 \\ 3 & 11 & 6 & 24 \end{pmatrix} \qquad x \stackrel{\text{def}}{=} \begin{pmatrix} 1 \\ -1 \\ 2 \\ 0 \end{pmatrix}
$$

Fig. 1. A four-dimensional discrete linear dynamical system.

---

[1] All of the results we present in this paper carry over to the more general setting of *real-algebraic* LDS, whose entries are allowed to be real algebraic numbers. Nevertheless, we stick here to rationals for simplicity of exposition.

J. Ouaknine—Also affiliated with Keble College, Oxford as emmy.network Fellow, and supported by DFG grant 389792660 as part of TRR 248 (see https://perspicuous-computing.science).

J.-F. Raskin and K. Chatterjee (Eds.): Principles of Systems Design, LNCS 13660, pp. 21–38, 2022.
https://doi.org/10.1007/978-3-031-22337-2_2

One of the most natural and fundamental computational questions concerning linear dynamical systems is the *Point-to-Point Reachability Problem*, also known as the *Kannan-Lipton Orbit Problem*: given a d-dimensional LDS (M, x) together with a point target $y \in \mathbb{Q}^d$, does the orbit of the LDS ever hit the target? The decidability of this question was settled affirmatively in the 1980s in the seminal work of Kannan and Lipton [35,36]. In fact, Kannan and Lipton showed that this problem is solvable in polynomial time, answering an earlier open problem of Harrison from the 1960s on reachability for linear sequential machines [33].

Interestingly, one of Kannan and Lipton's motivations was to propose a line of attack to the well-known *Skolem Problem*, which had itself been famously open since the 1930s. The Skolem Problem remains unsolved to this day, although substantial advances have recently been made—more on this shortly. Phrased in the language of linear dynamical systems, the Skolem Problem asks whether it is decidable, given (M, x) as above, together with a $(d - 1)$-dimensional subspace H of $\mathbb{R}^d$, to determine if the orbit of (M, x) ever hits H. Kannan and Lipton suggested that, in ambient space $\mathbb{R}^d$ of arbitrary dimension, the problem of hitting a low-dimensional subspace might be decidable. Indeed, this was eventually substantiated by Chonev *et al.* for linear subspaces of dimension at most 3 [21,23].

Subsequent research focussed on the decidability of hitting targets of increasing complexity, such as half-spaces [32,39,46–48], polytopes [5,22,52], and semialgebraic sets [6,7]. It is also worth noting that discrete linear dynamical systems can equivalently be viewed as linear (or affine) simple, branching-free while loops, where reachability corresponds to loop termination. There is a voluminous literature on the topic, albeit largely focussing on heuristics and semi-algorithms (via spectral methods or the synthesis of ranking functions, in particular), rather than exact decidability results. Relevant papers include [10–13,18–20,24,34,50,51,54]. Several of these approaches have moreover been implemented in software verification tools, such as Microsoft's Terminator [26,27].

In recent years, motivated in part by verification questions for stochastic systems and linear loops, researchers have begun investigating more sophisticated decision problems than mere reachability: for example, the paper [1] studies approximate LTL model checking of Markov chains (which themselves can be viewed as particular kinds of linear dynamical systems), whereas [38] focusses on LTL model checking of low-dimensional linear dynamical systems with semialgebraic predicates.[2] In [4], the authors solve the semialgebraic model-checking problem for diagonalisable linear dynamical systems in arbitrary dimension against prefix-independent MSO[3] properties, whereas [37] investigates semialge-

---

[2] Semialgebraic predicates are Boolean combinations of polynomial equalities and inequalities.

[3] Monadic Second-Order Logic (MSO) is a highly expressive specification formalism that subsumes the vast majority of temporal logics employed in the field of automated verification, such as Linear Temporal Logic (LTL). "Prefix independence" is a quality of properties that are *asymptotic* in nature—we provide a precise definition shortly.

braic MSO model checking of linear dynamical systems in which the dimensions of predicates are constrained. To illustrate this last approach, recall the dynamical system (M, x) from Fig. 1, and consider the following three semialgebraic predicates:

$$P_1(x_1, x_2, x_3, x_4) \stackrel{\text{def}}{=} x_1 + x_2 + x_3 - x_4 = 0 \wedge (x_1^3 = x_2^2 \vee x_4 \geq 3x_1^2 + x_2)$$

$$P_2(x_1, x_2, x_3, x_4) \stackrel{\text{def}}{=} x_1 + x_2 + 2x_3 - 2x_4 = 0 \wedge x_1^3 + x_3^2 + x_3 > x_4$$

$$P_3(x_1, x_2, x_3, x_4) \stackrel{\text{def}}{=} x_1^4 - x_2^2 = 3 \wedge 2x_3^2 = x_4 \wedge x_1^2 - 2x_2^3 = 4x_3 \, .$$

Recall that the ambient space is $\mathbb{R}^4$. We identify the above predicates with the corresponding subsets of $\mathbb{R}^4$, and wish to express assertions about the orbit of (M, x) as it traces a trajectory through $\mathbb{R}^4$. For example (in LTL notation),

$$\mathbf{G}(P_1 \Rightarrow \mathbf{F}\neg P_2) \wedge \mathbf{F}(P_3 \vee \neg P_1)$$

asserts that whenever the orbit visits P_1, then it must eventually subsequently visit the complement of P_2, and moreover that the orbit will eventually either visit P_3 or the complement of P_1. The reader will probably agree that whether or not the above assertion holds for our LDS (M, x) is not immediately obvious to determine (even, arguably, in principle). Nevertheless, this example falls within the scope of [37], as the semialgebraic predicates P_1, P_2, and P_3 are each either contained in some three-dimensional subspace (this is the case for P_1 and P_2), or have intrinsic dimension at most 1 (this is the case of P_3, which is 'string-like', or a curve, as a subset of $\mathbb{R}^4$). Naturally, we shall return to these notions in due course, and articulate the relevant results in full details.

A recent and closely related line of inquiry concerns the study of algebraic model checking of linear dynamical systems [42]. The setting is similar to the above, the only difference being that the allowable predicates are the *constructible* ones, i.e., built from *algebraic* sets[4] using arbitrary Boolean operations (including complementation). The paper [42] introduces in addition the key notion of *Skolem oracle*, which we discuss next.

1.1   Skolem Oracles

There is an intimate connection between linear dynamical systems and linear recurrence sequences. An *(integer) linear recurrence sequence (LRS)* $\boldsymbol{u} = \langle u_n \rangle_{n=0}^{\infty}$ is an infinite sequence of integers satisfying

$$u_{n+d} = c_1 u_{n+d-1} + \cdots + c_{d-1} u_{n+1} + c_d u_n \tag{1}$$

for all $n \in \mathbb{N}$, where the coefficients $c_1, \ldots, c_d$ are integers and $c_d \neq 0$. We say that the above recurrence has *order* d. We moreover say that an LRS is *simple* if the characteristic polynomial[5] of its minimal-order recurrence has no repeated

---

[4] Algebraic sets correspond to positive Boolean combinations of polynomial equalities.

[5] The characteristic polynomial associated with recurrence (1) is $X^d - c_1 X^{d-1} - \ldots - c_d$.

roots. The sequence of Fibonacci numbers $\langle f_n \rangle_{n=0}^{\infty} = \langle 0, 1, 1, 2, 3, 5, \ldots \rangle$, which obeys the recurrence $f_{n+2} = f_{n+1} + f_n$, is perhaps the most emblematic LRS, and also happens to be simple.

The celebrated theorem of Skolem, Mahler, and Lech (see [31]) describes the structure of the set $\{n \in \mathbb{N} : u_n = 0\}$ of zero terms of an LRS as follows:

Theorem 1. *Given a linear recurrence sequence $\boldsymbol{u} = \langle u_n \rangle_{n=0}^{\infty}$, its set of zero terms is a semilinear set, i.e., it consists of a union of finitely many full arithmetic progressions,[6] together with a finite set.*

As shown by Berstel and Mignotte [14], in the above one can effectively extract all of the arithmetic progressions; we refer herein to the corresponding procedure as the 'Berstel-Mignotte algorithm'. Nevertheless, how to compute the leftover finite set of zeros remains open, and is easily seen to be equivalent to the *Skolem Problem*: given an LRS $\boldsymbol{u}$, does $\boldsymbol{u}$ contain a zero term?

The paper [42] therefore introduces the notion of a *Skolem oracle*: given an LRS $\boldsymbol{u} = \langle u_n \rangle_{n=0}^{\infty}$, such an oracle returns the finite set of indices of zeros of $\boldsymbol{u}$ that do not already belong to some infinite arithmetic progression of zeros. Likewise, a *Simple-Skolem oracle* is a Skolem oracle restricted to simple LRS.

As mentioned earlier, the decidability of the Skolem Problem is a longstanding open question [31,49], with a positive answer for LRS of order at most 4 known since the mid-1980s [53,55]. Very recently, two major conditional advances on the Skolem Problem have been made, achieving decidability subject to certain classical number-theoretic conjectures: in [40], Lipton *et al.* established decidability for LRS of order 5 assuming the *Skolem Conjecture* (also known as the *Exponential Local-Global Principle*); and in [15], Bilu *et al.* showed decidability for simple LRS of arbitrary order, subject to both the Skolem Conjecture and the *p-adic Schanuel Conjecture* (we refer the reader to [15] for the precise definitions and details). It is interesting to note that in both cases, the procedures in question rely on the conjectures *only* for termination; correctness is unconditional. In fact, these procedures are *certifying algorithms* (in the sense of [45]) in that, upon termination, they produce an independent certificate (or witness) that their output is correct. Such a certificate can be checked algorithmically by a third party with no reliance on any unproven conjectures. The authors of [15] have implemented their algorithm within the SKOLEM tool, available online.[7]

In view of the above, Simple-Skolem oracles *can* be implemented with unconditional correctness, and guaranteed termination subject to the Skolem and p-adic Schanuel conjectures. Whether full Skolem oracles can be devised is the subject of active research (see, e.g., [41,43]); at the time of writing, to the best of our knowledge, no putative procedure is even conjectured in the general (non-simple) case.

---

[6] A full arithmetic progression is a set of non-negative integers of the form $\{a + bm : m \in \mathbb{N}\}$, with $a, b \in \mathbb{N}$ and $a < b$.

[7] https://skolem.mpi-sws.org/.

1.2 Paper Outline

Questions of reachability and model checking for linear dynamical systems constitute one of the central foci of this paper. In Sect. 2, we cover the state of the art and beyond, both unconditionally and relative to Skolem oracles. We paint what is essentially a complete picture of the landscape, in each situation establishing either decidability (possibly conditional on Skolem oracles), or hardness with respect to longstanding open problems. An important theme in the classical theory of dynamical systems concerns the study of *asymptotic* properties (e.g., stability, convergence, or divergence of orbits), and we therefore consider both MSO along with its *prefix-independent* fragment piMSO. Section 3 then focusses on questions of robustness through the notion of pseudo-orbit. In Sect. 4, we discuss the algorithmic synthesis of inductive invariants for linear dynamical systems, and Sect. 5 examines the situation in which orbits originate from an initial set rather than a single point. Finally, Sect. 6 concludes with a brief summary and a glimpse of several research directions.

2 Model Checking

Throughout this section, we assume familiarity with the rudiments of Monadic Second-Order Logic (MSO); an excellent reference is the text [16].

Let us work in fixed ambient space $\mathbb{R}^d$, and consider a d-dimensional LDS (M, x) (i.e., $M \in \mathbb{Q}^{d \times d}$ and $x \in \mathbb{Q}^d$). Recall that the orbit $\mathcal{O} = \mathcal{O}(M, x)$ of our LDS is the infinite sequence $\langle x, Mx, M^2x, \ldots \rangle$ in $\mathbb{Q}^d$. Let us write $\mathcal{O}[n]$ for the nth term of the orbit.

Given an MSO formula φ over the collection of semialgebraic predicates $\mathcal{P} = \{P_1, \ldots, P_m\}$, where each $P_i \subseteq \mathbb{R}^d$, the model-checking problem consists in determining whether the orbit (more precisely, the characteristic word $\alpha \in (2^{\mathcal{P}})^\omega$ of the orbit $\mathcal{O}(M, x)$ with respect to $\mathcal{P}$, where $P_i \in \alpha[n]$ iff $\mathcal{O}[n] \in P_i$) satisfies φ. Reachability problems for LDS constitute special cases of the model-checking problem, and already the questions of determining whether a given orbit reaches a hyperplane (Skolem Problem) or a halfspace (the *Positivity Problem* [46]) are longstanding open problems in number theory, couched in the language of linear dynamical systems. Recent research has, however, succeeded in uncovering several important decidable subclasses of the model-checking problem and in demarcating the boundary between what is decidable and what is hard with respect to longstanding open mathematical problems.

In order to present the main results, we require some further definitions to specify the classes of predicates that are allowed within MSO formulas. Let us write $\mathcal{S} \subseteq 2^{\mathbb{R}^d}$ and $\mathcal{C} \subseteq 2^{\mathbb{R}^d}$ to denote respectively the collections of all semialgebraic subsets of $\mathbb{R}^d$ and of all constructible subsets of $\mathbb{R}^d$.[8] We also define the collection $\mathcal{T} \subseteq 2^{\mathbb{R}^d}$ of *tame* sets as follows: $\mathcal{T}$ comprises all semialgebraic

---

[8] Recall that $\mathcal{C}$ is the smallest set containing all algebraic subsets of $\mathbb{R}^d$, and which is closed under finite union, finite intersection, and complement. (The terminology of "constructible" originates from algebraic geometry.).

subsets of $\mathbb{R}^d$ that are either contained in a three-dimensional subspace of $\mathbb{R}^d$, or that have intrinsic dimension at most one.[9] Moreover, $\mathcal{T}$ is defined to be the smallest such set which is in addition closed under finite union, finite intersection, and complement. Finally, we define the set $\mathcal{T} \oplus \mathcal{C}$ to be the smallest superset of $\mathcal{T} \cup \mathcal{C}$ that is closed under finite union, finite intersection, and complement.

Note that all of $\mathcal{S}$, $\mathcal{C}$, $\mathcal{T}$, and $\mathcal{T} \oplus \mathcal{C}$ are closed under all Boolean operations; this is in keeping with their intended use as collections of predicates for MSO formulas, bearing in mind that MSO itself possesses all Boolean operators.

The motivation for considering the collection $\mathcal{T}$ of tame predicates has origins in the results of [6,9,21,38]. A common theme is that for tame predicates, the proofs that establish how to decide reachability also provide one with a means of representing, in a finitary manner, all the time steps at which the orbit of a given LDS is in a particular predicate set T. The authors of [37] show how to combine these representations (one for each predicate) to obtain structural information about the characteristic word α that is sufficient for determining whether a deterministic automaton $\mathcal{A}$ accepts α, leading to the following.

Theorem 2. *Let (M, x) be an LDS, $\mathcal{P} = \{T_1, \dots, T_m\} \subseteq \mathcal{T}$ be a collection of tame predicates and φ be an MSO formula over $\mathcal{P}$. It is decidable whether $(M, x) \vDash \varphi$ (i.e., whether the characteristic word α of the orbit $\mathcal{O}(M, x)$ with respect to $\mathcal{P}$ satisfies φ).*

Let us note in passing that Theorem 2 subsumes the decidability of the Kannan-Lipton Point-to-Point Reachability Problem, since points are singleton sets and the latter are evidently tame.

It is also worth pointing out, absent other restrictions, that this delineation of the decidable fragment of the model-checking problem is tight as trying to expand the definition of tame predicates runs into open problems already for formulas that describe mere reachability properties. In particular, the Skolem Problem in dimension 5 is open and can be encoded (i) as a reachability problem with a four-dimensional LDS and a three-dimensional affine subspace [21] (that is, in general, not contained in a three-dimensional linear subspace) and (ii) as a reachability problem with a target of intrinsic dimension two [9].

To sidestep these obstacles, in [4] the authors restrict φ to formulas that define *prefix-independent* properties. A property is prefix-independent if the infinite words that satisfy it are closed under the operations of insertion and

---

[9] The intrinsic dimension of a semialgebraic set is formally defined via cell decomposition; intuitively, one-dimensional semialgebraic sets can be viewed as 'strings' or 'curves', whereas zero-dimensional semialgebraic sets are finite collections of singleton points.

deletion of finitely many letters.[10] Such properties capture behaviours that are intrinsically asymptotic in nature (for example: "does the orbit enter P infinitely often?"); note that the property of reachability is *not* prefix-independent. The main theorem of [4] in this direction concerns *diagonalisable* linear dynamical systems:[11]

Theorem 3. *Let (M, x) be a diagonalisable LDS and φ be a prefix-independent MSO formula over a collection of semialgebraic predicates $S_1, \ldots, S_m \in \mathcal{S}$. It is decidable whether $(M, x) \vDash \varphi$.*

Note in the above that the semialgebraic predicates are entirely unrestricted (in particular, not required to be tame). However, the restrictions to prefix-independent formulas and to diagonalisable systems both again turn out to be essential. Since the Skolem Problem is open for diagonalisable systems (in dimensions $d \geq 5$), the (non-prefix-independent) model-checking problem for diagonalisable LDS is Skolem-hard already for four-dimensional systems and affine subspace targets, as discussed earlier. On the other hand, if we allow non-diagonalisable systems, then the problem of determining whether the orbit of an LDS is eventually trapped in a given half-space H (known as the *Ultimate Positivity Problem*, corresponding to the prefix-independent formula $\varphi = \mathbf{F} \mathbf{G} H$) is hard with respect to certain longstanding open problems in Diophantine approximation [46].

This last observation however suggests that it might be possible to orchestrate a trade-off between the type of LDS under consideration and the class of allowable specification predicates. Indeed, it turns out that one can lift the restriction to diagonalisable LDS if one agrees to restrict the class of predicates:

Theorem 4. *Let (M, x) be an LDS and φ be a prefix-independent MSO formula over a collection of predicates $P_1, \ldots, P_m \in \mathcal{T} \oplus \mathcal{C}$. It is decidable whether $(M, x) \vDash \varphi$.*

Theorem 4 goes beyond both Theorem 2 (in that constructible predicates are allowed into the mix) as well as [42, Thm. 7.3] (in that tame predicates are allowed).

Let us provide a brief proof sketch of Theorem 4. Let (M, x) and φ be as above. Observe first (as a straightforward exercise) that any $P \in \mathcal{T} \oplus \mathcal{C}$

---

[10] It is interesting to note that whether an MSO formula φ is prefix-independent or not is decidable. To see this, for $A = (Q, q_0, \Sigma, \Delta, F)$ a deterministic Müller automaton, define $A(q)$, for $q \in Q$, to be the same as A, except that the initial state of $A(q)$ is q (rather than q_0). We say that a deterministic Müller automaton A (as above) is *prefix-independent* if, for all $q \in Q$ that are reachable from q_0, $A(q)$ recognises the same language as A. Write $L(A)$ to denote the language recognised by A. It is now straightforward to show that A is prefix-independent iff $L(A)$ is prefix-independent. Since any MSO formula is encodable as a deterministic Müller automaton, and equality of ω-regular languages is decidable, the desired decidability result follows.

[11] An LDS (M, x) is *diagonalisable* if the matrix M is diagonalisable (over $\mathbb{C}$). In a measure-theoretic sense, most LDS are diagonalisable.

can be written in conjunctive normal form, i.e., as an expression of the form $P = \bigcap_{i=1}^{a} \bigcup_{j=1}^{b} B_{i,j}$, where each $B_{i,j}$ is either a tame predicate or a constructible predicate. Without loss of generality, one may therefore assume that each predicate appearing in φ is either tame or constructible.

We now invoke [42, Prop. 5] to conclude that, for each constructible predicate B_ℓ appearing in φ, the Boolean-valued word α_ℓ tracking the passage of the orbit of (M, x) through B_ℓ is ultimately periodic. Moreover, thanks to the Berstel-Mignotte algorithm, the attendant arithmetic progressions can all be effectively elicited. For each such α_ℓ, one can therefore construct a (fully) periodic word α'_ℓ which differs from α_ℓ in at most finitely many places. In other words, for all sufficiently large n, $M^n x \in B_\ell$ iff $\alpha'_\ell[n] = true$. Being periodic, α'_ℓ can in turn be described by an MSO subformula ψ_ℓ. Let us therefore replace within φ every occurrence of a constructible predicate B_ℓ by the subformula ψ_ℓ, obtaining in this process a new MSO formula φ' that comprises exclusively tame predicates. As φ is prefix-independent, it is immediate that $(M, x) \vDash \varphi$ iff $(M, x) \vDash \varphi'$. But the latter is of course decidable thanks to Theorem 2, concluding the proof sketch of Theorem 4.

Once again, Theorem 4 is tight: in Appendix A, we show that the ability to solve the model-checking problem for prefix-independent MSO specifications making use of semialgebraic predicates in ambient space $\mathbb{R}^4$ would necessarily entail major breakthroughs in Diophantine approximation.

Let us now turn to the question of the extent to which the above results can be enhanced through the use of Skolem oracles. The key result is as follows, in effect enabling us to drop the restriction of prefix-independence from Theorem 4:

Theorem 5. *Let (M, x) be an LDS and φ be an MSO formula over a collection of predicates $P_1, \ldots, P_m \in \mathcal{T} \oplus \mathcal{C}$. It is decidable whether $(M, x) \vDash \varphi$, subject to the existence of a Skolem oracle.*

The same result also holds for diagonalisable LDS, assuming the existence of a Simple-Skolem oracle.

The proof of Theorem 5 is similar to that of Theorem 4; we provide a brief sketch below.

Let (M, x) and φ be as above, and assume, thanks to the representation of $(\mathcal{T} \oplus \mathcal{C})$-predicates in conjunctive normal form, that every predicate occurring in φ is either tame of constructible. Thanks to [42, Cor. 6], for each constructible predicate B_ℓ appearing in φ, the Boolean-valued word α_ℓ tracking the passage of the orbit of (M, x) through B_ℓ is effectively ultimately periodic (this requires the use of a Skolem oracle, or a Simple-Skolem oracle if M is diagonalisable). In other words, we have a finitary exact representation of α_ℓ, and can therefore describe it via an MSO subformula ψ_ℓ.

We can now replace within φ every occurrence of a constructible predicate B_ℓ by its corresponding subformula ψ_ℓ, obtaining in this process an equivalent MSO formula φ' that comprises exclusively tame predicates. The desired result then immediately follows from Theorem 2, concluding the proof sketch of Theorem 5.

As noted earlier, Simple-Skolem oracles can be implemented into provably correct certifying procedures which terminate subject to classical number-theoretic conjectures [15]. Let us therefore separately record an important corollary:

Corollary 1. *Let (M, x) be a diagonalisable LDS and φ be an MSO formula over a collection of predicates $P_1, \ldots, P_m \in \mathcal{T} \oplus \mathcal{C}$. It is decidable whether $(M, x) \models \varphi$, assuming the Skolem Conjecture and the p-adic Schanuel Conjecture. Moreover, correctness of the attendant procedure is unconditional, and independent correctness certificates can be produced upon termination.*

Let us point out that Theorem 5 is, once again, tight. For arbitrary LDS, a similar argument as that put forth in Appendix A applies, since it is not known (or even believed) that Skolem oracles are of any use in tackling Ultimate Positivity problems. For diagonalisable LDS, we can invoke the order-10 Simple Positivity Problem, which remains open to this day (see [46]); it can be modelled straightforwardly as a half-space reachability problem in ambient space $\mathbb{R}^{10}$ (or even $\mathbb{R}^9$, by considering an affine half-space). In fact, critical unsolved cases of order-10 Positivity can even be formulated as semialgebraic reachability problems in ambient space $\mathbb{R}^4$; we omit the details in the interests of space and simplicity of exposition.

We summarise the main results of this section in Fig. 2 below.

Diagonalisable LDS:

	unconditional	Simple-Skolem oracle
piMSO	$\mathcal{S}$ (Thm. 3)	$\mathcal{S}$ (Thm. 3)
MSO	$\mathcal{T}$ (Thm. 2)	$\mathcal{T} \oplus \mathcal{C}$ (Thm. 5)

Arbitrary LDS:

	unconditional	Skolem oracle
piMSO	$\mathcal{T} \oplus \mathcal{C}$ (Thm. 4)	$\mathcal{T} \oplus \mathcal{C}$ (Thm. 4 or Thm. 5)
MSO	$\mathcal{T}$ (Thm. 2)	$\mathcal{T} \oplus \mathcal{C}$ (Thm. 5)

Fig. 2. A summary of the decidable model-checking fragments for both diagonalisable and arbitrary linear dynamical systems. The prefix-independent fragment of MSO is denoted piMSO. $\mathcal{S}$ is the collection of semialgebraic predicates, $\mathcal{T}$ is the collection of tame predicates (Boolean closure of semialgebraic sets that either are contained in a three-dimensional subspace, or have intrinsic dimension at most one), $\mathcal{C}$ is the collection of constructible predicates (Boolean closure of algebraic sets), and $\mathcal{T} \oplus \mathcal{C}$ is the Boolean closure of $\mathcal{T} \cup \mathcal{C}$. The right-hand columns in both tables assume access to Skolem or Simple-Skolem oracles.

Taken together, Theorems 2–5, along with Corollary 1, not only subsume— to the best of our knowledge—all existing results regarding model-checking and reachability problems for discrete linear dynamical systems, but moreover paint an essentially complete picture of what is (even in principle) feasible, barring major breakthroughs in longstanding open problems. It is noteworthy that, in this characterisation, there appears to be very little difference between being able to decide mere reachability for a given class of predicates, and being able to decide the whole of MSO over the same class of predicates.

3   Pseudo-Reachability and Robustness

In this section we discuss decision problems about pseudo-orbits that are related to robustness of computation. Given an LDS (M, x), recall that the orbit of x under M is the sequence $\langle x, Mx, M^2 x, \ldots \rangle$. We say that the sequence $\langle x_n : n \in \mathbb{N} \rangle$ is an ε-*pseudo-orbit* of x under M if $x_0 = x$ and $x_{n+1} = Mx_n + d_n$ for some perturbation d_n with $||d_n|| < \epsilon$. The *pseudo-orbit* of x under M is then defined as the set of points that are reachable from x via an ε-pseudo-orbit for every $\epsilon > 0$. This notion of an $(\varepsilon$-)pseudo-orbit, introduced and studied by Anosov [8], Bowen [17] and Conley [25], is an important conceptual tool in dynamical systems. From the computational perspective, an ε-pseudo-orbit can be viewed as a trajectory after a rounding error of magnitude at most ϵ is applied at each step.

Given these definitions, we can consider the reachability and model-checking problems for pseudo-orbits. A natural analogy to the Kannan-Lipton Orbit Problem is the *Pseudo-Orbit Problem*, which is to determine whether a target point y belongs to the pseudo-orbit of x under M. In [28] the authors show that, just like the Orbit Problem, the Pseudo-Orbit Problem is decidable in polynomial time. Generalising from points to sets, let us say that a target set T is pseudo-reachable if for every $\epsilon > 0$ there exists an ε-pseudo-orbit of x under M that reaches T. We can then define the *Pseudo-Skolem Problem* and the *Pseudo-Positivity Problem* to be the pseudo-reachability problems with a hyperplane and a halfspace as target sets, respectively. Surprisingly, [28] shows that both of these problems are in fact decidable! Moreover, [29] establishes decidability of pseudo-reachability with arbitrary semialgebraic targets for diagonalisable linear dynamical systems.

Inspired by the above results, one might consider the model-checking problem for pseudo-orbits, namely the problem of determining, given (M, x) and a formula φ, whether for every $\varepsilon > 0$, there exists an ε-pseudo-orbit that satisfies φ. After all, as discussed in the preceding section, for genuine orbits the fragments of the reachability problem and the full MSO model-checking problem that are known to be decidable (i.e., the restrictions on the class of predicates and the property φ that make the problems decidable) are essentially the same. This optimism is, however, quickly shattered by the following observation. Let H be a closed halfspace and φ be the property $\mathbf{G} H$ ("the trajectory always remains inside H"). Then the pseudo-orbits satisfy φ (in the sense defined above) if and only the (genuine) orbit satisfies φ. The problem of determining whether the orbit $\mathcal{O}(M, x)$ always remains in H, is however, equivalent to the problem of determining whether the orbit ever hits an open halfspace, which itself is the Positivity Problem (a longstanding open question).

4   Invariant Generation

In the absence of fully general algorithms to decide whether the orbit of a given LDS reaches targets of arbitrary forms, much effort has been expended on sound—but possibly incomplete—techniques, and particularly on constructing certificates of (non-)reachability. This splits into two broad lines of attack: ranking functions and invariants. The former are certificates of reachability, demonstrating that progress is being made towards the target. Inductive invariants are, on the other hand, certificates of non-reachability, establishing that the orbit will not reach the target by enclosing the former within a set that is itself disjoint from the latter. We focus in this section on the algorithmic generation of invariants.

More precisely, a set $\mathcal{I} \subseteq \mathbb{R}^d$ is said to be an *inductive invariant* of (M, x) if it contains x ($x \in \mathcal{I}$), and is stable under M, that is:

$$M\mathcal{I} \overset{\text{def}}{=} \{My : y \in \mathcal{I}\} \subseteq \mathcal{I}.$$

Clearly there are some trivial invariants, such as $\mathbb{R}^d$ and the orbit $\mathcal{O}(M, x)$ itself. They are not particularly useful in the sense that the ambient space $\mathbb{R}^d$ is never disjoint from whatever target might be under consideration, whereas for various classes of targets (such as hyperplanes or half-spaces; or more generally arbitrary semialgebraic sets) we do not in general know how to decide whether $\mathcal{O}(M, x)$ is disjoint from the target. Hence one does not seek *any* invariant, but rather an invariant that can be algorithmically established to be disjoint from the target.

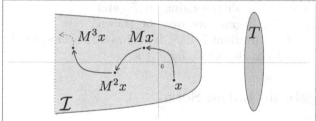

We therefore seek a sufficiently large, or expressive, class of invariants $\mathcal{F}$ which moreover exhibits favourable algorithmic properties. A natural family to consider is the collection of all semialgebraic sets. We now have:

Theorem 6 ([3]). *Given an LDS (M, x) in ambient space $\mathbb{R}^d$, together with a semialgebraic target $T \subseteq \mathbb{R}^d$, it is decidable whether there exists a semialgebraic invariant of (M, x) that is disjoint from T.*

Furthermore, the algorithm explicitly constructs the invariant when it exists, in the form of a Boolean combination of polynomial inequalities.

Theorem 6 holds for an even larger class $\mathcal{F}$, namely that of o-minimal sets. We give an informal definition. Recall the contents of Tarski's quantifier-elimination theorem, to the effect that semialgebraic subsets of $\mathbb{R}^d$ are closed under projections. Moreover, semialgebraic subsets of $\mathbb{R}$ are quite simple: they are finite unions of intervals. Other families of sets that enjoy these two properties exist, notably those definable in the first-order theory of the real numbers augmented with a symbol for the exponential function, an important result due to Wilkie [56]. Structures of $\mathbb{R}^d$ that are induced by such logical theories are called *o-minimal*, and an *o-minimal set* is a set that belongs to such a structure [30].

These include semialgebraic sets, as well as sets definable in the first-order theory of the reals with restricted analytic functions.

In [2], it is shown that it is decidable whether there exists an o-minimal invariant (for a given LDS (M, x)) that is disjoint from a semialgebraic target T; and moreover, when such an invariant exists, it is always possible to exhibit one that is in fact semialgebraic [3]. Once again, these results are effective, and the invariants can always be explicitly produced.

Varying the class of invariants and the class of targets gives rise to a number of natural questions that—for the most part—remain unexplored. Let us however mention a further desirable property enjoyed both by the class of o-minimal sets and that of semialgebraic sets: in either case, they admit *minimal families* of invariants, a notion which we now explain. Let $\mathcal{F}$ be a class of sets—either the class of o-minimal sets or that of semialgebraic sets. It is easy to verify that, in general, $\mathcal{F}$ does not possess minimal invariants. Nevertheless, [2,3] show how to produce a sequence of (M, x)-invariants $\langle \mathcal{C}_k : k \in \mathbb{N} \rangle$, all belonging to $\mathcal{F}$, and such that $\mathcal{C}_{k+1} \subset \mathcal{C}_k$. It can moreover be shown 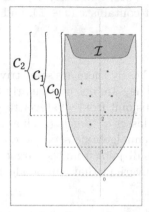 that, given any (M, x)-invariant $\mathcal{I} \in \mathcal{F}$, it is always the case that $\mathcal{I}$ contains one of the $\mathcal{C}_k$, and *ipso facto* also all $\mathcal{C}_j$ for $j \geq k$.

5   Semialgebraic Initial Sets

Up until now we have exclusively considered problems concerning the orbit $\mathcal{O}(M, x)$ of a *single* initial point x. It is natural to ask whether the algorithmic problems which we have discussed remain solvable if one instead considers an entire *set* of initial points $S \subseteq \mathbb{R}^d$. Unfortunately the answer is negative. We sketch below the proof of the undecidability of a natural model-checking problem.

Theorem 7. *The following problem is undecidable. Given a natural number $k \in \mathbb{N}$, a semialgebraic set $S \subseteq \mathbb{R}^d$, a $d \times d$ rational matrix M, and a hyperplane H in $\mathbb{R}^d$ (having rational normal vector), determine whether there exists $x \in S$ such that the orbit generated by (M, x) hits H at least k times.*

In symbols, whether there is some $x \in S$ such that

$$|\mathcal{O}(M, x) \cap H| \geq k$$

is undecidable.

It is worth noting that all the problems that we have discussed so far (including the Skolem and Positivity Problems) are not known to be undecidable, and are in fact widely conjectured to be decidable. It is therefore perhaps somewhat surprising that this natural generalisation of our setting immediately leads to undecidability.

The proof of Theorem 7 proceeds by reduction from a variant of Hilbert's tenth problem. Recall that Hilbert's tenth problem asks whether a given polynomial $P \in \mathbb{Z}[Y_1, Y_2, \ldots, Y_{d-1}]$ with integer coefficients and $d - 1$ variables has a root with all unknowns taking integer values. This problem is undecidable, as shown by Davis, Putnam, Robinson, and Matiyasevich [44].

The variant that we will reduce from asks whether the polynomial has roots with the unknowns being distinct natural numbers. It is straightforward to show that this variant is also undecidable.

Let $d \in \mathbb{N}$, $d > 1$, and $P \in \mathbb{Z}[Y_1, Y_2, \ldots, Y_{d-1}]$ be an arbitrary polynomial. We define the subset $S \subseteq \mathbb{R}^d$ via a formula of the first-order theory of the reals:

$$S(x_1, x_2, \ldots, x_d) \overset{\text{def}}{=} \exists y_1, y_2, \ldots y_{d-1} \begin{cases} 0 & = P(y_1, y_2, \ldots, y_{d-1}), \\ x_1 & = (1 - y_1)(1 - y_2) \cdots (1 - y_{d-1}), \\ x_2 & = (2 - y_1)(2 - y_2) \cdots (2 - y_{d-1}), \\ & \vdots \\ x_d & = (d - y_1)(d - y_2) \cdots (d - y_{d-1}). \end{cases}$$

A point $x := (x_1, \ldots, x_d) \in \mathbb{R}^d$ is in the set S if and only if one can find real numbers $y_1, \ldots, y_{d-1}$ for which the above equations hold. The idea behind this definition comes from the fact that, for $x, y_1, \ldots, y_{d-1}$ as above, one can construct a $d \times d$ matrix M with rational entries such that

$$(M^n x)_1 = (n - y_1)(n - y_2) \cdots (n - y_{d-1}),$$

for all $n \in \mathbb{N}$, where $(\cdot)_1$ refers to the first entry of the vector. Admitting the existence of such a matrix, let H be the hyperplane having normal vector $(1, 0, \ldots, 0)$ and going through the origin. Then clearly $\mathcal{O}(M, x)$ enters H at least $d - 1$ times if and only if the reals $y_1, \ldots, y_{d-1}$ are distinct natural numbers, because only then is the first entry of $M^n x$—the polynomial $(n - y_1) \cdots (n - y_{d-1})$—equal to zero.

The existence of the matrix M rests on the fact that the expression $u_n = (n - y_1) \cdots (n - y_{d-1})$ (for fixed $y_1, \ldots, y_{d-1}$) can be obtained as a linear recurrence sequence of order d, and in turn such a linear recurrence sequence can be represented as the sequence of fixed-position entries of increasing powers of a fixed $d \times d$ matrix M. In the standard construction of this matricial representation, one must in addition set $x_1 = u_1$, $x_2 = u_2$, $\ldots$, $x_d = u_d$, which is achieved through the definition of our initial semialgebraic set S.

It is worth noting that Theorem 7 holds even if k is fixed, due to the fact that Hilbert's tenth problem remains undecidable for a fixed number of variables. Furthermore, if k is fixed to be 1, then the problem becomes decidable in low dimensions, however even in the case where the ambient space has dimension 2 and $k = 2$, the problem does not seem to be trivially decidable.

6   Research Directions and Open Problems

We have presented an overview of the state of the art regarding decidability and solvability of a range of algorithmic problems for discrete linear dynamical systems, focussing on reachability, model-checking, and invariant-generation questions. In the case of model checking in particular, we have painted an essentially complete picture of what is achievable, both unconditionally as well as relative to Skolem oracles. We pointed out that extending the existing results further runs up against formidable mathematical obstacles (longstanding open problems in number theory); the work presented here therefore appears to lie at the very frontier of what is attainable, barring major breakthroughs in mathematics.

A central open question is whether Skolem oracles can actually be devised and implemented. As remarked earlier, a certifying algorithm for the Simple-Skolem Problem has recently been proposed, with termination relying on classical (and widely believed) number-theoretic conjectures. Whether similar algorithms can be obtained for the general Skolem Problem is the subject of active research.

An even more difficult question is whether oracles for the Positivity Problem (or Simple-Positivity Problem) can be devised. This would enable one to circumvent the mathematical obstacles mentioned earlier, and allow one to substantially extend the scope of semialgebraic model checking for linear dynamical systems. For the time being, this goal appears to be well out of reach.

In the present paper we have entirely confined ourselves to matters of decidability, largely on account of space limitations, but also because the complexity-theoretic picture is not nearly as clear-cut as its decidability counterpart. Providing a comprehensive account of the complexity landscape for linear dynamical systems would be an interesting and promising research direction.

A   Prefix-Independent Model Checking for LDS

The goal of this appendix is to exhibit boundaries on the extent to which Theorem 4 can be improved. More precisely, we show that the ability to solve the model-checking problem for arbitrary LDS against prefix-independent MSO specifications making use of semialgebraic predicates in ambient space $\mathbb{R}^4$ would necessarily entail major breakthroughs in Diophantine approximation.

We build upon the framework developed in [47, Sec. 5]. To this end, consider the class of order-6 rational LRS of the form

$$u_n = -n + \frac{1}{2}(n - ri)\lambda^n + \frac{1}{2}(n + ri)\overline{\lambda}^n = r\,\text{Im}(\lambda^n) - n(1 - \text{Re}(\lambda^n)),$$

where $\lambda \in \mathbb{Q}(i)$ and $|\lambda| = 1$, and $r \in \mathbb{Q}$. Let us write $\mathcal{L}$ to denote this class of LRS.

It is shown in [47] that solving the *Ultimate Positivity Problem* for LRS in $\mathcal{L}$, i.e., providing an algorithm which, given an LRS $\langle u_n \rangle_{n=0}^{\infty} \in \mathcal{L}$, determines whether there exists some integer N such that, for all $n \geq N$, $u_n \geq 0$, would necessarily entail major breakthroughs in the field of Diophantine approximation.

The purpose of the present section is to reduce the Ultimate Positivity Problem for LRS in $\mathcal{L}$ to the prefix-independent semialgebraic MSO model-checking problem for 4-dimensional LDS.

Given λ and r as above, let

$$
M = \begin{bmatrix} \operatorname{Re}(\lambda) & -\operatorname{Im}(\lambda) & 1 & 0 \\ \operatorname{Im}(\lambda) & \operatorname{Re}(\lambda) & 0 & 1 \\ 0 & 0 & \operatorname{Re}(\lambda) & -\operatorname{Im}(\lambda) \\ 0 & 0 & \operatorname{Im}(\lambda) & \operatorname{Re}(\lambda) \end{bmatrix} \text{ and } x = \begin{bmatrix} 1 \\ 1 \\ 1 \\ 1 \end{bmatrix}.
$$

Observe that M has rational entries. We have that

$$
M^n x = \begin{bmatrix} \operatorname{Re}(\lambda^n) - \operatorname{Im}(\lambda^n) + n\operatorname{Re}(\lambda^{n-1}) - n\operatorname{Im}(\lambda^{n-1}) \\ \operatorname{Im}(\lambda^n) + \operatorname{Re}(\lambda^n) + n\operatorname{Im}(\lambda^{n-1}) + n\operatorname{Re}(\lambda^{n-1}) \\ \operatorname{Re}(\lambda^n) - \operatorname{Im}(\lambda^n) \\ \operatorname{Im}(\lambda^n) + \operatorname{Re}(\lambda^n) \end{bmatrix}.
$$

As a semialgebraic target consider the set $S = \{x : p(x) > 0\}$, where

$$
p(x_1, x_2, x_3, x_4) = \frac{r}{2}(x_4 - x_3) - \frac{x_1 - x_3}{\operatorname{Re}(\lambda^{-1})x_3 - \operatorname{Im}(\lambda^{-1})x_4}\left(1 - \frac{x_3 + x_4}{2}\right).
$$

We now have that $p(M^n x) = r\operatorname{Im}(\lambda^n) - n(1 - \operatorname{Re}(\lambda^n))$, and that $\langle u_n \rangle_{n=0}^{\infty}$ is ultimately positive if and only if the orbit of x under M eventually gets trapped in S. This can be expressed by the prefix-independent LTL formula $\varphi = \mathbf{F}\,\mathbf{G}\,S$.

References

1. Agrawal, M., Akshay, S., Genest, B., Thiagarajan, P.S.: Approximate verification of the symbolic dynamics of Markov chains. J. ACM **62**(1), 2:1–2:34 (2015)
2. Almagor, S., Chistikov, D., Ouaknine, J., Worrell, J.: O-minimal invariants for linear loops. In: 45th International Colloquium on Automata, Languages, and Programming, ICALP 2018. LIPIcs, vol. 107, pp. 114:1–114:14. Schloss Dagstuhl - Leibniz-Zentrum für Informatik (2018)
3. Almagor, S., Chistikov, D., Ouaknine, J., Worrell, J.: O-minimal invariants for discrete-time dynamical systems. ACM Trans. Comput. Log. **23**(2), 9:1–9:20 (2022)
4. Almagor, S., Karimov, T., Kelmendi, E., Ouaknine, J., Worrell, J.: Deciding ω-regular properties on linear recurrence sequences. In: Proceedings of the ACM Programming Language 5(POPL), 1–24 (2021)
5. Almagor, S., Ouaknine, J., Worrell, J.: The polytope-collision problem. In: 44th International Colloquium on Automata, Languages, and Programming, ICALP 2017. LIPIcs, vol. 80, pp. 24:1–24:14. Schloss Dagstuhl - Leibniz-Zentrum für Informatik (2017)
6. Almagor, S., Ouaknine, J., Worrell, J.: The semialgebraic Orbit Problem. In: 36th International Symposium on Theoretical Aspects of Computer Science, STACS 2019. LIPIcs, vol. 126, pp. 6:1–6:15. Schloss Dagstuhl - Leibniz-Zentrum für Informatik (2019)
7. Almagor, S., Ouaknine, J., Worrell, J.: First-order orbit queries. Theory Comput. Syst. **65**(4), 638–661 (2021)

8. Anosov, D.V.: Geodesic flows on closed Riemannian manifolds of negative curvature. Proc. Steklov Inst. Math. **90** (1967)
9. Baier, C., et al.: The Orbit Problem for parametric linear dynamical systems (2021)
10. Ben-Amram, A.M., Doménech, J.J., Genaim, S.: Multiphase-linear ranking functions and their relation to recurrent sets. In: Chang, B.-Y.E. (ed.) SAS 2019. LNCS, vol. 11822, pp. 459–480. Springer, Cham (2019). https://doi.org/10.1007/978-3-030-32304-2_22
11. Ben-Amram, A.M., Genaim, S.: On the linear ranking problem for integer linear-constraint loops. In: The 40th Annual ACM SIGPLAN-SIGACT Symposium on Principles of Programming Languages, POPL 2013, pp. 51–62. ACM (2013)
12. Ben-Amram, A.M., Genaim, S.: Ranking functions for linear-constraint loops. J. ACM **61**(4), 26:1–26:55 (2014)
13. Ben-Amram, A.M., Genaim, S.: On multiphase-linear ranking functions. In: Majumdar, R., Kunčak, V. (eds.) CAV 2017. LNCS, vol. 10427, pp. 601–620. Springer, Cham (2017). https://doi.org/10.1007/978-3-319-63390-9_32
14. Berstel, J., Mignotte, M.: Deux propriétés décidables des suites récurrentes linéaires. Bull. Soc. Math. France **104**, 175–184 (1976)
15. Bilu, Y., Luca, F., Nieuwveld, J., Ouaknine, J., Purser, D., Worrell, J.: Skolem meets Schanuel. In: Szeider, S., Ganian, R., Silva, A. (eds.) 47th International Symposium on Mathematical Foundations of Computer Science, MFCS 2022, August 22–26, 2022, Vienna, Austria. LIPIcs, vol. 241, pp. 62:1–62:15. Schloss Dagstuhl - Leibniz-Zentrum für Informatik (2022)
16. Börger, E., Grädel, E., Gurevich, Y.: The Classical Decision Problem. Perspectives in Mathematical Logic, Springer, Heidelberg (1997)
17. Bowen, R.: Equilibrium States and the Ergodic Theory of Anosov Diffeomorphisms, Lecture Notes in Mathematics, vol. 470. Springer, Heidelberg (1975)
18. Bradley, A.R., Manna, Z., Sipma, H.B.: Termination analysis of integer linear loops. In: Abadi, M., de Alfaro, L. (eds.) CONCUR 2005. LNCS, vol. 3653, pp. 488–502. Springer, Heidelberg (2005). https://doi.org/10.1007/11539452_37
19. Braverman, M.: Termination of integer linear programs. In: Ball, T., Jones, R.B. (eds.) CAV 2006. LNCS, vol. 4144, pp. 372–385. Springer, Heidelberg (2006). https://doi.org/10.1007/11817963_34
20. Chen, H.Y., Flur, S., Mukhopadhyay, S.: Termination proofs for linear simple loops. Int. J. Softw. Tools Technol. Transf. **17**(1), 47–57 (2015)
21. Chonev, V., Ouaknine, J., Worrell, J.: The Orbit Problem in higher dimensions. In: Symposium on Theory of Computing Conference, STOC 2013, pp. 941–950. ACM (2013)
22. Chonev, V., Ouaknine, J., Worrell, J.: The polyhedron-hitting problem. In: Proceedings of the Twenty-Sixth Annual ACM-SIAM Symposium on Discrete Algorithms, SODA 2015, pp. 940–956. SIAM (2015)
23. Chonev, V., Ouaknine, J., Worrell, J.: On the complexity of the Orbit Problem. J. ACM **63**(3), 23:1–23:18 (2016)
24. Colóon, M.A., Sipma, H.B.: Synthesis of linear ranking functions. In: Margaria, T., Yi, W. (eds.) TACAS 2001. LNCS, vol. 2031, pp. 67–81. Springer, Heidelberg (2001). https://doi.org/10.1007/3-540-45319-9_6
25. Conley, C.C.: Isolated invariant sets and the Morse index, CBMS Regional Conference Series in Mathematics, vol. 25. American Mathematical Society (1978)
26. Cook, B., Podelski, A., Rybalchenko, A.: Termination proofs for systems code. In: Proceedings of the ACM SIGPLAN 2006 Conference on Programming Language Design and Implementation, pp. 415–426. ACM (2006)

27. Cook, B., Podelski, A., Rybalchenko, A.: TERMINATOR: beyond safety. In: Ball, T., Jones, R.B. (eds.) CAV 2006. LNCS, vol. 4144, pp. 415–418. Springer, Heidelberg (2006). https://doi.org/10.1007/11817963_37
28. D'Costa, J., et al.: The Pseudo-Skolem problem is decidable. In: Bonchi, F., Puglisi, S.J. (eds.) 46th International Symposium on Mathematical Foundations of Computer Science (MFCS 2021). Leibniz International Proceedings in Informatics (LIPIcs), vol. 202, pp. 34:1–34:21. Schloss Dagstuhl - Leibniz-Zentrum für Informatik, Dagstuhl, Germany (2021)
29. D'Costa, J., Karimov, T., Majumdar, R., Ouaknine, J., Salamati, M., Worrell, J.: The pseudo-reachability problem for diagonalisable linear dynamical systems. In: Szeider, S., Ganian, R., Silva, A. (eds.) 47th International Symposium on Mathematical Foundations of Computer Science, MFCS 2022, August 22–26, 2022, Vienna, Austria. LIPIcs, vol. 241, pp. 40:1–40:13. Schloss Dagstuhl - Leibniz-Zentrum für Informatik (2022)
30. Van den Dries, L.: Tame Topology and O-Minimal Structures, vol. 248. Cambridge University Press, Cambridge (1998)
31. Everest, G., van der Poorten, A.J., Shparlinski, I.E., Ward, T.: Recurrence Sequences, Mathematical Surveys and Monographs, vol. 104. American Mathematical Society (2003)
32. Halava, V., Harju, T., Hirvensalo, M.: Positivity of second order linear recurrent sequences. Discret. Appl. Math. **154**(3), 447–451 (2006)
33. Harrison, M.A.: Lectures on Linear Sequential Machines. Academic Press, New York (1969)
34. Hosseini, M., Ouaknine, J., Worrell, J.: Termination of linear loops over the integers. In: 46th International Colloquium on Automata, Languages, and Programming, ICALP 2019. LIPIcs, vol. 132, pp. 118:1–118:13. Schloss Dagstuhl - Leibniz-Zentrum für Informatik (2019)
35. Kannan, R., Lipton, R.J.: The Orbit Problem is decidable. In: Proceedings of the 12th Annual ACM Symposium on Theory of Computing 1980, pp. 252–261. ACM (1980)
36. Kannan, R., Lipton, R.J.: Polynomial-time algorithm for the Orbit Problem. J. ACM **33**(4), 808–821 (1986)
37. Karimov, T., et al.: What's decidable about linear loops? In: Proceedings of the ACM Programming Languages 6(POPL), pp. 1–25 (2022)
38. Karimov, T., Ouaknine, J., Worrell, J.: On LTL model checking for low-dimensional discrete linear dynamical systems. In: 45th International Symposium on Mathematical Foundations of Computer Science, MFCS 2020. LIPIcs, vol. 170, pp. 54:1–54:14. Schloss Dagstuhl - Leibniz-Zentrum für Informatik (2020)
39. Laohakosol, V., Tangsupphathawat, P.: Positivity of third order linear recurrence sequences. Discrete Appl. Math. **157**(15), 3239–3248 (2009)
40. Lipton, R.J., Luca, F., Nieuwveld, J., Ouaknine, J., Worrell, D.P.J.: On the Skolem Problem and the Skolem Conjecture. In: 37th Annual ACM/IEEE Symposium on Logic in Computer Science, LICS 2022, Haifa, Israel, 2 August– 5 August 2022. ACM (2022)
41. Luca, F., Ouaknine, J., Worrell, J.: Universal Skolem sets. In: 36th Annual ACM/IEEE Symposium on Logic in Computer Science, LICS 2021, Rome, Italy, 29 June–2 July 2021, pp. 1–6. IEEE (2021)
42. Luca, F., Ouaknine, J., Worrell, J.: Algebraic model checking for discrete linear dynamical systems. In: Bogomolov, S., Parker, D. (eds.) FORMATS 2022. LNCS, vol .13465, pp. 3–15. Springer, Cham (2022). https://doi.org/10.1007/978-3-031-15839-1_1

43. Luca, F., Ouaknine, J., Worrell, J.: A universal Skolem set of positive lower density. In: Szeider, S., Ganian, R., Silva, A. (eds.) 47th International Symposium on Mathematical Foundations of Computer Science, MFCS 2022, Vienna, Austria, 22–26 August 2022, LIPIcs, vol. 241, pp. 73:1–73:12. Schloss Dagstuhl - Leibniz-Zentrum für Informatik (2022)

44. Matiyasevich, Y.V.: Hilbert's Tenth Problem. MIT Press, Cambridge (1993)

45. McConnell, R.M., Mehlhorn, K., Näher, S., Schweitzer, P.: Certifying algorithms. Comput. Sci. Rev. **5**(2), 119–161 (2011)

46. Ouaknine, J., Worrell, J.: On the positivity problem for simple linear recurrence sequences'. In: Esparza, J., Fraigniaud, P., Husfeldt, T., Koutsoupias, E. (eds.) ICALP 2014. LNCS, vol. 8573, pp. 318–329. Springer, Heidelberg (2014). https://doi.org/10.1007/978-3-662-43951-7_27

47. Ouaknine, J., Worrell, J.: Positivity problems for low-order linear recurrence sequences. In: Proceedings of the Twenty-Fifth Annual ACM-SIAM Symposium on Discrete Algorithms, SODA 2014, pp. 366–379. SIAM (2014)

48. Ouaknine, J., Worrell, J.: Ultimate positivity is decidable for simple linear recurrence sequences. In: Esparza, J., Fraigniaud, P., Husfeldt, T., Koutsoupias, E. (eds.) ICALP 2014. LNCS, vol. 8573, pp. 330–341. Springer, Heidelberg (2014). https://doi.org/10.1007/978-3-662-43951-7_28

49. Ouaknine, J., Worrell, J.: On linear recurrence sequences and loop termination. ACM SIGLOG News **2**(2), 4–13 (2015)

50. Podelski, A., Rybalchenko, A.: A complete method for the synthesis of linear ranking functions. In: Steffen, B., Levi, G. (eds.) VMCAI 2004. LNCS, vol. 2937, pp. 239–251. Springer, Heidelberg (2004). https://doi.org/10.1007/978-3-540-24622-0_20

51. Podelski, A., Rybalchenko, A.: Transition invariants. In: 19th IEEE Symposium on Logic in Computer Science (LICS 2004), pp. 32–41. IEEE Computer Society (2004)

52. Tarasov, S., Vyalyi, M.: Orbits of linear maps and regular languages. In: Kulikov, A., Vereshchagin, N. (eds.) CSR 2011. LNCS, vol. 6651, pp. 305–316. Springer, Heidelberg (2011). https://doi.org/10.1007/978-3-642-20712-9_24

53. Tijdeman, R., Mignotte, M., Shorey, T.N.: The distance between terms of an algebraic recurrence sequence. J. für die reine und angewandte Mathematik **349**, 63–76 (1984)

54. Tiwari, A.: Termination of linear programs. In: Alur, R., Peled, D.A. (eds.) CAV 2004. LNCS, vol. 3114, pp. 70–82. Springer, Heidelberg (2004). https://doi.org/10.1007/978-3-540-27813-9_6

55. Vereshchagin, N.: The problem of appearance of a zero in a linear recurrence sequence. Mat. Zametki **38**(2), 609–615 (1985)

56. Wilkie, A.J.: Model completeness results for expansions of the ordered field of real numbers by restricted Pfaffian functions and the exponential function. J. Am. Math. Soc. **9**(4), 1051–1094 (1996)

Symbolic Analysis of Linear Hybrid Automata – 25 Years Later

Goran Frehse[1]($\boxtimes$)(iD), Mirco Giacobbe[2](iD), and Enea Zaffanella[3](iD)

[1] U2IS, ENSTA Paris, Institut Polytechnique de Paris, Paris, France
goran.frehse@ensta-paris.fr
[2] School of Computer Science, University of Birmingham, Birmingham, UK
m.giacobbe@bham.ac.uk
[3] Department of Mathematical, Physical and Computer Sciences,
University of Parma, Parma, Italy
enea.zaffanella@unipr.it

Abstract. We present a collection of advances in the algorithmic verification of hybrid automata with piecewise linear derivatives, so-called Linear Hybrid Automata. New ways to represent and compute with polyhedra, in combination with heuristic algorithmic improvements, have led to considerable speed-ups in checking safety properties through set propagation. We also showcase a CEGAR-style approach that iteratively constructs a polyhedral abstraction. We illustrate the efficiency and scalability of both approaches with two sets of benchmarks.

1 Introduction

Hybrid automata are a modeling paradigm that combines finite state machines with differential equations in order to capture processes in which discrete, event-based, behavior interacts with continuous, time-based behavior. They came to rise in the beginning of the 1990s, throughout a collaboration of scientists from various disciplines, notably computer scientists and control theorists. By that time, formal methods such as abstract interpretation [19] and model checking [18,44] had demonstrated their potential to increase the trustworthiness of safety critical software and digital hardware designs. The goal was to develop similar techniques for discrete systems that interact with processes that can be described by differential equations, like some mechanical or biological processes, so-called *hybrid systems*. In *The Theory of Hybrid Automata*, whose first version was published 25 years ago in 1996, Tom Henzinger pointed out a class of hybrid automata that hit a particular sweet spot for the purposes of symbolic (set-based) analysis: *linear hybrid automata* (LHA). LHA are characterized by linear predicates over the continuous variables and the evolution of the continuous variables is governed by differential inclusions that depend only on the discrete state, not the continuous variables themselves. LHA readily lend themselves as sound abstractions of complex natural and technical processes and as asymptotically complete approximations of a large class of hybrid automata [35]. While properties like safety are not decidable for LHA, the states reachable over a given

© Springer Nature Switzerland AG 2022
J.-F. Raskin and K. Chatterjee (Eds.): Principles of Systems Design, LNCS 13660, pp. 39–60, 2022.
https://doi.org/10.1007/978-3-031-22337-2_3

finite path can be computed exactly and symbolically, in the form of continuous sets associated to discrete states. In a sense, the continuous time domain can be abstracted away for LHA, so that the symbolic analysis resembles that of linear programs. Consequently, techniques from linear program analysis, such as the polyhedral computations in [30], could be applied. This led to symbolic analysis tools such as the pioneering model checker HyTech [33]. Since then, much research effort has been invested in making symbolic analysis more efficient, in order to scale up to systems of practical interest.

In this paper, we present a selection of techniques that, applied to the symbolic analysis of LHA, have led to performance improvements of several orders of magnitude since the days of HyTech. We focus entirely on safety properties encoded as *reachability* problems, i.e., whether a state is reachable from any state in a given set of initial states. We start with a simple fixed-point algorithm for computing reachable sets of states, using convex polyhedra as set representations. We then present various advances in polyhedral computations as well as efficient abstractions that serve as heuristics to speed up the fixed-point algorithm, and illustrate the performance gains with experiments. As an alternative approach, we also present a technique based on the CEGAR (Counter-Example Guided Abstraction Refinement) paradigm. Starting from an initial, coarse abstraction, the finite-path encoding of LHA is used to iteratively refine the abstraction until either a counterexample has been found or the system is proved safe. Our overview is far from exhaustive and limited to work by the authors. We point the reader to the references in [1,3,40,51] for related work. Other CEGAR approaches are implemented, e.g., in the tools HARE [46] and HyCOMP/IC3 [13]. To take an instance of an entirely different approach, we point to the work in [43], where LHA are encoded as linear programs, which are then analyzed by the software model checker ARMC. Bounded model checking for LHA has been implemented in the tool BACH [14].

The remainder of the paper is structured as follows. In Sect. 2, we define linear hybrid automata and give a brief overview on set-based reachability. In Sect. 3 we show how set-based reachability can be implemented efficiently, either exactly or by resorting to overapproximations. In Sect. 4 we present a CEGAR framework than can further enhance scalability. In Sect. 5, a series of experiments illustrates the impact of the different approaches and techniques on performance. Finally, we conclude in Sect. 6.

2   Symbolic Analysis of Linear Hybrid Automata

Hybrid automata describe the evolution of a set of real-valued variables over time. In this section, we give a formal definition of hybrid automata and their behaviors, and illustrate the concept with an example. But first, we introduce some notation for describing real-valued variables and sets of these values in the form of predicates and polyhedra.

2.1 Preliminaries

Variables: Let $X = \{x_1, \ldots, x_n\}$ be a finite set of *variables*. A *valuation* over X is written as $x \in \mathbb{R}^X$ or $x : X \to \mathbb{R}$. We use the primed variables $X' = \{x'_1, \ldots, x'_n\}$ to denote successor values and the dotted variables $\dot{X} = \{\dot{x}_1, \ldots, \dot{x}_n\}$ to denote the derivatives of the variables with respect to time. Given a set of variables $Y \subseteq X$, the *projection* $y = x \downarrow_Y$ is a valuation over Y that maps each variable in Y to the same value that it has in x. We may simply use a vector $x \in \mathbb{R}^n$ if it is clear from the context which index of the vector corresponds to which variable. We denote the i-th element of a vector x as x_i or $x(i)$ if the former is ambiguous. In the following, we use $\mathbb{R}^n$ instead of $\mathbb{R}^X$ except when the correspondence between indices and variables is not obvious, e.g., when valuations over different sets of variables are involved.

Predicates: A *predicate* over X is an expression that, given a valuation x over X, can be evaluated to either true or false. A *linear constraint* is a predicate $a_1 x_1 + a_2 x_2 + \cdots + a_n x_n \bowtie b$, where $a_1, \ldots a_n$ and b are real-valued constants, and whose sign may be strict or nonstrict (i.e., $\bowtie \in \{<, \leq\}$). A linear constraint is written in vector notation as $a^\mathsf{T} x \bowtie b$, with coefficient vector $a \in \mathbb{R}^n$ and inhomogeneous coefficient $b \in \mathbb{R}$. A *halfspace* $\mathcal{H} \subseteq \mathbb{R}^n$ is the set of points satisfying a linear constraint. A predicate over X defines a continuous set, which is the subset of $\mathbb{R}^X$ on which the predicate evaluates to true.

Polyhedra: A conjunction of finitely many linear constraints defines a polyhedron in *constraint form*, also called $\mathcal{H}$-*polyhedron*,

$$\mathcal{P} = \left\{ x \ \Big| \ \bigwedge_{i=1}^{m} a_i^\mathsf{T} x \bowtie_i b_i \right\}, \text{ with } \bowtie_i \in \{<, \leq\},$$

with *facet normals* $a_i \in \mathbb{R}^n$ and *inhomogeneous coefficients* $b_i \in \mathbb{R}$. A bounded polyhedron is called a *polytope*. Note that the set of constraints defining $\mathcal{P}$ is not necessarily unique. The representation of a polyhedron has a big impact on the computational cost of different geometric operations. Other representations for polyhedra can be more efficient for model checking, and will be discussed in detail in Sect. 3.

2.2 Linear Hybrid Automata

We now give a formal definition of a linear hybrid automaton and its run semantics.

Definition 1 (Linear Hybrid Automaton). *[2, 32, 36] A linear hybrid automaton $H = (X, \mathsf{Loc}, \mathsf{Edg}, \mathsf{Lab}, \mathsf{Init}, \mathsf{Inv}, \mathsf{Flow}, \mathsf{Jump}, \mathsf{Event})$ consists of*

- *a finite set of variables $X = \{x_1, \ldots, x_n\}$, partitioned into uncontrolled variables U and controlled variables Y;*
- *a finite directed multigraph $(\mathsf{Loc}, \mathsf{Edg})$, called the control graph, which consists of a set of locations $\mathsf{Loc} = \{\ell_1, \ldots, \ell_m\}$ that represent discrete modes, and a set of edges Edg that represent discrete transitions between modes;*

- *a finite set of synchronization labels* Lab*;*
- *a polyhedral constraint over variables* Inv$(\ell) \in \mathbb{R}^X$ *called invariant or staying condition, which restricts the values the variables can possibly take over location* $\ell \in$ Loc*; a state of H consists of a location* ℓ *and a value* $x \in$ Inv(ℓ) *for the variables, and is denoted by* $s = (\ell, x)$*;*
- *a polyhedral constraint* Init$(\ell) \subseteq$ Inv(ℓ) *called initial condition, which determines the set of initial values for the variables at location* $\ell \in$ Loc*; every behavior of H must start in one of the initial conditions;*
- *a polyhedral constraint over dotted variables* Flow$(\ell) \subseteq \mathbb{R}^{\dot{X}}$ *called flow condition, which gives for each location* $\ell \in$ Loc *the set of possible derivatives a trajectory can possibly take using a differential inclusion such as* $\dot{x} \in$ Flow(ℓ)*;*
- *a polyhedral constraint* Jump$(e) \subseteq \mathbb{R}^X \times \mathbb{R}^{X'}$ *over unprimed and primed variables called jump relation, which defines the set of possible successors* x' *of* x *when transition* $e \in$ Edg *is taken; jump relations are typically given by a polyhedral guard constraint* $\mathcal{G}_e \subseteq \mathbb{R}^X$ *and an affine assignment (or reset)* $x' = r_e(x)$ *as* Jump$(e) = \{(x, x') \mid x \in \mathcal{G}_e \wedge x' = r_e(x)\}$*; also, under certain definitions, every location* ℓ *is associated with an uncontrolled transition* $\bar{e} \in$ Edg *from* l *to itself and jump relation defined as* Jump$(\bar{e}) = \{(x, x') \mid x' \downarrow_Y = x \downarrow_Y \wedge x' \in$ Inv$(\ell)\}$*, which represents arbitrary assignments that the environment might perform on the uncontrolled variables* $U = X \setminus Y$*;*
- *an event function* Event$(e) \in$ Lab$\cup \{\tau\}$ *that maps every edge* $e \in$ Edg *to either a synchronization label or the internal event* τ*; uncontrolled transitions are always mapped to* τ*.*

We define the behavior of a hybrid automaton with a *run*: starting from one of the initial states, the state evolves according to the differential equations whilst time passes, and according to the jump relations when taking an (instantaneous) transition.

Definition 2 (Run semantics). *A run of H is a sequence*

$$(\ell_0, x_0) \xrightarrow[e_1]{\delta_0} (\ell_0, y_0) \xrightarrow[e_1]{\alpha_1} (\ell_1, x_1) \xrightarrow[e_2]{\delta_1} (\ell_1, y_1) \xrightarrow[e_2]{\alpha_2} \dots \xrightarrow{\delta_k} (\ell_k, y_k),$$

that satisfies for the three conditions listed below.

1. Initialisation: *the first state satisfies an initial condition, i.e.,* $x_0 \in$ Init(ℓ_0).
2. Continuous flow: *for every* $i = 0, \dots, k$, *there exist a trajectory* $\xi : [0, \delta_i] \to \mathbb{R}^X$ *from* x_i *to* y_i *and with dwell time* $\delta_i \in \mathbb{R}_{\geq 0}$ *over location* l_i, *that is,* ξ *is a continuously differentiable function such that* $\xi(0) = x_i$, $\xi(\delta_i) = y_i$, *and it holds true that* $\dot{\xi}(t) \in$ Flow(ℓ_i) *and* $\xi(t) \in$ Inv(ℓ_i) *for all* $t \in [0, \delta_i]$.
3. Discontinuous jumps: *for every* $i = 1, \dots, k$ *we have that* $e_i \in$ Edg *has source* ℓ_{i-1} *and destination* ℓ_i, $\alpha_i =$ Event(e_i), *and* $(y_{i-1}, x_i) \in$ Jump(e_i).

A state (ℓ, x) *is reachable if there exists a run with* $(\ell_i, x_i) = (\ell, x)$ *for some* i.

The existence of a run can be reduced to satisfiability of a conjunction of linear constraints. This has been exploited to synthesise parameters [27] and in Counter Example Guided Abstraction Refinement (CEGAR) frameworks [38], which we

data: lists of symbolic states W and R, initially empty

1 **foreach** $\ell \in$ Loc *s.t.* Init$(\ell) \neq \emptyset$ **do**
2       $\mathcal{P} \leftarrow \mathsf{post}_C(l, \mathsf{Init}(\ell))$;
3   push $(\ell, \mathcal{P})$ into the waiting list W;

4 **while** $W \neq \emptyset$ **do**
5   pop $(\ell, \mathcal{P})$ from W;
6   **if** $\mathcal{P} \subseteq \mathcal{P}''$ *and* $\ell = \ell''$ *for some* $(\ell'', \mathcal{P}'') \in R \cup W$ **then**
7   **continue**;

8   **foreach** $e \in$ Edg *with source* l *and destination* l' **do**
9           $\mathcal{P}' \leftarrow \mathsf{post}_C(\ell', \mathsf{post}_D(e, \mathcal{P}))$;
10   push $(\ell', \mathcal{P}')$ into W;

11   add $(\ell, \mathcal{P})$ to the passed list R;

Algorithm 1: Symbolic analysis procedure.

will discuss in more detail in Sect. 4. It also follows from these semantics that with a simple model transformation,[1] a LHA can be verified by model checkers able to handle linear constraints over the rationals, see [43].

2.3   Symbolic Analysis

A standard method to compute the reachable states is to iterate the following *one-step successor* operators for discrete and continuous transitions. Given a set of variables valuations $S \subseteq \mathbb{R}^n$, let $\mathsf{post}_C(\ell, S)$ be the set of valuations reachable by letting time elapse from any valuation in S over location $\ell \in$ Loc,

$$\mathsf{post}_C(\ell, S) = \left\{ y \,\middle|\, \exists x \in S, \delta \in \mathbb{R}_{\geq 0} : (\ell, x) \xrightarrow{\delta} (\ell, y) \right\}. \tag{1}$$

Let $\mathsf{post}_D(e, S)$ be the set of valuations resulting from transition $e \in$ Edg from any valuation in S

$$\mathsf{post}_D(e, S) = \left\{ x' \,\middle|\, \exists x \in S : (\ell, x) \xrightarrow[e]{\alpha} (\ell', x') \right\}, \tag{2}$$

where ℓ and ℓ' are source and target locations of e and $\alpha = $ Event(e).

Starting from the initial states, post_C and post_D are applied in alternation along the structure of the control graph. In model checkers such as HyTech [33], PHAVer [22] and SpaceEx [28], the symbolic analysis of a linear hybrid automaton is performed using *symbolic states* $s = (\ell, \mathcal{P})$, where $\ell \in$ Loc and $\mathcal{P}$ is a polyhedron. Computing the timed successors post_C of a symbolic state $s = (\ell, \mathcal{P})$ produces a new symbolic state $s' = (\ell, \mathcal{P}')$. Computing the jump successors post_D of $s = (\ell, \mathcal{P})$ involves iterating over all outgoing transitions of ℓ, and produces a set of symbolic states, each in one of the target locations. A *waiting list* contains the symbolic states whose successors still need to be explored, and a *passed list* contains all symbolic states computed so far. The fixed-point computation proceeds according to the steps below.

---
[1] It suffices to introduce a variable for the elapsed time in each location.

1. Initialization: compute the continuous successors of the initial states, put them on the waiting list, and proceed to step 2.
2. Containment checking: pop a symbolic state $s = (\ell, \mathcal{P})$ from the waiting list and check whether it has been encountered before, i.e., it is subsumed by some symbolic state in passed or waiting list. Repeat step 2 until either the waiting list is empty or a never encountered state is found. If the waiting list is empty, terminate and return. If a new state is found, proceed to step 3.
3. Post computation: compute all one-step successors $\mathsf{post}_C(\ell', \mathsf{post}_D(e, \mathcal{P}))$ of s along all transition e that are outgoing from ℓ (and have destination ℓ') and push them to the waiting list. Add s to the passed list and repeat step 2.

Upon termination of the procedure (which happens empirically, and is not guaranteed in general), the passed list R represents the whole set of reachable states.

An important aspect of the fixed point algorithm outlined above is that it attempts to reduce redundant exploration. This is taken care of by step 2, resp. line 6 in Algorithm 1, which implicitly performs the following operations:

2.1 it discards states that are contained in any symbolic state on the passed list,
2.2 it discards states that are contained in any remaining symbolic state on the waiting list—this is known as *waiting list filtering*.

Note that filtering the waiting list is a heuristic, which may or may not lead to an efficiency improvement with respect to a containment check over the passed list only; however, in practice, it leads to savings in computational time which compensates for the overhead of comparing a large number of symbolic states.

3   Implementing Symbolic Analysis Using Polyhedra

In this section we briefly describe how to implement the symbolic analysis outlined in Sect. 2.3 when adopting a domain of convex polyhedra for the representation of symbolic states.

The Double Description Method

Even though there exist polyhedra libraries that are exclusively based on the constraint form,[2] the classical approach [20] is based on the Double Description (DD) method [42], where the constraint form is paired with a *generator form* and conversion algorithms [16] can compute each representation from the other, removing redundancies so as to obtain minimal descriptions, as well as keeping them in synch after an incremental update. Polyhedra libraries based on the DD method include PolyLib (www.irisa.fr/polylib/), ELINA [50], NewPolka in Apron [37], PPL (Parma Polyhedra Library) [6], and PPLite [10]; the last three also support strict linear constraints.

---

[2] For instance, VPL (Verified Polyhedron Library) [12].

Generator Form and $\mathcal{V}$-Polyhedra. The classical definition of generators for closed polyhedra has been extended in [6] to the case of NNC (not necessarily closed) polyhedra. Namely, an $\mathcal{H}$-polyhedron can be equivalently represented in generator form by three finite sets (P, C, R), where $P \subseteq \mathbb{R}^n$ is a set of *points* of $\mathcal{P}$ (including its vertices), $C \subseteq \mathbb{R}^n$ is a set of *closure points*, and $R \subseteq \mathbb{R}^n$ is a set of *rays*. The generator form defines a $\mathcal{V}$ *-polyhedron* as

$$\mathcal{P} = \left\{ \sum_{p_i \in P} \pi_i \cdot p_i + \sum_{c_j \in C} \gamma_j \cdot c_j + \sum_{r_k \in R} \rho_k \cdot r_k \; \middle| \; \begin{array}{l} \pi_i \geq 0, \gamma_j \geq 0, \rho_k \geq 0, \\ \sum_i \pi_i + \sum_j \gamma_j = 1, \sum_i \pi_i \neq 0, \end{array} \right\}$$

which consists of the convex hull of points and closure points, extended towards infinity along the directions of the rays; the requirement that at least one point p_i positively contributes to the convex combination means that the closure points, which are in the topological closure of $\mathcal{P}$, are not necessarily contained in $\mathcal{P}$.

Both NewPolka and PPL, following the approach outlined in [30,31] and further developed in [5], use an additional slack variable (usually named ϵ) to encode the strict constraints as nonstrict ones, obtaining closed ϵ-*representations* of the NNC polyhedra. While allowing for a simple reuse of the classical conversion algorithms, this choice easily leads to a significant computation overhead. In contrast, the PPLite library is based on a *direct representation* for the strict constraints, leveraging on enhanced versions of the Chernikova procedures [7,8] fully supporting the use of strict constraints and closure points.

Converting Between $\mathcal{H}$ and $\mathcal{V}$ Representations. No matter if using the direct or the slack variable representation, the core algorithmic step of the DD method $\langle \mathcal{H}, \mathcal{V} \rangle \xrightarrow{\beta} \langle \mathcal{H}', \mathcal{V}' \rangle$ modifies a DD pair by adding a single constraint (resp., generator) β. From this, the conversion procedure computing the generator form $\mathcal{V} = \mathcal{V}_m$ for a given constraint form $\mathcal{H} = \{\beta_0, \ldots, \beta_m\}$ is obtained by *incrementally* processing the constraints, starting from a DD pair $\langle \mathcal{H}_0, \mathcal{V}_0 \rangle \equiv \mathbb{R}^n$ representing the whole vector space:

$$\langle \mathcal{H}_0, \mathcal{V}_0 \rangle \xrightarrow{\beta_0} \ldots \xrightarrow{\beta_{k-1}} \langle \mathcal{H}_k, \mathcal{V}_k \rangle \xrightarrow{\beta_k} \langle \mathcal{H}_{k+1}, \mathcal{V}_{k+1} \rangle \xrightarrow{\beta_{k+1}} \ldots \xrightarrow{\beta_m} \langle \mathcal{H}_m, \mathcal{V}_m \rangle.$$

The conversion from generators to constraints works similarly, starting from a DD pair representing the empty polyhedron and incrementally adding the generators. The same approach can also be used to compute the *set intersection* $\mathcal{P}_1 \cap \mathcal{P}_2$ (resp., the *convex polyhedral hull* $\mathcal{P}_1 \uplus \mathcal{P}_2$) of polyhedra $\mathcal{P}_1 \equiv \langle \mathcal{H}_1, \mathcal{V}_1 \rangle$ and $\mathcal{P}_2 \equiv \langle \mathcal{H}_2, \mathcal{V}_2 \rangle$: the constraints in $\mathcal{H}_2$ (resp., the generators in $\mathcal{V}_2$) are incrementally added to the DD pair describing $\mathcal{P}_1$.

Cartesian Factoring. Converting between $\mathcal{H}$ and $\mathcal{V}$ polyhedra has a worst case complexity that is exponential in the size of the input representation; it is therefore essential to keep representations small, e.g., by removing redundancies. Cartesian factoring [29] can greatly reduce the space needed to represent a $\mathcal{V}$-polyhedron. The space dimensions $X = \{x_1, \ldots, x_n\}$ are *partitioned* into a sequence of blocks $(B_1, \ldots, B_k)$ so that each linear constraint

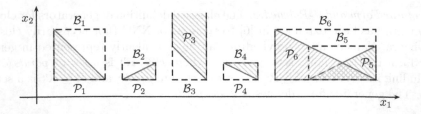

Fig. 1. Incomplete decision procedures speed up the containment checks.

in the $\mathcal{H}$-representation mentions the dimensions of a single block B_i; then, the $\mathcal{H}$-polyhedron $\mathcal{P}$ is factored into k polyhedra $(\mathcal{P}_1, \ldots, \mathcal{P}_k)$; if needed, these $\mathcal{H}$-polyhedra are converted to a sequence of $\mathcal{V}$-polyhedra. This can be much more efficient in time and space compared to a direct conversion. The ELINA library [50] uses a very efficient implementation of Cartesian factoring; the technique is also implemented in PPLite.

Implementation of Containment Checks

The overall efficiency of the procedure computing the set of reachable states is deeply affected by the efficiency of the polyhedra containment check. When using the DD method, the inclusion test $\mathcal{P}_1 \subseteq \mathcal{P}_2$ is implemented by checking that all the m_1 generators of $\mathcal{P}_1$ satisfy all the m_2 constraints of $\mathcal{P}_2$. In the worst case, i.e., when the inclusion holds, this amounts to the computation of $m_1 \cdot m_2$ scalar products, each one requiring $\mathcal{O}(n)$ arbitrary precision multiplications and additions, where n is the number of variables.

As shown in [9], impressive efficiency improvements can be obtained by exploiting the fact that each one-step successor state s'_i is checked against all the states stored in the passed list before being added to the passed and waiting lists. It is therefore possible to compute, and cache for reuse, simpler abstractions of the polyhedra that are enough to quickly semi-decide the containment check. The *boxed polyhedra* proposal in [9] uses a two-level scheme, where each polyhedron $\mathcal{P}_i$ is abstracted into its bounding box $\mathcal{B}_i$, which in turn is further abstracted in the *pseudo-volume* information.[3]

Figure 1 shows a few examples, where for each polyhedron $\mathcal{P}_i$ (solid blue) we draw the corresponding bounding box $\mathcal{B}_i$ (dashed black). Intuitively, we know that $\mathcal{P}_1 \not\subseteq \mathcal{P}_2$ because $\mathrm{vol}(\mathcal{B}_1) > \mathrm{vol}(\mathcal{B}_2)$; we know that $\mathcal{P}_3 \not\subseteq \mathcal{P}_1$ because num_rays$(\mathcal{B}_3) = 1 > 0 =$ num_rays$(\mathcal{B}_1)$; we know that $\mathcal{P}_2 \not\subseteq \mathcal{P}_4$ because $\mathcal{B}_2 \not\subseteq \mathcal{B}_4$ (even though $\mathrm{vol}(\mathcal{B}_2) = \mathrm{vol}(\mathcal{B}_4)$ and num_rays$(\mathcal{B}_2) =$ num_rays$(\mathcal{B}_4)$); finally, when checking whether or not $\mathcal{P}_5 \subseteq \mathcal{P}_6$, since $\mathcal{B}_5 \subseteq \mathcal{B}_6$ no semi-decision procedure applies and we need to resort to the more expensive polyhedra containment check.

---

[3] Roughly speaking, the volume of the box, in the case of a polytope; or the number of rays of the box, in the case of an unbounded polyhedron.

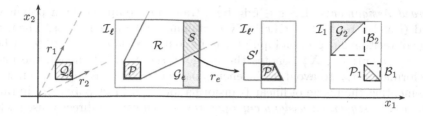

Fig. 2. Continuous and discrete post operators.

Implementing the Continuous Post Operator

For a fixed location ℓ, the flow relation of an LHA is specified by a polyhedron $\mathcal{Q}_\ell = \mathsf{Flow}(\ell)$ describing the possible values of the first time derivatives of the system variables. The possible trajectories starting from the states in polyhedron $\mathcal{P}$ are obtained by the *time-elapse* operator:

$$\mathcal{P} \nearrow \mathcal{Q}_\ell = \{\, p + t \cdot q \mid p \in \mathcal{P}, q \in \mathcal{Q}_\ell, t \in \mathbb{R}, t \geq 0 \,\}. \tag{3}$$

Assuming that $\mathcal{Q}_\ell$ is a closed $\mathcal{V}$-polyhedron described by generators (P, C, R), where $C = \emptyset$, the set $\mathcal{P} \nearrow \mathcal{Q}_\ell$ is a convex polyhedron that can be computed by (incrementally) adding to $\mathcal{P}$ the finite set of *rays* $R' = P \cup R$ [30].[4]

An example of applying the continuous post operator to a symbolic state $(\ell, \mathcal{P})$ is shown on the left hand side of Fig. 2. Suppose that $\mathcal{I}_\ell = \mathsf{Inv}(\ell)$ and $\mathcal{Q}_\ell = \mathsf{Flow}(\ell)$ are the polyhedra representing the invariant and the flow condition for location ℓ. Then, $\mathsf{post}_C(\ell, \mathcal{P}) = (\mathcal{P} \nearrow \mathcal{Q}_\ell) \cap \mathcal{I}_\ell = \mathcal{R},$[5] is computed by first adding rays r_1 and r_2 to $\mathcal{P}$ and then computing set intersection to restore the invariant $\mathcal{I}_\ell$.

Implementing the Discrete Post Operator

The discrete post operator can be implemented by combining several lower level operators on the polyhedra domain.

Uncontrolled Assignments. Consider first the case of an uncontrolled assignment to the variables in the set $U \subseteq X$. In order to avoid projection (which would imply a change of space dimension), this can be implemented by the existential quantification of the variables in U, followed by the intersection with the location invariant. When using the DD method, existential quantification is obtained by (incrementally) adding the set of rays $R_U = \{\, e_u, -e_u \mid u \in U \,\}$, where each e_u is the standard basis vector for variable u.[6]

---

[4] Not all polyhedra libraries directly support this operator: PPL/PPLite provide an operator named *time_elapse_assign*; the Apron interface defines an equivalent function named *add_ray_array*; the operator is not available in ELINA and VPL.

[5] Polyhedron $\mathcal{R}$ is shown with a blue border; it contains both $\mathcal{P}$ and $\mathcal{S}$.

[6] Polyhedra libraries often directly support the existential quantification operator; e.g., the *unconstrain* operator in PPL/PPLite and the *forget* operator in Apron.

48   G. Frehse et al.

Guarded Assignments. Let $e \in \mathsf{Edg}$ be a transition composed by a polyhedral guard $\mathcal{G}$ and a reset $x' = r_e(x)$ only containing affine assignments. Then, the image of relation $\mathsf{Jump}(e)$ on input $\mathcal{P}$ can be computed as $\mathcal{P}' = r_e[\mathcal{P} \cap \mathcal{G}_e]$, where $r_e[X] = \{r_e(x) : x \in X\}$ denotes the image of set $X \subseteq \mathbb{R}^n$ though the linear transformation r_e. To avoid inefficiencies, particular care has to be taken when implementing the image of linear transformation $r_e[\cdot]$. Most polyhedra libraries implement a *sequential assignment* operator, which can be directly used when the (parallel) reset operator r_e does not contain cyclic dependencies, so that the assignments can be topologically sorted without affecting their semantics. The sequential assignment further distinguishes between invertible and non-invertible assignments. In the invertible case (e.g., $x_1' = 2 \cdot x_1 + x_2$), both the constraint and the generator forms can be updated by simply applying r_e^{-1} and r_e, respectively. In the non-invertible case (e.g., $x_1' = x_2 + 3$), only the generator form is updated (using r_e), while the constraint form has to be recomputed from scratch using the conversion procedure. An alternative approach, better exploiting the incrementality of the DD method, implements the non-invertible assignment by temporarily adding a fresh variable. Letting $X' = X \setminus \{x_1\} \cup \{x_1'\}$, the assignment $x_1' = $ rhs can be computed as[7]

$$((\mathcal{P} \uparrow_{\{x_1'\}}) \cap \{x_1' - \text{rhs} \le 0, \text{rhs} - x_1' \le 0\}) \downarrow_{X'}, \qquad (4)$$

followed by a renaming of x_1' into x_1. This approach has been extended in [9] so as to be also applicable to parallel assignments having cyclic dependencies: the parallel assignment is compiled into an equivalent sequence of sequential assignments, taking care to introduce a minimal number of fresh variables (only when breaking a dependency cycle).

An example of application of the discrete post operator is shown in the middle of Fig. 2. Suppose that there exists a single transition e exiting from source location ℓ to target location ℓ', having the polyhedron $\mathcal{G}_e$ as guard component and a reset component modeled by affine transformation r_e (which combines a rotation and a translation); let also $\mathcal{I}_{\ell'}$ be the invariant for the target location ℓ'. Then, starting from $\mathcal{R}$, we obtain $\mathsf{post}_D(e, \mathcal{R}) = r_e[\mathcal{R} \cap \mathcal{G}_e] \cap \mathcal{I}_{\ell'} = r_e[\mathcal{S}] \cap \mathcal{I}_{\ell'} = \mathcal{S}' \cap \mathcal{I}_{\ell'} = \mathcal{P}'$. On the right hand side of Fig. 2 we also show an example where, by using the boxed polyhedra proposal of [9], it is sometimes possible to efficiently detect *disabled* transitions. Namely, the cheaper (but incomplete) check for disjointness $\mathcal{B}_1 \cap \mathcal{B}_2 = \emptyset$ on the bounding boxes $\mathcal{B}_1$ and $\mathcal{B}_2$ for the polyhedron state $\mathcal{P}_1$ and the polyhedral guard $\mathcal{G}_2$, when successful, is enough to conclude that $\mathcal{P}_1$ and $\mathcal{G}_2$ are disjoint too.

Computing Overapproximations for Scalability

While some verification tasks require the *exact* symbolic computation of the set of reachable states, there exists cases where an overapproximation may be good enough (e.g., when trying to prove a safety property of the hybrid automaton).

---

[7] We denote by $\mathcal{P} \uparrow_Y$ the addition to polyhedron $\mathcal{P}$ of the fresh, i.e., unconstrained, variables in Y, where $X \cap Y = \emptyset$.

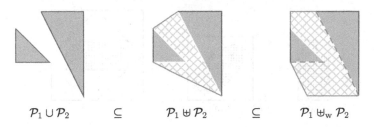

$$\mathcal{P}_1 \cup \mathcal{P}_2 \qquad \subseteq \qquad \mathcal{P}_1 \uplus \mathcal{P}_2 \qquad \subseteq \qquad \mathcal{P}_1 \uplus_{\mathrm{w}} \mathcal{P}_2$$

Fig. 3. Set union overapproximations: polyhedral hull vs. constraint hull.

One possibility is to choose a less precise symbolic domain, such as octagons [41] or template polyhedra [48]. A less radical alternative is to maintain the full generality of the domain of convex polyhedra and give up some precision in specific contexts or on specific operators. As a classical example, in [31] all symbolic states $(\ell_i, \mathcal{P}_i)$ for location ℓ_i are merged into a single state $(\ell_i, \uplus\{\mathcal{P}_i\})$. Since the computation of the convex polyhedral hull might still be expensive, it can be further approximated by computing, for instance, their *constraint hull* $(\ell_i, \uplus_{\mathrm{w}}\{\mathcal{P}_i\})$ (also called *weak join* [47]): this resembles the join operator defined on template polyhedra, since it is restricted to only use those constraint slopes that already occur in the arguments. Figure 3 shows a simple example of the different levels of overapproximation obtained. At the implementation level, the constraint hull of a set of polyhedra can be computed either by solving many Linear Programming problems or by enumerating the generators of the arguments. The latter approach is adopted in PPLite, which is the only library based on the DD method directly supporting this operator. Some tools (e.g., PHAVer) allow for the user to choose *if* and *how* to approximate set union by using a single polyhedron per location.

4 Symbolic Analysis Using CEGAR

An exact reachability analysis using polyhedra provides strong soundness guarantees in the sense that, if a counterexample to a safety property is identified over the symbolic representation, then corresponding a trajectory must exist in the system. Also, if the analysis finds a fixed point without identifying any counterexample, then the system is safe. However, an exact symbolic analysis is computationally costly. Computing the image of a post operator amounts to a projection of a system of linear inequalities over the output variables of the operator. Methods for computing projections include quantifier elimination methods as, e.g., the Fourier-Motzkin algorithm [52], or double-description methods (see Sect. 3), which suffer from exponential complexity blow-ups in the worst case. Moreover, tight representations of the reachable states may in some cases prevent the reachability algorithm from identifying a fixed point and, therefore, produce an answer at all; conversely, coarser abstractions can help reaching a fixed point. A method that tackles the above shortcomings is abstraction.

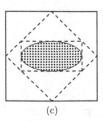

    (a)   (b)   (c)

Fig. 4. The wrapping effect.

Abstractions for hybrid systems come with a wide variety of flavors, which typically depend both on the kind of systems under analysis and the safety specifications of interest. Examples are abstractions based on interval arithmetic, which enjoy a high generality as they can even account for system dynamics described using polynomial and transcendental functions (that is, more general than LHA) and also enjoy high efficiency. On the other hand, interval analysis suffers from the wrapping effect. An example for the wrapping effect is shown in Fig. 4. The system in this example rotates an ellipse counterclockwise by 45° in discrete time steps, that is, a two-dimensional systems whose dynamic is governed by a linear difference equation. An abstraction based on interval analysis constructs rectangles (1) whose facets are orthogonal to the axes of the state space of interest and (2) that over-approximate the initial set of states (the init set) and the result of every computation of the post operator. In this instance, at the first step (Fig. 4a) the abstraction constructs a rectangle that encloses the init but also includes states that do not belong to it, introducing a small error. At the second step (Fig. 4b) the post operator is first applied to the abstract set of states (depicted with dashed lines) and then abstracted again within a larger rectangle, which introduces a further error with respect to the original set of states (the ellipse). The process is repeated over the third (Fig. 4c) and all successive steps, and this causes an ever increasing accumulation of over-approximation error.

Abstract safety analysis based on over-approximation conserves soundness in the sense that, upon termination, if the abstract reach set is disjoint from an unsafe region then the system is safe. However, it loses the property for which counterexamples are always genuine. An example can be constructed over Fig. 4, considering a bad region that intersect an abstract set of states (a rectangle) but does not intersect the concrete set of states (the ellipse). In this case, an abstract safety analyser would produce a spurious counterexample to safety. On the other hand, it should be clear that if a bad region is disjoint from the abstract states then it is also disjoint from the concrete states.

Abstractions are lightweight to compute, but may produce spurious counterexamples. Exact safety analysis always produces genuine counterexamples, but relies on heavy machinery. The approach that capitalises over the advantages of both worlds is counterexample-guided abstraction refinement (CEGAR) [17]. It consists of two phases, one that abstracts the system and another which

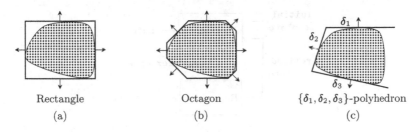

Rectangle	Octagon	$\{\delta_1, \delta_2, \delta_3\}$-polyhedron
(a)	(b)	(c)

Fig. 5. Template polyhedra.

refines the abstraction, which interact in a loop. The fundamental ingredient of a CEGAR loop is an abstraction that admits refinement, that is, an abstraction whose precision can be made tighter and tighter by changing some parameters. One example of parameterised abstraction is that of *template polyhedra*, which has been successfully applied not only to the verification of LHA [21], but also computer programs [49], hybrid automata with linear ODEs [39,48], and more recently neural network control [4]. Formally, template polyhedra are defined in terms of supporting halfspaces, which are in turn defined in terms of support functions. Given a convex set of states $\mathcal{X} \subseteq \mathbb{R}^n$, the support function of $\mathcal{X}$ in a direction $\delta \in \mathbb{R}^n$ is

$$\rho_{\mathcal{X}}(\delta) = \sup\{\langle x, \delta \rangle \colon x \in \mathcal{X}\}, \tag{5}$$

namely, the supremum of the inner product of δ with all elements of $\mathcal{X}$ [45]. This gives the offset with respect to the origin of the tightest halfspace containing $\mathcal{X}$—the supporting halfspace—that is orthogonal to δ. Finally, a template polyhedron of $\mathcal{X}$ is a finite intersections of supporting halfspaces of $\mathcal{X}$ that are orthogonal to a finite set of directions $\Delta \subset \mathbb{R}^n$. We call Δ a template and define the Δ-polyhedron of $\mathcal{X}$ as the following set:

$$\cap \underbrace{\{\{x \colon \langle x, \delta \rangle \le \rho_{\mathcal{X}}(\delta)\}}_{\text{supporting halfspace}} \colon \delta \in \Delta\}. \tag{6}$$

Rectangular and octagonal abstractions are special cases of templates polyhedra, as Fig. 5a and b exemplify; an arbitrary template parameterizes the shape of the polyhedron as shown in Fig. 5c.

In this section, abstract safety analysis can be seen as the procedure in Algorithm 1, but where $\mathcal{P}$ and $\mathcal{P}'$ are over-approximated as template polyhedra at respectively lines 2 and 9. Similarly to Sect. 3, we interpret the post operators as operators over sets of states in $\mathbb{R}^n$ as follows:

$$\text{post}_C(\ell, \mathcal{P}) = ((\mathcal{P} \cap \mathcal{I}_\ell) + \text{coni} \, \mathcal{Q}_\ell) \cap \mathcal{I}_\ell \tag{7}$$

$$\text{post}_D(e, \mathcal{R}) = A_e[\mathcal{R} \cap \mathcal{G}_e] + \{b_e\}, \tag{8}$$

where $\mathcal{I}_\ell = \text{Inv}(\ell)$ are invariant and $\mathcal{Q}_\ell = \text{Flow}(\ell)$ and flow constraint of location ℓ, and transition $e \in \text{Edg}$ is modeled as a guarded assignment with guard $\mathcal{G}_e$ and affine reset function $r_e(x) = A_e x + b_e$, with $A_e \in \mathbb{R}^{n \times n}$ and $b_e \in \mathbb{R}^n$

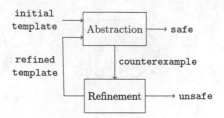

Fig. 6. Architecture of a CEGAR loop.

(a post operator for general jump conditions is described in [11]). Operator $\text{post}_C(\ell, \mathcal{P})$ in Eq. 7 represents time elapse over a mode ℓ, and is equivalent to $((\mathcal{P} \cap \mathcal{I}_\ell) \nearrow \mathcal{Q}_\ell) \cap \mathcal{I}_\ell$ as defined in Eq. 3; operator $\text{post}_D(e, \mathcal{R})$ in Eq. 8 is a rewriting of $r_e[\mathcal{R} \cap \mathcal{G}]$. Here, post operators are defined as combinations of four basic operations over sets:

$$
\begin{aligned}
&\mathcal{X} \cap \mathcal{Y} &&\text{(intersection)}\\
&\text{coni}\,\mathcal{X} = \{t \cdot x \colon x \in \mathcal{X}, t \geq 0\} &&\text{(conical hull)}\\
&\mathcal{X} + \mathcal{Y} = \{x + y \colon x \in \mathcal{X}, y \in \mathcal{Y}\} &&\text{(Minkowski sum)}\\
&A[\mathcal{X}] = \{Ax \colon x \in \mathcal{X}\} &&\text{(linear map)}
\end{aligned}
$$

where $\mathcal{X}$ and $\mathcal{Y}$ are sets in $\mathbb{R}^n$ and $A \in \mathbb{R}^{n \times n}$. Computing template polyhedra for our post operators consists of building the respective support function— inductively—over these operations over sets; a method to inductively construct support functions was introduced in [39], and later extended in [11] with exact intersection and conical hull operations. Abstract safety analysis computes an abstraction of the reach set by Algorithm 1 as a union of template polyhedra, until either it terminates or a counterexample is found; in the latter case, we refine the template polyhedra in a CEGAR loop.

Refining a template polyhedron amounts to adding directions to the template [15,25]. Intuitively, the more the directions are, the tighter the abstraction is. The objective of an abstraction refinement scheme for template polyhedra is identifying a template that avoids finding any spurious counterexamples [11,26]. A CEGAR loop constructs this template incrementally. As depicted in Fig. 6, the initial phase computes an abstraction using some initial template. If the abstraction is determined safe then the system is also safe and then the loop terminates and returns safe. If the abstraction identifies a counterexample then this is passed to the refinement phase. Refinement determines whether the counterexample is genuine or proposes a new template. In the earlier case the loop terminates and returns unsafe. In the latter case, refinement computes a template, that is, adds new directions to the existing template, which excludes the latest spurious counterexample from the abstraction. This refined template is passed to the abstraction phase and the loop is repeated. As a result, the loop enumerates spurious counterexamples and adds directions to the template until either all counterexamples are eliminated or some genuine counterexample is

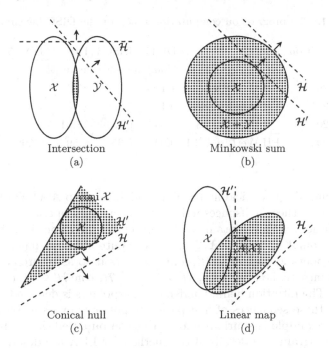

Intersection
(a)

Minkowski sum
(b)

Conical hull
(c)

Linear map
(d)

Fig. 7. Halfspace interpolants.

found. While this loop may in general not terminate, the same counterexample can never be encountered twice; this ensures progress.

A counterexample is a finite path $\ell_0, e_1, \ell_1, \ldots, e_k, \ell_k$ over the control graph of the hybrid automaton for which the respective sequence of abstract template polyhedra encounters a bad state, that is,

$$\mathcal{P}_0 = \Delta\text{-polyhedron of } \mathsf{post}_0(\mathcal{X}_0), \ldots, \mathcal{P}_k = \Delta\text{-polyhedron of } \mathsf{post}_k(\mathcal{P}_{k-1}),$$

and $\mathcal{P}_k \cap \mathcal{B} \neq \emptyset$, where $\mathcal{X}_0 = \mathsf{Init}(\ell_0)$ denotes the initial condition, $\mathcal{B} \subseteq \mathbb{R}^n$ denotes the bad region, $\mathsf{post}_0(\mathcal{X}) = \mathsf{post}_C(\ell_0, \mathcal{X})$, and $\mathsf{post}_i(\mathcal{X}) = \mathsf{post}_C(\ell_i, \mathsf{post}_D(e_i, \mathcal{X}))$ for $i = 1, \ldots, k$. The region that results from this path can be seen as a concatenation of post operators from initial to bad state. Refining the template so as to eliminate the counterexample amounts to identifying exactly one direction for each step along the counterexample. In turn, this amounts to identifying a sequence of *halfspace interpolants* along these steps such that the last halfspace separates the result from the bad region. More precisely, we want to construct a sequence of halfspaces $\mathcal{H}_0, \ldots, \mathcal{H}_k \subseteq \mathbb{R}^n$ such that

$$\mathsf{post}_0(\mathcal{X}_0) \subseteq \mathcal{H}_0, \mathsf{post}_1(\mathcal{H}_0) \subseteq \mathcal{H}_1 \ldots, \mathsf{post}_k(\mathcal{H}_{k-1}) \subseteq \mathcal{H}_k, \mathcal{H}_k \cap \mathcal{B} = \emptyset. \qquad (9)$$

To compute these halfspaces we break down these post operators into combinations of basic operations over sets. As indicated above, four operations are sufficient for the symbolic analysis of LHA: intersection between sets $\mathcal{X} \cap \mathcal{Y}$,

Table 1. The progress on computation times for the DISC benchmarks.

Edition	Tool	DISC2	DISC3	DISC4	DISC5
		Computation time in [s]			
2017	PHAVer/SX	1.1	—	—	—
2018	PHAVer-lite/SX	0.1	548.0	—	—
2019	PHAVerLite-0.1	0.04	0.68	77.51	—
2020	PHAVerLite-0.3.1	0.04	0.35	2.59	27.99

Minkowski sum $\mathcal{X} + \mathcal{Y}$, conical hull coni $\mathcal{X}$, and linear map $A[\mathcal{X}]$. For this reason, we can construct these halfspaces inductively over every operation. Specifically, for any halfspace $\mathcal{H}$ that contains the result of an operation, i.e., $\mathcal{X} \cap \mathcal{Y} \subseteq \mathcal{H}$, $\mathcal{X} + \mathcal{Y} \subseteq \mathcal{H}$, coni $\mathcal{X} \subseteq \mathcal{H}$, or $A\mathcal{X} \subseteq \mathcal{H}$, we compute a second halfspace $\mathcal{H}'$ that includes one operand, i.e., $\mathcal{X} \subseteq \mathcal{H}'$, and abstracts it so as to preserve inclusion of the result into H, i.e., $\mathcal{H}' \cap \mathcal{Y} \subseteq \mathcal{H}$, $\mathcal{H}' + \mathcal{Y} \subseteq \mathcal{H}$, coni $\mathcal{H}' \subseteq \mathcal{H}$, or $A[\mathcal{H}'] \subseteq \mathcal{H}$ respectively. The intuition behind halfspace interpolants is depicted in Fig. 7. As it turns out, these sequences of halfspace interpolants always exists if and only if the counterexample is spurious and can be computed efficiently by solving a large linear program; the details of the method for LHA are described in [11], and extended to hybrid automata with linear ODEs in [26]. The performance of this CEGAR approach is illustrated by some experiments in the next section.

5   Experiments

We provide some experiments to illustrate the above approaches for the analysis of Linear Hybrid Automata. They are based on results collected for the ARCH-COMP friendly verification competitions since 2017, in the category of hybrid system with piecewise constant dynamics of the [13], where different implementation techniques have been evaluated over the years. The following implementations are used:

- PHAVer [22] uses the fixed-point algorithm in Sect. 2.3 and calls the Parma Polyhedra Library [5] for the polyhedral computations in Sect. 3. PHAVer/SX is a subset of PHAVer, included as a plugin in the tool SpaceEx [28].
- PHAVerLite is a variant of PHAVer using the polyhedra library PPLite [8], which employs a novel representation and conversion algorithm [7] for NNC (Not Necessarily Closed) polyhedra. PHAVer-lite is an earlier version, implemented as a SpaceEx plugin.
- Lyse [24] is a tool for the reachability analysis of convex hybrid automata, whose constraints can be linear or non-linear but are required to be convex, as outlined in Sect. 4.

5.1   Distributed Controller

In Table 1 we provide some evidence of the incremental efficiency improvements that have been obtained in recent years. To this end, we consider the Distributed Controller (DISC) benchmarks [34], which model a distributed controller for a robot, reading data from multiple sensors and processing them according to multiple priorities. The instances DISCn are parametric on $n \in \{2, 3, 4, 5\}$, which is the number of sensors: the product automaton has $1 + 4n$ variables and $4 \times (1 + n) \times 4^n$ locations. The verification goal is to prove a safety property, so that overapproximations are allowed. The rows in Table 1 are labeled by a year corresponding to the edition of the competition; they provide the overall execution time spent by the corresponding model checking tool. In 2017 and 2018, the tools computed the exact reachable states, so that instances with $n > 3$ were timing out. The time improvement in 2018 is due to replacing the PPL library with PPLite. In 2019, PHAVerLite-0.1 overapproximated set unions using the constraint hull operator, thereby also solving the instance with $n = 4$; finally, in 2020 the adoption of Cartesian factoring solved the instance with $n = 5$.

In Table 2, we present a more detailed evaluation of the techniques from in Sect. 3, focussing on the instance DISC3. The first four columns show the tool configuration: (filter w-list) whether redundant polyhedra are removed from the waiting list; (boxing) whether polyhedra are boxed to speed up inclusion tests; (con-hull) whether set union is approximated using the constraint hull; and (factoring) whether polyhedra are represented using Cartesian factoring. For each of the considered combinations, in the next columns show: (iter) the number of iterations of the algorithm; (p-list) the final length of the passed list of polyhedra; (r-loc) the number of the reachable locations of the automaton; (time) the overall time spent by the tool.

When the *exact* reachable set needs to be computed, the filtering and boxing techniques are quite effective in improving efficiency. The constraint hull approximation provides another significant efficiency improvement; note that precision is degraded (78 reachable locations instead of 67 in the exact case), but the overapproximation is precise enough to prove safety. While here the Cartesian factoring technique only yields a marginal improvement, its effects become more relevant when considering bigger instances, as shown in Table 1, where for $n = 4$ the time drops from 77.51 to 2.59 s.

The above-mentioned progress is not specific to the considered benchmark: In the 2017 edition the corresponding tool verified 13 out of 20 tasks in 4:40 h, the 2020 edition solved 27 out of 28 tasks in less than 3 min.

5.2   Adaptive Cruise Controller

With this next benchmark, we compare the performance of the set-propagation approach implemented in PHAVer with the CEGAR approach implemented in the tool Lyse. The adaptive cruise controller is a distributed system for assuring that safety distances in a platoon of cars are satisfied [11]. For n cars, the number of discrete states is 2^n and the number of continuous variables is n. Each variable

Table 2. The effect of implementation techniques on DISC3.

filter w-list	boxing	con-hull	factoring	iter	p-list	r-loc	time
No	No	No	No	63805	63805	67	1379.4
Yes	No	No	No	9652	5506	67	93.1
Yes	Yes	No	No	9652	5506	67	10.3
—	—	Yes	No	189	78	78	0.7
—	—	Yes	Yes	189	78	78	0.4

Table 3. Computation times of the adaptive cruise controller [23,24].

Edition	Instance (n)	5-safe	5-unsafe	6-safe	6-unsafe	7-safe	7-unsafe	8-safe	8-unsafe
	#locs.	32	32	64	64	128	128	256	256
	Tool	Computation time in [s]							
2017	Lyse	1.08	≈0	–	–	573.35	0.233	–	–
2017	PHAVer/SX	9.4	13.7	461	13430	∞	∞	–	–
2018	PHAVer-lite	1.0	0.9	38.1	22.4	–	–	–	–
2019	PHAVerLite	0.10	0.06	0.55	0.27	4.26	1.39	47.10	7.15

x_i encodes the relative position of the i-th car and the relative velocities are subject to drift. The specification is that the distance between adjacent cars should be positive.

Table 3 shows the computation times for instances of different complexity. First, we observe that the set propagation approach shows similar performance characteristics as in the DISC benchmark: the advances associated with the polyhedra library PPLite, as well as the heuristic improvements to the fixed-point algorithm led to drastic gains in speed. The CEGAR approach clearly outshines the early versions of the set propagation approach. It also has a clear advantage in unsafe instances, where a counterexample can be found by solving a SAT instance. Somewhat surprisingly, however, the latest generation of set propagation tools seems to outperform CEGAR.

6   Conclusions

In this paper, we tried to draw the arc from straightforward to more sophisticated symbolic analysis methods for linear hybrid automata (LHA). We presented two flavors, one based on set propagation and one based on counterexample-guided abstraction refinemend (CEGAR). The performance of the set propagation approach depends on how efficiently the required operations can be realized on the chosen set representation. A natural choice for LHA are convex polyhedra in constraint representation. Despite the fact that convex polyhedra are used, e.g., in program analysis, since the seventies, we remark that several advances were made over the years that led to progressively more efficient libraries. In particular, a novel representation for polyhedra with strict as well as nonstrict inequalities has led to gains on this fundamental level. Further gains have been achieved through heuristics that use of multiple levels of abstraction: A property like containment is decided by going progressively through different levels of abstraction, so that the most precise and expensive checks are only carried out when cheaper checks have failed.

The CEGAR approach constructs an abstraction in the form of polyhedra iteratively, by checking whether the abstraction admits a path from the initial states to a given bad set of states, and then refining the abstraction to exclude this path if it turns out to be spurious. CEGAR easily outperformed earlier versions of the set propagation approach and in our experiments it outperforms for unsafe instances, quickly returning an unsafe path as a witness. Compared to more recent implementations of set propagation that leverage efficient encodings and a series of heuristics, CEGAR seems to lose some of the advantage.

This paper provided a small sample of implementations and benchmark instances in order to outline some of the improvements that can be had through clever encodings and heuristics. Further experimentation is needed to evaluate in which application domains such gains translate to successful analysis results.

References

1. Alur, R.: Formal verification of hybrid systems. In: Chakraborty, S., Jerraya, A., Baruah, S.K., Fischmeister, S. (eds.) EMSOFT, pp. 273–278. ACM (2011)
2. Alur, R., et al.: The algorithmic analysis of hybrid systems. Theor. Comput. Sci. **138**(1), 3–34 (1995)
3. Alur, R., Giacobbe, M., Henzinger, T.A., Larsen, K.G., Mikučionis, M.: Continuous-time models for system design and analysis. In: Steffen, B., Woeginger, G. (eds.) Computing and Software Science. LNCS, vol. 10000, pp. 452–477. Springer, Cham (2019). https://doi.org/10.1007/978-3-319-91908-9_22
4. Bacci, E., Giacobbe, M., Parker, D.: Verifying reinforcement learning up to infinity. In: IJCAI, pp. 2154–2160. ijcai.org (2021)
5. Bagnara, R., Hill, P.M., Zaffanella, E.: Not necessarily closed convex polyhedra and the double description method. Formal Aspects Comput. **17**(2), 222–257 (2005)
6. Bagnara, R., Hill, P.M., Zaffanella, E.: The parma polyhedra library: toward a complete set of numerical abstractions for the analysis and verification of hardware and software systems. Sci. Comput. Program. **72**(1–2), 3–21 (2008)
7. Becchi, A., Zaffanella, E.: A direct encoding for NNC polyhedra. In: Chockler, H., Weissenbacher, G. (eds.) CAV 2018, Part I. LNCS, vol. 10981, pp. 230–248. Springer, Cham (2018). https://doi.org/10.1007/978-3-319-96145-3_13
8. Becchi, A., Zaffanella, E.: An efficient abstract domain for not necessarily closed polyhedra. In: Podelski, A. (ed.) SAS 2018. LNCS, vol. 11002, pp. 146–165. Springer, Cham (2018). https://doi.org/10.1007/978-3-319-99725-4_11
9. Becchi, A., Zaffanella, E.: Revisiting polyhedral analysis for hybrid systems. In: Chang, B.-Y.E. (ed.) SAS 2019. LNCS, vol. 11822, pp. 183–202. Springer, Cham (2019). https://doi.org/10.1007/978-3-030-32304-2_10
10. Becchi, A., Zaffanella, E.: PPLite: zero-overhead encoding of NNC polyhedra. Inf. Comput. **275**, 104620 (2020)

11. Bogomolov, S., Frehse, G., Giacobbe, M., Henzinger, T.A.: Counterexample-guided refinement of template polyhedra. In: Legay, A., Margaria, T. (eds.) TACAS 2017. LNCS, vol. 10205, pp. 589–606. Springer, Heidelberg (2017). https://doi.org/10.1007/978-3-662-54577-5_34

12. Boulmé, S., Maréchal, A., Monniaux, D., Périn, M., Yu, H.: The verified polyhedron library: an overview. In: 20th International Symposium on Symbolic and Numeric Algorithms for Scientific Computing, SYNASC 2018, Timisoara, Romania, 20–23 September 2018, pp. 9–17. IEEE (2018)

13. Bu, L., et al.: ARCH-COMP20 category report: hybrid systems with piecewise constant dynamics and bounded model checking. In: ARCH20. 7th International Workshop on Applied Verification of Continuous and Hybrid Systems (ARCH20), Berlin, Germany, 12 July 2020. EPiC Series in Computing, vol. 74, pp. 1–15. EasyChair (2020)

14. Bu, L., Li, Y., Wang, L., Chen, X., Li, X.: BACH 2 : Bounded reachability checker for compositional linear hybrid systems. In: Design, Automation and Test in Europe, DATE 2010, Dresden, Germany, 8–12 March 2010, pp. 1512–1517 (2010)

15. Chen, X., Ábrahám, E.: Choice of directions for the approximation of reachable sets for hybrid systems. In: Moreno-Díaz, R., Pichler, F., Quesada-Arencibia, A. (eds.) EUROCAST 2011. LNCS, vol. 6927, pp. 535–542. Springer, Heidelberg (2012). https://doi.org/10.1007/978-3-642-27549-4_69

16. Chernikova, N.V.: Algorithm for discovering the set of all solutions of a linear programming problem. U.S.S.R. Computational Mathematics and Mathematical Physics 8(6), 282–293 (1968)

17. Clarke, E., Grumberg, O., Jha, S., Lu, Y., Veith, H.: Counterexample-guided abstraction refinement. In: Emerson, E.A., Sistla, A.P. (eds.) CAV 2000. LNCS, vol. 1855, pp. 154–169. Springer, Heidelberg (2000). https://doi.org/10.1007/10722167_15

18. Clarke, E.M., Emerson, E.A.: Design and synthesis of synchronization skeletons using branching time temporal logic. In: Kozen, D. (ed.) Logic of Programs 1981. LNCS, vol. 131, pp. 52–71. Springer, Heidelberg (1982). https://doi.org/10.1007/BFb0025774

19. Cousot, P., Cousot, R.: Abstract interpretation: a unified lattice model for static analysis of programs by construction or approximation of fixpoints. In: Proceedings of the 4th ACM SIGACT-SIGPLAN Symposium on Principles of Programming Languages, POPL 1977, New York, NY, USA, pp. 238–252. Association for Computing Machinery (1977)

20. Cousot, P., Halbwachs, N.: Automatic discovery of linear restraints among variables of a program. In: Aho, A.V., Zilles, S.N., Szymanski, T.G. (eds.) Conference Record of the Fifth Annual ACM Symposium on Principles of Programming Languages, Tucson, Arizona, USA, January 1978, pp. 84–96. ACM Press (1978)

21. Dang, T., Gawlitza, T.M.: Template-based unbounded time verification of affine hybrid automata. In: Yang, H. (ed.) APLAS 2011. LNCS, vol. 7078, pp. 34–49. Springer, Heidelberg (2011). https://doi.org/10.1007/978-3-642-25318-8_6

22. Frehse, G.: PHAVer: algorithmic verification of hybrid systems past HyTech. STTT 10(3), 263–279 (2008)

23. Frehse, G., et al.: ARCH-COMP19 category report: hybrid systems with piecewise constant dynamics. In: Frehse, G., Althoff, M. (eds.) ARCH19 6th International Workshop on Applied Verification of Continuous and Hybrid Systems. EPiC Series in Computing, vol. 61, pp. 1–13. EasyChair (2019)

24. Frehse, G., et al.: ARCH-COMP18 category report: hybrid systems with piecewise constant dynamics. In: Frehse, G. (eds.) ARCH18 5th International Workshop on Applied Verification of Continuous and Hybrid Systems. EPiC Series in Computing, vol. 54, pp. 1–13. EasyChair (2018)

25. Frehse, G., Bogomolov, S., Greitschus, M., Strump, T., Podelski, A.: Eliminating spurious transitions in reachability with support functions. In: Girard, A., Sankaranarayanan, S. (eds.) Proceedings of the 18th International Conference on Hybrid Systems: Computation and Control, HSCC 2015, Seattle, WA, USA, 14–16 April 2015, pp. 149–158. ACM (2015)

26. Frehse, G., Giacobbe, M., Henzinger, T.A.: Space-time interpolants. In: Chockler, H., Weissenbacher, G. (eds.) CAV 2018. LNCS, vol. 10981, pp. 468–486. Springer, Cham (2018). https://doi.org/10.1007/978-3-319-96145-3_25

27. Frehse, G., Jha, S.K., Krogh, B.H.: A counterexample-guided approach to parameter synthesis for linear hybrid automata. In: Egerstedt, M., Mishra, B. (eds.) HSCC 2008. LNCS, vol. 4981, pp. 187–200. Springer, Heidelberg (2008). https://doi.org/10.1007/978-3-540-78929-1_14

28. Frehse, G., et al.: SpaceEx: scalable verification of hybrid systems. In: Gopalakrishnan, G., Qadeer, S. (eds.) CAV 2011. LNCS, vol. 6806, pp. 379–395. Springer, Heidelberg (2011). https://doi.org/10.1007/978-3-642-22110-1_30

29. Halbwachs, N., Merchat, D., Gonnord, L.: Some ways to reduce the space dimension in polyhedra computations. Formal Methods Syst. Des. **29**(1), 79–95 (2006)

30. Halbwachs, N., Proy, Y.-E., Raymond, P.: Verification of linear hybrid systems by means of convex approximations. In: Le Charlier, B. (ed.) SAS 1994. LNCS, vol. 864, pp. 223–237. Springer, Heidelberg (1994). https://doi.org/10.1007/3-540-58485-4_43

31. Halbwachs, N., Proy, Y., Roumanoff, P.: Verification of real-time systems using linear relation analysis. Formal Methods Syst. Des. **11**(2), 157–185 (1997)

32. Henzinger, T.: The theory of hybrid automata. In: Proceedings of the 11th Annual IEEE Symposium on Logic in Computer Science, pp. 278 (1996)

33. Henzinger, T., Ho, P.-H., Wong-Toi, H.: HyTech: a model checker for hybrid systems. Softw. Tools Technol. Transf. **1**, 110–122 (1997)

34. Henzinger, T.A., Ho, P.-H.: HyTech: the Cornell hybrid technology tool. In: Antsaklis, P., Kohn, W., Nerode, A., Sastry, S. (eds.) HS 1994. LNCS, vol. 999, pp. 265–293. Springer, Heidelberg (1995). https://doi.org/10.1007/3-540-60472-3_14

35. Henzinger, T.A., Ho, P.-H., Wong-Toi, H.: Algorithmic analysis of nonlinear hybrid systems. IEEE Trans. Autom. Control **43**, 540–554 (1998)

36. Henzinger, T.A., Kopke, P.W., Puri, A., Varaiya, P.: What's decidable about hybrid automata? J. Comput. Syst. Sci. **57**, 94–124 (1998)

37. Jeannet, B., Miné, A.: APRON: a library of numerical abstract domains for static analysis. In: Bouajjani, A., Maler, O. (eds.) CAV 2009. LNCS, vol. 5643, pp. 661–667. Springer, Heidelberg (2009). https://doi.org/10.1007/978-3-642-02658-4_52

38. Jha, S.K., Krogh, B.H., Weimer, J.E., Clarke, E.M.: Reachability for linear hybrid automata using iterative relaxation abstraction. In: HSCC, pp. 287–300 (2007)

39. Le Guernic, C., Girard, A.: Reachability analysis of linear systems using support functions. Nonlinear Anal. Hybrid Syst. **4**(2), 250–262 (2010). IFAC World Congress 2008

40. Maler, O.: Algorithmic verification of continuous and hybrid systems. In: International Workshop on Verification of Infinite-State System (Infinity) (2013)

41. Miné, A.: The octagon abstract domain. High. Order Symb. Comput. **19**(1), 31–100 (2006)

42. Motzkin, T.S., Raiffa, H., Thompson, G.L., Thrall, R.M.: The double description method. In: Kuhn, H.W., Tucker, A.W. (eds.) Contributions to the Theory of Games – Volume II, no. 28. Annals of Mathematics Studies, pp. 51–73. Princeton University Press, Princeton, New Jersey (1953)
43. Podelski, A., Rybalchenko, A.: ARMC: the logical choice for software model checking with abstraction refinement. In: PADL, pp. 245–259 (2007)
44. Queille, J.P., Sifakis, J.: Specification and verification of concurrent systems in CESAR. In: Dezani-Ciancaglini, M., Montanari, U. (eds.) Programming 1982. LNCS, vol. 137, pp. 337–351. Springer, Heidelberg (1982). https://doi.org/10.1007/3-540-11494-7_22
45. Rockafellar, R.T. : Convex Analysis. Princeton University Press, Princeton (1970)
46. Roohi, N., Prabhakar, P., Viswanathan, M.: Hybridization based CEGAR for hybrid automata with affine dynamics. In: Chechik, M., Raskin, J.-F. (eds.) TACAS 2016. LNCS, vol. 9636, pp. 752–769. Springer, Heidelberg (2016). https://doi.org/10.1007/978-3-662-49674-9_48
47. Sankaranarayanan, S., Colón, M.A., Sipma, H., Manna, Z.: Efficient strongly relational polyhedral analysis. In: Emerson, E.A., Namjoshi, K.S. (eds.) VMCAI 2006. LNCS, vol. 3855, pp. 111–125. Springer, Heidelberg (2005). https://doi.org/10.1007/11609773_8
48. Sankaranarayanan, S., Dang, T., Ivančić, F.: Symbolic model checking of hybrid systems using template polyhedra. In: Ramakrishnan, C.R., Rehof, J. (eds.) TACAS 2008. LNCS, vol. 4963, pp. 188–202. Springer, Heidelberg (2008). https://doi.org/10.1007/978-3-540-78800-3_14
49. Sankaranarayanan, S., Sipma, H.B., Manna, Z.: Scalable analysis of linear systems using mathematical programming. In: Cousot, R. (ed.) VMCAI 2005. LNCS, vol. 3385, pp. 25–41. Springer, Heidelberg (2005). https://doi.org/10.1007/978-3-540-30579-8_2
50. Singh, G., Püschel, M., Vechev, M.T.: Fast polyhedra abstract domain. In: Castagna, G., Gordon, A.D. (eds.) Proceedings of the 44th ACM SIGPLAN Symposium on Principles of Programming Languages, POPL 2017, Paris, France, 18–20 January 2017, pp. 46–59. ACM (2017)
51. Tabuada, P.: Verification and Control of Hybrid Systems: A Symbolic Approach. Springer, New York (2009). https://doi.org/10.1007/978-1-4419-0224-5
52. Williams, H.P.: Fourier's method of linear programming and its dual. Am. Math. Mon. **93**(9), 681–695 (1986)

An Architecture for Safe Driving Automation

Hermann Kopetz[✉]

Technical University of Vienna, Vienna, Austria
h.kopetz@gmail.com

Abstract. This paper presents a novel distributed computer architecture that supports the incremental development and validation of a safe and secure *SAE level-four Driving Automation System* out of an existing *SAE level-two driver assistance system* (*called L2-system*). A strict separation—both logical and physical—of the *functional concerns* from the *safety and security concerns* characterizes this architecture. An existing *L2-system* is enhanced by a new independent *safety assurance system* that performs the functions that are provided by the human driver at SAE level two. The *safety assurance system* comprises three independent fault-containment units: a *monitoring subsystem* (*M-system*) that checks the trajectory provided by the L2-system, a *fallback subsystem* (*F-system*) that calculates a trajectory that brings the car from a critical state to a safe state, and a simple *decision subsystem* (*D-system*), that decides whether the *trajectory* from the L2-system or the *trajectory* from the F-system must be sent to the actuators. A single failure of any one of the three complex subsystems (the *L2-system*, the *F-system* or the *M-system*) caused by either a hardware failure, a design error in the software, or an intrusion, is detected and mitigated by the redundancy and design diversity that is inherent in the proposed architecture. Since the architecture restores autonomously the normal operation of the vehicle after the successful mitigation of a transient fault, it reduces significantly the number of disengagements of a vehicle. We give an estimate of the *Safety-Improvement Factor* of this architecture over an existing *SAE level-two Driving Automation System*.

Keywords: Intelligent transportation · Safety · Automotive systems · System architecture · Fault-tolerance

1 Introduction

The vision of a self-driving car is transforming the automotive industry. Today, advanced computer and sensor technologies make it possible to support the driver of a vehicle in routine situations and help to reduce the number of traffic accidents. At the end of this transformation, a new type of car that finds it way autonomously from the start of a journey to its destination is envisioned. Although more than 80 billion US $ have already been spent on developing autonomous vehicles, the goal of a *driver-less car* is still far away [Mim21]. In our opinion, the main obstacle to achieve this goal is the *guaranteed safety*, the topic of this paper.

To bring more structure into this transformation process of the automotive industry, the Society of Automotive Engineers has published the standard SAEJ 3016 (revised in

© Springer Nature Switzerland AG 2022
J.-F. Raskin and K. Chatterjee (Eds.): Principles of Systems Design, LNCS 13660, pp. 61–84, 2022.
https://doi.org/10.1007/978-3-031-22337-2_4

2018) [SAE18] that introduces six levels on the route from *no automation* (level zero) to a *fully autonomous vehicle* (level five). At present, *level-two vehicles* with *advanced driver assistance systems* (we call them *L2-systems*) are widely available on the market. An L2-system provide semi-autonomous longitudinal and lateral vehicle control under well-specified *nominal conditions*, called the *operational design domain (ODD)*. During the operation of an L2-system, the driver must continuously monitor the traffic and the operation of the car in order that she/he can detect an *off-nominal condition*, such as a violation of the ODD, a misbehavior of the car caused by software or hardware failure of the L2-system or an intrusion into the L2-system.

The main challenge in SAE level four Driving Automation is the achievement of *assured safety and security* without a supervising driver. This paper focuses on this preeminent safety and security challenge. The proposed architecture partitions an SAE level four Driving Automation System at the next lower level into *two major subsystems:* the existing *L2-system* and a new independent *safety assurance subsystem* (we call it the *SA-system*) that performs the functions that are provided by the human driver at SAE level two. The SA-system comprises three independent subsystems that must be *fault-containment units:* a *monitoring subsystem (M-system),* a *fault-tolerant decision subsystem (D-system),* and a *fallback system (F-system).*

A *fault-containment unit (FCU)* is a *unit of failure* [Kop12, p. 155]. It is an encapsulated subsystem with its own hardware and software that hides the immediate effects of an *internal fault* and exhibits a defined failure mode at the output message boundary of the FCU to its environment. It is up to quality engineering to ensure that FCUs fail independently. If a system is not partitioned into well-defined FCUs, we call it a *monolithic* system.

This paper is structured as follows: Section two explains the chosen terminology and elaborates on the six level of driving automation proposed in the SAE J3016 Standard (see Fig. 1). Since SAE level-two driver-assistance systems have already been on the road since a number of years, the safety record of these SAE level-two systems is examined. In Section three we survey related literature. In Section four we establish the required safety parameters for the future SAE level-four systems, review the practical experience with safety-relevant computer systems in other disciplines, summarize these experiences in *five impossibility results,* and argue that it is not possible to provide a flawless monolithic software system with millions of lines of code. In order to achieve the required safety, we introduce concurrently operating nearly independent subsystems that form independent Fault Containment Units (FCUs). The redundant FCUs are characterized by diverse designs in order to mask residual design errors [Avi86]. In the main Section of this paper, Section five, we present the proposed architecture for SAE level-four driving automation, describe the functions of each one of the proposed subsystems, discuss the autonomic system recovery after a transient fault, and estimate the Safety-Improvement Factor of this architecture over an existing *L2-system.* Section six discusses security aspects, the new approach to validation, and the evolution of the architecture to meet changing requirements.

	Role of Driver	Role of the Computer
Level zero: No Driving Automation	Performs all driving tasks	None
Level one: Driver Assistance	Supervises the CCDSS and intervenes as necessary	**Either** longitudinal or lateral vehicle motion within the ODD
Level two: Partial Driving Automation	Supervises the CCDSS and intervenes as necessary	**Both** longitudinal and lateral vehicle motion within the ODD
Level three: Conditional Driving Automation	Fallback ready driver is always ready to accept a *takeover request* from the CCDSS	**Both** longitudinal and lateral vehicle motion within the ODD Issue of a *takeover request.*
Level four: High Driving Automation	No fallback ready driver required	Sustained vehicle control in a limited ODD
Level five: Full Driving Automation	No fallback ready driver required	Sustained vehicle control in an unlimited ODD

Fig. 1. The six levels of *Driving Automation* according to SAE J3016.

2 The SAE J3016 Standard for *Driving Automation*

The purpose of the six levels of the SAE J3016 standard (Fig. 1) is to provide a logical taxonomy for classifying *driving automation features* along with a set of terms and definitions that support the taxonomy. It tries to standardize related concepts, terms and usage in order to facilitate clear communications. As such, SAE J3016 is a *"convention based upon reasoned agreement, rather than a technical specification"* [SAE18, p. 29].

2.1 Some Terminology

Figure 1 describes the characteristics of the different levels of automation distinguished in the SAE J3016 Standard. In SAE level-two, the *human driver* performs the functions of the *SA-system* (safety assurance system) to detect, handle and mitigate critical events that are not properly handled by the *existing L2-system*. S/he takes over the control of the car in the case of a computer failure or an abnormal driving situation. In SAE level-four automation the functionality of the SA-system must be provided by a *computerized SA-system*. Since this computerized SA-system is required to detect and mitigate its own computer system failures, it must be composed of a number of distributed and independent FCUs.

The *L2-system* is expected to handle all driving tasks in *normal driving situations*. A *normal driving situation* prevails if the *L2-system* and the mechanics of the vehicle function as specified, all other drivers observe the traffic code, and the vehicle is either travelling within its well-defined *Operational Design Domain* (*ODD*) or the *L2-system* recognizes that it cannot handle the current situation and brings the vehicle autonomously to a safe state. Otherwise we speak about an *abnormal driving situation*. This distinction between a *normal driving situation* and an *abnormal driving situation* is crucial for understanding the rationale behind this novel architecture for driving automation.

On page 14 of SAE J3016 the concept of an *Operational Design Domain (ODD)* is explained in detail: *"Operating conditions under which a given driving automation system or feature thereof is specifically designed to function, including, but not limited to, environmental, geographical, and time-of-day restrictions, and/or the requisite presence or absence of certain traffic or roadway characteristics."* The *Operational Design Domain* (ODD) thus specifies the conditions that have been assumed to prevail during *normal driving situations*.

In every-day traffic *normal driving situations* are encountered most of the time. A normal driving scenario prevails if the vehicle operates within its ODD specification and all computer systems are working properly. However, in rare circumstances, one of the multitudes of seldomly occurring unexpected events—we call it an *edge case*—will be encountered that leads to an *abnormal driving scenario* that cannot be handled by the existing *L2-system*. It is impossible to specify in detail all edge cases that can occur in a real-life environment. Examples of edge cases are the *appearance of a suicide driver*, a *suddenly encountered black ice on the road* or a *single event upset (SEU)* that leads to a silent data corruption in the computer hardware. The detection and handling of all edge cases are the main challenges in the design of an SAE level-four Driving Automation System.

The transition from a *normal driving situation* to an *abnormal driving situation* is called a *critical event*.

Examples of *critical events* are:

- A catastrophic hardware or software failure of the *L2-system*
- An edge case that is not part of the *L2-system* specification.
- A malign change of behavior of the *L2-system* caused by an intrusion.
- A mechanical failure of the vehicle that is not mitigated by the *L2-system*.
- An exit from the Operational Design Domain that is not recognized by the *L2-system*
- The appearance of a *suicide driver*.

The detection, handling and mitigation of critical events is the responsibility of the SA-System (*Safety Assurance Subsystem*).

2.2   Experience with SAE J3016 Level-Two Automation

Vehicles with L2-systems have been on the road since more than ten years. The computer system performs longitudinal and lateral vehicle control in normal situations under the supervision of an always attentive human driver. The human driver embodies the SA-system at SAE level-two.

In an *L2-systems* the human driver must perform the following safety-relevant tasks:

- Authoritative decision about the state of the system.
- Critical-event detection.
- Immediate takeover of control of the vehicle after the recognition of a critical event.
- Manual drive of the vehicle after a critical event, i.e., in an *abnormal driving situation*.

From a systems perspective, there are two independent subsystems operating concurrently in SAE level-two: The *L2*-system and the *human driver*. In normal situations the *L2-system* navigates the vehicle and must also supervise the attentiveness of the human driver (e.g., the *L2-system* checks if the driver is holding the steering wheel).

The human driver embodies the *SA-system* and must supervise the performance of the *L2-system*. In an *L2-system*, the human driver must always be attentive in order to detect the occurrence of a critical event. Based on inputs from her/his independent biological sensors (eyes, ears, haptic, smell, etc.) and referring to her/his *conscious* and *unconscious* driving experiences, the attentive human driver must react in the sub-second range to a critical event. S/he takes over the manual control of the car to mitigate the consequences of a critical event in an *abnormal driving situation*.

If there is a conflict between the decisions of the *L2-system* and the *human driver*, the design of a level-two system is clear on how this conflict is resolved: the human driver always prevails. In an *L2-system*, the human driver is the *authoritative decision maker*.

The concurrent operation of two independent control subsystems contributes positively to a safer operation. For example, if a driver falls asleep on a boring freeway trip, the *L2-system* will keep the car in lane, keep a safe distance from the car ahead, and sound an alarm to wake the driver. Another example: if a car is driven in dense fog, a preceding car is displayed on the dash-port (sensed via the radar sensor) before this preceding car is visible to the human eye. These positive safety effects of a level-two system are documented in a study on the safety benefits of an advanced driver assistance system [Yue18]. In this study it is shown that the deployment of these systems reduces the number of severe accidents by about a third.

However, if the human driver is of the erroneous opinion that a level-two system is a trustworthy autopilot that needs no human supervision, it can happen that after a critical event the vehicle exhibits an erratic behavior with potentially tragic consequences.

Function	Level two	Level three	Level four
Normal Driving	*L2-system*	*L2-system*	*L2-system*
Critical Event Detection	Driver	*L2-system*	*SA-system*
Critical Event Handling	Driver	Driver	*SA-system*

Fig. 2. Functions of SAE level two, three and four.

2.3 The Deep Divide Between SAE Level Two and the Higher Levels

Let us first compare *level-two* and *level-four automation* and *discuss level-three automation* afterwards. In a level-four system, all of the critical judgmental tasks of the human driver (see Fig. 2) have to be performed by the computerized *safety-assurance subsystem* (*SA-system*). Let us now look in some detail at the tasks of a human diver that must be realized by the computerized *SA-system* of level-four.

Critical-Event Detection: Critical-event detection is one of the most challenging tasks of a *Driving Automation System*. There are two types of critical events that must be distinguished: *external critical events* and *internal critical events*. Critical events that relate to software failures, hardware failures or intrusions into the computer system are called *internal critical events*. Critical events that are caused by phenomena external to the computer systems, such as an ODD exit, an unforeseen edge case, or an abrupt mechanical failure of the car, are called *external critical events*. *External critical-event detection* must be part of the application software of the *L2-system*. If the *L2-system* fails to properly handle a critical event, then the *SA-system* must mitigate the failure. The precise specification of the ODD provides the starting point for external critical-event detection of the *L2-system*. *Internal critical events* can only be detected if the computer system is decomposed into redundant *fault containment units* that are assumed to fail independently. The topic of internal critical-event detection is discussed in detail in Section five of this document.

Critical-Event Handling: Whereas the subsystem that is supposed to *detect* an ODD-exit can refer to a precise ODD specification, the subsystem that is supposed to handle the situation after an *ODD-exit* cannot refer to such a precise ODD specification, but must assume "*any driver-manageable road condition within its region of the world. This means, for example, that there are no design-based weather, time-of-day, or geographical restrictions on where and when the Driving Automation system can operate the vehicle*" [SAE18, p. 25]. If the *L2-system* fails to handle an ODD-exit properly, then the *computerized SA-system* must first try to immediately (within fractions of a second) bring the vehicle out of the dangerous situation to a safe state and afterwards implement a *recovery action* or a *limp-home strategy* until the vehicle is at a safe place to stop. As mentioned above, *internal critical-event handling*—the mitigation of hardware and software failures—requires a redundant FCU computer architecture of the *Driving Automation System* as introduced in Section five.

Resolution of Decision Conflicts: In any computer architecture that contains redundant subsystems the results of these redundant subsystems may differ, e.g. because of different inputs or a failure of a subsystem. In a level-two system with two partners (two subsystems)—the *human driver* and the *Computer Controlled Driving System* (*L2-system*)—the decision of the human driver is final and overrides any action from the *L2-system*. In a level-four system, the situation is involved and requires *architectural support* as outlined in Section five.

2.4   SAE Level-Three Systems

The main difference between an SAE level-two system and an SAE level-three system is the *critical-event detection* by the computer system in level three. After the computer system signals the detection of a critical event, the human driver must take over the driving task, i.e., the *critical-event handling* (see Fig. 2). In a level-three system *critical-event detection* is the responsibility of the *L2-system*. SAE18 states on p. 24 … "*the fallback-ready user **need not** supervise a level 3 Driving Automation System while it is engaged*".

Let us assume that the challenging task of *critical-event detection* is working properly. Immediately after a critical event has been detected, the Driving Automation System sends an alarm signal to the driver in order that the driver can start *critical-event handling*. On recognition of this alarm signal, the driver must shift attention from the current activity (e.g., working on email) to controlling the car. According to human factor studies [Ege97, p. 285] *"The deployment of attention from one stimulus to another is by no means instantaneous"*. *Attention shift time* can take from hundreds of milliseconds up to more than several seconds, depending of the specific environment. In a dangerous edge-case situation or after the occurrence of an internal critical event (a failure of the computer system), this total loss of control during the *attention shift time* can have catastrophic consequences. Based on the presented arguments we feel that the idea of an *SAE level-three Driving Automation system* without a mechanism that controls the vehicle during the unavoidable *attention shift time* is problematic.

3 Related Work

In order to establish worldwide unified terms and procedures for functional safety of electronic systems in production vehicles, the automotive industry has developed the ISO standard 26262 with the title *"Road vehicles—functional safety"* as an extension of the IEC standard 61508. This standard covers the specification, design, implementation, integration, and validation of automotive software and hardware for safety-critical systems. The ISO standard 26262 includes a risk classification scheme of a safety function called the *Automotive Safety integrity Level (ASIL)*. The four levels of ASILs (ASIL A, ASIL B, ASIL C, and ASIL D) are ordered according to the integrity requirement, where ASIL D is the highest level with the most stringent procedures for the development and validation of a safety function. In the last three years the additional ISO standard 21448 (*SOTIF—Safety of the Intended Functionality*) has been published that covers safety aspects during the operation of a Driving Automation System that arise from the handling of edge cases or human misjudgments that are not adequately covered by the ISO standard 26262.

The National Highway Traffic Safety Administration of the US Department of Transportation (NHTS) administers the Web Site *"A Vision for Safety"* [NHT20] for the voluntary safety self-assessment of Automated Driving Systems. On this Web Site companies publish their *Vision for Safety*. However, in many of the published documents a detailed presentation of the technical mechanisms that assure a safe behavior of an automated vehicle is missing.

The Department of Motor Vehicles (DMV) of the state of California, USA, publishes ever year a *Disengagement Report* [Her20] that documents the kind and number of disengagements of autonomous vehicles that have been observed on public roads in California. In [Her20] it is stated on p. 8: *"With the Disengagement Report, California is currently the only region in the world where this type of report is prescribed and published. This means that the interested public has no better and other data to inform them about the current state of development of autonomous cars."*

The extensive academic literature on driving automation deals predominantly with the structure, the algorithms and the validation of the *L2-systems*, i.e., the SAE level-two

Driving Automation System (see e.g., the review of the literature in [Sha19]). Although in nearly all papers the topic of *safety* is mentioned as a decisive characteristic of any Driving Automation System, only a small number of publications discuss an independent safety subsystem that detects and mitigates a failure of the *L2-system*.

S.M. Shah, in his master thesis on *"Save-AV, A fault-tolerant safety architecture for autonomous vehicles"* [Sha19], starts with a thorough analysis of six reported traffic accidents involving autonomous vehicles with an engaged *L2-system* at the instant of the accident. He concludes that the inattentiveness of the human drivers played an eminent role in the evolution of the disasters. All reported accidents could have been avoided if a *computerized L2-system* with the capability of an attentive human driver would have monitored the operation of the *L2-system* and interfered in case of the failure of the *L2-system*.

The topic of supervising the operation of the *L2-system* by an independent subsystem, a *monitor*, is considered, among others, in [Sha19], and [Meh20]. The monitor must decide, whether the trajectory provided by the *L2-system* is safe. This decision requires an independent monitor subsystem of about the same size and complexity as the *L2-system*. The important question of *"Who monitors the correct operation of the monitor?"* must be answered in an ultra-dependable system. The frequent argument that a periodic cross check between the monitor and the *L2-system* can solve this intricate failure detection problem breaks down when the monitor exhibits a *Byzantine failure*. In a *Byzantine failure mode,* the *L2-system* mimics to the observing monitor correct behavior and does bad things on its own.

This brings us the question of *Byzantine failures* of an FCU. A Byzantine failure of an FCU (see the definition of an FCU in the introduction of this paper) is the most general failure mode of an FCU that makes *no assumption whatsoever* about the behavior of a malfunctioning FCU [Lal94]. It is often argued that the Byzantine failure mode of an FCU is an academic invention without any practical relevance. This is contrary to evidence from ultra-dependable systems outside the automotive domain. Kevin Driscoll, who was involved in the design of the control system for the Boeing 777 aircraft, says in [Dri03]: *"Drawing from the authors' experiences with Byzantine failures in real-world systems, this paper shows that Byzantine problems are real, have nasty properties, and are likely to increase in frequency with emerging technology trends."* The justification of the assumption (the determination of the *assumption coverage* [Pow95]) that an FCU will not exhibit a Byzantine failure during the lifetime of the ultra-dependable system— i.e., in the order of more than 10^8 h of operation—is *more than difficult*. It is thus a wise decision to conceptualize an architecture that will mitigate any single Byzantine failure of any-one of its complex constituent FCUs.

An architecture that can mitigate *Byzantine failures* of its FCUs deals with the topics of safety and security in a single stroke. If an intrusion into the core of an FCU is successful, then the intruder can produce *any kind of behavior of the compromised FCU*, which is precisely the definition of a *Byzantine failure of an FCU*. Safety and Security, which are often discussed in different communities, are thus the two sides of a single coin in the domain of ultra-dependable systems.

In 1982 Lamport, Shostak and Pease published the archival paper on the *Byzantine Generals Problem* [Lam82]. In this paper they present a number of solutions for handing a Byzantine failure of a node in a distributed computing system. These solutions are expensive in terms of the number of nodes, the amount of time, and in the number of messages that must be exchanged: *"The only way to reduce the cost is to make assumptions about the type of failure that may occur"* [Lam82, p. 401]. In the architecture proposed in this paper we make such an assumption about one of the four FCUs that form the Driving Automation System. We justify this assumption by the simplicity of the software and the fault-tolerance of the execution platform of this FCU. This assumption significantly reduces the cost of mitigating a Byzantine failure in any one of the remaining three complex FCUs of the architecture.

4 Requirements and Constraints of a Driving Automation Architecture

In this Section we elaborate on the requirements that a *Driving Automation System* Architecture of SAE level-four must satisfy and the constraints that must be dealt with in a real-world environment. Neither an external critical event, nor an internal critical event, such as a design error in the software, a transient or permanent failure of the computer hardware, or an intrusion should lead to an accident in an ultra-dependable system, such as a Driving Automation system [Koo17].

4.1 Required Dependability

As noted in Sect. 2.2, the field record of the safety-improvement of level-two Driving-Automation Systems is positive. However, all fatal accidents cannot be eliminated since it is estimated that about *2% of the fatal traffic accidents are suicide behaviors* [Pom12].

To get an order of magnitude estimate for the required dependability we start from the traffic accident statistics in Austria. In Austria, with about 5 million cars on the road, there are about 35 000 reported traffic accidents/year with about 500 traffic fatalities/year [Sta19] (1 reported accident/150 cars per year and 1 traffic fatality/10 000 cars per year). Let us assume that every car is driven for 12 000 km/year with an average speed of about 60 km/h resulting, as a gross estimate, in 200 h of car usage per year. This implies that a reported traffic accident is encountered every 1 800 000 driven km or about every 30 000 h of car-operation and a traffic fatality is encountered every 120 000 000 km or every 2 000 000 h of operation.

Ultra-dependable computer systems are fundamentally different from conventional computer systems which have an MTTF of less than 10^4 h. For example, a failure caused by single event upsets (SEUs) in the hardware [Con02] must be dealt with in an ultra-dependable system, whereas SEUs are of little concern in conventional computer systems.

4.2 Five Impossibility Results

Most dependability engineers that are working on the design and validation of ultra-high dependable systems in other industries would agree that there is strong experimental evidence that it is impossible to overcome the constraints that are summed up in the following *five impossibility results.*

(i)   **It is impossible to find all design faults in a large and complex monolithic Software System.** According to a study [Dvo09] from the US NASA, a software system is considered large and complex if it contains more than 10 000 lines of source code. Experience with NASA systems has shown that it is practically impossible to eliminate all design faults, particularly of the *Heisenbug type* [Gra65], in a complex software system. Heisenbugs have the appearance of a transient malfunction. Although most design faults that occur during normal operation can be eliminated during operational testing, some design faults in the code that deal with the extremely rare *edge-cases* often remain undetected. This phenomenon is also observed in operating systems. According to [Cho01] there are hundreds of residual design faults in the widely used LINUX operating system. If we move from conventional deterministic algorithms to software systems that are using artificial neural networks and machine learning, the complexity problems are exacerbated. The certification of these systems for ultra-dependable applications is beyond the current state of the arts [Bha15, pp. 53–58].

(ii) **It is impossible to avoid single event upsets in non-redundant hardware during the life-time of an ultra-dependable system.** A single-event upset (SEU) is a hardware failure that can be caused by cosmic radiation. Normally, an SEU does not permanently damage the hardware. It causes a transient *change of value* of a single bit, called a *bitflip* [Con02]. If the hardware is not fault-tolerant, then such a bitflip is difficult to detect and may result in phenomena that are similar to a *Heisenbug* in the software. Li et al. [Li17] have shown that a single bitflip in a middle layer of a machine learning convolution network can cause the misclassification of a *truck* as a *bird*.

(iii) **It is impossible to establish the ultra-high dependability of a large monolithic system by testing and simulation.** In an archival paper on *Validation of Ultra-high Dependability for Software based systems*, Littlewood and Strigini [Lit93] argue that no solution exists for the validation of ultra-high dependability in monolithic systems relying on complex software. A complex monolithic subsystem, such as a Computer Controlled Driving Subsystem (*L2-system*) with million lines of code which is developed and validated according to the *ASIL B* standard will, after careful testing and simulation, achieve a validated MTTF of 10^4 h, which is three orders of magnitude short of the required 10^7 h for an ultra-high dependable Driving Automation system.

(iv) **It is impossible to precisely specify all edge cases that can be encountered in driving situations.** Uncovered edge cases, such as a weird failure of a sensor, are often the cause of an airline accident. Over the past fifty years, the airline industry has scrutinized every accident to find its root cause and extend the ODD accordingly. Conceivable edge-cases in automatic driving are much more plentiful than in the control of an airplane.

(v)   **It is impossible to shift human attention without a significant *attention shift time*.** This issue has been discussed in Sect. 2.4 above.

4.3   Consequences for Architecture Design

The implications of the *required dependability* and the *impossibility results* discussed above on the design of a system architecture for Driving Automation are manifold [Kop06]:

Independent Subsystems That Form Fault Containment Units (FCU): The allocation of separable functions of a large system to nearly independent subsystems is the most powerful technique for the reduction of the complexity at the system level [Kop19, p. 77]. At the top level of the architecture, the *Automatic Driving System* of a vehicle should be decomposed into a number of nearly independent subsystems with simple and well-defined interfaces. Every subsystem should form an independent Fault-Containment Unit (FCU) and constitute a unit of stand-alone validation.

Separation of *Simple* and *Complex* Subsystems: It is justified to assume that a simple subsystem that contains formally specified software of a limited size and where the software is developed according to ASIL D and executed on fault-tolerant hardware will meet the ultra-high dependability requirements. This assumption is not justified if the subsystem is complex, i.e., it contains millions of lines of code and is executed on standard hardware. It cannot be ruled out, that during the operation of a complex subsystem a Byzantine failure will occur. A deep neural network (DNN) is definitely a *complex subsystem* that cannot be developed according to the rules of ASIL D.

Design Diversity and Redundancy to mask a Failure of a Complex FCU: If we accept that it is impossible to avoid a failure of a non-redundant complex FCU caused by a design error in the complex software, a failure of the hardware, or an intrusion during the lifetime of an ultra-dependable system, then we have to implement redundancy and design diversity in order to detect and mitigate the consequences of a failure of a complex FCU. The diverse FCUs must be developed and validated by separate development organization using different algorithms and development tools in order to achieve a high-level of design diversity.

Provably correct Decision System: Whenever two independent redundant subsystems are involved in a decision in a complex environment there is the possibility of two different *correct* outcomes. The introduction of a third subsystem will only mask a single fault if the involved systems are *replica determinate* [Kop12, p. 125].

Consider a hypothetical example where a vehicle can avoid a collision with a rock in the middle of the road by passing the rock either on the left side or on the right side. A TMR (triple-modular redundancy) system consisting of three independent subsystems that send their results to a dependable voter is used in this example. The first subsystem decides to pass the rock on the right side. The second subsystem decides to pass the rock on the left side. The third subsystem decides to stop the vehicle before the rock which in this case causes an accident, because the speed of the car and the conditions of the road do not allow the halt of the car before the rock. In this TMR system the two-out-of-three voting algorithm is confused because it finds three different results from the three different subsystems and cannot decide which one of the three results is in error.

Since *replica determinism* cannot be achieved if large computer systems with their own independent sensor inputs operate concurrently a TMR system configuration will not provide fault tolerance in driving automation (see the example in Sect. 4.3), Alternatively, a *single version of a correct decision algorithm* that acts as an authoritative decision maker and executes on fault-tolerant hardware solves the decision problem. This decision algorithm must be as simple as possible (less than 10000 lines of code) and should be developed according to the ASIL level D standard which aims to eliminate all design errors before it is put into operation.

Avoidance of Unintended Emergent Behavior: Since it is impossible to establish the required ultra-high dependability of a monolithic Driving Automation System at the system level by testing and simulation [Kal16], the safety case must be based on the experimental evidence about the dependability of the isolated subsystems, the FCUs, and the analysis of the interactions among these subsystems. Unintended emergent behavior, which can be evoked by causal loops in the interactions among the subsystem, *destroys this route to validation* [Kop16]. In order to avoid unintended emergent behavior, the interactions among the subsystems should be reduced as far as possible and the remaining unavoidable interactions must be carefully analyzed to detect hidden causal loops that could generate unintended emergent behavior.

5   An Ideal Top-Level Architecture for *Driving* Automation

We assume that a human determines the desired destination for an automated vehicle and selects the relevant waypoints before s/he activates the Driving Automation System. From there onwards, the Driving Automation System navigates the car autonomously to the desired destination or brings the car to a safe stop-state in case a critical event that causes an abnormal driving situation cannot be mitigated in any other way. All subsystems of the Driving Automation System must have access to a fault-tolerant global time and must observe the environment at the same instant.

5.1   Architecture Overview

In our architecture proposal for Driving Automation at SAE level four (see Fig. 3) an existing *L2-system*, which is *complex*, is enhanced by a completely separated safety-assurance subsystem (the *SA-system*) that implements the functionality that is provided by the human driver at SAE level-two. The *SA-system* consists of *three independent subsystems, the simple fault-tolerant decision subsystem (D-system), the complex monitoring subsystem (M-system)* and *the complex fallback subsystem (F-system)* that mitigates critical events that cannot be handled by the *L2-system*. Each one of the subsystems of the proposed architecture must form an independent Fault-Containment Unit (FCU) with its own sensors, computer hardware and diverse software and must have access to fault-tolerant global time. According to our fault-hypothesis one out of the three complex subsystems (the *L2-system, the M-system, and* the *F-system*) can fail in a Byzantine failure mode within a single frame without causing an accident. However, an accident can occur if two out of these three subsystems fail within a single frame.

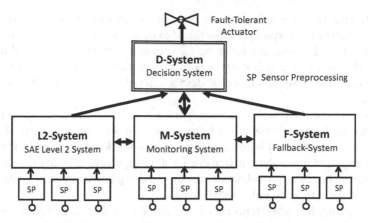

Fig. 3. Structure of the *Driving Automation System.*

In every frame the prospective trajectory—i.e. a sequence of timed *waypoints*—for a normal driving situation, calculated by the *L2-system*, is sent to the monitoring subsystem (*M-system*) via the *time-triggered* channel of Fig. 3 for a safety check. The *M-system* checks the safety of this prospective trajectory and reports the result of the safety check—*SAFE* or *UNSAFE*—in every frame to the fault-tolerant decision subsystem (*D-system*) at the top of the hierarchy.

The *D-system* at the top of the hierarchy (see Fig. 3) contains simple software, assumed to be free of design errors, that is executed on fault-tolerant hardware. In every frame the *D-system* receives three time-triggered input messages:

- A message from the *L2-system* that contains the setpoints for *normal driving situations.*
- A message from the *F-system* that contains the setpoints for *abnormal driving situations.*
- A message from the *M-system* that contains the results of a safety check.

The *D-system* checks in every frame whether the setpoints for a normal driving situation submitted by the *L2-system* have passed the safety check performed by the *M-system*. If this condition is SAFE, then the *D-system* assumes that a *normal driving situation prevails* and will deliver the setpoints calculated by the *L2-system* to the actuators. If this condition is UNSAFE, then the *D-system* does not know whether the *L2-system* or the *M-system* have failed. In any case, the D-system will assume that a *critical event has caused an abnormal driving situation*. Therefore, it will take the setpoint values received from the *F-system* and send them to the actuators. From there onwards, the *D-system* will take the setpoints provided by the *F-system* until a recovery of the *L2-system* is successful, the vehicle is in a safe state, or the human driver has taken over the manual control of the vehicle.

Additionally, the *D-system* sends the setpoints received from the *L2-system* in every frame to the *M-system* in order that the *M-system* can detect a Byzantine failure of the *L2-system*. The *D-system* sends the setpoints received from the *F-system* to the *M-system* in order that the *M-system* can detect an error in the setpoints from the *F-system* or a fail-silent failure of the *F-system*. In case the *M-system* detects such a failure, it will send a message to the *L2-system* and order the *L2-system* to terminate the normal operation and bring the vehicle to a safe state. A normal operation of the *L2-system* should not continue in case the subsystem that provides the safety fallback, i.e., the *F-system*, is out of service.

Each one of the three nearly *independent complex systems,* the *L2-system,* the *M-system,* and the *F-system* contains a large amount of software (millions of lines of code) executed on standard hardware. Since it is considered impossible that such a complex subsystem meets the requirement for ultra-high dependability (see Sect. 4.2), the proposed architecture provides redundancy and design diversity to mitigate a failure in any one of these three complex subsystems.

The three complex subsystems are characterized by a diverse design. They acquire their input information from their own sensors at the bottom of the hierarchy and produce the output information to the *D-system* at the top of the hierarchy. In essence, the structure of Fig. 3 resembles a *formal hierarchy.* A formal hierarchy supports perfectly the decomposition of a large system into nearly independent subsystems and avoids unintended emergent behavior. A clear separation of concerns is the most powerful technique to reduce the complexity of a large system [see the extended discussion on a *formal architecture* in Kop19, pp. 56–59 and on p. 78].

5.2 The Four Subsystems

The *D-system*: The purpose of the *D-system* is to decide on the basis of the data received from the *M-system* whether a *normal driving situation* or an *abnormal driving situation* prevails and to select the provided setpoints either from the *L2-system* (in normal driving situations) or from the *F-system* (in abnormal driving situations). The *D-system* at the top of the hierarchy is a small and simple system that must meet the ultra-high dependability requirement.

In the conception of this architecture we tried to reduce the functionality of the *D-system* to the necessary minimum and to allocate all complex software functions to one of the three complex subsystems below the *D-system* (see Fig. 3). The small and simple cyclic software of the *D-system* (without an underlying general-purpose operating system) must be developed according to ASIL D and is assumed to be free of residual design errors. Since the cyclic input data, the cyclic output data and the small internal state of the *D-system* are precisely specified and the logic of the *D-system* is easy to comprehend, the validation of the software can—in addition to extensive testing and simulation—also be supported by formal techniques. We do not see a need to modify the simple software of the *D-system* during the lifetime of a Driving Automation System within a vehicle, even if new functions are added to anyone of the complex subsystems. In order to avoid any intrusion, the *D-system* should be an encapsulated subsystem that is not connected to the Internet.

The hardware of the *D-system* must be fault tolerant. We propose a hardware design that consists of two *fail-silent compact Fault-Containment Units (FCU),* where each FCU consists of a self-checking pair with its own power supply. The two FCUs should be installed at different sites in the vehicle in order to tolerate a spatial proximity fault.

Both FCUs execute the identical simple software. Form a hardware point of view, the fail-silent failure of one FCU is masked by the correct result of the other FCU.

The L2-system: The purpose of the *L2-system* is to provide a trajectory in normal driving situations and to detect adverse events, such as an ODD exit, that makes it impossible to continue the autonomous driving mode. In case such an adverse event is detected, the *L2-system* terminates the autonomous driving mode and brings the vehicle to a safe state.

The functionality of the *L2-system* in an SAE level-four system is the same as the functionality of the *L2-system* of an SAE level-two system. The *L2-system* is an enclosed fault-containment unit (FCU) with its own hardware, software and sensors to calculate a trajectory for the movement of the vehicle from its current position in the direction towards its specified destination in normal driving situations.

At the end of each frame, the *L2-system* sends the following two time-triggered unidirectional messages to other subsystems.

- A message containing the setpoints and the prospective trajectory to the *M-system* in order that the *M-system* can establish the safety of this prospective trajectory.
- A message containing the setpoints for a *normal driving situation* to the *D-system*.

The unidirectionality of the message transmission is important to avoid the formation of causal loops. In order to detect a Byzantine error of the *L2-system*, the setpoints sent to the *D-system* must be relayed from the *D-system* to the *M-system*.

The M-system: The purpose of the *M-system* (Monitoring System) is to check the safety of the prospective trajectory provided by the *L2-system* and the setpoints provided by the *F-system*. The *M-system* is an enclosed fault-containment unit (FCU) with its own hardware, software and sensors to observe the environment. The *M-system* builds its own world model and first checks whether anyone of the assumptions that characterize the Operational Design Domain (ODD) of the *L2-system* is violated. It then constructs a map of the environment of the vehicle and examines whether the prospective trajectory received from the *L2-system* meets all required safety assertions and identified constraints when placed into this current map of the environment. The *M-system* does not have to calculate a trajectory.

The *M-system* also checks the safety of the setpoints received from the *F-system* via the *D-system* and reports a failure to the *L2-system*.

We distinguish between the following two failure modes of the *M-system*:

(i) *fail negative:* A safe trajectory is judged to be unsafe. This means that a correct trajectory is rejected. From a safety perspective, this failure mode is not critical since it will only cause an avoidable activation of the critical event handler, the *F-system*.

(ii) *fail positive:* An unsafe trajectory is judged to be safe. Since this implies that a failure of the *L2-system* is not detected by the *M-system*, this failure mode is critical and can cause an accident. However, this failure mode can only occur if two out of the three complex systems (the L2 system and the M-system) fail at the same time, which is outside the fault hypothesis.

Since there is a tradeoff between the probabilities for *fail positive* and *fail negative* of the *M-system,* a careful design will minimize the *fail-positive failures,* even at the expense of more *fail-negative* failures.

The F-system: The purpose of the *F-system* (the fallback system) is to provide a safe trajectory in an *abnormal driving situation.* The *F-system* is an enclosed FCU with its own hardware, software and sensors. Although the services of the *F-system* are only required *on demand,* i.e., after a *critical event* has been detected, the *F-system* must always be ready to control the vehicle.

The *F-system* must be able to properly handle a scenario that has not been encountered up to now. The logic of the *F-system* must support kno*wledge-based reasoning* [Ras83] and cannot rely solely on machine learning.

Figure 4 depicts the state transition in case of a failure of a complex subsystem. After the occurrence of a critical event the human driver has the option to take over the control of the vehicle, but is not required to take over the control, since the *F-system* will bring the vehicle to a safe state autonomously even if the human driver is not engaged.

The safe state will transition to a *stop state* if a permanent fault in the *L2-system* or in the *M-system* or if a permanent violation of the ODD has been identified. If the cause for the critical event was transient, e.g., an SEU, then an *L2-system* and *M-system* recovery, as described in Sect. 5.3, will be attempted.

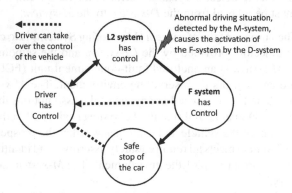

Fig. 4. State transitions after a critical event.

The *F-system* cannot refer to a detailed ODD specification, but must assume "*any driver-manageable road condition within its region of the world*" [SAE18, p. 25]. The *F-system* must calculate a safe trajectory in every frame, although this trajectory is not needed most of the time. After the occurrence of a critical event, the *D-system* decides that the *F-system* must take over the control of the vehicle. In a first phase, the *F-system* must bring the vehicle from its current dangerous state to a safe state—this can be a *stop-state* (at a safe location), or, preferably, a *steady moving state* where the vehicle is in a controlled out-of-danger movement until either the *L2-system* recovery is successful, a safe parking position has been reached, or the human driver disables the Automatic Driving System and takes over the control of the vehicle by manual operation. In case the human driver takes over the control of the car, s/he will provide the two setpoints for braking/accelerating and steering via the conventional driver interface, i.e., the pedals and the steering wheel.

5.3 L2-System and M-system Recovery

After the occurrence of a critical event that causes the *F-system* to take over the control of the vehicle, (see Fig. 4), the *L2-system* and the *M-system* will try to regain control of the vehicle. Such a resumption of normal operation is possible, if the fault that caused the critical event was transient. Since the majority of faults that cause a switch to the *F-system* are assumed to be transient (e.g., either a *bit-flip* in the hardware [Con02], or the manifestation of a Heisenbug in the software [Gra85], or an unforeseen external critical event) the probability that a recovery action will be successful is considerable. The autonomous *L2-system* and *M-system* recovery in case of a transient fault reduces very significantly the number of disengagements of an *SAE level-four Driving Automation System.*

In a first phase after the loss of control, the *L2-system* and the *M2-system* will perform a reset and self-test to confirm the internal integrity of the subsystems. If these tests are successful, then the *L2-system* will check whether a permanent external cause, such as an ODD exit or a mechanical fault of the vehicle, is present. If no permanent fault is present, then the *L2-system* will execute a restart and start to produce new trajectories. The *M-system* will execute a restart and validate the trajectories produced by the *L2-system*. If the *M2-system* decides that the new trajectory provided by the *L2-system* is SAFE, it will report this positive decision to the *D-system*. If the vehicle is in a safe mode (see Fig. 4), the *D-system* will switch to normal operation by taking from now on the setpoints from the *L2-system*.

If the *D-system* does not receive a positive decision from the *M-system* within a specified time-interval after it has entered the safe mode it will continue to take the setpoints from the *F-system* until the car is at a safe stop.

5.4 Fault Masking in the Architecture

Figure 5 summarized the failure detection and failure mitigation mechanisms in the proposed architecture. The small and simple *D-system* at the top of the formal hierarchy (Fig. 3) is assumed to be *correct*, i.e., *free of failure*. It contains *simple software* executed on *fault-tolerant hardware*.

At the next level down in Fig. 3 there are the three complex subsystems. The two complex subsystems *L2-system* and *F-system* calculate trajectories with complex software on standard hardware and the third complex subsystem, the *M-system* checks whether the prospective trajectory calculated by the *L2-system* and the *F-system* is safe. The fault hypothesis assumes that at any one time a **single one** of these three independently developed subsystems can fail, either due to a design error in the software or due to a hardware failure or due to an intrusion.

If we assume that there is no correlation between a failure or the L2-system and a failure of the M-system, then the probability of a fault-positive failure of the M-system at the same time as an L2-system failure is negligible. However, even if the L2-system and the M-system have their own sensors and diverse software there is a correlation between a failure of the L2- system and a failure the M-system caused by the sameness of the external environment.

Faulty Subsystem	Failure Detection	Failure Mitigation
L2-system	*M-system* detects the failure and reports the failure to the *D-system*.	*D-system* selects the set-points from *F-system*
F-system	*M-system* detects the failure and reports the failure to the *L2-system*.	*L2-system* brings the vehicle to a safe state.
M-system	*D-system* detects the failure. A critical *fail positive failure* of the M-system is only possible, if the L2 system has failed at the same time. Two simultaneous failures are not part of the fault hypothesis.	*D-system* selects the set-points from *F-system*
D-system	No failure detection, because *D-system* is assumed to be correct.	No failure mitigation.

Fig. 5. Failure detection and failure mitigation of a single FCU failure.

The services of the *F-system* are only needed *on demand*, when the *D-system* selects the set-points from *F-system*. According to [Lit93, p. 76] a *probability of failure on demand* of 10^{-4} is the best that is achievable with a complex software system in the nuclear industry.

During normal operation, the *M-system* receives the setpoints calculated by the *F-system* via the D-system. This detour is needed to detect a Byzantine failure of the *F-system*. The *M-system* checks whether these setpoints are safe. If the F-system fails, the M-system will detect the failure and will inform the L2-system that the fall-back mechanism is out of service and that it should terminate the autonomous operation.

The environment of every critical event must be recorded in order that this event can be analyzed off-line to improve the dependability of the Driving Automation System. This regular and systematic failure analysis is of great value in the airline industry.

5.5 Safety Improvement

The fault-hypothesis of the architecture states that only one out of the three complex subsystems of the architecture is assumed to fail at the same time. If this is the case, no accident will occur. However in reality there is a probability that two systems will fail at the same time, implying that the coverage of this assumption is less than one. Let us make the following guess of the *assumption coverage* in order to get a *rough estimate* of the *Safety Improvement* that can be achieved with the proposed safety architecture:

1. A critical situation that the *L2-system* cannot manage, i.e. a *critical event*, occurs on the average after a mean time of *a* hours of operation of the vehicle.

2. The *M-system* identifies with a probability of (*1-b*) the critical event correctly and *fails positively* with a probability of *b* per critical event. In case a critical event is not recognized by the *M-system* an accident may occur.
3. The *F-system* will fail to mitigate a correctly identified critical event with probability *c*, resulting in an accident.

Given that b << 1 and c << 1, then the *Mean-time-to-a-Reported Traffic-Accident* is approximately given by $a/(b + c)$. The term $1/(b + c)$ denotes the approximate *Safety Improvement Factor (SIF)* that is achieved by the *SA-system* (the safety assurance system) of the proposed architecture. Figure 6 shows the SIF for a set of parameters for an *L2-system* with a mean time to a critical event of 500 h or 30 000 km *driven* under the assumption that an average vehicle speed is 60 km/h.

Case		A	B	C	D
M-system fail positive probability	b	0,005	0,001		
F-system failure probability on demand	c	0,005	0,001		
Safety Improvement Factor (SIF)		100	500		
Mean time to an accident in hours		50 000	250 000	**30 000**	300 000
Mean km to an accident in 1000 km		3 000	15 000	**1 800**	18 000

Fig. 6. Safety improvement factor (SIF) of the proposed architecture

Under the stated assumptions we need an *SA-system* with a SIF of 100 (column A of Fig. 6) to arrive at a level of safety that is better than the one attained today by a human driver (column C in Fig. 6). If the Automated Driving System is required to be about ten times better than a human driver of today (column D in Fig. 6), then a SIF of better than 500 is needed (column B of Fig. 6)

Company	Number of Vehicles	Miles Driven in 2019	Mean Miles between Disengagements	Mean km between Disengagements
Baidu	4	108300	18050	29260
Waymo	148	1454137	13219	21175
Cruise	228	831040	12221	19626

Fig. 7. Some data from the 2019 California Disengagement Report [Her20].

If we consider the number of disengagements of current Drive-by-Wire Systems that are documented in the 2019 California Disengagement Report [Her20], then the assumption of a mean distance of 30 000 km between the occurrence of critical events of the L2-sxstem, (i.e., about once in every other year of vehicle operation) seems optimistic (Fig. 7).

6   Implementation Considerations

The safety architecture sketched in Section four assumes that the *D-system* and each one of the three complex subsystems, the *L2-system*, the *M-system* and the *F-system* with their own sensors, hardware and software, form independent Fault-Containment Units (FCUs) and that unintended emergent effects during the integration are avoided.

6.1   Security

Form the point of view of safety, an undetected intrusion is just as critical as a hardware or software failure. In the proposed architecture, a safety relevant security incident can only occur, if two independent intrusions are successful in two of the three complex subsystems at the same time. No intrusion is possible into the simple *D-system* at the top of the hierarchy since this simple subsystem is not connected to the Internet.

A safety-critical system that is connected to the Internet—such as an *L2-system*—must contain firewalls to fend off security attacks and must include internal intrusion detection mechanisms to detect an intrusion that managed to circumvent the firewall.

Each one of the three complex subsystems, the *L2-system*, the *M-system* and the *F-system* should have its own independent security firewall and its own diverse intrusion detection system. A good survey of intrusion detection techniques is given in [Khr19]. If an intrusion is detected in the *L2-system* or the *M-system* then the *L2-system* or the *M-system* should fail silently. In case of a silent failure of one of these two subsystems, the *D-system* will activate the *F-system* to bring the car to a safe state and deactivate the automation system. If an intrusion is detected in the *F-system*, then the failure will be detected by the *M-system* and reported to the *L2-system* to terminate the Driving Automation mode and bring the car to a safe state.

6.2   Validation

According to [Lit93] a testing duration of more than the envisioned MTTF is required in order to establish the envisioned MTTF of a system by testing. In the case of a Driving Automation System with a monolithic structure, a driving distance of about 1 800 000 km without a single reported accident must be mastered in the autonomous mode to demonstrate that a system has the envisioned dependability (measured by the occurrence of a reported accident, see Sect. 4.1), which is comparable to the dependability attained by a human driver. Since a Byzantine failure of a monolithic Driving Automation System can be caused by a single event upset (SEU) in the hardware [Con02], a *software simulation* of millions of kilometers driven does not provide the needed robust evidence for the correct operation of a *L2-system* in the physical world.

In the presented architecture the interactions among the independent FCUs by the exchange of well-defined time-triggered unidirectional state messages in cyberspace as well as the interactions among the FCUs by stigmergic channels in the environment [Kop15] have been designed to avoid causal loops that may lead to *unintended emergent phenomena* during system integration. If no *unintended emergent phenomena* are present then it is possible to establish the system level dependability out of the dependability of the isolated subsystems and the given structural redundancy of the architecture. This is kind of a gray box approach. We combine the known redundant structure of our solution with evidence about the dependability of the parts. This leads to an enormous reduction of the required validation effort compared to the validation effort for a comparable monolithic system.

During the validation and operation of the proposed architecture for Driving Automation it is crucial to distinguish between *incidents* and *accidents*. An incident occurs if a critical event causes a transfer of control from the *L2-system* to the *F-system*. An accident occurs if the *M-system fail positively* or the *F-system* is not capable to bring the car to a safe state. By carefully monitoring the relation between the number of incidents and the number of accidents in a multitude of cars, one can arrive at the following *measures for the dependability*: the *mean number of kilometers* driven between incidents, the *mean number of fail-positive classifications* by the *M-system*, the *mean number of failures by the F-system* and the *mean number of successful recoveries* of the *L2-system* and the *M-system*. These numbers must be carefully analyzed to arrive at an overall estimation of the dependability.

6.3 System Evolution

Every successful system must be continuously modified to remain relevant in the ever-changing world: latent design errors must be corrected, new functionality should be added to meet new requirements, and the technology base that is moving forward at an amazing pace opens new options for system implementations. These changes are particularly true for Driving Automation Systems, that learn to manage up-to-today novel edge-cases and take advantage of the capabilities of newly developed sensors and processing hardware. These repeated modifications of a system are subsumed under the term *system evolution* [Fur19].

An evolvable architecture should analyze the probability of change requests at the time of architecture conception and design the subsystems and their interfaces in such a way that the consequences of a change request are limited to the internals of a subsystem. This design principle has been observed in the proposed architecture for Driving Automation. In this architecture, the *pressure for evolution* is quite different for the subsystems of Fig. 3. The *D-system* at the top of the hierarchy is simple and stable with interfaces that are unlikely to change over the lifetime of a vehicle. On the other side, the functionality of the *L2-system* is the candidate for most modifications. The *pressure for evolution* on the other two subsystems, the M-system and the F-system, is between these two extremes.

The safety of the autonomous vehicle is the responsibility of the *SA-system* that comprises of the *M-system* the *F-system* and the *D-system*. The strict separation of the *SA-system* from the *L2-system*, simplifies the evolution of the *L2-system*. It ensures that a fault in a new version of the *L2-system* will not impact the safety of the vehicle as long as the functionality of a mature *SA-system* is not modified. It follows that only a limited revalidation of the safety of the architecture will be required if a new version of the *L2-system* is implemented—this is a major advantage of this distributed architecture over a monolithic architecture.

The novel architecture proposed in this paper opens the route to industry-wide cooperation, since the interfaces among the subsystems are simple and well-defined in the value domain and the temporal domain. For example, the independent *F-system* with its own sensors can be provided by a company that is an expert in this domain. It can be integrated with a small integration effort in many different proprietary driving automation systems.

Note that the hierarchy of Fig. 3 is nearly a *formal* hierarchy, i.e., there is a limited number of unidirectional horizontal interaction among the three independent subsystems. This independence is also important from the point of view of the *required design diversity* [Avi86] of the three complex subsystems. The total system development can be partitioned into nearly independent projects that are implemented by separate development teams. Since the interfaces among the complex subsystems are well-defined at the level of the system architecture, the coordination effort among the teams will be small.

6.4 Shared Sensors

From an economic perspective it is advantageous to share the sensors among the subsystems to avoid the duplication of expensive sensors.

From an engineering point of view, it is an advantage, if every-one of the three complex subsystems can access the information captured by all sensors. Every sensor sends the preprocessed results via a fault-tolerant time-triggered communication system to all information-consuming subsystems. The unidirectional information flow should be enforced by a fault-tolerant time-triggered communication subsystem in order that any backward error propagation from a receiver to a sender is avoided.

A severe problem of such a configuration is that the independence of the subsystems is compromised and a failure of a single sensor can result in a common mode failure of more than one of the complex subsystems. *Even a small increase in the probability of a common mode failure in participating subsystems has a very large effect on the dependability at the system level.*

7 Conclusion

It is a tremendous challenge to increase the dependability of a Driving Automation System by a factor of more than one hundred over the dependability obtained at present, in order to arrive at a level of dependability that is commensurate with the dependability that is achieved by an attentive human driver. This paper proposes a route to tackle this challenge by partitioning a Driving Automation System into four self-contained subsystems, where each one forms an independent fault-containment unit (FCU).

Only the top-level FCU, the *Fault-tolerant Decision Subsystem* (*the D-System*) must meet the ultra-high dependability requirement. It contains simple software that is executed on fault-tolerant hardware. The other three large subsystems, the *L2-System*, the *M-system*, and the *F-System*, contain complex software that is executed on standard hardware. A single failure of anyone of these large subsystems—caused either by the software, the hardware, or an intrusion—is tolerated by the redundancy and design diversity that is inherent in this architecture.

The restricted vertical information flow from the bottom to the top and the small well-defined horizontal information flow between the subsystems of this novel architecture avoids causal chains that can lead to *unintended emergent phenomena*. It is thus possible to develop and validate the three large and complex subsystems independently of each other and to a arrive at the system reliability by the experimentally established reliability of the subsystems and the analytical analysis of the redundancy structure of the architecture. This results in a very substantial reduction of the design and validation effort of the ultra-dependable Driving Automation System presented in this paper.

Acknowledgements. There have been many friends who commented on earlier drafts of this paper and made valuable contributions to improve the contents and the presentation. I am particularly grateful for the comments from Tom Anderson, Ricky Hudy, Stefan Poledna, Rob Siegel and Winfried Steiner and from the anonymous reviewers.

References

[Avi86] Avizienis, A., Laprie, J.C.: Dependable computing: from concepts to design diversity. Proc. IEEE **54**(5), pp. 629–638 (1986)

[Bha15] Bhattacharyya, S., Cofer, D.: Certification considerations for adaptive systems. NASA Report NASA/CR-2015–218702, March 2015

[Cho01] Chou, A., et al.: An empirical study of operating system errors. In: Proceedings of the ACM SOPS 2001, pp. 73–88 (2001)

[Con02] Constantinescu, C.: Impact of deep submicron technology on dependability of VLSI circuits. In: Proceedings International Conference on Dependable Systems and Networks, Washington, DC, USA, pp. 205–209 (2002)

[Dri03] Driscoll, K., Hall, B., Sivencrona, H., Zumsteg, P.: Byzantine fault tolerance, from theory to reality. In: Anderson, S., Felici, M., Littlewood, B. (eds.) SAFECOMP 2003. LNCS, vol. 2788, pp. 235–248. Springer, Heidelberg (2003). https://doi.org/10.1007/978-3-540-39878-3_19

[Dvo09] Dvorak, D.L.: NASA study on flight software complexity. Jet Propulsion Laboratory, California Institute of Technology (2009)

[Ege97] Egerth, H.E., Yantis, S.: Visual attention: control, representation and time course. Annu. Rev. Psychol. **48**, 269–297 (1997)

[Fur19] Furrer, F.: Future-Proof Software Systems: A sustainable Evolution Strategy. Springer, Wiesbaden (2019). https://doi.org/10.1007/978-3-658-19938-8

[Gra85] Gray, J.: Why do computers fail and what can be done about it? Technical report 85/7. Tandem Computer Corporation, June 1985

[Her20] Herger, M.: Disengagement Report 2019. https://thelastdriverlicenseholder.com/2020/02/26/disengagement-report-2019/. Accessed 22 Dec 2020

[Kal16] Kalra, N., Paddock, S.M.: Driving to safety: how many miles of driving would it take to demonstrate autonomous vehicle reliability? Transp. Res. Part A Policy Pract. **94**, 182–193 (2016)

[KHR19] Khraisat, A., et al.: Survey of intrusion detection systems: techniques, data sets, and challenges (2019). https://doi.org/10.1186/s42400-019-0038-7. Accessed 31 July 2020

[Koo17] Koopman, P.: Autonomous vehicle safety: an interdisciplinary challenge. IEEE Intell. Transp. Mag. **9**(1), 90–96 (2017)

[Kop06] Kopetz, H.: On the fault hypothesis for a safety-critical real-time system. In: Broy, M., Krüger, I.H., Meisinger, M. (eds.) ASWSD 2004. LNCS, vol. 4147. Springer, Heidelberg (2006). https://doi.org/10.1007/11823063_3

[Kop12] Kopetz, H., Real Time Systems—Design Principles for Distributed Embedded Applications, 2nd edn. Springer, New York (2012). https://doi.org/10.1007/978-1-4419-8237-7

[Kop15] Kopetz, H., et al.: Direct versus stigmergic information flows in systems-of-systems. In: Proceedings of the 10th System of Systems Engineering Conference (SoSE), pp. 36–41. IEEE Press (2015)

[Kop16] Kopetz, H., Bondavalli, A., Brancati, F., Frömel, B., Höftberger, O., Iacob, S.: Emergence in cyber-physical systems-of-systems (CPSoSs). In: Bondavalli, A., Bouchenak, S., Kopetz, H. (eds.) Cyber-Physical Systems of Systems. LNCS, vol. 10099, pp. 73–96. Springer, Cham (2016). https://doi.org/10.1007/978-3-319-47590-5_3

[Kop19] Kopetz, H.: Simplicity is Complex—Foundations of Cyber-Physical System Design. Springer, Cham (2019). https://doi.org/10.1007/978-3-030-20411-2

[Lal94] Lala, J., Harper, R.: Architectural principles for safety-critical real-time applications. Proc. IEEE **82**(1), 25–40 (1994)

[Lam82] Lamport, L., et al.: The byzantine generals problem. ACM Trans. Program. Lang. Syst. **4**(3), 382–401 (1982)

[Li17] Li, G., et al.: Understanding error propagation in deep learning neural networks (DNN) accelerators and applications. In: Proceedings of the International Conference for High Performance Computing, Networking, Storage and Analysis, pp.1–12. ACM Press (2017)

[Lit93] Littlewood, B., Strigini, L.: Validation of ultrahigh dependability for software-based systems. Commun. ACM **36**(11), 69–80 (1993)

[Mat19] Mat19 et al. White Paper: Safety First for Driving Automation. https://www.dai mler.com/innovation/case/autonomous/safety-first-for-automated-driving-2.html. Accessed 22 May 2020

[Meh20] Mehmed, A., et al.: The monitor as a key architectural element for safe self-driving. In: Proceedings of the DSN 2020, vol. DSN-S, Valencia, Spain. IEEE Press (2020)

[Mim21] Mims, C.: Self-driving cars could be decades away, no matter what Elon Musk said. Wall Street J. (2021)

[NHT20] A Vision for Safety.https://www.nhtsa.gov/automated-driving-systems/voluntary-saf ety-self-assessment. Accessed 16 Dec 2020

[Pom12] Pompili, M., et al.: Car accidents as a method of suicide: a comprehensive overview. Forensic Sci. Int. **223**(1–3), 1–9 (2012)

[Pow95] Powell, D.: Failure mode assumptions and assumption coverage. In: Randell, B., Laprie, J.C., Kopetz, H., Littlewood, B. (eds.) Predictably Dependable Computing Systems, p. 1995. Springer Verlag, ESPRIT Basic Research Series (1995)

[Ras83] Rasmussen, J.: Skills, rules and knowledge; signals, signs and symbols, and other distinctions in human performance models. IEEE Trans. Syst. Man Cybern. **smc-13**(3), 257–266 (1983)

[SAE18] SAE, Standard J3016. *Surface Vehicle Recommended Practice*. SAE International, 2018

[Sha19] Sha, S.A.: Save-AV, A fault-tolerant safety architecture for autonomous vehicles.https:// macsphere.mcmaster.ca/handle/11375/24205. Accessed 3 Feb 2021

[Sta19] Traffic Statistics in Austria 2018. https://www.statistik.at/web_de/statistiken/ene rgie_umwelt_innovation_mobilitaet/verkehr/strasse/unfaelle_mit_personenschaden/ index.html. Accessed 26 May 2019

[Yue18] Yue, L., et al.: Assessment of the safety benefits of vehicles' advanced driver assistance, connectivity and low-level automation systems. Accid. Anal. Prev. **117**, 55–64 (2018)

Specification and Validation of Autonomous Driving Systems: A Multilevel Semantic Framework

Marius Bozga[✉][iD] and Joseph Sifakis[iD]

Univ. Grenoble Alpes, CNRS, Grenoble INP, VERIMAG, 38000 Grenoble, France
{Marius.Bozga,Joseph.Sifakis}@univ-grenoble-alpes.fr
http://www-verimag.imag.fr/

Abstract. Autonomous Driving Systems (ADS) are critical dynamic reconfigurable agent systems whose specification and validation raises extremely challenging problems. The paper presents a multilevel semantic framework for the specification of ADS and discusses associated validation problems. The framework relies on a formal definition of maps modeling the physical environment in which vehicles evolve. Maps are directed metric graphs whose nodes represent positions and edges represent segments of roads. We study basic properties of maps including their geometric consistency. Furthermore, we study position refinement and segment abstraction relations allowing multilevel representation from purely topological to detailed geometric. We progressively define first order logics for modeling families of maps and distributions of vehicles over maps. These are Configuration Logics, which in addition to the usual logical connectives are equipped with a coalescing operator to build configurations of models. We study their semantics and basic properties. We illustrate their use for the specification of traffic rules and scenarios characterizing sequences of scenes. We study various aspects of the validation problem including run-time verification and satisfiability of specifications. Finally, we show links of our framework with practical validation needs for ADS and advocate its adequacy for addressing the many facets of this challenge.

Keywords: Autonomous Driving System · Map modeling · Configuration logic · Traffic rule specification · Scene and scenario description · Runtime verification · Simulation and validation in the large

1 Introduction

The validation of ADS raises challenges far beyond the current state of the art because of their overwhelming complexity and the integration of non-explainable AI components. Providing sufficient evidence that these systems are safe enough

---

Institute of Engineering Univ. Grenoble Alpes.

© Springer Nature Switzerland AG 2022
J.-F. Raskin and K. Chatterjee (Eds.): Principles of Systems Design, LNCS 13660, pp. 85–106, 2022.
https://doi.org/10.1007/978-3-031-22337-2_5

is a hot and critical need, given the underlying economic and societal stakes. This objective mobilizes considerable investments and efforts by key players including big tech companies and car manufacturers. The efforts focus on the development of efficient simulation technology and common infrastructure for modelling the physical environment of ADS and their desired properties. They led in particular to the definition of common formats such as OpenDRIVE [1] for the description of road networks, and OpenSCENARIO [2] for the description of complex, synchronized maneuvers that involve multiple entities like vehicles, pedestrians and other traffic participants. Additionally, several open simulation environments such as CARLA [9] and LGSVL [23] are available for modelling and validation.

The paper proposes a semantic framework for the specification and validation of ADS. The framework provides a precise semantic model of the environment of ADS based on maps. It also includes logics for the specification and validation of properties of the semantic model and of the system dynamic behavior. Maps have been the object of numerous studies focusing on the formalization of the concept and its use for the analysis of ADS. A key research issue is to avoid monolithic representations and build maps by composition of components and heterogeneous data. This motivated formalizations using ontologies and logics with associated reasoning mechanisms to check consistency of descriptions and their correctness with respect to desired properties [3,5] or to generate scenarios [3,7]. Other works propose open source map frameworks for highly automated driving [1,19].

A different research line focuses on the validation of ADS either to verify satisfaction of safety and efficiency properties or even to check that vehicles respect given traffic rules. Many works deal with safety verification in a simple multilane setting. In [16] a dedicated Multi-Lane Spatial Logic inspired by interval temporal logic is used to specify safety and provide proofs for lane change controllers. The work in [21] presents a motion planner formally verified in Isabelle/HOL. The planner is based on manoeuver automata, a variant of hybrid automata, and properties are expressed in linear temporal logic.

Other works deal with scenarios for modeling the behavior of ADS. Open-SCENARIO [2] defines a data model and a derived file format for the description of scenarios used in driving and traffic simulators, as well as in automotive virtual development, testing and validation. The work in [8] proposes a visual formal specification language for capturing scenarios inspired from Message Charts and shows possible applications to specification and testing of autonomous vehicles. In [24] a scenario-based methodology for functional safety analysis is presented using the example of automated valet parking. The work in [14] presents an approach to automated scenario-based testing of the safety of autonomous vehicles, based on Metric Temporal Logic. Finally, the probabilistic language Scenic for the design and analysis of cyber physical systems allows the description of scenarios used to control and validate simulated systems of self-driving cars. The Scenic programming environment provides a big variety of constructs making possible modeling anywhere in the spectrum from concrete scenes to broad classes of abstract scenarios [13].

Other works focus on checking compliance of vehicles with traffic rules. A formalization of traffic rules in linear temporal logic is proposed in [11]. Runtime verification is applied to check that maneuvers of a high-level planner comply with the rules. Works in [20,22] formalize a set of traffic rules for highway scenarios in Isabelle/HOL; they show that traffic rules can be used as requirements to be met by autonomous vehicles and propose a verification procedure. A formalization of traffic rules for uncontrolled intersections is provided in [18] using the CLINGO logic programming language. Furthermore, the rules are applied by a simulator to safely control traffic across intersections. The work in [12] proposes a methodology for the formalization of traffic rules in Linear Temporal Logic; it is shown how evaluation of formalized rules on recorded drives of humans provides insight on what extent drivers respect the rules.

This work is an attempt to provide a minimal framework unifying the concepts for the specification of ADS and the associated validation problems. The proposed semantic framework clearly distinguishes between a static part consisting of the road network with its equipment and a dynamic part involving objects. We progressively introduce three logics to express properties of the semantic model at different levels. The *Metric Configuration Logic* (*MCL*) allows the compositional and parametric description of metric graphs. This is a first order logic with variables ranging over positions and segments. It uses in addition to logical connectives, a coalescing operator for the compositional construction of maps from segments. A *MCL* formula represents configurations of maps sharing a common set of locations. We discuss a specification methodology and show how various road patterns such as roundabouts, intersections, mergers of roads can be specified in *MCL*.

The *Mobile Metric Configuration Logic* (*M2CL*) is an extension of *MCL* with object variables and primitives for the specification of scenes as the distribution of objects over maps. *M2CL* formulas can be written as the conjunction of formulas describing: i) static map contexts; ii) dynamic relations between objects; iii) addressing relations between objects and maps. Last, we define *Temporal M2CL* (*TM2CL*), a linear temporal logic whose atomic propositions are formulas of *M2CL*. We illustrate the use of these logics for the specification of safety properties including traffic rules as well as the description of dynamic scenarios.

Additionally, we study the validation of properties expressed in the three logics and provide a classification of problems showing that validation of general dynamic properties boils down to constraint checking on metric graphs. Checking that a finite model satisfies a formula of *MCL* or *M2CL* amounts to eliminate quantifiers by adequate instantiation of variables. We argue that satisfiability of *M2CL* formulas can be reduced to satisfiability of *MCL* formulas which is an undecidable problem. We identify a reasonably expressive decidable subset of *MCL* and propose a decision procedure. Furthermore, we discuss the problem of runtime verification of *TM2CL* formulas and sketch a principle of solution inspired from a recent work with a similar configuration logic [10]. We complete the presentation on ADS validation with an analysis of practical needs for a rigorous validation methodology. We describe a general validation environment and show how the proposed framework provides insight into the different aspects of validation and related methodological issues.

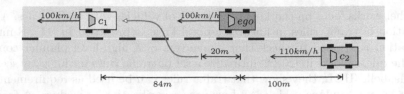

Fig. 1. A scenario example

To illustrate the specification and validation methodology based on the combined use of these three logics, let us consider a concrete example from [2] describing a scenario involving three cars moving on a two-lane road with their speeds and distances. We use *MCL* to describe the static environment in which the cars move. In this example, it is a two-lane road, but in the general case it can be a parametric map obtained by composing road segments. To describe a scene, such as the distribution of vehicles on a map, we use *M2CL* formulas. In this example, a scene is specified by the relative positions of the cars on the map and their speeds. Finally, to specify system properties, which are sequences of scenes, we use *TM2CL*. In this example, a scene sequence could be: car c_2 passes the *ego* car and moves to the right lane in front of it. The formulas in *TM2CL* can be used to specify traffic rules that must be satisfied by vehicle maneuvers.

The paper is structured as follows. In Sect. 2, we study metric graphs and their relevant properties for the representation of map models as well as the logic *MCL*, its main properties and application for map specification. Section 3 deals with the study of logics *M2CL* and *TM2CL* and their application to the specification of safety properties and the description of scenarios. Then, Sect. 4 discusses a classification of validations problems and approaches for their solution. Section 5 concludes with a summary of main results and a discussion about future developments. A long version of the paper is available in [6].

2   Metric Graphs and Metric Configuration Logic

2.1   Segments and Metric Graphs

Segments. We build contiguous road segments from a set $\mathcal{S}$ equipped with a partial concatenation operator $\cdot : \mathcal{S} \times \mathcal{S} \to \mathcal{S} \cup \{\bot\}$ and a length norm $\|.\| : \mathcal{S} \to \mathbb{R}_{\geq 0}$ satisfying the following properties:

(i) *associativity:* for any segments s_1, s_2, s_3 either both $(s_1 \cdot s_2) \cdot s_3$ and $s_1 \cdot (s_2 \cdot s_3)$ are defined and equal, or both undefined;

(ii) *length additivity wrt concatenation:* for any segments s_1, s_2 whenever $s_1 \cdot s_2$ defined it holds $\|s_1 \cdot s_2\| = \|s_1\| + \|s_2\|$;

(iii) *segment split:* for any segment s and non-negative a_1, a_2 such that $\|s\| = a_1 + a_2$ there exist unique s_1, s_2 such that $s = s_1 \cdot s_2$, $\|s_1\| = a_1$, $\|s_2\| = a_2$.

The last property allows us to define consistently a subsegment operation: $s[a_1, a_2]$ is the unique segment of length $a_2 - a_1$ satisfying $s = s_1 \cdot s[a_1, a_2] \cdot s_2$ where s_1, s_2 are such that $\|s_1\| = a_1$, $\|s_2\| = \|s\| - a_2$, for any $0 \leq a_1 \leq a_2 \leq \|s\|$. For brevity, we use the shorthand notation $s[a, \text{-}]$ to denote the subsegment $s[a, \|s\|]$. Moreover, we define $s_1 \preccurlyeq s_2$ iff $s_1 = s_2[0, a]$ for some non-negative a.

Segments will be used to model building blocks of roads in maps considering three different interpretations. Interval segments simply define the length of a segment. Curve segments define the precise geometric form of the trajectory of a mobile object along the segment. Region segments are 2D-regions of given width around a center curve segment.

Interval Segments. Consider $S_{interval} \stackrel{def}{=} \{[0, a] \mid a \in \mathbb{R}_{\geq 0}\}$, that is, the set of closed intervals on reals with lower bound 0, concatenation defined by $[0, a_1] \cdot [0, a_2] \stackrel{def}{=} [0, a_1 + a_2]$ and length $\|[0, a]\| \stackrel{def}{=} a$.

Curve Segments. Consider $S_{curve} \stackrel{def}{=} \{c : [0, 1] \to \mathbb{R}^2 \mid c(0) = (0, 0),\ c \text{ curve}\} \cup \{\epsilon\}$ that is, the set of curves that are continuous smooth[1] and uniformly progressing[2] functions c, starting at the origin, plus a designated single point curve ϵ. The length is defined by taking respectively the length of the curve $\|c\| \stackrel{def}{=} \int_0^1 |\dot{c}(t)| dt$ and $\|\epsilon\| = 0$. The concatenation $c_1 \cdot c_2$ of two curves c_1 and c_2 is a partial operation that consists in joining the final endpoint of c_1 with the initial endpoint of c_2 provided the slopes at these points are equal. This condition preserves smoothness of the curve $c_1 \cdot c_2$ defined by $c_1 \cdot c_2 : [0, 1] \to \mathbb{R}^2$ where:

$$(c_1 \cdot c_2)(t) \stackrel{def}{=} \begin{cases} c_1(\frac{t}{\lambda}) & \text{if } t \in [0, \lambda] \\ c_1(1) + c_2(\frac{t-\lambda}{1-\lambda}) & \text{if } t \in [\lambda, 1] \end{cases} \text{ where } \lambda = \frac{\|c_1\|}{\|c_1\| + \|c_2\|}$$

Note that in this definition, c_1 and c_2 are scaled on sub-intervals of $[0, 1]$ respecting their length ratio. We additionally take $c \cdot \epsilon \stackrel{def}{=} \epsilon \cdot c \stackrel{def}{=} c$, for any c. For practical reasons, one can further restrict the set S_{curve} to curves of some form e.g., finite concatenation of parametric line segments and circle arcs. That is, for any $a, r \in \mathbb{R}_{\geq 0}^*$, $\varphi \in \mathbb{R}$, $\theta \in \mathbb{R}^*$ the curves $line[a, \varphi]$, $arc[r, \varphi, \theta]$ are defined as

$$line[a, \varphi](t) \stackrel{def}{=} (at \cos \varphi, at \sin \varphi) \ \forall t \in [0, 1]$$
$$arc[r, \varphi, \theta](t) \stackrel{def}{=} (r(\sin(\varphi + t\theta) - \sin \varphi), r(-\cos(\varphi + t\theta) + \cos \varphi)) \ \forall t \in [0, 1]$$

Note that a and r are respectively the length of the line and the radius of the arc, φ is the slope of the curve at the initial endpoint and θ is the degree of the arc. Figure 2 illustrates the composition of three segments of this parametric form.

---

[1] the derivative $\dot{c}$ exists and is continuous on $[0, 1]$.
[2] the instantaneous speed $|\dot{c}|$, that is, the Euclidean norm of the derivative is constant.

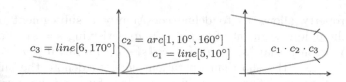

Fig. 2. Curve segments and their composition

Region Segments. Consider $\mathcal{S}_{region} \stackrel{def}{=} \mathcal{S}_{curve} \times \mathbb{R}^*_{\geq 0}$, that is, the set of pairs (c, w) where c is a curve and w a positive number, denoting respectively the region center curve and the region width. Region segments can be concatenated iff their curves can be concatenated and if their widths are equal, that is, $(c_1, w) \cdot (c_2, w) \stackrel{def}{=} (c_1 \cdot c_2, w)$ if $c_1 \cdot c_2 \neq \perp$. The length of a region segment is defined as the length of its center curve, $\|(c, w)\| \stackrel{def}{=} \|c\|$.

Region segments can be equally understood as sets of points in $\mathbb{R}^2$ defined by algebraic constraints. More precisely, for any curve c and width w the region segment (c, w) corresponds to the subset of $\mathbb{R}^2$ defined as $\{c(t) + \lambda \cdot \frac{ortho(\dot{c}(t))}{|\dot{c}(t)|} \mid t \in [0, 1], \lambda \in [-\frac{w}{2}, \frac{w}{2}]\}$ where *ortho* is the orthogonal operator on $\mathbb{R}^2$ defined as $ortho((a, b)) \stackrel{def}{=} (-b, a)$. In particular, the region generated by the curve $line[a, \varphi]$ is a rectangle containing the set of points $\{(at \cos \varphi - \lambda \sin \varphi, at \sin \varphi + \lambda \cos \varphi) \mid t \in [0, 1], \lambda \in [-\frac{w}{2}, \frac{w}{2}]\}$. The region generated by the curve $arc[r, \varphi, \theta]$ is a ring sector containing the set of points $\{((r + \lambda)(\sin(\varphi + t\theta) - r \sin \varphi, -(r + \lambda) \cos(\varphi + t\theta) + r \cos \varphi) \mid t \in [0, 1], \lambda \in [-\frac{w}{2}, \frac{w}{2}]\}$.

Metric Graphs. We use metric graphs $G \stackrel{def}{=} (V, \mathcal{S}, E)$ to represent maps, where V is a finite set of *vertices*, $\mathcal{S}$ is a set of segments and $E \subseteq V \times \mathcal{S}^* \times V$ is a finite set of *edges* labeled by non-zero length segments in $\mathcal{S}^*$. We also denote an edge $e = (v, s, v') \in E$ by $v \stackrel{s}{\to}_G v'$ and we define $\bullet e \stackrel{def}{=} v$, $e^\bullet \stackrel{def}{=} v'$, $e.s \stackrel{def}{=} s$. For a vertex v, we define $\bullet v \stackrel{def}{=} \{e \mid e^\bullet = v\}$ and $v^\bullet \stackrel{def}{=} \{e \mid \bullet e = v\}$. We denote by E^+_{ac} the finite set of non-empty *acyclic*[3] directed paths with edges from E. We call a metric graph *strongly* (resp. *weakly*) connected if a *directed* (resp. *undirected*) path exists between any pair of vertices. A metric graph is called *acyclic* if at most one path, directed or undirected, exist between any pairs of vertices.

We consider the set $Pos_G \stackrel{def}{=} V \cup \{(e, a) \mid e \in E, \ 0 < a < \|e.s\|\}$ of *positions* defined by a metric graph. Note that $(e, 0)$ and $(e, \|e.s\|)$ are respectively the positions $\bullet e$ and $e^\bullet$. Moreover, a s-labelled *ride* between positions (e, a) and (e', a') is an acyclic path denoted by $(e, a) \stackrel{s}{\leadsto}_G (e', a')$ and defined as follows:

(i) $e = e'$, $0 \leq a \leq a' \leq \|e.s\|$, $s = e.s[a, a']$
(ii) $e = e'$, $0 \leq a' \leq a \leq \|e.s\|$, $e^\bullet = \bullet e$, $s = e.s[a, -] \cdot e.s[0, a'] \neq \perp$

---

[3] every edge occurs at most once in the path.

(iii) $e = e'$, $0 \leq a' \leq a \leq \|e.s\|$, $w \in E_{ac}^+$, $e \not\subseteq w$, $e^\bullet = {}^\bullet w$, $w^\bullet = {}^\bullet e$,
$s = e.s[a,\text{-}] \cdot w.s \cdot e.s[0,a'] \neq \bot$
(iv) $e \neq e'$, $e^\bullet = {}^\bullet e'$, $s = e.s[a,\text{-}] \cdot e'.s[0,a'] \neq \bot$
(v) $e \neq e'$, $w \in E_{ac}^+$, $e,e' \not\subseteq w$, $e^\bullet = {}^\bullet w$, $w^\bullet = {}^\bullet e'$, $s = e.s[a,\text{-}] \cdot w.s \cdot e'.s[0,a'] \neq \bot$

Figure 3 illustrates the five cases of the above definition for a simple graph with segments s_1, s_2 and s_3. Cases (i) and (ii) correspond to rides on the same segment. Case (iii) corresponds to rides originating and terminating in fragments of the same segment and also involving other segments between them. Finally cases (iv) and (v) are rides originating and terminating at different segments.

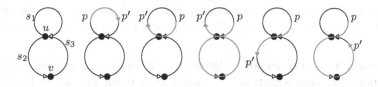

Fig. 3. Rides in metric graphs - cases (i)–(v) illustrated

We define the distance d_G between positions p, p' as 0 whenever $p = p'$ or the minimum length among all segments labeling rides from p to p' and otherwise $+\infty$ if no such ride exists. It can be checked that d_G is an *extended quasi-metric* on the set Pos_G and therefore, (Pos_G, d_G) is an extended quasi-metric space.

2.2 Properties of Metric Graphs

Contraction/Refinement. A metric graph $G' = (V', \mathcal{S}, E')$ is a *contraction* of a metric graph $G = (V, \mathcal{S}, E)$ (or dually, G is a *refinement* of G'), denoted by $G \sqsubseteq G'$, iff G is obtained from G' by transformations replacing some of its edges e by acyclic sequences of interconnected edges $e_1 e_2 ... e_n$ while preserving the segment labeling i.e., $e.s = e_1.s \cdot e_2.s \cdot ... \cdot e_n.s$. In Fig. 4, the graph on the right is a contraction of the one on the left iff $s_{12} = s_{14} \cdot s_{45} \cdot s_{52}$, $s'_{12} = s'_{16} \cdot s'_{62}$ and $s_{31} = s_{37} \cdot s_{78} \cdot s_{81}$.

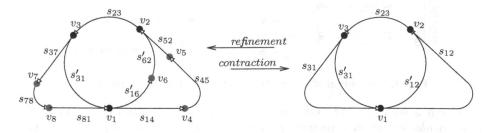

Fig. 4. Illustration of contraction/refinement on metric graphs

Note that metric graphs where all vertices have input or output degree greater than one cannot be contracted. Such vertices correspond to *junctions* (confluence of divergence of roads) when metric graphs represent maps. The following proposition states some key properties on contraction/refinement of metric graphs.

Proposition 1. *Let* $Con(G) \stackrel{def}{=} \{G' \mid G \sqsubseteq G'\}$, $Ref(G) \stackrel{def}{=} \{G' \mid G' \sqsubseteq G\}$ *be respectively the set of contractions, refinements of a metric graph* G.

   (i) the refinement relation $\sqsubseteq$ *is a partial order on the set of metric graphs;*
   (ii) for any metric graph G, *both* $(Con(G), \sqsubseteq)$ *and* $(Ref(G), \sqsubseteq)$ *are complete lattices, moreover,* $(Con(G), \sqsubseteq)$ *is finite;*
   (iii) for any metric graphs G, G' *if* $G \sqsubseteq G'$ *then (1) the labelled transition systems* $(Pos_G, \mathcal{S}, \leadsto_G)$ *and* $(Pos_{G'}, \mathcal{S}, \leadsto_{G'})$ *are strongly bisimilar and (2) the quasi-metric spaces* (Pos_G, d_G) *and* $(Pos_{G'}, d_{G'})$ *are isometric;*

Abstraction/Concretization. Consider $\mathcal{S}$, $\mathcal{S}'$ as sets of segments associated with respectively concatenation $\cdot$, $\cdot'$, and length norm $\|.\|$, $\|.\|'$. A function $\alpha : \mathcal{S} \to \mathcal{S}'$ is a *segment abstraction* if it satisfies the following properties: (i) *length preservation*: $\|s\| = \|\alpha(s)\|'$, forall $s \in \mathcal{S}$ (ii) *homomorphism wrt concatenation*: $\alpha(s_1 \cdot s_2) = \alpha(s_1) \cdot' \alpha(s_2)$ for all $s_1, s_2 \in \mathcal{S}$ such that $s_1 \cdot s_2 \neq \bot$.

For example, the function $\alpha^{CI} : \mathcal{S}_{curve} \to \mathcal{S}_{interval}$ defined by $\alpha^{CI}(s) \stackrel{def}{=} [0, \|s\|]$ for all $s \in \mathcal{S}_{curve}$ is a an abstraction of curve segments as interval segments. Similarly, the function $\alpha^{RC} : \mathcal{S}_{region} \to \mathcal{S}_{curve}$ defined by $\alpha^{RC}((s, w)) \stackrel{def}{=} s$ for all $(s, w) \in \mathcal{S}_{region}$ is an abstraction of region segments as curve segments.

Dually, we can define concretization functions γ that go from intervals to curves, and from curves to regions. For example, for any angles φ, θ consider $\gamma^{IC}_{\varphi, \theta} : \mathcal{S}_{interval} \to \mathcal{S}_{curve}$ where respectively, $\gamma^{IC}_{\varphi, \theta}([0, a]) \stackrel{def}{=} arc[\frac{a}{\theta}, \varphi, \theta]$ if $\theta \neq 0$ or $\gamma^{IC}_{\varphi, \theta}([0, a]) \stackrel{def}{=} line[a, \varphi]$ if $\theta = 0$. Or, for any positive real w consider $\gamma^{CR}_w : \mathcal{S}_{curve} \to \mathcal{S}_{regions}$ where $\gamma^{CR}_w(s) \stackrel{def}{=} (s, w)$.

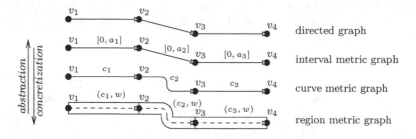

Fig. 5. Illustration of abstraction/concretization on metric graphs

Given a segment abstraction $\alpha : \mathcal{S} \to \mathcal{S}'$, a metric graph $G' = (V, \mathcal{S}', E')$ is an α-*abstraction* of a metric graph $G = (V, \mathcal{S}, E)$, denoted by $G' = \alpha(G)$, iff G' is obtained from G by replacing segments s by their abstractions $\alpha(s)$. That is, any edge $u \stackrel{s}{\to}_G v$ is transformed into an edge $u \stackrel{\alpha(s)}{\longrightarrow}_{G'} v$. In a similar way, γ-concretization on metric graphs is defined for a segment concretization $\gamma : \mathcal{S}' \to \mathcal{S}$. Figure 5 illustrates the use of the three segment abstraction levels (respectively as intervals, curves, regions) and their associated metric graphs. Interval metric graphs are α^{CI}-abstractions of curve metric graphs, which in turn are α^{RC}-abstractions of region metric graphs. Propositions 2 and 3 state some key properties on abstraction on metric graphs.

Proposition 2. *For a segment abstraction $\alpha : \mathcal{S} \to \mathcal{S}'$ and metric graphs G, G' such that $G' = \alpha(G)$, the labelled transition system $(Pos_{G'}, \mathcal{S}', \leadsto_{G'})$ simulates the labelled transition system $(Pos_G, \mathcal{S}, \leadsto_G)$ renamed by α.*

Proposition 3. *Contraction and abstraction commute, that is, for any metric graphs G, G', for any segment abstraction α, if $G \sqsubseteq G'$ then $\alpha(G) \sqsubseteq \alpha(G')$.*

2.3   The Metric Configuration Logic

Syntax. Let consider a fixed set of segments $\mathcal{S}$ and assume there exists a finite set $\mathcal{S}^T$ of segment constructors s^T (or segment types), that is, partial functions $s^T : \mathbb{R}^m \to \mathcal{S}^\perp$ for some natural m. For example, we can take $\mathcal{S}^T_{curve} = \{line : \mathbb{R}^2 \to \mathcal{S}^\perp, arc : \mathbb{R}^3 \to \mathcal{S}^\perp\}$ as the set of constructor curve segments $\mathcal{S}_{curve}$.

Let K, Z, X be distinct finite sets of *variables* denoting respectively reals, segments and vertices of a metric graph. The syntax of the *metric configuration logic* (*MCL*) is defined in Table 1.

Table 1. *MCL* Syntax

$t ::= a \in \mathbb{R} \mid k \in K \mid t + t \mid t \cdot t$	*arithmetic terms*
$\psi_K ::= t \leq t'$	*arithmetic constraints*
$s ::= s^T(t_1, ..., t_m) \mid z \in Z \mid s \cdot s$	*segment terms*
$\psi_S ::= s = s' \mid s \preccurlyeq s' \mid \|s\| = t$	*segment constraints*
$p ::= x \in X \mid (x, s, t) \mid (t, s, x)$	*position terms*
$\psi_G ::= x \xrightarrow{s} x' \mid p = p' \mid p \overset{s}{\leadsto} p' \mid d(p, p') = t$	*position constraints*
$\phi ::= \psi_K \mid \psi_S \mid \psi_G$	*atomic formula*
$\quad \mid \phi \oplus \phi \mid \phi \vee \phi \mid \neg\phi$	*non-atomic formula*
$\quad \mid \exists k.\ \phi(k) \mid \exists z.\ \phi(z) \mid \exists x.\ \phi(x)$	*quantifiers*

Semantics. Let $G = (V, \mathcal{S}, E)$ be a metric graph fixed in the context, and let σ be an assignment of variables K, Z, X to respectively reals $\mathbb{R}$, segments $\mathcal{S}$, vertices V. As usual, we extend σ for evaluation of arithmetic terms (with variables from K) into reals. Moreover, we extend σ for the partial evaluation of segment terms (with variables from Z) and position terms (with variables from Z and X) into respectively segments $\mathcal{S}$ and positions Pos_G as defined by the rules in Table 2.

Table 2. Evaluation of *MCL* terms

$$\sigma s^T(t_1, ..., t_m) \stackrel{def}{=} s^T(\sigma t_1, ..., \sigma t_m) \qquad \sigma(x, s, t) \stackrel{def}{=} pos_G^{fwd}(\sigma x, \sigma s, \sigma t)$$

$$\sigma \, s \cdot s' \stackrel{def}{=} \sigma s \cdot \sigma s' \qquad \sigma(t, s, x) \stackrel{def}{=} pos_G^{bwd}(\sigma x, \sigma s, \sigma t)$$

where $pos_G^{fwd}, pos_G^{bwd} : V \times S \times \mathbb{R} \to Pos_G^{\perp}$ are defined as

$$pos_G^{fwd}(v, s, a) \stackrel{def}{=} (e, a) \qquad \text{only if } \exists! \ e = (v, s, v') \in E, \ 0 < a < \|s\|$$

$$pos_G^{bwd}(v, s, a) \stackrel{def}{=} (e, \|s\| - a) \quad \text{only if } \exists! \ e = (v', s, v) \in E, \ 0 < a < \|s\|$$

We tacitly restrict to terms which evaluate successfully in their respective domains. The semantics of *MCL* is defined by the rules in Table 3. Note that a formula represents a configuration of metric graphs sharing common characteristics. Besides the logic connectives with the usual set-theoretic meaning, the coalescing operator $\oplus$ allows building graphs by grouping elementary constituents characterized by atomic formulas relating positions via segments. Hence, the formula $\phi_1 \oplus \phi_2$ represents the graph configurations obtained as the union of configurations satisfying ϕ_1 and ϕ_2 respectively. It differs from $\phi_1 \vee \phi_2$ in that this formula satisfies configurations that satisfy either ϕ_1 or ϕ_2.

Table 3. *MCL* Semantics

$\sigma, G \models t \leq t'$	iff	$\sigma t \leq \sigma t'$
$\sigma, G \models s = s'$	iff	$\sigma s = \sigma s'$
$\sigma, G \models s \preccurlyeq s'$	iff	$\sigma s \preccurlyeq \sigma s'$
$\sigma, G \models \|s\| = t$	iff	$\|\sigma s\| = \sigma t$
$\sigma, G \models x \xrightarrow{s} x'$	iff	$E = \{(\sigma x, \sigma s, \sigma x')\}$
$\sigma, G \models p = p'$	iff	$\sigma p = \sigma p'$
$\sigma, G \models p \xrightarrow{s} p'$	iff	$\sigma p \xrightarrow{\sigma s}_G \sigma p'$
$\sigma, G \models d(p, p') = t$	iff	$d_G(\sigma p, \sigma p') = \sigma t$
$\sigma, G \models \phi_1 \oplus \phi_2$	iff	$\sigma, (V, E_1) \models \phi_1$ and $\sigma, (V, E_2) \models \phi_2$
		for some E_1, E_2 such that $E_1 \cup E_2 = E$
$\sigma, G \models \phi_1 \vee \phi_2$	iff	$\sigma, G \models \phi_1$ or $\sigma, G \models \phi_2$
$\sigma, G \models \neg \phi$	iff	$\sigma, G \not\models \phi$
$\sigma, G \models \exists k. \ \phi$	iff	$\sigma[k \mapsto a], G \models \phi$ for some $a \in \mathbb{R}$
$\sigma, G \models \exists z. \ \phi$	iff	$\sigma[z \mapsto s], G \models \phi$ for some $s \in S$
$\sigma, G \models \exists x. \ \phi$	iff	$\sigma[x \mapsto v], G \models \phi$ for some $v \in V$

Properties. Table 4 provides a set of theorems giving insight into the characteristic properties of the logic. Theorems $(A.i)$–$(A.v)$ illustrate important properties of the $\oplus$ operator that is associative and commutative but not idempotent. As explained below, of particular interest for writing specifications are formulas of the form $\sim\phi \stackrel{def}{=} \phi \oplus true$. These are satisfied by configurations with graphs that contain a subgraph satisfying ϕ. Hence, while the formula $x \xrightarrow{s} x'$ characterizes the graphs with two vertices and a single edge labeled by s, the formula

Table 4. *MCL* Theorems

(A.i)	$(\phi_1 \oplus \phi_2) \oplus \phi_3 \equiv \phi_1 \oplus (\phi_2 \oplus \phi_3)$
(A.ii)	$\phi_1 \oplus \phi_2 \equiv \phi_2 \oplus \phi_1$
(A.iii)	$\phi \oplus \textit{false} \equiv \textit{false}$
(A.iv)	$\phi \oplus \phi \not\equiv \phi \ (\textit{in general})$
(A.v)	$\phi_1 \oplus (\phi_2 \vee \phi_3) \equiv (\phi_1 \oplus \phi_2) \vee (\phi_1 \oplus \phi_3)$
(B.i)	$\sim\sim\phi \equiv \sim\phi$
(B.ii)	$\phi \implies \sim\phi$
(B.iii)	$\sim(\phi_1 \vee \phi_2) \equiv \sim\phi_1 \vee \sim\phi_2$
(B.iv)	$\sim(\phi_1 \oplus \phi_2) \equiv \sim\phi_1 \oplus \sim\phi_2 \equiv \sim\phi_1 \wedge \sim\phi_2$
(C.i)	$x \xrightarrow{s} x' \wedge (\phi_1 \oplus \phi_2) \equiv (x \xrightarrow{s} x' \wedge \phi_1) \oplus (x \xrightarrow{s} x' \wedge \phi_2)$
(C.ii)	$\textit{true} \equiv (x \xrightarrow{s} x' \oplus \neg(\sim x \xrightarrow{s} x')) \vee \neg(\sim x \xrightarrow{s} x')$
(D.i)	$d(p,p') = t \wedge p \xrightarrow{s} p' \implies t \leq \|s\|$
(D.ii)	$d(p,p') = t \wedge d(p',p'') = t' \implies \exists k. \ d(p,p'') = k \wedge k \leq t + t'$

$\sim x \xrightarrow{s} x'$ characterizes the set of graphs containing such an edge. Thus $\sim$ is a closure operator which moreover satisfies theorems (B.i)–(B.iv). Finally, theorems (C.i)–(C.ii) relate the atomic formula $x \xrightarrow{s} x'$ to coalescing and the complement of their closure. The two last theorems (D.i)–(D.ii) differ from the others in that they express specific properties of segment and position constraints.

Proposition 4. *Position constraints not involving edge constraints of the form $x \xrightarrow{s} x'$ are insensitive to metric graph contraction and refinement.*

Note that stronger preservation results for (even simple fragments of) *MCL* are hard to obtain because the domain of vertex variables is a fixed set of vertices. This makes *MCL* sensitive to both contraction and refinement. For example, the formula $\exists x. \ \exists y. \ x \xrightarrow{s} y$ may not hold before and hold after refinement i.e., if a pair of vertices u, v satisfying the constraint is added by refinement.

We provide below abstraction preservation results for MCL formulas. Any segment abstraction $\alpha : \mathcal{S} \to \mathcal{S}'$ can be lifted to segment terms by taking respectively $\alpha(s^T(t_1, ..., t_m)) \overset{def}{=} (\alpha s^T)(t_1, ..., t_n)$, $\alpha(s_1 \cdot s_2) \overset{def}{=} \alpha(s_1) \cdot' \alpha(s_2)$, $\alpha(z) \overset{def}{=} z$. Moreover, α can be further lifted to *MCL* formulas on $\mathcal{S}$. We denote by $\alpha(\phi)$ the *MCL* formula on $\mathcal{S}'$ obtained by rewriting all the segment terms s occurring in ϕ by $\alpha(s)$. The following proposition relates abstractions on formulas to abstractions on metric graphs.

Proposition 5. *Let ϕ be an existential positive MCL formula. Then $G \models \phi$ implies $\alpha(G) \models \alpha(\phi)$ whenever:*

(i) ϕ does not contain distance constraints or
(ii) for any connected edges e_1, e_2 such that $e_1{}^\bullet =^\bullet e_2$ their segments compose, that is, $e_1.s \cdot e_2.s \neq \bot$.

3   ADS Specification

The results of the previous section provide a basis for the definition of both a dynamic model for ADS and of logics for the expression of their properties. The model is a timed transition system with states defined as the distribution of objects over of a metric graph representing a map. Objects may be mobile such as vehicles and pedestrians or static such as signaling equipment. The logics are two extensions of *MCL*, one for the specification of predicates representing sets of states and the other for the specification of its behavior.

We introduce first the concept of map and its properties. Then we define the dynamic model and the associated logics. Finally, we discuss the validation problem and its possible solutions.

3.1   Map Specification

A weakly connected metric graph $G = (V, \mathcal{S}, E)$ can be interpreted as a map with a set of roads R and a set of junctions J, defined in the following manner:

- a *road* r of G is a maximal directed path $r = v_0 \xrightarrow{s_1}_G v_1,\ v_1 \xrightarrow{s_2}_G v_2,\ ...,$ $v_{n-1} \xrightarrow{s_n}_G v_n$ where all the vertices $v_1, ..., v_{n-1}$ have indegree and outdegree equal to one. We say that v_0 is the *entrance* and v_n is the *exit* of r. Let $R = \{r_i\}_{i \in I}$ be the set of roads of G.
- a junction j of G is any maximal weakly connected sub-graph G' of G, obtained from G by removing from its roads all the vertices (and connecting edges) except their entrances and exits. Note that for a junction, its set of vertices of indegree (resp. outdegree) one are exits (resp. entrances) of some roads. Let $J = \{j_\ell\}_{\ell \in L}$ be the set of junctions of G.

Note that G is the union of the subgraphs representing its roads and junctions. For every junction, the strong connectivity of G implies that from any entrance there exists at least one path leading to an exit. Additionally, we assume that maps include information about features of roads, junctions that are relevant to traffic regulations:

- roads and junctions are *typed*: road types can be highway, built-up area roads, carriage roads, etc. Junctions types can be roundabouts, crossroads, highway exit, highway entrance, etc. We use standard notation associating a road or junction to its type e.g., $r : highway$, $j : roundabout$.
- roads, junctions and their segments have *attributes*. We use the dot notation $a.x$ and $a.X$ to denote respectively the attribute x or the set of attributes X of a. In particular, we denote by $r.en$ and $r.ex$ respectively the entrance and the exit of a road r and by $j.En$ and $j.Ex$ the sets of entrances and exits of a junction j. Similarly, $r.lanes$ is the number of lanes of the road r.

Note that contraction and refinement transform maps into maps. A road may be refined into a road while a junction may be decomposed into a set of roads and junctions. Furthermore, abstraction and concretization transform maps into maps as they preserve their connectivity.

Given a map with sets of roads and junctions R and J respectively, it is possible to derive compositionally its bottom-up and top-down specifications. We show first how we can get formulas ζ_j, ζ_r and ξ_j, ξ_r for the bottom-up and top-down specifications of j and r, respectively. Let us consider the junctions illustrated in Fig. 6:

- if ra is a roundabout with n entrances $ra.En = \{en_k\}_{k \in [1,n]}$ alternating with n exits $ra.Ex = \{ex_k\}_{k \in [1,n]}$ then its bottom-up specification is $\zeta_{ra} \overset{def}{=} \bigoplus_{k=1}^{n} \zeta_k \oplus \bigoplus_{k=1}^{n} \zeta_{k,k+1}$, where $\zeta_k \overset{def}{=} ex_k \overset{s_k}{\longrightarrow} en_k$ and $\zeta_{k,k+1} \overset{def}{=} en_k \overset{s_{k,k+1}}{\longrightarrow} ex_{k+1}$. The top-down specification is $\xi_{ra} \overset{def}{=} \bigwedge_{k=1}^{n} \xi_k \wedge \bigwedge_{k=1}^{n} \xi_{k,k+1}$ where $\xi_k \overset{def}{=} {\sim}\zeta_k$ and $\xi_{k,k+1} \overset{def}{=} {\sim}\zeta_{k,k+1}$.
- if in is an intersection with n entrances $in.En = \{en_k\}_{k=1,n}$ and n exits $in.Ex = \{ex_k\}_{k \in [1,n]}$ then its bottom-up specification is $\zeta_{in} \overset{def}{=} \bigoplus_{k=1}^{n} \zeta_k$ with $\zeta_k \overset{def}{=} \bigoplus_{j \in J_k} en_k \overset{s_{k,j}}{\longrightarrow} ex_j$ and J_k is the set of indices of the exits of $j.Ex$ connected to the entrance en_k. Hence, the top-down specification is $\xi_{in} \overset{def}{=} \bigwedge_{k=1}^{n} \xi_k$ where $\xi_k \overset{def}{=} {\sim}\zeta_k$.
- the formulas for a merger mg and a fork fk with respectively n entrances and n exits and unique exit and entrance respectively, can be obtained as a particular case of an intersection.
- finally, for a road r the specifications are $\xi_r \overset{def}{=} {\sim}\zeta_r$ with $\zeta_r \overset{def}{=} r.en \overset{s_r}{\longrightarrow} r.ex$.

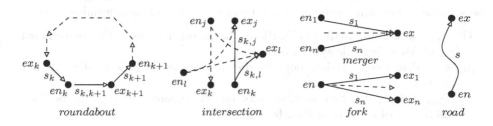

Fig. 6. Junctions and roads

3.2 Mobile *MCL* and Scenario Description for ADS

Mobile MCL (shorthand *M2CL*) is an extension of *MCL* for the specification of states of dynamic ADS models as distributions of objects over maps. Given a metric graph G representing a map, the state of an ADS is a tuple $\mathbf{s} \overset{def}{=} \langle \mathbf{s}_o \rangle_{o \in \mathcal{O}}$ representing the distribution of a finite set of objects $\mathcal{O}$ with their relevant dynamic attributes on the map G. The set of objects $\mathcal{O}$ includes a set of vehicles $\mathcal{C}$ and sets of immobile equipment such as lights, road signs, gates, etc.

For a vehicle c, its state $\mathbf{s}_c \overset{def}{=} \langle it, pos, sp, wt, ln, ...\rangle$ includes respectively its *itinerary* (from the set of segments $\mathcal{S}$), its *position* on the map (from Pos_G), its *speed* (from $\mathbb{R}_{\geq 0}$), the *waiting time* (from $\mathbb{R}_{\geq 0}$) which is the time elapsed since the speed of c became zero, the *lane* it is traveling (from $\mathbb{R}_{\geq 0}$), etc. For a traffic light lt, its state $\mathbf{s}_{lt} \overset{def}{=} \langle pos, cl, ...\rangle$ includes respectively its *position* on the map (from Pos_G), and its *color* (with values *red* and *green*), etc. For a map G and an initial state $\mathbf{s}^{(t_0)}$ we define a *run* as a sequence of consecutive states $[\mathbf{s}^{(t_i)}]_{i \geq 0}$ parameterized by an increasing sequence of time points $t_i \in \mathbb{R}_{\geq 0}$, equal to the sum of the time intervals elapsed for reaching the i-th state.

M2CL is equipped with object variables Y with attributes allowing to express constraints on object states. Object variables in Y are typed and denote objects from a finite set $\mathcal{O}$. Constraints are obtained by extending the syntax of *MCL* to include object attribute terms. For example, if y is a "vehicle" variable then $y.it$ is a segment term, $y.pos$ is a position term, and $y.ln$, $y.sp$, $y.wt$ are arithmetic terms of *M2CL*. Moreover, *M2CL* allows for equality $y = y'$ and existential quantification $\exists y$ of object variables.

The semantics of *M2CL* formulas is defined on distributions $\langle \sigma, G, \mathbf{s}\rangle$ where σ provides an interpretation of variables (including object variables) to their respective domains, G is a metric graph representing the map, and $\mathbf{s}$ is the system state vector for objects in $\mathcal{O}$. The evaluation of terms is extended to include object attributes, that is, for any object variable y with attribute *attr* we define $\sigma\, y.attr \overset{def}{=} \mathbf{s}_{\sigma y}(attr)$. Equality and existential elimination on objects variables are interpreted with the usual meaning, that is, $y = y'$ holds on $\langle \sigma, G, \mathbf{s}\rangle$ iff $\sigma y = \sigma y'$ and respectively $\exists y.\ \psi$ holds on $\langle \sigma, G, \mathbf{s}\rangle$ iff ψ holds on $\langle \sigma[y \mapsto o], G, \mathbf{s}\rangle$ for some object $o \in \mathcal{O}$.

From a methodological point of view, we restrict to *M2CL* formulas that can be written as boolean combinations of three categories of sub-formulas:

(i) ψ_{map} describing map specifications characterizing the static environment in which a dynamic system evolves,

(ii) ψ_{dyn} describing relations between distributions of the objects of a dynamic system,

(iii) ψ_{add} linking itinerary attributes of objects involved in ψ_{dyn} to position addresses of maps described by ψ_{map}.

The following set of primitives used respectively in sub-formulas of the above categories is needed to express ADS scenarios and specifications:

(i) for x, x' vertex variables, X set of vertex variables, $[x\ right\text{-}of\ x'\ in\ X]$, $[x\ opposite\ x'\ in\ X]$ express constraints on the positioning of x, x' with respect to the map restricted to vertices in X (typically a junction):

$$[x\ right\text{-}of\ x'\ in\ X] \overset{def}{=} \exists a.\exists r.\exists \varphi.\exists_{(0,\pi)}\theta.\ \bigvee_{x'' \in X} x' \xrightarrow{line[a,\varphi]} x'' \wedge x \xrightarrow{arc[r,\varphi+\theta,-\theta]} x''$$

$$[x\ opposite\ x'\ in\ X] \overset{def}{=} \exists a.\exists \varphi.\ \bigvee_{x'',x''' \in X} x \xrightarrow{line[a,\varphi]} x'' \wedge x' \xrightarrow{line[a,\varphi+\pi]} x'''$$

(ii) for c, o respectively vehicle, object variables, d arithmetic term, $[c\ meets(d)\ o]$ means that c reaches the position of o at distance d:

$$[c\ meets(d)\ o] \overset{def}{=} \exists z.\ z \prec c.it \wedge c.pos \overset{z}{\leadsto} o.pos \wedge \|z\| = d$$

(iii) a) for c a vehicle variable, X a set of vertex variables, $[c\ go\text{-}straight\ X]$, $[c\ turn\text{-}right\ X]$, $[c\ turn\text{-}left\ X]$ express constraints on the itinerary of c within the map restricted to vertices in X (typically, a junction):

$$[c\ go\text{-}straight\ X] \overset{def}{=} \exists a.\exists \varphi.\ line[a,\varphi] \preccurlyeq c.it \wedge \bigvee_{x,x' \in X} c.pos = x \wedge x \xrightarrow{line[a,\varphi]} x'$$

$$[c\ turn\text{-}right\ X] \overset{def}{=} \exists r.\exists \varphi.\exists_{(-\pi,0)}\theta.\ arc[r,\varphi,\theta] \preccurlyeq c.it \wedge \bigvee_{x,x' \in X} c.pos = x \wedge x \xrightarrow{arc[r,\varphi,\theta]} x'$$

$$[c\ turn\text{-}left\ X] \overset{def}{=} \exists r.\exists \varphi.\exists_{(0,\pi)}\theta.\ arc[r,\varphi,\theta] \preccurlyeq c.it \wedge \bigvee_{x,x' \in X} c.pos = x \wedge x \xrightarrow{arc[r,\varphi,\theta]} x'$$

b) for o an object variable, X a set of vertex variables, l an optional arithmetic term, $[o@X, l]$ means that the position of o belongs to the map subgraph restricted to vertices in X and the lane of o is l:

$$[o@X, l] \overset{def}{=} \left(\exists d.\exists s. \bigvee_{x,x' \in X} x \xrightarrow{s} x' \wedge o.pos = (x, s, d) \vee o.pos = x \right) \wedge o.ln = l$$

Scenario Description for ADS. We define a scene as a triplet $\langle \psi_{map}, \psi_{add}, \psi_{dyn} \rangle$ of $M2CL$ formulas without universal quantifiers where ψ_{add} defines the addresses of the objects involved in ψ_{dyn} in the map specified by ψ_{map}. As for maps, a scene can have a top-down and a bottom-up specification defined respectively by the formulas, $\sim\psi_{map} \Rightarrow \psi_{add} \wedge \psi_{dyn}$ and $\psi_{map} \wedge \psi_{add} \wedge \psi_{dyn}$.

A scenario is a sequence of scenes sharing a common map context and intended to describe relevant partial states of an ADS run. There are several proposals for scenario description languages [2,8,13]. Figure 1 presents a scenario of two scenes taken from [2]. The initial scene is defined by:

$$\psi_{map} = [r : road(x, s, y)] \wedge [s.lanes = 2]$$
$$\psi_{add} = [ego@r, 1] \wedge [c_1@r, 1] \wedge [c_2@r, 2]$$
$$\psi_{dyn} = [ego\ meets(84)\ c_1] \wedge [c_2\ meets(100)\ ego] \wedge [ego.sp = c_1.sp = 100 \wedge c_2.sp = 110]$$

The second scene after the vehicle c_2 passes the ego vehicle is:

$$\psi'_{map} = [r : road(x, s, y)] \wedge [s.lanes = 2]$$
$$\psi'_{add} = [ego@r, 1] \wedge [c_1@r, 1] \wedge [c_2@r, 1]$$
$$\psi'_{dyn} = [ego\ meets(20)\ c_2] \wedge [c_2\ meets(64)\ c_1] \wedge [ego.sp = c_1.sp = 100 \wedge c_2.sp = 110]$$

Note that from a semantic point of view, a scene is characterized by minimal models of $M2CL$ $\langle \sigma, G, \mathbf{s} \rangle$ that satisfy the formula and where all irrelevant components of $\mathbf{s}$ are omitted. For instance, in the minimal models of the two scenes only the components of $\mathbf{s}$ corresponding to c_1, c_2 and ego are taken.

3.3   Temporal $M2CL$ and Specification of ADS

Temporal M2CL (shorthand *TM2CL*) is defined as the linear time temporal extension of $M2CL$. The syntax is as follows:

$$\Phi ::= \phi \mid \mathbf{N}\ \Phi \mid \Phi\ \mathbf{U}\ \Phi \mid \Phi \wedge \Phi \mid \exists c.\ \Phi \mid \neg\Phi$$

where ϕ is $M2CL$ formula. We consider moreover the *eventually* operator $\Diamond\Phi \overset{def}{=} true\ \mathbf{U}\ \Phi$, and *always* operator $\Box\Phi \overset{def}{=} \neg\Diamond\neg\Phi$. The semantics of $TM2CL$ is defined on triples $(\sigma,\ G,\ [\mathbf{s}^{(t_i)}]_{i \geq 0})$ containing respectively an assignment σ of

Table 5. Semantics of *TM2CL*

$$\sigma, G, [\mathbf{s}^{(t_i)}]_{i\geq0} \models \phi \qquad \text{iff } \sigma, G, \mathbf{s}^{(t_0)}) \models \phi$$

$$\sigma, G, [\mathbf{s}^{(t_i)}]_{i\geq0} \models \mathbf{N}\,\Phi \qquad \text{iff } \sigma, G, [\mathbf{s}^{(t_i)}]_{i\geq1} \models \Phi$$

$$\sigma, G, [\mathbf{s}^{(t_i)}]_{i\geq0} \models \Phi_1\,\mathbf{U}\,\Phi_2 \text{ iff } \exists k \geq 0.\ \forall j \in [0, k-1].\ \sigma, G, [\mathbf{s}^{(t_i)}]_{i\geq j} \models \Phi_1$$
$$\text{and } \sigma, G, [\mathbf{s}^{(t_i)}]_{i\geq k} \models \Phi_2$$

$$\sigma, G, [\mathbf{s}^{(t_i)}]_{i\geq0} \models \Phi_1 \wedge \Phi_2 \text{ iff } \sigma, G, [\mathbf{s}^{(t_i)}]_{i\geq0} \models \Phi_1 \text{ and } \sigma, G, [\mathbf{s}^{(t_i)}]_{i\geq0} \models \Phi_2$$

$$\sigma, G, [\mathbf{s}^{(t_i)}]_{i\geq0} \models \exists o.\ \Phi \qquad \text{iff } \sigma[o \mapsto u], G, [\mathbf{s}^{(t_i)}]_{i\geq0} \models \Phi, \text{ for some } u \in \mathcal{O}$$

$$\sigma, G, [\mathbf{s}^{(t_i)}]_{i\geq0} \models \neg\Phi \qquad \text{iff } \sigma, G, [\mathbf{s}^{(t_i)}]_{i\geq0} \not\models \Phi$$

vehicle variables defined in the *TM2CL* context, a map G and a run $[\mathbf{s}^{(t_i)}]_{i\geq0}$ on G for a finite set of objects $\mathcal{O}$. The semantic rules are defined in Table 5.

We use *TM2CL* for both the specification of system properties and traffic rules. The difference between the two concepts is not clear-cut although it is implicit in many works. System properties characterize the desired ADS behavior in terms of relations between speeds and distances taking into account relevant dynamic characteristics. These include properties such as keeping safe distance or keeping acceleration and deceleration rates between some bounds.

Traffic rules are higher-level specifications for enhanced safety and efficiency that usually depend on the driving context. They deal not only with obligations such as yielding right of way and traffic control at junctions but also advice on how to drive sensibly and safely in situations disrupting traffic flow such as congestion, accidents and works in progress. We provide below a formalization of system properties and traffic rules showing the expressiveness of our modeling framework. We formalize a set of traffic rules for an intersection j with all-way stop provided in [26]. The rules are implications of the form $\sim \zeta(j) \Rightarrow \Phi(j)$ where $\zeta(j)$ is the *MCL* formula characterizing j and $\Phi(j)$ is a *TM2CL* formula describing contraints on the driver behavior. We provide below the constraints in English and the corresponding *TM2CL* formulas:

(i) "If a driver arrives at the intersection and no other vehicles are present, then the driver can proceed":
$$\forall c.\forall st.\ \Box\ [st@j.en] \wedge [c@j.en] \wedge [\neg\exists c'.\ c' \neq c \wedge [c'@j]] \Rightarrow \Diamond[c@j]$$

(ii) "If, on approach of the intersection, there are one or more cars already there, let them proceed, then proceed yourself":
$$\forall c.\forall st.\ \Box\ [st@j.en] \wedge [c\ meets(d)\ st] \wedge [d \leq d_{min}] \Rightarrow [\neg[c@j]]\ \mathbf{U}\ [\neg\exists c'.c' \neq c \wedge [c'@j]]$$

(iii) "If a driver arrives at the same time as another vehicle, the vehicle on the right has the right-of-way":
$$\forall c.\forall c'.\ \Box\ [c@j.en] \wedge [c'@j.en'] \wedge [c.wt = c'.wt] \wedge [j.en\ right\text{-}of\ j.en'\ in\ j] \Rightarrow$$
$$[c'@j.en']\ \mathbf{U}\ [c@j]$$

(iv) "(a) If two vehicles arrive opposite each other at the same time, and no vehicles are on the right, then they may proceed at the same time if they are going straight ahead. (b) If one vehicle is turning and one is going straight, the right-of-way goes to the car going straight:"

$\forall c.\forall c'.\ \Box\ [c@j.en] \land [c'@j.en'] \land [c.wt = c'.wt = 0] \land [j.en\ opposite\ j.en'\ in\ j] \land$
$\qquad \neg [\exists c''.\ [c''@j.en''] \land [j.en''\ right\mbox{-}of\ j.en\ in\ j] \lor [j.en''\ right\mbox{-}of\ j.en'\ in\ j]] \land$
$\qquad [c\ go\mbox{-}straight\ j] \land [c'\ go\mbox{-}straight\ j] \;\Rightarrow\; \Diamond [c@j] \land [c'@j]$

$\forall c.\forall c'.\ \Box\ [c@j.en] \land [c'@j.en'] \land [c.wt = c'.wt = 0] \land [j.en\ opposite\ j.en'\ in\ j] \land$
$\qquad \neg [\exists c''.\ [c''@j.en''] \land [j.en''\ right\mbox{-}of\ j.en] \lor [j.en''\ right\mbox{-}of\ j.en']] \land$
$\qquad [c\ go\mbox{-}straight\ j] \land \neg [c'\ go\mbox{-}straight\ j] \;\Rightarrow\; \Diamond [c@j]$

(v) "If two vehicles arrive opposite each other at the same time and one is turning right and one is turning left, the right-of-way goes to the vehicle turning right. Since they are both trying to turn into the same road, priority should be given to the vehicle turning right as they are closest to the lane":

$\forall c.\forall c'.\ \Box\ [c@j.en] \land [c'@j.en'] \land [c.wt = c'.wt = 0] \land [j.en\ opposite\ j.en'\ in\ j] \land$
$\qquad [c\ turn\mbox{-}right\ j] \land [c'\ turn\mbox{-}left\ j] \;\Rightarrow\; \Diamond [c@j]$

4 ADS Validation

4.1 Classification of Validation Problems

The following categories of validation problems can arise in our framework:

MCL and *M2CL* **Model-Checking:** (i) Given a map specification ϕ as a closed *MCL* formula and a metric graph G decide if G is a model of ϕ. The problem boils down to checking satisfiability of a *segment logic (SL)* formula obtained by quantifier elimination of vertex variables and partial evaluation of graph constraints in ϕ according to G. We present later in this section a decision procedure for *SL*. (ii) Similarly, given a distribution specification ϕ as a closed *M2CL* formula, a map G and a state **s** for a *finite* set of objects $\mathcal{O}$, decide if $\langle G, \mathbf{s} \rangle$ is a model of ϕ. Again, the problem boils down to checking satisfiability of a *SL* formula obtained by quantifier elimination of vertex and object variables an and partial evaluation of attribute terms.

TM2CL **Runtime Verification:** Given a temporal specification Φ as a *TM2CL* formula, a map G and a run $[\mathbf{s}^{(t_i)}]_{i \geq 0}$ of an ADS, check if $G, [\mathbf{s}^{(t_i)}]_{i \geq 0}$ is a model of Φ. This problem boils down to evaluating the semantics of Φ on the run. In [10] we consider a similar runtime verification problem for temporal configuration logic and runs of dynamic reconfigurable systems. We have shown that the evaluation of linear-time temporal operators and the model-checking of state/configuration specifications can be dealt separately. The same idea can be applied here: on one hand, the temporal formulas can be handled by LamaConv [17] to generate FSM monitors and on the other hand, the model-checking of distribution specifications can be handled by a SMT solver (such as Z3) by using an encoding into a decidable theory.

MCL and *M2CL* **Satisfiability Checking:** (i) Given a map specification ϕ as a closed *MCL* formula decide if ϕ is satisfiable, that is, it has at least one model.

We then show in this section that the problem can be effectively solved for a significant fragment of MCL including a restricted form of bottom-up map specifications. Notice that entailment checking, that is, deciding validity of $\forall \mathbf{x}.\ \phi_1 \Rightarrow \phi_2$ for map specifications ϕ_1, ϕ_2 where $fv(\phi_1) = fv(\phi_2) = \mathbf{x}$, boils down to checking satisfiability of $\exists \mathbf{x}.\ \phi_1 \wedge \neg\phi_2$, and can be solved under the same restrictions. (ii) Similarly, given a distribution specification ϕ as a closed $M2CL$ formula decide if ϕ is satisfiable, that is, it has at least one model. The problem can be reduced to the satisfiability checking of MCL specifications whenever ϕ is of the restricted form $\exists y_1...\exists y_k.\ \phi'$ where y_1, ... y_k are the only object variables occurring in ϕ'. In this case, every object variable y can be *substituted* by a finite number of MCL variables y_{attr} encoding its identity and attributes. As example, for a vehicle variable y consider an identity (real) variable y_{id}, a segment variable y_{it}, a position variable y_{pos}, real variables y_{ln}, y_{sp}, y_{wt}, etc. After replacement, we obtain an equisatisfiable MCL formula by enforcing the additional constraints that state attributes are consistently assigned (e.g., $(y_{id} = y'_{id}) \Rightarrow y_{it} = y'_{it}$) for all pairs y, y' of vehicle variables among y_1, ..., y_k. Finally, notice also that entailment checking between distributed specifications can be solved as well, by reduction to satisfiability checking as explained above.

4.2 Satisfiability Checking

Satisfiability Checking of MCL. The satisfiability checking for MCL formula is undecidable in general. Actually, the combined use of edge constraints $x \xrightarrow{s} x'$, equalities on vertex positions $x = x'$, boolean operators and quantifiers leads to undecidability, as it allows the embedding of first order logic on directed graphs.

Nevertheless, for a significant class of MCL formulas, their satisfiability checking can be reduced to satisfiability checking of *segment logic* (SL), that is, the fragment of MCL without vertex variables, which is a first order logic combining only arithmetic and segment constraints.

A *complete metric graph specification* ψ^* is a MCL formula of the form:

$$(\wedge_{1 \le i < j \le n}\ x_i \ne x_j) \wedge (\forall y.\ \vee_{i=1}^{n}\ y = x_i) \wedge$$
$$(\bigoplus_{i=1}^{n} \bigoplus_{j=1}^{n} \bigoplus_{h=1}^{m_{ij}}\ x_i \xrightarrow{s_{ijh}} x_j) \wedge (\wedge_{i=1}^{n} \wedge_{j=1}^{n} \wedge_{1 \le h < h' \le m_{ij}}\ s_{ijh} \ne s_{ijh'})$$

that is, where the set of free vertex variables is $\mathbf{x} = \{x_1, ..., x_n\}$. Note that a complete metric specification characterizes a metric graph with precisely n vertices (in correspondence with vertex variables $x_1, \ldots, x_n$) and, with precisely m_{ij} distinct edges (that is, defined by the constraints $x_i \xrightarrow{s_{ijh}} x_j$ for $h = 1, m_{ij}$), for every pair of vertices x_i, x_j.

Theorem 1. *Let ψ^* be a complete metric graph specification with free variables $\mathbf{x} \uplus \mathbf{z} \uplus \mathbf{k}$. For any MCL formula ϕ with $fv(\phi) \subseteq \mathbf{x} \uplus \mathbf{z} \uplus \mathbf{k}$ holds*

1. *the closed MCL formula $\exists \mathbf{x}.\ \exists \mathbf{z}.\ \exists \mathbf{k}.\ \psi^* \wedge \phi$ is satisfiable iff*
2. *the closed SL formula $\exists \mathbf{z}.\ \exists \mathbf{k}.\ (\wedge_{i=1}^{n} \wedge_{j=1}^{n} \wedge_{1 \le h < h' \le m_{ij}}\ s_{ijh} \ne s_{ijh'}) \wedge (\wedge_{i=1}^{n} \wedge_{j=1}^{n} \wedge_{h=1}^{m_{ij}}\ \|s_{ijh}\| > 0) \wedge tr(n, E^*, \mu^*, \phi)$ is satisfiable, where $n = \mathrm{card}\ \mathbf{x}$, $E^* = \cup_{i=1}^{n} \cup_{j=1}^{n} \{(i, s_{ijh}, j)\}_{h=1,m_{ij}}$, $\mu^* = \{x_i \mapsto i\}_{i=1,n}$ and the translation $tr(n, E, \mu, \phi)$ is defined in Table 6.*

Table 6. Translation rules for Theorem 1. (complete definition in [6])

$$tr(n, E, \mu, \psi_K) \stackrel{def}{=} \psi_K$$

$$tr(n, E, \mu, \psi_S) \stackrel{def}{=} \psi_S$$

$$tr(n, E, \mu, x \stackrel{s}{\rightarrow} y) \stackrel{def}{=} \begin{cases} s = s_{ijh} \text{ if } E = \{(i, s_{ijh}, j)\}, \ \mu x = i, \ \mu y = j \\ false \qquad \text{otherwise} \end{cases}$$

$$tr(n, E, \mu, p = p') \stackrel{def}{=} \textbf{eq-pos}(n, E, \mu, p, p')$$

$$tr(n, E, \mu, p \stackrel{s}{\rightsquigarrow} p') \stackrel{def}{=} \textbf{acyclic-path}(n, E, \mu, p, s, p')$$

$$tr(n, E, \mu, \phi_1 \oplus \phi_2) \stackrel{def}{=} \bigvee_{E_1 \cup E_2 = E} tr(n, E_1, \mu, \phi_1) \wedge tr(n, E_2, \mu, \phi_2)$$

$$tr(n, E, \mu, \phi_1 \vee \phi_2) \stackrel{def}{=} tr(n, E, \mu, \phi_1) \vee tr(n, E, \mu, \phi_2)$$

$$tr(n, E, \mu, \neg\phi) \stackrel{def}{=} \neg tr(n, E, \mu, \phi)$$

$$tr(n, E, \mu, \exists k. \ \phi) \stackrel{def}{=} \exists k. \ tr(n, E, \mu, \phi)$$

$$tr(n, E, \mu, \exists z. \ \phi) \stackrel{def}{=} \exists z. \ tr(n, E, \mu, \phi)$$

$$tr(n, E, \mu, \exists x. \ \phi) \stackrel{def}{=} \bigvee_{i=1}^{n} tr(n, E, \mu[x \mapsto i], \phi)$$

Proof. $(1 \Rightarrow 2)$ If the formula $\psi^* \wedge \phi$ is satisfiable, then it has a metric graph model isomorphic to the (unique up to edge labeling) metric graph G_{ψ^*} specified by ψ^*. The translated formula $tr(n, E^*, \mu^*, \phi)$ represents the evaluation of the semantics of ϕ on the metric graph G_{ψ^*} according to the rules defined in Table 3. It must be therefore satisfiable as well, as initially $\psi^* \wedge \phi$ is satisfiable. $(2 \Rightarrow 1)$ If the conjunction of the translated formula $tr(n, E^*, \mu^*, \phi)$ and the additional constraints has a model, ones can use it to build a metric graph, isomorphic to G_{ψ^*}, satisfying both ψ^* and ϕ. In particular the additional constraints ensure that the metric graph is well formed, that is, all edges are labeled by non-zero length segments, and there are no replicated edges between any pairs of vertices.

Satisfiability Checking of SL. If segments S are restricted to particular interpretations, the satisfiability checking of formula of SL can be further reduced to satisfiability checking of formulas of extended arithmetic on reals.

Theorem 2. *If segments S are defined as intervals*

1. *the closed SL formula ϕ is satisfiable iff*
2. *the closed real arithmetic formula $tr_1(\phi)$ is satisfiable, where the translation $tr_1(\phi)$ is defined in Table 7.*

Proof. With interval interpretation, segments are precisely determined by their length and all segment operations and constraints boil down to operations and constraints on reals. Moreover, we remark that the transformation does not require multiplication[4] on real terms, henceforth, the translated formula $tr_1(\phi)$ belongs to linear arithmetic iff all arithmetic constraints ψ_K within ϕ were linear.

---

[4] Except if needed for encoding the length of segment types.

Table 7. Translation rules for Theorem 2

$tr_1(\|s^T(t_1,...,t_m)\|) \stackrel{def}{=} len\text{-}s^T(t_1,...,t_m)$	$tr_1(s = s') \stackrel{def}{=} tr_1(\|s\|) = tr_1(\|s'\|)$
$tr_1(\|z\|) \stackrel{def}{=} k_z$	$tr_1(s \preccurlyeq s') \stackrel{def}{=} tr_1(\|s\|) \leq tr_1(\|s'\|)$
$tr_1(\|s \cdot s'\|) \stackrel{def}{=} tr_1(\|s\|) + tr_1(\|s'\|))$	$tr_1(\|s\| = t) \stackrel{def}{=} tr_1(\|s\|) = t$

5   Discussion

The proposed framework relies on a minimal set of semantically integrated concepts. It is expressive and modular as it introduces progressively the basic concepts and carefully separates concerns. It supports a well-defined specification and validation methodology without semantic gaps as discussed in [6]. Using configuration logic allows the specification of behavioral properties taking into account map contexts. This is a main difference from approaches relying on temporal logics that cannot account for map configurations and where formulas characterize sets of runs in some implicit map environment, usually a simple multi-lane setting. Configuration logic specifies scenes as conjunctions of formulas describing map configurations and vehicle distributions linked by an addressing relation. It enables enhanced expressiveness by combining static and dynamic aspects while retaining the possibility to consider them separately. It considers maps as the central concept of the semantic model and emphasizes the needs for multilevel representation depending on the type of goals to be met including long-term mission goals, mid-term maneuver goals and short-term safety and trajectory tracking goals. Among the three abstraction levels, curve segment models play a central role. Interval segment models can account for simple properties depending only on relative distances between the involved mobiles. For properties depending on topological and geometric relations, curve segment models are needed. The expression of such properties involves primitives such as go-straight, turn-right, turn-left, right-of and opposite. Region segment models are needed for low level properties taking into account the dimensions of the objects and their movement in the 2D space.

The paper is the culmination of work developed over the past three years both on foundations of autonomous systems [15,25] and on modelling and validation of reconfigurable dynamic systems using the DR-BIP component framework [4,10]. We plan to extend this work in two directions. The first is to leverage on the DR-BIP execution semantics and formalize ADS dynamics as the composition of object behavior acting on maps. The second is to extend our work on runtime verification of dynamic reconfigurable systems [10] by developing adaptive validation techniques driven by adequate model coverage criteria. These techniques should provide model-based evidence that a good deal of the many and diverse driving situations are covered (e.g. different types of roads, of junctions, of traffic conditions, etc.). Finally, we will investigate diagnostics generation techniques linking failures to their causes emerging from risk factors such as violations of traffic regulations and unpredictable events.

References

1. ASAM OpenDRIVE® - open dynamic road information for vehicle environment. Technical report, V 1.6.0, ASAM e.V., Mar 2020. https://www.asam.net/standards/detail/opendrive
2. ASAM OpenScenario® - dynamic content in driving simulation, UML modeling rules. Technical report, V 1.0.0, ASAM e.V., Mar 2020. https://www.asam.net/standards/detail/openscenario
3. Bagschik, G., Menzel, T., Maurer, M.: Ontology based scene creation for the development of automated vehicles. In: Intelligent Vehicles Symposium, pp. 1813–1820. IEEE (2018)
4. El Ballouli, R., Bensalem, S., Bozga, M., Sifakis, J.: Four exercises in programming dynamic reconfigurable systems: methodology and solution in DR-BIP. In: Margaria, T., Steffen, B. (eds.) ISoLA 2018. LNCS, vol. 11246, pp. 304–320. Springer, Cham (2018). https://doi.org/10.1007/978-3-030-03424-5_20
5. Beetz, J., Borrmann, A.: Benefits and limitations of linked data approaches for road modeling and data exchange. In: Smith, I., Domer, B. (eds.) EG-ICE 2018. LNCS, vol. 10864, pp. 245–261. Springer, Cham (2018). https://doi.org/10.1007/978-3-319-91638-5_13
6. Bozga, M., Sifakis, J.: Specification and validation of autonomous driving systems: a multilevel semantic framework. CoRR abs/2109.06478 (2021). https://arxiv.org/abs/2109.06478
7. Chen, W., Kloul, L.: An ontology-based approach to generate the advanced driver assistance use cases of highway traffic. In: KEOD, pp. 73–81. SciTePress (2018)
8. Damm, W., Kemper, S., Möhlmann, E., Peikenkamp, T., Rakow, A.: Using traffic sequence charts for the development of HAVs. In: ERTS 2018, Proceedings (2018)
9. Dosovitskiy, A., Ros, G., Codevilla, F., López, A.M., Koltun, V.: CARLA: an open urban driving simulator. In: Proceedings of Machine Learning Research, vol. 78, pp. 1–16. PMLR (2017). CoRL
10. El-Hokayem, A., Bozga, M., Sifakis, J.: A temporal configuration logic for dynamic reconfigurable systems. In: SAC, pp. 1419–1428. ACM (2021)
11. Esterle, K., Aravantinos, V., Knoll, A.C.: From specifications to behavior: maneuver verification in a semantic state space. In: IV, pp. 2140–2147. IEEE (2019)
12. Esterle, K., Gressenbuch, L., Knoll, A.C.: Formalizing traffic rules for machine interpretability. In: CAVS, pp. 1–7. IEEE (2020)
13. Fremont, D.J., et al.: Scenic: a language for scenario specification and data generation. CoRR abs/2010.06580 (2020). https://arxiv.org/abs/2010.06580
14. Fremont, D.J., et al.: Formal scenario-based testing of autonomous vehicles: from simulation to the real world. In: ITSC, pp. 1–8. IEEE (2020)
15. Harel, D., Marron, A., Sifakis, J.: Autonomics: in search of a foundation for next-generation autonomous systems. Proc. Natl. Acad. Sci. USA **117**(30), 17491–17498 (2020)
16. Hilscher, M., Linker, S., Olderog, E.-R., Ravn, A.P.: An abstract model for proving safety of multi-lane traffic manoeuvres. In: Qin, S., Qiu, Z. (eds.) ICFEM 2011. LNCS, vol. 6991, pp. 404–419. Springer, Heidelberg (2011). https://doi.org/10.1007/978-3-642-24559-6_28
17. Institute for Software Engineering and Programming Languages, University of Lübeck: LamaConv - Logics and Automata Converter Library (2020). https://www.isp.uni-luebeck.de/lamaconv

18. Karimi, A., Duggirala, P.S.: Formalizing traffic rules for uncontrolled intersections. In: ICCPS, pp. 41–50. IEEE (2020)
19. Poggenhans, F., et al.: Lanelet2: a high-definition map framework for the future of automated driving. In: ITSC, pp. 1672–1679. IEEE (2018)
20. Rizaldi, A., Althoff, M.: Formalising traffic rules for accountability of autonomous vehicles. In: ITSC, pp. 1658–1665. IEEE (2015)
21. Rizaldi, A., Immler, F., Schürmann, B., Althoff, M.: A formally verified motion planner for autonomous vehicles. In: Lahiri, S.K., Wang, C. (eds.) ATVA 2018. LNCS, vol. 11138, pp. 75–90. Springer, Cham (2018). https://doi.org/10.1007/978-3-030-01090-4_5
22. Rizaldi, A., et al.: Formalising and monitoring traffic rules for autonomous vehicles in Isabelle/HOL. In: Polikarpova, N., Schneider, S. (eds.) IFM 2017. LNCS, vol. 10510, pp. 50–66. Springer, Cham (2017). https://doi.org/10.1007/978-3-319-66845-1_4
23. Rong, G., et al.: LGSVL simulator: a high fidelity simulator for autonomous driving. CoRR abs/2005.03778 (2020). https://arxiv.org/abs/2005.03778
24. Schönemann, V., et al.: Scenario-based functional safety for automated driving on the example of valet parking. In: Arai, K., Kapoor, S., Bhatia, R. (eds.) FICC 2018. AISC, vol. 886, pp. 53–64. Springer, Cham (2019). https://doi.org/10.1007/978-3-030-03402-3_5
25. Sifakis, J.: Autonomous systems – an architectural characterization. In: Boreale, M., Corradini, F., Loreti, M., Pugliese, R. (eds.) Models, Languages, and Tools for Concurrent and Distributed Programming. LNCS, vol. 11665, pp. 388–410. Springer, Cham (2019). https://doi.org/10.1007/978-3-030-21485-2_21
26. Wikipedia. https://en.wikipedia.org/wiki/All-way_stop

On Specifications and Proofs of Timed Circuits

Matthias Függer[1] ⓘ, Christoph Lenzen[2] ⓘ, and Ulrich Schmid[3]([✉]) ⓘ

[1] CNRS, LMF, ENS Paris-Saclay, Université Paris-Saclay, Inria,
Gif-sur-Yvette, France
[2] CISPA Helmholtz Center for Information Security, Saarbrücken, Germany
[3] TU Wien, Vienna, Austria
s@ecs.tuwien.ac.at

Abstract. Given a discrete-state continuous-time reactive system, like a digital circuit, the classical approach is to first model it as a state transition system and then prove its properties. Our contribution advocates a different approach: to directly operate on the input-output behavior of such systems, without identifying states and their transitions in the first place. We discuss the benefits of this approach at hand of some examples, which demonstrate that it nicely integrates with concepts of self-stabilization and fault-tolerance. We also elaborate on some unexpected artefacts of module composition in our framework, and conclude with some open research questions.

1 Motivation and Overview

Many physical systems dealt with by computational methods today do not operate on discrete values. Examples range from electronic circuits to mechanical systems to chemical processes, which all share that analog information is continuously processed. Whereas natural and engineering sciences, in particular, control theory, have been successful in finding and using accurate models for such continuous systems, primarily based on systems of differential equations, the complexity both involved in model development and model usage is often prohibitive: Model composition and hierarchical modeling is usually difficult, and large simulation times and memory consumption as well as numerical instability typically limit the applicability of the resulting models in practice.

Discrete-Valued Abstractions. Applying discrete-valued abstractions for modeling continuous-valued systems is hence an attractive alternative, and much of the big success of computer science is owed to their introduction. Apart from being easily specified and understood, discrete abstractions usually involve all-digital

This project has received funding from the European Research Council (ERC) under the European Union's Horizon 2020 research and innovation programme (grant agreement 716562). The work was also supported by the Austrian Science Fund project DMAC (P32431) and by the ANR project DREAMY (ANR-21-CE48-0003).

J.-F. Raskin and K. Chatterjee (Eds.): Principles of Systems Design, LNCS 13660, pp. 107–130, 2022.
https://doi.org/10.1007/978-3-031-22337-2_6

information and finite (typically small) state-spaces that can be efficiently processed, transmitted, and stored. Among the many success stories of this approach is digital circuit design, which is one of the key enablers of modern computer systems (and also our main source of application examples): While it is out of question to perform analog simulations of the billions of transistors and other analog electronic components that implement the logic gates in a modern *very-large scale integration* (VLSI) circuit, applying digital timing simulations and verification techniques is common practice.

The Need for Accurate Timed Circuit Models. Given the tremendous advances in VLSI technology, with clock speeds in the GHz range and voltage swings well below 1 V [31], modeling accuracy becomes a concern [10]. Additionally, manufacturing *process, temperature, and supply-voltage* (PVT) variations cause a large variability in switching and signal propagation delays. Furthermore, reduced critical charges make the circuits more susceptible to ionizing particles [7,13] and electromagnetic interference [40], and feature sizes in the 10 nm range also increase the likelihood of permanent errors due to manufacturing defects and wear-out [33,43]. All these effects together make non-conservative delay predictions, which are required for digital modeling of fast synchronous circuits, difficult to obtain.

Indeed, none of these effects is adequately captured by existing timed digital circuit models. Besides the lack of modeling and analysis support for fault-tolerance, it was shown in [26] that none of the classic digital channel models, including the widely used pure and inertial delay channels [49], faithfully model the propagation of short pulses. The same is true for more advanced models like PID channels [8] (with the notable exception of involution channels [24], though). Since existing digital simulators exclusively use classic delay models, their predictions are hence not always accurate. Moreover, existing digital design tools lack an adequate support for metastability[1] [39] modeling and analysis.

Modeling Approaches: State-Based and State-Oblivious. A natural and powerful tool for modeling such systems are transition systems. A transition system is defined by a set of states, transitions between these states, and rules how *executions*, i.e., (timed) state sequences, are generated by such a system. Transition systems can be white-box or black-box: white-box approaches try to follow the actual implementation and model the dynamics of a system's state, while black-box models just try to capture the dynamics of the system's inputs and outputs. In the latter case, states are merely used as equivalence classes of execution pre-

---

[1] Metastable upsets can occur in any state-holding device with discrete stable states, such as memory cells. If a new state transition is triggered before the state change caused by the previous one has settled, an intermediate output value may be observed arbitrarily late. Even Byzantine (i.e., "worst-case") fault-tolerance techniques are incapable of containing the effects of metastable upsets perfectly [22], since a signal outside the (discrete) value domain is not just an arbitrary regular signal. Metastability is not restricted to electrical systems. For example, an engineered genetic toggle switch [28], acting as a memory cell storing 0 or 1, was observed to exhibit metastable behavior besides its two stable states.

fixes (histories), to abstract away individual execution prefixes that do not need to be further distinguished when capturing the system's behavior. We will refer to both variants as *state-based specifications* in the following.

On the other hand, the correct behavior of a system can be directly specified by the set of valid executions. For convenience, this is typically done in terms of an input-output function that maps a (timed) input state sequence to a set of allowed (timed) output state sequences. We will refer to this as a *state-oblivious specification*.

While the distinction is not strict, as a state-oblivious specification is easily translated to a state-based specification with the set of states being the set of all execution prefixes, i.e., trivial equivalence classes taken as states, the approaches tend to lead to quite different formalizations and proofs. In computer science, state-based specifications have received lots of attention, and can nowadays draw from a rich set of techniques, e.g., for showing that one system implements another system via simulation relations, or reasoning about properties of compositions of systems.

A Take on a State-Oblivious Modeling Framework. In this work, we advocate the considerably less popular alternative of state-oblivious specifications and discuss some of its properties, building on the framework originally presented in [16].

In Sects. 2, 3, 4 and 5, we review the cornerstones of state-oblivious formalizations of continuous-time, discrete-valued circuits as introduced in [16]. Like in some existing approaches for reactive systems, such as Broy and Stølen's FOCUS [9], a *module* is specified directly in terms of the output behaviors that it may exhibit in response to a given input signal. As already said, this is very different from existing frameworks that follow a state-based approach, including Alur-Dill Timed Automata [4], Lamport's TLA [35], Timed IO Automatons by Keynar et. al. [32], and discrete abstractions for hybrid systems [3], as well as state-space-based control theory [36], which all act on the (sometimes uncountable) state-space of the underlying system.

We demonstrate that typical timing constraints and fault-tolerance properties (e.g. Byzantine behavior [42]) are easily expressed and dealt with in a state-oblivious framework. In Sect. 6, we also demonstrate that self-stabilizing systems [18], in which the initial internal state is assumed to be completely arbitrary after a catastrophic (but transient) event, can be described and proved correct appropriately.

In Sect. 3, we address composition of modules. Composition has been extensively studied in state-based approaches. In general, however, it is even difficult to decide whether behavioral specifications match at interface boundaries [2]. While one can prove some generic properties about composition of state-oblivious specifications, they apply to quite restricted settings only. In Sect. 7, we will show that there are indeed some unexpected module composition artefacts for state-oblivious specifications when one considers more general settings. In particular, the *eventual short pulse filter* (eSPF) module introduced in [26, Sec. 7] reveals that composing modules with bounded delay in a feedback loop may result in a module with finite delay. Even worse, whereas the feedback-free composition of bounded-delay modules is always bounded delay, it turns out that the *feedback-free* composition of finite-delay modules need not always be finite-delay. Some conclusions and problems open for future research are provided in Sect. 8.

Applications Beyond VLSI Circuits. Although our framework emerged in the context of digital circuits [16], its applicability extends to other domains. It needs to be stressed, though, that we do not aim at typical application domains of classic control theory. Despite some similarities, like considering systems as function transformers, our continuous-time discrete-value (typically binary) signals and their properties of interest are very different from the signals considered in either continuous or discrete control theory.

However, the idea to model continuous dynamical systems by discrete-state timed circuits has been successfully applied to genetics as well: Rather than analyzing dependencies of transcription and protein levels by means of differential equations, genetic circuit models have been used for descriptive [1,48] and synthetic [6,28,30,46] purposes. In the meantime, a body of genetic circuit design principles has been established [29,41,44]. For a discussion on differences between classical circuits in silicon and genetic circuits, we refer the reader to [25]. Further, as many biological systems are fault-tolerant and even self-stabilizing to a certain extent, a unified model bears the promise of cross-fertilization between different application domains. Earlier work on biologically inspired self-stabilizing Byzantine fault-tolerant clock synchronization [11,45] is a promising example of the benefit of this approach.

2   Timed Circuit Models

Before discussing basic properties of state-oblivious specifications via some examples, we very briefly recall the standard synchronous, asynchronous, and partially synchronous timing models for specifying distributed systems. Obviously, they can be also used for modeling gates in a circuit that communicate with each other via interconnecting wires.

In *synchronous systems*, components act in synchronized lock-step *rounds*, each comprising a communication phase and a single computing step of every component. The strict constraints on the order of computing steps thus facilitate algorithms that are simple to analyze and implement, yet can leverage time to, e.g., avoid race conditions and implement communication by time [34]. Unfortunately, implementing the synchronous abstraction, e.g., by central clocking or causal relations enforced by explicit communication [5], can be too inefficient or plainly infeasible.

This fact fuels the interest in *asynchronous systems*, for which no assumptions are made on the order in which computation and communication steps are executed. The standard way of modeling asynchronous executions is to associate a local state with each component, and let a *(fair) scheduler* decide in which order components communicate and update their states (i.e., receive information and perform computation). Viewing synchrony as the temporally most ordered execution model of distributed computations, asynchronous systems are at the other extreme end of the spectrum. Since it is impossible to distinguish very slow components from such that have suffered from a crash fault, however, proving correct asynchronous distributed algorithms is difficult and often impossible.[2]

To circumvent this problem, a number of intermediate *partially-synchronous* state-based models have been defined (e.g. [14,19]). However, such models typically serve either special applications or as a vehicle to better understand the fundamental differences between synchronous and asynchronous systems.

2.1 When State-Based Formalizations Are Unnecessarily Complicated

While synchronous and asynchronous systems are easy to specify within state-based frameworks, the situation becomes different for systems with more complicated timing constraints like partially synchronous systems. The challenge in allowing for general timing constraints is that the elegant and convenient separation of time and the evolution of the system state cannot be maintained. The situation becomes even more involved when the goal is to model circuits, as opposed to software-based computer systems. A major difference is that software-based systems typically reside at a level of abstraction where discrete, well-separated actions are taken naturally by an underlying machine. The evolution of the internal state of this machine is then modeled as a transition system. By contrast, real circuits are analog devices that continuously transform inputs into outputs.

We demonstrate the differences between the state-based and the state-oblivious approach at the example of the arguably simplest circuit, namely, a bounded-delay channel, as instantiated e.g. by an (ideal) wire.

A Channel. We consider a binary bounded-delay first-in first-out (FIFO) channel, which has a single input port (=connector) and a single output port. Whereas such channels are also employed in various state-based models, they are usually *part* of the model and typically also the only means of communication. By contrast, we describe the channel as an object in a (to-be-defined) model.

Informally, we require the following: The *input port* is fed by an input signal given as a function IN : $\mathbb{R} \to \{0, 1\}$. Note that the restriction to binary-valued signals is for simplicity only and could be replaced by arbitrary discrete ranges. The reason why the domain of IN is $\mathbb{R}$ instead of, e.g., the non-negative reals $\mathbb{R}_0^+$, will be explained later. Typically, some further restrictions are made on (input) signals for modeling real circuits, e.g., only a finite number of transitions within each finite interval. For each input signal, the *output port* produces an output signal such that: (i) for each input transition there is exactly one output transition within some time $d > 0$, and (ii) output transitions occur in the same temporal order as their corresponding input transitions.

The State-Based Approach: The Channel as a Transition System. A state-based description would model the state of the channel at some time t, as well as the

---

[2] Consensus [42], a basic fault-tolerance task, can be solved deterministically in synchronous systems, but not in asynchronous systems [21].

rules for transitioning between states. Obviously, this would allow us to infer the correct behavior of the channel at times greater than t as valid traces of this transition system. However, a state-based description would be at odds with our goal of a simple and modular specification of the system:

- Both a physical wire connecting sender and receiver and reliable multi-hop wireless channel are implementations of our channel. Specifications with one of them in mind may differ significantly.
- The state space of the channel would be infinitely large, as it must be able to record an arbitrarily long sequence of alternating input transitions that may have occurred within $[t - d, t]$
- The strategy of breaking down a difficult-to-describe state-based description into smaller building blocks does not help here.

The above problems become even more pronounced when it comes to more interesting modules. Even if we were not discouraged by the above difficulties and went for a state-based definition of the channel, e.g. in terms of Timed I/O Automata [32], we argue that the original advantage of a state-based approach would be lost: the canonical description of the global state of the system as the product of the components' states.

The State-Oblivious Approach: The Channel as an Input-Output Function. We conclude that our preferred option is (i) to treat the channel as a blackbox, and (ii) not to bother with finding states, i.e., equivalence classes of histories, in the first place. That is, we infer the possible output not from some internal state, but rather directly from the input history. By the nature of a channel, however, the feasible output values at time t cannot be determined from IN alone: the *output* at times smaller than t enters the bargain as well. Hence, we naturally end up directly relating input and output signals: For each (possible) input signal IN, there must be a non-empty *set* of *feasible* output functions $\phi(\text{IN})$, where the *module specification* ϕ maps inputs signals to such feasible output signals. Note that we allow the adversary to choose which of the feasible output signals a module generates in some execution, i.e., we just assume non-determinism here.[3] This also allows to express any given restriction on the inputs, e.g., one that is considered suitable for a given module, simply by permitting *any* output signal for input signals that violate such a restriction.

A state-oblivious specification of our channel can be given in terms of an input-output function ϕ. For every input signal IN, the output signal OUT is feasible, i.e., $\text{OUT} \in \phi(\text{IN})$ if $\text{OUT}(t) = \text{IN}\left(\delta^{-1}(t)\right)$, where the delay function $\delta : \mathbb{R} \to \mathbb{R}$ is continuous, strictly increasing (hence invertible), and satisfies $t \leq \delta(t) \leq t + d$ for all $t \in \mathbb{R}$.

As we model signals as functions of real-time, we do not need special signal values (as in FOCUS [9]) that report the progress of time, and relating different (input, output) signals to each other becomes simple.

---

[3] Whereas one could extend our framework to restrict the adversary here, e.g., to capture probabilistic choice, we will not consider this possibility in this work.

It remains to explain why we chose the whole set of reals $\mathbb{R}$ as the (time) domain of our input and output functions. Again, in principle, nothing prevents us from using functions $\mathbb{R}_0^+ \to \{0, 1\}$. For the considered channel, it would be reasonably easy to adapt the description: $\text{OUT} \in \phi(\text{IN})$ is arbitrary on $[0, \delta(0))$ and $\text{OUT}(t) = \text{IN}(\delta^{-1}(t))$ on $[\delta(0), \infty)$, for some continuous, strictly increasing delay function $\delta : \mathbb{R}_0^+ \to \mathbb{R}_0^+$ satisfying that $t \le \delta(t) \le t + d$ for all $t \in \mathbb{R}_0^+$.

However, given that our "equivalent" to the channel's state is its input history, it is more natural to rely on input signals with a time domain that contains $[-d, \infty)$ when specifying feasible outputs on $\mathbb{R}_0^+$. Extending the range by a finite value only would not cover all possible values of d, though. Moreover, there are modules whose output may depend on events that lie arbitrarily far in the past, e.g., a memory cell. For simplicity and composability, picking $\mathbb{R}$ as domain is thus preferred here. We remark that this convention does not prevent suitable initialization of a module, say at time $t = 0$, however.

3   Composition

In the previous section, we demonstrated the use of state-oblivious specifications in terms of directly providing input-output functions ϕ for a simple channel. In general, we define:

Definition 1 (Module). *A signal is a function from $\mathbb{R}$ to $\{0, 1\}$. A module M has a set of input ports $I(M)$ and a set of output ports $O(M)$, which are the connectors where input signals are supplied to M and output signals leave M. The module specification ϕ_M maps the input signals $(\text{IN}_p : \mathbb{R} \to \{0, 1\})_{p \in I(M)}$ to sets of allowed output signals $(\text{OUT}_p : \mathbb{R} \to \{0, 1\})_{p \in O(M)}$. An execution of a module is a member of the set*

$$\left\{ \left((\text{IN}_p)_{p \in I(M)}, \phi_M((\text{IN}_p)_{p \in I(M)}) \right) \mid (\text{IN}_p : \mathbb{R} \to \{0, 1\})_{p \in I(M)} \right\}.$$

Note that we typically assume that modules are *causal*, i.e., that images of ϕ_M for two inputs that are identical until time t, are identical until time t.

Specifying a module M this way, i.e., by providing ϕ_M, can either be viewed as stating an assumption, in the sense that it is already known how to build a module with the respective behavior, or as stating a problem, i.e., expressing a desired behavior of a module that still needs to be built. We call a module specified this way a *basic module*.

Implementing such a module can be done in two different ways: (i) directly within a target-technology, which leaves the scope of our modeling framework, or (ii) by decomposition into smaller modules within the modeling framework.

Let us now formalize what the latter means in the context of our approach. Intuitively, we will take a set of modules and connect their input and output ports to form a larger *compound module*, whose inputs and outputs are subsets of the ports of these modules (cp. Fig. 1). The input-output function of the compound module is then derived from the ones of the submodules and their interconnection.

Definition 2 (Compound module). *A compound module M is defined by:*

1. *Decide on the sets of* input ports $I(M)$ *and* output ports $O(M)$ *of M.*
2. *Pick the set S_M of* submodules *of M. Each submodule $S \in S_M$ has input ports $I(S)$, output ports $O(S)$, and a specification ϕ_S that maps tuples $(\text{IN}_p : \mathbb{R} \to \{0,1\})_{p \in I(S)}$ of functions to sets of tuples $(\text{OUT}_p : \mathbb{R} \to \{0,1\})_{p \in O(S)}$ of functions, satisfying the following well-formedness constraints:*
   - *For each output port $p \in O(M)$, there is exactly one submodule $S \in S_M$ such that $p \in O(S)$.*
   - *For each input port $p \in I(S)$ of some submodule $S \in S_M$, either $p \in I(M)$ or there is exactly one submodule $S' \in S_M$ so that $p \in O(S')$.*
3. *For each $(\text{IN}_p : \mathbb{R} \to \{0,1\})_{p \in I(M)}$, we require $(\text{OUT}_p : \mathbb{R} \to \{0,1\})_{p \in O(M)} \in \phi_M\big((\text{IN}_p)_{p \in I(M)}\big)$ iff there exist functions $(f_p : \mathbb{R} \to \{0,1\})_{p \in \bigcup_{S \in S_M} I(S) \cup O(S)}$ with*
   - *$\forall S \in S_M : (f_p)_{p \in O(S)} \in \phi_S((f_p)_{p \in I(S)})$;*
   - *$\forall p \in I(M) : f_p = \text{IN}_p$; and*
   - *$\forall p \in O(M) : f_p = \text{OUT}_p$.*

Note that choices are made only in Steps 1 and 2, whereas ϕ_M is defined implicitly and non-constructively in Step 3. Informally, the latter just says that any execution, i.e., any pair of input and output signals, of M that leads to feasible executions of all submodules, must be in ϕ_M.

Example 1 (Oscillator). Figure 1 shows an example compound module: a simple resettable digital oscillator. It is composed of an inverter, an AND gate, and a fixed unit delay channel, i.e., a FIFO channel with $\delta(t) := t + 1$. Both gates operate in zero-time, i.e., all delays have been lumped into the FIFO channel.

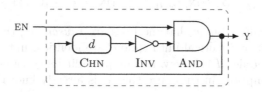

Fig. 1. Compound oscillator module.

The module's behavior is characterized by the fact that it oscillates at its output Y = CHN IN while input EN is 1, and outputs a constant 0 while EN is 0. Up to time 4, the signal trace depicted in Fig. 2 shows part of a correct execution of the oscillator module.

The same conceptual design of a negative feedback-loop with delay was used by Stricker et al. [46] in the context of genetic circuits, for synthesizing a genetic oscillator in *Escherichia coli* with an output period in the order of an hour. Figure 3 depicts the genetic design of the feedback-loop of the simplified (second)

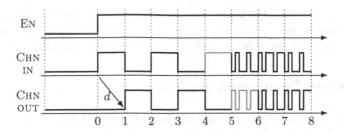

Fig. 2. Execution of oscillator module with transient channel fault (signal mismatch marked red). (Color figure online)

design proposed by Stricker et al. It shows the DNA segement that is introduced into the bacterial host. The DNA comprises of a promoter (bold arrow in the figure) and a downstream lacI gene (flanked by a ribosome binding site and a terminator that are not shown for simplicity). The lacI gene is transcribed and translated into LacI protein. The promoter is activated if no inhibiting LacI proteins are present (shown as an inhibitory arrow from lacI to the promoter) and externally introduced IPTG molecules are present (not shown in the figure, and assumed to be present throughout). The activation of the promoter leads to transcription and subsequent translation of the downstream lacI gene, resulting in increasing LacI protein levels, which then inactivate the promoter. Only when the concentration of the LacI protein has fallen to a sufficiently low level due to degradation and dilution, the promoter becomes active again. The result is an oscillation of the LacI protein concentration.

A Note on State-Oblivious Specifications: The Absence of an Initial State. In the previous section, we have argued that, when specifying the channel input-output behavior in a state-oblivious way, we resort to input output signals as functions $\mathbb{R} \to \{0, 1\}$. In this section, we followed this approach in Definitions 2 and 1. We will later see (in Sect. 5) that such specifications are also well-suited for specifying so-called self-stabilizing systems.

However, state-oblivious specifications also introduce difficulties that lead to open research questions. More specifically, a useful vehicle for showing that some module implements another one in classical state-based frameworks is by induction on a sequence of input events, starting from some initial state. Simulation and bi-simulation relations are proved this way, with implications on what can be said about using one module instead of the other. These proof techniques fail in our case, however, since signals are defined on the time domain $\mathbb{R}$, without

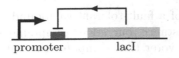

promoter   lacI

Fig. 3. Negative feedback loop of a genetic oscillator presented by Stricker et al. [46].

an initial time and "state". While one can argue that induction from a common time, say 0, can be done into the positive an negative direction, questions about what this means for one module replacing/implementing another are open.

4   Modeling Permanent Faults

Viewed from an outside perspective, all that a faulty module can do is deviating from its specification. Depending on the type of faults considered, there may or may not be constraints on this deviation. In other words, a faulty module M simply follows a *weaker* module specification than ϕ_M, i.e., some module specification $\bar{\phi}_M$ such that $\forall (\text{IN}_p)_{p \in I(M)} : \bar{\phi}_M \left((\text{IN}_p)_{p \in I(M)} \right) \supseteq \phi_M \left((\text{IN}_p)_{p \in I(M)} \right)$.

Definition 3 (Crash and Byzantine fault types). *For the fault type* crash faults *[20], a faulty component simply ceases to operate at some point in time. In this case, $\bar{\phi}_M ((\text{IN}_p)_{p \in I(M)})$ can be constructed from $\phi_M ((\text{IN}_p)_{p \in I(M)})$ by adding, for each $(\text{OUT}_p)_{p \in O(M)} \in \phi_M ((\text{IN}_p)_{p \in I(M)})$ and each $t \in \mathbb{R}$, the output signal*

$$\left(t' \in \mathbb{R} \mapsto \begin{cases} \text{OUT}_p(t') & \text{if } t' < t \\ \text{OUT}_p(t) & \text{else} \end{cases} \right)_{p \in O(M)}$$

to $\bar{\phi}_M ((\text{IN}_p)_{p \in I(M)})$. This just keeps ("stuck-at") the last output value before the crash.

The fault-type of Byzantine faults *[42] is even simpler to describe: The behavior of a faulty module is arbitrary, i.e., $\bar{\phi}_M$ is the constant function returning the set of* all *possible output signals, irrespective of the input signal.*

Having defined a faulty type $\bar{\phi}_S$ for a module S accordingly, it seems obvious how to define a fault-tolerant compound module: A compound module M with submodules S_M tolerates failures of a subset $F \subset S_M$, iff $\phi_M = \bar{\phi}_{M,F}$, where $\bar{\phi}_{M,F}$ is the specification of the compound module in which we replace each submodule $S \in F$ by the one with specification $\bar{\phi}_S$.

Example 2 (Fault-tolerant 1-bit adder module). Figure 4 shows an example of a 1-bit adder module. It is built from three (zero-time) 1-bit adder submodules, a (zero-time) majority voter, and FIFO channels with maximal delay d connecting the module's inputs to the adder submodules. The channels account for the module's propagation delay and potentially desynchronized arrivals of input transitions at the submodules. If the module inputs have been stable for d time, however, its output yields the sum of the two inputs, tolerating failure of any one of its three adder submodules and the associated input channels.

While this definition of a fault-tolerant compound module can be useful, it is very restrictive. For instance, our adder compound module cannot tolerate a failure of the majority voter that computes the output. More generally, no matter how a compound module M is constructed, it can never tolerate even a single crash failure of an arbitrary submodule S, unless M is trivial: If S has an

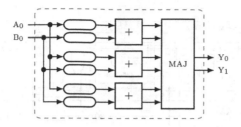

Fig. 4. Fault-tolerant 1-bit adder.

output port in common with M, i.e., if S generates this output for M, the only possible guarantee M could make for this output port is a fixed output value at all times, as this is what the crash of S would lead to.

To address this issue, we introduce the concept of a *fault-tolerant implementation* of a module.

Definition 4 (Fault-tolerant implementation). *We say that module M implements module M' iff*

$$\forall (\text{IN}_p)_{p \in I(M)} : \phi_M \left((\text{IN}_p)_{p \in I(M)} \right) \subseteq \phi_{M'} \left((\text{IN}_p)_{p \in I(M')} \right).$$

This requires that $I(M) = I(M')$ and $O(M) = O(M')$. Similarly, for a given fault type $\bar{\cdot}$, M is an implementation *of M' that tolerates failures of $F \subset S_M$ iff*

$$\forall (\text{IN}_p)_{p \in I(M)} : \bar{\phi}_{M,F} \left((\text{IN}_p)_{p \in I(M)} \right) \subseteq \phi_{M'} \left((\text{IN}_p)_{p \in I(M')} \right),$$

where $\bar{\phi}_{M,F}$ is defined according to the fault type. Finally, M is an f-tolerant implementation of M', iff it tolerates faults of $F \subset S_M$ for any F satisfying $|F| \leq f$.

Example 3 (Fault-tolerant adder). For an adder implementation that is 1-tolerant to Byzantine faults (and thus also any other fault type), *triple-modular redundancy* (TMR) can be used. Here, not just the adders, but also the pair of input and output signals is triplicated. Moreover, the single majority voter at the adder outputs is replaced by three majority voters at the adder inputs: Since they vote on the replicated input signals, we can guarantee that all three adders receive identical inputs if no voter fails, whereas two adders receive identical inputs and produce identical outputs if one voter is faulty. Note that relaxing the specification and using an implementation relation is necessary here, as otherwise the same reasoning as before would prevent a 1-tolerant solution.

The problem of developing a fault-tolerant implementation of an oscillator was addressed in the DARTS project [23,27]: Using a predecessor of the proposed modeling framework, it was shown that a circuit comprising $3f + 1$ tick generator nodes, in which the output of each node is fed back as input to all nodes (including the node itself), tolerates up to f Byzantine faulty nodes. The circuitry of a single tick generator node for $n = 4$ and $f = 1$ is depicted in Fig. 5.

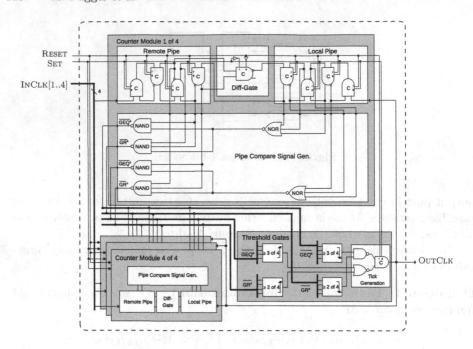

Fig. 5. Node of the fault-tolerant DARTS oscillator.

Informally, it counts the difference of clock transitions generated by itself (Local Pipe) and those received from other nodes (Remote Pipe) by means of Counter Modules implemented via elastic pipelines [47]. When sufficiently many nodes (not all, since there might be a fault) are not too far behind (determined by the Threshold Gates), it generates a new local clock transition (Tick Generation).

5   Modeling Transient Faults and Self-stabilization

Transient faults are assumed to be temporary in nature, in the sense that the *cause* of the fault eventually vanishes. Suitable recovery techniques can hence be used to resume correct operation later on. The most extreme requirement is *self-stabilization* [12], where the system must eventually resume correct operation even after all of its components experienced arbitrary transient faults. Since the latter results in arbitrary states, this is equivalent to requiring that the system re-establishes correct operation from arbitrary initial states in finite time. The maximal time it may take to do so is called *stabilization time*.

Self-stabilization plays a crucial role in mission-critical systems, where even the assumption that a certain fraction (e.g., less than a third, as in DARTS) of the subcomponents can fail is too optimistic, or for applications that cannot afford the amount of redundancy needed for fully masking faults. Unsurprisingly, self-stabilization and related concepts also play a vital role in biological systems. For example, Albert and Othmer [1] modeled part of the control circuit that regulates gene expression in the fruit fly Drosophila Melanogaster by a binary circuit, and observed that a considerable number of initial circuit states finally lead to the wild-type stable state. For the lobster heart, it has been established that it is, in essence, self-stabilizing even in the presence of ongoing Byzantine behavior [11, 45].

Transferring the idea of self-stabilization to our state-oblivious framework requires some effort, but we will demonstrate that it can be integrated very well. Most notably, there is no notion of a state (besides from trivial states), which means that we cannot define self-stabilization in the conventional state-based manner.

The first important observation underlying input-output functions in a state-oblivious specification of self-stabilization is that, since a basic module specification describes the desired behavior *from the viewpoint of an external observer*, we consider a module correct even if it merely *seems* to be operating correctly in terms of its input-output behavior. In other words, it does not matter whether the module internally operates as intended, as long as it produces correct results.

Second, when defining basic modules (Definition 1), we only resorted to input and output signals from $\mathbb{R} \to \{0, 1\}$. The input-output function ϕ_M of a module M then maps input signals to allowed output signals. For modules that are intended to be self-stabilizing (or that suffer from transient faults), this is not anymore convenient since they are not either correct or faulty during all of the execution. Merely, we would like to define how they should behave if they were *correct during a time interval* $[t^-, t^+]$.

Redefining Correctness for Transient Faults. An immediate solution to this is to define ϕ_M on all signal restrictions to all sub-intervals $I = [t^-, t^+] \subseteq \mathbb{R}$. To make such interval-restrictions explicit, we will sometimes write σ^I, IN^I, OUT^I, E^I etc. Note that such intervals I could also be open (t^-, t^+), closed $[t^-, t^+]$, or half-open, but are always contiguous.

Definition 5 (Basic module—interval-restricted specification). *An interval-restricted execution E^I of a basic module is correct during $I = [t^-, t^+]$ if its interval-restricted output signals OUT^I are within the image $\phi_M(\text{IN}^I)$ of its interval-restricted input signals.*

We termed this the *interval-restricted specification*, since it requires the definition of ϕ_M on all these sub-intervals.

However, care has to be taken: the input-output function ϕ_M has to be restricted to ensure that it adheres to an intuitive notion of correctness. For example, we expect an execution of M that is correct within $[t^-, t^+]$ to be also correct within all subintervals of $[t^-, t^+]$. One possibility is to add all those restrictions explicitly. Indeed, such specifications are powerful in expressiveness [16], but at the same time our experience in the early stages of [16] was that using this approach is tedious for simple modules, and practically guarantees mistakes for complex modules. The reason for this is that the subset-closedness of the correctness definition is easily violated in an interval-restricted specification even for simple modules like channels.

We thus primarily resort to another definition, which does not change the domain of ϕ_M, i.e., where the domain of all signals is $\mathbb{R}$, which we call a *definition by extension.* With this definition, correctness is subset-closed for time intervals by construction (see [16, Lem. 3.3]), such that the natural notion of correctness is also guaranteed by construction.

Definition 6 (Basic module, correct during time interval—definition by extension). *An interval-restricted execution E^I of a basic module M is correct during $I = [t^-, t^+]$, iff there is a (complete, i.e., with time domain $\mathbb{R}$) execution E' of a basic module M such that: (i) the input and output signals of E^I and E' are identical during $[t^-, t^+]$, and (ii) for execution E', letting i be the input signals and o the output signals of E', $o \in \phi_M(i)$.*

If not stated otherwise, we will resort to the definition by extension for basic modules. For ease of notation, we will, however, extend ϕ_M to input and output signals with time domains that are sub-intervals $[t^-, t^+]$ of $\mathbb{R}$ in the following: Writing $\mathrm{OUT}^I \in \phi_M(\mathrm{IN}^I)$ where $\mathrm{IN}^I, \mathrm{OUT}^I$ have time domain $I = [t^-, t^+]$ is just a short-hand notation for: For any execution E of M that behaves according to $\mathrm{IN}^I, \mathrm{OUT}^I$ during I, basic module M is correct during I.

Definition 7 (Extendible module).   *We say that a basic module is extendible, if its input-output function ϕ_M has the properties of a definition by extension. That is, executions that are correct on a subinterval can be extended to executions that are correct on $\mathbb{R}$.*

The above definition of correctness introduced above also implies that a sub-execution on some interval $[t^-, t^+] \subset \mathbb{R}$ that is considered correct can be extended to a (complete) correct execution on $\mathbb{R}$. This is natural for basic modules, but inappropriate for self-stabilizing compound modules: these take the role of algorithms, and making this a requirement would be equivalent to disallowing transient faults—or, more precisely, to implicitly turn them into persistent faults. To illustrate this issue, consider again the compound module implementing the oscillator shown in Fig. 1 and the signal trace shown in Fig. 2: The execution segment during time interval $[6, 8]$ must be considered correct, since it fulfills all input-output constraints of the involved circuit components during this interval. We know, however, that such a high-frequency oscillation can never occur in a (complete) correct execution of the compound module on $\mathbb{R}$, for which the only possible oscillator frequency is one transition per time unit.

To allow for a meaningful notion of self-stabilization, we will hence treat compound modules differently: When analyzing their stabilizing behavior, we assume that all sub-modules themselves operate correctly, whereas the "convergence" of the compound module's externally visible behavior to a correct one must be enforced. This is captured by defining correct executions of compound modules on time intervals $[t^-, t^+] \subset \mathbb{R}$ by the same process as in Definition 2, except that we replace $\mathbb{R}$ by $[t^-, t^+]$.

Definition 8 (Compound module—interval-restriced specification).
For any $I = [t^-, t^+]$ and any interval-restricted input signal $(\mathrm{IN}_p^I)_{p \in I(M)}$, we require that the interval-restricted output signal $(\mathrm{OUT}_p^I)_{p \in O(M)} \in \phi_M((\mathrm{IN}_p^I)_{p \in I(M)})$ iff

there exist interval-restricted input and output signals $(f_p^I)_{p \in \bigcup_{S \in S_M} I(S) \cup O(S)}$ *for all submodules S of M so that all the properties below hold:*

- $\forall S \in S_M : (f_p^I)_{p \in O(S)} \in \phi_S((f_p^I)_{p \in I(S)})$
- $\forall p \in I(M) : f_p = \mathrm{IN}_p^I$
- $\forall p \in O(M) : f_p = \mathrm{OUT}_p^I$

Note that this definition is recursive; we can iteratively extend all module specifications to inputs on arbitrary intervals $[t^-, t^+] \subseteq \mathbb{R}$, starting from the specifications of basic modules for inputs on $\mathbb{R}$.

With these definitions in place, we can now proceed to defining a suitable notion of self-stabilization in our framework.

Definition 9 (Self-stabilizing implementation). *A module M is called a T-stabilizing implementation of module M', iff $I(M) = I(M')$, $O(M) = O(M')$ and, for all $I = [t^-, t^+] \subseteq \mathbb{R}$ with $t^+ \geq t_- + T$, $I' = [t^- + T, t^+]$ and each $(\mathrm{OUT}_p^I)_{p \in O(M)} \in \phi_M \left((\mathrm{IN}_p^I)_{p \in I(M)} \right)$, it holds that*

$$\left(\mathrm{OUT}_p^{I'} \right)_{p \in O(M)} \in \phi_{M'} \left((\mathrm{IN}_p^{I'})_{p \in I(M')} \right).$$

Informally, cutting off the first T time units from any interval-restricted execution of M must yield a correct interval-restricted execution of M'.

Module M is a self-stabilizing implementation of M', iff it is a T-stabilizing implementation of M' for some $T < \infty$.

Example 4 (Self-stabilization). According to Defintion 9, the oscillator implementation from Fig. 1 is not self-stabilizing, as illustrated by Fig. 2: After a transient fault of the channel component during time $[5, 6]$, all circuit components operate correctly again from time 6 on, but the behavior of circuit output $Y = \mathrm{CHN\ IN}$ never returns to the behavior of Y that could be observed in an execution on $\mathbb{R}$.

For a positive example, recall the 1-bit adder depicted in Fig. 4. Its self-stabilization properties follow, without the need of a custom analysis, from a general principle (called forgetfulness), which will be introduced in the next section.

6   Example: A Self-stabilizing Oscillator

In view of the state-obliviousness and generality of our modeling framework, one might ask whether it indeed allows to derive meaningful results. As a proof of concept, we will thus elaborate more on self-stabilizing compound modules.

First, we will formalize the statement that if a compound module M is made up of submodules S whose output at time t depends only on the input during $[t - T_S, t]$ (for $T_S \in \mathbb{R}_0^+$) and contains no feedback-loops (like, e.g., the adder in Fig. 4, but unlike the oscillator in Fig. 1), then M is self-stabilizing. Interestingly, this result sometimes *does* also apply to systems that do have internal feedback loops; this holds true whenever we can contain the loop in a submodule and (separately) show that it is self-stabilizing.

Definition 10 (Forgetfulness). *For $F \geq 0$, module M is F-forgetful iff:*

1. *For any $I = [t^-, t^+] \subseteq \mathbb{R}$ with $t^+ \geq t^- + F$, pick any interval-restricted output $(\text{OUT}_p^I)_{p \in O(M)} \in \phi_M \left((\text{IN}_p^I)_{p \in I(M)} \right)$.*
2. *For each input port $p \in I(M)$, pick any input signal $\text{IN}_p' : \mathbb{R} \to \{0, 1\}$ so that IN_p' restricted to I equals IN_p^I.*
3. *Then $\left(\text{OUT}_p' : \mathbb{R} \to \{0, 1\} \right)_{p \in O(M)} \in \phi_M \left((\text{IN}_p' : \mathbb{R} \to \{0, 1\})_{p \in I(M)} \right)$ exists so that for all output ports $p \in O(M)$ the restrictions of OUT_p and OUT_p' to the interval $[t^- + F, t^+]$ are equal.*

In other words, the output of a F-forgetful module during $[t^- + F, t^+]$ reveals no information regarding the input during $(-\infty, t^-)$.

Example 5. A simple example of a d-forgetful module is a FIFO channel with maximum delay d.

Definition 11 (Feedback-free module). *Let the circuit graph of a compound module M be the directed graph whose nodes are the submodules S_M of M, and for each output port p of $S \in S_M$ that is an input port of another submodule $S' \in S_M$, there is a directed edge from S to S'. We say M is feedback-free iff all its submodules are forgetful and its circuit graph is acyclic.*

One can then show that feedback-free compound modules made up of forgetful submodules are self-stabilizing:

Theorem 1 ([16], **Theorem 3.7**). *Given a feedback-free compound module M, denote by $\mathcal{P}$ the set of paths in its circuit graph. Suppose that each submodule $S \in S_M$ is F_S-forgetful for some $F_S \in \mathbb{R}_0^+$. Then, M is F-forgetful with*

$$F = \max_{(S_1, \ldots, S_k) \in \mathcal{P}} \left\{ \sum_{i=1}^{k} F_{S_i} \right\}.$$

Using this theorem (possibly recursively applied, in the case of compound modules made up of compound submodules), one can show that a given feedback-free compound module is forgetful. Moreover, for such a module M, it is sufficient to show that it behaves like another module M' in correct executions (i.e., those on $\mathbb{R}$, rather than on certain time intervals) for proving that M is a self-stabilizing implementation of M'.

Corollary 1. *Suppose that compound module M satisfies the prerequisites of Theorem 1. Moreover, for a module M' with $I(M') = I(M)$ and $O(M') = O(M)$, assume that: For all input signals $(\text{IN}_p : \mathbb{R} \to \{0, 1\})_{p \in I(M)}$, it holds for its output signals that $\phi_M \left((\text{IN}_p)_{p \in I(M)} \right) \subseteq \phi_{M'} \left((\text{IN}_p)_{p \in I(M)} \right)$. Then, M is a self-stabilizing implementation of M'.*

These results ensure that self-stabilization follows without further ado not only in trivial cases where an erroneous state is *instantaneously* forgotten and overwritten by new input. By using compound modules in a hierarchical manner, one can encapsulate the heart of a proof of self-stabilization in the appropriate system layer and separate aspects from different layers that are unrelated. This plays along nicely with the standard approach for proving self-stabilization of complex systems, which is to establish properties of increasing strength and complexity in a bottom-up fashion, advancing from very basic aspects to high-level arguments.

Beyond Feedback-Free Compound Modules. Unfortunately, however, it is not hard to see that if (the circuit graph of) a compound module M is not feedback-free, self-stabilization of M does not necessarily follow from the fact that all submodules are forgetful. An example of such a circuit is the oscillator in Fig. 1. There are, however, circuits with feedback loops that stabilize.

Example 6. Figure 6 shows a self-stabilizing variant of the oscillator from Fig. 1 (without enable input). The module consists of (i) a watchdog-timed memory-cell MEM whose output MEM OUT $= Y$; the output is 1 at time t iff there is a time $t' \in (t-T, t)$ where output $Y(t') = 0$ and input $X(t') = 1$, (ii) a succeeding fixed delay channel with delay $d \leq T$, and (iii) an inverter. Note that (i) implies that the set $\{t \in \mathbb{R}_0^+ \mid Y(t) = 0\}$ is closed.

We now demonstrate how to formalize this example and its proof in our state-oblivious framework. The (basic) module OSC has no input and one output Y. Recall that, for basic modules, specifications involve defining ϕ_M on executions on $\mathbb{R}$ only. Hence, the module specification ϕ_{osc} is fully defined by deciding whether some function $(\text{OUT}_Y : \mathbb{R} \to \mathbb{R}) \in \phi_{osc}(\emptyset)$ or not. We define this to be the case for all functions satisfying that $\exists \delta \in [0, T+d)$ so that

$$\text{OUT}_Y(t) = \begin{cases} 1 & \text{if } \exists z \in \mathbb{Z}, \exists \tau \in (0, T) : t = \delta + z(T+d) + \tau \\ 0 & \text{else.} \end{cases}$$

Intuitively, δ denotes the fixed time offset of the signal, and τ the time the signal is 1 during the period $t + d$.

If restricted to times $[0, 5]$, Fig. 7 shows the execution for $\delta = 0$, $d = 1$ and $T = 1.5d = 1.5$. The channel incorrectly forwards the red signal at its input during time $[4, 5]$ to the red signal at its output during $[5, 6]$, i.e., is not correct during $[5, 6]$. However, the module quickly recovers: Starting from time 6.3, the circuit has returned to a feasible periodic behavior with $\delta = 0.3$ and $\tau = T$. We next show that this stabilizing behavior is guaranteed.

Lemma 1. *If $T \geq d$, the compound module given in Fig. 6 is a $(T + 2d)$-stabilizing implementation of* OSC.

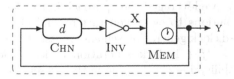

Fig. 6. Self-stabilizing oscillator module.

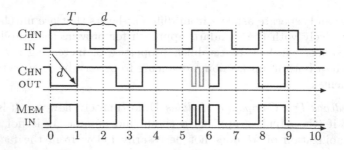

Fig. 7. Execution part of self-stabilizing oscillator module with transient channel fault (incorrect propagation in red). (Color figure online)

Proof. Wlog., assume that the compound module follows its specification during $[t^-, t^+) = [0, \infty)$.

1. There is some time $t^* \in [0, T + d]$ when $Y(t^*) = 0$. (Otherwise, the input to MEM at every time $t \in [d, T + d]$ would be $X(t) = \overline{Y}(t - d) = 0$ (with $\overline{Y}$ denoting negation), entailing $Y(T + d) = 0$ by the specification of MEM—a contradiction.)
2. Let $t_0 \in [t^*, t^* + d]$ be maximal with the property that $Y(t) = 0$ for all $t \in [t^*, t_0]$ (t_0 exists because $Y(t^*) = 0$ and $\{t \in \mathbb{R}_0^+ \mid Y(t) = 0\}$ is closed).
3. $X(t) = 0 \vee Y(t) = 1$ for every $t \in (t_0 - T, t_0)$ (specification of MEM).
4. (a) $t_0 < t^* + d$: Then, $Y(t_0^+) = \lim_{\varepsilon \to 0+} Y(t_0 + \varepsilon) = 1$ by maximality of t_0; hence $X(t_0) = 1$ by the specification of MEM and 3.
   (b) $t_0 = t^* + d$: Then, the channel ensures $X(t_0) = \overline{Y}(t^*) = 1$.
5. $Y(t) = 1$ for $t \in (t_0, t_0 + T)$ (specification of MEM).
6. $X(t) = \overline{Y}(t - d) = 0$ for $t \in (t_0 + d, t_0 + T + d) \supseteq (t_0 + T, t_0 + T + d)$ (as $T \geq d$).
7. $Y(t) = 0$ for $t \in [t_0 + T, t_0 + T + d]$ (specification of MEM).

We can now determine Y for larger times inductively, showing for $t_i := t_0 + i(T + d)$, $i \in \mathbb{N}$, that $Y(t) = 1$ for $t \in (t_i + d, t_i + T + d)$ and $Y(t) = 0$ for $t \in [t_i + T, t_i + T + d]$. Hence, the execution is feasible for module OSC during $[t_0, \infty)$. As $t_0 \leq t^* + d \leq T + 2d$, the claim follows.

By contrast, choosing $d > T$ leads to a circuit that does not necessarily self-stabilize.

   While the circuit in Fig. 6 is a self-stabilizing implementation of OSC, it is not fault-tolerant. A single permanent fault will stop it from operating correctly. However, the principle of using "forgetful" memory to achieve self-stabilization of oscillatory circuits can be carried over to fault-tolerant *distributed* oscillators like DARTS: In [16,17], we leveraged the approach in the design of fault-tolerant and self-stabilizing solutions to clock generation (and clock distribution [15]). FATAL$^+$, the proposed clock generation scheme, is essentially a distributed oscillator composed of $n \geq 3f + 1$ clock generation nodes, which self-stabilizes in time $\mathcal{O}(n)$ with probability $1 - 2^{-\Omega(n)}$ even in the presence of up to f Byzantine faults [17].

7   Module Composition Artefacts: The Weird Module

In this section, we will show that module composition in our framework some-times leads to surprising effects. As a consequence, one has to be careful when composing innocently looking modules that hide their true complexity behind deceptively simple specifications.

Like in Sect. 5, we will restrict signals and feasible executions in module specifications from $\mathbb{R}$ to arbitrary subintervals $I = [t^-, t^+] \subseteq \mathbb{R}$. To make such interval-restrictions explicit, we will sometimes write σ^I, IN^I, OUT^I, E^I etc. Note that such intervals I could also be open (t^-, t^+), closed $[t^-, t^+]$, or half-open, but are always contiguous.

A sequence of signals $(\sigma_i)_{i \in C}$ defined on intervals $I_1 \subseteq I_2 \subseteq \ldots$ with $I_i \subseteq I_{i+1}$ for all $i \in C$, for $C = \{1, \ldots, n\}$ or $C = \mathbb{N}$, is called a *covering* of a signal σ defined on $I = \bigcup_{i \in C} I_i$ if, for all $i \in C$, $\sigma_i = \sigma^{I_i}$. Clearly, any sequence of signals $(\sigma_i)_{i \in C}$ on $I_1 \subseteq I_2 \subseteq \ldots$ with the property that $\sigma_i = \sigma_{i+1}^{I_i}$ for all $i \in C$ defines a unique σ on $I = \bigcup_{i \in C} I_i$ such that $(\sigma_i)_{i \in C}$ is a covering of σ. For $C = \mathbb{N}$, we can hence set $\lim_{i \to \infty} \sigma_i = \sigma$, where σ is defined on $\lim_{i \to \infty} I^i = I$. These definitions and results naturally carry over to interval-restricted executions, i.e., pairs of sets of input and output signals of a module.

Definition 12 (Limit-closure). *Module M is* limit-closed *iff, for every covering $(E_i)_{i \in \mathbb{N}}$ consisting of interval-restricted executions E_i in the set $\mathcal{E}_M$ of all interval-restricted executions of M, it holds that $\lim_{i \to \infty} E_i \in \mathcal{E}_M$.*

Not every module is limit-closed, as the following example demonstrates.

Example 7. Consider the module specification WM, subsequently called the *weird module*: It has no inputs and only a single output, which is required to switch from 0 to 1 within finite time and have no other transitions.

The WM can be seen as an archetypal asynchronous module, as the transition must occur in finite time, but there is no known bound on the time until this happens.

For every $i \in \mathbb{N}$, the execution E_i defined on $[-i, i]$ with the output signal being constant 0 is feasible for WM, as it can be extended to some execution on $\mathbb{R}$ where the transition to 1 occurs, e.g., at time $i + 1$; it is thus an extendible module according to Definition 7. However, the limit of $E = \lim_{i \to \infty} E_i$ is the unique execution on $\mathbb{R}$ with output constant 0, which is infeasible for WM. According to Defintion 12, the specification of WM is hence extendable but not limit-closed. Conversely, limit-closure does not necessarily imply extendibility either, as the latter requires that *every* execution defined on some interval I can be extended to an execution on $\mathbb{R}$; limit-closure guarantees this only for interval-restricted executions that are part of coverings.

Definition 13 (Finite-delay & bounded-delay module). *Module M has* finite delay *(FD), iff every infeasible execution $E_M \notin \mathcal{E}_M$ has a finite infeasible restriction, i.e., $(E_M \notin \mathcal{E}_M) \Rightarrow (\exists \text{ finite } I \subset \mathbb{R} : E_M^I \notin \mathcal{E}_M)$. An FD module M*

is a bounded-delay module (BD), if I may not depend on the particular E_M in the FD definition. Finally, M is a bounded delay module with delay bound $B \in \mathbb{R}_0^+$, if it is BD and $|I| \leq B$.

Recall that if a module is correct in an execution during an interval I it is always also correct within a subinterval of I in the same execution. On the other hand, the other implication $(\exists \text{ finite } I \subset \mathbb{R} : E_M^I \notin \mathcal{E}_M) \Rightarrow (E_M \notin \mathcal{E}_M)$ always holds, by our definition of a restriction. Thus, for FD modules, it holds that $(E_M \notin \mathcal{E}_M) \Leftrightarrow (\exists \text{ finite } I \subset \mathbb{R} : E_M^I \notin \mathcal{E}_M)$.

According to Defintion 13, WM is not a finite-delay module, as any finite restriction of the infeasible all-zero trace on $\mathbb{R}$ is feasible. More generally, we have the following lemma:

Lemma 2. *A module is limit-closed iff it has finite delay.*

Proof. Suppose M is limit-closed. Given an arbitrary $E \notin \mathcal{E}_M$, defined on $I \subseteq \mathbb{R}$, consider the covering $E_i = E^{I \cap [-i,i]}$, $i \in \mathbb{N}$. Then, either there is some i so that $E_i \notin \mathcal{E}_M$, or we reach the contradiction that $E = \lim_{i \to \infty} E_i \in \mathcal{E}_M$ as M is limit-closed.

Conversely, suppose that M is a finite delay module. Consider an arbitrary infinite covering $\{E_i \mid E_i \in \mathcal{E}_M\}_{i \in \mathbb{N}}$, and denote by E its limit. If $E \notin \mathcal{E}_M$, then by Defintion 13 there is a finite $E^I \notin \mathcal{E}_M$ that is a restriction of E. As $\{E_i\}_{i \in \mathbb{N}}$ is a covering, for sufficiently large i, it holds that the interval I on which E^I is defined is contained in the interval on which E_i is defined. Hence, $E^I \notin \mathcal{E}_M$ is a restriction of $E_i \in \mathcal{E}_M$, which is a contradiction to the fact that E^I must be feasible.

At that point, the question arises whether and when the composition of modules preserves bounded resp. finite delays. The following Corollary 2 shows that this is the case for feedback-free compositions of BD modules:

Corollary 2 (Preservation of BD). *Suppose compound module M is feed-back-free with circuit graph G_M and each of its submodules $S \in \mathcal{S}_M$ is FD. Then, M is FD. Moreover, if $S \in \mathcal{S}_M$ is BD with delay bound B_S, then $\mathcal{S}_M$ is BD with delay bound*

$$B = \max_{\substack{(S_1,\ldots,S_k) \\ \text{path in } G_M}} \left\{ \sum_{i=1}^{k} B_S \right\}.$$

BD Is not Preserved in Arbitrary Compound Modules. Unfortunately, the above corollary does not hold if feedback-loops are allowed. A compound module made up of BD submodules in a feedback-loop need not be BD, and sometimes not even FD.

As an example of the former, consider the *eventual short-pulse filter* (eSPF) introduced in [26], which has a single input and a single output port, initially 0. Given a single pulse of duration $\Delta > 0$ at time 0 at the input, there is a time $T = T(\Delta)$ with $\lim_{\Delta \to 0} T = \infty$ such that the output $o(t) = 1$ for all $t \geq T$. Yet, the execution where the output never settles to 1 is not feasible (unless there is no input pulse). eSPF can be implemented as a compound module consisting of a two-input zero-time OR gate and a two pure-delay channels (with delay 1 and $\sqrt{2}$, respectively) in a feedback-loop. By adding an inertial delay channel [24] to the output of eSPF, which suppresses all pulses with duration less than 1 (and is hence also a BD module[4]), we obtain a module eSPF' that generates exactly one transition from 0 to 1 at the output. Module eSPF' is FD, as a finite interval $I = [0, T]$ that guarantees $E^I \in \mathcal{E}_{\text{eSPF}'}$ can be computed from the known Δ in every given execution E. However, eSPF' is not BD, albeit all its submodules are BD. Consequently, for compound modules that are not feedback-free, Corollary 2 need not hold.

Unexpected Properties of the WM *Module.* While the results on BD align with our intuition, similar properties do not hold for FD modules. To show this, let us add another BD basic submodule that acts as a random generator (which is of course also BD) for generating an input pulse of duration $\Delta > 0$ to eSPF (now considered a basic module). We obtain a feedback-free compound module implementation of WM, which is not even FD! Consequently, and surprisingly, one cannot generalize Corollary 2 to the preservation of FD: Feedback-free compound modules composed from FD submodules are *not* always FD: eSPF' is FD, and the random generator is even BD, yet the resulting WM is not FD.

The problem can be traced back to the fact that compound modules hide internal ports (the input port of eSPF fed by the random generator in our WM compound module), which does no longer allow to identify appropriate infeasible finite executions in infinite executions according to Defintion 13. Our modeling framework allows to completely abstract away this important submodule-internal information, which in turn creates this artefact. This intuitively suggests that one should not entirely discard the internal structure of a compound module, but rather simulate a "glass box view" of a submodule as advocated in [9] by exposing important submodule-signals when composing modules. A formal understanding of these problems is open, however.

8   Outlook

We discussed an alternative to the classical state-based modeling and analysis approach. In particular, we reviewed the state-oblivious modeling and analysis framework introduced in [16], and argued its utility by means of some examples, in particular, a self-stabilizing oscillator. We also showed that it may create some subtle artefacts when composing modules, which need careful consideration and possibly mitigation.

While we believe that the modeling framework discussed in this article is a sound basis for the formal study of digital circuits and even biological systems, it currently lacks several important features that are left open for further research:

---

[4] Since we can consider the inertial delay channel to be a basic module here, we need not care about implementability at that point.

The first one is the choice of a formal language for describing signals and module specifications. Whereas our simple signals could of course be described within a first-order theory on $\mathbb{R}$, it is not clear whether this is the most appropriate formalism for concisely expressing the most relevant properties of interest. Moreover, module specifications often require (all-)quantification over signals, which suggests the need for a second-order theory.

A somewhat related open problem is the definition of a proper notion of simulation equivalence for modules with *different* interfaces, and simulation-type proof techniques similar to the ones known for both untimed [37] and timed [38] distributed systems. Unfortunately, the state-obliviousness and the unconventional domain $\mathbb{R}$ of our framework does not allow one to just take over state-based simulation techniques.

Another open issue is the explicit handling of metastability, which can currently only be expressed by mapping a metastable state to a (high-frequency) pulse train. An obvious alternative is to use a three-valued logic, also providing a dedicated metastable state M, as advocated in [22]. While this extension appears relatively straightforward at the specification level, it should also be accompanied by ways of specifying metastable upsets and metastability propagation.

References

1. Albert, R., Othmer, H.G.: The topology of the regulatory interactions predicts the expression pattern of the segment polarity genes in drosophila melanogaster. J. Theor. Biol. **223**(1), 1–18 (2003)
2. de Alfaro, L., Henzinger, T.A., Stoelinga, M.: Timed interfaces. In: Sangiovanni-Vincentelli, A., Sifakis, J. (eds.) EMSOFT 2002. LNCS, vol. 2491, pp. 108–122. Springer, Heidelberg (2002). https://doi.org/10.1007/3-540-45828-X_9
3. Alur, R., Henzinger, T., Lafferriere, G., Pappas, G.: Discrete abstractions of hybrid systems. Proc. IEEE **88**(7), 971–984 (2000). https://doi.org/10.1109/5.871304
4. Alur, R., Dill, D.L.: A theory of timed automata. Theor. Comput. Sci. **126**(2), 183–235 (1994). https://doi.org/10.1016/0304-3975(94)90010-8. http://www.sciencedirect.com/science/article/pii/0304397594900108
5. Awerbuch, B.: Complexity of network synchronization. JACM **32**(4), 804–823 (1985)
6. Bartocci, E., Bortolussi, L., Nenzi, L.: A temporal logic approach to modular design of synthetic biological circuits. In: Gupta, A., Henzinger, T.A. (eds.) CMSB 2013. LNCS, vol. 8130, pp. 164–177. Springer, Heidelberg (2013). https://doi.org/10.1007/978-3-642-40708-6_13
7. Baumann, R.: Radiation-induced soft errors in advanced semiconductor technologies. IEEE Trans. Device Mater. Reliab. **5**(3), 305–316 (2005)
8. Bellido-Diaz, M.J., Juan-Chico, J., Acosta, A., Valencia, M., Huertas, J.L.: Logical modelling of delay degradation effect in static CMOS gates. IEE Proc. Circuits Devices Syst. **147**(2), 107–117 (2000)
9. Broy, M., Stølen, K.: Specification and Development of Interactive Systems: Focus on Streams, Interfaces, and Refinement. Springer, New York (2001). https://doi.org/10.1007/978-1-4613-0091-5
10. Constantinescu, C.: Trends and challenges in VLSI circuit reliability. IEEE Micro **23**(4), 14–19 (2003)

11. Daliot, A., Dolev, D., Parnas, H.: Self-stabilizing pulse synchronization inspired by biological pacemaker networks. In: Huang, S.-T., Herman, T. (eds.) SSS 2003. LNCS, vol. 2704, pp. 32–48. Springer, Heidelberg (2003). https://doi.org/10.1007/3-540-45032-7_3

12. Dijkstra, E.W.: Self-stabilizing systems in spite of distributed control. CACM **17**(11), 643–644 (1974)

13. Dixit, A., Wood, A.: The impact of new technology on soft error rates. In: Proceedings of IRPS, pp. 5B.4.1–5B.4.7 (2011)

14. Dolev, D., Dwork, C., Stockmeyer, L.: On the minimal synchronism needed for distributed consensus. JACM **34**(1), 77–97 (1987)

15. Dolev, D., Függer, M., Lenzen, C., Perner, M., Schmid, U.: HEX: scaling honeycombs is easier than scaling clock trees. In: Proceedings of the 25th ACM Symposium on Parallelism in Algorithms and Architectures (SPAA 2013), pp. 164–175 (2013)

16. Dolev, D., Függer, M., Lenzen, C., Posch, M., Schmid, U., Steininger, A.: Rigorously modeling self-stabilizing fault-tolerant circuits: an ultra-robust clocking scheme for systems-on-chip. JCSS **80**(4), 860–900 (2014)

17. Dolev, D., Függer, M., Lenzen, C., Schmid, U.: Fault-tolerant algorithms for tick-generation in asynchronous logic: robust pulse generation. J. ACM **61**(5), 30:1–30:74 (2014). https://doi.org/10.1145/2560561

18. Dolev, S.: Self-Stabilization. MIT Press, Cambridge (2000)

19. Dwork, C., Lynch, N., Stockmeyer, L.: Consensus in the presence of partial synchrony. JACM **35**(2), 288–323 (1988)

20. Fischer, M.J.: The consensus problem in unreliable distributed systems (a brief survey). In: Karpinski, M. (ed.) FCT 1983. LNCS, vol. 158, pp. 127–140. Springer, Heidelberg (1983). https://doi.org/10.1007/3-540-12689-9_99

21. Fischer, M., Lynch, N., Paterson, M.: Impossibility of distributed consensus with one faulty process. JACM **32**(2), 374–382 (1985)

22. Friedrichs, S., Függer, M., Lenzen, C.: Metastability-containing circuits. IEEE Trans. Comput. **67**(8), 1167–1183 (2018). https://doi.org/10.1109/TC.2018.2808185. https://doi.org/10.1109/TC.2018.2808185

23. Fuchs, G., Steininger, A.: VLSI implementation of a distributed algorithm for fault-tolerant clock generation. J. Electr. Comput. Eng. **2011**, 936712 (2011)

24. Függer, M., Najvirt, R., Nowak, T., Schmid, U.: A faithful binary circuit model. IEEE Trans. Comput. Aided Des. Integr. Circuits Syst. **39**(10), 2784–2797 (2020). https://doi.org/10.1109/TCAD.2019.2937748

25. Függer, M., Kushwaha, M., Nowak, T.: Digital circuit design for biological and silicon computers. In: Singh, V. (ed.) Advances in Synthetic Biology, pp. 153–171. Springer, Singapore (2020). https://doi.org/10.1007/978-981-15-0081-7_9

26. Függer, M., Nowak, T., Schmid, U.: Unfaithful glitch propagation in existing binary circuit models. IEEE Trans. Comput. **65**(3), 964–978 (2016). https://doi.org/10.1109/TC.2015.2435791. http://ieeexplore.ieee.org/stamp/stamp.jsp?tp=&arnumber=7110587

27. Függer, M., Schmid, U.: Reconciling fault-tolerant distributed computing and systems-on-chip. Distrib. Comput. **24**(6), 323–355 (2012)

28. Gardner, T.S., Cantor, C.R., Collins, J.J.: Construction of a genetic toggle switch in Escherichia coli. Nature **403**, 339–342 (2000)

29. Gorochowski, T.E., et al.: Genetic circuit characterization and debugging using RNA-SEQ. Mol. Syst. Biol. **13**(11), 952 (2017)

30. Hasty, J., McMillen, D., Collins, J.J.: Engineered gene circuits. Nature **420**, 224–230 (2002)

31. International Technology Roadmap for Semiconductors (2012). http://www.itrs. net
32. Kaynar, D.K., Lynch, N., Segala, R., Vaandrager, F.: The Theory of Timed I/O Automata. Morgan & Claypool Publishers, San Francisco (2006)
33. Koren, I., Koren, Z.: Defect tolerance in VLSI circuits: techniques and yield analysis. Proc. IEEE **86**(9), 1819–1838 (1998). https://doi.org/10.1109/5.705525
34. Lamport, L.: Time, clocks, and the ordering of events in a distributed system. CACM **21**(7), 558–565 (1978)
35. Lamport, L.: The temporal logic of actions. ACM Trans. Program. Lang. Syst. **16**(3), 872–923 (1994)
36. Lee, E.A., Varaiya, P.: Structure and Interpretation of Signals and Systems, 2nd edn. LeeVaraiya.org (2011)
37. Lynch, N., Vaandrager, F.: Forward and backward simulations, I: untimed systems. Inf. Comput. **121**(2), 214–233 (1995)
38. Lynch, N., Vaandrager, F.: Forward and backward simulations, II: timing-based systems. Inf. Comput. **128**(1), 1–25 (1996)
39. Marino, L.: General theory of metastable operation. IEEE Trans. Comput. **C30**(2), 107–115 (1981)
40. Maza, M.S., Aranda, M.L.: Analysis of clock distribution networks in the presence of crosstalk and groundbounce. In: Proceedings of ICECS, pp. 773–776 (2001)
41. Nielsen, A.A., et al.: Genetic circuit design automation. Science **352**(6281), aac7341 (2016)
42. Pease, M., Shostak, R., Lamport, L.: Reaching agreement in the presence of faults. JACM **27**, 228–234 (1980)
43. Peercy, M., Banerjee, P.: Fault tolerant VLSI systems. Proc. IEEE **81**(5), 745–758 (1993)
44. Santos-Moreno, J., Tasiudi, E., Stelling, J., Schaerli, Y.: Multistable and dynamic CRISPRI-based synthetic circuits. Nat. Commun. **11**(1), 1–8 (2020)
45. Sivan, E., Parnas, H., Dolev, D.: Fault tolerance in the cardiac ganglion of the lobster. Biol. Cybern. **81**(1), 11–23 (1999)
46. Stricker, J., Cookson, S., Bennett, M.R., Mather, W.H., Tsimring, L.S., Hasty, J.: A fast, robust and tunable synthetic gene oscillator. Nature **456**, 516–519 (2008)
47. Sutherland, I.E.: Micropipelines. CACM **32**(6), 720–738 (1989)
48. Thomas, R.: Boolean formalization of genetic control circuits. J. Theor. Biol. **42**(3), 563–585 (1973)
49. Unger, S.H.: Asynchronous sequential switching circuits with unrestricted input changes. IEEE Trans. Comput. **20**(12), 1437–1444 (1971)

Asynchronous Correspondences Between Hybrid Trajectory Semantics

Patrick Cousot$^{(\boxtimes)}$ (iD)

CS, CIMS, New York University, New York, USA
pcousot@cims.nyu.edu
https://cs.nyu.edu/~pcousot/

Dedicated to Thomas Henzinger
for his 60th birthday

Abstract. We formalize the semantics of hybrid systems as sets of
hybrid trajectories, including those generated by an hybrid transition
system. We study the abstraction of hybrid trajectory semantics for verification, static analysis, and refinement. We mainly consider abstractions
of hybrid semantics which establish a correspondence between trajectories derived from a correspondence between states such as homomorphisms, simulations, bisimulations, and preservations with progress. We
also consider abstractions that cannot be defined stepwise like discretization. All these abstractions are Galois connections between concrete and
abstract hybrid trajectory or discrete trace semantics. In contrast to
semantic based abstractions, we investigate the problematic trace-based
composition of abstractions.

Keywords: Hybrid systems · Semantics · Abstraction ·
Homomorphism · Simulations · Bisimulations · Preservations ·
Progress · Discretization · Verification · Refinement · Abstract
interpretation · Galois connection · Galois relation · Logical relation

1 Introduction

State and transition-based abstractions such as homomorphisms, simulations,
bisimulations [26], and preservations with progress (as used in type theory [38])
formalize a correspondence between concrete and abstract discrete semantics.
They have been successfully applied to the verification, analysis, and refinement
of programs. In program refinement, such state and transition-based abstractions
are used to transform specifications into implementations. In program verification and analysis they are used to simplify the reasoning on properties of program
executions.

All these abstractions have two fundamental properties. The first is that a
reasoning on computation steps (via a transition system) is sufficient to establish a correspondence between program semantics (which is the set of all their

© Springer Nature Switzerland AG 2022
J.-F. Raskin and K. Chatterjee (Eds.): Principles of Systems Design, LNCS 13660, pp. 131–159, 2022.
https://doi.org/10.1007/978-3-031-22337-2_7

possible maximal executions). The second is that they compose. For example the composition of simulations is a simulation. This allows, for example, for stepwise refinement in program construction or composing successive sound abstractions in program verification.

Our objective is to extend and study these state and transition-based abstractions for dynamical systems that exhibits both continuous and discrete dynamic behavior as found in cyber-physical systems. We consider concrete and abstract hybrid semantics (that is sets of sequences of configurations specifying continuous behaviors between discrete changes of modes) that allow for arbitrary timings, arbitrary continuous dynamic mode changes, and arbitrary evolutions of the states over time. We also consider hybrid semantics generated by hybrid transition systems hoping that, as in the discrete case, the abstraction of transition systems will induce the abstraction of the hybrid semantics. But contrary to the discrete case, this is problematic.

Such hybrid trajectory semantics can be understood as specifications, implementations, or abstractions of hybrid dynamical systems. They are more general than particular abstract models of hybrid systems such as synchronous systems [7], timed automata [2], switched systems (for which the sequence of modes and mutation times are known in advance) [22], hybrid automata [1], including restrictions for decidability subclasses [4,18], Simulink [24], and so on. Hybrid trajectory semantics can also be used to specify the semantics of these abstract models, that is, the set of possible behaviors that they describe.

We study homomorphisms, simulations, (bisimulations, preservations with progress in the ArXiv version) between concrete and abstract hybrid semantics as well as discretization of hybrid semantics to establish a correspondence between an hybrid system and a discrete system (such as a computer). Considered as semantic transformers they all form Galois connections and so do compose. However, when considering individual concrete and abstract trajectories, the problem is that in full generality, these abstraction may not compose well. For examples the discretization of two trajectories of (bi)simular hybrid systems may not be (bi)simular discrete traces. We investigate sufficient conditions to solve this compositionally problem when reasoning on individual trajectories.

The paper organized as follows. In Sect. 2 we recall the definitions of Galois connections, Galois relations (ordered logical relations), and tensor products. In Sect. 3, we introduce hybrid trajectory semantics to define the arbitrary evolution of hybrid systems over time. In Sect. 4, we introduce hybrid transition systems that can be used to generate hybrid trajectory semantics (the same way that discrete transition systems generate a discrete trace-based operational semantics for discrete systems). In Sect. 5, we consider the abstraction of hybrid trajectory semantics by reasoning on trajectories, that is executions of the hybrid system as defined by its semantics. It is often considered that reasoning on states, or consecutive states, is simpler that reasoning on full trajectories (although less general). This is the objective of Sect. 6, where an abstraction of states is shown to induce an abstraction of hybrid trajectories, hence of hybrid semantics (which are sets of hybrid trajectories). In case the hybrid semantics is defined by a transition system, we consider in Sect. 7 the abstraction of transition systems by homomorphisms, simulations, (bisimulation and preservation with progress in the ArXiv version) and study which abstraction of trajectories and hybrid semantics they induce. The main difficulty is that concrete and abstract trajectories may have different, not necessarily comparable timelines, that is timings for mode changes. A difficulty, in particular for discretization, is that the abstraction of transition systems may not be an abstraction of their hybrid semantics (which is never the case for discrete systems). We solve the problem under sufficient conditions. We conclude in Sect. 8.

2 Galois Connections and Relations

2.1 Galois Connections

A Galois connection $\langle C, \sqsubseteq \rangle \xrightarrow[\alpha]{\gamma} \langle A, \preccurlyeq \rangle$[1] between posets $\langle C, \sqsubseteq \rangle$ and $\langle A, \preccurlyeq \rangle$ is a pair of an abstraction function α and a concretization function γ such that

$$\langle C, \sqsubseteq \rangle \xrightarrow[\alpha]{\gamma} \langle A, \preccurlyeq \rangle \triangleq \begin{cases} \alpha \in C \xrightarrow{} A & \text{is increasing} & (1.a) \\ \gamma \in A \xrightarrow{} C & \text{is increasing} & (1.b) \\ \gamma \circ \alpha & \text{is an upper closure} & (1.c) \\ \alpha \circ \gamma & \text{is a lower closure} & (1.d) \end{cases} \quad (1)$$

where an upper closure is increasing, idempotent, and extensive ($\forall c \in C \,.\, x \sqsubseteq \gamma \circ \alpha(x)$) while a lower closure is increasing, idempotent, and reductive ($\forall y \in A \,.\, \alpha \circ \gamma(y) \preccurlyeq y$). An equivalent definition of a Galois connection is a pair of increasing functions satisfying

$$\forall x \in C \,.\, \forall y \in A \,.\, \alpha(x) \preccurlyeq y \implies x \sqsubseteq \gamma(y) \quad \wedge \qquad (2)$$
$$\alpha(x) \preccurlyeq y \impliedby x \sqsubseteq \gamma(y) \qquad (3)$$

Example 1 (Classic examples of Galois connections). Set transformers form Galois connections

$$\langle \wp(\mathsf{S}), \subseteq \rangle \xleftarrow[\mathsf{pre}[r]]{\widetilde{\mathsf{post}[r]}} \langle \wp(\overline{\mathsf{S}}), \subseteq \rangle \quad \text{and} \quad \langle \wp(\mathsf{S}), \subseteq \rangle \xleftarrow[\mathsf{post}[r]]{\widetilde{\mathsf{pre}[r]}} \langle \wp(\overline{\mathsf{S}}), \subseteq \rangle \qquad (4)$$

where $r \in \wp(\mathsf{S} \times \overline{\mathsf{S}})$, $\mathsf{post}[r]P \triangleq \{y \mid \exists x \in P \,.\, \langle x, y \rangle \in r\}$, $\mathsf{pre}[r] = \mathsf{post}[r^{-1}]$, $r^{-1} \triangleq \{\langle y, x \rangle \mid \langle x, y \rangle \in r\}$, $\tilde{f} \triangleq \neg \circ f \circ \neg$, and $(f \circ g)(x) = f(g(x))$ is function composition.

Another classic example is an homomorphic abstraction, where given $h \in \mathsf{S} \to \overline{\mathsf{S}}$, $\alpha_h(X) \triangleq \{h(x) \mid x \in X\}$, and $\gamma_h(Y) \triangleq \{x \in \mathsf{S} \mid h(x) \in Y\}$, we have

$$\langle \wp(\mathsf{S}), \subseteq \rangle \xrightarrow[\alpha_h]{\gamma_h} \langle \wp(\overline{\mathsf{S}}), \subseteq \rangle \qquad (5)$$

□

Interpreting C in (1) as a concrete semantics (e.g. a set of execution discrete traces or hybrid trajectories) and A as an abstract semantics, the concretization $\gamma(y)$ is the concrete semantics corresponding to the abstract semantics $y \in A$,

---

[1] see an introduction in [11, Ch. 11].

that is its concrete meaning. Conversely, $\alpha(x)$ is the abstraction of the concrete semantics $x \in C$.

The conditions (1.a) and (1.b) of order preservation express that the notions of over approximation in the concrete and the abstract are the same.

Condition (1.c) implies $x \sqsubseteq \gamma(\alpha(x))$. This expresses that $\alpha(x)$ is an abstract sound over approximation of x.

Condition (1.c) with $y = \alpha(x)$ implies (3) which expresses that $\alpha(x)$ is the best abstraction of x (since given any other abstraction of x which is sound, that is $x \sqsubseteq \gamma(y)$, $\alpha(x)$ is more precise since $\alpha(x) \preccurlyeq y$).

2.2   Galois Relations

Any Galois connection $\langle C, \sqsubseteq \rangle \xleftrightarrow[\alpha]{\gamma} \langle A, \preccurlyeq \rangle$ can be encoded by a *Galois relation* $R_\alpha \in \wp(C \times A)$ (also called ordered logical relations) defined as

$$R_\alpha \triangleq \{\langle x, y \rangle \in C \times A \mid \alpha(x) \preccurlyeq y\} = \{\langle x, y \rangle \in C \times A \mid x \sqsubseteq \gamma(y)\} \quad (6)$$

If $\langle C, \sqsubseteq, \sqcup \rangle$ and $\langle A, \preccurlyeq, \curlywedge \rangle$ are complete lattices such relations R_α satisfy the following characteristic properties of Galois relations R.

$$(x \sqsubseteq x' \wedge \langle x', y' \rangle \in R \wedge y' \preccurlyeq y) \Longrightarrow (\langle x, y \rangle \in R) \quad \text{(a)}$$

$$(\forall i \in \Delta . \langle x_i, y \rangle \in R) \Longrightarrow \langle \bigsqcup_{i \in \Delta} x_i, y \rangle \in R \quad \text{(b)} \quad (7)$$

$$(\forall i \in \Delta . \langle x, y_i \rangle \in R) \Longrightarrow \langle x, \bigcurlywedge_{i \in \Delta} y_i \rangle \in R \quad \text{(c)}$$

The tensor product $\langle C, \sqsubseteq \rangle \otimes \langle A, \preccurlyeq \rangle$ of two complete lattices $\langle C, \sqsubseteq \rangle$ and $\langle A, \preccurlyeq \rangle$ is [34]

$$\langle C, \sqsubseteq \rangle \otimes \langle A, \preccurlyeq \rangle \triangleq \{R \in \wp(C \times A) \mid R \text{ is a relation satisfying (7)}\} \quad (8)$$

Galois connections and relations are mathematically equivalent. If $\langle C, \sqsubseteq \rangle$ and $\langle A, \preccurlyeq \rangle$ be complete lattices then $\langle C, \sqsubseteq \rangle \xleftrightarrow[\alpha]{\gamma} \langle A, \preccurlyeq \rangle$ if and only if $R_\alpha \in \langle C, \sqsubseteq \rangle \otimes \langle A, \preccurlyeq \rangle$ where R_α is defined in (6) and, conversely, $\alpha(x) \triangleq \curlywedge \{y \mid \langle x, y \rangle \in R_\alpha\}$ and $\gamma(y) \triangleq \bigsqcup \{x \mid \langle x, y \rangle \in R_\alpha\}$.

Dual definitions of Galois connections and relations can be used to cope with under approximation.

3   Hybrid Trajectory Semantics

Time. We let the time t run over the set $\mathbb{R}_{\geqslant 0}$ of all positive reals.

States and Flows. We let S be a set of states. In our pictures, we use Cartesian coordinates where the horizontal axis is time and the vertical axis is the set of states (which we take to be S = $\mathbb{R}$).

Flows. A flow $f \in \mathsf{F} \triangleq \mathbb{R}_{\geqslant 0} \rightsquigarrow \mathsf{S}$ is a partial map from time to states representing the evolution of the state over time. Flows can be specified e.g. by ODEs over a period of time (with appropriate hypothesis, see e.g. [21, Ch. XIX], [19, ch. 8 & 9], [20], and [30]).

Time Intervals. If $t_1 \in \mathbb{R}_{\geqslant 0}$, $t_2 \in \mathbb{R}_{\geqslant 0} \cup \{\infty\}$, and $t_1 < t_2$ then $[t_1, t_2[\triangleq \{t \in \mathbb{R}_{\geqslant 0} \mid t_1 \leqslant t < t_2\}$ is the interval of time between t_1 and t_2, the lower bound $\mathsf{b}([t_1, t_2[) \triangleq t_1$ being included while the upper bound $\mathsf{e}([t_1, t_2[) \triangleq t_2$ is excluded. The set of all such time intervals is

$$i \in \mathsf{I} \triangleq \{[t_1, t_2[\mid t_1 \in \mathbb{R}_{\geqslant 0} \wedge t_2 \in \mathbb{R}_{\geqslant 0} \cup \{\infty\} \wedge t_1 + \zeta \leqslant t_2\} \tag{9}$$

where $\zeta > 0$ is any arbitrarily chosen infinitesimal defining the minimal duration $\mathsf{d}(i) \triangleq \mathsf{e}(i) - \mathsf{b}(i)$ of a time interval i. This implies that the duration of successive configurations cannot tend to 0 so we exclude *zeno* systems (with infinitely many successive configurations in a finite interval of time [39]).

The closure of an interval $\mathsf{cl}([t_1, t_2[) \triangleq [t_1, t_2]$ if $t_2 \neq \infty$ and $\mathsf{cl}([t_1, \infty[) = [t_1, \infty[$ includes the upper bound unless it is infinite. By convention, $[t_1, \infty] = [t_1, \infty[= \{t \in \mathbb{R}_{\geqslant 0} \mid t_1 \leqslant t\}$. We let $\mathsf{cl}(\mathsf{I}) \triangleq \{\mathsf{cl}(i) \mid i \in \mathsf{I}\}$.

Configurations. A configuration is a pair of a flow and a time interval

$$c \in \mathsf{C} \triangleq \{\langle f, i \rangle \in \mathsf{F} \times \mathsf{I} \mid \forall t \in i \,.\, f(t) \in \mathsf{S}\} \tag{10}$$

while final configurations include the upper bound

$$c \in \mathsf{cl}(\mathsf{C}) \triangleq \{\langle f, i \rangle \in \mathsf{F} \times \mathsf{cl}(\mathsf{I}) \mid \forall t \in i \,.\, f(t) \in \mathsf{S}\} \tag{11}$$

such that the flow is well-defined in the set of states S on the time interval, i.e. $i \subseteq \mathsf{dom}(f)$. A configuration $c = \langle f, i \rangle$ starts a time $\mathsf{b}(c) = \mathsf{b}(i)$ and ends at time $\mathsf{e}(c) = \mathsf{e}(i)$, excluded in (10) and included in (11). We call $\mathsf{dom}(c) = i$ the time interval of configuration c. Notice that by the choice of the infinitesimal $\zeta > 0$ and the definition (9) of I, the intervals $i \in \mathsf{I}$ in (10) and (11) cannot be empty.

Configurations c record the evolution of the state as specified by the flow during the period of time $\mathsf{dom}(c)$. During that time interval the definition of the flow f, which is the law of continuous evolution of the system as a function of the time, is fixed. It may be different in the next configuration of the system. In that case, it is common to say that the mode of the hybrid system has changed. The duration $\mathsf{d}(c) = \mathsf{e}(c) - \mathsf{b}(c) \geqslant \zeta$ of the configuration is lower-bounded by $\zeta > 0$ so that infinite sequences of configurations are always nonzeno. Additional hypotheses might be necessary on the flow f of configurations $\langle f, i \rangle$ such as continuity, uniform continuity, Lipschitz continuity, etc. However, discontinuities are always allowed (but not mandatory) when changing mode between consecutive configurations.

By convention the state of a configuration c at time $t \in \mathbb{R}_{\geqslant 0}$ is

$$\begin{aligned} c(t) &\triangleq f(t) & &\text{if } c = \langle f, i \rangle \text{ and } \mathsf{t} \in i \\ &\triangleq \text{undefined} & &\text{otherwise} \end{aligned} \tag{12}$$

Let us define the concatenation of two consecutive configurations $\langle f, i \rangle \in C$ and $\langle f', i' \rangle \in C \cup cl(C)$ where $e(i) = b(i')$ (i.e. the concatenation is undefined for non-consecutive intervals).

$$\langle f, i \rangle \,\fatsemi\, \langle f', i' \rangle \triangleq \langle f'', i \cup i' \rangle \text{ where } \begin{cases} f''(t) = f(t) \text{ when } t \in i \\ f''(t) = f'(t) \text{ when } t \in i' \end{cases} \quad (13)$$

Since the state at the beginning of a configuration may be different from the state at the end of the previous configuration at the same time, definitions (13), (15), and (23) favor states at the beginning of configurations (because intervals are left closed and open right).

To simplify notations, the empty configuration is, by convention, $\varepsilon \triangleq \langle \emptyset, \emptyset \rangle$ where $\emptyset$ is the empty set, that is, the everywhere undefined function. By convention, $b(\varepsilon) \triangleq +\infty$ and $e(\varepsilon) = -\infty$ so that $\min(t, b(\varepsilon)) = \max(t, e(\varepsilon)) = t$ when $t \in \mathbb{R}_{\geqslant 0}$. Observe that although $\varepsilon \notin C \cup cl(C)$ since the time interval is empty, we nevertheless have $\langle f, i \rangle \,\fatsemi\, \varepsilon \triangleq \varepsilon \,\fatsemi\, \langle f, i \rangle \triangleq \langle f, i \rangle$, for ease of writing.

The selection of a time slice during the configuration time interval.

$$\langle f, i \rangle (\!(t_1, t_2)\!) \triangleq \langle f, i \cap [t_1, t_2] \rangle \quad \text{where} \quad b(i \cap [t_1, t_2]) + \zeta \leqslant e(i \cap [t_1, t_2]) \,(14)$$
$$\langle f, i \rangle (\!(t_1, t_2(\!) \triangleq \langle f, i \cap [t_1, t_2[\rangle \qquad\qquad b(i \cap [t_1, t_2[) + \zeta \leqslant e(i \cap [t_1, t_2[)$$

In particular, we define $\varepsilon(\!(t_1, t_2)\!) \triangleq \varepsilon(\!(t_1, t_2(\!) \triangleq \varepsilon$.

Trajectories. The trajectories over configurations C are nonempty finite or infinite sequences of contiguous configurations.

$$T_C^n \triangleq \{\sigma \in [0, n] \to cl(C) \mid b(\sigma_0) = 0 \land \forall i \in [0, n[. \sigma_i \in C \land \quad e(\sigma_i) = b(\sigma_{i+1}) \land \sigma_n \in cl(C)\}$$

finite trajectories $\sigma \in T_C^n$ of length $|\sigma| = n + 1$, $n \in \mathbb{N}$

$$T_C^+ \triangleq \bigcup_{n \in \mathbb{N}} T_C^n \qquad \text{finite nonempty trajectories}$$

$$T_C^\infty \triangleq \{\sigma \in \mathbb{N} \to C \mid b(\sigma_0) = 0 \land \forall i \in \mathbb{N} . e(\sigma_i) = b(\sigma_{i+1})\}$$

infinite trajectories $\sigma \in T_C^\infty$ of length $|\sigma| = \infty$

$$T_C^{+\infty} \triangleq T_C^+ \cup T_C^\infty \qquad \text{nonempty trajectories} \qquad\qquad\qquad (15)$$

A finite or infinite trajectory $\sigma \in [0, |\sigma|[\to C$ is a sequence of configurations that will be denoted $\sigma = \langle \sigma_i, i \in [0, |\sigma|[\rangle$. Such a trajectory σ records the evolution of the state along discrete changes of the flows encoded by configurations. The state at the end of a configuration is that of the next state, if any. Therefore, the configuration intervals are open right and consecutive except for the last one in finite trajectories which is closed. No configuration in a trajectory can be empty.

We let $\sigma[i, j]$ denote the subsequence of configurations in σ of ranks i to j, $i, j \in [0, |\sigma|[. \sigma[i, j[$ excludes j (usually ∞).

Traces. We let traces $\varsigma \in \mathsf{T}_\mathsf{S}^{+\infty}$ be discrete finite or infinite untimed sequences of states in S and use the same notations for continuous trajectories and discrete traces. The homomorphic timeline abstraction $((\_?\_ : \_)$ is the conditional)

$$\alpha_{tl}(\sigma) \triangleq \lambda i \in [[0, |\sigma|]] \cdot (i = 0 ? 0 : (i = \infty ? \infty : \mathsf{e}(\sigma_{i-1})))$$
$$\alpha_{tl}(T) \triangleq \{\alpha_{tl}(\sigma) \mid \sigma \in T\}$$

such that, by (5), $\langle \mathsf{T}_\mathsf{C}^{+\infty}, \subseteq \rangle \xrightarrow[\alpha_{tl}]{\gamma_{tl}} \langle \mathsf{T}_{\mathbb{R}_{\geqslant 0}\cup\{\infty\}}^{+\infty}, \subseteq \rangle$ is an example of abstraction of trajectories into traces (by projection of the mode change timings).

Hybrid Trajectory Semantics and Properties. Given a set S of states and the corresponding configurations C in (10), a hybrid trajectory semantics $\mathcal{S}_\mathsf{C} \in \wp(\mathsf{T}_\mathsf{C}^{+\infty})$ is a subset of all possible trajectories (15). Properties of hybrid trajectory semantics belong to $\wp(\wp(\mathsf{T}_\mathsf{C}^{+\infty}))$ (sometimes called hyper properties) while their abstraction $\alpha_\cup(P) = \bigcup P$ into trajectory properties belong to $\wp(\mathsf{T}_\mathsf{C}^{+\infty})$.

Similarly a trace semantics $\mathcal{S}_\mathsf{S} \in \wp(\mathsf{T}_\mathsf{S}^{+\infty})$ is a subset of all possible traces.

Trajectory States. The duration $[\![\sigma]\!]$ of a trajectory σ is

$$[\![\sigma]\!] \triangleq \sum_{k=0}^{n} \mathsf{e}(\sigma_i) - \mathsf{b}(\sigma_i) = \mathsf{e}(\sigma_n) \qquad \text{when} \quad \sigma \in \mathsf{T}_\mathsf{C}^n \tag{16}$$

$$\triangleq \sum_{k=0}^{\infty} \mathsf{e}(\sigma_i) - \mathsf{b}(\sigma_i) = \infty \qquad \text{when} \quad \sigma \in \mathsf{T}_\mathsf{C}^\infty \qquad \text{(nonzeno hypothesis)}$$

as indicated by the time at which the last configuration in the trajectory ends or ∞ for infinite trajectories.

Time-evolution Law Abstraction. A trajectory σ can be abstracted into a function $\alpha_{tr}(\sigma) \in \mathbb{R}_{\geqslant 0} \to \mathsf{S}$ mapping time to a state such that

$$\mathrm{dom}(\alpha_{tr}(\sigma)) \triangleq [0, [\![\sigma]\!]] \qquad \text{(by convention, excluding } \infty \text{ if } [\![\sigma]\!] = \infty)$$
$$\alpha_{tr}(\sigma)(t) \triangleq f(t) \text{ such that } \exists k \in [0, |\sigma|[. \sigma_k = \langle f, i \rangle \wedge t \in i \tag{17}$$
$$\sigma_t \triangleq \alpha_{tr}(\sigma)(t) \qquad \text{(abbreviated notation)}$$

So we have two different representations of trajectories, σ in (15) and $\alpha_{tr}(\sigma)$ in (17), this second representation being closer to the time-evolution law of the theory of dynamical systems [20]. Notice that $\alpha_{tr}(\sigma)$ is a function defined by parts on the timeline abstraction $\alpha_{tl}(\sigma)$ of the trajectory σ so the time-evolution law $\alpha_{tr}(\sigma)$ is not simpler that the trajectory σ to reason upon, in particular because the timeline information is abstracted away.

We leave this α_{tr} abstraction implicit and use the same notation for both cases. Therefore a trajectory σ is either a discrete sequence of configurations

$\sigma = \langle \sigma_i, i \in [0, |\sigma|[\rangle$ or a state function of the time $\sigma = \langle \sigma_t, t \in [0, []\sigma[]] \rangle$ where $\sigma_t \triangleq \alpha_{tr}(\sigma)(t)$. By homomorphic abstraction (5), this extends to hybrid trajectory semantics T with $\alpha_{tr}(T) \triangleq \{\alpha_{tr}(\sigma) \mid \sigma \in T\}$

$$\langle \wp(T_C^{+\infty}), \subseteq \rangle \xrightleftharpoons[\alpha_{tr}]{\gamma_t} \langle \wp(\mathbb{R}_{\geq 0} \to S), \subseteq \rangle \tag{18}$$

Maximal Trajectory Semantics. A trajectory semantics $T \in \wp(T_C^{+\infty})$ on configurations C is a set of finite or infinite trajectories. Let us define the maximal trajectories of T as those without strict prefixes

$$\max(T) \triangleq \{\langle \sigma_i, i \in [0, |\sigma|[\rangle \in T \mid \forall n < |\sigma| . \langle \sigma_i, i \in [0, n[\rangle \notin T\}$$

A maximal trajectory semantics has no strict prefixes, that is $\max(T) = T$.

Example 2 (Specification of a water tank [17]). A water tank (or water dam) runs for ever with a continuous inflow and a valve (or spillway floodgate) than can be opened or shut to control the outflow. The objective is to design a controller to maintain the water level y between 0 and 3 (for some length unit). When the valve is opened, the water level y decreases while, when the valve is shut down, the water level y increases. The tank should never remain empty more than ζ units of time.

Define states

$$s \in S \triangleq \mathbb{R} \times \{open, shut\} \tag{19}$$

such that $s.y \in \mathbb{R}$ and $s.v \in \{open, shut\}$. Let C be the corresponding set (10) of configurations. The above informal specification can be formalized by the following abstract hybrid semantics of the water tank.

$$P(\sigma) \triangleq \forall t \in \mathbb{R}_{\geq 0} . 0 \leqslant \sigma(t).y \leqslant 3 \wedge \forall t_2 > t_1 \geqslant 0 . \tag{a) (20}$$
$$\forall t \in [t_1, t_2] . \sigma(t).v = open \implies \sigma(t_1).y > \sigma(t_2).y \wedge \tag{b}$$
$$\forall t \in [t_1, t_2] . \sigma(t).v = shut \implies \sigma(t_1).y < \sigma(t_2).y \wedge \tag{c}$$
$$\forall t \in \mathbb{R}_{\geq 0} . \sigma(t).y = 0 \implies \sigma(t + \zeta).y > 0 \tag{d}$$

The hybrid semantics specification the water tank is then

$$\mathcal{S}^2 \triangleq \{\sigma \in \{0\} \to C \mid b(\sigma_0) = 0 \wedge e(\sigma_0) = \infty \wedge P(\sigma_0)\} \tag{21}$$

with only one configuration, or using the homomorphic abstraction (17),

$$\mathcal{S}^2 \triangleq \{\sigma \in \mathbb{R}_{\geq 0} \to S \mid P(\sigma)\}$$

□

4 Transition-based Hybrid Trajectory Semantics

As in the discrete case, a simple way to define a hybrid trajectory semantics, is to first define a hybrid transition system and then to consider the hybrid semantic defined as the set of all possible trajectories generated by the hybrid transition system. As is the case for discrete trace semantics, not all hybrid semantics can be generated by a hybrid transition system on the same set of configurations (which cannot e.g. express fairness without adding a scheduler to the transition system or adding conditions on the generated traces).

Hybrid Transition System. A hybrid transition system is defined by a triple $\langle C, C^0, \tau \rangle$ of a set of configurations C, initial configurations C^0 and a transition relation $\tau \in \wp(C \times (C \cup \mathrm{cl}(C)))$ such that

$$\text{initial configurations} \qquad C^0 \subseteq \{c \in C \mid b(c) = 0\} \tag{22}$$
$$\text{consecutiveness} \qquad \forall \langle c, c' \rangle \in \tau . c \in C \wedge e(c) = b(c')$$
$$\text{closeness of final configurations} \qquad \forall c . (\forall c' . \langle c, c' \rangle \notin \tau) \iff c \in \mathrm{cl}(C)$$

Maximal Trajectory Semantics of a Transition System. A transition semantics $\langle C, C^0, \tau \rangle$ is usually used to define a hybrid trajectory semantics $[\![\langle C, C^0, \tau \rangle]\!]$ abbreviated $[\![\tau]\!]$, for example the maximal one.

$$[\![\tau]\!]^n \triangleq \{\sigma \in T_C^n \mid \sigma_0 \in C^0 \wedge \forall i \in [0, n[. \langle \sigma_i, \sigma_{i+1} \rangle \in \tau \wedge \forall c . \langle \sigma_n, c \rangle \notin \tau \}$$
$$[\![\tau]\!]^+ \triangleq \bigcup_{n \in \mathbb{N}} [\![\tau]\!]^n$$
$$[\![\tau]\!]^\infty \triangleq \{\sigma \in T_C^\infty \mid \sigma_0 \in C^0 \wedge \forall i \in \mathbb{N} . \langle \sigma_i, \sigma_{i+1} \rangle \in \tau \}$$
$$[\![\tau]\!] \triangleq [\![\tau]\!]^+ \cup [\![\tau]\!]^\infty \tag{23}$$

The trajectories of $[\![\tau]\!]$ are maximal, that is,

$$\max([\![\tau]\!]) = [\![\tau]\!] \tag{24}$$

Example 3 (Water tank automaton [17]). Continuing 2, the water tank specification can be implemented as described by the following hybrid automaton.

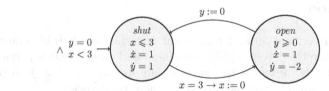

As soon as the tank is empty, the valve is shut down. The valve is reopened after 3 units of time.

The states, configurations, initial configurations, and transitions are (we write $\dot{x}$ for the derivative $\frac{dx}{dt}$ of the everywhere differentiable (hence continuous) real-valued function $x(t)$ of the time t).

$$S \triangleq \{open, shut\} \times \mathbb{R} \times \mathbb{R}$$
$$C^{shut} \triangleq \{\langle f, [t_1, t_2[\rangle \mid \exists x, y . \forall t \in [t_1, t_2] . f(t) = \langle shut, x(t), y(t) \rangle \wedge$$
$$(t = t_1 \implies y(t) = 0) \wedge x(t) \leqslant 3 \wedge (x(t) = 3 \implies t = t_2)$$
$$\wedge \dot{x}(t) = 1 \wedge \dot{y}(t) = 1\}$$
$$C^{open} \triangleq \{\langle f, [t_1, t_2[\rangle \mid \exists x, y . \forall t \in [t_1, t_2] . f(t) = \langle open, x(t), y(t) \rangle \wedge$$
$$(t = t_1 \implies x(t) = 0) \wedge y(t) \geqslant 0 \wedge (y(t) = 0 \implies t = t_2)$$
$$\wedge \dot{x}(t) = 1 \wedge \dot{y}(t) = -2\}$$
$$C \triangleq C^{shut} \cup C^{open}$$

$$C^0 \triangleq \{\langle f, \ [0,t[\rangle \in C^{shut} \mid t > 0 \wedge \exists x < 3 \ . \ f(0) = \langle shut, \ x, \ 0 \rangle\} \in C^{shut}$$

$$\tau^3 \triangleq (C^{shut} \times C^{open}) \cup (C^{open} \times C^{shut}) \text{ as restricted by (22)} \tag{25}$$

Notice that the final time t_2 is not part of the time interval of configurations in C^{shut} but, by (22), the starting time of the next configuration in C^{open}. Therefore, at that time the value of x is 0, not 3. So in this example, f is continuous on $[t_1, t_2[$ that is continuous on $]t_1, t_2[$ and right continuous at t_1. Same for y in C^{open}. An example of execution is given in figure (5.b). The hybrid semantics $[\![\tau^3]\!]$ of the water tank automaton is given by (23). □

Lemma 1. [2]   *If $\tau \subseteq \tau'$ and the blocking condition holds, i.e.*

$$\forall c \ . \ (\forall c' \ . \ \langle c, \ c' \rangle \notin \tau) \Longrightarrow (\forall c' \ . \ \langle c, \ c' \rangle \notin \tau') \tag{26}$$

then $[\![\tau]\!] \subseteq [\![\tau']\!]$.

(so if $[\![\tau']\!]$ has trajectory property $P \in \wp(T_C^{+\infty})$ (i.e. $[\![\tau']\!] \subseteq P$) then Lemma 1 implies that $[\![\tau]\!]$ has the same property P.)

Observe that the transition of one configuration to the next in (22) requires the specification of the time at which the next configuration will terminate. As shown by the water tank automaton 3 of [17], this is not a problem when the duration of the configuration is specified by a condition on the flow.

5   Trajectory-based Hybrid Trajectory Semantics Abstraction

In many program verification and refinement methods, the hybrid semantics is abstracted or concretized to simplify soundness and completeness proofs. One way of simplifying the proofs is to reason on an abstraction of trajectories, by applying an homomorphic abstraction (5) to these trajectories.

A classic example is sampling in signal processing, to reduce a continuous-time signal to a discrete-time signal. For an hybrid semantics, this is defined as follows.

Let $\delta > 0$ be a sampling interval (see [29, Ch. 9] for an adequate choice of the sampling rate). Define

$$h_\delta(\sigma) \triangleq \langle \sigma_{n\delta}, \ n \in \mathbb{N} \wedge n\delta \leqslant [\![\sigma]\!] \rangle \tag{27}$$

$$\alpha_\delta(T) \triangleq \{h_\delta(\sigma) \mid \sigma \in T\}$$

which, by (5), is an homomorphic Galois connection

$$\langle \wp(T_C^{+\infty}), \ \subseteq \rangle \xleftarrow[\alpha_\delta]{\gamma_\delta} \langle \wp(T_S^{+\infty}), \ \subseteq \rangle \tag{28}$$

where $\gamma_\delta(\Theta) \triangleq \{\sigma \in T_C^{+\infty} \mid h_\delta(\sigma) \in \Theta\}$.

---

[2] Underlined equation or theorem numbers link to proofs given in the ArXiv version.

(In general a trajectory σ cannot be regained from its discretization $h_\delta(\sigma)$. This might be possible under specific hypotheses. For example, the Nyquist-Shannon sampling theorem [28,33] establishes a sufficient condition for a sample rate that permits a discrete sequence of samples to capture all the information from a continuous-time signal of finite bandwidth.)

Trajectory based abstractions are useful to prove trajectory properties of hybrid systems by considering one possible trajectory at a time (but inadequate to prove (hyper) properties relating two of more trajectories). But reasoning on a complete trajectory is often complicated, in which case local reasonings relating states or transitions locally are preferred.

6   State-Based Hybrid Trajectory Semantics Abstraction

Since reasoning on discrete execution traces (hence on hybrid trajectories) is difficult, a number of proof techniques have been developed to reduce the reasoning on trajectories to reasonings on states (or pairs of states, that is transitions). Examples are discrete simulations that we extend to hybrid trajectories (and bisimulation [26] as well as preservation with progress [38] considered in the ArXiv version). Sampling in (28) is a counter example since, in general, sampling must be defined by reasoning on trajectories, not states and transitions.

Our objective is to show that a relation between states can be extended to configurations, then to trajectories, and then to hybrid semantics (independently of whether trajectories are generated by transition systems or not).

6.1   Relation Between States

For timed trajectories, the relation r between concrete states S to abstract states $\overline{\mathsf{S}}$ is a function of the time.

$$r \in \mathbb{R}_{\geqslant 0} \to \wp(\mathsf{S} \times \overline{\mathsf{S}}) \tag{29}$$

For simplicity, we assume r to be a total function of the time. If necessary, a partial function could be encoded using an undefined element (like $\perp$ in denotational semantics).

6.2   Relation Between Configurations

Let us define a partial relation between configurations with related states

$$\gamma(r) \triangleq \{\langle\langle f, i\rangle, \langle \overline{f}, \overline{i}\rangle\rangle \mid i \cap \overline{i} \neq \emptyset \wedge \forall t \in i \cap \overline{i} \ . \ \langle f(t), \overline{f}(t)\rangle \in r(t)\} \tag{30}$$

(which is said to be total when $i = \overline{i}$ e.g. for homomorphic abstractions or well-nested when $i \subseteq \overline{i}$). Define

$$\alpha(R) \triangleq \lambda t \cdot \{\langle f(t), \overline{f}(t)\rangle \mid \exists i, \overline{i} \ . \ t \in i \cap \overline{i} \wedge \langle\langle f, i\rangle, \langle \overline{f}, \overline{i}\rangle\rangle \in R\} \tag{31}$$

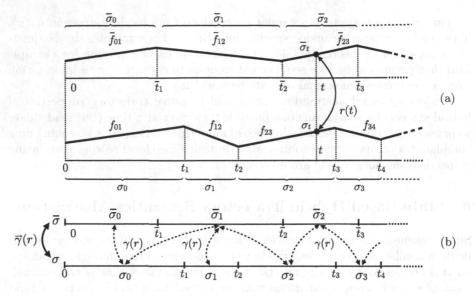

Fig. 1. Relations r between states in (a), and relations $\gamma(r)$ between configurations and $\vec{\gamma}(r)$ between trajectories in (b)

Define the set of all relations between overlapping configurations as

$$\mathsf{R_C} \triangleq \{R \in \wp(\mathsf{C} \times (\mathsf{C} \cup \mathsf{cl}(\mathsf{C}))) \mid \forall \langle \langle f, i \rangle, \langle \bar{f}, \bar{i} \rangle \rangle \in R . i \cap \bar{i} \neq \emptyset\} \quad (32)$$

We have a Galois isomorphism

$$\langle \mathsf{R_C}, \subseteq \rangle \xleftrightarrow[\alpha]{\gamma} \langle \mathbb{R}_{\geqslant 0} \to \wp(\mathsf{S} \times \mathsf{S}), \dot{\subseteq} \rangle \quad (33)$$

where $\dot{\subseteq}$ is the pointwise extension of set inclusion $\subseteq$. So when abstracting trajectories by abstraction of their configurations, we can equivalently start from a relation r between states and use the relation $\gamma(r) \in \mathsf{R_C}$ or start from a relation between configurations $R \in \mathsf{R_C}$ which induces a relation $\alpha(R)$ between states. In discrete systems, the two notions of state and configuration coincide.

6.3 Relation Between Trajectories

Let us also define a relation between trajectories so as to relate states of trajectories

$$\vec{\gamma}(r) \triangleq \{\langle \sigma, \bar{\sigma} \rangle \mid \forall t \in [0, \min(\llbracket \sigma \rrbracket, \llbracket \bar{\sigma} \rrbracket)[\, . \, \langle \sigma_t, \bar{\sigma}_t \rangle \in r(t)\} \quad (34)$$

as illustrated in figure (1.a) Notice that in the definition (34) of related trajectories, we do not use the relation $\gamma(r)$ in (30) between configurations since the states of the configurations with the same ranks in the concrete and abstract in trajectories may be unrelated while the timings are (i.e. the concrete and abstract configurations of same rank k may not even overlap in time).

However, we have the following equivalent definition using ranks of configurations in trajectories, as illustrated in figures (1.b) and (2).

$$\vec{\gamma}(r) \triangleq \vec{\gamma}_c(r) \cap \vec{\gamma}_a(r) \tag{35}$$
$$\vec{\gamma}_c(r) \triangleq \{\langle \sigma, \overline{\sigma} \rangle \mid \forall j < |\sigma| \,.\, (e(\sigma_j) \leqslant \llbracket \overline{\sigma} \rrbracket) \implies (\exists k < |\overline{\sigma}| \,.\, \langle \sigma_j, \overline{\sigma}_k \rangle \in \gamma(r))\} \quad \text{(a)}$$
$$\vec{\gamma}_a(r) \triangleq \{\langle \sigma, \overline{\sigma} \rangle \mid \forall k < |\overline{\sigma}| \,.\, (e(\overline{\sigma}_k) \leqslant \llbracket \sigma \rrbracket) \implies (\exists j < |\sigma| \,.\, \langle \sigma_j, \overline{\sigma}_k \rangle \in \gamma(r))\} \quad \text{(b)}$$

(By the isomorphism (33), there is a definition equivalent to (35) using $R \in \mathsf{R_C}$ instead of $\gamma(r)$.)

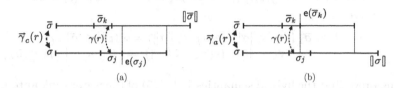

(a)   (b)

Fig. 2. Relations $\vec{\gamma}_c(r)$ and $\vec{\gamma}_a(r)$ between traces

Defining $\vec{\alpha}(\vec{R}) \triangleq \lambda t \cdot \{\langle \sigma_t, \overline{\sigma}_t \rangle \mid \langle \sigma, \overline{\sigma} \rangle \in \vec{R} \wedge t \in [0, \min(\llbracket \sigma \rrbracket, \llbracket \overline{\sigma} \rrbracket)]\}$, this is a Galois connection

$$\langle \wp(\mathsf{T_C^{+\infty}} \times \mathsf{T_{\overline{C}}^{+\infty}}), \subseteq \rangle \xleftrightarrow[\vec{\alpha}]{\vec{\gamma}} \langle \mathbb{R}_{\geqslant 0} \to \wp(\mathsf{S} \times \overline{\mathsf{S}}), \dot{\subseteq} \rangle \tag{36}$$

6.4   Relation Between Hybrid Trajectory Semantics

The abstraction (36) is then extended to hybrid trajectory semantics through a preorder, a common one being the overapproximation in verification ($\overline{T}$ is an abstraction of T since $\overline{T}$ has more possible behaviors than T) and underapproximation in refinement (T is a refinement of $\overline{T}$ since T has less behaviors that the specification $\overline{T}$), that is

$$\vec{\gamma}(R) \triangleq \{\langle T, \overline{T} \rangle \mid T \subseteq \mathsf{pre}[R]\overline{T}\} \tag{37}$$
$$= \{\langle T, \overline{T} \rangle \mid \forall \sigma \in T \,.\, \exists \overline{\sigma} \in \overline{T} \,.\, \langle \sigma, \overline{\sigma} \rangle \in R\}$$

Defining $\vec{\alpha}(P) \triangleq \{\langle \sigma, \overline{\sigma} \rangle \mid \exists \overline{T} \,.\, \langle \{\sigma\}, \overline{T} \rangle \in P \wedge \overline{\sigma} \in \overline{T}\}$, we have the Galois connection

$$\langle \{\langle T, \overline{T} \rangle \in \wp(\mathsf{T_C^{+\infty}}) \otimes \wp(\mathsf{T_{\overline{C}}^{+\infty}}) \mid \overline{T} = \emptyset \implies T = \emptyset\}, \supseteq \rangle \xleftrightarrow[\vec{\alpha}]{\vec{\gamma}} \langle \wp(\mathsf{T_C^{+\infty}} \times \mathsf{T_{\overline{C}}^{+\infty}}), \supseteq \rangle \tag{38}$$

where by (37), (4), and (8), the concrete domain is a tensor product.

Example 4 (The water tank automaton is a state-based refinement of the specification). Le us define the state-based relation

$$r^{(39)}(t) \triangleq \{\langle \langle v, x, y \rangle, \langle v, y \rangle \rangle \mid v \in \{shut, open\} \wedge x, y \in \mathbb{R}\} \tag{39}$$

between states (19) and (25) of the water tank specification and automaton. This induces a relation (30) between configurations, as follows.

$$\gamma(r^{(39)}) = \{\langle\langle\langle\boldsymbol{\lambda}t \cdot \langle v(t), x(t), y(t)\rangle, i\rangle, \langle\boldsymbol{\lambda}t \cdot \langle\overline{v}(t), \overline{y}(t)\rangle, \overline{i}\rangle\rangle \mid i \cap \overline{i} \neq \emptyset \wedge \quad (\underline{40})$$
$$\forall t \in i \cap \overline{i} \cdot v(t) = \overline{v}(t) \in \{shut, open\} \wedge y(t) = \overline{y}(t)\}$$

i.e. at any time in overlapping configurations, the water height and the state of the valve coincide. This induces a relation (35) between trajectories, as follows.

$$\vec{\gamma}(r^{(39)}) = \mathsf{let}\ \rho(c, \overline{c}) \triangleq \exists v, x, y, i, \overline{v}, \overline{y}, \overline{i} \cdot c = \langle\boldsymbol{\lambda}t \cdot \langle v(t), x(t), y(t)\rangle, i\rangle \wedge \quad (\underline{41})$$
$$\overline{c} = \langle\boldsymbol{\lambda}t \cdot \langle\overline{v}(t), \overline{y}(t)\rangle, i\rangle \wedge i \cap \overline{i} \neq \emptyset \wedge \forall t \in i\ \cap i \cdot v(t) = \overline{v}(t) \wedge$$
$$y(t) = \overline{y}(t)\ \mathsf{in}$$
$$\{\langle\sigma, \overline{\sigma}\rangle \mid \forall j < |\sigma| \cdot (\mathsf{e}(\sigma_j) \leqslant \rrbracket\overline{\sigma}\llbracket) \Longrightarrow (\exists k < |\overline{\sigma}| \cdot \rho(\sigma_j, \overline{\sigma}_k) \wedge$$
$$\forall k < |\overline{\sigma}| \cdot (\mathsf{e}(\overline{\sigma}_k) \leqslant \rrbracket\sigma\llbracket) \Longrightarrow (\exists j < |\sigma| \cdot \rho(\sigma_j, \overline{\sigma}_k)\}$$

Let us prove that the hybrid semantics $\llbracket\tau^3\rrbracket$ (25) of the water tank automaton of 3 is a state based refinement of the water tank specification $\mathcal{S}^2$ of 2 for $r^{(39)}$ in (39) (denoted $r^{(39)}$ to avoid confusions), meaning that

$$\langle\llbracket\tau^3\rrbracket, \mathcal{S}^2\rangle \in \vec{\gamma}(\vec{\gamma}(r^{(39)}))$$

or equivalently

$$\forall \sigma \in \llbracket\tau^3\rrbracket \cdot \exists \overline{\sigma} \cdot P(\overline{\sigma}) \wedge \forall t \geqslant 0 \cdot \sigma(t).y = \overline{\sigma}(t).y \wedge \sigma(t).v = \overline{\sigma}(t).v \quad (\underline{42})$$

By definition (20) of P, we have to show that $\forall t \in \mathbb{R}_{\geqslant 0} \cdot 0 \leqslant \sigma(t).y \leqslant 3$. In a shut configuration of C^{shut}, $y(t) = 0$ at the beginning, y evolves as the same rate as x, and $x(t)$ is bounded by 3 so that that $y(t)$ is also bounded by 3. By definition of initial configurations C^0, any trajectory of $\llbracket\tau^3\rrbracket$ starts with a *shut* configuration, and so, by definition (25) of the transition relation τ^3, any open configuration of C^{open} follows a *shut* configuration. At the end t of this *shut* configuration, and so at the beginning t of the following *open* configuration, we have shown that $\sigma(t).y \leqslant 3$. In the *open* configuration, y decreases by $\dot{y} = -2$ and remains positive, so the invariant holds.

Moreover, we must show that if the valve remains opened, then y decreases. If $\forall t \in [t_1, t_2] \cdot \sigma(t).v = open$ then t is within an open configuration, so $\dot{y} = -2$ implies that y decreases between t_1 and t_2. Similarly, if $\forall t \in [t_1, t_2] \cdot \sigma(t).v = shut$ then t is within a shut configuration, so $\dot{y} = 1$ implies that y increases.

Finally, if at some point t of time, $y(t) = 0$ then if we are in an *open* configuration, the system instantaneously moves to a *shut* configuration which last at least ζ by the nonzeno hypothesis, and so, by $\dot{y} = 1$, we have $\sigma(t + \zeta).y > 0$. $\square$

7   Transition-Based Hybrid Trajectory Semantics Abstraction

Reasonings on trajectories is often considered difficult and reasonings involving only one computation step at a time are preferred. An example is Turing/Naur/Floyd/Hoare invariance proof method where verification conditions involve only one computation step at a time.

So we assume that the concrete and abstract semantics are generated by transitions systems $\langle C, C^0, \tau \rangle$ and $\langle \overline{C}, \overline{C}^0, \overline{\tau} \rangle$, that is $T = [\![\tau]\!]$ and $\overline{T} = [\![\overline{\tau}]\!]$, and, given a relation (29) between states, we study relations between transition relations which enable us to define relations (34) between trajectories hence relations (38) between trajectory semantics. In the literature of abstraction of discrete transition systems, basic state and transition-based abstractions are homomorphisms, simulations, bisimulations, and preservations with progress, which we extend to hybrid transition systems, adding discretization.

7.1 Homomorphisms

Homomorphisms are the case when relation r in (29) is given by a function $h(t) \in S \rightarrow \overline{S}$ at time t. Following (30), the homomorphism is extended to configurations as

$$\alpha_h(\langle f, i \rangle) \triangleq \langle h \circ f, i \rangle \tag{43}$$

The function h is composed with the flow and the timings remain the same. The extension to trajectories is

$$\alpha_h(\langle \sigma_i, i \in [0, |\sigma|[\rangle) \triangleq \langle \alpha_h(\sigma_i), i \in [0, |\sigma|[\rangle \tag{44}$$

and to trajectory semantics

$$\alpha_h(T) \triangleq \{\alpha_h(\sigma) \mid \sigma \in T\} \tag{45}$$

which, by (5), is a Galois connection

$$\langle \wp(T_C^{+\infty}), \subseteq \rangle \xleftarrow[\alpha_h]{\gamma_h} \langle \wp(T_{\overline{C}}^{+\infty}), \subseteq \rangle \tag{46}$$

The homomorphic abstraction of a transition system is

$$\alpha_h(\langle C, C^0, \tau \rangle) \triangleq \langle \{h(c) \mid c \in C\}, \{h(c) \mid c \in C^0\}, \{\langle h(c), h(c') \rangle \mid \langle c, c' \rangle \in \tau\} \rangle \tag{47}$$

For brevity, we write $\alpha_h(\tau)$ for $\alpha_h(\langle C, C^0, \tau \rangle)$. The homomorphic abstraction of the trajectory semantics generated by the concrete transition system is the abstract trajectory semantics generated by the homomorphic abstraction of the concrete transition system

Theorem 1.

$$\alpha_h([\![\tau]\!]) = [\![\alpha_h(\tau)]\!] \tag{48}$$

The *verification* of a property of an hybrid system $[\![\tau]\!]$ defined by a transition relation τ can be done in the abstract, as follows.

Theorem 2. For any abstract hybrid trajectory property $\overline{P} \in \wp(\mathsf{T}_{\overline{\mathsf{C}}}^{+\infty})$,

$$\frac{\alpha_h(\tau) \subseteq \overline{\tau}, \quad (26), \quad [\![\overline{\tau}]\!] \subseteq \overline{P}}{[\![\tau]\!] \subseteq \gamma_h(\overline{P})} \tag{49}$$

i.e. a sound abstract small-step semantics $\overline{\tau}$ overapproximating the concrete semantics τ is designed so that the concretization $\gamma_h(\overline{P})$ of its trace properties $\overline{P}$ holds for the concrete semantics $[\![\tau]\!]$.

Given a specification in the form of an abstract transition system $\overline{\tau}$, *refinement* consists in designing a concrete transition system τ such that $[\![\tau]\!] \subseteq \gamma_h(\{[\![\overline{\tau}]\!]\})$. By induction principle (49) where $\overline{P} = \{[\![\overline{\tau}]\!]\}$, it is sufficient to ensure that $\alpha_h(\tau) \subseteq \overline{\tau}$ and the blocking condition (26).

Finally, the homomorphic abstraction is preserved by discretization (27).

Theorem 3.

$$\alpha_\delta(\alpha_h(T)) = \alpha_h(\alpha_\delta(T)) \tag{50}$$

In conclusion of this Sect. 7.1, homomorphic abstractions are very simple since they compose (because $h(t) \in \mathsf{S} \to \overline{\mathsf{S}}$ and $\overline{h}(t) \in \overline{\mathsf{S}} \to \overline{\overline{\mathsf{S}}}$ implies $\overline{h}(t) \circ h(t) \in \mathsf{S} \to \overline{\overline{\mathsf{S}}}$), there is a unique best abstract homomorphic abstract hybrid semantics (by (46)), they extend from hybrid transition systems to hybrid semantics (by theorem 1), allow proofs of trajectory properties by abstraction (by theorem 2), and are preserved by discretization (by theorem 3). Homomorphic abstractions seem to be almost the only ones considered in model-checking [5, pp. 499–504].

However, homomorphic abstractions are very restrictive in that the relation between flows is deterministic and the concrete and abstract timelines must be exactly the same[3].

7.2   Simulations

Simulations were introduced by Robin Milner [26] to relate discrete transitions systems hence, implicitly, their trace semantics or abstractions of these trace semantics. They have been used for program verification and refinement. Notice that Robin Milner originally used (bi)simulation relations to abstract reachability/invariance properties for which reasoning on transitions and their reflexive closure is sound and complete. So there was no need to consider (bi)similar traces.

---

[3] One could argue that the time-evolution low abstraction of (17) applied to the concrete and abstract trajectories would solve the problem of having the same timeline by merging the trajectories into a single configuration, but then the original timelines are hidden in the flow functions, which does not make time-dependent reasonings simpler.

Various extensions to continuous and hybrid systems have been proposed such as [3,6,9,12–15,15,16,23,25,31,35,36] among others. In contrast with this previous work, our definition of (bi)simulation takes into account the fact that concrete and abstract trajectories may have different durations and not necessarily comparable timelines for mode changes.

Definition of Asynchronous Hybrid Simulations. A relation $R \in \wp(\mathsf{C} \times \overline{\mathsf{C}})$ between concrete and abstract configurations (which can be the extension (30) $R = \gamma(r)$ of the timed relation r between states in (29)) is a *hybrid simulation* between the transition relations τ and $\overline{\tau}$ if and only if

$$\forall c, \overline{c}, c' . \exists \overline{c}' . (\langle c, \overline{c} \rangle \in R \wedge (\langle c, c' \rangle \in \tau \vee c' = \varepsilon)) \Longrightarrow \tag{51}$$
$$((\langle \overline{c}, \overline{c}' \rangle \in \overline{\tau} \vee \overline{c}' = \varepsilon) \wedge \langle c \,\mathring{,}\, c'(\!|\min(\mathsf{b}(c'), \mathsf{b}(\overline{c}')), \min(\mathsf{e}(c'), \mathsf{e}(\overline{c}'))|\!),$$
$$\overline{c} \,\mathring{,}\, \overline{c}'(\!|\min(\mathsf{b}(c'), \mathsf{b}(\overline{c}')), \min(\mathsf{e}(c'), \mathsf{e}(\overline{c}'))|\!)\rangle \in R)$$

To simplify notations, we write $c' = \varepsilon$ for $\mathsf{e}(\overline{c}') \leqslant \mathsf{e}(c) \wedge c' = \varepsilon$ and similarly $\overline{c}' = \varepsilon$ stands for $\mathsf{e}(c') \leqslant \mathsf{e}(\overline{c}) \wedge \overline{c}' = \varepsilon$, see Fig. 3.

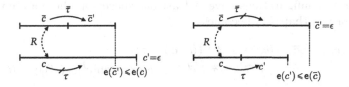

Fig. 3. Empty successor configurations

As shown in Fig. 4, this definition of an *asynchronous simulation* takes into account the fact that the concrete and abstract configurations may correspond

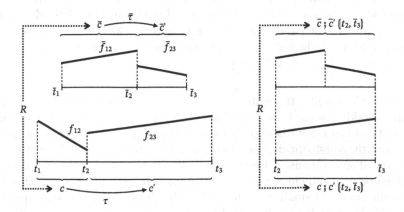

Fig. 4. Asynchronous hybrid simulation

to different timelines. Concrete and abstract configurations $\langle c, \overline{c} \rangle \in R$ are related and there is a concrete transition $\langle c, c' \rangle \in \tau$ from c to c' so there must exists an abstract transition $\langle \overline{c}, \overline{c}' \rangle \in \overline{\tau}$ such that c' and $\overline{c}'$ are related. But since c' and $\overline{c}'$ may have different timings, one of them is extended in the past by the previous configuration ($\overline{c}'$ extended to $t_2 = \min(t_2, \overline{t}_2) = \min(\mathsf{b}(c'), \mathsf{b}(\overline{c}'))$ using the previous $\overline{c}$ in Fig. 4) while one of them, maybe the same, is truncated in the future to the first terminating configuration (c' truncated to $\overline{t}_3 = \min(t_3, \overline{t}_3) = \min(\mathsf{e}(c'), \mathsf{e}(\overline{c}'))$ in Fig. 4).

The simulation $R = \{\langle c, \alpha_h(c) \rangle \mid c \in \mathsf{C}\}$ may be the homomorphic abstraction (43) which would enforce the concrete and abstract timings to be the same. More generally, the simulation R may be many-to-many. For example the concrete states can be equipped with a distance and R would ensure that, at each time instant, the concrete state is in a ball around the abstract state [9,16], the size of the ball evolving over time (this would, for example, account for cumulated rounding errors when the abstract states are reals and the refined concrete states are floats).

Another particular case is that of a *synchronous simulation* of well-nested configurations when concrete timelines are subdivisions of the abstract timelines (that is, if $\langle f, i \rangle \in \mathsf{C}$, $\langle \overline{f}, \overline{i} \rangle \in \overline{\mathsf{C}}$, and $i \cap \overline{i} \neq \emptyset$ then $\mathsf{b}(\overline{i}) \leqslant \mathsf{b}(i) < \mathsf{e}(i) \leqslant \mathsf{e}(\overline{i})$). If moreover all configurations have at least one successor, there are no blocking configurations so that (51) becomes

$$\forall c, \overline{c}, c' . \exists \overline{c}' . (\langle c, \overline{c} \rangle \in R \wedge (\langle c, c' \rangle \in \tau)) \Longrightarrow \qquad (52)$$
$$((\langle \overline{c}, \overline{c}' \rangle \in \overline{\tau} \vee \overline{c}' = \varepsilon) \wedge \langle c', \overline{c}'(\!|\mathsf{b}(c'), \mathsf{e}(c')|\!)\rangle \in R)$$

Example 5 (Change of variables). Let $\langle c_i, i \in [0, |c|[\rangle$ be a concrete semantics with concrete configurations $c_i = \langle \boldsymbol{\lambda} t \cdot f_i(t - t_i^\ell), [t_i^\ell, t_i^h[\rangle$ where $f_i(t)$ is given by the Cauchy-Euler implicit ordinary differential (ODE) equation $t^2 f_i''(t) + a_i t f_i'(t) + b_i f_i(t) = 0$. Under appropriate continuity hypotheses, a classic resolution method [30, ch.19, p. 170] consists in applying the change of variable $t = \ln(\overline{t})$, that is $\overline{t} = e^t$ to get $\varphi_i(\overline{t})$ solution of $\varphi_i''(\overline{t}) + (a_i - 1)\varphi_i'(\overline{t}) + b_i \varphi_i(\overline{t}) = 0$ which is a linear ODE solved via its characteristic polynomial. Let the abstract hybrid semantics be $\langle \overline{c}_i, i \in [0, |c|[\rangle$ with abstract configurations $\overline{c}_i = \langle \boldsymbol{\lambda} \overline{t} \cdot \varphi_i(\overline{t} - e^{t_i^\ell}), [e^{t_i^\ell}, e^{t_i^h}[\rangle$. This is a hybrid simulation (indeed a bisimulation) $\gamma(r)$ for $r(t) = \{\langle f_i(t - t_i^\ell), \varphi_i(e^t - e^{t_i^\ell})\rangle \mid i \in [0, |c|[\wedge t \in [t_i^\ell, t_i^h[\}.$ $\qquad\qquad\square$

Example 6. Continuing the water tank automaton 3, we refine the tank specification by taking some time ϵ to close (in *off* configuration) and open (in *on* configuration) the valve while in *shut* mode. We assume $\epsilon > \zeta$ to ensure that the duration of the valve opening and closing is not infinitesimal. The water inflow $\dot{y}$ is increased to compensate for this delay. We assume that ϵ is large enough for the valve opening and closing to be mechanically feasible in this period of time. We assume that ϵ is small enough so that the duration of the *shut* configuration in (25) is much larger than 2ϵ. In particular it must be chosen so that the increase of the inflow is physically possible.

Fig. 5. Concrete (a) and abstract (b) tank trajectories

The *open* mode is unchanged, as shown in figure (5.a). A formal definition of example $\underline{6}$ is given in the ArXiv version.

The relation $R^{(53)}$ between configurations of concrete trajectories in (Fig. 5.a) and the configurations of abstract trajectories in (Fig. 5.b) is the following.

$$R^{(53)} \triangleq \{\langle\langle \boldsymbol{\lambda} t \cdot \langle m_t,\, x_t,\, y_t\rangle,\, [t_1, t_2[\rangle,\, \langle \boldsymbol{\lambda} t \cdot \langle \overline{m}_t,\, \overline{x}_t,\, \overline{y}_t\rangle,\, [\overline{t}_1, \overline{t}_2[\rangle \mid \tag{53}$$
$$P^{(53)}(m, x, y, t_1, t_2, \overline{m}, \overline{x}, \overline{y}, \overline{t}_1, \overline{t}_2)\}$$

$$P^{(53)}(m, x, y, t_1, t_2, \overline{m}, \overline{x}, \overline{y}, \overline{t}_1, \overline{t}_2) \triangleq \forall t \in [\overline{t}_1, \overline{t}_2[\, .\, x_t = \overline{x}_t \wedge \tag{54}$$
$$((\overline{m}_t = shut \wedge$$
$$((m_t = off \wedge y = 0 \wedge \overline{y}_t = t - t_1 \wedge t_1 = \overline{t}_1 \wedge t_2 = \overline{t}_1 + \epsilon)$$
$$\vee\, (m_t = shut \wedge t_1 = \overline{t}_1 + \epsilon \wedge t_2 = \overline{t}_2 - \epsilon \wedge \overline{y}_t = y_t + \epsilon\Big(1 - \frac{2(t_2 - t)}{t_2 - t_1}\Big))$$
$$\vee\, (m_t = on \wedge t_1 = \overline{t}_2 - \epsilon \wedge t_2 = \overline{t}_2 \wedge y_t = \overline{y}_t + \epsilon\Big(\frac{\overline{t}_2 - t}{\overline{t}_2 - t_2}\Big))))$$
$$\vee\, (\overline{m}_t = m_t = open \wedge y_t = \overline{y_t} \wedge t_1 = \overline{t}_1 \wedge t_2 = \overline{t}_2))$$

By the Galois isomorphism (33), the relation $R^{(53)}$ between configurations defines the relation $r^{(53)}$ between states as a function of the time.

$$r^{(53)} \triangleq \{\langle\langle m_t,\, x_t,\, y_t\rangle,\, \langle \overline{m}_t,\, \overline{x}_t,\, \overline{y}_t\rangle\rangle \mid \exists [t_1, t_2[\subseteq [\overline{t}_1, \overline{t}_2[\, .\, t \in [t_1, t_2[\tag{55}$$
$$\wedge\, P^{(53)}(m, x, y, t_1, t_2, \overline{m}, \overline{x}, \overline{y}, \overline{t}_1, \overline{t}_2)\}$$

$R^{(53)}$, that is $\gamma(r^{(53)})$, is a synchronous simulation (52), where in *shut* mode the concrete level is within ϵ of the abstract water level while in *open* mode they are the same.   □

Trace Abstraction by Asynchronous Hybrid Simulations. Our objective is now to generalize the results of Sect. 7.1 on homomorphisms to (weaker ones for) simulations. Similar to (48) for homomorphic abstractions, simulations induce related hybrid trajectory semantics.

Theorem $\underline{4}$. *If the timed relation r between states in (29) is such that its extension $\gamma(r)$ to configurations in (30) is a simulation (51) between $\langle C, C^0, \tau\rangle$ and $\langle \overline{C}, \overline{C}^0, \overline{\tau}\rangle$ satisfying the initialization hypothesis*

$$\forall c \in \mathsf{C}^0 \ . \ \exists \bar{c} \in \overline{\mathsf{C}}^0 \ . \ \langle c, \bar{c} \rangle \in \gamma(r) \tag{56}$$

then $\langle [\![\tau]\!], [\![\bar{\tau}]\!] \rangle \in \vec{\gamma}(\vec{\gamma}_c(r))$. If moreover, the *blocking hypothesis*

$$\forall c, \bar{c} \ . \ (\langle c, \bar{c} \rangle \in \gamma(r) \wedge \forall c' \ . \ \langle c, c' \rangle \notin \tau) \implies (\forall \bar{c}' \ . \ \langle \bar{c}, \bar{c}' \rangle \notin \bar{\tau}) \tag{57}$$

holds then

$$\langle [\![\tau]\!], [\![\bar{\tau}]\!] \rangle \in \vec{\gamma}(\vec{\gamma}(r)) \tag{58}$$

(that is, by (37), $\forall \sigma \in [\![\tau]\!] \ . \ \exists \bar{\sigma} \in [\![\bar{\tau}]\!] \ . \ \langle \sigma, \bar{\sigma} \rangle \in \vec{\gamma}(r)$ and so, by (34), $\forall t \in [0, \min(\rbrack\sigma\lbrack, \rbrack\bar{\sigma}\lbrack)\lbrack\mathsf{\cap dom}(r) \ . \ \langle \sigma_t, \bar{\sigma}_t \rangle \in r(t))$.

Example 7. Continuing the water tank automaton in examples 3 and 6, $R^{(53)}$ is a synchronous simulation (52). So the hybrid semantics of example 6 is a simulation of (58) of the hybrid semantics $[\![\tau^3]\!]$ of example 3.　　　　□

Simulations are Abstractions. Observe that 4 implies that hybrid simulations are Galois connection-based abstractions (38).

Compositionality of Simulations. The composition of simulations may not, in general, correspond to the composition of their timed relations between states (defined as $(r_1 \circ r_2)(t) = r_1(t) \circ r_2(t)$). This is because the intermediate trajectories may be shorter that those in the composition, as shown in Fig. 6.

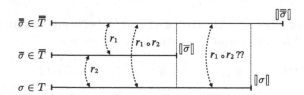

Fig. 6. Non-composition due to short intermediate trajectory duration

Another problem is that of interval mismatches where the intervals along trajectories thus leaving some states time-unrelate in the composition, see Fig. 7.

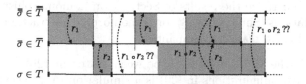

Fig. 7. Non-nested intervals

A sufficient condition for compositionally is that the involved trajectories be all infinite with well nested interval, meaning

$$\forall \langle \langle f_j, i_j \rangle, \ j \in \mathbb{N} \rangle \in T \ . \ \forall \langle \langle \bar{f}_k, \bar{i}_k \rangle, \ k \in \mathbb{N} \rangle \in \overline{T} \ . \tag{59}$$
$$\forall j, k \in \mathbb{N} \ . \ (i_j \cap \bar{i}_k \neq \emptyset) \implies (i_j \subseteq \bar{i}_k)$$

Theorem 5. If $T \in \mathsf{T}_\mathsf{C}^\infty$, $\overline{T} \in \mathsf{T}_{\overline{\mathsf{C}}}^\infty$, $\overline{\overline{T}} \in \mathsf{T}_{\overline{\overline{\mathsf{C}}}}^\infty$ are well-nested, $\langle T, \overline{T} \rangle \in \vec{\gamma}(\vec{\gamma}_c(r_1))$ and $\langle \overline{T}, \overline{\overline{T}} \rangle \in \vec{\gamma}(\vec{\gamma}_c(r_2))$ then $\langle T, \overline{\overline{T}} \rangle \in \vec{\gamma}(\vec{\gamma}_c(r_1 \circ r_2))$.

Example 8 (Composition of the water tank simulations). Continuing the water tank specification in example 2, automaton in example 3, and implementation in example 6, the hybrid trajectory semantics are well-nested according to (59). The hybrid semantics $[\![\tau^6]\!]$ of example 6 is a simulation of the hybrid semantics $[\![\tau^3]\!]$ of example 3 by $r^{(53)}$, which itself is a simulation of the specification $\mathcal{S}^2$ by $r^{(39)}$. So, by theorem 5, their composition $r^{(53)} \circ r^{(39)}$ holds at any time between the implementation $[\![\tau^6]\!]$ and the specification $\mathcal{S}^2$.

This may look paradoxical because if $\epsilon > \zeta$ then water in the implementation will remain at the zero level longer than prescribed by the specification (20.d).

However, this is not an anomaly since the composition is

$$r^{(53)} \circ r^{(39)} \triangleq \{ \langle \langle m_t, x_t, y_t \rangle, \langle \overline{m}_t, \overline{y}_t \rangle \rangle \mid \exists [t_1, t_2[\subseteq [\overline{t}_1, \overline{t}_2[\ . \ t \in [t_1, t_2[\wedge \quad (60)$$
$$P^{(53)}(m_t, x_t, y_t, t_1, t_2, \overline{m}_t, x_t, \overline{y}_t, \overline{t}_1, \overline{t}_2) \}$$

By definition (53), this expresses that the height $\overline{y}_t$ of the water in the specification when the valve is *off* for ϵ units of time is equal to $t - t_1 = t - \overline{t}_1$, not to the level of water $y_t = 0$ in the implementation. So, although each simulation $r^{(39)}$ and $r^{(53)}$ is a satisfactory specification, their composition is an incomplete refinement of the expected water tank behavior.   □

Greatest Simulation. (51) can be rewritten as

$$R \subseteq F_{\tau, \overline{\tau}}^s(R) \qquad \text{with} \qquad (61)$$
$$F_{\tau, \overline{\tau}}^s(R) \triangleq \{ \langle c, \overline{c} \rangle \mid \forall c' \ . \ (\langle c, c' \rangle \in \tau) \Longrightarrow$$
$$(\exists \overline{c}' \ . \ \langle \overline{c}, \overline{c}' \rangle \in \overline{\tau} \wedge \langle c \, \mathbin{;} c' \, (\!| \min(\mathsf{b}(c'), \mathsf{b}(\overline{c}')), \min(\mathsf{e}(c'), \mathsf{e}(\overline{c}')) |\!),$$
$$\overline{c} \, \mathbin{;} \overline{c}' \, (\!| \min(\mathsf{b}(c'), \mathsf{b}(\overline{c}')), \min(\mathsf{e}(c'), \mathsf{e}(\overline{c}')) |\!) \rangle \in R) \}$$

where $F_{\tau, \overline{\tau}}^s$ is increasing on the complete lattice $\langle \wp(\mathsf{C} \times \overline{\mathsf{C}}), \subseteq \rangle$ so that by Tarski's fixpoint theorem [37] there exists a greatest simulation between τ and $\overline{\tau}$, thus extending Robin Milner's classic result [27, Proposition 16, Sect. 4.6] to hybrid simulations (and the least fixpoint is $\emptyset$).

Verification of Trace Properties by Simulation. The homomorphic induction principle (49) can be generalized to hybrid asynchronous simulations $\vec{\gamma}(r)$ as follows

$$\frac{\vec{\gamma}(r) \subseteq F_{\tau, \overline{\tau}}^s(\vec{\gamma}(r)), \quad (56), \quad (57), \quad [\![\overline{\tau}]\!] \subseteq \overline{P}}{\langle [\![\tau]\!], \overline{P} \rangle \in \vec{\gamma}(\vec{\gamma}(r))} \qquad (62)$$

Discretization by Sampling

Discretization of a hybrid transition system. We have defined the discretization
(27) of a hybrid trajectory semantics. In general the discretization of a hybrid
transition system (22) and that of the generated trajectories (23) do not coincide,
as shown by the following counterexample (for which the discretization of the
trajectory and that of the configurations $c_1, c_2, c_3, \ldots$ in the transition relation
τ do not coincide).
To solve this dependency, it is generally assumed that the start time and duration
of configurations is a multiple of the discretization step

$$\forall c \in \mathsf{C} \, . \, \exists k, k' \in \mathbb{N} \, . \, \mathsf{b}(c) = k\delta < k'\delta = \mathsf{e}(c). \tag{63}$$

The relation (29) between states is time-dependent. Simply ignoring the discrete
time $\langle n\delta, \, n \in \mathbb{N}\rangle$ might create circularities (see example 10 thereafter).
    One solution is to incorporate the time (or at least the rank $n \in \mathbb{N}$) into
states to make the relation time-independent as in classic simulations. So (27)
becomes

$$\alpha_\delta(\sigma) \triangleq \langle\langle\sigma_{n\delta}, \, n\rangle, \, n \in \mathbb{N} \wedge n\delta \in [0, \llbracket\sigma\rrbracket]\rangle \tag{64}$$

and (29) becomes

$$\alpha_\delta(r) \triangleq \{\langle\langle s, \, n\rangle, \, \langle\overline{s}, \, n\rangle\rangle \mid n \in \mathbb{N} \wedge n\delta \in \mathsf{dom}(r) \wedge \langle s, \, \overline{s}\rangle \in r(n\delta)\}. \tag{65}$$

The timeful discretization of the hybrid transition system is

$$\alpha_\delta(\tau) \triangleq \{\langle\langle s, \, n\rangle, \, \langle s', \, n+1\rangle\rangle \mid \tag{66}$$
$$(\exists c \, . \, (c \in \mathsf{C}^0 \vee \exists c' \, . \, \langle c', \, c\rangle \in \tau) \wedge \tag{a}$$
$$\mathsf{b}(c) \leqslant n\delta < (n+1)\delta < \mathsf{e}(c) \wedge s = c_{n\delta} \wedge s' = c_{(n+1)\delta})$$
$$\vee (\exists\langle c, \, c'\rangle \in \tau \, . \, (n+1)\delta = \mathsf{e}(c) \wedge s = c_{n\delta} \wedge s' = c'_{(n+1)\delta}) \tag{b}$$
$$\vee (\exists c \in \mathsf{C} \, . \, \forall c' \, . \, \langle c, \, c'\rangle \notin \tau \wedge (n+1)\delta = \mathsf{e}(c) \wedge \tag{c}$$
$$s = c_{n\delta} \wedge s' = c_{(n+1)\delta})\}$$
$$\alpha_\delta(\mathsf{C}^0) \triangleq \{\langle c_0, \, 0\rangle \mid c \in \mathsf{C}^0\} \tag{d}$$

which is well-defined by (22) and since the durations of the configurations are
assumed to be multiples of δ. (66.a) covers discrete transitions within a configuration but the last one. The last transition is either to the first state of the next
configurations (66.b), or in absence of any successor configuration, to the last
state of the current configuration (66.c). This condition (66.c) solves the problem
of having open right time intervals in configurations by defining the last state
of the last configuration of finite trajectories. This discretization applies to both
concrete and abstract transition systems.

Example 9 (hybrid transition discretization). The various cases in (66 are illustrated below.

– By (66.a), the initial configuration $c = \langle f, \; [0, 2\delta] \rangle$ starting at time 0 of duration 2δ has an internal discrete transition $\langle \langle f(0), \; 0 \rangle, \; \langle f(\delta), \; 1 \rangle \rangle \in \alpha_\delta(\tau)$ between its states at times 0 and δ;
– Similarly, by (66.a), the successor configuration $c' = \langle f', \; [2\delta, 4\delta] \rangle$ starting at time 2δ of duration 2δ has an internal discrete transition $\langle \langle f'(2\delta), 2 \rangle, \langle f'(3\delta), 3 \rangle \rangle \in \alpha_\delta(\tau)$;
– By (66.b), the last discrete transition of configuration c is toward the beginning state $\langle f'(2\delta), \; 2 \rangle$ of its successor configuration(s) c' (and not toward its final state $\langle f(2\delta), \; 2 \rangle$);
– In contrast, by (66.c), the last discrete transition for configuration c' which has no possible successor by τ is toward its final state $\langle f'(4\delta), \; 4 \rangle$.

Observe that $f(\delta) = f'(4\delta)$ but they are distinguished by incorporating the rank n of discrete times $n\delta$. □

Example 10 (timeful and timeless abstraction). Consider $\mathsf{S} = \{s\}$, $\mathsf{C} = \mathsf{C}^0 = \{c\}$, $\tau = \emptyset$ where $c = \langle f, \; [0, 2] \rangle$ with $\forall t \in [0, 2] \; . \; f(t) = s$, and $\delta = 1$. We have $[\![\tau]\!] = \{c\}$ and $\alpha_\delta([\![\tau]\!]) = \{\langle s, \; 0 \rangle \langle s, \; 1 \rangle\}$ as well as $\alpha_\delta(\tau) = \emptyset$ and $[\![\alpha_\delta(\tau)]\!] = \{\langle s, \; 0 \rangle \langle s, \; 1 \rangle\}$, that is, (67).

Ignoring time, we would have $\widetilde{\alpha}_\delta([\![\tau]\!]) = \{ss\}$ while the transition abstraction $\widetilde{\alpha}_\delta(\tau) = \{\langle s, \; s \rangle\}$ yields a circularity so that $[\![\widetilde{\alpha}_\delta(\tau)]\!] = s^+ | s^\infty$ and in general $\widetilde{\alpha}_\delta([\![\tau]\!]) \subseteq [\![\widetilde{\alpha}_\delta(\tau)]\!]$ which would be a rather imprecise overapproximation. □

By definition of α_δ, it follows that

Theorem 6. The timed discretization of the semantics is the semantics of the timeful discretized transition system, formally

$$\alpha_\delta([\![\tau]\!]) = [\![\alpha_\delta(\tau)]\!] \tag{67}$$

Is the Discretization of a Hybrid Simulation a Discrete Simulation? If the simulation of a hybrid transition system is a generalization of Robin Milner's simulation of discrete transition systems [26] there should be an abstraction of time mapping the hybrid simulation of the hybrid transition system into a discrete simulation for the discretized transition system. This is our next objective.

Sampling in (28) is a discretization. But this discretization of a hybrid simulation may not be a discrete simulation, even when configuration durations are a multiples of a base duration δ, as assumed in (63).

For a counter example, on figure (8.a), we have a hybrid simulation since states are related by r on the common interval of time of c and $\bar{c}$. But in the discretization, concrete state s has a successor while the related state $\bar{s}$ has none, so this is not a discrete simulation.

A second counterexample is given in figure (8.b) when $t_0 = \bar{t}_0$. We have $\langle s, \; \bar{s}_0 \rangle \in r(\bar{t}_0)$ but $\bar{s}_0$ does not belong to any configuration and so has no successor by $\alpha_\delta(\bar{\tau})$. So the discretization of the hybrid simulation is not a discrete simulation.

A third counterexample is also given on figure (8.b) Configurations c and $\bar{c}$ are related because relation r between their states during the first period of

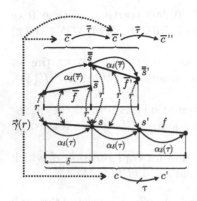

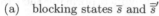

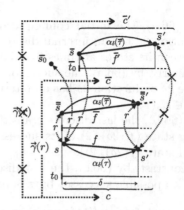

(a)   blocking states $\bar{\bar{s}}$ and $\bar{\bar{s}}'$ (b)   related states s and isolated state $\bar{\bar{s}}_0$ or
                                                                 s and $\bar{\bar{s}}$ of **unrelated** configurations c and $\bar{\bar{c}}'$

Fig. 8. Effects of asynchronous discretization

time (end included in successor) while c and $\bar{\bar{c}}'$ are not since r holds between s and $\bar{\bar{s}}$ whereas it does not hold between s' and $\bar{\bar{s}}'$. After discretization, the configuration $\bar{\bar{c}}'$ generates a transition $\alpha_\delta(\bar{\tau})$ from $\bar{\bar{s}}$ to $\bar{\bar{s}}'$. Now $\langle s, \bar{\bar{s}} \rangle \in r^{-1} \wedge \langle s, s' \rangle \in \alpha_\delta(\tau)$ but the only successor $\bar{\bar{s}}'$ of $\bar{\bar{s}}$ by $\alpha_\delta(\bar{\tau})$ is not related to s'. So the discretization of the hybrid simulation is not a discrete simulation.

Moreover, the relation r in (29) is the partial function of the time, whereas its abstraction $\alpha_\delta(r)^{-1}$ in Robin Milner's simulation $\alpha_\delta(r)^{-1} \circ \alpha_\delta(\tau) \dot{\subseteq} \alpha_\delta(\bar{\tau}) \circ \alpha_\delta(r)^{-1}$ is a well-defined relation between states. So, in case r in (29) is not total, and to be compatible with Robin Milner's definition, we must assume that r is well-defined at the discretization points

$$\forall n \in \mathbb{N} . (\exists c \in \mathsf{C} . n\delta \in \mathsf{dom}(c)) \implies (n\delta \in \mathsf{dom}(r)). \tag{68}$$

To prevent the case of isolated state $\bar{\bar{s}}_0$ in (Fig. 8.b), we assume that related states must come from related configurations (either initial or successor ones).

$$\forall c \in \mathsf{C}, \bar{\bar{s}} \in \bar{\bar{\mathsf{S}}}, n \in \mathbb{N} . (n\delta \in \mathsf{dom}(c) \cap \mathsf{dom}(r) \wedge \langle c_{n\delta}, \bar{\bar{s}} \rangle \in r(n\delta)) \implies \tag{69}$$
$$(\exists \bar{\bar{c}} \in \bar{\bar{\mathsf{C}}} . (\bar{\bar{c}} \in \bar{\bar{\mathsf{C}}}^0 \vee \exists \bar{\bar{c}}' . \langle \bar{\bar{c}}', \bar{\bar{c}} \rangle \in \bar{\tau}) \wedge n\delta \in \mathsf{dom}(\bar{\bar{c}}) \wedge \bar{\bar{c}}_{n\delta} = \bar{\bar{s}})$$

Beyond an initialization hypothesis (similar to (56)), a common hypothesis for discrete simulations is the *non-blocking condition*, which, for hybrid simulations, translates into

$$\forall c \in \mathsf{C}, \bar{\bar{c}} \in \bar{\bar{\mathsf{C}}} . (\exists t \in \mathsf{dom}(c) \cap \mathsf{dom}(\bar{\bar{c}}) \cap \mathsf{dom}(r) . \langle c_t, \bar{\bar{c}}_t \rangle \in r(t) \wedge \tag{70}$$
$$\forall \bar{\bar{c}}' . \langle \bar{\bar{c}}, \bar{\bar{c}}' \rangle \notin \bar{\tau}) \implies (\mathsf{e}(\bar{\bar{c}}) = \mathsf{e}(c))$$

The non-blocking condition (70) will avoid the blocking state $\bar{\bar{s}}$ in Fig. 8, on the left, since concrete blocking configurations can only be related to abstract configurations with the same ending time.

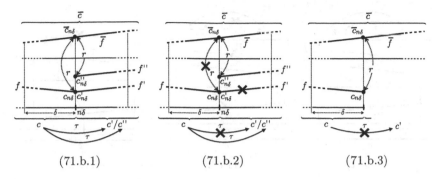

Fig. 9. Relation between states after discretization of concrete configuration transitions

Moreover, we request the relation r between states to be compatible with the discretization (66) of transition relations. If a concrete configuration c and an abstract one $\bar{c}$ have related states at some time t then their states must be related at any time $n\delta$ in their common time intervals, except maybe at the end of these time intervals (71.a).

$$\forall c \in \mathsf{C}, \bar{c} \in \overline{\mathsf{C}} \ . \ (\exists t \in \mathrm{dom}(c) \cap \mathrm{dom}(\bar{c}) \cap \mathrm{dom}(r) \ . \ \langle c_t, \bar{c}_t \rangle \in r(t)) \Longrightarrow \qquad (71)$$

$$(\forall n\delta \in (\mathrm{dom}(c) \cap \mathrm{dom}(\bar{c})) \setminus \{e(c), e(\bar{c})\} \ . \ \langle c_{n\delta}, \bar{c}_{n\delta} \rangle \in r(n\delta)) \wedge \qquad (a)$$

$$(\forall n \ . \ n\delta = e(c) \in \mathrm{dom}(\bar{c})) \Longrightarrow \qquad (b)$$

$$(\forall c' \ . \ (\langle c, c' \rangle \in \tau) \Longrightarrow (\langle c'_{n\delta}, \bar{c}_{n\delta} \rangle \in r(n\delta))) \wedge \qquad (b.1)$$

$$((\forall c' \ . \ \langle c, c' \rangle \in \tau \Longrightarrow c_{n\delta} \neq c'_{n\delta}) \Longrightarrow (\langle c_{n\delta}, \bar{c}_{n\delta} \rangle \notin r(n\delta))) \wedge \ (b.2)$$

$$((\forall c' \ . \ \langle c, c' \rangle \notin \tau) \Longrightarrow (\langle c_{n\delta}, \bar{c}_{n\delta} \rangle \in r(n\delta))) \wedge \qquad (b.3)$$

$$(\forall n \ . \ (n\delta = e(\bar{c}) \in \mathrm{dom}(c)) \Longrightarrow \qquad (c)$$

$$(\forall \bar{c}' \ . \ (\langle \bar{c}, \bar{c}' \rangle \in \bar{\tau}) \Longrightarrow (\langle c_{n\delta}, \bar{c}'_{n\delta} \rangle \in r(n\delta))) \wedge \qquad (c.1)$$

$$((\forall \bar{c}' \ . \ \langle \bar{c}, \bar{c}' \rangle \in \bar{\tau} \Longrightarrow \bar{c}_{n\delta} \neq \bar{c}'_{n\delta}) \Longrightarrow (\langle c_{n\delta}, \bar{c}_{n\delta} \rangle \notin r(n\delta))) \wedge \ (c.2)$$

$$((\forall \bar{c}' \ . \ \langle \bar{c}, \bar{c}' \rangle \notin \bar{\tau}) \Longrightarrow (\langle c_{n\delta}, \bar{c}_{n\delta} \rangle \in r(n\delta)))) \qquad (c.3)$$

The relations between states at the end of a concrete configuration c are illustrated in Fig. 9. In case (71.b.1), the state $c'_{n\delta}$ at the beginning of the next concrete configuration c' is related to the abstract state $\bar{c}_{n\delta}$ at the end of this concrete configuration c.

Case (71.b.2) states that if there is no concrete configuration c' which initial state $c'_{n\delta}$ is equal to the last state $c_{n\delta}$ of the previous configuration c then $c_{n\delta}$ should *not* be related to the abstract state $\bar{c}_{n\delta}$ at the end of this concrete configuration c.

Case (71.b.3) states that if the concrete configuration c ending at time $n\delta$ has no successor then its last state should be related to the abstract state $\bar{c}_{n\delta}$ at the end of this concrete configuration c.

Cases (71.c) in Fig. 10 are symmetrical.

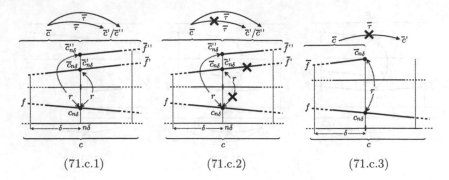

(71.c.1)   (71.c.2)   (71.c.3)

Fig. 10. Relation between states after discretization of abstract configuration transitions

Then, we have the following result (72) that supports the intuition that state-based hybrid simulations $\vec{\gamma}(r)$ satisfying (51) (or equivalently (61)) are a meaningful generalization of Robin Milner discrete simulations (i.e. $R \circ t \subseteq \bar{t} \circ R$).

Theorem 7.

$$(\vec{\gamma}(r) \subseteq F^s_{\tau,\overline{\tau}}(\vec{\gamma}(r)) \wedge (68) \wedge (69) \wedge (70) \wedge (71)) \implies \tag{72}$$
$$\alpha_\delta(r)^{-1} \circ \alpha_\delta(\tau) \stackrel{.}{\subseteq} \alpha_\delta(\overline{\tau}) \circ \alpha_\delta(r)^{-1}$$

8   Conclusion

We have studied correspondences between trajectory semantics of hybrid systems with possibly different durations and timelines (that is different timing for mode changes), including the case where the hybrid semantics is generated by an hybrid transition system.

The abstraction relation between semantics can be derived from relations between trajectories, possibly themselves derived from relations between configurations, possibly themselves derived from timed relations between states. Such correspondences include the particular cases of homomorphisms, simulations, and discretization (as well as bisimulations, preservation, progress considered in the ArXiv version). They induce abstractions of the hybrid semantics that are Galois connections. So the abstractions between hybrid semantics defined by the correspondences between trajectories do compose.

However, contrary to the discrete case [26,32] and with the exception of homomorphic trajectory abstraction in Sect. 7.1, the correspondences between trajectories or configurations do not necessarily compose with the correspondence between states. For example, the discretization of similar hybrid trajectories may not be similar discrete traces. The problem does not appear in Milner's original discrete definition [26] because the notion of state and configuration as well as timings do coincide. We have studied sufficient conditions for composability of trajectory correspondences to hold.

Like in the case of discrete systems [10], further abstractions of the hybrid trajectory semantics will lead to a hierarchy of semantics, verification, and static analysis methods. The most common abstraction is the reachability abstraction $\alpha(\{\langle \sigma_{ij}^j, i^j \in [0, |\sigma^j|[\rangle \mid j \in \Delta\}) \triangleq \{\sigma_{ij}^j(t) \mid j \in \Delta \wedge i^j \in [0, |\sigma^j|[\wedge t \in [0, |\sigma^j|[\}$, see [8] for a documented and comprehensive survey.

Acknowledgements. I thank Dominique Méry for his suggestions and encouragements, "la discrétisation, c'est coton". I thank the two anonymous referees for their constructive criticisms.

References

1. Alur, R., Courcoubetis, C., Henzinger, T.A., Ho, P.-H.: Hybrid automata: an algorithmic approach to the specification and verification of hybrid systems. In: Grossman, R.L., Nerode, A., Ravn, A.P., Rischel, H. (eds.) HS 1991-1992. LNCS, vol. 736, pp. 209–229. Springer, Heidelberg (1993). https://doi.org/10.1007/3-540-57318-6_30
2. Alur, R., Dill, D.L.: A theory of timed automata. Theor. Comput. Sci. **126**(2), 183–235 (1994)
3. Alur, R., Henzinger, T.A., Lafferriere, G., Pappas, G.J.: Discrete abstractions of hybrid systems. Proc. IEEE **88**(7), 971–984 (2000)
4. Alur, R., Madhusudan, P.: Decision problems for timed automata: a survey. In: Bernardo, M., Corradini, F. (eds.) SFM-RT 2004. LNCS, vol. 3185, pp. 1–24. Springer, Heidelberg (2004). https://doi.org/10.1007/978-3-540-30080-9_1
5. Baier, C., Katoen, J.P.: Principles of Model Checking. MIT Press, Cambridge (2008)
6. Banach, R., Butler, M.J., Qin, S., Verma, N., Zhu, H.: Core hybrid Event-B I: single hybrid Event-B machines. Sci. Comput. Program. **105**, 92–123 (2015)
7. Caspi, P., Halbwachs, N.: An approach to real time systems modeling. In: ICDCS. IEEE Computer Society, pp. 710–716 (1982)
8. Chen, X., Sankaranarayanan, S.: Reachability analysis for cyber-physical systems: are we there yet? In: Deshmukh, J.V., Havelund, K., Perez, I. (eds.) NFM 2022. LNCS, vol. 13260. Springer, Cham (2022). https://doi.org/10.1007/978-3-031-06773-0_6
9. Cheng, Z., Méry, D.: A refinement strategy for hybrid system design with safety constraints. In: Attiogbé, C., Ben Yahia, S. (eds.) MEDI 2021. LNCS, vol. 12732, pp. 3–17. Springer, Cham (2021). https://doi.org/10.1007/978-3-030-78428-7_1
10. Cousot, P.: Constructive design of a hierarchy of semantics of a transition system by abstract interpretation. Theor. Comput. Sci. **277**(1–2), 47–103 (2002)
11. Cousot, P.: Principles of Abstract Interpretation. MIT Press, Cambridge (2021)
12. D'Innocenzo, A., Julius, A.A., Pappas, G.J., Di Benedetto, M.D., Di Gennaro, S.: Verification of temporal properties on hybrid automata by simulation relations. In: CDC, pp. 4039–4044. IEEE (2007)
13. Doyen, L., Henzinger, T.A., Raskin, J.-F.: Automatic rectangular refinement of affine hybrid systems. In: Pettersson, P., Yi, W. (eds.) FORMATS 2005. LNCS, vol. 3829, pp. 144–161. Springer, Heidelberg (2005). https://doi.org/10.1007/11603009_13

14. Frehse, G.: On timed simulation relations for hybrid systems and compositionality. In: Asarin, E., Bouyer, P. (eds.) FORMATS 2006. LNCS, vol. 4202, pp. 200–214. Springer, Heidelberg (2006). https://doi.org/10.1007/11867340_15

15. Girard, A., Julius, A.A., Pappas, G.J.: Approximate simulation relations for hybrid systems. Discret. Event Dyn. Syst. **18**(2), 163–179 (2008). https://doi.org/10.1007/s10626-007-0029-9

16. Girard, A., Pappas, G.J.: Approximate bisimulation: a bridge between computer science and control theory. Eur. J. Control. **17**(5–6), 568–578 (2011)

17. Henzinger, T.A., Ho, P.-H.: A note on abstract interpretation strategies for hybrid automata. In: Antsaklis, P., Kohn, W., Nerode, A., Sastry, S. (eds.) HS 1994. LNCS, vol. 999, pp. 252–264. Springer, Heidelberg (1995). https://doi.org/10.1007/3-540-60472-3_13

18. Henzinger, T.A., Kopke, P.W., Puri, A., Varaiya, P.: What's decidable about hybrid automata? In: STOC, pp. 373–382. ACM (1995)

19. Isaacson, E., Keller, H.B.: Analysis of Numerical Methods. Dover, Mineola (1994)

20. Katok, A., Hasselblatt, B.: Introduction to the Theory of Dynamical Systems. Cambridge University Press, Cambridge (1999)

21. Lang, S.: Undergraduate Analysis, 2nd edn. Springer, Heidelberg (1997)

22. Liberzon, D.: Switching in Systems and Control. Birkhäuser, Basel (2003)

23. Lynch, N.: Simulation techniques for proving properties of real-time systems. In: de Bakker, J.W., de Roever, W.-P., Rozenberg, G. (eds.) REX 1993. LNCS, vol. 803, pp. 375–424. Springer, Heidelberg (1994). https://doi.org/10.1007/3-540-58043-3_24

24. MathWorks. Simulation and model-based design. https://www.mathworks.com/products/simulink.html (2022)

25. Meinicke, L., Hayes, I.J.: Continuous action system refinement. In: Uustalu, T. (ed.) MPC 2006. LNCS, vol. 4014, pp. 316–337. Springer, Heidelberg (2006). https://doi.org/10.1007/11783596_19

26. Milner, R.: An algebraic definition of simulation between programs. In: Proceedings IJCAI, vol. 1971, pp. 481–489 (1971)

27. Milner, R.: Communication and Concurrency. PHI Series in Computer Science, Prentice Hall, Hoboken (1989)

28. Nyquist, H.: Certain topics in telegraph transmission theory. Proc. IEEE **47**(2), 617–644 (1928)

29. Proakis, J.G., Manolakis, D.G.: Digital Signal Processing. Pearson, 4th (edn) (2006)

30. Robinson, J.C.: An Introduction to Ordinary Differential Equations. Cambridge University Press, Cambridge (2004)

31. Rökkö, M., Ravn, A.P., Sere, K.: Hybrid action systems. Theor. Comput. Sci. **290**(1), 937–973 (2003)

32. Sangiorgi, D.: Introduction to Bisimulation and Coinduction. Cambridge University Press, Cambridge (2011)

33. Shannon, C.E.: Communication in the presence of noise. In: Proceedings of the I.R.E., pp. 10–21 (1949)

34. Shmuely, Z.: The structure of Galois connections. Pac. J. Math. **54**(2), 209–225 (1974)

35. Wen, S., Abrial, J.-R., Zhu, H.: Formalizing hybrid systems with Event-B and the Rodin platform. Sci. Comput. Program. **94**, 164–202 (2014)

36. Tan, Y.K., Platzer, A.: An axiomatic approach to liveness for differential equations. In: ter Beek, M.H., McIver, A., Oliveira, J.N. (eds.) FM 2019. LNCS, vol. 11800, pp. 371–388. Springer, Cham (2019). https://doi.org/10.1007/978-3-030-30942-8_23

37. Tarski, A.: A lattice theoretical fixpoint theorem and its applications. Pacific J. of Math. **5**, 285–310 (1955)
38. Wright, A.K., Felleisen, M.: A syntactic approach to type soundness. Inf. Comput. **115**(1), 38–94 (1994)
39. Zhang, J., Johansson, K.H., Lygeros, J., Sastry, S.: Dynamical systems revisited: hybrid systems with Zeno executions. In: Lynch, N., Krogh, B.H. (eds.) HSCC 2000. LNCS, vol. 1790, pp. 451–464. Springer, Heidelberg (2000). https://doi.org/10.1007/3-540-46430-1_37

Generalizing Logical Execution Time

Edward A. Lee$^{(\boxtimes)}$ and Marten Lohstroh

UC Berkeley, Berkeley, CA, USA
{eal,marten}@berkeley.edu

Abstract. In the Logical Execution Time (LET) principle, concurrent software components interact deterministically, reading their inputs atomically at the start of a task and producing outputs atomically after a fixed elapsed logical time. In addition to deterministic concurrency, LET programs yield more deterministic timing when they interact with their physical environment through sensors and actuators. This paper shows through a series of examples that the LET principle can be realized flexibly and generalized using the LINGUA FRANCA coordination language.

Keywords: Concurrent software · Distributed systems · Logical execution time

1 Motivation

The Logical Execution Time (LET) principle was pioneered by Tom Henzinger and Christoph Kirsch (with, as always, significant contributions from others), who demonstrated its efficacy and realizability for the design of cyber-physical systems (CPSs) well before the term CPS had been coined [12]. The Giotto programming language, introduced in the very first EMSOFT conference [11] (of which Henzinger and Kirsch were founders), elegantly realized the LET principle in the form of a coordination language, where the business logic of programs was realized in a conventional language (such as C), but the modal behavior, concurrency, and timing were orchestrated by a runtime engine that closely followed the LET principle. This work inspired quite a bit follow-up work, including applications to distributed real-time automotive software [9] and automotive multicore software [3,8]. The LET principle has also been applied to programming time-predictable multicore processors [15], has been used to facilitate parallel execution of legacy software on multicore [29], and has been leveraged for schedulability analysis [14]. Whereas in Giotto execution of components is time driven, the language extensions in xGiotto support asynchronous events [10]. The Timing Definition Language (TDL) applies the LET principle in the context of Matlab/Simulink models [28].

According to Henzinger, et al., the LET principle enables "abstract, platform-independent real-time programming," and is an important step toward separating "reactivity from schedulability" [12,13]. They say,

© Springer Nature Switzerland AG 2022
J.-F. Raskin and K. Chatterjee (Eds.): Principles of Systems Design, LNCS 13660, pp. 160–181, 2022.
https://doi.org/10.1007/978-3-031-22337-2_8

The term reactivity expresses what we mean by control-systems aspects: the system's functionality, in particular, the control laws, and the system's timing requirements. The term schedulability expresses what we mean by platform-dependent aspects, such as platform performance, platform utilization (scheduling), and fault tolerance. Giotto decomposes the development process of embedded control software into high-level real-time programming of reactivity and low-level real-time scheduling of computation and communication. Programming in Giotto is real-time programming in terms of the requirements of control designs, i.e., their reactivity, not their schedulability. [12]

In this paper, we focus on this separation. Reactivity specifies what the designer intends to achieve, whereas schedulability specifies how an execution platform achieves that intent. We begin in Sect. 2 by interpreting this separation as distinct uses of models. In Sect. 3, we review the LET principle. In Sect. 4, we provide a formalism for logical and physical timelines. In Sect. 5, we briefly introduce the LINGUA FRANCA coordination language, and then, in Sect. 6, we give a series of examples of LINGUA FRANCA programs that flexibly apply the LET principle, allowing, for example, mitigation of the data age problem [4]. We make some concluding remarks in Sect. 7.

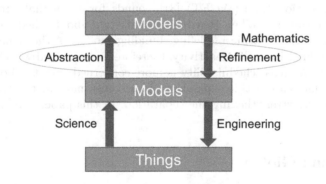

Fig. 1. Relations between models and between models and things.

2 Science, Engineering, and Mathematics

A Giotto program, and indeed any computer program that forms part of a cyber-physical system, is a **model** for the behavior of the electronic part of the system. A microcontroller, with electrons sloshing around inside, is a "thing-in-itself" (to use Kant's term), yet it is expected to behave as specified by programs it executes.

In *Plato and the Nerd*, one of us (Lee) makes a distinction between an **engineering model**, where the thing-in-itself is expected to behave like the model, and a **scientific model**, where the model is expected to behave like the thing-in-itself [20]. These mirror-image relationships are depicted in Fig. 1. While science is concerned with establishing models that capture characteristics of physical things, the goal of engineering is to craft physical things that share properties with models. The disciplines of science and engineering are in a symbiotic relationship with one another; designs are often evaluated through scientific experimentation, and many scientific experiments are enabled by carefully engineered tools.

Models also have utility beyond their relationship to things. Mathematics treats the properties of models and relationships between models unhindered by constraints of physical realizability. In mathematics, **abstraction** is used to derive simpler models from more elaborate ones, and **refinement** is used to elaborate simpler models by adding more specificity. The operations of abstraction and refinement are key in model-based system design, an idea that has been codified in the theory of contracts [2].

When Henzinger, et al., say that Giotto specifies reactivity, what they mean is that the Giotto program serves as an engineering model (as opposed to a scientific model). It is incumbent on the compiler and the execution platform to deliver the timing and concurrency behavior that is specified by the program. Determining whether a particular execution platform can deliver the specified behavior requires a certain amount of scientific modeling, for example to find worst-case execution time (WCET) [31] bounds for tasks that are scheduled by the Giotto runtime. When Henzinger, et al., talk about schedulability, they are concerned with scientific modeling, building models of the behavior of the platform, the thing-in-itself. Reactivity, therefore, is concerned with the bottom right of Fig. 1, whereas schedulability is more concerned with the bottom left.

Once we understand this separation, it becomes natural to generalize the LET principle by strengthening the separation. In this paper, we show how to do that.

3   LET and Giotto

Software for cyber-physical systems is inevitably concurrent and timing sensitive. The time of its interactions with its physical environment is important for determining system behavior, and, unlike many information processing tasks, the goal is not simply to finish as quickly as possible. Concurrency inevitably arises because of the need to react to a multiplicity of sensors and to drive a multiplicity of actuators, and the timing of the stimulus from the sensors and the actuations cannot be arbitrary.

Traditional methods for handling concurrency and timing in software are difficult to make deterministic [17]. Consider Toyota's unintended acceleration case, where in the early 2000s, there were a number of car accidents involving Toyota vehicles that appeared to suffer from unintended acceleration. The US Department of Transportation contracted NASA to study Toyota software to determine whether software was capable of causing unintended acceleration. The

NASA study [27] was unable to find a definitive cause, but they indicted the software architecture [16]. The software used a style of design that tolerates a seemingly innocuous form of nondeterminism. Specifically, many state variables, representing for example the most recent readings from a sensor, were accessed unguarded by a variety of threads. This style of design appeals to control-system engineers because it always uses the most recent value of a sensor or shared variable, minimizing "data age" [4]. But the result is a very large number of possible behaviors that manifest nondeterministically in the field.

Logical execution time (LET) is a principle that delivers both deterministic concurrency and more controllable timing of the interactions with the physical components of the system. However, these two properties, deterministic concurrency and controllable timing, tend to be lumped together. We contend here that interactions between a software component and another software component should be distinguished from interactions between a software component and a physical component. Separating these two types of interaction helps to generalize the LET principle and expand its applicability.

In a LET design, the interaction between software components is defined by a logical timing model, where each task behaves as if it reads its inputs instantaneously at the start of its execution period and writes its output instantaneously after a prespecified amount of logical time has elapsed. If the inputs to the task are coming from a physical component, then the logical time of the start of execution should align reasonably precisely with some local measure of physical time. Similarly, if the outputs from the task are driving actuators, then aligning the logical time of the task completion with the physical time of actuation results in much more precisely controlled timing than we would get if we simply drive the actuator whenever the task completes.

However, if the inputs to a task are coming from another *software* component, or the outputs are going to another software component, there is no need to align these logical times with physical time as long all interactions occur in the *order* specified by their logical timing. For such interactions, for example, a logical execution time of *zero* becomes reasonable and realizable. Synchronous-reactive languages [1] are based on a hypothesis of zero execution time.

In this paper, we observe that the physical timing of interactions between software components is not an important feature of their interaction. Timing of software only matters when interaction is with the physical environment through sensors and actuators. For the interaction between software components, what really matters is determinism, not timing. Controlling their timing is one way to achieve determinism, but it is not the only way. We will give a generalization to LET that preserves determinism but reduces the use of physical timing for governing interactions between software components. Physical timing comes into play only when interacting with the physical world through timers, sensors, and actuators.

4   Logical and Physical Time

In their papers, Henzinger, et al., do not go as far as they could in separating logical and physical time. There are good reasons for this. First, every embedded system designer has a strong intuitive understanding of time, usually governed by the Newtonian model, where time is a continuum and "now" is a pointer into that continuum that advances smoothly and uniformly everywhere.

Here, we will take a different stance and distinguish logical time (a semantic property of programs) from physical time (a measurement by a physical clock). We will insist that the only access to physical time is through imperfect measurements realized by physical clocks. Newtonian time is not available to us. Logical time and physical time will be expected to align at well-chosen points in the execution of programs, only at those points, and only imperfectly.

We are interested in times of events and time intervals between events. A **physical time** $T \in \mathbb{T}$ is an imperfect measurement of time taken from some clock somewhere in the system. The set $\mathbb{T}$ contains all the possible times that a physical clock can report. We assume that $\mathbb{T}$ is totally ordered and includes two special members: $\infty \in \mathbb{T}$ is larger than any time any clock can report, and $-\infty \in \mathbb{T}$ is smaller than any time any clock can report. For example, $\mathbb{T}$ could be the set of integers $\mathbb{Z}$ augmented with the two infinite members.

Given any $T_1, T_2 \in \mathbb{T}$, the **physical time interval** (or just **time interval** if there is no ambiguity) between the two times is written $i = T_1 - T_2$. Time intervals are assumed to be members of a group $\mathbb{I}$ with a largest member ∞ and smallest member $-\infty$ and a commutative and associative addition operation. For example, $\mathbb{I}$ could be the set of integers $\mathbb{Z}$ augmented with the two infinite members. Addition involving the infinite members behaves in the expected way in that for any $i \in \mathbb{I} \setminus \{\infty, -\infty\}$,

$$i + \infty = \infty$$
$$i + (-\infty) = -\infty.$$

We also assume that addition of infinite intervals saturates, as in

$$\infty + \infty = \infty$$
$$(-\infty) + (-\infty) = -\infty$$
$$\infty + (-\infty) \quad \text{is undefined.}$$

Note that we use the same symbols ∞ and $-\infty$ for the special members of both the set of physical times $\mathbb{T}$ and the set of intervals $\mathbb{I}$. We hope this will not create confusion.

Intervals can be added to a physical time value, and we assume that this addition is associative. I.e., for any $T \in \mathbb{T}$ and any $i_1, i_2 \in \mathbb{I}$,

$$T + (i_1 + i_2) = (T + i_1) + i_2 \in \mathbb{T}. \tag{1}$$

Addition of infinite intervals to a time value saturates in a manner similar to addition of infinite intervals.

These idealized requirements for physical times and time intervals can be efficiently approximated in practical implementations. First, it is convenient to have the set $\mathbb{T}$ represent a common definition of physical time, such as Coordinated Universal Time (UTC) because, otherwise, comparisons between times will not correlate with physical reality. In the LINGUA FRANCA language that we use in Sect. 6, $\mathbb{T}$ and $\mathbb{I}$ are both the set of 64-bit integers. A $T \in \mathbb{T}$ is a POSIX-compliant representation of time, where T represents the number of nanoseconds that have elapsed since midnight, January 1, 1970, Greenwich mean time. In the LINGUA FRANCA realization, the largest and smallest 64-bit integers represent ∞ and $-\infty$, respectively, and addition and subtraction respect the above saturation requirements. Note, however, the set of 64-bit integers is not the same as the set $\mathbb{Z}$ because it is finite. As a consequence, addition can overflow. In LINGUA FRANCA, such overflow saturates at ∞ or $-\infty$, and as a consequence, addition is no longer associative. For example, $T + (i_1 + i_2)$ may not overflow while $(T + i_1) + i_2$ does overflow. As a practical matter, however, this will only become a problem with systems that are running near the year 2270. Only then will the behavior deviate from the ideal given by our theory.

For *logical* time, we use an element that we call a **tag** g of a totally-ordered set $\mathbb{G}$. Each event in a distributed system is associated with a tag $g \in \mathbb{G}$. From the perspective of any component of a distributed system, the order in which events occur is defined by the order of their tags. If two distinct events have the same tag, we say that they are **logically simultaneous**. We assume the tag set $\mathbb{G}$ has an element ∞ that is larger than any other tag and another $-\infty$ that is smaller than any other tag.

In the LINGUA FRANCA language, $\mathbb{G} = \mathbb{T} \times \mathbb{U}$, where $\mathbb{U}$ is the set of 32-bit unsigned integers representing the microstep of a superdense time system [5, 7,25]. We use the term **tag** rather than timestamp to allow for such a richer model of logical time. For the purposes of this paper, however, the microsteps will not matter, and hence you can think of a tag as a timestamp and ignore the microstep. We will consistently denote tags with a lower case $g \in \mathbb{G}$ and measurements of physical time $T \in \mathbb{T}$ with upper case.

We will need operations that combine tags and physical times. To do this, we assume a monotonically nondecreasing function $\mathcal{T} \colon \mathbb{G} \to \mathbb{T}$ that gives a physical time interpretation to any tag. For any tag g, we call $\mathcal{T}(g)$ its **timestamp**. In LINGUA FRANCA, for any tag $g = (t, m) \in \mathbb{G}$, $\mathcal{T}(g) = t$. Hence, to get a timestamp from a tag, you just have to ignore the microstep.

The set $\mathbb{G}$ also includes infinite elements such that $\mathcal{T}(\infty_{\mathbb{G}}) = \infty_{\mathbb{T}}$ and $\mathcal{T}(-\infty_{\mathbb{G}}) = -\infty_{\mathbb{T}}$, where the subscripts disambiguate which infinity we are referring to.

An external input from outside the system, such as a user input or query, will be assigned a tag g such that $\mathcal{T}(g) = T$, where T is a measurement of physical time taken from the local clock where the input first enters the system. In LINGUA FRANCA, this tag is normally given microstep 0, $g = (T, 0)$.

To simplify notation, we will assume a **physical time origin** $T = 0$ when a program begins executing, and will set the logical time initially to g_0, where

```
1  target L;
2  reactor ReactorClass {
3      input name:type;
4      ...
5      output name:type;
6      ...
7      state name:type(init);
8      ...
9      ... timers, actions, if any ...
10     ...
11     reaction(trigger, ...) -> effect, ... {=
12         ... code in language L ...
13     =}
14     ... more reactions ...
15 }
16 ...
17 main reactor {
18     instance = new ReactorClass();
19     ...
20     instance.name -> instance.name;
21     ...
22 }
```

Fig. 2. Structure of a LINGUA FRANCA program for target language L.

$T(g_0) = 0$. On POSIX-compliant platforms, this is not what LINGUA FRANCA does. Instead, physical time is the Unix epoch time, the number of nanoseconds that have elapsed since January 1, 1970. Those numbers, however, are difficult to read, so we will give all times relative to the start of program execution.

5   Introduction to LINGUA FRANCA

LINGUA FRANCA (or LF, for short)[1] is a coordination language developed jointly at UC Berkeley, TU Dresden, UT Dallas, and Kiel University [24]. Applications are defined as concurrent compositions of components called **reactors** [21,22]. Figure 2 outlines the structure of a LINGUA FRANCA program. One or more **reactor classes** are defined with **input ports** (line 3), **output ports** (line 5), **state variables** (line 7), and timers and actions. We will elaborate on actions later. Inputs are handled by **reactions**, as shown on line 11. Reactions declare their **triggers**, as on line 11, which can be input ports, timers, or actions. If a reaction lists an output port among its **effects**, then it can produce tagged output messages via that output port. The routing of messages is specified by **connections**, as shown on line 20. The syntax and semantics will become clearer as we develop our specific examples.

6   LET and More in LINGUA FRANCA

In this section, we show through a series of examples how LINGUA FRANCA can realize concurrent programs under the LET principle, but is also more flexible.

---

[1] https://lf-lang.org.

```
1  reactor Sensor(p:time(10 ms)) {
2      output out:int;
3      timer t(0,p);
4      reaction(t) -> out {=
5          ... retrieve sensor data and produce it ...
6      =}
7  }
8  reactor Task1 {
9      input in:int;
10     output out:int;
11     reaction(in) -> out {=
12         ... process sensor data ...
13     =}
14 }
15 reactor Task2 {
16     input in:int;
17     output out:int;
18     reaction(in) -> out {=
19         ... further process sensor data ...
20     =}
21 }
22 reactor Actuator {
23     input in:int;
24     reaction(in) {=
25         ... drive actuator ...
26     =}
27 }
28 main reactor(p:time(10 ms)) {
29     s = new Sensor(p = p);
30     t1 = new Task1();
31     t2 = new Task2();
32     a = new Actuator();
33     s.out -> t1.in;
34     t1.out -> t2.in;
35     t2.out -> a.in;
36 }
```

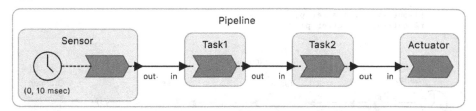

Fig. 3. Basic pipeline.

The key to this flexibility is that LINGUA FRANCA distinguishes logical time from physical time and enables alignment at cyber-physical interaction points [23]. As we go through the examples, we explain in more detail how execution of LINGUA FRANCA programs works.

6.1   Periodic Polled Control System

Consider a pipeline of tasks between a sensor and actuator shown in Fig. 3. One might find this example in the software portion of a feedback control system. The figure on the bottom is automatically generated and displayed by the development tools.[2] The chevrons in the figure represent reactions, and their dependencies on inputs and their ability to produce outputs is shown using dashed lines.

In this example, a sensor is polled with a period given by the parameter p, which has a default value of 10 ms. By default, LINGUA FRANCA reactions are logically instantaneous, so this program is more like a synchronous-reactive program than like a LET program. The timer t produces a sequence of events with tags g_i, $i = 0, 1, 2, \cdots$, where $T(g_i) = 10i$ ms. The runtime system first advances its **current tag** to g_0 and executes all reactions that are triggered at that tag with ordering constraints implied by data dependencies. In this example, it executes the Sensor reaction, and if that reaction produces an output, then it will execute the Task1 reaction. If Task1 produces an output, it will then execute Task2, and finally, if Task2 produces an output, it will execute Actuator. All of these executions will occur at tag g_0, and all will complete before the runtime advances its current tag to g_1.

Note that unlike a LET program, there is no parallelism in this program. Task2 cannot begin executing until Task1 has completed. Moreover, the logical time $T(g_0)$ of the actuation is *the same* as the logical time of sensing, which would not be the case with LET. The physical time at which the actuation occurs will be determined by the execution times of the tasks, again a feature one would not find in a LET design.

```
1  main reactor(p:time(10 ms)) {
2      ...
3      t1.out -> t2.in after p;
4      t2.out -> a.in after p;
5  }
```

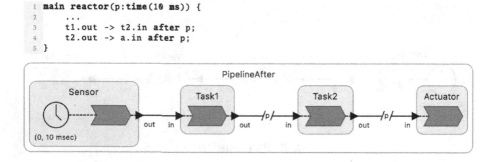

Fig. 4. Pipeline with logical delays, emulating LET.

In Fig. 4 we modify the last two lines of the program in Fig. 3, thereby converting this program to use the LET principle. The syntax "`after p`" specifies that the output produced by `t1.out` at tag g should be received by `t2.out` with tag g', where $T(g') = T(g) + p$. This has several consequences.

---

[2] The diagram synthesis feature was created by Alexander Schulz-Rosengarten of Kiel University using the graphical layout tools from the KIELER Lightweight Diagrams framework [30] (see https://rtsys.informatik.uni-kiel.de/kieler).

First, Task1 and Task2 can execute in parallel, exploiting a multicore architecture. While Task1 is handling sensor data at tag g_i, for $i \geq 1$, Task2 is processing its previous result computed with the sensor data from g_{i-1}.

Second, the latency between sensing and actuation is more constant now and less dependent on execution time. Assuming that Task1 and Task2 each are able to complete within time p, the runtime system will advance its current tag to g_i at physical time $T_i \geq \mathcal{T}(g_i)$, but T_i will be very close to $\mathcal{T}(g_i)$ because the system will have gone idle prior to that physical time. Hence, the physical latency between sensing and actuation will be close to 20 ms with the default value for the parameter $p = 10$ ms.

Compared to Fig. 3, the data delivered to the Actuator is based on older sensor input, so the designer is faced with a tradeoff between data age [4] and predictable, repeatable timing. In many safety-critical systems, repeatable timing is extremely valuable; for one, it greatly enhances the value of testing [18, 26].

Assuming all reactions produce outputs, at each tag g_i for $i \geq 2$, there are three computations that can proceed in parallel. The first is to invoke the Sensor reaction followed by Task1, the second is to invoke Task2, and the third is to invoke the Actuator. If there are at least three cores, then they can all execute in parallel. If there are fewer than three cores, however, we may wish to prioritize the execution the Actuator reaction so that actuation occurs as closely as possible to 20 ms after sensing. In LINGUA FRANCA, a simple way to do this is to assign a deadline to the reaction of the Actuator, as shown in Fig. 5. The LINGUA FRANCA runtime uses an earliest-deadline-first (EDF) scheduling policy, and hence, the mere presence of a deadline ensures that the Actuator reaction will execute before the others.

```
1  ...
2  reactor Actuator {
3      input in:int;
4      reaction(in) {=
5          ... drive actuator ...
6      =} deadline (1 ms) {=
7          ... handle a deadline miss ...
8      =}
9  }
10 main reactor(p:time(10 ms)) {
11     ...
12     t1.out -> t2.in after p;
13     t2.out -> a.in after p;
14 }
```

Fig. 5. Pipeline with deadline.

In addition, the deadline construct provides a **fault handling** mechanism. Line 6 in Fig. 5 specifies a deadline $d = 1$ ms. The meaning of this specification is that if the physical time T at which the runtime system invokes the reaction to an input with tag g is larger than $\mathcal{T}(g)$ by more than d, i.e. $T > \mathcal{T}(g) + d$, then a **deadline miss** has occurred, and the runtime system will invoke the code on line 7 rather than the code on line 5.

There is a subtle difference between these LINGUA FRANCA pipelines and the LET principle as realized in Giotto. The reactions in LINGUA FRANCA are still logically instantaneous even if their outputs are subjected to a logical delay using the `after` keyword. In LINGUA FRANCA, an input or output port is modeled as a function $P\colon \mathbb{G} \to V \cup \{\epsilon\}$, where V is a set of **values** (a data type) and ϵ represents **absent**, the absence of a value. Because P is a function, at each tag g, a port cannot have more than one value. Since reactions are logically instantaneous, therefore, input values do not change during their execution, exactly as in LET. But any output values that are produced during that execution have the same tag as the input that triggered them. This is why downstream reactions have to be executed after completion of upstream reactions if the connection has no logical delay, like the connection between Sensor and Task1. Only then is the input to the downstream reaction known.

6.2   Federated Execution

When executing on a single machine, the current LINGUA FRANCA runtime system completes execution of all reactions at any given tag g before advancing its **current tag** to some $g' > g$. In effect, this imposes a **barrier synchronization** between threads that might be executing in parallel on multiple cores (see Sect. 6.3 for our proposed extension that relaxes this barrier synchronization). The "after" clauses in Fig. 4 enable parallel execution by making available multiple input events to distinct reactors at the same tag.

Another way to achieve parallel execution in LINGUA FRANCA is to remove the barrier synchronization and allow reactors to maintain separate and distinct current tags. This requires that messages between reactors be queued and explicitly tagged so that each reactor can process events in tag order. This can be accomplished by declaring the top-level reactor to be a **federated reactor**, as shown in Fig. 6.[3] When the top-level reactor is declared to be federated, the LINGUA FRANCA code generator produces a separate program for each reactor instantiated within that top level. To get the same degree of parallelism as in Fig. 4, Fig. 6 creates two intermediate reactors called "Bundle1" and "Bundle2." The code generator will produce two programs, one for each Bundle. Each of these programs maintains its own current tag, and, as a consequence, Bundle2 can be processing an earlier tag while Bundle1 is processing a later one. A third program, a **runtime infrastructure** (RTI), coordinates startup and shutdown and possibly mediates communication and regulates advancement of the current tag.

---

[3] Federated execution of LINGUA FRANCA was largely created by Soroush Bateni.

```
1  ...
2  reactor Bundle1 {
3      output out:int;
4      s = new Sensor(p = p);
5      t1 = new Task1();
6      s.out -> t1.in;
7      t1.out -> out;
8  }
9  reactor Bundle2 {
10     input in:int;
11     t2 = new Task2();
12     a = new Actuator();
13     in -> t2.in;
14     t2.out -> a.in;
15 }
16 federated reactor(p:time(10 ms)) {
17     b1 = new Bundle1();
18     b2 = new Bundle2();
19     b1.out -> b2.in;
20 }
```

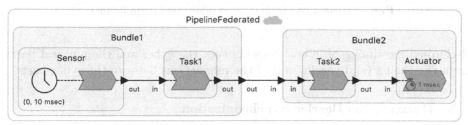

Fig. 6. Federated pipeline.

LINGUA FRANCA provides two distinct mechanisms for coordinating the execution of federated reactors [19]. The default mechanism is **centralized**, where each federate (each Bundle) consults with the RTI before advancing its current tag. This mechanism makes use of knowledge of the interconnection topology. In this example, there are no cycles in the communication pattern, and, consequently, Bundle1 can advance its current tag with no constraints. It has no inputs that might later see messages with earlier tags. Bundle2, however, cannot advance to tag g until it has been assured by the RTI that it has seen all inputs with tags less than g.

In **decentralized** coordination, federates rely on clock synchronization and assumed bounds on communication latencies and advance their current tag to g when their physical clock has advanced sufficiently that, given these assumptions, they have seen all inputs with tags less than g. This principle has been previously used in PTIDES [32] and Google Spanner [6]. For details, see Lee, et al. [19].

In Fig. 6, there are no "after" logical delays, so the timing of actuation relative to sensing will depend on execution times of the task and communication latency between bundles. The latency is bounded by a specified deadline. A single "after" delay on the connection between Task2 and Actuator would be sufficient to get the effect of a logical execution time. But now, this LET represents the logical execution time of the entire pipeline from Sensor to Actuator. We have effectively

```
1  ...
2  main reactor(p:time(10 ms)) {
3      ...
4      timer t(0, 1 ms);
5      reaction(t) {=
6          // ... handle quick reaction ...
7      =} deadline(500 usec) {=
8          // ... handle deadline violation ...
9      =}
10 }
```

Fig. 7. Variant of Fig. 5 with an additional periodic task.

decoupled the timing of interactions between the cyber and the physical parts from the timing (and parallelism) of the interactions between the cyber parts.

6.3   Relaxing the Barrier Synchronization

Consider the variant of Fig. 5 shown in Fig. 7. The only change is the addition of one more reaction that reacts to a timer with a period of one millisecond. When executed on a single machine with one or more cores, the current implementation of the LINGUA FRANCA runtime, with its barrier synchronization, has a major difficulty with this program. In this section, we show how to use the LET principle to eliminate this difficulty.

First, we explain the difficulty with the current runtime system. The reaction shown at the left in the figure is triggered at intervals of one ms and has a deadline of 500 microseconds. The reactions in the pipeline are triggered at intervals of 10 ms, and actuation has a deadline of one ms. At the one-out-of-ten reactions where these periodic events align, tags with 0, 10, 20, ... ms, the unnamed reaction at the left will be given priority over any other reaction because of its tighter deadline. So far so good. But what if the reactions in Task1 or Task2 take more than 1.5 ms to execute? What happens at tags with 1, 11, 21, ... ms? With the barrier synchronization, the execution of the Task1 and Task2 reactions will prevent the advancement of time to 1, 11, 21, ... and will thereby cause a deadline violation in the invocation of the unnamed reaction at those tags!

We could use federated execution to eliminate this problem, but, in practice, a new difficulty will arise because thread priorities will now have to be coordinated across *processes*, not just threads within a process. Moreover, federated execution introduces additional inefficiencies because of the need to send data across processes and the added overhead of coordinating the advancement of tags across processes. It would be better to solve this problem within a single multithreaded process.

We can use the LET principle to eliminate this problem within a single process. In particular, the reactions in Task1 and Task2 have the property that their effects (the outputs they produce) are all delayed by $p = 10$ ms. As a consequence, these two reactions can be temporarily withdrawn from the barrier synchronization to rejoin it only when the tag is to advance to the next 10 ms period. Hence, the tag can be advanced to 1, 11, 21, ... even though these reactions at tags with 0, 10, 20, ... have not yet completed. In a multithreaded execution, even if there is only a single core, the Task1 and Task2 reactions can proceed concurrently and can be preempted by a thread that is to execute the unnamed reaction, thereby avoiding the deadline violation. All that is required is that the underlying thread scheduler respect priorities, and that priorities be assigned to worker threads according to the deadlines of the reactions assigned to them.

The general principle is simple. For any reaction that produces outputs, it can be treated as a LET task with the LET equal to the minimum **after** delay of all of its outputs. The specific treatment is that if the LET is greater than zero, then the worker thread executing the reaction need not participate in the barrier synchronization until the time comes to advance the tag to $t + \text{LET}$. That worker thread can continue executing at logical time t while the rest of the program advances its logical time.

With this enhancement, we claim that LINGUA FRANCA will be capable of everything a classical LET system can do. But it can also do more, a property that becomes obvious when we consider less regular, aperiodic executions, as we do next.

6.4 Event Triggered Execution

In the examples given so far, the sensor input is periodic, polled using a timer. A more interesting scenario arises when inputs from the physical world are events with uncontrolled timing, for example arising through an interrupt request. In LINGUA FRANCA, such an external event is realized with a **physical action**, shown in Fig. 8, which is depicted in the diagram as a triangle with a "P". Line 4 defines the physical action and line 5 defines a reaction that reacts to the physical action. This reactor will also need some additional code (not shown) to interface to some physical device and call a built-in lf_schedule() function to schedule the physical action when an external event occurs. This could be done, for example, in a callback function or an interrupt service routine.

When an external event triggers a call to lf_schedule(), the LINGUA FRANCA runtime system consults the local physical clock, reading from it a time T, and creates an event with tag g such that $T(g) = T$. The reaction on line 5, therefore, will be invoked at tag g, and the timestamp of the tag will represent the physical time of the external event as measured by a local clock.

```
1  ...
2  reactor Event {
3      output out:int;
4      physical action a:int;
5      reaction(a) -> out {=
6          ... retrieve sensor data and produce it ...
7      =}
8  }
9  main reactor(p:time(10 ms)) {
10     s = new Event();
11     t1 = new Task1();
12     t2 = new Task2();
13     a = new Actuator();
14     s.out -> t1.in;
15     t1.out -> t2.in;
16     t2.out -> a.in;
17 }
```

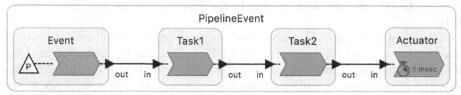

Fig. 8. Event-triggered pipeline.

Notice that, now, using the "after" logical delays of Fig. 4 will *not* yield parallel execution without the enhancement described in the previous section, Sect. 6.3. This is because when a new event with tag g' arrives, it is unlikely to have timestamp $\mathcal{T}(g') = \mathcal{T}(g) + a$, where g is the tag of the previous event and a is the "after" delay. Only if that coincidence occurs can the pipelined reactions execute in parallel (in the absence of our enhancement). Without the enhancement, to get parallel execution, we will have to use a federated program like that of Fig. 6. In this case, parallel execution *is* possible because Task2 may be still processing the previous event when a new event arrives.

This situation, however, reveals a subtlety about the enhancement of Sect. 6.3. Suppose Fig. 8 has **after** delays of 10 ms, like Fig. 4. Suppose that Task1's reaction has withdrawn from the barrier synchronization at tag 10 ms, say, and a new event occurs at tag 12 ms. In this case, it will not do for the reaction to remain withdrawn until 20 ms because this could result in Task1's reaction being invoked at tag 12 while it is still processing the event at tag 10 in some other thread. In LINGUA FRANCA, any two reactions belonging to the same reactor must have mutually exclusive invocations because they share state and there is no assurance that users have written reentrant code. Hence, our enhancement must be careful advancing tags while there are executing reactions that have withdrawn from the barrier synchronization. In particular, if any event at a tag t is about to trigger a reaction belonging to a reactor that has an executing reaction at tag $t' < t$, then that triggered reaction must be blocked until the executing reaction at t' completes. By blocking that reaction, we will also block any reactions that depend on it, thereby preserving determinism.

This raises an interesting and subtle semantic property of LINGUA FRANCA that is not shared with any LET system. Specifically, logically, a reaction *always* executes in zero time in that its local state gets updated without logical time advancing during that updating. Hence, the term "logical execution time" is no longer quite adequate, even though it can match the same concurrency properties of a classical LET system. In a classical LET system, the *local state* takes time to update, not just the externally visible effects, and hence, a classical LET task cannot be interrupted with a new execution during its logical execution time. In LINGUA FRANCA, it *can* be interrupted without undermining its determinism, which is a strict generalization over LET.

Such interruptions, however, may not be a good idea in practical applications. An unconstrained physical action like that of Fig. 8 runs a risk of overwhelming the software system and disrupting timing. If lf_schedule() is called while an earlier event is still being processed, the new event will simply be queued to be handled when prior tags have been fully processed. This could result in an unbounded buildup of queued events, for example if the physical action is triggered by a network input and the system is under a denial-of-service attack.

Fortunately, LINGUA FRANCA provides mechanisms to prevent such eventualities. First, a physical action can have a **minimum spacing** parameter, a minimum logical time interval between tags assigned to events. When the environment tries to violate this constraint by issuing requests too quickly, the programmer can specify one of three policies: drop, replace, or defer. The drop policy simply ignores the event. The replace policy replaces any previously unhandled event, or if the event has already been handled, defers. The defer policy assigns a tag g to the event with timestamp $\mathcal{T}(g)$ that is larger than the previous event by the specified minimum spacing.

While the minimum spacing parameter ensures that tags are sufficiently spaced, it does not, by itself, ensure that the scheduler will prioritize execution of the reaction in the Actuator reactor. We can again specify a **deadline** associated with that reaction, thereby ensuring that the Actuator reaction will execute first, resulting in greater precision in Sensor-to-Actuator latency.

We can further combine minimum spacing, deadlines, and "after" delays to maximize parallelism and timing precision under overload conditions, when the physical action repeatedly triggers with the minimum spacing. The resulting program is shown in Fig. 9. Line 4 declares the physical action to have minimum delay of 0 and a minimum spacing of 10 ms (the minimum delay argument is not relevant to our discussion here). Under burst conditions, this program will experience input events every 10 ms, and after the first two such events, at each 10 ms boundary, the Actuator reaction will have top priority. If two cores are available, then one will execute Actuator followed by Task2 while the other executes Sensor followed by Task1. The latency from Sensor to Actuator will be close to 20 ms, thereby realizing the goals of LET, but now in an event-triggered system rather than a periodic one.

```
1      ...
2      reactor Event {
3          output out:int;
4          physical action a(0, 10 ms);
5          reaction(a) -> out {=
6              ... retrieve sensor data and produce it ...
7          =}
8      }
9      main reactor(p:time(10 ms)) {
10         s = new Event();
11         t1 = new Task1();
12         t2 = new Task2();
13         a = new Actuator();
14         s.out -> t1.in;
15         t1.out -> t2.in after 10 ms;
16         t2.out -> a.in after 10 ms;
17     }
```

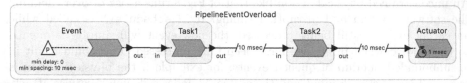

Fig. 9. Event-triggered pipeline optimized for overload conditions.

6.5   Merging Events with Periodic Tasks

A common scenario in cyber-physical systems is that asynchronous events are mixed with periodic actions. For example, a feedback control system may operate with a regular sample rate, but sporadic events may result in changes in the control laws. LINGUA FRANCA provides mechanisms for again achieving regular, tightly controlled timing.

Figure 10 shows an example where a **logical action** (depicted as a triangle with an "L") is used to precisely align the asynchronous events of a physical action with the periodic events of a pipeline. Here, the source code listing gives the details of the modified Event reactor as realized in the C target. This reactor accepts asynchronous events via its physical action, but then delays production of an output until the next logical time that will align with the timer driving the Sensor reactor. Specifically, the reaction defined on line 10 calculates the time interval to the next multiple of 10 ms and schedules a logical action b to trigger at that next multiple of 10 ms. Line 14 calculates a waiting time that is assured to be between 1 ns and 10 ms, where the latter value is chosen in the (unlikely) event that the physical action triggers at exactly the time of one of the timer triggers. That call to lf_schedule() will result in an invocation of the reaction defined on line 6 that will be precisely aligned with the next periodic sensor data, such that the reaction in Task2 will see two simultaneous inputs. The reaction in Task2 checks for the presence of an event on in1. This reaction is guaranteed to be invoked every 10 ms by this program, regardless of the timing of asynchronous inputs, thereby yielding highly deterministic timing. This design relies on the associativity of addition of time intervals.

```
1   target C;
2   reactor Event {
3       output out:int;
4       physical action a(0, 10 ms):int;
5       logical action b:int;
6       reaction(b) -> out {=
7           // Produce as output previously received event.
8           SET(out, b->value);
9       =}
10      reaction(a) -> b {=
11          // Get the time assigned to the physical action.
12          instant_t current_time = get_elapsed_logical_time();
13          // Calculate the time to the next multiple of 10 ms.
14          interval_t wait = MSEC(10) - current_time % MSEC(10);
15          // Schedule a logical action to trigger an output.
16          schedule_int(b, wait, a->value);
17      =}
18  }
19  reactor Task2 {
20      input in1:int;
21      input in2:int;
22      output out:int;
23      reaction(in1, in2) -> out {=
24          if (in1->is_present) {
25              // ... react to asynchronous event ...
26          } else if (in2->is_present) {
27              // ... react to periodic event ...
28          }
29      =}
30  }
31  ...
```

Fig. 10. Merging of asynchronous events with periodic ones.

6.6 Shared State

In Giotto, there is an assumption that tasks do not interact except through their input and output ports. In LINGUA FRANCA, in contrast, reactions within the same reactor can share state variables. Figure 11 shows a variant of Fig. 10 that takes advantage of this feature to realize a common pattern, where an asynchronous event changes the control law used to process periodic events.

The new version of Task2 now has two distinct reactions, one of which reacts to the asynchronous event by changing the control law, and the other of which reacts to the periodic inputs to apply the control law. On line 6, a state variable named "control_law" is defined. In LINGUA FRANCA semantics, if the two input ports have simultaneous input events, then the first reaction executes to completion before the second reaction executes, so access to the state variable is mutually exclusive and deterministically ordered. No such ordering is enforced between reactions across different reactors, enabling parallel execution of logically simultaneously triggered reactions that do not share state.

Notice in Fig. 11 that we no longer need the logical action of Fig. 10. The effect of the new control law is guaranteed to align with the 10 ms timing of the periodic events.

```
1   ...
2   reactor Task2 {
3       input in1:int;
4       input in2:int;
5       output out:int;
6       state control_law:int;
7       reaction(in1) {=
8           // Change control law.
9           self->control_law = in1->value;
10      =}
11      reaction(in2) -> out {=
12          // ... process sensor data using control_law state variable ...
13      =}
14  }
15  reactor Event {
16      output out:int;
17      physical action a(0, 10 ms):int;
18      reaction(a) -> out {=
19          SET(out, a->value);
20      =}
21  }
22  ...
```

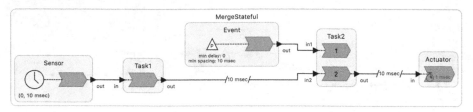

Fig. 11. Reactor with a state variable.

7   Conclusions

The LET principle accomplishes two distinct things. First it specifies the timing of the interaction between a software component and its environment, which consists of other software components and physical sensors and actuators. Second, perhaps even more importantly, it provides a deterministic concurrency model. That is, the interaction between software components does not depend on their execution time (as long as WCET bounds are respected).

We have shown that these two principles can be better separated. In LINGUA FRANCA, the deterministic concurrency model is provided by the use of tags that realize a logical timeline. This logical timeline is decoupled from physical time except at points where the program interacts with its physical environment by explicitly invoking timers, physical actions, and deadlines.

The result generalizes the LET principle, enabling combinations of logical execution time with the zero execution time semantics of synchronous languages while preserving the ability to precisely control the timing of interactions with the physical environment. LINGUA FRANCA also does not restrict the use of LET to periodic systems.

Acknowledgments. The authors would like to acknowledge and thank the following people for their contributions to the design and implementation of LINGUA FRANCA: Soroush Bateni, Peter Donovan, Clément Fournier, Hokeun Kim, Shaokai Lin, Christian Menard, Alexander Schulz-Rosengarten, Matt Weber, and Steven Wong. We also thank Libero Nigro and anonymous reviewers for constructive suggestions. The work in this paper was supported in part by iCyPhy (the Industrial Cyber-Physical Systems) research center, supported by Denso, Siemens, and Toyota.

References

1. Benveniste, A., Berry, G.: The synchronous approach to reactive and real-time systems. Proc. IEEE **79**(9), 1270–1282 (1991)
2. Benveniste, A., et al.: Contracts for system design. Research Report RR-8147, INRIA, November 2012. https://hal.inria.fr/hal-00757488
3. Biondi, A., Natale, M.D.: Achieving predictable multicore execution of automotive applications using the LET paradigm. In: IEEE Real-Time and Embedded Technology and Applications Symposium (RTAS), April 2018. https://doi.org/10.1109/RTAS.2018.00032
4. Bradatsch, C., Kluge, F., Ungerer, T.: Data age diminution in the logical execution time model. In: Hannig, F., Cardoso, J.M.P., Pionteck, T., Fey, D., Schröder-Preikschat, W., Teich, J. (eds.) ARCS 2016. LNCS, vol. 9637, pp. 173–184. Springer, Cham (2016). https://doi.org/10.1007/978-3-319-30695-7_13
5. Cataldo, A., Lee, E.A., Liu, X., Matsikoudis, E., Zheng, H.: A constructive fixed-point theorem and the feedback semantics of timed systems. In: Workshop on Discrete Event Systems (WODES) (2006)
6. Corbett, J.C., et al.: Spanner: Google's globally-distributed database. In: OSDI (2012). https://doi.org/10.1145/2491245
7. Cremona, F., Lohstroh, M., Broman, D., Lee, E.A., Masin, M., Tripakis, S.: Hybrid co-simulation: it's about time. Softw. Syst. Model. **18**(3), 1655–1679 (2017). https://doi.org/10.1007/s10270-017-0633-6
8. Ernst, R., Kuntz, S., Quinton, S., Simons, M.: The logical execution time paradigm: new perspectives for multicore systems (Dagstuhl Seminar 18092). Dagstuhl Rep. **8**, 122–149 (2018). https://doi.org/10.4230/DagRep.8.2.122. https://hal.inria.fr/hal-01956964
9. Gemlau, K.B., Köhler, L., Ernst, R., Quinton, S.: System-level logical execution time: augmenting the logical execution time paradigm for distributed real-time automotive software. ACM Trans. Cyber-Phys. Syst. **5**(2), 1–27 (2021). https://doi.org/10.1145/3381847
10. Ghosal, A., Henzinger, T.A., Kirsch, C.M., Sanvido, M.A.A.: Event-driven programming with logical execution times. In: Alur, R., Pappas, G.J. (eds.) HSCC 2004. LNCS, vol. 2993, pp. 357–371. Springer, Heidelberg (2004). https://doi.org/10.1007/978-3-540-24743-2_24
11. Henzinger, T.A., Horowitz, B., Kirsch, C.M.: Giotto: a time-triggered language for embedded programming. In: Henzinger, T.A., Kirsch, C.M. (eds.) EMSOFT 2001. LNCS, vol. 2211, pp. 166–184. Springer, Heidelberg (2001). https://doi.org/10.1007/3-540-45449-7_12

12. Henzinger, T.A., Horowitz, B., Kirsch, C.M.: Giotto: a time-triggered language for embedded programming. Proc. IEEE **91**(1), 84–99 (2003). https://doi.org/10.1109/JPROC.2002.805825

13. Henzinger, T.A., Kirsch, C.M., Sanvido, M.A.A., Pree, W.: From control models to real-time code using Giotto. IEEE Control Syst. Mag. **23**(1), 50–64 (2003). https://doi.org/10.1109/MCS.2003.1172829

14. Hladik, P.E.: A brute-force schedulability analysis for formal model under logical execution time assumption. In: ACM Symposium on Applied Computing (SAC), pp. 609–615 (2018). https://doi.org/10.1145/3167132.3167199

15. Kluge, F., Schoeberl, M., Ungerer, T.: Support for the logical execution time model on a time-predictable multicore processor. ACM SIGBED Rev. **13**(4), 61–66 (2016). https://doi.org/10.1145/3015037.3015047

16. Koopman, P.: A case study of Toyota unintended acceleration and software safety (2014). http://betterembsw.blogspot.com/2014/09/a-case-study-of-toyota-unintended.html

17. Lee, E.A.: The problem with threads. Computer **39**(5), 33–42 (2006)

18. Lee, E.A.: Determinism. ACM Trans. Embed. Comput. Syst. (TECS) **20**(5), 1–34 (2021). https://doi.org/10.1145/3453652

19. Lee, E.A., Bateni, S., Lin, S., Lohstroh, M., Menard, C.: Quantifying and generalizing the CAP theorem. arXiv:2109.07771 [cs.DC], 16 September 2021

20. Lee, E.A.: Plato and the Nerd - The Creative Partnership of Humans and Technology. MIT Press, Cambridge (2017)

21. Lohstroh, M.: Reactors: a deterministic model of concurrent computation for reactive systems. Ph.D. thesis, EECS Department, University of California, Berkeley, December 2020. http://www2.eecs.berkeley.edu/Pubs/TechRpts/2020/EECS-2020-235.html

22. Lohstroh, M., et al.: Reactors: a deterministic model for composable reactive systems. In: Chamberlain, R., Edin Grimheden, M., Taha, W. (eds.) CyPhy/WESE 2019. LNCS, vol. 11971, pp. 59–85. Springer, Cham (2020). https://doi.org/10.1007/978-3-030-41131-2_4

23. Lohstroh, M., Lee, E.A.: A language for deterministic coordination across multiple timelines. In: 2020 Forum for Specification and Design Languages, FDL 2020, Kiel, Germany, pp. 1–8. IEEE, 15–17 September 2020

24. Lohstroh, M., Menard, C., Bateni, S., Lee, E.A.: Toward a Lingua Franca for deterministic concurrent systems. ACM Trans. Embed. Comput. Syst. (TECS) **20**(4), Article 36 (2021). https://doi.org/10.1145/3448128

25. Maler, O., Manna, Z., Pnueli, A.: From timed to hybrid systems. In: de Bakker, J.W., Huizing, C., de Roever, W.P., Rozenberg, G. (eds.) REX 1991. LNCS, vol. 600, pp. 447–484. Springer, Heidelberg (1992). https://doi.org/10.1007/BFb0032003

26. Martinez, J., Sañudo, I., Bertogna, M.: Analytical characterization of end-to-end communication delays with logical execution time. IEEE Trans. Comput. Aided Des. Integr. Circuits Syst. **37**(11), 2244–2254 (2018). https://doi.org/10.1109/TCAD.2018.2857398

27. NASA Engineering and Safety Center: National highway traffic safety administration Toyota unintended acceleration investigation. Technical assessment report, NASA, 18 January 2011

28. Pree, W., Templ, J.: Modeling with the timing definition language (TDL). In: Broy, M., Krüger, I.H., Meisinger, M. (eds.) ASWSD 2006. LNCS, vol. 4922, pp. 133–144. Springer, Heidelberg (2008). https://doi.org/10.1007/978-3-540-70930-5_9

29. Resmerita, S., Naderlinger, A., Lukesch, S.: Efficient realization of logical execution times in legacy embedded software. In: ACM-IEEE International Conference on Formal Methods and Models for System Design (MEMOCODE), pp. 36–45, September 2017. https://doi.org/10.1145/3127041.3127054
30. Schneider, C., Spönemann, M., von Hanxleden, R.: Just model! - putting automatic synthesis of node-link-diagrams into practice. In: Proceedings of the IEEE Symposium on Visual Languages and Human-Centric Computing (VL/HCC 2013), San Jose, CA, USA, pp. 75–82, September 2013
31. Wilhelm, R., et al.: The worst-case execution-time problem-overview of methods and survey of tools. ACM Trans. Embed. Comput. Syst.(TECS) 7(3), 1–53 (2008)
32. Zhao, Y., Lee, E.A., Liu, J.: A programming model for time-synchronized distributed real-time systems. In: Real-Time and Embedded Technology and Applications Symposium (RTAS), pp. 259–268. IEEE (2007)

Automata, Logic and Games

Towards a Grand Unification of Büchi Complementation Constructions

Moshe Y. Vardi[1], Seth Fogarty[2], Yong Li[3]([✉]), and Yih-Kuen Tsay[4]

[1] Department of Computer Science, Rice University, Houston, USA
[2] Department of Computer Science, Trinity University, San Antonio, USA
[3] State Key Laboratory of Computer Science, Institute of Software, Chinese Academy of Sciences, Beijing, China
`liyong@ios.ac.cn`
[4] National Taiwan University, Taipei, Taiwan

Abstract. The complementation construction for nondeterministic word automata has numerous applications in formal verification. In particular, the language-containment problem, to which many verification problems are reduced, involves complementation. For automata on finite words, which correspond to safety properties, complementation is typically done by determinization using the subset construction. For Büchi automata on infinite words, which are required for the modeling of liveness properties, optimal complementation constructions are quite complicated, as the subset construction is not sufficient. Over the years, three different constructions have been developed for Büchi complementation, based on congruence relations (via Ramsey analysis), progress ranks, and profiles. In this work we unify the three constructions, by showing how profiles can also yield both optimal congruence relations and progress ranks.

1 Introduction

Complementation of nondeterministic word automta is a fundamental operation for both the automata-based model checking [40] and program termination checking [14]. In particular, in the automata-based model checking [40] framework, the verification problem of whether the behavior of a system A satisfies a specification B reduces to a language-containment problem between the corresponding automata modelling A and B, which is then reduced to the intersection of A and the complement of B. For verifying safety properties, automata on finite words [22] are sufficient, while for liveness properties, nondeterministic Büchi automata on *infinite* words (NBWs) [6], are usually utilized [40], as verification requires to represent the properties of nonterminating systems with infinite-length behaviors. This work focuses on the *complementation* of NBWs.

It is known that for automata on finite words, complementation involves determinization via the standard subset construction [18]. For NBWs, however, optimal complementation constructions are quite complicated, as the subset construction is not sufficient [34]. NBWs were originally proposed to prove the decidability of a restricted monadic second-order logic [6]. In previous work [6], Büchi

J.-F. Raskin and K. Chatterjee (Eds.): Principles of Systems Design, LNCS 13660, pp. 185–207, 2022.
https://doi.org/10.1007/978-3-031-22337-2_9

formulated the first proof of the existence of a complementary NBW implicitly using second-order formulae. Büchi's idea for complementation relies on a congruence relation and one can associate each equivalence class of the congruence relation with a state of the complementary automaton, similarly to the characterization provided by the Myhill-Nerode theorem for regular languages [18]. Due to the use of Ramsey's theorem in the proof, Büchi's complementation is widely referred to as *Ramsey-based* Büchi complementation. In this work, we will refer Büchi's complementation to as the *congruence-based* construction because it is defined with congruence relations. The congruence-based construction was later improved by Sistla *et al.* in 1987 with a blow-up of $2^{\mathcal{O}(n^2)}$ [34]. In 1988, Safra described a $2^{\mathcal{O}(n \log n)}$ complementation [32], widely known as the *determinization-based* complementation, matching the lower bound $2^{\Omega(n \log n)}$ established by Michel [27]. Work on complementation since then has focused on either providing simpler complementation algorithms with optimal complexity $2^{\mathcal{O}(n \log n)}$, such as *rank-based* complementation [22] and *slice-based* complementation [19], or further tightening the lower and upper bounds [33,41].

Over the past few decades, there are mainly three types of complementation constructions that have been actively studied, namely the congruence-based (alternatively Ramsey-based) [1,2,5,13,14,24,32], rank-based [8,12,15–17,20,22,33], and slice-based [3,12,19,36] constructions. Existing *direct* complementation constructions, in contrast to those going through determinization, all fall into one of the three types. The core idea of a complementation construction for NBWs is to identify the set of words rejected by the input NBW. To that end, rank-based constructions rely on progress ranks [21], while slice-based constructions were originally based on the construction of reduced split trees. In [12], the rank-based construction and slice-based construction are unified with a profile-based analysis, yielding a construction based on retrospective ranking.

Both rank-based and slice-based complementation constructions are based on tracking the (reduced) run DAG of an ω-word and determine whether the corresponding ω-word is accepted. Both constructions see an ω-word as a whole, while the congruence-based construction decomposes an ω-word into a finite prefix and a periodic finite word. This is why the congruence-based approach seems difficult to be related or unified with the rank-based and slice-based constructions so far. In this work, we further show that the profile-based analysis can also be applied to the congruence-based construction. This novel insight shows the connection between profiles and congruences, concluding that the three major constructions can all be unified based on profiles.

2   Preliminaries

We fix an *alphabet* Σ, and define a *word* as a finite or infinite sequence of letters from Σ. Let Σ^* and Σ^ω denote the set of all finite and infinite words (or ω-words), respectively. A *finitary language* is a subset of Σ^*; an ω-*language* is a subset of Σ^ω. Let L be a finitary language (resp., ω-language); the complementary language of L, written as $\overline{L}$, is $\Sigma^* \setminus L$ (resp., $\Sigma^\omega \setminus L$). Let ρ be a sequence; we denote by $\rho[i]$ the i-th element of ρ, and by $\rho[i..k]$ the subsequence of ρ starting at the i-th element and ending at the k-th element, inclusively. When $i > k$, then $\rho[i..k]$ is taken to be the empty sequence ϵ. We denote by $|\rho|$ the number of elements in ρ. We denote by $[m]$ the set $\{0, \cdots, m-1\}$ for $m > 0$. Given a finite word u and a word w, we denote by $u \cdot w$ (uw, for short) the concatenation of u and w. Given a finitary language L_1 and a finitary/ω-language L_2, the concatenation $L_1 \cdot L_2$ ($L_1 L_2$, for short) of L_1 and L_2 is the set $\{ u \cdot w \mid u \in L_1, w \in L_2 \}$ and L_1^ω the infinite concatenation of L_1.

Automata. A (nondeterministic) automaton is a tuple $\mathcal{A} = (Q, I, \delta, F)$, where Q is a finite set of states, $I \subseteq Q$ is a set of initial states, $\delta \colon Q \times \Sigma \to 2^Q$ is a transition function, and $F \subseteq Q$ is a set of accepting states. We extend δ to sets $S \subseteq Q$ of states, by letting $\delta(S, a) = \bigcup_{q \in S} \delta(q, a)$. We also extend δ to finite words, by letting $\delta(S, \epsilon) = S$ and $\delta(S, a_1 a_2 \cdots a_k) = \delta(\delta(S, a_1), \cdots, a_k)$ for $k \geq 1$. When running on finite words, an automaton is called a *nondeterministic automaton on finite words* (NFW), while an automaton on ω-words is called a *nondeterministic* Büchi *automaton on infinite words* (NBW). An automaton $\mathcal{A}$ is said to be *deterministic* if $|I| = 1$ and, for each $q \in Q$ and $a \in \Sigma$, it holds that $|\delta(q, a)| \leq 1$; when considered on finite words, $\mathcal{A}$ is called a DFW, while in the context of infinite words, it is called DBW.

A *run* of an NFW/NBW $\mathcal{A}$ on a finite word u of length $n \geq 0$ is a sequence of states $\rho = q_0 q_1 \cdots q_n \in Q^+$, such that $q_0 \in I$ and $q_i \in \delta(q_{i-1}, u[i])$ for every $0 < i \leq n$. A finite word $u \in \Sigma^*$ is *accepted* by an NFW $\mathcal{A}$ if there is a run $q_0 \cdots q_n$ over u such that $q_n \in F$. Similarly, an ω-*run* of an NBW $\mathcal{A}$ on an ω-word w is an infinite sequence of states $\rho = q_0 q_1 \cdots$ such that $q_0 \in I$ and, for every $i > 0$, $q_i \in \delta(q_{i-1}, w[i])$. Let $Inf(\rho)$ be the set of states that occur infinitely often in the run ρ. An ω-word $w \in \Sigma^\omega$ is *accepted* by an NBW $\mathcal{A}$ if there is an ω-run ρ of $\mathcal{A}$ over w such that $Inf(\rho) \cap F \neq \emptyset$. The *finitary language* recognized by an NFW $\mathcal{A}$, denoted by $\mathcal{L}_*(\mathcal{A})$, is defined as the set of finite words accepted by it. Similarly, we denote by $\mathcal{L}(\mathcal{A})$ the ω-*language* recognized by an NBW $\mathcal{A}$, i.e., the set of ω-words accepted by $\mathcal{A}$. The complementation construction of $\mathcal{A}$ is to construct an NBW that accepts the complementary language of $\mathcal{A}$, i.e., $\overline{\mathcal{L}(\mathcal{A})}$. We note that the index of words starts with 1, in contrast to 0 for other sequences, such as runs.

Directed acyclic graphs of runs (or run DAGs) were proposed by Kupferman and Vardi in [23] for reasoning about all runs of an NBW on a given ω-word w. Let $\mathcal{A} = (Q, I, \delta, F)$ be an NBW and w be an ω-word. The run DAG $\mathcal{G}_w = \langle V, E \rangle$ of $\mathcal{A}$ over w is defined as follows:

- The vertices $V \subseteq Q \times \mathbb{N}$ is the set $\{ \langle q, l \rangle \mid l \in \mathbb{N}, q \in \delta(I, w[1..l]) \}$.
- Edges: There is an edge from $\langle q, l \rangle$ to $\langle q', l' \rangle$ if $l' = l + 1$ and $q' \in \delta(q, w[l'])$.

A vertex $\langle q, l \rangle$ is said to be on level l; note there are at most $|Q|$ states on each level. A vertex $\langle q, l \rangle$ is called an *F-vertex* if $q \in F$. A finite (infinite) sequence of vertices $\hat{\rho} = \langle q_0, 0 \rangle \langle q_1, 1 \rangle \cdots$ is called a *branch* (resp. ω-*branch*) of $\mathcal{G}_w$ when for each $0 \leq l < k$ (resp. $0 \leq l$), there is an edge from $\langle q_l, l \rangle$ to $\langle q_{l+1}, l+1 \rangle$.

A vertex $\langle q_j, j \rangle$ is *reachable* from $\langle q_l, l \rangle$ if there is a path from $\langle q_l, l \rangle$ to $\langle q_j, j \rangle$. We call a vertex $\langle q, l \rangle$ *finite* in $\mathcal{G}_w$ if it is not on an ω-branch; we call a vertex $\langle q, l \rangle$ *F-free* if it is not finite and no F-vertices are reachable from $\langle q, l \rangle$ in $\mathcal{G}_w$. To a run $\rho = q_1 q_2 \cdots$ of $\mathcal{A}$ over w corresponds an ω-branch $\hat{\rho} = \langle q_0, 0 \rangle \langle q_1, 1 \rangle \cdots$. Therefore, w is accepted by $\mathcal{A}$ iff there is an ω-branch in $\mathcal{G}_w$ visiting F-vertices infinitely often; such an ω-branch is said to be *accepting*. $\mathcal{G}_w$ is accepting iff there is an accepting ω-branch in $\mathcal{G}_w$.

3 Complementation via Profiles

In this section we present the profile-based complementation algorithm introduced in [12], which is an alternative presentation of the slice-based complementation construction [19]. This construction uses a notion of *profiles* for the run DAGs, defined first over branches and then over vertices.

3.1 Profiles

Fix a run DAG $\mathcal{G}_w = \langle V, E \rangle$ of an NBW $\mathcal{A} = (Q, I, \delta, F)$ over a word $w \in \Sigma^\omega$. Let $\mathbf{f}_F : V \to \{0, 1\}$ be such that $\mathbf{f}_F(\langle q, i \rangle) = 1$ if $q \in F$ and $\mathbf{f}_F(\langle q, i \rangle) = 0$ otherwise. Thus, $\mathbf{f}_F$ labels F-vertices by 1 and all other vertices by 0. We first define the *profile* of a branch in $\mathcal{G}_w$ as the sequence of labels of vertices in the branch. For a finite branch $b = v_0 v_1 \ldots v_n$ in $\mathcal{G}_w$, define the profile of b, written as h_b, to be $\mathbf{f}_F(v_0) \mathbf{f}_F(v_1) \cdots \mathbf{f}_F(v_n)$. For an ω-branch $b = v_0 v_1 \ldots$, its profile is $h_b = \mathbf{f}_F(v_0) \mathbf{f}_F(v_1) \cdots$. We next define the profile of a vertex in $\mathcal{G}_w$ to be the lexicographically *maximal* profile of all branches that end in that vertex. Formally, let $\leq$ be the lexicographic ordering on $\{0, 1\}^* \cup \{0, 1\}^\omega$ such that $h_b < h_{b'}$ if there is a prefix $\alpha 0$ of h_b and $\alpha 1$ is a prefix of $h_{b'}$. We then say that h_b is lexicographically *smaller* than $h_{b'}$. Finally, the profile of a vertex v, written as h_v, is the lexicographically maximal element of $\{ h_b \mid b \text{ is a branch to } v \}$.

The lexicographic order of profiles induces a preorder over the vertices/states on the same level. The sequence of preorders $\preceq_i$ over the vertices/states on level $i \geq 0$ of $\mathcal{G}_w$ are defined as follows.

Definition 1 (Preorder $\preceq_i$). *For every two vertices u and v on level $i \geq 0$ in $\mathcal{G}_w$, we have that $u \prec_i v$ if $h_u < h_v$, $u \preceq_i v$ if $h_u \leq h_v$ and $u \approx_i v$ if $h_u = h_v$.*

By abuse of terminology, we can conflate vertices on level i of $\mathcal{G}_w$ with their underlying states and say $q \preceq_i r$ when $\langle q, i \rangle \preceq_i \langle r, i \rangle$.

One can verify that every two vertices/states on level i are comparable under $\preceq_i$ by definition. We also use the preorder $\preceq_i$ over states in Sects. 3.2 and 5.2. As $\preceq_i$ is transitive, $\approx_i$ is an equivalence relation.

For a vertex v on level i, its equivalence class under $\approx_i$ is denoted as $[v]_{\approx_i}$, or simply $[v]$ when it is clear from the context. Since the last element of a vertex's profile is 1 iff the vertex is an F-vertex, all vertices in an equivalence class of $\approx_i$ must agree on membership in F. We call an equivalence class an F-class when all its members are F-vertices, and a non-F-class when none of its members is an F-vertex.

We now use profiles in order to remove from $\mathcal{G}_w$ edges that are not on lexicographically maximal branches. Let $\mathcal{G}'_w = \langle V, E' \rangle$ be the subgraph of $\mathcal{G}_w$ induced by removing all edges (u, v) where there is an edge (u', v) such that $u \prec_{|u|} u'$.

Intuitively, we only keep the ω-branch with the maximal profile among the ω-branches that join together in the pruned run DAG $\mathcal{G}'_w$. Observe that the removal of such edges does not change the profiles of vertices, and further that vertices derive their profiles from their parents in $\mathcal{G}'_w$, as formalized here:

Lemma 1 ([12]). *For every two vertices u and v in $\mathcal{G}'_w$ (and hence $\mathcal{G}_w$), if $(u, v) \in E'$, then $h_v \in \{h_u 0, h_u 1\}$.*

While it is possible for two vertices with different profiles to share a child in $\mathcal{G}_w$, Lemma 1 precludes this possibility in $\mathcal{G}'_w$. If two vertices join in $\mathcal{G}'_w$, they must have the same profile and be in the same equivalence class. We can thus conflate vertices and equivalence classes, and for every edge $(u, v) \in E'$, consider the equivalence class $[v]$ of v to be the child of the equivalence class $[u]$ of u. Lemma 1 then entails that the class $[u]$ can have at most two children: the class of F-vertices with profile $h_u 1$, and the class of non-F-vertices with profile $h_u 0$. We call the first class the F-child, and the second class the non-F-child of $[u]$.

By using lexicographic ordering we can derive the preorder for level $i + 1$ of $\mathcal{G}_w$ solely from the preorder for the previous level i. To determine the ordering relation between two vertices, we need only know the relation between the parents of those vertices, and whether the vertices are F-vertices. Formally:

Lemma 2 ([12]). *For vertices u, v on level i, and vertices u', v' where $(u, u') \in E'$ and $(v, v') \in E'$ hold in $\mathcal{G}'_w$, we have:*

- *If $u \prec_i v$, then $u' \prec_{i+1} v'$.*
- *If $u \approx_i v$ and either both u' and v' are F-vertices, or neither are F-vertices, then $u' \approx_{i+1} v'$.*
- *If $u \approx_i v$ and v' is an F-vertex while u' is not, then $u' \prec_{i+1} v'$.*

We guarantee the correctness of the pruning on $\mathcal{G}_w$ with Lemma 3: an accepting ω-branch can only be pruned when it joins with another accepting ω-branch. Therefore we still capture an accepting ω-branch in $\mathcal{G}'_w$ for an accepting run DAG $\mathcal{G}_w$, as justified by Lemma 3.

Lemma 3 ([12]). *$\mathcal{G}'_w$ has an accepting branch iff $\mathcal{G}_w$ has an accepting branch.*

As a further step of pruning, we remove from $\mathcal{G}'_w$ all finite vertices. Let $\mathcal{G}''_w = \mathcal{G}'_w \setminus \{ v \mid v \text{ is finite in } \mathcal{G}'_w \}$. Note there may be vertices that are not finite in $\mathcal{G}_w$ but are finite in $\mathcal{G}'_w$. An important observation is that $\mathcal{G}_w$ may have infinitely many F-vertices, and still not contain an accepting branch: there may be infinitely many branches each with a finite number of F-vertices. Lemma 4 demonstrates that the transition from $\mathcal{G}_w$ via $\mathcal{G}'_w$ to $\mathcal{G}''_w$ removes this possibility, and the presence of infinitely many F-vertices in $\mathcal{G}''_w$ does imply the existence of an accepting branch.

Lemma 4 ([12]). $\mathcal{G}_w$ *has an accepting* ω-*branch iff* $\mathcal{G}''_w$ *has infinitely many* F-*vertices.*

The property of $\mathcal{G}''_w$ in Lemma 4 is vital for the profile-based complementation construction, as shown in Sect. 3.2.

3.2 Complementing with Profiles

We now complement the Büchi automaton $\mathcal{A} = (Q, I, \delta, F)$ by constructing an NBW $\mathcal{B}_p$ that employs Lemma 4 to determine if an ω-word w is in $L(\mathcal{A})$. The NBW $\mathcal{B}_p$ constructs $\mathcal{G}'_w$ level by level, while guessing which vertices are finite in $\mathcal{G}'_w$ and therefore not present in $\mathcal{G}''_w$. To build $\mathcal{G}'_w$, $\mathcal{B}_p$ encodes each level as a set S of states that occurs on the level. Every such set S is labeled with a guess of which vertices are finite and which are infinite. States that are guessed to be infinite, which are thus kept in $\mathcal{G}''_w$, are labeled $\top$. States that are guessed to be finite, which are thus omitted from $\mathcal{G}''_w$, are labeled $\bot$. In order to track the edges of $\mathcal{G}'_w$, $\mathcal{B}_p$ needs to know the lexicographic order of vertices. Thus $\mathcal{B}_p$ also maintains the preorder $\preceq_i$ as in Definition 1 over states on the corresponding level of $\mathcal{G}'_w$. To verify whether states labeled $\bot$ are indeed finite, $\mathcal{B}_p$ utilizes the cut-point construction of Miyano and Hayashi [28], keeping an "obligation set" of states currently being verified as finite. Finally, to ensure that w is rejected by $\mathcal{A}$, $\mathcal{B}_p$ enforces that there are finitely many F-vertices in $\mathcal{G}''_w$, using a bit b to guess the level from which no more F-vertices appear in $\mathcal{G}''_w$. From this point on, it enforces that all F-vertices are labeled $\bot$.

Before we define $\mathcal{B}_p$, we formalize *preordered subsets* in Definition 1 and operations over them. For a set Q of states, we define $\mathbf{Q} = \{\langle S, \preceq \rangle \mid S \subseteq Q\}$ to be the set of preordered subsets of Q where $\preceq$ is a preorder over S. Note that we write $\preceq_i$ as $\preceq$ here since the level number can be omitted. Let $\langle S, \preceq \rangle$ be an element in $\mathbf{Q}$. When considering the successors of a state, we only consider edges that remain in $\mathcal{G}'_w$. Formally, for every state $q \in S$ and $\sigma \in \Sigma$, define $\rho_{\langle S, \preceq \rangle}(q, \sigma) = \{r \in \delta(q, \sigma) \mid \text{for every} q' \in S, \text{if } r \in \delta(q', \sigma) \text{then} q' \preceq q\}$. Intuitively, $\rho_{\langle S, \preceq \rangle}(q, \sigma)$ defines the set of states at the next level in $\mathcal{G}'_w$ that can be reached by q.

Definition 2. *We define the* σ-*successor of* $\langle S, \preceq \rangle$ *as the tuple* $\langle \delta(S, \sigma), \preceq' \rangle$, *denoted as* $\langle \delta(S, \sigma), \preceq' \rangle = \mathcal{T}(\langle S, \preceq \rangle, \sigma)$, *where for every* $q, r \in S$, $q' \in \rho_{\langle S, \preceq \rangle}(q, \sigma)$, *and* $r' \in \rho_{\langle S, \preceq \rangle}(r, \sigma)$:

- *If* $q \prec r$, *then* $q' \prec' r'$.
- *If* $q \approx r$ *and either both* $r' \in F$ *and* $q' \in F$, *or both* $r' \notin F$ *and* $q' \notin F$, *then* $q' \approx' r'$.
- *If* $q \approx r$ *and one of* q' *and* r', *say* r', *is in* F *while the other,* q', *is not, then* $q' \prec' r'$.

One can see that the preorder $\preceq'$ over $\delta(S, \sigma)$ is exactly the one defined in Lemma 2 excluding the level number $i + 1$.

We now define $\mathcal{B}_p$. The states of $\mathcal{B}_p$ are tuples $\langle S, \preceq, \lambda, O, b \rangle$ where: $\langle S, \preceq \rangle \in$ **Q** is preordered subset of Q; $\lambda : S \rightarrow \{\top, \bot\}$ is a labeling indicating which states are guessed to be finite ($\bot$) or infinite ($\top$), $O \subseteq S$ is the obligation set, and $b \in \{0, 1\}$ is a bit indicating whether we have seen the last F-vertex in $\mathcal{G}''_w$. To transition between states of $\mathcal{B}_p$, say that $\mathbf{t}' = \langle S', \preceq', \lambda', O', b' \rangle$ *follows* $\mathbf{t} = \langle S, \preceq, \lambda, O, b \rangle$ *under* σ when:

1. $\langle S', \preceq' \rangle$ is the σ-successor of $\langle S, \preceq \rangle$, i.e., $\langle S', \preceq' \rangle = \mathcal{T}(\langle S, \preceq \rangle, \sigma)$.
2. λ' is such that for every $q \in S$:
   (a) If $\lambda(q) = \top$, then there exists $r \in \rho_{\langle S, \preceq \rangle}(q, \sigma)$ such that $\lambda'(r) = \top$,
   (b) If $\lambda(q) = \bot$, then for every $r \in \rho_{\langle S, \preceq \rangle}(q, \sigma)$, it holds that $\lambda'(r) = \bot$.
3. $O' = \begin{cases} \bigcup_{q \in O} \rho_{\langle S, \preceq \rangle}(q, \sigma) & O \neq \emptyset, \\ \{q \mid q \in S' \text{ and } \lambda'(q) = \bot\} & O = \emptyset. \end{cases}$
4. $b' \geq b$.

We can see that once b has been set to 1, then b will be 1 forever from this $\mathcal{B}_p$-state; that is, we guess that all its runs of $\mathcal{B}_p$ from this state reach a suffix where all F-vertices are labeled finite. Thus we also need to exploit a labeling λ that reflects this guess. To this end, given a $\mathcal{B}_p$-state $\langle S, \preceq, \lambda, O, b \rangle$, we say that λ is F-*free* if for every $q \in S \cap F$ we have $\lambda(q) = \bot$. We can now define the complementation construction, and state its theorem of correctness and complexity.

Definition 3 ([12]). *For an NBW $\mathcal{A} = \langle Q, I, \delta, F \rangle$, let $\mathcal{B}_p$ be the constructed NBW $\langle Q_p, I_p, \delta_p, F_p \rangle$ where:*

- $Q_p = \{\langle S, \preceq, \lambda, O, b \rangle \mid \text{if } b = 1 \text{ then } \lambda \text{ is } F\text{-free}, S \subseteq Q\}$,
- $I_p = \{\langle I, \preceq, \lambda, \emptyset, 0 \rangle \mid \}$ *for all* $q, r \in I, q \preceq r$ *iff* $q \notin F$ *or* $r \in F$,
- $\delta_p(\mathbf{t}, \sigma) = \{\mathbf{t}' \mid \mathbf{t}' \text{ follows } \mathbf{t} \text{ under } \sigma\}$, *and*
- $F_p = \{\langle S, \preceq, \lambda, \emptyset, 1 \rangle \mid S \subseteq Q\}$.

Theorem 1 ([12]). *Let $\mathcal{A}$ be an NBW with n states. Then we have that $\mathcal{L}(\mathcal{B}_p) = \overline{\mathcal{L}(\mathcal{A})}$ and $\mathcal{B}_p$ has at most $(2n)^n$ states.*

The correctness proof of Theorem 1 connects runs of $\mathcal{B}_p$ with $\mathcal{G}'_w$. For a more precise bound on the size, we note that if $n = |Q|$, the number of preordered subsets is roughly $(0.53n)^n$ [12]. As there are 2^n labellings, and a further 2^n obligation sets, the state space of $\mathcal{B}_p$ is at most $(2n)^n$. The slice-based automaton obtained in [19] coincides with $\mathcal{B}_p$, modulo the details of labeling states and the cut-point construction. The correctness proof in [19], however, is given by means of reduced split trees, whereas here we operate directly on the run DAG.

4   Complementation via Ranks

In this section, we present the rank-based complementation construction introduced in [23], and show how profiles can be used as a tool for this construction.

4.1   Rank-Based Complementation

Unlike the profile-based algorithm, the original rank-based complementation proposed by Kupferman and Vardi [23] constructs the complementary NBW by tracking the nonaccepting run DAGs, without pruning.

As shown in [38], checking whether a run DAG $\mathcal{G}_w$ is nonaccepting can be reduced to verifying fair termination; the core idea is that $\mathcal{G}_w$ can be viewed as a fair transition system [39] that fairly terminates if none of its runs satisfies the fair condition. Let $\mathcal{G}_w = \langle V, E \rangle$. The corresponding fair transition system is $M_w = (V, I \times \{0\}, E, F \times \mathbb{N})$ where $F \times \mathbb{N}$ is the fair condition. Clearly, $\mathcal{G}_w$ is nonaccepting iff M_w fairly terminates, i.e., all ω-branches in $\mathcal{G}_w$ visit only finitely many F-vertices.

To identify nonaccepting run DAGs, we use the model checking algorithm called One-Way-Catch-Them-Young (henceforth OWCTY) [10], an improvement of the Emerson-Lei algorithm (henceforth EL) [9]. A run DAG $\mathcal{G}_w$ can be seen as a fair transition system $M = (W, W_0, R, F) = M_w$, the input of OWCTY. Let $X, Y \subseteq W$ be two sets of states. We denote by $next(X)$ the states who have successors in X, i.e., for each state $x \in next(X)$, there is a state $y \in X$ such that $(x, y) \in R$. We represent $until(X, Y)$ as the set of states in X that can properly reach Y while still staying in X. That is, for each state $x \in until(X, Y)$, there is a sequence $x_0, \cdots, x_k, k > 0$, where $x_k \in Y$, $x_i \in X$ and $(x_i, x_{i+1}) \in R$ for $0 \leq i < k$. We give the OWCTY version presented in [39] as follows:

```
Q ← W
repeat
        repeat
                Q ← Q ∩ next(Q)
        until Q not changed
        Q ← Q ∩ until(Q, Q ∩ F)
until Q not changed
return (W₀ ∩ Q = ∅)
```

Intuitively, the inner loop deletes the states that have only finitely many successors; such states surely cannot lie on a fair infinite trace (i.e., trace with infinitely many F-states). The outer loop removes all states that cannot reach accepting states in F. It is shown in [23] that the outer loop of OWCTY always converges in at most n iterations when applied to fair transition systems of the form M_w for an NBW $\mathcal{A}$ with n states. Intuitively, each level of $\mathcal{G}_w$ has at most n vertices, and each iteration of the outer loop either halts or removes an infinite trace with finitely many accepting states. This allows us to assign finite ranks to the vertices of $\mathcal{G}_w$ as follows:

– Assign a vertex v rank $2i$ if it is deleted in the i-th iteration of the outer loop by the statement $Q \leftarrow Q \cap next(Q)$.
– Assign a vertex v rank $2i + 1$ if it is deleted in the i-th iteration of the outer loop by the statement $Q \leftarrow Q \cap until(Q, Q \cap F)$.

Intuitively, ranks measure the "progress" made by a vertex towards acceptance [21]. While, in general, transfinite ranks for a fair-transition system are required, we can use here exactly the ranks $0, \cdots, 2n - 2$ in the above procedure for a run DAG of an n-state NBW $\mathcal{A}$, according to [16,23]. Thus, given a run DAG $\mathcal{G}_w$, we can obtain a function $f : V \to \{0, \dots, 2n - 2\}$ for $\mathcal{G}_w$ in terms of ranks assigned by OWCTY. This is called in [39] the *C-ranking* of $\mathcal{G}_w$.

We can see that a vertex must be removed by OWCTY no sooner than its parents in $\mathcal{G}_w$ and the F-vertices are always removed in the inner loop. Therefore the ranks in the C-ranking f along a branch does not increase and F-vertices get only even ranks. Therefore, it is easy to see that all ω-branches in $\mathcal{G}_w$ eventually get trapped in odd ranks if $\mathcal{G}_w$ is nonaccepting. We say that the C-ranking f is *odd* if all the ω-branches of $\mathcal{G}_w$ eventually get trapped in odd ranks.

Lemma 5 ([23]). *$\mathcal{A}$ rejects w iff there is an odd C-ranking for $\mathcal{G}_w$.*

The odd C-ranking provides a unique way of rank assignments for identifying nonaccepting DAGs since the described OWCTY operates deterministically on a given run DAG. When constructing a complementary NBW $\mathcal{B}_r$ of $\mathcal{A}$, it is impossible to foresee the precise rank of C-ranking for a vertex in $\mathcal{G}_w$ and we have to guess the ranks level by level while reading the ω-word w. Recall that the maximum rank for $\mathcal{G}_w$ is $2n - 2$. So along an input word w, we can encode the ranking of a level in $\mathcal{G}_w$ by utilizing a *level-ranking* function $f : Q \to [2n-2] \cup \{\bot\}$ for the states S at a level of $\mathcal{G}_w$ such that if $q \in S \cap F$, then $f(q)$ is even, and $f(q) = \bot$ if $q \in Q \setminus S$. We denote by $\mathcal{R}$ the set of all possible level-ranking functions. In order to define a valid ranking for the next level, we define the following coverage relation for level-ranking functions.

Definition 4. *Let δ be the transition function of $\mathcal{A}$, σ a letter in Σ and f, f' two level-ranking functions. Let $\alpha(f) = \{q \in Q \mid f(q) \neq \bot\}$. We say f covers f' under letter σ, denoted by $f' \leq_\sigma^\delta f$, if $q' \in \delta(\alpha(f), \sigma)$, we have $0 \leq f'(q') \leq f(q)$ for every $q \in \alpha(f)$ such that $q' \in \delta(q, \sigma)$, otherwise $f'(q') = \bot$ if $q' \notin \delta(\alpha(f), \sigma)$.*

The coverage relation indicates that the level-rankings f and f' of two consecutive levels of $\mathcal{G}_w$ do not increase in ranks on a branch, as aforementioned.

In order to verify whether the guess about the ranking of $\mathcal{G}_w$ is correct, rank-based complementation also uses the *cut-point construction* in [28]. This construction employs a set of states $O \subseteq Q$ to check that the vertices assigned with even ranks are finite. That is, the ranking of a nonaccepting run DAG $\mathcal{G}_w$ eventually gets trapped in odd ranks. The formal definition of $\mathcal{B}_r$ is given below.

Definition 5 ([23]). *Let $\mathcal{A} = (Q, I, \delta, F)$ be an NBW. We define an NBW $\mathcal{B}_r = (Q_r, I_r, \delta_r, F_r)$ as follows.*

- $Q_r \subseteq \mathcal{R} \times 2^Q$,
- $I_r = (f, \emptyset)$ where $f(q) = 2n - 2$ if $q \in I$ and $f(q) = \bot$ otherwise.
- δ_r is defined as follows:
    1. *if $O \neq \emptyset$, then $\delta_r((f, O), \sigma) = \{ (f', \delta(O, \sigma) \setminus odd(f')) \mid f' \leq_\sigma^\delta f \}$,*
    2. *if $O = \emptyset$, then $\delta_r((f, O), \sigma) = \{ (f', even(f')) \mid f' \leq_\sigma^\delta f \}$*

– $F_r = \{\,(f, O) \in Q_r \mid O = \emptyset\,\}$.

where $odd(f) = \{\, q \in Q \mid f(q) \text{ is odd}\,\}$ and $even(f) = \{\, q \in Q \mid f(q) \text{ is even}\,\}$.

Here in (f, O), f is the guessed level-ranking for the current level and O contains vertices/states along the branches that have not visited a vertex with an odd rank since the last time O has been empty. Let w be an ω-word. Intuitively, every state (f, O) in $\mathcal{B}_r$ corresponds to a level of the DAG $\mathcal{G}_w$ over w. If w is accepted by $\mathcal{B}_r$, i.e., O becomes empty for infinitely many times, then we conclude that all the ω-branches of $\mathcal{G}_w$ eventually get trapped in odd ranks. It follows that no branches are accepting in $\mathcal{G}_w$, i.e., $w \notin \mathcal{L}(\mathcal{A})$. The other direction is also easy to prove: since we have guessed all possible rankings of $\mathcal{G}_w$, if $\mathcal{G}_w$ is nonaccepting, then at least one guess will be an odd C-ranking. Clearly, $\mathcal{B}_r$ will accept w since odd C-ranking will induce infinitely many $\mathcal{B}_r$-states with empty O. Thus we conclude that $\mathcal{L}(\mathcal{B}_r) = \Sigma^\omega \setminus \mathcal{L}(\mathcal{A})$. Since $f \in \mathcal{R}$ is a function from Q to $[2n-2] \cup \{\bot\}$, the number of possible f functions is at most $(2n)^n$. Therefore, the number of states in $\mathcal{A}$ is at most $2^n \times (2n)^n$.

Theorem 2 ([23]). *Let $\mathcal{A}$ be an NBW with n states and $\mathcal{B}_r$ the NBW defined in Definition 5. Then $\mathcal{L}(\mathcal{B}_r) = \overline{\mathcal{L}(\mathcal{A})}$ and $\mathcal{B}_r$ has $\mathcal{O}((4n)^n)$ states.*

With the optimizations proposed in [15,33], the number of states in $\mathcal{B}_r$ can be improved to $\mathcal{O}((0.76n)^n)$, matching the lower bound given in [41].

4.2   Connection Between Ranks and Profiles

In this subsection, we introduce a connection between the rank-based construction and the profile-based construction by defining a *retrospective ranking* of $\mathcal{G}_w$ based on profiles. We say a level $k \geq 1$ is a *stable level* in $\mathcal{G}'_w$ if all F-vertices starting from level k are finite. According to the proof of Lemma 7 in [12], we have that there is a stable level $k \geq 0$ in $\mathcal{G}'_w$ iff $\mathcal{G}'_w$ is nonaccepting. The following lemma is a reformulation of Corollary 10 in [12], adapted to our notations.

Lemma 6 (Adapted from [12]). *$\mathcal{A}$ does not accept w iff there exists a stable level $k \geq 0$ in $\mathcal{G}'_w$.*

Recall that we use the labeling function λ in Sect. 3.2 to indicate whether a vertex in $\mathcal{G}'_w$ is finite ($\bot$) or infinite ($\top$) for constructing $\mathcal{B}_p$; the function λ has to guess the labeling of every vertex in $\mathcal{G}'_w$ when constructing $\mathcal{B}_p$. With the existence of the stable level k for a nonaccepting $\mathcal{G}'_w$, we do not have to guess for each vertex but just guess the stable level of $\mathcal{G}'_w$. That is, we first guess a stable level k of $\mathcal{G}'_w$ and before the stable level k, every vertex is labelled with $\top$; after the stable level, all F-vertices and their descendants are labeled with $\bot$. We denote this labeling by λ^k since it is dependent on the stable level k. Let S_i be the set of vertices on level i of $\mathcal{G}_w$. Formally, for $i \geq 0$, the labeling function $\lambda^k : S_i \to \{\top, \bot\}$ is defined as follows:

– If $i \leq k$, then for every $u \in S_i$ we define $\lambda^k(u) = \top$.

– If $i > k$, then for every $u \in S_i$:
  • If u is an F-vertex, then $\lambda^k(u) = \perp$.
  • Otherwise, $\lambda^k(u) = \lambda^k(v)$, for a vertex v where $E'(v,u)$.

We note that λ^k is well defined when $i > k$ and u is not an F-vertex, since by Lemma 1, all its parents in $\mathcal{G}'$ belong to the same equivalence class; so $\lambda^k(u)$ does not depend on the choice of the vertex v where $E'(v,u)$; see [12] for detailed reasoning. The correctness of this labeling is justified by Lemma 6.

As a byproduct, the constructed NBW has nondeterminism only in the transition to stable level k, and is deterministic in the limit. Note that the labeling λ^k is defined on the edges of $\mathcal{G}'_w$ rather than on edges of $\mathcal{G}_w$ (see $E'(v,u)$ in the definition above). We say a labeling λ^k is *legal* if it correctly labels the finite/infinite vertices in the run DAG. Based on the definition of λ^k, Corollary 1 is a direct consequence of Lemma 6.

Corollary 1. $\mathcal{G}_w$ *is rejecting iff for some k, the labeling λ^k is legal.*

Now we are ready to derive an odd ranking for $\mathcal{G}_w$ from the function λ^k, thus relating the profile-based analysis behind λ^k with the rank-based analysis of [23]. We have defined in Sect. 4.1 the C-ranking for $\mathcal{G}_w$ such that the C-ranking is odd iff $\mathcal{G}_w$ is nonaccepting. In order to define such a ranking function for identifying nonaccepting run DAGs, we introduce below the so-called *retrospective ranking* for $\mathcal{G}_w$ [12]. Unlike C-ranking, which predicts the progress towards the acceptance in future, retrospective ranking is defined based on the past profiles we have seen. For the retrospective ranking to be odd for a nonaccepting run DAG $\mathcal{G}_w$, we only need to care about the ranks of vertices after stable level k in which all ω-branches get trapped in odd ranks.

Consider again $\mathcal{G}'_w$ and the labeling λ^k. We know that after the stable level k, if λ^k is legal, an ω-branch with only label $\top$ is nonaccepting. So, the retrospective ranking for $\mathcal{G}_w$ after level k, gives odd ranks to $\top$-labeled vertices and even ranks to $\perp$-labeled classes. Here the ranks increase in inverse lexicographic order, i.e., we define the rank of the maximal $\top$-labeled class as 1. A good property of this ranking is that we do not need to distinguish between two adjacent $\perp$-labeled classes. Formally, we have the following k-retrospective ranking for $\mathcal{G}_w$.

Definition 6. *Consider a run DAG $\mathcal{G}_w$, $k \in \mathbb{N}$, and a labeling $\lambda^k : \mathcal{G}_w \to \{\top, \perp\}$. Let $m = 2|Q \setminus F|$. For a vertex u on level i of $\mathcal{G}_w$, let $\alpha(u)$ be the number of $\top$-labeled classes larger than u; $\alpha(u) = |\{ [v] \mid \lambda^k(v) = \top \text{ and } u \prec_i v \}|$. The k-retrospective ranking of $\mathcal{G}'_w$ is the function $\mathbf{r}^k : V \to \{0..m\}$ defined for every vertex u on level i as follows.*

$$
\mathbf{r}^k(u) = \begin{cases} m & \text{if } i \leq k, \\ 2\alpha(u) & \text{if } i > k \text{ and } \lambda^k(u) = \perp, \\ 2\alpha(u) + 1 & \text{if } i > k \text{ and } \lambda^k(u) = \top. \end{cases}
$$

According to Lemma 1, every equivalence class $[u]$ has at most two child equivalence classes, one F-class and one non-F-class. So, on the same level, each

⊤-labeled class is given the odd rank greater by two than the rank of the next lexicographically larger ⊤-labeled class. The number of ⊤-labeled classes on each level is at most $\frac{m}{2} = |Q \setminus F|$. Moreover, since the number of larger ⊤-labeled classes does not increase, the ranks of child equivalence classes on the next level are no larger than the rank of their parent. Formally, we have the following.

Lemma 7 ([12]). *For a level $j \geq k$, we have*

- *If $u \prec_j u'$ then $\mathbf{r}^k(u) \geq \mathbf{r}^k(u')$, where u and u' are two vertices on level j.*
- *If $(u,v) \in E'$, then $\mathbf{r}^k(u) \geq \mathbf{r}^k(v)$, where u and v are two vertices on level j and $j+1$, respectively.*

Thus, the following lemma holds if λ^k is legal and $\mathcal{G}_w$ is nonaccepting, according to Lemma 15 of [12].

Lemma 8 ([12]). *$\mathcal{A}$ does not accept w iff the retrospective ranking $\mathbf{r}^k$ bounded by m for $\mathcal{G}_w$ is an odd ranking.*

4.3   Complementing with Retrospective Rankings

We have introduced in Sect. 4.2 about how to determine whether w is accepted by $\mathcal{A}$ by defining the retrospective rankings based on the profiles of branches after the stable level in $\mathcal{G}_w$ (cf. Lemma 7). Now we are ready to define the complementary NBW $\mathcal{A}_L$ based on the retrospective ranking.

First, we need to guess the stable level in $\mathcal{G}_w$ before we can define the retrospective ranking for checking whether the run DAG $\mathcal{G}_w$ is accepting. In order to correctly identify the stable level k for a given run DAG $\mathcal{G}_w$, we partition the construction of $\mathcal{A}_L$ into two phases, namely *initial phase* and *ranking phase*. In the initial phase, the NBW $\mathcal{A}_L$ deterministically tracks all preordered subsets and we assume all levels in this phase are before the stable level k. Once $\mathcal{A}_L$ nondeterministically moves to the ranking phase, we assume that we have reached the stable level k and need to deterministically track the ranks in order to check whether $\mathcal{G}_w$ is accepting. Therefore, the only nondeterminism in $\mathcal{A}_L$ lies in the guess of k, i.e., the transition between the initial phase and the ranking phase.

Recall that we denote by $\mathbf{Q}$ the set of preordered subsets of Q in Sect. 3.2. Let $\mathcal{R}^m$ be the set of level rankings bounded by m. There are three types of transitions in $\mathcal{A}_L$: transitions in the initial phase, transitions from the initial phase to the ranking phase, and transitions within the ranking phase. The first type of transitions is the σ-successor relation between preordered subsets for $\mathcal{B}_p$, as described in Sect. 3.2. We only give the other two types of transitions below.

Recall that the rank of a vertex u only depends on the number of ⊤-labeled classes larger than it, denoted $\alpha(u)$. The transitions moving between phases are transitions from a preordered set $\langle S, \preceq \rangle$ to the level ranking of its σ-successor, as defined below. For each $q \in S$, let $\beta(q) = |\{[p] \mid p \in S \setminus F, q \prec p\}|$ be the number of non-F-classes larger than q (On level $k+1$, a vertex is labeled with ⊤ iff it is an non-F-vertex and $\beta(q)$ is easy to compute). We define a function torank : $\mathbf{Q} \to \mathcal{R}^m$ that obtains from a preordered set $\langle S, \preceq \rangle$ a level-ranking function $f \in \mathcal{R}^m$ such that for each $q \in Q$:

$$f(q) = \begin{cases} \bot & \text{if } q \notin S, \\ 2\beta(q) & \text{if } q \in S \cap F, \\ 2\beta(q) + 1 & \text{if } q \in S \setminus F. \end{cases}$$

Now we define the transitions between the level rankings of $\mathcal{R}^m$. For a level ranking $f \in \mathcal{R}^m$, $\sigma \in \Sigma$, and $q' \in Q$, let $\text{pred}(q', \sigma, f) = \{ q \mid f(q) \neq \bot, \, q' \in \rho(q, \sigma) \}$ be the predecessors of q' with non-$\bot$ rank. One can see that the predecessor in $\text{pred}(q', \sigma, f)$ with the lowest rank has the maximal profile in $\mathcal{G}$ among $\text{pred}(q', \sigma, f)$. For $h \in \mathbb{N}$, let $\lfloor h \rfloor_{even}$ be h if h is even and be $h - 1$ if h is odd. Now we define the σ-successor of f to be f' where for each $q' \in Q$:

$$f'(q') = \begin{cases} \bot & \text{if } \text{pred}(q', \sigma, f) = \emptyset, \\ \lfloor \min(\{f(q) \mid q \in \text{pred}(q', \sigma, f)\}) \rfloor_{even} & \text{if } \text{pred}(q', \sigma, f) \neq \emptyset \text{ and } q' \in F, \\ \min(\{ f(q) \mid q \in \text{pred}(q', \sigma, f) \}) & \text{if } \text{pred}(q', \sigma, f) \neq \emptyset \text{ and } q' \notin F. \end{cases}$$

Here the rank of a vertex v is computed based on the rank of its predecessor u with maximal profile in $\mathcal{G}'_w$. Note, however, that λ^k may label a finite class $\top$; in such a case, a $\top$-labeled class larger than u has no children, thus $f(u) > f'(v)$. Hence we know that λ^k now is illegal, so an optimization is that we can just ignore the computation of following successors; this optimization is omitted in the construction for clarity. We formalize the construction of $\mathcal{A}_L$ as below.

Definition 7. *For an NBW* $\mathcal{A} = \langle Q, I, \delta, F \rangle$, *let* $\mathcal{A}_L$ *be the NBW* $\langle \mathbf{Q} \cup (\mathcal{R}^m \times 2^Q), I_L, \delta_L, \mathcal{R}^m \times \{\emptyset\} \rangle$, *where*

- $I_L = \{\langle I, \preceq_0 \rangle\}$, *where* $\preceq_0$ *is such that for all* $q, r \in I$, $q \preceq_0 r$ *iff* $q \notin F$ *or* $r \in F$.
- $\delta_L(\mathcal{S}, \sigma) = \{\mathcal{S}'\} \cup \{\langle torank(\mathcal{S}'), \emptyset \rangle\}$, *where* $\mathcal{S}'$ *is the* σ-*successor of* $\mathcal{S}$.
- $\delta_L(\langle f, O \rangle, \sigma) = \{\langle f', O' \rangle\}$ *where* f' *is the* σ-*successor of* f

$$\text{and } O' = \begin{cases} \rho(O, \sigma) \setminus odd(f') & \text{if } O \neq \emptyset, \\ even(f') & \text{if } O = \emptyset. \end{cases}$$

Theorem 3 ([12]). *For an NBW* $\mathcal{A}$ *with* n *states, we have that* $L(\mathcal{A}_L) = \overline{L(\mathcal{A})}$ *and* $\mathcal{A}_L$ *has* $\mathcal{O}((8n)^n)$ *states.*

The maximum rank of a state is $m = 2|Q \setminus F| \leq 2n$, so the number of states in the ranking phase is at most $(2n + 1)^n \times 2^n \leq (4n + 2)^n$. The number of states in the initial phase is at most $\mathcal{O}((0.53n)^n)$ [12]; so, in total $\mathcal{A}_L$ has at most $(4n + 2)^n + \mathcal{O}((0.53n)^n) \in \mathcal{O}((8n)^n)$ states. We remark that the level rankings can be further tightened, as done in [12], which, however, is not the goal of this section.

5   Complementation via Congruence Relations

In this section, we first give a general framework of complementation constructions from a language-theoretic perspective. We then recall the classical congruence relations defined in [34] and give optimal congruence relations based on
profiles [24]. Büchi [6] proposed a construction based on congruence relations for
complementing NBWs, involving a Ramsey-based analysis, which is why it is
widely known as the Ramsey-based complementation (RBC). His argument was
refined in [34], where the construction of congruence relation was optimized.
Later, Thomas showed that the Ramsey argument was not necessary [35].

The language-theoretic perspective to [6,34] offers the observation that every
ω-regular language (including the universe of all ω-words) is a finite union of
languages of the form UV^ω, where U and V (the latter does not contain the
empty word) are regular languages. One way to construct the complementary
language of an NBW $\mathcal{A}$, is to find a finite collection of languages $U_i V_i^\omega$ such
that (i) the union of the finite collection covers Σ^ω, the universe of all ω-words,
while (ii) the union of a subset of the finite collection equals $\mathcal{L}(\mathcal{A})$ and the union
of the rest of the collection equals the complement of $\mathcal{L}(\mathcal{A})$. We refer to these
properties below as Properties (i) and (ii).

When dealing with words from UV^ω, we can consider only the *ultimately
periodic* (UP)-words of the form uv^ω, where $u \in U$ and $v \in V$ and totally ignore
that there can be words that are not ultimately periodic [6,7,34]. We denote by
UP(L) the set of UP-words of L, i.e., $\{ uv^\omega \in L \mid u \in \Sigma^*, v \in \Sigma^+ \}$. With the
following theorem, UP(L) can be seen as the "fingerprint" of L.

Theorem 4 ([7]). *(1) Every non-empty ω-regular language L contains at least
one UP-word. (2) Let L, L' be two ω-regular languages. Then, $L = L'$ if and
only if UP(L) = UP(L').*

Therefore, we are concerned only with UP-words in the remainder of this paper.
In the following, we present a general framework for obtaining the complementary language of a given ω-language L.

To find a finite union of languages for constructing the complement of L, the
approach of [6,34] is to design first a finite partition of Σ^+ satisfying Property
(i). Assume that $\mathcal{P} = \{U_0, \cdots, U_{k-1}\}$, for $k \geq 1$, is a finite *partition* of Σ^+, so
$\Sigma^+ = \bigcup_{0 \leq i < k} U_i$ and $U_i \cap U_j = \emptyset$ for $0 \leq i < j < k$. We call each element of
$\mathcal{P}$ a *block* of $\mathcal{P}$. By Theorem 4, Lemma 9 holds since we can prove UP(Σ^ω) =
UP($\bigcup_{0 \leq i,j < k} U_i U_j^\omega$) from the fact that $\mathcal{P}$ is a partition of Σ^+.

Lemma 9 (Coverage of Σ^ω). $\Sigma^\omega = \bigcup_{0 \leq i,j < k} U_i U_j^\omega$.

In order to obtain the complement language of L, the partition $\mathcal{P}$ has to
satisfy Property (ii) as well, so we introduce the saturation property of $\mathcal{P}$. We
say $\mathcal{P}$ *saturates* L if each language $U_i U_j^\omega, 0 \leq i, j < k$ is either inside L or outside
L. To fulfill Property (ii), we can just let $\mathcal{P}$ saturate L. The following lemma
holds immediately.

Lemma 10 (Saturation of L). *Let $\mathcal{P}$ saturate L. Then for every $U_i U_j^\omega, 0 \leq
i, j < k$, $U_i U_j^\omega \cap L \neq \emptyset$ implies $U_i U_j^\omega \subseteq L$.*

With $\mathcal{P}$ saturating L, we finally obtain the complement of L by the following theorem, which is a direct consequence of Lemmas 9 and 10.

Theorem 5 (Complementary language of L). *Let $\mathcal{P}$ saturate L. Then* $\overline{L} = \bigcup\{ U_i U_j^\omega \mid U_i, U_j \in \mathcal{P}, U_i U_j^\omega \cap L = \emptyset \}$.

To obtain the partition $\mathcal{P}$ of Σ^+, we use a congruence relation $\backsim$. A *right congruence* (RC) relation $\backsim$ over Σ^* is an equivalence relation such that $x \backsim y$ implies $xv \backsim yv$ for all $v \in \Sigma^*$. A *congruence relation* $\backsim$ over Σ^* is an equivalence relation such that $x \backsim y$ implies $uxv \backsim uyv$ for every $x, y, u, v \in \Sigma^*$. We denote by $|\backsim|$ the *index* of the equivalence relation $\backsim$, i.e., the number of equivalence classes of $\backsim$. A *finite congruence relation* is a congruence relation with a finite index. We use $\Sigma^*/_\backsim$ to denote the set of equivalence classes of $\backsim$. Given $x \in \Sigma^*$, we denote by $[x]_\backsim$ the equivalence class of $\backsim$ that contains x.

A congruence relation $\backsim$ yields a finite partition $\Sigma^*/_\backsim$ of Σ^*; so we can also obtain a finite partition $\mathcal{P}$ of Σ^+. It follows that we can construct the complementary language of a given ω-language L, based on a congruence relation $\backsim$ if the partition induced by $\backsim$ satisfies Properties (i) and (ii), i.e., satisfying Lemmas 9 and 10. Below we introduce such a congruence relation.

5.1 Classical Congruence Relations

Sistla, Vardi, and Wolper [34] define the congruence relation $\backsim$ by distinguishing finite words in Σ^+ with the transition graph of $\mathcal{A}$. More precisely, given a word $u \in \Sigma^+$, for every two states $q, r \in Q$, we care about the following two questions:

– Is there a path in $\mathcal{A}$ from q to r over u? (we denote by $q \xrightarrow{u} r$ if so.)
– Is there a path in $\mathcal{A}$ from q to r over u that visits some accepting state? (we denote by $q \xRightarrow{u} r$ if so.)

Thomas [35] suggests to present the answers to these two questions as the following equivalence relation $\backsim$.

Definition 8 ([34, 35]). *For all $u_1, u_2 \in \Sigma^+$, $u_1 \backsim u_2$ if and only if for all $q, r \in Q$, (1) $q \xrightarrow{u_1} r$ iff $q \xrightarrow{u_2} r$; and (2) $q \xRightarrow{u_1} r$ iff $q \xRightarrow{u_2} r$.*

Let u_1 and u_2 be two finite words such that $u_1 \backsim u_2$. We have that $xu_1y \backsim xu_2y$ holds for all $x, y \in \Sigma^*$ because independently from the states reached by $\mathcal{A}$ after reading x, by Definition 8 $\mathcal{A}$ reaches the same state by reading u_1 and u_2, hence it can reach the same state after continuing with y. Therefore, we have following result.

Lemma 11. *The equivalence relation $\backsim$ is a (right-)congruence relation.*

Since $\backsim$ is defined by reachability between states, we can map each of the n^2 pairs of states (q, r) to either both $q \xRightarrow{u} r$ and $q \xrightarrow{u} r$, or just $q \xrightarrow{u} r$ or none of them. Thus, we have $|\backsim| = |\Sigma^+/_\backsim| \leq 3^{n^2}$. That is, the number of equivalence classes induced by $\backsim$, say $k \geq 1$, is at most 3^{n^2}, as stated in the following lemma.

Lemma 12 ([34,35]). *Let $\backsim$ be as given in Definition 8. Then $|\backsim| \leq 3^{n^2}$.*

Let $\mathcal{P}_\backsim = \{U_0, U_1, \cdots, U_{k-1}\}$ where U_i is $(i+1)$-th equivalence class induced by $\backsim$ in Σ^+ and k is the index of $\backsim$. By Lemma 9, for all partitions of Σ^+, including $\mathcal{P}_\backsim$, we can cover the universe of Σ^ω. Thus, we have:

Lemma 13 (Coverage of Σ^ω). $\Sigma^\omega = \bigcup_{U,V \in \mathcal{P}_\backsim} UV^\omega$.

An important property we want to have is that the finite partition $\mathcal{P}_\backsim$ saturates $\mathcal{L}(\mathcal{A})$, which indeed holds for $\backsim$.

Lemma 14 (Saturation of $\mathcal{L}(\mathcal{A})$ [34,35]). *For all $U, V \in \mathcal{P}_\backsim$, we have that $(UV^\omega) \cap \mathcal{L}(\mathcal{A}) \neq \emptyset$ implies $UV^\omega \subseteq \mathcal{L}(\mathcal{A})$.*

The intuition is that an accepting run ρ of the form $q_0 \xrightarrow{u} q_1 \xrightarrow{v} q_2 \cdots$ $q_i \xrightarrow{v} q_{i+1} \cdots$ for $uv^\omega \in (UV^\omega) \cap \mathcal{L}(\mathcal{A})$ with $u \in U$ and $v \in V$ induces an accepting run over $u'v'^\omega$ with $u' \in U$ and $v' \in V'$ of the form $q_0 \xrightarrow{u'} q_1 \xrightarrow{v'} q_2 \cdots q_i \xrightarrow{v'} q_{i+1} \cdots$, according to Definition 8. This means that for each $U, V \in \mathcal{P}$, either $UV^\omega \subseteq \mathcal{L}(\mathcal{A})$ or $UV^\omega \subseteq \Sigma^\omega \setminus \mathcal{L}(\mathcal{A})$. Thus, we obtain the complementary language of $\mathcal{A}$:

Theorem 6 (Complementary language of $\mathcal{L}(\mathcal{A})$ [34,35]). $\Sigma^\omega \setminus \mathcal{L}(\mathcal{A}) = \bigcup \{ UV^\omega \mid U, V \in \mathcal{P}_\backsim, UV^\omega \cap \mathcal{L}(\mathcal{A}) = \emptyset \}$.

Construction of complementary NBWs. For a given RC $\backsim$ of a regular language L, it is well-known that Myhill-Nerode theorem [30,31] defines a unique minimal DFW D of L, in which each state of D corresponds to an equivalence class defined by $\backsim$ over Σ^*. Therefore, we can construct a DFW $\mathcal{D}[\backsim]$ from $\backsim$ in a standard way [18]. We already have the congruence relation $\backsim$, which yields the finite collection of $U_i V_i^\omega$ that equals to $\overline{\mathcal{L}(\mathcal{A})}$ (cf. Theorem 6) where $U_i, V_i \in \mathcal{P}$. To obtain the complementary NBW of $\mathcal{A}$, we construct, for each language $U_i V_i^\omega$, its NBW $\mathcal{B}_{U_i, V_i}$ with two copies of the DFW $\mathcal{D}[\backsim]$ where the first copy accepts U_i while the second copy is modified from $\mathcal{D}[\backsim]$ to accept the words V_i^ω by adding a unique accepting state to connect the initial state and the original accepting states in $\mathcal{D}[\backsim]$. Each $\mathcal{D}[\backsim]$ has at most 3^{n^2} states, so $\mathcal{B}_{U_i, V_i}$ has at most $2 \times 3^{n^2} + 1$ states. Then the complementary NBW of $\mathcal{A}$, say $\overline{\mathcal{A}}$, can be obtained by computing the union of all such NBWs $\mathcal{B}_{U_i, V_i}$, where $U_i V_i^\omega \cap \mathcal{L}(\mathcal{A}) = \emptyset$. Moreover, the number of possible such NBWs $\mathcal{B}_{U_i, V_i}$ is $3^{n^2} \times 3^{n^2}$ according to Lemma 12. In total, the number of states in $\overline{\mathcal{A}}$ is in $2^{\mathcal{O}(n^2)}$. Therefore, we finally have the following theorem for the complementation algorithm based on congruence relation $\backsim$.

Theorem 7 ([34]). *For an NBW $\mathcal{A}$ with n states, we have that $\mathcal{L}(\overline{\mathcal{A}}) = \overline{\mathcal{L}(\mathcal{A})}$ and $\overline{\mathcal{A}}$ has at most $2^{\mathcal{O}(n^2)}$ states.*

In the remainder of the section, we show how to obtain tighter congruence relations for the complementary language $\Sigma^\omega \setminus \mathcal{L}(\mathcal{A})$ based on profiles.

5.2   Profile-Based Congruence Relations

In Theorem 5, we show that it is possible to obtain the complementary language of a given ω-regular language L from a finite partition $\mathcal{P}$ of Σ^+ that saturates and covers L. The congruence relation $\backsim$ defined in Sect. 5.1 implements such a partition $\mathcal{P}$ for a given ω-regular language $\mathcal{L}(\mathcal{A})$ specified with an NBW $\mathcal{A}$. The requirement of a full congruence relation is, however, too strong and contains redundant information, which may lead to unnecessary blow-up; see, e.g., [24]. In fact, the authors in [24] have shown that full congruence relations are not needed for obtaining partitions that saturate $\mathcal{L}(\mathcal{A})$, and RCs suffice. Since RC relations are coarser than full congruence relations, the complementation algorithms based on RCs can give us tighter constructions of the complementary NBWs.

In fact, the use of RCs in [24] dates back to earlier works [4, 26]. In [4, 26], the authors showed that one can define separate partitions for the finite prefixes U and the periodic words V for a given ω-regular language L. More precisely, one first defines a finite partition $\mathcal{P} = \{U_0, \cdots, U_{k-1}\}$ of Σ^+ for finite prefixes with an RC $\approx$. Then, for each block $U_i \in \mathcal{P}$, we define a finite partition $\mathcal{P}_i = \{V_{i,0}, \cdots, V_{i,k_i-1}\}$ of Σ^+ for the periodic words with an RC $\approx_{U_i}$. The families of partitions defined in [4, 26] satisfy certain properties of saturation and coverage, which we call *family coverage* and *family saturation*, as formalized below.

(1) FAMILY COVERAGE: $\Sigma^\omega = \bigcup_{U_i \in \mathcal{P}}(\bigcup_{\{V_{i,j} \in \mathcal{P}_i | U_i V_{i,j} = U_i\}} U_i V_{i,j}^\omega)$.
(2) FAMILY SATURATION: For every pair $U_i \in \mathcal{P}$ and $V_{i,j} \in \mathcal{P}_i$, if $U_i V_{i,j} = U_i$, it holds that either $U_i V_{i,j}^\omega \subseteq L$ or $U_i V_{i,j}^\omega \subseteq \Sigma^\omega \setminus L$.

Similarly to Theorem 6, we have the following result.

Theorem 8 (Complementary language of L [4, 26]). *Let $(\mathcal{P}, \{\mathcal{P}_i\}_{0 \le i < k})$ be a family of partitions satisfying family coverage and family saturation. Then* $\overline{L} = \bigcup_{U_i \in \mathcal{P}}\{U_i V_{i,j}^\omega \mid U_i \in \mathcal{P}, V_{i,j} \in \mathcal{P}_i, U_i V_{i,j} = U_i, U_i V_{i,j}^\omega \cap L = \emptyset\}$.

In this section, we introduce the RCs that define such families of partitions for an ω-regular language $\mathcal{L}(\mathcal{A})$ specified with an NBW $\mathcal{A} = (Q, I, \delta, F)$, using the framework of profiles described in Subsect. 3.1. We first define the RC $\approx$ that induces the finite partition $\mathcal{P}$ for finite prefixes. To that end, we first describe a profile-based preorder $\preceq_u$ on the set $\delta(I, u)$ of states for a given finite prefix $u \in \Sigma^*$ [11, 12].

Recall that when defining the congruence relation $\backsim$, we reasoned about the reachability relation between every pair of states of $\mathcal{A}$ over a finite word u (cf. Definition 8). Here, we focus on the set $\delta(I, u)$ of states reached from the initial states over a finite prefix $u \in \Sigma^*$, and we make use of the pruned run DAG as defined in Sect. 3. We show that one can define RCs to distinguish two finite prefixes u_1 and u_2 by the set of ordered states in their respective pruned run DAG $\mathcal{G}'_{u_1 w'}$ and $\mathcal{G}'_{u_2 w'}$, for an arbitrary $w' \in \Sigma^\omega$. We introduced in Subsect. 3.1 the preorder $\preceq_i$ for the states on level i in a run DAG $\mathcal{G}'_w$ for $w \in \Sigma^\omega$ (cf. Definition 1). Since the preorder $\preceq_i$ is only dependent on the prefix $w[1 \cdots i]$, we can just describe $\preceq_i$ with respect to the finite prefix $u = w[1 \cdots i]$, denoted $\preceq_u$ as below.

Definition 9 (Preorder $\preceq_{w[1\cdots i]}$). *Let* $w \in \Sigma^\omega$, $u = w[1\cdots i]$, *and* $q, r \in \delta(I, u)$. *We have that* $q \preceq_u r$ *iff* $q \preceq_i r$ *in* $\mathcal{G}'_w$. *Furthermore, we define an equivalence relation* $q \simeq_u r$ *if* $q \simeq_i r$ *in* $\mathcal{G}'_w$.

Let $w \in \Sigma^\omega$, $u = w[1\cdots i]$, and $P = \delta(I, u)$. Let $[q]_{\preceq_u} = \{ r \in P \mid q \simeq_u r \}$ be the equivalence class of $q \in P$ under $\preceq_u$; We denote by $P/_{\preceq_u}$ the family of such equivalence classes. Note that every two states q, r in P, rather than in the whole set Q, are comparable under the preorder $\preceq_u$ since every two states in P are comparable under $\preceq_i$ (cf. Definition 1). We denote by $\langle P, \preceq_u \rangle$ the ordered family of equivalence classes of P under $\preceq_u$. Recall that the preorder $\preceq_i$ of $\mathcal{G}'_w$ is equivalent to $\preceq_u$ (cf. Definition 9). Therefore, the a-successor of $\langle P, \preceq_u \rangle$ can be computed with $\mathcal{T}(\langle P, \preceq_u \rangle, a)$ as given in Definition 2. It is immediate that:

Corollary 2. *Let* $u \in \Sigma^*, a \in \Sigma$ *and* $P = \delta(I, u)$. *Then* $\langle \delta(I, ua), \preceq_{ua} \rangle = \mathcal{T}(\langle P, \preceq_u \rangle, a)$.

We are now ready to define the RC $\approx$ given in [24] with our notations. Instead of considering every pair of states (q, r) of $\mathcal{A}$ to define the congruence relation $\backsim$ (cf. Definition 8), we use the finite prefix u by tracing the reachable states $\delta(I, u)$ with the preorder $\preceq_u$ to get the RC $\approx$.

Definition 10 (RC $\approx$). *For* $u_1, u_2 \in \Sigma^*$, *we say* $u_1 \approx u_2$ *iff* $\langle \delta(I, u_1), \preceq_{u_1} \rangle = \langle \delta(I, u_2), \preceq_{u_2} \rangle$.

It is easy to see that $\approx$ is indeed an RC.

Lemma 15. *The equivalence relation* $\approx$ *is an RC.*

Since each equivalence class $[u]_\approx$, $u \in \Sigma^+$, can be uniquely encoded as the set $\langle \delta(I, u), \preceq_u \rangle$, i.e., an *ordered* partition of Q, by [12,37] we have that the number of possible ordered partitions over Q is approximately $(0.53n)^n \leq n^n$. Thus we have the following upper bound for $\approx$.

Lemma 16 ([24]). *Let* $\approx$ *be the RC in Definition 10. Then* $|\approx| \leq n^n$.

We now define the RC $\approx_u$ for processing the periodic words based on the reachability between equivalence classes in $\mathcal{G}'_{uw}$, where $w \in \Sigma^\omega$. More precisely, we define reachability between equivalence classes under the preorder $\preceq_u$ (at level $|u|$) and $\preceq_{uv}$ (at level $|uv|$) in the pruned run DAG $\mathcal{G}'_{uvw}$. We say that $[q]_{\preceq_u}$ v-reaches $[r]_{\preceq_{uv}}$, denoted by $[q]_{\preceq_u} \xrightarrow{v} [r]_{\preceq_{uv}}$, if there are two vertices $\tau \in [q]_{\preceq_u} \times \{|u|\}$ and $\tau' \in [r]_{\preceq_{uv}} \times \{|uv|\})$ in $\mathcal{G}'_{uvw}$ such that $\tau \xrightarrow{v} \tau'$. We write $[q]_{\preceq_u} \overset{v}{\Rightarrow} [r]_{\preceq_{uv}}$ if such path from τ to τ' also visits an F-vertex. One can see that the reachability relation between the equivalence classes does not depend on levels after $|uv|$ in $\mathcal{G}'_{uvw}$, i.e., w is not used there. So w can be an arbitrary ω-word in Σ^ω.

Definition 11 (RC $\approx_u$). *Given* $u, v_1, v_2 \in \Sigma^*$, *we say* $v_1 \approx_u v_2$ *if (1)* $uv_1 \approx uv_2$, *and (2) for all states* $q \in P, r \in P'$, *where* $P = \delta(I, u)$ *and* $P' = \delta(I, uv_1) = \delta(I, uv_2)$, *we have*

(i) $[q]_{\preceq_u} \overset{v_1}{\longrightarrow} [r]_{\preceq_{uv_1}}$ holds in $\mathcal{G}'_{uv_1 w}$ iff $[q]_{\preceq_u} \overset{v_2}{\longrightarrow} [r]_{\preceq_{uv_2}}$ holds in $\mathcal{G}'_{uv_2 w}$, and

(ii) $[q]_{\preceq_u} \overset{v_1}{\Rightarrow} [r]_{\preceq_{uv_1}}$ holds in $\mathcal{G}'_{uv_1 w}$ iff $[q]_{\preceq_u} \overset{v_2}{\Rightarrow} [r]_{\preceq_{uv_2}}$ holds in $\mathcal{G}'_{uv_2 w}$.

Note that under the assumption $uv_1 \approx uv_2$, we have that the ordered partitions $\langle \delta(I, uv_1), \preceq_{u_1} \rangle$ and $\langle \delta(I, uv_2), \preceq_{u_2} \rangle$ are equal by definition of $\approx$. It follows that $\delta(I, uv_1) = \delta(I, uv_2)$ also holds.

Definition 11 is designed to formalize the following idea for recognizing the ω-words accepted and rejected by $\mathcal{A}$. We want to use the RC $\approx$ for the finite prefixes and the RC $\approx_u$ for the periodic finite words of u to establish the family saturation property introduced before. That is, under the assumption that $u \approx uv_1$ and $u \approx uv_2$, we want to guarantee that if $v_1 \approx_u v_2$, then $uv_1^\omega \in \mathcal{L}(\mathcal{A})$ if and only if $uv_2^\omega \in \mathcal{L}(\mathcal{A})$. To achieve this, the first condition we impose – Item (1) of Definition 11 – is to ensure visiting infinitely often the same ordered partition under $\preceq_u$ over the ω-words uv_1^ω and uv_2^ω; so we require $uv_1 \approx uv_2$. The second condition is to guarantee that the profiles of branches in the pruned run DAG $\mathcal{G}'_{uv_1^k w}$ and $\mathcal{G}'_{uv_2^k w}$, $k \geq 1$, share visits to F-vertices; so, when extending to infinite words, their profiles either both have infinitely many 1s or neither of them does. This ensures that $uv_1^\omega \in \mathcal{L}(\mathcal{A})$ if and only if $uv_2^\omega \in \mathcal{L}(\mathcal{A})$. To guarantee that, we first require that the reachability relation between every pair of equivalence classes or blocks under $\preceq_u$ over finite words v_1 and v_2 either holds for both or neither of them (cf. condition (2)-(i)); then, we demand that they also share the visits to accepting states (cf. condition (2)-(ii)).

As stated before Definition 11, the index of $\approx_u$ is indeed in $2^{\mathcal{O}(n \log n)}$.

Lemma 17 ([24]). *Given* $u \in \Sigma^*$, *let* $\approx_u$ *be the RC from Definition 11. Then* $|\approx_u| \leq n^n \times (n+1)^n \times 2^n \in 2^{\mathcal{O}(n \log n)}$.

The upper bound for $|\approx_u|$ can be deduced from the encoding we use for $[v]_{\approx_u}$. $[v]_{\approx_u}$ is mapped to the pair $\langle \langle \delta(I, uv), \preceq_{uv} \rangle, f \rangle$ where the function f keeps track of the satisfaction of the pair of states $q, r \in Q$ of the conditions in Definition 11, i.e., whether $[q]_{\preceq_u} \overset{v}{\longrightarrow} [r]_{\preceq_{uv}}$ and $[q]_{\preceq_u} \overset{v}{\Rightarrow} [r]_{\preceq_{uv}}$ in Conditions (2)-(i) and (2)-(ii) for the such states. Each equivalence class $[r]_{\preceq_{uv}}$ can only be reached by exactly one equivalence class under $\preceq_u$. There are at most n equivalence classes defined by both $\preceq_u$ and $\preceq_{uv}$. Then the codomain of f has size $2n+1 < 2(n+1)$, so the possible different functions f are $(2(n+1))^n = 2^n \times (n+1)^n$, while by [12] the possible sets $\langle \delta(I, uv), \preceq_{uv} \rangle$ are n^n, hence $|\approx_u| \leq n^n \times (n+1)^n \times 2^n \in 2^{\mathcal{O}(n \log n)}$.

Let $\mathcal{P} = \{U_0, \cdots, U_{k-1}\}$ be a partition of Σ^+ induced by $\approx$. For each block $U_i \in \mathcal{P}$, let $\mathcal{P}_i = \{V_{i,0}, \cdots, V_{i,k_i-1}\}$ be the partition of Σ^+ induced by $\approx_u$, where $[u]_\approx = U_i$. We first show that to cover Σ^ω, we do not need to consider all U_i and $V_{i,j}$ pairs, i.e., the Property (1) as aforementioned. To that end, we first prove that the concatenation of an equivalence class U_i of $\mathcal{P}$ and an equivalence class $V_{i,j}$ of $\mathcal{P}_i$ is also an equivalence class of $\mathcal{P}$.

Lemma 18. *For all* $U_i \in \mathcal{P}$ *and* $V_{i,j} \in \mathcal{P}_i$, *we have* $U_i V_{i,j} \in \mathcal{P}$ *where* $0 \leq i < k$ *and* $0 \leq j < k_i$.

We now show that we can focus on a subset of pairs of equivalence classes $U_i \in \mathcal{P}$ and $V_{i,j} \in \mathcal{P}_i$ to cover the universe Σ^ω, i.e., Property (1).

Lemma 19 (Coverage of Σ^ω [24]). $\Sigma^\omega = \bigcup_{0 \leq i < k, 0 \leq j < k_i} \{ U_i V_{i,j}^\omega \mid U_i V_{i,j} = U_i \}$.

The proof idea of Lemma 19 is similar to that of Lemma 9 since one can just prove that the UP-words of the two sets of the equation are equivalent. We refer interested readers to [24] for the proof details.

Next we need to show that the partition $(\mathcal{P}, \{\mathcal{P}_i\})$ saturates the ω-regular language $\mathcal{L}(\mathcal{A})$, i.e., Property (2). The proof of Lemma 20 is similar to that of Lemma 14, except that we have to consider the reachability relation over equivalence classes in reduced run DAGs $\mathcal{G}'_w$ rather than over states.

Lemma 20 (Saturation of $\mathcal{L}(\mathcal{A})$ [24]). For $U_i \in \mathcal{P}, V_{i,j} \in \mathcal{P}_i$, if $U_i V_{i,j} = U_i$, $U_i V_{i,j}^\omega \cap \mathcal{L}(\mathcal{A}) \neq \emptyset$ implies $U_i V_{i,j}^\omega \subseteq \mathcal{L}(\mathcal{A})$.

Finally, we are ready to obtain the complementary language of $\mathcal{L}(\mathcal{A})$ based on the results of Lemma 19 and Lemma 20.

Theorem 9 (Complementary language of $\mathcal{L}(\mathcal{A})$ [24]). $\Sigma^\omega \setminus \mathcal{L}(\mathcal{A}) = \bigcup_{0 \leq i < k, 0 \leq j < k_i} \{ U_i V_{i,j}^\omega \mid U_i V_{i,j} = U_i, U_i V_{i,j}^\omega \cap \mathcal{L}(\mathcal{A}) = \emptyset \}$.

Breuers *et al.* [5] used a subset construction to define an RC for processing the finite prefix u of a UP-word uv^ω in $\Sigma^\omega \setminus \mathcal{L}(\mathcal{A})$; however, they still used the classical congruence relation $\backsim$ in Definition 8 for recognizing the periodic word v of uv^ω. The congruence relation for processing v in [5] has also been optimized with a preorder, leading to the same upper bound $2^{\mathcal{O}(n \log n)}$ as our work. As pointed out in [24], the complementation construction in [5] uses more than one congruences for recognizing v for a given u; instead, we need only one RC here since the equivalence class $[u]_\approx$ of $\approx$ only relates with one RC $\approx_u$.

In Theorem 7, we build a complementary NBW for $\mathcal{A}$ with the congruence relation $\backsim$, which in fact only requires $\backsim$ being an RC. Similarly, we can construct a complementary NBW $\mathcal{A}^c$ accepting $\Sigma^\omega \setminus \mathcal{L}(\mathcal{A})$ with $\approx$ and $\approx_u, u \in \Sigma^*$. Since the index of $\approx_u$ is in $2^{\mathcal{O}(n \log n)}$, the number of states in $\mathcal{A}^c$ is also in $2^{\mathcal{O}(n \log n)}$.

Theorem 10 ([24]). For an NBW $\mathcal{A}$ with n states, we have that $\mathcal{L}(\mathcal{A}^c) = \overline{\mathcal{L}(\mathcal{A})}$ and $\mathcal{A}^c$ has at most $2^{\mathcal{O}(n \log n)}$ states.

We remark that the RCs $\backsim$ and $\approx_u, u \in \Sigma^*$ allow us to construct a family of DFWs [4] that accept either $\mathcal{L}(\mathcal{A})$ or $\Sigma^\omega \setminus \mathcal{L}(\mathcal{A})$ [24]; we refer to [24] for the detailed construction.

6   Concluding Remarks

Over the past few decades, several different approaches have been proposed for complementing NBWs: congruence-based (alternatively Ramsey-based), rank-based and slice-based (alternatively profile-based) constructions. In this work we show that the profile-based analysis is the one tool underlying all of them.

Profiles have been used in [11] for the determinization-based complementation construction. As future work, we will look into the problem of whether profile-based analysis can also be used to explain determinization-based complementation constructions, such as Safra's [32] and Muller-Schupp's [29], possibly inspired by the unified approaches presented in [11,25].

Acknowledgements. We thank the anonymous reviewers for their valuable suggestions to this paper. This work is supported in part by the National Natural Science Foundation of China (Grant Nos. 62102407 and 61836005), CAS grant QYZDB-SSW-SYS019, NSF grants IIS-1527668, CCF-1704883, IIS-1830549, CNS-2016656, DoD MURI grant N00014-20-1-2787, and an award from the Maryland Procurement Office.

References

1. Abdulla, P.A., et al.: Simulation subsumption in Ramsey-based Büchi automata universality and inclusion testing. In: Touili, T., Cook, B., Jackson, P. (eds.) CAV 2010. LNCS, vol. 6174, pp. 132–147. Springer, Heidelberg (2010). https://doi.org/10.1007/978-3-642-14295-6_14

2. Abdulla, P.A., et al.: Advanced Ramsey-based Büchi automata inclusion testing. In: Katoen, J.-P., König, B. (eds.) CONCUR 2011. LNCS, vol. 6901, pp. 187–202. Springer, Heidelberg (2011). https://doi.org/10.1007/978-3-642-23217-6_13

3. Allred, J.D., Ultes-Nitsche, U.: A simple and optimal complementation algorithm for Büchi automata. In: Dawar, A., Grädel, E. (ed.) LICS, pp. 46–55. ACM (2018)

4. Angluin, D., Fisman, D.: Learning regular omega languages. Theor. Comput. Sci. **650**, 57–72 (2016)

5. Breuers, S., Löding, C., Olschewski, J.: Improved Ramsey-based Büchi complementation. In: Birkedal, L. (ed.) FoSSaCS 2012. LNCS, vol. 7213, pp. 150–164. Springer, Heidelberg (2012). https://doi.org/10.1007/978-3-642-28729-9_10

6. Büchi, J.R.: On a decision method in restricted second order arithmetic. In: Proceedings of International Congress on Logic, Method, and Philosophy of Science, pp. 1–12. Stanford University Press (1962)

7. Calbrix, H., Nivat, M., Podelski, A.: Ultimately periodic words of rational ω-languages. In: Brookes, S., Main, M., Melton, A., Mislove, M., Schmidt, D. (eds.) MFPS 1993. LNCS, vol. 802, pp. 554–566. Springer, Heidelberg (1994). https://doi.org/10.1007/3-540-58027-1_27

8. Chen, Y.-F., Havlena, V., Lengál, O.: Simulations in rank-based Büchi automata complementation. In: Lin, A.W. (ed.) APLAS 2019. LNCS, vol. 11893, pp. 447–467. Springer, Cham (2019). https://doi.org/10.1007/978-3-030-34175-6_23

9. Allen Emerson, E., Lei, C.-L.: Temporal reasoning under generalized fairness constraints. In: Monien, B., Vidal-Naquet, G. (eds.) STACS 1986. LNCS, vol. 210, pp. 21–36. Springer, Heidelberg (1986). https://doi.org/10.1007/3-540-16078-7_62

10. Fisler, K., Fraer, R., Kamhi, G., Vardi, M.Y., Yang, Z.: Is there a best symbolic cycle-detection algorithm? In: Margaria, T., Yi, W. (eds.) TACAS 2001. LNCS, vol. 2031, pp. 420–434. Springer, Heidelberg (2001). https://doi.org/10.1007/3-540-45319-9_29

11. Fogarty, S., Kupferman, O., Vardi, M.Y., Wilke, T.: Profile trees for Büchi word automata, with application to determinization. Inf. Comput. **245**, 136–151 (2015)

12. Fogarty, S., Kupferman, O., Wilke, T., Vardi, M.Y.: Unifying Büchi complementation constructions. Log. Methods Comput. Sci. **9**(1), 1–26 (2013)

13. Fogarty, S., Vardi, M.Y.: Efficient Büchi universality checking. In: Esparza, J., Majumdar, R. (eds.) TACAS 2010. LNCS, vol. 6015, pp. 205–220. Springer, Heidelberg (2010). https://doi.org/10.1007/978-3-642-12002-2_17

14. Fogarty, S., Vardi, M.Y.: Büchi complementation and size-change termination. Log. Methods Comput. Sci. **8**(1), 1–33 (2012)
15. Friedgut, E., Kupferman, O., Vardi, M.Y.: Büchi complementation made tighter. Int. J. Found. Comput. Sci. **17**(4), 851–868 (2006)
16. Gurumurthy, S., Kupferman, O., Somenzi, F., Vardi, M.Y.: On complementing nondeterministic Büchi automata. In: Geist, D., Tronci, E. (eds.) CHARME 2003. LNCS, vol. 2860, pp. 96–110. Springer, Heidelberg (2003). https://doi.org/10.1007/978-3-540-39724-3_10
17. Havlena, V., Lengál, O.: Reducing (to) the ranks: efficient rank-based Büchi automata complementation (technical report). CoRR, abs/2010.07834 (2020)
18. Hopcroft, J.E., Ullman, J.D.: Introduction to Automata Theory, Languages and Computation, 2nd edn. Addison-Wesley, Reading (2000)
19. Kähler, D., Wilke, T.: Complementation, disambiguation, and determinization of Büchi automata unified. In: Aceto, L., Damgård, I., Goldberg, L.A., Halldórsson, M.M., Ingólfsdóttir, A., Walukiewicz, I. (eds.) ICALP 2008. LNCS, vol. 5125, pp. 724–735. Springer, Heidelberg (2008). https://doi.org/10.1007/978-3-540-70575-8_59
20. Karmarkar, H., Chakraborty, S.: On minimal odd rankings for Büchi complementation. In: Liu, Z., Ravn, A.P. (eds.) ATVA 2009. LNCS, vol. 5799, pp. 228–243. Springer, Heidelberg (2009). https://doi.org/10.1007/978-3-642-04761-9_18
21. Klarlund, N.: Progress measures for complementation of omega-automata with applications to temporal logic. In: FOCS, pp. 358–367. IEEE Computer Society (1991)
22. Kupferman, O., Vardi, M.Y.: Model checking of safety properties. Formal Methods Syst. Des. **19**(3), 291–314 (2001)
23. Kupferman, O., Vardi, M.Y.: Weak alternating automata are not that weak. ACM Trans. Comput. Log. **2**(3), 408–429 (2001)
24. Li, Y., Tsay, Y.-K., Turrini, A., Vardi, M.Y., Zhang, L.: Congruence relations for Büchi automata. In: Huisman, M., Păsăreanu, C., Zhan, N. (eds.) FM 2021. LNCS, vol. 13047, pp. 465–482. Springer, Cham (2021). https://doi.org/10.1007/978-3-030-90870-6_25
25. Löding, C., Pirogov, A.: Determinization of Büchi automata: unifying the approaches of Safra and Muller-Schupp. In: Baier, C., Chatzigiannakis, I., Flocchini, P., Leonardi, S. (eds.) ICALP. LIPIcs, vol. 132, pp. 120:1–120:13. Schloss Dagstuhl - Leibniz-Zentrum für Informatik (2019)
26. Maler, O., Staiger, L.: On syntactic congruences for omega-languages. Theor. Comput. Sci. **183**(1), 93–112 (1997)
27. Michel, M.: Complementation is more difficult with automata on infinite words. Technical report, CNET, Paris (Manuscript) (1988)
28. Miyano, S., Hayashi, T.: Alternating finite automata on omega-words. Theor. Comput. Sci. **32**, 321–330 (1984)
29. Muller, D.E., Schupp, P.E.: Simulating alternating tree automata by nondeterministic automata: new results and new proofs of the theorems of Rabin, McNaughton and Safra. Theor. Comput. Sci. **141**(1&2), 69–107 (1995)
30. Myhill, J.: Finite automata and the representation of events. Technical report, WADD TR-57-624, pp. 112–137 (1957)
31. Nerode, A.: Linear automaton transformations. Am. Math. Soc. **9**, 541–544 (1958)
32. Safra, S.: On the complexity of ω-automata. In: FOCS, pp. 319–327. IEEE (1988)
33. Schewe, S.: Büchi complementation made tight. In: STACS. LIPIcs, vol. 3, pp. 661–672. Schloss Dagstuhl, Germany (2009)

34. Sistla, A.P., Vardi, M.Y., Wolper, P.: The complementation problem for Büchi automata with applications to temporal logic. Theor. Comput. Sci. **49**(2–3), 217–237 (1987)
35. Thomas, W.: Automata on infinite objects. In: Handbook of Theoretical Computer Science, Volume B: Formal Models and Semantics, pp. 133–191. Elsevier and MIT Press (1990)
36. Tsai, M.-H., Fogarty, S., Vardi, M.Y., Tsay, Y.-K.: State of Büchi complementation. Log. Methods Comput. Sci. **10**(4), 1–27 (2014)
37. Vardi, M.Y.: Expected properties of set partitions. Technical report, The Weizmann Institute of Science (1980)
38. Vardi, M.Y.: Verification of concurrent programs: the automata-theoretic framework. Ann. Pure Appl. Log. **51**(1–2), 79–98 (1991)
39. Vardi, M.Y.: The Büchi complementation Saga. In: Thomas, W., Weil, P. (eds.) STACS 2007. LNCS, vol. 4393, pp. 12–22. Springer, Heidelberg (2007). https://doi.org/10.1007/978-3-540-70918-3_2
40. Vardi, M.Y., Wolper, P.: An automata-theoretic approach to automatic program verification (preliminary report). In: LICS, pp. 332–344. IEEE (1986)
41. Yan, Q.: Lower bounds for complementation of ω-automata via the full automata technique. Log. Methods Comput. Sci. **4**(1:5), 1–20 (2008)

A Simple Rewrite System
for the Normalization of Linear Temporal
Logic

Javier Esparza[1] , Rubén Rubio[2(✉)] , and Salomon Sickert[3]

[1] Technical University of Munich, Munich, Germany
esparza@in.tum.de
[2] Universidad Complutense de Madrid, Madrid, Spain
rubenrub@ucm.es
[3] The Hebrew University, Jerusalem, Jerusalem, Israel
salomon.sickert@mail.huji.ac.il

Abstract. In the mid 80s, Lichtenstein, Pnueli, and Zuck showed that
every formula of Past LTL (the extension of Linear Temporal Logic with
past operators) is equivalent to a conjunction of formulas of the form
$\mathbf{GF}\varphi \vee \mathbf{FG}\psi$, where φ and ψ contain only past operators. Some years
later, Chang, Manna, and Pnueli derived a similar normal form for LTL.
Both normalization procedures have a non-elementary worst-case blow-
up, and follow an involved path from formulas to counter-free automata
to star-free regular expressions and back to formulas. In 2020, Sickert and
Esparza presented a direct and purely syntactic normalization procedure
for LTL yielding a normal form similar to the one by Chang, Manna, and
Pnueli, with a single exponential blow-up, and applied it to the problem
of constructing a succinct deterministic ω-automaton for a given formula.
However, their procedure had exponential time complexity in the best
case. In particular, it does not perform better for formulas that are almost
in normal form. In this paper we present an alternative normalization
procedure based on a simple set of rewrite rules.

1 Introduction

In the late 1970s,s, Amir Pnueli introduced Linear Temporal Logic (LTL) into
computer science as a framework for specifying and verifying concurrent programs [15,16], a contribution that earned him the 1996 Turing Award. During
the 1980s s and the early 1990s,s, Pnueli proceeded to study the properties
expressible in LTL in collaboration with other researchers. In 1985, Lichtenstein, Pnueli and Zuck introduced a classification of LTL properties [7], later

This work was partially supported by the Deutsche Forschungsgemeinschaft (DFG)
under projects 183790222, 317422601, and 436811179; by the European Research
Council (ERC) under the European Union's Horizon 2020 research and innovation
programme under grant agreement No 787367 (PaVeS); by the Spanish MCI project
ProCode (PID2019-108528RB-C22); and by the Spanish MU grants FPU17/02319 and
EST21/00536.

© Springer Nature Switzerland AG 2022
J.-F. Raskin and K. Chatterjee (Eds.): Principles of Systems Design, LNCS 13660, pp. 208–227, 2022.
https://doi.org/10.1007/978-3-031-22337-2_10

described in detail by Manna and Pnueli, who called it the *safety-progress* hierarchy in [11,12]. These works consider an extended version of LTL with past operators, called Past LTL. The safety-progress hierarchy consists of a *safety* class of formulas, and five *progress* classes. The classes are defined semantically in terms of their models, and the largest class, called the *reactivity* class in [11,12], contains all properties expressible in LTL. Manna and Pnueli provide syntactic characterizations of each class. In particular, they prove a fundamental theorem showing that every reactivity property is expressible as a conjunction of formulas of the form $\mathbf{GF}\varphi \vee \mathbf{FG}\psi$, where $\mathbf{F}\chi$ and $\mathbf{G}\chi$ mean that χ holds at some and at every point in the future, respectively, and φ, ψ only contain past operators.

In 1992, Chang, Manna, and Pnueli presented a different and very elegant characterization of the safety-progress hierarchy in terms of standard LTL without past operators, containing only the future operators $\mathbf{X}$ (next), $\mathbf{U}$ (until), and $\mathbf{W}$ (weak until) [4]. They show that every reactivity formula is equivalent to an LTL formula in negation normal form, such that every path through the syntax tree contains at most one alternation of $\mathbf{U}$ and $\mathbf{W}$. We call this fundamental result the Normalization Theorem. In the notation of [3,13,18], which mimics the definition of the Σ_i, Π_i, and Δ_i classes of the arithmetical and polynomial hierarchies, they proved that every LTL formula is equivalent to a Δ_2-formula.

While these normal forms have had large conceptual impact in model checking, automatic synthesis, and deductive verification (see e.g. [14] for a recent survey), the normalization *procedures* have had none. In particular, contrary to the case of propositional or first-order logic, they have not been implemented in tools. The reason is that they are not direct, have high complexity, and their correctness proofs are involved. The proof of the Normalization Theorem sketched in [4] (to the best of our knowledge, a full proof was never published) relies on the 1985 theorem by Lichtenstein, Pnueli and Zuck, a complete proof of which can be found in Zuck's PhD Thesis [19]. Zuck's proof translates the initial Past LTL formula into a counter-free semi-automaton, then applies the Krohn-Rhodes decomposition and other results to translate the automaton into a star-free regular expression, and finally translates this expression into a reactivity formula with a non-elementary blow-up. It is remarkable that, despite this prominence, only little progress has been made to improve Zuck's non-elementary normalization procedure, even though no lower bound was known.

On the one hand, Maler and Pnueli have presented a double-exponential[1] construction, based on the Krohn-Rhodes decomposition, translating a deterministic counter-free automaton into a Past LTL formula [8–10]. On the other hand, building upon this work, Boker, Lehtinen, and Sickert discovered a triple-exponential construction translating into a standard LTL formula without past operators [2]. Noticeably, both constructions yield formulas in the normal forms for Past LTL ([11,12]) and standard LTL ([3,4,13,18]), respectively.

In 2020, two of us presented a novel proof of the Normalization Theorem in [18] (based on [17]). We showed that every formula φ of LTL is equivalent to a

---

[1] For further details we refer the reader to [2, Remark 1].

formula of the form

$$\bigvee_{M \subseteq \mu(\varphi), N \subseteq \nu(\varphi)} \varphi_{M,N}$$

where $\mu(\varphi)$ and $\nu(\varphi)$ are the sets of subformulas of φ with top operator in $\{\mathbf{U}, \mathbf{M}\}$ and $\{\mathbf{W}, \mathbf{R}\}$, respectively, and $\varphi_{M,N}$ is a Δ_2-formula obtained from φ, M, and N by means of a few syntactic rewrite rules. This yields a normalization procedure with single exponential complexity, which was applied in [17,18] to the problem of translating LTL formulas into deterministic and limit-deterministic ω-automata.

Despite being a clear improvement on the previous indirect and non-elementary procedures, the normalization algorithm of [18] still has a problem: Since it has to consider all possible sets M and N, it has exponential time complexity *in the best case*. Moreover, the algorithm is not goal-oriented, in the sense that it does not only concentrate on those parts of the formula that do not belong to Δ_2. Consider for example a family of formulas

$$\varphi_n = ((a\mathbf{U}b)\mathbf{W}c)\mathbf{U}\psi_n$$

where a, b, c are atomic propositions and ψ_n is some very large formula containing only the $\mathbf{W}$ operator. Intuitively, ψ_n does not need to be touched by a normalization procedure, the only problem lies in the alternation $\mathbf{U}$-$\mathbf{W}$-$\mathbf{U}$ along the leftmost branch of the syntax tree. However, the procedure of [18] will be exponential in the number of $\mathbf{W}$-subformulas of ψ_n.

In this paper we provide a normalization procedure that solves these problems. The procedure is similar to the one for bringing a Boolean formula in conjunctive normal form (CNF). Recall that a Boolean formula is in CNF if in its syntax tree no conjunctions are below disjunctions, and only atomic propositions are below negations. The rewrite rules allow us to eliminate a node that violates one of these conditions; for example, if a conjunction is below a disjunction, we distribute the conjunction over the disjunction. In the case of LTL, instead of conjunctions and disjunctions we have to deal with different kinds of temporal operators, but we can still characterize the normal form in terms of constraints of the form "no X-node of the syntax tree is below a Y-node". Our rewrite rules eliminate nodes violating one of these constraints.

The paper is organized as follows. Section 2 introduces the syntax and semantics of LTL. Section 3 defines the Safety-Progress hierarchy, and recalls the Normalization Theorem of Chang, Manna, and Pnueli. Section 4 presents the rewrite system, and proves it correct. Section 5 summarizes the normalization algorithm derived from the rewrite system, and Sect. 6 introduces some derived results and some extensions of the algorithm. Finally, Sect. 7 reports on an experimental evaluation.

2   Preliminaries

Let Σ be a finite alphabet. A *word* w over Σ is an infinite sequence of letters $a_0 a_1 a_2 \ldots$ with $a_i \in \Sigma$ for all $i \geq 0$, and a language is a set of words. A *finite word* is a finite sequence of letters. The set of all words (finite words) is denoted

Σ^{ω} (Σ^*). We let $w[i]$ (starting at $i = 0$) denote the i-th letter of a word w. The finite infix $w[i]w[i+1]\ldots w[j-1]$ is abbreviated with w_{ij} and the infinite suffix $w[i]w[i+1]\ldots$ with w_i. We denote the infinite repetition of a finite word $a_0\ldots a_n$ by $(a_0\ldots a_n)^{\omega} = a_0\ldots a_n a_0\ldots a_n a_0\ldots$. A set of (finite or infinite) words is called a language.

Definition 2.1. *LTL formulas over a set Ap of atomic propositions are constructed by the following syntax:*

$$\varphi ::= \mathbf{tt} \mid \mathbf{ff} \mid a \mid \neg a \mid \varphi \wedge \varphi \mid \varphi \vee \varphi$$
$$\mid \mathbf{X}\varphi \mid \varphi\mathbf{U}\varphi \mid \varphi\mathbf{W}\varphi \mid \varphi\mathbf{R}\varphi \mid \varphi\mathbf{M}\varphi$$

where $a \in Ap$ is an atomic proposition and $\mathbf{X}$, $\mathbf{U}$, $\mathbf{W}$, $\mathbf{R}$, *and* $\mathbf{M}$ *are the next, (strong) until, weak until, (weak) release, and strong release operators, respectively.*

The inclusion of both the strong and weak until operators as well as the negation normal form are essential to our approach. The operators $\mathbf{R}$ and $\mathbf{M}$, however, are only added to ensure that every formula of length n in the standard syntax, with negation but only the until operator, is equivalent to a formula of length $O(n)$ in our syntax. They can be removed at the price of an exponential blow-up when translating formulas with occurrences of $\mathbf{R}$ and $\mathbf{M}$ into formulas without. The semantics is defined as usual:

Definition 2.2. *Let w be a word over the alphabet $\Sigma := 2^{Ap}$ and let φ be a formula. The satisfaction relation $w \models \varphi$ is inductively defined as the smallest relation satisfying:*

$$
\begin{aligned}
&w \models \mathbf{tt} && \text{for every } w \\
&w \not\models \mathbf{ff} && \text{for every } w \\
&w \models a && \text{iff } a \in w[0] \\
&w \models \neg a && \text{iff } a \notin w[0] \\
&w \models \varphi \wedge \psi && \text{iff } w \models \varphi \text{ and } w \models \psi \\
&w \models \varphi \vee \psi && \text{iff } w \models \varphi \text{ or } w \models \psi \\
&w \models \mathbf{X}\varphi && \text{iff } w_1 \models \varphi \\
&w \models \varphi\mathbf{U}\psi && \text{iff } \exists k.\, w_k \models \psi \text{ and } \forall j < k.\, w_j \models \varphi \\
&w \models \varphi\mathbf{M}\psi && \text{iff } \exists k.\, w_k \models \varphi \text{ and } \forall j \leq k.\, w_j \models \psi \\
&w \models \varphi\mathbf{R}\psi && \text{iff } \forall k.\, w_k \models \psi \text{ or } w \models \varphi\mathbf{M}\psi \\
&w \models \varphi\mathbf{W}\psi && \text{iff } \forall k.\, w_k \models \varphi \text{ or } w \models \varphi\mathbf{U}\psi
\end{aligned}
$$

We let $\mathcal{L}(\varphi) := \{w \in \Sigma^{\omega} : w \models \varphi\}$ denote the language of φ. We overload the definition of $\models$ and write $\varphi \models \psi$ as a shorthand for $\mathcal{L}(\varphi) \subseteq \mathcal{L}(\psi)$. Two formulas φ and ψ are equivalent, denoted $\varphi \equiv \psi$, if $\mathcal{L}(\varphi) = \mathcal{L}(\psi)$. Further, we use the abbreviations $\mathbf{F}\varphi := \mathbf{tt}\,\mathbf{U}\,\varphi$ (eventually) and $\mathbf{G}\varphi := \mathbf{ff}\,\mathbf{R}\,\varphi$ (always).

3   The Safety-Progress Hierarchy

We recall the hierarchy of temporal properties studied by Manna and Pnueli [11] following the formulation of Černá and Pelánek [3]. The definition formalizes the intuition that e.g. a safety property is violated by an execution iff one of its finite prefixes is "bad" or, equivalently, satisfied by an execution iff all its finite prefixes belong to a language of good prefixes.

Definition 3.1 ([3,11]). *Let $P \subseteq \Sigma^\omega$ be a property over Σ.*

- *P is a safety property if there exists a language of finite words $L \subseteq \Sigma^*$ such that $w \in P$ iff all finite prefixes of w belong to L.*
- *P is a guarantee property if there exists a language of finite words $L \subseteq \Sigma^*$ such that $w \in P$ iff there exists a finite prefix of w which belongs to L.*
- *P is an obligation property if it can be expressed as a positive Boolean combination of safety and guarantee properties.*
- *P is a recurrence property if there exists a language of finite words $L \subseteq \Sigma^*$ such that $w \in P$ iff infinitely many prefixes of w belong to L.*
- *P is a persistence property if there exists a language of finite words $L \subseteq \Sigma^*$ such that $w \in P$ iff all but finitely many prefixes of w belong to L.*
- *P is a reactivity property if P can be expressed as a positive Boolean combination of recurrence and persistence properties.*

The inclusions between these classes are shown in Fig. 1a. Chang, Manna, and Pnueli give in [4] a syntactic characterization of the classes in terms of the following fragments of LTL:

Definition 3.2 (Adapted from [3]**).** *We define the following classes of LTL formulas:*

- *The class $\Sigma_0 = \Pi_0 = \Delta_0$ is the least set of formulas containing all atomic propositions and their negations, and is closed under the application of conjunction and disjunction.*
- *The class Σ_{i+1} is the least set of formulas containing Π_i that is closed under the application of conjunction, disjunction, and the **X**, **U**, and **M** operators.*
- *The class Π_{i+1} is the least set of formulas containing Σ_i that is closed under the application of conjunction, disjunction, and the **X**, **R**, and **W** operators.*
- *The class Δ_{i+1} is the least set of formulas containing Σ_{i+1} and Π_{i+1} that is closed under the application of conjunction and disjunction.*

The following is a corollary of the proof of [4, Thm. 8]:

Theorem 3.1 (Adapted from [3]**).** *A property that is specifiable in LTL is a guarantee (safety, obligation, persistence, recurrence, reactivity, respectively) property if and only if it is specifiable by a formula from the class Σ_1, (Π_1, Δ_1, Σ_2, Π_2, Δ_2, respectively).*

Together with the result of [7], stating that every formula of LTL is equivalent to a reactivity formula, Chang, Manna, and Pnueli obtain:

Theorem 3.2 (Normalization Theorem [4,7,11]**).** *Every LTL formula is equivalent to a formula of Δ_2.*

(a) Safety-progress hierarchy [11]   (b) Syntactic-future hierarchy

Fig. 1. Both hierarchies, side-by-side, indicating the correspondence of Theorem 3.1

In [18], Sickert and Esparza obtain a new proof of the Normalization Theorem. They show that every formula φ is equivalent to a formula of the form

$$\bigvee_{M \subseteq \mu(\varphi), N \subseteq \nu(\varphi)} \varphi_{M,N}$$

where $\mu(\varphi)$ and $\nu(\varphi)$ are the sets of subformulas of φ with top operator in $\{\mathbf{U}, \mathbf{M}\}$ and $\{\mathbf{W}, \mathbf{R}\}$, respectively, and $\varphi_{M,N}$ is a Δ_2-formula obtained from φ, M, and N by means of a few syntactic rewrite rules. Further, $\varphi_{M,N}$ is at most exponentially longer than φ. While this is a big improvement with respect to previous procedures, it requires to iterate over all subsets of $\mu(\varphi)$ and $\nu(\varphi)$, and so the procedure *always* takes exponential time, even for simple families of formulas that have equivalent Δ_2-formulas with only a linear blow-up.

Example 3.1. Consider the family of formulas

$$\varphi_n = (\cdots ((((a_0 \mathbf{U} a_1)\mathbf{W} a_2)\mathbf{U} a_3)\mathbf{U} a_4) \cdots \mathbf{U} a_n)$$

for $n \geq 3$. The sets $\mu(\varphi_n)$ and $\nu(\varphi_n)$ have size $n - 1$ and 1, respectively. The procedure of [18] yields a disjunction of 2^{n+1} formulas $\varphi_{M,N}$, and so it takes exponential time in n. However, exhaustive application of a few simplification rules yields a short formula in normal form of length $\Theta(n)$:

$$\varphi_n \equiv (\mathbf{GF} a_1 \wedge (\cdots ((((a_0 \mathbf{U} a_1)\mathbf{U}(a_2 \vee \mathbf{G}(a_0 \vee a_1)))\mathbf{U} a_3)\mathbf{U} a_4)\cdots \mathbf{U} a_n)$$
$$\vee (\cdots ((((a_0 \mathbf{U} a_1)\mathbf{U} a_2)\mathbf{U} a_3)\mathbf{U} a_4) \cdots \mathbf{U} a_n)$$

Intuitively, in order to normalize φ_n it suffices to solve the "local" problem caused by the subformula $((a_0 \mathbf{U} a_1)\mathbf{W} a_2)\mathbf{U} a_3$ of φ_n, which is in Σ_3; however, the procedure of [18] is blind to this fact, and generates 2^{n+1} formulas, only to simplify them away later on.

4   A Normalizing Rewrite System

We present a rewrite system that allows us to normalize every LTL formula. As a corollary, we obtain an alternative proof of the Normalization Theorem.

The key idea is to treat the combinations **GF** (infinitely often) and **FG** (almost always) of temporal operators as *atomic* operators **GF** and **FG** (notice the typesetting with the two letters touching each other). We call them the *limit operators*; intuitively, whether a word satisfies a formula **GF**φ or **FG**φ depends only on its behaviour "in the limit", in the sense that $w'w$ satisfies **GF**φ or **FG**φ iff w does.[2] So we add the limit operators to the syntax. Moreover, in order to simplify the presentation, we also temporarily remove the operators **M** and **R** (we reintroduce them in Sect. 6). So we define:

Definition 4.1. *Extended LTL formulas over a set Ap of atomic propositions are generated by the syntax:*

$$\varphi ::= \mathbf{tt} \mid \mathbf{ff} \mid a \mid \neg a \mid \varphi \wedge \varphi \mid \varphi \vee \varphi$$
$$\mid \mathbf{X}\varphi \mid \varphi\mathbf{U}\varphi \mid \varphi\mathbf{W}\varphi \mid \mathbf{GF}\varphi \mid \mathbf{FG}\varphi$$

When determining the class of a formula in the syntactic future hierarchy, **GF** and **FG** are implicitly replaced by **GF** and **FG**. For example, **FGF**a is rewritten into **FGF**a, and so it is a formula of Σ_3. In the rest of the section we only consider extended formulas which are by construction negation normal form and call them just formulas.

Let us now define the precise shape of our normal form, which is a bit more strict than Δ_2. Formulas of the form $\varphi\mathbf{U}\psi$, $\varphi\mathbf{W}\psi$, $\mathbf{X}\varphi$, **GF**φ, and **FG**φ are called **U-**, **W-**, **X-**, **GF-**, and **FG-**formulas, respectively. We refer to these formulas as *temporal* formulas. The syntax tree T_φ of a formula φ is defined in the usual way, and $|\varphi|$ denotes the number of nodes of T_φ. A node of T_φ is a *U-node* if the subformula rooted at it is a **U**-formula. **W-**, **GF-**, **FG-** and temporal nodes are defined analogously.

Definition 4.2. *Let φ be an LTL formula. A node of T_φ is a* limit node *if it is either a* **GF***-node or a* **FG***-node. The formula φ is in* normal form *if T_φ satisfies the following properties:*

1. *No* **U***-node is under a* **W***-node.*
2. *No limit node is under another temporal node.*
3. *No* **W***-node is under a* **GF***-node, and no* **U***-node is under a* **FG***-node.*

Remark 4.1. Observe that formulas in normal form belong to Δ_2. Even a slightly stronger statement holds: a formula in normal form is a positive Boolean combination of formulas of Σ_2 and formulas of the form **GF**ψ such that $\psi \in \Sigma_1$ (and so **GF**$\psi \in \Pi_2$).

There is a dual normal form in which property 1. is replaced by "no **W**-node is under a U-node", and the other two properties do not change. Formulas in dual normal form are positive Boolean combination of formulas of Π_2 and formulas of the form **FG**ψ such that $\psi \in \Pi_1$. Once the Normalization Theorem for the primal normal form is proved, a corresponding theorem for the dual form follows as an easy corollary (see Sect. 6).

---

[2] Limit operators are called *suspendable* in [1].

In the following three subsections we incrementally normalize formulas by dealing with the three requirements of the normal form one by one. Intermediate normal forms are obtained between stages, which we define formally using the following two measures:

- $n_u(\varphi)$ is the number of **U**-nodes in T_φ that are under some **W**-node, but not under any limit node of T_φ. For example, if $\varphi = (a\mathbf{U}b)\mathbf{W}(\mathbf{FG}(c\mathbf{U}d))$ then $n_u(\varphi) = 1$.
- $n_{\lim}(\varphi)$ is the number of distinct limit subformulas under some temporal operator. Formally, $n_{\lim}(\varphi)$ is the number of limit formulas ψ' such that ψ' is a proper subformula of a temporal subformula (proper or not) of φ. For example, if $\varphi = (\mathbf{FG}a \, \mathbf{U} \, \mathbf{GF}b) \vee (\mathbf{GF}b \, \mathbf{W} \, \mathbf{FG}a)$ then $n_{\lim}(\varphi) = 2$.

Definition 4.3. *An LTL formula φ is in 1-form if $n_u(\varphi) = 0$, and in 1-2-form if $n_u(\varphi) = 0$ and $n_{lim}(\varphi) = 0$.*

We proceed in three stages:

1. We remove all **U**-nodes that are under some **W**-node, but not under any limit node. The resulting formula is in 1-form.
2. We remove all limit nodes under some other temporal node. The resulting formula is in 1-2-form.
3. We remove all **W**-nodes under some **GF**-node, and all **U**-nodes under some **FG**-node. The resulting formula is in normal form (Definition 4.2).

Stage 1: Removing U-nodes under W-nodes.

We consider formulas φ with placeholders, i.e., "holes" that can be filled with a formula. Formally, let [ ] be a symbol denoting a special atomic proposition. A formula with placeholders is a formula with one or more occurrences of [ ], all of them positive (i.e., the formula has no occurrence of ¬[ ]). We denote by $\varphi[\psi]$ the result of filling each placeholder of φ with an occurrence of ψ; formally, $\varphi[\psi]$ is the result of substituting ψ for [ ] in φ. For example, if $\varphi[\ ] = ([\ ]\mathbf{W}(a\mathbf{U}[\ ]))$, then $\varphi[\mathbf{X}b] = (\mathbf{X}b)\mathbf{W}(a\mathbf{U}\mathbf{X}b)$. We assume that [ ] binds more strongly than any operator, e.g. $\varphi_1\mathbf{W}\varphi_2[\psi] = \varphi_1\mathbf{W}(\varphi_2[\psi])$.

This lemma, proved in the Appendix, allows us to pull **U**-subformulas out of **W**-formulas:

Lemma 4.1.

(1) $$\varphi_1\mathbf{W}\varphi_2[\psi_1\mathbf{U}\psi_2] \equiv (\varphi_1\mathbf{U}\varphi_2[\psi_1\mathbf{U}\psi_2]) \vee \mathbf{G}\varphi_1$$
(2) $$\varphi_1[\psi_1\mathbf{U}\psi_2]\mathbf{W}\varphi_2 \equiv (\mathbf{GF}\psi_2 \wedge \varphi_1[\psi_1\mathbf{W}\psi_2]\mathbf{W}\varphi_2)$$
$$\vee \; \varphi_1[\psi_1\mathbf{U}\psi_2]\mathbf{U}(\varphi_2 \vee (\mathbf{G}\varphi_1[\mathbf{ff}]))$$

Proposition 4.1. *For every LTL formula φ there exists an equivalent formula φ' in 1-form such that $|\varphi'| \leq 4^{2|\varphi|} \cdot |\varphi|$. Moreover, for every subformula $\mathbf{GF}\psi$ of φ' the formula ψ is a subformula of φ, and every $\mathbf{FG}$-subformula of φ' is also a subformula of φ.*

Proof. We associate to each formula a rank, defined by $rank(\varphi) = |\varphi| + n_u(\varphi)$. Observe that a formula φ is in 1-form iff $rank(\varphi) = |\varphi|$. Throughout the proof we say that a formula φ' *satisfies the limit property* if for every subformula $\mathbf{GF}\psi$ of φ' the formula ψ is a subformula of φ and every $\mathbf{FG}$-subformula of φ' is also a subformula of φ (notice the asymmetry). Further, we say that a formula φ' *satisfies the size property* if $|\varphi'| \leq 4^{rank(\varphi)} \cdot |\varphi|$ from which the claimed size bound immediately follows.

We prove by induction on $rank(\varphi)$ that φ is equivalent to a formula φ' in 1-form satisfying the limit and size properties. Within the inductive step we proceed by a case distinction of φ:

If $\varphi = \mathbf{tt}, \mathbf{ff}, \mathbf{GF}\psi, \mathbf{FG}\psi$ then φ is already in 1-form, and satisfies the limit and size properties.

If $\varphi = \varphi_1 \wedge \varphi_2, \varphi_1 \vee \varphi_2, \varphi_1\mathbf{U}\varphi_2$ then by induction hypothesis φ_1 and φ_2 can be normalized into formulas φ_1' and φ_2' satisfying the limit and size properties. The formulas $\varphi_1' \wedge \varphi_2'$, $\varphi_1' \vee \varphi_2'$, $\varphi_1'\mathbf{U}\varphi_2'$ are then in 1-form (the latter because the additional $\mathbf{U}$-node is above any $\mathbf{W}$-node) and satisfy the limit property. The size property holds because:

$$|\varphi_1'| + |\varphi_2'| + 1 \leq 4^{rank(\varphi_1)} \cdot |\varphi_1| + 4^{rank(\varphi_2)} \cdot |\varphi_2| + 1$$
$$\leq 4^{rank(\varphi_1)+rank(\varphi_2)} \cdot (|\varphi_1| + |\varphi_2| + 1)$$
$$\leq 4^{rank(\varphi)} \cdot |\varphi|$$

If $\varphi = \mathbf{X}\varphi_1$, then by induction hypothesis there is a formula φ_1' equivalent to φ_1 in 1-form, and so φ is equivalent to $\mathbf{X}\varphi_1'$, which is in 1-form and satisfies the limit and size properties.

If $\varphi = \varphi_1\mathbf{W}\varphi_2$ and $n_u(\varphi) = 0$, then $\varphi_1\mathbf{W}\varphi_2$ is already in 1-form and satisfies the limit and size properties.

If $\varphi = \varphi_1\mathbf{W}\varphi_2$ and $n_u(\varphi) > 0$, then we proceed by a case distinction:

- φ_2 contains at least one $\mathbf{U}$-node that is not under a limit node. Let $\psi_1\mathbf{U}\psi_2$ be such a $\mathbf{U}$-node. We derive $\varphi_2[\ ]$ from φ_2 by replacing each $\mathbf{U}$-node labelled by $\psi_1\mathbf{U}\psi_2$ by the special atomic proposition $[\ ]$. By Lemma 4.1(1) we have:

$$\varphi_1\mathbf{W}\varphi_2[\psi_1\mathbf{U}\psi_2] \equiv \varphi_1\mathbf{U}\varphi_2[\psi_1\mathbf{U}\psi_2] \vee \varphi_1\mathbf{W}\mathbf{ff}$$

Since $rank(\varphi_1) < rank(\varphi)$, $rank(\varphi_2) < rank(\varphi)$, and $rank(\varphi_1\mathbf{W}\mathbf{ff}) < rank(\varphi)$ (the latter because φ_2 contains at least one $\mathbf{U}$-node), by induction hypothesis φ_1, φ_2, and $\varphi_1\mathbf{W}\mathbf{ff}$ can be normalized into formulas φ_1', φ_2', and φ_3' satisfying the limit and size properties. So φ can be normalized into $\varphi' = \varphi_1'\mathbf{U}\varphi_2' \vee \varphi_3'$. Moreover, φ' satisfies the limit property, because all $\mathbf{GF}$- and $\mathbf{FG}$-subformulas of φ' are subformulas of φ_1', φ_2', or φ_3'. For the size property we calculate:

$$|\varphi'| = |\varphi_1'| + |\varphi_2'| + |\varphi_3'| + 2$$
$$\leq 4^{rank(\varphi_1)} \cdot |\varphi_1| + 4^{rank(\varphi_2)} \cdot |\varphi_2| + 4^{rank(\varphi_1\mathbf{W}\mathbf{ff})} \cdot |\varphi_1\mathbf{W}\mathbf{ff}| + 2$$
$$\leq 4^{rank(\varphi)-1} \cdot (|\varphi_1| + |\varphi_2| + |\varphi_1\mathbf{W}\mathbf{ff}| + 2)$$
$$\leq 4^{rank(\varphi)-1} \cdot 4 \cdot |\varphi| = 4^{rank(\varphi)} \cdot |\varphi|$$

- Every **U**-node of φ_2 is under a limit node, and φ_1 contains at least one **U**-node that is not under any limit node. Then φ_1 contains a maximal subformula $\psi_1 \mathbf{U} \psi_2$ (with respect to the subformula order) that is not under a limit node. We derive $\varphi_1[\ \ ]$ from φ_1 by replacing each **U**-node labelled by $\psi_1 \mathbf{U} \psi_2$ that does not appear under a limit node by the special atomic proposition $[\ \ ]$. By Lemma 4.1(2), we have

$$\varphi_1[\psi_1 \mathbf{U} \psi_2] \mathbf{W} \varphi_2 \equiv$$
$$\left(\mathbf{GF} \psi_2 \wedge \underbrace{\varphi_1[\psi_1 \mathbf{W} \psi_2] \mathbf{W} \varphi_2}_{\rho_1} \right) \vee \left(\underbrace{\varphi_1[\psi_1 \mathbf{U} \psi_2]}_{\rho_2} \mathbf{U} \underbrace{(\varphi_2 \vee (\varphi_1[\mathbf{ff}] \mathbf{W} \mathbf{ff}))}_{\rho_3} \right)$$

In order to apply the induction hypothesis we argue that ρ_1, ρ_2, and ρ_3 have rank smaller than φ, and thus can be normalized to ρ_1', ρ_2' and ρ_3' satisfying the limit and size properties. The formula ρ_1 has the same number of nodes as φ, but fewer **U**-nodes under **W**-nodes; so $n_u(\rho_1) < n_u(\varphi)$ and thus $rank(\rho_1) < rank(\varphi)$. The same argument applies to ρ_3. Finally, $rank(\rho_2) < rank(\varphi)$ follows from the fact that ρ_2 has fewer nodes than φ. So φ can be normalized to $\varphi' = (\mathbf{GF} \psi_2 \wedge \rho_1') \vee (\rho_2' \mathbf{U} \rho_3')$.

We show that φ' satisfies the limit property. Let $\mathbf{GF} \psi$ be a subformula of φ'. If $\mathbf{GF} \psi = \mathbf{GF} \psi_2$, then we are done, because ψ_2 is a subformula of φ. Otherwise $\mathbf{GF} \psi$ is a subformula of ρ_1', ρ_2', or ρ_3'. Since all of them satisfy the limit property, ψ is a subformula of φ, and we are done. Further, every **FG**-subformula of φ' belongs to ρ_1', ρ_2', or ρ_3' and so it is also subformula of φ. For the size property we calculate:

$$|\varphi'| = |\rho_1'| + |\rho_2'| + |\rho_3'| + |\psi_2| + 4$$
$$\leq 4^{rank(\rho_1)} \cdot |\rho_1| + 4^{rank(\rho_2)} \cdot |\rho_2| + 4^{rank(\rho_3)} \cdot |\rho_3| + |\varphi_1| + 4$$
$$\leq 4^{rank(\varphi)-1} \cdot (|\varphi| + |\varphi| + |\varphi|) + |\varphi| + 4$$
$$\leq 4^{rank(\varphi)-1} \cdot 4 \cdot |\varphi| = 4^{rank(\varphi)} \cdot |\varphi|$$

Stage 2: Moving **GF**- and **FG**-subformulas up.

In this section, we address the second property of the normal form. The following lemma allows us to pull limit subformulas out of any temporal formula. (Note that the second rule is only necessary if the formula before stage 1 contained **FG**-subformulas, since stage 1 only creates new **GF**-formulas.)

Lemma 4.2.

(3) $$\varphi[\mathbf{GF} \psi] \equiv (\mathbf{GF} \psi \wedge \varphi[\mathbf{tt}]) \vee \varphi[\mathbf{ff}]$$
(4) $$\varphi[\mathbf{FG} \psi] \equiv (\mathbf{FG} \psi \wedge \varphi[\mathbf{tt}]) \vee \varphi[\mathbf{ff}]$$

We show using (3) and (4) that every formula in 1-form can be transformed into an equivalent formula in 1-2-form.

Proposition 4.2. *Every LTL formula φ in 1-form is equivalent to a formula φ' in 1-2-form such that $|\varphi'| \leq 3^{n_{\lim}(\varphi)} \cdot |\varphi|$. Moreover, the size of the limit subformulas does not increase: for every $b > 0$, if $|\psi| \leq b$ for every limit subformula of φ, then $|\psi'| \leq b$ for every limit subformula of φ'.*

Proof. We proceed by induction on the number of proper limit subformulas of φ. If φ does not contain any, then it is already in 1-2-form. Assume there exists such a proper limit subformula ψ that is smaller (or incomparable) to all other limit subformulas of φ according to the subformula order. We derive $\varphi[\ ]$ from φ by replacing each limit-node labelled by ψ by the special atomic proposition $[\ ]$. We then apply Lemma 4.2 to obtain:

$$\varphi[\psi] \equiv (\psi \wedge \varphi[\mathbf{tt}]) \vee \varphi[\mathbf{ff}] \qquad \text{where } \psi = \mathbf{GF}\psi', \mathbf{FG}\psi' \ .$$

Note that ψ does not properly contain any limit subformula, and so it is in 1-2-form. Both $\varphi[\mathbf{tt}]$ and $\varphi[\mathbf{ff}]$ are still in 1-form and they have one limit operator less than φ. Thus they can be normalized by the induction hypothesis into φ'_1 and φ'_2 in 1-2-form. Finally, $\varphi' = (\psi \wedge \varphi'_1) \vee \varphi'_2$ is a Boolean combination of formulas in 1-2-form, so it is in 1-2-form. The number of nodes of $T_{\varphi'}$ can be crudely bounded as follows:

$$|\varphi'| \leq |\varphi'_1| + |\varphi'_2| + |\psi| + 2$$
$$\leq 2 \cdot 3^{n_{\lim}(\varphi[\mathbf{tt}])} \cdot |\varphi[\mathbf{tt}]| + |\psi| + 2$$
$$\leq 3^{n_{\lim}(\varphi[\mathbf{tt}])} \cdot (2 \cdot (|\varphi| - |\psi| + 1) + |\psi| + 2)$$
$$\leq 3^{n_{\lim}(\varphi)-1} \cdot (2|\varphi| - |\psi| + 4)$$
$$\leq 3^{n_{\lim}(\varphi)-1} \cdot (3|\varphi|) = 3^{n_{\lim}(\varphi)} \cdot |\varphi|$$

where the induction hypothesis is used in the second inequality, and $|\psi| \geq 2$ and $|\varphi| \geq 2$ in the last one.

To show that the size of the limit subformulas does not increase, let b be a bound on the size of the $\mathbf{GF}$-subformulas of φ. We claim that the size of each $\mathbf{GF}$-subformula of φ' is also bounded by b (the case of $\mathbf{FG}\psi$ is analogous). Indeed, the $\mathbf{GF}$-subformulas of φ' are ψ (which is already in φ) and the $\mathbf{GF}$-subformulas of φ'_1 and φ'_2. Since the $\mathbf{GF}$-subformulas of $\varphi[\mathbf{tt}]$ and $\varphi[\mathbf{ff}]$ can only have decreased in size, by induction hypothesis the number of nodes of any $\mathbf{GF}$-subformula of φ'_1 and φ'_2 is bounded by b, and we are done.

Stage 3: Removing W-nodes (U-nodes) under GF-nodes (FG-nodes)

The normalization of LTL formulas is completed in this section by fixing the problems within limit subformulas. In order to do so, we introduce two new rewrite rules that allow us to pull $\mathbf{W}$-subformulas out of $\mathbf{GF}$-formulas, and $\mathbf{U}$-subformulas out of $\mathbf{FG}$-formulas.

Lemma 4.3.

(5) $\qquad \mathbf{GF}\varphi[\psi_1 \mathbf{W}\psi_2] \equiv \mathbf{GF}\varphi[\psi_1 \mathbf{U}\psi_2] \vee (\mathbf{FG}\psi_1 \wedge \mathbf{GF}\varphi[\mathbf{tt}])$

(6) $\qquad \mathbf{FG}\varphi[\psi_1 \mathbf{U}\psi_2] \equiv (\mathbf{GF}\psi_2 \wedge \mathbf{FG}\varphi[\psi_1 \mathbf{W}\psi_2]) \vee \mathbf{FG}\varphi[\mathbf{ff}]$

The following proposition repeatedly applies these rules to show that limit formulas can be normalized with an exponential blowup.

Proposition 4.3. *For every LTL formula φ without limit operators, $\mathbf{GF}\varphi$ and $\mathbf{FG}\varphi$ can be normalized into formulas with at most $|\varphi'| \leq 3^{|\varphi|} \cdot |\varphi|$ nodes.*

Proof. A $\mathbf{GF}$-obstacle of a formula is a $\mathbf{W}$-node or a $\mathbf{U}$-node under a $\mathbf{W}$-node inside a $\mathbf{GF}$-node. Similarly, a $\mathbf{FG}$-obstacle is a $\mathbf{U}$-node or a $\mathbf{W}$-node under a $\mathbf{U}$-node inside a $\mathbf{FG}$-node. Finally, an obstacle is either a $\mathbf{GF}$-obstacle or an $\mathbf{FG}$-obstacle. We proceed by induction on the number of obstacles of $\mathbf{GF}\varphi$ or $\mathbf{FG}\varphi$. If they have no obstacles, then they are already in normal form (Definition 4.2).

Assume $\mathbf{GF}\varphi$ has at least one obstacle. Then φ contains at least one maximal $\mathbf{W}$-node $\psi_1\mathbf{W}\psi_2$. We derive $\mathbf{GF}\varphi[\ \ ]$ from $\mathbf{GF}\varphi$ by replacing each $\mathbf{W}$-node labelled by $\psi_1\mathbf{W}\psi_2$ by the special atomic proposition $[\ \ ]$. By Lemma 5, $\mathbf{GF}\varphi[\psi_1\mathbf{W}\psi_2]$ is equivalent to

$$\mathbf{GF}\varphi[\psi_1\mathbf{U}\psi_2] \vee (\mathbf{FG}\psi_1 \wedge \mathbf{GF}\varphi[\mathbf{tt}])$$

We claim that each of $\mathbf{GF}\varphi[\psi_1\mathbf{U}\psi_2]$, $\mathbf{GF}\varphi[\mathbf{tt}]$, and $\mathbf{FG}\psi_1$ has fewer obstacles than $\mathbf{GF}\varphi[\psi_1\mathbf{W}\psi_2]$, and so can be normalized by induction hypothesis. Indeed, $\mathbf{GF}\varphi[\psi_1\mathbf{U}\psi_2]$, and $\mathbf{GF}\varphi[\mathbf{tt}]$ have at least one $\mathbf{W}$-node less than φ, and the number of $\mathbf{U}$-nodes under a $\mathbf{W}$-node, due to the maximality of $\psi_1\mathbf{W}\psi_2$, has not increased, and as a consequence it has fewer $\mathbf{GF}$-obstacles (and by definition no $\mathbf{FG}$-obstacles). For $\mathbf{FG}\psi_1$, observe first that every $\mathbf{FG}$-obstacle of $\mathbf{FG}\psi_1$ is a $\mathbf{GF}$-obstacle of $\mathbf{GF}\varphi[\psi_1\mathbf{W}\psi_2]$. Indeed, the obstacles of $\mathbf{FG}\psi_1$ are the $\mathbf{U}$-nodes and the $\mathbf{W}$-nodes under $\mathbf{U}$-nodes; the former were under $\mathbf{W}$-nodes in φ, and the latter were $\mathbf{W}$-nodes of φ, and so both $\mathbf{GF}$-obstacles of $\mathbf{GF}\varphi$. Moreover, $\psi_1\mathbf{W}\psi_2$ is a $\mathbf{GF}$-obstacle of φ, but not a $\mathbf{FG}$-obstacle of $\mathbf{FG}\psi_1$. Hence, the number of obstacles has decreased.

Assume now that $\mathbf{FG}\varphi$ has at least one obstacle. Then φ contains at least one maximal $\mathbf{U}$-node $\psi_1\mathbf{U}\psi_2$. We derive $\mathbf{FG}\varphi[\ \ ]$ from $\mathbf{FG}\varphi$ by replacing each $\mathbf{U}$-node labelled by $\psi_1\mathbf{U}\psi_2$ by the special atomic proposition $[\ \ ]$. By Lemma 6, $\mathbf{FG}\varphi[\psi_1\mathbf{U}\psi_2]$ is equivalent to

$$(\mathbf{GF}\psi_2 \wedge \mathbf{FG}\varphi[\psi_1\mathbf{W}\psi_2]) \vee \mathbf{FG}\varphi[\mathbf{ff}]$$

Each of $\mathbf{GF}\psi_2$, $\mathbf{FG}\varphi[\psi_1\mathbf{W}\psi_2]$, and $\mathbf{FG}\varphi[\mathbf{ff}]$ has fewer obstacles as $\mathbf{FG}\varphi[\psi_1\mathbf{U}\psi_2]$, and can be normalized by induction hypothesis. The proof is as above.

The size of the formula increases at most by a factor of 3 on each step, and the number of steps is bounded by the number of both $\mathbf{W}$-nodes and $\mathbf{U}$-nodes in φ, which is bounded by the total number of nodes in φ. So the formula has at most $3^{|\varphi|}|\varphi|$ nodes.

The Normalization Theorem

The main result directly follows from the previous propositions.

Theorem 4.1. *Every formula φ of LTL is normalizable into a formula with at most $4^{7|\varphi|}$ nodes.*

Proof. Any LTL formula φ can be transformed into an equivalent φ' in 1-form of size $|\varphi'| \leq 4^{2|\varphi|} \cdot |\varphi|$ by Proposition 4.1. Moreover, $n_{\lim}(\varphi') \leq 2 \cdot |\varphi|$, since every **FG**-subformula of ψ' and every argument ψ of a **GF**-subformula of φ' is a subformula of φ. In addition, $|\psi| \leq |\varphi|$ for every **GF**ψ subformula of φ.

According to Proposition 4.2, for every formula φ' in 1-form there is an equivalent formula φ'' in 1-2-form with

$$(\star) \qquad |\varphi''| \leq 3^{n_{\lim}(\varphi')} \cdot |\varphi'| \leq 3^{2|\varphi|} \cdot (4^{2|\varphi|} \cdot |\varphi|) \leq 3^{2|\varphi|} \cdot 4^{3|\varphi|}$$

This formula is a Boolean combination of limit formulas with at most $|\varphi|$ nodes, not containing any proper limit node, and other temporal formulas containing neither limit nodes nor **U**-nodes under **W**-nodes. The latter are in Σ_2 and Proposition 4.3 deals with the former. Notice that every **GF**ψ and **FG**ψ subformula has at most $|\varphi|$ nodes and thus can be normalized into a formula with at most $3^{|\varphi|}|\varphi|$ nodes. The result φ''' of replacing these limit subformulas by their normal forms within φ'' is a Boolean combination of normal forms, and so we are done. The number of nodes in the resulting formula φ''' is at most:

$$|\varphi'''| \leq |\varphi''| + n_{\lim}(\varphi'') \cdot 3^{|\varphi|} \cdot |\varphi| \qquad\qquad n_{\lim}(\varphi'') \leq |\varphi''|$$
$$\leq |\varphi''| \cdot 3^{2|\varphi|} \cdot (|\varphi| + 1) \qquad\qquad\qquad\qquad (\star)$$
$$\leq 4^{3|\varphi|} \cdot 3^{4|\varphi|} \cdot (|\varphi| + 1) \qquad\qquad |\varphi| + 1 \leq 4^{|\varphi|/2}$$
$$\leq 4^{3|\varphi|} \cdot 4^{(4\log_4 3 + \frac{1}{2})|\varphi|} \leq 4^{7|\varphi|}$$

5   Summary of the Normalization Algorithm

We summarize the steps of the normalization algorithm described and proven in Sect. 4. Recall that a formula is in normal form iff it satisfies the following properties:

1. No **U**-node is under a **W**-node.
2. No limit node is under another temporal node.
3. No **W**-node is under a **GF**-node, and no **U**-node is under a **FG**-node.

The normalization algorithm applies the rules in Table 1 as follows to fix any violation of these properties:

1. **U**-nodes under **W**-nodes and not under limit nodes are removed using rules (1) and (2). This may introduce new **GF**-subformulas. By applying (2) only to highest **U**-nodes of φ_1 the number of new **GF**-subformulas is only linear in the size of the original formula.

Table 1. Normalization rules.

Stage 1:
$$(1) \quad \varphi_1 \mathbf{W} \varphi_2 [\psi_1 \mathbf{U} \psi_2] \equiv \varphi_1 \mathbf{U} \varphi_2 [\psi_1 \mathbf{U} \psi_2] \vee \mathbf{G} \varphi_1$$

$$(2) \quad \varphi_1 [\psi_1 \mathbf{U} \psi_2] \mathbf{W} \varphi_2 \equiv (\mathbf{GF} \psi_2 \wedge \varphi_1 [\psi_1 \mathbf{W} \psi_2] \mathbf{W} \varphi_2)$$
$$\vee \ \varphi_1 [\psi_1 \mathbf{U} \psi_2] \mathbf{U} (\varphi_2 \vee \mathbf{G} \varphi_1 [\mathbf{ff}])$$

Stage 2:
$$(3) \quad \varphi [\mathbf{GF} \psi] \equiv (\mathbf{GF} \psi \wedge \varphi [\mathbf{tt}]) \vee \varphi [\mathbf{ff}]$$

$$(4) \quad \varphi [\mathbf{FG} \psi] \equiv (\mathbf{FG} \psi \wedge \varphi [\mathbf{tt}]) \vee \varphi [\mathbf{ff}]$$

Stage 3:
$$(5) \quad \mathbf{GF} \varphi [\psi_1 \mathbf{W} \psi_2] \equiv \mathbf{GF} \varphi [\psi_1 \mathbf{U} \psi_2] \vee (\mathbf{FG} \psi_1 \wedge \mathbf{GF} \varphi [\mathbf{tt}])$$

$$(6) \quad \mathbf{FG} \varphi [\psi_1 \mathbf{U} \psi_2] \equiv (\mathbf{GF} \psi_2 \wedge \mathbf{FG} \varphi [\psi_1 \mathbf{W} \psi_2]) \vee \mathbf{FG} \varphi [\mathbf{ff}]$$

2. Limit nodes under other temporal nodes are pulled out using rules (3) and (4). By applying the rules only to the lowest limit nodes, it only needs to be applied once for each limit subformula.
3. **W**-nodes under **GF**-nodes are removed using rule (5), and **U**-nodes under **FG**-nodes are removed using rule (6). This may produce new limit nodes of smaller size that are handled recursively. Choosing highest **W**- and **U**-nodes ensures that the process produces only a single exponential blowup over the initial size of the formula.

After the three steps, a formula in normal form is obtained with a single exponential blowup in the number of nodes.

Moreover, notice that ψ_1 itself does not play any role in rules (2) and (6), and neither does ψ_2 in (5). Hence, the application of (1) can be made mode efficient by replacing not only every occurrence of $\psi_1 \mathbf{U} \psi_2$ outside a limit subformula with $\psi_1 \mathbf{W} \psi_2$ and $\mathbf{ff}$, but also every occurrence of $\psi \mathbf{U} \psi_2$ for any formula ψ by $\psi \mathbf{W} \psi_2$ and by $\mathbf{ff}$. The same holds for rules (5) and (6).

Example 5.1. Let us apply the procedure to the formula φ_n in Example 3.1. In stage 1, rule (2) matches the subformula $(a_0 \mathbf{U} a_1) \mathbf{W} a_2$ and rewrites it to $\mathbf{GF} a_1 \wedge (a_0 \mathbf{W} a_1) \mathbf{W} a_2 \vee (a_0 \mathbf{U} a_1) \mathbf{U} (a_2 \vee \mathbf{ff} \mathbf{W} \mathbf{ff})$, where $\mathbf{ff} \mathbf{W} \mathbf{ff}$ can be simplified to $\mathbf{ff}$ and removed. The rewritten formula is in 1-form, because there is no **U**-node under a **W**-node, so we can continue to stage 2. Now, we must pull the **GF**-node $\mathbf{GF} a_1$ out the cascade of **U**-nodes using rule (3). This yields

$$\varphi_n \equiv (\mathbf{GF} a_1 \wedge (\cdots ((((a_0 \mathbf{W} a_1) \mathbf{W} a_2 \vee (a_0 \mathbf{U} a_1) \mathbf{U} a_2) \mathbf{U} a_3) \mathbf{U} a_4) \cdots \mathbf{U} a_n)$$
$$\vee ((\cdots ((((a_0 \mathbf{U} a_1) \mathbf{U} a_2) \mathbf{U} a_3) \mathbf{U} a_4) \cdots \mathbf{U} a_n)$$

Since the only remaining limit node is outside any temporal formula, we have obtained a formula in 1–2-form and the procedure arrives to stage 3. Again, the only limit subformula is $\mathbf{GF} a_1$, and a_1 does not contain any **W**-node, so the

Table 2. Normalization rules for **R** and **M**.

$$\varphi_1[\psi_1\mathbf{M}\psi_2]\mathbf{W}\varphi_2 \equiv (\mathbf{GF}\psi_1 \wedge \varphi_1[\psi_1\mathbf{R}\psi_2]\mathbf{W}\varphi_2) \vee \varphi_1[\psi_1\mathbf{M}\psi_2]\mathbf{U}(\varphi_2 \vee \mathbf{G}\varphi_1[\mathbf{ff}])$$

$$\varphi_1\mathbf{W}\varphi_2[\psi_1\mathbf{M}\psi_2] \equiv \varphi_1\mathbf{U}\varphi_2[\psi_1\mathbf{M}\psi_2] \vee \mathbf{G}\varphi_1$$

$$\varphi_1[\psi_1\mathbf{U}\psi_2]\mathbf{R}\varphi_2 \equiv \varphi_1[\psi_1\mathbf{U}\psi_2]\mathbf{M}\varphi_2 \vee \mathbf{G}\varphi_2$$

$$\varphi_1[\psi_1\mathbf{M}\psi_2]\mathbf{R}\varphi_2 \equiv \varphi_1[\psi_1\mathbf{M}\psi_2]\mathbf{M}\varphi_2 \vee \mathbf{G}\varphi_2$$

$$\varphi_1\mathbf{R}\varphi_2[\psi_1\mathbf{U}\psi_2] \equiv (\mathbf{GF}\psi_2 \wedge \varphi_1\mathbf{R}\varphi_2[\psi_1\mathbf{W}\psi_2]) \vee (\varphi_1 \vee \mathbf{G}\varphi_2[\mathbf{ff}])\mathbf{M}\varphi_2[\psi_1\mathbf{U}\psi_2]$$

$$\varphi_1\mathbf{R}\varphi_2[\psi_1\mathbf{M}\psi_2] \equiv (\mathbf{GF}\psi_1 \wedge \varphi_1\mathbf{R}\varphi_2[\psi_1\mathbf{R}\psi_2]) \vee (\varphi_1 \vee \mathbf{G}\varphi_2[\mathbf{ff}])\mathbf{M}\varphi_2[\psi_1\mathbf{M}\psi_2]$$

$$\mathbf{GF}\varphi[\psi_1\mathbf{R}\psi_2] \equiv \mathbf{GF}\varphi[\psi_1\mathbf{M}\psi_2] \vee (\mathbf{FG}\psi_2 \wedge \mathbf{GF}\varphi[\mathbf{tt}])$$

$$\mathbf{FG}\varphi[\psi_1\mathbf{M}\psi_2] \equiv (\mathbf{GF}\psi_1 \wedge \mathbf{FG}\varphi[\psi_1\mathbf{R}\psi_2]) \vee \mathbf{FG}\varphi[\mathbf{ff}]$$

formula is completely normalized and we have finished. Observe that φ_n has been normalized by exactly two rule applications for all $n \geq 3$, so the algorithm proceeds in linear-time for this family of formulas. The result is not identical, but very similar to the one in Example 3.1.

6 Extensions

The operators **R** *and* **M**. We have omitted these operators from the proof and the normalization procedure, since they can be expressed in terms of the subset of operators we have considered. However, this translation exponentially increases the number of nodes of the formula, so handling them directly is convenient for efficiency. Their role at every step of the procedure is analogous to that of the **U** and **W** operators, i.e. we treat **R** in the same as **W** and we treat **M** in the same way as **U**. The corresponding rules are shown in Table 2.

Dual Normal Form. Recall that a formula is in dual normal form if it satisfies conditions 2. and 3. of Definition 4.2 and no **W**-node is under a **U**-node. Given a formula φ, let $\overline{\varphi}$ be a formula in negation normal form equivalent to $\neg\varphi$, and let ψ be a formula in primal normal form equivalent to $\overline{\varphi}$. Since $\varphi \equiv \neg\overline{\varphi} \equiv \neg\psi$, pushing the negation into ψ yields a formula equivalent to φ in dual normal form.

Past LTL. Past LTL is an extension of LTL with past operators like yesterday (**Y**), since (**S**), etc. In an appendix of [5], Gabbay introduced eight rewrite rules to pull future operators out of past operators. Combining these rules with ours yields a procedure that transforms a Past LTL formula into a normalized LTL formula, where past operators are gathered in past-only subformulas, and so can be considered atomic propositions.

7   Experimental Evaluation

We have implemented the normalization procedure summarized in Sect. 5 as a C++ program,[3] and compared its performance and the size of the generated formulas with the implementation of the procedure of [18] included in the Owl tool [6].[4] In order to make the comparison as fair as possible, we have implemented the same basic simplification rules that are eagerly applied during the normalization process.

We consider the following test suites: TLSF(a-b) is the repertory of formulas of the 2021 Reactive Synthesis Competition of sizes between a and b; random formulas are a set of 1000 randomly generated formulas, $\mathbf{WU}^*$ is the family of formulas in Example 3.1 for $2 \leq n \leq 200$; finally, $(\mathbf{WU})^*$ is the family defined by $\varphi_0 = a_0$ and $\varphi_{n+1} = (\varphi_n \mathbf{U} a_{2n-1})\mathbf{W} a_{2n}$ for $1 \leq n \leq 5$. Notice that the last family is limited to $n = 5$ because Owl cannot handle φ_6 due to the size of the powersets involved, while this is not a limitation for the new procedure.

Table 3. Experimental comparison of our normalization procedure and the one of [18].

Test cases	Size blowup			Time	
	Mean (Tree)	Worst-case (Tree)	Worst-case (DAG)	(ms)	
Random formulas	1.38	28.47	4.64	67	New
	1.06	10.69	3.90	589	Owl
$\mathbf{WU}^*$	2.12	3.57	2.20	90	New
	2.12	4.00	2.60	32343	Owl
$(\mathbf{WU})^*$	193.58	744.29	17.81	11	New
	27.86	73.33	10.05	54	Owl
TLSF(-100)	1.04	4.60	3.14	65	New
	1.17	8.02	2.48	867	Owl
TLSF(100–300)	2.14	369.66	15.10	230	New
	1.14	12.54	2.47	8636	Owl

Table 3 shows the mean and worst-case blowup of the syntax tree of the formulas (i.e., the ratio between the sizes of the formulas before and after normalization), the worst-case blowup of their directed acyclic graphs, and the execution time. Generally, the new procedure is faster but generates larger formulas. However, the execution time and the size of the formulas can be strongly affected by slight changes in the procedure. For example, selecting an innermost instead of

---

[3] The implementation is available at https://github.com/ningit/ltl2delta2rs.
[4] We evaluate the tool build from commit **2fb342a09d3a9d7025b219404c764021d17b7 ebd** of https://gitlab.lrz.de/i7/owl/.

an outermost $\psi_1 \mathbf{U} \psi_2$ when matching $\varphi[\psi_1 \mathbf{U} \psi_2]$ in rule (1) yields much bigger formulas in some examples, like TLSF(-100), but produces the opposite effect in others, like $(\mathbf{WU})^*$. Applying stage 2 separately to each topmost temporal formula is generally better than applying it to the whole term, but it can sometimes be slightly worse. Characterizing these situations and designing a procedure that adapts to them is a subject for future experiments.

8 Conclusions

We have presented a simple rewrite system that transforms any LTL formula into an equivalent formula in Δ_2. We think that, together with [18], this result demystifies the Normalization Theorem of Chang, Manna, and Pnueli, which heavily relied on automata-theoretic results, and involved a nonelementary blowup. Indeed, the only conceptual difference between our procedure and a rewrite system for bringing Boolean formulas in CNF is the use of rewrite rules with contexts.

The normalization procedure of Sickert and Esparza has already found applications to the translation of LTL formulas into deterministic or limit-deterministic ω-automata [18]. Until now normalization had not been considered, because of the non-elementary blow-up, much higher than the double exponential blow-up of existing constructions. With the new procedure, translations that first normalize the formula, and then apply efficient formula-to-automaton procedures specifically designed for formulas in normal form, have become competitive. Our new algorithm, purely based on rewriting rules, makes this even more attractive. More generally, we think that the design of analysis procedures for formulas in normal form (to check satisfiability, equivalence, or other properties) should be further studied in the coming years.

A Appendix

Let $\varphi \equiv^w \psi$ denote $w_k \models \varphi$ iff $w_k \models \psi$ for all $k \in \mathbb{N}$. The next two straightforward lemmas will be used pervasively in the following proofs.

Lemma A.1. *For every formula φ in negation normal form (and thus for every LTL formula we consider in this article), and for every two formulas ψ and ψ', $\psi \models \psi'$ implies $\varphi[\psi] \models \varphi[\psi']$.*

Lemma A.2. *For every formula φ and word w, $\psi \equiv^w \psi'$ implies $\varphi[\psi] \equiv^w \varphi[\psi']$.*

Lemma 4.1. (1) $\varphi_1 \mathbf{W} \varphi_2[\psi_1 \mathbf{U} \psi_2] \equiv (\varphi_1 \mathbf{U} \varphi_2[\psi_1 \mathbf{U} \psi_2]) \vee \mathbf{G} \varphi_1$,
(2) $\varphi_1[\psi_1 \mathbf{U} \psi_2] \mathbf{W} \varphi_2 \equiv (\mathbf{GF} \psi_2 \wedge \varphi_1[\psi_1 \mathbf{W} \psi_2] \mathbf{W} \varphi_2) \vee \varphi_1[\psi_1 \mathbf{U} \psi_2] \mathbf{U} (\varphi_2 \vee (\mathbf{G} \varphi_1[\mathbf{ff}]))$

Proof. For Eq. (1) observe that, by the definition of the semantics of LTL, $\varphi_1 \mathbf{W} \varphi_2 \equiv \varphi_1 \mathbf{U} \varphi_2 \vee \mathbf{G} \varphi_2$ holds for arbitrary formulas φ_1, φ_2. For Eq. (2) we proceed as follows.

($\models$): Assume $w \models \varphi_1[\psi_1\mathbf{U}\psi_2]\mathbf{W}\varphi_2$. If $w \models \mathbf{GF}\psi_2$, then we have $w_k \models \psi_1\mathbf{W}\psi_2$ iff $w_k \models \psi_1\mathbf{U}\psi_2$ for every $k \in \mathbb{N}$; by Lemma A.2 we then have $w \models \varphi_1[\psi_1\mathbf{W}\psi_2]\mathbf{W}\varphi_2$, and we are done. If $w \not\models \mathbf{GF}\psi_2$, then there is $n \in \mathbb{N}$ such that $w_k \not\models \psi_2$ for all $k \geq n$, and so $\psi_1\mathbf{U}\psi_2 \equiv^{w_n} \mathbf{ff}$. Since w satisfies the left-hand side, there are two possible cases

- There is $m \in \mathbb{N}$ such that $w_m \models \varphi_2$ and $w_k \models \varphi_1[\psi_1\mathbf{U}\psi_2]$ for every $k < m$. Then, the second disjunct holds and we are done.
- $w_k \models \varphi_1[\psi_1\mathbf{U}\psi_2]$ for every $k \in \mathbb{N}$. Then $w_k \models \varphi_1[\mathbf{ff}]$ for all $k \geq n$ by Lemma A.2 with $\psi_1\mathbf{U}\psi_2 \equiv^{w_n} \mathbf{ff}$. So $w_n \models \varphi_2 \vee \mathbf{G}\varphi_1[\mathbf{ff}]$, and we are done.

($\Leftarrow$): Assume w satisfies the right-hand side formula. We consider two cases:

- $w \models \mathbf{GF}\psi_2 \wedge \varphi_1[\psi_1\mathbf{W}\psi_2]\mathbf{W}\varphi_2$. Then $w \models \mathbf{GF}\psi_2$ and, as above, we have $w_k \models \psi_1\mathbf{W}\psi_2$ iff $w_k \models \psi_1\mathbf{U}\psi_2$ for every $k \in \mathbb{N}$. Since $w \models \varphi_1[\psi_1\mathbf{W}\psi_2]\mathbf{W}\varphi_2$, we get $w \models \varphi_1[\psi_1\mathbf{U}\psi_2]\mathbf{W}\varphi_2$.
- $w \models \varphi_1[\psi_1\mathbf{U}\psi_2]\mathbf{U}(\varphi_2 \vee \mathbf{G}\varphi_1[\mathbf{ff}])$. Then there is $n \in \mathbb{N}$ such that $w_n \models \varphi_2 \vee \mathbf{G}\varphi_1[\mathbf{ff}]$ and $w_k \models \varphi_1[\psi_1\mathbf{U}\psi_2]$ for every $k < n$. We consider two cases: $w_n \models \varphi_2$ or $w_k \models \varphi_1[\mathbf{ff}]$ for all $k \geq n$. In the first case, $w_n \models \varphi_1[\psi_1\mathbf{U}\psi_2]\mathbf{W}\varphi_2$ by definition of $\mathbf{W}$. For the second, since $\mathbf{ff} \models \psi_1\mathbf{U}\psi_2$ and by Lemma A.1, $w_k \models \varphi_1[\mathbf{ff}]$ implies $w_k \models \varphi_1[\psi_1\mathbf{U}\psi_2]$. Therefore, we have $w_k \models \varphi_1[\psi_1\mathbf{U}\psi_2]$ for every $k < n$ and for every $k \geq n$, so $w \models \varphi_1[\psi_1\mathbf{U}\psi_2]\mathbf{W}\varphi_2$.

Lemma 4.2. (3) $\varphi[\mathbf{GF}\psi] \equiv (\mathbf{GF}\psi \wedge \varphi[\mathbf{tt}]) \vee \varphi[\mathbf{ff}]$, (4) $\varphi[\mathbf{FG}\psi] \equiv (\mathbf{FG}\psi \wedge \varphi[\mathbf{tt}]) \vee \varphi[\mathbf{ff}]$

Proof. We prove that $\varphi[\psi] \equiv (\psi \wedge \varphi[\mathbf{tt}]) \vee \varphi[\mathbf{ff}]$ for every ψ such that $\mathbf{G}\psi \equiv \psi$, i.e., $w \models \psi$ iff $w_k \models \psi$ for all $k \in \mathbb{N}$. This is a generalization of (3) and (4), since both $\mathbf{GF}\psi'$ and $\mathbf{FG}\psi'$ satisfy the requirement about ψ for any ψ'. Since ψ is satisfied by all suffixes or for no suffix of a word w, it follows that either $\psi \equiv^w \mathbf{tt}$ or $\psi \equiv^w \mathbf{ff}$ for any word w.

($\models$): If w satisfies ψ, we also have $w \models \varphi[\mathbf{tt}]$ by Lemma A.2, and so the first disjunct is satisfied. Otherwise, again by Lemma A.2, we have $w \models \varphi[\mathbf{ff}]$, so the second disjunct holds.

($\Leftarrow$): Suppose w satisfies the first disjunct, then $w \models \psi$ and $\varphi[\psi] \equiv^w \varphi[\mathbf{tt}]$ by Lemma A.2. Otherwise, the second disjunct holds, and then $w \models \varphi[\psi]$ by Lemma A.1 since $\mathbf{ff} \models \psi$.

Lemma 4.3.

(5) $\qquad \mathbf{GF}\varphi[\psi_1\mathbf{W}\psi_2] \equiv \mathbf{GF}\varphi[\psi_1\mathbf{U}\psi_2] \vee (\mathbf{FG}\psi_1 \wedge \mathbf{GF}\varphi[\mathbf{tt}])$

(6) $\qquad \mathbf{FG}\varphi[\psi_1\mathbf{U}\psi_2] \equiv (\mathbf{GF}\psi_2 \wedge \mathbf{FG}\varphi[\psi_1\mathbf{W}\psi_2]) \vee \mathbf{FG}\varphi[\mathbf{ff}]$

Proof. Proof of Eq. (5).
($\Leftarrow$): We prove the following claims, which immediately imply the result:

- $\mathbf{GF}\varphi[\psi_1\mathbf{U}\psi_2] \models \mathbf{GF}\varphi[\psi_1\mathbf{W}\psi_2]$.
  Follows from $\psi_1\mathbf{U}\psi_2 \models \psi_1\mathbf{W}\psi_2$ and Lemma A.1.

- $\mathbf{FG}\psi_1 \wedge \mathbf{GF}\varphi[\mathbf{tt}] \models \mathbf{GF}\varphi[\psi_1 \mathbf{W}\psi_2]$.

    Assume $w \models \mathbf{FG}\psi_1 \wedge \mathbf{GF}\varphi[\mathbf{tt}]$. On the one hand, there must be $n \in \mathbb{N}$ such that $w_k \models \mathbf{G}\psi_1$ for all $k \geq n$. Since $\mathbf{G}\psi_1 \models \psi_1 \mathbf{W}\psi_2$, $w_k \models \psi_1 \mathbf{W}\psi_2$ for all $k \geq n$. On the other hand, $\varphi[\mathbf{tt}]$ holds in infinitely many suffixes of w. By Lemma A.2 and $\psi_1 \mathbf{W}\psi_2 \equiv^{w_k} \mathbf{tt}$ for all $k \geq n$, $\varphi[\psi_1 \mathbf{W}\psi_2]$ holds infinitely often in w and we are done.

($\models$): Assume w satisfies $\mathbf{GF}\varphi[\psi_1 \mathbf{W}\psi_2]$, and so that $w' \models \varphi[\psi_1 \mathbf{W}\psi_2]$ for infinitely many suffixes w' of w. We prove the following three claims, which immediately imply the result:

- If $w \models \mathbf{FG}\psi_1$ then $w \models \mathbf{GF}\varphi[\mathbf{tt}]$.
    Since $w \models \mathbf{FG}\psi_1 \wedge \mathbf{GF}\varphi[\psi_1 \mathbf{W}\psi_2]$, infinitely many suffixes of w satisfy $\mathbf{G}\psi_1$ and $\varphi[\psi_1 \mathbf{W}\psi_2]$. Since $\mathbf{G}\psi_1 \models \psi_1 \mathbf{W}\psi_2$, these suffixes also satisfy $\psi_1 \mathbf{W}\psi_2$, and so also $\varphi[\mathbf{tt}]$.
- If $w \not\models \mathbf{FG}\psi_1$, then $\psi_1 \mathbf{U}\psi_2 \equiv^w \psi_1 \mathbf{W}\psi_2$ because $\mathbf{G}\psi_1$ never holds and $\psi_1 \mathbf{W}\psi_2 \equiv \psi_1 \mathbf{U}\psi_2 \vee \mathbf{G}\psi_1$. Therefore, $w \models \mathbf{GF}[\psi_1 \mathbf{W}\psi_2]$ by Lemma A.2 and the first clause of the disjunction.

Proof of Eq. (6).

($\models$): If the second clause of the right-hand side disjunction is satisfied, $\mathbf{FG}\varphi[\psi_1 \mathbf{U}\psi_2]$ holds since φ is in negation normal form and $\mathbf{ff} \models \psi_1 \mathbf{U}\psi_2$. Otherwise, the first disjunct must be true, so for any word w satisfying $\mathbf{GF}\psi_2$, $\psi_1 \mathbf{W}\psi_2 \equiv^w \psi_1 \mathbf{U}\psi_2$ and so they can be replaced inside the context by Lemma A.2.

($\models$): Assume w satisfies $\mathbf{FG}\varphi[\psi_1 \mathbf{U}\psi_2]$, i.e., there is an $n \in \mathbb{N}$ such that $w_k \models \varphi[\psi_1 \mathbf{U}\psi_2]$ for all $k \geq n$. We consider two cases whether $w \models \mathbf{GF}\psi_2$ or not.

- If $w \models \mathbf{GF}\psi_2$, $\psi_1 \mathbf{U}\psi_2 \equiv^w \psi_1 \mathbf{W}\psi_2$ for every $k \in \mathbb{N}$, so $w_k \models \varphi[\psi_1 \mathbf{W}\psi_2]$ for all $k \geq n$ by Lemma A.2. Hence, the first disjunct holds.
- Otherwise, there is an $m \geq n$ such that $w_k \not\models \psi_2$ for all $k \geq m$. As a result, $w_k \not\models \psi_1 \mathbf{U}\psi_2$ and $\psi_1 \mathbf{U}\psi_2 \equiv^{w_k} \mathbf{ff}$ for all $k \geq m$. Using that $w_k \models \varphi[\psi_1 \mathbf{U}\psi_2]$ and Lemma A.2, $w_k \models \varphi[\mathbf{ff}]$ for all $k \geq m$, so $\mathbf{FG}\varphi[\mathbf{ff}]$.

References

1. Babiak, T., Badie, T., Duret-Lutz, A., Křetínský, M., Strejček, J.: Compositional approach to suspension and other improvements to LTL translation. In: Bartocci, E., Ramakrishnan, C.R. (eds.) SPIN 2013. LNCS, vol. 7976, pp. 81–98. Springer, Heidelberg (2013). https://doi.org/10.1007/978-3-642-39176-7_6
2. Boker, U., Lehtinen, K., Sickert, S.: On the translation of automata to linear temporal logic. In: FoSSaCS 2022. LNCS, vol. 13242, pp. 140–160. Springer, Cham (2022). https://doi.org/10.1007/978-3-030-99253-8_8
3. Černá, I., Pelánek, R.: Relating hierarchy of temporal properties to model checking. In: Rovan, B., Vojtáš, P. (eds.) MFCS 2003. LNCS, vol. 2747, pp. 318–327. Springer, Heidelberg (2003). https://doi.org/10.1007/978-3-540-45138-9_26

4. Chang, E., Manna, Z., Pnueli, A.: Characterization of temporal property classes. In: Kuich, W. (ed.) ICALP 1992. LNCS, vol. 623, pp. 474–486. Springer, Heidelberg (1992). https://doi.org/10.1007/3-540-55719-9_97

5. Gabbay, D.: The declarative past and imperative future. In: Banieqbal, B., Barringer, H., Pnueli, A. (eds.) Temporal Logic in Specification. LNCS, vol. 398, pp. 409–448. Springer, Heidelberg (1989). https://doi.org/10.1007/3-540-51803-7_36

6. Křetínský, J., Meggendorfer, T., Sickert, S.: Owl: a library for ω-words, automata, and LTL. In: Lahiri, S.K., Wang, C. (eds.) ATVA 2018. LNCS, vol. 11138, pp. 543–550. Springer, Cham (2018). https://doi.org/10.1007/978-3-030-01090-4_34

7. Lichtenstein, O., Pnueli, A., Zuck, L.: The glory of the past. In: Parikh, R. (ed.) Logic of Programs 1985. LNCS, vol. 193, pp. 196–218. Springer, Heidelberg (1985). https://doi.org/10.1007/3-540-15648-8_16

8. Maler, O.: On the Krohn-Rhodes cascaded decomposition theorem. In: Manna, Z., Peled, D.A. (eds.) Time for Verification. LNCS, vol. 6200, pp. 260–278. Springer, Heidelberg (2010). https://doi.org/10.1007/978-3-642-13754-9_12

9. Maler, O., Pnueli, A.: Tight bounds on the complexity of cascaded decomposition of automata. In: Proceedings of FOCS, pp. 672–682 (1990). https://doi.org/10.1109/FSCS.1990.89589

10. Maler, O., Pnueli, A.: On the cascaded decomposition of automata, its complexity and its application to logic. Unpublished (1994). http://www-verimag.imag.fr/maler/Papers/decomp.pdf

11. Manna, Z., Pnueli, A.: A hierarchy of temporal properties. In: PODC, pp. 377–410. ACM (1990). https://doi.org/10.1145/93385.93442

12. Manna, Z., Pnueli, A.: Completing the temporal picture. Theor. Comput. Sci. **83**(1), 91–130 (1991). https://doi.org/10.1016/0304-3975(91)90041-Y

13. Pelánek, R., Strejček, J.: Deeper connections between LTL and alternating automata. In: Farré, J., Litovsky, I., Schmitz, S. (eds.) CIAA 2005. LNCS, vol. 3845, pp. 238–249. Springer, Heidelberg (2006). https://doi.org/10.1007/11605157_20

14. Piterman, N., Pnueli, A.: Temporal logic and fair discrete systems. In: Clarke, E., Henzinger, T., Veith, H., Bloem, R. (eds.) Handbook of Model Checking, pp. 27–73. Springer, Cham (2018). https://doi.org/10.1007/978-3-319-10575-8_2

15. Pnueli, A.: The temporal logic of programs. In: FOCS, pp. 46–57. IEEE Computer Society (1977). https://doi.org/10.1109/SFCS.1977.32

16. Pnueli, A.: The temporal semantics of concurrent programs. Theor. Comput. Sci. **13**, 45–60 (1981). https://doi.org/10.1016/0304-3975(81)90110-9

17. Sickert, S.: A unified translation of linear temporal logic to ω-automata. Ph.D. thesis, Technical University of Munich, Germany (2019). https://nbn-resolving.org/urn:nbn:de:bvb:91-diss-20190801-1484932-1-4

18. Sickert, S., Esparza, J.: An efficient normalisation procedure for linear temporal logic and very weak alternating automata. In: LICS, pp. 831–844. ACM (2020). https://doi.org/10.1145/3373718.3394743

19. Zuck, L.D.: Past temporal logic. Ph.D. thesis, The Weizmann Institute of Science, Israel, August 1986

A Survey on Satisfiability Checking for the μ-Calculus Through Tree Automata

Daniel Hausmann$^{(\boxtimes)}$ and Nir Piterman$^{(\boxtimes)}$

Gothenburg University, Gothenburg, Sweden
{hausmann,piterman}@chalmers.se

Abstract. Algorithms for model checking and satisfiability of the modal μ-calculus start by converting formulas to alternating parity tree automata. Thus, model checking is reduced to checking acceptance by tree automata and satisfiability to checking their emptiness. The first reduces directly to the solution of parity games but the second is more complicated.

We review the non-emptiness checking of alternating tree automata by a reduction to solving parity games of a certain structure, so-called *emptiness games*. Since the emptiness problem for alternating tree automata is ExpTime-complete, the size of these games is exponential in the number of states of the input automaton. We show how the construction of the emptiness games combines a (fixed) structural part with (history-)determinization of parity word automata. For tree automata with certain syntactic structures, simpler methods may be used to handle the treatment of the word automata, which then may be asymptotically smaller than in the general case.

These results have direct consequences in satisfiability and validity checking for (various fragments of) the modal μ-calculus.

1 Introduction

The modal μ-calculus extends modal logic with least and greatest fixpoint operators [16]. The μ-calculus is expressive enough to express many temporal logics, in particular it can capture CTL* and its fragments LTL and CTL [6]. At the same time, the μ-calculus has interesting algorithmic and algebraic properties. For example, the μ-calculus model-checking problem is equivalent to the solution of parity games, a well known (still) open problem attracting much research. This combination led to high interest in the μ-calculus, studying many aspects of the logic.

Here, we are interested in the question of satisfiability of the μ-calculus. The problem is ExpTime-complete and the first algorithms of this complexity were automata based [5]. Much like for other temporal logics, initial treatment of the logic was done through nondeterministic automata [26]. However, later,

This work is supported by the ERC Consolidator grant D-SynMA (No. 772459).

© Springer Nature Switzerland AG 2022
J.-F. Raskin and K. Chatterjee (Eds.): Principles of Systems Design, LNCS 13660, pp. 228–251, 2022.
https://doi.org/10.1007/978-3-031-22337-2_11

the richer structure of alternating automata enabled translations that are more natural and direct [20]. This translation defers the complicated handling of the satisfiability problem to standard automata constructions.

With this approach, the satisfiability problem for the modal μ-calculus reduces to the non-emptiness problem of alternating parity tree automata [20]. The latter problem is solved either by constructing equivalent nondeterministic parity tree automata [21] or by a direct reduction to two-player perfect information parity games [27].

We revisit the reduction and present it in a way that separates the tree acceptance and the parity acceptance aspects of a parity tree automaton A. The method creates an arena G_A (*strategy arena*), which captures all the decisions made at the same location by A and a nondeterministic parity word automaton T_A (*tracking automaton*) that "accepts" bad branches in run-trees of the original automaton. The original automaton then is non-empty if and only if the combination of G_A with T_A as losing condition is won by the existential player. By using a history deterministic (or fully deterministic) word automaton H_A that accepts the same language as T_A, we construct a parity game G_A^*.

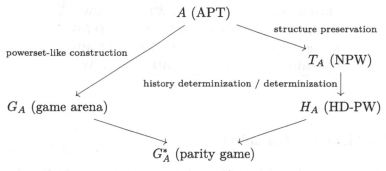

This approach reduces the algorithmic content of non-emptiness checking for alternating automata (and for satisfiability checking in the modal μ-calculus) to a fixed construction of a game arena and (history-)determinization of word automata that depend on the exact structure of the original automaton (μ-calculus formula).

We then show that as the structure of T_A strongly depends on the structure of A, specialized history determinization and determinization constructions lead to complexity results that match bespoke algorithms for different fragments of the μ-calculus. These results are summarized in the following table, where LL stands for limit linear, LD for limit deterministic, N for nondeterministic, HD for history deterministic, D for deterministic, W for weak, B for Büchi, C for co-Büchi, and P for parity. For example, LL-CW is a limit linear co-Büchi word automaton and LD-WT is a limit deterministic weak tree automaton.

		Type of T_A	Method	Type of H_A	Size of H_A
co-Büchi	Det.	LL-CW	circle method	DCW	$n^2 \cdot 2^n$
		NCW	Miyano-Hayashi	DCW	3^n
	History-det.	LD-CW	focus method	HD-CW	$n \cdot 2^n$
Büchi	Det.	LD-BW	permutation method	DPW	$\mathcal{O}(n!)$
		NBW	Safra-Piterman	DPW	$\mathcal{O}((n!)^2)$
	History-det.	NBW	Henzinger-Piterman	HD-PW	$\mathcal{O}(3^{n^2})$

Going back to the μ-calculus, the following table depicts relations between various syntactic properties of μ-calculus formulas (formally defined later) and automata. Thus, the separated treatment of the arena and the acceptance, and the different constructions for word automata summarize in one framework complexity results relating to various different fragments of the μ-calculus.

Property of φ	Type of A	Type of T_A
Limit-linear	LL-WT	LL-CW
Alternation-free	AWT	NCW
Aconjunctive alternation-free	LD-WT	LD-CW
Aconjunctive	LD-PT	LD-BW
Unrestricted	APT	NBW

2   The Modal μ-Calculus

We are concerned with satisfiability checking for different syntactical fragments of the branching-time μ-calculus, introduced by Kozen [16].

Syntax. Formulas of the μ-calculus are generated by the following grammar, where At and Var are countable sets of atoms and fixpoint variables, respectively:

$$\varphi, \psi := p \mid \neg p \mid \varphi \wedge \psi \mid \varphi \vee \psi \mid \Diamond \varphi \mid \Box \varphi \mid X \mid \xi X. \varphi \quad p \in \mathsf{At}, X \in \mathsf{Var}, \xi \in \{\mu, \nu\}$$

Fixpoint operators $\mu X.$ and $\nu X.$ *bind* their variable X, giving rise to standard notions of *bound* and *free variables*; for $\mu X. \psi$, free occurrences of X in ψ are *least fixpoint variables* and for $\nu X. \psi$, free occurrences of X in ψ are *greatest fixpoint variables*.

The *Fischer-Ladner closure* [16] $\mathsf{FL}(\varphi)$ (or just *closure*) of a closed formula φ is the least set of formulas that contains φ and is closed under taking subformulas for non-fixpoint operators and under unfolding for fixpoint operators; e.g. $\mu X. \psi \in \mathsf{FL}(\varphi)$ implies $\psi[X \mapsto \mu X. \psi] \in \mathsf{FL}(\varphi)$, where $\psi[X \mapsto \mu X. \psi]$ is the formula that is obtained from ψ by replacing every free occurrence of the variable X in ψ by the formula $\mu X. \psi$. We have $\mathsf{FL}(\varphi) \le |\varphi|$ where $|\varphi|$ is the number of operators that are required to write φ (that is, the number of nodes in the syntax tree of φ).

A formula φ is *clean*, if all fixpoint variables are bound at most once in it. Then we denote *the* fixpoint formula $\xi X.\psi$ that binds a variable X in φ by $\theta_\varphi(X)$. While transforming an arbitrary formula to a clean formula (by renaming bound variables accordingly) can increase the closure size, a translation to tree automata that does not rely on cleanness has recently been given in [17]. For brevity of presentation we assume throughout that target formulas are clean but remark that this does not affect the stated complexity results since the more involved translation from [17] can be used to obtain tree automata (of suitable size and rank) from arbitrary formulas.

$$[\![p]\!]_\eta = \{w \mid p \in L(w)\}$$
$$[\![\neg p]\!]_\eta = \{w \mid p \notin L(w)\}$$
$$[\![\varphi \vee \psi]\!]_\eta = [\![\varphi]\!]_\eta \cup [\![\psi]\!]_\eta$$
$$[\![\varphi \wedge \psi]\!]_\eta = [\![\varphi]\!]_\eta \cap [\![\psi]\!]_\eta$$
$$[\![\Diamond\varphi]\!]_\eta = \{w \mid R(w) \cap [\![\varphi]\!]_\eta \neq \emptyset\}$$
$$[\![\Box\varphi]\!]_\eta = \{w \mid R(w) \subseteq [\![\varphi]\!]_\eta\}$$
$$[\![X]\!]_\eta = \eta(X)$$
$$[\![\mu X.\varphi]\!]_\eta = \bigcap\{T \subseteq W \mid [\![\varphi]\!]_{\eta[X \leftarrow T]} \subseteq T\}$$
$$[\![\nu X.\varphi]\!]_\eta = \bigcup\{T \subseteq W \mid T \subseteq [\![\varphi]\!]_{\eta[X \leftarrow T]}\}$$

Fig. 1. Semantics of the μ-calculus

Remark 2.1. Another common constraint on the syntactic structure of formulas is *guardedness*, which requires that there is always at least one modal operator between a fixpoint operator and occurrences of the fixpoint variable that it binds. It is currently an open question whether there is a guardedness-transformation with polynomial blow-up of the closure size, and it has been shown that such a polynomial transformation would yield a polynomial algorithm for parity game solving [17]. Throughout this work, we assume that formulas are guarded.

Alternation-Depth. Given a clean formula φ, and two subformulas $\xi X.\psi$ and $\xi'Y.\chi$ of φ, $\xi'Y.\chi$ *depends* on $\xi X.\psi$ if X has a free occurrence in χ. We define the *dependent nesting order* $\succeq_\varphi$ to be the partial order on fixpoint subformulas of φ obtained by taking the reflexive-transitive closure of the dependency ordering. The *alternation-depth* $\mathsf{ad}(\varphi)$ of φ then is defined to be the maximal length of an alternating $\succ_\varphi$-path, where a $\succ_\varphi$-path is alternating if all its transitions switch the fixpoint type. Given a fixpoint subformula $\chi = \eta X.\psi$ of φ, let d be the maximal length of an alternating $\succeq_\varphi$-path that starts at χ. We define the *alternation-level* $\mathsf{al}(\chi)$ of χ to be $2\lceil d/2\rceil - 1$ if $\eta = \mu$ and $2\lfloor d/2\rfloor$ if $\eta = \nu$. Hence least fixpoint formulas have odd alternation-level while greatest fixpoint formulas have even alternation-level; furthermore, we always have $\mathsf{al}(\chi) \leq \mathsf{ad}(\varphi)$.

Semantics. Formulas of the μ-calculus are evaluated over pointed Kripke structures. A pointed Kripke structure is $K = (W, w_0, R, L)$, where W is a set of worlds, $w_0 \in W$ is an initial world, $R \subseteq W \times W$ is a transition relation, and $L : W \to \mathcal{P}(\text{At})$ is a labeling function. We denote by $R(w) = \{w' \in W \mid (w, w') \in R\}$ the set of worlds connected by R to w. We restrict attention to structures where for every $w \in W$ we have $R(w) \neq \emptyset$.

Given a μ-calculus formula φ and a pointed Kripke structure K, the semantics of the formula is defined based on a valuation function η assigning each variable appearing in φ to a set of worlds of K. Given such a function η we denote by $\eta[X \leftarrow S]$ the function η' where $\eta'(X) = S$ and $\eta'(Y) = \eta(Y)$ for every $Y \neq X$. The semantics of the μ-calculus is included in Fig. 1. It is simple to see that in the case that a formula φ is closed its semantics does not depend on the initial valuation η. Thus, for a closed formula we write $[\![\varphi]\!]$. A formula φ is satisfiable if there exists a structure $K = (W, w_0, R, L)$ such that $w_0 \in [\![\varphi]\!]$.

Theorem 2.2 ([5]). *Given a μ-calculus formula φ, deciding whether φ is satisfiable is* ExpTime-*complete.*

Fragments of the μ-calculus. We consider the following fragments of the μ-calculus:

- The *limit-linear* fragment of the μ-calculus consists of all formulas φ such that for all subformulas $\mu X. \psi$ of φ, X has exactly one occurrence in ψ, and this occurrence is not in the scope of a fixpoint subformula of ψ. Computation tree logic (CTL) is a fragment of the limit-linear μ-calculus.
- The *alternation-free* fragment of the μ-calculus consists of all formulas φ such that $\text{ad}(\varphi) \leq 1$. It has been shown that satisfiability checking for a guarded alternation-free formula of size n can be done by solving a Büchi game of size 3^n [9].
- The *aconjunctive* fragment of the μ-calculus consists of all formulas φ such that for all conjunctions $\psi \wedge \chi$ that occur as a subformula in φ, at most one of the conjuncts ψ or χ contains a free least fixpoint variable. Satisfiability checking for a (weakly) aconjunctive formula of size n and with k priorities can be done by solving a parity game of size $e \cdot (nk)!$ and with $2nk$ priorities [12].
- The *alternation-free aconjunctive* fragment of the μ-calculus is the intersection of the alternation-free fragment and the aconjunctive fragment. In particular, every limit-linear formula is alternation-free and aconjunctive.

3   Two-Player Games and Alternating Parity Tree Automata

We give background on two-player games and tree automata. Our notations are based on those developed by Wilke [27].

Definition 3.1. A *game* is $G = (V, V_\Diamond, V_\Box, E, \alpha)$, where V is a set of nodes, $V_\Diamond$ and $V_\Box$ form a partition of V to player $\Diamond$ and player $\Box$ nodes, $E \subseteq V \times V$ is a set of edges, and $\alpha \subseteq V^\omega$ is a winning condition. A *play* is a sequence $\pi = v_0, v_1, \ldots$ such that for every i we have $(v_i, v_{i+1}) \in E$. A play π is winning for player $\Diamond$ if $\pi \in \alpha$. A strategy for player $\Diamond$ is $\sigma : V^* \cdot V_\Diamond \to V$ such that $(v, \sigma(wv)) \in E$ for $wv \in V^* \cdot V_\Diamond$. A play π is *compatible* with σ if whenever $v_i \in V_\Diamond$ we have $v_{i+1} = \sigma(v_0, \ldots, v_i)$. A strategy for player $\Diamond$ is winning from node v if all the plays starting in v that are compatible with σ are winning for her. Strategies for player $\Box$ are defined similarly.

In a *parity* game, there exists a priority function $\Omega : V \to \mathbb{N}$ and a play π is winning for player $\Diamond$ if the maximal priority occurring infinitely often in π is even. A *Büchi* game is a parity game with just the priorities 1 and 2. Given an infinite sequence $\pi \in V^\omega$ let $\inf(\pi)$ denote the set of nodes occuring in π infinitely often and put $\inf_\Omega(\pi) = \{\Omega(v) \mid v \in \inf(\pi)\}$. Then the parity winning condition induced by Ω is $\alpha = \{\pi \in V^\omega \mid \max(\inf_\Omega(\pi)) \text{ is even}\}$. The complexity of analyzing parity games is a hot area of research [1,3,4]. Here we denote by PARITY(n, k)-TIME the time complexity of solving parity games with n nodes and k priorities. We do not refer to space complexity, however, a similar general dependency on space can be stated. Our results produce parity games of different parameters depending on the exact shape of a μ-calculus formula. We hence use this parametric form to give complexity results.

Theorem 3.2 (Parity and Büchi games [1,2]**).** *Parity games with n nodes and k priorities can be solved in time quasipolynomial in n and k, more specifically[1] in time $n^{2\log(k/\log n)+\mathcal{O}(1)}$, and in polynomial time if $k < \log n$. Büchi games with n nodes can be solved in time $\mathcal{O}(n^2)$.*

We sometimes consider games where edges are labeled. In such a case, there exists a set of labels D and we have $E \subseteq V \times D \times V$. Then, α can be a subset of $V \cdot (D \cdot V)^\omega$.

When the winning condition is not important, we call $(V, V_\Diamond, V_\Box, E)$ an *arena*.

Definition 3.3. An *alternating parity tree automaton* $A = (\Sigma, Q, q_0, \delta, \Omega)$ consists of a finite alphabet Σ, a finite set of states Q, an initial state $q_0 \in Q$, a transition function $\delta : Q \times \Sigma \to \mathcal{P}(Q)$, and a priority function $\Omega : Q \to \mathbb{N}$; furthermore, each state $q \in Q$ is marked as either local-existential, local-universal, modal-existential or modal-universal (denoted by $q \in Q_\vee$, $q \in Q_\wedge$, $q \in Q_\Diamond$, and $q \in Q_\Box$, respectively). We also denote $Q_l = Q_\vee \cup Q_\wedge$, where l stands for local, and $Q_m = Q_\Diamond \cup Q_\Box$, where m stands for modal. Without loss of generality, we assume that modal-existential and modal-universal states have exactly one successor, formally: $|\delta(q)| = 1$ if $q \in Q_\Diamond$ or $q \in Q_\Box$. We overload $\delta(q)$ to denote q' if $\delta(q) = \{q'\}$. The *rank* of A is the number $|\Omega(Q)|$ of priorities appearing in its priority function. We assume that A does not have local loops. That is, for every letter σ and for every sequence of states $q_1, \ldots, q_l \in Q_l^+$ such that for every $i \geq 1$ we have $q_{i+1} \in \delta(q_i, \sigma)$ we have $q_l \neq q_1$.

A tree automaton is *weak* if for all its strongly connected components C, either all states in C have priority 0 or all states in C have priority 1. A weak tree

---

[1] This improved bound has been shown in [14].

automaton is *limit-linear* if for each $q \in Q$ such that $\Omega(q) = 1$, there is exactly one path from q to q. That is, within rejecting strongly connected components the looping behavior is deterministic. A tree automaton is *limit-deterministic* if for each odd priority p and each state q such that $\Omega(q) = p$, we have that for all $a \in \Sigma$ and all states $q' \in Q_\wedge$ that are reachable from q by visiting nodes with priority at most p, $|\delta(q', a) \cap Q_{\leq p}| \leq 1$, where $Q_{\leq p} = \{q \in Q \mid \Omega(q) \leq p\}$. In particular, every limit-linear automaton is limit-deterministic.

Alternating tree automata read *pointed Kripke structures*. An alternating tree automaton A accepts a Kripke structure $K = (W, w_0, R, L)$ if player $\Diamond$ wins the node (w_0, q_0) in the acceptance game $G_{A,K}$. Formally, $G_{A,K} = (V, V_\Diamond, V_\Box, E, \alpha)$, where $V = W \times Q$, $V_\Diamond = W \times (Q_\vee \cup Q_\Diamond)$, $V_\Box = W \times (Q_\wedge \cup Q_\Box)$, α is induced by the priority function $\Omega'(w, q) = \Omega(q)$, and E is defined as follows.

$$
\begin{aligned}
E = \{&((w,q),(w,q')) \mid q \in Q_l \text{ and } q' \in \delta(q, L(w))\} \quad \cup \\
&\{((w,q),(w',q')) \mid q \in Q_m, q' \in \delta(q, L(w)), \text{ and } w' \in R(w)\}
\end{aligned}
$$

An automaton A is *non-empty* if there exists a Kripke structure that it accepts.

We now state (the well known result) that given a μ-calculus formula, we can construct an alternating tree automaton accepting exactly the models of the formula.

Definition 3.4. (Formula automaton). Given a closed and clean μ-calculus formula φ that mentions atoms $A \subseteq At$, we define an alternating parity tree automaton $A(\varphi) = (\Sigma, Q, q_0, \delta, \Omega)$ by putting $\Sigma = \mathcal{P}(A)$, $Q = FL(\varphi) \cup \{\top, \bot\}$, and $q_0 = \varphi$. We define a partial priority function $\Omega' : Q \rightharpoonup \{0, \ldots, ad(\varphi)\}$ by putting $\Omega'(\eta X. \psi) = al(\theta(X))$ (recalling that $\theta(X)$ is *the* subformula of φ that binds X), $\Omega'(\bot) = 1$ and $\Omega'(\top) = 0$; then Ω' assigns a priority to at least one state on each cycle in $A(\varphi)$. The total priority function $\Omega : V \to \{0, \ldots, ad(\varphi)\}$ is obtained by putting, for each state $q \in Q$ such that $\Omega'(q)$ is undefined, $\Omega(q) = p$ where p is the minimum priority such that all paths from q to q visit priority at most p; states that do not belong to a strongly connected component obtain priority 0. Furthermore, we put

$$
\delta(q, P) = \begin{cases}
\{\psi_0, \psi_1\} & \text{if } q = \psi_0 \wedge \psi_1 \text{ or } q = \psi_0 \vee \psi_1 \\
\{\psi\} & \text{if } q = \Diamond\psi \text{ or } q = \Box\psi \\
\{\psi[X \mapsto \eta X. \psi]\} & \text{if } q = \eta X. \psi \\
\{\top\} & \text{if } q = p \text{ and } p \in P \text{ or } q = \neg p \text{ and } p \notin P \\
\{\bot\} & \text{if } q = p \text{ and } p \notin P \text{ or } q = \neg p \text{ and } p \in P \\
\{q\} & \text{if } q = \top \text{ or } q = \bot
\end{cases}
$$

for $q \in Q$, $P \in \Sigma$. Finaly, we put

$$
\begin{aligned}
Q_\exists &= \{\psi_0 \vee \psi_1, \eta X. \psi \in FL(\varphi)\} \cup \{\bot\} & Q_\Diamond &= \{\Diamond\psi \in FL(\varphi)\} \\
Q_\forall &= \{\psi_0 \wedge \psi_1, p, \neg p \in FL(\varphi)\} \cup \{\top\} & Q_\Box &= \{\Box\psi \in FL(\varphi)\}.
\end{aligned}
$$

Theorem 3.5. ([17,27]). *We have $L(A(\varphi)) = \{(W, w_0, R, L) \mid w_0 \in [\![\varphi]\!]\}$. Furthermore, $|Q| \leq |\mathsf{FL}(\varphi)| + 2$ and $A(\varphi)$ has rank $\mathsf{ad}(\varphi) + 1$.*

Corollary 3.6. *Deciding if a Kripke structure with set of worlds W satisfies a μ-calculus formula φ is in $\mathrm{PARITY}(|W| \cdot (\mathsf{FL}(\varphi) + 2), \mathsf{ad}(\varphi) + 1)$-TIME.*

It follows from Theorem 3.5 that by checking whether the language of $A(\varphi)$ is empty we can decide whether φ is satisfiable. In the next section, we proceed to show how to determine whether the language of an automaton is empty.

Before proceeding, we show that in case the μ-calculus formula has a special structure, as defined in Sect. 2, the automaton resulting from the translation above has also a special structure.

Lemma 3.7. – *If φ is alternation-free, then $A(\varphi)$ is a weak tree automaton.*
– *If φ is limit linear, then $A(\varphi)$ is limit linear.*
– *If φ is aconjunctive, then $A(\varphi)$ is limit deterministic.*

Proof. – Let φ be alternation-free so that $\mathsf{ad}(\varphi) \leq 1$ and $\mathsf{al}(\psi) \leq 1$ for all $\psi \in \mathsf{FL}(\varphi)$. Hence $A(\varphi)$ uses just the priorities $\{0, 1\}$. Furthermore, every strongly connected component in $A(\varphi)$ belongs to either a greatest or a least fixpoint and hence consists only of states with priority 0 or only of states with priority 1, as claimed.
– Let φ be limit linear so that for all subformulas $\mu X. \psi$ of φ, X has exactly one occurrence in ψ. Then φ is alternation-free so that $A(\phi)$ is weak by the previous item. Furthermore, all states in the strongly connected component of $\theta(X)$ belong to $\mu X. \psi$ and hence have priority 1. Since φ is limit-linear, there is exactly one circular path in the strongly connected component of $\theta(X)$. Hence $A(\varphi)$ is limit linear.
– Let φ be aconjunctive, let p be an odd number, let $q \in Q$ such that $\Omega(q) = p$ and let $q' \in Q_\forall$ be a state that is reachable from q by visiting states with priority at most p. It remains to show that for all $a \in \Sigma$, we have $|\delta(q', \Sigma) \cap Q_{\leq p}| \leq 1$, where $Q_{\leq p} = \{q \in Q \mid \Omega(q) \leq p\}$. Since $q \in Q_\wedge$, we have $q = \psi_1 \wedge \psi_2$ for some $\psi_1, \psi_2 \in \mathsf{FL}(\varphi)$. As φ is aconjunctive, there is at most one i such that ψ_i contains a free least fixpoint variable, and such that an odd priority is reachable from ψ_i without first passing a priority greater than p. Hence $\Omega(\psi_1) > p$ or $\Omega(\psi_2) > p$, showing that $|\delta(q', \Sigma) \cap Q_{\leq p}| \leq 1$.
□

4   Emptiness of Alternating Tree Automata

We now show how the decision whether the language of an alternating automaton is non-empty can be reduced to deciding the winner in a two-player game. We start by constructing a game with labeled edges and an acceptance condition that is defined by a nondeterministic word automaton. We show that player ◇ wins in this game if the language of the alternating automaton is not empty. Then, by manipulating the word automaton, we construct a parity game with the same quality: player ◇ wins if the language of the alternating automaton is not empty. This is interesting because it unifies many results about fragments of the μ-calculus to results about word automata.

4.1   Nondeterministic Parity Word Automata

Before proceeding we introduce nondeterministic and history deterministic word automata.

Definition 4.1 (Nondeterministic Parity Word Automata). A nondeterministic parity word automaton is $N = (\Sigma, Q, q_0, \delta, \Omega)$, where Σ is a finite alphabet, Q a finite set of states, $q_0 \in Q$ an initial state, and $\delta : Q \times \Sigma \to \mathcal{P}(Q)$ a transition function. The *priority function* $\Omega : Q \to \mathbb{N}$ assigns priorities to states. Given an automaton N, the rank of N is its maximal priority, that is $\max\{\Omega(q) \mid q \in Q\}$. Given an infinite word $w = a_0 a_1 \ldots \in \Sigma^\omega$, a *run of N on* w is an infinite sequence $\tau = q_0, q_1, \ldots$ of states such that $q_{i+1} \in \delta(q_i, a_i)$ for all $i \geq 0$. A run $\tau = q_0, q_1, \ldots$ is *accepting* if the highest priority that occurs infinitely often in τ is even. Formally, reusing the notation $\inf_\Omega$ introduced for parity games, run τ is accepting if and only if $\max\{\inf_\Omega(\tau)\}$ is an even number. The language accepted by N is

$$L(N) = \{w \in \Sigma^\omega \mid \text{there is an accepting run of } N \text{ on } w\}.$$

Definition 4.2 (History-deterministic Word Automata [13]**).** Given a nondeterministic word automaton N, a *resolver* for N is a function $\sigma : \Sigma^* \to Q$ such that $\sigma(\epsilon) = q_0$ and for all sequences $wa \in \Sigma^+$, we have $\sigma(wa) \in \delta(\sigma(w), a)$. Given a word $w = a_0 a_1 \cdots \in \Sigma^\omega$ the outcome of σ on w, denoted $\sigma(w)$, is the run $r = q_0, q_1, \ldots$ such that for all $i \geq 0$ we have $q_i = \sigma(a_0 \ldots a_{i-1})$. We say that N is *history-deterministic* if there is a resolver σ such that for every word w we have that

$$w \in L(N) \text{ if and only if } \sigma(w) \text{ is an accepting run of } N.$$

A word automaton is *deterministic* if for every state $q \in Q$ and every letter $a \in \Sigma$ we have $|\delta(q, a)| \leq 1$. In particular, every deterministic automaton is history deterministic.

Theorem 4.3 ([13, 22, 23]). *Given a nondeterministic parity word automaton N, there exist a history deterministic parity automaton H and a deterministic parity automaton D such that $L(N) = L(H) = L(D)$.*

In Sect. 5 we mention several determinization and history determinization constructions that take nondeterministic word automata and construct equivalent (history) deterministic automata.

4.2   The Emptiness Games

Using these definitions we are ready to proceed with the construction of the games capturing emptiness of an alternating parity tree automaton.

Definition 4.4 (Strategy Arena). Given an alternating parity tree automaton $A = (\Sigma, Q, q_0, \delta, \Omega)$ we define the *strategy arena* $G_A = (V, V_\Diamond, V_\Box, E)$, where the components of G_A are as follows. We label the edges in E as we explain below.

- $V = (\mathcal{P}(Q) \times \Sigma) \cup \mathcal{P}(Q)$
- $V_\Diamond = \mathcal{P}(Q) \cup \{(s,\sigma) \mid s \cap Q_l \neq \emptyset\}$
- $V_\Box = \{(s,\sigma) \mid s \cap Q_l = \emptyset\}$

  That is, nodes correspond to either sets of states of A with a letter from Σ or just a set of states of A. A node is in $V_\Diamond$ if either it is a plain subset of states of A or if it contains local states of A. A node is in $V_\Box$ if it does not contain local states of A.
- A *choice function* for $a \in \Sigma$ is $d : Q_\lor \to Q$ such that for every $q \in Q_\lor$ we have $d(q) \in \delta(q,a)$. We denote by D_a all the choice functions for a and by D all the choice functions for all letters $a \in \Sigma$.

  Let $D_A = D \cup Q_\Diamond \cup \Sigma$ be the set of labels.

  Intuitively, an edge e from a node (set of states) s to set of states s' corresponds to one of three cases.

  - Either e corresponds to a set of transitions taken by local states of A, in which case e is labeled by the choice function associating each existential state in s to the successor chosen for it.
  - Edge e corresponds to a set of transitions taken by modal states of A. In this case the edge corresponds to the transitions of exactly *one* existential modal state and potentially many universal modal states. In this case e is labeled by the existential modal state whose transition was taken.
  - Or e corresponds to a choice of a letter in Σ.
- Given a set of states $s \subseteq Q$, $q \in s \cap Q_\Diamond$, a letter σ, and a choice $d \in D_\sigma$ we define the update of s as follows:

$$update_l(s,\sigma,d) = (s \setminus Q_l) \cup \left\{ q' \,\middle|\, \begin{matrix} \exists q \in s \cap Q_\land \text{ and } q' \in \delta(q,\sigma) \text{ or} \\ \exists q \in s \cap Q_\lor \text{ and } q' = d(q) \end{matrix} \right\}$$
$$update_m(s,\sigma,q) = \{q' \mid q' \in \delta(q,\sigma) \text{ or } \exists q'' \in s \cap Q_\Box \text{ and } q' \in \delta(q'',\sigma)\}$$

That is, a local update consists of the set of all the successors of all the local universal states in s and all the chosen successors of all the local existential states in s. A modal update consists of the successors of the (modal existential) state $q \in s$ and all the successors of all the modal universal states in s.

The set of edges is:

$$E = \left\{ ((s,\sigma),d,(s',\sigma)) \,\middle|\, \begin{matrix} (s,\sigma) \in V_\Diamond, d \in D_\sigma, \text{ and} \\ s' = update_l(s,\sigma,d) \end{matrix} \right\} \cup$$
$$\left\{ ((s,\sigma),q,s') \,\middle|\, \begin{matrix} (s,\sigma) \in V_\Box, q \in s \cap Q_\Diamond, \\ s' = update_m(s,\sigma,q) \end{matrix} \right\} \cup$$
$$\{ \quad (s,\sigma,(s,\sigma)) \mid \sigma \in \Sigma \}$$

That is, a node (s,σ), where s contains local states of A, has successors that correspond to taking a transition from all the local states. For existential local states only one successor is taken (according to the choice labeling the edge) and for universal local states all successors are taken. A node (s,σ), where s contains no local states, has successors that correspond to taking a transition from one existential modal state in s (according to the state labeling the edge) and taking the transitions of all the universal modal states in s. A node $s \subseteq Q$, has successors that correspond to choosing a letter $\sigma \in \Sigma$ (labeling the edge) and moving to (s, σ).

We now define the winning condition associated with the strategy arena. For a labeled arena, the winning condition is a subset of $V \cdot (D_A \cdot V)^\omega$. We construct a word automaton to define the winning condition.

Definition 4.5 (Tracking Automaton). Given an alternating parity tree automaton $A = (\Sigma, Q, q_0, \delta, \Omega)$, and the arena G_A, we define the *tracking automaton* $T_A = (\Sigma_A, Q, q_0, \Gamma, \overline{\Omega})$ to be a nondeterministic parity word automaton. The alphabet of T_A is $\Sigma_A = (\Sigma \times (D \cup Q_\Diamond)) \cup \Sigma$. That is T_A reads either a letter in Σ and either a choice function or a modal existential state or simply a letter in Σ. The transition function of T_A is defined by putting

$$\Gamma(q, (\sigma, d)) = \begin{cases} d(q) & \text{if } q \in Q_\vee \text{ and } d \in D \\ \emptyset & \text{if } q \in Q_\vee \text{ and } d \in Q_\Diamond \\ \delta(q, \sigma) & \text{if } q \in Q_\wedge \\ \delta(q, \sigma) & \text{if } q \in Q_\Diamond \text{ and } d = q \\ \emptyset & \text{if } q \in Q_\Diamond \text{ and } d \in Q \setminus \{q\} \\ q & \text{if } q \in Q_\Diamond \text{ and } d \notin Q \\ \delta(q, \sigma) & \text{if } q \in Q_\Box \text{ and } d \in Q \\ q & \text{if } q \in Q_\Box \text{ and } d \notin Q \end{cases}$$

for $q \in Q$, $\sigma \in \Sigma$, and $d \in D \cup Q_\Diamond$.
For $q \in Q$ and $\sigma \in \Sigma$ we put $\Gamma(q, \sigma) = \{q\}$.

Notice that the only transitions of T_A that lead to sets with more than one element are when $q \in Q_\wedge$. Indeed, when $q \in Q_m$, by assumption, we have $|\delta(q, \sigma)| = 1$. Finally, $\overline{\Omega}$ is obtained from Ω by setting $\overline{\Omega}(q) = \Omega(q) + 1$.

We are now ready to define the acceptance condition α. Recall, that a labeled play π in G_A is $\pi \in V \cdot (D_A \cdot V)^\omega$. Given a pair (v, d), their projection onto Σ_A, denoted $\lfloor v, d \rfloor$, is $\lfloor (s, \sigma), d \rfloor = (\sigma, d)$ and $\lfloor s, \sigma \rfloor = \sigma$. Given an infinite sequence $\pi = v_0 d_0 v_1 d_1 \cdots \in V \cdot (D_A \cdot V)^\omega$, we denote by $\lfloor \pi \rfloor$ the sequence $\lfloor v_0, d_0 \rfloor \lfloor v_1, d_1 \rfloor \cdots$. We define α_A as follows.

$$\alpha_A = \{\pi \mid \lfloor \pi \rfloor \notin L(T_A)\}$$

Let G_A^+ be the combination of the arena G_A with α_A. We sum up the relation between A and G_A^+ as follows.

Theorem 4.6 (Simulation). *Let A be an alternating tree automaton A. Then A is non-empty if and only if player $\Diamond$ wins G_A^+ from $\{q_0\}$.*

A proof is included in [11].

Consider the automaton T_A. By Theorem 4.3, there exists an equivalent history deterministic automaton H_A. Let $H_A = (\Sigma_A, T, t_0, \rho, \Omega')$. By using H_A we can turn the game G_A^+ to a parity game G_A^* capturing the non-emptiness of A.

Definition 4.7 (G_A^*). Consider the strategy arena $G_A = (V, V_\Diamond, V_\Box, E)$ and the automaton H_A. We construct the parity game $G_A^* = (V', V_\Diamond', V_\Box', E', \Omega'')$, where the components of G_A^* are as follows.

- $V' = (V \times T) \cup (\Sigma_A \times V \times T)$
- $V_\Diamond' = V_\Diamond \times T$
- $V_\Box' = (V_\Box \times T) \cup (\Sigma_A \times V \times T)$
- The set of edges is:

$$
\begin{aligned}
E' = \{ \quad &(((s,\sigma),t)\,,\,((\sigma,d),v',t)) \mid ((s,\sigma),d,v') \in E \} \quad \cup \\
\{ \quad &((s,t)\,,\,(\sigma,v',t)) \mid (s,\sigma,v') \in E \quad\} \quad \cup \\
\{ (((\sigma,d),v',t)\,,\,&(v',t')) \mid t' \in \rho(t,(\sigma,d)) \quad\} \quad \cup \\
\{ \quad ((\sigma,v',t)\,,\,&(v',t')) \mid t' \in \rho(t,\sigma) \quad\}
\end{aligned}
$$

- The priority function Ω'' is obtained from Ω' by setting $\Omega''(v,t) = \Omega'(t) + 1$ and $\Omega''(a,v,t) = \Omega'(t) + 1$.

Theorem 4.8 (Game Translation). *Player $\Diamond$ wins in G_A^+ from some state (s,σ) if and only if player $\Diamond$ wins in G_A^* from $((s,\sigma),t_0)$.*

Proof. We can show that player $\Box$ wins in G_A^* if and only if she wins in G_A^+. The proof follows the proof that history deterministic automata can be used in combination with games as in [13].

Remark 4.9. An alternative way to view the construction of T_A and H_A is to think about the dual of T_A as a universal automaton recognizing plays that are winning for player $\Diamond$. Then, the dual of H_A would be a history-deterministic universal parity automaton recognizing the same language. The resolution of the transition function of a history-deterministic universal automaton is delegated to player $\Box$ just like it is in the construction of G_A^*. In particular, every history-determinization for nondeterministic automata is, in fact, also a history-determinization for universal automata. This implies that the history-determinization construction of Henzinger and Piterman [13] can be also used for under-approximating the losing region in an LTL game, which was left as an open question in their paper.

The following is a direct implication of Theorems 4.6 and 4.8.

Corollary 4.10 (Emptiness). *Let A be an alternating tree automaton. Then A is non-empty if and only if player $\Diamond$ wins G_A^* from the node $(\{q_0\}, t_0)$.*

We now consider the complexity of the decision problem. Let A be an alternating tree automaton reading an alphabet of size m with n states and rank k. Then G_A has $(m+1) \cdot 2^n$ vertices and T_A has n states and rank k as well. Let $S_{HD}(n,k)$ denote the number of states and $R_{HD}(n,k)$ denote the rank of a history deterministic automaton obtained from a nondeterministic word automation with n states and rank k.

Corollary 4.11 (Complexity). *Let A be an alternating tree automaton reading an alphabet of size m, with n states and rank k. The complexity of emptiness of A is* PARITY$((m+1) \cdot 2^n \cdot S_{HD}(n,k), R_{HD}(n,k))$-TIME.

Remark 4.12. In case that H_A is a deterministic automaton, a winning strategy for player $\Diamond$ in G_A^* directly induces a Kripke structure K with set of worlds $W = V_\square \times T$ such that A accepts K. Hence non-empty alternating parity tree automata accept some structure of size at most $(m+1) \cdot 2^n \cdot S_{HD}(n,k)$ which is in $\mathcal{O}((m+1) \cdot 2^n \cdot ((nk)!)^2)$ by Lemma 5.1 and Lemma 5.11 below.

5 Transformations of Word Automata

We specialize parity acceptance conditions to the special cases of Büchi and co-Büchi conditions. In a Büchi condition the priority function uses only the priorities $1, 2$. In a co-Büchi condition the priority function uses only the priorities $0, 1$. For Büchi automata, we put $F = \{q \in Q \mid \Omega(q) = 2\}$; for co-Büchi automata, we put $F = \{q \in Q \mid \Omega(q) = 0\}$; in both cases, we put $\overline{F} = Q \setminus F$. The Büchi acceptance requires accepting runs to contain infinitely many accepting states, while co-Büchi acceptance requires accepting runs to contain only finitely many non-accepting states. A co-Büchi automaton is weak if for all its strongly connected components C, we have $C \subseteq F$ or $C \subseteq \overline{F}$. For deterministic automata, we extend δ from letters to finite words in the obvious way.

Lemma 5.1 ([15]). *Let $A = (\Sigma, Q, q_0, \delta, \Omega)$ be a nondeterministic parity word automaton of rank k. Then there is a nondeterministic Büchi word automaton $A' = (\Sigma, Q', q_0, \delta', F)$ such that $L(A) = L(A')$ and $|Q'| \leq (\lceil \frac{k+1}{2} \rceil + 1) \cdot |Q|$.*

Proof. We just recall the construction of A' and refer to [12,15] for the proof of $L(A) = L(A')$. Intuitively, the automaton A' nondeterministically guesses a position and an even priority p such that there is a run of A on the input word such that from the guessed position on, no state with priority greater than p is visited and some state with priority p is visited infinitely often. Formally, we put $Q'' = Q \times \{i \in \mathbb{N} \mid 0 \leq i \leq k \text{ and } i \text{ is even}\}$ and

$$Q' = Q \cup Q'' \qquad\qquad F = \{(q, i) \in Q'' \mid \Omega(q) = i\}$$

so that the claimed bound on the size of A' follows immediately. The transition function δ' is defined, for $q \in Q$, even i such that $0 \leq i \leq k$ and $a \in \Sigma$, by putting

$$\delta'(q, a) = \delta(q, a) \cup \{(q', i) \in Q'' \mid q' \in \delta(q, a) \text{ and } \Omega(q') = i\}$$

and

$$\delta'((q, i), a) = \{(q', i) \in \delta(q, a) \times \{i\} \mid \Omega(q') \leq i\}.$$

$\square$

Definition 5.2 (Limit-linear co-Büchi Automata). A co-Büchi automaton $A = (\Sigma, Q, q_0, \delta, F)$ is *limit-linear* if for all $q \in F$, there is exactly one δ-path that stays in F and leads from q to q.

Definition 5.3 (Limit-deterministic Word Automata). Fix a parity word automaton $A = (\Sigma, Q, q_0, \delta, \Omega)$. Given a state $q \in Q$, the *compartment* C_q of q consists of all states that are reachable from q by a path that visits states with priority at most $\Omega(q)$. We say that A is *limit-deterministic (LD)* if for all states q such that $\Omega(q)$ is even, C_q is *internally deterministic*, that is, $|\delta(q', a) \cap C_q| \leq 1$ for all $q' \in C_q$ and $a \in \Sigma$.

Thus a Büchi automaton is limit-deterministic if all its states that are reachable from an accepting state are deterministic. A co-Büchi automaton is limit-deterministic if all its accepting states are deterministic. In particular, every limit-linear co-Büchi automaton is limit-deterministic.

Lemma 5.4. *The construction in Lemma 5.1 preserves limit determinism.*

Proof. Let A be a limit-deterministic parity automaton. Then we claim that A' as constructed in Lemma 5.1 is limit-deterministic. Since A' is a Büchi automaton and since all states that are reachable from some state in F are contained in $Q \times \{p\}$ for some even p, it suffices to show that for all even p, all states $(q, p) \in Q \times \{p\}$ and all $a \in \Sigma$, we have $|\delta'((q, p), a)| \leq 1$. So let $(q, p) \in Q \times \{p\}$. Then, by construction of A', (q, p) is contained in the compartment C of some state with priority p in A. By definition of δ', we have $\delta'((q, p), a) \subseteq C$ since C is a compartment. Since A is limit-deterministic, C is internally deterministic which shows $|\delta'((q, p), a)| \leq 1$, as required. □

5.1 Determinizing Word Automata

We give specialized determinization constructions for limit-linear co-Büchi automata, nondeterministic co-Büchi automata, limit-deterministic Büchi automata, and finally for general Büchi automata and parity automata.

Lemma 5.5 (Circle method). *Let A be a limit-linear co-Büchi automaton with n states. Then there is a deterministic co-Büchi automaton A' with n' states such that $L(A) = L(A')$ and $n' \leq n^2 \cdot 2^n$.*

Proof. Let $A = (\Sigma, Q, q_0, \delta, F)$. If $F = Q$, then A is deterministic and we put $A' = A$. Otherwise, we have $|F| < n$ and proceed with the following construction, which is similar to the powerset construction, but additionally annotates macro-states with a single state and a counter. The states of accepting components are arranged in a cycle since A is limit-linear. Intuitively, the single state component of macro-states identifies exactly one state in exactly one accepting cycle that has a token. The determinized automaton then checks whether it is possible to stay within this cycle forever, moving the token according to the letters that are read. If this is not possible, the automaton reduces the counter by one and moves the token to *the* next state in the current cycle and again checks whether is possible to stay in the cycle forever when moving the token according to the read word. When this fails so often that the counter reaches 0, the automaton picks a state from another accepting cycle, moves the token to this state and resets the counter. It is crucial that the moving of tokens between accepting cycles is done in a fair way, so that if the token changes cycles infinitely often, the token visits every accepting cycle infinitely often. Then the token eventually stays forever within one accepting cycle if and only if there is an accepting run.

Formally, we proceed as follows. For moving the token between accepting cycles, we assume a function next : $Q \to Q$ such that for $q \in Q$, next(q) is some abitrary but fixed state from an accepting cycle of A such that iterative application of next cycles through all accepting cycles of A in a fair manner. We also assume a function step : $F \to F$ that cycles through the states of a single accepting cycle of A in a fair manner; formally, we put step$(q) = q'$ where q' is *the* state such that there is some $a \in \Sigma$ such that $\delta(q,a) \cap F = \{q'\}$. We define the deterministic co-Büchi automaton $A' = (\Sigma, Q', u_0, \delta', F')$ by putting

$$Q' = 2^Q \times Q \times \{0, \ldots, |F|\} \qquad F' = \{(U, q, c) \in Q' \mid c \neq 0\}$$

and $u_0 = (\{q_0\}, q_0, 0)$. The claimed bound on the size of A' follows immediately since $|F| < n$ so that $|\{0, \ldots, |F|\}| \leq n$. Finally, the transition relation δ' is defined by putting, for $(U, q, c) \in Q'$ and $a \in \Sigma$,

$$\delta'((U, q, c), a) = (\delta(U, a), q', c)$$

if $c \neq 0$, $\delta(q, a) \cap F = \{q'\}$ and $q \in U$; this moves the token within the current accepting cycle according to the input letter, if possible. Otherwise, the run represented by the token does not stay in the current accepting cycle and we move the token to another state. This is achieved by putting

$$\delta'((U, q, c), a) = \begin{cases} (\delta(U, a), \text{next}(q), |F|) & \text{if } c = 0 \\ (\delta(U, a), \text{step}(\text{step}(q)), c - 1) & \text{if } c > 0 \end{cases}$$

If $c = 0$, then the token is moved to the next accepting cycle and the counter is reset to $|F|$; if $c > 0$, then the token is moved to the next state in the current accepting cycle (to also incorporate the a-transition that takes place, we apply step twice) and the counter is reduced by 1. We show in [11] that $L(A) = L(A')$.
□

Example 5.6. Consider the limit-linear co-Büchi automaton A depicted below, and the equivalent deterministic co-Büchi automaton A' obtained by using the construction from Lemma 5.5; to be able show a complete example, A is picked to be a very simple automaton (accepting just the word $(ab)^\omega$). For brevity, we depict only the reachable part of A' and collapse all macro-states of the shape $(\emptyset, q, c)$ to a single non-accepting sink state $\bot$. Any macro-state in A' that has a nonzero counter value is accepting. We have step$(y) = u$ and step$(u) = y$. Since there is just one accepting strongly connected component in A, we assume that next$(x) = $ next$(y) = $ next$(z) = y$, and next$(u) = u$.

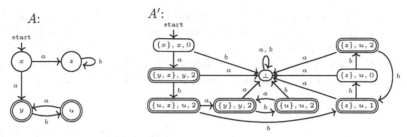

The automaton A' starts with the token at x and with counter value 0. When reading a, the token is moved to $\mathsf{next}(x) = y$ and the counter is reset to 2. Afterwards, there are two cases: If the automaton reads bb, it is not possible in A to move the token accordingly from y and stay in the accepting cycle between y and u. Thus A' transitions to $(\{z\}, u, 1)$, intuitively moving the token to the next accepting cycle, which in this example moves the token to u. This state however is not contained in the powerset component $\{z\}$ so that the automaton rejects the word, which is reflected by the fact that $(\{z\}, u, 1)$ accepts the empty language. The other option to proceed from $(\{y, z\}, y, 2)$ is by reading sequences $(ba)^*$, which results in repeatedly moving the token from y to u and back to y; if this continues forever, the word is accepted by A'. Otherwise, a sequence aa or bb is read eventually and the automaton transitions to the sink state and rejects the word.

Lemma 5.7 (Miyano-Hayashi [19]). *Given a nondeterministic co-Büchi automaton $A = (\Sigma, Q, q_0, \delta, F)$, there is a deterministic co-Büchi automaton $A' = (\Sigma, Q', u_0, \delta', F')$ such that $L(A) = L(A')$ and $|Q'| \leq 3^{|Q|}$.*

Proof. We just show the construction of A'; for the proof of $L(A) = L(A')$ we refer to [19]. The construction is similar to the powerset construction but additionally tracks subsets V of the accepting states $U \cap F$ of macro-states $U \subseteq Q$. Intuitively, there is, for each state in V, a run of A that has not left F recently. Whenever this set is the empty set, it is reset to all accepting states of the current macro-state. A run of A' then is accepting if such resetting steps happen only finitely often, ensuring the existence of a run of A that from some point on stays within F forever. Formally, we put

$$Q' = \{(U, V) \mid U \subseteq Q, V \subseteq U \cap F\} \qquad F' = \{(U, V) \in Q' \mid V \neq \emptyset\}$$

and $u_0 = (\{q_0\}, \emptyset)$. The claimed bound on the size of A' follows since macro-states $(U, V) \in Q'$ can be coded by functions $f : Q \rightarrow \{0, 1, 2\}$ where $f(q) = 0$ if $q \notin U$, $f(q) = 1$ if $q \in U$ but $q \notin V$ and $f(q) = 2$ if $q \in V$; the number of such functions is bounded by $3^{|Q|}$. We define δ' by putting

$$\delta'((U, V), a) = \begin{cases} (\delta(U, a), \delta(V, a) \cap F) & \text{if } V \neq \emptyset \\ (\delta(U, a), \delta(U, a) \cap F) & \text{if } V = \emptyset \end{cases}$$

for $(U, V) \in Q'$ and $a \in \Sigma$. $\qquad\qquad\qquad\qquad\qquad\qquad\qquad\qquad\qquad\qquad\square$

Example 5.8. Consider the nondeterministic co-Büchi automaton A depicted below, and the equivalent deterministic automaton A' obtained by using the construction from Lemma 5.7; both automata accept exactly the infinite words over $\Sigma = \{a, b\}$ that contain a finitely often. For brevity, we depict only the reachable part of A' and label macro-states (U, V) with $U \setminus V, V$.

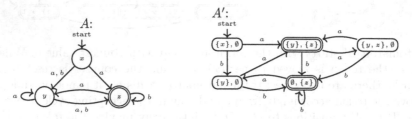

The a-transition from the accepting macro-state $(\{y\}, \{z\})$ in A' leads to the non-accepting macro-state $(\{y, z\}, \emptyset)$ and not to $(\{y\}, \{z\})$; the tracked set of accepting states is then reset to $\{z\}$ after a further a- or b-transition. This reflects the fact that no run of A can stay in the accepting state z by reading the letter a so that all words that contain a infinitely often are rejected by both A and A'.

Lemma 5.9 (Permutation method [7,12]). *Let A be a limit-deterministic Büchi automaton with n states. Then there is a deterministic parity automaton A' with n' states and $2n$ priorities such that $L(A) = L(A')$ and $n' \leq e(n+1)!$.*

Proof. We sketch just the construction of A' and refer to [7,12] for the proof of equivalence of A and A'. Intuitively, A' is similar to the powerset automaton of A, but additionally keeps a permutation on the deterministic states in macro-states, indicating the order in which runs leading to the respective states have last seen an accepting state. Additionally, states in A' contain a third component which indicates the leftmost position in the permutation that is *active* or *ending* by the transitions leading to the current state in A'. Here, a position is active in an a-transition, if the state at this position in the current permutation is accepting; a position is said to be ending if all runs of A that are represented by the state at this position end when reading the letter a or lead to a state at an older position. A parity condition then uses this information to detect a position in the permutation components that is active infinitely often but, from some point on, never ends. This ensures the existence of a continuous run of A that visits some accepting state infinitely often.

Formally, we proceed as follows. Given a limit-deterministic Büchi automaton $A = (\Sigma, Q, q_0, \delta, F)$ with sets $Q_D, Q_N \subseteq Q$ of deterministic and nondeterministic states, respectively, we have that every state reachable from F is contained in Q_D. We assume without loss of generality that $q_0 \in Q_N$. We let $\mathsf{perm}(Q_D)$ denote the set of partial permutations over Q_D, that is, $\mathsf{perm}(Q_D)$ consists of all partial functions $f : Q_D \rightharpoonup |Q_D|$ such that $f(q) \neq f(q')$ for all $q, q' \in \mathsf{dom}(f)$ such that $q \neq q'$. We denote the empty permutation by $[]$ ($\mathsf{dom}([]) = \emptyset$). Then we define the deterministic parity automaton $A' = (\Sigma, Q', u_0, \delta', \Omega)$ by putting

$$Q' = 2^{Q_N} \times \mathsf{perm}(Q_D) \times \{1, \ldots, 2|Q_D| + 1\} \qquad \Omega(U, f, p) = p$$

and $u_0 = (\{q_0\}, [], 1)$. The claimed bounds on the size and number of priorities of A' follows. The transition function δ' is defined by putting, for $(U, f, p) \in Q'$ and $a \in \Sigma$,

$$\delta'((U, f, p), a) = (\delta(U, a) \cap Q_N, f', p'),$$

where f' denotes the partial permutation that is obtained by applying a-transitions from δ to the partial permutation f, keeping the ordering intact but removing elements that do not have an outgoing a-transition; here it is crucial that all states in f are deterministic so that it is never the case that additional elements are inserted between any two elements of the permutation. Furthermore, we add all states from $\delta(U, a) \cap Q_D$ that do not already occur in this new permutation to the end of it (the order of these elements is irrelevant). Let $i \geq 1$ be the leftmost position in f' such that $f(i)$ is defined and $\delta(f(i), a) \neq f'(i)$ (including the case that $f'(i)$ is undefined), or we have $f'(i) \in F$. Thus i identifies the leftmost position in the partial permutation that is active or ending (possibly both). If no such i exists, put $p' = 1$. Otherwise, if $\delta(f(i), a) \neq f'(i)$, then put $p' = 2(|Q_D| - i) + 3$; if $\delta(f(i), a) = f(i) \in F$, then put $p' = 2(|Q_D| - i) + 2$. □

Example 5.10. For the limit-deterministic Büchi automaton A with $Q_N = \{x, z\}$ and $Q_D = \{y, u\}$ depicted below, we obtain the equivalent deterministic parity automaton A' using the construction from Lemma 5.9. For brevity, we depict A' with *edge priorities*, thus moving the priority component p of macro-states (U, f, p) to the edges.

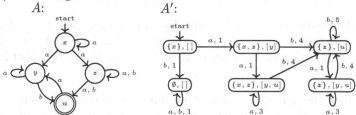

Let δ be the transition relation of A. In A' there is an a-transition with priority 1 from the initial state $(\{x\}, [])$ to $(\{x, z\}, [y])$. This is the case since $\delta(\{x\}, a) = \{x, y, z\}$ so that $\{x, y, z\} \cap Q_N = \{x, z\}$. Since $y \in \delta(\{x\}, a) \cap Q_D$, we add it to the end of the permutation component which thereby changes from $[]$ to $[y]$. We have $y \notin F$ so that there is no position in the permutation that ends or is active. Thus the priority of this transition is 1. There is an a-loop with priority 3 at $(\{x, z\}, [y, u])$. This is the case since $\delta(\{x, z\}, a) = \{x, y, z, u\}$ so that $\delta(\{x, z\}, a) \cap Q_N = \{x, z\}$. Also we update the permutation component $[y, u]$ according to reading the letter a: We have $\delta(y, a) = y$ and $\delta(u, a) = y$ and hence obtain a temporary permutation $[y]$. Now $\delta(\{x, z\}, a) \cap Q_D$ contains the state u that is appended to the permutation, resulting in $[y, u]$ as new permutation component. As $y \notin F$ and $\delta(y, a) = y$, the leftmost position in the permutation component is neither active nor ending. We also have $u \in F$ and $\delta(u, a) \neq u$ so that position 2 is both ending and active. Hence the priority of this transition is $2(|Q_D| - i) + 3 = 2(2 - 2) + 3 = 3$. This reflects the fact that even though an accepting state can be reached from $\{x, y, z, u\}$ by an a-transition in A (as $u \in \delta(z, a)$), all runs that have visited an accepting state at least once before are residing in the state y after reading a. Thus it is not possible to construct a continuous run that only reads the letter a and still visits u more than once. Intuitively, reading the letter a merges all runs leading to y or u, so that both positions in the permutation component $[y, u]$ are merged into the new first position containing just y; the second position thus is ending. The deterministic state u to which there is no a-transition from y or u then is appended as new (accepting) position to the permutation.

Lemma 5.11 (Safra-Piterman [22,23]). *Let* $A = (\Sigma, Q, q_0, \delta, F)$ *be a Büchi automaton. Then there is a deterministic parity automaton* $A' = (\Sigma, Q', u_0, \delta', \Omega)$ *such that* $L(A) = L(A')$, $|Q'| \in \mathcal{O}(|Q|!^2)$ *and* A' *has at most* $2|Q|$ *priorities.*[2]

Lemma 5.12 (Parity Determinization [25]). *Let* $A = (\Sigma, Q, q_0, \delta, \Omega)$ *be a parity automaton of rank* k. *Then there is a deterministic parity automaton* $A' = (\Sigma, Q', u_0, \delta', \Omega')$ *such that* $L(A) = L(A')$, $|Q'| \in \mathcal{O}(|Q|!^{2k})$ *and* A' *has at most* $2|Q|k$ *priorities.*

5.2 History-Determinizing Word Automata

Next we give specialized history determinization constructions for limit-deterministic co-Büchi automata and for general Büchi automata.

Lemma 5.13 (History-determinizing by focusing). *Let* $A = (\Sigma, Q, q_0, \delta, F)$ *be a limit-deterministic co-Büchi word automaton. Then there is a history-deterministic co-Büchi word automaton* $A' = (\Sigma, Q', u_0, \delta', F')$ *such that* $L(A) = L(A')$ *and* $|Q'| \leq (|F| + 1) \cdot 2^{|Q|}$.

Proof. Inituively, the determinization procedure is similar to the powerset construction but uses the limited nondeterminism that is allowed in history-deterministic automata to guess a run that eventually stays in F forever. Information about the guessed runs is kept by annotating macro-states with a *focus*, that is, the state in which the run currently resides. If the guess turns out to be wrong and the run leaves F, a new guess is taken (a refocusing step takes place). The resulting automaton then can be shown to be history-deterministic by using a resolver function that refocuses in a fair manner, guaranteeing that no run is overlooked.

Formally, we put $Q'' = \{(U, q) \in 2^Q \times F \mid q \in U\}$ and

$$Q' = 2^Q \cup Q'' \qquad\qquad u_0 = \{q_0\} \qquad\qquad F' = Q'',$$

---

[2] The tight complexity analysis of the construction in [22] is in [24].

from which the claimed bound on the size of A' follows since

$$|Q'| = |2^Q \cup Q''| = 2^{|Q|} + (2^{|Q|} \cdot |F|) = (|F| + 1) \cdot 2^{|Q|}.$$

The transition relation δ' is defined by putting, for $a \in \Sigma$ and $U \subseteq Q$,

$$\delta'(U, a) = \{\delta(U, a)\} \cup \{(\delta(U, a), q') \mid q' \in \delta(U, a) \cap F\}$$

and, for $a \in \Sigma$ and $(U, q) \in Q''$,

$$\delta'((U, q), a) = \begin{cases} \{(\delta(U, a), q')\} & \text{if } \delta(q, a) \cap F = \{q'\} \\ \{\delta(U, a)\} & \text{if } \delta(q, a) \cap F = \emptyset, \end{cases}$$

noting that since A is limit-deterministic, we have $|\delta(q, a) \cap F| \leq 1$ if $q \in F$, so that the case distinction above is exhaustive. Given $(U, q) \in Q''$, we refer to q as the *focus* and for $U \in Q'$ we say that the focus is *finished* at U. Outgoing transitions from $U \subseteq Q$ to $(U', q) \in Q''$ are *refocusing transitions*. We show in [11] that $L(A) = L(A')$.

$\square$

We note that the automaton A' in the above construction is not a weak automaton, even if A is a weak automaton.

Example 5.14. Consider the limit-deterministic co-Büchi automaton A depicted below, and the equivalent history-deterministic co-Büchi automaton A' obtained by using the construction from Lemma 5.13; both automata accept exactly the infinite words over $\Sigma = \{a, b\}$ that contain either a or b finitely often. For brevity, we depict only the reachable part of A' and label macro-states (U, q) with the elements of U with focus q underlined. Every macro-state in A' that has a focus is accepting.

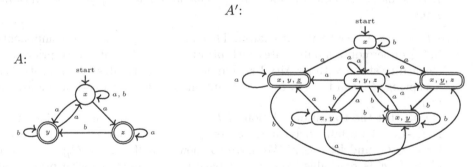

Let δ be the transition relation of A. Then we have a-transitions from x to $x, y, \underline{z}$, to x, y, z and to $x, \underline{y}, z$. This is the case since $\delta(x, a) = \{x, y, z\}$. Since both y and z are accepting states in A, A' has, when reading a at the state x, the history-deterministic choice to focus either y or z (or none of the two).

On the other hand, we have e.g. an a-transition from $x, \underline{y}$ to the non-accepting macro-state x, y, z since $\delta(y, a) = x$ is not an accepting state. Hence the a-transition from $x, \underline{y}$ finishes the focus and another refocusing step is necessary in order for a run to be accepting. Thus A' accepts for instance the word $(aba)b^\omega$ (also accepted by A) by staying unfocused when reading $abab$, leading to the partial run $x \xrightarrow{a} x, y, z \xrightarrow{b} x, y \xrightarrow{a} x, y, z \xrightarrow{b} x, y$; then the automaton can focus on y, continuing the run with $x, \underline{y} \xrightarrow{b} x, \underline{y} \xrightarrow{b} x, \underline{y} \ldots$, resulting in an overall accepting run. For the word a^ω however, there is a non-accepting run $x \xrightarrow{a} x, \underline{y}, z \xrightarrow{a} x, \underline{y}, z \xrightarrow{a} x, y, z \xrightarrow{a} x, \underline{y}, z$ in which y is focused infinitely often, but also finished infinitely often. This shows that fair order of focusing is crucial in resolving the history-determinism: Every run in which the automaton eventually focuses the state z is accepting.

Lemma 5.15 (Henzinger-Piterman [13]**).** *Let A be a nondeterministic Büchi word automaton with n states. Then there is a history-deterministic parity word automaton A' with n' states such that $L(A) = L(A')$ and $n' \in \mathcal{O}(3^{n^2})$.*

Notice that the size of a history-deterministic automaton, in the general case, is larger than the size of the deterministic automaton. The potential advantage of using history determinization would be to have a simpler structure of the resulting automaton.

5.3   Application to Emptiness Checking and μ-Calculus Satisfiability

To conclude this section, we state the connection between the structure of the alternating parity tree automaton A and the structure of the tracking automaton T_A.

Lemma 5.16.   – *If A is an alternating weak tree automaton, then the tracking automaton T_A is a weak word automaton.*
– *If A is limit deterministic, then the tracking automaton T_A is limit deterministic.*

Proof.   – Let A be a weak automaton. Then all strongly connected components in T_A either contain only states with priority 2 or only states with priority 1. Regarding states with priority 1 as non-accepting and states with priority 2 as accepting, T_A can be seen as a weak automaton (and as a co-Büchi automaton).
– Recall that the transition relation of T_A is Γ and the priority function of T_A is $\overline{\Omega}$. Let A be limit deterministic, let $q \in Q$ such that $\overline{\Omega}(q) = p$ is even, let $q' \in C_q$ and let $a \in \Sigma$. We have to show that $|\Gamma(q', a) \cap C_q| \leq 1$. Since $q' \in C_q$, q' is reachable from q by a path that visits states with priority at most p. The only case where we have $|\Gamma(q', a)| > 1$ is when $q' \in Q_\wedge$. Also $\Omega(q) = \overline{\Omega}(q) - 1 = p - 1$ is odd and q' is reachable in A by a path that visits nodes with priority at most $p - 1$. Since A is limit-deterministic, we have $|\delta(q', a) \cap Q_{\leq p-1}| \leq 1$ which implies $|\Gamma(q', a) \cap C_q| \leq 1$ since $C_q \subseteq Q_{\leq p-1}$ by definition of compartments and since $\Gamma(q', a) \subseteq \delta(q', a)$ by definition of Γ. $\qquad \square$

Remark 5.17. If A is limit linear, then A is weak. By the above lemma, T_A is a weak automaton with F being the states with priority 2. Given $q \in F$ so that $\Omega(q) = \overline{\Omega}(q) - 1 = 1$, there is exactly one path from q to q in A, since A is limit linear. Except for the self-loops introduced by non-manipulating transitions in T_A, there is exactly one path from q to q in T_A that stays in F. We note that the concept of limit-linear word automata can be slightly extended to accommodate self-loops, using a notion of *synchronizing* transitions in such a way that the method from Lemma 5.5 can be employed, obtaining the same complexity result. For brevity, we omit the technical details here and refer to [10] instead.

By using the bespoke determinization and history-determinization constructions stated above we achieve below better complexity bounds.

Corollary 5.18. *Let A be an alternating parity tree automaton reading an alphabet of size m, with n states and rank k. Depending on the structure of A, the complexity of emptiness checking for A is as follows (where $s = (nm+1)\cdot 2^n$).*

- *If A is limit-linear:*   PARITY($s \cdot n^2 \cdot 2^n, 2$)-TIME
- *If A is limit-deterministic and weak:*   PARITY($s \cdot n \cdot 2^n, 2$)-TIME
- *If A is weak:*   PARITY($s \cdot 3^n, 2$)-TIME
- *If A is limit-deterministic:*   PARITY($s \cdot e \cdot (nk)!, 2nk$)-TIME
- *In any case:*   PARITY($s \cdot \mathcal{O}((n)!^{2k}), 2nk$)-TIME

Remark 5.19. Given a formula φ, the automaton $A(\varphi)$ makes very limited use of the alphabet Σ (in fact, it is only used to check for satisfaction of propositional atoms). For satisfiability checking, the guessing and memorizing of letters in the emptiness game G_A^* can hence be avoided by letting player $\square$ immediately win all nodes whose state component $s \subseteq Q$ in the strategy arena contains $\{p, \neg p\}$ for some atom p. Furthermore, the state component $s \subseteq Q$ of nodes in the strategy arena is always contained in the label of states of the (history) deterministic variant of the tracking automaton H_A. Hence G_A^* can be slightly adapted to obtain the following complexity bounds, matching previously known results for guarded formulas.

Corollary 5.20. *Let φ be a μ-calculus formula and let $n = |\mathsf{FL}(\varphi)|$, $k = \mathsf{ad}(\varphi)$. Then the time complexity of deciding satisfiability of φ is as follows.*

- *If φ is limit-linear:*   PARITY($n^2 \cdot 2^n, 2$)-TIME
- *If φ is aconjunctive and alternation-free:* PARITY($n \cdot 2^n, 2$)-TIME
- *If φ is alternation-free:*   PARITY($3^n, 2$)-TIME
- *If φ is aconjunctive:*   PARITY($e \cdot (nk)!, 2nk$)-TIME
- *In any case:*   PARITY($\mathcal{O}((n)!^{2k}), 2nk$)-TIME

Let φ be satisfiable. Then φ has a model of size $2^{O(nk)\log n}$, and of size 3^n if φ is alternation-free.

Remark 5.21. In [8], the authors present a tableaux-based satisfiability algorithm for unguarded formulas; unguardedness is handled by an auxilliary tableau rule and by extending the tracking automaton with an additional priority to detect *inactive* traces. Using this approach however, the tracking automaton for unguarded alternation-free formulas is (in contrast to our framework) *not* a co-Büchi automaton and co-Büchi methods for (history)-determinization can not be used to obtain Büchi games that characterize satisfiability.

Our treatment of aconjunctive and alternation-free formulas employs a focusing method (Lemma 5.13) to history-determinize limit-deterministic co-Büchi automata. This generalizes the focus games for CTL [18] to the aconjunctive alternation-free μ-calculus and sheds light on the automata theoretic background of focus games.

6   Conclusions

We surveyed the approach to deciding the satisfiability of the modal μ-calculus through a reduction to alternating parity tree automata emptiness. We present the solution to the emptiness of alternating parity tree automata as a combination of a structural game construction with word automata for defining the winning condition. Interestingly the structural game construction remains fixed regardless of the exact structure of the automaton. The exact structure, however, greatly affects the properties of the word automata for the winning condition. This, in turn, can be exploited to give improved complexity results for various fragments of the μ-calculus by concentrating on bespoke word automata conversion constructions.

References

1. Calude, C., Jain, S., Khoussainov, B., Li, W., Stephan, F.: Deciding parity games in quasipolynomial time. In: Theory of Computing, STOC 2017, pp. 252–263. ACM (2017)
2. Chatterjee, K., Henzinger, M.: An $O(n^2)$ time algorithm for alternating büchi games. In: SODA, pp. 1386–1399. SIAM (2012)
3. Colcombet, T., Fijalkow, N.: Universal graphs and good for games automata: new tools for infinite duration games. In: Bojańczyk, M., Simpson, A. (eds.) FoSSaCS 2019. LNCS, vol. 11425, pp. 1–26. Springer, Cham (2019). https://doi.org/10.1007/978-3-030-17127-8_1
4. Czerwinski, W., Daviaud, L., Fijalkow, N., Jurdzinski, M., Lazic, R., Parys, P.: Universal trees grow inside separating automata: Quasi-polynomial lower bounds for parity games. In: SODA, pp. 2333–2349. SIAM (2019)
5. Emerson, E.A., Jutla, C.: The complexity of tree automata and logics of programs. SIAM J. Comput. **29**(1), 132–158 (1999)
6. Emerson, E.A., Lei, C.: Efficient model checking in fragments of the propositional mu-calculus (extended abstract). In: LICS, pp. 267–278. IEEE Computer Society (1986)
7. Esparza, J., Křetínský, J., Raskin, J.-F., Sickert, S.: From LTL and limit-deterministic Büchi automata to deterministic parity automata. In: Legay, A., Margaria, T. (eds.) TACAS 2017. LNCS, vol. 10205, pp. 426–442. Springer, Heidelberg (2017). https://doi.org/10.1007/978-3-662-54577-5_25

8. Friedmann, O., Lange, M.: Deciding the unguarded modal μ-calculus. J. Appl. Non-Class. Log. **23**, 353–371 (2013)
9. Friedmann, O., Latte, M., Lange, M.: Satisfiability games for branching-time logics. Log. Methods Comput. Sci. **9**, 1–36 (2013)
10. Hausmann, D.: Satisfiability checking for the coalgebraic μ-calculus. Ph.D. thesis, University of Erlangen-Nuremberg, Germany (2018). https://opus4.kobv.de/opus4-fau/frontdoor/index/index/docId/9932
11. Hausmann, D., Piterman, N.: A survey on satisfiability checking for the μ-calculus through tree automata. CoRR abs/2207.00517 (2022). https://arxiv.org/abs/2207.00517
12. Hausmann, D., Schröder, L., Deifel, H.-P.: Permutation games for the weakly aconjunctive μ-calculus. In: Beyer, D., Huisman, M. (eds.) TACAS 2018. LNCS, vol. 10806, pp. 361–378. Springer, Cham (2018). https://doi.org/10.1007/978-3-319-89963-3_21
13. Henzinger, T.A., Piterman, N.: Solving games without determinization. In: Ésik, Z. (ed.) CSL 2006. LNCS, vol. 4207, pp. 395–410. Springer, Heidelberg (2006). https://doi.org/10.1007/11874683_26
14. Jurdzinski, M., Morvan, R.: A universal attractor decomposition algorithm for parity games. CoRR abs/2001.04333 (2020). https://arxiv.org/abs/2001.04333
15. King, V., Kupferman, O., Vardi, M.Y.: On the complexity of parity word automata. In: Honsell, F., Miculan, M. (eds.) FoSSaCS 2001. LNCS, vol. 2030, pp. 276–286. Springer, Heidelberg (2001). https://doi.org/10.1007/3-540-45315-6_18
16. Kozen, D.: Results on the propositional μ-calculus. Theor. Comput. Sci. **27**, 333–354 (1983)
17. Kupke, C., Marti, J., Venema, Y.: Succinct graph representations of μ-calculus formulas. In: Computer Science Logic, CSL 2022. LIPIcs, vol. 216, pp. 29:1–29:18. Schloss Dagstuhl - Leibniz-Zentrum für Informatik (2022)
18. Lange, M., Stirling, C.: Focus games for satisfiability and completeness of temporal logic. In: Logic in Computer Science, LICS 2001, pp. 357–365. IEEE Computer Society (2001)
19. Miyano, S., Hayashi, T.: Alternating finite automata on ω-words. Theor. Comput. Sci. **32**, 321–330 (1984)
20. Muller, D.E., Saoudi, A., Schupp, P.E.: Weak alternating automata give a simple explanation of why most temporal and dynamic logics are decidable in exponential time. In: LICS, pp. 422–427. IEEE Computer Society (1988)
21. Muller, D.E., Schupp, P.E.: Alternating automata on infinite trees. Theor. Comput. Sci. **54**, 267–276 (1987)
22. Piterman, N.: From nondeterministic Büchi and Streett automata to deterministic parity automata. Log. Meth. Comput. Sci. **3**, 1–21 (2007)
23. Safra, S.: On the complexity of omega-automata. In: Foundations of Computer Science, FOCS 1988, pp. 319–327. IEEE Computer Society (1988)
24. Schewe, S.: Tighter bounds for the determinisation of Büchi automata. In: de Alfaro, L. (ed.) FoSSaCS 2009. LNCS, vol. 5504, pp. 167–181. Springer, Heidelberg (2009). https://doi.org/10.1007/978-3-642-00596-1_13
25. Schewe, S., Varghese, T.: Determinising parity automata. In: Csuhaj-Varjú, E., Dietzfelbinger, M., Ésik, Z. (eds.) MFCS 2014. LNCS, vol. 8634, pp. 486–498. Springer, Heidelberg (2014). https://doi.org/10.1007/978-3-662-44522-8_41
26. Streett, R.S., Emerson, E.A.: An automata theoretic decision procedure for the propositional mu-calculus. Inf. Comput. **81**(3), 249–264 (1989)
27. Wilke, T.: Alternating tree automata, parity games, and modal μ-calculus. Bull. Belgian Math. Soc. Simon Stevin **8**, 359–391 (2001)

Universal Algorithms for Parity Games and Nested Fixpoints

Marcin Jurdziński[1] , Rémi Morvan[2,3(✉)] , and K. S. Thejaswini[1]

[1] Department of Computer Science, University of Warwick, Coventry, England
{marcin.jurdzinski,thejaswini.raghavan.1}@warwick.ac.uk
[2] École normale supérieure Paris-Saclay, Cachan, France
remi.morvan@ens-paris-saclay.fr
[3] LaBRI, University Bordeaux, CNRS & Bordeaux INP, Bordeaux, France

Abstract. An attractor decomposition meta-algorithm for solving parity games is given that generalises the classic McNaughton-Zielonka algorithm and its recent quasi-polynomial variants due to Parys (2019), and to Lehtinen, Schewe, and Wojtczak (2019). The central concepts studied and exploited are attractor decompositions of dominia in parity games and the ordered trees that describe the inductive structure of attractor decompositions.

The universal algorithm yields McNaughton-Zielonka, Parys, and Lehtinen-Schewe-Wojtczak algorithms as special cases when suitable universal trees are given to it as inputs. The main technical results provide a unified proof of correctness and structural insights into those algorithms.

Suitably adapting the universal algorithm for parity games to fixpoint games gives a quasi-polynomial time algorithm to compute nested fixpoints over finite complete lattices.

The universal algorithms for parity games and nested fixpoints can be implemented symbolically. It is shown how this can be done with $O(\lg d)$ symbolic space complexity, improving the $O(d \lg n)$ symbolic space complexity achieved by Chatterjee, Dvořák, Henzinger, and Svozil (2018) for parity games, where n is the number of vertices and d is the number of distinct priorities in a parity game.

Keywords: Parity games · Universal trees · Attractor decompositions · Quasi-polynomial · Fixpoint equations · Symbolic algorithms

A full version of this paper can be found either on arXiv:2001.04333 or on hal-03762990.

1 Context

1.1 Parity Games and Their Significance

Parity games play a fundamental role in automata theory, logic, and their applications to verification [14], program analysis [3,25], and synthesis [22,30]. In particular, parity games are very intimately linked to the problems of emptiness and

© Springer Nature Switzerland AG 2022
J.-F. Raskin and K. Chatterjee (Eds.): Principles of Systems Design, LNCS 13660, pp. 252–271, 2022.
https://doi.org/10.1007/978-3-031-22337-2_12

complementation of non-deterministic automata on trees [14,35], model checking and satisfiability checking of fixpoint logics [4,14,15], fair simulation relations [16] or evaluation of nested fixpoint expressions [3,23,25]. It is a long-standing open problem whether parity games can be solved in polynomial time [15].

The impact of parity games goes well beyond their home turf of automata theory, logic, and formal methods. For example, an answer [18] of a question posed originally for parity games [34] has strongly inspired major breakthroughs on the computational complexity of fundamental algorithms in stochastic planning [17] and linear optimization [20,21], and parity games provide the foundation for the theory of nested fixpoint expressions used in program analysis [3,25] and coalgebraic model checking [23].

1.2   Related Work

The major breakthrough in the study of algorithms for solving parity games occurred in 2017 when Calude, Jain, Khoussainov, Li, and Stephan [6] have discovered the first quasi-polynomial algorithm. Three other—and seemingly distinctly different—techniques for solving parity games in quasi-polynomial time have been proposed in quick succession soon after: by Jurdziński and Lazić [26], Lehtinen [27], and Lehtinen, Parys, Schewe, and Wojtczak [28]. We would like to remark that [28] is journal paper—describing two quasi-polynomial time algorithms—combining a conference paper of Parys [32] and a preprint by Lehtinen, Schewe, and Wojtczak [29]. To distinguish between the two algorithms, we refer to these versions as the algorithms by Parys and the Lehtinen-Schewe-Wojtazak, respectively.

Czerwiński, Daviaud, Fijalkow, Jurdziński, Lazić, and Parys [9] have also uncovered an underlying combinatorial structure of universal trees as provably underlying the techniques of Calude et al., of Jurdziński and Lazić, and of Lehtinen. Czerwiński et al. have also established a quasi-polynomial lower bound for the size of smallest universal trees, providing evidence that the techniques developed in those three papers may be insufficient for leading to futher improvements in the complexity of solving parity games. The work of Lehtinen, Parys, Schewe, and Wojtczak [28], who noted that the tree of recursive calls of their algorithms is universal, has not been obviously subject to the quasi-polynomial barrier of Czerwiński et al. [9], making it a focus of current activity. Their algorithms are obtained by modifying the classic McNaughton-Zielonka algorithm [31,35], which has exponential running time in the worst case [19], but consistently outperforms most other algorithms in practice [13].

Using these universal trees as a crucial structure, there have also been further work to solve nested fixpoint expressions [2,25] in quasi-polynomial time.

1.3   Our Contributions

In this work we provide a meta-algorithm—the *universal attractor decomposition algorithm*—that generalizes McNaughton-Zielonka, Parys's, and Lehtinen-

Schewe-Wojtczak algorithms. There are multiple benefits of considering the universal algorithm.

Firstly, in contrast to Parys's and Lehtinen-Schewe-Wojtczak algorithms, the universal algorithm has a very simple and transparent structure that minimally departs from the classic McNaughton-Zielonka algorithm. Secondly, we observe that Lehtinen-Schewe-Wojtczak algorithm, as well as non-adaptive versions (see Sects. 3.2 and 4.4) of McNaughton-Zielonka and Parys's algorithms, all arise from the universal algorithm by using specific classes of universal trees, strongly linking the theory of universal trees to the only class of quasi-polynomial algorithms that had no established formal relationship to universal trees so far. Moreover, since our algorithm can be modified to use any trees, they can also run on several classes of universal trees like the Strahler universal trees introduced in the work of Daviaud, Jurdziński and Thejaswini [12].

Thirdly, we further develop the theory of dominia and their attractor decompositions in parity games, initiated by Daviaud, Jurdziński, and Lazić [10] and by Daviaud, Jurdziński, and Lehtinen [11], and we prove two new structural theorems (the embedabble decomposition theorem and the dominion separation theorem) about ordered trees of attractor decompositions.

Fourthly, we use the structural theorems to provide a unified proof of correctness of various McNaughton-Zielonka-style algorithms, identifying very precise structural conditions on the trees of recursive calls of the universal algorithm that result in it correctly identifying the largest dominia.

Fifthly, we identify a structure of nested fixpoint games, the parity games that arise naturally while solving fixpoint expressions which help us solve them in quasi-polynomial time using a modification of our universal algorithm.

Finally, we observe that thanks to its simplicity, the universal algorithm is particularly well-suited for solving parity games as well as nested fixpoint equations efficiently in a symbolic model of computation, when large sizes of input graphs prevent storing them explicitly in memory. Indeed, we argue that already a routine implementation of the universal algorithm for parity games improves the state-of-the-art symbolic space complexity of solving parity games in quasi-polynomial time from $O(d \lg n)$ to $O(d)$, but we also show that a more sophisticated symbolic data structure allows to further reduce the symbolic space of the universal algorithm to $O(\lg d)$.

2   Dominia and Decompositions

2.1   Strategies, Traps, and Dominia

A *parity game* $\mathcal{G}$ consists of a finite directed graph (V, E) together with a partition $(V_{\text{Even}}, V_{\text{Odd}})$ of the set of vertices V, and a function $\pi : V \to \{0, 1, \ldots, d\}$ that labels every vertex $v \in V$ with a non-negative integer $\pi(v)$ called its *priority*. We say that a cycle is *even* if the highest vertex priority on the cycle is even; otherwise the cycle is *odd*. We say that a parity game is (n, d)-*small* if it has at most n vertices and all vertex priorities are at most d.

For a set S of vertices, we write $\mathcal{G} \cap S$ for the substructure of $\mathcal{G}$ whose graph is the subgraph of (V, E) induced by the sets of vertices S. Sometimes, we also write $\mathcal{G} \setminus S$ to denote $\mathcal{G} \cap (V \setminus S)$. We assume throughout that every vertex has at least one outgoing edge, and we reserve the term *subgame* to substructures $\mathcal{G} \cap S$, such that every vertex in the subgraph of (V, E) induced by S has at least one outgoing edge. For a subgame $\mathcal{G}' = \mathcal{G} \cap S$, we sometimes write $V^{\mathcal{G}'}$ for the set of vertices S that the subgame $\mathcal{G}'$ is induced by. When convenient and if the risk of confusion is contained, we may simply write $\mathcal{G}'$ instead of $V^{\mathcal{G}'}$.

A (positional) *Even strategy* is a set $\sigma \subseteq E$ of edges such that:

- for every $v \in V_{\text{Even}}$, there is an edge $(v, u) \in \sigma$,
- for every $v \in V_{\text{Odd}}$, if $(v, u) \in E$ then $(v, u) \in \sigma$.

We sometimes call all the edges in such an Even strategy σ the *strategy edges*, and the definition of an Even strategy requires that every vertex in V_{Even} has an outgoing strategy edge, and every outgoing edge of a vertex in V_{Odd} is a strategy edge.

For a non-empty set of vertices T, we say that an Even strategy σ *traps Odd in T* if no strategy edge leaves T, that is, $w \in T$ and $(w, u) \in \sigma$ imply $u \in T$. We say that a set of vertices T is a *trap for Odd* if there is an Even strategy that traps Odd in T.

Observe that if T is a trap in a game $\mathcal{G}$ then $\mathcal{G} \cap T$ is a subgame of $\mathcal{G}$. For brevity, we sometimes say that a subgame $\mathcal{G}'$ is a trap if $\mathcal{G}' = \mathcal{G} \cap T$ and the set T is a trap in $\mathcal{G}$. Moreover, the following simple *"trap transitivity"* property holds: if T is a trap for Odd in game $\mathcal{G}$ and T' is a trap for Odd in subgame $\mathcal{G} \cap T$ then T' is a trap for Odd in $\mathcal{G}$.

For a set of vertices $D \subseteq V$, we say that an Even strategy σ is an *Even dominion strategy on D* if: σ traps Odd in D and every cycle in the subgraph (D, σ) is even. Finally, we say that a set D of vertices is an *Even dominion* if there is an Even dominion strategy on it.

Odd strategies, trapping Even, and Odd dominia are defined in an analogous way by swapping the roles of the two players. It is an instructive exercise to prove the following two facts about Even and Odd dominia.

Proposition 1 (Closure Under Union). *If D and D' are Even (resp. Odd) dominia then $D \cup D'$ is also an Even (resp. Odd) dominion.*

Proposition 2 (Dominion Disjointness). *If D is an Even dominion and D' is an Odd dominion then $D \cap D' = \emptyset$.*

From closure under union it follows that in every parity game, there is the largest Even dominion W_{Even} (which is the union of all Even dominia) and the largest Odd dominion W_{Odd} (which is the union of all Odd dominia), and from dominion disjointness it follows that the two sets are disjoint. The positional determinacy theorem states that, remarkably, the largest Even dominion and the largest Odd dominion form a partition of the set of vertices.

Theorem 3 (Positional Determinacy [14]). *Every vertex in a given parity game is either in the largest Even dominion or in the largest Odd dominion.*

2.2   Reachability Strategies and Attractors

In a parity game $\mathcal{G}$, for a target set of vertices B ("bullseye") and a set of vertices A such that $B \subseteq A$, we say that an Even strategy σ is an *Even reachability strategy to B from A* if every infinite path in the subgraph (V, σ) that starts from a vertex in A contains at least one vertex in B.

For every target set B, there is the largest (with respect to set inclusion) set from which there is an Even reachability strategy to B in $\mathcal{G}$; we call this set the *Even attractor to B in $\mathcal{G}$* and denote it by $\mathrm{Attr}_{\mathrm{Even}}^{\mathcal{G}}(B)$. *Odd reachability strategies* and *Odd attractors* are defined analogously.

We highlight the simple facts that if A is an attractor for a player in $\mathcal{G}$ then its complement $V \setminus A$ is a trap for her; and that attractors are monotone operators: if $B' \subseteq B$ then the attractor to B' is included in the attractor to B.

2.3   Attractor Decompositions

If $\mathcal{G}$ is a parity game in which all priorities do not exceed a non-negative even number d then we say that

$$\mathcal{H} = \langle A, (S_1, \mathcal{H}_1, A_1), \ldots, (S_k, \mathcal{H}_k, A_k) \rangle$$

is an *Even d-attractor decomposition* of $\mathcal{G}$ if:

- A is the Even attractor to the (possibly empty) set of vertices of priority d in $\mathcal{G}$;

and setting $\mathcal{G}_1 = \mathcal{G} \setminus A$, for all $i = 1, 2, \ldots, k$, we have:

- S_i is a non-empty trap for Odd in $\mathcal{G}_i$ in which every vertex priority is at most $d - 2$;
- $\mathcal{H}_i$ is a $(d - 2)$-attractor decomposition of subgame $\mathcal{G} \cap S_i$;
- A_i is the Even attractor to S_i in $\mathcal{G}_i$;
- $\mathcal{G}_{i+1} = \mathcal{G}_i \setminus A_i$;

and the game $\mathcal{G}_{k+1}$ is empty. If $d = 0$ then we require that $k = 0$.

The following proposition states that if a subgame induced by a trap for Odd has an Even attractor decomposition then the trap is an Even dominion. Indeed, a routine proof argues that the union of all the reachability strategies, implicit in the attractors listed in the decomposition, is an Even dominion strategy.

Proposition 4. *If d is even, T is a trap for Odd in $\mathcal{G}$, and there is an Even d-attractor decomposition of $\mathcal{G} \cap T$, then T is an Even dominion in $\mathcal{G}$.*

By symmetry, the dual proposition holds for player Even, assuming that d is odd.

Attractor decompositions are witnesses for the largest dominia and that the classic recursive McNaughton-Zielonka algorithm can be amended to produce such witnesses. We provide the details of this claim in the full version of the paper. Since McNaughton-Zielonka algorithm produces Even and Odd attractor decompositions, respectively, of subgames that are induced by sets of vertices that are complements of each other, a by-product of its analysis is a constructive proof of the positional determinacy theorem (Theorem 3).

Theorem 5. *McNaughton-Zielonka algorithm can be enhanced to produce both the largest Even and Odd dominia, and an attractor decomposition of each. Every vertex is in one of the two dominia.*

3   Universal Trees and Algorithms

The running time of the McNaughton-Zielonka algorithm is, up to a small polynomial factor, determined by the number of recursive calls it makes overall. While numerous experiments indicate that the algorithm performs very well on some classes of random games and on games arising from applications in model checking, temporal logic synthesis, and equivalence checking [13], it is also well known that there are families of parity games on which McNaughton-Zielonka algorithm performs exponentially many recursive calls [19].

Parys [32] has devised an ingenious modification of McNaughton-Zielonka algorithm that reduced the number of recursive calls of the algorithm to quasi-polynomial number $n^{O(\lg n)}$ in the worst case. Lehtinen, Schewe, and Wojt-czak [29] have slightly modified Parys's algorithm in order to improve the running time from $n^{O(\lg n)}$ down to $d^{O(\lg n)}$ for (n, d)-small parity games. They have also made an informal observation that the tree of recursive calls of their recursive procedure is universal.

In this paper, we argue that McNaughton-Zielonka algorithm, Parys's algorithm, and Lehtinen-Schewe-Wojtczak algorithm are special cases of what we call a *universal attractor decomposition algorithm.* The universal algorithm is parameterized by two ordered trees and we prove a striking structural result that if those trees are capacious enough to embed (in a formal sense explained later) ordered trees that describe the "shape" of some attractor decompositions of the largest Even and Odd dominia in a parity game, then the universal algorithm correctly computes the two dominia. It follows that if the algorithm is run on two universal trees then it is correct, and indeed we reproduce McNaughton-Zielonka, Parys's, and Lehtinen-Schewe-Wojtczak algorithms by running the universal algorithm on specific classes of universal trees. In particular, Lehtinen-Schewe-Wojtczak algorithm is obtained by using the succinct universal trees of Jurdziński and Lazić [26], whose size nearly matches the quasi-polynomial lower bound on the size of universal trees [9].

3.1   Universal Ordered Trees

Ordered Trees. Ordered trees are defined inductively; an ordered tree is the trivial tree $\langle \rangle$ or a sequence $\langle T_1, T_2, \ldots, T_k \rangle$, where T_i is an ordered tree for every $i = 1, 2, \ldots, k$. For an ordered tree T, we denote its *number of leaves* by leaves(T) and its *height* by height(T), with the convention that the height of the trivial tree is zero. Moreover, we denote by $\langle T \rangle^n$ the ordered tree $\langle T_1, \ldots, T_i \rangle$ where T_i is a copy of T for each $i = 1, 2, \ldots, n$.

Trees of Attractor Decompositions. The definition of an attractor decomposition is inductive and we define an ordered tree that reflects the hierarchical structure of an attractor decomposition. If d is even and

$$\mathcal{H} = \langle A, (S_1, \mathcal{H}_1, A_1), \ldots, (S_k, \mathcal{H}_k, A_k)\rangle$$

is an Even d-attractor decomposition then we define the *tree of attractor decomposition* $\mathcal{H}$, denoted by $\mathcal{T}_{\mathcal{H}}$, to be the trivial ordered tree $\langle\rangle$ if $k = 0$, and otherwise, to be the ordered tree $\langle \mathcal{T}_{\mathcal{H}_1}, \mathcal{T}_{\mathcal{H}_2}, \ldots, \mathcal{T}_{\mathcal{H}_k}\rangle$, where for every $i = 1, 2, \ldots, k$, tree $\mathcal{T}_{\mathcal{H}_i}$ is the tree of attractor decomposition $\mathcal{H}_i$. Trees of Odd attractor decompositions are defined analogously.

Observe that the sets $S_1, S_2, \ldots, S_k$ in an attractor decomposition as above are non-empty and pairwise disjoint, which implies that trees of attractor decompositions are small relative to the number of vertices and the number of distinct priorities in a parity game. More precisely, we say that an ordered tree is (n, h)-*small* if its height is at most h and it has at most n leaves. The following proposition can be proved by routine structural induction.

Proposition 6. *If $\mathcal{H}$ is an attractor decomposition of an (n, d)-small parity game then its tree $\mathcal{T}_{\mathcal{H}}$ is $(n, \lceil d/2 \rceil)$-small.*

Embedding Ordered Trees. Intuitively, an ordered tree *embeds* another if the latter can be obtained from the former by pruning some subtrees. More formally, every ordered tree embeds the trivial tree $\langle\rangle$, and $\langle \mathcal{T}_1, \mathcal{T}_2, \ldots, \mathcal{T}_k\rangle$ embeds $\langle \mathcal{T}_1', \mathcal{T}_2', \ldots, \mathcal{T}_\ell'\rangle$ if there are indices $i_1, i_2, \ldots, i_\ell$, such that $1 \leq i_1 < i_2 < \cdots < i_\ell \leq k$ and for every $j = 1, 2, \ldots, \ell$, we have that $\mathcal{T}_{i_j}$ embeds $\mathcal{T}_j'$.

Universal Ordered Trees. We say that an ordered tree is (n, h)-*universal* [9] if it embeds every (n, h)-small ordered tree. The complete n-ary tree of height h can be defined by induction on h: if $h = 0$ then $C_{n,0}$ is the trivial tree $\langle\rangle$, and if $h > 0$ then $C_{n,h}$ is the ordered tree $\langle C_{n,h-1}\rangle^n$. The tree $C_{n,h}$ is obviously (n, h)-universal but its size is exponential in h.

We define two further classes $P_{n,h}$ and $S_{n,h}$ of (n, h)-universal trees, introduced respectively by Parys [32] and by Jurdziński and Lazić [26], whose size is only quasi-polynomial, and hence they are significantly smaller than the complete n-ary trees of height h. Both classes are defined by induction on $n + h$.

If $h = 0$ then both $P_{n,h}$ and $S_{n,h}$ are defined to be the trivial tree $\langle\rangle$. If $h > 0$ then $P_{n,h}$ is defined to be the ordered tree

$$\left\langle P_{\lfloor n/2 \rfloor, h-1}\right\rangle^{\lfloor n/2 \rfloor} \cdot \left\langle P_{n,h-1}\right\rangle \cdot \left\langle P_{\lfloor n/2 \rfloor, h-1}\right\rangle^{\lfloor n/2 \rfloor},$$

and $S_{n,h}$ is defined to be the ordered tree

$$S_{\lfloor n/2 \rfloor, h} \cdot \left\langle S_{n,h-1}\right\rangle \cdot S_{\lfloor n/2 \rfloor, h}.$$

The following proposition can easily be proven by induction on (n, h).

Proposition 7. *Ordered trees $C_{n,h}$, $P_{n,h}$ and $S_{n,h}$ are (n, h)-universal.*

A proof of universality of $S_{n,h}$ is implicit in the work of Jurdziński and Lazić [26], whose *succinct multi-counters* are merely an alternative presentation of trees $S_{n,h}$. Parys [32] has shown that the number of leaves in trees $P_{n,h}$ is $n^{\lg n + O(1)}$ and Jurdziński and Lazić [26] have proved that the number of leaves in trees $S_{n,h}$ is $n^{\lg h + O(1)}$. Czerwiński et al. [9] have established a quasi-polynomial lower bound on the number of leaves in (n, h)-universal trees, which the size of $S_{n,h}$ exceeds only by a small polynomial factor.

3.2 Universal Algorithm

Every call of McNaughton-Zielonka algorithm (see appendix A of the full version) repeats the main loop until the set returned by a recursive call is empty. If the number of iterations for each value of d is large then the overall number of recursive calls may be exponential in d in the worst case, and that is indeed what happens for some families of hard parity games [19].

Algorithm 1: The universal algorithm

---

procedure $\mathrm{Univ}_{\mathrm{Even}}(\mathcal{G}, d, \mathcal{T}^{\mathrm{Even}}, \mathcal{T}^{\mathrm{Odd}})$:

  let $\mathcal{T}^{\mathrm{Odd}} = \langle \mathcal{T}_1^{\mathrm{Odd}}, \mathcal{T}_2^{\mathrm{Odd}}, \dots, \mathcal{T}_k^{\mathrm{Odd}} \rangle$

  $\mathcal{G}_1 \leftarrow \mathcal{G}$

  for $i \leftarrow 1$ **to** k **do**

   $D_i \leftarrow \pi^{-1}(d) \cap \mathcal{G}_i$

   $\mathcal{G}_i' \leftarrow \mathcal{G}_i \setminus \mathrm{Attr}_{\mathrm{Even}}^{\mathcal{G}_i}(D_i)$

   $U_i \leftarrow \mathrm{Univ}_{\mathrm{Odd}}(\mathcal{G}_i', d-1, \mathcal{T}^{\mathrm{Even}}, \mathcal{T}_i^{\mathrm{Odd}})$

   $\mathcal{G}_{i+1} \leftarrow \mathcal{G}_i \setminus \mathrm{Attr}_{\mathrm{Odd}}^{\mathcal{G}_i}(U_i)$

  return $V^{\mathcal{G}_{k+1}}$

procedure $\mathrm{Univ}_{\mathrm{Odd}}(\mathcal{G}, d, \mathcal{T}^{\mathrm{Even}}, \mathcal{T}^{\mathrm{Odd}})$:

  let $\mathcal{T}^{\mathrm{Even}} = \langle \mathcal{T}_1^{\mathrm{Even}}, \mathcal{T}_2^{\mathrm{Even}}, \dots, \mathcal{T}_\ell^{\mathrm{Even}} \rangle$

  $\mathcal{G}_1 \leftarrow \mathcal{G}$

  for $i \leftarrow 1$ **to** ℓ **do**

   $D_i \leftarrow \pi^{-1}(d) \cap \mathcal{G}_i$

   $\mathcal{G}_i' \leftarrow \mathcal{G}_i \setminus \mathrm{Attr}_{\mathrm{Odd}}^{\mathcal{G}_i}(D_i)$

   $U_i \leftarrow \mathrm{Univ}_{\mathrm{Even}}(\mathcal{G}_i', d-1, \mathcal{T}_i^{\mathrm{Even}}, \mathcal{T}^{\mathrm{Odd}})$

   $\mathcal{G}_{i+1} \leftarrow \mathcal{G}_i \setminus \mathrm{Attr}_{\mathrm{Even}}^{\mathcal{G}_i}(U_i)$

  return $V^{\mathcal{G}_{\ell+1}}$

In our *universal attractor decomposition algorithm* (Algorithm 1), every iteration of the main loop performs exactly the same actions as in McNaughton-Zielonka algorithm (see Fig. 2), but the algorithm uses a different mechanism to determine how many iterations of the main loop are performed in each recursive call. In the mutually recursive procedures $\mathrm{Univ}_{\mathrm{Odd}}$ and $\mathrm{Univ}_{\mathrm{Even}}$, this is determined by the numbers of children of the root in the input trees $\mathcal{T}^{\mathrm{Even}}$ (the third argument) and $\mathcal{T}^{\mathrm{Odd}}$ (the fourth argument), respectively. Note that the sole recursive call of $\mathtt{Univ_{Odd}}$ in the i-th iteration of the main loop in a call of $\mathtt{Univ_{Even}}$ is given subtree T_i^{Odd} as its fourth argument and, analogously, the sole recursive call of $\mathtt{Univ_{Even}}$ in the j-th iteration of the main loop in a call of $\mathtt{Univ_{Odd}}$ is given subtree T_j^{Even} as its third argument.

In order to characterise the tree of recursive calls, let us define the *inter-leaving* operation on two ordered trees inductively as follows: $\langle\rangle \bowtie T = \langle\rangle$ and $\langle T_1, T_2, \ldots, T_k \rangle \bowtie T = \langle T \bowtie T_1, T \bowtie T_2, \ldots, T \bowtie T_k \rangle$. Then the following simple proposition provides an explicit description of the tree of recursive calls of our universal algorithm. We state it only for the case where d is even, but a similar proposition holds when d is odd if trees T^{Even} and T^{Odd} are swapped in the statement.

Proposition 8. *If d is even then the tree of recursive calls to the procedure* $\mathtt{Univ_{Even}}\left(\mathcal{G}, d, T^{Even}, T^{Odd}\right)$ *is the interleaving* $T^{Odd} \bowtie T^{Even}$ *of trees* T^{Odd} *and* T^{Even}.

The following elementary proposition helps estimate the size of an interleaving of two ordered trees and hence the running time of a call of the universal algorithm that is given two ordered trees as inputs.

Proposition 9. *If T and T' are ordered trees then:*

- $\mathrm{height}(T \bowtie T') \leq \mathrm{height}(T) + \mathrm{height}(T')$;
- $\mathrm{leaves}(T \bowtie T') \leq \mathrm{leaves}(T) \cdot \mathrm{leaves}(T')$.

In contrast to the universal algorithm, the tree of recursive calls of McNaughton-Zielonka algorithm is not pre-determined by a structure separate from the game graph, such as the pair of trees T^{Even} and T^{Odd}. Instead, McNaughton-Zielonka algorithm determines the number of iterations of its main loop adaptively, using the adaptive *empty-set early termination rule*: terminate the main loop as soon as $U_i = \emptyset$. We argue that if we add the empty-set early termination rule to the universal algorithm in which both trees T^{Even} and T^{Odd} are the tree $C_{n,d/2}$ then its behaviour coincides with McNaughton-Zielonka algorithm.

Proposition 10. *The universal algorithm performs the same actions and produces the same output as McNaughton-Zielonka algorithm if it is run on an (n, d)-small parity game and with both trees T^{Even} and T^{Odd} equal to $C_{n,d/2}$, and if it uses the adaptive empty-set early termination rule.*

The idea of using rules for implicitly pruning the tree of recursive calls of a McNaughton-Zielonka-style algorithm that are significantly different from the adaptive empty-set early termination rule is due to Parys [32]. In this way, he has designed the first McNaughton-Zielonka-style algorithm that works in quasi-polynomial time $n^{O(\lg n)}$ in the worst case, and Lehtinen, Schewe, and Wojtczak [29] have refined Parys's algorithm, improving the worst-case running time down to $n^{O(\lg d)}$. Both algorithms use two numerical arguments (one for Even and one for Odd) and "halving tricks" on those parameters, which results in pruning the tree of recursive calls down to quasi-polynomial size in the worst case. We note that our universal algorithm yields the algorithms of Parys and of Lehtinen et al., respectively, if, when run on an (n, d)-small parity game and if both trees $\mathcal{T}^{\text{Even}}$ and $\mathcal{T}^{\text{Odd}}$ set to be the $(n, d/2)$-universal trees $P_{n,d/2}$ and $S_{n,d/2}$, respectively.

Proposition 11. *The universal algorithm performs the same actions and produces the same output as Lehtinen-Schewe-Wojtczak algorithm if it is run on an (n, d)-small parity game with both trees $\mathcal{T}^{\text{Even}}$ and $\mathcal{T}^{\text{Odd}}$ equal to $S_{n,d/2}$.*

The correspondence between the universal algorithm executed on $(n, d/2)$-universal trees $P_{n,d/2}$ and Parys's algorithm is a bit more subtle. While both run in quasi-polynomial time in the worst case, the former may perform more recursive calls than the latter. The two coincide, however, if the former is enhanced with a simple adaptive tree-pruning rule similar to the empty-set early termination rule. The discussion of this and other adaptive tree-pruning rules will be better informed once we have dicussed sufficient conditions for the correctness of our universal algorithm. Therefore, we will return to elaborating the full meaning of the following proposition in Sect. 4.4.

Proposition 12. *The universal algorithm performs the same actions and produces the same output as a non-adaptive version of Parys's algorithm if it is run on an (n, d)-small parity games with both trees $\mathcal{T}^{\text{Even}}$ and $\mathcal{T}^{\text{Odd}}$ equal to $P_{n,d/2}$.*

4 Correctness via Structural Theorems

The classical proof of the correctness of McNaughton-Zielonka algorithm [1] essentially relies on claim that when one reaches the empty-set condition, then this proves that we've precisely computed the opponent's winning region. The argument breaks down if the loop terminates before that empty-set condition obtains. Instead, Parys [32] has developed a novel *dominion separation technique* to prove correctness of his algorithm and Lehtinen et al. [29] use the same technique to justify theirs.

In this paper, we significantly generalize the dominion separation technique of Parys, which allows us to intimately link the correctness of our meta-algorithm to shapes (modelled as ordered trees) of attractor decompositions of largest Even and Odd dominia. We say that the universal algorithm is correct on a parity game if $\text{Univ}_{\text{Even}}$ returns the largest Even dominion and Univ_{Odd} returns the largest Odd dominion. We also say that an ordered tree $\mathcal{T}$ *embeds* a dominion D in a parity game $\mathcal{G}$ if it embeds the tree of some attractor decomposition of $\mathcal{G} \cap D$. The main technical result we aim to prove in this section is the sufficiency of the following condition for the universal algorithm to be correct.

Theorem 13 (Correctness of Universal Algorithm). *The universal algorithm is correct on a parity game $\mathcal{G}$ if it is run on ordered trees $\mathcal{T}^{\text{Even}}$ and $\mathcal{T}^{\text{Odd}}$, such that $\mathcal{T}^{\text{Even}}$ embeds the largest Even dominion in $\mathcal{G}$ and $\mathcal{T}^{\text{Odd}}$ embeds the largest Odd dominion in $\mathcal{G}$.*

4.1 Embeddable Decomposition Theorem

Before we prove Theorem 13, in this section we establish another technical result—the embeddable decomposition theorem—that enables our generalization of Parys's dominion separation technique. Its statement is intuitive: a subgame induced by a trap has a simpler attractor decomposition structure than the whole game itself; its proof, however, seems to require some careful surgery.

Theorem 14 (Embeddable Decomposition). *If T is a trap for Even in a parity game $\mathcal{G}$ and $\mathcal{G}' = \mathcal{G} \cap T$ is the subgame induced by T, then for every Even attractor decomposition $\mathcal{H}$ of $\mathcal{G}$, there is an Even attractor decomposition $\mathcal{H}'$ of $\mathcal{G}'$, such that $\mathcal{T}_{\mathcal{H}}$ embeds $\mathcal{T}_{\mathcal{H}'}$.*

In order to streamline the proof of the embeddable decomposition theorem, we state the following two propositions, which synthesize or generalize some of the arguments that were also used by Lehtinen, Parys, Schewe and Wojtczak [28]. Proofs are included in the full version.

Proposition 15. *Suppose that R is a trap for Even in game $\mathcal{G}$. Then if T is a trap for Odd in $\mathcal{G}$ then $T \cap R$ is a trap for Odd in subgame $\mathcal{G} \cap R$, and if T is an Even dominion in $\mathcal{G}$ then $T \cap R$ is an Even dominion in $\mathcal{G} \cap R$.*

The other proposition is illustrated in Fig. 1. Its statement is more complex than that of the first proposition. The statement and the proof describe the relationship between the Even attractor of a set B of vertices in a game $\mathcal{G}$ and the Even attractor of the set $B \cap T$ in subgame $\mathcal{G} \cap T$, where T is a trap for Even in $\mathcal{G}$.

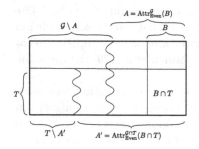
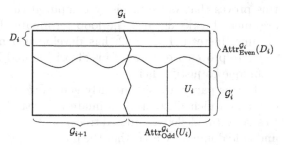

Fig. 1. Traps and attractors in Proposition 16.

Fig. 2. Attractors and subgames in one iteration of the loop in attractor decomposition algorithms.

Proposition 16. *Let $B \subseteq V^{\mathcal{G}}$ and let T be a trap for Even in game $\mathcal{G}$. Define $A = \operatorname{Attr}_{\mathrm{Even}}^{\mathcal{G}}(B)$ and $A' = \operatorname{Attr}_{\mathrm{Even}}^{\mathcal{G} \cap T}(B \cap T)$. Then $T \setminus A'$ is a trap for Even in subgame $\mathcal{G} \setminus A$.*

We prove the embeddable decomposition theorem by induction on the number of leaves of the tree of attractor decomposition $\mathcal{H}$. Note that our definition of an attractor decomposition allows for S_i to be any non-empty trap for Odd in $\mathcal{G}_i$ in which every vertex priority is at most $d-2$, whereas Daviaud, Jurdziński, and Lehtinen's definition [11] ask for S_i to be the *maximal* trap for Odd satisfying the aforementioned property. Relaxing the definition of attractor decompositions is crucial for Proposition 16 to hold.

4.2   Dominion Separation Theorem

The simple dominion disjointness property (Proposition 2) states that every Even dominion is disjoint from every Odd dominion. For two sets A and B, we say that another set X *separates* A *from* B if $A \subseteq X$ and $X \cap B = \emptyset$. In this section we establish a very general dominion separation property for subgames that occur in iterations of the universal algorithm. This allows us to prove one of the main technical results of this paper (Theorem 13) that describes a detailed structural sufficient condition for the correctness of the universal algorithm.

Theorem 17 (Dominion Separation). *Let $\mathcal{G}$ be an (n, d)-small parity game and let $\mathcal{T}^{\mathrm{Even}} = \langle \mathcal{T}_1^{\mathrm{Even}}, \ldots, \mathcal{T}_\ell^{\mathrm{Even}} \rangle$ and $\mathcal{T}^{\mathrm{Odd}} = \langle \mathcal{T}_1^{\mathrm{Odd}}, \ldots, \mathcal{T}_k^{\mathrm{Odd}} \rangle$ be trees of height at most $\lceil d/2 \rceil$ and $\lfloor d/2 \rfloor$, respectively.*

(a) *If d is even and $\mathcal{G}_1, \ldots, \mathcal{G}_{k+1}$ are the games that are computed in the successive iterations of the loop in the call $\mathrm{Univ}_{\mathrm{Even}}\left(\mathcal{G}, d, \mathcal{T}^{\mathrm{Even}}, \mathcal{T}^{\mathrm{Odd}}\right)$, then for every $i = 0, 1, \ldots, k$, we have that $\mathcal{G}_{i+1}$ separates every Even dominion in $\mathcal{G}$ that tree $\mathcal{T}^{\mathrm{Even}}$ embeds from every Odd dominion in $\mathcal{G}$ that tree $\langle \mathcal{T}_i^{\mathrm{Odd}}, \ldots, \mathcal{T}_i^{\mathrm{Odd}} \rangle$ embeds.*
(b) *If d is odd and $\mathcal{G}_1, \ldots, \mathcal{G}_{\ell+1}$ are the games that are computed in the successive iterations of the loop in the call $\mathrm{Univ}_{\mathrm{Odd}}\left(\mathcal{G}, d, \mathcal{T}^{\mathrm{Even}}, \mathcal{T}^{\mathrm{Odd}}\right)$, then for every $i = 0, 1, \ldots, \ell$, we have that $\mathcal{G}_{i+1}$ separates every Odd dominion in $\mathcal{G}$ that tree $\mathcal{T}^{\mathrm{Odd}}$ embeds from every Even dominion in $\mathcal{G}$ that tree $\langle \mathcal{T}_1^{\mathrm{Even}}, \ldots, \mathcal{T}_i^{\mathrm{Even}} \rangle$ embeds.*

4.3   Correctness and Complexity

The dominion separation theorem (Theorem 17) allows us to conclude the proof of the main universal algorithm correctness theorem (Theorem 13). Indeed, if trees $\mathcal{T}^{\mathrm{Even}}$ and $\mathcal{T}^{\mathrm{Odd}}$ satisfy the conditions of Theorem 13 then, by the dominion separation theorem, the set returned by the call $\mathrm{Univ}_{\mathrm{Even}}\left(\mathcal{G}, d, \mathcal{T}^{\mathrm{Even}}, \mathcal{T}^{\mathrm{Odd}}\right)$ separates the largest Even dominion from the largest Odd dominion, and hence—by the positional determinacy theorem (Theorem 3)—it is the largest Even dominion. The argument for procedure $\mathrm{Univ}_{\mathrm{Odd}}$ is analogous.

We note that the universal algorithm correctness theorem, together with Propositions 12 and 11, imply correctness of the non-adaptive version of Parys's algorithm [32] and of Lehtinen-Schewe-Wojtczak algorithm [29], because trees of attractor decompositions are $(n, d/2)$-small (Proposition 6) and trees $P_{n,d/2}$ and $S_{n,d/2}$ are $(n, d/2)$-universal.

The following fact, an alternative restatement of the conclusion of Lehtinen et al. [29], is a simple corollary of the precise asymptotic upper bounds on the size of the universal trees $S_{n,d/2}$ established by Jurdziński and Lazić [26], and of Propositions 11, 8, and 9.

Proposition 18 (Complexity). *The universal algorithm that uses universal trees $S_{n,d/2}$ (aka. Lehtinen-Schewe-Wojtczak algorithm) solves (n,d)-small parity games in polynomial time if $d = O(\log n)$, and in time $n^{2 \lg(d/\lg n) + O(1)}$ if $d = \omega(\log n)$.*

4.4 Acceleration by Tree Pruning

As we have discussed in Sect. 3.2, Parys [32] has achieved a breakthrough of developing the first quasi-polynomial McNaughton-Zielonka-style algorithm for parity games by pruning the tree of recursive calls down to quasi-polynomial size. Proposition 12 clarifies that Parys's scheme can be reproduced by letting the universal algorithm run on universal trees $P_{n,d/2}$, but as it also mentions, just doing so results in a "non-adaptive" version of Parys's algorithm. What is the "adaptive" version actually proposed by Parys?

Recall that the root of tree $P_{n,h}$ has $n + 1$ children, the first $n/2$ and the last $n/2$ children are the roots of copies of tree $P_{n/2,h-1}$, and the middle child is the root of a copy of tree $P_{n,h-1}$. The adaptive version of Parys's algorithm also uses another tree-prunning rule, which is adaptive and a slight generalization of the empty-set rule: whenever the algorithm is processing the block of the first $n/2$ children of the root or the last $n/2$ children of the root, if one of the recursive calls in this block returns an empty set then the rest of the block is omitted.

We expect that our structural results (such as Theorems 13 and 17) will provide insights to inspire development and proving correctness of further and more sophisticated adaptive tree-pruning rules, but we leave it to future work. This may be critical for making quasi-polynomial versions of McNaughton-Zielonka competitive in practice with its basic version that is exponential in the worst case, but remains very hard to beat in practice [13, 28].

5 Computing Nested Fixpoints

Computing fixpoints is fundamental in the study of computer science. Solving nested fixpoint equations (NFEs) over finite lattices are known to be computationally equivalent to solving parity games [3], however, most of the reductions involve an exponential increase in the size of the resulting parity game. The satisfiability problem of the coalgebraic μ-calculus has also been reduced to the same [24]. A corollary of Calude et al.'s breakthrough result was that specific kinds of fixpoint equations could be solved in quasi-polynomial time. Following this progress, there were several algorithms targeted at solving more general fixpoint equations by using universal graphs [25] and universal trees [2]. Hausman and Schröder gave a quasi-polynomial algorithm to solve NFEs using progress measures on universal graphs whereas Arnold, Niwinski and Parys solved NFEs using the key result on decompositions of dominions similar to an earlier version of this paper. Here, we provide a slightly different way of solving nested fixpoints by converting the equation to an exponentially sized fixpoint game, as in [25] but using our attractor decomposition algorithm, parameterised by two trees, as in [2]. The algorithm proposed by Arnold, Niwinski and Parys is similar to ours, in the sense that both algorithms use a pair of trees to guide the computation of a subset of a complete lattice and of a set of vertices in a parity game in our case, respectively. Since we can describe the set of winning vertices for some player in a parity game with a formula whose length is linear in the number of distinct priorities: d, the algorithm of [2] can be seen as a generalisation of Algorithm 1. On the other hand, we explain in this section how to, given a nested fixpoint equation, run the latter algorithm on a parity game—called a fixpoint game—, which has an exponential size compared to the size of the NFE, without having an exponential blowup. We thus obtain an algorithm to compute nested fixpoint equations in quasi-polynomial time. In this sense, we argue that the algorithm of Arnold, Niwinski and Parys is equivalent to ours. However, it should be noted that [2] provides an asymmetrical version of their algorithm—using a technique of Seidl [33]—which is quadratically faster, in the worse case, than Algorithm 1. In Sect. 6, a detailed description of how to implement symbolically both variants of the universal algorithm, for parity games and nested fixpoint, which require logarithmically less symbolic space than Chatterjee, Dvořák, Henzinger and Svozil quasi-polynomial symbolic algorithm [8] is provided.

We argue that we can directly apply our universal attractor decomposition algorithm on these exponential sized fixpoint games with the help of a carefully designed data structure, which ensures that we can in fact compute fixpoints using our algorithm in time proportional to $|\mathcal{T}_{\text{Odd}}| \cdot |\mathcal{T}_{\text{Even}}|$.

5.1   Nested Fixpoint Equations

In this subsection, we will define nested fixpoint equations over the powerset lattice. Consider a finite set of elements U and its powerset lattice $\mathcal{P}(U)$. Let f be a monotone function (component wise) from $\mathcal{P}(U)^d$ to $\mathcal{P}(U)^d$. The function f can be expressed as a tuple $(f_1, \ldots, f_d)$ of functions from $\mathcal{P}(U)^d$ to $\mathcal{P}(U)$, where f_i is the projection of f to the i-th component.

Since there is a natural bijection from d tuples of subsets of U to subsets of $(U \times [d])$, we instead denote f as a function from $\mathcal{P}(U \times [d])$ to $\mathcal{P}(U \times [d])$.

A nested fixpoint equation, is a system of d fixpoint equations of the form:

$$X_i =_{\eta_i} f_i(X_1, \ldots, X_d) \qquad (*)$$

for i ranging from $1, \ldots d$ and where $\eta_i = \nu$ if i is even, and $\eta_i = \mu$ otherwise. We refer to a system such as $(*)$ as a nested fixpoint equation and refer to it with the short hand: $X =_\eta f(X)$. One could consider a more general form of fixpoint equations where $\eta_i \in \{\mu, \nu\}$, but for simplicity of presentation, we restrict ourselves to the above.

The *solution* of a system of d equations as the one defined by $(*)$, is a subset of $U \times [d]$, defined recursively as follows. We say that the solution of the empty set of equations is the empty tuple. For a system of one or more fixpoint equations, we define a function f^{d-1} from subsets of U to subsets of $(U \times [d-1])$. This function f^{d-1} takes as input Y_d, a subset of U, and uses this input to fix $X_d = Y_d$ in the system of equations and the solution obtained to the system of $d-1$ equations by fixing X_d to be Y_d is the output of f^{d-1}. We finally say the solution of the system of equations is $\left(f^{d-1}(Y_d), Y_d\right)$, where $Y_d = \eta_d \left(\lambda X_d. f_d(f^{d-1}(X_d), X_d)\right)$.

5.2   Fixpoint Games

Let us now define an *equivalent* parity game $\mathcal{G}_f$, called a *fixpoint game*. Solving the parity game $\mathcal{G}_f$ correlates to finding the solution of the system of nested fixpoint equation defined by $X =_\eta f(X)$ [3,25].

Here, $\mathcal{G}_f = (V_f, E_f)$ with the priority function π_f, where V_f consists of the disjoint union $(U \times [d]) \cup \{v_A \mid A \subseteq U \times [d]\}$. The vertices corresponding to elements of the set $(U \times [d])$ belong to Even and the ones corresponding to subsets of the same set belong to Odd. The priority function π_f assigns Even's vertices (u, i) to i, and vertices Odd's vertices to priority 0. The edges from a vertex (u, i) belonging to Even in $\mathcal{G}_f$ lead to the set of Odd vertices $\{v_A \mid (u, i) \in f(A)\}$ and edges from a vertex v_A, belonging to Odd lead to the set of Even vertices $\{(u, i) \mid (u, i) \in A\}$.

Finding if (u, i) is in the solution of a nested fixpoint equation $X =_\eta f(X)$ is known to be equivalent to solving the corresponding fixpoint game $\mathcal{G}_f$ of the equation from the even vertex (u, i), as shown in Theorem 4.8 of [3].

5.3   Solving Fixpoint Games

We provide a way to solve a fixpoint game with the help of the attractor decomposition algorithm in Sect. 3.2.

We define a specific kind of subgames that we call *flowery* subgames and show that they are pertinent to solving fixpoint games using attractor decomposition algorithms. Given two subsets $\emptyset \subsetneq Y \subseteq X \subseteq U \times [d]$, we define the flowery subgame on (X, Y), denoted by $\mathcal{F}(X, Y)$, to be the subgame of $\mathcal{G}_f$ whose set of vertices consists of all Odd vertices v_A which is a subset of X intersecting non-trivially with Y, resembling the petal of a flower along with all vertices of Even belonging to Y, resembling the core of a flower. More formally, we define

$$\mathcal{F}(X, Y) = Y \uplus \{v_A \mid A \subseteq X \text{ and } A \cap Y \neq \emptyset\}.$$

In the game $\mathcal{G}_f$, on removing vertices that have no outgoing edges along with the respective attractors to these sets of vertices, i.e., Odd attractors to Even vertices with no outgoing edges and vice versa, we get a flowery subgame. Moreover, the following lemma reassures us that all significant operations performed by Algorithm 1 on flowery subgames, results in flowery subgames.

Lemma 19 (Floweriness Lemma). *If* UNIV-EVEN *(resp.,* UNIV-ODD*) is run on a flowery subgame, for all iterations in the for-loop, subgame $\mathcal{G}_i$ is also flowery. In particular, $\mathcal{G}_{k+1}$, which is the subgame returned, is flowery.*

The attractor to a set of vertices during a run of the algorithm can be computed by at most $d|U|$ many computation of f on subsets of $U \times [d]$. We can therefore solve nested fixpoint games in quasi-polynomial time using an attractor decomposition algorithm, by only keeping track of the sets X and Y representing each subgame, as stated below.

Theorem 20. *The modified universal algorithm that computes nested fixpoint equations on trees $\mathcal{T}_{\text{Odd}}$ and $\mathcal{T}_{\text{Even}}$ makes $|\mathcal{T}_{\text{Odd}}| \cdot |\mathcal{T}_{\text{Even}}|$ many recursive calls. Each recursive call makes at most $2d|U|$ many function evaluations of f.*

5.4   Concurrent Parity Games

Concurrent parity games have been well studied before. We consider the two player version as studied by Chatterjee, Alfredo and Henzinger in [7]. These games are played among two players—Even and Odd, but instead of partitioning the vertices among the two players, they take simultaneous actions at each vertex and the token moves to a neighbour depending on the actions of both players. One might also consider a stochastic version where the simultaneous actions are decided by a pre-decided probability distribution. Both the players are allowed to use a randomised strategy, i.e., a strategy where the next action is proposed with the help of a probability distribution. A state is called *limit-winning* for Even (respectively Odd) if Even has a strategy to win from that state with probability arbitrarily close to 1. The decision question we have at hand, is to determine if a state is a limit-winning state for a given input player. Concurrent parity games vary from original parity games in that, a player might need both infinite memory and randomisation to win these games. We refer the readers to the work of Chatterjee, Alfaro, and Henzinger [7] for a rigorous definition of the above games along with examples for the claims above. In their paper, they show that solving concurrent parity games is in NP∩co-NP as a corollary of the following theorem.

Theorem 21 ([7, Theorem 5, Lemma 29 and Lemma 30]). *Limit-winning in a concurrent parity game can be expressed as an NFE over the powerset lattice of the set of edges with alternation depth at most $2d$ for a function, whose evaluation involves solving another NFE also with depth at most $2d$.*

An easy corollary from Theorem 20 along with Theorem 21, we have the following.

Corollary 22. *Limit-winning in concurrent parity games can be solved in quasi-polynomial time.*

6   Symbolic Algorithms

Parity games that arise in applications, for example from the automata-theoretic model checking approaches to verification and automated synthesis, often suffer from the *state-space explosion problem*: the sizes of models are exponential (or worse) in the sizes of natural descriptions of the modelled objects, and hence the models obtained may be too large to store them explicitly in memory. One method of overcoming this problem that has been successful in the practice of algorithmic formal methods is to represent the models symbolically rather than explicitly, and to develop algorithms for solving the models that work directly on such succinct symbolic representations [5].

We adopt the *set-based symbolic model of computation* that was already considered for parity games by Chatterjee, Dvořák, Henzinger, and Svozil [8]. In this model, any standard computational operations on any standard data structures are allowed, but there are also the following symbolic resources available: *symbolic set variables* can be used to store sets of vertices in the graph of a parity game; basic set-theoretic operations on symbolic set variables are available as *primitive symbolic operations*; the *controllable predecessors* operations are available as primitive symbolic operations: the Even (resp. Odd) controllable predecessor, when applied to a symbolic set variable X, returns the set of vertices from which Even (resp. Odd) can force to move into the set X, by taking just one outgoing edge. Since symbolic set variables can represent possibly very large and complex objects, they should be treated as a costly resource.

Chatterjee et al. [8] have given a symbolic set-based algorithm that on (n, d)-small parity games uses $O(d \log n)$ of symbolic set variables and runs in quasi-polynomial time. While the dependence on n is only logarithmic, a natural question is whether this dependence is inherent. Given that n can be prohibitively large in applications, reducing dependence on n is desirable. In this section we argue that it is not only possible to eliminate the dependence on n entirely, but it is also possible to exponentially improve the dependence on d, resulting in a quasi-polynomial symbolic algorithm for solving parity games that uses only $O(\lg d)$ symbolic set variables.

In the set-based symbolic model of computation, it is routine to compute the attractors efficiently: it is sufficient to iterate the controllable predecessor operations. Using the results of Jurdziński and Lazić [26], one can also represent a path of nodes from the root to a leaf in the tree $S_{n,d/2}$ in $O(\lg n \cdot \lg d)$ bits, and for every node on such a path, to compute its number of children in $O(\lg n \cdot \lg d)$ standard primitive operations. This allows to run the whole universal algorithm (Algorithm 1) on an (n, d)-small parity game and two copies of trees $S_{n,d/2}$, using only $O(\lg n \cdot \lg d)$ bits to represent the relevant nodes in the trees $\mathcal{T}^{\mathrm{Even}}$ and $\mathcal{T}^{\mathrm{Odd}}$ throughout the execution.

The depth of the tree of recursive calls of the universal algorithm on an (n, d)-small parity game is at most d. Moreover, in every recursive call, only a small constant number of set variables is needed because only the latest sets $V^{\mathcal{G}_i}$, D_i, $V^{\mathcal{G}_i'}$, and U_i are needed at any time. It follows that the overall number of symbolic set variables needed to run the universal algorithm is $O(d)$. Also note that every recursive call can be implemented symbolically using a constant number of primitive symbolic operations and two symbolic attractor computations.

This improves the symbolic space from Chatterjee, Dvořák, Henzinger, and Svozil's $O(d \lg n)$ to $O(d)$, while keeping the running time quasi-polynomial. This symbolic algorithm is very simple and straightforward to implement, which makes it particularly promising and attractive for empirical evaluation and deployment in applications.

Theorem 23. *There exists a symbolic algorithm that solves (n, d)-small parity games using $O(\lg d)$ symbolic set variables, $O(\log d \cdot \log n)$ bits of conventional space, and whose running time is polynomial if $d = O(\log n)$, and quasi-polynomial, namely $n^{2 \lg(d/\lg n)+O(1)}$, if $d = \omega(\log n)$.*

The proof of the above appears in the full version. Moreover, using the same arguments, we obtain a symbolic algorithm to solve nested fixpoint equations in quasi-polynomial time and $O(\lg d)$ symbolic space.

Acknowledgements. The first and the third author had been supported by the EPSRC grant EP/P020992/1 (Solving Parity Games in Theory and Practice). The idea of the design of the universal algorithm has been discovered independently and later by Nathanaël Fijalkow; we thank him for sharing his conjectures with us and exchanging ideas about adaptive tree-pruning rules. We also thank our anonymous reviewers and Alexander Kozachinskiy for helpful comments on earlier drafts of the paper.

References

1. Apt, K.R., Grädel, E. (eds.): Lectures in Game Theory for Computer Scientists. Cambridge University Press (2011). http://www.cambridge.org/gb/knowledge/isbn/item5760379

2. Arnold, A., Niwiński, D., Parys, P.: A quasi-polynomial black-box algorithm for fixed point evaluation. In: CSL. LIPIcs, vol. 183, pp. 9:1–9:23. Schloss Dagstuhl - Leibniz-Zentrum für Informatik (2021). https://doi.org/10.4230/LIPIcs.CSL.2021.9, https://doi.org/10.4230/LIPIcs.CSL.2021.9

3. Baldan, P., König, B., Mika-Michalski, C., Padoan, T.: Fixpoint games on continuous lattices. Proc. ACM Program. Lang. **3**(POPL) (2019). https://doi.org/10.1145/3290339, https://doi.org/10.1145/3290339

4. Bradfield, J.C., Walukiewicz, I.: The mu-calculus and model checking. In: Clarke, E.M., Henzinger, T.A., Veith, H., Bloem, R. (eds.) Handbook of Model Checking, pp. 871–919. Springer (2018). https://doi.org/10.1007/978-3-319-10575-8_26, https://doi.org/10.1007/978-3-319-10575-8_26

5. Burch, J.R., Clarke, E.M., McMillan, K.L., Dill, D.L., Hwang, L.J.: Symbolic model checking: 10^20 states and beyond. Inf. Comput. **98**(2), 142–170 (1992). https://doi.org/10.1016/0890-5401(92)90017-A, https://doi.org/10.1016/0890-5401(92)90017-A

6. Calude, C.S., Jain, S., Khoussainov, B., Li, W., Stephan, F.: Deciding parity games in quasipolynomial time. In: STOC, pp. 252–263 (2017). https://doi.org/10.1145/3055399.3055409

7. Chatterjee, K., Alfaro, L.D., Henzinger, T.A.: Qualitative concurrent parity games. ACM Trans. Comput. Logic **12**(4) (2011). https://doi.org/10.1145/1970398. 1970404, https://doi.org/10.1145/1970398.1970404

8. Chatterjee, K., Dvořák, W., Henzinger, M., Svozil, A.: Quasipolynomial set-based symbolic algorithms for parity games. In: LPAR-22. EPiC Series in Computing, vol. 57, pp. 233–253 (2018). https://doi.org/10.29007/5z5k

9. Czerwiński, W., Daviaud, L., Fijalkow, N., Jurdziński, M., Lazić, R., Parys, P.: Universal trees grow inside separating automata: quasi-polynomial lower bounds for parity games. In: SODA, pp. 2333–2349 (2019). https://doi.org/10.1137/1. 9781611975482.142

10. Daviaud, L., Jurdziński, M., Lazić, R.: A pseudo-quasi-polynomial algorithm for mean-payoff parity games. In: Proceedings of the 33rd Annual ACM/IEEE Symposium on Logic in Computer Science, LICS 2018, 09–12 July 2018. pp. 325–334. ACM, Oxford, UK (2018). https://doi.org/10.1145/3209108.3209162, https://doi. org/10.1145/3209108.3209162

11. Daviaud, L., Jurdziński, M., Lehtinen, K.: Alternating weak automata from universal trees. In: CONCUR 2019, 27–30 August 2019, pp. 18:1–18:14. LIPIcs (2019). https://doi.org/10.4230/LIPIcs.CONCUR.2019.18, https://doi. org/10.4230/LIPIcs.CONCUR.2019.18

12. Daviaud, L., Jurdziński, M., Thejaswini, K.S.: The strahler number of a parity game. In: ICALP 2020, 8–11 July 2020, vol. 168, pp. 123:1–123:19. LIPIcs (2020). https://doi.org/10.4230/LIPIcs.ICALP.2020.123

13. Dijk, T.: Oink: an implementation and evaluation of modern parity game solvers. In: Beyer, D., Huisman, M. (eds.) TACAS 2018. LNCS, vol. 10805, pp. 291–308. Springer, Cham (2018). https://doi.org/10.1007/978-3-319-89960-2_16

14. Emerson, E.A., Jutla, C.: Tree automata, mu-calculus and determinacy. In: FOCS, pp. 368–377 (1991). https://doi.org/10.1109/SFCS.1991.185392

15. Emerson, E.A., Jutla, C.S., Sistla, A.P.: On model-checking for fragments of μ-calculus. In: Courcoubetis, C. (ed.) CAV 1993. LNCS, vol. 697, pp. 385–396. Springer, Heidelberg (1993). https://doi.org/10.1007/3-540-56922-7_32

16. Etessami, K., Wilke, T., Schuller, R.A.: Fair simulation relations, parity games, and state space reduction for Büchi automata. SIAM J. Comput. **34**(5), 1159–1175 (2005). https://doi.org/10.1137/S0097539703420675, https://doi.org/ 10.1137/S0097539703420675

17. Fearnley, J.: exponential lower bounds for policy iteration. In: Abramsky, S., Gavoille, C., Kirchner, C., Meyer auf der Heide, F., Spirakis, P.G. (eds.) ICALP 2010. LNCS, vol. 6199, pp. 551–562. Springer, Heidelberg (2010). https://doi.org/ 10.1007/978-3-642-14162-1_46

18. Friedmann, O.: An exponential lower bound for the parity game strategy improvement algorithm as we know it. In: Proceedings of the 24th Annual IEEE Symposium on Logic in Computer Science, LICS 2009, 11–14 August 2009,pp. 145–156. IEEE Computer Society, Los Angeles, CA, USA (2009). https://doi.org/10.1109/ LICS.2009.27, https://doi.org/10.1109/LICS.2009.27

19. Friedmann, O.: Recursive algorithm for parity games requires exponential time. RAIRO Theor. Inform. Appl. **45**(4), 449–457 (2011). https://doi.org/10.1051/ita/ 2011124, https://doi.org/10.1051/ita/2011124

20. Friedmann, O.: a subexponential lower bound for zadeh's pivoting rule for solving linear programs and games. In: Günlük, O., Woeginger, G.J. (eds.) IPCO 2011. LNCS, vol. 6655, pp. 192–206. Springer, Heidelberg (2011). https://doi.org/10. 1007/978-3-642-20807-2_16

21. Friedmann, O., Hansen, T.D., Zwick, U.: Subexponential lower bounds for randomized pivoting rules for the simplex algorithm. In: STOC, pp. 283–292. ACM (2011). https://doi.org/10.1145/1993636.1993675, https://doi.org/10.1145/1993636.1993675

22. Grädel, E., Thomas, W., Wilke, T. (eds.): Automata, Logics, and Infinite Games: A Guide to Current Research [outcome of a Dagstuhl seminar, February 2001], LNCS, vol. 2500. Springer (2002). https://doi.org/10.1007/3-540-36387-4, https://doi.org/10.1007/3-540-36387-4

23. Hasuo, I., Shimizu, S., Cîrstea, C.: Lattice-theoretic progress measures and coalgebraic model checking. In: POPL, pp. 718–732. ACM (2016). https://doi.org/10.1145/2837614.2837673, https://doi.org/10.1145/2837614.2837673

24. Hausmann, D., Schröder, L.: Optimal satisfiability checking for arithmetic μ-Calculi. In: Bojańczyk, M., Simpson, A. (eds.) FoSSaCS 2019. LNCS, vol. 11425, pp. 277–294. Springer, Cham (2019). https://doi.org/10.1007/978-3-030-17127-8_16

25. Hausmann, D., Schröder, L.: Quasipolynomial computation of nested fixpoints. In: TACAS 2021. LNCS, vol. 12651, pp. 38–56. Springer, Cham (2021). https://doi.org/10.1007/978-3-030-72016-2_3

26. Jurdziński, M., Lazić, R.: Succinct progress measures for solving parity games. In: LICS, pp. 1–9 (2017). https://doi.org/10.1109/LICS.2017.8005092

27. Lehtinen, K.: A modal μ perspective on solving parity games in quasi-polynomial time. In: LICS, pp. 639–648 (2018). https://doi.org/10.1145/3209108.3209115

28. Lehtinen, K., Parys, P., Schewe, S., Wojtczak, D.: A recursive approach to solving parity games in quasipolynomial time. Logical Methods Comput. Sci. **18**(1), 10 (2022). 46298/lmcs-18(1:8)2022, https://lmcs.episciences.org/8953

29. Lehtinen, K., Schewe, S., Wojtczak, D.: Improving the complexity of Parys' recursive algorithm. arXiv:1904.11810 (2019). https://doi.org/10.48550/arXiv.1904.11810

30. Luttenberger, M., Meyer, P.J., Sickert, S.: Practical synthesis of reactive systems from LTL specifications via parity games. Acta Informatica **57**(1-2), 3–36 (2020). https://doi.org/10.1007/s00236-019-00349-3, https://doi.org/10.1007/s00236-019-00349-3

31. McNaughton, R.: Infinite games played on finite graphs. Ann. Pure Appl. Logic **65**(2), 149–184 (1993). https://doi.org/10.1016/0168-0072(93)90036-D

32. Parys, P.: Parity games: Zielonka's algorithm in quasi-polynomial time. In: 44th International Symposium on Mathematical Foundations of Computer Science, MFCS 2019 (2019). https://doi.org/10.4230/LIPIcs.MFCS.2019.10

33. Seidl, H.: Fast and simple nested fixpoints. Inform. Process. Let. **59**(6), 303–308 (1996). https://doi.org/10.1016/0020-0190(96)00130-5

34. Vöge, J., Jurdziński, M.: a discrete strategy improvement algorithm for solving parity games. In: Emerson, E.A., Sistla, A.P. (eds.) CAV 2000. LNCS, vol. 1855, pp. 202–215. Springer, Heidelberg (2000). https://doi.org/10.1007/10722167_18

35. Zielonka, W.: Infinite games on finitely coloured graphs with applications to automata on infinite trees. Theoretical Comput. Sci. **200**, 135–183 (1998). https://doi.org/10.1016/S0304-3975(98)00009-7

Simulation Relations and Applications in Formal Methods

Kim G. Larsen⬤, Christian Schilling(✉)⬤, and Jiří Srba⬤

Department of Computer Science, Aalborg University, Aalborg, Denmark
{kgl,christianms,srba}@cs.aau.dk

Abstract. We survey the research on application of equivalence checking to formal methods, with a particular focus on the notion of simulation and bisimulation as well as of modal refinement on modal transition systems. We discuss the algorithmic aspects of efficiently computing (bi)simulation relations, the extension to infinite state systems, and existing tool support. We then present results related to simulation and bisimulation checking on timed and hybrid systems and highlight the connections to automata theory.

Keywords: Simulation · Bisimulation · Transition system · Hybrid system · Automata theory

1 Foreword and Outline

In this chapter we review simulation relations and their success story in formal methods. Written at the occasion of Tom Henzinger's 60th anniversary, we focus on three areas where he substantially contributed to this topic, and describe selected works in detail. Section 3 covers the general computation of simulation relations for finite and infinite transition systems. Section 4 covers simulation relations in timed and hybrid systems. Section 5 covers simulation relations in automata theory. We begin with a general introduction to simulation relations and related concepts in the next section.

2 Transition Systems, Simulation, and Bisimulation

In this section we outline the basic notions underlying the topics discussed in the later sections: transition systems, simulation and bisimulation relations, modal transition systems, and modal refinement. For a detailed introduction to these topics we refer to the literature [10,14,37,46].

2.1 Transition Systems

Simulation relations are defined over (labeled) transition systems. These are structures to abstractly describe the behavior of systems and coincide mathematically with directed edge-labeled graphs. A transition system consists of a

© Springer Nature Switzerland AG 2022
J.-F. Raskin and K. Chatterjee (Eds.): Principles of Systems Design, LNCS 13660, pp. 272–291, 2022.
https://doi.org/10.1007/978-3-031-22337-2_13

(finite or infinite) set of states (the nodes in the graph) and a set of transitions connecting pairs of states (the directed edges in the graph).

Definition 1 (Transition System). *A transition system is a triple* $TS = (S, \Lambda, T)$ *where* S *is a set of* states, Λ *is a set of* labels, *and* $T \subseteq S \times \Lambda \times S$ *is a transition relation whose elements are called* transitions.

We write $s \xrightarrow{a} t$ for transition $(s, a, t) \in T$ and generalize it to a sequence of transitions such that $s_0 \xrightarrow{a_1 \cdots a_n} s_n$ if there are states $s_1, \ldots, s_{n-1} \in S$ where $s_{i-1} \xrightarrow{a_i} s_i$ for all $i = 1, \ldots, n$. We use the following terminology: a sequence of transitions is a *path*, the projection of a path to the states is a *run*, and the projection of a path to the labels is a *trace*. Figure 1 shows an example transition system over labels a and b with seven states and eight transitions.

Transition systems are rather general models. Many systems encountered in computer science can be modeled with a transition system. Once a system has been modeled as a transition system, one can use all the tools that have been developed for their analysis. But this generality comes with a price: transition systems for most interesting systems are huge or even infinite. This implies that typical graph algorithms such as state space search are expensive or may not even terminate.

The main approach to reduce the size of transition systems, possibly even making an infinite transition system finite, is through quotienting. For an equivalence relation $\equiv \subseteq X \times X$ we denote the equivalence class of $e \in X$ by $[e]_\equiv$. Given a transition system and an equivalence relation over its states, the induced *quotient transition system* is obtained by merging all equivalent states and remapping the corresponding transitions. Formally:

Definition 2 (Quotient Transition System). *Given a transition system* $TS = (S, \Lambda, T)$ *and an equivalence relation* $\equiv \subseteq S \times S$, *the* quotient transition system *is* $TS/_\equiv = (S/_\equiv, \Lambda, T/_\equiv)$ *with states* $S/_\equiv = \{[s]_\equiv \mid s \in S\}$ *and transitions* $T/_\equiv = \{([s]_\equiv, a, [t]_\equiv) \mid (s, a, t) \in T\}$.

Note that we have not put any restriction on $\equiv$ above. Thus we cannot guarantee many properties about the quotient system. What is true for any relation $\equiv$ is that reachability is preserved: if there is a path $s \xrightarrow{w} t$ in TS, then there is a path $[s]_\equiv \xrightarrow{w} [t]_\equiv$ in $TS/_\equiv$. Guaranteeing more interesting properties, such as trace equivalence, requires more structure in the relation $\equiv$. Prominent families of relations that provide such structure are simulations and bisimulations.

2.2 Simulation and Bisimulation

The concept of simulation relations, or simulations for short, dates back to Milner [83]. Roughly speaking, a state s' simulates a state s if any transition from s to a state t can be matched by a transition with the same label leading from s' to a state t' such that t' again simulates the state t.

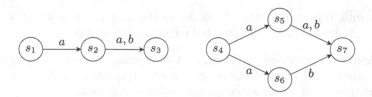

Fig. 1. A transition system.

Definition 3 (Simulation). *Given a transition system* $TS = (S, \Lambda, T)$, *a binary relation* $R \subseteq S \times S$ *is a* simulation *if for all* $a \in \Lambda$ *and* $s, s' \in S$ *with* $(s, s') \in R$ *the following holds: for all* $t \in S$ *such that* $s \xrightarrow{a} t$ *there exists* $t' \in S$ *such that* $s' \xrightarrow{a} t'$ *and* $(t, t') \in R$.

If $(s, s') \in R$, we say that s' simulates s. While simulations are locally defined, they also provide the global guarantee that, intuitively, s' has at least the same set of traces as s (and hence simulation implies trace inclusion). Note that for a given transition system there may exist multiple simulations, and that simulations need neither be reflexive nor transitive. However, the union of all simulations $\preccurlyeq$ is itself a simulation (namely the coarsest one), which is a reflexive and transitive relation called the *simulation preorder*. In the following, we are typically interested in the simulation preorder. The simulation preorder $\preccurlyeq$ induces a *similarity* relation $\simeq \subseteq S \times S$ such that $s \simeq t$ if and only if $s \preccurlyeq t$ and $t \preccurlyeq s$. Thus $\simeq$ is the maximal symmetric subset of $\preccurlyeq$ and hence an equivalence relation. A symmetric simulation $R \subseteq S \times S$ is called a *bisimulation* [86]. The following definition is equivalent:

Definition 4 (Bisimulation). *Given a transition system* $TS = (S, \Lambda, T)$, *a binary relation* $R \subseteq S \times S$ *is a* bisimulation *if for all* $a \in \Lambda$ *and* $s, s' \in S$ *with* $(s, s') \in R$ *the following holds:*

- *for all* $t \in S$ *such that* $s \xrightarrow{a} t$ *there exists* $t' \in S$ *such that* $s' \xrightarrow{a} t'$ *and* $(t, t') \in R$, *and*
- *for all* $t' \in S$ *such that* $s' \xrightarrow{a} t'$ *there exists* $t \in S$ *such that* $s \xrightarrow{a} t$ *and* $(t, t') \in R$.

As for simulations, bisimulations are not unique and they may be neither reflexive nor transitive. Again, the union of all bisimulations $\sim$ is itself a bisimulation (namely the coarsest one), which is an equivalence relation called *bisimilarity*. In the following, we are typically interested in the bisimilarity relation.

Observe that similarity $\simeq$ is generally coarser than bisimilarity $\sim$ (as witnessed in the example below). Thus computing the similarity relation may be more interesting; for instance, when used for quotienting, it yields a smaller transition system. However, computing a simulation relation is typically harder than computing the corresponding bisimulation relation [68].

Consider the transition system in Fig. 1. The states s_3 and s_7 have no outgoing transitions, so they cannot be distinguished and must be similar and bisimilar: $s_3 \preccurlyeq s_7 \preccurlyeq s_3$ and $s_3 \sim s_7$. The states s_2 resp. s_5 only have transitions with a

Table 1. Simulation preorder $\precsim$ and bisimilarity $\sim$ for the transition system in Fig. 1. A pair in the relation is marked with ✓. The shaded cells correspond to similarity $\simeq$.

$\precsim$	s_1	s_2	s_3	s_4	s_5	s_6	s_7		$\sim$	s_1	s_2	s_3	s_4	s_5	s_6	s_7
s_1	✓			✓					s_1	✓						
s_2		✓			✓				s_2		✓			✓		
s_3	✓	✓	✓	✓	✓	✓	✓		s_3			✓				✓
s_4	✓			✓					s_4				✓			
s_5		✓			✓				s_5		✓			✓		
s_6		✓			✓	✓			s_6						✓	
s_7	✓	✓	✓	✓	✓	✓	✓		s_7			✓				✓

and b to s_3 resp. s_7, which we already know are bisimilar; hence the same holds for s_2 and s_5: $s_2 \precsim s_5 \precsim s_2$ and $s_2 \sim s_5$. The state s_6 on the other hand has no outgoing a-transition and hence cannot simulate (nor bisimulate) s_2 and s_5, but those states simulate s_6: $s_6 \precsim s_2$ and $s_6 \precsim s_5$. The state s_1 clearly simulates s_4, but the converse also holds due to s_5: $s_1 \precsim s_4 \precsim s_1$. Yet s_1 and s_4 are not bisimilar because of s_6. The complete relations are given in Table 1. The shaded cells mark the similarity relation $\simeq$; observe that here similarity $\simeq$ is strictly coarser than bisimilarity $\sim$, as it includes the pairs (s_1, s_4) and (s_4, s_1).

There is also a game-theoretic characterization of the simulation preorder (see [93,95] for an early proposal and discussion and [82] for a detailed introduction). Consider the two-player "imitation game" where each player has a token on one state. In each round, the first player, called antagonist, moves their token along a transition and the second player, called protagonist, has to move the other token along a transition of the same label. The game ends if a player cannot move, making the other player win. Otherwise, the game is infinite and the protagonist wins. We have that $s \precsim t$ holds for states s and t if, in a game where the antagonist's token starts on s and the protagonist's token starts on t, the protagonist has a winning strategy. That means: a rational protagonist can always imitate the antagonist's move.

A similar characterization exists for bisimilarity. The only change of rules is that, at the beginning of each round, the antagonist may choose to swap the tokens. Hence the antagonist has more chances to win. From this characterization it is clear that bisimilarity is symmetric and generally finer than similarity.

In the context of model checking, simulation and bisimulation are alternatively defined for *Kripke structures*, which are transition systems with state labels. In that case, the additional requirement for a state s simulating a state t is that the labels of s and t are identical. If we consider the labels of a state "public information," this is in line with the original intuition that s simulates t if an observer cannot determine whether a trace starting from t may have started from s instead. See also [14] for a discussion of these two system models.

We have motivated simulations for the purpose of quotienting to reduce the size of a transition system. More generally, one can use simulations to establish a formal relation between transition systems. If we consider transition systems with initial states, then a transition system TS_1 simulates a transition system TS_2 if for each initial state of TS_2 there is a simulating initial state of TS_1. Simulation can be used as a formal proof that a reactive system, e.g., a controller, works correctly in an adversary environment: to stay in the game-theoretic view, the environment takes the role of the antagonist and the controller takes the role of the protagonist. Similarly, one can establish levels of abstractions of systems, e.g., a specification and an implementation, which are also called refinement mappings [1]. Quotienting is one way to find such abstractions (see [19,30,36] for some examples).

2.3   Modal Transition Systems and Modal Refinement

An important practical application of equivalence checking is a component-based software development and stepwise refinement process. Assuming that we have a system specification expressed as a transition system (that is usually generated from some higher-level specification language), our aim is to refine (possibly in several steps) the given component specification by adding more implementation details, while preserving a suitable equivalence/preorder with the initial specification. However, should bisimulation be used as the notion of equivalence, we are required to describe all the implementation details already in the specification because bisimulation is a too strict notion requiring that any action of the specification must be matched in the implementation and vice versa. On the other hand, the notion of simulation allows us to create several variants of the given specification, as it only requires that any refined process must be simulated by its specification (and hence every behavior of the refined process is guaranteed to be sound). The drawback is that an empty implementation (where the initial state is deadlocked) is trivially simulated by any given specification, whereas it is clearly not an intended product implementation.

It is hence clear that for a usable stepwise refinement process, we need to use a relation/preorder that is less strict than bisimulation but at the same time it must enforce some minimum system behavior that a simulation relation cannot guarantee. One possible answer to this problem was suggested by Larsen and Thomsen [75] (for an overview paper see also [10]) in terms of *modal transition systems* and the notation of *modal refinement*.

In a modal transition system, transitions are split into *may* and *must* transitions: any refinement of a specification is then allowed to implement any may-transition, and at the same time it is required to preserve any must-transition. This allows to encode some minimal required process behavior while at the same time allowing for different variants during the refinement process as may-transitions are not mandatory to be implemented.

Definition 5 (Modal Transition System). *A* modal transition system *is a tuple* $TS = (S, \Lambda, T_{may}, T_{must})$ *where S is a set of* states, *Λ is a set of* labels, *and $T_{must} \subseteq T_{may} \subseteq S \times \Lambda \times S$ are* may *resp.* must *transition relations.*

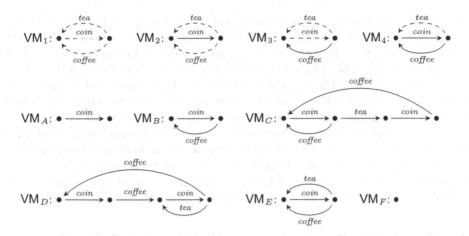

Fig. 2. Four specifications of a vending machine, VM_1-VM_4, and six different implementations VM_A-VM_F.

We write $s \xrightarrow{a} t$ for transition $(s, a, t) \in T_{must}$ and $s \dashrightarrow^{a} t$ for transition $(s, a, t) \in T_{may} \setminus T_{must}$. Intuitively, every must-transition of the specification must be matched in the refined process, and every may-transition of a refined process must be matched in the specification. This gives rise to a co-inductive definition of a modal refinement, generalizing the notion of bisimulation to modal transition systems.

Definition 6 (Modal Refinement). *Given a modal transition system $TS = (S, \Lambda, T_{may}, T_{must})$, a binary relation $R \subseteq S \times S$ is a modal refinement if for all $a \in \Lambda$ and $s, s' \in S$ with $(s, s') \in R$ the following holds:*

- *for all $t \in S$ such that $s \dashrightarrow^{a} t$ there exists $t' \in S$ such that $s' \dashrightarrow^{a} t'$ and $(t, t') \in R$, and*
- *for all $t' \in S$ such that $s' \xrightarrow{a} t'$ there exists $t \in S$ such that $s \xrightarrow{a} t$ and $(t, t') \in R$.*

We say that s is a modal refinement of s' if there exists a modal refinement relation R such that $(s, s') \in R$. The definition of modal refinement resembles that of simulation/bisimulation. Indeed, if every may-transition is also a must-transition ($T_{may} = T_{must}$), modal refinement and bisimulation coincide. On the other hand, if the modal transition system does not contain any must transitions, the obtained notion of modal refinement defines a simulation relation.

In Fig. 2 the authors of [16] demonstrate four possible specifications of a vending machine and six possible implementations. The first specification VM_1 does not require any behavior (contains no must-transitions), but it allows to execute a coin-transition, after which both tea and coffee-transitions may be executed. All six implementations $VM_A, \ldots, VM_F$ are refinements of VM_1. The second specification VM_2 requires that the coin-transition must be present but implementing the tea and coffee-transitions is optional. This excludes the machine

VM_F that contains only the deadlock state from being a refinement of VM_2. The third specification VM_3 requires that, if a coin is inserted, at least the coffee-transition must be implemented. This excludes VM_A from being a correct implementation of VM_3 while all other implementations (including VM_F) are in refinement with VM_3. Finally, the specification VM_4 ensures that inserting the coin and providing a coffee is mandatory while returning tea is optional. There are four valid refinements of VM_4, namely VM_B, VM_C, VM_D and VM_E.

Hence modal transition systems in connection with modal refinement relations allow for a stepwise refinement process in system modeling and generalize the notion of simulation and bisimulation, allowing to be more specific which transitions should be preserved in which direction. For further results about modal transition systems and its extensions, we refer to [10–12,15,17,73].

3   Computing Simulations on Finite and Infinite Graphs

In this section we review results about computing (bi)simulations for finite and infinite graphs. The work of Tom Henzinger we summarize here is [88]. That paper has two main contributions. The first contribution is an efficient algorithm to compute the simulation preorder on finite transition systems, together with an extension to infinite transition systems. The second contribution is an algorithm to compute the similarity relation for a class of hybrid automata, which is discussed in the next section.

Two states are *trace equivalent* if the set of outgoing traces coincide. Trace equivalence is coarser than similarity. The authors advocate similarity as a middle ground between bisimilarity and trace equivalence, for the following reasons.

First there is the aspect of computational complexity. Computing bisimilarity for finite transition systems with n states and m transitions is an $O(m \log n)$ problem [85]. Computing trace equivalence is a PSPACE-complete problem [94]. The authors propose an $O(mn)$ algorithm for computing the simulation preorder (a similar result has been independently obtained at the same time [20]). For an overview of the algorithms for computing bisimulation we refer to [4]. Similarly, deciding if two systems are in modal refinement can be done in polynomial time, while checking whether every implementation of one specification is also an implementation of another specification becomes EXPTIME-complete [18].

Second, similarity is coarser than bisimilarity, and so the corresponding quotient is smaller, but at the same time the quotient still preserves useful properties. On the one hand, two states are bisimilar if and only if they satisfy the same formulae in branching temporal logic (CTL or CTL*). Hence for such logics, similarity is not of interest. On the other hand, two states are trace equivalent if and only if they satisfy the same formulae in the widely used linear temporal logic (LTL). Moreover, two states are similar if and only if they satisfy the same formulae in branching temporal logic without quantifier switches. (See [14] for proofs of these statements.) Thus computing the similarity quotient is useful.

Third, as a consequence of the smaller quotient, transition systems with infinite bisimilarity quotient may still yield a finite similarity quotient, which allows for effective computations and decision procedures. The authors extend their algorithm to a symbolic algorithm applicable to infinite but "effectively presented" transition systems, in the line of [21,77]. The symbolic algorithm terminates if the similarity quotient is finite.

3.1   Further Results About Infinite State Systems

The decidability of bisimilarity, equivalence with a given finite state system, as well as the regularity problem (does there exist a finite state system equivalent to the given system) were extensively studied for different types of process algebra generating infinite state systems (for an overview see [91]; further details about the used techniques can be found in [24,70,84]). The classes of infinite state systems include the process algebras BPA (basic process algebra) and BPP (basic parallel processes) that support a pure sequential resp. parallel composition, their generalization PA (process algebra) allowing to mix both the sequential and parallel operators, as well as transition systems described by Petri nets (a model of parallel processes allowing for synchronization) and pushdown automata (adding a finite control-state unit to the BPA processes).

All these systems can be uniformly described by the formalism of *process rewrite systems* suggested by Mayr [80], and the results indicate (for references consult [91]) that for the simple process algebras BPA and BPP, bisimulation and regularity are decidable, and bisimilarity of a BPA or BPP process with a given finite state system can be decided even in polynomial time. Decidability of bisimulation, equivalence with a finite state system and regularity is preserved for the class of pushdown automata, however, with higher complexity bounds. Decidability of bisimulation and regularity for PA process algebra remains an open problem, while for Petri nets only regularity and equivalence with a finite state system remains decidable while bisimulation checking becomes undecidable by the application of the defender's forcing technique [64].

3.2   Tools for Equivalence Checking

There exist a number of tools supporting equivalence/bisimulation checking, including Edinburgh Concurrency Workbench and its successors [31–33], and tools like CADP [44], mCRL2 [23], TAPAs [26] and FDR3 [47]. Several of these tools rely on the fixed-point calculation of the bisimilarity. More recently, on-the-fly methods based on dependency graphs [40] have been used in tools like CAAL [9] and allow for an early termination without the need of enumerating the full state space.

4   Simulation Relations for Timed and Hybrid Systems

In this section we review simulation relations in the context of hybrid systems [5, 54], i.e., dynamical systems with mixed discrete and continuous behavior.

4.1   Timed Systems

The *timed automaton* model, introduced by Alur and Dill [6,7], is an established formalism for describing the behavior of real-time systems. Initially, the focus was on model checking with respect to a variety of logics, and only later the notions of (timed and untimed) bisimulation and simulation were considered.

Given a finite set of clocks C, we denote by $\Phi(C)$ all conjunctions of simple clock constraints of the form $x \bowtie k$, where $x \in C$, $\bowtie \in \{<, \leq, =, \geq, >\}$, $k \in \mathbb{N}$. The semantics of clocks is given by a *clock valuation* $v : C \to \mathbb{R}_{\geq 0}$ assigning non-negative real values to clocks. Thus a clock constraint ϕ denotes a set of clock valuations. By $v \in \phi$ we mean that the valuation v satisfies the constraint ϕ. If v is a clock valuation and $d \in \mathbb{R}_{\geq 0}$, $v + d$ is the clock valuation such that $(v + d)(x) = v(x) + d$ for all $x \in C$. Also, if $r \subseteq C$, we denote by $v[r]$ the clock valuation where $v[r](x) = 0$ if $x \in r$ and $v[r](x) = v(x)$ if $x \notin r$.

Definition 7. *A timed automaton is a tuple* $\mathcal{A} = (Loc, \ell_0, C, \Lambda, I, T)$ *where Loc is a finite set of locations,* $\ell_0 \in Loc$ *is the initial location, C is a finite set of clocks, Λ is a set of labels, $I : Loc \to \Phi(C)$ is a mapping assigning invariants to locations, and* $T \subseteq Loc \times \Phi(C) \times \Lambda \times 2^C \times Loc$ *is a set of transitions.*

The semantics of a timed automaton $\mathcal{A}$ is given by an infinite-state *timed* transition system, where states are location-valuation pairs (ℓ, v). Transitions are labeled with either discrete labels from Λ or delays from $\mathbb{R}_{\geq 0}$ as follows:

- $(\ell, v) \xrightarrow{a} (\ell', v')$ iff $v \in g$ and $v' = v[r]$ for some transition $(\ell, g, a, r, \ell') \in T$,
- $(\ell, v) \xrightarrow{d} (\ell, v + d)$ iff $v + d \in I(\ell)$.

We shall denote by $(\ell, v) \xrightarrow{\epsilon} (\ell, v')$ that $(\ell, v) \xrightarrow{d} (\ell, v')$ for some delay $d \in \mathbb{R}_{\geq 0}$, and refer to the transition as a *time-abstracted transition*, and the resulting transition system as the *untimed* transition system.

The notions of bisimulation and simulation may readily be applied to timed automata based on either the timed or untimed transition system semantics. Now consider the four timed automata from [3] depicted in Fig. 3. Here A and X are not timed bisimilar as $(X, y = 0) \xrightarrow{2} \xrightarrow{a}$ cannot be matched by $(A, y = 0)$. However, it can be seen that A and X are untimed bisimilar and that A is timed simulated by X. Considering A and U, it can be seen that they are not even untimed bisimilar (and hence not timed bisimilar): the transition $(A, y = 0) \xrightarrow{2} (A, y = 2)$ leads to a state that cannot perform a, while from $(U, y = 0)$, a is always enabled regardless of the delay. However, U timed simulates A. Finally, it can be argued that U and U' are timed bisimilar.

Several decision problems for timed automata are settled using the so-called *region* graph construction (see, e.g., [3]), essentially partitioning the infinite state-space of a timed automaton into a *finite* number of equivalence classes that are stable with respect to untimed bisimulation. From this region graph, the decidability of the untimed versions of bisimulation and simulation for timed automata follows (see, e.g., [76]).

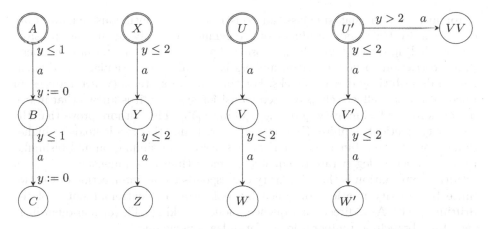

Fig. 3. Four timed automata. The initial locations are marked with double circles.

In contrast to the untimed setting, the decidability of timed bisimulation (and timed simulation) was for some time an open question, which was of particular importance to the several real-time process calculi that were developed in parallel with (and essentially equivalent to) timed automata at the time, e.g., the calculus of TCCS by Wang Yi [98]. However, in 1992 [28], Karlis Cerans conclusively demonstrated decidability of timed bisimulation through an elegant application of regions to a product construction, essentially constituting a timed game between two timed automata to be shown timed bisimilar. The decidability of synthesis for timed games in [13] provides a proof of decidability of timed bisimilarity. Another alternative proof can be obtained by reducing timed bisimulation to model checking using the characteristic formula construction given in [72].

4.2   Tools for Analyzing Timed Systems

The first tool supporting analysis of timed bisimulation (in fact a timed version of modal refinement) was the tool EPSILON [29], directly basing its implementation on the region construction by Cerans [28]. Only two years later, in 1995, the tool UPPAAL [74] was launched at the very first edition of TACAS [22]; UPPAAL is by now the standard tool for analyzing timed automata. Strongly encouraged by Tom Henzinger, the branch UPPAAL TIGA, supporting the synthesis for timed games, was launched in 2005 [27]. Later, supporting refinement between timed modal specification (in the shape of timed I/O automata), the branch ECDAR—effectively replacing EPSILON—was launched in 2010 [38].

4.3   Beyond Timed Systems

Recall Tom Henzinger's work in [88] from Sect. 3. As a concrete example for applying similarity, the authors discuss a subclass of rectangular hybrid automata [58]. In that subclass, all constraints and continuous dynamics are described by Cartesian products of (nonempty, possibly open, and possibly unbounded) intervals $[l, u] \subseteq \mathbb{R}_{\geq 0}$ whose end points $l, u \in \mathbb{N}$ are natural numbers. (The restriction to nonnegative numbers is crucial.) In particular, the dynamics are described by drifting clocks. For this class of systems (which induces an uncountable but effectively presented transition system), it is known that in two dimensions the bisimilarity quotient is infinite [53]. The authors prove that the similarity quotient is finite. (It was conjectured that this result holds in higher dimensions as well, but the authors later showed that simulation and bisimulation equivalence degenerate to equality in more than two dimensions [57].) An intuitive explanation is that similarity corresponds to the intersection of the two finite bisimilarity relations obtained by looking at the extremal slopes of the drifting clocks. As a direct consequence, model checking LTL (or non-quantifier-switching branching temporal logic) formulae is decidable.

The generalization to automata where the intervals in one dimension are not restricted to nonnegative reals yields infinite similarity quotients, but the quotient tiles the plane in a regular manner such that LTL model checking is possible with a procedure based on a pushdown ω-automaton that stores the integer part of the second dimension. When relaxing the nonnegativity constraints such that both dimensions can range into the negative reals, then already the bisimilarity quotient is finite [53]. The first model checker for rectangular and linear hybrid automata was HYTECH [55].

Simulation relations and abstraction have also been applied to general non-linear hybrid systems (e.g., [56,71,96]). A popular notion in the context of hybrid systems is *approximate (bi)simulation* [48,49]. The idea is that two systems need not be identical but remain bounded by some distance, possibly with two parameters [66]. Some notable use cases are control systems with inputs [87] and digital control systems [79].

5   Simulation Relations and Automata Theory

In this section we review simulation relations in the context of automata theory.

5.1   Fair Simulation

The work of Tom Henzinger we summarize here is [59]. The main contribution of that paper is a definition of *fair simulation*—a notion of simulation under fairness constraints—that can be computed in polynomial time. The paper presents an automata-theoretic algorithm to compute a fair simulation relation and also has applications in automata theory, which we shall describe later.

Determining trace inclusion (i.e., whether the set of traces starting in some state is included in the set of traces starting in another state) for a finite transition system is PSPACE-complete [94]. Analogously, one can define tree inclusion: A state s tree-includes a state t if every tree of observations that can be embedded in the unrolling of the transition system starting in t can also be embedded in the unrolling of the transition system starting in s. Tree inclusion happens to coincide with similarity.

For liveness properties, one typically only considers the fair behaviors of a transition system. A prominent example is Büchi fairness: an infinite trace is fair if some event (such as reading a certain label) repeats infinitely often.

One main benefit of (ordinary) simulation over trace inclusion is the computation in polynomial time. Fair trace inclusion is a straightforward generalization of trace inclusion. But the corresponding generalization of simulation is not obvious. There have been other proposals how to define fair simulation. Two of them [50, 78] are discussed in the paper, but they do not provide a practical computational advantage over fair trace inclusion: computing the fair simulation in [50] is PSPACE-complete [69] and computing the fair simulation in [78] is still NP-complete [62].

The newly suggested definition[1] of fair simulation uses a game-theoretic characterization and is based on a strategy: state t fairly simulates state s if there exists a strategy such that for every fair run $s_0 s_1 \cdots$ emerging from $s_0 = s$ the run $t_0 t_1 \cdots$ emerging from $t_0 = t$ of the same length and induced by the strategy is also fair and we have that t_i fairly simulates s_i for each $i \geq 0$.

The new definition of fair simulation lies strictly between those in [50, 78]. For vacuous fairness constraints, all three definitions coincide with simulation. For deterministic systems, all three definitions coincide with fair trace inclusion.

Fair simulation as defined above enjoys the theoretical property that it is monotonic: given a fair simulation, every (ordinary) simulation that is a superset is also a fair simulation. Then it follows that a finite-state strategy suffices, and even a memoryless strategy for Büchi fairness constraints. The authors reduce the problem of computing a fair simulation relation (respectively finding a winning strategy) to the nonemptiness problem of tree automata. The algorithm to check weak (Büchi) or strong (Streett) fairness constraints is polynomial in the size of the transition system, and in the latter case exponential in the size of the Streett constraint.

As an alternative characterization, the authors extend tree inclusion to fair tree inclusion: a computation tree is fair if all infinite paths correspond to fair behaviors. A state t fairly tree-includes a state s if every fair computation tree starting in s can also be started in t.

Yet another characterization of fair simulation is that fair similarity is the coarsest abstraction that preserves equivalence of all formulae in the fair universal fragment (defined by the authors) of the alternation-free μ-calculus [19].

Fair simulation has been applied in multiple contexts. In [61] the authors show that fair *bi*simulation preserves equivalence in the fair (but not necessarily universal) fragment of the alternation-free μ-calculus and in CTL*. Fair simulation can be checked in a compositional framework using assume-guarantee reasoning [60]. More recently, fair simulation has been extended to tree automata and probabilistic automata, both with Büchi acceptance condition [97]. In particular,

---

[1] The original definition is given for transition systems with labeled states. Here we use an adaptation to labeled transitions.

that approach models Büchi automata coalgebraically. In the next subsection, we describe common applications of fair simulation and other simulation relations in the broader context of automata theory.

5.2   Language Inclusion and Minimization

Simulation relations play a prominent role in automata theory as an efficient way to solve hard problems in practice. In particular, simulation is a sufficient condition for trace inclusion.

One hard problem in automata theory is language inclusion: is the language of automaton $\mathcal{A}$ included in the language of automaton $\mathcal{B}$? A candidate sufficient condition could be that the initial state of $\mathcal{B}$ simulates the initial state of $\mathcal{A}$. However, most automata have an acceptance condition, often represented by a set of accepting states F. In such cases, ordinary simulation of the initial state does not imply language inclusion. In addition, the acceptance condition needs to be taken into account in the definition of the simulation relation.

A second important problem in automata theory is to reduce the size (usually the number of states) of an automaton. Traditionally, such procedures are said to *minimize* the automaton, although many of them do not actually find a minimum result; this is however intended because exact minimization is typically a hard problem itself [45,65,89]. Minimization is motivated because many algorithms operating on automata scale with the automaton size. The common approach to minimization is quotienting: merging states according to an equivalence relation.

Consider the class of finite automata, for which the acceptance criterion is simple. In this case, one can resort to *direct simulation*: for p to directly simulate q, in addition to ordinary simulation we also require that $p \in F$ if $q \in F$. For deterministic finite automata (DFA), the corresponding direct bisimulation quotient coincides with the canonical minimal DFA, which can be found efficiently [63]. For nondeterministic finite automata, the direct simulation can be used for language inclusion and minimization [39].

A three-step algorithm to reduce a Kripke structure to a unique simulation-equivalent minimum is described in [25]. The algorithm first constructs a quotient structure, then eliminates transitions, and finally deletes unreachable states.

One of the most applied automaton classes in the literature is the Büchi automaton. It has its main application in the context of LTL model checking, where an LTL formula is converted to a Büchi automaton. This automaton can get very large, so minimization is an important tool.

The works in [90] and [42] use simulation relations to minimize Büchi automata. The authors of [90] use direct and backward simulation (essentially direct simulation, but swapping the direction of the transitions in the automaton). The authors of [42] use a notion of fair simulation that is stronger than the one in [59] but more efficient to implement.

A systematic study of simulation and bisimulation relations for minimization and language inclusion of Büchi automata is presented in [43]. The authors describe how to compute the direct simulation [39] and the fair simulation by

Henzinger et al. [59] in a unified framework by reduction to a parity game. The computation is more efficient than the previous algorithm in [59]. Fair simulation as defined before can be used for checking language inclusion but cannot be used for minimization (the obtained language may change). The authors propose a *delayed simulation* for the purpose of minimizing Büchi automata.

An alternative minimization algorithm based on fair simulation with some careful handling to preserve the language is proposed in [51]. An extension of fair and delayed simulation to generalized Büchi automata is given in [67].

Further works focus on stronger reductions for nondeterministic Büchi automata, which in the game view means to give more power to the protagonist.

Etessami proposes the extension to k-*simulation* [41]. The protagonist has k tokens that can all advance at the same time and be redistributed at any time. This can be seen as applying the subset construction with sets of size up to k. For a fixed k, computing k-simulations is polynomial. For $k = n$, k-simulation corresponds to trace inclusion. Since k-simulation is not transitive, so the transitive closure must be chosen for quotienting.

Clemente describes two simulation relations [34]. The first relation is *fixed-word simulation*: here the antagonist initially chooses a word. After that, both players need to move according to the next letter in the word, as usual. This gives more power to the protagonist because the suffix is known at any time. The author shows that adding multiple tokens (see k-simulation above) does not add more power. But fixed-word simulation is PSPACE-complete. The second relation is *proxy simulation*, which is a refinement of backward simulation. It can be seen as iteratively re-playing the game in the new quotient automaton until there is no change. Delayed proxy simulation allows for language-preserving quotienting. Computing a proxy simulation is polynomial.

Mayr and Clemente propose further simulation techniques both for transition pruning and state quotienting [81]. For the latter purpose, the authors introduce k-*lookahead simulation*: the antagonist takes k steps, then the protagonist takes up to k steps, and finally the antagonist backtracks the steps that were not taken. The advantage over k-simulation [41] is its efficiency: one only needs to store at most n^2 configurations. Notably, this approach works well to shrink random automata, which typically do not contain structure to exploit. In a recent work, the same authors use combinations of backward and forward trace inclusion and simulation relations for testing language inclusion [35]. The paper also contains a technical overview of different proposals from the literature.

Simulation relations have also been applied to other classes of automata. Tree automata generalize finite automata from words to tree structures. A minimization algorithm for bottom-up tree automata based on two types of simulation relations is proposed in [2]. The first type is *downward simulation*, which generalizes backward simulation for finite automata. The second type is *upward simulation*, which is however not language-preserving. The authors describe a combination that, in the worst case, leads to the same reduction as with downward simulation, but the additional knowledge from the upward simulation often yields better results.

The visibly pushdown automaton (VPA) [8] is a restricted form of a pushdown automaton where the stack access is determined by the input symbol. Srba considers several types of simulation and bisimulation [92]. The standard bisimulation game is used to determine bisimilarity. The problems of computing the respective preorders and equivalences are all EXPTIME-complete, and PSPACE-complete if the stack is a counter. For the purpose of minimization, Heizmann et al. extend bisimulation to visibly pushdown automata for quotient-based minimization [52]. One difficulty of VPA is that, unlike for finite automata, merging states (and hence simulation) is not transitive: given three states q_1, q_2, q_3, if merging q_1 and q_2 or q_2 and q_3 preserves the language, merging all three states may still alter the language.

Acknowledgments. This research was partly supported by DIREC - Digital Research Centre Denmark and the Villum Investigator Grant S4OS.

References

1. Abadi, M., Lamport, L.: The existence of refinement mappings. Theor. Comput. Sci. **82**(2), 253–284 (1991). https://doi.org/10.1016/0304-3975(91)90224-P
2. Abdulla, P.A., Holík, L., Kaati, L., Vojnar, T.: A uniform (bi-)simulation-based framework for reducing tree automata. Electron. Notes Theor. Comput. Sci. **251**, 27–48 (2009). https://doi.org/10.1016/j.entcs.2009.08.026
3. Aceto, L., Ingólfsdóttir, A., Larsen, K.G., Srba, J.: Reactive Systems: Modelling. Cambridge University Press, Specification and Verification (2007)
4. Aceto, L., Ingólfsdóttir, A., Srba, J.: The algorithmics of bisimilarity. In: Advanced Topics in Bisimulation and Coinduction, Cambridge tracts in theoretical computer science, vol. 52, pp. 100–172. Cambridge University Press (2012)
5. Alur, R., Courcoubetis, C., Henzinger, T.A., Ho, P.: Hybrid automata: an algorithmic approach to the specification and verification of hybrid systems. In: Hybrid Systems. LNCS, vol. 736, pp. 209–229. Springer, Cham (1992). https://doi.org/10.1007/3-540-57318-6_30
6. Alur, R., Dill, D.L.: Automata for modeling real-time systems. In: ICALP, LNCS, vol. 443, pp. 322–335. Springer, Cham (1990). https://doi.org/10.1007/BFb0032042
7. Alur, R., Dill, D.L.: A theory of timed automata. Theor. Comput. Sci. **126**(2), 183–235 (1994). https://doi.org/10.1016/0304-3975(94)90010--8
8. Alur, R., Madhusudan, P.: Visibly pushdown languages. In: STOC. pp. 202–211. ACM (2004). https://doi.org/10.1145/1007352.1007390
9. Andersen, J.R., et al.: CAAL: concurrency workbench, Aalborg edition. In: ICTAC. LNCS, vol. 9399, pp. 573–582. Springer, Cham (2015). https://doi.org/10.1007/978-3-319-25150-9_33
10. Antonik, A., Huth, M., Larsen, K.G., Nyman, U., Wasowski, A.: 20 years of modal and mixed specifications. Bull. EATCS **95**, 94–129 (2008)
11. Antonik, A., Huth, M., Larsen, K.G., Nyman, U., Wasowski, A.: Complexity of decision problems for mixed and modal specifications. In: FOSSACS. LNCS, vol. 4962, pp. 112–126. Springer, Cham (2008). https://doi.org/10.1007/978-3-540-78499-9_9

12. Antonik, A., Huth, M., Larsen, K.G., Nyman, U., Wasowski, A.: EXPTIME-complete decision problems for modal and mixed specifications. ENTCS **242**(1), 19–33 (2009). https://doi.org/10.1016/j.entcs.2009.06.011
13. Asarin, E., Maler, O., Pnueli, A.: Symbolic controller synthesis for discrete and timed systems. In: Hybrid Systems. LNCS, vol. 999, pp. 1–20. Springer, Cham (1994). https://doi.org/10.1007/3-540-60472-3_1
14. Baier, C., Katoen, J.: Principles of Model Checking. MIT Press (2008)
15. Bauer, S.S., Juhl, L., Larsen, K.G., Srba, J., Legay, A.: A logic for accumulated-weight reasoning on multiweighted modal automata. In: TASE, pp. 77–84. IEEE Computer Society (2012). https://doi.org/10.1109/TASE.2012.9
16. Benes, N., Křetínský, J., Larsen, K.G., Srba, J.: On determinism in modal transition systems. Theor. Comput. Sci. **410**(41), 4026–4043 (2009). https://doi.org/10.1016/j.tcs.2009.06.009
17. Beneš, N., Křetínský, J., Larsen, K.G., Møller, M.H., Srba, J.: Parametric modal transition systems. In: ATVA. LNCS, vol. 6996, pp. 275–289. Springer, Cham (2011). https://doi.org/10.1007/978-3-642-24372-1_20
18. Beneš, N., Křetínský, J., Larsen, K.G., Srba, J.: Checking thorough refinement on modal transition systems is EXPTIME-complete. In: ICTAC. LNCS, vol. 5684, pp. 112–126. Springer, Cham (2009). https://doi.org/10.1007/978-3-642-03466-4_7
19. Bensalem, S., Bouajjani, A., Loiseaux, C., Sifakis, J.: Property preserving simulations. In: CAV. LNCS, vol. 663, pp. 260–273. Springer, Cham (1992). https://doi.org/10.1007/3-540-56496-9_21
20. Bloom, B., Paige, R.: Transformational design and implementation of a new efficient solution to the ready simulation problem. Sci. Comput. Program. **24**(3), 189–220 (1995). https://doi.org/10.1016/0167-6423(95)00003-B
21. Bouajjani, A., Fernandez, J., Halbwachs, N.: Minimal model generation. In: Clarke, E.M., Kurshan, R.P. (eds.) CAV 1990. LNCS, vol. 531, pp. 197–203. Springer, Heidelberg (1991). https://doi.org/10.1007/BFb0023733
22. Brinksma, E., Cleaveland, R., Larsen, K.G., Margaria, T., Steffen, B. (eds.): Tools and Algorithms for Construction and Analysis of Systems, First International Workshop, TACAS '95, Aarhus, Denmark, 19–20 May 1995, Proceedings, LNCS, vol. 1019. Springer, Cham (1995). https://doi.org/10.1007/3-540-60630-0
23. Bunte, O., et al.: The mCRL2 toolset for analysing concurrent systems - improvements in expressivity and usability. In: TACAS. LNCS, vol. 11428, pp. 21–39. Springer, Cham (2019). https://doi.org/10.1007/978-3-030-17465-1_2
24. Burkart, O., Caucal, D., Moller, F., Steffen, B.: Verification on infinite structures. In: Handbook of Process Algebra, pp. 545–623. North-Holland/Elsevier (2001). https://doi.org/10.1016/b978-044482830-9/50027-8
25. Bustan, D., Grumberg, O.: Simulation based minimization. In: CADE. LNCS, vol. 1831, pp. 255–270. Springer, Cham (2000). https://doi.org/10.1007/10721959_20
26. Calzolai, F., Nicola, R.D., Loreti, M., Tiezzi, F.: TAPAs: a tool for the analysis of process algebras. Trans. Petri Nets Other Model. Concurr. **1**, 54–70 (2008). https://doi.org/10.1007/978-3-540-89287-8_4
27. Cassez, F., David, A., Fleury, E., Larsen, K.G., Lime, D.: Efficient on-the-fly algorithms for the analysis of timed games. In: CONCUR. LNCS, vol. 3653, pp. 66–80. Springer, Cham (2005). https://doi.org/10.1007/11539452_9
28. Cerans, K.: Decidability of bisimulation equivalences for parallel timer processes. In: CAV. LNCS, vol. 663, pp. 302–315. Springer, Cham (1992). https://doi.org/10.1007/3-540-56496-9_24

29. Cerans, K., Godskesen, J.C., Larsen, K.G.: Timed modal specification - theory and tools. In: CAV. LNCS, vol. 697, pp. 253–267. Springer, Cham (1993). https://doi.org/10.1007/3-540-56922-7_21

30. Clarke, E.M., Grumberg, O., Long, D.E.: Model checking and abstraction. ACM Trans. Program. Lang. Syst. **16**(5), 1512–1542 (1994). https://doi.org/10.1145/186025.186051

31. Cleaveland, R., Parrow, J., Steffen, B.: The concurrency workbench. In: Automatic Verification Methods for Finite State Systems. LNCS, vol. 407, pp. 24–37. Springer, Cham (1989). https://doi.org/10.1007/3-540-52148-8_3

32. Cleaveland, R., Parrow, J., Steffen, B.: The concurrency workbench: a semantics-based tool for the verification of concurrent systems. ACM Trans. Program. Lang. Syst. **15**(1), 36–72 (1993). https://doi.org/10.1145/151646.151648

33. Cleaveland, R., Sims, S.: The NCSU concurrency workbench. In: CAV. LNCS, vol. 1102, pp. 394–397. Springer, Cham (1996). https://doi.org/10.1007/3-540-61474-5_87

34. Clemente, L.: Büchi automata can have smaller quotients. In: ICALP. LNCS, vol. 6756, pp. 258–270. Springer, Cham (2011). https://doi.org/10.1007/978-3-642-22012-8_20

35. Clemente, L., Mayr, R.: Efficient reduction of nondeterministic automata with application to language inclusion testing. Log. Methods Comput. Sci. **15**(1) (2019). https://doi.org/10.23638/LMCS-15(1:12)2019

36. Dams, D., Gerth, R., Grumberg, O.: Abstract interpretation of reactive systems. ACM Trans. Program. Lang. Syst. **19**(2), 253–291 (1997). https://doi.org/10.1145/244795.244800

37. Dams, D., Grumberg, O.: Abstraction and abstraction refinement. In: Handbook of Model Checking, pp. 385–419. Springer, Cham (2018). https://doi.org/10.1007/978-3-319-10575-8_13

38. David, A., Larsen, K.G., Legay, A., Nyman, U., Wasowski, A.: ECDAR: an environment for compositional design and analysis of real time systems. In: ATVA. LNCS, vol. 6252, pp. 365–370. Springer, Cham (2010). https://doi.org/10.1007/978-3-642-15643-4_29

39. Dill, D.L., Hu, A.J., Wong-Toi, H.: Checking for language inclusion using simulation preorders. In: CAV. LNCS, vol. 575, pp. 255–265. Springer, Cham (1991). https://doi.org/10.1007/3-540-55179-4_25

40. Enevoldsen, S., Larsen, K.G., Mariegaard, A., Srba, J.: Dependency graphs with applications to verification. Int. J. Softw. Tools Technol. Transf. **22**(5), 635–654 (2020). https://doi.org/10.1007/s10009-020-00578-9

41. Etessami, K.: A hierarchy of polynomial-time computable simulations for automata. In: CONCUR. LNCS, vol. 2421, pp. 131–144. Springer, Cham (2002). https://doi.org/10.1007/3-540-45694-5_10

42. Etessami, K., Holzmann, G.J.: Optimizing Büchi automata. In: CONCUR. LNCS, vol. 1877, pp. 153–167. Springer, Cham (2000). https://doi.org/10.1007/3-540-44618-4_13

43. Etessami, K., Wilke, T., Schuller, R.A.: Fair simulation relations, parity games, and state space reduction for Büchi automata. SIAM J. Comput. **34**(5), 1159–1175 (2005). https://doi.org/10.1137/S0097539703420675

44. Garavel, H., Lang, F., Mateescu, R., Serwe, W.: CADP 2011: a toolbox for the construction and analysis of distributed processes. Int. J. Softw. Tools Technol. Transf. **15**(2), 89–107 (2013). https://doi.org/10.1007/s10009-012-0244-z

45. Gauwin, O., Muscholl, A., Raskin, M.: Minimization of visibly pushdown automata is NP-complete. Log. Methods Comput. Sci. **16**(1) (2020). https://doi.org/10. 23638/LMCS-16(1:14)2020
46. Gentilini, R., Piazza, C., Policriti, A.: From bisimulation to simulation: Coarsest partition problems. J. Autom. Reason. **31**(1), 73–103 (2003). https://doi.org/10. 1023/A:1027328830731
47. Gibson-Robinson, T., Armstrong, P.J., Boulgakov, A., Roscoe, A.W.: FDR3 - A modern refinement checker for CSP. In: TACAS. LNCS, vol. 8413, pp. 187–201. Springer, Cham (2014). https://doi.org/10.1007/978-3-642-54862-8_13
48. Girard, A., Julius, A.A., Pappas, G.J.: Approximate simulation relations for hybrid systems. Discret. Event Dyn. Syst. **18**(2), 163–179 (2008). https://doi.org/10.1007/ s10626-007-0029-9
49. Girard, A., Pappas, G.J.: Approximation metrics for discrete and continuous systems. IEEE Trans. Autom. Control. **52**(5), 782–798 (2007). https://doi.org/10. 1109/TAC.2007.895849
50. Grumberg, O., Long, D.E.: Model checking and modular verification. ACM Trans. Program. Lang. Syst. **16**(3), 843–871 (1994). https://doi.org/10.1145/177492. 177725
51. Gurumurthy, S., Bloem, R., Somenzi, F.: Fair simulation minimization. In: CAV. LNCS, vol. 2404, pp. 610–624. Springer, Cham (2002). https://doi.org/10.1007/3-540-45657-0_51
52. Heizmann, M., Schilling, C., Tischner, D.: Minimization of visibly pushdown automata using partial Max-SAT. In: TACAS. LNCS, vol. 10205, pp. 461–478 (2017). https://doi.org/10.1007/978-3-662-54577-5_27
53. Henzinger, T.A.: Hybrid automata with finite bisimulations. In: ICALP. LNCS, vol. 944, pp. 324–335. Springer, Cham (1995). https://doi.org/10.1007/3-540-60084-1_85
54. Henzinger, T.A.: The theory of hybrid automata. In: LICS. pp. 278–292. IEEE Computer Society (1996). https://doi.org/10.1109/LICS.1996.561342
55. Henzinger, T.A., Ho, P.: HYTECH: the Cornell HYbrid TECHnology tool. In: Hybrid Systems. LNCS, vol. 999, pp. 265–293. Springer, Cham (1994). https:// doi.org/10.1007/3-540-60472-3_14
56. Henzinger, T.A., Ho, P., Wong-Toi, H.: Algorithmic analysis of nonlinear hybrid systems. IEEE Trans. Autom. Control. **43**(4), 540–554 (1998). https://doi.org/10. 1109/9.664156
57. Henzinger, T.A., Kopke, P.W.: State equivalences for rectangular hybrid automata. In: CONCUR. LNCS, vol. 1119, pp. 530–545. Springer, Cham (1996). https://doi. org/10.1007/3-540-61604-7_74
58. Henzinger, T.A., Kopke, P.W., Puri, A., Varaiya, P.: What's decidable about hybrid automata? J. Comput. Syst. Sci. **57**(1), 94–124 (1998). https://doi.org/ 10.1006/jcss.1998.1581
59. Henzinger, T.A., Kupferman, O., Rajamani, S.K.: Fair simulation. Inf. Comput. **173**(1), 64–81 (2002). https://doi.org/10.1006/inco.2001.3085
60. Henzinger, T.A., Qadeer, S., Rajamani, S.K., Tasiran, S.: An assume-guarantee rule for checking simulation. ACM Trans. Program. Lang. Syst. **24**(1), 51–64 (2002). https://doi.org/10.1145/509705.509707
61. Henzinger, T.A., Rajamani, S.K.: Fair bisimulation. In: TACAS. LNCS, vol. 1785, pp. 299–314. Springer, Cham (2000). https://doi.org/10.1007/3-540-46419-0_21
62. Hojati, R.: A BDD-Based Environment for Formal Verification of Hardware Systems. Ph.D. thesis, EECS Department, University of California, Berkeley (1996). https://www2.eecs.berkeley.edu/Pubs/TechRpts/1996/3052.html

63. Hopcroft, J.E.: An n log n algorithm for minimizing states in a finite automaton. In: Theory of Machines and Computations, pp. 189–196. Academic Press (1971). https://doi.org/10.1016/B978-0-12-417750-5.50022-1

64. Jančar, P., Srba, J.: Undecidability of bisimilarity by defender's forcing. J. ACM **55**(1), 1–26 (2008). https://doi.org/10.1145/1326554.1326559

65. Jiang, T., Ravikumar, B.: Minimal NFA problems are hard. SIAM J. Comput. **22**(6), 1117–1141 (1993). https://doi.org/10.1137/0222067

66. Julius, A.A., D'Innocenzo, A., Benedetto, M.D.D., Pappas, G.J.: Approximate equivalence and synchronization of metric transition systems. Syst. Control. Lett. **58**(2), 94–101 (2009). https://doi.org/10.1016/j.sysconle.2008.09.001

67. Juvekar, S., Piterman, N.: Minimizing generalized Büchi automata. In: CAV. LNCS, vol. 4144, pp. 45–58. Springer, Cham (2006). https://doi.org/10.1007/11817963_7

68. Kucera, A., Mayr, R.: Why is simulation harder than bisimulation? In: CONCUR. LNCS, vol. 2421, pp. 594–610. Springer, Cham (2002). https://doi.org/10.1007/3-540-45694-5_39

69. Kupferman, O., Vardi, M.Y.: Verification of fair transition systems. Chic. J. Theor. Comput. Sci. 1998 (1998). https://cjtcs.cs.uchicago.edu/articles/1998/2/contents.html

70. Kučera, A., Jančar, P.: Equivalence-checking with infinite-state systems: Techniques and results. In: SOFSEM. LNCS, vol. 2540, pp. 41–73. Springer, Cham (2002). https://doi.org/10.1007/3-540-36137-5_3

71. Lanotte, R., Tini, S.: Taylor approximation for hybrid systems. Inf. Comput. **205**(11), 1575–1607 (2007), https://doi.org/10.1016/j.ic.2007.05.004

72. Laroussinie, F., Larsen, K.G., Weise, C.: From timed automata to logic - and back. In: MFCS. LNCS, vol. 969, pp. 529–539. Springer, Cham (1995). https://doi.org/10.1007/3-540-60246-1_158

73. Larsen, K.G., Nyman, U., Wasowski, A.: On modal refinement and consistency. In: CONCUR. LNCS, vol. 4703, pp. 105–119. Springer, Cham (2007). https://doi.org/10.1007/978-3-540-74407-8_8

74. Larsen, K.G., Pettersson, P., Yi, W.: UPPAAL in a nutshell. Int. J. Softw. Tools Technol. Transf. **1**(1–2), 134–152 (1997). https://doi.org/10.1007/s100090050010

75. Larsen, K.G., Thomsen, B.: A modal process logic. In: LICS, pp. 203–210. IEEE Computer Society (1988). https://doi.org/10.1109/LICS.1988.5119

76. Larsen, K.G., Yi, W.: Time abstracted bisimulation: Implicit specifications and decidability. In: MFPS. LNCS, vol. 802, pp. 160–176. Springer, Cham (1993). https://doi.org/10.1007/3-540-58027-1_8

77. Lee, D., Yannakakis, M.: Online minimization of transition systems (extended abstract). In: STOC, pp. 264–274. ACM (1992). https://doi.org/10.1145/129712.129738

78. Lynch, N.A., Tuttle, M.R.: Hierarchical correctness proofs for distributed algorithms. In: PODC, pp. 137–151. ACM (1987). https://doi.org/10.1145/41840.41852

79. Majumdar, R., Zamani, M.: Approximately bisimilar symbolic models for digital control systems. In: CAV. LNCS, vol. 7358, pp. 362–377. Springer, Cham (2012). https://doi.org/10.1007/978-3-642-31424-7_28

80. Mayr, R.: Process rewrite systems. Inf. Comput. **156**(1–2), 264–286 (2000). https://doi.org/10.1006/inco.1999.2826

81. Mayr, R., Clemente, L.: Advanced automata minimization. In: POPL, pp. 63–74. ACM (2013). https://doi.org/10.1145/2429069.2429079

82. Mazala, R.: Infinite games. In: Automata, Logics, and Infinite Games: a Guide to Current Research. LNCS, vol. 2500, pp. 23–42. Springer, Cham (2001). https:// doi.org/10.1007/3-540-36387-4_2

83. Milner, R.: An algebraic definition of simulation between programs. In: IJCAI, pp. 481–489 (1971). https://ijcai.org/Proceedings/71/Papers/044.pdf

84. Moller, F.: Infinite results. In: CONCUR. LNCS, vol. 1119, pp. 195–216. Springer, Cham (1996). https://doi.org/10.1007/3-540-61604-7_56

85. Paige, R., Tarjan, R.E.: Three partition refinement algorithms. SIAM J. Comput. 16(6), 973–989 (1987). https://doi.org/10.1137/0216062

86. Park, D.M.R.: Concurrency and automata on infinite sequences. In: Theoretical Computer Science. LNCS, vol. 104, pp. 167–183. Springer, Cham (1981). https:// doi.org/10.1007/BFb0017309

87. Pola, G., Girard, A., Tabuada, P.: Approximately bisimilar symbolic models for nonlinear control systems. Autom. 44(10), 2508–2516 (2008). https://doi.org/10. 1016/j.automatica.2008.02.021

88. Rauch Henzinger, M., Henzinger, T.A., Kopke, P.W.: Computing simulations on finite and infinite graphs. In: FOCS, pp. 453–462. IEEE Computer Society (1995). https://doi.org/10.1109/SFCS.1995.492576

89. Schewe, S.: Beyond hyper-minimisation–minimising DBAs and DPAs is NP-complete. In: FSTTCS. LIPIcs, vol. 8, pp. 400–411. Schloss Dagstuhl - Leibniz-Zentrum für Informatik (2010). https://doi.org/10.4230/LIPIcs.FSTTCS.2010.400

90. Somenzi, F., Bloem, R.: Efficient Büchi automata from LTL formulae. In: CAV. LNCS, vol. 1855, pp. 248–263. Springer, Cham (2000). https://doi.org/10.1007/ 10722167_21

91. Srba, J.: Roadmap of infinite results. In: Current Trends in Theoretical Computer Science: The Challenge of the New Century, vol. 2, pp. 337–350. World Scientific (2004)

92. Srba, J.: Beyond language equivalence on visibly pushdown automata. Log. Methods Comput. Sci. 5(1) (2009). https://arxiv.org/abs/0901.2068

93. Stirling, C.: Local model checking games. In: CONCUR. LNCS, vol. 962, pp. 1–11. Springer, Cham (1995). https://doi.org/10.1007/3-540-60218-6_1

94. Stockmeyer, L.J., Meyer, A.R.: Word problems requiring exponential time. In: STOC, pp. 1–9. ACM (1973). https://doi.org/10.1145/800125.804029

95. Thomas, W.: On the Ehrenfeucht-Fraïssé game in theoretical computer science. In: TAPSOFT. LNCS, vol. 668, pp. 559–568. Springer, Cham (1993). https://doi.org/ 10.1007/3-540-56610-4_89

96. Tiwari, A.: Abstractions for hybrid systems. Formal Methods Syst. Des. 32(1), 57–83 (2008). https://doi.org/10.1007/s10703-007-0044-3

97. Urabe, N., Hasuo, I.: Fair simulation for nondeterministic and probabilistic Büchi automata: a coalgebraic perspective. Log. Methods Comput. Sci. 13(3) (2017). https://doi.org/10.23638/LMCS-13(3:20)2017

98. Yi, W.: CCS + time = an interleaving model for real time systems. In: ICALP. LNCS, vol. 510, pp. 217–228. Springer, Cham (1991). https://doi.org/10.1007/3-540-54233-7_136

Fine-Grained Complexity Lower Bounds for Problems in Computer Aided Verification

Monika Henzinger[(✉)]

Department of Computer Science, Universität Wien, 1090 Wien, Austria
monika.henzinger@univie.ac.at

Abstract. This article presents two fine-grained complexity lower bounds with relevance to algorithmic problems in computer aided verification. We have chosen these lower bounds as the proofs are relatively simple, but the techniques can be extended to give lower bounds for many more algorithmic problems. The goal is to present the bounds with minimal notation, making the results accessible to a broad community and stimulating further research in the area.

Specifically, we first describe a lower bound on the symbolic complexity of computing strongly connected components, which can be extended to show lower bounds for fundamental model-checking questions in graphs, published in [CDHL16b]. Second we present a conditional lower bound for disjunctive safety problems on graphs from [CDHL18] in the RAM model of computation. This bound can be modified to give conditional lower bounds for disjunctive objectives for reachability, Büchi, coBüchi and Rabin objectives in MDPs. We also present various open questions.

1 Introduction

Directed graphs, Markov decision processes (MDPs), two-player games played on directed graphs (aka game graphs) provide a combinatorial framework to model a wide range of problems in computer science. Game algorithms are fundamental in many applications of formal methods such as the compatibility of interface automata [DAH01] and game logics [AHK02].

We focus in this article on algorithmic problems arising in the analysis of reactive systems where the vertices in the graph represent the states in the system and directed edges represent state transitions. The object of study are infinite

This project has received funding from the European Research Council (ERC) under the European Union's Horizon 2020 research and innovation programme (Grant agreement No. 101019564 "The Design of Modern Fully Dynamic Data Structures (MoDynStruct)" and from the Austrian Science Fund (FWF) project "Fast Algorithms for a Reactive Network Layer (ReactNet)", P 33775-N, with additional funding from the *netidee SCIENCE Stiftung*, 2020–2024.

© Springer Nature Switzerland AG 2022
J.-F. Raskin and K. Chatterjee (Eds.): Principles of Systems Design, LNCS 13660, pp. 292–305, 2022.
https://doi.org/10.1007/978-3-031-22337-2_14

walks in these graphs that fulfill certain properties, usually called *objectives*. Given a starting vertex s the question is usually whether there exists such a walk starting from s. Even though there can be infinitely many such walks for a given objective there are very efficient algorithms for certain objectives that can answer the existence questions in polynomial and sometimes even in linear time (in the size of the graph). This naturally leads to the research question what the exact complexity of answering the existence question for various objectives is. Research has mostly focused on whether the complexity is polynomial or not, but recently there has been significant progress on determining the exact complexity for objectives, i.e., what their fine-grained complexity is. For work in the RAM model see [CH14, CDHL16a, CDHL16b, CHS17, CDHL17, CDHS19, CHKS21], for work on symbolic computation see [CHL17, CDHS18, CDHL18, CHL+18, CDHS21b]).

In this survey we present two fine-grained lower bounds with relevance to algorithmic problems in computer aided verification.

(1) First we describe a lower bound on the symbolic complexity of computing strongly connected components using a reduction from the Set Disjointness problem in communication complexity from [CDHL16b]. Note that the importance of symbolic methods in model checking was shown e.g. in [HKQ03, HMR05]. Our lower bound is interesting as it can be extended to show (a) lower bounds of $\Omega(D)$ for reachability objectives in diameter-D graphs in graphs and (b) lower bounds of $\Omega(n)$ for safety, Büchi, and co-Büchi objectives in a n-node graph.

(2) Second we present a conditional lower bound for disjunctive safety problems on graphs in the RAM model from [CDHL18]. This lower bound can be extended to disjunctive coBüchi and Rabin objectives in graphs and to disjunctive reachability, Büchi, coBüchi, and Rabin objectives in MDPs.

Note that there are also lower bounds known for model-checking questions known in MDPs and game graphs (see e.g. [CDHS21a]. However, for simplicity we only present lower bounds for graphs here, but note that they all carry over to game graphs.

The field of fine-grain complexity lower bounds for various fields of computer science have been blossoming in the last decade. For example, fine-grained complexity lower bounds have been given edit-distance problem in string problems and language theory [BI15], for dynamic graph algorithms [AW14, HKNS15], and planning problems in artificial intelligence [CDHS21a]. For a survey on fine-grained complexity see e.g. [Wil15].

2 Preliminaries

We first need to introduce the necessary definitions.

2.1 Word RAM Model of Computation

The *word RAM model of word size w* is a model of computation where a random-access machine can use an unlimited number of *words* (or *registers*) of w bits to perform its computation. The computation performed by a *RAM algorithm* consists of a sequence of instructions that are executed one after another, with no concurrent execution. Commonly an instruction is an arithmetic (add, subtract, multiply, divide, remainder, floor, ceiling), logical (bitwise AND, bitwise OR, bitwise NOT), control (conditional and unconditional branch), or data movement (load, store, copy) operation. Each operation takes a constant amount of time.

2.2 Probabilistic Algorithms

A *probabilistic* (or *randomized*) algorithm is a RAM algorithm that additionally to the instructions of the word RAM model has access to an operation that returns a random number of w bits. A *probabilistic algorithm with error probability p* is a probabilistic algorithm that returns the correct answer with probability at least p and can return any other answer with probability $1 - p$. Such an algorithm is also called a *Monte-Carlo algorithm*.

2.3 Symbolic Computation

A *symbolic algorithm* is allowed to use the same mathematical, logical, and memory access operations as a regular algorithm in the word RAM model with word size $O(\log n)$, but its access to the input graph is restricted. The graph is not given in an adjacency list or adjacency matrix representation, but instead through two types of *symbolic operations*:

1. *One-step operations Pre and Post*: Each predecessor (Pre) (resp., successor (Post)) operation is given a set X of vertices and returns the set of vertices Y with an edge to (resp., edge from) some vertex of X, i.e., $Pre(S) = \{v \in V | \exists s \in S : (v, s) \in E\}$ and $Post(S) = \{v \in V | \exists s \in S : (s, v) \in E\}$. Note that this operation does not disclose information about individual edges if $|X| > 1$.
2. *Basic set operations*: Each basic set operation is given one or two sets of vertices and performs a union, intersection, or complement on these sets.

An initial set of vertices is given as part of the input. We usually assume that the whole set is given as well as that each individual vertex is given as a singleton set. In this way every subset of vertices can be constructed with $O(n)$ set operations.

Time and Space Complexity: Symbolic one-step operations are more expensive than the non-symbolic operations and, thus, we define the time complexity to consist of only the number of symbolic one-step operations. Moreover, as the symbolic model is motivated by the compact representation of huge graphs, the goal is to design for symbolic algorithms that only store $O(1)$ or $O(\log n)$ many sets of vertices as otherwise algorithms become impractical due to their space requirements.

Note that every computable graph-algorithmic question can be solved with $2n$ symbolic one-step operations storing $O(n)$ many sets (and allowing an unbounded number of non-symbolic operations): For every vertex v perform a Pre and a Post operation, store the resulting $2n$ sets (which represent the full graph), and then compute the solution on this graph, using only non-symbolic operations. Note, however, that the lower bounds on the time complexity that we present here, do not depend on the space requirement of the algorithm, i.e., they also apply to symbolic algorithms that store an arbitrary number of sets.

2.4 Lower Bounds

There are two types of lower bounds, *unconditional* lower bounds and lower bounds that are based on some popular complexity assumptions, called *conditional* lower bounds. We give the necessary definitions for both next.

Unconditional Lower Bounds. The unconditional lower bounds of [CDHL17] are based on results from the area of communication complexity. Specifically the lower bounds are based on the known lower bounds for the communication complexity of the *Set Disjointness problem*.

We first define the classical *symmetric two-party communication complexity model*, for more details see [KN97]. There are three finite sets X, Y, Z, the former two are inputs for a function $f : X \times Y \to Z$, and Z is the image of the function. Two players, called Alice and Bob, each want to evaluate the function $f(x, y)$ for some a $x \in X$ and a $y \in Y$. However, Alice does not know y and Bob does not know x, and, thus, their goal is to compute the function collaboratively while sending as few bits as possible to each other. Note that their communication happens according to a fixed protocol, known to both players beforehand, that determines at what time which player sends which bits, and when to stop.

In the *Set Disjointness problem* we have a universe $U = \{0, 1, ..., k - 1\}$ of k elements and both sets X, Y contain all possible bit vectors of length k, i.e., they represent all possible subsets of U of size k. Alice is given a vector $x \in X$ and Bob a vector $y \in Y$, and the function f is defined as $f(x, y) = 1$ if for all $0 \leq i \leq k - 1$ either $x_i = 0$ or $y_i = 0$. Otherwise $f(x, y) = 0$. We will use S_x to denote the set $\{i, x_i = 1\}$. Thus $f(x, y) = 1$ if and only if $S_x \cap S_y = \emptyset$. The lower bounds we present for symbolic algorithms in Sect. 3 are based on the following fundamental lower bound for the communication complexity of Set Disjointness.

Theorem 1. *[KS92] Any (probabilistic bounded error or deterministic) protocol for the Set Disjointness problem sends $\Omega(k)$ bits in the worst case over all inputs.*

Conditional Lower Bounds. Another way to show lower bounds is by basing them on a popular complexity assumption. There are quite a few such assumptions by now, we will state some of them. We start with the strong triangle conjecture as we will use it to show a conditional lower bound for disjunctive safety objectives in Sect. 4.

Conjecture 1 (Strong Triangle Conjecture (STC)). In the word RAM model with words of $O(\log n)$ bits, any combinatorial algorithm requires at least $n^{3-o(1)}$ time in expectation to detect whether an n-node graph contains a triangle.

There is also a weaker version of the triangle conjecture.

Conjecture 2 (No Almost Linear Time Triangle). There is a constant $\delta > 0$, such that in the word RAM model with words of $O(\log n)$ bits, any algorithm requires at least $m^{1+\delta-o(1)}$ time in expectation to detect whether an m-edge graph contains a triangle.

We will list a few more other popular conjectures that have been or might be useful for further conditional lower bounds for model-checking problems.

Conjecture 3 (Strong Exponential Time Hypothesis (SETH)). For every $\epsilon > 0$, there exists a k, such that SAT on k-CNF formulas on n variables cannot be solved in $O(2^{(1-\epsilon)n}n^c)$ time for any constant c.

Conjecture 4 (No Truly Subquadratic 3SUM). In the word RAM model with words of $O(\log n)$ bits, any algorithm requires at least $n^{2-o(1)}$ time in expectation to determine whether a set $S \subseteq \{-n^3, \ldots, n^3\}$ of $|S| = n$ integers contains three distinct elements $a, b, c \in S$ with $a + b = c$.

Conjecture 5 (No Truly Subcubic APSP). There is a constant c, such that in the Word RAM model with words of $O(\log n)$ bits, any algorithm requires at least $n^{3-o(1)}$ time in expectation to compute the distances between every pair of vertices in an n-node graph with edge weights in $\{1, \ldots, n^c\}$.

Conjecture 6 (Online Matrix Vector (OMv) [HKNS15]*).* For any constant $\epsilon > 0$, there is no $O(n^{3-\epsilon})$-time algorithm that solves OMv with error probability at most $1/3$ in the word RAM model with $O(\log n)$ bit words.

Conjecture 7 (Combinatorial k-Clique). For any constant $\epsilon > 0$, for an n-node graph there is no $O(n^{k-\epsilon})$ time combinatorial algorithm for k-clique detection with error probability at most $1/3$ in the word RAM model with $O(\log n)$ bit words.

2.5   Graph Properties

We also quickly review two graph properties that we will refer to in the following sections. Given a directed graph $G = (V, E)$ a *strongly connected component (SCC)* is a maximal set $C \subseteq V$ such that there is a path from every vertex $u \in C$ to every other vertex $v \in C$. It follows that the set of strongly connected components induces a partition of V.

Furthermore, we define the *diameter* D of $G = (V, E)$ to be $\max\{d(u, v), u, v \in V, d(u, v) < |V|\}$, where $d(u, v)$ is the length of the shortest path from u to v. Note that this definition allows for a finite diameter even if there is no path between all pairs of nodes u and v.

3   Unconditional Lower Bound for the Symbolic Computation of Strongly Connected Components

3.1   Problem Description and Statement of Main Result

Computing the strongly connected components is one of the fundamental problems in graph algorithms and can be solved in linear time in the word RAM model with word size $O(\log n)$ using depth-first search. However, its exact symbolic complexity was not well-understood until recently [CDHL18]. We present here their proof of a lower bound for computing the strongly connected components (SCCs) using a symbolic algorithm. The reason why we present this proof is that it can be extend to show lower bounds for liveness, reachability, safety, and coBüchi objectives in graphs [CDHL18]. However, the proof for SCCs is simpler and it nicely captures the main idea of the other lower bounds.

Specifically, in this section we will show the following theorem.

Theorem 2 ([CDHL18]). *Any (probabilistic bounded error or deterministic) symbolic algorithm that computes the SCCs of a graph with n vertices needs $\Omega(n)$ symbolic one-step operations, even in constant-degree graphs.*

Note that these lower bounds are tight, as Gentilini et al. [GPP08] gave an $O(n)$ upper bound. Furthermore, [CDHL18] give matching upper and lower bounds of $\Theta(\sum_{C \in SCC(G)} (diam(C) + 1))$ for this problem, where $SCC(G)$ is the set of strongly connected components of the given graph G and $diam(C)$ is the diameter of the graph induced by the vertices of the strongly connected component C.

3.2   Proof of Main Result

To prove the theorem we assume that there exists a symbolic algorithm $\mathcal{A}$ that violates the theorem. Then we use $\mathcal{A}$ to solve the Set Disjointness problem with universe size k using only $o(k)$ bits of communication, leading to a contradiction. Thus, we need to reduce an arbitrary instance of the Set Disjointness problem to an instance of the SCC computation problem that we then solve with $\mathcal{A}$. The reduction works as follows:

Let (x, y) be an instance of Set Disjointness with universe size k and w.l.o.g. let $k = \ell \cdot q$ for some positive integers ℓ and q. We construct a directed graph $G = (V, E)$ with $n = k + \ell = \Theta(k)$ vertices and $O(n^2)$ edges as follows.

(1) The vertex set V is the union of ℓ sets V_i with $0 \le i \le \ell - 1$, where each set V_i equals $\{v_{i,0}, ..., v_{i,q}\}$, i.e., $|V_i| = q + 1$.
(2) *Type-1 edges:* There is a directed edge from $v_{i,j}$ to $v_{i',j'}$ if either $i < i'$ or $i = i'$ and $j < j'$.
(3) *Type-2 edges:* For $0 \le i \le \ell - 1$, $0 \le j \le q - 1$ there is an edge from $v_{i,j+1}$ to $v_{i,j}$ iff $x_{i \cdot q + j} = 0$ or $y_{i \cdot q + j} = 0$.

Note that there are $\Theta(\ell^2 q^2) = \Theta(k^2)$ edges of the first type and at most k edges of the second type.

Imagine that all the vertices are placed on a horizontal line by lexicographic order of their index with $v_{0,0}$ being the leftmost vertex. Note that all edges of the first type are pointing from left to right while all edges of the second type of edges are pointing from right to left. Furthermore, for every edge $(v_{i,j+1}, v_{i,j})$ of the second type there is a corresponding edge $(v_{i,j}, v_{i,j+1})$ of the first type, leading to a cycle in the graph. Also note that there is no edge from V_j to V_i if $i < j$ and, thus, there are at least ℓ SCCs in the graph. Now if $f(x,y) = 1$, then every edge $(v_{i,j+1}, v_{i,j})$ for all $0 \le i \le \ell - 1$ and all $0 \le j < q$ exists, implying that every set V_i forms exactly one SCC. On the other side if $f(x,y) = 0$, then there exists an i^* with $0 \le i^* \le \ell - 1$ and a j^* with $0 \le j^* < q$ such that the edge $(v_{i^*,j^*+1}, v_{i^*,j^*})$ does not exist. This proves the following crucial property of our reduction:

Lemma 1. *The graph G has exactly ℓ SCCs iff $f(x,y) = 1$.*

Thus we can solve the Set Disjointness problem by computing the number of SCCs of the graph.

Next we need to show that any algorithm that counts the number of SCCs in T many symbolic one-step operations can be used to construct a communication protocol for Set Disjointness that requires $O(T)$ bits of communication. The lower bound of $\Omega(k)$ for Set Disjointness then implies a lower bound of $\Omega(k) = \Omega(n)$ on the number of symbolic one-step operations needed to count the number of SCCs. Of course, any algorithm that computes the SCCs can also count them, giving the desired lower bound for computing SCCs.

Thus we are left with showing the following lemma.

Lemma 2. *For any algorithm $\mathcal{A}$ that counts the number of SCCs in T symbolic one-step operations there is a communication protocol for Set Disjointness that requires $O(T)$ bits of communication.*

Proof. Recall that Alice only knows x and Bob only knows y. Both Alice and Bob will each execute $\mathcal{A}$ *simultaneously*. As both know all the vertices, they can execute set operations without communication. The same holds for non-symbolic operations.

However, the symbolic one-step operations depend on the graph and while type-1 edges are independent of x and y (and, thus, known to both of them), type-2 edges depend on x and y. More specifically, if a type-2 edge exists, it is possible that only one of them knows of its existence (namely the one whose corresponding bit is 0). Additionally, if a type-2 edge does not exist, neither of them knows that the edge does not exist. Thus, Alice and Bob need to communicate whenever their version of $\mathcal{A}$ performs a symbolic one-step operation whose outcome is influenced by the existence of a type-2 edge. As we argue next

1. each of them can independently determine (using only set operations) whether communication is needed, and if so, the existence of which exact edge needs to be communicated and

2. for each symbolic one-step operation knowledge about the existence of at most two edges is needed and Alice and Bob have agreed beforehand that whenever the existence of two edges needs to be communicated, they will first communicate about the leftmost of the two and then about the rightmost.

Thus, whenever Alice and Bob need to communicate to find out the existence of a given edge, both Alice and Bob send the corresponding bit to the other one. As they execute $\mathcal{A}$ simultaneously and can determine which edge is needed independently, they do not needed to also send the index of the corresponding bits (which would require $\Theta(\log k)$ bits. Thus 2 bits of communication suffice. As $\mathcal{A}$ only performs T symbolic one-step operations, it follows that the corresponding communication protocol uses only $O(T)$ bits of communication and solves the Set Disjointness problem.

It suffice to show (1) and (2) for each symbolic operation. For this it is more convenient to rename the vertices as follows: We use $v'_{i \cdot q + j}$ to denote vertex $v_{i,j}$.

(1) Whenever a symbolic Post operation receives as parameter a set X of nodes let min be the smallest index such that $v'_{\min} \in X$. Due to the special structure of the graph it holds that $\{v_{\min+1}, v_{\min+2}, \ldots, v_{k+\ell-1}\} \subseteq Post(X) \subseteq \{v_{\min-1}, v_{\min}, \ldots, v_{k+\ell-1}\}$. Said differently, the exact answer depends only on the existence of the directed edges $(v_{\min}, v_{\min-1})$ and $(v_{\min+1}, v_{\min})$. If (min) mod $q = 0$ then only one edge needs to be checked as the edge $(v_{\min}, v_{\min-1})$ cannot exist. If (min +1) mod $q = 0$ then only one edge needs to be checked as the edge $(v_{\min+1}, v_{\min})$ cannot exist. Note that Alice and Bob can determine independently the value of min and, thus, also which edges to check.

(2) Whenever a symbolic Pre operation receives as parameter a set X of nodes let max be the largest index such that $v'_{\max} \in X$. Due to the special structure of the graph it holds that $\{v_0, v_1, \ldots, v_{\max-1}\} \subseteq Post(X) \subseteq \{v_0, v_1, \ldots, v_{\max+1}\}$. Thus, the exact answer depends only on the existence of the edges $(v_{\max}, v_{\max-1})$ and $(v_{\max+1}, v_{\max})$. If (max) mod $q = 0$ or (max +1) mod $q = 0$ then only one edge needs to be checked. As before, Alice and Bob can determine independently the value of max and, thus, also which edges to check.

This shows the $\Omega(n)$ lower bound on the number of symbolic one-step operations. Furthermore note that the proof holds for any positive integers ℓ and q. Observe also that G has diameter at most q. Thus, choosing $q = 2$ (equivalently $\ell = n/2$) shows that the $\Omega(n)$ lower bound also holds for graphs with constant diameter.

This completes the proof of Theorem 2.

3.3   Open Questions

Let D be the diameter of the graph. This approach can be extended to show lower bounds linear in D for reachability, and linear in n for safety, Büchi and co-Büchi objectives in graphs. However, while intuitively other types of objectives such as Rabin and Streett objectives, should be "harder", there are no lower bounds for them and leave this as an open question.

For reachability objectives, the basic symbolic algorithm requires $O(D)$ symbolic one-step operations (and stores $O(D)$ sets). Thus, the lower bound shows that this is optimal. As mentioned in the preliminaries every objective can be solved with $O(n)$ symbolic one-step operations, when allowed to store $\Theta(n)$ sets. The lower bounds show that this is optimal for safety, Büchi and co-Büchi objectives. However, this is impractical leading to the challenging open question how many symbolic one-step operations are needed when the number of sets that are stored (simultaneously) is restricted to constant or $O(\log n)$. Is it possible to give super-linear lower bounds in that setting?

4   A Conditional Lower Bound for Disjunctive Safety Objectives

4.1   Problem Description and Statement of Main Result

We first give the necessary definition. For a vertex set $T \subseteq V$ the *safety objective* is the set of infinite paths that do not contain any vertex of T, i.e., $Safety(T) = \{v_0, v_1, v_2, \ldots i \in \Omega \mid \forall v_j \geq 0 : v_j \in T\}$. We say that an infinite path p *satisfies the safety objective* if $p \in \text{Safety}(T)$, i.e., if p contains no vertex of T.

Given k sets $T_1, T_2, \ldots, T_k$, the *disjunctive objective* consists of the union of the k individual objectives. A path p *satisfies the disjunctive safety objective* if it does not contain any vertex of T_j for at least one j, with $1 \leq j \leq k$. A vertex s is in the *winning set* of the disjunctive safety objective if there exists a path starting at s that satisfies the disjunctive safety objective, i.e., that does not contain any vertex of some set T_j.

We will show that assuming the strong triangle conjecture, i.e., Conjecture 1, then any combinatorial algorithm that computes the winning set of a disjunctive safety objective takes time at least $n^{3-\epsilon}$ in expectation in a graph with n vertices. Using the weaker no-linear-time triangle conjecture, i.e., Conjecture 2, our reduction shows that there is a constant $\delta > 0$ such that any algorithm for computing the winning set requires time $m^{1+\delta-o(1)}$ in expectation in a graph with m edges.

Theorem 3 ([CDHL16b]). *There is no combinatorial $O(n^{3-\epsilon})$ or $O((k \cdot n^2)^{1-\epsilon})$ time algorithm (for any $\epsilon > 0$) that computes the winning set for the disjunctive safety objective with k objectives in an n-vertex graph under Conjecture 1.*

Under Conjecture 2 there is a constant $\delta > 0$ such that any algorithm for computing the winning set for this problem requires time at least $m^{1+\delta-o(1)}$ in expectation in a graph with m edges.

In particular, under both conjectures there is no such algorithm deciding whether the winning set is non-empty or deciding whether a specific vertex is in the winning set.

Note that [CDHL16b] presented an upper bound of $O(km)$ for computing the winning set for the disjunctive safety objective in an n-vertex graph. As Conjecture 1 implicitly assumes that the graph used in the lower bound construction is dense, the first conditional lower bounds is almost tight.

4.2   Proof of Main Result

To prove the theorem we give a reduction from triangle detection in a graph $G = (V, E)$ to determining the emptiness of the winning set of disjunction safety objective in a suitable graph $G' = (V', E')$. The reduction works as follows:

- There are four sets V^i with $1 \leq i \leq 4$ such that $V^i = \{v^i, v \in V\}$. Now $V' = \{s\} \cup \bigcup_{i=1}^{4} V^i$, where s is an additional node, not belonging to V or any V^i.
- For each $1 \leq i \leq 3$ there is a directed edge (v^i, u^{i+1}) in E' iff $(v, u) \in E$. Additionally, E' contains a directed edge (s, v^1) and a directed edge (v^4, s) for every $v \in V$.

Note that $|V'| = 4|V| + 1$ and $|E'| = 3|E| + 2|V|$.

Furthermore we choose the following sets $T_v = (V^1 \setminus \{v^1\}) \cup (V^4 \setminus \{v^4\})$ for each $v \in V$ for the disjunctive safety objectives. This completes the description of the reduction. The important property is now as follows:

Lemma 3. *There is a triangle in G iff the winning set of the disjunctive safety objective with sets T_v for all $v \in V$ in the graph G' is non-empty.*

Proof. " $\rightarrow$": Given that there is a triangle a, b, c in G consider the path that starts at s and visits the loop s, a^1, b^2, c^3, a^4, s in this order infinitely often. Note that this path does not contain any vertex from V^1 except for a^1 and not any vertex from V^4 except for a^4, and, thus, fulfills the T_a safety objective. It follows that s belongs to the winning set of Safety(T_a) and, thus, the winning set of the disjunctive safety objective with sets T_v for all $v \in V$ in the graph G' is non-empty.

" $\leftarrow$": Note that when removing s from G' the resulting graph is acyclic. Thus every infinite path in G' must contain s infinitely often. Hence, if the winning set is non-empty there must be an infinite path p' in the winning set. This implies that there must be a vertex $a \in V$ such that p' contains no other vertex from V^1 except a^1 and no other vertex from V^4 except a^4. Furthermore, p must contain s infinitely often. Now trim p' to start at the first occurrence of s. The resulting path p still contains no other vertex from V^1 except a^1 and no other vertex from V^4 except a^4, i.e., it fulfills the disjunctive safety objective with sets T_v. As there are no self-loops in G, there must exist vertices b and c in V such that p contains the vertices b^2 and c^3. But this implies that there are the edges $(a, b), (b, c)$, and (c, a) in E, implying that there is a triangle in G.

As $|V'| = \Theta(|V|)$ and $k = |V|$, it follows under Conjecture 1 that there is no combinatorial algorithm with $O(n^{3-\epsilon})$ or $O((k \cdot n^2)^{1-\epsilon})$ time (for any $\epsilon > 0$)

that decides the emptiness of the winning set for the disjunctive safety objective in an n-vertex graph.

Recall that $|E'| = 3|E| + 2|V|$. Note that for triangle counting we can assume that $|E| \geq |V|/2$ as isolated vertices can be ignored. Thus it follows that $|E'| = \Theta(|E|)$. Hence Conjecture 2 implies that there is a constant $\delta > 0$ such that any algorithm for the computing the winning set requires time at least $m^{1+\delta-o(1)}$ in expectation in a graph with m edges.

4.3   Extensions and Open Questions

The above reduction can be modified to also give lower bounds for disjunctive coBüchi and Rabin objectives in graphs, disjunctive safety objectives in MDPs and game graphs under Conjecture 3, and for disjunctive reachability queries in MDPs under Conjecture 1. Another reduction can be used to give lower bounds for disjunctive reachability queries in MDPs under Conjecture 3 giving slightly different bounds [CDHL16b].

Note that, due to the recent process of computing the MEC decomposition [CH14, BPW19], there is a $\tilde{O}(m + n)^1$ upper bound for the corresponding conjunctive queries. For the corresponding conjunctive objectives in MDPs [CDHL16b] linear-time upper bounds for graphs are folklore. There also exists such an upper bound for Streett objectives in graphs and MPDs [CDHS19]. Thus for these problems no super-linear lower bounds can exist.

Resolving the complexity of parity objectives is one of the main open questions: There are no superlinear lower bounds for parity objectives with more than two parities in graphs, MDPs, or game graphs known and there is also no almost-linear time algorithm.

Another interesting question is to understand the complexity of 2-player games in graphs, for which no results are known, except for the above mentioned disjunctive safety objective. In Sect. 2 we presented a large number of other complexity conjectures. It is possible that one of them can be used to give lower bounds for game graphs?

Finally, incremental verification/synthesis consists of the analysis of systems where the system changes little due to small updates, and dynamic algorithms allowing edge insertions and deletions give the suitable theoretical algorithmic framework to study this setting. Based on Conjecture 6 there is an almost-linear time conditional lower bounds for determining the number of SCCs in a directed graph that is modified by a sequence of edge insertions and deletions [HKNS15]. This lower bound can be adapted to give a lower bound for the 1-vertex safety and the Büchi objective in dynamic graphs. Note that Chatterjee and Henzinger [CH14] gave a linear-time Büchi algorithm for dynamic graphs under restrictions on the type of updates that are allowed, even for game graphs. However, the question whether there is a linear-time algorithm in game graphs with arbitrary edge insertions and deletions and the question of how to efficiently other objectives can be maintained in the dynamic setting are still open.

---

[1] We use the $\tilde{O}(.)$-notation to suppress polylogarithmic factors.

References

[AHK02]   Alur, R., Henzinger, T.A., Kupferman, O.: Alternating-time temporal logic. J. ACM **49**(5), 672–713 (2002)

[AW14]   Abboud, A., Williams, V.V.: Popular conjectures imply strong lower bounds for dynamic problems. In: 2014 IEEE 55th Annual Symposium on Foundations of Computer Science, pp. 434–443. IEEE (2014)

[BI15]   Backurs, A., Indyk, P.: Edit distance cannot be computed in strongly sub-quadratic time (unless seth is false). In: Proceedings of the Forty-seventh Annual ACM Symposium on Theory pf Computing, pp. 51–58 (2015)

[BPW19]   Bernstein, A., Probst, M., Wulff-Nilsen, C.: Decremental strongly-connected components and single-source reachability in near-linear time. In: Charikar, M., Cohen, E. (eds). Proceedings of the 51st Annual ACM SIGACT Symposium on Theory of Computing, STOC 2019, 23–26 June 2019, pp. 365–376. Phoenix, AZ, USA. ACM (2019)

[CDHL16a] Chatterjee, K., Dvorák, W., Henzinger, M., Loitzenbauer, V.: Condition-ally optimal algorithms for generalized Büchi games. In: Faliszewski, P., Muscholl, A., Niedermeier, R. (eds.) 41st International Symposium on Mathematical Foundations of Computer Science, MFCS 2016, August 22–26, 2016 - Kraków, Poland, volume 58 of LIPIcs, pp. 25:1–25:15. Schloss Dagstuhl - Leibniz-Zentrum für Informatik (2016)

[CDHL16b] Chatterjee, K., Dvorák, W., Henzinger, M., Loitzenbauer, V.: Model and objective separation with conditional lower bounds: Disjunction is harder than conjunction. In: Grohe, M., Koskinen, E., Shankar, N. (eds.) Proceedings of the 31st Annual ACM/IEEE Symposium on Logic in Computer Science, LICS 2016, 5–8 July 2016, pp. 197–206. ACM, New York, NY, USA (2016)

[CDHL17] Chatterjee, K., Dvorák, W., Henzinger, M., Loitzenbauer, V.: Improved set-based symbolic algorithms for parity games. In: Goranko, V., Dam, M. (eds.) 26th EACSL Annual Conference on Computer Science Logic, CSL 2017, 20–24 Aug 2017, volume 82 of LIPIcs, pp. 18:1–18:21. Stockholm, Sweden, . Schloss Dagstuhl - Leibniz-Zentrum für Informatik (2017)

[CDHL18] Chatterjee, K., Dvorák, W., Henzinger, M., Loitzenbauer, V.: Lower bounds for symbolic computation on graphs: Strongly connected components, liveness, safety, and diameter. In: Czumaj, A., (ed.) Proceedings of the Twenty-Ninth Annual ACM-SIAM Symposium on Discrete Algorithms, SODA 2018, 7–10 Jan 2018, pp. 2341–2356. SIAM, New Orleans, LA, USA (2018)

[CDHS18] Chatterjee, K., Dvorák, W., Henzinger, M., Svozil, A.: Quasipolynomial set-based symbolic algorithms for parity games. In: Barthe, G., Sutcliffe, G., Veanes, M. (eds.) LPAR-22. 22nd International Conference on Logic for Programming, Artificial Intelligence and Reasoning, 16–21 Nov 2018, volume 57 of EPiC Series in Computing, pp. 233–253Awassa, Ethiopia, EasyChair (2018)

[CDHS19] Chatterjee, K., Dvorák, W., Henzinger, M., Svozil, A.: Near-linear time algorithms for streett objectives in graphs and MDPS. In: Fokkink, W.J., van Glabbeek, R., (eds.) 30th International Conference on Concurrency Theory, CONCUR 2019, 27–30 Aug 2019, volume 140 of LIPIcs, pp. 7:1–7:16. Amsterdam, the Netherlands, Schloss Dagstuhl - Leibniz-Zentrum für Informatik (2019)

[CDHS21a] Chatterjee, K., Dvorák, W., Henzinger, M., Svozil, A.: Algorithms and conditional lower bounds for planning problems. Artif. Intell. **297**, 103499 (2021)

[CDHS21b] Chatterjee, K., Dvorák, W., Henzinger, M., Svozil, A.: Symbolic time and space tradeoffs for probabilistic verification. CoRR, abs/2104.07466 (2021)

[CH14] Chatterjee, K., Henzinger, M.: Efficient and dynamic algorithms for alternating Büchi games and maximal end-component decomposition. J. ACM, **61**(3), 15:1–15:40 (2014)

[CHKS21] Chatterjee, K., Dvorák, W., Henzinger, M., Svozil, A.: Faster algorithms for bounded liveness in graphs and game graphs. In: Bansal, N., Merelli, E., Worrell, J. (eds.) 48th International Colloquium on Automata, Languages, and Programming, ICALP 2021, 12–16 July 2021, volume 198 of LIPIcs, pp. 124:1–124:21. Glasgow, Scotland (Virtual Conference). Schloss Dagstuhl - Leibniz-Zentrum für Informatik (2021)

[CHL17] Chatterjee, K., Henzinger, M., Loitzenbauer, V.: Improved algorithms for parity and streett objectives. Log. Methods Comput. Sci. **13**(3) (2017)

[CHL+18] Chatterjee, K., Henzinger, M., Loitzenbauer, V., Oraee, S., Toman, V.: Symbolic Algorithms for Graphs and Markov Decision Processes with Fairness Objectives. In: Chockler, H., Weissenbacher, G. (eds.) CAV 2018. LNCS, vol. 10982, pp. 178–197. Springer, Cham (2018). https://doi.org/10.1007/978-3-319-96142-2_13

[CHS17] Chatterjee, K., Henzinger, M., Svozil, A.: Faster algorithms for mean-payoff parity games. In: Larsen, K.G., Bodlaender, H.L., Raskin, J.-F. (eds.) 42nd International Symposium on Mathematical Foundations of Computer Science, MFCS 2017, 21–25 Aug 2017, volume 83 of LIPIcs, pp. 39:1–39:14 - Aalborg, Denmark. Schloss Dagstuhl - Leibniz-Zentrum für Informatik (2017)

[DAH01] De Alfaro, L., Henzinger, T.A.: Interface automata. ACM SIGSOFT Software Eng. Notes **26**(5), 109–120 (2001)

[GPP08] Gentilini, R., Piazza, C., Policriti, A.: Symbolic graphs: linear solutions to connectivity related problems. Algorithmica **50**(1), 120–158 (2008)

[HKNS15] Henzinger, M., Krinninger, S., Nanongkai, D., Saranurak, T.: Unifying and strengthening hardness for dynamic problems via the online matrix-vector multiplication conjecture. In: Servedio, R.A., Rubinfeld, R. (eds.) Proceedings of the Forty-Seventh Annual ACM on Symposium on Theory of Computing, STOC 2015, 14–17 June 2015, pp. 21–30. ACM, Portland, OR, USA (2015)

[HKQ03] Henzinger, T.A., Kupferman, O., Qadeer, S.: From pre-historic to post-modern symbolic model checking. Formal Methods Syst. Des. **23**(3), 303–327 (2003)

[HMR05] Henzinger, T.A., Majumdar, R., Raskin, J.-F.: A classification of symbolic transition systems. ACM Trans. Comput. Logic **6**(1):1–32 (2005)

[KN97] Kushilevitz, E., Nisan, N.: Communication Complexity. Cambridge University Press, 1997

[KS92] Kalyanasundaram, B., Schnitger, G.: The probabilistic communication complexity of set intersection. SIAM J. Discret. Math. **5**(4), 545–557 (1992)

[Wil15] Williams, V.V.: Hardness of easy problems: basing hardness on popular conjectures such as the strong exponential time hypothesis (invited talk). In: Husfeldt, T., Kanj, I.A. (eds.) 10th International Symposium on Parameterized and Exact Computation, IPEC 2015, 16–18 Sep 2015, volume 43 of LIPIcs, pp. 17–29. Patras, Greece. Schloss Dagstuhl - Leibniz-Zentrum für Informatik (2015)

Getting Saturated with Induction

Márton Hajdu[1], Petra Hozzová[1](✉), Laura Kovács[1], Giles Reger[2], and Andrei Voronkov[1,2,3]

[1] TU Wien, Vienna, Austria
{marton.hajdu,petra.hozzova}@tuwien.ac.at
[2] University of Manchester, Manchester, UK
[3] EasyChair, Manchester, UK

Abstract. Induction in saturation-based first-order theorem proving is a new exciting direction in the automation of inductive reasoning. In this paper we survey our work on integrating induction directly into the saturation-based proof search framework of first-order theorem proving. We describe our induction inference rules proving properties with inductively defined datatypes and integers. We also present additional reasoning heuristics for strengthening inductive reasoning, as well as for using induction hypotheses and recursive function definitions for guiding induction. We present exhaustive experimental results demonstrating the practical impact of our approach as implemented within Vampire.

Keywords: Induction · Formal verification · Theorem proving

1 Introduction

One commonly used theory in the development of imperative/functional programs is the theory of inductively defined data types, such as natural numbers (e.g. see Fig. 1(a)). Automating reasoning in formal verification therefore also needs to automate induction. Previous works on automating induction mainly focus on inductive theorem proving [3–5,17,21]: deciding when induction should be applied and what induction axiom should be used. Recent advances related to automating inductive reasoning, such as first-order reasoning with inductively defined data types [14], inductive strengthening [19] and structural induction in superposition [6,8,10,13,18], open up new possibilities for automating induction. In this paper we survey our recent results towards automating inductive reasoning for first-order properties with inductively defined data types and beyond.

Relation to the State-of-the-Art. Our work automates induction by integrating it directly in the saturation-based approach of first-order provers [15,20,24]. These provers implement saturation-based proof search using the superposition calculus [16]. Moreover, they rely on powerful indexing algorithms, notions of redundancy, selection functions and term orderings for making theorem proving efficient. First-order theorem provers complement SMT solvers in reasoning with theories and quantifiers, as evidenced in the annual system competitions of SMT solvers [2,23] and first-order provers [22].

© Springer Nature Switzerland AG 2022
J.-F. Raskin and K. Chatterjee (Eds.): Principles of Systems Design, LNCS 13660, pp. 306–322, 2022.
https://doi.org/10.1007/978-3-031-22337-2_15

Our approach towards automating induction is conceptually different from previous attempts to use induction with superposition [6,8,13], as we are not restricted to specific clause splitting algorithms and heuristics [6], nor are we limited to induction over inductively defined data types using a subterm ordering [8]. As a result, we stay within the standard saturation framework and do not have to introduce constraint clauses, additional predicates, nor change the notion of redundancy as in [8]. In addition, our approach can be used to automate induction over arbitrary, and not just inductively defined, data types, such as integers (Sect. 8). Our work is also fundamentally different from rewrite-based approaches automating induction [3–5,17,19,21], as we do not rely on external algorithms/heuristics to generate subgoals/lemmas of an inductive property. Instead, applications of induction become inference rules of the saturation process, adding instances of appropriate induction schemata. We extend superposition reasoning with new inference rules capturing inductive steps (Sects. 5-7), and optimize the saturation theorem proving process with induction. In addition, we instantiate induction axioms with logically stronger versions of the property being proved and use induction hypotheses as specialized rewrite rules (Sect. 8).

This combination of saturation with induction is very powerful. Our experimental results show that many problems previously unsolved by any system can be solved by our work, some resulting in very complex proofs of program properties and proofs of complex mathematical properties (Sect. 9).

Contributions. This paper serves as *a survey* of our recent progress in automating induction using a first-order theorem prover [9,10,12,18].

- We give a small tutorial of induction in saturation, helping non-experts in theorem proving to understand and further use our methodology. To this end, we describe saturation theorem proving and the main concepts of saturation with induction (Sects. 4–5).
- We overview technical considerations for turning saturation with induction into an efficient approach (Sect. 5) and discuss variants of induction inference rules (Sect. 6).
- We present extensions of induction inference rules with multiple premises (Sect. 7), generalizations and integer reasoning (Sect. 8).
- We report on exhaustive experiments comparing and analysing our approach to state-of-the-art methods (Sect. 9).

2   Motivating Example

We motivate the challenges of automating induction for formal verification using the functional program of Fig. 1(a). This program defines the inductively defined data type **nat** of natural numbers. In first-order logic, this data type corresponds to a term algebra with constructors 0 (zero) and s (successor); inductively defined data types, such as **nat**, are special cases of term algebras. The functional program in Fig. 1(a) implements **add**, **even** and **half** operations over naturals, by using recursive equations (function definitions) preceded by the **fun**

assume even(x)

datatype nat $= 0 \mid$ s(x)

fun add($0, y$) $= y$
  | add(s(z), y) = s(add(z, y));

fun even(0) = $\top$
  | even(s(z)) = $\neg$even(z);

fun half(0) $= 0$
  | half(s(0)) $= 0$
  | half(s(s(z))) = s(half(z));

assert $x =$ add(half(x), half(x))

(a)

Axiomatization of add, even and half:

$\forall y \in$ nat.(add($0, y$) $= y$)

$\forall z, y \in$ nat.(add(s(z), y) = s(add(z, y)))

even(0)

$\forall z \in$ nat.(even(s(z)) $\leftrightarrow \neg$even(z))

half(0) $= 0$

half(s(0)) $= 0$

$\forall z \in$ nat.(half(s(s(z))) = s(half(z)))

Verification task (conjecture):

$\forall x \in$ nat.(even(x) $\rightarrow x =$ add(half(x), half(x)))

(b)

Fig. 1. Motivating example over inductively defined data types.

construct. These recursive equations correspond to universally quantified equalities in first-order logic, as listed in the axioms of Fig. 1(b).

The expected behaviour of Fig. 1(a) is specified using program assertions in first-order logic: the pre-condition using the **assume** construct and the postcondition using **assert**. Figure 1(a) satisfies its requirements. Formally proving correctness of Fig. 1(a) essentially requires proving the conjecture of Fig. 1(b), establishing that half(x) of an **even** natural number x added to half(x) equals the original number x. That is,

$$\forall x \in \text{nat}.\big(\text{even}(x) \rightarrow x = \text{add}(\text{half}(x), \text{half}(x))\big). \tag{1}$$

Proving (1), and thus establishing correctness of Fig. 1(a), is however challenging as it requires induction over the naturals. As such, finding and using an appropriate induction schemata is needed. The following sound *structural induction schema* for a formula F could, for example, be used, where F contains (multiple occurrences of) a natural-valued variable x:

$$\Big(F[0] \wedge \forall z \in \text{nat}.(F[z] \rightarrow F[\text{s}(z)])\Big) \rightarrow \forall x \in \text{nat}.F[x] \tag{2}$$

We instantiate schema (2) by considering $\forall x \in \text{nat}.F(x)$ to be formula (1), yielding the induction formula:

(IB) $\big(\text{even}(0) \rightarrow 0 = \text{add}(\text{half}(0), \text{half}(0))\big) \wedge$

(IS) $\forall z \in \text{nat}. \left(\begin{array}{l} (\text{even}(z) \rightarrow z = \text{add}(\text{half}(z), \text{half}(z))) \rightarrow \\ (\text{even}(\text{s}(z)) \rightarrow \text{s}(z) = \text{add}(\text{half}(\text{s}(z)), \text{half}(\text{s}(z)))) \end{array} \right)$ (3)

  $\rightarrow \forall x \in \text{nat}.\text{even}(x) \rightarrow x = \text{add}(\text{half}(x), \text{half}(x)),$

where the subformulas denoted by (IB) and (IS) correspond to the *induction base case* and the *induction step case* of (3). Since schema (2) is sound, its instance (3) is valid. As such, the task of proving (1) is reduced to proving the base case and step case of (3).

Using the definitions of half and add from Fig. 1(b), the base case (IB) simplifies to the tautology $\top \to 0 = 0$. On the other hand, proving (IS) requires additional inductive reasoning. Yet, the induction scheme (2) cannot be used as $even(z)$ and $even(s(z))$ yield two different base cases. We overcome this limitation by using an additional induction schema with two base cases, as follows:

$$\big(F[0] \wedge F[s(0)] \wedge \forall z.(F[z] \to F[s(s(z))])\big) \to \forall x.F[x] \tag{4}$$

As before, by instantiating (4) with (1) and simplifying based on the axioms of Fig. 1(b), we are left with proving the step case:

$$
\begin{aligned}
\text{(IH)} \quad & \forall z \in \text{nat.}\Big(\big(even(z) \to z = add(half(z), half(z))\big) \to \\
\text{(IC)} \quad & \quad \big(even(s(s(z))) \to s(s(z)) = add(half(s(s(z))), half(s(s(z))))\big)\Big)
\end{aligned}
\tag{5}
$$

The antecedent (IH) and conclusion (IC) of (5) are called the *induction (step) hypothesis* and *induction step conclusion* of the step case, respectively. After rewriting $even(s(s(z)))$ to $even(z)$ in (IC), both (IH) and (IC) have the same assumption $even(z)$, which can be discarded. By rewriting the remaining conclusions in (IH) and (IC) using the definitions of half and add, as well as the injectivity of the term algebra constructor s, we obtain:

$$
\begin{aligned}
\text{(IH)} \quad & \forall z \in \text{nat.}\big(z = add(half(z), half(z)) \to \\
\text{(IC)} \quad & \qquad\qquad s(z) = add(half(z), s(half(z)))\big)
\end{aligned}
\tag{6}
$$

Since the more complex right-hand side of (IH) is not equal to any subterm of (IC) in (6), we have to use (IH) in the left-to-right direction – in order to preserve validity, our only option is to rewrite z on the left-hand side of (IC):

$$\forall z \in \text{nat.}\big(s(add(half(z), half(z))) = add(half(z), s(half(z)))\big) \tag{7}$$

Equation (7) is a special case of the formula $\forall x, y \in \text{nat.}s(add(x,y)) = add(x, s(y))$ which can be easily verified using the induction schema (2). This establishes the correctness of Fig. 1(a).

The verification task of Fig. 1(a) highlights the main difficulties in automating inductive reasoning: (i) incorporating induction into saturation (Sect. 5); (ii) finding suitable induction schemata (Sect. 6); and (iii) using extensions of induction inference rules to further push the boundaries of automating induction (Sects. 7–8). We next present our solutions to these challenges, based on our results from [9,10,12,18].

3   Preliminaries

We assume familiarity with *standard multi-sorted first-order logic with equality*. Functions are denoted with f, g, h, predicates with p, q, r, variables with x, y, z, w, and Skolem constants with σ, all possibly with indices. A term is *ground* if it contains no variables. We use the words *sort* and *type* interchangeably.

We distinguish special sorts called *term algebra sorts*, function symbols for term algebra sorts called *constructors* and *destructors*. For a term algebra sort τ, we denote its constructors with Σ_τ. For each $c \in \Sigma_\tau$, we denote its arity with n_c and the corresponding destructor returning the value of the ith argument of c by d_c^i. Moreover, we denote with P_c the set of argument positions of c of the sort τ. We say that c is a *recursive constructor* if P_c is non-empty, otherwise it is called a *base constructor*. We call the ground terms built from the constructor symbols of a sort its *term algebra*. We axiomatise term algebras using their *injectivity*, *distinctness*, *exhaustiveness* and *acyclicity* axioms [14]. We refer to term algebras also as algebraic data types or inductively defined data types. Additionally, we assume a distinguished *integer sort*, denoted by $\mathbb{Z}$. When we use standard integer predicates $<, \leq, >, \geq$, functions $+, -, \ldots$ and constants $0, 1, \ldots$, we assume that they denote the corresponding interpreted integer predicates and functions with their standard interpretations. All other symbols are uninterpreted.

We use the standard logical connectives $\neg, \vee, \wedge, \rightarrow$ and $\leftrightarrow$, and quantifiers $\forall$ and $\exists$. We write quantifiers like $\forall x \in \tau$ to denote that x has the sort τ where it is not clear from the context. A *literal* is an atom or its negation. For a literal L, we write $\overline{L}$ to denote its complementary literal. A disjunction of literals is a *clause*. We denote clauses by C, D and reserve the symbol $\square$ for the *empty clause* which is logically equivalent to $\bot$. We denote the *clausal normal form* of a formula F by $\mathtt{cnf}(F)$. We call every term, literal, clause or formula an *expression*.

We write $E[s]$ to denote that the expression E contains k distinguished occurrence(s) of the term s, with $k \geq 0$. For simplicity, $E[t]$ means that these occurrences of s are replaced by the term t. A *substitution* θ is a mapping from variables to terms. A substitution θ is a *unifier* of two terms s and t if $s\theta = t\theta$, and is a *most general unifier* (*mgu*) if for every unifier η of s and t, there exists substitution μ s.t. $\eta = \theta\mu$. We denote the mgu of s and t with $\mathtt{mgu}(s, t)$.

4   Saturation-Based Theorem Proving

We briefly introduce saturation-based proof search, which is the leading technology for automated first-order theorem proving. For details, we refer to [15].

First-order theorem provers work with clauses, rather than with arbitrary formulas. Given a set S of input clauses, first-order provers *saturate* S by computing all logical consequences of S with respect to a sound inference system $\mathcal{I}$. The saturated set of S is called the *closure* of S and the process of computing the closure of S is called *saturation*. If the closure of S contains the empty clause $\square$, the original set S of clauses is unsatisfiable. A simplified saturation algorithm for a sound inference system $\mathcal{I}$ is given in Algorithm 1, with a clausified goal B ($\neg B$ is also clausified) and clausified assumptions A as input.

Note that a saturation algorithm proves validity of B by establishing unsatisfiabiliy of $\neg B$ using the assumptions A; we refer to this proving process as a *refutation* of $\neg B$ from A. Completeness and efficiency of saturation-based reasoning rely heavily on properties of selection and addition of clauses from/to S, using the inference system $\mathcal{I}$ (lines 3–5). To organize saturation, first-order

Algorithm 1. The Saturation Loop.

```
1  initial set of clauses S := A ∪ {¬B}
2  repeat
3     Select clause G ∈ S
4     Derive consequences C₁,...,Cₙ of G and formulas from S using rules of 𝓘
5     S := S ∪ {C₁,...,Cₙ}
6     if □ ∈ S then return  A → B is UNSAT
8  return  A → B is SAT
```

Superposition:

$$\frac{l = r \vee C \quad L[l'] \vee D}{(L[r] \vee C \vee D)\theta} \qquad \frac{l = r \vee C \quad s[l'] \neq t \vee D}{(s[r] \neq t \vee C \vee D)\theta} \qquad \frac{l = r \vee C \quad s[l'] = t \vee D}{(s[r] = t \vee C \vee D)\theta}$$

where $\theta := \mathtt{mgu}(l, l')$, $r\theta \not\succeq l\theta$, (first rule only) $L[l']$ is not an equality literal, and (second and third rules only) $t\theta \not\succeq s[l']\theta$.

Binary resolution:	**Equality resolution:**	**Equality factoring:**

$$\frac{L \vee C \quad \neg L' \vee D}{(C \vee D)\theta} \qquad\qquad \frac{s \neq t \vee C}{C\theta} \qquad\qquad \frac{s = t \vee s' = t' \vee C}{(s = t \vee t \neq t' \vee C)\theta}$$

where $\theta := \mathtt{mgu}(L, L')$. where $\theta := \mathtt{mgu}(s, t)$. where $\theta := \mathtt{mgu}(s, s')$, $t\theta \not\succeq s\theta$, and $t'\theta \not\succeq t\theta$.

Fig. 2. The superposition calculus $\mathbb{S}$up for first-order logic with equality.

provers use simplification *orderings* on terms, which are extended to orderings over literals and clauses; for simplicity, we write $\succ$ for both the term ordering and its clause/multiset ordering extensions. Given an ordering $\succ$, a clause C is *redundant* with respect to a set S of clauses if there exists a subset S' of S such that S' is smaller than $\{C\}$, that is $\{C\} \succ S'$ and $S' \to C$.

The *superposition calculus*, denoted as $\mathbb{S}$up, is the most common inference system employed by saturation-based first-order theorem provers for first-order logic with equality [16]. A summary of superposition inference rules is given in Fig. 2. The superposition calculus $\mathbb{S}$up is *sound* and *refutationally complete*: for any unsatisfiable formula $\neg B$, the empty clause can be derived as a logical consequence of $\neg B$.

5 Saturation with Induction

We now describe our approach towards automating inductive reasoning within saturation-based proof search. We illustrate the key ingredients of our method using our motivating example from Fig. 1(a), that is proving (1) in order to establish correctness of Fig. 1(a). As mentioned in Sect. 4, proving (1) in a saturation-based approach means refuting the clausified negation of (1), that is, refuting the following two clauses:

$$\text{even}(\sigma_0) \tag{8}$$

$$\sigma_0 \neq \text{add}(\text{half}(\sigma_0), \text{half}(\sigma_0)) \tag{9}$$

We establish invalidity of inductive formulas, such as (8)–(9), by *integrating the application of induction as additional inference rules of the saturation process*. Our induction inference rules are used directly in Algorithm 1, as follows:

(i) we pick up an inductive property G in the search space S (line 3);
(ii) derive new induction axioms $C_1, \ldots, C_n$ (instances of *induction schemata*), aiming at refuting G, or sometimes a more general formula than G (line 4);
(iii) add the induction axioms $C_1, \ldots, C_n$ to the search space (line 5).

Our work therefore follows a different approach than the one used in inductive theorem provers, as we do not rely on external algorithms to generate subgoals/stronger formulas G' of an inductive property G nor do we replace G by subgoals/stronger formulas G'. Rather, new induction axioms C_i, and sometimes new induction axioms C_i' for more general formulas G', are derived from G and used in the search space S *in addition* to G.

Finding the right induction schema and developing efficient induction inference rules for deriving inductive axioms/formulas (steps (i)–(ii) above) are crucial for saturation with induction. In [18] we introduced the following induction inference rule, parametrized by a valid induction schema:

$$\frac{\overline{L}[t] \vee C}{\text{cnf}(F \to \forall x.L[x])} \text{ (Ind)},$$

where t is a ground term, L is a ground literal, C is a clause, and $F \to \forall x.L[x]$ is a valid induction schema. For example, the induction schema (2) for F can be used in (Ind). We call $\overline{L}[t]$ the *induction literal* and t the *induction term*. We note that (Ind) can naturally be generalized to handle multiple induction terms, as in [9]. In this paper, we only use the rule with one induction term.

Based on Algorithm 1 (the saturation-based proof search algorithm), note that the application of (Ind) adds new clauses to the search space by clausifying induction formulas (cnf() in (Ind)). These new clauses then become potential candidates to be selected in the next steps of the algorithm. As such, the selection of these new clauses are likely to be delayed, and thus their use in proving an inductive goal becomes highly inefficient. We therefore propose the application of (Ind) followed by a binary resolution step to "guide" induction over selected induction literals and terms. In particular, upon the application of (Ind), we do not add $\text{cnf}(F \to \forall x.L[x])$ to the search space. Instead, we binary resolve the conclusion literal $L[x]$ against $\overline{L}[t]$, allowing us to only add the formula $\text{cnf}(\neg F) \vee C$ to the search space, whenever (Ind) is applied.

In order to "guide" and combine the application of (Ind) with a binary resolution rule, we exploit instances of (Ind) for special cases of induction schemata over term algebras (Sect. 6) and integers (Sect. 8). We also consider extension of (Ind) for more general and efficient inductive reasoning (Sects. 7–8).

6   Induction with Term Algebras

We first consider the theory of term algebras and introduce instances of the induction rule (Ind), by exploiting properties of the induction literal $\overline{L}[t]$ and induction schemata over the induction term t. For now, the induction term t is a ground element from a term algebra.

Structural Induction. The first instance of (Ind) uses the following constructor-based structural induction schema, where $L[x]$ is a literal containing (possibly multiple occurrences of) x of a term algebra sort τ:

$$\Big(\bigwedge_{c \in \Sigma_\tau} \forall y_1, ..., y_{n_c}.(\wedge_{i \in P_c} L[y_i] \to L[c(y_1, ..., y_{n_c})])\Big) \to \forall x \in \tau.L[x] \qquad (10)$$

Note that the structural induction schema (2) over naturals is an instance of (10).

Example 1. By instantiating schema (10) with the sole literal of clause (9) and induction term σ_0, we obtain:

$$\left(\forall z \in \mathbf{nat}. \begin{pmatrix} 0 = \mathtt{add}(\mathtt{half}(0), \mathtt{half}(0)) \wedge \\ z = \mathtt{add}(\mathtt{half}(z), \mathtt{half}(z)) \to \\ \mathtt{s}(z) = \mathtt{add}(\mathtt{half}(\mathtt{s}(z)), \mathtt{half}(\mathtt{s}(z))) \end{pmatrix} \right) \to \forall x \in \mathbf{nat}.\begin{pmatrix} x = \\ \mathtt{add}(\mathtt{half}(x), \mathtt{half}(x)) \end{pmatrix}$$

$$(11)$$

The clausified form of (11) consists of the following two clauses:

$0 \neq \mathtt{add}(\mathtt{half}(0), \mathtt{half}(0)) \vee \sigma_1 = \mathtt{add}(\mathtt{half}(\sigma_1), \mathtt{half}(\sigma_1)) \vee x = \mathtt{add}(\mathtt{half}(x), \mathtt{half}(x))$

$0 \neq \mathtt{add}(\mathtt{half}(0), \mathtt{half}(0)) \vee \mathtt{s}(\sigma_1) \neq \mathtt{add}(\mathtt{half}(\mathtt{s}(\sigma_1)), \mathtt{half}(\mathtt{s}(\sigma_1)))$

$$\vee \, x = \mathtt{add}(\mathtt{half}(x), \mathtt{half}(x))$$

After applying (Ind) instantiated with (11) on (9), the above clauses are resolved with the literal in clause (9), adding to the search space the resulting clauses:

$0 \neq \mathtt{add}(\mathtt{half}(0), \mathtt{half}(0)) \vee \sigma_1 = \mathtt{add}(\mathtt{half}(\sigma_1), \mathtt{half}(\sigma_1))$

$0 \neq \mathtt{add}(\mathtt{half}(0), \mathtt{half}(0)) \vee \mathtt{s}(\sigma_1) \neq \mathtt{add}(\mathtt{half}(\mathtt{s}(\sigma_1)), \mathtt{half}(\mathtt{s}(\sigma_1)))$ □

Well-Founded Induction. Two other instances of (Ind) exploit well-founded induction schemata, by using a binary well-founded relation R on a term algebra τ. For such an R, if there does not exists a smallest value $v \in \tau$ w.r.t. R such that $L[v]$ does not hold, then $L[x]$ holds for any $x \in \tau$. This principle is formalized by the following schema:

$$\Big(\neg \exists y \in \tau.\big(\neg L[y] \wedge \forall z \in \tau.(R(y, z) \to L[z])\big) \Big) \to \forall x \in \tau.L[x] \qquad (12)$$

However, to instantiate (12), we need to find an R suitable for the considered τ.

Similarly to [19], we first consider the direct subterm relation expressed using term algebra constructors and destructors of the term algebra sort τ. We obtain the following instance of (12) to be applied in (Ind):

$$\Big(\neg \exists y.\big(\neg L[y] \wedge \bigwedge_{c \in \Sigma_\tau} (y = c(d_c^1(y), \dots, d_c^{n_c}(y)) \to \bigwedge_{i \in P_c} L[d_c^i(y)])\big) \Big) \to \forall x.L[x]$$

$$(13)$$

In the case of natural numbers, where p is the destructor for s, we have the following instance of (13) to be used in (Ind):

$$\left(\neg \exists y \in \mathbf{nat}.(\neg L[y] \wedge (y = \mathbf{s}(\mathbf{p}(y)) \rightarrow L[\mathbf{p}(y)]))\right) \rightarrow \forall x \in \mathbf{nat}.L[x] \qquad (14)$$

Another instance of (12) to be used in (Ind) employs a fresh predicate $\mathtt{less}_y$, as given next. The axiomatisation of such a predicate enables efficient reasoning over subterm properties withing saturation, as advocated in [14].

$$\begin{aligned} \left(\neg \exists y.(\neg F[y] \wedge \forall z.(\mathtt{less}_y(z) \rightarrow F[z]) \wedge (y = \mathbf{s}(\mathbf{p}(y)) \rightarrow \mathtt{less}_y(\mathbf{p}(y)))\right. \\ \left. \wedge \forall w.(\mathtt{less}_y(\mathbf{s}(\mathbf{p}(w))) \rightarrow \mathtt{less}_y(\mathbf{p}(w))))\right) \rightarrow \forall x.F[x] \end{aligned} \qquad (15)$$

Induction with Recursive Function Definitions. In formalizing the induction schemata instances given e.g. in (2) and (14), we considered the term algebra **nat** as an instance of τ. To come up with the "right" term algebra instance of τ, we can also use terminating recursive function definitions from the input problem to be proven, such as **add**, **even** and **half** from Fig. 1(a). The termination of such recursive functions naturally depends on a well-founded relation R.

Example 2. We can obtain schema (4) from **half** in Fig. 1(b) if we consider the well-founded relation based on its first argument. In particular, the third branch of **half** relates its first argument $\mathbf{s}(\mathbf{s}(z))$ to z in its recursive call for all $z \in \mathbf{nat}$. This relation gives the step case of schema (4), and the base cases can be obtained by considering the terms in the first argument positions for the other two branches of **half**.

Thus, based on the term $\mathtt{half}(\sigma_0)$ in clause (9), we can instantiate (4) inducting on term σ_0. However, this induction axiom does not yet lead to a refutation of (1), because for each clausified induction axiom, new Skolem constants are introduced. Thus, the literals in clauses resulting from applying (Ind) on (8) or (9), respectively, do not contain σ_0, and hence we cannot use (9) nor (8), respectively, to refute them. In the next section we therefore generalize (Ind) towards the use of induction schemata with multiple clauses.   □

7 Multi-clause Induction

Inducting on a single literal is sometimes not sufficient to get a refutation, as illustrated in Example 2 for Fig. 1(a). In general however, induction can be applied on literals from multiple clauses, similarly to formula (3) in Sect. 2. We generalize the inference rule (Ind) towards multi-clause induction (IndMC):

$$\frac{L_1[t] \vee C_1 \quad \dots \quad L_n[t] \vee C_n \quad \overline{L}[t] \vee C}{\mathtt{cnf}(F \rightarrow \forall x.(\bigwedge_{1 \leq i \leq n} L_i[x] \rightarrow L[x]))} \text{ (IndMC)}$$

where $F \rightarrow \forall x.(\bigwedge_{1 \leq i \leq n} L_i[x] \rightarrow L[x])$ is a valid induction formula, $\overline{L}$ and L_i are ground literals and C and C_i are clauses. Similarly to (Ind), our new rule (IndMC) is used within saturation-based proof as an additional inference rule, followed by an application of binary resolution for guiding inductive reasoning.

Example 3. We use schema (4) with formula (1) with induction term σ_0 to instantiate (IndMC) for premises (8) and (9). The induction formula is:

$$\left(\forall z \in \mathbf{nat}. \left(\begin{array}{c} \big(\mathtt{even}(0) \to 0 = \mathtt{add}(\mathtt{half}(0), \mathtt{half}(0))\big) \wedge \\ \big(\mathtt{even}(\mathtt{s}(0)) \to \mathtt{s}(0) = \mathtt{add}(\mathtt{half}(\mathtt{s}(0)), \mathtt{half}(\mathtt{s}(0)))\big) \wedge \\ \big(\mathtt{even}(z) \to z = \mathtt{add}(\mathtt{half}(z), \mathtt{half}(z))\big) \to \\ \big(\mathtt{even}(\mathtt{s}(\mathtt{s}(z))) \to \mathtt{s}(\mathtt{s}(z)) = \mathtt{add}(\mathtt{half}(\mathtt{s}(\mathtt{s}(z))), \mathtt{half}(\mathtt{s}(\mathtt{s}(z))))\big) \end{array} \right) \right) \qquad (16)$$
$$\to \forall x \in \mathbf{nat}.\big(\mathtt{even}(x) \to x = \mathtt{add}(\mathtt{half}(x), \mathtt{half}(x))\big)$$

Clausification of formula (16) results in twelve clauses, each containing the literals $\neg\mathtt{even}(x)$ and $x = \mathtt{add}(\mathtt{half}(x), \mathtt{half}(x))$, which we can binary resolve with clauses (8) and (9). After simplifications are applied to the clauses from formula (16), we are left with the following two clauses:

$$\sigma_2 = \mathtt{add}(\mathtt{half}(\sigma_2), \mathtt{half}(\sigma_2)) \qquad (17)$$

$$\mathtt{s}(\sigma_2) \neq \mathtt{add}(\mathtt{half}(\sigma_2), \mathtt{s}(\mathtt{half}(\sigma_2))) \qquad (18)$$

We now need to rewrite (18) with the induction hypothesis clause (17) in the left-to-right orientation. However, $\sigma_2 \prec \mathtt{add}(\mathtt{half}(\sigma_2), \mathtt{half}(\sigma_2))$, which holds for any simplification ordering $\prec$, contradicts the superposition ordering conditions. Moreover, even if we rewrote against the ordering, we would be left with

$$\mathtt{s}(\mathtt{add}(\mathtt{half}(\sigma_2), \mathtt{half}(\sigma_2))) \neq \mathtt{add}(\mathtt{half}(\sigma_2), \mathtt{s}(\mathtt{half}(\sigma_2))), \qquad (19)$$

which is hard to refute using induction due to the induction term σ_2 occurring in the second argument of $\mathtt{add}$, which does not change in the recursive definition of $\mathtt{add}$ (see Fig. 1(b)). We overcome this limitation by extensions of inductive reasoning in Sect. 8.   □

8   Extensions of Inductions in Saturation

Induction with Generalizations. It is common in mathematics that for proving a formula A, we prove instead a formula B such that $B \to A$. In other words, we prove a *generalization* B of A. Inductive theorem provers implement various heuristics to *guess formulas/lemmas* B and use B instead of A during proof search, see e.g. [3–5,17]. However, a saturation-based theorem prover would not/can not do this, since goals/conjectures are not replaced by sub-goals in saturation-based proof search. We thus propose a different approach for implementing the common generalization recipe of mathematical theorem proving. Namely, we introduce the inference rule (IndGen) of *induction with generalization*, allowing us to (i) add instances of induction schemata not only for A but also for versions of B and then (ii) perform saturation over these induction schemata instances, using superposition reasoning. Our (IndGen) rule inducts only on *some* occurrences of the induction term t, as follows:

$$\frac{\overline{L}[t] \vee C}{\mathtt{cnf}(F \to \forall x.L'[x])} \text{ (IndGen)},$$

where t is a ground term, L is a ground literal, C is a clause, $F \to \forall x.L'[x]$ is a valid induction schema and $L'[x]$ is obtained from $L[t]$ by replacing some occurrences of t with x.

Example 4. We illustrate induction with generalization on the unit clause (19). One generalization that would help refute (19) by eliminating $\mathtt{half}(\sigma_2)$ is:

$$\forall x, y \in \mathtt{nat}.\mathtt{s}(\mathtt{add}(x,y)) = \mathtt{add}(x, \mathtt{s}(y)) \qquad (20)$$

Instantiating schema (2) with (20) and variable x would lead to a refutation when used with rule $(\mathtt{IndGen})$ on (19). However, since we do not use y from the generalization in the induction, there is no need to replace the occurrences of $\mathtt{half}(\sigma_2)$ corresponding to it in the generalized literal. Our final generalized induction formula, also leading to the refutation of (19), is:

$$\left(\forall z \in \mathtt{nat}. \left(\begin{array}{l} \mathtt{s}(\mathtt{add}(0, \mathtt{half}(\sigma_2))) = \mathtt{add}(0, \mathtt{s}(\mathtt{half}(\sigma_2))) \wedge \\ \mathtt{s}(\mathtt{add}(z, \mathtt{half}(\sigma_2))) = \mathtt{add}(z, \mathtt{s}(\mathtt{half}(\sigma_2))) \to \\ \mathtt{s}(\mathtt{add}(\mathtt{s}(z), \mathtt{half}(\sigma_2))) = \mathtt{add}(\mathtt{s}(z), \mathtt{s}(\mathtt{half}(\sigma_2))) \end{array} \right) \right) \qquad (21)$$
$$\to \forall x \in \mathtt{nat}.\mathtt{s}(\mathtt{add}(x, \mathtt{half}(\sigma_2))) = \mathtt{add}(x, \mathtt{s}(\mathtt{half}(\sigma_2))) \qquad \square$$

Rewriting with Induction Hypotheses. For turning saturation-based proof search into an efficient process, one key ingredient is to ensure that bigger terms/literals are rewritten by small ones (big/small w.r.t. the simplification ordering $\succ$), and not vice versa. However, this often prohibits using induction hypotheses to rewrite their corresponding conclusions which would be the necessary step to proceed with the proof, To overcome this obstacle, we introduce the following inference rule which uses an induction hypothesis literal to rewrite its conclusion:

$$\frac{l = r \vee D \quad s[l] \neq t \vee C}{\mathtt{cnf}(F \to \forall x.(s[r] = t)[x])} \; (\mathtt{IndHRW})$$

where $s[l] \neq t$ is an induction conclusion literal with corresponding induction hypothesis literal $l = r$, $l \not\succ r$, and $F \to \forall x.(s[r] = t)[x]$ is a valid induction formula. Moreover, we resolve the clauses with the intermediate clause $s[r] \neq t \vee C \vee D$, obtained from the rewriting of the premises of $(\mathtt{IndHRW})$.

Example 5. Using unit clause (17) in a left-to-right orientation and rewriting the sides of unit clause (18) one after the other, we get intermediate clauses, which are then used for generating induction formulas. One such intermediate clause is (19), from which the induction formula (21) is generated. After clausifying (21), a subsequent binary resolution is performed with intermediate clause (19). By more simplifications using the definition of $\mathtt{add}$ and the injectivity of $\mathtt{s}$, we finally obtain a refutation of (1), concluding thus the correctness of Fig. 1(a). $\qquad \square$

Integer Induction. The last extension of our induction framework we introduce is *integer induction*, motivated by the need of inductive reasoning in program analysis and verification problems using integers. As the standard order $<$ (or

$>$) over integers $\mathbb{Z}$ is not well-founded, we work with *subsets of $\mathbb{Z}$ with a lower (and/or an upper) bound*. We therefore define the *downward, respectively upward, induction schema with symbolic bound b* as any formula of the form:

$$F[b] \land \forall y \in \mathbb{Z}.(y \leq b \land F[y] \rightarrow F[y-1]) \rightarrow \forall x \in \mathbb{Z}.(x \leq b \rightarrow F[x]); (downward)$$
$$F[b] \land \forall y \in \mathbb{Z}.(y \geq b \land F[y] \rightarrow F[y+1]) \rightarrow \forall x \in \mathbb{Z}.(x \geq b \rightarrow F[x]), (upward)$$

respectively, where $F[x]$ is a formula with one or more occurrences of an integer variable x and b is an integer term not containing x nor y. Further, we also define *interval downward, respectively upward, induction schema with symbolic bounds b_1, b_2* as any formula of the form:

$$F[b_2] \land \forall y \in \mathbb{Z}.(b_1 < y \leq b_2 \land F[y] \rightarrow F[y-1]) \rightarrow \forall x \in \mathbb{Z}.(b_1 \leq x \leq b_2 \rightarrow F[x]); (down.)$$
$$F[b_1] \land \forall y \in \mathbb{Z}.(b_1 \leq y < b_2 \land F[y] \rightarrow F[y+1]) \rightarrow \forall x \in \mathbb{Z}.(b_1 \leq x \leq b_2 \rightarrow F[x]), (up.)$$

respectively, where $F[x]$ is a formula with one or more occurrences of an integer variable x and b_1, b_2 are integer terms not containing x nor y.[1]

To automate inductive reasoning over integers, we need to automatically generate suitable instances of our integer induction schemata. To this end we introduce induction rules with the integer induction schemata in the conclusion, giving us the recipe for instantiating the schemata. Since our schemata are sound, all resulting induction rules are sound as well. When t, b are ground terms and $L[t]$ is a ground literal, the following is an *integer upward induction rule*:

$$\frac{\overline{L}[t] \lor C \quad t \geq b}{\mathtt{cnf}\Big(\big(L[b] \land \forall y \in \mathbb{Z}.(y \geq b \land L[y] \rightarrow L[y+1])\big) \rightarrow \forall x \in \mathbb{Z}.(x \geq b \rightarrow L[x])\Big)} (\mathtt{IntInd}_{\geq})$$

Our further integer induction rules using the other schemata are obtained similarly, as detailed in [12].

9 Implementation and Experiments

9.1 Implementation

Our approach for automating induction in saturation is implemented in the VAMPIRE prover. All together, our implementation consists of around 7,800 lines of C++ code and is available online at https://github.com/vprover/vampire/tree/int-induction. In the following, VAMPIRE* refers to the VAMPIRE version supporting induction.

Our induction rules allow us to derive many new clauses potentially leading to refutation of inductive properties. These new clauses – especially in combination with theory reasoning in case of integer induction – might however pollute the search space without advancing the proof. We therefore introduce options to control the use of induction rules by inducting only on negative literals, unit clauses or clauses derived from the goal. Further, for induction over algebraic

---

[1] The above schemata can be seen as a special case of the multi-clause schemata used in the (IndMC) rule from Sect. 7, tailored specifically for integers.

Table 1. Selected induction options or VAMPIRE. Default values are underlined.

Name & comma-separated values	Description
`--induction int, struct, both, none`	Enable induction on integers only, or induction on algebraic types only, or both, or none
`--induction_on_complex_terms on, off`	Apply induction also on complex terms
`--induction_multiclause   on, off`	Enable the (IndMC) form of induction rules
`--induction_gen         on, off`	Enable the (IndGen) form of induction rules

types, we only allow induction on terms containing a constant other than a base constructor. For integer induction, by default we disable rules with default bound, induction on interpreted constants, and induction on some comparison literals. Our most relevant induction options are summarized in Table 1.[2]

9.2   Experimental Setup

The main goal of our experiments was to evaluate how much induction improves VAMPIRE's performance. We therefore compared VAMPIRE* to VAMPIRE without induction. We also show the numbers of problems solved by the SMT solvers CVC4 [19], Z3 [7], where only CVC4 supports induction. In our experiments, we do not include other provers, such as ACL2 [3] or ZIPPERPOSITION [6], as these solvers do not support the SMT-LIB input format [1]; yet for further comparison we refer to [9,10,12].

We ran our experiments using (i) benchmarks over inductive data types (UFDT set of the SMT-LIB benchmark library and *dty* set of the inductive benchmarks [11]), (ii) benchmarks using integers (LIA, UFLIA, NIA and UFNIA of SMT-LIB and *int* of [11]), and (iii) benchmarks using both integers and data types (UFDTLIA of SMT-LIB). From these datasets, we excluded those problems that are marked satisfiable, as our work is meant for validity checking[3]

For our experiments, we used Z3 version 4.8.12 in the default configuration, and CVC4 version 1.8 with parameters `--conjecture-gen --quant-ind`. To extensively compare VAMPIRE and VAMPIRE*, we ran multiple instances of both for each experiment: we used a portfolio of 18 base configurations differing in the parameters not related to induction. Additionally, we varied the induction parameters of VAMPIRE* for each experiment: for (i) we used `--induction struct --structural_induction_kind one --induction_gen on -induction_on_complex_terms on`, for (ii) `--induction int --induction_multiclause off`, for (iii) `--induction both --structural_induction_kind one --induction_gen on -induction_on_complex_terms on`. In experiments (ii)

---

[2] VAMPIRE also offers a so-called portfolio mode, in which it sequentially tries different option configurations for short amounts of time.

[3] we have excluded all together 1562 satisfiable problems from LIA, UFLIA, NIA and UFNIA; and 86 satisfiable problems from UFDT.

Table 2. Comparison of the number of solved problems. The configuration of VAMPIRE and VAMPIRE* depends on the benchmark set.

Problem set	SMT-LIB						ind. set [11]		Sum
	UFDT	UFDTLIA	LIA	UFLIA	NIA	UFNIA	*dty*	*int*	
Total count	4483	327	404	10118	8	12181	3397	120	31038
VAMPIRE	1848	82	241	6125	3	3704	17	0	12020
VAMPIRE*	1792	186	241	6240	4	3679	464	76	12682
CVC4	2072	200	357	6911	7	3022	164	30	12763
Z3	1807	76	242	6710	2	4938	17	0	13792

and (iii), for each of the 18 base configurations we ran 7 instances of VAMPIRE* with different integer induction parameters, chosen based on preliminary experimentation on a smaller set of benchmarks. Each prover configuration was given 10 s and 16 GB of memory per each problem. The experiments were ran on computers with 32 cores (AMD Epyc 7502, 2.5 GHz) and 1 TB RAM.

9.3 Experimental Results

Results Overview. Our results are summarized in Table 2. For VAMPIRE and VAMPIRE* we show the number of problems solved by the most successful configuration. Note that for different benchmark sets the most successful configurations might be different. In the inductive problems, the maximum and average numbers of induction steps in a proof were 20 and 1.54, respectively, and the maximum number of nested induction steps was 9. Overall, Table 2 shows that VAMPIRE* outperforms VAMPIRE without induction. Moreover, VAMPIRE* is competitive with leading SMT solvers.

Comparison of VAMPIRE *and* VAMPIRE*. To evaluate the impact of inductive reasoning in VAMPIRE, we look at two key metrics: the *overall number of solved problems*; and the *number of newly solved problems*, which we define as the number of problems solved using induction[4] by some VAMPIRE*, but not solved by any VAMPIRE. The latter metric is especially important, since in practice, one can run multiple solvers or configurations in parallel, and thereby solve the union of all problems solved by individual solvers.

Table 3 summarizes our result. Column "Combined" lists the number of problems solved by any instance of the configuration, and in the parentheses the number of problems newly solved by the configuration. The other columns (most

---

[4] New rules change proof search organization and VAMPIRE* might solve a problem without using induction, while this problem was not solved by VAMPIRE. We do not consider such problems to be newly solved.

Table 3. Comparison of VAMPIRE and VAMPIRE* configurations; numbers given (in parentheses) indicate new problems solved using induction but not without induction.

Benchmarks	Configurations	Combined	Most solved	Most new	Default mode
UFDT	VAMPIRE	2082	1848	–	1827
	VAMPIRE*	2047	1792 (12)	1754 (17)	1761
dty	VAMPIRE	17	17	–	17
	VAMPIRE*	525	464 (453)	464 (453)	432
LIA, UFLIA,	VAMPIRE	11260	10073	–	9835
NIA, UFNIA	VAMPIRE*	11334 (81)	10051 (0)	9006 (41)	9773 (0)
int	VAMPIRE	0	0	–	0
	VAMPIRE*	118 (118)	76 (76)	76 (76)	49 (49)
UFDTLIA	VAMPIRE	91	82	–	65
	VAMPIRE*	197 (108)	186 (101)	186 (101)	136 (72)

solved, most new, default mode) give the numbers of solved problems, and in parentheses newly solved problems, for the corresponding VAMPIRE/VAMPIRE* instance. The "Default mode" columns shows results for the best induction configuration with all non-induction parameters set to default.

Induction helped most with the `dty`, `int` and UFDTLIA benchmark sets, as these sets contain a lot of problems focused on induction (induction was used in 91% of proofs for problems in `dty`, in all proofs in `int`, and in 71% of proofs in UFDTLIA), while the other sets contain a wide variety of problems (induction was only used in 2% of proofs in UFDT and 8.8% of proofs in LIA, UFLIA, NIA and UFNIA). Interestingly, the configuration which solved most problems in `int` solved the least in LIA, UFLIA, NIA, UFNIA combined, what illustrates the difficulty in choosing the right values for integer induction parameters for such a mixed benchmark set.

10   Conclusion

Motivated by application of program analysis and verification, we describe recent advances in automating inductive reasoning about first-order (program) properties using inductively defined data types and beyond. We integrate induction in the saturation-based proof engine of first-order theorem provers, without radical changes in the existing machinery of such provers. Our inductive inference rules and heuristics open up new research directions to be further studied in automating induction. Guiding and further extending the application of multi-clause induction with theory-specific induction schema variants is an interesting line of research. Combining induction schemas and rules and using lemma generation and rewriting procedures from inductive theorem provers are another ways to further improve saturation-based inductive reasoning.

Acknowledgements. We thank Johannes Schoisswohl for joint work related on experimenting with inductive theorem provers. This work was partially funded by the ERC CoG ARTIST 101002685, the EPSRC grant EP/P03408X/1, the FWF grant LogiCS W1255-N23, the Amazon ARA 2020 award FOREST and the TU Wien SecInt DK.

References

1. Barrett, C., Fontaine, P., Tinelli, C.: The Satisfiability Modulo Theories Library (SMT-LIB). www.SMT-LIB.org (2016)
2. Barrett, C., de Moura, L., Stump, A.: SMT-COMP: satisfiability modulo theories competition. In: Etessami, K., Rajamani, S.K. (eds.) CAV 2005. LNCS, vol. 3576, pp. 20–23. Springer, Heidelberg (2005). https://doi.org/10.1007/11513988_4
3. Boyer, R.S., Moore, J.S.: A Computational Logic Handbook. Academic Press (1988). https://doi.org/10.1016/C2013-0-10412-6
4. Bundy, A., Stevens, A., Harmelen, F.V., Ireland, A., Smaill, A.: Rippling: a heuristic for guiding inductive proofs. Artif. Intell. **62**, 185–253 (1993). https://doi.org/10.1016/0004-3702(93)90079-Q
5. Claessen, K., Johansson, M., Rosén, D., Smallbone, N.: Automating inductive proofs using theory exploration. In: Bonacina, M.P. (ed.) CADE-24. LNCS (LNAI), vol. 7898, pp. 392–406. Springer, Heidelberg (2013). https://doi.org/10.1007/978-3-642-38574-2_27
6. Cruanes, S.: Superposition with structural induction. In: Dixon, C., Finger, M. (eds.) Superposition with Structural Induction. LNCS (LNAI), vol. 10483, pp. 172–188. Springer, Cham (2017). https://doi.org/10.1007/978-3-319-66167-4_10
7. de Moura, L., Bjørner, N.: Z3: An Efficient SMT Solver. In: Ramakrishnan, C.R., Rehof, J. (eds.) TACAS 2008. LNCS, vol. 4963, pp. 337–340. Springer, Heidelberg (2008). https://doi.org/10.1007/978-3-540-78800-3_24
8. Echenheim, M., Peltier, N.: Combining induction and saturation-based theorem proving. J. Automated Reasoning **64**, 253–294 (2020)
9. Hajdu, M., Hozzová, P., Kovács, L., Voronkov, A.: Induction with recursive definitions in superposition. In: 2021 Formal Methods in Computer Aided Design (FMCAD), pp. 1–10 (2021). https://doi.org/10.34727/2021/isbn.978-3-85448-046-4_34
10. Hajdú, M., Hozzová, P., Kovács, L., Schoisswohl, J., Voronkov, A.: Induction with generalization in superposition reasoning. In: Benzmüller, C., Miller, B. (eds.) CICM 2020. LNCS (LNAI), vol. 12236, pp. 123–137. Springer, Cham (2020). https://doi.org/10.1007/978-3-030-53518-6_8
11. Hajdu, M., Hozzová, P., Kovács, L., Schoisswohl, J., Voronkov, A.: Inductive benchmarks for automated reasoning. In: Kamareddine, F., Sacerdoti Coen, C. (eds.) CICM 2021. LNCS (LNAI), vol. 12833, pp. 124–129. Springer, Cham (2021). https://doi.org/10.1007/978-3-030-81097-9_9
12. Hozzová, P., Kovács, L., Voronkov, A.: Integer Induction in Saturation. In: Platzer, A., Sutcliffe, G. (eds.) CADE 2021. LNCS (LNAI), vol. 12699, pp. 361–377. Springer, Cham (2021). https://doi.org/10.1007/978-3-030-79876-5_21
13. Kersani, A., Peltier, N.: Combining superposition and induction: a practical realization. In: Proceedings of FroCoS, pp. 7–22 (2013)
14. Kovács, L., Robillard, S., Voronkov, A.: Coming to terms with quantified reasoning. In: Castagna, G., Gordon, A.D. (eds.) POPL, pp. 260–270 (2017). https://doi.org/10.1145/3093333.3009887

15. Kovács, L., Voronkov, A.: First-order theorem proving and Vampire. In: Sharygina, N., Veith, H. (eds.) CAV, pp. 1–35. Springer (2013)
16. Nieuwenhuis, R., Rubio, A.: Paramodulation-based theorem proving. In: Robinson, J.A., Voronkov, A. (eds.) Handbook of Automated Reasoning, vol. I, chap. 7, pp. 371–443. North-Holland (2001)
17. Passmore, G., Cruanes, S., Ignatovich, D., Aitken, D., Bray, M., Kagan, E., Kanishev, K., Maclean, E., Mometto, N.: The Imandra automated reasoning system (system description). In: Peltier, N., Sofronie-Stokkermans, V. (eds.) IJCAR 2020. LNCS (LNAI), vol. 12167, pp. 464–471. Springer, Cham (2020). https://doi.org/10.1007/978-3-030-51054-1_30
18. Reger, G., Voronkov, A.: Induction in saturation-based proof search. In: Fontaine, P. (ed.) CADE. pp. 477–494. Springer (2019)
19. Reynolds, A., Kuncak, V.: Induction for SMT solvers. In: D'Souza, D., Lal, A., Larsen, K.G. (eds.) VMCAI 2015. LNCS, vol. 8931, pp. 80–98. Springer, Heidelberg (2015). https://doi.org/10.1007/978-3-662-46081-8_5
20. Schulz, S., Cruanes, S., Vukmirović, P.: Faster, higher, stronger: E 2.3. In: Fontaine, P. (ed.) CADE 2019. LNCS (LNAI), vol. 11716, pp. 495–507. Springer, Cham (2019). https://doi.org/10.1007/978-3-030-29436-6_29
21. Sonnex, W., Drossopoulou, S., Eisenbach, S.: Zeno: an automated prover for properties of recursive data structures. In: Flanagan, C., König, B. (eds.) TACAS 2012. LNCS, vol. 7214, pp. 407–421. Springer, Heidelberg (2012). https://doi.org/10.1007/978-3-642-28756-5_28
22. Sutcliffe, G.: The CADE ATP System Competition - CASC. AI Mag. **37**(2), 99–101 (2016)
23. Weber, T., Conchon, S., Déharbe, D., Heizmann, M., Niemetz, A., Reger, G.: The SMT competition 2015-2018. J. Satisf. Boolean Model. Comput. **11**(1), 221–259 (2019). https://doi.org/10.3233/SAT190123
24. Weidenbach, C., Dimova, D., Fietzke, A., Kumar, R., Suda, M., Wischnewski, P.: SPASS Version 3.5. In: Schmidt, R.A. (ed.) CADE 2009. LNCS (LNAI), vol. 5663, pp. 140–145. Springer, Heidelberg (2009). https://doi.org/10.1007/978-3-642-02959-2_10

Probabilistic and Quantitative Verification

On Probabilistic Monitorability

Luca Aceto[1,4](✉) ⓘ, Antonis Achilleos[1] ⓘ, Elli Anastasiadi[1] ⓘ,
Adrian Francalanza[2] ⓘ, Anna Ingólfsdóttir[1] ⓘ, Karoliina Lehtinen[3] ⓘ,
and Mathias Ruggaard Pedersen[1] ⓘ

[1] ICE-TCS, Department of Computer Science,
Reykjavík University, Reykjavik, Iceland
luca@ru.is
[2] Department of Computer Science, University of Malta, Msida, Malta
[3] CNRS, Aix-Marseille University and University of Toulon, LIS,
Marseille, France
[4] Gran Sasso Science Institute, L'Aquila, Italy

Abstract. This paper investigates monitorability in the context of probabilistic systems. We specify how monitor verdicts, reached over finite (partial) traces, can be given a probabilistic interpretation. For monitors that are used to verify properties at runtime, we also relate their probabilistic verdicts to the probability that a trace satisfies the property of interest. This leads us to define probabilistic monitor soundness and completeness, which are then used to formulate probabilistic monitorability. Surprisingly, we show that the resulting notions coincide with standard monitorability definitions from the literature. This allows us to transfer prior results from the standard setting to the probabilistic realm.

1 Introduction

Some of Thomas A. Henzinger's recent work has given seminal contributions to the field of runtime monitoring—see, for instance, the papers [18,21,22,29,30]. Moreover, in light of the new Advanced Grant he received from the European Research Council in April 2021 for the project 'Vigilant Algorithmic Monitoring Of Software (VAMOS)', we expect that, in the coming years, Thomas A. Henzinger and his group at IST Austria will contribute substantial new developments to both the theoretical foundations and the practice of runtime monitoring for modern software-based systems that rely on artificial intelligence and cloud computing, amongst other paradigms, and interact with an uncertain cyber-physical environment. To our mind, Thomas A. Henzinger cogently articulated the vision for the VAMOS project, and indeed for the field of runtime monitoring as a

This research was supported by the projects 'TheoFoMon: Theoretical Foundations for Monitorability' (no. 163406-051), 'Open Problems in the Equational Logic of Processes (OPEL)' (no. 196050-051) and 'MoVeMnt: Mode(l)s of Verification and Monitorability' (no. 217987-051) of the Icelandic Research Fund, project BehAPI, funded by the EU H2020 RISE programme under the Marie Skłodowska-Curie grant (no. 778233), and the Italian MIUR project PRIN 2017FTXR7S IT MATTERS 'Methods and Tools for Trustworthy Smart Systems'.

J.-F. Raskin and K. Chatterjee (Eds.): Principles of Systems Design, LNCS 13660, pp. 325–342, 2022.
https://doi.org/10.1007/978-3-031-22337-2_16

whole, in his keynote address at the 2020 edition of the conference on Runtime Verification. The key idea is to ensure that the runtime behaviour of critical software components be *always* observed and vetted online by other software devices, the so-called *monitors*, in order to identify possible misbehaviours at execution time in a timely fashion. Ideally, the monitors used for that purpose should be developed independently of the systems whose behaviour they observe and be synthesised automatically from system specifications. According to an IST Austria press release[1], the aim of the project VAMOS is to increase the robustness, dependability and trustworthiness of critical software systems by harnessing 'the increasing availability of hardware resources, from multicore processors to data centers.'

As we trust the above prefatory text makes clear, monitors are key components in runtime monitoring. They are passive computational entities that observe the execution of a system, *i.e.*, a finite trace of events, to determine properties about it [11,23–25]. When monitoring the behaviour of systems involving randomised choices, such as communication protocols and randomised algorithms, the observed systems are naturally equipped with probabilistic information about their branching behaviour and, due to their passivity, monitors intrinsically inherit this probabilistic behaviour. It is then natural, and fairly straightforward to ascribe the associated probability measure to monitor verdicts. However, when relating monitors to (linear-time) specifications, it is unclear whether the resulting probabilistic verdicts, reached by the monitor over finite trace observations, are in accordance with the probability that the completed trace (which may be infinite) satisfies the specification being monitored at runtime. This constitutes a monitorability problem that, to our mind, still deserves to be studied.

This paper investigates monitorability for probabilistic systems. Our results are modelled on the monitorability definition given in [4,25] which, opportunely, teases apart the monitor behaviour from the semantics of the properties being monitored, and relates them in terms of standard soundness and completeness criteria; it has also been formally related to other variants in the literature [6] and used for branching-time settings [2,3,5,26]. Our contributions in this celebratory article are as follows:

1. We define probabilistic versions of monitor soundness and completeness relating the probability of reaching each verdict after a finite prefix to the probability that a complete trace extending it satisfies the property (Definitions 8 and 9).
2. We show a surprising correspondence between probabilistic monitorability and its classical variant (Theorem 1), which allows us to inherit prior results such as syntactic characterisations of monitorable properties.
3. We show how this framework is general enough to be adapted to probabilistic settings that permit a margin of error (Definition 11 and Theorem 2).

---

[1] See https://ist.ac.at/en/news/erc-grants-beacon-of-scientific-success/.

4. Section 4 concludes our contribution with an application of these results to estimate probabilities in settings that allow for repeated monitored runs while still treating the observed system as a black box.

We end this article with some concluding remarks, a discussion of related literature and some avenues for future research (Sect. 5).

2 Preliminaries

We introduce the core concepts of measure and probability theory needed in this study. We refer the interested reader to [7, 10, 12] for a more in-depth presentation.

Definition 1 (σ-algebra [10, p. 754]). *For a set X, a σ-algebra on X is a set $\Sigma \subseteq 2^X$ such that*

- $X \in \Sigma$,
- *if $A \in \Sigma$ then $\overline{A} = X \setminus A \in \Sigma$ (closure under complement), and*
- *if $A_1, A_2, \ldots \in \Sigma$ then $\bigcup_{n \geq 1} A_n \in \Sigma$ (closure under countable unions).*

A pair (X, Σ) of a set X together with a σ-algebra Σ on X is known as a measurable space. If Σ is a σ-algebra and $A \in \Sigma$, we say that A is measurable for Σ, and if Σ is evident from the context, we simply say that A is measurable. With a σ-algebra on X at hand, we can define a probability measure on X.

Definition 2 (Probability measure [10, p. 754]). *Given a measurable space (X, Σ), a probability measure is a function $\mathbb{P} : \Sigma \to [0, 1]$ such that $\mathbb{P}(X) = 1$ and $\mathbb{P}(\bigcup_{i \in I} A_i) = \sum_{i \in I} \mathbb{P}(A_i)$ for any countable, pairwise disjoint collection $\{A_i\}_{i \in I} \subseteq \Sigma$. We denote by $\mathcal{D}(X)$ the set of all probability measures on X.*

Hence a probability measure assigns a probability to any measurable set in such a way that, for example, $\mathbb{P}(A \cup B) = \mathbb{P}(A) + \mathbb{P}(B)$, if A and B are disjoint sets, as well as ensuring that $\mathbb{P}(\emptyset) = 0$ and $\mathbb{P}(\overline{A}) = 1 - \mathbb{P}(A)$, for each A.

A probabilistic system is one in which the evolution of the system is governed by some probability distribution. We use here one of the simplest probabilistic systems, namely (generative) labelled Markov chains. Assume a fixed, finite set of actions Act.

Definition 3 (Labelled Markov chain). *A labelled Markov chain is a tuple $M = (S, s_*, \Delta)$, where S is a countable set of states, $s_* \in S$ is the start state, and $\Delta : S \to \mathcal{D}(\mathsf{Act} \times S)$ is the transition function assigning to each state a distribution over actions and states.*

Remark 1. The model defined above is essentially an action-based formulation of the hidden Markov chains considered in [34], which are called labelled Markov chains in [17]. Note, however, that the state-observation function in the models studied in those papers associates an observation with each state deterministically.

A labelled Markov chain $M = (S, s_*, \Delta)$ currently in state $s \in S$ evolves by choosing action a and state s' with probability $\Delta(s)(a, s')$, moving to s' while outputting the action a. In this paper we consider the trace-based behaviour of labelled Markov chains. A trace is an infinite sequence of actions $a_1 a_2 \cdots \in \mathsf{Act}^\omega$. We let π, π' range over traces. A finite trace is a sequence of actions $a_1 a_2 \ldots a_n \in \mathsf{Act}^*$, which we range over by w, w', and sets of finite traces are ranged over by F. We denote the empty trace by ε. Given two finite traces w and w', we write $w \preceq w'$ if w is a prefix of w', meaning that there exists a finite trace w'' such that $ww'' = w'$. For a trace $\pi = a_1 a_2 \ldots$, we let $\pi\langle i \rangle = a_i$, $\pi|_i = a_1 \ldots a_i$ and $\pi|^i = a_{i+1} \ldots$.

For a labelled Markov chain $M = (S, s_*, \Delta)$, we obtain a measurable space of traces $(\mathsf{Act}^\omega, \Sigma)$ using the cylinder construction (see e.g. [10, pp. 757–758]) as follows. Given a finite trace $a_1 \ldots a_n$, we define the cylinder of that trace as

$$\mathbb{C}(a_1 \ldots a_n) = \{\pi \in \mathsf{Act}^\omega \mid \pi|_n = a_1 \ldots a_n\}.$$

Thus $\mathbb{C}(a_1 \ldots a_n)$ is the set of infinite traces that all agree on the finite prefix $a_1 \ldots a_n$. In the following, we fix the σ-algebra Σ on Act^ω defined as the smallest σ-algebra containing all cylinders. For a given state s, we define a probability measure $\mathbb{P}_M^s$ on the measurable space $(\mathsf{Act}^\omega, \Sigma)$ inductively as $\mathbb{P}_M^s(\mathbb{C}(\varepsilon)) = 1$ and

$$\mathbb{P}_M^s(\mathbb{C}(a_1 a_2 \ldots a_n)) = \sum_{s' \in S} \Delta(s)(a_1, s') \cdot \mathbb{P}_M^{s'}(\mathbb{C}(a_2 \ldots a_n)).$$

Although we only define $\mathbb{P}_M^s$ on cylinders, the probability extends uniquely to the whole σ-algebra Σ using the Hahn-Kolmogorov theorem [36, Theorem 1.7.8]. Thus for any measurable set $A \in \Sigma$, the probability $\mathbb{P}_M^s(A)$ is well-defined.

3 Monitoring

Runtime verification employs monitors to observe the behaviour of some system, typically as a black box; the system emits sequences of events/actions from some set Act. A monitor accepts if the (finite) observations lead it to conclude that the system satisfies a property of interest, and rejects if it observes enough events to conclude that the property is violated. Our objective is to give an account of monitoring in the case where the system being monitored is a probabilistic system. In this case, the monitor itself is still non-probabilistic, and can only observe the actions emitted by the probabilistic system. Thus the monitored system is still a black box, and the monitor has no way of knowing the internal state or the transition probabilities of the system.

Definition 4 (Monitor). *A monitor $m = (F_{acc}, F_{rej})$ is a pair of sets of finite traces $F_{acc}, F_{rej} \subseteq \mathsf{Act}^*$ satisfying: (i) $F_{acc} \cap F_{rej} = \emptyset$; (ii) for $i \in \{acc, rej\}$:*

if $w \in F_i$ then for any $w' \in \mathsf{Act}^*$ where $w \preceq w'$ we also have $w' \in F_i$.

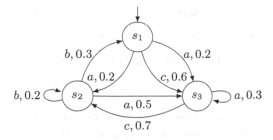

Fig. 1. A labelled Markov chain with three states, the initial state being s_1. The symbol and number above each transition indicates which action is taken and with what probability.

The traces in F_{acc} denote the finite observations accepted by the monitor whereas those in F_{rej} are the finite traces the monitor rejects. Condition (ii) in Definition 4 ensures that verdicts (i.e., acceptances and rejections) are irrevocable. For a set $F \subseteq \mathsf{Act}^*$ we define $\mathbb{C}(F) = \bigcup_{w \in F} \mathbb{C}(w)$, so that $\mathbb{C}(F)$ is the union of the cylinders generated by each finite trace in F. Since each cylinder $\mathbb{C}(w)$ is measurable by definition, $\mathbb{C}(F)$ is also measurable, being a countable union of measurable sets.

Example 1. Assume that $\mathsf{Act} = \{a, b, c\}$. Consider a monitor whose accepting set is

$$F_{acc} = \{w \in \mathsf{Act}^* \mid \exists w'.\ w = aaw' \text{ or } w = cw'\},$$

and let $M = (S, s_1, \Delta)$ be the labelled Markov chain describing the system depicted in Fig. 1. In order to calculate the probability of the monitor accepting when monitoring this system, we first note that $\mathbb{C}(F_{acc}) = \mathbb{C}(aa) \cup \mathbb{C}(c)$. Since these are disjoint sets, we can calculate the probability as

$$\mathbb{P}_M^{s_1}(\mathbb{C}(F_{acc})) = \mathbb{P}_M^{s_1}(\mathbb{C}(aa)) + \mathbb{P}_M^{s_1}(\mathbb{C}(c)) = (0.2 \cdot \mathbb{P}_M^{s_2}(\mathbb{C}(a)) + 0.2 \cdot \mathbb{P}_M^{s_3}(\mathbb{C}(a))) + 0.6$$
$$= (0.2 \cdot 0.5 + 0.2 \cdot 0.3) + 0.6 = 0.76.$$

Properties of systems will be described in the linear-time μ-calculus [4,38], whose formulas are given by the following grammar

$$\varphi, \psi ::= \mathbf{tt} \mid \mathbf{ff} \mid X \mid \varphi \wedge \psi \mid \varphi \vee \psi \mid [a]\varphi \mid \langle a \rangle \varphi \mid \mu X.\varphi \mid \nu X.\varphi,$$

where X comes from a countable set $\mathsf{L_{VAR}}$ of logical variables and $a \in \mathsf{Act}$. Formulas are interpreted over infinite traces using an interpretation $\rho : \mathsf{L_{VAR}} \to 2^{\mathsf{Act}^\omega}$ for variables. The semantics is standard; we present here only the cases dealing with the modal and the fixed-point operators.

$$[[a]\varphi]_\rho = \{\pi \in \mathsf{Act}^\omega \mid \pi|^1 \in [[\varphi]]_\rho \text{ whenever } \pi\langle 1 \rangle = a\}$$
$$[\langle a \rangle \varphi]_\rho = \{\pi \in \mathsf{Act}^\omega \mid \pi\langle 1 \rangle = a \text{ and } \pi|^1 \in [[\varphi]]_\rho\}$$
$$[[\mu X.\varphi]]_\rho = \bigcap\{S \subseteq \mathsf{Act}^\omega \mid [[\varphi]]_{\rho[X \mapsto S]} \subseteq S\}$$
$$[[\nu X.\varphi]]_\rho = \bigcup\{S \subseteq \mathsf{Act}^\omega \mid [[\varphi]]_{\rho[X \mapsto S]} \supseteq S\}$$

Henceforth, we only consider closed formulas, for which we may omit the subscript and simply write $[[\varphi]]$. Since the logic is semantically closed under complement, we define negation as complement, meaning that $[[\neg\varphi]] = \mathsf{Act}^\omega \setminus [[\varphi]]$. We next prove that each formula denotes a measurable property over infinite traces.

Lemma 1. *For each φ, the property $[[\varphi]]$ is measurable.*

Proof. The linear-time μ-calculus and Büchi automata are equivalent [16], and [37, Proposition 2.3] states that the set of traces recognisable by a given Büchi automaton is measurable. Therefore, $[[\varphi]]$ is measurable. $\square$

Lemma 1 means that the probability $\mathbb{P}_M^s([[\varphi]])$ of a property is well-defined.

Example 2. The property $\varphi = [a]\langle a \rangle \mathtt{tt} \wedge [b]\mathtt{ff}$ states that a trace cannot start with b, and whenever it starts with a, it must be followed by another a. Assume that $\mathsf{Act} = \{a, b, c\}$. The probability that $M = (S, s_1, \Delta)$, from Fig. 1, does *not* satisfy φ is

$$\begin{aligned}
\mathbb{P}_M^{s_1}([[\neg\varphi]]) &= \mathbb{P}_M^{s_1}(\mathbb{C}(b) \cup \mathbb{C}(ab) \cup \mathbb{C}(ac)) \\
&= \mathbb{P}_M^{s_1}(\mathbb{C}(b)) + \mathbb{P}_M^{s_1}(\mathbb{C}(ab)) + \mathbb{P}_M^{s_1}(\mathbb{C}(ac)) \\
&= 0 + (0.2 \cdot \mathbb{P}_M^{s_2}(\mathbb{C}(b)) + 0.2 \cdot \mathbb{P}_M^{s_3}(\mathbb{C}(b))) + (0.2 \cdot \mathbb{P}_M^{s_2}(\mathbb{C}(c)) + 0.2 \cdot \mathbb{P}_M^{s_3}(\mathbb{C}(c))) \\
&= 0 + (0.2 \cdot 0.5 + 0.2 \cdot 0) + (0.2 \cdot 0 + 0.2 \cdot 0.7) = 0.24.
\end{aligned}$$

It follows that $\mathbb{P}_M^{s_1}([[\varphi]]) = 0.76$, which is the 'acceptance probability' of a monitor of the type we considered in Example 1. In the subsequent section, we will explore the precise connections between monitors and properties in the setting we study in this paper.

3.1   Soundness, Completeness, and Monitorability

In the non-probabilistic setting [4], a monitor is sound with respect to some property of interest if any trace accepted by the monitor also satisfies the property, and any trace rejected by the monitor does not satisfy the property. In other words, soundness means that the monitor is an *underapproximation* of the property.

Definition 5 (Soundness). *A monitor $m = (F_{acc}, F_{rej})$ is sound for a formula φ if $\mathbb{C}(F_{acc}) \subseteq [[\varphi]]$ and $\mathbb{C}(F_{rej}) \subseteq [[\neg\varphi]]$.*

Dually, completeness requires the monitor to *overapproximate* the property being monitored: if a trace satisfies the property, the monitor must accept that trace, and if a trace violates the property, the monitor should reject the trace.

Definition 6 (Completeness). *A monitor* $m = (F_{acc}, F_{rej})$ *is*

- satisfaction complete *for a formula φ, if* $[\![\varphi]\!] \subseteq \mathbb{C}(F_{acc})$,
- violation complete *for φ if* $[\![\neg\varphi]\!] \subseteq \mathbb{C}(F_{rej})$, *and*
- complete *for φ if it is both satisfaction and violation complete for φ.*

Together, soundness and completeness require a monitor to fully agree with the property being monitored, i.e. $\mathbb{C}(F_{acc}) = [\![\varphi]\!]$ and $\mathbb{C}(F_{rej}) = [\![\neg\varphi]\!]$. Completeness is, in general, a strong condition for a monitor, which often cannot be met [4,6]. In fact, we observe that completeness implies soundness.

Lemma 2. *Every complete monitor for a closed formula φ is also sound for φ.*

Proof. Assume that $m = (F_{acc}, F_{rej})$ is complete for φ. To prove that m is also sound, let $\pi \in \mathbb{C}(F_{acc})$. This means that there is some $w \in F_{acc}$ such that $\pi \in \mathbb{C}(w)$. If $\pi \in [\![\neg\varphi]\!]$, then due to completeness, $\pi \in \mathbb{C}(F_{rej})$. Again, this means that there is some $w' \in F_{rej}$ such that $\pi \in \mathbb{C}(w')$. Since w and w' are both prefixes of π, either of them is contained in $F_{acc} \cap F_{rej}$, which is a contradiction, because $F_{acc} \cap F_{rej} = \emptyset$. Therefore, $\pi \in [\![\varphi]\!]$, because $[\![\varphi]\!] \cup [\![\neg\varphi]\!] = \mathsf{Act}^\omega$. The case for $\pi \in \mathbb{C}(F_{rej})$ is analogous. □

Lemma 2 only applies to complete monitors, and, in general, neither to satisfaction-complete nor to violation-complete monitors. For example, the monitor with $F_{rej} = \mathsf{Act}^*$ is violation complete for $[a][b]\mathtt{ff}$, but is not sound. We are interested in the properties that have sound, and complete, satisfaction- or violation-complete monitors.

Definition 7 (Monitorability). *A formula φ is*

- satisfaction monitorable *if there exists a monitor that is sound and satisfaction complete for φ,*
- violation monitorable *if there exists a monitor that is sound and violation complete for φ, and*
- fully monitorable *if there exists a monitor that is (sound and) complete for φ.*

Several properties are not fully monitorable, and therefore we often aim to show that they are either satisfaction or violation monitorable, and to synthesise corresponding monitors [4,26].

Example 3. For $\mathsf{Act} = \{a, b\}$, the formula $\varphi = \mu X.(\langle a \rangle \mathtt{tt} \vee [b]X)$ is true exactly for the traces that have some occurrence of a. It is not hard to see that φ is satisfaction monitorable, but not violation monitorable.

In the probabilistic setting, we change neither the monitors nor the properties, but we interpret them over probabilistic systems. Hence, whereas non-probabilistic soundness and completeness range over satisfaction of the property in *all* models, the probabilistic version will range over the probability of the property in *all probabilistic models*. In order to extend the notions of soundness and completeness to the probabilistic setting, we impose two criteria: (1) the extension should be conservative, so that if m is sound and complete for φ, it is also probabilistically sound and complete for φ; (2) the extension should preserve the idea of soundness being an underapproximation and completeness being an overapproximation, but in a probabilistic setting.

Definition 8 (Probabilistic soundness). *A monitor* $m = (F_{acc}, F_{rej})$ *is probabilistically sound for* φ *if* $\mathbb{P}_M^{s_*}(\mathbb{C}(F_{acc})) \leq \mathbb{P}_M^{s_*}(\llbracket \varphi \rrbracket)$ *and* $\mathbb{P}_M^{s_*}(\mathbb{C}(F_{rej})) \leq \mathbb{P}_M^{s_*}(\llbracket \neg \varphi \rrbracket)$ *for all labelled Markov chains* $M = (S, s_*, \Delta)$.

Definition 8 fulfills criterion (1), since the monotonicity property of probability measures, which states that if $A \subseteq B$, then $\mathbb{P}(A) \leq \mathbb{P}(B)$, gives us that if $\mathbb{C}(F_{acc}) \subseteq \llbracket \varphi \rrbracket$, then $\mathbb{P}_M^{s_*}(\mathbb{C}(F_{acc})) \leq \mathbb{P}_M^{s_*}(\llbracket \varphi \rrbracket)$, and likewise for rejection. It also fulfills criterion (2), since probabilistic soundness ensures that the probability of the monitor accepting is an underapproximation of the probability of the property being satisfied, and likewise for rejection.

Example 4. Assume $\mathsf{Act} = \{a, b, c\}$. Recall the formula $\varphi = [a]\langle a\rangle \mathsf{tt} \wedge [b]\mathsf{ff}$ we considered in Example 2. Let

$$F_{acc} = \{w \in \mathsf{Act}^* \mid \exists w'. \ w = aaw' \text{ or } w = cw'\} \quad \text{and}$$
$$F_{rej} = \emptyset.$$

For any $M = (S, s_*, \Delta)$, Examples 1–2 tell us that

$$\mathbb{P}_M^{s_*}(\mathbb{C}(F_{acc})) = \mathbb{P}_M^{s_*}(\{\pi \in \mathsf{Act}^\omega \mid (\pi\langle 1\rangle = a = \pi\langle 2\rangle) \text{ or } (\pi\langle 1\rangle = c)\}) = \mathbb{P}(\llbracket \varphi \rrbracket).$$

Moreover, $0 = \mathbb{P}_M^{s_*}(\emptyset) = \mathbb{P}_M^{s_*}(F_{rej}) \leq \mathbb{P}_M^{s_*}(\llbracket \neg \varphi \rrbracket)$, so $m = (F_{acc}, F_{rej})$ is sound for φ.

Definition 9 (Probabilistic completeness). *A monitor* $m = (F_{acc}, F_{rej})$ *is*

– *probabilistically satisfaction complete for a formula* φ *if*

$$\mathbb{P}_M^{s_*}(\mathbb{C}(F_{acc})) \geq \mathbb{P}_M^{s_*}(\llbracket \varphi \rrbracket) \quad \text{for all labelled Markov chains } M = (S, s_*, \Delta),$$

– *probabilistically violation complete for a formula* φ *if*

$$\mathbb{P}_M^{s_*}(\mathbb{C}(F_{rej})) \geq \mathbb{P}_M^{s_*}(\llbracket \neg \varphi \rrbracket) \quad \text{for all labelled Markov chains } M = (S, s_*, \Delta),$$

– *probabilistically complete for a formula* φ *if it is both probabilistically satisfaction and violation complete for the given formula.*

This definition also fulfills both of the stated criteria. Criterion (1) is satisfied for the same reason as for probabilistic soundness, and criterion (2) is satisfied because the probability that the monitor accepts is an overapproximation of the probability that the property is satisfied, and likewise for rejection.

Remark 2. At first glance, Definitions 8 and 9 for probabilistic soundness and completeness may seem arbitrary. Indeed, the comparison of the probabilities of two events does not in general indicate any causal relation between them. Note, however, that if the goal is to estimate the probability that a labelled Markov chain generates a trace that satisfies or violates a property, Definitions 8 and 9 describe exactly the appropriate notions of under- and over-approximation. Furthermore, as Theorem 1 demonstrates later in this section, in this case, due to the quantification over all labelled Markov chains, our probability requirements *do imply* a causal relation between the monitor verdict and the satisfaction of the formula.

Example 5. Assume $\mathsf{Act} = \{a, b, c\}$ and recall φ from Example 4 with

$$F_{acc} = \{w \in \mathsf{Act}^* \mid \exists w'.\ w = aaw' \text{ or } w = cw'\}, \text{ and}$$
$$F_{rej} = \{w \in \mathsf{Act}^* \mid \exists w'.\ w = bw' \text{ or } w = abw' \text{ or } w = acw'\}.$$

Then, for any system described by a labelled Markov chain $M = (S, s_*, \Delta)$, we get

$$\mathbb{P}_M^{s_*}(\mathbb{C}(F_{acc})) = \mathbb{P}_M^{s_*}(\{\pi \in \mathsf{Act}^\omega \mid (\pi\langle 1\rangle = a = \pi\langle 2\rangle) \text{ or } (\pi\langle 1\rangle = c)\}) = \mathbb{P}_M^{s_*}(\llbracket \varphi \rrbracket), \text{ and}$$
$$\mathbb{P}_M^{s_*}(\mathbb{C}(F_{rej})) = \mathbb{P}_M^{s_*}(\{\pi \in \mathsf{Act}^\omega \mid (\pi\langle 1\rangle = b) \text{ or } (\pi\langle 1\rangle = a \text{ and } (\pi\langle 2\rangle = b \text{ or } \pi\langle 2\rangle = c))\})$$
$$= \mathbb{P}_M^{s_*}(\{\pi \in \mathsf{Act}^\omega \mid (\pi\langle 1\rangle \neq a \text{ or } \pi\langle 2\rangle \neq a) \text{ and } (\pi\langle 1\rangle \neq c)\}) = \mathbb{P}_M^{s_*}(\llbracket \neg\varphi \rrbracket),$$

so $m = (F_{acc}, F_{rej})$ is both probabilistically sound and complete for φ.

Soundness and completeness together would then imply $\mathbb{P}_M^{s_*}(\mathbb{C}(F_{acc})) = \mathbb{P}_M^{s_*}(\llbracket \varphi \rrbracket)$ and $\mathbb{P}_M^{s_*}(\mathbb{C}(F_{rej})) = \mathbb{P}_M^{s_*}(\llbracket \neg\varphi \rrbracket)$ for all labelled Markov chains $M = (S, s_*, \Delta)$. This describes the probabilistic monitorability of a formula.

Definition 10 (Probabilistic monitorability). *A formula φ is*

- *probabilistically satisfaction monitorable if there exists a monitor m which is probabilistically sound and probabilistically satisfaction complete for φ,*
- *probabilistically violation monitorable if there exists a monitor m which is probabilistically sound and probabilistically violation complete for φ, and*
- *probabilistically fully monitorable if there exists a monitor m which is probabilistically sound and probabilistically complete for φ.*

It is interesting to consider the connections between the probabilistic and non-probabilistic version of soundness and completeness. Because probabilistic soundness and completeness are conservative extensions of their non-probabilistic counterparts, if m monitors soundly for φ in the non-probabilistic setting, then m also monitors soundly for φ in the probabilistic setting, and likewise for the various flavours of completeness. Surprisingly, it turns out that the reverse implication also holds.

Theorem 1. *For every monitor m and formula φ,*

- *m is sound for φ if and only if m is probabilistically sound for φ;*
- *m is satisfaction complete for φ if and only if m is probabilistically satisfaction complete for φ;*
- *m is violation complete for φ if and only if m is probabilistically violation complete for φ; and*
- *m is complete for φ if and only if m is probabilistically complete for φ.*

Proof. Soundness and completeness imply their probabilistic counterparts by monotonicity of probability measures. For the other direction, we only present the proof for the case of soundness, as all the others are similar—and the case of completeness is a consequence of the other ones. We prove the contrapositive, so assume that $m = (F_{acc}, F_{rej})$ is not sound for φ. Assume, without loss of generality, that $\mathbb{C}(F_{acc}) \not\subseteq \llbracket \varphi \rrbracket$. This means that there exists a trace $\pi \in \mathbb{C}(F_{acc})$ such that $\pi \notin \llbracket \varphi \rrbracket$. It is now immediate to exhibit a labelled Markov chain M such that $\mathbb{P}_M^{s*}(\mathbb{C}(F_{acc})) = 1$ but $\mathbb{P}_M^{s*}(\llbracket \varphi \rrbracket) = 0$ by constructing M such that it generates only the trace π. Then $1 = \mathbb{P}_M^{s*}(\mathbb{C}(F_{acc})) \not\leq \mathbb{P}_M^{s*}(\llbracket \varphi \rrbracket) = 0$, so m is not probabilistically sound for φ.   □

A corollary of Theorem 1 is that the probabilistically fully monitorable formulas are exactly those that are also non-probabilistically fully monitorable. In [4, Theorem 4.8] it was shown that the Hennessy-Milner logic [28], which is the recursion-free fragment of the μ-calculus, expresses exactly the fully monitorable properties—without assuming that these properties are expressed in the μ-calculus.

Corollary 1. *A property is probabilistically fully monitorable if and only if it can be expressed with a formula generated by the following grammar:*

$$\varphi, \psi ::= \mathsf{tt} \mid \mathsf{ff} \mid \varphi \wedge \psi \mid \varphi \vee \psi \mid [a]\varphi \mid \langle a \rangle \varphi.$$

The satisfaction- and violation-monitorable formulas were also characterized in [4] with maximally expressive fragments. However, in contrast to the case of full monitorability, there are violation-monitorable properties that cannot be expressed in the μ-calculus, as long as one assumes sufficiently powerful monitors.

Corollary 2. *A μ-calculus formula is*

- *probabilistically satisfaction monitorable, if and only if is equivalent to a formula of the fragment*

$$\varphi, \psi ::= \mathsf{tt} \mid \mathsf{ff} \mid \varphi \wedge \psi \mid \varphi \vee \psi \mid [a]\varphi \mid \langle a \rangle \varphi \mid \nu X.\varphi, \qquad and$$

- *probabilistically violation monitorable, if and only if is equivalent to a formula of the fragment*

$$\varphi, \psi ::= \mathsf{tt} \mid \mathsf{ff} \mid \varphi \wedge \psi \mid \varphi \vee \psi \mid [a]\varphi \mid \langle a \rangle \varphi \mid \mu X.\varphi.$$

3.2   Other Monitor Requirements

Example 1 may seem to imply that Definitions 9 and 8 are very restrictive. However, the theorem holds for other interpretations of soundness and completeness in a probabilistic setting. Fix two parameters $c, d > 0$.

Definition 11 (Probabilistic soundness and completeness with a margin of error). *A monitor* $m = (F_{acc}, F_{rej})$ *is probabilistically sound for* φ *with margin of error* c *if* $\mathbb{P}_M^{s_*}(\mathbb{C}(F_{acc})) \leq c \cdot \mathbb{P}_M^{s_*}(\llbracket \varphi \rrbracket)$ *and* $\mathbb{P}_M^{s_*}(\mathbb{C}(F_{rej})) \leq c \cdot \mathbb{P}_M^{s_*}(\llbracket \neg\varphi \rrbracket)$ *for all labelled Markov chains* $M = (S, s_*, \Delta)$. *Likewise,* m *is*

- *probabilistically satisfaction complete for* φ *with margin of error* d *if*

$$\mathbb{P}_M^{s_*}(\mathbb{C}(F_{acc})) \geq d \cdot \mathbb{P}_M^{s_*}(\llbracket \varphi \rrbracket) \quad \text{for all labelled Markov chains } M = (S, s_*, \Delta),$$

- *probabilistically violation complete for* φ *with margin of error* d *if*

$$\mathbb{P}_M^{s_*}(\mathbb{C}(F_{rej})) \geq d \cdot \mathbb{P}_M^{s_*}(\llbracket \neg\varphi \rrbracket) \quad \text{for all labelled Markov chains } M = (S, s_*, \Delta),$$

- *probabilistically complete for* φ *with margin of error* d *if it is both satisfaction and violation complete for* φ *with margin of error* d.

The two parameters, when $c > 1$ and $d < 1$, allow the monitor to occasionally give more or fewer verdicts than it should, but always within a set margin of error. Another candidate for soundness and completeness, parameterised with respect to c and d, is conditional soundness and completeness.

Definition 12 (Conditional soundness and completeness). *A monitor* $m = (F_{acc}, F_{rej})$ *is conditionally sound for* φ *with margin of error* c *if it holds that* $\mathbb{P}_M^{s_*}(\llbracket \varphi \rrbracket \mid \mathbb{C}(F_{acc})) \geq c$ *and* $\mathbb{P}_M^{s_*}(\llbracket \neg\varphi \rrbracket \mid \mathbb{C}(F_{rej})) \geq c$ *for all labelled Markov chains* $M = (S, s_*, \Delta)$. *Likewise,* m *is*

- *conditionally satisfaction complete with margin of error* d *for a formula* φ *if*

$$\mathbb{P}_M^{s_*}(\mathbb{C}(F_{acc}) \mid \llbracket \varphi \rrbracket) \geq d \quad \text{for all labelled Markov chains } M = (S, s_*, \Delta),$$

- *conditionally violation complete with margin of error* d *for a formula* φ *if*

$$\mathbb{P}_M^{s_*}(\mathbb{C}(F_{rej}) \mid \llbracket \neg\varphi \rrbracket) \geq d \quad \text{for all labelled Markov chains } M = (S, s_*, \Delta),$$

- *conditionally complete with margin of error* d *for a formula* φ *if it is both conditionally satisfaction and violation complete for* φ.

We observe that for these variations of probabilistic soundness and completeness, the arguments used in the proof of Theorem 1 can also be applied.

Theorem 2. *All the variants of soundness and completeness are equivalent. This means that Definitions 5, 8, 11, and 12 are equivalent, and that Definitions 6, 9, 11, and 12 are also equivalent.*

Proof. The first two items, both for soundness and completeness are equivalent, by Theorem 1. To show that each other item is equivalent to the first, we follow the proof of Theorem 1.   □

Theorem 2 allows us to treat monitorability uniformly for all the approaches described by Definitions 5, 6, 8, 9 and 11 to 12. For instance, the monitor synthesis defined in [4, 26] and implemented in [1, 8, 9] applies directly to the probabilistic setting (with margins of error).

Remark 3. One conclusion from the results of this section is that using the qualitative monitoring framework studied in [4,6] to monitor for properties of labelled Markov chains allows one to monitor the same collections of properties that are monitorable for labelled transition systems. Therefore, to use the probabilistic setting to monitor for more properties than in the qualitative setting, one must increase the power of monitors, *e.g.*, by using randomisation (as done in, *e.g.*, [34]), or by giving them some information about the monitored system.

4   An Application: Estimating Probabilities

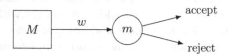

Fig. 2. A setup for estimating probabilities. M is a probabilistic system being monitored by the monitor m, which reads the trace w emitted by S to provide a verdict.

The theory we have described in Sect. 3 allows us to estimate the probabilities of properties over infinite traces, even if the system itself is a black box. To see this, consider the setup depicted in Fig. 2. Here we have a probabilistic system $M = (S, s_*, \Delta)$, of which we do not know the internal workings, and hence should be viewed as a black box. Using the monitor synthesis from [4], we can generate a monitor $m = (F_{acc}, F_{rej})$ which is both sound and complete for a monitorable property φ, whose probability in M we are interested in estimating. As m observes the behaviour of M given by a sequence of outputs $w = a_1 \dots a_n$, m will eventually, in finite time, produce either an accept or a reject verdict. This is guaranteed because m is both sound and complete.

In a setting where a system is executed repeatedly (*e.g.*, once every morning), we can estimate the probability $\mathbb{P}_M^{s_*}(\llbracket \varphi \rrbracket)$. Concretely, every time the system M is run (with passive monitor m), the verdict reached for an exhibited trace is recorded (here we assume that we can reset the system to its initial state, as is done in, for instance, [19]). After some number of iterations, say n iterations, we will have observed some number n_{acc} of accept verdicts and some number n_{rej} of reject verdicts. We can then estimate the probabilities $\mathbb{P}_M^{s_*}(\mathbb{C}(F_{acc}))$ and

$\mathbb{P}_M^{s_*}(\mathbb{C}(F_{rej}))$ by $\frac{n_{acc}}{n}$ and $\frac{n_{rej}}{n}$, respectively. By Theorem 1, the probability of satisfying the property is equal to the probability of the monitor accepting, and likewise for not satisfying the property and rejecting. This means that $\frac{n_{acc}}{n}$ and $\frac{n_{rej}}{n}$ are also estimates of $\mathbb{P}_M^{s_*}(\llbracket\varphi\rrbracket)$ and $\mathbb{P}_M^{s_*}(\llbracket\neg\varphi\rrbracket)$, respectively, so we can use these to estimate the probability that φ is satisfied in M.

This approach to estimating only works for the monitorable fragment of the logic (see Corollary 1). However, even for non-monitorable properties, we can use the approach to give estimates of the probability in terms of lower and upper bounds. For some non-monitorable property φ, one could construct a sound monitor $m_1 = (F_{acc}^1, F_{rej}^1)$ and a complete monitor $m_2 = (F_{acc}^2, F_{rej}^2)$. Then $\mathbb{P}_M^{s_*}(\mathbb{C}(F_{acc}^1)) \leq \mathbb{P}_M^{s_*}(\llbracket\varphi\rrbracket) \leq \mathbb{P}_M^{s_*}(\mathbb{C}(F_{acc}^2))$, and similarly for $\llbracket\neg\varphi\rrbracket$ and the rejection parts of the monitors. Hence m_1 gives a lower bound on the probability of φ, and m_2 gives an upper bound. Now we can use the approach from before to estimate the probabilities of m_1 accepting and rejecting and of m_2 accepting and rejecting, thus giving us estimates on lower and upper bounds on the probability that M satisfies φ. The downside is that in this case we have no guarantee that m_1 will give a verdict in finite time.

5   Conclusions

In this article, we have applied the monitoring framework studied in [4,6] to verify properties of labelled Markov chains at runtime. We have considered a variety of notions of probabilistic monitorability that arise naturally in this setting and proved that they are all equivalent to the corresponding 'purely qualitative' notions in the above-mentioned references. The main conclusion of our study is, therefore, that the power of monitors observing systems with probabilistic dynamics must be increased if one wants to monitor more properties of such systems than in the qualitative setting from [4,6].

Related Work. Runtime monitoring for probabilistic systems has been an active research area for some time and is currently the subject of considerable activity—see, for instance, the papers [14,19,27,31,34,35] to name but a few. To our mind, the work that is closest to our study is the one presented by Sistla and Srinivas in [34]. In that article, the authors investigate runtime monitoring of qualitative properties for systems modelled as Hidden Markov Chains, namely Markov chains that have outputs associated with their states. (The labelled Markov chains we consider can be viewed as an action-based counterpart of Hidden Markov Chains.) In the above-mentioned paper, Sistla and Srinivas study both deterministic and probabilistic monitors. They give deterministic monitors that use counters to monitor properties that can be expressed as deterministic Büchi automata with a desired accuracy. However, the monitoring algorithm needs to know the Hidden Markov Chain defining the system and is therefore not black box. This deficiency is remedied in *op. cit.* by means of probabilistic monitors. A probabilistic monitor for a property is a randomised algorithm that rejects with probability one every system computation that does not satisfy the property. On the other hand, a strong probabilistic monitor for a property is a probabilistic monitor that accepts every system computation that satisfies the property with some positive probability. Sistla and Srinivas prove an expressive completeness result for strong probabilistic monitors that characterises the class of properties that have such monitors, namely the class of properties whose complements can be recognised by (infinite-state) Büchi automata. The above-mentioned paper also gives some techniques that can be used to combine deterministic and probabilistic approaches to monitoring Hidden Markov Chains.

Junges et al. study runtime monitors for systems modelled as Markov Decision Processes in [31]. These are systems that are partially observable and, unlike (Hidden) Markov Chains, exhibit both nondeterministic and probabilistic dynamics. The observation function for Markov Decision Processes, which describes the observations that can be made at each system state, is also probabilistic. Moreover, each system state has an associated non-negative real number that describes how risky that state is. In the above-mentioned paper, Junges et al. study the following monitoring problem:

> Decide whether, for any possible scheduler used to resolve the nondeterminism in the observed system, the 'weighted trace risk' of a given trace of observations is larger than some given threshold.

Two algorithms are given for solving the above problem and are evaluated on a range of benchmark applications. One is based on using forward filtering and employs vertices of a convex hull to represent a possibly exponential set of distributions. The other is based on model checking and runs in polynomial time. Both algorithms, however, require knowledge of the observed Markov Decision Process and therefore do not treat the system as a black box.

The runtime monitoring problem studied in [31] is conceptually related to the predictive monitoring problem for hybrid systems [15], namely the problem of predicting, at runtime, whether the system can reach some unsafe state in the future within a given time bound. Unlike other approaches to runtime verification, predictive monitoring aims at detecting potentially bad system executions before a violation occurs. In [33], Phan et al. have proposed a method they call Neural State Classification to train deep neural networks to classify observed executions of hybrid systems as unsafe if they can be extended to reach an unsafe state. Bortolussi et al. build on that work in [13] to develop a framework called Neural Predictive Monitoring that provides efficiency, accuracy, and statistical guarantees on the prediction error, which were not provided by the methods from [33]. It would be very interesting to apply some of the methods in those two papers to the setting described in Sect. 4.

Esparza et al. study the enforcement of ω-regular properties over labelled Markov chains by means of universal restarting strategies in [19]. The key requirement on the restarting strategy is that, for each Markov chain, the number of restarts is finite and the execution of the Markov chain after the last restart satisfies the desired property, with probability 1. Two algorithms are given for this task, a cautious and a more efficient bold one, and are evaluated experimentally using models from the PRISM Benchmark Suite [32]. In the work by

Esparza *et al.*, both the Markov chain and its set of states are unknown to the algorithms. However, the authors assume that the algorithms can detect whether the current state has been observed previously, but cannot pinpoint which state of the observed chain it is.

In [14], Bartolo *et al.* investigate monitoring for probabilistic, automata-based specifications expressed as (binary) session types where choice points are augmented with a probability distribution. Their monitors employ statistical inference techniques to detect (partial) executions that deviate considerably from the prescribed probabilities as they pass repeatedly through these choice points. Since detections in this work are interpreted with respect to a pre-specified confidence level, it is worth investigating whether Definition 12 can be used to assess the soundness and completeness of the approach; the margin of error c might be used to accommodate errors induced by said confidence level.

Future Work. The work presented in this paper paves the way to several interesting avenues for future research. First of all, following [34], it is natural to study the expressive power of randomised versions of the monitors considered in [4,6] and to characterise precisely the collection of properties they can monitor and with what guarantees. It would also be interesting to investigate how repeated monitor observations of some probabilistic system can be used to learn models of it and how well those models approximate the system under observation. Moreover, building on the work by Esparza *et al.* on the enforcement of ω-regular properties over labelled Markov chains in [19], one might attempt to develop a general theory of runtime enforcement for probabilistic systems akin to the one presented in, for instance, [20]. Last, but by no means least, it would be fitting to accompany the above mentioned theoretical work with tool development, and applications to benchmarks from the literature and to case studies. We would not be surprised if Thomas A. Henzinger and his group at IST Austria did all this work and much more. VAMOS Tom!

Acknowledgments. We thank the anonymous reviewers for their comments, and Thomas A. Henzinger for the inspiration his scientific work has provided over many years and for his leadership within the scientific community.

References

1. Aceto, L., Achilleos, A., Attard, D.P., Exibard, L., Francalanza, A., Ingólfsdóttir, A.: A monitoring tool for linear-time μHML. In: ter Beek, M., Sirjani, M. (eds.) Proceedings of Coordination Models and Languages – 24th IFIP WG 6.1 International Conference, COORDINATION 2022. LNCS. Springer, Cham (2022). (to appear)
2. Aceto, L., Achilleos, A., Francalanza, A., Ingólfsdóttir, A.: Monitoring for silent actions. In: Lokam, S.V., Ramanujam, R. (eds.) 37th IARCS Annual Conference on Foundations of Software Technology and Theoretical Computer Science, FSTTCS 2017. LIPIcs, Kanpur, India, 11–15 December 2017, vol. 93, pp. 7:1–7:14. Schloss Dagstuhl - Leibniz-Zentrum für Informatik (2017)

3. Aceto, L., Achilleos, A., Francalanza, A., Ingólfsdóttir, A.: A framework for parameterized monitorability. In: Baier, C., Dal Lago, U. (eds.) FoSSaCS 2018. LNCS, vol. 10803, pp. 203–220. Springer, Cham (2018). https://doi.org/10.1007/978-3-319-89366-2_11

4. Aceto, L., Achilleos, A., Francalanza, A., Ingólfsdóttir, A., Lehtinen, K.: Adventures in monitorability: from branching to linear time and back again. Proc. ACM Program. Lang. **3**(POPL), 52:1–52:29 (2019)

5. Aceto, L., Achilleos, A., Francalanza, A., Ingólfsdóttir, A., Lehtinen, K.: The best a monitor can do. In: Baier, C., Goubault-Larrecq, J. (eds.) 29th EACSL Annual Conference on Computer Science Logic, CSL 2021. LIPIcs, Ljubljana, Slovenia, 25–28 January 2021, (Virtual Conference), vol. 183, pp. 7:1–7:23. Schloss Dagstuhl - Leibniz-Zentrum für Informatik (2021)

6. Aceto, L., Achilleos, A., Francalanza, A., Ingólfsdóttir, A., Lehtinen, K.: An operational guide to monitorability with applications to regular properties. Softw. Syst. Model. **20**(2), 335–361 (2021). https://doi.org/10.1007/s10270-020-00860-z

7. Ash, R.B., Doléans-Dade, C.A.: Probability & Measure Theory, 2nd edn. Harcourt/Academic Press, Cambridge (1999)

8. Attard, D.P., Aceto, L., Achilleos, A., Francalanza, A., Ingólfsdóttir, A., Lehtinen, K.: Better late than never or: verifying asynchronous components at runtime. In: Peters, K., Willemse, T.A.C. (eds.) FORTE 2021. LNCS, vol. 12719, pp. 207–225. Springer, Cham (2021). https://doi.org/10.1007/978-3-030-78089-0_14

9. Attard, D.P., Francalanza, A.: Trace partitioning and local monitoring for asynchronous components. In: Cimatti, A., Sirjani, M. (eds.) SEFM 2017. LNCS, vol. 10469, pp. 219–235. Springer, Cham (2017). https://doi.org/10.1007/978-3-319-66197-1_14

10. Baier, C., Katoen, J.-P.: Principles of Model Checking. MIT Press, Cambridge (2008)

11. Bartocci, E., Falcone, Y., Francalanza, A., Reger, G.: Introduction to runtime verification. In: Bartocci, E., Falcone, Y. (eds.) Lectures on Runtime Verification. LNCS, vol. 10457, pp. 1–33. Springer, Cham (2018). https://doi.org/10.1007/978-3-319-75632-5_1

12. Billingsley, P.: Probability and Measure, 3rd edn. Wiley-Interscience, Hoboken (1995)

13. Bortolussi, L., Cairoli, F., Paoletti, N., Smolka, S.A., Stoller, S.D.: Neural predictive monitoring. In: Finkbeiner, B., Mariani, L. (eds.) RV 2019. LNCS, vol. 11757, pp. 129–147. Springer, Cham (2019). https://doi.org/10.1007/978-3-030-32079-9_8

14. Bartolo Burlò, C., Francalanza, A., Scalas, A., Trubiani, C., Tuosto, E.: Towards probabilistic session-type monitoring. In: Damiani, F., Dardha, O. (eds.) COORDINATION 2021. LNCS, vol. 12717, pp. 106–120. Springer, Cham (2021). https://doi.org/10.1007/978-3-030-78142-2_7

15. Chen, X., Sankaranarayanan, S.: Model predictive real-time monitoring of linear systems. In: Proceedings of the 2017 IEEE Real-Time Systems Symposium, RTSS 2017, pp. 297–306. IEEE Computer Society (2017)

16. Dam, M.: Fixed points of Büchi automata. In: Shyamasundar, R. (ed.) FSTTCS 1992. LNCS, vol. 652, pp. 39–50. Springer, Heidelberg (1992). https://doi.org/10.1007/3-540-56287-7_93

17. Doyen, L., Henzinger, T.A., Raskin, J.-F.: Equivalence of labeled Markov chains. Int. J. Found. Comput. Sci. **19**(3), 549–563 (2008)

18. Elgyütt, A., Ferrère, T., Henzinger, T.A.: Monitoring temporal logic with clock variables. In: Jansen, D.N., Prabhakar, P. (eds.) FORMATS 2018. LNCS, vol. 11022, pp. 53–70. Springer, Cham (2018). https://doi.org/10.1007/978-3-030-00151-3_4

19. Esparza, J., Kiefer, S., Kretínský, J., Weininger, M.: Enforcing ω-regular properties in Markov chains by restarting. In: Haddad, S., Varacca, D. (eds.) Proceedings of the 32nd International Conference on Concurrency Theory, CONCUR 2021. LIPIcs, vol. 203, pp. 5:1–5:22. Schloss Dagstuhl - Leibniz-Zentrum für Informatik (2021)

20. Falcone, Y., Fernandez, J.-C., Mounier, L.: What can you verify and enforce at runtime? Int. J. Softw. Tools Technol. Transfer **14**(3), 349–382 (2012)

21. Ferrère, T., Henzinger, T.A., Kragl, B.: Monitoring event frequencies. In: Fernández, M., Muscholl, A. (eds.) Proceedings of the 28th EACSL Annual Conference on Computer Science Logic, CSL 2020. LIPIcs, vol. 152, pp. 20:1–20:16. Schloss Dagstuhl - Leibniz-Zentrum für Informatik (2020)

22. Ferrère, T., Henzinger, T.A., Saraç, N.E.: A theory of register monitors. In: Dawar, A., Grädel, E. (eds.) Proceedings of the 33rd Annual ACM/IEEE Symposium on Logic in Computer Science, LICS 2018, pp. 394–403. ACM (2018)

23. Francalanza, A.: Consistently-detecting monitors. In: Meyer, R., Nestmann, U. (eds.) 28th International Conference on Concurrency Theory, CONCUR 2017. LIPIcs, Berlin, Germany, 5–8 September 2017, vol. 85, pp. 8:1–8:19. Schloss Dagstuhl - Leibniz-Zentrum für Informatik (2017)

24. Francalanza, A.: A theory of monitors. Inf. Comput. **281**, 104704 (2021)

25. Francalanza, A., et al.: A foundation for runtime monitoring. In: Lahiri, S., Reger, G. (eds.) RV 2017. LNCS, vol. 10548, pp. 8–29. Springer, Cham (2017). https://doi.org/10.1007/978-3-319-67531-2_2

26. Francalanza, A., Aceto, L., Ingólfsdóttir, A.: Monitorability for the Hennessy-Milner logic with recursion. Formal Methods Syst. Des. **51**(1), 87–116 (2017)

27. Gondi, K., Patel, Y., Sistla, A.P.: Monitoring the full range of ω-regular properties of stochastic systems. In: Jones, N.D., Müller-Olm, M. (eds.) VMCAI 2009. LNCS, vol. 5403, pp. 105–119. Springer, Heidelberg (2008). https://doi.org/10.1007/978-3-540-93900-9_12

28. Hennessy, M., Milner, R.: Algebraic laws for nondeterminism and concurrency. J. ACM **32**(1), 137–161 (1985)

29. Henzinger, T.A., Saraç, N.E.: Monitorability under assumptions. In: Deshmukh, J., Ničković, D. (eds.) RV 2020. LNCS, vol. 12399, pp. 3–18. Springer, Cham (2020). https://doi.org/10.1007/978-3-030-60508-7_1

30. Henzinger, T.A., Saraç, N.E.: Quantitative and approximate monitoring. In: Proceedings of the 36th Annual ACM/IEEE Symposium on Logic in Computer Science, LICS 2021, pp. 1–14. IEEE (2021)

31. Junges, S., Torfah, H., Seshia, S.A.: Runtime monitors for Markov decision processes. In: Silva, A., Leino, K.R.M. (eds.) CAV 2021. LNCS, vol. 12760, pp. 553–576. Springer, Cham (2021). https://doi.org/10.1007/978-3-030-81688-9_26

32. Kwiatkowska, M.Z., Norman, G., Parker, D.: The PRISM benchmark suite. In: Proceedings of the Ninth International Conference on Quantitative Evaluation of Systems, QEST 2012, pp. 203–204. IEEE Computer Society (2012)

33. Phan, D., Paoletti, N., Zhang, T., Grosu, R., Smolka, S.A., Stoller, S.D.: Neural state classification for hybrid systems. In: Lahiri, S.K., Wang, C. (eds.) ATVA 2018. LNCS, vol. 11138, pp. 422–440. Springer, Cham (2018). https://doi.org/10.1007/978-3-030-01090-4_25

34. Sistla, A.P., Srinivas, A.R.: Monitoring temporal properties of stochastic systems. In: Logozzo, F., Peled, D.A., Zuck, L.D. (eds.) VMCAI 2008. LNCS, vol. 4905, pp. 294–308. Springer, Heidelberg (2008). https://doi.org/10.1007/978-3-540-78163-9_25

35. Sistla, A.P., Žefran, M., Feng, Y.: Runtime monitoring of stochastic cyber-physical systems with hybrid state. In: Khurshid, S., Sen, K. (eds.) RV 2011. LNCS, vol. 7186, pp. 276–293. Springer, Heidelberg (2012). https://doi.org/10.1007/978-3-642-29860-8_21

36. Tao, T.: An Introduction to Measure Theory. Graduate Studies in Mathematics. American Mathematical Society, Providence (2013)

37. Vardi, M.Y.: Automatic verification of probabilistic concurrent finite-state programs. In: 26th Annual Symposium on Foundations of Computer Science, Portland, Oregon, USA, 21–23 October 1985, pp. 327–338. IEEE Computer Society (1985)

38. Vardi, M.Y.: A temporal fixpoint calculus. In: Ferrante, J., Mager, P. (eds.) Conference Record of the Fifteenth Annual ACM Symposium on Principles of Programming Languages, San Diego, California, USA, 10–13 January 1988, pp. 250–259. ACM Press (1988)

On the Foundations of Cycles in Bayesian Networks

Christel Baier[1], Clemens Dubslaff[1], Holger Hermanns[2,3], and Nikolai Käfer[1(✉)]

[1] TU Dresden, Dresden, Germany
{christel.baier,clemens.dubslaff,nikolai.kaefer}@tu-dresden.de
[2] Saarland University, Saarbrücken, Germany
hermanns@cs.uni-saarland.de
[3] Institute of Intelligent Software, Guangzhou, China

Abstract. Bayesian networks (BNs) are a probabilistic graphical model widely used for representing expert knowledge and reasoning under uncertainty. Traditionally, they are based on directed acyclic graphs that capture dependencies between random variables. However, directed cycles can naturally arise when cross-dependencies between random variables exist, e.g., for modeling feedback loops. Existing methods to deal with such cross-dependencies usually rely on reductions to BNs without cycles. These approaches are fragile to generalize, since their justifications are intermingled with additional knowledge about the application context. In this paper, we present a foundational study regarding semantics for cyclic BNs that are generic and conservatively extend the cycle-free setting. First, we propose constraint-based semantics that specify requirements for full joint distributions over a BN to be consistent with the local conditional probabilities and independencies. Second, two kinds of limit semantics that formalize infinite unfolding approaches are introduced and shown to be computable by a Markov chain construction.

1 Introduction

A *Bayesian network* (BN) is a probabilistic graphical model representing a set of random variables and their conditional dependencies. BNs are ubiquitous across many fields where reasoning under uncertainties is of interest [10]. Specifically, a BN is a directed acyclic graph with the random variables as nodes and edges manifesting conditional dependencies, quantified by *conditional probability tables* (CPTs). The probability of any random variable can then be deduced by the CPT entries along all its predecessors. Here, these probabilities are independent of all variables that are no (direct or transitive) predecessors in the graph. Acyclicity is hence crucial and commonly assumed to be rooted in some sort of causality [23].

This work was partially supported by the DFG in projects TRR 248 (CPEC, see https://perspicuous-computing.science, project ID 389792660) and EXC 2050/1 (CeTI, project ID 390696704, as part of Germany's Excellence Strategy), and the Key-Area Research and Development Program Grant 2018B010107004 of Guangdong Province.

J.-F. Raskin and K. Chatterjee (Eds.): Principles of Systems Design, LNCS 13660, pp. 343–363, 2022.
https://doi.org/10.1007/978-3-031-22337-2_17

Y	$X=T$	$X=F$
F	s_1	$1-s_1$
T	s_2	$1-s_2$

X	$Y=T$	$Y=F$
F	t_1	$1-t_1$
T	t_2	$1-t_2$

Fig. 1. A cyclic GBN with CPTs for X and Y

A classical use of BNs is in expert systems [22] where BNs aggregate statistical data obtained by several independent studies. In the medical domain, e.g., they can capture the correlation of certain symptoms, diseases, and human factors [11, 15, 26].

Imagine for instance an expert system for supporting diagnosis of Covid-19, harvesting multiple clinical studies. One study might have investigated the percentage of patients who have been diagnosed with fever also having Covid-19, while another study in turn might have investigated among the Covid-19 patients whether they have fever, too. Clearly, both studies investigate the dependency between fever and Covid-19, but under different conditions. Fever may weaken the immune system and could increase the risk of a Covid-19 infection, while Covid-19 itself has fever as a symptom. In case there is uniform knowledge about "which symptom was first" in each of the constituent studies, then *dynamic Bayesian networks* (DBNs) [19] could be used as a model for the expert system, breaking the interdependence of fever and Covid-19 through a precedence relation. However, this implies either to rely only on studies where these temporal dependencies are clearly identified or to introduce an artificial notion of time that might lead to spurious results [18]. A naive encoding into the BN framework always yields a graph structure that contains cycles, as is the case in our small example shown in Fig. 1 where X and Y stand for the random variables of diagnosing Covid-19 and fever, respectively.

That cycles might be unavoidable has already been observed in seminal papers such as [15, 22]. But acyclicity is crucial for computing the joint probability distribution of a BN, and thereby is a prerequisite for, e.g., routine inference tasks. Existing literature that considers cycles in BNs mainly recommends to reduce questions on the probability values to properties in acyclic BNs. For instance, in [11] nodes are collapsed towards removing cycles, while [22] suggests to condition on each value combination on a cycle, generating a decomposition into tree-like BNs and then averaging over the results to replace cycles. Sometimes, application-specific methods that restructure the cyclic BN towards an acyclic BN by introducing additional nodes [8, 26] or by unrolling cycles up to a bounded depth [2, 17] have been reported to give satisfactory results. Other approaches either remove edges that have less influence or reverse edges on cycles (see, e.g., [10]). However, such approaches are highly application dependent and hinge on knowledge about the context of the statistical data used to construct the BN. Furthermore, as already pointed out by [30], they usually reduce the solution space of families of joint distributions to a single one, or introduce solutions not consistent with the CPTs of the original cyclic BN. While obviously many practitioners have stumbled on the problem how to treat cycles in BNs and on the foundational question "What is the meaning of a cyclic BN?", there is very little work on the foundations of Bayesian reasoning with cycles.

In this paper, we approach this question by presenting general semantics for BNs with cycles, together with algorithms to compute families of joint distributions for such BNs. First, we investigate how the two main constituents of classical BNs, namely consistency with the CPTs and independencies induced by the graph structure, influence the joint distributions in the presence of cycles. This leads to *constraints semantics* for cyclic BNs that comprise all those joint distributions respecting the constraints, being either a single uniquely defined one, none, or infinitely many distributions. Second, we present semantics that formalize unfolding approaches and depend on the choice of a *cutset*, a set of random variables that break every cycle in a cyclic BN. Intuitively, such cutsets form the seams along which feedback loops can be unraveled. These semantics are defined in terms of the limit (or limit average) of a sequence of distributions at descending levels in the infinite unfolding of the BN. We show that the same semantics can be defined using a Markov chain construction and subsequent long-run frequency analysis, which enables both precise computation of the semantics as well as deep insights in the semantics' behavior. Among others, an immediate result is that the family of distributions induced with respect to the limit semantics is always non-empty. As we will argue, the limit semantics have obvious relations to a manifold of approaches that have appeared in the literature, yet they have not been spelled out and studied explicitly.

1.1   Notation

Let $\mathcal{V}$ be a set of Boolean random variables[1] over the domain $\mathbb{B} = \{\mathsf{F}, \mathsf{T}\}$. We usually denote elements of $\mathcal{V}$ by X, Y, or Z. An *assignment* over $\mathcal{V}$ is a function $b\colon \mathcal{V} \to \mathbb{B}$ which we may specify through set notation, e.g., $b = \{X{=}\mathsf{T}, Y{=}\mathsf{F}\}$ for $b(X) = \mathsf{T}$ and $b(Y) = \mathsf{F}$, or even more succinctly as $X\overline{Y}$. The set of all possible assignments over $\mathcal{V}$ is denoted by $Asg(\mathcal{V})$. We write $b_{\mathcal{U}}$ for the restriction of b to a subset $\mathcal{U} \subseteq \mathcal{V}$, e.g., $b_{\{X\}} = \{X{=}\mathsf{T}\}$, and may omit set braces, e.g., $b_{X,Y} = b_{\{X,Y\}}$.

A *distribution* over a set $\mathcal{S}$ is a function $\mu\colon \mathcal{S} \to [0,1]$ where $\sum_{s\in\mathcal{S}} \mu(s) = 1$. The set of all distributions over $\mathcal{S}$ is denoted by $Dist(\mathcal{S})$. For $|\mathcal{S}| = n$, μ will occasionally be represented as a vector of size n for some fixed order on $\mathcal{S}$. In the following, we are mainly concerned with distributions over assignments, that is distributions $\mu \in Dist(Asg(\mathcal{V}))$ for some set of random variables $\mathcal{V}$. Each such distribution μ induces a probability measure (also called μ) on $2^{Asg(\mathcal{V})}$. Thus, for a set of assignments $\phi \subseteq Asg(\mathcal{V})$, we have $\mu(\phi) = \sum_{b\in\phi} \mu(b)$. We are often interested in the probability of a *partial assignment* $d \in Asg(\mathcal{U})$ on a subset $\mathcal{U} \subsetneq \mathcal{V}$ of variables, which is given as the probability of the set of all full assignments $b \in Asg(\mathcal{V})$ that agree with d on $\mathcal{U}$. As a shorthand, we define

---

[1]   We use Boolean random variables for simplicity of representation, an extension of the proposed semantics over random variables with arbitrary finite state spaces is certainly possible.

$$\mu(d) \; := \; \mu(\{b \in Asg(\mathcal{V}) : b_{\mathcal{U}} = d\}) \; = \sum_{\substack{b \in Asg(\mathcal{V}) \\ \text{s.t. } b_{\mathcal{U}} = d}} \mu(b).$$

The special case $\mu(X{=}\top)$ is called the *marginal probability* of X. The restriction of $\mu \in Dist(Asg(\mathcal{V}))$ to $\mathcal{U}$, denoted $\mu|_{\mathcal{U}} \in Dist(Asg(\mathcal{U}))$, is given by $\mu|_{\mathcal{U}}(d) := \mu(d)$. For a set $\mathcal{W}$ disjoint from $\mathcal{V}$ and $\nu \in Dist(Asg(\mathcal{W}))$, the *product distribution* of μ and ν is given by $(\mu \otimes \nu)(c) := \mu(c_{\mathcal{V}}) \cdot \nu(c_{\mathcal{W}})$ for every $c \in Asg(\mathcal{V} \cup \mathcal{W})$. μ is called a *Dirac distribution* if $\mu(b) = 1$ for some assignment $b \in Asg(\mathcal{V})$ and thus $\mu(c) = 0$ for all other assignments $c \neq b$. A Dirac distribution derived from a given assignment b is denoted by $Dirac(b)$.

Graph Notations. For a graph $\mathcal{G} = \langle \mathcal{V}, \mathcal{E} \rangle$ with nodes $\mathcal{V}$ and directed edges $\mathcal{E} \subseteq \mathcal{V} \times \mathcal{V}$, we may represent an edge $(X, Y) \in \mathcal{E}$ as $X \to Y$ if $\mathcal{E}$ is clear from context. $Pre(X) := \{Y \in \mathcal{V} : Y \to X\}$ denotes the set of *parents* of a node $X \in \mathcal{V}$, and $Post^*(X) := \{Y \in \mathcal{V} : X \to \cdots \to Y\}$ is the set of nodes *reachable* from X. A node X is called *initial* if $Pre(X) = \varnothing$, and $Init(\mathcal{G})$ is the set of all nodes initial in $\mathcal{G}$. A graph $\mathcal{G}$ is *strongly connected* if each node in $\mathcal{V}$ is reachable from every other node. A set of nodes $\mathcal{D}$ is a *strongly connected component* (SCC) of $\mathcal{G}$ if all nodes in $\mathcal{D}$ can reach each other and $\mathcal{D}$ is not contained in another SCC, and a *bottom SCC* (BSCC) if no node in $\mathcal{V} \setminus \mathcal{D}$ can be reached from $\mathcal{D}$.

Markov Chains. A *discrete-time Markov chain* (DTMC) is a tuple $\mathcal{M} = \langle \mathcal{S}, \mathbf{P} \rangle$ where $\mathcal{S}$ is a finite set of states and $\mathbf{P} \colon \mathcal{S} \times \mathcal{S} \to [0, 1]$ a function such that $\mathbf{P}(s, \cdot) \in Dist(\mathcal{S})$ for all states $s \in \mathcal{S}$. The underlying graph $\mathcal{G}_{\mathcal{M}} = \langle \mathcal{S}, \mathcal{E} \rangle$ is defined by $\mathcal{E} = \{(s, t) \in \mathcal{S} \times \mathcal{S} : \mathbf{P}(s, t) > 0\}$. The transient distribution $\pi_n^\iota \in Dist(\mathcal{S})$ at step n is defined through the probability $\pi_n^\iota(s)$ to be in state s after n steps if starting with initial state distribution ι. It satisfies (in matrix-vector notation) $\pi_n^\iota = \iota \cdot \mathbf{P}^n$. We are also interested in the long-run frequency of state occupancies when n tends to infinity, defined as the Cesàro limit $\mathrm{lrf}^\iota \colon \mathcal{S} \to [0, 1]$:

$$\mathrm{lrf}^\iota(s) \; := \; \lim_{n \to \infty} \frac{1}{n+1} \sum_{i=0}^{n} \pi_n^\iota(s). \tag{LRF}$$

This limit always exists and corresponds to the long-run fraction of time spent in each state [12]. The limit probability $\lim_{n \to \infty} \pi_n^\iota$ is arguably more intuitive as a measure of the long-run behavior, but may not exist (due to periodicity). In case of existence, it agrees with the Cesàro limit lrf^ι. If $\mathcal{G}_{\mathcal{M}}$ forms an SCC, the limit is independent of the choice of ι and the superscript can be dropped. We denote this limit by $\mathrm{lrf}_{\mathcal{M}}$.

2   Generalized Bayesian Networks

We introduce *generalized Bayesian networks* (GBNs) as a BN model that does not impose acyclicity and comes with a distribution over initial nodes.

Definition 1 (Generalized BN). *A GBN $\mathcal{B}$ is a tuple $\langle \mathcal{G}, \mathcal{P}, \iota \rangle$ where*

- $\mathcal{G} = \langle \mathcal{V}, \mathcal{E} \rangle$ *is a directed graph with nodes $\mathcal{V}$ and an edge relation $\mathcal{E} \subseteq \mathcal{V} \times \mathcal{V}$,*
- $\mathcal{P}$ *is a function that maps all non-initial nodes $X \in \mathcal{V} \backslash Init(\mathcal{G})$ paired with each of their parent assignments $b \in Asg(Pre(X))$ to a distribution*

$$\mathcal{P}(X, b) \colon Asg(\{X\}) \to [0, 1],$$

- ι *is a distribution over the assignments for the initial nodes $Init(\mathcal{G})$, i.e., $\iota \in Dist(Asg(Init(\mathcal{G})))$.*

The distributions $\mathcal{P}(X, b)$ have the same role as the entries in a *conditional probability table* (CPT) for X in classical BNs: they specify the probability for $X=\textsf{T}$ or $X=\textsf{F}$ depending on the assignments of the predecessors of X. To this end, for $X \in \mathcal{V} \backslash Init(\mathcal{G})$ and $b \in Asg(Pre(X))$, we also write $\Pr(X=\textsf{T} \mid b)$ for $\mathcal{P}(X, b)(X=\textsf{T})$. In the literature, initial nodes are often assigned a marginal probability via a CPT as well, assuming independence of all initial nodes. Differently, in our definition of GBNs, it is possible to specify an arbitrary distribution ι over all initial nodes. If needed, $\mathcal{P}$ can be easily extended to initial nodes by setting $\mathcal{P}(X, \varnothing) := \iota|_{\{X\}}$ for all $X \in Init(\mathcal{G})$. Hence, classical BNs arise as a special instance of GBNs where the graph $\mathcal{G}$ is acyclic and initial nodes are pairwise independent. In that case, the CPTs given by $\mathcal{P}$ are a compact representation of a single unique full joint distribution $dist_{\mathrm{BN}}(\mathcal{B})$ over all random variables $X \in \mathcal{V}$. For every assignment $b \in Asg(\mathcal{V})$, we can compute $dist_{\mathrm{BN}}(\mathcal{B})(b)$ by the so-called *chain rule*:

$$dist_{\mathrm{BN}}(\mathcal{B})(b) := \iota\big(b_{Init(\mathcal{G})}\big) \cdot \prod_{X \in \mathcal{V} \backslash Init(\mathcal{G})} \Pr\big(b_X \mid b_{Pre(X)}\big). \qquad \text{(CR)}$$

In light of the semantics introduced later on, we define the *standard BN-semantics* of an acyclic GBN $\mathcal{B}$ as the set $[\![\mathcal{B}]\!]_{\mathrm{BN}} := \{dist_{\mathrm{BN}}(\mathcal{B})\}$, and $[\![\mathcal{B}]\!]_{\mathrm{BN}} := \varnothing$ if $\mathcal{B}$ contains cycles.

The distribution $dist_{\mathrm{BN}}(\mathcal{B})$ satisfies two crucial properties: First, it is consistent with the CPT entries given by $\mathcal{P}$ and the distribution ι, and second, it observes the independencies encoded in the graph $\mathcal{G}$. In fact, those two properties are sufficient to uniquely characterize $dist_{\mathrm{BN}}(\mathcal{B})$. We briefly review the notion of independence and formally define CPT consistency later on in Section 3.

Independence. Any full joint probability distribution $\mu \in Dist(Asg(\mathcal{V}))$ may induce a number of conditional independencies among the random variables in $\mathcal{V}$. For $\mathcal{X}$, $\mathcal{Y}$, and $\mathcal{Z}$ disjoint subsets of $\mathcal{V}$, the random variables in $\mathcal{X}$ and $\mathcal{Y}$ are independent under μ given $\mathcal{Z}$ if the conditional probability of each assignment over the nodes in $\mathcal{X}$ given an assignment for $\mathcal{Z}$ is unaffected by further conditioning on any assignment of $\mathcal{Y}$. Formally, the set $Indep(\mu)$ contains the triple $(\mathcal{X}, \mathcal{Y}, \mathcal{Z})$ iff for all $a \in Asg(\mathcal{X})$, $b \in Asg(\mathcal{Y})$, and $c \in Asg(\mathcal{Z})$, we have

$$\mu(a \mid b, c) = \mu(a \mid c) \quad \text{or} \quad \mu(b, c) = 0.$$

We also write $(\mathcal{X} \perp \mathcal{Y} \mid \mathcal{Z})$ for $(\mathcal{X}, \mathcal{Y}, \mathcal{Z}) \in Indep(\mu)$ and may omit the set brackets of $\mathcal{X}$, $\mathcal{Y}$, and $\mathcal{Z}$.

d-separation. For classical BNs, the graph topology encodes independencies that are necessarily satisfied by any full joint distribution regardless of the CPT entries. Given two random variables X and Y as well as a set of observed variables $\mathcal{Z}$, then X and Y are conditionally independent given $\mathcal{Z}$ if the corresponding nodes in the graph are *d-separated* given $\mathcal{Z}$ [6]. To establish *d*-separation, all simple undirected paths[2] between X and Y need to be *blocked* given $\mathcal{Z}$. Let $\mathbb{W}$ denote such a simple path $W_0, W_1, \ldots, W_k$ with $W_0 = X$, $W_k = Y$, and either $W_i \to W_{i+1}$ or $W_i \leftarrow W_{i+1}$ for all $i < k$. Then $\mathbb{W}$ is blocked given $\mathcal{Z}$ if and only if there exists an index i, $0 < i < k$, such that one of the following two conditions holds: (1) W_i is in $\mathcal{Z}$ and is situated in a *chain* or a *fork* in $\mathbb{W}$, i.e.,

- $W_{i-1} \to W_i \to W_{i+1}$ (forward chain)
- $W_{i-1} \leftarrow W_i \leftarrow W_{i+1}$ (backward chain)   and $W_i \in \mathcal{Z}$,
- $W_{i-1} \leftarrow W_i \to W_{i+1}$ (fork)

(2) W_i is in a *collider* and neither W_i nor any descendant of W_i is in $\mathcal{Z}$, i.e.,

- $W_{i-1} \to W_i \leftarrow W_{i+1}$ (collider)   and $Post^*(W_i) \cap \mathcal{Z} = \varnothing$.

Two sets of nodes $\mathcal{X}$ and $\mathcal{Y}$ are *d*-separated given a third set $\mathcal{Z}$ if for each $X \in \mathcal{X}$ and $Y \in \mathcal{Y}$, X and Y are *d*-separated given $\mathcal{Z}$. Notably, the *d*-separation criterion is applicable also in presence of cycles [28]. For a graph $\mathcal{G} = \langle \mathcal{V}, \mathcal{E} \rangle$ of a GBN, we define the set *d-sep*$(\mathcal{G})$ as

$$d\text{-}sep(\mathcal{G}) := \{(\mathcal{X}, \mathcal{Y}, \mathcal{Z}) \in (2^{\mathcal{V}})^3 : \mathcal{X} \text{ and } \mathcal{Y} \text{ are } d\text{-separated given } \mathcal{Z}\}.$$

For acyclic Bayesian networks it is well known that the independencies evident from the standard BN semantics' distribution include the independencies derived from the graph. That is, for acyclic GBNs $\mathcal{B}_\emptyset = \langle \mathcal{G}, \mathcal{P}, \iota \rangle$ where all initial nodes are pairwise independent under ι, we have

$$d\text{-}sep(\mathcal{G}) \subseteq Indep(dist_{\mathrm{BN}}(\mathcal{B}_\emptyset)).$$

For an arbitrary initial distribution, the above relation does not necessarily hold. However, we can still find a set of independencies that are necessarily observed by the standard BN semantics and thus act as a similar lower bound. We do so by assuming the worst case, namely that each initial node depends on every other initial node under ι. Formally, given a graph $\mathcal{G} = \langle \mathcal{V}, \mathcal{E} \rangle$, we define a closure operation *Close*$(\cdot)$ as follows and compute the set *d-sep*$(Close(\mathcal{G}))$:

$$Close(\mathcal{G}) := \langle \mathcal{V}, \mathcal{E} \cup \{(A, B) \text{ for } A, B \in Init(\mathcal{G}), A \neq B\} \rangle.$$

Lemma 1. *Let $\mathcal{B}_\emptyset = \langle \mathcal{G}, \mathcal{P}, \iota \rangle$ be an acyclic GBN. Then*

$$d\text{-}sep(Close(\mathcal{G})) \subseteq Indep(dist_{\mathrm{BN}}(\mathcal{B}_\emptyset)).$$

As intuitively expected, the presence of cycles in $\mathcal{G}$ generally reduces the number of graph independencies, though note that also in strongly connected graphs independencies may exist. For example, if $\mathcal{G}$ is a four-node cycle with nodes W, X, Y, and Z, then $d\text{-}sep(\mathcal{G}) = \{(W \perp Y \mid X, Z), (X \perp Z \mid W, Y)\}$.

---

[2] A path is simple if no node occurs twice in the path. "Undirected" in this context means that edges in either direction can occur along the path.

3   Constraints Semantics

For classical acyclic BNs there is exactly one distribution that agrees with all CPTs and satisfies the independencies encoded in the graph. This distribution can easily be constructed by means of the chain rule (CR). For cyclic GBNs, applying the chain rule towards a full joint distribution is not possible in general, as the result is usually not a valid probability distribution. Still, we can look for distributions consistent with a GBN's CPTs and the independencies derived from its graph. Depending on the GBN, we will see that there may be none, exactly one, or even infinitely many distributions fulfilling these constraints.

3.1   CPT-consistency

We first provide a formal definition of CPT consistency in terms of linear constraints on full joint distributions.

Definition 2 (Strong and weak CPT-consistency). *Let $\mathcal{B}$ be a GBN with nodes $\mathcal{V}$ and $X \in \mathcal{V}$. Then μ is called strongly CPT-consistent for X in $\mathcal{B}$ (or simply CPT-consistent) if for all $c \in Asg(Pre(X))$*

$$\mu(X{=}\mathsf{T}, c) \;=\; \mu(c) \cdot \Pr(X{=}\mathsf{T} \mid c). \tag{CPT}$$

We say that μ is weakly CPT-consistent for X in $\mathcal{B}$ if

$$\mu(X{=}\mathsf{T}) \;=\; \sum_{c \in Asg(Pre(X))} \mu(c) \cdot \Pr(X{=}\mathsf{T} \mid c). \tag{wCPT}$$

Intuitively, the constraint (CPT) is satisfied for μ if the conditional probability $\mu(X{=}\mathsf{T} \mid c)$ equals the entry in the CPT for X under assignment c, i.e., $\mu(X{=}\mathsf{T} \mid c) = \Pr(X{=}\mathsf{T} \mid c)$. In the weak case (wCPT), only the resulting marginal probability of X needs to agree with the CPTs.

Definition 3 (CPT and wCPT semantics). *For a GBN $\mathcal{B} = \langle \mathcal{G}, \mathcal{P}, \iota \rangle$, the CPT-semantics $[\![\mathcal{B}]\!]_{\mathrm{CPT}}$ is the set of all distributions $\mu \in Dist(Asg(\mathcal{V}))$ where $\mu|_{Init(\mathcal{G})} = \iota$ and μ is CPT-consistent for every node $X \in \mathcal{V} \backslash Init(\mathcal{G})$. The weak CPT-semantics $[\![\mathcal{B}]\!]_{\mathrm{wCPT}}$ is defined analogously.*

Clearly, we have $[\![\mathcal{B}]\!]_{\mathrm{CPT}} \subseteq [\![\mathcal{B}]\!]_{\mathrm{wCPT}}$ for all $\mathcal{B}$. The next example shows that depending on the CPT values, the set $[\![\mathcal{B}]\!]_{\mathrm{CPT}}$ may be empty, a singleton, or of infinite cardinality.

Example 1. To find CPT-consistent distributions for the GBN from Fig. 1, we construct a system of linear equations whose solutions form distributions $\mu \in Dist(Asg(\{X, Y\}))$, represented as vectors in the space $[0, 1]^4$:

$$
\begin{pmatrix}
s_1 & 0 & s_1{-}1 & 0 \\
0 & s_2 & 0 & s_2{-}1 \\
t_1 & t_1{-}1 & 0 & 0 \\
0 & 0 & t_2 & t_2{-}1 \\
1 & 1 & 1 & 1
\end{pmatrix}
\cdot
\begin{pmatrix}
\mu_{\overline{XY}} \\
\mu_{\overline{X}Y} \\
\mu_{X\overline{Y}} \\
\mu_{XY}
\end{pmatrix}
=
\begin{pmatrix}
0 \\
0 \\
0 \\
0 \\
1
\end{pmatrix}
$$

where, e.g., $\mu_{X\overline{Y}}$ abbreviates $\mu(X{=}\mathsf{T}, Y{=}\mathsf{F})$. The first line of the matrix states the (CPT) constraint for node X and the parent assignment $c = \{Y{=}\mathsf{F}\}$:

$$0 = s_1 \cdot \mu_{\overline{X}\,\overline{Y}} + 0 \cdot \mu_{\overline{X}Y} + (s_1{-}1) \cdot \mu_{X\overline{Y}} + 0 \cdot \mu_{XY}$$
$$\mu_{X\overline{Y}} = (\mu_{X\overline{Y}} + \mu_{\overline{X}\,\overline{Y}}) \cdot s_1$$
$$\mu_{X\overline{Y}} = \mu_{\overline{Y}} \cdot \Pr(X{=}\mathsf{T} \mid Y{=}\mathsf{F})$$
$$\mu(X{=}\mathsf{T}, c) = \mu(c) \cdot \Pr(X{=}\mathsf{T} \mid c).$$

Analogously, the following three rows encode the CPT constraints for X, Y, and their remaining parent assignments. The last equation ensures that solutions are indeed probability distributions satisfying $\sum_c \mu(c) = 1$.

The number of solutions for the system now depends on the CPT entries s_1, s_2, t_1, and t_2. For $s_1 = t_2 = 0$ and $s_2 = t_1 = 1$, no solution exists as the first four equations require $\mu(b) = 0$ for all $b \in Asg(\{X, Y\})$, while the last equation ensures $\mu_{\overline{X}\,\overline{Y}} + \mu_{\overline{X}Y} + \mu_{X\overline{Y}} + \mu_{XY} = 1$. For $s_1 = t_1 = 0$ and $s_2 = t_2 = 1$, all distributions with $\mu_{XY} = 1 - \mu_{\overline{X}\,\overline{Y}}$ and $\mu_{X\overline{Y}} = \mu_{\overline{X}Y} = 0$ are solutions. Finally, e.g., for $s_1 = t_1 = 3/4$ and $s_2 = t_2 = 1/2$, there is exactly one solution with $\mu_{\overline{X}\,\overline{Y}} = 1/10$ and $\mu(b) = 3/10$ for the other three assignments.

3.2   Independence-consistency

We extend CPT semantics with a set of independencies that need to be observed by all induced distributions.

Definition 4 (CPT-$\mathcal{I}$ semantics). *For a GBN $\mathcal{B} = \langle \mathcal{G}, \mathcal{P}, \iota \rangle$ and a set of independencies $\mathcal{I}$, the CPT-$\mathcal{I}$semantics $[\![\mathcal{B}]\!]_{\text{CPT-}\mathcal{I}}$ is defined as the set of all CPT-consistent distributions μ for which $\mathcal{I} \subseteq Indep(\mu)$ holds.*

Technically, the distributions in $[\![\mathcal{B}]\!]_{\text{CPT-}\mathcal{I}}$ have to fulfill the following polynomial constraints in addition to the CPT-consistency constraints:

$$\mu(b) \cdot \mu(b_{\mathcal{W}}) = \mu(b_{\{X\}\cup\mathcal{W}}) \cdot \mu(b_{\mathcal{U}\cup\mathcal{W}}) \tag{CPT-$\mathcal{I}$}$$

for each independence $(X \perp \mathcal{U} \mid \mathcal{W}) \in \mathcal{I}$ with variable $X \in \mathcal{V}$ and sets of variables $\mathcal{U}, \mathcal{W} \subseteq \mathcal{V}$, and for each assignment $b \in Asg(\{X\} \cup \mathcal{U} \cup \mathcal{W})$. Note that in case $\mu(b_{\mathcal{W}}) > 0$, (CPT-$\mathcal{I}$) is equivalent to the constraint $\mu(b_X \mid b_{\mathcal{U}\cup\mathcal{W}}) = \mu(b_X \mid b_{\mathcal{W}})$.

We can now formally state the alternative characterization of the standard BN semantics as the unique CPT-consistent distribution that satisfies the d-separation independencies of the graph. For each classical BN $\mathcal{B}$ with acyclic graph $\mathcal{G}$ and $\mathcal{I} = d\text{-}sep(\mathcal{G})$, we have $[\![\mathcal{B}]\!]_{\text{BN}} = \{ dist_{\text{BN}}(\mathcal{B}) \} = [\![\mathcal{B}]\!]_{\text{CPT-}\mathcal{I}}$. Thus, the CPT-$\mathcal{I}$ semantics provides a conservative extension of the standard BN semantics to GBNs with cycles. However, in practice, its use is limited since there might be no distribution that satisfies all constraints. In fact, the case where $[\![\mathcal{B}]\!]_{\text{CPT-}\mathcal{I}} = \varnothing$ is to be expected for most cyclic GBNs, given that the resulting constraint systems tend to be heavily over-determined.

The next section introduces semantics that follow a more constructive approach. We will see later on in Section 5.1 that the families of distributions induced by these semantics are always non-empty and usually singletons.

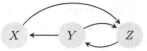

Fig. 2. The graph of a strongly connected GBN

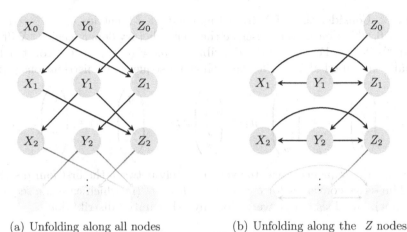

(a) Unfolding along all nodes   (b) Unfolding along the Z nodes

Fig. 3. Two infinite unfoldings of the graph in Fig. 2

4   Limit and Limit Average Semantics

We first develop the basic ideas underling the semantics by following an example, before giving a formal treatment in Section 4.2.

4.1   Intuition

Consider the GBN $\mathcal{B}$ whose graph $\mathcal{G}$ is depicted in Fig. 2. One way to get rid of the cycles is to construct an infinite unfolding of $\mathcal{B}$ as shown in Fig. 3a. In this new graph $\mathcal{G}_\infty$, each level contains a full copy of the original nodes and corresponds to some $n \in \mathbb{N}$. For any edge $X \to Y$ in the original graph, we add edges $X_n \to Y_{n+1}$ to $\mathcal{G}_\infty$, such that each edge descends one level deeper. Clearly any graph constructed in this way is acyclic, but this fact alone does not aid in finding a matching distribution since we dearly bought it by giving up finiteness. However, we can consider what happens when we plug in some initial distribution μ_0 over the nodes X_0, Y_0, and Z_0. Looking only at the first two levels, we then get a fully specified acyclic BN by using the CPTs given by $\mathcal{P}$ for X_1, Y_1, and Z_1. For this sub-BN, the standard BN semantics yields a full joint distribution over the six nodes from X_0 to Z_1, which also induces a distribution μ_1 over the three nodes at level 1. This procedure can then be repeated to construct a distribution μ_2 over the nodes X_2, Y_2, and Z_2, and, more generally, to get a distribution μ_{n+1} given a distribution μ_n. Recall that each of those distributions can be viewed as vector of size 2^3. Considering the sequence $\mu_0, \mu_1, \mu_2, \ldots$, the question naturally arises whether a limit exists, i.e., a distribution/vector μ such that

$$\mu = \lim_{n \to \infty} \mu_n.$$

Example 2. Consider the GBN from Fig. 1 with CPT entries $s_1 = t_2 = 1$ and $s_2 = t_1 = 0$, which intuitively describe the contradictory dependencies "X iff not Y" and "Y iff X". For any initial distribution $\mu_0 = \langle e\ f\ g\ h \rangle$, the construction informally described above yields the following sequence of distributions μ_n:

$$\mu_0 = \begin{pmatrix} e \\ f \\ g \\ h \end{pmatrix}, \ \mu_1 = \begin{pmatrix} f \\ h \\ e \\ g \end{pmatrix}, \ \mu_2 = \begin{pmatrix} h \\ g \\ f \\ e \end{pmatrix}, \ \mu_3 = \begin{pmatrix} g \\ e \\ h \\ f \end{pmatrix}, \ \mu_4 = \begin{pmatrix} e \\ f \\ g \\ h \end{pmatrix}, \ \ldots$$

As $\mu_4 = \mu_0$, the sequence starts to cycle infinitely between the first four distributions. The series converges for $e = f = g = h = 1/4$ (in which case the sequence is constant), but does not converge for any other initial distribution.

The example shows that the existence of the limit depends on the given initial distribution. In case no limit exists because some distributions keep repeating without ever converging, it is possible to determine the *limit average* (or *Cesàro limit*) of the sequence:

$$\tilde{\mu} = \lim_{n \to \infty} \frac{1}{n+1} \sum_{i=0}^{n} \mu_i.$$

The limit average has three nice properties: First, if the regular limit μ exists, then the limit average $\tilde{\mu}$ exists as well and is identical to μ. Second, in our use case, $\tilde{\mu}$ in fact always exists for any initial distribution μ_0. And third, as we will see in Section 5, the limit average corresponds to the long-run frequency of certain Markov chains, which allows us both to explicitly compute and to derive important properties of the limit distributions.

Example 3. Continuing Ex. 2, the limit average of the sequence $\mu_0, \mu_1, \mu_2, \ldots$ is the uniform distribution $\tilde{\mu} = \langle 1/4\ 1/4\ 1/4\ 1/4 \rangle$, regardless of the choice of μ_0.

Before we formally define the infinite unfolding of GBNs and the resulting limit semantics, there is one more observation to be made. To ensure that the unfolded graph $\mathcal{G}_\infty$ is acyclic, we redirected every edge of the GBN $\mathcal{B}$ to point one level deeper, resulting in the graph displayed in Fig. 3a. As can be seen in Fig. 3b, we also get an acyclic unfolded graph by only redirecting the edges originating in the Z nodes to the next level and keeping all other edges on the same level. The relevant property is to pick a set of nodes such that for each cycle in the original GBN $\mathcal{B}$, at least one node in the cycle is contained in the set. We call such sets the *cutsets* of $\mathcal{B}$.

Definition 5 (Cutset). *Let $\mathcal{B}$ be an GBN with graph $\mathcal{G} = \langle \mathcal{V}, \mathcal{E} \rangle$. A subset $\mathcal{C} \subseteq \mathcal{V}$ is a cutset for $\mathcal{B}$ if every cycle in $\mathcal{G}$ contains at least one node from $\mathcal{C}$.*

Example 4. The GBN in Fig. 2 has the following cutsets: $\{Y\}$, $\{Z\}$, $\{X, Y\}$, $\{X, Z\}$, $\{Y, Z\}$, and $\{X, Y, Z\}$. Note that $\{X\}$ does not form a cutset as no node from the cycle $Y \to Z \to Y$ is contained.

So far we implicitly used the set $\mathcal{V}$ of all nodes for the unfolding, which always trivially forms a cutset. The following definitions will be parameterized with a cutset, as the choice of cutsets influences the resulting distributions as well as the time complexity.

4.2 Formal Definition

Let $\mathcal{V}_n := \{X_n : X \in \mathcal{V}\}$ denote the set of nodes on the nth level of the unfolding in $\mathcal{G}_\infty$. For $\mathcal{C} \subseteq \mathcal{V}$ a cutset of the GBN, the subset of cutset nodes on that level is given by $\mathcal{C}_n := \{X_n \in \mathcal{V}_n : X \in \mathcal{C}\}$. Then a distribution $\gamma_n \in Dist(Asg(\mathcal{C}_n))$ for the cutset nodes in $\mathcal{C}_n$ suffices to get a full distribution $\mu_{n+1} \in Dist(Asg(\mathcal{V}_{n+1}))$ over all nodes on the next level, $n + 1$: We look at the graph fragment $\mathcal{G}_{n+1}$ of $\mathcal{G}_\infty$ given by the nodes $\mathcal{C}_n \cup \mathcal{V}_{n+1}$ and their respective edges. In this fragment, the cutset nodes are initial, so the cutset distribution γ_n can be combined with the initial distribution ι to act as new initial distribution. For the nodes in $\mathcal{V}_{n+1}$, the corresponding CPTs as given by $\mathcal{P}$ can be used, i.e., $\mathcal{P}_n(X_n, \cdot) = \mathcal{P}(X, \cdot)$ for $X_n \in \mathcal{V}_n$. Putting everything together, we obtain an acyclic GBN $\mathcal{B}_{n+1} = \langle \mathcal{G}_{n+1}, \mathcal{P}_{n+1}, \iota \otimes \gamma_n \rangle$. However, GBNs constructed in this way for each level $n > 0$ are all isomorphic and only differ in the given cutset distribution γ. For simplicity and in light of later use, we thus define a single representative GBN $Dissect(\mathcal{B}, \mathcal{C}, \gamma)$ that represents a dissection of $\mathcal{B}$ along a given cutset $\mathcal{C}$, with $\iota \otimes \gamma$ as initial distribution.

Definition 6 (Dissected GBN). *Let $\mathcal{B} = \langle \mathcal{G}, \mathcal{P}, \iota \rangle$ be a GBN with graph $\mathcal{G} = \langle \mathcal{V}, \mathcal{E} \rangle$ and $\mathcal{C} \subseteq \mathcal{V}$ a cutset for $\mathcal{B}$ with distribution $\gamma \in Dist(Asg(\mathcal{C}))$. Then, the $\mathcal{C}$-dissected GBN $Dissect(\mathcal{B}, \mathcal{C}, \gamma)$ is the acyclic GBN $\langle \mathcal{G}_\mathcal{C}, \mathcal{P}_\mathcal{C}, \iota \otimes \gamma \rangle$ with graph $\mathcal{G}_\mathcal{C} = \langle \mathcal{V} \cup \mathcal{C}', \mathcal{E}_\mathcal{C} \rangle$ where*

- *$\mathcal{C}' := \{X' : X \in \mathcal{C}\}$ extends $\mathcal{V}$ by fresh copies of all cutset nodes;*
- *incoming edges to nodes in $\mathcal{C}$ are redirected to their copies, i.e.,*

$$\mathcal{E}_\mathcal{C} := \{(X, Y') : (X, Y) \in \mathcal{E}, Y \in \mathcal{C}\} \cup \{(X, Y) : (X, Y) \in \mathcal{E}, Y \notin \mathcal{C}\};$$

- *the function $\mathcal{P}_\mathcal{C}$ uses the CPT entries given by $\mathcal{P}$ for the cutset nodes as entries for their copies and the original entries for all other nodes, i.e., we have $\mathcal{P}_\mathcal{C}(Y', a) = \mathcal{P}(Y, a)$ for each node $Y' \in \mathcal{C}'$ and parent assignment $a \in Asg(Pre(Y'))$, and $\mathcal{P}_\mathcal{C}(X, b) = \mathcal{P}(X, b)$ for $X \in \mathcal{V} \backslash \mathcal{C}$ and $b \in Asg(Pre(X))$.*

As any dissected GBN is acyclic by construction, the standard BN semantics yields a full joint distribution over all nodes in $\mathcal{V} \cup \mathcal{C}'$. We restrict this distribution to the nodes in $(\mathcal{V} \setminus \mathcal{C}) \cup \mathcal{C}'$, as those are the ones on the "next level" of the

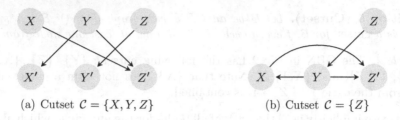

(a) Cutset $C = \{X, Y, Z\}$ (b) Cutset $C = \{Z\}$

Fig. 4. Dissections of the GBN in Fig. 2 for two cutsets

unfolding, while re-identifying the cutset node copies with the original nodes to get a distribution over $\mathcal{V}$. Formally, we define the distribution $Next(\mathcal{B}, \mathcal{C}, \gamma)$ for each assignment $b \in Asg(\mathcal{V})$ as

$$Next(\mathcal{B}, \mathcal{C}, \gamma)(b) := dist_{\mathrm{BN}}\big(Dissect(\mathcal{B}, \mathcal{C}, \gamma)\big)(b')$$

where the assignment $b' \in Asg\big((\mathcal{V} \backslash \mathcal{C}) \cup \mathcal{C}'\big)$ is given by $b'(X) = b(X)$ for all $X \in \mathcal{V} \backslash \mathcal{C}$ and $b'(Y') = b(Y)$ for all $Y \in \mathcal{C}$. In the unfolded GBN, this allows us to get from a cutset distribution γ_n to the next level distribution $\mu_{n+1} = Next(\mathcal{B}, \mathcal{C}, \gamma_n)$. The next cutset distribution γ_{n+1} is then given by restricting the full distribution to the nodes in $\mathcal{C}$, i.e., $\gamma_{n+1} = Next(\mathcal{B}, \mathcal{C}, \gamma_n)|_{\mathcal{C}}$.[3] Vice versa, a cutset distribution γ suffices to recover the full joint distribution over all nodes $\mathcal{V}$. Again using the standard BN semantics of the dissected GBN, we define the distribution $Extend(\mathcal{B}, \mathcal{C}, \gamma) \in Dist(Asg(\mathcal{V}))$ as

$$Extend(\mathcal{B}, \mathcal{C}, \gamma) := dist_{\mathrm{BN}}\big(Dissect(\mathcal{B}, \mathcal{C}, \gamma)\big)\big|_{\mathcal{V}}.$$

With these definitions at hand, we can formally define the limit and limit average semantics described in the previous section. Figure 4 shows two examples of dissections on the GBN of Fig. 2.

Definition 7 (Limit and limit average semantics). *Let $\mathcal{B}$ be a GBN over nodes $\mathcal{V}$ with cutset $\mathcal{C}$. The* limit semantics *of $\mathcal{B}$w.r.t. $\mathcal{C}$ is the partial function*

$$Lim(\mathcal{B}, \mathcal{C}, \cdot) : \; Dist\big(Asg(\mathcal{C})\big) \rightharpoonup Dist\big(Asg(\mathcal{V})\big)$$

from initial cutset distributions γ_0 to full distributions $\mu = Extend(\mathcal{B}, \mathcal{C}, \gamma)$ where

$$\gamma = \lim_{n \to \infty} \gamma_n \qquad and \qquad \gamma_{n+1} = Next(\mathcal{B}, \mathcal{C}, \gamma_n)|_{\mathcal{C}}.$$

The set $[\![\mathcal{B}]\!]_{\mathrm{LIM\text{-}}\mathcal{C}}$ is given by the image of $Lim(\mathcal{B}, \mathcal{C}, \cdot)$, i.e.,

$$[\![\mathcal{B}]\!]_{\mathrm{LIM\text{-}}\mathcal{C}} := \{Lim(\mathcal{B}, \mathcal{C}, \gamma_0) : \gamma_0 \in Dist(Asg(\mathcal{C})) \; s.t. \; Lim(\mathcal{B}, \mathcal{C}, \gamma_0) \; is \; defined\}.$$

---

[3] Recall that we may view distributions as vectors which allows us to equate distributions over different but isomorphic domains.

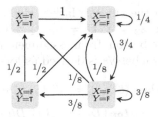

Fig. 5. A cutset Markov chain for a cutset $\mathcal{C} = \{X, Y\}$

The limit average semantics of $\mathcal{B}$ *w.r.t.* $\mathcal{C}$ *is the partial function*

$$LimAvg(\mathcal{B}, \mathcal{C}, \cdot) \ : \ Dist\big(Asg(\mathcal{C})\big) \rightharpoonup Dist\big(Asg(\mathcal{V})\big)$$

from γ_0 to distributions $\mu = Extend(\mathcal{B}, \mathcal{C}, \gamma)$ where

$$\gamma = \lim_{n \to \infty} \frac{1}{n+1} \sum_{i=0}^{n} \gamma_n \qquad \text{and} \qquad \gamma_{n+1} = Next(\mathcal{B}, \mathcal{C}, \gamma_n)|_{\mathcal{C}}.$$

The set $[\![\mathcal{B}]\!]_{\text{LimAvg-}\mathcal{C}}$ is likewise given by the image of $LimAvg(\mathcal{B}, \mathcal{C}, \cdot)$.

We know that the limit average coincides with the regular limit if the latter exists, so for every initial cutset distribution γ_0, we have $Lim(\mathcal{B}, \mathcal{C}, \gamma_0) = LimAvg(\mathcal{B}, \mathcal{C}, \gamma_0)$ if $Lim(\mathcal{B}, \mathcal{C}, \gamma_0)$ is defined. Thus, $[\![\mathcal{B}]\!]_{\text{Lim-}\mathcal{C}} \subseteq [\![\mathcal{B}]\!]_{\text{LimAvg-}\mathcal{C}}$.

5 Markov Chain Semantics

While we gave some motivation for the limit and limit average semantics, their definitions do not reveal an explicit way to compute their member distributions. In this section we introduce the *(cutset) Markov chain semantics* which offers explicit construction of distributions and is shown to coincide with the limit average semantics. It further paves the way for proving several properties of both limit semantics in Section 5.1.

At the core of the cutset Markov chain semantics lies the eponymous *cutset Markov chain* which captures how probability mass flows from one cutset assignment to the others. To this end, the Dirac distributions corresponding to each assignment are used as initial distributions in the dissected GBN. With the *Next* function we then get a new distribution over all cutset assignments, and the probabilities assigned by this distribution are used as transition probabilities for the Markov chain.

Definition 8 (Cutset Markov chain). *Let $\mathcal{B}$ be a GBN with cutset $\mathcal{C}$. The cutset Markov chain $CMC(\mathcal{B}, \mathcal{C}) = \langle Asg(\mathcal{C}), \mathbf{P} \rangle$ w.r.t. $\mathcal{B}$ and $\mathcal{C}$ is a DTMC where the transition matrix $\mathbf{P}$ is given for all cutset assignments $b, c \in Asg(\mathcal{C})$ by*

$$\mathbf{P}(b, c) := Next\big(\mathcal{B}, \mathcal{C}, Dirac(b)\big)(c).$$

Example 5. Figure 5 shows the cutset Markov chain for the GBN from Fig. 1 with CPT entries $s_1 = 1/4$, $s_2 = 1$, $t_1 = 1/2$, $t_2 = 0$, and cutset $\mathcal{C} = \{X, Y\}$. Exemplarily, the edge at the bottom from assignment $b = \{X{=}\text{F}, Y{=}\text{F}\}$ to assignment $c = \{X{=}\text{F}, Y{=}\text{T}\}$ with label $3/8$ is derived as follows:

$$
\begin{aligned}
\mathbf{P}(b,c) \ &= \ \mathit{Next}\big(\mathcal{B}, \mathcal{C}, \mathit{Dirac}(b)\big)(c) \ = \ \mathit{dist}_{\mathrm{BN}}\big(\mathit{Dissect}(\mathcal{B}, \mathcal{C}, \mathit{Dirac}(b))\big)(c') \\
&= \ \sum_{\substack{a \in \mathit{Asg}(\mathcal{V}_c) \\ \text{s.t. } c' \subseteq a}} \mathit{dist}_{\mathrm{BN}}\big(\mathit{Dissect}(\mathcal{B}, \mathcal{C}, \mathit{Dirac}(b))\big)(a) \\
&= \ \sum_{\substack{a \in \mathit{Asg}(\mathcal{V}_c) \\ \text{s.t. } c' \subseteq a}} \mathit{Dirac}(b)(a_{X,Y}) \cdot \Pr(X'{=}\text{F} \mid a_Y) \cdot \Pr(Y'{=}\text{T} \mid a_X) \\
&= \ \Pr(X'{=}\text{F} \mid Y{=}\text{F}) \cdot \Pr(Y'{=}\text{T} \mid X{=}\text{F}) \ = \ (1 - s_1) \cdot t_1 \ = \ 3/8.
\end{aligned}
$$

Note that in the second-to-last step, in the sum over all full assignments a which agree with the partial assignment c', only the assignment which also agrees with b remains as for all other assignments we have $\mathit{Dirac}(b)(a_{X,Y}) = 0$.

Given a cutset Markov chain with transition matrix $\mathbf{P}$ and an initial cutset distribution γ_0, we can compute the uniquely defined long-run frequency distribution lrf^{γ_0} (see Section 1.1). Then the Markov chain semantics is given by the extension of this distribution over the whole GBN.

Definition 9 (Markov chain semantics). *Let $\mathcal{B}$ be a GBN over nodes $\mathcal{V}$ with a cutset $\mathcal{C} \subseteq \mathcal{V}$ and cutset Markov chain $\mathit{CMC}(\mathcal{B}, \mathcal{C}) = \langle \mathit{Asg}(\mathcal{C}), \mathbf{P} \rangle$. Then the Markov chain semantics of $\mathcal{B}$ w.r.t. $\mathcal{C}$ is the function*

$$
MCS(\mathcal{B}, \mathcal{C}, \cdot) : \ \mathit{Dist}\big(\mathit{Asg}(\mathcal{C})\big) \to \mathit{Dist}\big(\mathit{Asg}(\mathcal{V})\big)
$$

from cutset distributions γ_0 to full distributions $\mu = \mathit{Extend}(\mathcal{B}, \mathcal{C}, \mathrm{lrf}^{\gamma_0})$ where

$$
\mathrm{lrf}^{\gamma_0} \ = \ \lim_{n \to \infty} \frac{1}{n+1} \sum_{i=0}^{n} \gamma_i \qquad \text{and} \qquad \gamma_{i+1} = \gamma_i \cdot \mathbf{P}.
$$

The set $[\![\mathcal{B}]\!]_{\mathrm{MC\text{-}}\mathcal{C}}$ is defined as the image of $MCS(\mathcal{B}, \mathcal{C}, \cdot)$.

In the following lemma, we give four equivalent characterizations of the long-run frequency distributions of the cutset Markov chain.

Lemma 2. *Let $\mathcal{B}$ be a GBN with cutset $\mathcal{C}$, cutset distribution $\gamma \in \mathit{Dist}(\mathit{Asg}(\mathcal{C}))$, and $\mathcal{M} = \langle \mathit{Asg}(\mathcal{C}), \mathbf{P} \rangle$ the cutset Markov chain $\mathit{CMC}(\mathcal{B}, \mathcal{C})$. Then the following statements are equivalent:*

(a) $\gamma = \gamma \cdot \mathbf{P}$.

(b) There exists $\gamma_0 \in \mathit{Dist}(\mathit{Asg}(\mathcal{C}))$ such that for $\gamma_{i+1} = \gamma_i \cdot \mathbf{P}$, we have

$$
\gamma \ = \ \lim_{n \to \infty} \frac{1}{n+1} \sum_{i=0}^{n} \gamma_i.
$$

(c) γ belongs to the convex hull of the long-run frequency distributions $\mathrm{lrf}_{\mathcal{D}}$ of the bottom SCCs $\mathcal{D}$ of $\mathcal{M}$.

(d) $\gamma = Next(\mathcal{B}, \mathcal{C}, \gamma)|_{\mathcal{C}}$.

Following Lemma 2, we can equivalently define the cutset Markov chain semantics as the set of extensions of all stationary distributions for $\mathbf{P}$:

$$[\![\mathcal{B}]\!]_{\text{MC-}\mathcal{C}} := \{Extend(\mathcal{B}, \mathcal{C}, \gamma) : \gamma \in Dist(Asg(\mathcal{C})) \text{ s.t. } \gamma = \gamma \cdot \mathbf{P}\}.$$

Example 6. Continuing Ex. 5, there is a unique stationary distribution γ with $\gamma = \gamma \cdot \mathbf{P}$ for the cutset Markov chain in Fig. 5: $\gamma = \langle {}^{48}/_{121} \; {}^{18}/_{121} \; {}^{40}/_{121} \; {}^{15}/_{121} \rangle$. As in this case the cutset $\mathcal{C} = \{X, Y\}$ equals the set of all nodes $\mathcal{V}$, we have $Extend(\mathcal{B}, \mathcal{C}, \gamma) = \gamma$ and thus $[\![\mathcal{B}]\!]_{\text{MC-}\{X,Y\}} = \{\gamma\}$.

As shown by Lemma 2, the behavior of the *Next* function is captured by multiplication with the transition matrix $\mathbf{P}$. Both the distributions in the limit average semantics and the long-run frequency distributions of the cutset Markov chain are defined in terms of a Cesàro limit, the former over the sequence of distributions obtained by repeated application of *Next*, the latter by repeated multiplication with $\mathbf{P}$. Thus both semantics are equivalent.

Theorem 1. *Let $\mathcal{B}$ be a GBN. Then for any cutset $\mathcal{C}$ of $\mathcal{B}$ and initial distribution $\gamma_0 \in Dist(Asg(\mathcal{C}))$, we have*

$$MCS(\mathcal{B}, \mathcal{C}, \gamma_0) = LimAvg(\mathcal{B}, \mathcal{C}, \gamma_0).$$

We know that $Lim(\mathcal{B}, \mathcal{C}, \gamma_0)$ is not defined for all initial distributions γ_0. However, the set of all limits that do exist contains exactly the distributions admitted by the Markov chain and limit average semantics.

Lemma 3. *Let $\mathcal{B}$ be a GBN. Then for any cutset $\mathcal{C}$ of $\mathcal{B}$, we have*

$$[\![\mathcal{B}]\!]_{\text{MC-}\mathcal{C}} = [\![\mathcal{B}]\!]_{\text{LimAvg-}\mathcal{C}} = [\![\mathcal{B}]\!]_{\text{Lim-}\mathcal{C}}.$$

5.1   Properties

By the equivalences established in Theorem 1 and Lemma 3, we gain profound insights about the limit and limit average distributions by Markov chain analysis. As every finite-state Markov chain has at least one stationary distribution, it immediately follows that $[\![\mathcal{B}]\!]_{\text{MC-}\mathcal{C}}$—and thus $[\![\mathcal{B}]\!]_{\text{LimAvg-}\mathcal{C}}$ and $[\![\mathcal{B}]\!]_{\text{Lim-}\mathcal{C}}$—is always non-empty. Further, if the cutset Markov chain is *irreducible*, i.e., the graph is strongly connected, the stationary distribution is unique and $[\![\mathcal{B}]\!]_{\text{MC-}\mathcal{C}}$ is a singleton. The existence of the limit semantics for a given initial distribution γ_0 hinges on the *periodicity* of the cutset Markov chain.

Example 7. We return to Example 2 and construct the cutset Markov chain $CMC(\mathcal{B}, \mathcal{C}) = \langle Asg(\mathcal{C}), \mathbf{P} \rangle$ for the (implicitly used) cutset $\mathcal{C} = \{X, Y\}$:

The chain is strongly connected and has a period of length 4, which explains the observed behavior that for any initial distribution γ_0, we got the sequence

$$\gamma_0, \gamma_1, \gamma_2, \gamma_3, \gamma_0, \gamma_1, \ldots$$

This sequence obviously converges only for initial distributions that are stationary, i.e., if we have $\gamma_0 = \gamma_0 \cdot \mathbf{P}$.

The following lemma summarizes the implications that can be drawn from close inspection of the cutset Markov chain.

Lemma 4 (Cardinality). *Let $\mathcal{B}$ be a GBN with cutset $\mathcal{C}$ and cutset Markov chain $CMC(\mathcal{B}, \mathcal{C}) = \langle Asg(\mathcal{C}), \mathbf{P} \rangle$. Further, let $k > 0$ denote the number of bottom SCCs $\mathcal{D}_1, \ldots, \mathcal{D}_k$ of $CMC(\mathcal{B}, \mathcal{C})$. Then*

1. the cardinality of the cutset Markov chain semantics is given by

$$\left| [\![\mathcal{B}]\!]_{\text{MC-}\mathcal{C}} \right| = \begin{cases} 1 & \text{if } k = 1, \\ \infty & \text{if } k > 1; \end{cases}$$

2. $Lim(\mathcal{B}, \mathcal{C}, \gamma_0)$ is defined for all $\gamma_0 \in Dist(Asg(\mathcal{C}))$ if all $\mathcal{D}_i$ are aperiodic;
3. $Lim(\mathcal{B}, \mathcal{C}, \gamma)$ is only defined for stationary distributions γ with $\gamma = \gamma \cdot \mathbf{P}$ if $\mathcal{D}_i$ is periodic for any $1 \leqslant i \leqslant k$.

A handy sufficient (albeit not necessary) criterion for both aperiodicity and the existence of a single bottom SCC in the cutset Markov chain is the absence of zero and one entries in the CPTs and the initial distribution of a GBN.

Definition 10 (Smooth GBNs). *A GBN $\mathcal{B} = \langle \mathcal{G}, \mathcal{P}, \iota \rangle$ is called smooth iff all CPT entries as given by $\mathcal{P}$ and all values in ι are in the open interval $]0, 1[$.*

Lemma 5. *Let $\mathcal{B}$ be a smooth GBN and $\mathcal{C}$ a cutset of $\mathcal{B}$. Then the graph of the cutset Markov chain $CMC(\mathcal{B}, \mathcal{C})$ is a complete digraph.*

Corollary 1. *The limit semantics of a smooth GBN $\mathcal{B}$ is a singleton for every cutset $\mathcal{C}$ of $\mathcal{B}$ and $Lim(\mathcal{B}, \mathcal{C}, \gamma_0)$ is defined for all $\gamma_0 \in Dist(Asg(\mathcal{C}))$.*

As noted in [14], one rarely needs to assign a probability of zero (or, conversely, of one) in real-world applications; and doing so in cases where some event is extremely unlikely but not impossible is a common modeling error. This observation gives reason to expect that most GBNs encountered in practice are smooth and their semantics is thus, in a sense, well-behaved.

5.2   Relation to Constraints Semantics

We take a closer look at how the cutset semantics relates to the CPT-consistency semantics defined in Section 3. CPTs of nodes outside cutsets remain unaffected in the dissected BNs from which the Markov chain semantics is computed. Since there are cyclic GBNs for which no CPT-consistent distribution exists (cf. Example 1) while Markov chain semantics always yields at least one solution due to Lemma 4, it cannot be expected that cutset nodes are necessarily CPT-consistent. However, they are always weakly CPT-consistent.

Lemma 6. *Let $\mathcal{B}$ be a GBN over nodes $\mathcal{V}$, $\mathcal{C} \subseteq \mathcal{V}$ a cutset for $\mathcal{B}$, and $\mu \in [\![\mathcal{B}]\!]_{\mathrm{MC}\text{-}\mathcal{C}}$. Then μ is strongly CPT-consistent for all nodes in $\mathcal{V}\backslash\mathcal{C}$ and weakly CPT-consistent for the nodes in $\mathcal{C}$.*

The lemma shows a way to find fully CPT consistent distributions: Consider there is a distribution $\mu \in [\![\mathcal{B}]\!]_{\mathrm{MC}\text{-}\mathcal{C}} \cap [\![\mathcal{B}]\!]_{\mathrm{MC}\text{-}\mathcal{D}}$ for two disjoint cutsets $\mathcal{C}$ and $\mathcal{D}$. Then by Lemma 6 the nodes in $\mathcal{V} \setminus \mathcal{C}$ and $\mathcal{V} \setminus \mathcal{D}$ are CPT consistent, so in fact μ is CPT consistent. In general, we get the following result.

Lemma 7. *Let $\mathcal{B}$ be a GBN over nodes $\mathcal{V}$ and $\mathcal{C}_1, \ldots, \mathcal{C}_k$ cutsets of $\mathcal{B}$ s.t. for each node $X \in \mathcal{V}$ there is an $i \in \{1, \ldots, k\}$ with $X \notin \mathcal{C}_i$. Then*

$$\bigcap_{0 \leqslant i \leqslant k} [\![\mathcal{B}]\!]_{\mathrm{MC}\text{-}\mathcal{C}_i} \subseteq [\![\mathcal{B}]\!]_{\mathrm{CPT}}.$$

We take a look at which independencies are necessarily observed by the distributions in $[\![\mathcal{B}]\!]_{\mathrm{MC}\text{-}\mathcal{C}}$. Let $\gamma \in Dist(Asg(\mathcal{C}))$ be the cutset distribution and let $\mathcal{G}[\mathcal{C}]$ denote the graph of $Dissect(\mathcal{B}, \mathcal{C}, \gamma)$ restricted to the nodes in $\mathcal{V}$ such that the cutset nodes in $\mathcal{C}$ are initial. Then by Lemma 1, the d-separation independencies of the closure of $\mathcal{G}[\mathcal{C}]$ hold in all distributions $\mu \in [\![\mathcal{B}]\!]_{\mathrm{MC}\text{-}\mathcal{C}}$, i.e., $d\text{-}sep(Close(\mathcal{G}[\mathcal{C}])) \subseteq Indep(\mu)$. The next lemma states that any CPT-consistent distribution that satisfies these independence constraints for some cutset $\mathcal{C}$ also belongs to $[\![\mathcal{B}]\!]_{\mathrm{MC}\text{-}\mathcal{C}}$.

Lemma 8. *Let $\mathcal{B}$ be a GBN with cutset $\mathcal{C}$ and $\mathcal{I}_{\mathcal{C}} = Close(\mathcal{G}[\mathcal{C}])$. Then we have*

$$[\![\mathcal{B}]\!]_{\mathrm{CPT}\text{-}\mathcal{I}_{\mathcal{C}}} \subseteq [\![\mathcal{B}]\!]_{\mathrm{MC}\text{-}\mathcal{C}}.$$

Combining Lemma 7 and Lemma 8 yields the following equivalence.

Corollary 2. *For a GBN $\mathcal{B}$ with cutsets $\mathcal{C}_1, \ldots, \mathcal{C}_k$ as in Lemma 7 and the independence set $\mathcal{I} = \bigcup_{0 \leqslant i \leqslant k} Close(\mathcal{G}[\mathcal{C}_i])$, we have*

$$\bigcap_{0 \leqslant i \leqslant k} [\![\mathcal{B}]\!]_{\mathrm{MC}\text{-}\mathcal{C}_i} = [\![\mathcal{B}]\!]_{\mathrm{CPT}\text{-}\mathcal{I}}.$$

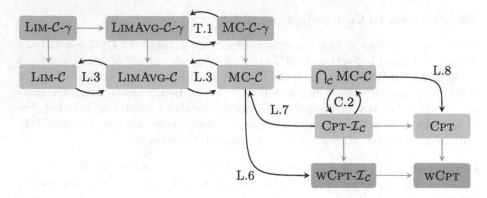

Fig. 6. Relations between different variations of limit, limit average, and Markov chain semantics (blue) as well as strong and weak CPT-consistency semantics (yellow resp. orange)

5.3 Overview

Fig. 6 gives an overview of the relations between all proposed semantics. Boxes represent the set of distributions induced by the respective semantics and arrows stand for set inclusion. For the non-trivial inclusions the arrows are annotated with the respective lemma or theorem. As an example, CPT→wCPT states that $[\mathcal{B}]_{\text{CPT}} \subseteq [\mathcal{B}]_{\text{wCPT}}$ holds for all GBNs $\mathcal{B}$. The three semantics in the top row parameterized with a cutset $\mathcal{C}$ and a distribution γ stand for the singleton set containing the respective function applied to γ, i.e., $[\mathcal{B}]_{\text{LIM-}\mathcal{C}\text{-}\gamma} = \{Lim(\mathcal{B}, \mathcal{C}, \gamma)\}$. $\bigcap_{\mathcal{C}}$ MC-$\mathcal{C}$ stands for the intersection of the Markov chain semantics for various cutsets as in Lemma 7, and the incoming arrow from CPT-$\mathcal{I}_{\mathcal{C}}$ holds for the set of independencies $\mathcal{I}_{\mathcal{C}}$ as in Lemma 8.

6   Related Work

That cycles in a BN might be unavoidable when learning its structure is well known for more than 30 years [15,22]. During the learning process of BNs, cycles might even be favorable as demonstrated in the context of *gene regulatory networks* where cyclic structures induce monotonic scores [32]. That work only discusses learning algorithms, but does not deal with evaluating the joint distribution of the resulting cyclic BNs. In most applications, however, cycles have been seen as a phenomenon to be avoided to ease the computation of the joint distribution in BNs. By an example BN comprising a single isolated cycle, [30] showed that reversing or removing edges to avoid cycles may reduce the solution space from infinitely many joint distributions that are (weakly) consistent with the CPTs to a single one. In this setting, our results on weak CPT-semantics also provide that wCPT cannot express conditions on the relation of variables like implications or mutual exclusion. This is rooted in the fact that the solution space of weak CPT-semantics always contains at least one full joint distribution with pairwise independent variables. An example where reversing edges led to satisfactory results has been considered in [3], investigating the impact of reinforced defects by steel corrosion in concrete structures.

Unfolding cycles up to a bounded depth has been applied in the setting of a robotic sensor system by [2]. In their use case, only cycles of length two may appear, and only the nodes appearing on the cycles are implicitly used as cutset for the unfolding. In [13], the set of all nodes is used for unfolding (corresponding to a cutset $\mathcal{C} = \mathcal{V}$ in our setting) and subsequent limit construction, but restricted to cases where the limit exists.

There have been numerous variants of BNs that explicitly or implicitly address cyclic dependencies. *Dynamic Bayesian networks* (DBNs) [19] extend BNs by an explicit notion of discrete time steps that could break cycles through timed ordering of random variables. Cycles in BNs could be translated to the DBN formalism by introducing a notion of time, e.g., following [13]. Our cutset approach is orthogonal, choosing a time-abstract view on cycles and treating them as stabilizing feedback loops. Learning DBNs requires "relatively large time-series data" [32] and thus, may be computationally demanding. In [18] *activator random variables* break cycles in DBNs to circumvent spurious results in DBN reasoning when infinitesimal small time steps would be required.

Causal BNs [23] are BNs that impose a meaning on the direction of an edge in terms of causal dependency. Several approaches have been proposed to extend causal BNs for modeling feedback loops. In [25], an equilibrium semantics is sketched that is similar to our Markov chain semantics, albeit based on variable orderings rather than cutsets. Determining independence relations, Markov properties, and joint distributions are central problems addressed for cyclic causal BNs [2,5,20,24,29]. Markov properties and joint distributions for extended versions of causal BNs have been considered recently, e.g., in *directed graphs with hyperedges* (HEDGes) [5] and *cyclic structural causal models* (SCMs) [2]. Besides others, they show that in presence of cycles, there might be multiple solutions for a joint distribution or even no solution at all [7]. While we consider all random variables to be observable, the latter approaches focus on models with latent variables. Further, while our focus in this paper is not on causality, our approach is surely also applicable to causal BNs with cycles.

Recursive relational Bayesian networks (RRBNs) [9] allow representing probabilistic relational models where the random variables are given by relations over varying domains. The resulting first-order dependencies can become quite complex and may contain cycles, though semantics are given only for the acyclic cases by the construction of corresponding standard BNs.

Bayesian attack graphs (BAGs) [16] are popular to model and reason about security vulnerabilities in computer networks. Learned graphs and thus their BN semantics frequently contain cycles, e.g., when using the tool MULVAL [21]. In [27], "handling cycles correctly" is identified as "a key challenge" in security risk analysis. Resolution methods for cyclic patterns in BAGs [1,4,17,31] are mainly based on context-specific security considerations, e.g., to break cycles by removing edges. The semantic foundations for cyclic BNs laid in this paper do not require graph manipulations and decouple the probability theoretic basis from context-specific properties.

7 Conclusion

This paper has developed a foundational perspective on the semantics of cycles in Bayesian networks. Constraint-based semantics provide a conservative extension of the standard BN semantics to the cyclic setting. While conceptually important, their practical use is limited by the fact that for many GBNs, the induced constraint system is unsatisfiable. On the other hand, the two introduced limit semantics echo in an abstract and formal way what practitioners have been devising across a manifold of domain-specific situations. In this abstract perspective, cutsets are the ingredients that enable a controlled decoupling of dependencies. The appropriate choice of cutsets is where, in our view, domain-specific knowledge is confined to enter the picture. Utilizing the constructively defined Markov chain semantics, we established key results relating and demarcating the different semantic notions and showed that for the ubiquitous class of smooth GBNs a unique full joint distribution always exists.

References

1. Aguessy, F., Bettan, O., Blanc, G., Conan, V., Debar, H.: Bayesian attack model for dynamic risk assessment. CoRR (2016)
2. Castellano-Quero, M., Fernández-Madrigal, J.A., García-Cerezo, A.: Improving bayesian inference efficiency for sensory anomaly detection and recovery in mobile robots. Expert Systems with Applications **163** (2021)
3. Castillo, E., Gutiérrez, J.M., Hadi, A.S.: Modeling probabilistic networks of discrete and continuous variables. Journal of Multivariate Analysis **64**(1), 48–65 (1998)
4. Doynikova, E., Kotenko, I.: Enhancement of probabilistic attack graphs for accurate cyber security monitoring. In: 2017 IEEE SmartWorld/SCALCOM/UIC/ATC/CBDCom/IOP/SCI. pp. 1–6 (2017)
5. Forré, P., Mooij, J.M.: Markov properties for graphical models with cycles and latent variables (2017)
6. Geiger, D., Verma, T., Pearl, J.: d-separation: From theorems to algorithms. In: Machine Intelligence and Pattern Recognition, vol. 10, pp. 139–148. Elsevier (1990)
7. Halpern, J.Y.: Axiomatizing causal reasoning. J. Artif. Int. Res. **12**, 317–337 (2000)
8. Han, S.H.: A top-down iteration algorithm for monte carlo method for probability estimation of a fault tree with circular logic. NET **50**(6), 854–859 (2018)
9. Jaeger, M.: Complex probabilistic modeling with recursive relational bayesian networks. Ann. Math. Artif. Intell. **32**(1-4), 179–220 (2001)
10. Jensen, F., Nielsen, T.: Bayesian Network and Decision Graphs. Springer (2007)
11. Jensen, F.V., Andersen, S.K., Kjærulff, U., Andreassen, S.: Munin – on the case for probabilities in medical expert systems – a practical exercise. In: AIME 87. pp. 149–160. Springer Berlin Heidelberg (1987)
12. Kemeny, J., Snell, J.: Finite Markov chains. University series in undergraduate mathematics, VanNostrand, New York, repr edn (1969)

13. Kłopotek, M.A.: Cyclic Bayesian network: Markov process approach. Studia Informatica: systems and information technology **1**(7), 47–55 (2006)
14. Koller, D., Friedman, N.: Probabilistic Graphical Models: Principles and Techniques. Adaptive Computation and Machine Learning, MIT Press (2009)
15. Lauritzen, S.L., Spiegelhalter, D.J.: Local computations with probabilities on graphical structures and their application to expert systems. Journal of the Royal Statistical Society. Series B (Methodological) **50**(2), 157–224 (1988)
16. Liu, Y., Man, H.: Network vulnerability assessment using Bayesian networks. In: Data Mining, Intrusion Detection, Information Assurance, and Data Networks Security. vol. 5812, pp. 61–71. SPIE (2005)
17. Matthews, I., Mace, J., Soudjani, S., van Moorsel, A.: Cyclic bayesian attack graphs: A systematic computational approach (2020)
18. Motzek, A.: Indirect Causes, Dependencies and Causality in Bayesian Networks. Ph.D. thesis, University of Lübeck (2017)
19. Murphy, K.P.: Dynamic Bayesian Networks: Representation, Inference and Learning. Ph.D. thesis, University of California, Berkeley (2002)
20. Neal, R.M.: On deducing conditional independence from d-separation in causal graphs with feedback. Journal of Artificial Intelligence Research **12**, 87–91 (2000)
21. Ou, X., Govindavajhala, S., Appel, A.W.: Mulval: A logic-based network security analyzer. In: Proceedings of the 14th Conference on USENIX Security Symposium-Volume 14. p. 8. SSYM'05, USENIX Association, USA (2005)
22. Pearl, J.: Fusion, Propagation, and Structuring in Belief Networks, pp. 366–413. Morgan Kaufmann Publishers Inc. (1990)
23. Pearl, J.: Causality: Models, Reasoning and Inference. CUP (2009)
24. Pearl, J., Dechter, R.: Identifying independencies in causal graphs with feedback. In: Proceedings of the Twelfth International Conference on Uncertainty in Artificial Intelligence. pp. 420–426. UAI'96, Morgan Kaufmann Publishers Inc. (1996)
25. Poole, D., Crowley, M.: Cyclic causal models with discrete variables: Markov chain equilibrium semantics and sample ordering. In: IJCAI International Joint Conference on Artificial Intelligence (2013)
26. Robert F. Nease, J., Owens, D.K.: Use of influence diagrams to structure medical decisions. Medical Decision Making **17**(3), 263–275 (1997)
27. Singhal, A., Ou, X.: Security Risk Analysis of Enterprise Networks Using Probabilistic Attack Graphs, pp. 53–73. Springer International Publishing, Cham (2017)
28. Spirtes, P.: Conditional independence in directed cyclic graphical models for feedback. Tech. Rep. CMU-PHIL-53, Carnegie Mellon University (1994)
29. Spirtes, P.: Directed cyclic graphical representations of feedback models. In: Proceedings of the Eleventh Conference on Uncertainty in Artificial Intelligence. pp. 491–498. UAI'95, Morgan Kaufmann Publishers Inc. (1995)
30. Tulupyev, A.L., Nikolenko, S.I.: Directed cycles in bayesian belief networks: Probabilistic semantics and consistency checking complexity. In: MICAI 2005: Advances in Artificial Intelligence. pp. 214–223. Springer Berlin Heidelberg (2005)
31. Wang, L., Islam, T., Long, T., Singhal, A., Jajodia, S.: An attack graph-based probabilistic security metric. In: Data and Applications Security XXII. pp. 283–296. Springer Berlin Heidelberg (2008)
32. Wiecek, W., Bois, F.Y., Gayraud, G.: Structure learning of bayesian networks involving cyclic structures (2020)

Satisfiability of Quantitative Probabilistic CTL: Rise to the Challenge

Miroslav Chodil[1], Antonín Kučera[1], and Jan Křetínský[2(✉)]

[1] Masaryk University, Brno, Czechia
[2] TU München, Munich, Germany
jan.kretinsky@tum.de

Abstract. The decidability of PCTL satisfiability is a challenging open problem in logic and formal verification. We give an overview of the existing results and proof techniques, and we also present some new results documenting the subtlety of the problem.

Keywords: Probabilistic temporal logics · Satisfiability · PCTL

1 Introduction

The main purpose of formal verification is to prevent erroneous behaviour of systems. Unfortunately, even if the verification techniques were perfect, the systems never are. As the old saying goes, every programme contains an error (and can be one line shorter, so by induction...). Anyway, even if it did not, cyber-physical systems, which are the truly safety-critical examples, may fail in their hardware parts, no matter how much redundancy is implemented. Consequently, the notion of correct and incorrect systems is too naïve. Instead, a finer, quantitative notion is in place. Tom Henzinger has been a prime example of a convincing systematic "quantivizer" of all notions of the classic verification: be it the mentioned quantitative notion of correctness [32], or more generally quantitative languages [16] generated by quantitative models [33] quantitatively synthesized [13] via quantitative games [17] and then checked against quantitative properties [14] or at least quantitatively monitored [34]. Not a single notion survived Tom's gentle but critical eye, even the quality is better quantitative [6]. The personal collaboration with Tom, however pleasant, has often been probably approximately correct, so at least doubly quantitative, whether it concerned distances [21] or probabilistic linear temporal logic (pLTL) [20]. And it is the temporal logic that we focus on in this paper, an omnipresent theme in Tom's work, starting in his first paper, in FOCS [1]. The quantitative extension is here, as often, probabilistic; the logic is, for a change, of branching time.

Probabilistic computation-tree logic (PCTL) has been born from CTL in several stages during 1982–1989, as we detail below. The most important problem for logics in the early 80's was the satisfiability problem, with the tempting vision of specifying system's behaviour and asking for a model of the formula. Aiming

J.-F. Raskin and K. Chatterjee (Eds.): Principles of Systems Design, LNCS 13660, pp. 364–387, 2022.
https://doi.org/10.1007/978-3-031-22337-2_18

at synthesis has turned out to be a bit ahead of time and in the late 80's, an easier task of checking models has gained more attention.

Satisfiability Problem. As for the *non-probabilistic* predecessors of PCTL, the satisfiability problem is known to be EXPTIME-complete for CTL [24] as well as the more general modal μ-calculus [3,27]. Both logics have the small model property [24,36]. More precisely, every satisfiable formula φ has a finite-state model whose size is exponential in the size of φ. The complexity of the satisfiability problems has been investigated also for fragments of CTL [40] and the modal μ-calculus [31]. However, the decidability of the satisfiability problem for probabilistic CTL is a long-standing open problem. In this paper, we survey the results achieved for various fragments and special settings, prove high "degree" of absence of the small model property (the model sizes for a single formula may need to grow depending on the quantity appearing within), and finally set several concrete goals in sight to further stimulate the current interest in this challenging task.

Related Problems. The PCTL *model checking problem* is the task to determine whether a given system satisfies a given formula, i.e. whether it is a model of the formula. This problem has been studied both for finite and infinite Markov chains and decision processes, see e.g. [11,19,25,26,35]. The PCTL *strategy synthesis* problem asks whether the non-determinism in a given Markov decision process can be resolved so that the resulting Markov chain satisfies the formula [2,7,10, 39].

2 Preliminaries

We use $\mathbb{N}$, $\mathbb{Q}$, $\mathbb{R}$ to denote the sets of non-negative integers, rational numbers, and real numbers, respectively. We use the standard notation for writing intervals of real numbers, e.g., $[0,1)$ denotes the set of all $r \in \mathbb{R}$ such that $0 \leq r < 1$.

The logic PCTL [28] is a probabilistic version of Computational Tree Logic [23] obtained by replacing the existential and universal path quantifiers with the probabilistic operator $P(\Phi) \bowtie r$, where Φ is a path formula, $\bowtie$ is a comparison, and $r \in [0,1]$ is a constant. In addition to the standard until connective U, the logic PCTL also includes a bounded until connective $U^{\leq k}$, where $\varphi U^{\leq k} \psi$ means "after at most k transitions, a state satisfying ψ is visited, and all preceding states satisfy φ". Note that the path formula $\varphi U^{\leq k} \psi$ is equivalent to

$$\psi \lor (\varphi \land X\psi) \lor (\varphi \land X\varphi \land XX\psi) \lor \ldots \lor (\varphi \land X\varphi \land \ldots \land \underbrace{XX \cdots X}_{k} \psi).$$

Hence, the $U^{\leq k}$ connective is redundant if the set of path formulae is closed under Boolean connectives, which holds for the logic CTL* but not for CTL.

Definition 1 (PCTL). *Let AP be a set of atomic propositions. The syntax of PCTL state and path formulae is defined by the following abstract syntax equations:*

$$\varphi \ ::= \ a \mid \neg a \mid \varphi \wedge \varphi \mid \varphi \vee \varphi \mid P(\varPhi) \bowtie r$$
$$\varPhi \ ::= \ \mathrm{X}\varphi \mid \mathrm{F}\varphi \mid \mathrm{F}^{\leq k}\varphi \mid \mathrm{G}\varphi \mid \varphi \mathrm{U}\varphi \mid \varphi \mathrm{U}^{\leq k}\varphi$$

Here, $a \in AP$, $\bowtie \in \{\geq, >, \leq, <\}$, $r \in [0,1]$, and $k \in \mathbb{N}$.

For simplicity, the trivial probability constraints '≥ 0', '>1', '<0', and '≤ 1' are syntactically forbidden. Furthermore, the probabilistic operator in $P(\varPhi) \bowtie r$ is sometimes omitted, and the probability constraint $\bowtie r$ is written as a lower index of the topmost path connective of $\varPhi$. For example, we write $\varphi \mathrm{U}_{\bowtie r}\varphi$ instead of $P(\varphi \mathrm{U}\varphi) \bowtie r$.

Observe that the negation is applicable only to atomic propositions. This causes no loss of generality because negations can be pushed inside towards the probabilistic operator where the probability constraint is negated. As we shall see, the path connectives F, $\mathrm{F}^{\leq k}$, and G are in fact redundant, but we include them into the PCTL syntax for the sake of clarity.

PCTL formulae are interpreted over Markov chains where every state s is assigned a subset $v(s) \subseteq AP$ of atomic propositions valid in s.

Definition 2 (Markov chain). *A Markov chain is a triple $M = (S, P, v)$, where S is a finite or countably infinite set of states, $P \colon S \times S \to [0,1]$ is a function such that $\sum_{t \in S} P(s,t) = 1$ for every $s \in S$, and $v \colon S \to 2^{AP}$.*

A *path* in M is a finite sequence $w = s_0 \ldots s_n$ of states such that $P(s_i, s_{i+1}) > 0$ for all $i < n$. A *run* in M is an infinite sequence $\pi = s_0 s_1 \ldots$ of states such that every finite prefix of π is a path in M. We also use $\pi(i)$ to denote the state s_i of π.

For every path $w = s_0 \ldots s_n$, let $Run(w)$ be the set of all runs starting with w, and let $\mathbb{P}(Run(w)) = \prod_{i=0}^{n-1} P(s_i, s_{i+1})$. To every state s, we associate the probability space $(Run(s), \mathcal{F}_s, \mathbb{P}_s)$, where $\mathcal{F}_s$ is the σ-field generated by all $Run(w)$ where w starts in s, and $\mathbb{P}_s$ is the unique probability measure obtained by extending $\mathbb{P}$ in the standard way (see, e.g., [5]).

The *validity* of a PCTL state/path formula for a given state/run of M is defined inductively as follows:

$$
\begin{aligned}
s &\models a & \text{iff} \quad & a \in v(s), \\
s &\models \neg a & \text{iff} \quad & a \notin v(s), \\
s &\models \varphi_1 \wedge \varphi_2 & \text{iff} \quad & s \models \varphi_1 \text{ and } s \models \varphi_2, \\
s &\models \varphi_1 \vee \varphi_2 & \text{iff} \quad & s \models \varphi_1 \text{ or } s \models \varphi_2, \\
s &\models P(\varPhi) \bowtie r & \text{iff} \quad & \mathbb{P}_s(\{\pi \in Run(s) \mid \pi \models \varPhi\}) \bowtie r, \\[6pt]
\pi &\models \mathrm{X}\varphi & \text{iff} \quad & \pi(1) \models \varphi, \\
\pi &\models \mathrm{F}^{\leq k}\varphi & \text{iff} \quad & \text{there is } j \leq k \text{ s.t. } \pi(j) \models \varphi, \\
\pi &\models \mathrm{F}\varphi & \text{iff} \quad & \pi \models \mathrm{F}^{\leq k}\varphi \text{ for some } k \geq 0, \\
\pi &\models \mathrm{G}\varphi & \text{iff} \quad & \pi(j) \models \varphi \text{ for all } j \geq 0, \\
\pi &\models \varphi_1 \mathrm{U}^{\leq k}\varphi_2 & \text{iff} \quad & \text{there is } j \leq k \text{ s.t. } \pi(j) \models \varphi_2 \text{ and } \pi(i) \models \varphi_1 \text{ for all } i < j, \\
\pi &\models \varphi_1 \mathrm{U}\varphi_2 & \text{iff} \quad & \pi \models \varphi_1 \mathrm{U}^{\leq k}\varphi_2 \text{ for some } k \geq 0.
\end{aligned}
$$

We say that M is a *model* of φ if $s \models \varphi$ for some state s of M.

3   PCTL Satisfiability

Non-probabilistic temporal logics such as CTL, CTL*, or the modal μ-calculus satisfy the *small model property*, i.e., every satisfiable formula has a finite model (transition system) of bounded size. This immediately implies the decidability of the satisfiability problem for these logics. However, PCTL does not have the small model property. There even exist satisfiable PCTL formulae with only infinite-state models.

Example 1. Consider the formula

$$\varphi \equiv G_{=1}F_{>0}a \wedge F_{<1}a$$

To see that φ does not have a finite model, realize that for every finite Markov chain M there exists a fixed $\delta > 0$ such that $t \models F_{>0}a$ implies $t \models F_{\geq\delta}a$ for every state t of M. Hence, for every state s of M such that $s \models G_{=1}F_{>0}a$ we also have that $s \models F_{=1}a$, which means that $s \not\models \varphi$. (In other words, if there was a finite model $\mathcal{M}$ of φ, there would be a bottom strongly connected component satisfying $F_{=0}a$ reachable with probability $p > 0$ implying $P(GF_{>0}a) \leq 1 - p < 1$.)

However, $s_0 \models \varphi$ in the infinite-state Markov chain of Fig. 1, where $s_i \models \neg a$ and $t_i \models a$ (indicated by a double circle) for all i. Indeed, on the one hand, $s_i \models F_{>0}a$ for all i and thus $s_0 \models G_{=1}F_{>0}a$; on the other hand, $s_0 \models P(Fa) = p$ where $p = 1/4 + 3/4(1/8 + 7/8(\cdots)) < 1/4 + 1/8 + 1/16 + \cdots = 1/2 < 1$.   □

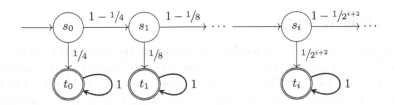

Fig. 1. An infinite-state model of φ

Deciding Model Existence. Hence, the PCTL satisfiability problem naturally arises in several variants. Apart, from the *(general) satisfiability*, where we ask about the existence of an unrestricted model, *finite satisfiability* asks about the existence of a finite model and *bounded satisfiability* rules out arbitrarily small probabilities in a model (occurring, e.g., in the Markov chain of Fig. 1). More generally, we can consider the satisfiability problem for a given PCTL fragment $\mathcal{L}$ (a subset of PCTL formulae, typically defined syntactically) and a given class of Markov chains $\mathcal{C}$.

Problem: GENERALIZED PCTL SATISFIABILITY
Parameters: A PCTL fragment $\mathcal{L}$ and a class $\mathcal{C}$ of Markov chains.

Instance: A formula $\varphi \in \mathcal{L}$.
Question: Does φ have a model in $\mathcal{C}$?
    In particular,

- for *(general) satisfiability*, $\mathcal{C}$ is the class of all Markov chains;
- for *bounded satisfiability*, $\mathcal{C}$ is the class of all Markov chains M such that all positive transition probabilities in M are bounded away from 0 by some $\delta_M > 0$;
- for *finite satisfiability*, $\mathcal{C}$ is the class of all finite-state Markov chains.

    For brevity, we also refer to the above problems as g-satisfiability, b-satisfiability, and f-satisfiability, respectively.

Model Synthesis. If φ has a model in $\mathcal{C}$, another natural problem is the *algorithmic synthesis* of such a model. This is particularly challenging for PCTL fragments containing formulae that are not finitely satisfiable, because here one needs to devise an appropriate formalism for representing infinite Markov chains.

Structure of Models. A problem closely related to generalized PCTL satisfiability is classifying the *structural model complexity* for PCTL fragments. For a given fragment $\mathcal{L}$, we aim to identify a class $\mathcal{C}$ of Markov chains such that every satisfiable (or finitely satisfiable) formula $\varphi \in \mathcal{L}$ has a model in $\mathcal{C}$. Results about structural model complexity are useful for solving the generalized PCTL satisfiability problem and they also bring a deeper understanding of the PCTL expressive power.

4   Existing Results

In this section, we survey the decidability results on the satisfiability problem for various PCTL fragments. So far, the most explored fragment is the *qualitative PCTL (qPCTL)*, obtained by constraining the constants used to be only 0 and 1. In fact, qPCTL was introduced already in early 80's [30] as the probabilistic variant of the branching-time logic CTL [22] where the existential and universal path quantifiers are replaced with the qualitative probabilistic operator. The quantitative extension (with constants between 0 and 1) has been considered significantly later [28].

4.1   Qualitative PCTL

Decidability and Complexity of Satisfiability. The satisfiability problem for qPCTL and actually for a richer logic qPCTL* [41] was investigated immediately after the introduction of these logics, together with the existence of sound and complete axiomatic systems, the traditional tool for deciding validity of formulae. Note that a formula φ is *not* satisfiable iff $\neg\varphi$ is valid. Here qPCTL* denotes the qualitative probabilistic variant of CTL*, freely combining linear-time operators and the qualitative probabilistic operator. The main results for qPCTL can be summarized as follows:

Theorem 1 ([8,41]). *General, bounded, and finite satisfiability problems for qPCTL are in* **EXPTIME**.

While the decidability of satisfiability problems on qPCTL follows from the decidability for the more general qPCTL* [37], establishing their complexity requires finer argumentation since the upper bounds established for the three variants for qPCTL* are all **2-NEXPTIME** [37].

Interestingly, each of the three results above has been proven by a different technique, which we detail on in the next section. Firstly, finite satisfiability for qPCTL can be reduced to satisfiability of (non-probabilistic) CTL because, intuitively, the actual values of positive transition probabilities do not matter. Secondly, the complexity of bounded satisfiability has been established in [30] through a sound and complete axiomatization of the logic, yielding a tableaux-based decision procedure. Thirdly, the complexity of general satisfiability was not examined until [8], which takes the approach based on the existence of "canonic" models constructible from the syntax of qPCTL formulae.

g- vs. b- vs. f-Satisfiability. Trivially, every f-satisfiable formula is also b-satisfiable and every b-satisfiable formula is also g-satisfiable. Moreover, the inclusions are strict. While Example 1 shows only the difference between finite and general satisfiability, the following two modified examples refine the hierarchy.

Example 2. The formula $\varphi \equiv G_{=1}X_{>0}a \wedge F_{<1}a$ is g-satisfiable, but not b-satisfiable. For the former consider the model of Example 1. For the latter, if there was a model of φ where all positive transition probabilities are bounded away from 0 by some $\delta > 0$, then all reachable states satisfy $P(X\neg a) \le 1 - \delta$ and hence also $P(G\neg a) \le \lim_{n\to\infty}(1 - \delta)^n = 0$.

Example 3. The formula $\varphi = G_{=1}F_{>0}a \wedge F_{<1}a$ is not f-satisfiable as seen in Example 1, yet it is b-satisfiable. Indeed, the bounded model of Fig. 2 (with uniform probabilities $1/2$ or 1) uses stuttering to simulate the decreasing probabilities of the exits in the model of Fig. 1.

However, some simple sound criteria for the equivalence of different versions of satisfiability can be stated. To this end, it is useful to consider the *canonical form* of qPCTL formulae [29] given by the following syntax:

$$\varphi ::= p \mid \neg p \mid \varphi_1 \vee \varphi_2 \mid \varphi_1 \wedge \varphi_2 \mid X_{=1}\varphi \mid X_{>0}\varphi \mid$$
$$\varphi_1 U_{=1}\varphi_2 \mid \varphi_1 U_{>0}\varphi_2 \mid F_{=1}\varphi \mid G_{>0}\varphi$$

In [29], a formula is called *finitary*, if, when written in canonical form, it contains at most one subformula of the form $G_{>0}\varphi$ and, if it contains such a subformula, then it contains no subformulae of the form $\varphi_0 U_{>0}\varphi_1$.

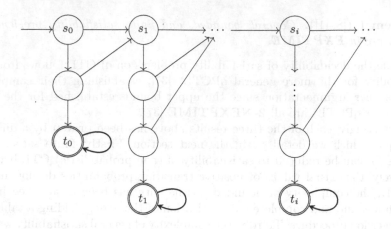

Fig. 2. A bounded (uniform) model of φ

Theorem 2 ([29]). *Let φ be a finitary qPCTL formula. Then φ is b-satisfiable iff φ is f-satisfiable.*

In Example 2, the difference between g- and b-satisfiability has been demonstrated using the next operator. A qPCTL formula is *next-free* if it contains no $X_{\bowtie \varrho}$ operators. Intuitively, small transition probabilities in models of next-free formulae can be "simulated" using longer auxiliary paths with stuttering as in Example 3. Technically, this result can be proven using the structural properties of the particular models for g-satisfiable formulae derived in [8].

Theorem 3. *Let φ be a next-free qPCTL formula. Then φ is g-satisfiable iff φ is b-satisfiable.*

4.2 Quantitative PCTL

The satisfiability problem for PCTL is open for each of the three variants of general, bounded, and finite models, yet there are restrictions known to yield decidability. They can be classified into bounding the model size and restricting to a PCTL fragment, either structurally or by altering the semantics, namely imposing a bound on the *horizon* of the operators. Due to the different nature of the restrictions, the respective techniques vary and are discussed in more detail in Sect. 5, whereas here we again only summarize the results.

Bounded Size. The *bounded satisfiability problem* is to determine whether there exists a model of a given finite size (number of states) for a given formula. This problem can be solved by encoding it into an SMT problem, an idea explored in [4] with restrictions on the models, such as transition probabilities being always $1/2$. We provide a complete proof of the general case in Sect. 5.3.

There is an important implication of this result. Namely, if we are able to determine a maximum required model size for some formula, then it follows that the satisfiability of that formula can also be determined.

While in general the size of the smallest model cannot be bounded by any constant, the result of [8] states that the *branching degree* (maximum number of successors) for a model of a formula φ can be bounded by $|\varphi| + 2$, where $|\varphi|$ is the length of φ.

Bounded Horizon. Similar in spirit, *bounded PCTL* limits the scope of the operators by a step bound to a given time horizon, i.e., eventualities are to occur within given k steps, and always modalities only apply in the first k steps. The decidability result follows again by bounding the size of the models [15].

Structural Fragments. Another class of restrictions focuses on possible interactions of various operators and limits their combinations. This yields more understanding of the expressive power of PCTL and seems more hopeful concerning prospective decidability for the general PCTL.

A systematic study of simpler fragments is conducted in [38], where the set of admissible temporal connectives is restricted to F and G. Its summary is schematically depicted in Fig. 3. Since already the satisfiability for propositional logic in negation normal form has nontrivial instances only when all the constructs $a, \neg a$ and conjunction are present, only fragments with all three included are considered; see the bottom of the Hasse diagram. The fragments are named by the list of constructs they use, where we omit the three constructs above to avoid clutter. We use f and g to abbreviate finite and general satisfiability, respectively, and the equality denotes that the problems are equivalent.

For all the fragments, the decidability follows by establishing a bound $b(|\varphi|)$ on the size of a model, written as "$f = b(|\varphi|)$". Alternatively, one can bound only the height of tree models, denoted by "H:$b(|\varphi|)$". In such a case, since for every satisfiable PCTL formula φ its model can be pruned to have branching degree bounded by $|\varphi| + 2$, the size of the model is bounded by $(|\varphi| + 2)^{b(|\varphi|)}$. This yields the decidability for the lower part of the diagram.

Progressive Fragments. In general, an f-satisfiable PCTL formula φ may enforce the existence of non-bottom SCCs in every finite model of φ. Nevertheless, there always exists a model M of φ where the height of the corresponding DAG of SCCs is *minimal*, and we use $\mathscr{H}(\varphi)$ to denote this minimal height (in particular, if φ has a strongly connected model, then $\mathscr{H}(\varphi) = 0$). For simplicity, let us again consider the simplified variant of PCTL where the temporal connectives are restricted to F and G. Then, every formula can be rewritten so that negations are pushed towards atomic propositions and the probabilistic operator takes the form $P(\Phi) \rhd r$ where $\rhd \in \{>, \geq\}$. Hence, if $s \models \varphi$ and s' is another state such that s and s' satisfy the same set of atomic propositions and for every path subformula Φ of φ we have that $\mathbb{P}_{s'}(\{\pi \in Run(s') \mid \pi \models \Phi\}) \geq \mathbb{P}_s(\{\pi \in Run(s) \mid \pi \models \Phi\})$, then $s' \models \varphi$.

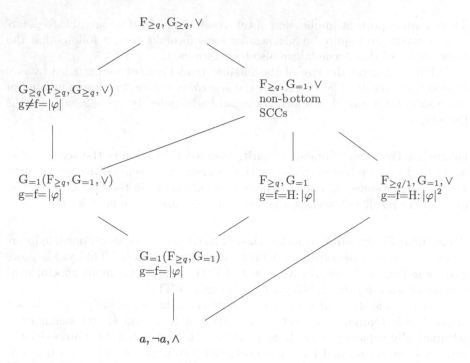

Fig. 3. A Hasse diagram summarizing the satisfiability results [38] for the considered fragments of PCTL based on the F and G operators. All fragments contain literals and conjunctions, and some form of quantitative comparisons. The fragments are described by the list of operators they allow (excluding the constructs of the minimal fragment at the bottom). The subscript denotes the possible constraints on probabilistic operators. $G(list)$ denotes formulae in the fragment described by $list$ with G-operators at the top-level; $F_{\geq q/1}$ denotes the use of $F_{\geq q}$ with the restriction that inside G only $q = 1$ can be used.

The formulae φ where $\mathscr{H}(\varphi) = 0$ are effectively recognizable and their f-satisfiability is easy to check. More precisely, we have the following:

Theorem 4 ([18]). *For every φ we have that $\mathscr{H}(\varphi) = 0$ iff φ has a strongly connected model with at most $2^{AP(\varphi)}$ states ($AP(\varphi)$ is the set of all atomic propositions occurring in φ).*

If $\mathscr{H}(\varphi) \geq 1$, then the top SCC C of a model M with DAG height equal to $\mathscr{H}(\varphi)$ must achieve some "progress" in satisfying φ before entering one of the C-descendants $t_1, \ldots, t_n$ (a C-descendant is a state $t \notin C$ such that $s \to t$ for some $s \in C$). An *effectively progressive PCTL fragment* $\mathcal{L}$ [18] consists of formulae where the progress is effectively measurable. More precisely, there must be computable functions $c, h : \mathbb{N} \to \mathbb{N}$ such that for every f-satisfiable $\varphi \in \mathcal{L}$ there exists a finite Markov chain M_φ satisfying the following conditions (see Fig. 4):

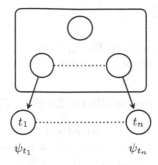

Fig. 4. The structure of M_φ.

- M_φ has one top SCC C with at most $c(|\varphi|)$ states, where all C-descendants $t_1, \ldots, t_n$ are absorbing.
- For every C-descendant t there is an f-satisfiable formula $\psi_t \in \mathcal{L}$ such that $c(\psi_t) \leq c(\varphi)$, $h(\psi_t) < h(\varphi)$, and the following condition holds: If every C-descendant t is replaced with a state u_t such that $u_t \models \psi_t$, then $s \models \varphi$ for some $s \in C$.

Note that the functions c, h determine a computable upper bound on the number of states in a model of φ. Hence, the finite satisfiability problem is decidable for every progressive PCTL fragment. This technique has been used in [18] to demonstrate the decidability of several PCTL fragments that are not covered by the results of [38]. Examples are given below.

Fragment $\mathcal{L}_1$

$$\varphi ::= a \mid \neg a \mid \varphi_1 \wedge \varphi_2 \mid \varphi_1 \vee \varphi_2 \mid F_{\rhd r}\varphi \mid G_{\rhd r}\psi$$
$$\psi ::= a \mid \neg a \mid \psi_1 \wedge \psi_2 \mid \psi_1 \vee \psi_2 \mid G_{\rhd r}\psi$$

Fragment $\mathcal{L}_2$

$$\varphi ::= a \mid \neg a \mid \varphi_1 \wedge \varphi_2 \mid \varphi_1 \vee \varphi_2 \mid F_{\rhd r}\varphi \mid G_{=1}\psi$$
$$\psi ::= a \mid \neg a \mid \psi_1 \wedge \psi_2 \mid \psi_1 \vee \psi_2 \mid F_{\rhd w}\psi$$

Fragment $\mathcal{L}_3$

$$\varphi ::= a \mid \neg a \mid \varphi_1 \wedge \varphi_2 \mid \varphi_1 \vee \varphi_2 \mid F_{\rhd r}\varphi \mid G_{=1}\psi \mid G_{=1}\varrho$$
$$\psi ::= a \mid \neg a \mid \psi_1 \wedge \psi_2 \mid \psi_1 \vee \psi_2 \mid F_{\rhd w}\psi$$
$$\varrho ::= \varrho_1 \wedge \varrho_2 \mid \varrho_1 \vee \varrho_2 \mid F_{\rhd w}\psi \mid G_{=1}\psi \mid G_{=1}\varrho$$

Fragment $\mathcal{L}_4$

$$\varphi ::= a \mid \neg a \mid \varphi_1 \wedge \varphi_2 \mid \varphi_1 \vee \varphi_2 \mid F_{\rhd r}\varphi \mid G_{=1}\psi$$
$$\psi ::= a \mid \neg a \mid \psi_1 \wedge \psi_2 \mid \psi_1 \vee \psi_2 \mid F_{>0}\psi \mid G_{=1}\psi$$

5   Proof Techniques

Here we survey the techniques used. The first two subsections focus on techniques applicable to qPCTL, the rest on quantitative settings.

5.1   Reduction to Non-probabilistic Logic CTL

Observe that when checking the satisfiability of formulae such as $X_{=1}\varphi$ or $\varphi U_{>0}\psi$, we are not interested in actual values of transition probabilities. It is only important which of them are positive. Such operators are also called *non-probabilistic*. On the other hand, when considering $F^{=1}\varphi$ over infinite models, the actual probability values matter (recall Example 1). The operators for which the probability values are relevant are called *probabilistic*. In order to isolate the probabilistic features of qPCTL, one can equivalently define qPCTL via the W (weak until) and F operators instead of U (the semantics of W is defined so that $\varphi_1 W \varphi_2$ is equivalent to $(\varphi_1 U \varphi_2) \vee G\varphi_1$):

$$\varphi ::= a \quad | \quad \neg\varphi \quad | \quad \varphi_1 \vee \varphi_2 \quad | \quad X_{=1}\varphi \quad | \quad \varphi_1 W_{=1}\varphi_2 \quad | \quad F_{=1}\varphi$$

The operators $X_{=1}$ and $W_{=1}$ are non-probabilistic. Now observe that for qPCTL over *finite* models, the probabilistic $F_{=1}$ operator is actually expressible using $W_{=1}$ because

$$F_{=1}\varphi \quad \equiv \quad (F_{>0}\varphi)W_{=1}\varphi \quad \equiv \quad (\neg(\neg\varphi W_{=1}\textbf{false}))W_{=1}\varphi$$

Thus, one can reduce the f-satisfiability of qPCTL to the satisfiability of CTL. In one direction, it suffices to forget the probabilities. For the opposite direction, arbitrary (e.g., uniform) distributions serve well.

5.2   Axiomatization and Tableaux

The traditional logical perspective on satisfiability is that of establishing a deductive system to prove validity of tautologies.

Axiomatic Systems. In [30] the following systems are proposed and shown to be sound and complete.

- Axioms
    A0 axioms of the propositional calculus
    A1 $X_{=1}(\varphi \rightarrow \psi) \rightarrow (X_{=1}\varphi \rightarrow X_{=1}\psi)$
    A2 $\varphi W_{=1}\psi \rightarrow \psi \vee (p \wedge X_{=1}(\varphi W_{=1}\psi))$
- Inference rules
    R0 modus ponens
    R1 if $\vdash \varphi$ then $\vdash X_{=1}\varphi$
    R2 if $\chi \rightarrow \psi \vee (\varphi \wedge X_{=1}\chi)$ then $\vdash \chi \rightarrow \varphi W_{=1}\psi$
    R3 if $\vdash \varphi$ then $\vdash \neg F_{=1}\neg\varphi$

- Additional axioms for finite models interpretation
  A3 $F_{=1}\varphi \leftrightarrow (\mathbf{true}W_{>0}\varphi)W_{=1}\varphi$
- Additional axioms and rules for bounded models interpretation
  A4 $F_{=1}\varphi \leftrightarrow \varphi \vee X_{=1}F^{=1}\varphi$
  A5 $F_{=1}F^{=1}\varphi \rightarrow F_{=1}\varphi$
  A6 $\varphi W_{=1}\psi \wedge F_{=1}\neg\varphi \rightarrow F_{=1}\psi$
  R4 if $\vdash \chi \rightarrow \varphi \vee (X_{=1}F_{=1}\chi \wedge X_{>0}\varphi)$ then $\vdash \chi \rightarrow F_{=1}\varphi$.

The following axiomatic systems are then defined:

b-qPCTL R0–R3 and A0–A2 and A3
f-qPCTL R0–R3 and A0–A2 and A4–A6 and R4.

While A3 holds in the finite case only, A4–A6 apply also to the general unbounded case, whereas R4 captures the essence of bounded models interpretation.

Tableaux Method. A tableaux is a directed graph with nodes labelled by sets of formulae to be satisfied. Satisfaction of such a node (set of formulae) is guaranteed if at least one of the node's children is satisfied. For example $a \vee b$ is satisfied iff either a or b is satisfied. Hence, we expand the formulae according to the rules that preserve this property, see the following few examples of a node r expanded into its children r_i:

r	r_1	r_2	r_3
$\varphi \vee \psi$	φ	ψ	
$G_{>0}\varphi$	φ	$X_{>0}G_{>0}\varphi$	$X_{=1}(\mathbf{true} \vee G_{>0}\varphi)$
$F_{=1}\varphi$	φ	$X_{=1}F_{=1}\varphi \wedge X_{>0}F_{=1}\varphi$	

The main differences to CTL tableaux are underlined. These are actually the only probabilistic cases and require special handling. Although they contain logically redundant subformulae, these are needed for the method to work properly.

Following the expansion, we build a directed graph from a root labelled with the given formula by expanding the leaves repetitively. To finish the expansion of a branch, at least one of the following conditions must hold:

- the leaf cannot be expanded;
- the branch is contradictory (contains a proposition and its negation);
- nodes repeat, more precisely, the to-be-created son has the same label as one of its ancestors; here an edge is set to lead to the ancestor rather than to the new son.

Therefore, the tableau is finite and its size is singly exponential in the size of the formula put in the root. After finishing the tableaux, we mark unsatisfiable nodes: we start with the contradictory ones and propagate appropriately to the respective predecessors. This results in either marking the root as well—here a proof of the negated formula can be read off—, or leaving it unmarked—such a tableau yields a model of the formula.

Theorem 5 ([30])**.** *A formula φ of qPCTL is b-satisfiable iff the root $\{\varphi\}$ of the tableau has not been marked. Moreover:*

- *if the root has not been marked, a b-model of φ can be obtained mechanically from the tableau;*
- *if the root has been marked, a proof of $\neg\varphi$ in b-qPCTL axiomatization can be obtained mechanically from the tableau.*

For f-satisfiability, using A3 we can transform the given formula into a non-probabilistic formula containing only $X_{=1}, X_{>0}, W_{=1}, W_{>0}$ operators. Then the tableaux method can be applied and it coincides with the tableau method for CTL.

For g-satisfiability, such result has not been established yet. The axiomatization b-qPCTL without the rule R4 gives a sound axiomatization of the general model interpretation, though to the best of our knowledge it has not been shown whether it is also complete.

5.3   Bounding the Size of a Model

So far, most of the decidability results for the generalized PCTL satisfiability problem involving a non-qualitative PCTL fragments have been obtained by bounding the size of a model. The existence of a model with n states where all transition probabilities are equal to $1/2$ can be formulated as an SMT problem [4]. The general case (with arbitrary probabilities) is solvable by encoding the problem into the existential fragment of first order theory of the reals. Since we are not aware of an explicit full proof of this folklore result, we include a proof here.

Theorem 6. *Let φ be a PCTL formula and $n \in \mathbb{N}$. The existence of a model of φ with at most n states is decidable in space polynomial in n and the size of φ.*

Proof. Let φ be a PCTL formula and $n \in \mathbb{N}$ a bound on the size of the model. Without restrictions, we assume that φ does not contain the redundant $F^{\leq k}$, F, and G operators. We use $sub(\varphi)$ and $Psub(\varphi)$ to denote the sets of all state/path subformulae of φ.

The algorithm starts by guessing a finite directed graph $G = (V, \rightarrow)$, where $V = \{v_1, \ldots, v_m\}$ and $m \leq n$. Furthermore, for every $\psi \in sub(\varphi)$, the algorithm guesses a subset $V(\psi) \subseteq V$ so that

- $V(a) = V \setminus V(\neg a)$ for every atomic proposition a such that $\neg a \in sub(\varphi)$;
- $V(\xi_1 \wedge \xi_2) = V(\xi_1) \cap V(\xi_2)$ for every $\xi_1 \wedge \xi_2 \in sub(\varphi)$;
- $V(\xi_1 \vee \xi_2) = V(\xi_1) \cup V(\xi_2)$ for every $\xi_1 \vee \xi_2 \in sub(\varphi)$;
- $V(\varphi) \neq \emptyset$.

Then, the algorithm constructs the following formula of existential theory of the reals, where k is the number of edges of G.

$$\exists x_1, \ldots, x_k : \bigwedge_{i=1}^{k} 0 < x_i \leq 1 \ \wedge \ \bigwedge_{v \in V} Distr(v) \ \wedge \ \bigwedge_{\psi \in Psub(\varphi)} Correct(\psi) \quad (1)$$

The variables $x_1, \ldots, x_k$ represent the (positive) probability of edges. The variable representing the probability of an edge $v \to u$ is denoted by $x[v \to u]$.

The formula $Distr(v)$ says that the sum of the variables associated with the outgoing edges of v is equal to 1, i.e.,

$$Distr(v) \quad \equiv \quad \sum_{v \to u} x[v \to u] = 1$$

The formula $Correct(\psi)$ says that the set of vertices satisfying the formula ψ is precisely $V(\psi)$, assuming that this claim holds for all subformulae of ψ. Hence, the formula (1) is valid iff the sets $V(\psi)$, $\psi \in sub(\varphi)$ were guessed correctly.

Now we show how to construct the formula $Correct(\psi)$. We distinguish three possibilities.

- $\psi \equiv X_{\bowtie r} \xi$. Then $Correct(X_{\bowtie r} \xi)$ takes the form

$$\bigwedge_{v \in V(X_{\bowtie r} \xi)} \left(\sum_{\substack{v \to u, \\ u \in V(\xi)}} x[v \to u] \right) \bowtie r \quad \wedge \quad \bigwedge_{v \in V \setminus V(X_{\bowtie r} \xi)} \left(\sum_{\substack{v \to u, \\ u \in V(\xi)}} x[v \to u] \right) \not\bowtie r.$$

- $\psi \equiv \varrho U_{\bowtie r} \xi$. Consider a directed graph $G(\varrho, \xi)$ obtained from G by replacing the outgoing edges of all vertices in $V(\xi)$ and outside $V(\varrho)$ with a self-loop. The probability of each such self-loop is 1, and the other edges keep the probability defined by the $x[v \to u]$ variables. Furthermore, consider two auxiliary atomic propositions $\bar{\varrho}$ and $\bar{\xi}$ that are valid precisely in the vertices of $V(\varrho)$ and $V(\xi)$, respectively. Then, the probability of satisfying $\bar{\varrho} U \bar{\xi}$ in a vertex v_i of G is the same as the probability y_i of satisfying $F(\bar{\xi})$ in the vertex v_i of $G(\varrho, \psi)$. The trivial recursive dependency among $y_1, \ldots, y_n$ is captured by the standard system of linear equations with *unique solution* in $[0, 1]$. Our construction of $Correct(\varrho U_{\bowtie r} \xi)$ is based on encoding this equational system. Let $Zero(\varrho U \xi)$ be the set of all $v \in V$ such that G contains no finite path of the form $v_0, \ldots, v_m$ where $m \geq 1$, $v = v_0$, $v_i \in V(\varrho)$ for all $0 \leq i < m$, and $v_m \in V(\xi)$. Note that $Zero(\varrho U \xi)$ is computable in time polynomial in n, and contains precisely all vertices satisfying the formula $\varrho U_{=0} \xi$ (assuming the sets $V(\varrho)$ and $V(\xi)$ were guessed correctly). The formula $Correct(\varrho U_{\bowtie r} \xi)$ looks as follows:

$$\exists y_1, \ldots, y_n \quad : \quad \bigwedge_{i=1}^{n} 0 \leq y_i \leq 1 \quad \wedge \quad \bigwedge_{v_i \in V(\xi)} y_i = 1 \quad \wedge \quad \bigwedge_{v_i \in Zero(\varrho U \xi)} y_i = 0$$

$$\wedge \quad \bigwedge_{v_i \in V \setminus Zero(\varrho U \xi)} y_i = \sum_{v_i \to v_j} x[v_i \to v_j] \cdot y_j$$

$$\wedge \quad \bigwedge_{v_i \in V(\varrho U_{\bowtie r} \xi)} y_i \bowtie r \quad \wedge \quad \bigwedge_{v_i \notin V(\varrho U_{\bowtie r} \xi)} y_i \not\bowtie r$$

- $\psi \equiv \varrho U^{\leq \ell}_{\bowtie r} \xi$. Since the bound ℓ is written in binary, we must ensure that the formula $Correct(\varrho U^{\leq \ell}_{\bowtie r} \xi)$ is computed in time polynomial in $\log(\ell)$. Recall the definition of the directed graph $G(\varrho, \xi)$ and the propositions $\bar{\varrho}$ and $\bar{\xi}$. Observe that the probability of satisfying $\bar{\varrho} U^{\leq \ell} \bar{\xi}$ in a vertex v of G is the same as the probability of visiting a vertex satisfying $\bar{\xi}$ in *precisely* ℓ transitions from the vertex v of $G(\varrho, \xi)$.

For all $t \in \mathbb{N}$ and $v, u \in V$, we inductively construct a formula $R(t)$ defining variables of the form $y[v, u, t]$ representing the probability of visiting u from v in exactly t transitions in $G(\varrho, \xi)$.

- $R(0) \equiv \bigwedge_{v,u \in V} y[v, u, 0] = e_{v,u}$, where $e_{v,u}$ is either 1 or 0 depending on whether $v = u$ or not, respectively.
- $R(1) \equiv \bigwedge_{v,u \in V} y[v, u, 1] = f_{v,u}$, where $f_{v,u}$ is defined as follows. If $v \in V(\xi)$ or $v \notin V(\varrho)$, then $f_{v,u}$ is either 1 or 0, depending on whether $v = u$ or not, respectively. Otherwise, $f_{v,u}$ is the variable $x[v, u]$.
- $R(2t)$ is defined as

$$R(t) \wedge \bigwedge_{v,u \in V} y[v, u, 2t] = \sum_{w \in V} y[v, w, t] \cdot y[w, u, t]$$

- $R(2t+1)$ is defined as

$$R(t) \wedge \bigwedge_{v,u \in V} y[v, u, 2t+1] = \sum_{w,z \in V} y[v, w, t] \cdot y[w, z, t] \cdot y[z, u, 1]$$

Let $V(\xi) = \{u_1, \ldots, u_b\}$. The formula $Correct(\varrho U^{\leq \ell}_{\bowtie r} \xi)$ is defined as

$$R(\ell) \wedge \bigwedge_{v \in V(\varrho U^{\leq \ell}_{\bowtie r} \xi)} \left(\sum_{j=1}^{b} y[v, u_j, \ell] \right) \bowtie r \wedge \bigwedge_{v \notin V(\varrho U^{\leq \ell}_{\bowtie r} \xi)} \left(\sum_{j=1}^{b} y[v, u_j, \ell] \right) \not\bowtie r$$

Note that the above formula is computable in time polynomial in $\log(\ell)$.

Observe that the constructed formula (1) belongs to existential theory of the reals and its size is polynomial in n and the size of φ. Our algorithm outputs 'yes' or 'no' depending on whether the formula is valid or not (which is decidable in space polynomial in n and the size of φ [12]). Thus, the existence of a model of φ with at most n states is decided in polynomial space. $\qquad \square$

5.4   Filtration

Filtration is the prominent technique for establishing the small model property of non-probabilistic temporal logics. The basic idea is to "filter" a model M of φ through a finite set $Cl(\varphi)$ of formulae determined by φ, i.e., to construct the quotient $M/\sim$ where two states of M are related by $\sim$ iff they satisfy the same formulae of $Cl(\varphi)$. A variant of this technique is applicable to the qualitative fragment of PCTL, and it can be used to construct an exponential-size model for every finite-satisfiable qPCTL formula, and also a finite description of a (possibly infinite-state) model of every satisfiable qPCTL formula [8].

Intuitively, the reason why filtration still works for qPCTL is that the validity of a qualitative formula in a state s is determined by the validity of the subformulae of φ in s and its immediate successors. For example, $s \models F_{=1}\psi$ iff either $s \models \psi$ or $t \models F_{=1}\psi$ for every immediate successor t of s. However, a quantitative formula such as $F_{=0.7}\psi$ does not admit such a simple "unfolding". Here, we need to know the *precise* probabilities of satisfying the path formula $F\psi$ in the immediate successors of s. Clearly, it does not make much sense to filter a model through *all* formulae of the form $F_{=x}\psi$. Nevertheless, one may "copy" the relevant quantities from the considered model and use them to enlarge the sets of formulae that need to be satisfied in successor states. If the growth of these sets is kept under control, this may lead to establishing a computable bound on the size of a model. This approach has been used in [18] to establish the decidability of finite satisfiability for several PCTL fragments.

5.5   Undecidability Results

Some variants of the generalized PCTL satisfiability problem are known to be undecidable. For a given $k \geq 2$, let $\mathcal{C}_k$ be the class of all Markov chains (S, P, v) where for every state s there are at most k pairwise different states u such that $P(s, u) > 0$. Furthermore, let $\mathcal{F}_k$ be the set of all finite-state Markov chains in $\mathcal{C}_k$. The next theorem has been proven in [8] (a detailed proof can be found in [9]).

Theorem 7. *Let $k \geq 2$. For a given PCTL formula φ,*

- *the problem whether φ has a model in $\mathcal{C}_k$ is highly undecidable (i.e., beyond the arithmetical hierarchy);*
- *the problem whether φ has a finite model in $\mathcal{F}_k$ is undecidable.*

A proof of Theorem 7 is obtained by reduction of the strategy synthesis problem for Markov decision processes and PCTL objectives. An instance of this problem is a finite-state Markov decision problem $\mathcal{D}$, a state s_0 of $\mathcal{D}$, and a PCTL formula φ. The question is whether there exists a strategy σ such that $s_0 \models \varphi$ in the Markov chain $\mathcal{D}^\sigma$ obtained by applying the strategy σ to $\mathcal{D}$. For *unrestricted* (i.e., history dependent and randomized) strategies, this problem is *highly undecidable*; and for *finite-memory* strategies, where $\mathcal{D}^\sigma$ is a finite-state Markov chain, the problem is *undecidable* [7].

Let $k \geq 2$. First, it is shown that one can safely assume that

(a) every *stochastic* vertex s of $\mathcal{D}$ has precisely k pairwise different successors t such that $P(s, t) > 0$;

(b) every *non-deterministic* vertex s of $\mathcal{D}$ has precisely $k + 1$ pairwise different successors, and the strategy σ must select precisely k of these successors with positive probability in order to satisfy φ.

For every vertex s of $\mathcal{D}$, a fresh atomic proposition a_s is fixed, and the structure of $\mathcal{D}$ is encoded by a PCTL formula

$$\psi \equiv a_{s_0} \; \wedge \; \mathbf{G}_{=1}\left(\bigvee_{a_s}\left(a_s \wedge \bigwedge_{t \neq s} \neg a_t\right)\right) \; \wedge \; \mathbf{G}_{=1}\left(\bigwedge_s a_s \Rightarrow \xi_s\right)$$

Intuitively, the formula ψ says that we start in a state satisfying s_0, the propositions a_s are mutually exclusive, and whenever a state satisfying a_s in visited, the formula ξ_s holds. If s is a stochastic state with successors $t_1, \ldots, t_k$, we put

$$\xi_s \; \equiv \; \bigwedge_{i=1}^{k} \mathbf{X}_{=P(s,t_i)} a_{t_i}$$

Hence, ξ_s enforces the structure of immediate successors as in $\mathcal{D}$ *if the model of ψ belongs to $\mathcal{F}_k$.* If v is a non-deterministic state with successors $t_1, \ldots, t_{k+1}$, then ξ_s says that there is a subset A of $\{a_{t_1}, \ldots, a_{t_{k+1}}\}$ with precisely k elements such that all propositions in A are satisfied with positive probability in the next state. Now one can show that

- $\psi \wedge \varphi$ has a model in $\mathcal{F}_k$ iff there is an unrestricted strategy σ such that $s_0 \models \varphi$ in the Markov chain $\mathcal{D}^\sigma$;
- $\psi \wedge \varphi$ has *finite* model in $\mathcal{F}_k$ iff there is a finite-memory strategy σ such that $s_0 \models \varphi$ in the Markov chain $\mathcal{D}^\sigma$.

This proves Theorem 7.

6   Enforcing Large Models by the Probabilistic Operator

One intrinsic but not fully understood feature of PCTL formulae is the way how concrete numerical values in probability constraints influence the structure and the size of a model. In this section, we present a (perhaps surprising) result documenting the subtlety of this question.

A *parameterized PCTL formula* is a PCTL formula where the numerical constant r in some occurrences of the probabilistic operator $P(\Phi) \bowtie r$ is represented symbolically by a parameter p (for our purposes, it suffices to consider only one such parameter). For a parameterized PCTL formula φ and $\kappa \in [0,1]$, we use $\varphi(\kappa)$ to denote the (standard) PCTL formula obtained by replacing every occurrence of p with κ in φ.

For a given $k \in \mathbb{N}$, we say that a Markov chain $M = (S, P, v)$ is *k-cycle-free* if the length of every executable simple cycle in M is strictly bounded by k. More precisely, for every finite sequence of states $s_0, \ldots, s_\ell$ such that $s_0 = s_\ell$, $s_i \neq s_j$ for all $i \neq j$ smaller than ℓ, and $P(s_i, s_{i+1}) > 0$ for all $0 \leq i < \ell$, we have that $\ell < k$.

One simple class of 2-cycle-free Markov chains are *tree-like* Markov chains, where the underlying graph is a directed finite tree with self-loops at every leaf.

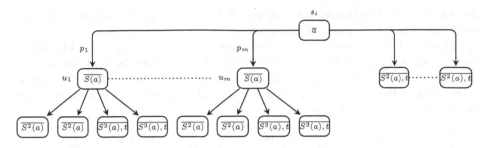

Fig. 5. The successors of s_i.

Intuitively, the question whether a given PCTL formula has a tree-like model appears easier than other variants of the generalized PCTL satisfiability problem. One is tempted to conjecture the existence of some simple function f bounding the height of a tree-like model for a given φ (if a tree-like model of φ exists). Note that a construction of f would already imply the decidability of PCTL satisfiability in the class of tree-like models due to the bound on the branching degree. The next theorem provides a parameterized formula φ such that $f(\varphi(\kappa))$ is *unbounded* when interpreted as a function of κ. This implies that f cannot be based on simplistic structural measures, and the same holds for an *arbitrary* class of k-cycle-free Markov chains subsuming tree-like models.

Theorem 8. *For every $k \in \mathbb{N}$, there is a parameterized PCTL formula φ satisfying the following condition: For every $n \in \mathbb{N}$, there is a rational $B(n) \in (0,1)$ such that $\varphi(B(n))$ has a tree-like model with $2n+3$ states, and every k-cycle-free model of $\varphi(B(n))$ has at least n states.*

Proof. For the rest of this proof, we fix constants

- $q \in (\frac{3}{4}, 1)$,
- $x \in (\frac{1-\sqrt{4q-3}}{2}, \frac{1+\sqrt{4q-3}}{2})$.

Furthermore, we define an infinite sequence of numbers $B(0), B(1), \dots$ inductively as follows:

- $B(0) = x$,
- $B(i+1) = \frac{q-1+B(i)}{B(i)}$.

Using the defining properties of q and x, a straightforward induction on i shows that, for all $i \in \mathbb{N}$,

- $B(i) < B(i+1)$,
- $B(i) \in (\frac{1-\sqrt{4q-3}}{2}, \frac{1+\sqrt{4q-3}}{2})$.

The formula φ guarantees the existence of a sequence of $s_0, \dots, s_n$ where every subsequence of k consecutive states contains pairwise different states. For

k-cycle-free Markov chains, this implies that *all* states in the sequence are pairwise different, which proves Theorem 8.

The set of atomic propositions occurring in φ is $\{a_0, \ldots, a_{k-1}, t\}$. The subset $\{a_0, \ldots, a_{k-1}\}$ is denoted by A. Intuitively, the propositions of A are used to enforce a certain "circular pattern" in a model of φ, and t marks "terminal" states where the pattern is no longer enforced. For notation convenience, for every $\alpha \in \{a_0, \ldots, a_{k-1}\}$ we use

- $S(\alpha)$ to denote the "successor" of α, where $S(a_i) = a_{i+1 \bmod k}$;
- $S^j(\alpha)$ to denote $S(\ldots S(\alpha) \ldots)$ composed j times (in particular, $S^0(\alpha) = \alpha$);
- $\overline{\alpha}$ to denote the formula $\alpha \wedge \neg t \wedge \bigwedge_{j=1}^{k-1} \neg S^j(\alpha)$;
- $\overline{\alpha, t}$ to denote the formula $\alpha \wedge t \wedge \bigwedge_{j=1}^{k-1} \neg S^j(\alpha)$.

Hence, $\overline{\alpha}$ says that α is valid and the other atomic propositions are invalid in a given state.

The parameterized formula φ is defined as

$$\varphi \equiv init \wedge G_{=1}(end \vee succ)$$

where

$$init \equiv \overline{a_0} \wedge F_{=B(0)}^{\leq 1} S(a_0)$$

$$end \equiv t \vee \bigvee_{\alpha \in A} (\overline{\alpha} \wedge F_{=p}^{\leq 1} S(\alpha))$$

$$succ \equiv \bigvee_{\alpha \in A} (\overline{\alpha} \wedge F_{=q}^{\leq 2} S^2(\alpha) \wedge F_{=1}^{\leq 1}(\overline{S(\alpha)} \vee \overline{S^2(\alpha), t}))$$

Note that the parameter p appears only in the subformula *end*.

Let $M = (S, P, v)$ be a model of $\varphi(B(n))$. We show that there exists a sequence of states $s_0, \ldots, s_n$ satisfying the following conditions:

- $P(s_i, s_{i+1}) > 0$ for all $0 \leq i < n$;
- $s_i \models \overline{S^i(a_0)} \wedge F_{\leq B(i)}^{\leq 1} S^{i+1}(a_0)$.

Note that every subsequence of $s_0, \ldots, s_n$ of length k consists of pairwise different states, because each state in the subsequence satisfies a different $\overline{a_i}$. Hence, if M is k-cycle-free, then M has at least n states. Furthermore, we show that $\varphi(B(n))$ has a 2-cycle-free model.

Let s be a state of M such that $s \models \varphi(B(n))$. The sequence $s_0, \ldots, s_n$ is constructed inductively.

- $s_0 = s$. Clearly, $s_0 \models \overline{a_0} \wedge F_{\leq B(0)}^{\leq 1} S(a_0)$ because $s \models init$.
- Suppose that $s_0, \ldots, s_i$ has already been constructed for $i < n$. By induction hypothesis, $s_i \models \overline{a_i} \wedge F_{\leq B(i)}^{\leq 1} S(a_i)$, which implies $s_i \not\models end$. Since $s_0 \models G_{=1}(end \vee succ)$ and s_i is reachable from s_0 with positive probability, we have that $s_i \models succ$. Let a be the proposition $S^i(a_0)$. Then,

$$s_i \models \overline{a} \wedge F_{=q}^{\leq 2} S^2(a) \wedge F_{=1}^{\leq 1}(\overline{S(a)} \vee \overline{S^2(a), t}).$$

Hence, every state u such that $P(s_i, u) > 0$ satisfies either $\overline{S(a)}$ or $\overline{S^2(a)}, t$. Let $u_1, \ldots, u_m$ be the states satisfying $\overline{S(a)}$, and let $p_j = P(s_i, u_j)$ for every $j \leq m$ (see Fig. 5). Let $p = \sum_{j=1}^{m} p_j$. Since $s_i \models F^{\leq 1}_{\leq B(i)} S(a)$, we obtain $p \leq B(i)$.

Observe that for every $j \leq m$, we have that $u_j \models succ$, i.e.,

$$u_j \models \overline{S(a)} \wedge F^{\leq 2}_{=q} S^3(a) \wedge F^{\leq 1}_{=1}(\overline{S^2(a)} \vee \overline{S^3(a)}, t).$$

Let r_j be the probability of satisfying $F^{\leq 1}\overline{S^2(a)}$ in u_j. Then, the probability of satisfying the formula $F^{\leq 2}S^2(a)$ in s_i is equal to

$$(1 - p) + \sum_{j=1}^{m} p_j \cdot r_j \tag{2}$$

Since $s_i \models F^{\leq 2}_{=q} S^2(a)$, we have that (2) is equal to q, yielding

$$\sum_{j=1}^{m} p_j \cdot r_j = q - 1 + p \tag{3}$$

We claim that there is $j \leq m$ such that $r_j \leq B(i+1)$. Suppose the converse. Then

$$\sum_{j=1}^{m} p_j \cdot r_j \ > \ \sum_{j=1}^{m} p_j \cdot B(i+1) \ = \ p \cdot B(i+1) \tag{4}$$

By combining (3) and (4), we obtain

$$B(i+1) \ < \ \frac{q - 1 + p}{p} \tag{5}$$

Since $B(i+1) = \frac{q-1+B(i)}{B(i)}$ and $p \leq B(i)$, we also have $B(i+1) \geq \frac{q-1+p}{p}$, which is a contradiction. Hence, there exists u_j such that

$$u_j \models \overline{S(a)} \wedge F^{\leq 1}_{\leq B(i+1)} S^2(a)$$

and we put $s_{i+1} = u_j$ (recall that $S(a) = S^{i+1}(a_0)$).

A tree-like model of $\varphi(B(n))$ with $2n + 3$ states is shown in Fig. 6.   □

7 Some Challenges for Future Work

The PCTL satisfiability problem is a difficult question resisting numerous research attempts. Due to the many subtle features of PCTL (and probabilistic logics in general), trying to solve the whole problem 'at once' is perhaps not the best way to achieve real progress. Alternatively, one can concentrate on special variants of the problem representing barriers more realistic to overcome. In this section, we give several concrete proposals.

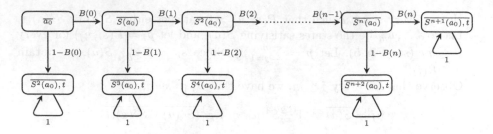

Fig. 6. A 2-cycle-free model of $\varphi(B(n))$.

Problem 1. Solve PCTL satisfiability for the F, G-fragment and tree-like models.

To solve Problem 1, it suffices to give a computable upper bound in the height of a tree-like model for a given formula φ (assuming a tree-like model of φ exists). However, such a bound must inevitably depend on the precise values of constants used in the probabilistic operator, as it is shown in Sect. 6.

Problem 2. Show the decidability of the satisfiability problem for PCTL fragments containing quantitative formulae with only infinite-state models.

One possible approach to Problem 2 is to show that every satisfiable formula of the considered fragment has a model with finite symbolic representation of bounded size (whose existence is decidable). This might bring new insights into the structural model complexity for the fragment.

Problem 3. Construct a parameterized PCTL formula φ such that for every $n \in \mathbb{N}$ there is $\kappa \in (0,1)$ such that $\varphi(\kappa)$ has a finite model but every model of $\varphi(\kappa)$ has at least n states. Alternatively, show that such a φ does not exist.

In other words, can the result of Sect. 6 be extended from tree-like models to general models?

Problem 4. Extend the undecidability of PCTL satisfiability beyond the classes of models with bounded branching degree.

Acknowledgments. Miroslav Chodil and Antonín Kučera are supported by the Czech Science Foundation, Grant No. 21-24711S. Jan Křetínský is supported by the German Research Foundation (DFG), project 427755713 (KR 4890/3-1) *Group-By Objectives in Probabilistic Verification (GOPro)*.

References

1. Alur, R., Henzinger, T.A.: A really temporal logic. In: FOCS, pp. 164–169. IEEE Computer Society (1989)
2. Baier, C., Größer, M., Leucker, M., Bollig, B., Ciesinski, F.: Controller synthesis for probabilistic systems. In: Proceedings of IFIP, TCS 2004, pp. 493–506. Kluwer (2004)

3. Banieqbal, B., Barringer, H.: Temporal logic with fixed points. In: Banieqbal, B., Barringer, H., Pnueli, A. (eds.) Temporal Logic in Specification. LNCS, vol. 398, pp. 62–74. Springer, Heidelberg (1989). https://doi.org/10.1007/3-540-51803-7_22
4. Bertrand, N., Fearnley, J., Schewe, S.: Bounded satisfiability for PCTL. In: Proceedings of CSL 2012. Leibniz International Proceedings in Informatics, vol. 16, pp. 92–106. Schloss Dagstuhl-Leibniz-Zentrum für Informatik (2012)
5. Billingsley, P.: Probability and Measure. Wiley, Hoboken (1995)
6. Bloem, R., Chatterjee, K., Henzinger, T.A., Jobstmann, B.: Better quality in synthesis through quantitative objectives. In: Bouajjani, A., Maler, O. (eds.) CAV 2009. LNCS, vol. 5643, pp. 140–156. Springer, Heidelberg (2009). https://doi.org/10.1007/978-3-642-02658-4_14
7. Brázdil, T., Brožek, V., Forejt, V., Kučera, A.: Stochastic games with branching-time winning objectives. In: Proceedings of LICS 2006, pp. 349–358. IEEE Computer Society Press (2006)
8. Brázdil, T., Forejt, V., Křetínský, J., Kučera, A.: The satisfiability problem for probabilistic CTL. In: Proceedings of LICS 2008, pp. 391–402. IEEE Computer Society Press (2008)
9. Brázdil, T., Forejt, V., Křetínský, J., Kučera, A.: The satisfiability problem for probabilistic CTL. Technical report FIMU-RS-2008-03. Faculty of Informatics, Masaryk University (2008)
10. Brázdil, T., Forejt, V., Kučera, A.: Controller synthesis and verification for Markov decision processes with qualitative branching time objectives. In: Aceto, L., Damgård, I., Goldberg, L.A., Halldórsson, M.M., Ingólfsdóttir, A., Walukiewicz, I. (eds.) ICALP 2008. LNCS, vol. 5126, pp. 148–159. Springer, Heidelberg (2008). https://doi.org/10.1007/978-3-540-70583-3_13
11. Brázdil, T., Kučera, A., Stražovský, O.: On the decidability of temporal properties of probabilistic pushdown automata. In: Diekert, V., Durand, B. (eds.) STACS 2005. LNCS, vol. 3404, pp. 145–157. Springer, Heidelberg (2005). https://doi.org/10.1007/978-3-540-31856-9_12
12. Canny, J.: Some algebraic and geometric computations in PSPACE. In: Proceedings of STOC 1988, pp. 460–467. ACM Press (1988)
13. Cerný, P., Henzinger, T.A.: From boolean to quantitative synthesis. In: EMSOFT, pp. 149–154. ACM (2011)
14. Chakrabarti, A., Chatterjee, K., Henzinger, T.A., Kupferman, O., Majumdar, R.: Verifying quantitative properties using bound functions. In: Borrione, D., Paul, W. (eds.) CHARME 2005. LNCS, vol. 3725, pp. 50–64. Springer, Heidelberg (2005). https://doi.org/10.1007/11560548_7
15. Chakraborty, S., Katoen, J.: On the satisfiability of some simple probabilistic logics. In: LICS, pp. 56–65. ACM (2016)
16. Chatterjee, K., Doyen, L., Henzinger, T.A.: Quantitative languages. In: Kaminski, M., Martini, S. (eds.) CSL 2008. LNCS, vol. 5213, pp. 385–400. Springer, Heidelberg (2008). https://doi.org/10.1007/978-3-540-87531-4_28
17. Chatterjee, K., Jurdzinski, M., Henzinger, T.A.: Quantitative stochastic parity games. In: SODA, pp. 121–130. SIAM (2004)
18. Chodil, M., Kučera, A.: The satisfiability problem for a quantitative fragment of PCTL. In: Bampis, E., Pagourtzis, A. (eds.) FCT 2021. LNCS, vol. 12867, pp. 149–161. Springer, Cham (2021). https://doi.org/10.1007/978-3-030-86593-1_10
19. Courcoubetis, C., Yannakakis, M.: The complexity of probabilistic verification. J. Assoc. Comput. Mach. **42**(4), 857–907 (1995)

20. Daca, P., Henzinger, T.A., Křetínský, J., Petrov, T.: Faster statistical model checking for unbounded temporal properties. In: Chechik, M., Raskin, J.-F. (eds.) TACAS 2016. LNCS, vol. 9636, pp. 112–129. Springer, Heidelberg (2016). https://doi.org/10.1007/978-3-662-49674-9_7

21. Daca, P., Henzinger, T.A., Kretínský, J., Petrov, T.: Linear distances between Markov chains. In: CONCUR. LIPIcs, vol. 59, pp. 20:1–20:15. Schloss Dagstuhl - Leibniz-Zentrum für Informatik (2016)

22. Emerson, E.A., Clarke, E.M.: Using branching time temporal logic to synthesize synchronization skeletons. Sci. Comput. Program. **2**(3), 241–266 (1982)

23. Emerson, E.: Temporal and modal logic. In: Handbook of Theoretical Computer Science B, pp. 995–1072 (1991)

24. Emerson, E., Halpern, J.: Decision procedures and expressiveness in the temporal logic of branching time. In: Proceedings of STOC 1982, pp. 169–180. ACM Press (1982)

25. Esparza, J., Kučera, A., Mayr, R.: Model-checking probabilistic pushdown automata. Log. Methods Comput. Sci. **2**(1:2), 1–31 (2006)

26. Etessami, K., Yannakakis, M.: Recursive Markov chains, stochastic grammars, and monotone systems of non-linear equations. In: Diekert, V., Durand, B. (eds.) STACS 2005. LNCS, vol. 3404, pp. 340–352. Springer, Heidelberg (2005). https://doi.org/10.1007/978-3-540-31856-9_28

27. Fischer, M., Ladner, R.: Propositional dynamic logic of regular programs. J. Comput. Syst. Sci. **18**, 194–211 (1979)

28. Hansson, H., Jonsson, B.: A logic for reasoning about time and reliability. Formal Aspects Comput. **6**, 512–535 (1994)

29. Hart, S., Sharir, M.: Probabilistic propositional temporal logics. Inf. Control **70**(2–3), 97–155 (1986)

30. Hart, S., Sharir, M.: Probabilistic temporal logics for finite and bounded models. In: STOC, pp. 1–13. ACM (1984)

31. Henzinger, T., Kupferman, O., Majumdar, R.: On the universal and existential fragments of the μ-calculus. Theoret. Comput. Sci. **354**(2), 173–186 (2006)

32. Henzinger, T.A.: From boolean to quantitative notions of correctness. In: POPL, pp. 157–158. ACM (2010)

33. Henzinger, T.A.: Quantitative reactive models. In: France, R.B., Kazmeier, J., Breu, R., Atkinson, C. (eds.) MODELS 2012. LNCS, vol. 7590, pp. 1–2. Springer, Heidelberg (2012). https://doi.org/10.1007/978-3-642-33666-9_1

34. Henzinger, T.A., Saraç, N.E.: Quantitative and approximate monitoring. In: LICS, pp. 1–14. IEEE (2021)

35. Huth, M., Kwiatkowska, M.: Quantitative analysis and model checking. In: Proceedings of LICS 1997, pp. 111–122. IEEE Computer Society Press (1997)

36. Kozen, D.: A finite-model theorem for the propositional μ-calculus. Stud. Logica **47**(3), 233–241 (1988)

37. Kraus, S., Lehmann, D.: Decision procedures for time and chance. In: Proceedings of FOCS 1983, pp. 202–209. IEEE Computer Society Press (1983)

38. Křetínský, J., Rotar, A.: The satisfiability problem for unbounded fragments of probabilistic CTL. In: Proceedings of CONCUR 2018. Leibniz International Proceedings in Informatics, vol. 118, pp. 32:1–32:16. Schloss Dagstuhl-Leibniz-Zentrum für Informatik (2018)

39. Kučera, A., Stražovský, O.: On the controller synthesis for finite-state Markov decision processes. In: Sarukkai, S., Sen, S. (eds.) FSTTCS 2005. LNCS, vol. 3821, pp. 541–552. Springer, Heidelberg (2005). https://doi.org/10.1007/11590156_44
40. Kupferman, O., Vardi, M.: An automata-theoretic approach to modular model checking. ACM Trans. Program. Lang. Syst. **22**, 87–128 (2000)
41. Lehmann, D., Shelah, S.: Reasoning with time and chance. Inf. Control **53**, 165–198 (1982)

Symbolic Verification and Strategy Synthesis for Turn-Based Stochastic Games

Marta Kwiatkowska[1], Gethin Norman[1,2], David Parker[1,3(✉)],
and Gabriel Santos[1]

[1] Department of Computer Science, University of Oxford, Oxford, UK
david.parker@cs.ox.ac.uk
[2] School of Computing Science, University of Glasgow, Glasgow, UK
[3] School of Computer Science, University of Birmingham, Birmingham, UK

Abstract. Stochastic games are a convenient formalism for modelling systems that comprise rational agents competing or collaborating within uncertain environments. Probabilistic model checking techniques for this class of models allow us to formally specify quantitative specifications of either collective or individual behaviour and then automatically synthesise strategies for the agents under which these specifications are guaranteed to be satisfied. Although good progress has been made on algorithms and tool support, efficiency and scalability remain a challenge. In this paper, we investigate a symbolic implementation based on multi-terminal binary decision diagrams. We describe how to build and verify turn-based stochastic games against either zero-sum or Nash equilibrium based temporal logic specifications. We collate a set of benchmarks for this class of games, and evaluate the performance of our approach, showing that it is superior in a number of cases and that strategies synthesised in a symbolic fashion can be considerably more compact.

1 Introduction

Games have long been used as an underlying modelling formalism for the design and verification of computerised systems. For example, they naturally model the interaction between a system, whose behaviour can be controlled, and its environment whose actions cannot. Another example is the interplay between the defender and attacker in a computer security scenario.

In the context of *model checking*, where the required behaviour of a system is specified using temporal logic, we can use, for example, alternating-time temporal logic (ATL) [4] to formalise the capabilities of a player (or a coalition of players) acting in the context of another, adversarial player (or coalition) in a game model. Yet further expressive logics such as strategy logic [19] can also reason about the existence of, for instance, Nash equilibria.

Another important tool for modelling and verification is *stochasticity*. Probability is often essential to effectively quantify uncertain aspects of systems, from the presence of hardware failures to the unreliability of physical sensors.

J.-F. Raskin and K. Chatterjee (Eds.): Principles of Systems Design, LNCS 13660, pp. 388–406, 2022.
https://doi.org/10.1007/978-3-031-22337-2_19

Stochastic games [24,28,49] are a well studied model for the dynamic execution of multiple players in a probabilistic setting. Results and algorithms for many verification problems on such models have also been presented, e.g., [17,18].

Building on these foundations, progress has since been made on the practical applicability of probabilistic model checking using stochastic games. This includes logics and algorithms for both *turn-based* stochastic games (TSGs) [21] and *concurrent* stochastic games (CSGs) [39]. The logic rPATL, a quantitative extension of ATL, allows specification of zero-sum properties for stochastic games, and extensions [39] also permit reasoning about the existence of Nash equilibria. A modelling formalism and tool support for TSGs and CSGs have been developed, in the form of PRISM-games [38], and this framework has been successfully applied to the analysis of, for example, human-robot collaborations [27,29], self-adaptive software systems [14] and computer security [6].

However, as usual for model checking approaches, efficiency and scalability are key challenges. So, in this paper, we consider *symbolic* implementations, in particular using binary decision diagrams (BDDs) and multi-terminal BDDs (MTBDDs), previously deployed for the compact representation and efficient manipulation of various models. Well known tools for verifying multi-agent systems such as MOCHA [3] and MCMAS [41] incorporate symbolic implementations of model checking, and probabilistic model checkers such as PRISM [34] and STORM [26] support symbolic techniques for simpler classes of stochastic models, such as Markov chains and Markov decision processes (MDPs).

As a first step in this direction, we consider a symbolic implementation of model checking and strategy synthesis for *turn-based* stochastic games. This also provides symbolic verification of (turn-based) probabilistic timed games, via the digital clocks translation [36]. We describe how to encode TSGs as MTBDDs and how to perform verification symbolically, in particular using value iteration. We also describe how to perform strategy synthesis, and how to extend this approach to compute Nash equilibria for TSGs.

In order to evaluate this, we collate a set of TSG model checking benchmarks of varying sizes, and add them to the PRISM benchmark suite [35]. We show that the symbolic approach offers significant gains in terms of the time required for model construction, for qualitative (graph-based) verification and, in some cases, for numerical solution of TSGs. We also show that optimal strategies can be represented more compactly symbolically rather than explicitly.

Related Work. Various methods have been proposed for solving stochastic games [24,28,49] and for verifying them against logical specifications, e.g., [17,18]. GIST [16] implements qualitative verification against ω-regular specifications and PRISM-games [38] supports various quantitative properties. In [33], a wider range of methods for solving TSGs are implemented and explored, offering significant speed-ups. However, none of these provide symbolic implementations.

Multiple MTBDD-based implementations of probabilistic model checking for simpler (non-game) stochastic models have been developed. Originally, this focused on PCTL model checking for Markov chains or MDPs [8,9,48]. A so-called *hybrid* approach [48] improves performance through a combination of symbolic model storage and explicit-state algorithms, and is the default model checking engine in PRISM. Enhancements by others include automatic variable reordering and model checking of quantile-based properties [32]. MTBDDs and BDDs have also been applied to the solution of energy games [5], which are *non-probabilistic* games with integer weights. Extensions of MTBDDs (XADDs) have been used for symbolic analysis of continuous-state MDPs [50].

Interpreting "symbolic" verification more widely, i.e., beyond BDD-based approaches, [42] considers symbolic methods for stochastic parity games, and [10] presents a probabilistic variant of the well known IC3 approach to model checking. Also relevant are methods to use, and learn, decision trees to succinctly represent strategies for probabilistic models [11].

2   Preliminaries

We begin with some background material, first on model checking of turn-based stochastic games, and then on (multi-terminal) binary decision diagrams.

Notation. We use $Dist(X)$ to denote the set of probability distributions over a set X, and we use $\mathbb{B} = \{0, 1\}$ for the set of Boolean values, with 0 denoting false and 1 denoting true.

2.1   Model Checking for Stochastic Games

Several variants of stochastic games exist. In this paper, we focus on (finite, multi-player) turn-based stochastic games.

Definition 1 (Turn-based stochastic game). *A turn-based stochastic game (TSG) is a tuple* $\mathcal{G} = (N, S, (S_i)_{i \in N}, \bar{s}, A, \delta, L)$ *where:*

- N *is a finite set of players;*
- S *is a finite set of states;*
- $(S_i)_{i \in N}$ *is a partition of* S;
- $\bar{s} \in S$ *is an initial state;*
- A *is a finite set of actions;*
- $\delta : S \times A \to Dist(S)$ *is a (partial) transition probability function;*
- $L : S \to 2^{AP}$ *is a labelling function.*

We now fix an n-player TSG $\mathcal{G}$ for the remainder of the section. The TSG $\mathcal{G}$ starts in its initial state $\bar{s} \in S$. In each state s, a player $i \in N$ selects an action from the set of *available* actions, which is denoted by $A(s) = \{a \in A \mid \delta(s, a) \text{ is defined}\}$. We assume that $A(s) \neq \varnothing$ for all states s. The choice of action to take in each state s is under the control of exactly one player, namely the player $i \in N$ for which $s \in S_i$. Once action $a \in A(s)$ is selected, the successor state is chosen according to the probability distribution $\delta(s, a)$, i.e., the game moves to state s' with probability $\delta(s, a)(s')$. We augment $\mathcal{G}$ with *reward structures*, which are tuples of the form $r = (r_A, r_S)$ where $r_A : S \times A \to \mathbb{R}$ and $r_S : S \to \mathbb{R}$ are action and state reward functions, respectively.

A *path* through $\mathcal{G}$ is a sequence $\pi = s_0 \xrightarrow{a_0} s_1 \xrightarrow{a_1} \cdots$ such that $s_i \in S$, $a_i \in A(s_i)$ and $\delta(s_i, a_i)(s_{i+1}) > 0$ for all $i \geqslant 0$. The sets of finite and infinite paths (starting in state s) of $\mathcal{G}$ are given by $FPaths_{\mathcal{G}}$ and $IPaths_{\mathcal{G}}$ ($FPaths_{\mathcal{G},s}$ and $IPaths_{\mathcal{G},s}$).

Strategies of $\mathcal{G}$ are used to resolve the choices of the players. Formally, a strategy for player i is a function $\sigma_i \colon FPaths_{\mathcal{G}} \to Dist(A)$ such that, if $\sigma_i(\pi)(a_i) > 0$, then $a_i \in A(last(\pi))$ where $last(\pi)$ is the final state of path π. A *strategy profile* is a tuple $\sigma = (\sigma_1, \ldots, \sigma_n)$ of strategies for all players. The set of strategies for player i and set of profiles are denoted $\Sigma_{\mathcal{G}}^i$ and $\Sigma_{\mathcal{G}}$. Given a profile σ and state s, let $IPaths_{\mathcal{G},s}^{\sigma}$ denote the infinite paths with initial state s corresponding to σ. We can then define, using standard techniques [31], a probability measure $Prob_{\mathcal{G},s}^{\sigma}$ over $IPaths_{\mathcal{G},s}^{\sigma}$ and, for a random variable $X \colon IPaths_{\mathcal{G}} \to \mathbb{R}$, the expected value $\mathbb{E}_{\mathcal{G},s}^{\sigma}(X)$ of X from s under σ.

In $\mathcal{G}$, the utility or *objective* of player i is represented by a random variable $X_i \colon IPaths_{\mathcal{G}} \to \mathbb{R}$. Such variables can encode, for example, the probability of reaching a target or the expected cumulative reward before reaching a target.

We now introduce the notion of Nash equilibrium (NE) [46] for $\mathcal{G}$ given objectives $(X_i)_{i=1}^n$ for the players. We restrict our attention to subgame-perfect NE [47], which are NE in every state of $\mathcal{G}$. For profile $\sigma = (\sigma_1, \ldots, \sigma_n)$ and player i strategy σ_i', we define the sequence $\sigma_{-i} \stackrel{\text{def}}{=} (\sigma_1, \ldots, \sigma_{i-1}, \sigma_{i+1}, \ldots, \sigma_n)$ and profile $\sigma_{-i}[\sigma_i'] \stackrel{\text{def}}{=} (\sigma_1, \ldots, \sigma_{i-1}, \sigma_i', \sigma_{i+1}, \ldots, \sigma_n)$.

Definition 2 (Best response). *For objectives $(X_i)_{i=1}^n$, player i, strategy sequence σ_{-i} and state s, a best response for player i to σ_{-i} in state s is a strategy $\sigma_i^{\star}$ for player i such that $\mathbb{E}_{\mathcal{G},s}^{\sigma_{-i}[\sigma_i^{\star}]}(X_i) \geqslant \mathbb{E}_{\mathcal{G},s}^{\sigma_{-i}[\sigma_i]}(X_i)$ for all $\sigma_i \in \Sigma_{\mathcal{G}}^i$.*

Definition 3 (Nash equilibrium). *For objectives $(X_i)_{i=1}^n$, a strategy profile $\sigma^{\star} = (\sigma_1^{\star}, \ldots, \sigma_n^{\star})$ of $\mathcal{G}$ is a subgame-perfect Nash equilibrium (NE) if $\sigma_i^{\star}$ is a best response to $\sigma_{-i}^{\star}$ for all $i \in N$ and $s \in S$. Furthermore, a NE $\sigma^{\star}$ of $\mathcal{G}$ is a social welfare optimal NE (SWNE) for objectives $X_1, \ldots, X_n$ if $\mathbb{E}_{\mathcal{G},s}^{\sigma^{\star}}(X_1) + \cdots + \mathbb{E}_{\mathcal{G},s}^{\sigma^{\star}}(X_n) \geqslant \mathbb{E}_{\mathcal{G},s}^{\sigma}(X_1) + \cdots + \mathbb{E}_{\mathcal{G},s}^{\sigma}(X_n)$ for all NE σ of $\mathcal{G}$.*

We can also define the dual concept of *social cost optimal NE* (SCNE) [39], for which the players of $\mathcal{G}$ try to minimise, rather than maximise, their expected utilities by considering equilibria for the objectives $-X_1, \ldots, -X_n$.

To formally specify properties of TSGs, we use the PRISM-games logic presented in [39], which extends the logic rPATL previously defined for zero-sum properties of TSGs [21]. The logic uses the *coalition* operator $\langle\!\langle C \rangle\!\rangle$ from alternating temporal logic (ATL) [4] to define *zero-sum* formulae and allows *nonzero-sum* properties, using (social welfare or social cost) NE.

Definition 4 (PRISM-games logic syntax). *The syntax of the PRISM-games logic is given by the grammar:*

$$\phi ::= \mathtt{true} \mid a \mid \neg\phi \mid \phi \wedge \phi \mid \langle\!\langle C \rangle\!\rangle \mathtt{P}_{\bowtie p}[\psi] \mid \langle\!\langle C \rangle\!\rangle \mathtt{R}_{\bowtie q}^r[\rho] \mid \langle\!\langle C_1 \colon \cdots \colon C_m \rangle\!\rangle_{\mathrm{opt} \bowtie q}(\theta)$$

$$\psi ::= \mathtt{X}\phi \mid \phi\, \mathtt{U}^{\leqslant k}\, \phi \mid \phi\, \mathtt{U}\, \phi$$

$$\rho ::= \mathtt{I}^{=k} \mid \mathtt{C}^{\leqslant k} \mid \mathtt{F}\, \phi$$

$$\theta ::= \mathtt{P}[\psi] + \cdots + \mathtt{P}[\psi] \mid \mathtt{R}^r[\rho] + \cdots + \mathtt{R}^r[\rho]$$

where C and $C_1,\ldots,C_m$ are coalitions of players such that $C_i \cap C_j = \varnothing$ for all $1 \leqslant i \neq j \leqslant m$ and $\cup_{i=1}^{m} C_i = N$, $\bowtie \in \{<,\leqslant,\geqslant,>\}$, $p \in [0,1] \cap \mathbb{R}$, r is a reward structure, $q \in \mathbb{R}_{\geqslant 0}$, opt $\in \{\min,\max\}$, a is an atomic proposition and $k \in \mathbb{N}$.

The syntax of the PRISM-games logic distinguishes between state (ϕ), path (ψ), reward (ρ) and nonzero-sum (θ) formulae. State formulae are evaluated over states of a TSG, while path, reward and nonzero-sum formulae are evaluated over paths. *Zero-sum* state formula have the following meaning:

- $\langle\!\langle C \rangle\!\rangle \mathsf{P}_{\bowtie q}[\psi]$ is satisfied in a state if the coalition of players C can ensure that the probability of the path formula ψ being satisfied is $\bowtie q$, regardless of the actions of the other players;
- $\langle\!\langle C \rangle\!\rangle \mathsf{R}_{\bowtie x}^{r}[\rho]$ is satisfied in a state if the players in C can ensure that the expected value of the reward formula ρ for reward structure r is $\bowtie x$, regardless of the actions of the other players.

On the other hand, for a *nonzero-sum* state formula:

- $\langle\!\langle C_1{:}\cdots{:}C_m \rangle\!\rangle_{\max \bowtie x}(\theta)$ is satisfied if there exists a subgame-perfect SWNE profile between coalitions $C_1,\ldots,C_m$ under which the *sum* of the objectives of $C_1,\ldots,C_m$ in θ is $\bowtie x$;
- $\langle\!\langle C_1{:}\cdots{:}C_m \rangle\!\rangle_{\min \bowtie x}(\theta)$ is satisfied if there exists a subgame-perfect SCNE profile between coalitions $C_1,\ldots,C_m$ under which the *sum* of the objectives of $C_1,\ldots,C_m$ in θ is $\bowtie x$.

For all of the above formulae, we also allow *numerical* variants, which directly yield an optimal value, rather than checking whether a threshold can be met. For example, $\langle\!\langle C \rangle\!\rangle \mathsf{P}_{\max=?}[\psi]$ gives the maximum probability with which the players in C can guarantee that ψ is satisfied.

Both zero-sum and nonzero-sum formulae are composed of *path* (ψ) and *reward* (ρ) formulae, used in the probabilistic and reward objectives included within P and R operators, respectively. The path formulae include: *next* $(\mathtt{X}\,\phi)$, *bounded until* $(\phi \, \mathtt{U}^{\leqslant k} \, \phi)$ and *unbounded until* $(\phi \, \mathtt{U} \, \phi)$. There are also the standard equivalences including: *probabilistic reachability* $(\mathtt{F}\,\phi \equiv \mathtt{true} \, \mathtt{U} \, \phi)$ and *bounded probabilistic reachability* $(\mathtt{F}^{\leqslant k}\,\phi \equiv \mathtt{true} \, \mathtt{U}^{\leqslant k} \, \phi)$.

The reward formulae include: *instantaneous (state) reward* at the kth step $(\mathtt{I}^{=k})$, *bounded cumulative reward* over k steps $(\mathtt{C}^{\leqslant k})$, and *reachability reward* until a formula ϕ is satisfied $(\mathtt{F}\,\phi)$. In the case of reachability reward formulae, several variants have previously been introduced [21], differing in how they treat paths that do not reach a state satisfying ϕ. We restrict our attention to the most common one, the default in PRISM, which assigns the reward value infinity to paths that never reach a state satisfying ϕ.

We next define the semantics of the PRISM-games logic for TSGs. However, we first need to define the concept of a coalition game.

Definition 5 (Coalition game). *For TSG $\mathcal{G}$ and a partition of its players into m coalitions $\mathcal{C} = \{C_1,\ldots,C_m\}$, we define the coalition game $\mathcal{G}^{\mathcal{C}} = (\{1,\ldots,m\}, S, (S_i^{\mathcal{C}})_{i \in M}, \bar{s}, A, \delta, L)$ as an m-player TSG where $S_i^{\mathcal{C}} = \cup_{j \in C_i} S_j$.*

To simplify notation, for any coalition C of $\mathcal{G}$, we use the notation $\mathcal{G}^C$ to represent the 2-player coalition game $\mathcal{G}^{\mathcal{C}}$ where $\mathcal{C} = \{C, N \backslash C\}$.

Definition 6 (PRISM-games logic semantics). *For a TSG $\mathcal{G}$ and formula ϕ, we define the satisfaction relation $\models$ inductively over the structure of ϕ. The propositional logic fragment (true, a, $\neg$, $\wedge$) is defined in the usual way. For a PRISM-games logic formula and state $s \in S$ of TSG $\mathcal{G}$, we have:*

$$s \models \langle\!\langle C \rangle\!\rangle \mathrm{P}_{\bowtie q}[\psi] \quad \Leftrightarrow \quad \exists \sigma_1 \in \Sigma^1. \forall \sigma_2 \in \Sigma^2. \mathbb{E}_{\mathcal{G}^C, s}^{\sigma_1, \sigma_2}(X^\psi) \bowtie q$$

$$s \models \langle\!\langle C \rangle\!\rangle \mathrm{R}_{\bowtie x}^r[\rho] \quad \Leftrightarrow \quad \exists \sigma_1 \in \Sigma^1. \forall \sigma_2 \in \Sigma^2. \mathbb{E}_{\mathcal{G}^C, s}^{\sigma_1, \sigma_2}(X^{r,\rho}) \bowtie x$$

$$s \models \langle\!\langle C_1 : \cdots : C_m \rangle\!\rangle_{\mathrm{opt} \bowtie q}(\theta) \quad \Leftrightarrow \quad \exists \sigma^\star \in \Sigma_{\mathcal{G}^{\mathcal{C}}}. \Big(\sum_{i=1}^{m} \mathbb{E}_{\mathcal{G}^{\mathcal{C}}}^{\sigma^\star}(X_i^\theta) \Big) \bowtie q$$

and $\sigma^\star$ is an SWNE if opt = max, and an SCNE if opt = min, for the objectives $(X_i^\theta)_{i=1}^m$ in the coalition game $\mathcal{G}^{\mathcal{C}}$.

For an objective X^ψ, $X^{r,\rho}$ and path $\pi \in IPaths_{\mathcal{G}^{\mathcal{C}}, s}$:

$$X^\psi(\pi) \;=\; 1 \text{ if } \pi \models \psi \text{ and } 0 \text{ otherwise}$$
$$X^{r,\rho}(\pi) \;=\; rew(r, \rho)(\pi).$$

The semantics for satisfaction of path formulae ($\pi \models \psi$) and the random variable $rew(r, \rho)(\pi)$ for a reward formula can be found in, e.g., [39].

As the zero-sum objectives appearing in the logic are either finite-horizon or infinite-horizon and correspond to either probabilistic until or expected reachability formulae, we have that TSGs are *determined* with respect to these objectives [43], which yields the following equivalences:

$$\langle\!\langle C \rangle\!\rangle \mathrm{P}_{\max=?}[\psi] \equiv \langle\!\langle N \backslash C \rangle\!\rangle \mathrm{P}_{\min=?}[\psi]$$
$$\langle\!\langle C \rangle\!\rangle \mathrm{R}_{\max=?}^r[\rho] \equiv \langle\!\langle N \backslash C \rangle\!\rangle \mathrm{R}_{\min=?}^r[\rho].$$

Also, as for other probabilistic temporal logics, we can represent negated path formulae by inverting the probability threshold, e.g.:

$$\langle\!\langle C \rangle\!\rangle \mathrm{P}_{\geqslant q}[\neg \psi] \equiv \langle\!\langle C \rangle\!\rangle \mathrm{P}_{\leqslant 1-q}[\psi]$$

notably allowing the 'globally' operator $\mathsf{G}\, \phi \equiv \neg(\mathsf{F}\, \neg \phi)$ to be defined.

Since the logic is branching-time, the model checking algorithm for the logic works by recursively computing the set $Sat(\phi)$ of states satisfying formula ϕ over the structure of ϕ. The main step in the algorithm requires computation of values for zero-sum and nonzero-sum formulae. The standard approach is to use *value iteration* [15], which we discuss below.

Note that the PRISM logic used here, which includes non-zero sum formulae, was first considered for CSGs [37,39]. Our focus here is on TSGs, where the computation of values is simpler: because only one coalition has a choice in each state, value iteration need only take the minimum or maximum over actions, whereas for CSGs matrix games need to be solved in each state.

For the case of zero-sum formulae, efficiency and accuracy can be improved through the use of graph-based *precomputation algorithms* [4], which identify the states that have values 0 and 1 in the case of probabilistic properties and value ∞ in the case of expected reward properties.

Value Iteration. Below, we illustrate value iteration for the zero-sum formula $\phi = \langle\langle C \rangle\rangle P_{\max=?}[\, F\, \phi' \,]$; the remaining cases have a similar structure. The value of ϕ in state s is given by the limit $val(s, \phi) = \lim_{k \to \infty} x_s^k$, where for any $k \in \mathbb{N}$:

$$
x_s^k = \begin{cases} 1 & \text{if } s \in Sat(\phi') \\ 0 & \text{else if } k = 0 \\ \max\limits_{a \in A(s)} \sum_{s' \in S} \delta(s, a)(s') \cdot x_{s'}^{k-1} & \text{else if } s \in \cup_{i \in C} S_i \\ \min\limits_{a \in A(s)} \sum_{s' \in S} \delta(s, a)(s') \cdot x_{s'}^{k-1} & \text{otherwise} \end{cases}
$$

In practice, a suitable convergence criterion needs to be chosen to terminate the computation. Here, we use the simple but common approach of checking the maximum relative difference between values for states in successive iterations, but more sophisticated approaches have been devised for TSGs [30].

2.2   Binary Decision Diagrams

A *binary decision diagram* (BDD) [12] is a rooted, directed acyclic graph used to provide a compact representation of a Boolean function over a particular set of Boolean variables. A BDD b over n Boolean variables $\underline{x} = (x_1, \ldots, x_n)$ represents a function $f_b : \mathbb{B}^n \to \mathbb{B}$. BDDs have two types of nodes: (i) *non-terminal* nodes, which are labelled with a variable x_i, and whose outgoing edges are labelled 1 ("then") and 0 ("else"); and (ii) *terminal* (leaf) nodes, labelled with 0 or 1. For a valuation $\underline{v} = (v_1, \ldots, v_n) \in \mathbb{B}^n$ of $\underline{x}$, the value of $f_b(\underline{v})$ can be found by traversing the BDD b from its root to a terminal node, taking at each non-terminal node the edge matching the value v_i for its variable x_i. The value of $f_b(\underline{v})$ is taken as the value of the terminal node that is reached.

By requiring that variables are ordered, from the root node downwards, and by storing the graph in reduced form (merging isomorphic subgraphs, and removing redundant nodes), BDDs can represent structured Boolean functions very compactly and can be manipulated efficiently, i.e., with operations whose complexity is proportional to the number of nodes in the graph rather than the size of the function. This includes all standard Boolean operators, for example, $\textsc{Or}(b_1, b_2)$, which returns the BDD representing the function $f_{b_1} \vee f_{b_2}$. We also use $\textsc{And}(b_1, b_2)$ and $\textsc{Not}(b)$, defined analogously.

Multi-terminal BDDs (MTBDDs) [23], which are also sometimes known as algebraic decision diagrams (ADDs) [7], generalise BDDs by allowing terminal nodes to be labelled with values from an arbitrary set D. Hence, they represent functions of the form $f : \mathbb{B}^n \to D$. Typically, we are interested in real-valued functions and so an MTBDD m over n Boolean variables $\underline{x} = (x_1, \ldots, x_n)$ represents a function $f_m : \mathbb{B}^n \to \mathbb{R}$. Like for BDDs, a variety of useful operators for MTBDDs can be implemented. In particular, we use:

– APPLY(op, m_1, m_2), where op is a binary operation over the reals: returns the MTBDD representing the function $f_{m_1} \; op \; f_{m_2}$.

– IFTHENELSE(b, m_1, m_2), where b is a BDD and m_1, m_2 are MTBDDs: returns the MTBDD for the function with value f_{m_1} if f_b is true and f_{m_2} otherwise.

– CONST(c), where $c \in \mathbb{R}$: returns the MTBDD representing the constant function with value c.

– ABSTRACT($op, \underline{y}, m$), where op is a commutative and associative binary operation over the reals (here, we often use min or max) and $\underline{y} \subset \underline{x}$ is a subset of the variables of m: returns an MTBDD over variables $\underline{x}\backslash\underline{y}$ representing the result of abstracting all the variables in $\underline{y}$ from m by applying op over all possible values taken by the variables in $\underline{y}$.

BDDs were popularised thanks to the success of *symbolic model checking* [13,45], which uses them to provide an efficient and scalable implementation of model checking, for example of the temporal logic CTL on labelled transition systems. Assume that we have an encoding $enc_S : S \to \mathbb{B}^k$ of the state space S of a transition system into k Boolean variables. We can represent a subset $S' \subseteq S$ as a BDD, by using it to encode the characteristic function $\chi_{S'} : S \to \mathbb{B}$. A transition relation $\to \subseteq S \times S$ can be represented similarly as a BDD over 2 sets of k Boolean variables, i.e., by a BDD b where $f_b(enc_S(s), enc_S(s')) = 1$ if and only if $(s, s') \in \to$. The key operations for model checking such as (pre or post) image computation can be performed efficiently on these BDD representations.

Symbolic implementations of probabilistic model checking [9,48] build on the fact that real-value vectors and matrices can be represented as MTBDDs in similar fashion. A key operation used in the numerical computation required for probabilistic model checking (i.e., for value iteration) is matrix-vector multiplication, which can be performed symbolically [22,23]:

– MVMULT(m, v), where m is an MTBDD over variables $\underline{x}, \underline{y}$ representing a matrix $\mathbf{M}$ and v is an MTBDD over variables $\underline{x}$ representing a vector $\mathbf{v}$: returns the MTBDD over variables $\underline{x}$ representing the vector $\mathbf{Mv}$.

3   Symbolic Model Checking for Stochastic Games

We now describe a symbolic implementation for the representation, construction and verification of TSGs.

3.1   Symbolic Representation and Construction of TSGs

We begin by discussing how to represent TSGs symbolically, as MTBDDs. The key components of a TSG, as required to perform model checking, are the transition probability function $\delta : S \times Act \to Dist(S)$ and the partition $(S_i)_{i \in N}$ of the state space amongst players. We consider two different symbolic encodings, one which represents δ and $(S_i)_i$ separately, and one which uses a single MTBDD.

For the first, we can use the standard approach for MDPs [1,8], which considers $\delta : S \times Act \to Dist(S)$ as a function $\delta' : S \times Act \times S \to [0, 1]$ in the obvious

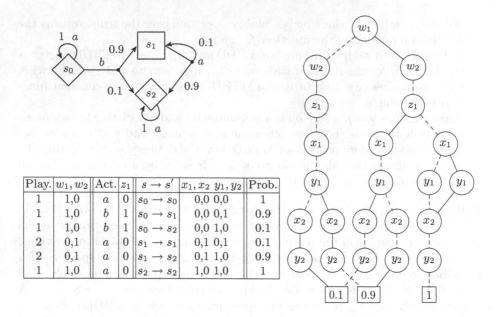

Fig. 1. A TSG with its MTBDD representation and an explanation of the encoding.

way, i.e., for states s, s' and action a, we have $\delta'(s, a, s') = \delta(s, a)(s')$. Then, given an encoding $\text{enc}_S : S \to \mathbb{B}^k$ of the state space into k Boolean variables, and an encoding $\text{enc}_{Act} : Act \to \mathbb{B}^l$ of the action set into l Boolean variables, δ can be represented by an MTBDD over $2k + l$ variables. Reusing the same encoding enc_S, each set S_i is represented by a BDD over k variables.

For the second encoding, we assume that the TSG is represented by a single function $\delta'' : N \times S \times Act \times S \to [0, 1]$ such that, for player i, states s, s' and action a, $\delta''(i, s, a, s')$ equals $\delta(s, a)(s')$ if $s \in S_i$ and 0 otherwise. Given encodings $\text{enc}_S : S \to \mathbb{B}^k$ and $\text{enc}_{Act} : Act \to \mathbb{B}^l$ as above, plus an encoding $\text{enc}_N : N \to \mathbb{B}^m$ of the player set, we can represent the TSG as an MTBDD over $2k + l + m$ Boolean variables. In our experiments, we found minimal difference between the two encodings, in terms of the size of storage for δ, but the first option incurs some additional overhead relating to the representation of the sets S_i. Hence, in this paper, we focus on the second, single-MTBDD encoding.

From now on, we will assume the use of variables $\underline{x} = (x_1, \ldots, x_k)$ and $\underline{y} = (y_1, \ldots, y_k)$ to encode the state space S (both $\underline{x}$ and $\underline{y}$ are used when representing the transition function; only one, usually $\underline{x}$, is needed when representing a subset of S or a real-valued vector indexed over S). We will use variables $\underline{z} = (z_1, \ldots, z_l)$ to encode actions and variables $\underline{w} = (w_1, \ldots, w_m)$ to encode players.

Example 1. Figure 1 shows a simple TSG with 2 players and its symbolic representation, using the second (single MTBDD) encoding described above. Top left is the TSG, in which player 1 states are drawn as diamonds and player 2 states as squares. Below that is a table explaining the representation: the details of each transition in the TSG and how it is encoded into Boolean variables.

For players, we use a one-hot encoding to two Boolean variables (w_1, w_2), i.e., $\text{enc}_N(1) = (1,0)$ and $\text{enc}_N(2) = (0,1)$. For the (two) actions, we use just a single variable z_1, where $\text{enc}_{Act}(a) = (0)$ and $\text{enc}_{Act}(b) = (1)$. The state space S is encoded with 2 variables using the usual binary encoding of the integer index i of each state s_i. In a transition, variables (x_1, x_2) and (y_1, y_2) represent the source and destination states, respectively.

To the right of the figure is the MTBDD representation. The 1 ("then") and 0 ("else") edges from each non-terminal node are drawn as solid and dashed lines, respectively. The zero terminal and edges to it are omitted for clarity. Each row of the table corresponds to a unique path through the MTBDD. The variable order used places $\underline{w}$ and $\underline{z}$ first, followed by $\underline{x}$ and $\underline{y}$, where, as usual in symbolic model checking, the variables in the latter two are interleaved.   ∎

In order to be effective in practice, symbolic representations of TSGs need to be *constructed* in an efficient manner. In the context of this paper, we work with games that are described in the modelling language of the PRISM-games tool [38], which is inspired by the Reactive Modules formalism [2], proposed for specifying concurrent, multi-component systems.

We omit full details here, but note that this can be done by extending the existing approach used for the symbolic implementation of model checking for simpler probabilistic models in PRISM [34]. The basics for model construction from the PRISM modelling language can be found in [48]. The key idea is to construct the MTBDD in a compositional fashion, based on the structure of the model description. We also note that the second MTBDD encoding, building a single MTBDD, is better suited for this task, since it facilitates the detection of modelling errors (such as multiple players controlling actions in the same state).

3.2 Symbolic Model Checking of TSGs

Next, we describe a symbolic approach to performing probabilistic model checking of TSGs. We focus here on the PRISM-games logic described in Sect. 2.1. Essentially, since this is a branching-time logic, the model checking problem for a TSG $\mathcal{G}$ and a formula ϕ amounts to determining the set $Sat(\phi) = \{s \in S \mid s \models \phi\}$. Furthermore, this set is computed in a recursive fashion, following the structure of the parse tree of the formula ϕ.

In a symbolic setting, the set $Sat(\phi)$ will be represented as a BDD. The propositional fragment of the logic is treated in the usual way for symbolic model checking [13,45], using standard BDD implementations of Boolean operators. The key parts of the model checking algorithm are those for the P and R operators. In particular, we need to compute an MTBDD representing the real-valued vector of probability or expected reward values for each state s.

Computing these values can be done in a variety of ways. Here, we use *value iteration*, since iterative methods are known to be typically better suited to symbolic implementation [7,9,48]. This is because it requires minimal changes

---

Algorithm 1. Value iteration and strategy synthesis for reachability probabilities

---
Input: BDD target (over variables $\underline{x}$) for set of target states
Output: MTBDD sol (over variables $\underline{x}$) giving the probability from each state, and a BDD strat (over variables $\underline{x}, \underline{z}'$) representing an optimal strategy

1: **procedure** PROBREACH(target)
2:    $S_0 \leftarrow$ PROB0(target)
3:    $S_1 \leftarrow$ PROB1(target)
4:    $S_? \leftarrow$ NOT(APPLY($\lor, S_1, S_0$))
5:    trans$_? \leftarrow$ APPLY($\times$, trans, $S_?$)
6:    sol $\leftarrow S_1$; done $\leftarrow$ **false**
7: **while** $\neg$done **do**
8:    tmp $\leftarrow$ sol
9:    sol $\leftarrow$ MVMULT(trans$_?$, sol)
10:    $p_1 \leftarrow$ OR($\{$CUBE(enc$_N(i), \underline{w}) : i \in N\}$)
11:    $p_2 \leftarrow$ OR($\{$CUBE(enc$_N(i), \underline{w}) : i \in N \backslash C\}$)
12:    sol$_1 \leftarrow$ ABSTRACT(max, ABSTRACT($+$, APPLY($\times$, sol, p_1), $\underline{w}$), $\underline{z}$)
13:    sol$_2 \leftarrow$ ABSTRACT(min, ABSTRACT($+$, APPLY($\times$, sol, p_2), $\underline{w}$), $\underline{z}$)
14:    sol $\leftarrow$ APPLY($+$, sol$_1$, sol$_2$)
15:    sol $\leftarrow$ IFTHENELSE(S_1, CONST(1), sol)
16:    done $\leftarrow$ SUPNORM(sol, tmp) $< \varepsilon$
17: **end while**
18: strat $\leftarrow$ APPLY($\approx$, MVMULT(trans$_?$, sol), sol)
19: strat $\leftarrow$ ABSTRACT($\lor$, strat, $\underline{w}$)
20: strat $\leftarrow$ REPLACEVARS(strat, $\underline{z}, \underline{z}'$)
21: **return** sol, strat
22: **end procedure**

---

to be made to the representation of the model during solution, which could cause a blow-up in storage size due to the introduction of irregularities. This means that some alternative methods for solving stochastic games such as quadratic programming are unlikely to be well suited to a symbolic implementation.

To simplify presentation, we restrict our attention to computing reachability probabilities, assuming that they are maximised by a coalition of players C (and minimised by $N \backslash C$). The process for other computations, such as expected reward values, is similar. In other words, we consider the construction of an MTBDD sol representing a vector $\underline{sol}$ indexed over S with $sol(s) = val(s, \langle\!\langle C \rangle\!\rangle P_{\max=?}[F \ target])$ for some atomic proposition $target$ labelling the states to be reached (see Sect. 2.1).

Algorithm 1 shows an MTBDD implementation that performs both the numerical solution, using value iteration, and synthesis of an optimal strategy. The input is a BDD target representing the target set $Sat(target)$, and we assume that MTBDD trans encodes the TSG. PROB0 and PROB1 are BDD-based implementations of the precomputation algorithms [4] for finding states with probability 0 and 1; we omit the details and focus on the numerical part.

The key part of value iteration can be done using matrix multiplication, treating the TSG as a non-square matrix with rows over $N \times Act \times S$ and columns over S, followed by maximising and minimising over action choices for players in C and $N\backslash C$, respectively. Function $\textsc{Cube}(\underline{v}, \underline{w})$ builds a *cube*, i.e., a BDD b over variables $\underline{w}$ such that $f_{\mathsf{b}} = 1$ for precisely one valuation $\underline{v}$ of $\underline{w}$. We check termination of value iteration using a function $\textsc{SupNorm}$ which performs a pointwise calculation of the relative difference for pairs of elements in two vectors represented as MTBDDs and returns the maximum difference. This is compared against a pre-specified convergence criterion threshold $\varepsilon \in \mathbb{R}_{>0}$.

Strategy Synthesis. Lines 18–20 compute an optimal strategy, where $\approx$ represents an approximate equality check to the same level of accuracy as the convergence check (i.e., relative difference less than ε), and $\underline{z}'$ is a fresh copy of the variables $\underline{z}$ that encode actions, but appearing after $\underline{x}$ and $\underline{y}$ in the variable ordering. The result is a BDD strat over variables $\underline{x}$ and $\underline{z}$, representing an optimal strategy: for any state s, we traverse the top part of the BDD by following valuation $\mathrm{enc}_S(s)$. Any path (we allow multiple) from that node to the 1 terminal represents an optimal action a in that state (read from its encoding $\mathrm{enc}_{Act}(a)$). We leave as future work the possibility of selecting single optimal actions for states in a way that further reduces the size of the strategy representation.

Nash Equilibria. Lastly, we briefly sketch how our symbolic model checking implementation also extends to nonzero-sum formulas, i.e., the synthesis of (social welfare) Nash equilibria. The process is again based on value iteration but, as mentioned in Sect. 2.1, this is simpler for TSGs than the CSG-based algorithm of [39]. Essentially we adapt Algorithm 1, first maximising for individual coalitions, as in the existing value iteration loop, then selecting all actions that are optimal, as in the strategy synthesis part, and then further maximising those choices over the sum of values for all players. The latter part means that we maintain a solution vector for each player as MTBDDs during the process. For the 2-coalition case, part of the computation reduces to symbolic model checking for MDPs, where we can reuse existing implementations.

4   Case Studies and Experimental Results

We have developed a symbolic implementation of model checking for TSGs within PRISM-games [38], leveraging parts of PRISM's existing symbolic engines for other models (Markov chains and Markov decision processes). This builds upon the CUDD decision diagram library by Fabio Somenzi, which supports both BDDs and MTBDDs, and a Java wrapper contained within PRISM which extends this library. Our experiments were carried out using a 2.10 GHz Intel Xeon Gold with 16 GB maximum heap space for Java.

4.1 TSG Benchmarks

In order to evaluate the approach, we first present a set of benchmark TSG models. We have collated these and added them to the PRISM Benchmark Suite [35], which provides a selection of probabilistic models and associated properties for performing model checking. To facilitate benchmarking, most models and properties are parameterised, allowing a wide range of model checking instances to be considered. Python scripts are also included to automate the process of selecting and executing instances, and for extracting information from tool logs.

The benchmarks are listed below:

- *avoid*: a TSG example from [20] modelling a game between an intruder and an observer in a grid-world (also used in [33]);
- *dice*: a simple 2-player dice game TSG distributed with PRISM-games;
- *hallway_human*: a TSG variant (from [20]) of a standard benchmark from the AI literature [40] modelling a robot moving through a hallway environment which is both probabilistic and adversarial (also used in [33]);
- *investors*: the futures market investor TSG example from [44], adapted and extended to more investors;
- *safe_nav*: a TSG modelling safe navigation in a human-robot system, from [29].
- *task_graph*: an extended version of the task-graph scheduling problem with faulty processors from [36], converted from a (turn-based) probabilistic timed game to a TSG using the digital clocks translation of [36].

4.2 Experimental Results

Table 1 shows statistics for a selection of TSG model instances that we use for our evaluation (see [35,51] for more details). We also give the time required to build a representation of the TSG, from its PRISM-games modelling language description, either symbolically, as an MTBDD, or explicitly, as a sparse matrix, as done in the existing implementation of PRISM-games. The faster time is in bold. For the symbolic case, we also show the MTBDD size. We see that the symbolic approach is considerably faster. The explicit implementation of model construction (in Java) is not highly optimised but the difference in performance is clear nonetheless. For some instances, where the explicit engine took several hours, the symbolic one requires no more than a few seconds.

Table 1. Model building statistics for the TSG case studies.

Case study [parameters]	Param. values	Players	States	MTBDD nodes	Constr. time (s) Symbolic	Explicit
avoid [X_MAX, Y_MAX]	10, 10	2	106,524	19,298	**0.2**	1.6
	15, 15		480,464	36,178	**0.4**	6.4
	20, 20		1,436,404	69,407	**1.0**	18.8
dice [N]	10	2	5,755	1,717	**0.02**	0.2
	25		34,645	4,046	**0.04**	0.5
	50		136,795	7,958	**0.09**	1.5
hallway_human [X_MAX, Y_MAX]	5, 5	2	25,000	1,334	**0.03**	0.6
	8, 8		163,840	1,234	**0.04**	2.8
	10, 10		400,000	1,752	**0.07**	6.7
investors [N, vmax]	2, 10	3	172,240	5,846	**0.04**	2.0
	2, 20		568,790	11,325	**0.06**	6.5
	2, 40		2,041,690	22,191	**0.1**	23.4
	3, 10	4	1,229,001	7,434	**0.06**	13.7
	3, 20		4,058,751	12,913	**0.1**	48.5
	3, 40		14,569,251	23,779	**0.2**	Memout
safe_nav [N, feat]	8, D	2	2,592,845	28,008	**1.0**	1,602
	8, C		5,078,029	44,973	**1.7**	4,588
	8, B		8,732,493	67,735	**2.7**	10,010
	8, A		17,052,941	118,262	**4.8**	Memout
task_graph [N, k1, k2]	6, 10, 10	2	467,638	19,881	**0.6**	6.7
	6, 15, 15		1,010,318	22,350	**1.0**	13.8
	6, 20, 20		1,759,348	22,350	**1.8**	25.1
	9, 10, 10	2	2,567,638	36,014	**1.4**	46.5
	9, 15, 15		5,533,288	36,745	**2.8**	100.0
	9, 20, 20		9,6231,38	39,349	**4.6**	169.2

Secondly, Table 2 shows the performance of model checking for the symbolic and explicit implementations on a range of example properties for the benchmarks (again, see [35,51] for full details). We break down the time required into qualitative analysis (graph-based precomputation) and quantitative analysis (numerical solution with value iteration). Again, the faster time is highlighted in bold. We also show the total memory required to store the resulting optimal strategy in each case (these are omitted for qualitative probabilistic reachability and expected reward, since they are not yet included in the implementation).

Pre-computation has shown to be more efficient for all model/property combinations in the table, and in some cases this is a decisive factor in terms of the overall model checking time. Results for value iteration generally favour the explicit engine, although there are instances where the symbolic one performs better. In terms of representing optimal strategies, we see that the symbolic one is more compact in all cases.

Table 2. Statistics for TSG verification instances.

Case study [parameters] Property (type)	Param. values	Verification time and strategy memory							
		Symbolic				Explicit			
		Qual. (s)	Quant. (s)	Total (s)	Strat. (MB)	Qual. (s)	Quant. (s)	Total (s)	Strat. (MB)
avoid [X_MAX, Y_MAX] exit (P[F])	10, 10	4.4	4.0	8.4	0.1	33.2	0.9	34.2	0.4
	15, 15	20.4	23.0	43.6	0.2	407.2	9.1	416.3	1.8
	20, 20	77.7	82.8	161.2	0.4	1,544	14.5	1,558	5.5
avoid [X_MAX, Y_MAX] find (P[F])	10, 10	8.3	4.0	12.3	0.2	17.4	0.5	18.0	0.4
	15, 15	37.8	21.9	60.0	0.4	224.9	3.7	228.7	1.8
	20, 20	152.7	66.7	220.0	0.7	1,145	9.2	1,155	5.5
dice [N] p1wins (P[F])	10	0.02	0.02	0.02	0.02	0.07	0.04	0.1	0.02
	25	0.2	0.2	0.4	0.05	0.5	0.2	0.8	0.1
	50	0.6	0.5	1.1	0.1	5.3	2.6	7.9	0.5
hallway_human [X_MAX, Y_MAX] save (P[F])	5, 5	0.06	–	0.06	–	0.2	–	0.2	–
	8, 8	0.2	–	0.2	–	2.0	–	2.0	–
	10, 10	0.6	–	0.6	–	6.9	–	7.0	–
investors [N, vmax] greater (P[F])	2, 10	0.04	1.0	1.1	0.06	3.1	3.1	6.4	0.7
	2, 20	0.04	5.4	5.6	0.1	19.7	22.3	42.2	2.2
	2, 40	0.05	22.6	22.8	0.2	27.8	97.1	125.3	7.8
	3, 10	0.1	3.4	3.6	0.2	27.6	30.9	58.9	4.7
	3, 20	0.1	16.0	16.2	0.3	83.8	169.8	255.5	15.5
	3, 40	0.2	62.5	62.9	0.4	–	–	Memout	–
safe_nav [N, feat] reach (P[F])	8, D	12.7	4.1	17.1	1.8	134.9	2.5	138.0	9.9
	8, C	26.1	7.6	34.4	2.9	145.8	3.6	150.4	19.4
	8, B	48.8	12.0	62.1	4.6	313.8	7.6	323.1	33.3
	8, A	138.7	27.1	169.3	8.7	–	–	Memout	–
task_graph [N, k1, k2] time (R[F])	6, 10, 10	0.8	116.8	117.7	–	14.3	34.2	48.9	–
	6, 15, 15	1.1	346.6	348.1	–	27.9	63.4	91.8	–
	6, 20, 20	1.4	826.5	828.6	–	52.9	116.8	170.8	–
	9, 10, 10	4.1	1,117	1,122	–	90.9	179.3	271.5	–
	9, 15, 15	5.7	3,304	3,312	–	250.9	515.9	769.9	–
	9, 20, 20	7.8	6,624	6,636	–	660.2	1,268	1,934	–

5   Conclusions

We have presented a symbolic version of probabilistic model checking for turn-based stochastic games, using BDDs and MTBDDs to implement model construction, model checking (via value iteration) and optimal strategy synthesis. There are some significant gains to be had, particularly in terms of model construction, but also further improvements to be made.

Future work includes studying different encodings more thoroughly, as well as variable orderings. There is also scope to investigate more efficient symbolic strategy representations. Another possibly interesting extension is providing support for Büchi, co-Büchi and Rabin-chain objectives [25], where a symbolic implementation could also allow for better scalability.

Acknowledgements. This project was funded by the ERC under the European Union's Horizon 2020 research and innovation programme (FUN2MODEL, grant agreement No. 834115).

References

1. de Alfaro, L., Kwiatkowska, M., Norman, G., Parker, D., Segala, R.: Symbolic model checking of probabilistic processes using MTBDDs and the Kronecker representation. In: Graf, S., Schwartzbach, M. (eds.) TACAS 2000. LNCS, vol. 1785, pp. 395–410. Springer, Heidelberg (2000). https://doi.org/10.1007/3-540-46419-0_27
2. Alur, R., Henzinger, T.: Reactive modules. Formal Methods Syst. Des. **15**(1), 7–48 (1999)
3. Alur, R., Henzinger, T.A., Mang, F.Y.C., Qadeer, S., Rajamani, S.K., Tasiran, S.: MOCHA: modularity in model checking. In: Hu, A.J., Vardi, M.Y. (eds.) CAV 1998. LNCS, vol. 1427, pp. 521–525. Springer, Heidelberg (1998). https://doi.org/10.1007/BFb0028774
4. Alur, R., Henzinger, T.A., Kupferman, O.: Alternating-time temporal logic. J. ACM **49**(5), 672–713 (2002)
5. Amram, G., Maoz, S., Pistiner, O., Ringert, J.O.: Efficient algorithms for omega-regular energy games. In: Huisman, M., Păsăreanu, C., Zhan, N. (eds.) FM 2021. LNCS, vol. 13047, pp. 163–181. Springer, Cham (2021). https://doi.org/10.1007/978-3-030-90870-6_9
6. Aslanyan, Z., Nielson, F., Parker, D.: Quantitative verification and synthesis of attack-defence scenarios. In: Proceedings of the 29th IEEE Computer Security Foundations Symposium (CSF 2016), pp. 105–119. IEEE (2016)
7. Bahar, I., et al.: Algebraic decision diagrams and their applications. Formal Methods Syst. Des. **10**(2/3), 171–206 (1997)
8. Baier, C.: On algorithmic verification methods for probabilistic systems. Habilitation thesis. Fakultät für Mathematik & Informatik, Universität Mannheim (1998)
9. Baier, C., Clarke, E.M., Hartonas-Garmhausen, V., Kwiatkowska, M., Ryan, M.: Symbolic model checking for probabilistic processes. In: Degano, P., Gorrieri, R., Marchetti-Spaccamela, A. (eds.) ICALP 1997. LNCS, vol. 1256, pp. 430–440. Springer, Heidelberg (1997). https://doi.org/10.1007/3-540-63165-8_199
10. Batz, K., Junges, S., Kaminski, B.L., Katoen, J.-P., Matheja, C., Schröer, P.: PrIC3: property directed reachability for MDPs. In: Lahiri, S.K., Wang, C. (eds.) CAV 2020. LNCS, vol. 12225, pp. 512–538. Springer, Cham (2020). https://doi.org/10.1007/978-3-030-53291-8_27
11. Brázdil, T., Chatterjee, K., Chmelík, M., Fellner, A., Křetínský, J.: Counterexample explanation by learning small strategies in Markov decision processes. In: Kroening, D., Păsăreanu, C.S. (eds.) CAV 2015. LNCS, vol. 9206, pp. 158–177. Springer, Cham (2015). https://doi.org/10.1007/978-3-319-21690-4_10
12. Bryant, R.: Graph-based algorithms for Boolean function manipulation. IEEE Trans. Comput. C **35**(8), 677–691 (1986)
13. Burch, J., Clarke, E., McMillan, K., Dill, D., Hwang, J.: Symbolic model checking: 10^{20} states and beyond. In: Proceedings of the 5th Annual IEEE Symposium on Logic in Computer Science (LICS 1990), pp. 428–439. IEEE Computer Society Press (1990)
14. Caámara, J., Garlan, D., Schmerl, B., Pandey, A.: Optimal planning for architecture-based self-adaptation via model checking of stochastic games. In: Proceedings of the 30th ACM Symposium on Applied Computing (SAC 2015) (2015)
15. Chatterjee, K., Henzinger, T.A.: Value iteration. In: Grumberg, O., Veith, H. (eds.) 25 Years of Model Checking. LNCS, vol. 5000, pp. 107–138. Springer, Heidelberg (2008). https://doi.org/10.1007/978-3-540-69850-0_7

404   M. Kwiatkowska et al.

16. Chatterjee, K., Henzinger, T.A., Jobstmann, B., Radhakrishna, A.: GIST: a solver for probabilistic games. In: Touili, T., Cook, B., Jackson, P. (eds.) CAV 2010. LNCS, vol. 6174, pp. 665–669. Springer, Heidelberg (2010). https://doi.org/10.1007/978-3-642-14295-6_57

17. Chatterjee, K., Jurdzinski, M., Henzinger, T.: Quantitative stochastic parity games. In: Munro, J.I. (ed.) Proceedings of the 15th Annual ACM-SIAM Symposium on Discrete Algorithms (SODA 2004), pp. 121–130. SIAM (2004)

18. Chatterjee, K., Henzinger, T.A.: A survey of stochastic ω-regular games. J. Comput. Syst. Sci. **78**(2), 394–413 (2012)

19. Chatterjee, K., Henzingera, T.A., Piterman, N.: Strategy logic. Inf. Comput. **208**(6), 677–693 (2010)

20. Chatterjee, K., Katoen, J.-P., Weininger, M., Winkler, T.: Stochastic games with lexicographic reachability-safety objectives. In: Lahiri, S.K., Wang, C. (eds.) CAV 2020. LNCS, vol. 12225, pp. 398–420. Springer, Cham (2020). https://doi.org/10.1007/978-3-030-53291-8_21

21. Chen, T., Forejt, V., Kwiatkowska, M., Parker, D., Simaitis, A.: Automatic verification of competitive stochastic systems. Formal Methods Syst. Des. **43**(1), 61–92 (2013)

22. Clarke, E., Fujita, M., McGeer, P., McMillan, K., Yang, J., Zhao, X.: Multiterminal binary decision diagrams: an efficient data structure for matrix representation. In: Proceedings of the International Workshop on Logic Synthesis (IWLS 1993), pp. 1–15 (1993). Also available in Formal Methods Syst. Des. **10**(2/3), 149–169 (1997)

23. Clarke, E., McMillan, K., Zhao, X., Fujita, M., Yang, J.: Spectral transforms for large Boolean functions with applications to technology mapping. In: Proceedings of the 30th Design Automation Conference (DAC 1993), pp. 54–60. ACM Press (1993). Also available in Formal Methods Syst. Des. **10**(2/3), 137–148 (1997)

24. Condon, A.: The complexity of stochastic games. Inf. Comput. **96**(2), 203–224 (1992)

25. de Alfaro, L., Majumdar, R.: Quantitative solution of omega-regular games. J. Comput. Syst. Sci. **68**(2), 374–397 (2004)

26. Dehnert, C., Junges, S., Katoen, J.-P., Volk, M.: A STORM is coming: a modern probabilistic model checker. In: Majumdar, R., Kunčak, V. (eds.) CAV 2017. LNCS, vol. 10427, pp. 592–600. Springer, Cham (2017). https://doi.org/10.1007/978-3-319-63390-9_31

27. Feng, L., Wiltsche, C., Humphrey, L., Topcu, U.: Synthesis of human-in-the-loop control protocols for autonomous systems. IEEE Trans. Autom. Sci. Eng. **13**(2), 450–462 (2016)

28. Filar, J., Vrieze, K.: Competitive Markov Decision Processes. Springer, New York (1997). https://doi.org/10.1007/978-1-4612-4054-9

29. Junges, S., Jansen, N., Katoen, J.-P., Topcu, U., Zhang, R., Hayhoe, M.: Model checking for safe navigation among humans. In: McIver, A., Horvath, A. (eds.) QEST 2018. LNCS, vol. 11024, pp. 207–222. Springer, Cham (2018). https://doi.org/10.1007/978-3-319-99154-2_13

30. Kelmendi, E., Krämer, J., Křetínský, J., Weininger, M.: Value iteration for simple stochastic games: stopping criterion and learning algorithm. In: Chockler, H., Weissenbacher, G. (eds.) CAV 2018. LNCS, vol. 10981, pp. 623–642. Springer, Cham (2018). https://doi.org/10.1007/978-3-319-96145-3_36

31. Kemeny, J., Snell, J., Knapp, A.: Denumerable Markov Chains. Springer, New York (1976). https://doi.org/10.1007/978-1-4684-9455-6

32. Klein, J., et al.: Advances in symbolic probabilistic model checking with PRISM. In: Chechik, M., Raskin, J.-F. (eds.) TACAS 2016. LNCS, vol. 9636, pp. 349–366. Springer, Heidelberg (2016). https://doi.org/10.1007/978-3-662-49674-9_20
33. Kretínský, J., Ramneantu, E., Slivinskiy, A., Weininger, M.: Comparison of algorithms for simple stochastic games. In: Proceedings of the 11th International Symposium on Games, Automata, Logics, and Formal Verification (GandALF 2020), pp. 131–148. EPTCS (2020)
34. Kwiatkowska, M., Norman, G., Parker, D.: PRISM 4.0: verification of probabilistic real-time systems. In: Gopalakrishnan, G., Qadeer, S. (eds.) CAV 2011. LNCS, vol. 6806, pp. 585–591. Springer, Heidelberg (2011). https://doi.org/10.1007/978-3-642-22110-1_47
35. Kwiatkowska, M., Norman, G., Parker, D.: The PRISM benchmark suite. In: Proceedings of the 9th International Conference on Quantitative Evaluation of SysTems (QEST 2012), pp. 203–204. IEEE CS Press (2012). https://www.prismmodelchecker.org/benchmarks/
36. Kwiatkowska, M., Norman, G., Parker, D.: Verification and control of turn-based probabilistic real-time games. In: Alvim, M.S., Chatzikokolakis, K., Olarte, C., Valencia, F. (eds.) The Art of Modelling Computational Systems: A Journey from Logic and Concurrency to Security and Privacy. LNCS, vol. 11760, pp. 379–396. Springer, Cham (2019). https://doi.org/10.1007/978-3-030-31175-9_22
37. Kwiatkowska, M., Norman, G., Parker, D., Santos, G.: Multi-player equilibria verification for concurrent stochastic games. In: Gribaudo, M., Jansen, D.N., Remke, A. (eds.) QEST 2020. LNCS, vol. 12289, pp. 74–95. Springer, Cham (2020). https://doi.org/10.1007/978-3-030-59854-9_7
38. Kwiatkowska, M., Norman, G., Parker, D., Santos, G.: PRISM-games 3.0: stochastic game verification with concurrency, equilibria and time. In: Lahiri, S.K., Wang, C. (eds.) CAV 2020. LNCS, vol. 12225, pp. 475–487. Springer, Cham (2020). https://doi.org/10.1007/978-3-030-53291-8_25
39. Kwiatkowska, M., Norman, G., Parker, D., Santos, G.: Automatic verification of concurrent stochastic systems. Formal Methods Syst. Des. **58**, 1–63 (2021)
40. Littman, M., Cassandra, A., Kaelbling, L.: Learning policies for partially observable environments: scaling up. In: Proceedings of the 12th International Conference on Machine Learning (ICML 1995), pp. 362–370 (1995)
41. Lomuscio, A., Qu, H., Raimondi, F.: MCMAS: a model checker for the verification of multi-agent systems. In: Bouajjani, A., Maler, O. (eds.) CAV 2009. LNCS, vol. 5643, pp. 682–688. Springer, Heidelberg (2009). https://doi.org/10.1007/978-3-642-02658-4_55
42. Majumdar, R., Mallik, K., Schmuck, A.K., Soudjani, S.: Symbolic qualitative control for stochastic systems via finite parity games. IFAC **54**(5), 127–132 (2021)
43. Martin, D.: The determinacy of Blackwell games. J. Symb. Log. **63**(4), 1565–1581 (1998)
44. McIver, A., Morgan, C.: Results on the quantitative mu-calculus qMu. ACM Trans. Comput. Log. **8**(1), 3-es (2007)
45. McMillan, K.: Symbolic Model Checking. Kluwer Academic Publishers, Amsterdam (1993)
46. von Neumann, J., Morgenstern, O., Kuhn, H., Rubinstein, A.: Theory of Games and Economic Behavior. Princeton University Press, Princeton (1944)
47. Osborne, M., Rubinstein, A.: An Introduction to Game Theory. Oxford University Press, Oxford (2004)
48. Parker, D.: Implementation of symbolic model checking for probabilistic systems. Ph.D. thesis. University of Birmingham (2002)

49. Shapley, L.: Stochastic games. In: Proceedings of the National Academy of Science, vol. 39, pp. 1095–1100 (1953)
50. Zamani, Z., Sanner, S., Fang, C.: Symbolic dynamic programming for continuous state and action MDPs. In: Proceedings of the AAAI 2012, pp. 1839–1845. AAAI Press (2012)
51. Supporting material. https://www.prismmodelchecker.org/files/pgsym/

Parameter Synthesis in Markov Models: A Gentle Survey

Nils Jansen[1], Sebastian Junges[1], and Joost-Pieter Katoen[2(✉)]

[1] Radboud University, Nijmegen, The Netherlands
[2] RWTH Aachen University, Aachen, Germany
katoen@cs.rwth-aachen.de

Abstract. This paper surveys the analysis of parametric Markov models whose transitions are labelled with functions over a finite set of parameters. These models are symbolic representations of uncountable many concrete probabilistic models, each obtained by instantiating the parameters. We consider various analysis problems for a given logical specification φ: do all parameter instantiations within a given region of parameter values satisfy φ?, which instantiations satisfy φ and which ones do not?, and how can all such instantiations be characterised, either exactly or approximately? We address theoretical complexity results and describe the main ideas underlying state-of-the-art algorithms that established an impressive leap over the last decade enabling the fully automated analysis of models with millions of states and thousands of parameters.

1 Introduction

Markov models are ubiquitous. Markov chains (MCs) are central in performance and dependability analysis, whereas Markov decision processes (MDPs) are key in stochastic decision making and planning in AI. A standard assumption in these models is that all probabilities are precisely known. This assumption is often too severe. System quantities such as component fault rates, molecule reaction rates, packet loss ratios, etc. are often not, or at best partially, known.

A Motivating Example. In early stages of reliable system design, the concrete failure rate of components [28] is deliberately left unspecified. Let us illustrate this by considering a multiplexed NAND integrated circuit. As such circuits are built at ever smaller scale, they are prone to defects and/or to exhibit transient failures. The analysis of a parametric

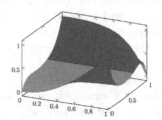

Fig. 1. For which gate failure rates is the circuit reliable? (Color figure online)

This work has been supported by the DFG RTG 2236 "UnRAVeL" and the ERC Advanced Grant 787914 "FRAPPANT".

J.-F. Raskin and K. Chatterjee (Eds.): Principles of Systems Design, LNCS 13660, pp. 407–437, 2022.
https://doi.org/10.1007/978-3-031-22337-2_20

Markov chain model of the NAND circuit [44] can provide insights into the effect of failure probabilities of the gates on the overall circuit's reliability. The unknown random gate failure rates are the model's parameters. Questions of interest are e.g., for which gate failure rates are at least 70% of the NAND outputs correct, or which failure rates minimise the circuit's reliability? More advanced objectives are to determine either exactly or approximately *all* possible failure rates such that the NAND's failure probability is below $3/10$, or even to provide a closed-form formula of how the circuit's reliability depends on the vulnerability of its gates. Figure 1, for instance, plots exact synthesis results (obtained in a few minutes) for two gates with unknown failure rate (x- and y-axis) indicating all gate's failure rates leading to circuit failure probabilities (z-axis) above (red) and below (green) the threshold $3/10$.

Aims of this Paper. Our aim is to provide insight in the underlying algorithmic techniques and the complexity to answer the above questions of interest. We do so by surveying the automated analysis of parametric Markov models. For the sake of simplicity, we consider *parametric Markov chains (pMCs)* and do not consider parametric versions of MDPs. Yet, various of the presented techniques are also applicable to non-deterministic models. Parametric MCs are classical discrete-time Markov chains where the transition probabilities are specified by polynomials over real-valued parameters, e.g., x, $1-x$, and $1-x \cdot y+z$. Intervals over parameters are simple instances imposing constant lower and upper bounds on each parameter [38,58]. The setting here is more liberal as it includes the possibility to express parameter dependencies: a parameter can occur at several transitions. This often leads to solving trade-offs: for some states it may beneficial to have a small value of parameter x, whereas for other states a large value of x is better, e.g., to increase the probability to reach a certain target state.

Parameter Synthesis Problems. We consider various problems for parametric MCs and a given logical specification φ: (1) do all parameter instantiations, within a given region of parameter values, satisfy φ?, (2) which instantiations satisfy φ and which ones do not?, and (3) how can all such instantiations be characterised, either exactly or approximately? These questions are intrinsically hard: parameters can take uncountable many different values and the parameters may depend on each other. We address theoretical complexity results and describe the main ideas underlying state-of-the-art algorithms for (1) through (3). For the sake of simplicity, we focus on specifications φ that impose thresholds on infinite-horizon reachability probabilities; e.g., can a bad state be reached with a probability at most 10^{-6}? The presented algorithms can however also be generalised in a straightforward manner to total expected reward objectives such as: is the expected cost to reach a goal state at most 10^3? This survey aims to give an insight into the main advances during the last decade. Whereas initial algorithms could only handle a handful of parameters[1], these advancements enable

---

[1] And this was viewed by quite some scepticism, e.g., our initial paper on this topic received reviews saying "this is a fun problem that is unlikely to ever result in practical advancements.".

the fully automated analysis of models with millions of states and thousands of parameters.

POMDP Controller Synthesis. Parametric MCs can be seen as Markov chains with partial information about the transition probabilities. Indeed, these transition probabilities are solutions of functions over the parameters. As the choice of the parameter values is assumed to be fully non-deterministic (these values are e.g., not subject to a probability distribution), pMCs can be seen as a kind of MDP with partial information. This raises the question whether there is a relation to the well-known model of partially-observable MDPs (POMDPs) [57,71,75]. POMDPs are a prominent model in sequential decision-making under uncertainty: decisions have to be made under partial knowledge about the environment. Intuitively, POMDP policies (aka: controllers) have to make optimal decisions based on partial information about the visited states. Indeed, there exists a direct link between parameter synthesis for pMCs and controller synthesis for POMDPs. In fact, finding a finite-memory policy that guarantees the satisfaction of a reachability property φ in a POMDP is equivalent to feasibility—find a parameter instantiation satisfying φ—in a corresponding pMC.

Highlights. Section 4 shows that the decision problem of feasibility, does there exist a parameter instantiation such that specification φ is satisfied, is ETR-complete. In particular, the fact that ETR-satisfiability problems can be encoded as reachability problems in pMCs is of interest. Section 5.4 describes how convex optimisation can be used to solve feasibility approximatively and how a tight integration with model checking improves this further. Section 5.2 describes an abstraction-based approach that reduces checking whether a region of parameter instantiations satisfies φ on a pMC to a parameter-less model checking problem on an MDP. Section 6 details the connection between feasibility in pMCs to POMDP controller synthesis. This link closes a complexity gap in POMDP controller synthesis, and enables using parameter synthesis algorithms such as the integrated model checking–convex optimisation for POMDP controller synthesis. Almost all sections include indications about the kind of synthesis problems (in terms of model size, number of parameters, and precision) that can be solved using current algorithms and software tools.

2   Parametric Markov Chains

Let X be a set of n real-valued parameters (or variables) $x_1, \ldots, x_n$. The parameters x_i should be considered as symbols. Their values are defined by a parameter instantiation, i.e., a function $v \colon X \to \mathbb{R}$. The set $V \subseteq \mathbb{R}^n$ of all parameter values is called the parameter space. A set $R \subseteq V$ of instantiations is a *region*.

Let $\mathbb{Q}[X]$ denote the set of multivariate polynomials over X with rational coefficients. A polynomial $f \in \mathbb{Q}[X]$ can be interpreted as a function $f \colon \mathbb{R}^n \to \mathbb{R}$ where $f(v)$ is obtained by replacing each occurrence of x_i in f by $v(x_i)$; e.g., for $f = 2x_1 \cdot x_2 + x_1^2$ with $v(x_1) = 2$ and $v(x_2) = 3$, we have $f(v) = 16$. To make clear where substitution occurs, we write $f[v]$ instead of $f(v)$ from now on.

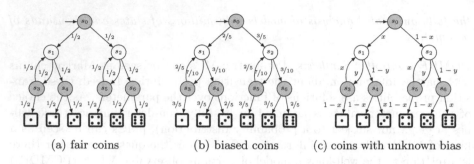

(a) fair coins   (b) biased coins   (c) coins with unknown bias

Fig. 2. Three variations of the Knuth-Yao die

Definition 1. *A pMC $\mathcal{D}$ is a tuple $(S, s_I, X, \mathcal{P})$ with a finite set S of states, an initial state $s_I \in S$, a finite set X of real-valued variables (parameters) and a transition function $\mathcal{P}\colon S \times S \to \mathbb{Q}[X]$.*

The parametric transition probability of going from state s to t is given by $\mathcal{P}(s, t)$. Intuitively, instead of a concrete probability, a transition is equipped with a polynomial over the parameters X, e.g., $\mathcal{P}(s, t) = x^2 + 2 \cdot y$. A pMC with $X = \varnothing$ is a classical Markov chain (MC). Applying an instantiation v to a pMC $\mathcal{D}$ yields MC $\mathcal{D}[v]$ by replacing each transition $\mathcal{P}(s, t) = f \in \mathbb{Q}[X]$ in $\mathcal{D}$ by $f[v]$. In general, a pMC defines an uncountable infinite family of MCs where each family member is obtained by a parameter instantiation. We assume every instantiation v of $\mathcal{D}$ to yield well-defined MCs, i.e., $\mathcal{P}(s, \cdot)[v]$ is a probability distribution over the set S of states; e.g., values $v(x)$ and $v(y)$ for $\mathcal{P}(s, t) = x^2 + 2y$ should be such that $0 \leqslant v(x)^2 + 2 \cdot v(y) \leqslant 1$. For a detailed treatment we refer to [50,51]. An instantiation v is *graph-preserving* (for $\mathcal{D}$) if the topology of $\mathcal{D}$ is preserved, i.e., $\mathcal{P}(s, s') \neq 0$ implies $\mathcal{P}(s, s')[v] \neq 0$ for all $s, s' \in S$. A region R is graph-preserving if every $v \in R$ is graph preserving.

Example 1. Figure 2a depicts an MC with 13 states representing the Knuth-Yao algorithm [56] that mimics a six-sided die by repeatedly flipping a fair coin. Figure 2b shows a version that uses two coins (in the white and gray states respectively) with different but fixed biases. Figure 2c provides a parametric version where the two coins have an unknown bias. The parameters x and y represent the probability to throw heads in the gray and white states, respectively. The parameter space is $\{(x, y) \mid 0 < x, y < 1\}$. The instantiation v with $v(x) = 2/5$ and $v(y) = 7/10$ results in the MC in Fig. 2b. The region of "almost fair" coins x and y, say the coins that are fair up to a possible deviation of $1/10$, is given by $\{v\colon X \to \mathbb{R} \mid 9/20 \leqslant v(x), v(y) \leqslant 11/20\}$.

3 Parameter Synthesis Problems

A typical specification φ requires to eventually reach a set of target states in pMC $\mathcal{D}$ with at least (or at most) a certain probability. A non-parametric MC D satisfies φ, denoted $D \models \varphi$, if the reachability probability of the target states meets this threshold for its fixed transition probabilities. In the presence of parameters, the validity of φ is considered with respect to a given region R of admissible parameter values. Although this survey focuses on reachability probabilities this is not a severe restriction. For instance, reacha-

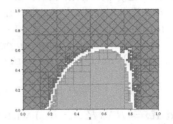

Fig. 3. Approximate partitioning to reach ☐ with probability $< \;^3/_{20}$ (Color figure online)

bility probabilities suffice to determine the probability to satisfy an ω-regular specification. Such specifications contain LTL formulas and coincide with languages accepted by automata on infinite words such as non-deterministic Büchi automata. The probability to satisfy ω-regular specification φ in a non-parametric MC D equals the reachability probability of certain[2] bottom strongly connected components [80] in the synchronous product of D with a deterministic automaton on infinite words corresponding to φ. Similar holds for the parametric setting. Alternative specifications involve rewards (where $\mathcal{D}$ may have parametric rewards), bounded (aka: finite-horizon) reachability, etc.

Let pMC $\mathcal{D}$ over $X = \{x_1, \ldots, x_n\}$, specification φ, and region $R \subseteq \mathbb{R}^n$. Let $v \in R$ stand for instantiation $v \colon X \to \mathbb{R}$ with $v(x_i) \in R{\restriction}i$ for all i, and let:

$$\mathcal{D}, R \models \varphi \quad \text{iff} \quad (\forall v \in R.\, \mathcal{D}[v] \models \varphi).$$

We consider the following parameter synthesis problems:

- The *feasibility problem* is to check whether: $\exists v \in R.\, \mathcal{D}[v] \models \varphi$. Feasibility for φ in R is equivalent to not $(\mathcal{D}, R \models \neg\varphi)$.
- The *optimal* feasibility problem is to find an instantiation $v \in R$ that maximises (or dually minimises) the probability to satisfy φ.
- The *region verification problem* is to check whether:

$$\underbrace{\mathcal{D}, R \models \varphi}_{R \text{ is accepting}} \quad \text{or} \quad \underbrace{\mathcal{D}, R \models \neg\varphi}_{R \text{ is rejecting}} \quad \text{or} \quad \underbrace{\mathcal{D}, R \not\models \varphi \wedge \mathcal{D}, R \not\models \neg\varphi}_{R \text{ is inconclusive}}.$$

- The *exact partitioning problem* is to partition (measurable) R into R_+ and R_- such that:

$$R_+ = \{v \in R \mid \mathcal{D}[v] \models \varphi\} \quad \text{and} \quad R_- = \{v \in R \mid \mathcal{D}[v] \models \neg\varphi\}.$$

---

[2] The ones that are accepting according to the type (e.g., Muller, Rabin) of deterministic automaton to encode φ.

Instead of checking whether a region R is accepting or rejecting, the exact partitioning problem aims to find the largest subset of R that is accepting (or, dually, rejecting). As finding an exact partitioning is hard, often a relaxed version is considered.

- The *approximate partitioning problem* is to partition (measurable) R into R_+, R_-, and $R_?$ such that for some given $0 \leqslant \eta \leqslant 1$:

$$R_+ \subseteq \{v \in R \mid \mathcal{D}[v] \models \varphi\} \quad \text{and} \quad R_- \subseteq \{v \in R \mid \mathcal{D}[v] \models \neg\varphi\},$$

and $R_? = R \setminus (R_+ \cup R_-)$ with $\|R_?\| \leqslant (1-\eta) \cdot \|R\|$ where $\|\cdot\|$ denotes the volume of R. Here, $R_?$ is the fragment of R that is inconclusive for φ. It is required that this fragment occupies at most a factor $1-\eta$ of the volume of R. Stated differently, the accepting and rejecting region cover at least a factor η of the region. Exact partitioning is obtained if $\eta = 1$.

Example 2. Consider the parametric die from Fig. 2c and let φ be the specification that the probability to reach state ▢ is at least $3/20$. There exists a feasible solution, e.g., $x = y = 1/2$. Let region R be all valuations with $1/10 \leqslant v(x) \leqslant 9/10$ and $3/4 \leqslant v(y) \leqslant 5/6$. It follows that R is accepting for $\neg\varphi$ (and thus rejecting φ) as for all $v \in R$ the probability to reach ▢ is at most $3/20$. The function:

$$f(x,y) = \frac{x \cdot (1 - y) \cdot (1 - x)}{1 - x \cdot y} \tag{1}$$

describes the probability to reach ▢. For $\neg\varphi$, $R_+ = \{v \mid f[v] < 3/20\}$ and $R_- = R \setminus R_+$. Figure 3 shows an approximation (for $\eta = 0.95$) of the function f for $\neg\varphi$. The set of rectangular accepting (green) regions indicate R_+ for $\neg\varphi$, whereas the red (hatched) area indicates R_-. The white area indicates $R_?$.

The synthesis problems are complex as—in contrast to interval MCs [58]—parameters may depend on each other and may occur at several transitions in a pMC. These dependencies lead to trade-offs: increasing a parameter value may raise a reachability probability in one state but lower such probability in another state. The next section addresses the theoretical complexity of the feasibility problem.

4   Complexity of the Feasibility Problem

The ETR-SAT (Existential Theory of the Reals) decision problem consists of deciding whether a given existentially quantified formula $\exists x_1 \ldots \exists x_n . F(x_1, \ldots, x_n)$ holds, where F is a Boolean combination of polynomial inequalities over the real-valued parameters x_1 through x_n.[3] The complexity class ETR contains all decision problems for which a polynomial many-to-one reduction to the ETR-SAT decision problem exists. The class ETR contains NP and is contained in PSPACE [17]. Given that the Boolean structure of an ETR formula can be

---

[3] In SAT modulo theories, ETR is referred to as the quantifier-free fragment of non-linear real arithmetic (QFNRA, for short).

encoded into a polynomial, solving an ETR-SAT problem is equally hard as determining whether a polynomial over x_1 through x_n has a real root.

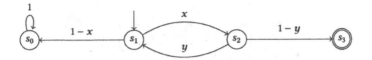

Fig. 4. A sample pMC for reachability probabilities

Encoding Feasibility as ETR-SAT. The following example illustrates that the feasibility problem can be reduced to the ETR-SAT problem.

Example 3. Consider the pMC $\mathcal{D}$ in Fig. 4 with region $R = \{v \mid 0 < v(x), v(y) < 1\}$ and target state s_3. There exists a parameter instantiation such that the specification φ holds, i.e., s_3 is reached with probability at least $3/4$, whenever the following ETR-formula holds:

$$\exists p_0, \ldots, p_3, x, y. \underbrace{0 < x < 1 \wedge 0 < y < 1}_{\text{region } R} \wedge \underbrace{p_1 \geqslant 3/4}_{\text{spec. } \varphi}$$
$$\wedge \; p_3 = 1 \; \wedge \; p_0 = 0$$
$$\wedge \; p_1 = x{\cdot}p_2 + \underbrace{(1{-}x){\cdot}p_0}_{=0} \; \wedge \; p_2 = y{\cdot}p_1 + \underbrace{(1{-}y){\cdot}p_3}_{=1-y} \, .$$

A variable p_i is introduced for each state s_i in $\mathcal{D}$ that intuitively represents the probability to eventually reach state s_3 from s_i. Variables x and y represent the equally named parameters in $\mathcal{D}$. The first line encodes the region R and that φ has to hold for state s_1. The second line encodes that s_3 reaches itself almost surely, and that s_3 can almost surely not be reached from s_0. The equations in the last line express the recursive equations for reachability probabilities. They conform to the form:

$$p_s \; = \; \sum_{s' \in S_{>0}} \mathcal{P}(s, s') \cdot p_{s'} \quad \text{for all } s \in S_{>0} \setminus G \tag{2}$$

where $S_{>0} = \{s_1, s_2, s_3\}$ is the set of states that can reach a state in the set of target states $G = \{s_3\}$. The size of the ETR-formula is linear in the size of $\mathcal{D}$. The set $S_{>0}$ can be computed by efficient graph analysis methods.

Encoding ETR-SAT as Feasibility. Interestingly, this reduction also works (under mild conditions) in the reverse direction. We illustrate by example how to obtain an acyclic pMC $\mathcal{D}_F$ from a given ETR-formula F such that a target state can be reached with probability at least λ in $\mathcal{D}_F$ for some variable instantiation v if F holds for v. This reduction relies on important observations in [26]. The size of $\mathcal{D}_F$ is polynomial in the degree of F, the number of terms in F, and the maximal number of bits to encode the threshold λ and F's coefficients.

Example 4. Consider the ETR-formula $F = \exists x, y. -2 \cdot x^2 \cdot y + y \geqslant 5$. We adapt this formula so as to remove the negative coefficients. Simplification yields:

$$2 \cdot (1-x) \cdot x \cdot y + 2 \cdot (1-x) \cdot y + 2 \cdot (1-y) + y - 2 \geqslant 5.$$

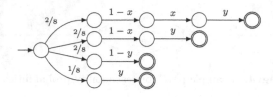

Fig. 5. Sample construction for ETR-hardness for feasibility checking

By adding 2 and dividing by 8, the coefficients describe a probability distribution:

$$2/8 \cdot (1-x) \cdot x \cdot y + 2/8 \cdot (1-x) \cdot y + 2/8 \cdot (1-y) + 1/8 \cdot y \geqslant 7/8.$$

The left-hand side of this inequation induces the pMC in Fig. 5, where the missing transitions all lead to a sink state (omitted in the figure). The probability to reach a target state is at least $7/8$ if the ETR-formula F holds.

Theorem 1. *[53] The feasibility problem for pMCs is ETR-complete.*

A few remarks are in order. The reduction already applies to very simple classes of pMCs, e.g., acyclic ones, and pMCs that only contain expressions such as x and $1-x$ on the transitions. Our next remark concerns the complexity of related feasibility problems. The above results apply to reachability objectives with non-strict conditions (i.e., either $\leqslant$ or $\geqslant$) on the probability thresholds. For strict conditions, the feasibility problem is NP-hard. The feasibility problem for qualitative reachability, i.e., thresholds 0 or 1, is NP-complete for most cases and in P for specific cases such as graph-preserving instantiations. Our third remark concerns pMCs with non-deterministic choices. The complexity class ETR is also relevant for synthesis problems on parametric MDPs; e.g., the feasibility problem "does there exist a parameter valuation such that for some (or, dually, for all possible) resolution(s) of the non-determinism a reachability probability meets a non-strict threshold" is ETR-complete too. Full details can be found in [53]. As a fourth remark, we point out that the above result holds for the setting with arbitrarily many parameters. If the number of parameters is fixed, the feasibility problem for pMCs can be solved in polynomial time [7,48]. The complexity of the fixed parameter case for parametric MDPs is still open. Finally, we note that the above result indicates that solving the feasibility problem is difficult in general. This motivates the search for heuristics and approximate techniques; such techniques are discussed in Sect. 5.4.

5   Algorithms

This section describes the main underlying principles of algorithmic approaches to tackle the aforementioned synthesis problems: exact and approximate parameter space partitioning, region verification, and (optimal) feasibility checking.

5.1   Exact Partitioning

Exact partitioning amounts to computing the rational function f as e.g., given in Eq. (1). This function is commonly referred to as the *solution* function (for the reachability objective "eventually ◻"). Computing a closed-form solution function has been one of the first problems considered for pMCs [32] and has been subject to several practical efficiency improvements, see e.g., [7, 26, 35, 36, 40, 48, 49]. Solution functions map parameter values onto reachability probabilities. For pMCs with polynomial transition functions as in this survey, solution functions are lower semi-continuous; for acyclic pMCs they are continuous.

Complexity. The functions can be obtained by successively eliminating the state variables from the characteristic equation system, e.g., the equations shown in Example 3. This procedure is in fact a Gaussian elimination procedure on the parametric transition probability function. Phrased differently, one solves a linear equation system with rational functions as coefficients.

Example 5. Consider again the pMC $\mathcal{D}$ in Fig. 4. The rational function for reaching s_3 is obtained by solving the non-linear equation system:

$$p_0 = 0 \ \wedge \ p_1 = x{\cdot}p_2 \ \wedge \ p_2 = y{\cdot}p_1 + (1{-}y) \ \wedge \ p_3 = 1.$$

The unique solution of this equation system yields:

$$p_0 = 0 \ \wedge \ p_1 = \frac{x{\cdot}(1{-}y)}{1 - x{\cdot}y} \ \wedge \ p_2 = \frac{1{-}y}{1 - x{\cdot}y} \ \wedge \ p_3 = 1.$$

The function of pMC $\mathcal{D}$ to reach s_3 from its initial state s_1 is thus $\frac{x{\cdot}(1{-}y)}{1-x{\cdot}y}$.

The challenge is that elimination over the ring of polynomials results in large functions—a problem that unfortunately cannot be avoided in general.

Theorem 2. *[7,48] Computing the solution function (for reachability objectives) is exponential in the number of parameters, and polynomial in the number of states and the maximal degree of the polynomial transition probability functions.*

This result is a direct consequence of one-step fraction-free Gaussian elimination. Standard Gaussian elimination does not suffice. The point is that during triangulation, an elementary step in Gaussian elimination, the total degree of the involved factors is doubled in the worst case. The growth of the fractions can be often limited by eliminating common factors, i.e., by keeping the numerator and denominator co-prime. This, however, requires computing greatest common divisors which is expensive.[4] Fraction-free elimination avoids a fractional representation of the intermediate matrix entries altogether. This does not avoid the exponential growth, but in combination with the one-step variant, it avoids gcd-computations. This keeps the coefficients during the elimination process polynomially large. Experiments [7] indicate that this seems beneficial for pMCs with a dense topology.

---

[4] Data structures to avoid computing gcd's have been proposed in [49].

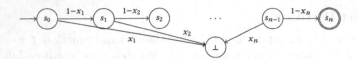

Fig. 6. Small multivariate pMC with an exponentially large solution function

Example 6. The solution function for the family $(\mathcal{D})_n$ of pMCs with $n \geqslant 2$ parameters, $n+2$ states and target state s_n in Fig. 6 is of the form:

$$\prod_{i=1}^{n}(1 - x_i) = \sum_{J \subseteq \{1,\ldots,n\}} -1^{|J|} \cdot \prod_{j \in J} x_j$$

whose shortest sum-of-monomial representation has 2^n monomials.

State Elimination. Rather than using (one-step fraction-free) Gaussian elimination, tools such as PARAM [40], PRISM [60] and Prophesy [33] use state elimination on the pMC as originally proposed in [32]. This approach is analogous to computing regular expressions from non-deterministic finite automata (NFA) [47] and has also been applied in other contexts such as probabilistic workflow nets [34]. The core idea behind state elimination is based on two operations:

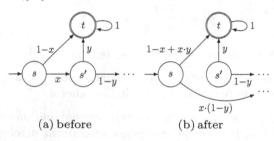

(a) before   (b) after

Fig. 7. Adding short-cuts

(1) *Adding short-cuts:* Consider the pMC-fragment in Fig. 7a. The reachability probabilities from any state to t are as in Fig. 7b where the transitions from s to t via s' are replaced by a short-cut from s to t and similar for all other direct successors of s', thus bypassing s'. By successively creating short-cuts, eventually any path from the initial state to the target state consists of a single transition.

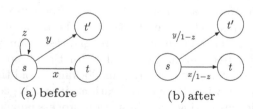

(a) before   (b) after

Fig. 8. Self-loop removal

(2) *Eliminating self-loops:* In order to bypass a state, it needs to be free of self-loops. As the probability of staying forever in a non-absorbing state s is zero, self-loops at s can be eliminated by rescaling all outgoing transitions of s, cf. the change from Fig. 8a to Fig. 8b.

As for computing regular expressions from NFA, the elimination order of states is essential. Computing an optimal order with respect to minimality of the result, however, is already NP-hard for acyclic NFA, see [42]. Practical approaches resort to heuristics that are e.g., based on the pMC's topology, the in-degree of states, and so forth. These heuristics can be static i.e., once fixed for the entire computation, or dynamic in which the ordering is re-considered during the computation depending on e.g., the complexity of transition probability functions.

Experimental Experiences. Extensive experiments are reported in [51, Section 10.2]. While solution functions can grow prohibitively large, medium-sized functions can still be computed. E.g., for a variant of the NAND-example from the introduction with about 300K states and 400K transitions, the solution function consisting of 4640 monomials of degree up to 200 could be computed in about 90 s. Experiments also reveal that the heuristic to determine the order of state elimination is essential and depends on the pMC at hand. For most cases, state elimination (significantly) outperforms Gaussian elimination. Recent experiments [72] indicate that the techniques described above significantly outperform similar techniques used for probabilistic graphical models; e.g., for Bayesian network win95pts[5] with 76 random variable and 200 parameters spread randomly over the graph, the solution function with about 7,5 million monomials of maximal degree 16 could be computed in about 400 s. It is also beneficial to compute solution functions in a compositional way rather than on a monolithic pMC. This has been advocated for each strongly connected component separately [49] and more recently for more liberal decompositions of the graphical structure of the pMC [35]. Experiments in [35] indicate possible speed-ups of several orders of magnitude and more compact closed forms.

5.2 Region Verification

A direct approach to check whether $\mathcal{D}, R \models \varphi$ is to use the ETR-formulation: one exploits a satisfiability modulo theory (SMT) checker for non-linear real arithmetic to check whether the conjunction of the ETR-formula F as described in Sect. 4 and a formula encoding the region R is satisfiable. The number of variables in the ETR-formula can be reduced significantly by pre-computing the solution function using the techniques described in the previous section. The advantage of this approach is that it is exact and complete, but practically this SMT approach does not scale beyond a few parameters.

Example 7. For the pMC in Fig. 4, this procedure amounts to check whether the ETR-formula in Example 3 holds, or equivalently whether, phrased using the solution function, $\frac{x\cdot(1-y)}{1-x\cdot y} \geqslant 3/4$ for some $0 < x, y < 1$.

---

[5] A network with a relatively high average Markov blanket, i.e., with relatively many causal dependencies between the random variables.

A Brief Intermezzo: MDPs. An alternative is to exploit a *dedicated abstraction technique.* To that end, we require the notion of a (non-parametric) Markov decision process. Let $Distr(S)$ be the set of discrete probability distributions over the set S of states.

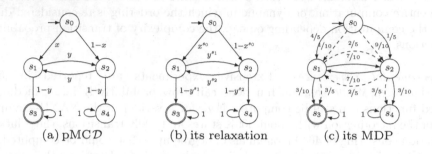

(a) pMC$\mathcal{D}$ (b) its relaxation   (c) its MDP

Fig. 9. A two-phase procedure to transform a pMC into an MDP

Definition 2 (MDP). *A Markov decision process (MDP) is a tuple $M = (S, s_I, Act, P)$ with a finite set S of* states, *an initial state $s_I \in S$, a finite set Act of* actions, *and a (partial) transition probability function $P \colon S \times Act \to Distr(S)$.*

An MDP exhibits nondeterministic choices of actions at each state, where an action corresponds to a probability distribution over successor states, as in Markov chains. So-called *policies*, also referred to as schedulers or strategies, resolve this nondeterminism. For the type of specifications in this survey, it suffices to consider deterministic memoryless policies, specified by $\sigma \colon S \to Act$. Essentially, a policy σ picks a unique action at each state of an MDP. Model checking for MDPs employs techniques like value iteration or linear programming and aims to compute the maximal or minimal probability to satisfy a specification under any policy [9,69]. For surveys on MDP model checking, we refer to [6,8].

Parameter Lifting. Coming back to parametric models, a viable and efficient method that works for a large class of pMCs is to transform a pMC $\mathcal{D}$ into an MDP whose minimal (maximal) reachability probability under-approximates (over-approximates) the reachability probability in $\mathcal{D}$ for all instantiations in a region. The key steps of this so-called *parameter lifting* approach [70] are to:

(1) relax the parameter dependencies (as inspired by [15]), and
(2) consider lower and upper bounds of parameters as worst cases.

Put in a nutshell, it reduces a region verification query on a pMC onto a verification query for an abstract probabilistic model, viz. an MDP representing an interval MC [74].

Example 8. Consider the pMC $\mathcal{D}$ in Fig. 9a and let region $R = [1/10, 4/5] \times [2/5, 7/10]$[6]. The parameter y occurs at transitions emanating from two states. This leads to the following trade-off. To maximise reaching the state s_3 from s_1, the value of y should be low. However, from state s_2, y's value should be large so as to avoid reaching s_4 from which s_3 is unreachable. The optimal y-value depends on the probability to visit s_1 and s_2 and thus directly on x's value.

(1) The first conceptual step in parameter lifting is to remove parameter dependencies: We make all parameters occurrences unique for each state. Parameter y at state s_1 becomes y^{s_1} and at s_2 becomes y^{s_2}, etc. Figure 9b shows the resulting pMC rel($\mathcal{D}$). The corresponding 3-dimensional relaxed version of R is:

$$\text{rel}(R) \;=\; \underbrace{[1/10, 4/5]}_{\text{range of } x^{s_0}} \times \underbrace{[2/5, 7/10]}_{\text{range of } y^{s_1}} \times \underbrace{[2/5, 7/10]}_{\text{range of } y^{s_2}} \;.$$

On instantiating the pMC rel($\mathcal{D}$), the "local" copies of y get the same value. Thus, e.g., $(v(x), v(y)) = (4/5, 3/5) \in R$ becomes $(\text{rel}(v)(x^{s_0}), \text{rel}(v)(y^{s_1}), \text{rel}(v)(y^{s_2})) = (4/5, 3/5, 3/5) \in \text{rel}(R)$. The region rel($R$) contains spurious instantiations, e.g., $(4/5, 1/2, 3/5)$, where the two copies of y have distinct values. These instantiations do not have a counterpart in R. *Removing parameter dependencies is thus an over-approximation.*

(2) The second conceptual step creates the MDP in Fig. 9c. It has the same state space as the pMC rel($\mathcal{D}$). States s_0 through s_2 are equipped with actions for upper (lower) bounds in the region rel(R), indicated by solid (dashed) lines. For instance, state s_2 has a solid (dashed) transition with probability $7/10$ ($2/5$) to s_1. These transitions represent the largest (smallest) probability to go from s_2 to s_1 in rel(R). As each value between these two extreme values can be selected, the resulting MDP is in fact an interval MC [74]. Choices in s_3 and s_4 are unique, as the outgoing transitions in rel($\mathcal{D}$) are constant.

How is an analysis of the resulting MDP related to checking whether $\mathcal{D}, R \models \varphi$? Assume that φ requires to reach state s_3 with at most probability $4/5$, i.e., $48/60$. Verifying the resulting MDP using standard probabilistic model checking (PMC) techniques [6,8,55] yields a maximal probability to reach s_3 of $47/60$. This is achieved by a policy that selects solid transitions in s_0 and s_2 and dashed transitions in s_1. As $47/60 \leqslant 48/60$, and the MDP over-approximates pMC $\mathcal{D}$, it follows that $\mathcal{D}, R \models \varphi$. If φ would impose a lower bound (rather than an upper bound) on the reachability objective, the minimal probability to reach s_3 in the MDP is considered.

Correctness. For the following result, we use the notion of the Markov chain M^σ that is *induced* by an MDP M and a policy σ.

Theorem 3. *[70] Let $\mathcal{D}$ be a locally monotone pMC, R a rectangular and closed region*[7], *φ a reachability specification, and M the resulting MDP from lifting $\mathcal{D}$ and R. Then:*

---

[6] More precisely, $R = \{v \mid v(x) \in [1/10, 4/5], v(y) \in [2/5, 7/10]\}$.

[7] A rectangular and closed region is of the form $\prod_i [\ell_i, u_i]$ where the value of parameter x_i lies in the closed interval $[\ell_i, u_i]$.

1. *(for all policies σ on M: $M^\sigma \models \varphi$)*   *implies* $\mathcal{D}, R \models \varphi$, *and*
2. *(for all policies σ on M : $M^\sigma \models \neg\varphi$)*   *implies* $\mathcal{D}, R \models \neg\varphi$,

where σ ranges over all possible policies for the MDP M.

Note that the (graph-preserving) region R is required to be rectangular and closed, and that pMC $\mathcal{D}$ is locally monotone, i.e., the transition probability functions in $\mathcal{D}$ are monotonic. Examples of such functions are e.g., multi-linear polynomials. The first constraint makes the bounds of the parameters independent of other parameter instantiations and ensures the maximum (and minimum) over the region R to exist. Due to the local monotonicity and the absence of parameter dependencies after relaxation, maximal reachability probabilities are easy to determine: it suffices to consider instantiations that set the value of each parameter to either the lowest or highest possible value. These two constraints on $\mathcal{D}$ and R are quite mild; in fact, almost all examples from the literature comply to these constraints.

Region Refinement. If the over-approximation $\mathrm{rel}(R)$ of region R is too coarse for a conclusive answer, R can be refined into smaller regions. Intuitively, by excluding more potential parameter values, the actual choice of the parameter value has lesser impact on reachability probabilities. The smaller the region, the smaller the over-approximation: the optimal instantiation on the pMC $\mathcal{D}$ is over-approximated by some policy on the MDP M. The approximation error originates from choices where an optimal policy on M chooses actions v_1 and v_2 at states s_1 and s_2, respectively, with $v_1(x_i^{s_1}) \neq v_2(x_i^{s_2})$ for some parameter x_i, and therefore intuitively disagree on its value. The probability mass that is affected by these choices decreases if the region is smaller.

Experimental Results. Experiments [51,70] show that parameter lifting is an excellent approach for region verification if the influence of the parameter dependencies is minor, or if the number of parameters is relatively low (at most 15, say). For more parameters, the refinement in exponentially many regions often yields a prohibitive number of sub-regions that have to be analysed.

The beauty of parameter lifting is threefold: (1) it is conceptually simple, (2) its principle is applicable to other models such as parametric MDPs (which are then transformed into two-player stochastic games), and (3) it reduces a verification problem on parametric probabilistic models to a model-checking query on non-parametric probabilistic models for which efficient algorithms exist.

5.3   Approximate Parameter Space Partitioning

The approximate parameter space partitioning problem requests to partition region R into accepting and rejecting fragments together with an unknown fragment which covers at most fraction $1-\eta$ of R's volume. This section presents an iterative approach to this problem that builds on top of region verification discussed just above. The basic idea of this approach was first presented in [33] and has substantially been refined and extended in [50, Ch. 8].

The Basic Idea. Approximate parameter space partitioning can be viewed as a *counter-example guided abstraction* refinement (CEGAR)-like [27] approach to successively divide the parameter space into accepting and rejecting regions. The basic idea is to compute a sequence $\left(R_+^i\right)_{i\in\mathbb{N}}$ of simple (read: rectangular) accepting regions that successively extend each other. Similarly, an increasing sequence $\left(R_-^i\right)_{i\in\mathbb{N}}$ of simple rejecting regions is computed. At the i-th iteration, $R^i = R_+^i \cup R_-^i$ is the covered fragment of the parameter space. The iterative approach halts when R^i covers at least $100\cdot\eta\%$ of the entire region R. Termination is guaranteed: in the limit a solution to the exact synthesis problem is obtained as $\lim_{i\to\infty} R_+^i = R_+$ and $\lim_{i\to\infty} R_-^i = R_-$.

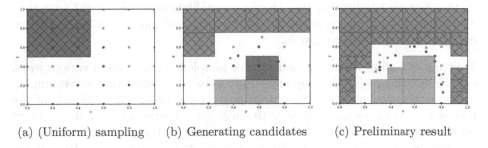

(a) (Uniform) sampling   (b) Generating candidates   (c) Preliminary result

Fig. 10. Parameter space partitioning in progress (using PROPhESY [33].) (Color figure online)

Issues are e.g., how to find good region candidates, how to refine a region, and how to effectively use diagnostic feedback if a region is found to be inconclusive.

Example 9 (A naive procedure). Consider the parametric die from Example 1. Suppose we want to synthesise the partitioning in Fig. 3 on page 5. We start by verifying the full parameter space R against φ. The verifier returns false, as R is not accepting. Since R might be rejecting, we invoke the verifier with R and $\neg\varphi$, yielding false too. Thus, the full parameter space R is inconclusive. Let us now split R into four equally-sized regions, all of which turn out to be inconclusive. Only after splitting again by the same principle, the first accepting and rejecting regions are found. After various iterations, this procedure leads to the partitioning in Fig. 3.

Finding Region Candidates. Rather than starting with the entire (typically large and inconclusive) initial region R, a better strategy is to first do some *sampling*. Here, sampling means identifying an instantiation $v \in R$ and verifying using an off-the-shelf probabilistic model checker for MCs whether $\mathcal{D}[v] \models \varphi$. One can e.g., start by uniformly sampling the region R, see Fig. 10a. A red cross at point $v = (v(x), v(y))$ indicates that $\mathcal{D}[v] \models \neg\varphi$, while a green dot indicates $\mathcal{D}[v] \models \varphi$. The sampling results can be used to steer the selection of a candidate region that is consistent with all samples contained in it; e.g., the blue rectangle in

Fig. 10a is a candidate region for the hypothesis $\neg\varphi$ (indicated by the hatching) as it only contains red crosses.

How to Split Regions? A simple strategy is to split regions that sampling or region verification revealed to be inconsistent.

Example 10. After several iterations, the iterative refinement proceeded to the situation in Fig. 10b. The blue candidate region in Fig. 10a turned out to be not rejecting; the region verifier provided the counterexample $(p, q) = (0.45, 0.52)$. Further iterations with smaller regions had some success, but some additional samples (the dots and circles that are off-grid points) were obtained as counterexamples. The blue region in Fig. 10b is a candidate for φ. Figure 10c shows a further snapshot indicating that this blue candidate region is indeed accepting. The white box on the right border has been checked but its verification timed out without any counterexample.

Splitting of regions based on the available samples can be done in various ways, e.g., by splitting regions into equally-sized regions (as used in the above example), or by attempting to gradually obtain larger candidates. The rationale of the former is to obtain small regions with small bounds whereas the latter is based on the rationale to quickly cover a vast fragment of the parameter space. For the construction of region candidates, a good practical strategy is to split the initial regions according to a heuristic until none of the regions is inconclusive. Candidate regions are sorted in descending size. Regions are preferred where verification seems less costly: candidate regions that are supposed to be accepting and are further away from samples or regions that are rejecting are preferred over those regions which have rejecting samples or are close to rejecting regions.

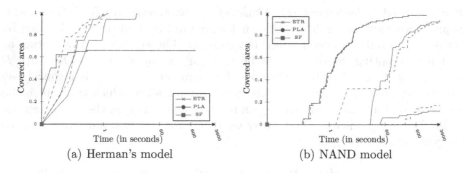

(a) Herman's model   (b) NAND model

Fig. 11. Covered parameter space during partitioning for two benchmarks

Experimental Experiences. Figure 11a depicts results for parameter space partitioning on Herman's randomised self-stabilisation algorithm [45] for a distributed system with five processes and threshold $\lambda = 5$. This model has one parameter, 33 states and 276 transitions. The plot depicts the covered parameter space for three techniques with both quads (straight lines) and rectangles (dashed lines) as region representations. A point (x, y) indicates that y percent of the parameter space could be covered within x seconds. The three techniques are parameter lifting (PLA), the ETR-encoding, and the solution function (SF) encoded as ETR-formula. Recall that the ETR-encoding contains a variable for each state and each parameter, whereas the SF only contains a variable for each parameter, cf. Eq. (1).

For Herman's distributed algorithm, SMT-based techniques perform better than PLA. PLA was able to cover 64% of the parameter space within milliseconds but only 2% more space was covered in the remaining hour. SMT was able to cover at least 99% of the parameter space within 15 s. Moreover, rectangles cover the parameter space faster than quads. The results on the NAND model [44] are a bit different, see Fig. 11b. This model has two parameters, 178 states and 243 transitions. Here, PLA outperforms SMT. Rectangles and quads perform on par, although for smaller

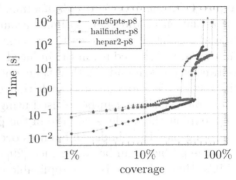

Fig. 12. Approximate parameter partitioning on three Bayesian networks with each eight parameters

thresholds their performance does differ. Applications on various benchmarks reveals that parameter lifting is almost always superior but not on all benchmarks and all (sub-)regions. There can be substantial differences between the heuristics for candidate generation, especially in settings where single region verification calls are expensive. To indicate the scalability of the approach, we report on some recent experiments [73] on parametric Bayesian networks. Figure 12 shows that 80–90% of the 8-dimensional parameter space for three parametric Bayesian networks (`win95pts`, `hailfinder`, and `hepar-2`) can be covered in about 100–1,000 s.

5.4 Feasibility Checking

We now return to the ETR-complete feasibility problem of before and describe how techniques from mathematical optimisation can be exploited to obtain a scalable approach.

Two "Extreme" Approaches: Sampling and ETR-Solving. To find a satisfiable parameter instantiation it suffices to guess an instantiation v such that $\mathcal{D}[v] \models \varphi$. Checking whether $\mathcal{D}[v] \models \varphi$ can be done using PMC techniques [6,55] or, alternatively, by instantiating the solution function efficiently [37]. This insight has led to an adaptation of sampling-based techniques to the parameter synthesis problem, most prominently particle swarm optimisation (PSO) [24]. These techniques can handle millions of states but their efficiency is limited for models with more than roughly ten parameters, see the left part of Fig. 13. Rather than pure sampling-based techniques such as PSO, one can pursue an exact (but costly) approach by computing the ETR-formula and checking whether it is satisfiable. This is exact, but costly as indicated on the right part of Fig. 13.

A Middle Ground: Mathematical Optimisation. An approach that is suitable compromise between sampling and exact solution techniques is to exploit techniques from *mathematical optimisation.* The basic idea is to guess a parameter instantiation v, and then optimise around this v in the parameter space so as to find a point that improves the reachability probability (or whatever specification we are interested in) in the induced MC. This is repeated until an accepting instantiation is found. Rather than optimising on the original ETR formula, the formula is approximated such that every iteration step is computationally tractable. This idea can be realised using different ideas. These ideas share that they exploit the model structure of the pMC $\mathcal{D}$, and need fewer iterations than sampling-based methods. Differences occur due to the choice of approximation, e.g., the problem can be convexified [29] or linearised [30]. Although we consider pMCs, this technique is also applicable to parametric MDPs.

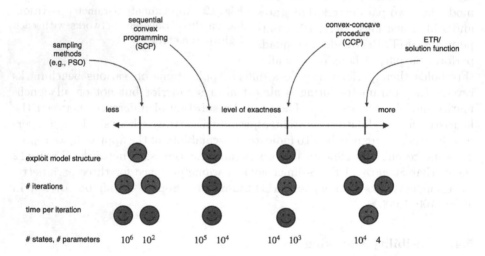

Fig. 13. Comparing various techniques for feasibility for different levels of precision

Feasibility as an Optimisation Problem. The first step is to formulate the feasibility problem as an optimisation problem. Assuming that all transition probabilities are linear in the parameters, the ETR-formula can be represented as a *quadratically-constrained quadratic program* (QCQP [14]), an optimisation problem with a quadratic objective that is to be achieved under a set of quadratic constraints[8]. We show this for a key part of the ETR encoding:

---

[8] For readers familiar with the LP encoding for reachability objectives for MDPs, this QCQP is the straightforward representation of this LP where the transition probabilities (parameters) are multiplied with the state-variables.

minimise p_{s_I} s.t.

$$p_s \geqslant \underbrace{\sum_{s' \in S_{>0}} \mathcal{P}(s, s') \cdot p_{s'}}_{= h(s, s')} \quad \text{for all } s \in S_{>0} \setminus G, \tag{3}$$

where $S_{>0}$ and $G \subseteq S$ are as before in Eq. (2). Note that the QCQP formulation is exact: its solutions coincide with the solutions to the ETR-formulation. However, in general, the QCQP is a non-convex optimisation problem—witnessed by the encoding of the pMC in Fig. 14—and thus not directly amenable to efficient methods (which is a trivial consequence of the ETR-completeness of the problem).

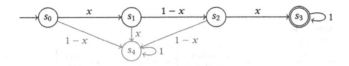

Fig. 14. A sample pMC to illustrate the use of mathematical optimisation

Example 11. The ETR constraints for the pMC in Fig. 14 to reach state s_3 with threshold $\leqslant \lambda$ are:

$$p_0 \leqslant \lambda, \quad \varepsilon \leqslant x \leqslant 1-\varepsilon, \quad p_3 = 1, \quad p_0 \geqslant x \cdot p_1, \quad p_1 \geqslant (1-x) \cdot p_2, \quad p_2 \geqslant x \cdot p_3.$$

Quadratic constraints are e.g., $(1-x) \cdot p_2$ and $x \cdot p_1$.

Turning the QCQP into a Series of LP Problems. We present a *sequential-convex-optimisation* (SCP) approach that iteratively solves LPs to find a solution of the QCQP. This approach is originally presented in [25,62,85] and has been adapted for pMCs in [30]. Eventually, the solution of one of these LPs will provide a solution to the original QCQP. Checking whether this is indeed the case can be done by model checking the instantiated pMC. Given an assignment $\hat{v}$ to v, we obtain an affine approximation in the form of a linearisation $\hat{f}$ of the polynomial f around $\hat{v}$:

$$\hat{f}_{\hat{v}} = f[\hat{v}] + \nabla f[\hat{v}]^T \cdot (v - \hat{v}) \tag{4}$$

where $\nabla f[\hat{v}]$ is the gradient of the polynomial f at $\hat{v}$. Consequently, the LP approximation around $\hat{v}$ of the constraint (3) then reads:

$$p_s \geqslant \sum_{s' \in S_{>0}} h_{\hat{v}}(s, s') \quad \text{for all } s \in S_{>0} \setminus G.$$

However, the LP from the conjunction of these variables is not necessarily feasible. To remedy this, we relax the LP by introducing a penalty variable k_s for each state s that intuitively allows violating the constraints up to some degree.

By adapting the objective function, we encourage the solver to not violate the constraints, turning (3) into:

$$\text{minimise } p_{s_I} + \tau \cdot \sum_s k_s \text{ s.t.}$$

$$k_s + p_s \geqslant \sum_{s' \in S_{>0}} h_{\hat{v}}(s, s') \quad \text{for all } s \in S_{>0} \setminus G. \tag{5}$$

The constant τ is chosen sufficiently large. To ensure that the linearisation is accurate, we enforce that the solution is sufficiently close to $\hat{v}$ using *trust regions* [85].

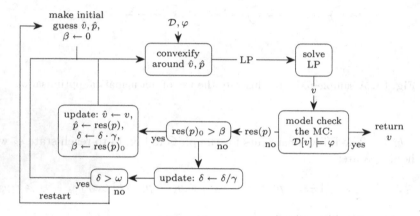

Fig. 15. Feasibility checking using an integrated SCP-PMC approach

Example 12. After a linearisation around an assignment for the parameter instantiation $\hat{x}$, $\hat{p}_0$ through $\hat{p}_2$, the resulting LP formulation for our example pMC requires to minimise $p_0 + \tau \cdot \sum k_i$ under $k_i \geqslant 0$, $p_3 = 1$, $p_0 \leqslant \lambda$, and the linear constraints:

$$k_0 + p_0 \geqslant \hat{x} \cdot \hat{p}_1 + \hat{p}_1 \cdot (x - \hat{x}) + \hat{x} \cdot (p_1 - \hat{p}_1)$$
$$k_1 + p_1 \geqslant p_2 - \hat{x} \cdot \hat{p}_2 - \hat{p}_2 \cdot (x - \hat{x}) - \hat{x} \cdot (p_2 - \hat{p}_2)$$
$$k_2 + p_2 \geqslant \hat{x} \cdot \hat{p}_3 + \hat{p}_3 \cdot (x - \hat{x}) + \hat{x} \cdot (p_3 - \hat{p}_3),$$

and some constraints on the trust region with radius $\delta > 0$, where $\delta' = \delta + 1$:

$$\hat{p}_0 / \delta' \geqslant p_0 \geqslant \hat{p}_0 \cdot \delta', \quad \hat{p}_1 / \delta' \geqslant p_1 \geqslant \hat{p}_1 \cdot \delta', \quad \hat{p}_2 / \delta' \geqslant p_2 \geqslant \hat{p}_2 \cdot \delta', \quad \text{and } \hat{x} / \delta' \geqslant x \geqslant \hat{x} \cdot \delta'.$$

Integration with Probabilistic Model Checking. These methods can ensure the correctness of the solution only when the initial point is feasible, which amounts to solving the parameter synthesis problem. Thus, this assumption cannot be made. Instead, we employ the following scheme. A PMC step is integrated into the SCP approach, see details in [30] to verify whether the instantiated pMC by the solutions for x, $v = \text{res}(x)$, obtained from the LP improves upon the previous instantiation. If indeed the computed reachability probability from the initial state (by convention: $\text{res}(p)_0$) increases over the result (β) from the previous iteration, then these values are used in the next iteration. Otherwise, the radius of the trust region is contracted (by a factor $\gamma < 1$) and the LP is solved again. If the trust region becomes too large ($> \omega$), we may have hit a local optimum and restart. A schematic overview of the resulting iterative procedure is given in Fig. 15. Trust region methods converge under regularisation assumptions such as Lipschitz continuity for the gradients of the functions in the objective and constraints. These conditions are satisfied for our QCQP formulation.

What is Different in CCP? Above, we outlined the SCP approach from Fig. 13. The figure also mentions the CCP procedure, which approximates the QCQP using a series of convex programs rather than a series of linear programs. The main trick is to write the quadratic terms as a sum of a convex and a concave part, and then to linearise the concave part. Contrary to the SCP approach, this construction ensures that the constraints all (in some sense) overapproximate the original solution, and thus that (whenever the penalty variables are assigned to zero) a solution to the convexified QCQP is a solution to the original QCQP.

Experimental Evaluation. Experiments [30] on several benchmarks indicate that the SCP-PMC technique can solve feasibility for pMCs with hundreds of thousands of states and tens of thousands of parameters. Why not use plain SCP? The integration of PMC techniques yields an improvement of multiple orders of magnitude in run time compared to plain SCP, and guarantees the solution's correctness.

6   Controller Synthesis Under Partial Observability

As indicated in the introduction of this survey, the feasibility problem for parametric MCs—find a parameter instantiation satisfying reachability objective φ— is equivalent to the finite-memory controller synthesis problem for φ in POMDPs. A POMDP is in fact a finite-state MDP in which to each state a set of observations is associated. States with the same observations have the same set of enabled actions.

A policy for a POMDP, e.g., to maximise the probability to eventually reach a given state, has to base its decisions on the sequence of observations seen so far. This contrasts policies for MDPs that have the sequence of states visited so far at their disposal to make a decision. Deciding whether there exists an observation-based policy satisfying an infinite-horizon reachability specification φ is undecidable [61]. Optimal policies need infinite memory. For computational tractability, policies are therefore often restricted to finite memory and are randomised: an enabled action is taken with some probability. Let us for simplicity restrict ourselves to memory-less (aka: positional) policies. These policies have memory size one.

Theorem 4. *[52] The decision problem whether there exists a memory-less policy for a POMDP satisfying φ is polynomial-time equivalent to the feasibility checking problem for φ on a corresponding pMC.*

Together with Theorem 1, this yields that finding a policy for a POMDP satisfying φ is ETR-complete. This improves the known complexity results for the POMDP controller synthesis decision problem: being NP-hard, SQRT-SUM-hard and being in PSPACE [81]. How to obtain a corresponding pMC? One can obtain a pMC for a POMDP under an arbitrary randomised memory-less policy in a simple way. The topology of the pMC and POMDP are identical. The parametric transition probabilities in the pMC are obtained from the (unknown) probabilities to select actions in the POMDP by an arbitrary randomised policy. The following example illustrates this for a memory-less policy.

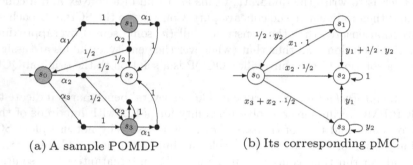

(a) A sample POMDP   (b) Its corresponding pMC

Fig. 16. The connection between POMDPs and pMCs

Example 13. Figure 16a depicts a sample POMDP where colors indicate the observations at a state, and actions are indicated by α_i. Now consider the following memory-less randomised policy. In any red colored state, it takes action α_1 with probability y_1, and action α_2 with probability y_2. At any blue colored state, action α_i is taken with probability x_i. This perspective directly yields the pMC of Fig. 16b.

The connection and construction for memory-less policies can be extended to finite-memory controllers. We employ *randomised finite-state controllers (FSCs)* [67], that are essentially extensions of Moore machines. A POMDP satisfies φ under some k-FSC (an FSC with k memory states) if and only if a POMDP that is obtained by a k-*unfolding* of the original POMDP satisfies φ under a memory-less policy. This unfolding can be viewed as the synchronous product construction of the POMDP and the k-FSC. The induced pMC of the unfolded POMDP has a state space that is linear in k and its number of parameters is quadratic in k and linear in the total number of observations as well as the maximal number of actions over all observations.

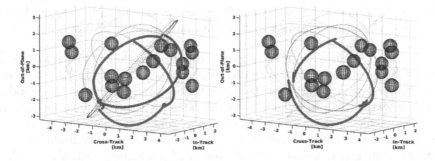

Fig. 17. Satellite trajectories obtained by pMC feasibility checking

A Satellite Collision Avoidance Example. We consider a swarm of satellites following circular orbits with a radius of 7728 km. A satellite can follow its current trajectory with no fuel usage. A trajectory is discretised in numerous (7200) time steps. Based on regularly obtained observations, at every observation the satellite can either stay in its current trajectory or can switch to a close ($\leqslant 250$ km apart) trajectory. In total 36 trajectories are possible. The objective is to compute a switching policy that ensures the satellite to avoid collisions with other objects with high (0.995) probability. The POMDP for this scenario ranges from 6K states and a few hundred observations for $k = 0$ (memory-less) to 288K states and thousands of observations for $k = 5$. The feasibility of the resulting pMC is analysed using the SCP-PMC approach from Sect. 5.4. Figure 17 indicates the obtained policies for a memory-less policy (left) and a policy with memory size five (right) obtained in about 20 s and five minutes of computation time respectively. The initial satellite position is indicated by a fat red circle. The black spheres represent the obstacles to be avoided. The average length of the trajectory with the finite-memory policy is about half the length for the for the memory-less policy.

7   Epilogue

Finally, we present some interesting research directions on parameter synthesis along with some first results in these directions.

Monotonicity Checking. It is often the case that perturbing parameter values has a monotonic influence on the induced reachability probability. Consider, e.g., a network protocol where increasing the channel quality typically decreases the protocol's packet drop rate. Increasing parameter values that encode the reliability of hardware components will typically increase the system's reliability. The decision problem whether the reachability probability function is monotonic in a given parameter is however ETR-hard [77]. Nevertheless, checking sufficient properties on the topology of the pMC yields effective methods to establish monotonicity [77]. Whenever monotonicity (in some parameter) is established, region verification and feasibility checking become significantly cheaper. In general, however, the overhead of first establishing monotonicity does not always pay off.

Recently, [78] intertwined the region verification method outlined in Sect. 5.2 with establishing monotonicity (within that region). The main benefit is that when the over-approximation of the region verification is too coarse, the obtained bounds from the verification help to establish monotonicity whereas on the other hand monotonicity results simplify the refinement loop in region verification. This yields an effective method to solve the *optimal*[9] feasibility problem.

When assuming monotonicity, hill climbing (gradient descent, GD) methods for feasibility checking perform especially well: the optimal value will be in a corner of the parameter space and the GD methods will accelerate sampling towards that corner. We furthermore observe that the performance here neither requires establishing monotonicity a priori, nor does it require monotonicity in all parameters. The key step to enable GD methods is to efficiently compute the gradient. The recent paper [76] shows that this is possible and additionally empirically compares various GD methods in the context of feasibility checking.

Transfer to Other Models. Various approaches in this survey carry over to parametric MDPs[10]. This applies e.g., to complexity results for feasibility, parameter lifting, and mathematical optimisation for feasibility. Various works consider even richer models. In particular, the methods described here can be extended towards parametric probabilistic timed automata [43] and to controller synthesis for uncertain POMDPs, see below. Similarly, there exist various approaches for parametric continuous-time MCs, see, e.g., [16,18,39] and parameter synthesis has been applied to stochastic population models [41] and to accelerate solving hierarchical MDPs [54].

Beyond Markov models, probabilistic graphical models in general and Bayesian networks in particular are widespread to describe complex conditional probability distributions. Recent work [72,73] shows that ideas and methods for parameter synthesis in Markov chains as described in this survey significantly improve upon existing methods for parametric Bayesian networks [21]. Vice versa, some inference techniques do yield interesting alternatives for the analysis of (finite-horizon properties in) pMCs [46].

Synthesis techniques explained in this survey are also used for stochastic hybrid systems. The approach advocated in [65] takes a parametric stochastic differential equation (SDE) and a specification φ, computes a parametric formal abstraction, yielding a (parametric) abstract model, and synthesises parameters on the abstract model in order to satisfy φ for the SDE. The abstraction can be iteratively refined to increase its precision.

---

[9] In fact, ε-optimal feasibility, i.e., finding a parameter instantiation that achieves the maximal or minimal reachability probability up to a given accuracy $\varepsilon > 0$.

[10] Solution functions for pMDPs are challenging, but can be thought of as the maximum over the solution functions for the induced pMCs.

Parameter synthesis has recently also been considered for the richer type of probabilistic hyper-properties [1], properties that are relevant in e.g., security.

Topology Synthesis. The methods presented here are tailored towards continuous parameter values with a continuous solution function (which means that most methods assume graph-preserving regions or acyclic pMCs). A related setting studies discrete parameters and varying topologies. Such settings naturally occur when synthesising implementations of probabilistic programs and controllers in probabilistic settings. In a nutshell, methods rely either on abstraction-refinement [20], similar to Sect. 5.2, or on inductive synthesis [19] inspired by ideas such as programming-by-example and program synthesis. These two methods can be efficiently combined [2]. Despite a slightly different focus, the integration of the discrete and continuous setting seems a natural next step.

Variations. Beyond the problem statements discussed in this paper, there are various related problem statements.

Robust Policies. For parametric MDPs, one can either quantify:

- (*robust policies*) first over the policies and then over the parameters, or
- (*robust parameters*) first over the parameters and then over the policies.

The generalisation of the approaches in this paper consider the latter. While some ideas carry over, there are some differences. Furthermore, finding memory-less robust policies is theoretically harder than finding robust parameters and, in general, optimal robust policies require memory [3,53]. We remark that the notion of robustness itself can also be considered on pMCs, using, e.g., perturbation analysis [23].

Interval and Other Uncertainty Models. Many models assume a more local notion of uncertainty in transition probabilities. Typically, the verification problem for such models aims at robustness against all probability distributions within the uncertainty sets; this may also mean robust policies as discussed above. The transitions of *uncertain MCs or MDPs* are equipped with, e.g., *probability intervals, likelihood functions*, or form even more general uncertainty sets [10,38,59,63,68,84]. For a detailed handling of different types of uncertainty sets, we refer to [83]. Extensions to uncertain POMDPs also exist [31,79].

Distributions over Parameters. Rather than assuming the best or worst case for parameter values, one can equip parameters with a parameter distribution [3]. For pMCs, this assumption then enables sampling-based approaches that yield probably-approximately-correctness (PAC) style guarantees [4]. Finally, one may integrate Bayesian updates on parameter distributions with the analysis of pMCs [66]. For parametric continous-time MCs, both scenario-based approaches [5] and a variety of approaches around Gaussian processes exist [12,13].

Model Repair and Optimisation. Parameter synthesis plays an important role in model repair [11,64]: how can the transition probabilities in a given parameterless MC that refutes a given specification φ be changed such that an MC is obtained satisfying φ? Model repair reduces to a feasibility checking problem. To deal with large state spaces, model repair has been combined with abstraction [22]. Optimal feasibility has been applied to find the optimal bias of coin flips used in self-stabilisation algorithms for distributed systems [82].

Acknowledgements. We thank all our co-authors in the work(s) surveyed in this paper: Erika Ábrahám, Christel Baier, Bernd Becker, Harold Bruintjes, Florian Corzilius, Murat Cubuktepe, Christian Hensel, Lisa Hutschenreiter, Joachim Klein, Guillermo Pérez, Tim Quatmann, Ufuk Topcu, Matthias Volk, Ralf Wimmer, Tobias Winkler and Leonore Winterer. We thank Bahare Salmani, Jip Spel, and Tobias Winkler as well as the reviewers of this volume for their thoughtful feedback on a draft version of this survey.

References

1. Ábrahám, E., Bartocci, E., Bonakdarpour, B., Dobe, O.: Parameter synthesis for probabilistic hyperproperties. In: LPAR. EPiC Series in Computing, vol. 73, pp. 12–31. EasyChair (2020)
2. Andriushchenko, R., Češka, M., Junges, S., Katoen, J.-P.: Inductive synthesis for probabilistic programs reaches new horizons. In: Groote, J.F., Larsen, K.G. (eds.) TACAS 2021. LNCS, vol. 12651, pp. 191–209. Springer, Cham (2021). https://doi.org/10.1007/978-3-030-72016-2_11
3. Arming, S., Bartocci, E., Chatterjee, K., Katoen, J.-P., Sokolova, A.: Parameter-independent strategies for pMDPs via POMDPs. In: McIver, A., Horvath, A. (eds.) QEST 2018. LNCS, vol. 11024, pp. 53–70. Springer, Cham (2018). https://doi.org/10.1007/978-3-319-99154-2_4
4. Badings, T., Cubuktepe, M., Jansen, N., et al.: Scenario-based verification of uncertain parametric MDPs. Int. J. Softw. Tools Technol. Transf. **24**, 803–819 (2022). https://doi.org/10.1007/s10009-022-00673-z
5. Badings, T.S., Jansen, N., Junges, S., Stoelinga, M., Volk, M.: Sampling-based verification of CTMCs with uncertain rates. In: CAV (2022, to appear)
6. Baier, C., de Alfaro, L., Forejt, V., Kwiatkowska, M.: Model checking probabilistic systems. In: Clarke, E., Henzinger, T., Veith, H., Bloem, R. (eds.) Handbook of Model Checking, pp. 963–999. Springer, Cham (2018). https://doi.org/10.1007/978-3-319-10575-8_28
7. Baier, C., Hensel, C., Hutschenreiter, L., Junges, S., Katoen, J.P., Klein, J.: Parametric Markov chains: PCTL complexity and fraction-free Gaussian elimination. Inf. Comput. **272**, 104504 (2020)
8. Baier, C., Hermanns, H., Katoen, J.-P.: The 10,000 facets of MDP model checking. In: Steffen, B., Woeginger, G. (eds.) Computing and Software Science. LNCS, vol. 10000, pp. 420–451. Springer, Cham (2019). https://doi.org/10.1007/978-3-319-91908-9_21
9. Baier, C., Katoen, J.P.: Principles of Model Checking. MIT Press, Cambridge (2008)

10. Bart, A., Delahaye, B., Fournier, P., Lime, D., Monfroy, E., Truchet, C.: Reachability in parametric interval Markov chains using constraints. Theor. Comput. Sci. **747**, 48–74 (2018)
11. Bartocci, E., Grosu, R., Katsaros, P., Ramakrishnan, C.R., Smolka, S.A.: Model repair for probabilistic systems. In: Abdulla, P.A., Leino, K.R.M. (eds.) TACAS 2011. LNCS, vol. 6605, pp. 326–340. Springer, Heidelberg (2011). https://doi.org/10.1007/978-3-642-19835-9_30
12. Bortolussi, L., Milios, D., Sanguinetti, G.: Smoothed model checking for uncertain continuous-time Markov chains. Inf. Comput. **247**, 235–253 (2016)
13. Bortolussi, L., Silvetti, S.: Bayesian statistical parameter synthesis for linear temporal properties of stochastic models. In: Beyer, D., Huisman, M. (eds.) TACAS 2018. LNCS, vol. 10806, pp. 396–413. Springer, Cham (2018). https://doi.org/10.1007/978-3-319-89963-3_23
14. Boyd, S., Vandenberghe, L.: Convex Optimization. Cambridge University Press, Cambridge (2004)
15. Brim, L., Češka, M., Dražan, S., Šafránek, D.: Exploring parameter space of stochastic biochemical systems using quantitative model checking. In: Sharygina, N., Veith, H. (eds.) CAV 2013. LNCS, vol. 8044, pp. 107–123. Springer, Heidelberg (2013). https://doi.org/10.1007/978-3-642-39799-8_7
16. Calinescu, R., Ceska, M., Gerasimou, S., Kwiatkowska, M., Paoletti, N.: Efficient synthesis of robust models for stochastic systems. J. Syst. Softw. **143**, 140–158 (2018)
17. Canny, J.F.: Some algebraic and geometric computations in PSPACE. In: STOC, pp. 460–467. ACM (1988)
18. Češka, M., Dannenberg, F., Kwiatkowska, M., Paoletti, N.: Precise parameter synthesis for stochastic biochemical systems. In: Mendes, P., Dada, J.O., Smallbone, K. (eds.) CMSB 2014. LNCS, vol. 8859, pp. 86–98. Springer, Cham (2014). https://doi.org/10.1007/978-3-319-12982-2_7
19. Češka, M., Hensel, C., Junges, S., Katoen, J.-P.: Counterexample-driven synthesis for probabilistic program sketches. In: ter Beek, M.H., McIver, A., Oliveira, J.N. (eds.) FM 2019. LNCS, vol. 11800, pp. 101–120. Springer, Cham (2019). https://doi.org/10.1007/978-3-030-30942-8_8
20. Češka, M., Jansen, N., Junges, S., Katoen, J.-P.: Shepherding hordes of Markov chains. In: Vojnar, T., Zhang, L. (eds.) TACAS 2019. LNCS, vol. 11428, pp. 172–190. Springer, Cham (2019). https://doi.org/10.1007/978-3-030-17465-1_10
21. Chan, H., Darwiche, A.: When do numbers really matter? J. Artif. Intell. Res. **17**, 265–287 (2002)
22. Chatzieleftheriou, G., Katsaros, P.: Abstract model repair for probabilistic systems. Inf. Comput. **259**(1), 142–160 (2018)
23. Chen, T., Feng, Y., Rosenblum, D.S., Su, G.: Perturbation analysis in verification of discrete-time Markov chains. In: Baldan, P., Gorla, D. (eds.) CONCUR 2014. LNCS, vol. 8704, pp. 218–233. Springer, Heidelberg (2014). https://doi.org/10.1007/978-3-662-44584-6_16
24. Chen, T., Hahn, E.M., Han, T., Kwiatkowska, M., Qu, H., Zhang, L.: Model repair for Markov decision processes. In: TASE, pp. 85–92. IEEE Computer Society (2013)
25. Chen, X., Niu, L., Yuan, Y.: Optimality conditions and a smoothing trust region Newton method for non-Lipschitz optimization. SIAM J. Optimiz. **23**(3), 1528–1552 (2013)
26. Chonev, V.: Reachability in augmented interval Markov chains. CoRR abs/1701.02996 (2017)

27. Clarke, E., Grumberg, O., Jha, S., Lu, Y., Veith, H.: Counterexample-guided abstraction refinement. In: Emerson, E.A., Sistla, A.P. (eds.) CAV 2000. LNCS, vol. 1855, pp. 154–169. Springer, Heidelberg (2000). https://doi.org/10.1007/10722167_15

28. Cousineau, D.: Fitting the three-parameter Weibull distribution: review and evaluation of existing and new methods. IEEE DEIS **16**(1), 281–288 (2009)

29. Cubuktepe, M., Jansen, N., Junges, S., Katoen, J.-P., Topcu, U.: Synthesis in pMDPs: a tale of 1001 parameters. In: Lahiri, S.K., Wang, C. (eds.) ATVA 2018. LNCS, vol. 11138, pp. 160–176. Springer, Cham (2018). https://doi.org/10.1007/978-3-030-01090-4_10

30. Cubuktepe, M., Jansen, N., Junges, S., Katoen, J.P., Topcu, U.: Convex optimization for parameter synthesis in MDPs. IEEE Trans. Autom. Control (2022)

31. Cubuktepe, M., Jansen, N., Junges, S., Marandi, A., Suilen, M., Topcu, U.: Robust finite-state controllers for uncertain POMDPs. In: AAAI, pp. 11792–11800. AAAI Press (2021)

32. Daws, C.: Symbolic and parametric model checking of discrete-time Markov chains. In: Liu, Z., Araki, K. (eds.) ICTAC 2004. LNCS, vol. 3407, pp. 280–294. Springer, Heidelberg (2005). https://doi.org/10.1007/978-3-540-31862-0_21

33. Dehnert, C., et al.: PROPhESY: a PRObabilistic ParamEter SYnthesis tool. In: Kroening, D., Păsăreanu, C.S. (eds.) CAV 2015. LNCS, vol. 9206, pp. 214–231. Springer, Cham (2015). https://doi.org/10.1007/978-3-319-21690-4_13

34. Esparza, J., Hoffmann, P., Saha, R.: Polynomial analysis algorithms for free choice probabilistic workflow nets. Perform. Eval. **117**, 104–129 (2017)

35. Fang, X., Calinescu, R., Gerasimou, S., Alhwikem, F.: Fast parametric model checking through model fragmentation. In: ICSE, pp. 835–846. IEEE (2021)

36. Filieri, A., Tamburrelli, G., Ghezzi, C.: Supporting self-adaptation via quantitative verification and sensitivity analysis at run time. IEEE Trans. Softw. Eng. **42**(1), 75–99 (2016)

37. Gainer, P., Hahn, E.M., Schewe, S.: Accelerated model checking of parametric Markov chains. In: Lahiri, S.K., Wang, C. (eds.) ATVA 2018. LNCS, vol. 11138, pp. 300–316. Springer, Cham (2018). https://doi.org/10.1007/978-3-030-01090-4_18

38. Givan, R., Leach, S.M., Dean, T.L.: Bounded-parameter Markov decision processes. Artif. Intell. **122**(1–2), 71–109 (2000)

39. Gouberman, A., Siegle, M., Tati, B.: Markov chains with perturbed rates to absorption: theory and application to model repair. Perform. Eval. **130**, 32–50 (2019)

40. Hahn, E.M., Hermanns, H., Zhang, L.: Probabilistic reachability for parametric Markov models. STTT **13**(1), 3–19 (2010)

41. Hajnal, M., Nouvian, M., Petrov, T., Šafránek, D.: Data-informed parameter synthesis for population Markov chains. In: Bortolussi, L., Sanguinetti, G. (eds.) CMSB 2019. LNCS, vol. 11773, pp. 383–386. Springer, Cham (2019). https://doi.org/10.1007/978-3-030-31304-3_32

42. Han, Y.: State elimination heuristics for short regular expressions. Fundam. Inform. **128**(4), 445–462 (2013)

43. Hartmanns, A., Katoen, J.-P., Kohlen, B., Spel, J.: Tweaking the odds in probabilistic timed automata. In: Abate, A., Marin, A. (eds.) QEST 2021. LNCS, vol. 12846, pp. 39–58. Springer, Cham (2021). https://doi.org/10.1007/978-3-030-85172-9_3

44. Haselman, M., Hauck, S.: The future of integrated circuits: a survey of nanoelectronics. Proc. IEEE **98**(1), 11–38 (2010)

45. Herman, T.: Probabilistic self-stabilization. Inf. Process. Lett. **35**(2), 63–67 (1990)

46. Holtzen, S., Junges, S., Vazquez-Chanlatte, M., Millstein, T., Seshia, S.A., Van den Broeck, G.: Model checking finite-horizon Markov chains with probabilistic inference. In: Silva, A., Leino, K.R.M. (eds.) CAV 2021. LNCS, vol. 12760, pp. 577–601. Springer, Cham (2021). https://doi.org/10.1007/978-3-030-81688-9_27
47. Hopcroft, J.E., Motwani, R., Ullman, J.D.: Introduction to Automata Theory, Languages, and Computation. Addison-Wesley (2003)
48. Hutschenreiter, L., Baier, C., Klein, J.: Parametric Markov chains: PCTL complexity and fraction-free Gaussian elimination. In: GandALF. EPTCS, vol. 256, pp. 16–30 (2017)
49. Jansen, N., et al.: Accelerating parametric probabilistic verification. In: Norman, G., Sanders, W. (eds.) QEST 2014. LNCS, vol. 8657, pp. 404–420. Springer, Cham (2014). https://doi.org/10.1007/978-3-319-10696-0_31
50. Junges, S.: Parameter synthesis in Markov models. Dissertation, RWTH Aachen University (2020)
51. Junges, S., et al.: Parameter synthesis for Markov models. CoRR abs/1903.07993 (2019)
52. Junges, S., et al.: Finite-state controllers of POMDPs using parameter synthesis. In: UAI, pp. 519–529. AUAI Press (2018)
53. Junges, S., Katoen, J.P., Pérez, G.A., Winkler, T.: The complexity of reachability in parametric Markov decision processes. J. Comput. Syst. Sci. **119**, 183–210 (2021)
54. Junges, S., Spaan, M.T.J.: Abstraction-refinement for hierarchical probabilistic models. In: Shoham, S., Vizel, Y. (eds.) CAV 2022. LNCS, vol. 13371, pp. 102–123. Springer, Cham (2022). https://doi.org/10.1007/978-3-031-13185-1_6
55. Katoen, J.P.: The probabilistic model checking landscape. In: LICS, pp. 31–45. ACM (2016)
56. Knuth, D., Yao, A.: The complexity of nonuniform random number generation (chap). In: Algorithms and Complexity: New Directions and Recent Results. Academic Press (1976)
57. Kochenderfer, M.J.: Decision Making Under Uncertainty: Theory and Application. MIT Press, Cambridge (2015)
58. Kozine, I., Utkin, L.V.: Interval-valued finite Markov chains. Reliab. Comput. **8**(2), 97–113 (2002)
59. Krak, T.E., T'Joens, N., Bock, J.D.: Hitting times and probabilities for imprecise Markov chains. In: ISIPTA. PMLR, vol. 103, pp. 265–275. PMLR (2019)
60. Kwiatkowska, M., Norman, G., Parker, D.: PRISM 4.0: verification of probabilistic real-time systems. In: Gopalakrishnan, G., Qadeer, S. (eds.) CAV 2011. LNCS, vol. 6806, pp. 585–591. Springer, Heidelberg (2011). https://doi.org/10.1007/978-3-642-22110-1_47
61. Madani, O., Hanks, S., Condon, A.: On the undecidability of probabilistic planning and related stochastic optimization problems. Artif. Intell. **147**(1–2), 5–34 (2003)
62. Mao, Y., Szmuk, M., Xu, X., Acikmese, B.: Successive Convexification: A Superlinearly Convergent Algorithm for Non-convex Optimal Control Problems. arXiv preprint arXiv:1804.06539 (2018)
63. Nilim, A., El Ghaoui, L.: Robust control of Markov decision processes with uncertain transition matrices. Oper. Res. **53**(5), 780–798 (2005)
64. Pathak, S., Ábrahám, E., Jansen, N., Tacchella, A., Katoen, J.-P.: A greedy approach for the efficient repair of stochastic models. In: Havelund, K., Holzmann, G., Joshi, R. (eds.) NFM 2015. LNCS, vol. 9058, pp. 295–309. Springer, Cham (2015). https://doi.org/10.1007/978-3-319-17524-9_21

65. Peruffo, A., Abate, A.: Formal abstraction and synthesis of parametric stochastic processes. In: Dima, C., Shirmohammadi, M. (eds.) FORMATS 2021. LNCS, vol. 12860, pp. 135–153. Springer, Cham (2021). https://doi.org/10.1007/978-3-030-85037-1_9

66. Polgreen, E., Wijesuriya, V.B., Haesaert, S., Abate, A.: Automated experiment design for data-efficient verification of parametric Markov decision processes. In: Bertrand, N., Bortolussi, L. (eds.) QEST 2017. LNCS, vol. 10503, pp. 259–274. Springer, Cham (2017). https://doi.org/10.1007/978-3-319-66335-7_16

67. Poupart, P., Boutilier, C.: Bounded finite state controllers. In: NIPS, pp. 823–830. MIT Press (2003)

68. Puggelli, A., Li, W., Sangiovanni-Vincentelli, A.L., Seshia, S.A.: Polynomial-time verification of PCTL properties of MDPs with convex uncertainties. In: Sharygina, N., Veith, H. (eds.) CAV 2013. LNCS, vol. 8044, pp. 527–542. Springer, Heidelberg (2013). https://doi.org/10.1007/978-3-642-39799-8_35

69. Puterman, M.L.: Markov Decision Processes: Discrete Stochastic Dynamic Programming. Wiley (1994)

70. Quatmann, T., Dehnert, C., Jansen, N., Junges, S., Katoen, J.-P.: Parameter synthesis for Markov models: faster than ever. In: Artho, C., Legay, A., Peled, D. (eds.) ATVA 2016. LNCS, vol. 9938, pp. 50–67. Springer, Cham (2016). https://doi.org/10.1007/978-3-319-46520-3_4

71. Russell, S.J., Norvig, P.: Artificial Intelligence - A Modern Approach (3. internat. edn.). Pearson Education (2010)

72. Salmani, B., Katoen, J.-P.: Fine-tuning the odds in Bayesian networks. In: Vejnarová, J., Wilson, N. (eds.) ECSQARU 2021. LNCS (LNAI), vol. 12897, pp. 268–283. Springer, Cham (2021). https://doi.org/10.1007/978-3-030-86772-0_20

73. Salmani, B., Katoen, J.P.: Automatically finding the right probabilities in Bayesian networks. arXiv preprint (2022, to appear)

74. Skulj, D.: Discrete time Markov chains with interval probabilities. Int. J. Approx. Reason. **50**(8), 1314–1329 (2009)

75. Spaan, M.T.J.: Partially observable Markov decision processes. In: Wiering, M., van Otterlo, M. (eds.) Reinforcement Learning. ALO, vol. 12, pp. 387–414. Springer, Heidelberg (2012). https://doi.org/10.1007/978-3-642-27645-3_12

76. Heck, L., Spel, J., Junges, S., Moerman, J., Katoen, J.-P.: Gradient-descent for randomized controllers under partial observability. In: Finkbeiner, B., Wies, T. (eds.) VMCAI 2022. LNCS, vol. 13182, pp. 127–150. Springer, Cham (2022). https://doi.org/10.1007/978-3-030-94583-1_7

77. Spel, J., Junges, S., Katoen, J.-P.: Are parametric Markov chains monotonic? In: Chen, Y.-F., Cheng, C.-H., Esparza, J. (eds.) ATVA 2019. LNCS, vol. 11781, pp. 479–496. Springer, Cham (2019). https://doi.org/10.1007/978-3-030-31784-3_28

78. Spel, J., Junges, S., Katoen, J.-P.: Finding provably optimal Markov chains. In: TACAS 2021. LNCS, vol. 12651, pp. 173–190. Springer, Cham (2021). https://doi.org/10.1007/978-3-030-72016-2_10

79. Suilen, M., Jansen, N., Cubuktepe, M., Topcu, U.: Robust policy synthesis for uncertain POMDPs via convex optimization. In: IJCAI, pp. 4113–4120 (2020). ijcai.org

80. Vardi, M.Y.: Automatic verification of probabilistic concurrent finite-state programs. In: FOCS, pp. 327–338. IEEE Computer Society (1985)

81. Vlassis, N., Littman, M.L., Barber, D.: On the computational complexity of stochastic controller optimization in POMDPs. ACM Trans. Comput. Theory **4**(4), 12:1–12:8 (2012)

82. Volk, M., Bonakdarpour, B., Katoen, J.P., Aflaki, S.: Synthesizing optimal bias in randomized self-stabilization. Distrib. Comput. **35**(1), 37–57 (2022)
83. Wiesemann, W., Kuhn, D., Rustem, B.: Robust Markov decision processes. Math. Oper. Res. **38**(1), 153–183 (2013)
84. Wolff, E.M., Topcu, U., Murray, R.M.: Robust control of uncertain Markov decision processes with temporal logic specifications. In: CDC, pp. 3372–3379. IEEE (2012)
85. Yuan, Y.: Recent advances in trust region algorithms. Math. Program. **151**(1), 249–281 (2015). https://doi.org/10.1007/s10107-015-0893-2

Convex Lattice Equation Systems

Giorgio Bacci[✉], Giovanni Bacci, Mathias Claus Jensen, and Kim G. Larsen

Department of Computer Science, Aalborg University, Aalborg, Denmark
grbacci@cs.aau.dk

Abstract. In this paper we revisit the paradigm shift *"From Boolean to Quantitative Notions of Correctness"* proposed by Henzinger more than 10 years ago. In particular, we present the notion of Convex Lattice Equation Systems as a universal framework for encoding and inferring behavioural metrics between quantitative system behaviours. We demonstrate how the framework may be applied to infer bounds on values of stochastic games and distances between timed systems.

1 Introduction

In the seminal talk *"From Boolean to Quantitative Notions of Correctness"* [20] at POPL10, Henzinger challenged the classical Boolean treatment of systems and properties: e.g. a property is either true or false of a system. In particular, within the well-established research field of concurrent and reactive systems, so-called implementation verification involves checking the behavioural equivalence (or preorder) between implementations and specifications. This approach requires a suitable model of the system and specification, as well as procedure for checking whether the two are related with respect to the given equivalence or preorder. And again the verdict is either true or false.

The *"Embedded Design Challenge"* [22] presented by Henzinger and Sifakis in 2006, emphasizes the importance of quantitative models in order to capture in an adequate manner physical constraints, timing requirements and probabilistic uncertainties, etc. Even in this quantitative setting, the Boolean view has been prevalent: two timed automata are either (timed) bisimilar [38] or not, two Markov chains are either (probabilistic) bisimilar [27] or not. There has been some research into better describing inconsistent models of systems by extending the *true-false* dichotomy to being part of some larger lattice structure. E.g. Easterbrook and Chechik develop a general framework for reasoning about such inconsistent viewpoints using multi-valued logics [16] and Kupferman and Lustig give a notion of *latticed* simulation for multi-valued Kripke structures [24].

The paradigm shift to quantitative notions of correctness, as advocated by Henzinger [20], was motivated by the need of a more refined view, where a system if not fully correct may still be correct up to a certain degree, and where two systems if not fully equivalent may still be close according to a behavioural distance. The proposed paradigm shift to quantitative verdicts has been pursued by several researchers, leading – among others – to notions of timed bisimulation

J.-F. Raskin and K. Chatterjee (Eds.): Principles of Systems Design, LNCS 13660, pp. 438–455, 2022.
https://doi.org/10.1007/978-3-031-22337-2_21

$$\mathbf{A_1}\ \dfrac{x \in \Gamma}{\Gamma \vdash_\varepsilon x} \qquad \mathbf{A_2}\ \dfrac{}{\Gamma \vdash_\varepsilon tt}$$

(a) BES $\mathcal{E}$

$x_1 = x_1 \wedge x_1$

$x_2 = x_1 \vee x_3$

$x_3 = ff$

$$\mathbf{A_3}\ \dfrac{\Gamma, x \vdash_\varepsilon \phi}{\Gamma \vdash_\varepsilon x}\ x =_\varepsilon \phi, x \notin \Gamma$$

$$\mathbf{A_4}\ \dfrac{\Gamma \vdash_\varepsilon x \quad \Gamma \vdash_\varepsilon y}{\Gamma \vdash_\varepsilon x \wedge y}$$

$$\mathbf{A_5}\ \dfrac{\Gamma \vdash_\varepsilon x}{\Gamma \vdash_\varepsilon x \vee y} \qquad \mathbf{A_6}\ \dfrac{\Gamma \vdash_\varepsilon y}{\Gamma \vdash_\varepsilon x \vee y}$$

(b) Proof System $\mathcal{A}$

$$\dfrac{\dfrac{x_1 \in \{x_1\}}{\{x_1\} \vdash x_1}\ \mathbf{A_1} \quad \dfrac{x_1 \in \{x_1\}}{\{x_1\} \vdash x_1}\ \mathbf{A_1}}{\dfrac{\{x_1\} \vdash_\varepsilon x_1 \wedge x_1}{\emptyset \vdash_\varepsilon x_1}\ \mathbf{A_3}}\ \mathbf{A_4}$$

(c) Proof of $\vdash_\varepsilon x$

Fig. 1. A BES, the proof system $\mathcal{A}$ and proof of $\vdash_\varepsilon x$ from [26]

distances [21,32,35], weighted bisimulation distances [17,25], and probabilistic bisimulation metrics [14,15]. Here a key question has been the design of complete proof systems respectively effective procedures for inferring respectively computing the distance between (timed, weighted or probabilistic) models, e.g. [4–6,10] [7,8]. However, in this effort one is facing the very same challenge as for the corresponding Boolean equivalence checking problems: the *state-space explosion problem*. That is, in many cases enumeration of the full state-space may be infeasible. To deal with this problem, the development of *on-the-fly* algorithms have been made in the hope that answers about the degree of equivalence between systems behaviour can be made by exploring only a fraction of the state-space.

The idea of local or on-the-fly model checking was discovered simultaneously and independently by various people in the end of the 1980s s all engaged in making (Boolean) model-checking and equivalence-checking tools for various process algebras and tools (Concurrency Workbench CWB [11], CADP [18], VESAR [1], TAV-EPSILON [9]). In this process, it was realized that a very simple formalism, Boolean Equation Systems (BES), can provide a universal framework for efficiently encoding and solving (essentially) all model-checking and equivalence problems in a local manner. In a BES, a finite number of Boolean variables are defined recursively (maximally or minimally) by Boolean expressions over the variables. Whereas [26] provides a complete proof system and the first local algorithms, the work in [2,29] provides the first optimal (linear-time) local algorithms. See Fig. 1 for a BES, the proof system and its application from [26]. Later extensions and adaptations of BES have been implemented in the tools CADP, muCRL [30] and the educational tool CAAL [3].

Aiming at providing the foundation for a similar universal framework for computing behavioural metrics in a local manner, we introduce in this paper the notion of *Convex Lattice Equation Systems* (CLES). Here, variables $\mathcal{X} = \{x_1, \ldots, x_n\}$ range over values from a convex (complete) lattice (generalizing Boolean as well as a range of numeric domains) and are defined recursively by expressions $\{E_1, \ldots, E_n\}$ over $\mathcal{X}$ involving lattice constructs (join and meet) and convex combinations. We present a sound and complete proof system for checking consistency of statements of the form $E \leq \varepsilon$, where E is an expression over $\mathcal{X}$ and ε is an element from the complete lattice expressing a bound. As for BES, this proof system will provide the basis of a generic on-the-fly algorithm. Finally, we show how values of stochastic games and distances between timed systems may be encoded using CLES over the complete lattices $([0,1], \leq)$ respectively $([0, \infty], \leq)$.

2   Convex Lattice Equation Systems

A *convex (complete) lattice* is a structure $\langle \mathbb{D}, \sqsubseteq, \{+_\alpha \mid \alpha \in [0,1]\} \rangle$ consisting of a complete partial order $(\mathbb{D}, \sqsubseteq)$ (hence, with joins $\bigsqcup D$ and meets $\bigsqcap D$ for arbitrary subsets $D \subseteq \mathbb{D}$) and a convex space $\langle \mathbb{D}, \{+_\alpha \mid \alpha \in [0,1]\} \rangle$, where $w +_\alpha w'$ denotes the binary convex combination of two elements $w, w' \in \mathbb{D}$, subject to the following distributive laws

$$\bigsqcup D +_\alpha w = \bigsqcup \{w' +_\alpha w \mid w' \in D\}$$
$$\bigsqcap D +_\alpha w = \bigsqcap \{w' +_\alpha w \mid w' \in D\}$$

When the partial order and convex structure of $\langle \mathbb{D}, \sqsubseteq, \{+_\alpha \mid \alpha \in [0,1]\} \rangle$ are clear from the context, we will refer to the convex lattice simply as $\mathbb{D}$.

Simple examples of convex lattices are the unit interval $[0,1]$ and the extended non-negative reals $[0, \infty]$, with order $\leq$ and convex combination interpreted as $a +_\alpha b = \alpha a + (1 - \alpha)b$. A less trivial example of convex lattice is the space of convex sets of probability distributions which have been used in the literature to combine non-determinism and probabilistic choice (see e.g. [19,31,36,37]).

Note that, if $\mathbb{D}$ is a convex lattice, also the set $\mathbb{D}^X$ of functions from X to $\mathbb{D}$ can be turned into a convex lattice $\langle \mathbb{D}^X, \dot{\sqsubseteq}, \{\dot{+}_\alpha \mid \alpha \in [0,1]\} \rangle$ by point-wise extension of the order and convex combinator:

$$\dot{\sqsubseteq} = \{(f, g) \mid \forall x \in X. f(x) \sqsubseteq g(x)\}, \qquad (f \dot{+}_\alpha g)(x) = f(x) +_\alpha g(x).$$

Remark 1. Any complete partial order $(\mathbb{D}, \sqsubseteq)$ can be also seen as a (trivial) convex lattice by simply interpreting the convex combination as

$$w +_\alpha w' = w \sqcup w' \quad (\text{for } \alpha \in (0,1)), \qquad w +_1 w' = w, \qquad w +_0 w' = w'.$$

This means that the theory we shall develop in the following sections can be applied also on complete partial orders with no (nontrivial) convex structure.

Hereafter, we fix a convex lattice $\langle \mathbb{D}, \sqsubseteq, \{+_\alpha \mid \alpha \in [0,1]\} \rangle$ and denote by $\top = \bigsqcup \mathbb{D}$ and $\bot = \bigsqcap \mathbb{D}$ its top and bottom elements, respectively.

Convex Lattice Expressions. Let $\mathcal{X}$ be a set of variables. The set $\mathcal{L}_\mathcal{X}$ of *convex lattice expressions* over $\mathcal{X}$ is given by the following grammar:

$$\phi ::= x \mid w \mid \phi_1 \sqcup \phi_2 \mid \phi_1 \sqcap \phi_2 \mid \phi_1 +_\alpha \phi_2.$$

where $x \in \mathcal{X}$, $w \in \mathbb{D}$, and $\alpha \in [0,1]$. We say that an expression is *simple* if it is of the form, w, $x_1 \sqcup x_2$, $x_1 \sqcap x_2$, or $x_1 +_\alpha x_2$, where x_1 and x_2 are variables.

Semantically, we interpret convex lattice expressions with respect to an environment $\rho \colon \mathcal{X} \to \mathbb{D}$ mapping variables to elements in $\mathbb{D}$. Formally, for ρ and environment and ϕ a convex lattice expression we define the value $[\![\phi]\!]\rho \in \mathbb{D}$ inductively on ϕ as follows:

$$[\![x]\!]\rho = \rho(x)$$
$$[\![w]\!]\rho = w$$
$$[\![\phi_1 \sqcup \phi_2]\!]\rho = [\![\phi_1]\!]\rho \sqcup [\![\phi_2]\!]\rho$$
$$[\![\phi_1 \sqcap \phi_2]\!]\rho = [\![\phi_1]\!]\rho \sqcap [\![\phi_2]\!]\rho$$
$$[\![\phi_1 +_\alpha \phi_2]\!]\rho = [\![\phi_1]\!]\rho +_\alpha [\![\phi_2]\!]\rho$$

Example 1. Consider the convex lattice $\langle [0,1], \leq, \{+_\alpha \mid \alpha \in [0,1]\}$, where convex combinations are interpreted as $a +_\alpha b = \alpha a + (1-\alpha)b$. Under the environment $\rho = [x \mapsto 0.2, y \mapsto 0.5]$, the expression $x \sqcap y$, and $(x \sqcup y) +_{0.2} y$ are interpreted as follows

$$[\![x \sqcap y]\!]\rho = \min(0.2, 0.5) = 0.2 \,,$$
$$[\![(x \sqcup y) +_{0.1} y]\!]\rho = 0.1 \cdot \max(0.2, 0.5) + 0.9 \cdot 0.5 = 0.5 \,.$$

The desired semantics of variables is specified recursively through the use of an equation system, which assigns with each variable $x \in \mathcal{X}$ a defining expression.

Definition 1. *A convex lattice equation system (CLES) is a pair $\mathcal{E} = (\mathcal{X}, E)$ where $\mathcal{X}$ is a finite set of variables and $E \colon \mathcal{X} \to \mathcal{L}_{\mathcal{X}}$ is a mapping from variables to expressions over $\mathcal{X}$. We will write $x =_{\mathcal{E}} \phi$ to indicate that $E(x) = \phi$.*

An equation system specifies a semantic requirement to an environment ρ. We say that ρ is a *model* of the equation system $\mathcal{E} = (\mathcal{X}, E)$ if and only if for all $x \in \mathcal{X}$, $[\![x]\!]\rho = [\![E(x)]\!]\rho$.

Example 2. Consider the convex lattice from Example 1. Let $\mathcal{E} = (\{x, y\}, E)$ be the CLES where $E(x) = 0.2 \sqcup (x \sqcap y)$ and $E(y) = (x \sqcup y) +_{0.1} y$. One can verify that, an interpretation ρ is a model of $\mathcal{E}$ whenever $0.2 \leq \rho(x) \leq \rho(y)$.

Given an equation system $\mathcal{E}$, we are interested in checking statements of the form $\phi \leq \varepsilon$, for for $\phi \in \mathcal{L}$ and $\varepsilon \in \mathbb{D}$.

Definition 2 (Consistency). *Let $\mathcal{E} = (\mathcal{X}, E)$ be a CLES. A statement $\phi \leq \varepsilon$ is consistent for $\mathcal{E}$, written $\models_{\mathcal{E}} \phi \leq \varepsilon$, if $[\![\phi]\!]\rho \sqsubseteq \varepsilon$ for some model ρ of $\mathcal{E}$.*

Example 3. Consider the CLES $\mathcal{E}$ from Example 2. The statement $x \sqcap y \leq 0.5$ is consistent for $\mathcal{E}$, and the model $\rho = [x \mapsto 0.2, y \mapsto 0.2]$ is a witnesses for that. In contrast, the statement $x \sqcap y \leq 0.1$ is not consistent for $\mathcal{E}$ because no model ρ of $\mathcal{E}$ satisfies $[\![x \sqcap y]\!]\rho \leq 0.1$.

The models of $\mathcal{E}$ are exactly the fixed points of functional $F_{\mathcal{E}} \colon \mathbb{D}^{\mathcal{X}} \to \mathbb{D}^{\mathcal{X}}$ defined as follows, for $\rho \colon \mathcal{X} \to \mathbb{D}$ an environment and $x \in \mathcal{X}$ a variable:

$$F_{\mathcal{E}}(\rho)(x) = [\![E(x)]\!]\rho \,.$$

$$(A_1) \frac{}{\Gamma \vdash_{\mathcal{E}} \phi \leq \top} \qquad (A_2) \frac{\Gamma \vdash_{\mathcal{E}} \phi \leq \varepsilon'}{\Gamma \vdash_{\mathcal{E}} \phi \leq \varepsilon} \text{ if } \varepsilon' \sqsubseteq \varepsilon$$

$$(A_3) \frac{}{\Gamma \vdash_{\mathcal{E}} x \leq \Gamma(x)} \qquad (A_4) \frac{\Gamma \cup \{x \leq \varepsilon\} \vdash_{\mathcal{E}} \Gamma(x) \sqcap E(x) \leq \varepsilon}{\Gamma \vdash_{\mathcal{E}} x \leq \varepsilon}$$

$$(A_5) \frac{}{\Gamma \vdash_{\mathcal{E}} w \leq w} \qquad (A_6) \frac{\Gamma \vdash_{\mathcal{E}} \phi_1 \leq \varepsilon \quad \Gamma \vdash_{\mathcal{E}} \phi_2 \leq \varepsilon}{\Gamma \vdash_{\mathcal{E}} \phi_1 \sqcup \phi_2 \leq \varepsilon}$$

$$(A_7) \frac{\Gamma \vdash_{\mathcal{E}} \phi_1 \leq \varepsilon_1 \quad \Gamma \vdash_{\mathcal{E}} \phi_2 \leq \varepsilon_2}{\Gamma \vdash_{\mathcal{E}} \phi_1 \sqcap \phi_2 \leq \varepsilon_1 \sqcap \varepsilon_2} \qquad (A_8) \frac{\Gamma \vdash_{\mathcal{E}} \phi_1 \leq \varepsilon_1 \quad \Gamma \vdash_{\mathcal{E}} \phi_2 \leq \varepsilon_2}{\Gamma \vdash_{\mathcal{E}} \phi_1 +_\alpha \phi_2 \leq \varepsilon_1 +_\alpha \varepsilon_2}$$

Fig. 2. The proof system $\mathcal{CL}$ for inferring the (relative) consistency of statements of the form $\phi \leq \varepsilon$ w.r.t. a CLES $\mathcal{E} = (\mathcal{X}, E)$.

It can be shown that $F_{\mathcal{E}}$ is monotone—this is an immediate consequence of the fact that, for all $\phi \in \mathcal{L}_{\mathcal{X}}$, $\rho \stackrel{.}{\sqsubseteq} \rho'$ implies $[\![\phi]\!]\rho \sqsubseteq [\![\phi]\!]\rho'$—therefore, since $\mathbb{D}^{\mathcal{X}}$ is a complete lattice, by Knaster-Tarski's fixed point theorem, the set of fixed points of $F_{\mathcal{E}}$ is also a complete lattice. In particular, there are least and greatest fixed points, denoted $\mu F_{\mathcal{E}}$ and $\nu F_{\mathcal{E}}$, respectively, and a model of $\mathcal{E}$ always exists. It is therefore clear that $\models_{\mathcal{E}} \phi \leq \varepsilon$ if and only if $[\![\phi]\!]\mu F_{\mathcal{E}} \sqsubseteq \varepsilon$.

Example 4. BESs as introduced in [26] may be recast as CLESs over the complete lattice $\mathbb{B} = (\{\texttt{tt}, \texttt{ff}\}, \leq)$, with $\texttt{tt} \leq \texttt{ff}$. With this ordering, $\sqcup$ will be represented by conjunction and $\sqcap$ by disjunction. Given a Boolean expression ϕ (resp. equation system $\mathcal{E}$), we denote by ϕ^* (resp. $\mathcal{E}^*$) the corresponding complete lattice expression (resp. equation system)[1]. Moreover given a BES $\mathcal{E}$ the notion of *consistency* of a Boolean expression ϕ in [26] is captured precisely by $\models_{\mathcal{E}^*} \phi^* \leq \texttt{tt}$.

3   Complete Proof System for Consistency Checking

In Fig. 2, we present the proof system $\mathcal{CL}$ for checking the (relative) consistency of a statement $\phi \leq \varepsilon$ by exploring the equation system $\mathcal{E} = (\mathcal{X}, E)$ in a minimal fashion. This is done by allowing one to make assumptions on the values of variables along the derivation proof when needed.

The statements of the proof system are of the form

$$\{x_1 \leq \varepsilon_1, \dots, x_n \leq \varepsilon_n\} \vdash_{\mathcal{E}} \phi \leq \varepsilon. \tag{1}$$

where $x_1, \dots, x_n \in \mathcal{X}$ are variables, $\varepsilon_1, \dots, \varepsilon_n \in \mathbb{D}$, and $\phi \in \mathcal{L}_{\mathcal{X}}$.

The statement (1) may informally be interpreted as: $\phi \leq \varepsilon$ is consistent under the assumption of consistency of $x_i \leq \varepsilon_i$, for all $i = 1, \dots, n$.

Most of the rules in Fig. 2 are obvious. The only non-obvious one is (A_4) that allows one to infer the consistency of a variable x from the consistency of

---

[1] Note that convex combinations are treated as described in Remark 1.

its definition $E(x)$, under an assumption set updated with a new assumption on the variable itself. The way we interpret a set of assumptions Γ is essential to understand how the rule (A_4) operates. Augmenting an assumption set Γ with a new assumption $x \leq \varepsilon$ should be interpreted as updating our belief on what the tightest bound should be for the value of x. In this respect, we see a set of assumption as a function $\Gamma \colon \mathcal{X} \to \mathbb{D}$ mapping each $x \in \mathcal{X}$ to the tightest upper-bound $\Gamma(x) = \bigsqcap \{\varepsilon \mid (x \leq \varepsilon) \in \Gamma\}$ that can be inferred from Γ. In the following, we will use these two equivalent interpretations of Γ (as a function or a set of statements) interchangeably, as convenient.

Example 5. Returning to BES and the proof system $\mathcal{A}$ from [26]. Here judgements are of the form $\Gamma \vdash_{\mathcal{E}} \phi$, where ϕ is a Boolean formula, $\mathcal{E}$ is a BES and Γ is a set of Boolean variables (assumptions). Now let $\Gamma^* = \{x \leq \mathtt{tt} \mid x \in \Gamma\} \cup \{x \leq \mathtt{ff} \mid x \notin \Gamma\}$, we may consider $\Gamma^* \vdash_{\mathcal{E}^*} \phi^* \leq \mathtt{tt}$ as the corresponding judgment in $\mathcal{CL}$. With this correspondence it can be seen that the inference rules of $\mathcal{A}$ are captured by the rules of $\mathcal{CL}$ in the following way:

$$\mathbf{A_1} \equiv (A3),$$
$$\mathbf{A_2} \equiv (A5) \text{ with } \omega = \mathtt{tt},$$
$$\mathbf{A_3} \equiv (A4),$$
$$\mathbf{A_4} \equiv (A6),$$
$$\mathbf{A_5} \equiv (A7) \text{ with } \varepsilon_2 = \mathtt{ff},$$
$$\mathbf{A_6} \equiv (A7) \text{ with } \varepsilon_1 = \mathtt{ff}.$$

It follows that $\Gamma \vdash_{\mathcal{E}} \phi$ are provable in $\mathcal{A}$ if and only if $\Gamma^* \vdash_{\mathcal{E}^*} \phi^* \leq \mathtt{tt}$ is provable in $\mathcal{CL}$.

To interpret semantically the conditional statements used in the proof system, we are looking for a notion of consistency that is relative to a set of assumptions. To this end we need to define what it means for an environment to be a model relative to some assumptions. We say that an environment ρ is a *model* of an equation system $\mathcal{E} = (\mathcal{X}, E)$ *relative to a set of assumptions* Γ, if for all $x \in \mathcal{X}$, $[\![x]\!]\rho = \Gamma(x) \sqcap [\![E(x)]\!]\rho$.

Definition 3 (Relative Consistency). *Let $\mathcal{E} = (\mathcal{X}, E)$ be a convex lattice equation system. A statement $\phi \leq \varepsilon$ is consistent for $\mathcal{E}$ relative to Γ, written $\Gamma \models_{\mathcal{E}} \phi \leq \varepsilon$, if there exists a model ρ of $\mathcal{E}$ relative to Γ such that $[\![\phi]\!]\rho \sqsubseteq \varepsilon$.*

Note that when the set of assumptions Γ is empty, relative consistency corresponds to standard consistency (i.e., $\emptyset \models_{\mathcal{E}} \phi \leq \varepsilon$ iff $\models_{\mathcal{E}} \phi \leq \varepsilon$).

The models of $\mathcal{E}$ relative to Γ are exactly the fixed points of the functional $F_{\mathcal{E},\Gamma} \colon \mathbb{D}^{\mathcal{X}} \to \mathbb{D}^{\mathcal{X}}$ defined as follows, for ρ an environment and $x \in \mathcal{X}$ a variable:

$$F_{\mathcal{E},\Gamma}(\rho)(x) = \Gamma(x) \sqcap [\![E(x)]\!]\rho.$$

Also $F_{\mathcal{E},\Gamma}$ is monotone, thus, by Knaster-Tarski's fixed point theorem, $F_{\mathcal{E},\Gamma}$ has least fixed point, denoted as $\mu F_{\mathcal{E},\Gamma}$. In particular, $\Gamma \models_{\mathcal{E}} \phi \leq \varepsilon$ is equivalent to $[\![\phi]\!]\mu F_{\mathcal{E},\Gamma} \sqsubseteq \varepsilon$.

The next two theorems prove the soundness and completeness of the proof system w.r.t. relative consistency.

Theorem 1 (Soundness). *If $\Gamma \vdash_{\mathcal{E}} \phi \leq \varepsilon$, then $\Gamma \models_{\mathcal{E}} \phi \leq \varepsilon$.*

Proof. By structural induction on the derivation tree for $\Gamma \vdash_{\mathcal{E}} \phi \leq \varepsilon$.

Case (A_1): if $\Gamma \vdash_{\mathcal{E}} \phi \leq \varepsilon$ has been established using the axiom (A_1), then $\varepsilon = \top$. Clearly, $[\![\phi]\!]\mu F_{\mathcal{E},\Gamma} \sqsubseteq \top$. Thus, $\Gamma \models_{\mathcal{E}} \phi \leq \top$.

Case (A_2): if $\Gamma \vdash_{\mathcal{E}} \phi \leq \varepsilon$ has been established using the axiom (A_2), then $\Gamma \vdash_{\mathcal{E}} \phi \leq \varepsilon'$ for some $\varepsilon' \sqsubseteq \varepsilon$. By inductive hypothesis, $\Gamma \models_{\mathcal{E}} \phi \leq \varepsilon'$. As this is equivalent to $[\![\phi]\!]\mu F_{\mathcal{E},\Gamma} \sqsubseteq \varepsilon'$, by transitivity of $\sqsubseteq$ we have $[\![\phi]\!]\mu F_{\mathcal{E},\Gamma} \sqsubseteq \varepsilon$. Thus, $\Gamma \models_{\mathcal{E}} \phi \leq \varepsilon$.

Case (A_3): if $\Gamma \vdash_{\mathcal{E}} \phi \leq \varepsilon$ has been established using the axiom (A_3), then $\phi = x$ and $\varepsilon = \Gamma(x)$. Since $\mu F_{\mathcal{E},\Gamma}(x)$ is a fixed point of $F_{\mathcal{E},\Gamma}$, we have $\mu F_{\mathcal{E},\Gamma}(x) \sqsubseteq \Gamma(x)$. By definition, $[\![x]\!]\mu F_{\mathcal{E},\Gamma}(x) = \mu F_{\mathcal{E},\Gamma}(x)$ and, by transitivity of $\sqsubseteq$, we get $[\![x]\!]\mu F_{\mathcal{E},\Gamma}(x) \sqsubseteq \Gamma(x)$. Thus, $\Gamma \models_{\mathcal{E}} x \leq \Gamma(x)$.

Case (A_4): if $\Gamma \vdash_{\mathcal{E}} \phi \leq \varepsilon$ has been established using the axiom (A_4), then $\phi = x$ and $\Gamma \cup \{x \leq \varepsilon\} \vdash_{\mathcal{E}} \Gamma(x) \sqcap E(x) \leq \varepsilon$. By inductive hypothesis, we have that $\Gamma \cup \{x \leq \varepsilon\} \models_{\mathcal{E}} \Gamma(x) \sqcap E(x) \leq \varepsilon$, which, in turn, it is equivalent to $\Gamma(x) \sqcap [\![E(x)]\!]\mu F_{\mathcal{E},\Gamma \cup \{x \leq \varepsilon\}} \sqsubseteq \varepsilon$. As $\mu F_{\mathcal{E},\Gamma \cup \{x \leq \varepsilon\}}$ is a fixed point of $F_{\mathcal{E},\Gamma \cup \{x \leq \varepsilon\}}$, we have $\mu F_{\mathcal{E},\Gamma \cup \{x \leq \varepsilon\}}(x) = \Gamma(x) \sqcap \varepsilon \sqcap [\![E(x)]\!]\mu F_{\mathcal{E},\Gamma \cup \{x \leq \varepsilon\}}$. Thus, $\mu F_{\mathcal{E},\Gamma \cup \{x \leq \varepsilon\}}(x) \sqsubseteq \varepsilon$.

We prove that $[\![x]\!]\mu F_{\mathcal{E},\Gamma} = \mu F_{\mathcal{E},\Gamma}(x) \sqsubseteq \varepsilon$, by showing that $\mu F_{\mathcal{E},\Gamma \cup \{x \leq \varepsilon\}}$ is a prefix point of $F_{\mathcal{E},\Gamma}$, i.e., $F_{\mathcal{E},\Gamma}(\mu F_{\mathcal{E},\Gamma \cup \{x \leq \varepsilon\}})(y) \sqsubseteq \mu F_{\mathcal{E},\Gamma \cup \{x \leq \varepsilon\}}(y)$ for all $y \in \mathcal{X}$. We consider only the case $y = x$, since the others are trivial.

$$
\begin{aligned}
F_{\mathcal{E},\Gamma}(\mu F_{\mathcal{E},\Gamma \cup \{x \leq \varepsilon\}})(x) &= \Gamma(x) \sqcap [\![E(x)]\!]\mu F_{\mathcal{E},\Gamma \cup \{x \leq \varepsilon\}} &&\text{(def. } F_{\mathcal{E},\Gamma}) \\
&= \Gamma(x) \sqcap \varepsilon \sqcap [\![E(x)]\!]\mu F_{\mathcal{E},\Gamma \cup \{x \leq \varepsilon\}} &&\text{(ind. hp.)} \\
&= \mu F_{\mathcal{E},\Gamma \cup \{x \leq \varepsilon\}}(x). &&\text{(fixed point of } F_{\mathcal{E},\Gamma \cup \{x \leq \varepsilon\}})
\end{aligned}
$$

From the above, we conclude that $\Gamma \models_{\mathcal{E}} x \leq \varepsilon'$.

Case (A_5): if $\Gamma \vdash_{\mathcal{E}} \phi \leq \varepsilon$ has been established using the axiom (A_5), then $\phi = w$ and $\varepsilon = w$. By definition, $[\![w]\!]\mu F_{\mathcal{E},\Gamma} = w$, thus $\Gamma \models_{\mathcal{E}} w \leq w$.

Case (A_6): if $\Gamma \vdash_{\mathcal{E}} \phi \leq \varepsilon$ has been established using the axiom (A_6), then $\phi = \phi_1 \sqcup \phi_2$ and $\Gamma \vdash_{\mathcal{E}} \phi_i \leq \varepsilon$, for $i = 1, 2$. By inductive hypothesis, $\Gamma \models_{\mathcal{E}} \phi_i \leq \varepsilon$, for $i = 1, 2$. This is equivalent to $[\![\phi_1]\!]\mu F_{\mathcal{E},\Gamma} \sqcup [\![\phi_2]\!]\mu F_{\mathcal{E},\Gamma} \sqsubseteq \varepsilon$. By definition, $[\![\phi_1 \sqcup \phi_1]\!]\mu F_{\mathcal{E},\Gamma} = [\![\phi_1]\!]\mu F_{\mathcal{E},\Gamma} \sqcup [\![\phi_2]\!]\mu F_{\mathcal{E},\Gamma}$. Thus, $\Gamma \models_{\mathcal{E}} \phi_1 \sqcup \phi_2 \leq \varepsilon$.

Case (A_7): if $\Gamma \vdash_{\mathcal{E}} \phi \leq \varepsilon$ has been established using the axiom (A_7), then $\phi = \phi_1 \sqcap \phi_2$, $\varepsilon = \varepsilon_1 \sqcap \varepsilon_2$, and $\Gamma \vdash_{\mathcal{E}} \phi_i \leq \varepsilon$, for $i = 1, 2$. By inductive hypothesis, $\Gamma \models_{\mathcal{E}} \phi_i \leq \varepsilon_i$, for $i = 1, 2$. This is equivalent to $[\![\phi_i]\!]\mu F_{\mathcal{E},\Gamma} \sqsubseteq \varepsilon_i$, for $i = 1, 2$. Therefore $[\![\phi_1]\!]\mu F_{\mathcal{E},\Gamma} \sqcap [\![\phi_2]\!]\mu F_{\mathcal{E},\Gamma} \sqsubseteq \varepsilon_1 \sqcap \varepsilon_2$. By definition and transitivity of $\sqsubseteq$, $[\![\phi_1 \sqcap \phi_1]\!]\mu F_{\mathcal{E},\Gamma} = [\![\phi_1]\!]\mu F_{\mathcal{E},\Gamma} \sqcap [\![\phi_2]\!]\mu F_{\mathcal{E},\Gamma} \sqsubseteq \varepsilon_1 \sqcap \varepsilon_2$. Thus, $\Gamma \models_{\mathcal{E}} \phi_1 \sqcap \phi_2 \leq \varepsilon_1 \sqcap \varepsilon_2$.

Case (A_8): if $\Gamma \vdash_\varepsilon \phi \leq \varepsilon$ has been established using the axiom (A_8), then $\phi = \phi_1 +_p \phi_2$, $\varepsilon = \varepsilon_1 +_p \varepsilon_2$ and $\Gamma \vdash_\varepsilon \phi_i \leq \varepsilon_i$, for $i = 1, 2$. By inductive hypothesis, $\Gamma \models_\varepsilon \phi_i \leq \varepsilon_i$, which is equivalent to $[\![\phi_i]\!]\mu F_{\varepsilon,\Gamma} \sqsubseteq \varepsilon_i$ for $i = 1, 2$. We show that $[\![\phi_1 +_p \phi_2]\!]\mu F_{\varepsilon,\Gamma} \sqsubseteq \varepsilon_1 +_p \varepsilon_2$ in two steps.

$$
\begin{aligned}
& [\![\phi_1]\!]\mu F_{\varepsilon,\Gamma} +_p [\![\phi_2]\!]\mu F_{\varepsilon,\Gamma} \\
&= ([\![\phi_1]\!]\mu F_{\varepsilon,\Gamma} \sqcap \varepsilon_1) +_p [\![\phi_2]\!]\mu F_{\varepsilon,\Gamma} && ([\![\phi_1]\!]\mu F_{\varepsilon,\Gamma} \sqsubseteq \varepsilon_1) \\
&= ([\![\phi_1]\!]\mu F_{\varepsilon,\Gamma} +_p [\![\phi_2]\!]\mu F_{\varepsilon,\Gamma}) \sqcap (\varepsilon_1 +_p [\![\phi_2]\!]\mu F_{\varepsilon,\Gamma}) && \text{(distributive law)}
\end{aligned}
$$

Hence, $[\![\phi_1]\!]\mu F_{\varepsilon,\Gamma} +_p [\![\phi_1]\!]\mu F_{\varepsilon,\Gamma} \sqsubseteq \varepsilon_1 +_p [\![\phi_2]\!]\mu F_{\varepsilon,\Gamma}$. Moreover,

$$
\begin{aligned}
\varepsilon_1 +_p \varepsilon_2 &= \varepsilon_1 +_p (\varepsilon_2 \sqcup [\![\phi_2]\!]\mu F_{\varepsilon,\Gamma}) && ([\![\phi_2]\!]\mu F_{\varepsilon,\Gamma} \sqsubseteq \varepsilon_2) \\
&= (\varepsilon_1 +_p \varepsilon_2) \sqcup (\varepsilon_1 +_p [\![\phi_2]\!]\mu F_{\varepsilon,\Gamma}) && \text{(distributive law)}
\end{aligned}
$$

Hence, $\varepsilon_1 +_p [\![\phi_2]\!]\mu F_{\varepsilon,\Gamma} \sqsubseteq \varepsilon_1 +_p \varepsilon_2$. Thus, by transitivity of $\sqsubseteq$ we have

$$
[\![\phi_1 +_p \phi_2]\!]\mu F_{\varepsilon,\Gamma} = [\![\phi_1]\!]\mu F_{\varepsilon,\Gamma} +_p [\![\phi_1]\!]\mu F_{\varepsilon,\Gamma} \sqsubseteq \varepsilon_1 +_p \varepsilon_2 \,.
$$

Therefore, $\Gamma \models_\varepsilon \phi_1 +_p \phi_2 \leq \varepsilon_1 +_p \varepsilon_2$. $\qquad\square$

Theorem 2 (Completeness). *If $\Gamma \models_\varepsilon \phi \leq \varepsilon$, then $\Gamma \vdash_\varepsilon \phi \leq \varepsilon$.*

Proof. In the following we will prove that $\Gamma \vdash_\varepsilon \phi \leq [\![\phi]\!]\mu F_{\varepsilon,\Gamma}$. To simplify the exposition, we will make use of a semantically equivalent variant of the proof system in Fig. 2 where we add the following rule derivable from (A_4)

$$
(A_4^*) \quad \frac{\Gamma' \cup \{\bar{x} \leq [\![x]\!]\mu F_{\varepsilon,\Gamma}\} \vdash_\varepsilon \Gamma'(x) \sqcap E(x) \leq [\![x]\!]\mu F_{\varepsilon,\Gamma}}{\Gamma' \vdash_\varepsilon x \leq [\![x]\!]\mu F_{\varepsilon,\Gamma}}
$$

Note that in the premise of (A_4^*), the variable x in the assumption set is "marked". The markings have no additional semantic meaning (i.e., $x = \bar{x}$). We will use them in our proof to keep track of the assumptions that have been introduced by applying (A_4^*).

We prove the following stronger statement: $\Gamma \cup \bar{\Gamma} \vdash_\varepsilon \phi \leq [\![\phi]\!]\mu F_{\varepsilon,\Gamma}$ for all $\bar{\Gamma}$ containing only marked assumptions of the form $\bar{x} \leq [\![x]\!]\mu F_{\varepsilon,\Gamma}$. We proceed by induction on $n = |\mathcal{X} \setminus \{x \mid (\bar{x} \leq \varepsilon) \in \bar{\Gamma}\}|$.

Base Case (n = 0). By hypothesis $(\bar{x} \leq [\![x]\!]\mu F_{\varepsilon,\Gamma}) \in \bar{\Gamma}$ for all $x \in \mathcal{X}$. We proceed by induction on the structure of ϕ.

($\phi = w$) Recall that $[\![w]\!]\mu F_{\varepsilon,\Gamma} = w$. By axiom ($A_5$), $\Gamma \cup \bar{\Gamma} \vdash_\varepsilon w \leq [\![w]\!]\mu F_{\varepsilon,\Gamma}$.

($\phi = x$) Recall that $(\bar{x} \leq [\![x]\!]\mu F_{\varepsilon,\Gamma}) \in \bar{\Gamma}$, hence $(\Gamma \cup \bar{\Gamma})(x) \sqsubseteq [\![x]\!]\mu F_{\varepsilon,\Gamma}$. Thus, using ($A_3$) and ($A_2$) we prove $\Gamma \cup \bar{\Gamma} \vdash_\varepsilon x \leq [\![x]\!]\mu F_{\varepsilon,\Gamma}$.

($\phi = \phi_1 \sqcap \phi_2$) By inductive hypothesis we have $\Gamma \cup \bar{\Gamma} \vdash_\varepsilon \phi_i \leq [\![\phi_i]\!]\mu F_{\varepsilon,\Gamma}$ for $i = 1, 2$. Thus, by def. of $[\![\cdot]\!]$, via (A_7) we get $\Gamma \cup \bar{\Gamma} \vdash_\varepsilon \phi_1 \sqcap \phi_2 \leq [\![\phi_1 \sqcap \phi_2]\!]\mu F_{\varepsilon,\Gamma}$.

($\phi = \phi_1 \sqcup \phi_2$) By inductive hypothesis we have $\Gamma \cup \bar{\Gamma} \vdash_\varepsilon \phi_i \leq [\![\phi_i]\!]\mu F_{\varepsilon,\Gamma}$ for $i = 1, 2$. Thus, by def. of $[\![\cdot]\!]$, via (A_2) we get $\Gamma \cup \bar{\Gamma} \vdash_\varepsilon \phi_i \leq [\![\phi_1 \sqcup \phi_2]\!]\mu F_{\varepsilon,\Gamma}$. Then, via ($A_6$) we get $\Gamma \cup \bar{\Gamma} \vdash_\varepsilon \phi_1 \sqcup \phi_2 \leq [\![\phi_1 \sqcup \phi_2]\!]\mu F_{\varepsilon,\Gamma}$.

($\phi = \phi_1 +_\alpha \phi_2$) By inductive hypothesis we have $\Gamma \cup \bar{\Gamma} \vdash_{\mathcal{E}} \phi_i \leq [\![\phi_i]\!] \mu F_{\mathcal{E},\Gamma}$ for $i = 1, 2$. Thus, by def. of $[\![\cdot]\!]$, via (A_8) we get $\Gamma \cup \bar{\Gamma} \vdash_{\mathcal{E}} \phi_1 +_\alpha \phi_2 \leq [\![\phi_1 +_\alpha \phi_2]\!] \mu F_{\mathcal{E},\Gamma}$.

Inductive Case. Again, we proceed by induction on the structure of ϕ. We only show the case $\phi = x$. All other cases carry over exactly as in the base case.

We distinguish two cases: some marked assumption on x is present in $\bar{\Gamma}$, or not. In the former of the two cases we proceed exactly as done in the base case.

For the latter case, by inductive hypothesis on n we have that

$$\Gamma \cup \bar{\Gamma} \cup \{\bar{x} \leq [\![x]\!] \mu F_{\mathcal{E},\Gamma}\} \vdash_{\mathcal{E}} \Gamma(x) \sqcap E(x) \leq [\![\Gamma(x) \sqcap E(x)]\!] \mu F_{\mathcal{E},\Gamma}. \quad (2)$$

By def. of $[\![\cdot]\!]$ and the fact that $\mu F_{\mathcal{E},\Gamma}$ is a fixed point of $F_{\mathcal{E},\Gamma}$ we have

$$[\![\Gamma(x) \sqcap E(x)]\!] \mu F_{\mathcal{E},\Gamma} = \Gamma(x) \sqcap [\![E(x)]\!] \mu F_{\mathcal{E},\Gamma} = [\![x]\!] \mu F_{\mathcal{E},\Gamma}. \quad (3)$$

Therefore, by (2) and (3) via (A_4^*) we get $\Gamma \cup \bar{\Gamma} \vdash_{\mathcal{E}} x \leq [\![x]\!] \mu F_{\mathcal{E},\Gamma}$. □

4 Simple Stochastic Games

In this section we show how convex lattice equation systems encompass the powerful formalism of simple stochastic games [12,13].

A *simple stochastic game* (SSG) is a directed graph $G = (V, E)$ with the following properties. Vertices are partitioned into sets of *0-sinks*, *1-sinks*, *max vertices*, *min vertices*, and *average vertices*. Except the sink vertices, each vertex v of V, has two successors nodes that for convenience we call the left and the right successor of v, respectively denoted by *left(v)* and *right(v)*.

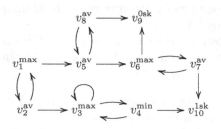

Fig. 3. A simple stochastic game (from [13]).

The game is played by two players, the *max player* and the *min player*, with a single token. At each step of the game, the token is moved from a vertex to one of its two successors. At a min vertex the min player chooses the successor, at a max vertex the max player chooses the successor, and at an average vertex the successor is chosen at random by tossing a fair coin. The max player wins a play of the game if the token reaches a 1-sink and the min player wins if the play reaches a 0-sink or continues forever without reaching a sink. Since the game is stochastic, the max player tries to maximize the probability of reaching a 1-sink whereas the min player tries to minimize that probability.

A *strategy*, a.k.a. *policy*, for the min player is a function $\sigma\colon V_{\min} \to V$ that assigns the target of an outgoing edge to each min vertex, that is, for all $v \in V_{\min}$, $(v, \sigma(v)) \in E$. Likewise, a strategy for the max player is a function $\tau\colon V_{\max} \to V$ that assigns the target of an outgoing edge to each max vertex. These strategies are known as *pure stationary* strategies. We can restrict ourselves to these strategies since both players of a simple stochastic game have optimal strategies of this type (see, for example, [28]).

Such strategies determine a sub-game in which each max vertex and each min vertex has out-degree one. We write $\nu_{\sigma,\tau}\colon V \to [0,1]$ for the function that gives the probability of a vertex in this sub-game to reach a 1-sink (see [13, Section 2] for details). The *value function* $\nu^*\colon V \to [0,1]$ of a SSG is defined as

$$\nu^* = \min_{\sigma} \max_{\tau} \nu_{\sigma,\tau} .$$

It is folklore that the value function of a simple stochastic game can be characterised as the least fixed point of the following function $\Psi_G\colon [0,1]^V \to [0,1]^V$ (see, for example, [23, Section 2.2 and 2.3]) defined by

$$\Psi_G(\nu)(v) = \begin{cases} 0 & \text{if } v \text{ is a 0-sink} \\ 1 & \text{if } v \text{ is a 1-sink} \\ \max\{\nu(\mathit{left}(v)), \nu(\mathit{right}(v))\} & \text{if } v \text{ is a max vertex} \\ \min\{\nu(\mathit{left}(v)), \nu(\mathit{right}(v))\} & \text{if } v \text{ is a min vertex} \\ 1/2(\nu(\mathit{left}(v)) + \nu(\mathit{right}(v))) & \text{if } v \text{ is an average vertex} \end{cases}$$

4.1   Value Function of an SSGs as a Consistency Checking

Let $G = (V, E)$ be a SSG. Consider the convex lattice $([0,1], \leq, \{+_\alpha \mid \alpha \in [0,1]\})$ where $a +_\alpha b = \alpha a + (1-\alpha)b$. We define the equation system $\mathcal{E}_G = (V, E_G)$ by

$$E_G(v) = \begin{cases} 0 & \text{if } v \text{ is a 0-sink} \\ 1 & \text{if } v \text{ is a 1-sink} \\ \mathit{left}(v) \sqcup \mathit{right}(v) & \text{if } v \text{ is a max vertex} \\ \mathit{left}(v) \sqcap \mathit{right}(v) & \text{if } v \text{ is a min vertex} \\ \mathit{left}(v) +_{1/2} \mathit{right}(v) & \text{if } v \text{ is an average vertex} \end{cases}$$

The following result relates the value of a SSG to consistency checking w.r.t. its corresponding equation system.

Theorem 3. *Let $G = (V, E)$ be a SSG and $\mathcal{E}_G = (V, E_G)$ the corresponding equation system. Then $\nu^*(v) \leq \varepsilon$ iff $\vdash_{\mathcal{E}_G} v \leq \varepsilon$.*

Proof. It is immediate to show that $F_{\mathcal{E}_G} = \Psi_G$, thus $\nu^* = \mu F_{\mathcal{E}_G}$. From this it follows that $\nu^*(v) \le \varepsilon$ if and only if $\models_{\mathcal{E}_G} v \le \varepsilon$, as $\models_{\mathcal{E}_G} v \le \varepsilon$ is equivalent to $[\![v]\!]\mu F_{\mathcal{E}_G} = \mu F_{\mathcal{E}_G}(v) \le \varepsilon$. The thesis follows by soundness and completeness of the proof system (Theorems 1 and 2).

We can now provide a first concrete application of the proof system in Fig. 2. Example 6 showcases a proof for a (tight) upper bound of the value of a vertex in a SSG made through consistency checking.

Example 6. Consider the SSG in Fig. 3. In [13] it is shown that the value of the vertex v_3 under the strategies $\tau = (v_1 \mapsto v_5, v_3 \mapsto v_4, v_6 \mapsto v_7)$ and $\sigma = (v_4 \mapsto v_3)$ is $\nu_{\sigma,\tau}(v_3) = 0$. As these are optimal strategies for the players, we also have $\nu^*(v_3) = 0$. Next we show the inference tree for $\vdash_{\mathcal{E}_G} v_3 \le 0$.

$$
\cfrac{
\cfrac{
\cfrac{
\cfrac{\{v_3, v_4 \le 0\} \vdash_{\mathcal{E}_G} v_3 \le 0}{}(A_3) \quad \cfrac{\{v_3, v_4 \le 0\} \vdash_{\mathcal{E}_G} v_{10} \le 1}{}(A_1)
}{\{v_3, v_4 \le 0\} \vdash_{\mathcal{E}_G} v_3 \sqcap v_{10} \le 0}(A_7)
}{\{v_3 \le 0\} \vdash_{\mathcal{E}_G} v_4 \le 0}(A_4)
}{
\cfrac{\{v_3 \le 0\} \vdash_{\mathcal{E}_G} v_3 \le 0}{}(A_3) \qquad\quad
}
{\{v_3 \le 0\} \vdash_{\mathcal{E}_G} v_3 \sqcup v_4 \le 0}(A_6)
}{\vdash_{\mathcal{E}_G} v_3 \le 0}(A_4)
$$

Remarkably, the consistency of $v_3 \le 0$ could be proven without exploring the entire equation system (only the equations for v_3, v_4 are used).

Remark 2. Many interesting optimization problems can be encoded as simple stochastic games. In particular, Tang and van Breugel [33] showed that the probabilistic bisimilarity distance for Markov chains proposed by Desharnais et al. [14] can be characterized as the value of a simple stochastic game (without max vertices). Later, this result was generalised to the case of probabilistic automata [8] which combine non-determinism with probabilistic choice.

Thus, thanks to Theorem 3, one can prove upper bounds for the above mentioned probabilistic bisimilarity distances using the proof system of Fig. 2.   □

5   Timed Bisimulation Distance

In this section we introduce the novel notion of *timed bisimulation distance*, the natural extension of Wang Yi's timed bisimulation equivalence [38] to a metric setting. We provide rudimentary results for this distance and we provide an encoding in terms of equation systems that allow us to check for upper-bounds of this distance for regular timed systems.

Towards this let us recall the basic notions of time domains and timed transition systems along with some properties regarding them.

Definition 4 (Time Domain). *A time domain is a monoid $\langle \mathbb{T}, +, 0 \rangle$ satisfying the following axioms*

$$\forall t, r, v \in \mathbb{T}: \quad t = t + r + v \implies t = t + r \qquad \text{(irreversibility)}$$

$$\forall t, r, v \in \mathbb{T}: \quad t + r = t + v \implies r = v \qquad \text{(left-cancellation)}$$

Time domains yield a canonical preorder $\leq$ given for $t, r \in \mathbb{T}$ by $t \leq r$ iff there exists $v \in \mathbb{T}$ such that $t + v = r$. Note that due to *left-cancellation* this v is unique and we can therefore derive substraction as $r - t = v$ whenever $t \leq r$. We can further generalize this substraction by truncating at 0 whenever $t > r$, i.e. $r \doteq t = 0$. A distance $d\colon \mathbb{T} \times \mathbb{T} \to [0, \infty]$ over $\mathbb{T}$ is said to respect the time domain $\langle \mathbb{T}, +, 0 \rangle$ if it makes $+$ non-expansive:

$$\forall t, r, v \in \mathbb{T}: \quad d(t, r) \geq d(t + v, r + v) \qquad \text{(non-expansiveness)}$$

The usual example of a time domain would be the non-negative reals, i.e. $\langle [0, \infty], +, 0 \rangle$, along with the distance given by the absolute difference, i.e. $|t - r|$.

For the remainder of this section we fix a time domain $\langle \mathbb{T}, +, 0 \rangle$ and a distance $d_{\mathbb{T}}\colon \mathbb{T} \times \mathbb{T} \to [0, \infty]$ respecting it.

Definition 5 (TTS). *A timed transition system is a tuple* $\mathcal{M} = (M, \mathbf{A}, \to)$ *where, M is a set of states, $\mathbf{A}$ is a countable set of action labels disjoint from $\mathbb{T}$, $\to \subseteq (M \times \mathbb{T} \times M) \cup (M \times \mathbf{A} \times M)$ is a transition relation describing timed and labelled behaviour, satisfying the following, for all $m, m', m'' \in M$ and $t, t' \in \mathbb{T}$*

$$m \xrightarrow{\ 0\ } m \qquad \text{(zero delay)}$$

$$m \xrightarrow{t} m' \wedge t' \leq t \implies \exists n.\, m \xrightarrow{t'} n \xrightarrow{t - t'} m' \qquad \text{(time additivity)}$$

$$m \xrightarrow{t} m' \wedge m \xrightarrow{t} m'' \implies m' = m'' \qquad \text{(time determinism)}$$

We will use $\to^*$ to denote the transitive and reflexive closure of $\to$ and we write $m \not\to$ whenever there are no labelled transitions from the state $m \in M$.

Now, for a given $m \in M$, we define the set of possible timed behaviour of m, denoted $\delta_{\mathcal{M}}(m)$, by

$$\delta_{\mathcal{M}}(m) = \left\{ \langle t, \dagger, m' \rangle \in \mathbb{T} \times \{\dagger\} \times M \;\middle|\; m \xrightarrow{t} m' \not\to \right\}$$

$$\cup \left\{ \langle t, a, m' \rangle \in \mathbb{T} \times \mathbf{A} \times M \;\middle|\; m \xrightarrow{t} \xrightarrow{a} m' \right\}$$

where we use the special symbol $\dagger \notin \mathbf{A}$ to denote deadlocks. With this we can now define a preliminary distance between timed behaviour.

Definition 6. *Let $d\colon M \times M \to [0, \infty]$ be a distance over the states of M, then the behavioural distance of $\mathcal{M}$ wrt. to d is the distance $\Lambda_{\mathcal{M}}(d)\colon (\mathbb{T} \times \mathbf{A}_{\dagger} \times M)^2 \to [0, \infty]$ defined for arbitrary $\langle t, a, m \rangle, \langle r, b, n \rangle \in \mathbb{T} \times \mathbf{A}_{\dagger} \times M$ by*

$$\Lambda_{\mathcal{M}}(d)(\langle t, a, m \rangle, \langle r, b, n \rangle) = \max \{ d_{\mathbb{T}}(t, r), \iota(a, b), d(m, n) \}$$

where $\iota(a, b) = 0$ if $a = b$ and $\iota(a, b) = \infty$ otherwise.

We can now define the iterator of which we take the least fixed point to be our timed bisimilarity distance.

Definition 7 (Iterator). $\Psi_{\mathcal{M}} : [M \times M \to [0, \infty]] \to [M \times M \to [0, \infty]]$ *defined for arbitrary* $d : M \times M \to [0, \infty]$ *by*

$$\Psi_{\mathcal{M}}(d)(m, n) = \mathcal{H}(\Lambda_{\mathcal{M}}(d))(\delta_{\mathcal{M}}(m), \delta_{\mathcal{M}}(n))$$

where $\mathcal{H}(\Lambda_{\mathcal{M}}(d))$ *is the Hausdorff lifting of* $\Lambda_{\mathcal{M}}(d)$.

Lemma 1 (Monotonicity). *If* $d, d' : M \times M \to [0, \infty]$ *such that* $d \le d'$, *then* $\Psi_{\mathcal{M}}(d) \le \Psi_{\mathcal{M}}(d')$.

As the space of distances over M forms a complete lattice wrt. to pairwise comparison and as $\Psi_{\mathcal{M}}$ is monotonic over this space, we have by the Knaster-Tarski fixed point theorem [34] that $\Psi_{\mathcal{M}}$ yields a unique least fixed point, denoted $\mu\Psi_{\mathcal{M}}$.

To justify our timed bisimilarity distance, we state the following two rudimentary results. Firstly, that $\mu\Psi_{\mathcal{M}}$ indeed behaves like a distance, in this case an (extended) pseudo-metric. Secondly, that $\mu\Psi_{\mathcal{M}}$ agrees with timed bisimilarity, that is whenever two states are bisimilar then $\mu\Psi_{\mathcal{M}}$ puts those states at distance zero.

Theorem 4. *If* d_T *is a pseudo-metric, then* $\mu\Psi_{\mathcal{M}}$ *is a pseudo-metric.*

Theorem 5. *If* m *and* n *are timed bisimilar then* $\mu\Psi_{\mathcal{M}}(m, n) = 0$.

5.1 Encoding for Regular Timed Processes

For the encoding we will only consider TTS induced by the regular fragment of TCCS (e.g. no use of parallel composition). We will not formally define TCCS here but instead refer to [39]. The restriction to regular TCCS permits an easy characterisation of the timed bisimulation distance on a finite set of timed behaviour and thereby allowing us to encode it using convex lattice equation systems.

For any $m \in M$, let us define the minimal timed behaviour as

$$\delta_{\mathcal{M}}^{\min}(m) = \left\{ \langle t, a, m' \rangle \in \delta_{\mathcal{M}} \;\middle|\; t = \min_{\langle r, a, m' \rangle \in \delta_{\mathcal{M}}(m)} r \right\}$$

For TTS induced by TCCS expressions, the above set is finite regardless of choice of state. Furthermore, we have the following lemma stating that we only need to consider these finite subsets of timed behaviour for the timed bisimulation distance.

Lemma 2. *For arbitrary* $d : M \times M \to [0, \infty]$ *and* $m, n \in M$,

$$\Psi_{\mathcal{M}}(d)(m, n) = \mathcal{H}(\Lambda)(\delta_{\mathcal{M}}^{\min}(m), \delta_{\mathcal{M}}^{\min}(n))$$

Consider now the complete partial order $([0,\infty],\leq)$. For a given TTS $\mathcal{M}$ induced by a TTS expression we define the equation system $\langle \mathcal{X}_{\mathcal{M}}, E_{\mathcal{M}} \rangle$ where $\mathcal{X}_{\mathcal{M}}$ is given by $x_{m,n} \in \mathcal{X}_{\mathcal{M}}$ whenever $m, n \in M$ and $E_{\mathcal{M}}$ is given for $x_{m,n} \in \mathcal{X}_{\mathcal{M}}$ by

$$x_{m,n} =_{E_{\mathcal{M}}} \bigsqcup_{\langle t,a,m' \rangle \in \delta^-(m)} \bigsqcap_{\langle r,b,n' \rangle \in \delta^-(n)} (d_{\mathbb{T}}(t,r) \sqcup \iota(a,b) \sqcup x_{m',n'})$$

$$\sqcup \bigsqcup_{\langle r,b,n' \rangle \in \delta^-(n)} \bigsqcap_{\langle t,a,m' \rangle \in \delta^-(m)} (d_{\mathbb{T}}(t,r) \sqcup \iota(a,b) \sqcup x_{m',n'})$$

where $\bigsqcap \emptyset = \infty$ and $\bigsqcup \emptyset = 0$.

Here $\mathcal{X}_{\mathcal{M}}$ may be infinite, but the formulae given by $E_{\mathcal{M}}$ are finite and depend only on finite subsets of $\mathcal{X}_{\mathcal{M}}$. This is because you can only describe finite branching using TCCS and that the target states of labelled transitions remain the same regardless of further delays due to the TTS induced by TCCS expressions satisfying persistency. Hence, one need only consider a finite sub-equation system of $E_{\mathcal{M}}$ when checking for consistency.

Example 7. As an example, consider the two TCCS expressions

$$P = \epsilon(4).a.P + b.\text{Nil} \quad \text{and} \quad Q = \epsilon(3).(a.Q + b.\text{Nil})$$

over the time domain $\mathbb{T} = \mathbb{R}_{\geq 0}$. Let $d_{\mathbb{T}}$ be given by the absolute difference, then P and Q have distance $\mu \Psi_{\mathcal{M}}(P,Q) = \max(d_{\mathbb{T}}(4,3), d_{\mathbb{T}}(0,3)) = 3$. For the given TCCS expressions we have that their minimal time behaviour is

$$\delta_{\mathcal{M}}^{\min}(P) = \{\langle 4, a, \text{Nil} \rangle, \langle 0, b, \text{Nil} \rangle\}$$

$$\delta_{\mathcal{M}}^{\min}(Q) = \{\langle 3, a, \text{Nil} \rangle, \langle 3, b, \text{Nil} \rangle\}$$

and hence the formula associated with them is

$$x_{P,Q} = ((d_{\mathbb{T}}(4,3) \sqcup \iota(a,a) \sqcup x_{P,Q}) \sqcap (d_{\mathbb{T}}(4,3) \sqcup \iota(a,b) \sqcup x_{P,\text{Nil}}))$$

$$\sqcup ((d_{\mathbb{T}}(0,3) \sqcup \iota(b,a) \sqcup x_{\text{Nil},Q}) \sqcap (d_{\mathbb{T}}(0,3) \sqcup \iota(b,b) \sqcup x_{\text{Nil},\text{Nil}}))$$

$$\sqcup ((d_{\mathbb{T}}(4,3) \sqcup \iota(a,a) \sqcup x_{P,Q}) \sqcap (d_{\mathbb{T}}(0,3) \sqcup \iota(b,a) \sqcup x_{\text{Nil},Q}))$$

$$\sqcup ((d_{\mathbb{T}}(4,3) \sqcup \iota(a,b) \sqcup x_{P,\text{Nil}}) \sqcap (d_{\mathbb{T}}(0,3) \sqcup \iota(b,b) \sqcup x_{\text{Nil},\text{Nil}}))$$

As $\iota(a,b) = \iota(b,a) = \infty$, $\iota(a,a) = \iota(b,b) = 0$, and $d_{\mathbb{T}}(4,3) \leq d_{\mathbb{T}}(0,3) = 3$ we can even reduce the above formulae to the semantically equivalent formulae

$$3 \sqcup x_{\text{Nil},\text{Nil}} \sqcup x_{P,Q}$$

Of course it is no coincidence that we arrive at more less the exact distance between P and Q, as the equations of $E_{\mathcal{M}}$ exactly encode the definition of $\Psi_{\mathcal{M}}$. Hence, we can even state the following lemma

Lemma 3. *If* $d(m,n) = \rho(x_{m,n})$ *for arbitrary* $m, n \in M$, *then* $\llbracket E(x_{m,n}) \rrbracket \rho = \Psi(d)(m,n)$

Using this, one quickly arrives at the main result of this section, namely that we can encode our timed bisimilarity distance using Convex Lattice Equation Systems.

Theorem 6. $\mu\Psi_{\mathcal{M}}(m,n) \leq \varepsilon$ *iff* $\models_{E_{\mathcal{M}}} x_{m,n} \leq \varepsilon$.

Corollary 1. $\mu\Psi_{\mathcal{M}}(m,n) \leq \varepsilon$ *iff* $\vdash_{E_{\mathcal{M}}} x_{m,n} \leq \varepsilon$.

Example 8. Let us finally reconsider the TCCS processes P and Q from Example 7. Here we give the proof tree for $\vdash_{E_{\mathcal{M}}} x_{P,Q} \leq 3$ under the reduced defining Convex Lattice Equation System:

$$x_{P,Q} = 3 \sqcup x_{\text{Nil,Nil}} \sqcup x_{P,Q}$$
$$x_{\text{Nil,Nil}} = 0$$

$$
\cfrac{
\cfrac{
x_{P,Q} \leq 3 \vdash_{E_{\mathcal{M}}} 3 \leq 3 \; (A_5) \qquad
\cfrac{
\cfrac{
\cfrac{
\cfrac{
x_{\text{Nil,Nil}}, x_{P,Q} \leq 3 \vdash_{E_{\mathcal{M}}} 0 \leq 0 \;(A_5)
}{x_{\text{Nil,Nil}}, x_{P,Q} \leq 3 \vdash_{E_{\mathcal{M}}} 0 \leq 3}\;(A_2)
}{x_{P,Q} \leq 3 \vdash_{E_{\mathcal{M}}} x_{\text{Nil,Nil}} \leq 3}\;(A_4)
}{x_{P,Q} \leq 3 \vdash_{E_{\mathcal{M}}} 3 \sqcup x_{\text{Nil,Nil}} \leq 3}\;(A_6) \qquad
\cfrac{}{x_{P,Q} \leq 3 \vdash_{E_{\mathcal{M}}} x_{P,Q} \leq 3}\;(A_3)
}{x_{P,Q} \leq 3 \vdash_{E_{\mathcal{M}}} (3 \sqcup x_{\text{Nil,Nil}}) \sqcup x_{P,Q} \leq 3}\;(A_6)
}{\vdash_{E_{\mathcal{M}}} x_{P,Q} \leq 3}\;(A_4)
$$

□

6   Conclusion

More than 10 years ago, Henzinger advocated the use of *quantitative* notions of correctness, as opposed to *Boolean*, for a more refined view of a quantitative system which, if not fully correct, can still be correct up to a certain degree. Taking to hear Henzinger's suggestion, in this paper we proposed a quantitative extension of [26]. The result of this effort is *Convex Lattice Equation Systems* (CLES), a universal framework for encoding abstract quantitative notions of correctness, such as behavioral metrics for probabilistic and timed systems. We presented a sound and complete proof system for checking consistency of statements of the form $E \leq \varepsilon$ over a CLES, where E is an convex lattice expression expressing some property of the CLES and ε is an element from the complete lattice expressing a bound. To demonstrate the generality of this framework, we showed how value functions of Simple Stochastic Games and behavioural distances between timed systems may be encoded using CLES. We also showed examples of proof derivations which exploits the local exploration of the equations of a CLES to check consistency statements. As in [26], this proof system paves the way for an on-the-fly algorithm for checking consistency statements over a CLES.

References

1. Algayres, B., Coelho, V., Doldi, L., Garavel, H., Lejeune, Y., Rodríguez, C.: VESAR: a pragmatic approach to formal specification and verification. Comput. Netw. ISDN Syst. **25**(7), 779–790 (1993)
2. Andersen, H.R.: Model checking and Boolean graphs. In: Krieg-Brückner, B. (ed.) ESOP 1992. LNCS, vol. 582, pp. 1–19. Springer, Heidelberg (1992). https://doi.org/10.1007/3-540-55253-7_1
3. Andersen, J.R., et al.: CAAL: concurrency workbench, Aalborg edition. In: Leucker, M., Rueda, C., Valencia, F.D. (eds.) ICTAC 2015. LNCS, vol. 9399, pp. 573–582. Springer, Cham (2015). https://doi.org/10.1007/978-3-319-25150-9_33
4. Bacci, G., Bacci, G., Larsen, K.G., Mardare, R.: Computing behavioral distances, compositionally. In: Chatterjee, K., Sgall, J. (eds.) MFCS 2013. LNCS, vol. 8087, pp. 74–85. Springer, Heidelberg (2013). https://doi.org/10.1007/978-3-642-40313-2_9
5. Bacci, G., Bacci, G., Larsen, K.G., Mardare, R.: On-the-fly exact computation of bisimilarity distances. In: Piterman, N., Smolka, S.A. (eds.) TACAS 2013. LNCS, vol. 7795, pp. 1–15. Springer, Heidelberg (2013). https://doi.org/10.1007/978-3-642-36742-7_1
6. Bacci, G., Bacci, G., Larsen, K.G., Mardare, R.: Complete axiomatization for the bisimilarity distance on Markov chains. In: Desharnais, J., Jagadeesan, R. (eds.) 27th International Conference on Concurrency Theory, CONCUR 2016, Québec City, Canada, 23–26 August 2016, volume 59 of LIPIcs, pp. 21:1–21:14. Schloss Dagstuhl - Leibniz-Zentrum für Informatik (2016)
7. Bacci, G., Bacci, G., Larsen, K.G., Mardare, R.: Complete axiomatization for the total variation distance of Markov chains. In: Staton, S. (ed.) Proceedings of the Thirty-Fourth Conference on the Mathematical Foundations of Programming Semantics, MFPS 2018, Dalhousie University, Halifax, Canada, 6–9 June 2018, volume 341 of Electronic Notes in Theoretical Computer Science, pp. 27–39. Elsevier (2018)
8. Bacci, G., Bacci, G., Larsen, K.G., Mardare, R., Tang, Q., van Breugel, F.: Computing probabilistic bisimilarity distances for probabilistic automata. Log. Methods Comput. Sci. **17**(1) (2021)
9. Čerāns, K., Godskesen, J.C., Larsen, K.G.: Timed modal specification—Theory and tools. In: Courcoubetis, C. (ed.) CAV 1993. LNCS, vol. 697, pp. 253–267. Springer, Heidelberg (1993). https://doi.org/10.1007/3-540-56922-7_21
10. Chen, D., van Breugel, F., Worrell, J.: On the complexity of computing probabilistic bisimilarity. In: Birkedal, L. (ed.) FoSSaCS 2012. LNCS, vol. 7213, pp. 437–451. Springer, Heidelberg (2012). https://doi.org/10.1007/978-3-642-28729-9_29
11. Cleaveland, R., Parrow, J., Steffen, B.: The concurrency workbench. In: Sifakis, J. (ed.) CAV 1989. LNCS, vol. 407, pp. 24–37. Springer, Heidelberg (1990). https://doi.org/10.1007/3-540-52148-8_3
12. Condon, A.: On algorithms for simple stochastic games. In: Advances in Computational Complexity Theory, volume 13 of DIMACS Series in Discrete Mathematics and Theoretical Computer Science, pp. 51–72. DIMACS/AMS (1990)
13. Condon, A.: The complexity of stochastic games. Inf. Comput. **96**(2), 203–224 (1992)
14. Desharnais, J., Gupta, V., Jagadeesan, R., Panangaden, P.: Metrics for labelled Markov processes. Theor. Comput. Sci. **318**(3), 323–354 (2004)

15. Desharnais, J., Laviolette, F., Tracol, M.: Approximate analysis of probabilistic processes: logic, simulation and games. In: Fifth International Conference on the Quantitative Evaluaiton of Systems (QEST 2008), Saint-Malo, France, 14–17 September 2008, pp. 264–273. IEEE Computer Society (2008)
16. Easterbrook, S.M., Chechik, M.: A framework for multi-valued reasoning over inconsistent viewpoints. In: Müller, H.A., Harrold, M.J., Schäfer, W. (eds.) Proceedings of the 23rd International Conference on Software Engineering, ICSE 2001, Toronto, Ontario, Canada, 12–19 May 2001, pp. 411–420. IEEE Computer Society (2001)
17. Fahrenberg, U., Thrane, C.R., Larsen, K.G.: Distances for weighted transition systems: games and properties. In: Massink, M., Norman, G. (eds.) Proceedings Ninth Workshop on Quantitative Aspects of Programming Languages, QAPL 2011, Saarbrücken, Germany, 1–3 April 2011, volume 57 of EPTCS, pp. 134–147 (2011)
18. Garavel, H., Lang, F., Mateescu, R., Serwe, W.: CADP 2010: a toolbox for the construction and analysis of distributed processes. In: Abdulla, P.A., Leino, K.R.M. (eds.) TACAS 2011. LNCS, vol. 6605, pp. 372–387. Springer, Heidelberg (2011). https://doi.org/10.1007/978-3-642-19835-9_33
19. Goubault-Larrecq, J.: Prevision domains and convex powercones. In: Amadio, R. (ed.) FoSSaCS 2008. LNCS, vol. 4962, pp. 318–333. Springer, Heidelberg (2008). https://doi.org/10.1007/978-3-540-78499-9_23
20. Henzinger, T.A.: From Boolean to quantitative notions of correctness. In: Hermenegildo, M.V., Palsberg, J. (eds.) Proceedings of the 37th ACM SIGPLAN-SIGACT Symposium on Principles of Programming Languages, POPL 2010, Madrid, Spain, 17–23 January 2010, pp. 157–158. ACM (2010)
21. Henzinger, T.A., Majumdar, R., Prabhu, V.S.: Quantifying similarities between timed systems. In: Pettersson, P., Yi, W. (eds.) FORMATS 2005. LNCS, vol. 3829, pp. 226–241. Springer, Heidelberg (2005). https://doi.org/10.1007/11603009_18
22. Henzinger, T.A., Sifakis, J.: The embedded systems design challenge. In: Misra, J., Nipkow, T., Sekerinski, E. (eds.) FM 2006. LNCS, vol. 4085, pp. 1–15. Springer, Heidelberg (2006). https://doi.org/10.1007/11813040_1
23. Juba, B.: On the hardness of simple stochastic games. Master's thesis, Carnegie Mellon University, Pittsburgh, PA, USA, May 2005
24. Kupferman, O., Lustig, Y.: Latticed simulation relations and games. Int. J. Found. Comput. Sci. **21**(2), 167–189 (2010)
25. Larsen, K.G., Fahrenberg, U., Thrane, C.R.: Metrics for weighted transition systems: axiomatization and complexity. Theoret. Comput. Sci. **412**(28), 3358–3369 (2011)
26. Larsen, K.G.: Efficient local correctness checking. In: von Bochmann, G., Probst, D.K. (eds.) CAV 1992. LNCS, vol. 663, pp. 30–43. Springer, Heidelberg (1993). https://doi.org/10.1007/3-540-56496-9_4
27. Larsen, K.G., Skou, A.: Bisimulation through probabilistic testing. In: Conference Record of the Sixteenth Annual ACM Symposium on Principles of Programming Languages, Austin, Texas, USA, 11–13 January 1989, pp. 344–352. ACM Press (1989)
28. Liggett, T., Lippman, S.A.: Stochastic games with perfect information and time average payoff. SIAM Rev. **11**(4), 604–607 (1969)
29. Liu, X., Smolka, S.A.: Simple linear-time algorithms for minimal fixed points. In: Larsen, K.G., Skyum, S., Winskel, G. (eds.) ICALP 1998. LNCS, vol. 1443, pp. 53–66. Springer, Heidelberg (1998). https://doi.org/10.1007/BFb0055040
30. Man, K.L.: μCRL: a computer science based approach for specification and verification of hardware circuits, vol. 01, pp. I-387–I-390 (2008)

31. Mislove, M.: Nondeterminism and probabilistic choice: obeying the laws. In: Palamidessi, C. (ed.) CONCUR 2000. LNCS, vol. 1877, pp. 350–365. Springer, Heidelberg (2000). https://doi.org/10.1007/3-540-44618-4_26

32. Rosenmann, A.: On the distance between timed automata. In: André, É., Stoelinga, M. (eds.) FORMATS 2019. LNCS, vol. 11750, pp. 199–215. Springer, Cham (2019). https://doi.org/10.1007/978-3-030-29662-9_12

33. Tang, Q., van Breugel, F.: Computing probabilistic bisimilarity distances via policy iteration. In: CONCUR, volume 59 of LIPIcs, pp. 22:1–22:15. Schloss Dagstuhl - Leibniz-Zentrum für Informatik (2016)

34. Tarski, A.: A lattice-theoretical fixpoint theorem and its applications. Pac. J. Math. **5**(2), 285–309 (1955)

35. Thrane, C.R., Fahrenberg, U., Larsen, K.G.: Quantitative analysis of weighted transition systems. J. Log. Algebr. Methods Program. **79**(7), 689–703 (2010)

36. Tix, R., Keimel, K., Plotkin, G.D.: Semantic domains for combining probability and non-determinism. Electron. Notes Theoret. Comput. Sci. **222**, 3–99 (2009)

37. Varacca, D., Winskel, G.: Distributing probability over non-determinism. Math. Struct. Comput. Sci. **16**(1), 87–113 (2006)

38. Wang, Y.: Real-time behaviour of asynchronous agents. In: Baeten, J.C.M., Klop, J.W. (eds.) CONCUR 1990. LNCS, vol. 458, pp. 502–520. Springer, Heidelberg (1990). https://doi.org/10.1007/BFb0039080

39. Yi, W.: CCS + time = an interleaving model for real time systems. In: Albert, J.L., Monien, B., Artalejo, M.R. (eds.) ICALP 1991. LNCS, vol. 510, pp. 217–228. Springer, Heidelberg (1991). https://doi.org/10.1007/3-540-54233-7_136

Variance Reduction in Stochastic Reaction Networks Using Control Variates

Michael Backenköhler[1,2](✉), Luca Bortolussi[1,3], and Verena Wolf[1]

[1] Saarland University, Saarbrücken, Germany
`michael.backenkoehler@uni-saarland.de`
[2] Saarbrücken Graduate School of Computer Science, Saarbrücken, Germany
[3] University of Trieste, Trieste, Italy

Abstract. Monte Carlo estimation in plays a crucial role in stochastic reaction networks. However, reducing the statistical uncertainty of the corresponding estimators requires sampling a large number of trajectories. We propose control variates based on the statistical moments of the process to reduce the estimators' variances. We develop an algorithm that selects an efficient subset of infinitely many control variates. To this end, the algorithm uses resampling and a redundancy-aware greedy selection. We demonstrate the efficiency of our approach in several case studies.

Keywords: Chemical reaction network · Stochastic Simulation Algorithm · Moment equations · Control variates · Variance reduction · Monte Carlo

1 Introduction

Stochastic reaction networks that are used to describe cellular processes are often subject to inherent stochasticity. The dynamics of gene expression, for instance, is influenced by single random events (e.g. transcription factor binding) and hence, models that take this randomness into account must monitor discrete molecular counts and reaction events that change these counts. Discrete-state continuous-time Markov chains have successfully been used to describe networks of chemical reactions over time that correspond to the basic events of such processes. The time-evolution of the corresponding probability distribution is given by the chemical master equation, which is a system of differential equations with one equation for each possible molecular count. However, its numerical solution is extremely challenging because of the enormous size of the underlying state-space.

In contrast, analysis approaches based on sampling, such as the Stochastic Simulation Algorithm (SSA) [23], can be applied independent of the size of the model's state-space. However, statistical approaches are costly since a large

© Springer Nature Switzerland AG 2022
J.-F. Raskin and K. Chatterjee (Eds.): Principles of Systems Design, LNCS 13660, pp. 456–474, 2022.
https://doi.org/10.1007/978-3-031-22337-2_22

number of simulation runs is necessary to reduce the statistical inaccuracy of estimators. This problem is particularly severe if reactions occur on multiple time scales or if the event of interest is rare. A particularly popular technique to speed up simulations is τ-leaping which applies multiple reactions in one step of the simulation. However, such multi-step simulations rely on certain assumptions about the number of reactions in a certain time interval. These assumptions are typically only approximately fulfilled and therefore introduce approximation errors on top of the statistical uncertainty of the considered point estimators.

Variance reduction techniques are an alternative to approaches that decrease the computational costs of each SSA run. Instead of focusing on making sample generation more efficient, most variance reduction methods modify the estimator. The modified estimate has the same expected value as the original one. However its variance is (hopefully) equal or lower than the original estimator's variance. This means, that "better" estimates with comparable confidence are possible at lower cost. For control variates this means, that the estimation of the expected value $\mathbb{E}(X)$ of some random variable X is replaced. If another correlated random variable with $\mathbb{E}(Y) = 0$, i.e. a control variate, is known we are in luck. Then, we can estimate $\mathbb{E}(X + bY)$ instead which is more efficient because the variance of $X + bY$ is lower when choosing b wisely. By reducing the variance of the estimators, these methods need fewer runs to achieve high statistical accuracy.

In this work, we approach the variance reduction problem by considering a (infinite) set of differential equations for the evolution of the statistical moments of the molecular counts. Instead of applying a moment closure and performing numerical integration [1,15], we use these equations to derive a combination of moment constraints. Such moment constraints have already been used for for parameter estimation [4] and for computing moment bounds using semi-definite programming [14,18]. Here, we interpret these constraints as random variables that are correlated with the estimators of interest usually given as functions of population variables. These constraints can be used as (linear) control variates in order to improve the final estimate and reduce its variance [28,43]. The method is easy on an intuitive level. If a control variate is positively correlated with the function to be estimated then we can use the estimate of the variate to adjust the target estimate.

The incorporation of control variates into the SSA introduces additional simulation costs for the calculation of the constraint values. These values are integrals over time, which we accumulate based on the piece-wise constant trajectories. This introduces a trade-off between the variance reduction that is achieved by using control variates versus the increased simulation cost. This trade-off is expressed as the product of the variance reduction ratio and the cost increase ratio.

For a good trade-off, it is crucial to find an appropriate set of control variates. Here we propose a class of constraints which is parameterized by a moment vector and a weighting parameter, resulting in infinitely many choices.

In previous work [5], we have proposed an algorithm that learns a set of control variates through refinement of an initial set. This initial set of control variates is based on samples of the time-weighting λ. Each control variate is then checked for effectiveness in isolation. Furthermore, the set is refined by considering variables pairwise to determine redundancies.

In this work, we improve on the initial selection of control variates. This initial set is build using a splitting approach akin to sequential Monte Carlo methods. Over multiple rounds, new control variates are sampled based on their performance in prior iterations. This way, we construct a set of candidate variates and select a subset using a greedy approach, which takes into account the correlation between variates. A benefit of this algorithm is that it is less sensitive to user input. In particular, no heuristic redundancy threshold has to be fixed, making this approach more flexible.

This approach applies to the Monte Carlo estimation of any quantity deal with any property that can be expressed in terms of expected values such as probabilities of complex path properties. Another advantage of our technique is that increased efficiency is achieved without the price of an additional approximation error as is the case for methods based on moment approximations or multi-step simulations.

This paper is structured as follows. In Sect. 2 we give a brief survey of methods and tools related to efficient stochastic simulation and moment techniques. In Sect. 3 we introduce the common stochastic semantics of stochastic reaction networks. From these semantics we show in Sect. 4 how to derive constraints on the moments of the transient distribution. The variance reduction technique of control variates is described in Sect. 5. We show the design of an algorithm using moment constraints to reduce sample variance in Sect. 6. The efficiency and other characteristics of this algorithm are evaluated on four non-trivial case studies in Sect. 7. Finally, we discuss the findings and give possibilities for further work in Sect. 8.

2   Related Work

Much research has been directed at the efficient analysis of stochastic reaction networks. Usually research focuses on improving efficiency by making certain approximations.

If the state-space is finite and small enough one can deal with the underlying Markov chain directly. But there are also cases where the transient distribution has an infinitely large support and one can still deal with explicit state probabilities. To this end, one can fix a finite state-space, that should contain most of the probability [31]. Refinements of the method work dynamically and adjust the state-space according to the transient distributions [3,25,30].

On the other end of the spectrum there are mean-field approximations, which model the mean densities faithfully in the system size limit [7]. In between there are techniques such as moment closure [40], that not only consider the mean, but also the variance and other higher order moments. These methods depend on ad-hoc approximations of higher order moments to close the ODE system given by the moment equations. Yet another class of methods approximate molecular counts continuously and approximate the dynamics in such a continuous space, e.g. the system size expansion [44] and the chemical Langevin equation [21].

While the moment closure method uses ad-hoc approximations for high order moments to facilitate numerical integration, they can be avoided in some contexts. For the equilibrium distribution, for example, the time-derivative of all moments is equal to zero. This directly yields constraints that have been used for parameter estimation at steady-state [4] and bounding moments of the equilibrium distribution using semi-definite programming [17,18,27]. The latter technique of bounding moments has been successfully adapted in the context of transient analysis [14,37,38]. We adapt the constraints proposed in these works to improve statistical estimations via stochastic simulation (cf. Sect. 4).

While the above techniques give a deterministic output, stochastic simulation generates single executions of the stochastic process [23]. This necessitates accumulating large numbers of simulation runs to estimate quantities. This adds a significant computational burden. Consequently, some effort has been directed at lowering this cost. A prominent technique is τ-leaping [22], which in one step performs multiple instead of only a single reaction. Another approach is to find approximations that are specific to the problem at hand, such as approximations based on time-scale separations [8,9].

Multilevel Monte Carlo methods have been applied in to time-inhomogeneous SRNs [2]. In this techniques estimates are combined using estimates of different approximation levels.

In the case of rare events, approaches based on importance sampling [20,36] and importance splitting [26] have been adapted to the setting of reaction networks. Importance sampling relies on a suitable change of the underlying probability measure, which is often handcrafted for each model, continually refined using the cross-entropy method [12,35], or derived from Gaussian approximations of the process [19]. Importance splitting decomposes the state space into level sets and estimates the rare event probability by a level-based splitting of sample paths before reaching the set of interest. It requires to construct a model-specific level function together with the corresponding splitting thresholds.

Recently, randomized quasi-Monte Carlo (RQMC) approaches have been adapted to the application area of stochastic reaction networks [6] and improved for the case of long simulation horizons with an extension to array-RQMC [34]. It is based on a tau-leaping approach where time is discretized and requires a level/importance function or a costly multivariate sort.

3   Stochastic Reaction Networks

A stochastic reaction network (SRN) describes the interactions between a set of species $S_1, \ldots, S_{n_S}$ in a well-stirred reactor. Since we assume that all reactant molecules are spatially uniformly distributed, we just keep track of the overall amount of each molecule. Therefore the state-space is given by $\mathcal{S} \subseteq \mathbb{N}^{n_S}$. These interactions are expressed a set of *reactions* with a certain inputs and outputs, given by the vectors v_j^- and v_j^+ for reaction $j = 1, \ldots, n_R$, respectively. Further-more, for reaction j the overall stoichiometric vector $v_j = v_j^+ - v_j^-$. A reactions are denoted as

$$\sum_{i=1}^{n_S} v_{ji}^- S_i \xrightarrow{c_j} \sum_{i=1}^{n_S} v_{ji}^+ S_i . \tag{1}$$

The reaction rate constant $c_j > 0$ gives us information on the propensity of the reaction. If just a constant is given, *mass-action* propensities are assumed. In a stochastic setting for some state $x \in S$ these are

$$\alpha_j(x) = c_j \prod_{i=1}^{n_S} \binom{x_i}{v_{ji}^-} . \tag{2}$$

The system's behavior is described by a stochastic process $\{X_t\}_{t \geq 0}$. The propensity function gives the infinitesimal probability of a reaction occurring, given a state x. That is, for a small time step $\delta t > 0$

$$\Pr(X_{t+\delta t} = x + v_j \mid X_t = x) = \alpha_j(x)\delta t + o(\delta t) . \tag{3}$$

This induces a corresponding continuous-time Markov chain (CTMC) on S with generator matrix[1]

$$Q_{x,y} = \begin{cases} \sum_{j:x+v_j=y} \alpha_j(x), & \text{if } x \neq y \\ -\sum_{j=1}^{n_R} \alpha_j(x), & \text{otherwise.} \end{cases} \tag{4}$$

Accordingly, the time-evolution of the process' distribution, given an initial distribution π_0, is given by the Kolmogorov forward equation, i.e. $\frac{d\pi_t}{dt} = Q\pi_t$, where $\pi_t(x) = \Pr(X_t = x)$. For a single state, it is commonly referred to as the *chemical master equation* (CME)

$$\frac{d}{dt}\pi_t(x) = \sum_{j=1}^{n_R} (\alpha_j(x - v_j)\pi_t(x - v_j) - \alpha_j(x)\pi_t(x)) . \tag{5}$$

A direct solution of (5) is usually not possible. If the state-space with non-negligible probability is suitably small, a state space truncation could be performed. That is, (5) is integrated on a possibly time-dependent subset $\hat{S}_t \subseteq S$ [25,31,41]. Instead of directly analyzing (5), one often resorts to simulating trajectories. A trajectory $\tau = x_0 t_1 x_1 t_1 \ldots t_n x_n$ over the interval $[0, T]$ is a sequence of states x_i and corresponding jump times t_i, $i = 1, \ldots, n$ and $t_n = T$. We can sample trajectories of X by using stochastic simulation [23].

Consider the birth-death model below as an example.

Model 1 (Birth-death process). *A single species* A *has a constant production and a decay that is linear in the current amount of molecules. Therefore the model consists of two mass-action reactions*

$$\varnothing \xrightarrow{\gamma} A, \quad A \xrightarrow{\delta} \varnothing ,$$

where $\varnothing$ denotes no reactant or no product, respectively.

---

[1] Assuming a fixed enumeration of the state space.

For Model 1 the change of probability mass in a single state $x > 0$ is described by expanding (5) and

$$\frac{d}{dt}\pi_t(x) = \gamma\pi_t(x-1) + \delta\pi_t(x+1) - (\gamma+\delta)\pi_t(x) .$$

We can generate trajectories of this model by choosing either reaction, with a probability that is proportional to its rate given the current state x_i. The jump time $t_i - t_{i+1}$ is determined by sampling from an exponential distribution with rate $\gamma + x_i\delta$.

4 Moment Constraints

The time-evolution of the expected value $\mathbb{E}\left(f(X_t)\right)$ of some function f can be directly derived from (5) by computing the sum $\sum_{x \in \mathcal{S}} f(x)\frac{d}{dt}\pi_t(x)$, which yields

$$\frac{d}{dt}\mathbb{E}\left(f(X_t)\right) = \sum_{j=1}^{n_R} \mathbb{E}\left((f(X_t + v_j) - f(X_t))\, \alpha_j(X_t)\right) . \tag{6}$$

While many choices of f are possible, for this work we will restrict ourselves to monomial functions $f(x) = x^m$, $m \in \mathbb{N}^{n_S}$ i.e. the *non-central moments* of the process. The *order* $|m|$ of a moment $\mathbb{E}\left(X^m\right)$ is the sum over the exponents, i.e. $|m| = \sum_i m_i$. The integration of (6) with such functions f is well-known in the context of moment approximations of SRN models. For most models the arising ODE system is infinitely large, because the time-derivative of low order moments usually depends on the values of higher order moments. To close this system, *moment closures*, i.e. ad-hoc approximations of higher order moments are applied [39]. The main drawback of this kind of analysis is that it is not known whether the chosen closure gives an accurate approximation for the case at hand. Here, such approximations are not necessary, since we will apply the moment dynamics in the context of stochastic sampling instead of trying to integrate (6).

Apart from integration strategies, setting (6) to zero has been used as a constraint for parameter estimation at steady-state [4] and bounding moments at steady-state [13,18,27]. The extension of the latter has recently lead to the adaption of these constraints to a transient setting [14,38]. These two transient constraint variants are analogously derived by multiplying (6) by a time-dependent, differentiable weighting function $w(t)$ and integrating:

Multiplying with $w(t)$ and integrating on $[t_0, T]$ yields [14,38]

$$w(T)\mathbb{E}\left(f(X_T)\right) - w(t_0)\mathbb{E}\left(f(X_{t_0})\right) - \int_{t_0}^{T} \frac{dw(t)}{dt}\mathbb{E}\left(f(X_t)\right) dt$$

$$= \sum_{j=1}^{n_R} \int_{t_0}^{T} w(t)\mathbb{E}\left((f(X_t + v_j) - f(X_t))\, \alpha_j(X_t)\right) dt \tag{7}$$

In the context of computing moment bounds via semi-definite programming the choices $w(t) = t^s$ [38] and $w(t) = e^{\lambda(T-t)}$ [14] have been proposed. While both choices proved to be effective in different case studies, relying solely on the latter choice, i.e. $w(t) = e^{\lambda(T-t)}$ was sufficient. We can further forgo the time inversion such that $w(t) = e^{\lambda t}$.

By expanding the rate functions and f in (7) and substituting the exponential weight function we can re-write (7) as

$$0 = e^{\lambda T} \mathbb{E}\left(f(X_T)\right) - \mathbb{E}\left(f(X_{t_0})\right) + \sum_k c_k \int_{t_0}^{T} e^{\lambda t} \mathbb{E}\left(X_t^{m_k}\right) dt \qquad (8)$$

with coefficients c_k and vectors m_k defined accordingly. Assuming the moments remain finite on $[0, T]$, we can define the random variable

$$Z = e^{\lambda T} f(X_T) - f(X_{t_0}) + \sum_k c_k \int_{t_0}^{T} e^{\lambda t} X_t^{m_k} dt \qquad (9)$$

with $\mathbb{E}(Z) = 0$.

Note, that a realization of Z depends on the whole trajectory $\tau = x_0 t_1 x_1 t_1 \dots t_n x_n$ over $[t_0, T]$. Thus, for the integral terms in (9) we have to compute sums

$$\frac{1}{\lambda} \sum_{i=1}^{n} \left(e^{\lambda t_{i+1}} - e^{\lambda t_i}\right) x_i^{m_k}, \qquad (10)$$

over a given trajectory. This accumulation is best done during the simulation to avoid storing the whole trajectory. Algorithm 1 specifies the stochastic simulation of system trajectories while computing the values of integrals (10) alongside the trajectory itself. The cost of a simulation using this algorithm is more expensive. For the method to be efficient, the variance reduction (Sect. 5) needs to overcompensate for this increased cost of a simulation run.

For Model 1 the moment equation for $f(x) = x$ becomes

$$\frac{d}{dt} \mathbb{E}(X_t) = \gamma - \delta \mathbb{E}(X_t) .$$

The corresponding constraint (8) with $\lambda = 0$ gives

$$0 = \mathbb{E}(X_T) - \mathbb{E}(X_0) - \gamma T + \delta \int_0^T \mathbb{E}(X_t) \, dt.$$

In this instance the constraint leads to an explicit function of the moment over time. If $X_0 = 0$ w.p. 1, then (8) becomes

$$\mathbb{E}(X_T) = \frac{\gamma}{\delta}\left(1 - e^{-\delta T}\right) \qquad (11)$$

when choosing $\lambda = \delta$.

Algorithm 1: SSA with accumulator updates

---

    input : π_0, T, P, n
    output: trajectory τ
1 initialize accumulator map A **for** $i = 1, \ldots, n$ **do**
2      $\tau \leftarrow$ empty list, $s \leftarrow$ sample from π_0, $t \leftarrow 0$;
3   **while** $t < T$ **do**
4          $\tau \leftarrow$ append$(\tau, (s, t))$;
5          $k \leftarrow$ sample reaction i with probability $\propto \alpha_i(s)$;
6          $\delta \sim \mathrm{Exp}\left(\sum_i \alpha_i(s)\right)$;
7   **for** $(m, \lambda) \in keys(A)$ **do**
8              $A[(m, \lambda)] \leftarrow A[(m, \lambda)] + \frac{1}{\lambda}\left(e^{\lambda(t+\delta)} - e^{\lambda t}\right)x^m$;
9          $s \leftarrow s + v_k$;
10         $t \leftarrow t + \delta$;
11   update means $\hat{V}$, $\hat{Z}$ and covariances $\hat{\Sigma}$ using A;
12   **for** $(m, \lambda) \in keys(A)$ **do**
13         $A[(m, \lambda)] \leftarrow 0$
14 **return** $(\hat{\Sigma}, \hat{V}, \hat{Z})$;

---

5 Control Variates

Before using the moment constraints derived above, we now discuss control variates in general. To this end let V be some random variable with finite moments. We are interested in the estimation of some quantity $\mathbb{E}(V)$ by stochastic simulation. Let $V_1, \ldots, V_n$ be independent samples of V. Then the sample mean $\hat{V}_n = \frac{1}{n}\sum_{i=1}^n V_k$ is an estimate of $\mathbb{E}(V)$. By the central limit theorem

$$\sqrt{n}\hat{V}_n \xrightarrow{d} N\left(\mathbb{E}(V), \sigma_V^2\right).$$

Now suppose, we know of a random variable Z with $0 = \mathbb{E}(Z)$. The variable Z is called a *control variate*. If a control variate Z is correlated with V, we can use it to reduce the variance of $\hat{V}_n$ [24,32,43,45]. For example, consider we are running a set of simulations and consider a single constraint. If the estimated value of this constraint is larger than zero and we estimate a positive correlation between the constraint Z and V, we would, intuitively, like to decrease our estimate $\hat{V}_n$ accordingly. This results in an estimation of the mean of the random variable

$$Y_\beta = V - \beta Z$$

instead of V. The variance

$$\sigma_{Y_\beta}^2 = \sigma_V^2 - 2\beta\mathrm{Cov}(V, Z) + \beta^2\sigma_Z^2.$$

The optimal choice β can be computed by considering the minimum of $\sigma_{Y_\beta}^2$. Then

$$\beta^* = \mathrm{Cov}(V, Z)/\sigma_Z^2.$$

Therefore $\sigma_{Y_{\beta^*}} = \sigma_Z^2(1 - \rho_{VZ}^2)$, where ρ_{VZ} is the correlation of Z and V.

If we have multiple control variates, we can proceed in a similar fashion. Now, let Z denote a vector of d control variates and let

$$\Sigma = \begin{bmatrix} \Sigma_Z & \Sigma_{VZ} \\ \Sigma_{ZV} & \sigma_V^2 \end{bmatrix}$$

be the covariance matrix of (Z, V). As above, we estimate the mean of $Y_\beta = V - \beta^\top Z$. The ideal choice of β is the result of an ordinary least squares regression between V and Z_i, $i = 1, \ldots, n$. Specifically, $\beta^* = \Sigma_Z^{-1}\Sigma_{ZV}$. Then, asymptotically the variance of this estimator is [43],

$$\sigma_{\hat{Y}_{\beta^*}}^2 = (1 - R_{ZV}^2)\sigma_V^2, \quad R_{ZV}^2 = \Sigma_{ZV}\Sigma_Z^{-1}\Sigma_{ZV}/\sigma_V^2. \tag{12}$$

This is commonly known as the fraction of variance unexplained [16]. In practice, however, β^* is unknown and needs to be replaced by an estimate $\hat{\beta}$. This leads to an increase in the estimator's variance. Under the assumption of Z and V having a multivariate normal distribution [11,28], the variance of the estimator is $\hat{Y}_{\hat{\beta}} = \hat{V} - \hat{\beta}^\top \hat{Z}$

$$\sigma_{\hat{Y}_{\hat{\beta}}}^2 = \frac{n-2}{n-2-d}(1 - R_{ZV}^2)\sigma_V^2. \tag{13}$$

Clearly, a control variate is "good" if it is highly correlated with V. The constraint in (11) is an example of the extreme case. When we use this constraint as a control variate for the estimation of the mean at some time point t, it has a correlation of ± 1 since it describes the mean at that time precisely. Therefore the variance is reduced to zero. We thus aim to pick control variates that are highly correlated with V (Fig. 1).

Consider, for example, the above case of the birth-death process. If we choose (11) as a constraint, it would always yield the exact difference of the exact mean to the sample mean and therefore have a perfect correlation. Clearly, $\hat{\beta}$ reduces to 1 and $\hat{Y}_1 = \mathbb{E}(X_t)$.

6   Finding Efficient Control Variates

In this work, we propose a novel algorithm to synthesize an efficient set of control variates. As we have seen in the previous section, effective control variates have a high correlation with the target random variable. In the case of a single variate, the variance reduction is directly proportional to $1 - \rho^2$, where ρ is the correlation. In our case, infinitely many choices of Z are available. Our goal is to choose a subset that satisfies two objectives. Firstly, every selected control variate should reduce the estimator's variance. Secondly, the subset should not be too large, i.e. we want to avoid redundancies to achieve a good overall computational efficiency of the variance reduction.

Accordingly, we define an *efficiency* value to estimate whether the reduction in variance is compensating for the associated cost increase. A natural baseline of

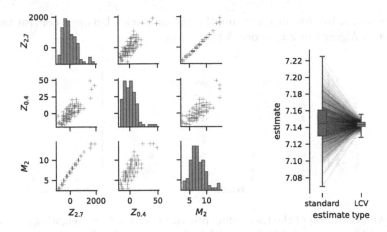

Fig. 1. (left) The correlation structure of control variates $Z_{0.4}$ and $Z_{2.7}$ with the objective random variable M_2 in Model 3. (right) Estimates using the same trajectories with and without using the control variates.

any variance reduction is that it outweighs its associated additional costs. Let σ_Y^2 be the variance of Y. The *efficiency* of the method is the ratio of the necessary cost to achieve a similar reduction with the CV estimate Y_{CV} compared to the standard estimate Y [29,33], i.e.

$$E = \frac{c_0 \sigma_Y^2}{c_1 \sigma_{Y_{CV}}^2} . \tag{14}$$

The cost ratio c_0/c_1 depends on both the specific implementation and the technical setup. The cost increase is mainly due to the computation of the integrals in (10). The accumulation over the trajectory directly increases the cost of a single simulation, which is the critical part of the estimation.

If the computation of a variate does not adequately compensate for its computation with variance reduction, we do not want to include it. Balancing both objectives is challenging because control variates often correlate with each other. Such correlations expose redundancy between different variates. This also becomes clear, when considering that the overall variance reduction depends on the coefficient of multiple correlation.

Here we follow a resampling paradigm. We start by building up a set of candidates using a particle splitting approach. After each splitting step, we generate a small number of SSA samples to estimate correlations. Promising candidates are chosen based on the *improvement* they provide and their time-weighting parameter λ is resampled (see Fig. 2). The main benefit of this bottom-up approach is its lower dependence on the initial sampling distribution of λ. Moreover, the procedure spends less time evaluating unpromising candidates. After generating a set of control variates, the overall covariance matrix is estimated using stochastic simulations. Using this information, we construct an efficient subset using a greedy scheme, taking into account the redundancies between control variates. We discuss Algorithm 2 in more detail below.

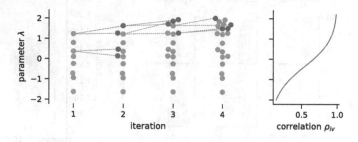

Fig. 2. An illustration of the resampling procedure for the time-weighting parameter λ using Model 3. Areas giving higher correlations are resampled through multiple rounds. The newly sampled values are given in blue. In each round only the new candidates are evaluated. (Color figure online)

Initialization. A tuple (m_k, λ_k) of a moment vector m_k and a time-weighting parameter λ_k uniquely identifies a control variate k. The algorithm starts out with an initial small set of control variates. That is, we use $w(t) = e^{\lambda_k t}$ and $f(x) = x^{m_k}$ in (7). For a given set of time-weighting parameters L, we use all moments up to some fixed order $n_{\max}$ (line 2). For a fixed moment vector m_k the time-weighting parameter λ_k can lead to vastly different correlations ρ_{kv} with the quantity of interest. The best choices of λ are usually not known beforehand. Therefore, we sample an initial set of λ's from a fixed distribution π_λ (line 1). Here, we use a standard normal distribution because its mean is the neutral weighting of $\lambda = 0$ and extreme values are unlikely.

Resampling. Promising candidates are chosen from all control variates based on the estimated *improvement ratio* they provide, i.e.

$$\hat{\gamma}_{kv} = (1 - \hat{\rho}_{kv}^2)^{-1} \tag{15}$$

following (13). Specifically, control variate k is chosen with probability proportional to $\hat{\gamma}_{kv}$ (line 8). The covariances of (only) the new variates are roughly estimated using very few (e.g., $d = 10$) SSA samples. For the selected variates I_{cands}, the time-weighting parameter is resampled using a step distribution. There is some freedom in the specifics of this resampling procedure. In particular, the number of splits n_c and descendants n_s for each candidate control the number of additional candidates. The algorithm performs n_r rounds of resampling. Figure 2 illustrates this part of the algorithm.

Covariance Estimation. After sampling a set of candidates this way, we need to select the most promising ones. For this, we are interested in covariances between

---

Algorithm 2: Estimate the mean of species i at time T

---

input : $n, d, n_{\max}, n_\lambda, n_c, n_s, n_r$
output: estimate using linear control variates

1   $L \leftarrow \{\lambda_i \sim \pi_\lambda \mid 1 \le i < n_\lambda\} \cup \{0\};$ `// initialization`
2   $P \leftarrow \{(m, \lambda) \mid 1 \le |m| \le n_{\max}, \lambda \in L\};$
3   $P_{\text{all}} = \emptyset;$
4   **for** $i = 1, \ldots, n_r$;   `// resampling`
5   **do**
6     $(\hat{\Sigma}, \hat{V}, \hat{Z}) \leftarrow \text{SSA}(\pi_0, T, P, d);$
7     $P_{\text{all}} \leftarrow P_{\text{all}} \cup P;$
8     $I_{\text{cands}} \leftarrow \{k \sim \hat{\gamma}_{kv} / \sum_\ell \hat{\gamma}_{\ell v} \mid 1 \le k \le |P_{\text{all}}|, j = 1, \ldots, n_c\};$
9     $P \leftarrow \bigcup_{k \in I_{\text{cands}}} \bigcup_{l=1}^{n_s} \{(m_k, \lambda_k') \mid \lambda_k' \sim N(\lambda_k, 0.5)\};$
10 $(\hat{\Sigma}, \hat{V}, \hat{Z}) \leftarrow \text{SSA}(\pi_0, T, P_{\text{all}}, 5d);$ `// covariance estimation`
11 $P^* = \emptyset;$
12 **while** $\exists i : (m_i, \lambda_i) \in P_{\text{all}} \setminus P^* \wedge \hat{\gamma}_{iv} \prod_{j=1; (m_j, \lambda_j) \in P^*}^{|P_{\text{all}}|} \hat{\gamma}_{ij}^{-1} > \epsilon;$ `// selection`
13 **do**
14     $k \leftarrow \arg\max_i \hat{\gamma}_{iv} \prod_{j=1; (m_j, \lambda_j) \in P^*}^{|P_{\text{all}}|} \hat{\gamma}_{ij}^{-1};$
15     $P^* \leftarrow P^* \cup \{(m_k, \lambda_k)\};$
16 $(\hat{\Sigma}, \hat{V}, \hat{Z}) \leftarrow \text{SSA}(\pi_0, T, P^*, n);$ `// estimation`
17 **return** $\hat{V} - (\hat{\Sigma}_Z^{-1} \hat{\Sigma}_{ZV})^\top \hat{Z}$

---

all control variates, as well. Since the resampling does not provide us with such estimates, we evaluate all candidates together for a fixed number of simulations (line 10).

Selection. The selection part of the algorithm (line 12) proceeds in a greedy fashion wrt. the potential estimated improvement $\hat{\gamma}_{iv}$ given by any variate. However, covariates often have high mutual correlations. For example, Z_λ and $Z_{\lambda+\epsilon}$ for a small ϵ are typically highly correlated — often more with each other than with the objective. We want to avoid this unnecessary computational overhead from computing nearly redundant information and numerical problems due to the covariance matrix inversion (see (12)). As a solution, we normalize the estimated improvement vector $(\hat{\gamma}_{iv})_i$ by the product of the fractions of explained variances by the already selected covariates. Therefore we choose the most promising candidate given a selection P^* as

$$\arg\max_{1 \le i \le |P_{\text{all}}|} \hat{\gamma}_{iv} \prod_{\substack{1 \le j \le |P_{\text{all}}| \\ (m_j, \lambda_j) \in P^*}} \hat{\gamma}_{ij}^{-1} \tag{16}$$

in line 14. This selection is done, until some lower threshold ϵ is reached (line 12).

Estimation. Finally, we simulate the model n times (line 16). The resulting information enables an LCV estimation (line 17).

7   Case Studies

The simulation is implemented in the Rust programming language[2]. The model description is parsed from a high level specification. Rate functions are compiled to stack programs for fast evaluation. To estimate the base-line cost c_0, 1000 estimations were performed without considering any control variates.

We first consider two case studies that have already been used in previous work [5]. The first model is a simple dimerization process, albeit with an countably infinite state-space. The second model is a switch model with a more complex bi-modal behavior. We now describe the models and the estimated quantities in detail.

Model 2 (Dimerization). *We first examine a simple dimerization model on an unbounded state-space*

$$\varnothing \xrightarrow{10} M, \quad 2M \xrightarrow{0.1} D$$

with initial condition $X_0^{(M)} = 0$.

Despite the models simplicity, the moment equations are not closed for this system due to the second reaction which is non-linear. Therefore a direct analysis of the expected value would require a closure. For this model we will estimate $\mathbb{E}(X_2^{(M)})$.

The following models is bimodal, i.e. they each posses two stable regimes among which they can switch stochastically. We choose the initial conditions such that the process will move towards either attracting region with equal probability.

Model 3 (Distributive Modification). *This model was introduced in [10]. It consists of the reactions*

$$X + Y \xrightarrow{.001} B + Y, \quad B + Y \xrightarrow{.001} 2Y,$$

$$Y + X \xrightarrow{.001} B + X, \quad B + X \xrightarrow{.001} 2X$$

with initial conditions $X_0^X = X_0^Y = X_0^{(B)} = 100$.

The expected value of interest here is $\mathbb{E}(X_{50}^{(X)})$.

We executed the presented estimation algorithm for 1000 times using $n = 10000$ simulations. Initially $n_\lambda = 10$ samples for the time-weighting parameter were drawn from a standard normal distribution ($\pi_\lambda = N(0,1)$). Constraints corresponding to each first-order moment, i.e. the process' expectations were

---

[2] https://www.rust-lang.org.

generated ($n_{max} = 1$). The covariance estimation during resampling used $d = 10$ samples.

We evaluated the algorithm both with and without resampling for these first two case studies. The algorithm without resampling leaves out lines 4–9 from Algorithm 2. The evaluation without resampling provides a good point of comparison to our previous heuristics performance on these cases. In the case of dimerization we observe a variance reduction of ≈ 27.67 compared to a best case reduction of ≈ 28.75 in our previous work. This close performance however has to balance very different slowdown factors. With our new heuristic the slowdown is a factor of ≈ 1.34 while in the previous case it was ≈ 1.95. Therefore the new method clearly outperforms in terms of efficiency (≈ 20.5 (new) versus ≈ 14.86 (old)). This is mainly due to the higher number of covariates used by the simple threshold heuristic. In contrast the new method takes into account redundancies between covariances while still retaining good performance. This becomes apparent when comparing the average number of used variates (≈ 3.34 (old) versus ≈ 1.98 (new)).

The variance reduction factor for the distributive modification model is similar at ≈ 2.63 (old) versus ≈ 2.66 (new). Noticeably, the new method uses on average fewer CVs (≈ 2.74) than the previous heuristic with the best efficiency (≈ 3.23). The overall efficiency of the new algorithm with 1.72 is slightly lower than the previous best value of 1.77, due to a higher slowdown. It is however important to note, that the trade-off differs significantly between different heuristics used in the previous algorithm. Furthermore, the lower average number of control variates would reduce the slowdown factor further, if more trajectories are generated.

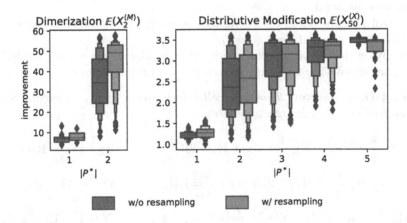

Fig. 3. The variance reduction factor $\sigma_Y^2/\sigma_{Y_{LCV}}^2$ over different numbers of selected covariates with and without the resampling procedure.

In Fig. 3 we contrast the variance improvement ratio with and without the resampling algorithm. For the dimerization model, we see a clear improvement of variance reduction. This improvement is due to the fact that the strongest correlations are present for $\lambda \approx 2.5$ (cf. Fig. 2). This region of the time-weighting parameter space is less likely to be sampled by the initial samples from the standard normal distribution. Therefore the resampling procedure is especially beneficial if the better parameters λ are farther from the origin. In case of the distributive modification case study, we see a slight improvement. Here, the best parameters λ are close to zero and thereby more likely to be sampled by a standard normal. Still, the resampling improves covariate performance for the most frequent cases of 2–4 covariates being selected (the case of 5 covariates has only a few instances). Note, that the additional cost incurred by the resampling procedure is comparatively small, because at most 4 candidates are evaluated in each iteration.

Next, we turn to the estimation of probabilities. In particular, we consider the event of a species being below a threshold ℓ at time t (species M for the dimerization and X for the distributive modification). In Fig. 4 we summarize the results of this study for varying levels ℓ. In both case studies we observe that control variates are efficient for probabilities not close to either zero or one. In this case control variates are able to reduce the variance of the estimated probabilities whilst maintaining a beneficial reduction-slowdown trade-off. This region is larger for the distributive modification model because of its bimodal behavior. If the probability to be estimated is close to either one or zero, the event occurs too rarely or too often, respectively, to adequately explain variance using linear correlations. We note, that the worst case efficiency is close to one. This is due to the algorithm throwing out all covariate candidates leaving us with a standard estimation. Only the initial covariate evaluation and resampling causes a slowdown, driving efficiency slightly below one. Naturally this cost decreases with more samples n.

Control variates based on test functions restricted to intervals did not lead to an improvement (data not shown).

Finally, with the lac operon model we consider a larger case study. This model consists of 11 species and 25 partly non-linear reactions.

Model 4 (Lac operon). *This is a well-known model of genetic regulation with positive feedback [42]. Its reactions are*

$$\varnothing \underset{k_1 9}{\overset{k_1}{\rightleftharpoons}} M_R, \quad M_R \overset{k_2}{\longrightarrow} M_R + R, \quad 2R \underset{k_4}{\overset{k_3}{\rightleftharpoons}} R_2, \quad R_2 + O \underset{k_6}{\overset{k_5}{\rightleftharpoons}} R_2O,$$

$$2I + R_2 \underset{k_8}{\overset{k_7}{\rightleftharpoons}} I_2R_2, \quad 2I + R_2O \underset{k_{10}}{\overset{k_9}{\rightleftharpoons}} I_2R_2 + O, \quad O \overset{k_{11}}{\longrightarrow} O + M_Y,$$

$$M_Y \overset{k_{13}}{\longrightarrow} M_Y + Y, \quad Y + I_{ex} \underset{k_{15}}{\overset{k_{14}}{\rightleftharpoons}} YI_{ex}, \quad YI_{ex} \overset{k_{16}}{\longrightarrow} Y + I, \quad I_{ex} \underset{k_{18}}{\overset{k_{17}}{\rightleftharpoons}} I,$$

$$M_Y \overset{k_{20}}{\longrightarrow} \varnothing, \quad R \overset{k_{21}}{\longrightarrow} \varnothing, \quad R_2 \overset{k_{22}}{\longrightarrow} \varnothing, \quad Y \overset{k_{23}}{\longrightarrow} \varnothing,$$

$$YI_{ex} \overset{k_{24}}{\longrightarrow} I, \quad I_2R_2 \overset{k_{25}}{\longrightarrow} 2I, \quad R_2O \overset{k_{12}}{\longrightarrow} R_2O + M_Y.$$

Initially, $X_0^{(O)} = 1$ and $X^{(I_{ex})} = 48177$ while all other abundancies are zero. The parameters are $k_1 = 0.111$, $k_2 = 15.0$, $k_3 = 103.8$, $k_4 = 0.001$, $k_5 = 1992.7$,

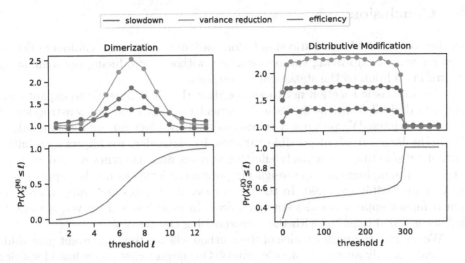

Fig. 4. The methods efficiency for the estimation of threshold probabilities. For each threshold ℓ at least 200 estimations were performed.

$k_6 = 2.4$, $k_7 = k_9 = 1.293d - 7$ $k_8 = 12$, $k_{10} = 9963.2$, $k_{11} = 0.5$, $k_{12} = 0.01$, $k_{13} = 30.0$, $k_{14} = 0.249$, $k_{15} = 0.1$, $k_{16} = 6.0d4$, $k_{17} = k_{18} = 0.92$, $k_{19} = k_{20} = 0.462$, $k_{21} = k_{22} = k_{23} = k_{24} = k_{25} = 0.2$.

We estimate the abundancy of LacY after one time unit, i.e. $\mathbb{E}(X_1^{(Y)})$. It is encoded by Y and facilitates the lactose import via reactions 14 and 16. A typical simulation of the system up to time-horizon $T = 1$ takes well above one minute of computational time. Therefore we reduce the number of used trajectories to $n = 1000$. The other settings remain as above.

Despite the high dimensionality, we observe a good efficiency value of $E \approx 4.85$. The slowdown caused by the method is approximately 1.98. A big part of this slowdown is due to the initial search of covariates. Initially 10 covariates are generated for each first order moment, i.e. each of the 11 species. The number of additionally resampled covariates is similar to previous case studies. Thus the main cost of the initial resampling and selection is due to the first iteration of the resampling loop and the simulation loop of the selection procedure. This part naturally has still potential for optimization: Not all known covariates need to be reconsidered at the selection stage. Instead, unpromising candidates could be discarded prior to that stage.

Still, the high variance reduction by a factor of approx. 9.64^{-1} more than compensates for this increase in computational cost, leading to the good overall efficiency. This shows that, even for more complex models, the method is applicable and can extremely beneficial for Monte Carlo estimation.

8   Conclusion

In the context of Monte Carlo simulation, variance reduction techniques offer an elegant way of improving the performance without introducing approximation errors in addition to the statistical uncertainty.

For stochastic reaction networks, we show that it is possible to exploit constraints derived from the statistical moment equations for the construction of control variates. We propose a robust method to select an appropriate subset from the large set of all possible variates. In particular, we improve an initial subset by selecting particularly effective variates and removing redundant variates. By resampling the time-weighting parameter λ we ensure that appropriate values are flexibly explored. In the worst case, all variates are dropped and the performance approaches the standard SSA. In most cases, however, a suitable subset is found together with the corresponding choices of λ.

We analyze the performance of the method when estimating event probabilities and not only average molecule counts. Our largest case study has 11 species and 24 reactions.

In the future, we will further explore the algorithmic design space. For example, the resampling distribution could be adjusted using decaying standard deviations. Furthermore, we will look at different test functions weighting the state space more flexibly.

Acknowledgements. This work was supported by the DFG project MULTIMODE.

References

1. Ale, A., Kirk, P., Stumpf, M.P.: A general moment expansion method for stochastic kinetic models. J. Chem. Phys. **138**(17), 174101 (2013)
2. Anderson, D.F., Yuan, C.: Low variance couplings for stochastic models of intracellular processes with time-dependent rate functions. Bull. Math. Biol. 1–29 (2018)
3. Andreychenko, A., Mikeev, L., Spieler, D., Wolf, V.: Parameter identification for Markov models of biochemical reactions. In: Gopalakrishnan, G., Qadeer, S. (eds.) CAV 2011. LNCS, vol. 6806, pp. 83–98. Springer, Heidelberg (2011). https://doi.org/10.1007/978-3-642-22110-1_8
4. Backenköhler, M., Bortolussi, L., Wolf, V.: Moment-based parameter estimation for stochastic reaction networks in equilibrium. IEEE/ACM Trans. Comput. Biol. Bioinform. (TCBB) **15**(4), 1180–1192 (2018)
5. Backenköhler, M., Bortolussi, L., Wolf, V.: Control variates for stochastic simulation of chemical reaction networks. In: Bortolussi, L., Sanguinetti, G. (eds.) CMSB 2019. LNCS, vol. 11773, pp. 42–59. Springer, Cham (2019). https://doi.org/10.1007/978-3-030-31304-3_3
6. Beentjes, C.H., Baker, R.E.: Quasi-Monte Carlo methods applied to tau-leaping in stochastic biological systems. Bull. Math. Biol. **81**(8), 2931–2959 (2019)
7. Bortolussi, L., Hillston, J., Latella, D., Massink, M.: Continuous approximation of collective system behaviour: a tutorial. Perform. Eval. **70**(5), 317–349 (2013)

8. Bortolussi, L., Milios, D., Sanguinetti, G.: Efficient stochastic simulation of systems with multiple time scales via statistical abstraction. In: Roux, O., Bourdon, J. (eds.) CMSB 2015. LNCS, vol. 9308, pp. 40–51. Springer, Cham (2015). https://doi.org/10.1007/978-3-319-23401-4_5

9. Cao, Y., Gillespie, D.T., Petzold, L.R.: The slow-scale stochastic simulation algorithm. J. Chem. Phys. **122**(1), 014116 (2005)

10. Cardelli, L., Csikász-Nagy, A.: The cell cycle switch computes approximate majority. Sci. Rep. **2**, 656 (2012)

11. Cheng, R.C.: Analysis of simulation experiments under normality assumptions. J. Oper. Res. Soc. **29**(5), 493–497 (1978)

12. Daigle Jr, B.J., Roh, M.K., Gillespie, D.T., Petzold, L.R.: Automated estimation of rare event probabilities in biochemical systems. J. Chem. Phys. **134**(4), 01B628 (2011)

13. Dowdy, G.R., Barton, P.I.: Bounds on stochastic chemical kinetic systems at steady state. J. Chem. Phys. **148**(8), 084106 (2018)

14. Dowdy, G.R., Barton, P.I.: Dynamic bounds on stochastic chemical kinetic systems using semidefinite programming. J. Chem. Phys. **149**(7), 074103 (2018)

15. Engblom, S.: Computing the moments of high dimensional solutions of the master equation. Appl. Math. Comput. **180**(2), 498–515 (2006)

16. Freedman, D.A.: Statistical Models: Theory and Practice. Cambridge University Press, Cambridge (2009)

17. Ghusinga, K.R., Lamperski, A., Singh, A.: Estimating stationary characteristic functions of stochastic systems via semidefinite programming. In: 2018 European Control Conference (ECC), pp. 2720–2725. IEEE (2018)

18. Ghusinga, K.R., Vargas-Garcia, C.A., Lamperski, A., Singh, A.: Exact lower and upper bounds on stationary moments in stochastic biochemical systems. Phys. Biol. **14**(4), 04LT01 (2017)

19. Gillespie, C.S., Golightly, A.: Guided proposals for efficient weighted stochastic simulation. J. Chem. Phys. **150**(22), 224103 (2019)

20. Gillespie, D.T., Roh, M., Petzold, L.R.: Refining the weighted stochastic simulation algorithm. J. Chem. Phys. **130**(17), 174103 (2009)

21. Gillespie, D.T.: The chemical Langevin equation. J. Chem. Phys. **113**(1), 297–306 (2000)

22. Gillespie, D.T.: Approximate accelerated stochastic simulation of chemically reacting systems. J. Chem. Phys. **115**(4), 1716–1733 (2001)

23. Gillespie, D.: Exact stochastic simulation of coupled chemical reactions. J. Phys. Chem. **81**(25), 2340–2361 (1977)

24. Glasserman, P., Yu, B.: Large sample properties of weighted Monte Carlo estimators. Oper. Res. **53**(2), 298–312 (2005)

25. Henzinger, T.A., Mateescu, M., Wolf, V.: Sliding window abstraction for infinite Markov chains. In: Bouajjani, A., Maler, O. (eds.) CAV 2009. LNCS, vol. 5643, pp. 337–352. Springer, Heidelberg (2009). https://doi.org/10.1007/978-3-642-02658-4_27

26. Jegourel, C., Legay, A., Sedwards, S.: Importance splitting for statistical model checking rare properties. In: Sharygina, N., Veith, H. (eds.) CAV 2013. LNCS, vol. 8044, pp. 576–591. Springer, Heidelberg (2013). https://doi.org/10.1007/978-3-642-39799-8_38

27. Kuntz, J., Thomas, P., Stan, G.B., Barahona, M.: Rigorous bounds on the stationary distributions of the chemical master equation via mathematical programming. arXiv preprint arXiv:1702.05468 (2017)

28. Lavenberg, S.S., Moeller, T.L., Welch, P.D.: Statistical results on control variables with application to queueing network simulation. Oper. Res. **30**(1), 182–202 (1982)
29. L'Ecuyer, P.: Efficiency improvement and variance reduction. In: Proceedings of the 26th Conference on Winter Simulation, pp. 122–132. Society for Computer Simulation International (1994)
30. Mateescu, M., Wolf, V., Didier, F., Henzinger, T.: Fast adaptive uniformisation of the chemical master equation. IET Syst. Biol. **4**(6), 441–452 (2010)
31. Munsky, B., Khammash, M.: The finite state projection algorithm for the solution of the chemical master equation. J. Chem. Phys. **124**(4), 044104 (2006)
32. Nelson, B.L.: Control variate remedies. Oper. Res. **38**(6), 974–992 (1990)
33. Owen, A.B.: Monte Carlo theory, methods and examples (2013)
34. Puchhammer, F., Abdellah, A.B., L'Ecuyer, P.: Variance reduction with array-RQMC for tau-leaping simulation of stochastic biological and chemical reaction networks. Bull. Math. Biol. **83**(8), 1–31 (2021)
35. Roh, M.K., Daigle, B.J., Jr., Gillespie, D.T., Petzold, L.R.: State-dependent doubly weighted stochastic simulation algorithm for automatic characterization of stochastic biochemical rare events. J. Chem. Phys. **135**(23), 234108 (2011)
36. Roh, M.K., Gillespie, D.T., Petzold, L.R.: State-dependent biasing method for importance sampling in the weighted stochastic simulation algorithm. J. Chem. Phys. **133**(17), 174106 (2010)
37. Sakurai, Y., Hori, Y.: A convex approach to steady state moment analysis for stochastic chemical reactions. In: 2017 IEEE 56th Annual Conference on Decision and Control (CDC), pp. 1206–1211. IEEE (2017)
38. Sakurai, Y., Hori, Y.: Bounding transient moments of stochastic chemical reactions. IEEE Control Syst. Lett. **3**(2), 290–295 (2019)
39. Schnoerr, D., Sanguinetti, G., Grima, R.: Comparison of different moment-closure approximations for stochastic chemical kinetics. J. Chem. Phys. **143**(18), 11B610_1 (2015)
40. Singh, A., Hespanha, J.P.: Lognormal moment closures for biochemical reactions. In: Proceedings of the 45th IEEE Conference on Decision and Control, pp. 2063–2068. IEEE (2006)
41. Spieler, D.: Numerical analysis of long-run properties for Markov population models. Ph.D. thesis, Saarland University (2014)
42. Stamatakis, M., Mantzaris, N.V.: Comparison of deterministic and stochastic models of the lac operon genetic network. Biophys. J. **96**(3), 887–906 (2009)
43. Szechtman, R.: Control variate techniques for Monte Carlo simulation. In: Proceedings of the 35th Conference on Winter Simulation: Driving Innovation, pp. 144–149. Winter Simulation Conference (2003)
44. Van Kampen, N.G.: Stochastic Processes in Physics and Chemistry, vol. 1. Elsevier (1992)
45. Wilson, J.R.: Variance reduction techniques for digital simulation. Am. J. Math. Manag. Sci. **4**(3–4), 277–312 (1984)

Software Systems Theory

From Interface Automata
to Hypercontracts

Inigo Incer[1,2(✉)], Albert Benveniste[2], Alberto Sangiovanni-Vincentelli[1],
and Sanjit A. Seshia[1]

[1] University of California, Berkeley, USA
inigo@berkeley.edu
[2] INRIA/IRISA, Rennes, France

Abstract. de Alfaro and Henzinger's interface automata brought renewed vigor to the tasks of specifying software formally and reasoning about systems compositionally. The key ingredients to this approach were the separation of concerns between environment and implementation, a light-weight behavioral interface that enabled more comprehensive compatibility checks than those allowed by type checking, and the notion of *optimistic* composition of specifications. This new impetus helped launch a research program of formally analyzing and designing general cyber-physical systems compositionally, where contract-based design has been playing a fundamental role. In this paper, we discuss the path connecting interface automata to the theory of contracts, with a special emphasis on hypercontracts, a recent development of contract theory.

1 Introduction

The task of formally verifying software was first enunciated by Turing in 1949. His three-page document starts with a familiar paradigm: "How can one check a routine in the sense of making sure that it is right? In order that the man who checks may not have too difficult a task the programmer should make a number of definite assertions which can be checked individually, and from which the correctness of the whole programme easily follows" [36]. The software verification agenda gained force and focus some twenty years later with Floyd [15] and Hoare [19]. An important part of the verification effort is writing the specifications that programs should satisfy. A methodology for this task was reported by Parnas in 1972 [28]. Concurrency introduced a new angle to writing specifications: it is no longer sufficient to specify an input/output relation for a concurrently-executing routine, as this maintains an ongoing relation with its environment. This realization led to the definition of a reactive system by Harel and Pnueli in 1985 [17]. Interface automata find a home in this context.

In 1998, de Alfaro and Henzinger introduced Interface Automata (IA), a "light-weight formalism for capturing temporal aspects of software component interfaces which are beyond the reach of traditional type systems" [2]. The formalism used by the authors has several distinguishing traits: the choice of an

---

This paper is based on [20] and [22].

© Springer Nature Switzerland AG 2022
J.-F. Raskin and K. Chatterjee (Eds.): Principles of Systems Design, LNCS 13660, pp. 477–493, 2022.
https://doi.org/10.1007/978-3-031-22337-2_23

automata-based language, the partition of symbols into inputs and outputs, a new refinement relation, the separation of concerns between assumptions from the environment and responsibilities of the object under specification, and an optimistic approach to composing automata.

IA gave rise to a series of *interface theories* which extended it in multiple ways, for example, modal I/O automata [24], resource interfaces [8], timed interfaces [3], timed IO automata [12], permissive interfaces [18], modal interfaces [33], and interfaces with support for component reuse [14]. Moreover, IA influenced approaches to formally design and analyze cyber-physical systems.

From a practical standpoint, a difficulty with interface theories is the tight coupling between assumptions on the environment and guarantees expected from the component. However, the explicit expression of assumptions and guarantees seems to be a conceptually simpler approach to system specification (see [7] Chap. 12). Assume-guarantee contract-based design can then be seen as an alternative to formal system specification with a friendlier formalism for practicing designers.

Recognizing the fundamental contributions by Tom Henzinger, this paper is about establishing a relationship between the two approaches and generalizing contracts to a more powerful formalism to extend their applicability.

2 Interface Automata

Let Σ be a fixed set of actions[1]. We partition Σ into sets or input and output actions, I and O, respectively.

Definition 1. *An interface automaton [2] is a tuple $A = (I, O, Q, q_0, \rightarrow)$, where Q is a finite set whose elements we call states, $q_0 \in Q$ is the initial state, and $\rightarrow \subseteq Q \times \Sigma \times Q$ is a deterministic transition relation.*

In the original definition, interface automata (IA) also use the concept of internal actions, which can be represented as output actions in the synchronous case. Syntactically, interface automata are indistinguishable from IO automata [25]. They, however, differ in their associated semantic concepts of refinement and parallel composition. Also, in contrast to IO automata, which require their implementations to be receptive to input actions, IA state the assumptions on the environments in which valid implementations run. In other words, certain moves by the environment may not be allowed by the IA.

Definition 2. *Given two interface automata (IA) $A_i = (I, O, Q_i, q_{i,0}, \rightarrow_i) \in \mathcal{A}_I$ for $i \in \{1, 2\}$, the state $q_1 \in Q_1$ refines $q_2 \in Q_2$, written $q_1 \leq q_2$, if*

- $\forall \sigma \in O, q_1' \in Q_1.\ q_1 \xrightarrow{\sigma}_1 q_1' \Rightarrow \exists q_2' \in Q_2.\ q_2 \xrightarrow{\sigma}_2 q_2'$ *and* $q_1' \leq q_2'$ *and*
- $\forall \sigma \in I, q_2' \in Q_2.\ q_2 \xrightarrow{\sigma}_2 q_2' \Rightarrow \exists q_1' \in Q_1.\ q_1 \xrightarrow{\sigma}_1 q_1'$ *and* $q_1' \leq q_2'$.

A_1 *refines* A_2, *written* $A_1 \leq A_2$, *if* $q_{1,0} \leq q_{2,0}$.

---

[1] To simplify our development, we assume that all interface automata share the same action alphabet.

Note that this is the definition of alternating simulation by Alur et al. [4]. Compared to the usual definition of simulation for automata, alternating simulation builds on a game view of automata, in which inputs are seen as adversarial.

IA are composed according to an optimistic approach: for two IA to be composed, it suffices that there be an environment that allows both to operate.

Definition 3. *Let $A_1 = (I_1, O_1, Q_1, q_{1,0}, \rightarrow_1)$ and $A_2 = (I_2, O_2, Q_2, q_{2,0}, \rightarrow_2)$ be two IA. Let $I_1 \cup I_2 = \Sigma.^2$ Then, the composition of A_1 and A_2, $A_1 \parallel A_2$, is an IA $(I, O, Q, (q_{1,0}, q_{2,0}), \rightarrow_c)$, where $I = I_1 \cap I_2$, $O = O_1 \cup O_2$, and the set of states and the transition relation are obtained as follows:*

- *Initialize $Q := Q_1 \times Q_2$. For every $\sigma \in \Sigma$, $(q_1, q_2) \xrightarrow{\sigma}_c (q'_1, q'_2)$ if $q_1 \xrightarrow{\sigma}_1 q'_1$ and $q_2 \xrightarrow{\sigma}_2 q'_2$.*
- *Initialize the set of invalid states to those states where one interface automaton can generate an output action that the other interface automaton does not accept:*

$$
N := \left\{ (q_1, q_2) \in Q_1 \times Q_2 \;\middle|\; \begin{array}{l} \exists q'_2 \in Q_2, \sigma \in O_2 \, \forall q'_1 \in Q_1. \; q_2 \xrightarrow{\sigma}_2 q'_2 \wedge \neg \left(q_1 \xrightarrow{\sigma}_1 q'_1 \right) \; or \\ \exists q'_1 \in Q_1, \sigma \in O_1 \, \forall q'_2 \in Q_2. \; q_1 \xrightarrow{\sigma}_1 q'_1 \wedge \neg \left(q_2 \xrightarrow{\sigma}_2 q'_2 \right) \end{array} \right\}.
$$

- *Also consider invalid any state in which an output action of one of the interface automata makes a transition to an invalid state, i.e., iterate this rule until convergence:*

$$
N := N \cup \left\{ (q_1, q_2) \in Q_1 \times Q_2 \;\middle|\; \begin{array}{l} \exists (q'_1, q'_2) \in N, \sigma \in O_1 \cup O_2. \\ (q_1, q_2) \xrightarrow{\sigma}_c (q'_1, q'_2) \end{array} \right\}.
$$

- *Remove the invalid states from the IA to obtain*

$$
Q := Q \setminus N \; and
$$
$$
\rightarrow_c := \rightarrow_c \setminus \{ (q, \sigma, q') \in \rightarrow_c \mid q \in N \; or \; q' \in N \}.
$$

Abadi and Lamport [1] studied the composition of specifications split into assumptions on the environment and responsibilities of the object under specification. As shown by Benveniste et al. [7], the composition of interface automata follows the composition principle enunciated by Abadi and Lamport.

3   Cyber-Physical Systems and Assume-Guarantee Contracts

Cyber-Physical Systems and the Practical Relevance of Traces. The control community had developed since the early 1990's a hybrid system modeling approach based on ODEs plus discrete-time dynamical systems. Solution

---

[2] Since the sets of input and output actions for a given IA partition Σ, this condition is equivalent to requiring that the two IA don't share outputs.

trajectories of such models are called *traces* in the computer science community. The concept of trace is indeed playing a fundamental role in CPS.

Referring to a paper by Dijkstra from 1965 [13], Lamport writes, "Dijkstra was aware from the beginning of how subtle concurrent algorithms are and how easy it is to get them wrong. He wrote a careful proof of his algorithm. The computational model implicit in his reasoning is that an execution is represented as a sequence of states... I have found this to be the most generally useful model of computation—for example, it underlies a Turing machine. I like to call it the standard model" [23]. During the 70s, making statements over the standard model became well established. The trace was the object that enabled us to conclude whether a program satisfied a certain requirement. Traces were given convenient syntactical representations with temporal logic, notably Pnueli's LTL [30] and Clarke and Emerson's CTL [9]. Many algebraic formalisms were also introduced to reason about systems whose components were modeled as collections of traces.

Component-Based Design. By refocusing on the interfaces of reactive systems, interface automata brought new vigor to research in compositional design. Damm [11] introduced to systems engineering the notion of a *rich component* where functional and non-functional aspects of the design can be captured. This idea motivated the agenda of applying the techniques of formal methods to any kind of CPS, a theory and methodology called contract-based design [6,34]. An agenda for further development of component-based design for software is given in Sifakis's book on rigorous design [35], Sect. 5.3.

Assumptions and Guarantees as First Class Citizens: Assume-Guarantee contracts. Building on top of trace-based modeling, Assume-Guarantee (AG) contracts [6,7] provide a formal framework of contract-based design, in which assumptions and guarantees are first-class citizens. AG contracts assume that all functional and non-functional behaviors of the system have been modeled in advance. We assume an underlying set $\mathcal{B}$ of behaviors, generalizing traces or executions typical in the computer science literature.

Definition 4. *An assume-guarantee contract is a pair $\mathcal{C} = (A, G)$, where $A \subseteq \mathcal{B}$ models the assumptions made on the environment, and $G \subseteq \mathcal{B}$ the guarantees required of the object under specification.*

An *environment* $E \subseteq \mathcal{B}$ of $\mathcal{C}$ is a component that satisfies the assumptions of the contract, i.e., $E \subseteq A$. An *implementation* $M \subseteq \mathcal{B}$ of $\mathcal{C}$ is a component that satisfies the guarantees of the contract provided that it operates in an environment that satisfies the contract specifications, i.e., if $M \cap E \subseteq G$ for all environments E of $\mathcal{C}$.

Two contracts are *equivalent* if they have the same environments and the same implementations. By observing that the set of implementations is the set of all subsets of $G \cup \neg A$, we deduce that any contract (A, G) has the same environments and implementations as the contract $(A, G \cup \neg A)$. Moreover, we cannot increase the guarantees of this last contract without increasing its implementation set. For this reason, when a contract satisfies the constraint $G = G \cup \neg A$ (which is equivalent to $A \cup G = B$), the contract is *in canonical form* (some authors call it *saturated form*).

We say that a contract $\mathcal{C}$ *refines* a contract $\mathcal{C}'$ if the environments of $\mathcal{C}'$ are also environments of $\mathcal{C}$ and the implementations of $\mathcal{C}$ are also implementations of $\mathcal{C}'$. That is, the notion of refinement of AG contracts is covariant for implementations and contravariant for environments, just like in interface automata.

Definition 5. *If contracts $\mathcal{C} = (A, G)$ and $\mathcal{C}' = (A', G')$ are in canonical form, we say that $\mathcal{C} \leq \mathcal{C}'$ if $G \subseteq G'$ and $A' \subseteq A$.*

AG contracts are composed according to the composition principle of Abadi and Lamport [1]. When contracts $\mathcal{C}_i$ are composed, this principle states that the composite is the smallest specification satisfying the following constraints:

- any composition of implementations of all $\mathcal{C}_i$ is an implementation of $\mathcal{C}'$; and
- for any $1 \leq j \leq n$, any composition of an environment of $\mathcal{C}'$ with implementations of all $\mathcal{C}_i$ (for $i \neq j$) yields an environment for $\mathcal{C}_j$.

Instantiating this composition for contracts $\mathcal{C}_1 = (A_1, G_1)$ and $\mathcal{C}_2 = (A_2, G_2)$ in canonical form yields

$$\mathcal{C}_1 \parallel \mathcal{C}_2 = ((A_1 \cap A_2) \cup \neg(G_1 \cap G_2), G_1 \cap G_2).$$

It may be the case that the same design element is assigned multiple specifications corresponding to multiple viewpoints, or design concerns [6,29] (e.g., functionality and a performance criterion). Therefore, AG contracts also support an operation of conjunction, which can be used to enforce simultaneously multiple specifications over the same design element. This operation is the least-upper bound with respect to the refinement order of contracts in canonical form. For contracts in canonical form, this operation is

$$\mathcal{C}_1 \wedge \mathcal{C}_2 = (A_1 \cup A_2, G_1 \cap G_2).$$

In 1997, Negulescu introduced the formalism of process spaces [27]. Process spaces are mathematically the same objects as AG contracts. While Negulescu thought of process spaces are representing specifications for arbitrary software components, AG contracts were introduced to model arbitrary functional and non-functional aspects of CPSs.

3.1   Issues with AG Contracts

Algorithmic Issues. Core operations for AG contracts require all contracts to be in canonical form. Putting a contract in canonical form is by itself an expensive operation (see, e.g., [7], Chap. 6). In contrast, interface theories in general come with efficient algorithms, making them excellent candidates for internal representations of specifications. Some authors ([7] Chap. 10) have therefore proposed to translate contracts expressed as pairs (assumptions, guarantees) into suitable interface models, where the available algorithms are applied. This approach has the drawback that results cannot be traced back to the original (assumptions, guarantees) formulation.

Trace Properties Cannot Express Certain Important Specifications.
AG contracts are capable of expressing any environment and implementation as
a set of traces. These are sometimes also called *trace properties* to emphasize
the centrality of the trace in their definition. A trace property P can be defined
as follows:

$$P = \{b \in \mathcal{B} \mid \phi(b)\},$$

that is, P contains all traces satisfying a certain predicate ϕ. Observe that the
traces contained in any subset of P meet predicate ϕ; these subsets thus correspond to components having property P. Safety and liveness properties are
trace properties.

However, not all attributes of a system behave in this way. Consider the
component with behaviors $M = \{1, 2, 3\}$. Suppose we state the property $P = $
"the average of the behaviors is 2." M clearly satisfies this property, but M
has subsets that do not: P is not a trace property. A statement like P is a
perfectly reasonable property one may wish to verify in a system. In order to
apply assume-guarantee reasoning to properties of this sort, we must extend the
theory of contracts.

4   The Theory of Hypercontracts

4.1   Hyperproperties

The core concept on top of which specifications, interfaces, or contracts can
be expressed, is that of *property*. The most basic definition of a property in
the formal methods community is "a set of traces." This notion is based on the
behavioral approach to system modelling: we assume we start with an underlying
set of behaviors $\mathcal{B}$, and properties are defined as subsets of $\mathcal{B}$. In this approach,
design elements or components (or environments) are also defined as subsets of
$\mathcal{B}$. The difference between properties and components is semantics: a component collects the behaviors that can be observed from that component, while
a property collects the behaviors meeting some criterion of interest. We say a
component M satisfies a property P, written $M \models P$, when $M \subseteq P$, that is,
when the behaviors of M meet the criterion that determines P. Properties of this
sort are also called *trace properties*. Many design qualities are of this type, such
as *safety*. But there are many system attributes that can only be determined by
analyzing multiple traces such as mean response times, reliability, and security
attributes. The following running example illustrates this.

Example 1 (Running example).   Consider the digital system shown in Fig. 1a;
this system is similar to those presented in [26,31] to illustrate the non-
interference property in security. Here, we have an s-bit secret data input S
and an n-bit public input P. The system has an output O. There is also an
input H that is equal to zero when the system is being accessed by a user with
low-privileges, i.e., a user not allowed to use the secret data, and equal to one

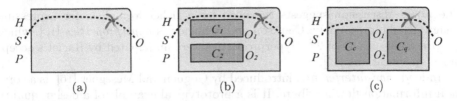

Fig. 1. (a) A digital system with a secret input S and a public input P. The overall system must meet the requirement that the secret input does not affect the value of the output O when the signal H is deasserted (this signal is asserted when a privileged user uses the system). Our agenda for this running example is the following: (b) we will start with two components C_1 and C_2 satisfying respective hypercontracts $\mathcal{C}_1$ and $\mathcal{C}_2$ characterizing information-flow properties of their own; (c) the composition of these two hypercontracts, $\mathcal{C}_c$, will be derived. Through the quotient hypercontract $\mathcal{C}_q$, we will discover the functionality that needs to be added in order for the design to meet the top-level information-flow specification $\mathcal{C}$.

otherwise. We wish the overall system to satisfy the property that for all environments with $H = 0$, the implementations can only make the output O depend on P, the public data, not on the secret input S.

A prerequisite for writing this requirement is to be able to express the property that "the output O depends on P, the public data, not on the secret input S". We claim that this property cannot be captured by a trace property. To see this, suppose for simplicity that O, P, and S are 1-bit-long. A trace property that aims at expressing the independence from the secret by making the output O equal to P is

$$P_C = \left\{ \begin{array}{l} (P = 1, S = 1, O = 1), \\ (P = 0, S = 1, O = 0), \\ (P = 1, S = 0, O = 1), \\ (P = 0, S = 0, O = 0) \end{array} \right\} .$$

A valid implementation $M \subseteq P_C$ is the following set of traces

$$M = \left\{ \begin{array}{l} (P = 1, S = 1, O = 1), \\ (P = 0, S = 0, O = 0) \end{array} \right\} .$$

However, the component M leaks the value of S in its output, showing that the independence does not behave as a trace property. Therefore, neither does non-interference.

To overcome this, reformulate the property by simply listing all the subsets of P_C that satisfy the independence requirement, namely:

$$\left\{ \left\{ \begin{array}{l} (P{=}1, S{=}1, O{=}1), \\ (P{=}0, S{=}1, O{=}0), \\ (P{=}1, S{=}0, O{=}1), \\ (P{=}0, S{=}0, O{=}0) \end{array} \right\}, \left\{ \begin{array}{l} (P{=}1, S{=}1, O{=}1), \\ (P{=}1, S{=}0, O{=}1) \end{array} \right\}, \left\{ \begin{array}{l} (P{=}0, S{=}1, O{=}0), \\ (P{=}0, S{=}0, O{=}0) \end{array} \right\} \right\}$$

This rather defines a subset of 2^B.   □

The above discussion suggests the need for a richer formalism for expressing design attributes, namely: Clarkson and Schneider's *hyperproperties* [10], which are precisely subsets of 2^B. Hyperproperties were anticipated by Raclet's acceptance specifications [32].

Indeed, *non-interference*, introduced by Goguen and Meseguer [16], is a common information-flow attribute. It is a prototypical example of a design quality which trace properties are unable to capture. It can be expressed with hyperproperties, and is in fact one reason behind their introduction. Suppose σ is one of the behaviors that our system can display. The behaviors will be defined as sequences of the states of memory locations through time. For example, if the system has a memory of two bits, the first element of σ will be the initial values of these memory locations; the next element will be the state of these two bits at the next step, and so on. Some of those memory locations we call *privileged*, some *unprivileged*. Let $L_0(\sigma)$ and $L_f(\sigma)$ be the projections of the behavior σ to the unprivileged memory locations of the system, at time zero, and at the final time (when execution is done). We say that a component M meets the non-interference hyperproperty when

$$\forall \sigma, \sigma' \in M.\ L_0(\sigma) = L_0(\sigma') \Rightarrow L_f(\sigma) = L_f(\sigma'),$$

i.e., if two traces begin with the unprivileged locations in the same state, the final state of the unprivileged locations matches. Non-interference is a downward-closed hyperproperty with respect to the subset order [26,31], and a 2-safety hyperproperty—hyperproperties called *k-safety* are those for the refutation of which one must provide at least k traces. In our example, to refute the hyperproperty, it suffices to show two traces that share the same unprivileged initial state, but which differ in the unprivileged final state.

To summarize, many statements of interest are beyond the scope of AG contracts, as AG contracts only support trace properties. Our objective is to develop a theory of assume-guarantee reasoning capable of expressing all attributes of CPSs that have been so far formalized. As hyperproperties have this expressive capability, we focused on an assume-guarantee theory capable of expressing environments and implementations as hyperproperties. We do this in three steps:

1. we consider components coming with notions of preorder (e.g., simulation) and parallel composition;
2. we introduce the notion of a *compset*, a variation of the notion of hyperproperty, equipped with substantial algebraic structure;
3. we build *hypercontracts* as pairs of compsets specifying legal environments and implementations.

4.2   Components

In the theory of hypercontracts, the most primitive concept is the component. Let $(\mathbb{M}, \leq)$ be a preorder. The elements $M \in \mathbb{M}$ are called *components*. We say that M is a subcomponent of M' when $M \leq M'$. If we represented components as automata, the statement "is a subcomponent of" would correspond to "is simulated by."

There exists a partial binary operation, $\|: \mathbb{M}, \mathbb{M} \to \mathbb{M}$, monotonic in both arguments, called *composition*. If $M \| M'$ is not defined, we say that M and M' are *non-composable* (and *composable* otherwise). A component E is an environment for component M if E and M are composable. We assume that composition is associative and commutative. We say that a set of components $\{M_i\}_{i=1}^n$ is a decomposition of component M if $M_1 \| \dots \| M_n \leq M$.

Example 2 (running example, cont'd). In order to reason about possible decompositions of the system shown in Fig. 1a, we introduce the internal variables O_1 and O_2, as shown in Fig. 1b. They have lengths o_1 and o_2, respectively. The output O has length o. For simplicity, we will assume that the behaviors of the entire system are stateless (i.e., we don't analyze their change over a notion of a progression or time). In that case, the underlying set of components $\mathbb{M}$ must contain at least the following components:

– For $i \in \{1, 2\}$, components with inputs H, S, P, and output O_i, i.e.,

$$\{(H, S, P, O_1, O_2, O) \mid \exists f \in (2^1 \times 2^s \times 2^n \to 2^{o_i}). O_i = f(H, S, P)\} .$$

– Components with inputs H, S, P, O_1, O_2, and output O, i.e.,

$$\{(H, S, P, O_1, O_2, O) \mid \exists f \in (2^1 \times 2^s \times 2^n \times 2^{o_1} \times 2^{o_2} \to 2^o). O = f(H, S, P, O_1, O_2)\} .$$

– Any subset of these components, as these correspond to restricting inputs to subsets of their domains.

In this theory of components, composition is carried out via set intersection. So for example, if for $i \in \{1, 2\}$ we have functions $f_i \in (2^1 \times 2^s \times 2^n \to 2^{o_i})$ and components $M_i = \{(H, S, P, O_1, O_2, O) \mid O_i = f_i(H, S, P)\}$, the composition of these objects is

$$M_1 \| M_2 = \left\{ (H, S, P, O_1, O_2, O) \,\middle|\, \begin{matrix} O_1 = f_1(H, S, P) \\ O_2 = f_2(H, S, P) \end{matrix} \right\} ,$$

which is the set intersection of the components's behaviors. $\square$

4.3 Compsets

CmpSet is a lattice whose objects, called *compsets*, are sets of components. The order of **CmpSet** is set inclusion. In general, not every set of components is an object of **CmpSet**. Compsets boil down to hyperproperties when the underlying component theory represents components as sets of behaviors. Since we assume **CmpSet** is a lattice, the greatest lower bounds and least upper bounds of finite sets are defined. Observe, however, that although the partial order of **CmpSet** is given by the subset order, the meet and join of **CmpSet** are not necessarily intersection and union, respectively, as the union or intersection of any two elements are not necessarily elements of **CmpSet**. In other words, **CmpSet** is a sublattice of $2^{\mathbb{M}}$.

CmpSet comes with a notion of satisfaction. Suppose $M \in \mathbb{M}$ and H is a compset. We say that M *satisfies* H or conforms to H, written $M \models H$, when $M \in H$. For compsets H, H', we say that H *refines* H', written $H \leq H'$, when $\forall M \models H. M \models H'$, i.e., when $H \subseteq H'$.

Example 3 (Running example: non-interference). Regarding the system shown in Fig. 1a, we require the top level component to generate the output O independently from the secret input S. We build our theory of compsets by letting the set of elements of **CmpSet** be the set $2^{\mathbb{M}}$. This means that any set of components is a valid compset. The components meeting the top-level non-interference property are those belonging to the compset

$$\{(H, S, P, O_1, O_2, O) \mid \exists f \in (2^1 \times 2^n \to 2^o). O = f(H, P)\},$$

i.e., those components for which H and P are sufficient to evaluate O. This corresponds exactly to those components that are insensitive to the secret input S. The join and meet of these compsets is given by set union and intersection, respectively.   □

Composition and Quotient. Composition in **CmpSet** is element-wise:

$$H \parallel H' = \left\{ M \parallel M' \; \middle| \; \begin{array}{l} M \models H, M' \models H', \text{ and} \\ M \text{ and } M' \text{ are composable} \end{array} \right\}. \tag{1}$$

Composition is total and monotonic, i.e., if $H' \leq H''$, then $H \parallel H' \leq H \parallel H''$. It is also commutative and associative, by the commutativity and associativity, respectively, of component composition.

In order to define composition for hypercontracts, we need to assume the existence of a second (but partial) binary operation on the objects of **CmpSet**. This operation is the right adjoint of composition: for compsets H and H', the residual H/H' (also called *quotient*), is given by

$$H/H' = \{M \in \mathbb{M} \mid \{M\} \parallel H' \subseteq H\}. \tag{2}$$

The definition of quotient for compsets does not require a notion of quotient for components. However, when such a notion exists, and depending on the structure of **CmpSet**, it can be used to simplify the computation of (2).

Downward-Closed Compsets. The set of components was introduced with a partial order. We say that a compset H is *downward-closed* when $M' \leq M$ and $M \models H$ imply $M' \models H$, i.e., if a component satisfies a downward-closed compset, so does its subcomponent.

4.4   Hypercontracts

A hypercontract is a specification for a design element that tells what is required from the design element when it operates in an environment that meets the expectations of the hypercontract. Several ways of specifying hypercontracts can be considered.

Hypercontracts as Pairs (Environments, Closed-System Specification). In this setting, a hypercontract is a pair of compsets:

$$C = (\mathcal{E}, \mathcal{S}) = (\text{environments, closed-system specification}).$$

$\mathcal{E}$ states the environments in which the object being specified must adhere to the specification. $\mathcal{S}$ states the requirements that the design element must fulfill when operating in an environment which meets the expectations of the hypercontract. We say that a component E *is an environment of hypercontract* C, written $E \models^E C$, if $E \models \mathcal{E}$. We say that a component M *is an implementation of* C, written $M \models^I C$, when $M \parallel E \models \mathcal{S}$ for all $E \models \mathcal{E}$. Note that we can use the quotient of compsets to define the set of implementations $\mathcal{I}$ of C as the compset containing all implementations, i.e., as the quotient:

$$\text{implementations} = \mathcal{I} = \mathcal{S}/\mathcal{E}.$$

A hypercontract with a nonempty set of environments is called *compatible*. If it has a nonempty set of implementations, it is called *consistent*. For $\mathcal{S}$ and $\mathcal{I}$ as above, the compset $\mathcal{E}'$ defined as $\mathcal{E}' = \mathcal{S}/\mathcal{I}$ contains all environments in which the implementations of C satisfy the specifications of the hypercontract. Thus, we say that a hypercontract is *saturated* if its environments compset is as large as possible in the sense that adding more environments to the hypercontract would reduce its implementations. This means that C satisfies the following fixpoint equation:

$$\mathcal{E} = \mathcal{S}/\mathcal{I} = \mathcal{S}/(\mathcal{S}/\mathcal{E}).$$

At a first sight, this notion of saturation may seem to go against what for assume-guarantee contracts are called contracts in canonical or saturated form, as we make the definition based on the environments instead of on the implementations. This, however, is a wrong guess: the two definitions for AG contracts and hypercontracts agree. Indeed, for AG contracts, this notion means that the contract $C = (A, G)$ satisfies $G = G \cup \neg A$. For this AG contract, we can form a hypercontract as follows: if we take the set of environments to be $\mathcal{E} = 2^A$ (i.e., all subsets of A) and the closed system specs to be $\mathcal{S} = 2^G$, we get a hypercontract whose set of implementations is $2^{G \cup \neg A}$, which means that the hypercontract $(2^A, 2^G)$ is saturated.

Hypercontracts as Pairs (Environments, Implementations). Another way to interpret a hypercontract is by telling explicitly which environments and implementations it supports. Thus, we would write the hypercontract as

$\mathcal{C} = (\mathcal{E}, \mathcal{I})$. Assume-guarantee theories can differ as to the most convenient representation for their hypercontracts. Moreover, some operations on hypercontracts find their most convenient expression in terms of implementations (e.g., parallel composition), and some in terms of the closed system specifications (e.g., strong merging), as discussed below.

The Lattice. Contr of hypercontracts. Just as with **CmpSet**, we define **Contr** as a lattice formed by putting together two compsets in one of the above two ways. Not every pair of compsets is necessarily a valid hypercontract. We will now define the operations that give rise to this lattice.

Preorder. We define a preorder on hypercontracts as follows: we say that $\mathcal{C}$ *refines* $\mathcal{C}'$, written $\mathcal{C} \le \mathcal{C}'$, when every environment of $\mathcal{C}'$ is an environment of $\mathcal{C}$, and every implementation of $\mathcal{C}$ is an implementation of $\mathcal{C}'$, i.e., $E \models^E \mathcal{C}' \Rightarrow E \models^E \mathcal{C}$ and $M \models^I \mathcal{C} \Rightarrow M \models^I \mathcal{C}'$. Using the notation introduced for compsets, we can express this as

$$\mathcal{E}' \le \mathcal{E} \text{ and } \mathcal{S}/\mathcal{E} = \mathcal{I} \le \mathcal{I}' = \mathcal{S}'/\mathcal{E}'.$$

Any two $\mathcal{C}, \mathcal{C}'$ with $\mathcal{C} \le \mathcal{C}'$ and $\mathcal{C}' \le \mathcal{C}$ are said to be *equivalent* since they have the same environments and the same implementations. We now obtain some operations using preorders which are defined as the LUB or GLB of **Contr**. We point out that the expressions we obtain are unique up to the preorder, i.e., up to hypercontract equivalence.

GLB and LUB. From the preorder just defined, the GLB of $\mathcal{C}$ and $\mathcal{C}'$ satisfies: $M \models^I \mathcal{C} \wedge \mathcal{C}'$ if and only if $M \models^I \mathcal{C}$ and $M \models^I \mathcal{C}'$; and $E \models^E \mathcal{C} \wedge \mathcal{C}'$ if and only if $E \models^E \mathcal{C}$ or $E \models^E \mathcal{C}'$.

Conversely, the least upper bound satisfies $M \models^I \mathcal{C} \vee \mathcal{C}'$ if and only if $M \models^I \mathcal{C}$ or $M \models^I \mathcal{C}'$, and $E \models^E \mathcal{C} \vee \mathcal{C}'$ if and only if $E \models^E \mathcal{C}$ and $E \models^E \mathcal{C}'$.

The lattice **Contr** has hypercontracts for objects (up to contract equivalence), and meet and join as just described.

Parallel Composition. The composition of hypercontracts $\mathcal{C}_i = (\mathcal{E}_i, \mathcal{I}_i)$ for $1 \le i \le n$, denoted $\|_i \mathcal{C}_i$, is defined using the Abadi-Lamport composition principle discussed in Sect. 2:

$$\|_i \mathcal{C}_i = \bigwedge \left\{ \begin{array}{l} (\mathcal{E}', \mathcal{I}') \\ \in \mathbf{Contr} \end{array} \middle| \begin{bmatrix} \mathcal{I}_1 \| \dots \| \mathcal{I}_n \le \mathcal{I}', \text{ and} \\ \mathcal{E}' \| \mathcal{I}_1 \| \dots \| \hat{\mathcal{I}}_j \| \dots \| \mathcal{I}_n \le \mathcal{E}_j \\ \text{for all } 1 \le j \le n \end{bmatrix} \right\}$$

$$= \bigwedge \left\{ \begin{array}{l} (\mathcal{E}', \mathcal{I}') \\ \in \mathbf{Contr} \end{array} \middle| \begin{bmatrix} \mathcal{I}_1 \| \dots \| \mathcal{I}_n \le \mathcal{I}', \text{ and} \\ \mathcal{E}' \le \bigwedge_{1 \le j \le n} \frac{\mathcal{E}_j}{\mathcal{I}_1 \| \dots \| \hat{\mathcal{I}}_j \| \dots \| \mathcal{I}_n} \end{bmatrix} \right\}, \qquad (3)$$

where the notation $\hat{\mathcal{I}}_j$ indicates that the composition $\mathcal{I}_1 \| \dots \| \hat{\mathcal{I}}_j \| \dots \| \mathcal{I}_n$ includes all terms $\mathcal{I}_i$, except for $\mathcal{I}_j$.

Example 4 (Running example, parallel composition). Consider the example shown in Fig. 1. We want to state the following requirement for the top-level component: for all environments with $H = 0$, valid implementations can only make the output O depend on P, the public data. We will write a hypercontract for the top-level. We let $\mathcal{C} = (\mathcal{E}, \mathcal{I})$, where

$$\mathcal{E} = \{M \in \mathbb{M} \mid \forall(H, S, P, O_1, O_2, O) \in M.\, H = 0\}$$
$$\mathcal{I} = \{M \in \mathbb{M} \mid \exists f \in (2^n \to 2^o).\forall(H, S, P, O_1, O_2, O) \in M.\, H = 0 \to O = f(P)\}.$$

The environments are all those components only defined for $H = 0$. The implementations are those such that the output is a function of P when $H = 0$.

Let $f^* : 2^n \to 2^o$. Suppose we have two hypercontracts that require their implementations to satisfy the function $O_i = f^*(P)$, one implements it when $S = 0$, and the other when $S \neq 0$. For simplicity of syntax, let s_1 and s_2 be the propositions $S = 0$ and $S \neq 0$, respectively. Let the two hypercontracts be $\mathcal{C}_i = (\mathcal{E}_i, \mathcal{I}_i)$ for $i \in \{1, 2\}$. We won't place restrictions on the environments for these hypercontracts, so we obtain $\mathcal{E}_i = \mathbb{M}$ and

$$\mathcal{I}_i = \{M \in \mathbb{M} \mid \forall(H, S, P, O_1, O_2, O) \in M.s_i \to O_i = f^*(P)\}.$$

We now evaluate the composition of these two hypercontracts: $\mathcal{C}_c = \mathcal{C}_1 \parallel \mathcal{C}_2 = (\mathcal{E}_c, \mathcal{I}_c)$, yielding $\mathcal{E}_c = \mathbb{M}$ and

$$\mathcal{I}_c = \left\{ M \in \mathbb{M} \,\middle|\, \begin{array}{l} \forall(H, S, P, O_1, O_2, O) \in M. \\ (s_1 \to O_1 = f^*(P)) \wedge (s_2 \to O_2 = f^*(P)) \end{array} \right\}$$

Mirror or Reciprocal. We assume we have an additional operation on hypercontracts, called both mirror and reciprocal, which flips the environments and implementations of a hypercontract: $\mathcal{C}^{-1} = (\mathcal{E}, \mathcal{I})^{-1} = (\mathcal{I}, \mathcal{E})$ and $\mathcal{C}^{-1} = (\mathcal{E}, \mathcal{S})^{-1} = (\mathcal{S}/\mathcal{E}, \mathcal{S})$. This notion gives us, so to say, the hypercontract obeyed by the environment. The introduction of this operation assumes that for every hypercontract $\mathcal{C}$, its reciprocal is also an element of **Contr**. Moreover, we assume that, when the infimum of a collection of hypercontracts exists, the following identity holds:

$$(\textstyle\bigwedge_i \mathcal{C}_i)^{-1} = \bigvee_i \mathcal{C}_i^{-1}. \tag{4}$$

Hypercontract Quotient. Now we consider an operation which answers the following question: given a top-level hypercontract $\mathcal{C}''$ that we want to implement and the hypercontract $\mathcal{C}$ of a partial implementation of the design, what is the largest hypercontract that we can compose with $\mathcal{C}$ in order to meet the top-level specification $\mathcal{C}''$? The *quotient* or residual for hypercontracts $\mathcal{C}$ and $\mathcal{C}''$, written $\mathcal{C}''/\mathcal{C}$, has the universal property $\forall \mathcal{C}'.\, \mathcal{C} \parallel \mathcal{C}' \leq \mathcal{C}''$ if and only if $\mathcal{C}' \leq \mathcal{C}''/\mathcal{C}$. We can obtain a closed-form expression using the reciprocal:

Proposition 1. *The hypercontract quotient obeys* $\mathcal{C}''/\mathcal{C} = ((\mathcal{C}'')^{-1} \parallel \mathcal{C})^{-1}$.

Example 5 (Running example, quotient). We use the quotient to find the specification of the component that we need to add to the system shown in Fig. 1c in order to meet the top level contract $\mathcal{C}$. To compute the quotient, we use (11) from [21]. We let $\mathcal{C}/\mathcal{C}_c = (\mathcal{E}_q, \mathcal{I}_q)$ and obtain $\mathcal{E}_q = \mathcal{E} \wedge \mathcal{I}_c$ and

$$\mathcal{I}_q = \left\{ M \in \mathbb{M} \;\middle|\; \begin{array}{l} \exists f \in (2^n \to 2^o) \; \forall (H, S, P, O_1, O_2, O) \in M. \\ ((s_1 \to O_1 = f^*(P)) \wedge (s_2 \to O_2 = f^*(P))) \to (H = 0 \to O = f(P)) \end{array} \right\}.$$

We can refine the quotient by lifting any restrictions on the environments, and picking from the implementations the term with $f = f^*$. Observe that f^* is a valid choice for f. This yields the hypercontract $\mathcal{C}_3 = (\mathcal{E}_3, \mathcal{I}_3)$, defined as $\mathcal{E}_3 = \mathbb{M}$ and

$$\mathcal{I}_3 = \left\{ M \in \mathbb{M} \;\middle|\; \begin{array}{l} \forall (H, S, P, O_1, O_2, O) \in M. \\ ((s_1 \to O_1 = f^*(P)) \wedge (s_2 \to O_2 = f^*(P))) \to O = f^*(P) \end{array} \right\}.$$

A further refinement of this hypercontract is $\mathcal{C}_r = (\mathcal{E}_r, \mathcal{I}_r)$, where $\mathcal{E}_r = \mathbb{M}$ and

$$\mathcal{I}_r = \{ M \in \mathbb{M} \mid \forall (H, S, P, O_1, O_2, O) \in M. ((s_1 \to O = O_1) \wedge (s_2 \to O = O_2)) \}.$$

By the properties of the quotient, composing this hypercontract, which knows nothing about f^*, with $\mathcal{C}_c$ will yield a hypercontract which meets the non-interference hypercontract $\mathcal{C}$. Note that this hypercontract is consistent, i.e., it has implementations (in general, refining may lead to inconsistency).

Merging. Another important operation on hypercontracts is viewpoint merging, or *merging* for short. This operation is used to summarize into a single hypercontract multiple specifications of the same design element (e.g., functionality and performance). Suppose $\mathcal{C}_1 = (\mathcal{E}_1, \mathcal{S}_1)$ and $\mathcal{C}_2 = (\mathcal{E}_2, \mathcal{S}_2)$ are the hypercontracts we wish to merge. Two slightly different operations can be considered as candidates for formalizing viewpoint merging:

- A *weak merge* which is the GLB; and
- A *strong merge* which states that environments of the merger should be environments of both $\mathcal{C}_1$ and $\mathcal{C}_2$ and that the closed systems of the merger are closed systems of both $\mathcal{C}_1$ and $\mathcal{C}_2$. If we let $\mathcal{C}_1 \bullet \mathcal{C}_2 = (\mathcal{E}, \mathcal{I})$, we have

$$\mathcal{E} = \vee \{ \mathcal{E}' \in \mathbf{CmpSet} \mid \mathcal{E}' \le \mathcal{E}_1 \wedge \mathcal{E}_2 \text{ and } \exists \mathcal{C}'' = (\mathcal{E}'', \mathcal{I}'') \in \mathbf{Contr}. \; \mathcal{E}' = \mathcal{E}'' \}$$

$$\mathcal{I} = \vee \left\{ \mathcal{I}' \in \mathbf{CmpSet} \;\middle|\; \begin{array}{l} \mathcal{I}' \le (\mathcal{S}_1 \wedge \mathcal{S}_2)/\mathcal{E} \text{ and} \\ (\mathcal{E}, \mathcal{I}) \in \mathbf{Contr} \end{array} \right\}.$$

The difference is that, whereas the commitment to satisfy $\mathcal{S}_2$ survives under the weak merge when the environment fails to satisfy $\mathcal{E}_1$, no obligation survives under the strong merge. This distinction was proposed in [34] under the name of weak/strong assumptions.

5   Concluding Remarks

We introduced hypercontracts. In hypercontracts, we kept the separation of assumptions and guarantees explicit, as we have found this approach to be the most intuitive for expressing specifications in applications. Hypercontracts extend the scope of AG reasoning to arbitrary, structured hyperproperties, where the structure is dictated by the modeling needs of the adopter of the theory. Imposing no structure allows the development of a theory that supports all hyperproperties. However, limiting expressivity has the advantage of a reduced algorithmic complexity when applying the theory.

Our running example was developed by hand, not aided by a tool. However, having hypercontracts theory was useful in guiding us in this task. For example, atomic properties were easily checked manually with reasonable confidence. However, doing the right chaining was difficult: there, contract theory provided adequate guidelines.

Hypercontracts are a meta-theory: before hypercontracts are used, one must choose a theory of components and a theory of compsets. In this sense, hypercontracts are akin to the meta-theory of Benveniste et al. [7]. This meta-theory builds contracts out of a theory of components, while hypercontracts are built using compsets. This additional algebraic layer allows defining the structured sets of compsets that the theory will use. Moreover, the additional algebraic structure gives hypercontracts the ability to express their formulas using more closed-form expressions than the meta-theory of contracts.

So far, we showed how to instantiate, as hypercontracts, AG contracts and interface automata. Hypercontracts were also used to introduce two new theories of AG reasoning: *interval contracts*, which are similar to AG contracts but come with a "must modality," and more importantly, *conic contracts*, which support arbitrary subset-closed hyperproperties, needed for reasoning about security. The details of these developments are provided in [20,21].

The scope of hypercontracts intersects that of information-flow interfaces [5]. Information-flow interfaces enable assume-guarantee reasoning over information-flow properties. Hypercontracts are complementary to this theory, as they support arbitrary classes of hyperproperties. It is future work to explore the links between these two concepts.

Tom's influence is identifiable in the theory of hypercontracts. We look forward to continue to get inspiration from his work. Happy festschrift, Tom!

Acknowledgments. This work was supported by NSF Contract CPS Medium 1739816, by the DARPA LOGiCS project under contract FA8750-20-C-0156, and by the Chateaubriand Fellowship of the Office for Science & Technology of the Embassy of France in the United States.

References

1. Abadi, M., Lamport, L.: Composing specifications. ACM Trans. Program. Lang. Syst. **15**(1), 73–132 (1993)

2. de Alfaro, L., Henzinger, T.A.: Interface automata. In: Proceedings of the 8th European Software Engineering Conference Held Jointly with 9th ACM SIGSOFT International Symposium on Foundations of Software Engineering, pp. 109–120 ESEC/FSE-9, Association for Computing Machinery, New York, NY, USA (2001)
3. de Alfaro, L., Henzinger, T.A., Stoelinga, M.: Timed interfaces. In: Sangiovanni-Vincentelli, A., Sifakis, J. (eds.) EMSOFT 2002. LNCS, vol. 2491, pp. 108–122. Springer, Heidelberg (2002). https://doi.org/10.1007/3-540-45828-X_9
4. Alur, R., Henzinger, T.A., Kupferman, O., Vardi, M.Y.: Alternating refinement relations. In: Sangiorgi, D., de Simone, R. (eds.) CONCUR 1998. LNCS, vol. 1466, pp. 163–178. Springer, Heidelberg (1998). https://doi.org/10.1007/BFb0055622
5. Bartocci, E., Ferrère, T., Henzinger, T.A., Nickovic, D., Da Costa, A.O.: Information-flow interfaces. In: Johnsen, E.B., Wimmer, M. (eds.) Fundamental Approaches to Software Engineering. FASE 2022. LNCS, vol. 13241, pp. 3–22. Springer, Cham (2022). https://doi.org/10.1007/978-3-030-99429-7
6. Benveniste, A., Caillaud, B., Ferrari, A., Mangeruca, L., Passerone, R., Sofronis, C.: Multiple viewpoint contract-based specification and design. In: de Boer, F.S., Bonsangue, M.M., Graf, S., de Roever, W.-P. (eds.) FMCO 2007. LNCS, vol. 5382, pp. 200–225. Springer, Heidelberg (2008). https://doi.org/10.1007/978-3-540-92188-2_9
7. Benveniste, A., et al.: Contracts for system design. Foundations and Trends® in Electronic Design Automation, vol. 12(2–3), pp. 124–400 (2018)
8. Chakrabarti, A., de Alfaro, L., Henzinger, T.A., Stoelinga, M.: Resource Interfaces. In: Alur, R., Lee, I. (eds.) EMSOFT 2003. LNCS, vol. 2855, pp. 117–133. Springer, Heidelberg (2003). https://doi.org/10.1007/978-3-540-45212-6_9
9. Clarke, E.M., Emerson, E.A.: Design and synthesis of synchronization skeletons using branching time temporal logic. In: Kozen, D. (ed.) Logic of Programs 1981. LNCS, vol. 131, pp. 52–71. Springer, Heidelberg (1982). https://doi.org/10.1007/BFb0025774
10. Clarkson, M.R., Schneider, F.B.: Hyperproperties. J. Comput. Secur. 18(6), 1157–1210 (2010)
11. Damm, W.: Controlling speculative design processes using rich component models. In: Fifth International Conference on Application of Concurrency to System Design (ACSD2005), pp. 118–119 (2005)
12. David, A., Larsen, K.G., Legay, A., Nyman, U., Wasowski, A.: Timed I/O automata: a complete specification theory for real-time systems. In: Proceedings of the 13th ACM International Conference on Hybrid Systems: Computation and Control, pp. 91–100. HSCC 2010, Association for Computing Machinery, New York, NY, USA (2010)
13. Dijkstra, E.W.: Solution of a problem in concurrent programming control. Commun. ACM 8(9), 569 (1965)
14. Doyen, L., Henzinger, T.A., Jobstmann, B., Petrov, T.: Interface theories with component reuse. In: Proceedings of the 8th ACM International Conference on Embedded Software, pp. 79–88 EMSOFT 2008, Association for Computing Machinery, New York, NY, USA (2008)
15. Floyd, R.W.: Assigning meanings to programs. Proceed. Symp. Appl. Math. 19, 19–32 (1967)
16. Goguen, J.A., Meseguer, J.: Security policies and security models. In: 1982 IEEE Symposium on Security and Privacy. Oakland, CA, USA, April 26–28, 1982, pp. 11–20 IEEE Computer Society, Oakland, CA, USA (1982)

17. Harel, D., Pnueli, A.: On the development of reactive systems. In: Apt, K.R. (ed.) Logics and Models of Concurrent Systems. NATO ASI Series, vol. 13, pp. 477–498. Springer, Heidelberg (1985). https://doi.org/10.1007/978-3-642-82453-1_17

18. Henzinger, T.A., Jhala, R., Majumdar, R.: Permissive interfaces. SIGSOFT Softw. Eng. Notes 30(5), 31–40 (2005)

19. Hoare, C.A.R.: An axiomatic basis for computer programming. Commun. ACM 12(10), 576–580 (1969)

20. Incer, I.: The algebra of contracts, Ph. D. thesis, EECS Department, University of California, Berkeley (2022)

21. Incer, I., Benveniste, A., Sangiovanni-Vincentelli, A., Seshia, S.A.: Hypercontracts. arXiv preprint arXiv:2106.02449 (2021)

22. Incer, I., Benveniste, A., Sangiovanni-Vincentelli, A., Seshia, S.A.: Hypercontracts. In: Deshmukh, J.V., Havelund, K., Perez, I. (eds.) NASA Formal Methods, pp. 674–692. Springer International Publishing, Cham (2022)

23. Lamport, L.: The computer science of concurrency: the early years. Commun. ACM 58(6), 71–76 (2015)

24. Larsen, K.G., Nyman, U., Wąsowski, A.: Modal I/O automata for interface and product line theories. In: De Nicola, R. (ed.) ESOP 2007. LNCS, vol. 4421, pp. 64–79. Springer, Heidelberg (2007). https://doi.org/10.1007/978-3-540-71316-6_6

25. Lynch, N.A., Tuttle, M.R.: An introduction to input/output automata. CWI Quarterly 2, 219–246 (1989)

26. Mastroeni, I., Pasqua, M.: Verifying bounded subset-closed hyperproperties. In: Podelski, A. (ed.) SAS 2018. LNCS, vol. 11002, pp. 263–283. Springer, Cham (2018). https://doi.org/10.1007/978-3-319-99725-4_17

27. Negulescu, R.: Process spacess. Tech. Rep. CS-95-48, University of Waterloo (1995)

28. Parnas, D.L.: A technique for software module specification with examples. Commun. ACM 15(5), 330–336 (1972)

29. Passerone, R., Incer, I., Sangiovanni-Vincentelli, A.L.: Coherent extension, composition, and merging operators in contract models for system design. ACM Trans. Embed. Comput. Syst. 18(5s), 1–23 (2019)

30. Pnueli, A.: The temporal logic of programs. In: 18th Annual Symposium on Foundations of Computer Science (sfcs 1977)(FOCS), pp. 46–57 (1977)

31. Rabe, M.N.: A temporal logic approach to information-flow control, Ph. D. thesis, Universität des Saarlandes (2016)

32. Raclet, J.: Residual for component specifications. Electr. Notes Theor. Comput. Sci. 215, 93–110 (2008)

33. Raclet, J.B., Badouel, E., Benveniste, A., Caillaud, B., Legay, A., Passerone, R.: A modal interface theory for component-based design. Fund. Inform. 108(1–2), 119–149 (2011)

34. Sangiovanni-Vincentelli, A., Damm, W., Passerone, R.: Taming Dr. Frankenstein: contract-based design for cyber-physical systems. Eur. J. Control 18(3), 217–238 (2012)

35. Sifakis, J.: Rigorous system design. Foundations and Trends® in Electronic Design Automation, vol. 6, no. 4, pp. 293–362 (2013)

36. Turing, A.M.: On checking a large routine. In: Report of a Conference on High-Speed Automatic Calculating Machines, pp. 67–69. University Mathematical Laboratory, Cambridge (1949)

Consistency and Persistency in Program Verification: Challenges and Opportunities

Parosh Aziz Abdulla[1]($\boxtimes$), Mohamed Faouzi Atig[1], Ahmed Bouajjani[2],
Bengt Jonsson[1], K. Narayan Kumar[3,5], and Prakash Saivasan[4,5]

[1] Uppsala University, Uppsala, Sweden
parosh@it.uu.se
[2] Paris Diderot University, Paris, France
[3] Chennai Mathematical Institute, Chennai, India
[4] Institute of Mathematical Sciences, HBNI, Chennai, India
[5] CNRS UMI ReLaX, Chennai, India

Abstract. We consider the verification of concurrent programs and, in particular, the challenges that arise because modern platforms only guarantee *weak semantics*, i.e., semantics that are weaker than the classical Sequential Consistency (SC). We describe two architectural concepts that give rise to weak semantics, namely *weak consistency* and *weak persistency*. The former defines the order in which operations issued by a given process become visible to the rest of the processes. The latter prescribes the order in which data becomes persistent. To deal with the extra complexity in program behaviors that arises due to weak semantics, we propose translating the program verification problem under weak semantics to SC. The main principle is to augment the program with a set of (unbounded) data structures that guarantee the equivalence of the source program's behavior under the weak semantics with the augmented program's behavior under the SC semantics. Such an equivalence opens the door to leverage, albeit in a non-trivial manner, the rich set of techniques that we have developed over the years for program verification under the SC semantics. We illustrate the framework's potential by considering the persistent version of the well-known Total Store Order semantics. We show that we can capture the program behaviors on such a platform using a finite set of unbounded monotone FIFO buffers. The use of monotone FIFO buffers allows the use of the well-structured-systems framework to prove the decidability of the reachability problem.

1 Introduction

Parallelism is almost as old as computing, but its early use was restricted to a few specialized areas such as operating systems, computer networking, scientific computing, and database systems. During the last decade, parallel systems

Would like to acknowledge the support of Infosys Foundation and IndoSwedish Project DST/INT/SWD/VR/P-04/2019.

© Springer Nature Switzerland AG 2022
J.-F. Raskin and K. Chatterjee (Eds.): Principles of Systems Design, LNCS 13660, pp. 494–510, 2022.
https://doi.org/10.1007/978-3-031-22337-2_24

have become a critical part of the infrastructure of our society due to the emergence of modern platforms such as multicores and cloud technology. Nowadays, multicores are available on mobile phones, laptops, embedded systems, servers, and numerous other devices that are integral parts of our daily life. Furthermore, cloud technology is increasingly based on efficient storage and exchange of data across large-scale networks. Such networks include enterprise services (e.g., Google Cloud or Microsoft Azure), banking systems, on-line markets (e.g., Amazon), and social networks (e.g., Facebook).

The ubiquity of parallel systems means that their efficiency and correctness are vital goals both from the security and economical points of view. To achieve these goals, program verification methodologies have, in recent years, encountered a new set of challenges. The principal reason is that such methodologies are often conducted under the fundamental assumption of *Sequential Consistency (SC)* where all components are strongly synchronized so that they all have a *uniform view* of the global state of the system.

SC interleaves the parallel executions of different processes while preserving the order of actions performed by a single process [21]. The SC model is intuitive and programmers usually assume that it is guaranteed by the platforms on which they run their applications. However, nowadays most parallel software run on platforms that do not guarantee SC. More precisely, to satisfy demands on efficiency and energy saving, such platforms implement optimizations that lead to the relaxation of the inter-component synchronization, hence offering only *weak* semantic guarantees. There are two main sources of weak semantics, namely *weak consistency* and *weak persistency*.

A consistency model defines the order in which memory operations are made visible to the application processes. In SC, such an operation is made visible as soon as it is issued by the executing process. However, almost all currently available platforms offer only weaker forms of consistency. We find such platforms at all levels of system design:

- Multiprocessor architectures: At the bottom level, multiprocessors such as x86-TSO, Sparc, IBM POWER, and ARM, use sophisticated techniques to achieve efficiency such as store buffers and speculative executions. Processes in programs running on such architectures may have different views of the memory thus giving rise to complicated non-SC behaviors [25,26].
- Cache protocols: Traditional cache coherence protocols such as MESI and MOESI are transparent to the programmer in the sense that they do not affect the order in which operations access memory. However, to meet increasing demands on energy efficiency, developers have recently proposed ways to simplify coherence. This comes at the price of allowing reorderings of memory accesses which means that new generations of cache protocols do not guarantee SC any more [24] (and de facto the transparency property).

- Language level concurrency: Semantical models for languages such as C11 or Java formalize the behaviors of multithreaded programs taking into account the effect of both the hardware architectures and compiler optimizations [20]. For instance, C11 allows several types of non-SC operations such as *Release/Acquire* accesses, which can be used to perform "message passing" between processes, and *Relaxed* accesses which are intended to be compiled down to the machine level and hence only provide the minimal synchronization guaranteed by the hardware.
- Distributed data stores: At the application level, data stores on the cloud are often implemented as distributed servers that store copies of the data at geographically distinct locations. The famous CAP theorem [16] shows that it is impossible to create a system that satisfies three important properties, namely *strong consistency* (i.e., applications get the illusion that each operation occurs atomically without being interrupted), *availability* (i.e., front-end servers can always respond to client requests), and *partition tolerance* (i.e., the system can continue operating even when datacenters cannot communicate with one another). Faced with the choice of at most two of these three properties, many system designers have chosen to sacrifice strong consistency and instead implement weaker consistency criteria such as *eventual consistency* [13], used in Amazon's Dynamo, LinkedIn's Project Voldemort, and Facebook Apache's Cassandra, and *causal consistency* used in the COPS and EIGER projects at Princeton.

Another source of weak semantics comes from *weak persistence*. The matter prescribes the order in which data stored inside the memory of the system. In many applications, the underlying platform does not guarantee that data is stored in the same order in which it is generated. There are numerous examples of applications that provide weak persistency, e.g., NVRAMs, intermittent computing systems, and file storage protocols. Let us consider the example of NVRAMs. The current data storage hierarchy paradigm, consisting of a *memory layer* and a *store layer*, has been around for several decades, and it has obviously worked well. The memory layer consists of the processor registers, followed by several cache levels, and finally the DRAM. It offers high performance and low latency but it is *volatile*, i.e., it loses its data when a system failure occurs. The storage layer, typically a disk or a flash, has large capacity, and is *non-volatile*, i.e., it keeps its data across system failures such as power interruption, OS crashes, and program crashes. Furthermore, the data movement between the store and the memory is performed within the system, and hence it does not need the involvement of a programmer. On the other hand, the store is slow and has very high latency, making file-based operations a bottleneck in many applications.

Emerging *Non-Volatile Random-Access Memories (NVRAM)* provide the best of the two worlds, i.e., the efficiency of DRAM, and the data persistency of the store [18,22]. In particular, NVRAMs offer byte addressability, i.e., it can be addressed directly by the CPU through read and write operations, thus giving programs direct and low-latency access to persistent data without any assistance from the operating system. Upon a crash, the volatile state of the system, including the DRAM content and process registers are lost while, in contrast, the NVRAM state is preserved. This is why NVRAMs are often referred to as *Persistent Memories (PM)*, a term that we will use in the sequel.

To deal with concurrency, we need to take into consideration *both* the behavior of the processor (consistency) and the memory (persistency) into consideration. To deal with the extra complexity in program behaviors that arises due to weak semantics, we propose translating the program verification problem under weak semantics to SC. The main principle is to augment the program with a set of (unbounded) data structures that guarantee the equivalence of the source program's behavior under the weak semantics with the augmented program's behavior under the SC semantics. Such an equivalence opens the door to leverage, albeit in a non-trivial manner, the rich set of techniques that we have developed over the years for program verification under the SC semantics. We illustrate the framework's potential by considering the persistent version of the well-known Total Store Order semantics. The model corresponds to the recent Intel chip that augments the x86 architecture with persistent memory [17], resulting in an extension of the classical Total Store Order (TSO) semantics [26]. The manner in which data is persisted in the chip does not conform to TSO, and program runs, along which crashes occur, follow a weaker memory model than TSO. This is reflected in the operational model defined in [23], called there Px86. We show that we can capture the program behaviors on such a platform using a finite set of unbounded monotone FIFO buffers. The use of monotone FIFO buffers allows the use of the well-structured-systems framework to prove the decidability of the reachability problem i.e. the problem of determining whether a given set of program locations is realisable through an execution.

In Sect. 2, we describe sequential consistency. In the Sects. 3, 4 we describe the semantics of TSO and persistent TSO respectively. In the Sect. 5, we describe well structured systems, in Sects. 6 and 7 we show how to obtain decidability using the well structured system framework.

2   Sequential Consistency (SC)

We consider concurrent programs consisting of processes that share a set of (global) variables.

Figure 1 depicts a typical program with two processes p_1 and p_2 that perform read and write operations on two shared

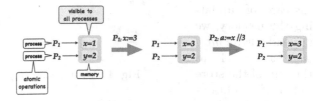

Fig. 1. SC transitions.

variables x and y. The fundamental property of SC is that the process operations are atomic. If a process performs a write operation on a variable x then we update the value of x in the memory, and the new value of x will be immediately readable by the other processes. In Fig. 1, the process p_1 assigns the value 3 to x in the first transition. When p_2 reads the value of x in the second transitions, it sees the latest value written to x, namely 3.

Figure 2 depicts the classical Dekker protocol where we have two processes p_1 and p_2 sharing two variables x and y.

Furthermore, each process has one local variable, namely a resp. b. The goal of the protocol is to guarantee *mutual exclusion*, i.e., to prevent the processes from entering their crucial section, CS_1 and CS_2, at the same time. Under the SC semantics, the program will satisfy mutual exclusion. To see this assume, without loss of generality, p_1 executes the first instruction. Since the transition assigns 1 to x, process p_2 assigns the value 1 to its local variable b when it executes its read instruction, and hence it will not be able to cross to its critical section.

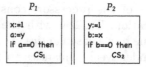

Fig. 2. The Dekker Protocol

3   Total Store Order

The semantics of Total Store Order (TSO) inserts an unbounded FIFO buffer, called the *store buffer*, between each process and the memory (Fig. 3). Figure 4 illustrates a typical run following the TSO semantics in a program with processes p_1 and p_2 and two shared variables x and y. The run starts in a configuration γ_0 where the store buffers are empty and where the values of the variables in the memory are all equal to 0.

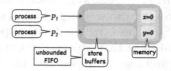

Fig. 3. The TSO architecture.

Write operations are not atomic anymore. In the first step, the process p_1 writes the value 1 to the variable x. Instead of updating the memory, we append a *write message* $x = 1$ to the end of the store buffer of p_1, obtaining the configuration γ_1. From γ_1, the process p_1 writes the value 2 to the variable

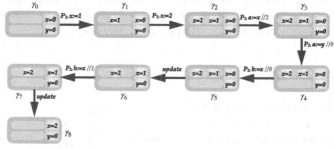

Fig. 4. A run according to the TSO semantics

x, so we append $x = 2$ to the store buffer. In γ_2, the store buffer of p_1 now contains two messages, while the store buffer of p_2 is still empty. When p_1 tries to read the value of x in γ_2, it checks its store buffer. If the buffer contains a message on x, then p_1 fetches the value of the latest such a value (2, in this case). We call this a *read-own-write* operation. Since there is no pending write messages on y in the buffer of p_1 γ_2, it fetches the value 0 of y from the memory. We all this a *read-from-memory* operation.

The same applies when p_2 reads the value of y from γ_3, or the value of x from γ_4. Although p_1 has already performed the write operations on x, their effects are not visible to p_2 since the corresponding message have still not reached the memory. From γ_5, the program performs an *update* operation, where it takes the message $x = 1$ at the *head* of the buffer of p_1 and uses it to update the value of x in the memory. This value will be visible to p_2 in γ_7. Finally, the program performs the last update operation changing the value of x in the memory to 2.

In summary, the TSO semantics is characterized by the following four operations: (i) appending fresh write operations to the tail of the store buffer. (ii) reading-own-writes. (iii) reading-from-memory. (iv) updating the memory.

We re-consider the Dekker protocol of Sect. 2 and explain why it does not satisfy mutual exclusion under the TSO semantics. The processes p_1 and p_2 perform their write operations appending the corresponding messages to their buffers. When p_1 performs its read operations, it does not find any pending write messages on y in its buffer and hence it fetches the value of y from the memory. Since the write message of y in the buffer of p_2 has not reached the memory, it is yet not visible to p_1 and p_1 will read the value $y = 0$. Analogously, p_2 reads the value $x = 0$ and hence both processes can enter their critical sections.

To help programmers eliminate bad behaviors such as the one in the case of Dekker's protocol, weakly consistent platforms provide synchronization primitives that help retrieve part of the SC behavior. In the case of TSO one such synchronization primitive is the

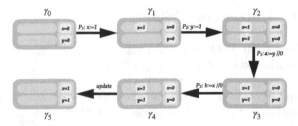

Fig. 5. A run of the Dekker Protocol under the TSO semantics.

memory fence (mfence) instruction. The instruction can be performed by a process only if its store buffer is empty. Equivalently, the mfence instruction *flushes* the buffer contents when it is executed by the process. Figure 6 depicts a new version of the Dekker protocol where we have inserted an mfence instruction between the write and read instructions of the processes p_1 and p_2.

Since each process must flush its buffer before it reads the value of the shared variable, we guarantee that at least one of the processes (the process that executes its mfence last) will fail to reach its critical section, and hence the fenced version of the protocol guarantees mutual exclusion.

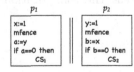

Fig. 6. The Dekker Protocol with memory fences.

The TSO semantics induces an infinite transition system even in the case where the given program is finite-state. In Fig. 7, we show a simple program with a single process which performs a self-loop performing a write instruction. Under the SC semantics, this program has a finite state space. However, under the TSO semantics, there is no bound on the size of the store buffer. The process may execute the loop an unbounded number of times, and the generated write messages may all get stored in the buffer. Therefore, the state space of the program under the TSO semantics is not finite.

We observe that the TSO semantics is weaker than SC since it allows read instructions to overtake write instructions. More precisely, a read operation on a variable x can overtake a write operation on a *different* variable y, through the read-own-write mechanism. However, the

Fig. 7. Program with an infinite state space under the TSO semantics.

semantics respects the order of write/write operations and read/read operations. Furthermore, it does not allow write operations to overtake read operations, and it does not allow a read operation to overtake a write operation on the same variable.

4   Persistent TSO

Persistent TSO (PTSO) adds another stage, called the *persistency stage* to the TSO architecture (Fig. 8). The persistency stage consists of two components, namely the *persistent memory*, and the *persistency buffer*. The persistent memory contains a copy of each shared variable. The

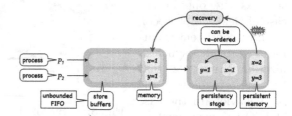

Fig. 8. The PTSO architecture.

content of the persistent memory survives a system crash. We can therefore use the data in the persistent memory to re-start the program after the crash, using a *recovery* program. The recovery program decides, based on the persistent memory's content, the configuration from which the program re-starts running after the crash.

The persistency stage induces additional weak behaviors on the top of the read/write re-ordering of TSO. More precisely, write instructions on different variables can overtake each other. This means that, even for a sequential program, we cannot guarantee that we preserve the program behavior. In Fig. 9 assume that the shared variables x and y have initial values that are equal to 0; and that the (single) process have issued a write instruction $x := 1$ followed by a write instruction $y := 1$; and hence the write message $x = 1$ and $y = 1$ are inside the buffer (in that order).

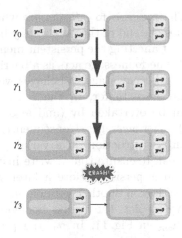

Fig. 9. An example of weak persistency.

The write messages preserves the order when updated to the memory and then cross to the persistency stage. However, inside the persistency stage, the write message $y = 1$ can overtake $x = 1$, i.e., the former can persist before the latter. If a crash happens at the point where only $y = 1$ has persisted then, after recovery, the program will see the values $x = 0$ resp. $y = 1$.

In a similar manner to the case of TSO, the instruction set of PTSO contains fence/flush instructions that we can use to limit the orderings that can arise. PTSO provides several types of fences that cover different trade-offs between strength (the amount of re-orderings they prevent) and efficiency (how much time it costs to execute the instruction). Below,

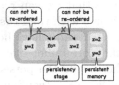

Fig. 10. The cache line flush optimized in the persistency stage.

we give two examples. Figure 10 illustrates the flush instruction $\texttt{flush}_{opt}$, referred to as *cache line flush optimized* in the Intel Manual [17,23].

For a variable x, when a process p executes the $\texttt{flush}_{opt} x$ instruction, a corresponding message $\texttt{fo}^x$ is added to the store buffer of p. The message $\texttt{fo}^x$ will eventually move to the persistency buffer, where it acts as a *barrier* that prevents write messages on x that lie before it in the persistency buffer to be overtaken by write messages on other variables that lie after it in the buffer (cf. Fig. 10).

The message fo^x *disappears* when it reaches the end of the persistency buffer without affecting the persistent memory. While the fo message acts as a barrier in the persistency stage, it behaves weakly in the store buffer, in the sense that it can be overtaken by (and also overtake) other messages. Consequently, the $\text{flush}_{\text{opt}}$ instruction on a variable x is too weak to ensure that a write instruction on x persists before a later write instruction on another variable y.

We depict the weak behavior of $\text{flush}_{\text{opt}}$ in Fig. 11. In γ_0, the process has executed three instructions, namely two write instructions on x resp. y, with a $\text{flush}_{\text{opt}}$ instruction on x in between; and has put the corresponding messages in the store buffer. A write message is allowed to *overtake* an fo message on a different variable in the store buffer.

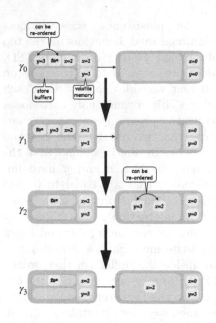

Fig. 11. The weak behavior of $\text{flush}_{\text{opt}}$.

This means that we can reach the configuration γ_1 in which we have swapped the write on y with the $\text{flush}_{\text{opt}}$ instruction, and hence reach γ_2 where the write messages on x and y have both crossed to the persistency buffer, while the fo^x is still in the store buffer. Since write messages on different variables can overtake each other inside the persistency buffer, the message $y = 3$ can persist before the message $x = 2$ (configuration γ_3). If the system crashes at this point, after recovery, the program will see the new value 3 of y while it sees the old value 0 of x.

Despite the weak behavior of the $\text{flush}_{\text{opt}}$ instruction in the store buffer, it plays a role restricting the order in which writes persist, particularly when used in conjunction with the *store fence* sfence instruction.

The sfence and $\text{flush}_{\text{opt}}$ combine together to enforce persistence in a given order as follows. The sfence instruction generates the message sf in the store buffer. The sf message *disappears* when it reaches the end of the store buffer. However, it acts as a barrier *inside* the store buffer. Since fo generates a barrier in the persistency buffer, the two messages can enforce that persistency between write messages occurs in a given order. We illustrate the combined effect of sfence with $\text{flush}_{\text{opt}}$ in the program run in Fig. 12.

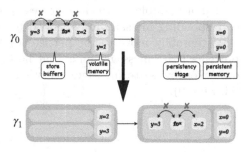

Fig. 12. Combining $\text{flush}_{\text{opt}}$ with sfence.

trate the combined effect of sfence with $\text{flush}_{\text{opt}}$ in the program run in Fig. 12.

In γ_0, the process has executed the same instructions as in Fig. 11 with an additional sfence after the flush$_{opt}$$x$. In the persistency semantics, the message fo^x cannot overtake a write message on the same variable x. Given this, and the fact that the message sf cannot be re-ordered with any other messages in the store buffer means that the messages move from the store to the persistency buffer in the order shown in γ_1. Hence the addition of the sfence after the flush$_{opt}$$x$ has enforced that writes persist in the same order as they are issued by the process.

5   Well-Structured Systems

The goal of the well-structured system (WSS) framework is to allow algorithmic verification of programs with infinite state spaces [4,15]. One instantiation of the framework is programs consisting of finite-state processes that communicate

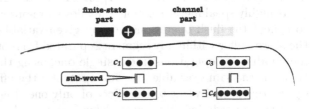

Fig. 13. Monotone Channels.

through unbounded channels that (i) respect the FIFO semantics, and (ii) have *monotonic behaviors* [7] (Fig. 13). Monotonicity means that inserting additional messages to the channels does not limit the program behavior. Put differently, configurations with *larger* channel contents can *simulate* configurations with *smaller* channel contents. We consider a channel c_1 to be smaller than another channel c_2 if the content of c_1 is a (not necessarily contiguous) subword of c_2.

As we describe in the following two sections, several aspects of the PTSO semantics prevents instantiation of the framework: (i) monotonicity: The store buffers in TSO are not monotone since adding a write message may make some memory states unreachable. (ii) FIFO behavior: flush instructions can be re-ordered in the TSO stage, write operations can be re-ordered in the persistency stage. To apply the WSS framework, we need to propose an architecture for PTSO that (i) is equivalent up reachability to the original architecture of [23] (cf. Sect. 4); and (ii) can be described as a set of finite-state processes operating on a set of channels that are FIFO and monotone.

6   Fixing FIFO Behaviors

The write messages in the TSO store buffers are FIFO by definition. However, as we explained in Sect. 4 (Fig. 8), write operations on different variables can be re-ordered in the persistency stage, and hence they violate the FIFO semantics. Furthermore, the

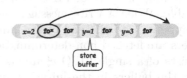

Fig. 14. Reorderings of the flush operations in the store buffers.

flush and fence operations can be re-ordered with write operations and among each other even in the store buffers (Figs. 11 and 14).

In the TSO stage we add a finite-state protocol that (i) simulates all possible re-orderings of the flush oper-ations, and (ii) collapses multiple occurrences of the flush operations in the buffers so that there is an upper bounded on the number of non-write operations that we need to maintain

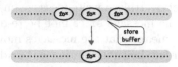

Fig. 15. Collapsing the flush operations in the store buffers.

in the store buffers. We refer to [1] for the full description of the protocol.

Roughly speaking, we exploit the allowed re-orderings of the flush operations to collect the flush operations on any given variable in a single position inside the store buffer within any segment separated from others by sfences. Then, we merge all these operations into a single one, using the fact that the flush operations on the same variable are "idempotent": the effect of multiple consecutive operations is equivalent to the effect of only one (Fig. 15). The protocol encodes operation re-orderings through a *delay/promise* scheme. When a flush operation reaches the end of the store buffer, we can delay its transfer to the persistency state. In such a manner we allow other operations to overtake it. Furthermore, we allow a process to *promise* that it will issue a flush operation in the future. This allows the flush operations to overtake other operations

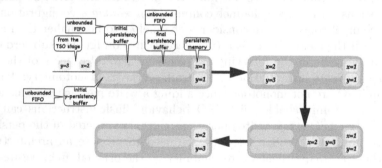

Fig. 16. The two-stage persistency buffer system.

In the persistency stage we use a two-stage channel system (Fig. 16). The *initial* stage is a set of FIFO buffers each with the write messages on a given variable. When a write message, on a variable x, enters the persistency stage we append it to the end of the initial x-buffer. The channels from the initial buffers are fetched non-deterministically and added to the second stage, which consists of a single FIFO channel. The non-deterministic transfer of messages from the buffers in the initial stage to the buffer in the final stage allows to encode the re-ordering of messages in the persistency stage without violating the FIFO semantics. The behaviour of flush_{opt} as a barrier in the persistency stage is arranged in this semantics as follows: the transfer of an $\texttt{flush}_{\texttt{opt}}x$ to the persistent stage is permitted if the initial buffer corresponding to x is empty.

7   Fixing Monotonicity

Neither the store buffer nor the final persistency buffer is monotone. The reason is identical in both cases. We explain the case of the final persistency buffer (Fig. 17). Consider the configurations γ_1 and γ_2 where the content of the buffer is larger in γ_2 than in γ_1. By moving the write messages from the buffer to the persistent memory, we can obtain the con-

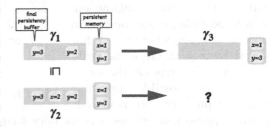

Fig. 17. Non-monotonicity of the final persistency buffer.

figuration γ_3 from γ_1 where the value of the variables x and y are 1 and 3 respectively. However, we cannot obtain the same configuration from γ_2 since at the point whether we move the message assigning $y = 3$ we have already also moved the message $x = 2$.

To retrieve monotonicity of the final persistency buffer, we provide a different but equivalent model of the buffer. The messages inside the buffer will now represent memory snapshots rather than individual messages. A message represents the memory content at the time point when the message has reached the persistent memory (Fig. 18). This means that the larger configuration γ_3 can simulate all the steps that are possible from γ_1.

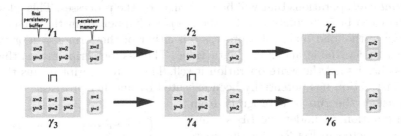

Fig. 18. Fixing the monotonicity of the final persistency buffer.

More precisely, when we perform a transition from γ_1 to update the memory using a memory snapshot, we can use the same memory snapshot to obtain an identical memory content while still preserving a larger (or equal) buffer content.

Achieving monotonicity for the TSO stage is more complicated. The reason is that the write operations, performed by the different processes, interfere with each other. Therefore, using memory snapshots per buffer will introduce inconsistency.

Consider the configuration in Fig. 19 where the processes have performed the write operations $x = 1$ resp. $y = 1$ whose messages are traveling in the store buffers. From this configuration, it is impossible for any process to observe the sequence $x = 1$ followed by $x = 0$. Once the write message $x = 1$ has hit the memory, the only possible value of x that the processes can read is 1.

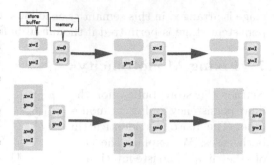

Fig. 19. Non-monotonicity of the store buffers.

Now, suppose that we use the memory snapshot abstraction. Recall that the memory snapshots encode the state of the memory at the time point where the corresponding write message hits the memory, so we have the snapshots $x = 1$, $y = 0$, resp. $x = 0$, $y = 1$ in the buffers (Fig. 19). When the snapshot $x = 1$, $y = 0$ hits the memory the value of x in the memory is 1. At this point the first process sees the value $x = 1$. In the next step, the snapshot in the buffer of the second process hits the memory, assigning the value 0 to x (and 1 to y). This means that the first process will now see the value $x = 0$ again.

In order to achieve monotonicity in the TSO stage, we use an alternative formulation of TSO [3], called the Load Buffer (LB) semantics. We *reverse* the flow of messages between the processes and the memory. Recall that in the store buffer semantics, the reads were instantaneous and the writes were buffered. In the load buffer semantics, the writes are instantaneous and the reads are from what is called the *load buffer*. Concretely, we replace the store buffer between each process and the memory by a load buffer (Fig. 20). The load buffers carry *potential read* operations that will be performed by the processes. This allows for the writes to be immediate and for the reads to happen from the buffer. Each message in the load buffer of a process p is either of the form $x = v$ or $x = v^s$ where x is a variable and v is a data value. The s-superscript means that the process has issued the write operation it self. The o-superscript means that the write instruction has potentially been executed by another process.

Consider the run of a program from a configuration γ_0 under the LB semantics, as depicted in Fig. 21. A write operation $x := 1$ by a process p_1 immediately updates the shared memory and, at the same time, appends a new message of the form $x = 1^s$ to the tail of the load buffer of p_1, obtaining γ_1. We use the s-subscript since the write operation is performed by the process itself. Analogously, the process p_2 performs the write operation $y := 1$, updating the value of y in the memory and appending the message $y = 1^s$ to the tail of its load buffer (γ_2). We can, at any time, perform, a *read*

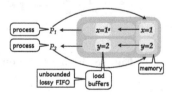

Fig. 20. The Load Buffer architecture.

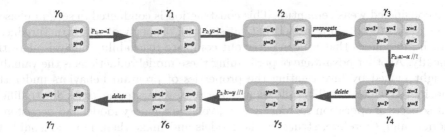

Fig. 21. A run under the Load Buffer semantics.

propagation by non-deterministically choosing a variable and append its value in the memory to the tail of the buffer of one of the processes. From γ_2 we can propagate $y = 1^o$ to the process p_1. We use the o-superscript since the write operation is performed by a different process. A *read-self-write* operation by a process p_1 on a variable x can performed on the most recent own write on x in the buffer of p. Accordingly, the process p_1 can read the value $x = 1$ taking the program from the configuration γ_3 to the configuration γ_4. A process can always delete the message at the head of its buffer, this crucially provides the monotonicity requirement. In transition from γ_4 to γ_5, the process p_1 deletes the message $x = 1^s$ from the head of its buffer. In a *read-other-write* transition, a process p reads the value of a variable x, at the head of its buffer, provided there are not self-write-messages on x in the buffer of p_1. Following this rule, the process p_1 can read the value $y = 1$ from γ_5.

In summary, the LB TSO semantics is characterized by the following four operations: (i) updating the memory and simultaneously appending fresh self-write messages to the tail of the load buffer. (ii) reading-self-writes. (iii) propagating other-write messages from the memory to the load buffers. (iv) deleting the message at the head of a buffer. (v) reading an other-write message. Then, through a somewhat technical argument one can show that the load buffer semantics is equivalent w.r.t. reachability to the store buffer semantics and further the former satisfies the monotonicity property needed by the well structured framework to obtain decidability.

8   Conclusions and Future Work

While strong consistency is desirable since it offers (to application programmers) the best abstraction for concurrency reasoning it is, for performance reasons, not guaranteed by storage systems implementations. This is visible at all levels of the system design (from the hardware memory level to one of the cloud infrastructures). In this paper, we presented issues that arise in the verification of applications running over weakly consistent storage systems that may reorder operations of processes at different stages, and we have described an approach for tackling these issues. The method we presented is based on constructing suitable operational models capturing the behaviors of programs running under the considered weak semantics. This construction is conducted in several phases. The goal is to obtain a model that satisfies the property of well-structuredness, which guarantees that we can carry out complete reachability analysis algorithmically. Another advantage of performing these model reductions is the valuable insight gained by investigating the properties of program behaviors under the considered semantics. This allows, in general, to separate the issues due to different sources of operation reordering (e.g., volatile memory model and persistency model) and, therefore, structure the models and make them more amenable to automated verification.

We consider one particular case: Persistent TSO, the model adopted in Intel x86 architectures. However, as said earlier, dealing with weakly consistent storage systems is a general issue that has many instances, and the approach we advocate in this paper could apply to them as well. It has been applied to several weak consistency models, e.g., [9,10,19]. The verification problem for models with persistency, other than Persistent TSO [1], has not yet been addressed as far as we know. In the existing work in this line of research, the reductions leading to well-structured systems need to be adapted to each specific weak semantics. A challenging question is to develop generic methods that allow systematically derived operational models with data structures encoding various action reorderings with desired properties such as monotonicity.

We have focused on the reachability problem, and we have provided an approach for showing that this problem is decidable. However, solving reachability in well-structured systems is highly complex. For instance, for the model we considered in this paper, the complexity is non-primitive recursive. Nevertheless, using the operational model we have defined, it is possible to adopt approximate analysis approaches such as context-bounded analysis [2,11]. Defining such strategies taking into account weak persistency models is an interesting problem for future work.

A crucial related property to consider for the verification of applications running over weakly consistent storage systems is their *robustness* against some weak consistency model. For a given application program, this property means that all its observable behaviors under the considered weak model are also observable under a more robust reference model, typically the sequential consistency model. In other words, that means that this particular program is not sensitive to (or is immune against) the relaxation of the consistency guarantees that the storage system implementation may do. This property is essential since a program that has been designed and proved correct under the strong model remains necessarily correct under the weaker model against which it is robust. Here, the notion of "observable behavior" is important. Typically it corresponds to the notion of *trace* that is an abstraction of a computation where only relevant order relations between operations (such as reads and writes) are kept, capturing the essence of the considered consistency model. It has been shown that verifying robustness in this sense can be reduced in some cases to verifying the reachability problem under the *strong* model [12,14]. This is important because the strong model has fewer behaviors than the weaker one. Its reachability problem may be easier to verify; for instance, checking reachability under sequential consistency is PSPACE-complete while solving the same problem under TSO is non-primitive recursive.

Other interesting directions for future work include parameterized systems on weak memory models [5,6], and applying symbolic partial order techniques [8] to increase efficiency.

References

1. Abdulla, P.A., Atig, M.F., Bouajjani, A., Kumar, K.N., Saivasan, P.: Deciding reachability under persistent x86-tso. In: Proceedings of the ACM on Programming Languages, vol. 5, no. POPL, pp. 1–32 (2021)
2. Abdulla, P.A., Atig, M.F., Bouajjani, A., Ngo, T.P.: Context-bounded analysis for power. In: Legay, A., Margaria, T. (eds.) TACAS 2017. LNCS, vol. 10206, pp. 56–74. Springer, Heidelberg (2017). https://doi.org/10.1007/978-3-662-54580-5_4
3. Abdulla, P.A., Atig, M.F., Bouajjani, A., Ngo, T.P.: A load-buffer semantics for total store ordering. Log. Methods Comput. Sci. **14**(1), 9 (2018)
4. Abdulla, P.A., Cerans, K., Jonsson, B., Tsay, Y.-K.: General decidability theorems for infinite-state systems. In: Proceedings, 11th Annual IEEE Symposium on Logic in Computer Science, New Brunswick, New Jersey, USA, July 27–30 1996, pp. 313–321. IEEE Computer Society (1996)
5. Abdulla, P.A., Deneux, J., Mahata, P.: Multi-clock timed networks. In: 19th IEEE Symposium on Logic in Computer Science (LICS 2004), 14–17 July 2004, Turku, Finland, Proceedings, pp. 345–354. IEEE Computer Society (2004)
6. Abdulla, P.A., Ben Henda, N., Delzanno, G., Rezine, A.: Handling parameterized systems with non-atomic global conditions. In: Logozzo, F., Peled, D.A., Zuck, L.D. (eds.) VMCAI 2008. LNCS, vol. 4905, pp. 22–36. Springer, Heidelberg (2008). https://doi.org/10.1007/978-3-540-78163-9_7
7. Abdulla, P.A., Jonsson, B.: Verifying programs with unreliable channels. In: Proceedings of the Eighth Annual Symposium on Logic in Computer Science (LICS 1993), Montreal, Canada, 19–23 June 1993, pp. 160–170. IEEE Computer Society (1993)
8. Abdulla, P.A., Jonsson, B., Kindahl, M., Peled, D.: A general approach to partial order reductions in symbolic verification. In: Hu, A.J., Vardi, M.Y. (eds.) CAV 1998. LNCS, vol. 1427, pp. 379–390. Springer, Heidelberg (1998). https://doi.org/10.1007/BFb0028760
9. Atig, M.F., Bouajjani, A., Burckhardt, S., Musuvathi, M.: On the verification problem for weak memory models. In: Hermenegildo, M.V., Palsberg, J., (eds.), Proceedings of the 37th ACM SIGPLAN-SIGACT Symposium on Principles of Programming Languages, POPL 2010, Madrid, Spain, 17–23 Jan 2010, pp. 7–18. ACM (2010)
10. Atig, M.F., Bouajjani, A., Burckhardt, S., Musuvathi, M.: What's decidable about weak memory models? In: Seidl, H. (ed.) ESOP 2012. LNCS, vol. 7211, pp. 26–46. Springer, Heidelberg (2012). https://doi.org/10.1007/978-3-642-28869-2_2
11. Atig, M.F., Bouajjani, A., Parlato, G.: Context-bounded analysis of TSO systems. In: From Programs to Systems. The Systems perspective in Computing - ETAPS Workshop, FPS 2014, in Honor of Joseph Sifakis, Grenoble, France, 6 Apr 2014. Proceedings, pp. 21–38 (2014)

12. Bouajjani, A., Derevenetc, E., Meyer, R.: Checking and enforcing robustness against TSO. In: Felleisen, M., Gardner, P. (eds.) ESOP 2013. LNCS, vol. 7792, pp. 533–553. Springer, Heidelberg (2013). https://doi.org/10.1007/978-3-642-37036-6_29

13. Burckhardt, S.: Principles of eventual consistency. Found. Trends Program. Lang. **1**(1–2), 1–150 (2014)

14. Derevenetc, E., Meyer, R.: Robustness against Power is PSpace-complete. In: Esparza, J., Fraigniaud, P., Husfeldt, T., Koutsoupias, E. (eds.) ICALP 2014. LNCS, vol. 8573, pp. 158–170. Springer, Heidelberg (2014). https://doi.org/10.1007/978-3-662-43951-7_14

15. Finkel, A., Schnoebelen, P.: Well-structured transition systems everywhere! Theor. Comput. Sci. **256**(1–2), 63–92 (2001)

16. Gilbert, S., Lynch, N.A.: Brewer's conjecture and the feasibility of consistent, available, partition-tolerant web services. SIGACT News **33**(2), 51–59 (2002)

17. Intel. Architectures software developer's manual (combined volumes) Software.intel.com (2019)

18. Intel. Intel Optane Technology (2019). www.intel.com/content/www/us/en/architecture-and-technology/intel-optane-technology.html

19. Lahav, O., Boker, U.: Decidable verification under a causally consistent shared memory. In: Donaldson, A.F., Torlak, E., (eds.) Proceedings of the 41st ACM SIGPLAN International Conference on Programming Language Design and Implementation, PLDI 2020, London, UK, 15–20 June 2020, pp. 211–226. ACM (2020)

20. Lahav, O., Giannarakis, N., Vafeiadis, V.: Taming release-acquire consistency. In: Bodík, R., Majumdar, R., (eds.) Proceedings of the 43rd Annual ACM SIGPLAN-SIGACT Symposium on Principles of Programming Languages, POPL 2016, St. Petersburg, FL, USA, 20–22 Jan 2016, pp. 649–662. ACM (2016)

21. Lamport, L.: How to make a multiprocessor that correctly executes multiprocess programs. IEEE Trans. Comput. **C-28**, 690–691 (1979)

22. Liu, S., Seemakhupt, K., Wei, Y., Wenisch, T.F., Kolli, A., Khan, S.: Cross failure bug detection in persistent memory programs. In: ASPLOS (2020)

23. Raad, A., Wickerson, J., Neiger, G., Vafeiadis, V.: Persistency semantics of the intel-x86 architecture. In: PACMPL, vol. 4, no. POPL, pp. 1–31 (2020)

24. Ros, A., Kaxiras, S.: Racer: TSO consistency via race detection. In: MICRO (2016)

25. Sarkar, S., Sewell, P., Alglave, J., Maranget, L., Williams, D.: Understanding Power Multiprocessors. In: PLDI **2011**, 175–186 (2011)

26. Sewell, P., Sarkar, S., Owens, S., Nardelli, F.Z., Myreen, M.O.: x86-TSO: a rigorous and usable programmer's model for x86 multiprocessors. Commun. ACM **53**(7), 89–97 (2010)

Automated Program Repair Using Formal Verification Techniques

Hadar Frenkel[1], Orna Grumberg[2], Bat-Chen Rothenberg[2(✉)], and Sarai Sheinvald[3]

[1] CISPA Helmholtz Center for Information Security, Saarbrücken, Germany
[2] Department of Computer Science, The Technion, Haifa, Israel
batcheni89@gmail.com
[3] Department of Software Engineering, Braude College of Engineering, Karmiel, Israel

Abstract. We focus on two different approaches to automatic program repair, based on formal verification methods. Both repair techniques consider infinite-state C-like programs, and consist of a generate-validate loop, in which potentially repaired programs are repeatedly generated and verified. Both approaches are *incremental* – partial information gathered in previous verification attempts is used in the next steps. However, the settings of both approaches, including their techniques for finding repairs, are quite distinct. The first approach uses syntactic mutations to repair sequential programs with respect to assertions in the code. It is based on a reduction to the problem of finding unsatisfiable sets of constraints, which is addressed using an interplay between SAT and SMT solvers. A novel notion of *must-fault-localization* enables efficient pruning of the search space, without losing any potential repair. The second approach uses an Assume-Guarantee (AG) style reasoning in order to verify large programs, composed of two concurrent components. The AG reasoning is based on automata-learning techniques. When verification fails, the procedure repeatedly repairs one of the components, until a correct repair is found. Several different repair methods are considered, trading off precision and convergence to a correct repair.

1 Introduction

This work is concerned with automated program repair. It focuses on two specific approaches, presented in [48,50] and [21,22], that demonstrate many of the guiding principles in program repair, when it is based on formal methods. While the two approaches have much in common, they are also quite distinct, due to their different settings, including their type of programs, specifications and repair mechanisms.

Both approaches handle infinite-state C-like programs, for which both the syntax and the semantics must be taken into account. The syntax refers to the program code, which might be updated for the purpose of repair. In [50] a predefined set of mutations is used for syntactic update, where [22] uses *abduction* to derive constraints that are added to the program code. In both cases, SMT solvers are used to answer semantic questions that arise during verification.

As often with program repair, the entire process can be seen as a *generate-validate* loop. *Generate* produces a candidate program, and *validate* checks whether it is a *good repair*, that is, whether the candidate program satisfies the given specification.

© Springer Nature Switzerland AG 2022
J.-F. Raskin and K. Chatterjee (Eds.): Principles of Systems Design, LNCS 13660, pp. 511–534, 2022.
https://doi.org/10.1007/978-3-031-22337-2_25

In order to prune the search space of candidate programs when validation fails, the goal is not only to remove the failed candidate program, but also to remove "similar" candidates that are likely to fail as well.

In [50] the search space consists of all mutated programs and the goal is to return *all* good repairs that are minimal. A notion of *must-fault localization* is developed in order to guarantee that similarly failed programs will not be considered in the future. This makes the repair process much more efficient.

In [22], the search space consists of sets of executions of the original program, which can be represented by a Control Flow Graph (CFG). Once the current program fails to satisfy the specification, faulty executions are removed by altering the CFG of the program. Several repair methods are proposed, some may remove more executions than necessary. This allows to trade efficiency for completeness. This approach too is *incremental*, meaning that the current validation step makes use of previous validation steps, thus increasing efficiency.

As stated, the differences between the two approaches are quite significant. [50] exploits a predefined set of mutations for repair. Its goal is to return all minimal repairs and its focus is on the notion of must-fault localization, which achieves efficiency and completeness. Its verification notion is bounded. [22], on the other hand, focuses on making the validation step more scalable. To this end, it exploits the Assume-Guarantee (AG) learning-based paradigm for compositional verification [39,46] and adapts it to the setting of infinite-state communicating C programs. The CFG of the verified program is viewed as an automaton, in order to enable automata-learning (e.g., via $\mathbf{L}^*$ [4]). Its verification is unbounded.

Next, we present a high-level description of each of the approaches, followed by a more detailed description.

1.1   The Must-Fault Localization Approach

The first approach we present focuses on repair of imperative, sequential, programs with respect to assertions in the code. We use a bounded notion of correctness. That is, for a given bound wb, we consider only *bounded computations*, along which the body of each loop is entered at most wb times and the maximum depth of the call stack is wb. We say that a program is *repaired* if whenever a bounded computation reaches an assertion, the assertion is evaluated to true.

Our repair method is *sound*, meaning that every returned program is repaired (i.e., no violation occurs in it up to the given bound). Just like Bounded Model Checking, this increases our confidence in the returned program.

Our programs are repaired using a predefined set of mutations, applied to expressions in conditionals and assignments (e.g., replacing a $+$ operator by a $-$), as was shown useful in previous work [16,47]. We impose no assumptions on the number of mutations needed to repair the program and are able to produce repairs involving multiple buggy locations, possibly co-dependent. To make sure that our suggested repairs are as close to the original program as possible, the candidate repaired programs are examined and returned in increasing number of mutations. In addition, only *minimal* sets of mutations are taken into account. That is, if a program can be repaired by applying a set of mutations *Mut*, then no superset of *Mut* is later considered. Intuitively, this is our way to make sure all changes made to the program by a certain repair are indeed necessary.

Our method is *complete* in the sense of returning *all* minimal sets of mutations that create a repaired program. Specifically, if no repair is found, one can conclude that the given set of mutations is not enough to repair the program.

Our algorithm, FL-AllRepair, is based on the translation of the program into a set of SMT constraints called the *program formula*, which is satisfiable iff the program contains an assertion violation. This was originally done for the purpose of bounded model checking in [11]. Our key observation is that mutating an expression in the program corresponds to replacing a constraint in the set of constraints encoding the program. Thus, searching the space of mutated programs is reduced to searching unsatisfiable sets of constraints.

The search is conducted using an interplay between SAT and SMT solvers, which realizes a generate-validate loop: The SAT solver is used to sample the search space of mutated programs and to efficiently block sets of undesired programs. The SMT solver is used to verify whether a mutated program is repaired.

Two key factors make this search process efficient: incremental solving, and pruning via blocking. Incremental solving is used in both the SAT solver and the SMT solver, which means that each of them retains learned information between successive calls. Using an SMT solver incrementally constitutes a novel way to exploit information learned while checking the correctness of one program for the process of checking correctness of another program. Note, that if the programs are similar, their encoding as sets of SMT constraints will also be similar (due to our observation presented above), resulting in bigger savings when using incremental SMT.

The second key contributing factor to efficiency is pruning. Pruning occurs after the validate stage, based on its results. Whenever a program is found to be repaired, we use it to prune other mutated programs based on non-minimality. If, however, the program is found to be buggy (i.e., not repaired) our algorithm makes use of fault localization to prune other buggy programs.

Although fault localization and automated program repair have long been combined, our use of fault localization to block undesired programs is non-standard. Traditionally, fault localization suggests a set of locations F in the program that might be the cause of the bug. Then, repair attempts to change those suspicious locations in order to eliminate the bug. Pruning based on such an approach would mean blocking mutated programs where lines outside of F are changed. However if fault localization is too restrictive (i.e., F is too small), we will be missing potential repairs. In fact, a recent study has shown that for test-based repair imprecise fault localizations happen very often in practice [34]. On the other hand, if fault localization is too permissive, this blocking might cause redundant search work.

This identifies the need for fault localization that can narrow down the space of candidates while still promising not to lose potential causes for a bug. For this purpose, we define the concept of a *must* location set. Intuitively, such a set includes at least one location from every repair for the bug. Thus, it *must* be used for repair. In other words, **it is impossible to fix the bug using only locations outside this set**. A fault localization technique is considered a *must* algorithm if it returns a must location set for every buggy program and every bug in the program.

The blocking done in our repair process whenever a buggy mutated program is discovered is based on a must-fault-localization algorithm. This blocking ensures that we do not lose repairs, and therefore do not damage completeness.

We implemented FL-AllRepair in an open-source tool available on GitHub[1], compared it with the methods of [29,30] and got very encouraging results.

1.2   The Assume-Guarantee-Repair (AGR) Approach

The second approach focuses on the Assume-Guarantee (AG) style compositional verification [39,46], which enables making the verification of large systems more scalable. The simplest AG rule checks whether a system composed of components M_1 and M_2 satisfies a property P by checking that M_1 along with an assumption A satisfies P, and that any system containing M_2 as a component satisfies A. Several frameworks have been proposed to support this style of reasoning. Finding a suitable assumption A is a common challenge in such frameworks.

Our fully-automated framework, called *Assume-Guarantee-Repair* (AGR), applies the Assume-Guarantee rule, and while seeking a suitable assumption A, iteratively repairs the given program in case the verification fails. Our framework is inspired by [44], which presented a learning-based method for finding an assumption A for finite-state programs represented by labeled transition systems (LTS). The assumptions are found using the $\mathbf{L}^*$ [4] algorithm for learning regular languages.

In contrast to [44], our AGR framework handles *communicating programs*. These are infinite-state C-like programs, extended with the ability to synchronously read and write data over communication channels. We model such programs as finite-word automata over an *action alphabet*, which reflects the program statements. The accepting states in the automaton model points of interest in the program that the specification can relate to. The automata representation, which enables exploiting automata-learning algorithms, is similar in nature to that of control-flow graphs.

The composition of the two program components M_1 and M_2, denoted $M_1\|M_2$, synchronizes on read-write actions on the same channel. Between two synchronized actions, the individual actions of both systems interleave. Figure 1 presents the code of a communicating program (left) and its corresponding automaton M_2 (right). The automaton alphabet consists of constraints, assignment actions, and communication actions. For example, $enc!x_{pw}$ sends the value of variable x_{pw} over channel enc, and $getEnc?x_{pw2}$ reads a value to x_{pw2} on channel $getEnc$.

The specification P is modeled as an automaton that does not contain assignment actions. It may contain communication actions in order to specify behavioral requirements, as well as constraints over the variables of both system components, that express requirements on their values in various points in the runs.

Consider, for example, the program M_1 and the specification P seen in Fig. 2, and the program M_2 of Fig. 1. M_2 reads a password on channel $read$ to the variable x_{pw}, and once the password is long enough (at least four digits), M_2 sends the value of x_{pw}

---

[1] Fl-AllRepair is an extension of the AllRepair tool, available here: https://github.com/batchenRothenberg/AllRepair. FL-AllRepair is currently enabled by adding the `--blockrepair slicing` option to the AllRepair tool.

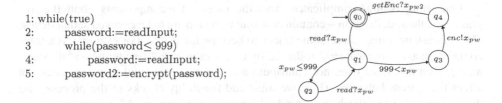

```
1: while(true)
2:     password:=readInput;
3      while(password≤ 999)
4:        password:=readInput;
5:     password2:=encrypt(password);
```

Fig. 1. Modeling a communicating program as an automaton M_2

to M_1 through channel *enc*. The component M_1 reads this value to variable y_{pw} and then applies a simple function that changes its value, and sends the changed variable back to M_2. The property P reasons about the parallel run of the two programs. The pair $(getEnc?x_{pw2}, getEnc!y_{pw})$ denotes a synchronization of M_1 and M_2 on channel *getEnc*. The specification P requests that the parallel run of M_1 and M_2 first reads a value and only then encrypts it – a temporal requirement. In addition, it makes sure that the value after encryption is different from the original value, and that there is no overflow – both are semantic requirements on the program variables. In case that one of the requirements does not hold, P reaches the error state r_4. Note that P here is not complete, for simplicity of presentation.

The **L*** algorithm aims at learning a regular language U. Its entities consist of a *teacher* – an oracle that answers *membership queries* ("is the word w in U?") and *equivalence queries* ("is $\mathcal{A}$ an automaton whose language is U?"), and a *learner*, which iteratively constructs a finite deterministic automaton $\mathcal{A}$ for U by submitting a sequence of membership and equivalence queries to the teacher. In using the **L*** algorithm for learning an assumption A for the AG-rule, membership queries are answered according to the specification P: A trace t should be in A iff $M_1||t$ satisfies P. Once the learner constructs a stable system A, it submits an equivalence query. The teacher then checks whether $M_1||A$ satisfies P, and whether the language of M_2 is contained in the language of A. According to the results, the process either continues or halts with an answer to the verification problem. The learning procedure aims at learning the weakest assumption A_w, which contains all the traces that in parallel with M_1 satisfy P. The key observation that guarantees termination in [44] is that the components in this procedure – M_1, M_2, P and A_w – are all regular.

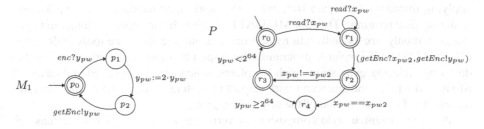

Fig. 2. The program M_1 and the specification P

Our setting is more complicated, since the traces in the components – both the programs and the specification – contain constraints, which are to be checked semantically. These constraints may cause some traces to become infeasible. For example, if a trace contains an assignment $x := 3$ followed by a constraint $x \geq 4$ (modeling an "if" statement), then this trace does not contribute any concrete runs, and therefore does not affect the system behavior. Thus, we must add feasibility checks to the process, and there is more here to check than standard language containment. Moreover, in our setting A_w above may no longer be regular, see Example 3. However, our method manages overcoming this problem.

We proceed to describe the repair process in case that the verification fails. An AG-rule can either conclude that $M_1 \| M_2$ satisfies P, or return a counterexample, which is a computation t of $M_1 \| M_2$ that violates P. Instead of returning t, we repair M_2 in a way that eliminates it. Our repair is either syntactic or semantic. For semantic repair we use *abduction* [45] to infer a new constraint, which makes the counterexample t infeasible.

Consider again M_1 and P of Fig. 2 and M_2 of Fig. 1. The composition $M_1 \| M_2$ does not satisfy P. For example, if the initial value of x_{pw} is 2^{63}, then after encryption the value of y_{pw} is 2^{64}, violating P. Our algorithm finds a bad trace t during the AG stage, which captures this bad behavior. In the repair stage, the abduction finds a constraint $x_{pw} < 2^{63}$ that eliminates t, and adds it to M_2.

Following this step we now have an updated M_2, and we apply the AG-rule again, using information we have gathered in the previous steps. In addition to removing the error trace, we update the alphabet of M_2 with the new constraint. Continuing our example, in a following iteration AGR will verify that the repaired M_2 together with M_1 satisfy P, and terminate.

In case that the current system does satisfy P, we return the repaired M_2 together with an assumption A that abstracts M_2 and acts as a smaller proof for correctness.

We have implemented a tool for AGR and evaluated it on examples of various sizes and of various types of errors. Our experiments show that for most examples, AGR converges and finds a repair after 2–5 iterations of verify-repair. Moreover, our tool generates assumptions that are significantly smaller than the (possibly repaired) M_2, thus constructing a compact and efficient proof of correctness.

1.3 Related Work

There is a wide range of techniques for automated program repair using formal methods [6, 14, 27, 28, 38, 41, 42, 53]. Both [16] and [47] also use fault localization followed by applying mutations for repair. But, unlike this work, fault localization is applied only to the original program. The tool MUT-APR [5] fixes binary operator faults in C programs, but only targets faults that require one line modification. The tools FORENSIC [7] and MAPLE [43] repair C programs with respect to a formal specification, but they do so by replacing expressions with templates, which are then patched and analysed. SEMGRAFT [37] conducts repair with respect to a reference implementation, but relies on tests for fault localization of the original program.

Assume-guarantee style compositional verification [39, 46] has been extensively studied, using learning-based approaches [8, 10, 13, 19, 20, 23, 25, 26, 36, 40]. All these works are limited to finite state systems, and do not repair the system but only address the verification problem. [33] addresses $\mathbf{L}^*$-based compositional verification and synthesis, but it only targets finite-state systems.

The work of [2,32] use logical abduction for synthesis and repair, however, their setting is sequential, while here we target concurrent systems. [51] computes the *interface* of an infinite-state component, but it only analyzes one component at a time. In contrast, we use both components of a system to compute the necessary assumptions.

2   Mutation-Based Repair with Iterative Fault Localization

2.1   Setting

Programs and Program Correctness. For our purposes, a *program* is a sequential program composed of standard statements: assignments, conditionals, loops and function calls with their standard semantics. Each statement is located at a certain *location* (or *line*) l_i, and all statements are defined over the set of program variables X. The desired behavior of the program is expressed through `assume` and `assert` statements. An `assume` statement is used to restrict executions to only those of interest (if an `assume` is violated, execution ends without an error), and an `assert` statement is used to express a desired property (if an `assert` is violated, execution ends in an error).

A program P has a *bug on input I* if an assertion violation occurs during the execution of P on I. If no assertion violation occurs during the execution of P on I, then the program is *correct for I*. If P has a bug on some input I then P is said to be *erroneous*, otherwise it is *correct*.

In this work, we focus on bounded executions of the program. A wb-bounded execution of a program P, for some integer bound wb, is an execution of P where the body of each loop is entered at most wb times and the maximum depth of the call stack is wb. A program P where no assertion violation occurs during any of its wb-bounded executions is said to be wb-*violation-free*. Our algorithm repairs programs with respect to a fixed, user-supplied, bound wb. Therefore, we refer to a wb-violation-free program as a *repaired program*, for short.

The Mutation Repair Scheme. We use the notion of a *repair scheme* to define which changes to a program are allowed by a repair method. A repair scheme $\mathcal{S}$ is a function mapping a statement to a set of statements. Intuitively, the image of a statement in this function represents all options to replace it allowed by the repair method.

The repair scheme used in our algorithm is the *mutation scheme*. The mutation scheme, $\mathcal{S}_{mut}$, is a repair scheme constructed using a finite list of mutation operations, $M_1, \cdots, M_k$. A mutation operator M_i can be any partial function mapping a program expression to another program expression of the same type. Applying a mutation operator M_i to a statement st, denoted $M_i(st)$, means applying M_i to the expression of st^2. This application is only defined if the expression of st is in the domain of M_i, in which case we say that M_i is *applicable* to st. For a program statement st, $\mathcal{S}_{mut}(st)$ is defined as $\{M_{i_1}(st), \cdots, M_{i_n}(st)\}$, where $M_{i_1}, \cdots, M_{i_n}$ are all the mutation operators from $M_1, \cdots, M_k$ applicable to st.

---

^{2} If st is an assignment of the form x:=e then its expression is e. If st is a conditional statement, then its expression is the condition.

Example 1. Suppose we have M_1 which replaces a + operator with a – operator, M_2 which replaces a < operator with a > operator, and M_3 which allows increasing a numerical constant by 1. Let st be the statement $\mathtt{x:=y+1}$. The expression of st is thus $\mathtt{y+1}$, and the mutation operators applicable to st are M_1 and M_3. Therefore,

$$\mathcal{S}_{mut}(st) = \{\mathtt{x:=y-1}, \mathtt{x:=y+2}\}$$

Let $\mathcal{S}$ be a repair scheme. An $\mathcal{S}$-*patch* of a program P is thus a set of pairs, $\{(l_1, st_1^r), \cdots, (l_k, st_k^r)\}$, where l_i is a program location and st_i^r is a statement, for which the following holds: for all $1 \leq i \leq k$, let st_i be the statement in location l_i in P, then $st_i^r \in \mathcal{S}(st_i)$. In addition, for every $i \neq j$, $l_i \neq l_j$. Applying an $\mathcal{S}$-*patch* τ to a program P means replacing the statement st_i with st_i^r in every location l_i in τ. The *size* of the patch is the number of mutated statements (k).

We refer to the result of applying an $\mathcal{S}_{mut}$-*patch* to a program as a *mutated program*. The set of all mutated programs created from a program P is the *search space* of P.

2.2 The FL-AllRepair Algorithm

In this section we present algorithm FL-AllRepair, which gets a program P and returns all minimal repairs from within the search space of P, where minimality is defined with respect to inclusion between patches. A high level description of the algorithm is presented in Fig. 3. The algorithm follows a generate-validate loop: the *generate* stage chooses a mutated program P' from the search space and the *validate* stage checks whether P' is correct. In both cases, a blocking stage occurs that removes irrelevant programs from the search space. If the program was correct, blocking is based on non-minimality. Otherwise, it is based on the results of a fault localization component.

The following subsections dive into the details of the individual components.

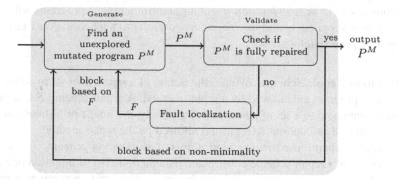

Fig. 3. Outline of algorithm FL-AllRepair for iterative mutation-based program repair.

2.3 Generate

To choose a mutated program from the search space we need to choose which mutation operator to apply to which line. We encode this choosing process in a propositional formula. Specifically, for every mutation operator M and line l, there is a boolean variable

$B_M(l)$ in the formula, which is true if and only if M is applied to line l. Additionally, for every line l there is a variable $B_O(l)$, which is true if and only if line l is not mutated. Then, the formula is constructed by requiring that for every line l exactly one of the variables $B_O(l), B_{M_1}(l), \cdots, B_{M_k}(l)$ be true. This way, there is a 1–1 correspondence between models of the formula and mutated programs in the search space. Hence, the generate stage can be realized using a SAT solver that solves this formula.

The advantage of this SAT encoding is that it allows an easy removal (blocking) of mutated programs from the search space. Such a removal can be realized by simply adding a blocking clause to the propositional formula. For example, to prevent all programs where mutation operator M is applied to line l from being considered, one can simply add the clause $\neg B_M(l)$.

Another advantage of this encoding is that it let's us easily control the size of patches being explored: we can limit the number of variables allowed to be set to true to at most s, for the desired size s. We then explore patches in increasing size by repeatedly increasing s as soon as the formula becomes unsatisfiable.

2.4 Validate

The validation of a mutated program P^M is based on a translation of the program P into a set of constraints, whose conjunction constitutes the *program formula*. In addition to representing assignments and conditionals, the program formula includes constraints representing assumptions, and a constraint representing the negated conjunction of all assertions. Thus, a satisfying assignment (a *model*) of the program formula represents an execution of P that satisfies all assumptions but violates at least one assertion.

From Programs to Program Formulas. Next, we explain how the program is translated into a set of constraints. The translation, following [11], goes through four stages. Figure 4 demonstrates certain steps of the translation. First, the program is simplified and each of the branch conditions is replaced with a fresh boolean variable. In the example, g replaces the condition $w > 3$. Second, the body of each loop and each function is inlined wb times. Next, the program is converted to static single assignment (SSA) form. In particular, variables are indexed so that each indexed variable is assigned at most once. Finally, the program in SSA form is translated to a set of constraints, whose conjunction forms the formula φ_P^{wb}.

For a more detailed description see [50].

Theorem 1 ([12]). *A program P is repaired iff the formula φ_P^{wb} is unsatisfiable.*

Validation via SMT Solving. Based on Theorem 1, we realize the validate stage using an SMT solver that solves the program formula $\varphi_{P^M}^{wb}$ of the mutated program P^M in question. If $\varphi_{P^M}^{wb}$ is determined unsatisfiable, P^M is added to the list of possible repairs returned to the user.

Incrementality. To facilitate the repeated verification of mutated programs during different iterations, we make use of incrementality. A naive, non-incremental, approach would require translating each mutated program into a formula and solving it from

proc. foo(x, w)	proc. simFoo(x, w)	proc. SSAFoo(x, w)	$\varphi_{foo} = \{$
1: t := 0	t := 0	t0 := 0	$t_0 = 0,$
2: y := x - 3	y := x - 3	y0 := x0 - 3	$y_0 = x_0 - 3,$
3: z := x + 3	z := x + 3	z0 := x0 + 3	$z_0 = x_0 + 3,$
4: if (w > 3) then	g := w > 3	g0 := w0 > 3	$g_0 = w_0 > 3,$
5: t := z + w	if (g) then	t1 := z0 + w0	$t_1 = z_0 + w_0,$
6: assert (t < x)	t := z + w	assert (g0 → t1 < x0)	
7: y := y + 10	assert (t < x)	y1 := y0 + 10	$y_1 = y_0 + 10,$
8: assert (y > z)	y := y + 10	t2 := g0 ? t1 : t0	$t_2 = ite(g_0, t_1, t_0),$
	assert (y > z)	y2 := g0 ? y1 : y0	$y_2 = ite(g_0, y_1, y_0),$
		assert (y2 > z0)	$\neg(y_2 > z_0) \lor$
			$\neg(g_0 \rightarrow t_1 < x_0)\}$

Fig. 4. Example of the translation process of a simple program

scratch during each iteration. Instead, we translate only the original program into a formula as a preliminary step, before the generate-validate loop begins. Then, during each iteration we make the necessary changes to the formula and use incremental SMT solving, which reuses relevant partial results from the previous iteration.

The key observation that makes this process efficient is that replacing one mutated program with another requires making only small changes to the program formula. Consider, for example, the foo program of Fig. 4. Replacing y := x - 3 with y := x * 3 on line number 2 would only require replacing the constraint $y_0 = x_0 - 3$ with the constraint $y_0 = x_0 * 3$ in the program formula. Similarly, any changes made to the right-hand-side of an assignment or to the expression in a condition only require replacing a single constraint in the formula. Therefore, this is a promising application for incremental SMT solving.

2.5 Blocking Based on Non-minimality

As mentioned, FL-AllRepair aims at returning all minimal repairs. Next, we formally define minimality: Let $P^M, P^{M'}$ be two mutated programs constructed using patches pat, pat', resp. We say that $P^M \subseteq P^{M'}$ if $pat \subseteq pat'$. This intuitively means that all lines that are mutated in P^M are mutated in $P^{M'}$, using the same mutation operators, but $P^{M'}$ contains additional mutated lines.

Definition 1 (minimal repair). *A mutated program P^M is said to be a* minimal repair *if it is a repair, and there is no other mutated program $P^{M'}$ s.t. $P^{M'} \subseteq P^M$ and $P^{M'}$ is a repair.*

The rationale for considering only minimal repairs is the observation that the program should remain as syntactically close to the original program as possible (we should avoid making changes to the code if they are not necessary for repair).

Constructing a Blocking Clause. Once a program P^M is found to be correct during the validate stage, we block every mutated program $P^{M'}$ s.t. $P^M \subseteq P^{M'}$. This, together with the fact that programs are explored in increasing patch size, guarantees that only minimal repairs are returned. The blocking is realized as follows: let

$pat = \{(l_1, M_{i_1}), \cdots, (l_n, M_{i_n})\}$ be the patch used in creating P^M. Then, the following clause is added to the propositional formula of the generate stage:

$$\neg B_{M_{i_1}}(l_1) \vee \cdots \vee \neg B_{M_{i_n}}(l_n).$$

This clause restricts the search space to those mutated programs where there exists an index i for which line l_i is not mutated using mutation operator M_{l_i}. This will prune from the search space all mutated programs created using a patch pat' s.t. $pat \subseteq pat'$.

2.6 Blocking Based on Fault Localization

When a program P^M is determined buggy by the validate stage, it is passed on to a fault localization component in order to find the root cause of the bug and block other unexplored programs that exhibit the same bug. Specifically, we want fault localization to return a set of locations F whose content alone ensures the recurrence of the bug. This way, all programs in which the content of F remains the same (as in P^M) can be safely blocked. To formalize the above intuition we use the notions of a *must-location-set* and *must-fault-localization*[3].

Let P be a program with a bug on input I. A *repair for I* is a mutated program that is (bounded) correct for I. A *repairable location set (RLS) for I* is a set of locations F such that there exists a repair for I defined over F. An RLS for I is *minimal* if removing any location from it makes it no longer an RLS for I. A location is *relevant to I* if it is a part of a minimal RLS for I.

The aim of fault localization is to focus the programmer's attention on locations that are relevant for the bug. But, returning the exact set of locations relevant to I as defined above can be computationally hard. In practice, what many fault localization algorithms return is a set of locations that *may* be relevant: The returned locations have a higher chance of being relevant to I than those that are not, but there is no guarantee that all returned locations are relevant to I, nor that all locations that are relevant to I, are returned. We call such an algorithm *may fault localization*. In contrast, we define *must fault localization*, as follows:

Definition 2 (must location set). *A* must location set *for I is a set of locations that contains at least one location from each minimal RLS for I.*[4]

Definition 3 (must fault localization). *A* must fault localization *algorithm is an algorithm that for every program P and every buggy input I, returns a must location set.*

Note that a must location set is not required to contain all locations relevant to I, but only one location from each minimal RLS for I. This notion is still powerful, since it guarantees that no repair is possible without including at least one such element.

Also note, that the set of all locations visited by P during its execution on I is always a must location set. This is because any patch where none of these locations is included is definitely **not** a repair for I, since the same assertion will be violated along the same path. However, this set of locations may not be minimal.

---

[3] For brevity, the definitions brought here are an instantiation of the original definitions from [50] to the mutation scheme. Originally, the definitions of both a must-location-set and must-fault-localization depend on the repair scheme.

[4] This is, in fact, a hitting set of the set of all minimal RLS for I.

Fault Localization Algorithm. Going back to FL-AllRepair, Let P^M be a program found to be buggy by the validate stage, and let μ be the model of the program formula φ_{PM} obtained by the SMT solver. P^M is then passed to a fault localization component, which receives the formula φ_{PM} and the model μ and returns a set of locations F. This component is realized using a formula slicing-based algorithm that agrees with the definition of a must-fault-localization algorithm. For brevity, we omit the details of this algorithm and refer the reader to section 5 in [50].

Constructing a Blocking Clause. Let F be the set of locations returned by the fault localization component. Since the fault localization algorithm is a must-fault-localization algorithm, F is a must-location-set. This means that all mutated programs which are identical to P^M on the locations in F can be safely removed from the search space. We remove them by adding a blocking clause to the propositional formula, encoding that at least one location from F should be changed. For example, suppose that F consists of $\{l_1, l_2, l_3\}$, where l_1 was mutated with M_1, where l_2 was not mutated, and l_3 was mutated with M_3. The constructed blocking clause will then be $\neg B_{M_1}(l_1) \lor \neg B_O(l_2) \lor \neg B_{M_3}(l_3)$. The blocking clause restricts the search space to those mutated programs that either do not apply mutation M_1 to l_1, or do mutate l_2, or do not apply M_3 to l_3.

2.7 Experimental Results

We have implemented the FL-AllRepair algorithm on top of the AllRepair open source tool. This tool previously implemented an earlier version of the algorithm, presented in [49], which avoids the use of fault localization and instead blocks only the one incorrect mutated program found during that iteration.

This early version of the algorithm was recently compared against 4 other repair tools in [43] and was found to be very efficient. The tools participating in the experiment were: ANGELIX [38], GENPROG [31], FORENSIC [7] and MAPLE [43]. All tools were run on the TCAS benchmark [18], but with different specifications: ANGELIX and GEN-PROG use a test suite while the rest of the tools use a formal specification. The results showed a significant

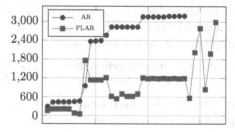

Fig. 5. Time to find a repair using FL-AllRepair and AllRepair (in seconds). Each point along the x axis represents a repair for a single input and the y axis value represents the time to find that repair.

advantage to the ALLREPAIR tool in terms of efficiency: ALLREPAIR was found to be faster by an order of magnitude than all of the compared tools, taking only 16.9 s to find a repair on average, where the other tools take 1540.7, 325.4, 360.1, and 155.3 s, respectively. On the other hand, ALLREPAIR's repair ability is limited, due to the use of the mutation scheme: it is only able to repair 18 versions (out of 41), while ANGELIX, GENPROG, FORENSIC and MAPLE repair 32, 11, 23, and 26, respectively.

In [50] we have conducted an experiment to check the impact of adding fault-localization-based blocking on efficiency (repair ability is not affected, since must-fault-localization guarantees that we will not lose any of the potential good repairs). We ran FL-AllRepair on the TCAS benchmark as well as a small subset of the Code-flaws benchmark [52]. The Codeflaws benchmark is a collection of programs taken from buggy user submissions to the programming contest site Codeforces[5]. We compared the time to find a repair in FL-AllRepair and All-Repair, using various unwinding bounds and mutation sets. Overall, the experiment consisted of 186 *inputs*, where an input is a combination of buggy program, mutation set, and unwinding bound.

Our conclusion was that FL-AllRepair is able to acheive significant speed-ups, especially for cases of interest where AllRepair struggles to find a repair in the first place. To demonstrate, Fig. 5 shows the time it took to find a repair using both algorithms, for all the repairs where AllRepair took more than 5 min. Observe that FL-AllRepair saves time for all but one of these repairs, and the savings go up to dozens of minutes.

For a more detailed description of our experiments, see [48,50]

3 Verification and Repair of Communicating Systems (AGR)

We now describe our second approach to automatic repair, based on compositional verification.

3.1 Communicating Programs

We first present our programs, which are modeled as *communicating systems*.

The alphabet α of a communicating system uses a set of variables X (whose ordered vector is $\bar{x}$), ranging over a (possibly infinite) data domain $\mathbb{D}$. The alphabet α consists of a set $\mathcal{C}$ of *constraints*, which are quantifier-free first-order formulas over $X \cup \mathbb{D}$, representing the conditions in *if* and *while* statements. It also includes a set of *assignment statements* $\mathcal{E}$, consisting of statements of the type $x := e$, where e is an expression over $X \cup \mathbb{D}$. Finally, α includes a set $\mathcal{G}$ of *communication actions*, over a set G of communication channels. The action $g?x$ is a *read* action of a value to the variable x through channel g, and $g!x$ is a *write* action of the value of x on g. We use $g * x$ to indicate some action, either *read* or *write*, through g. The pairs $(g?x_1, g!x_2)$ and $(g!x_1, g?x_2)$ then represent a synchronization of two programs on read-write actions over g.

Definition 1. *A* communicating program *(or, a program) is* $M = \langle Q, X, \alpha, \delta, q_0, F \rangle$, *where:*

1. *Q is a finite set of states and $q_0 \in Q$ is the initial state.*
2. *X is a finite set of variables over $\mathbb{D}$.*
3. *$\alpha = \mathcal{G} \cup \mathcal{E} \cup \mathcal{C}$ is the action alphabet of M.*
4. *$\delta \subseteq Q \times \alpha \times Q$ is the transition relation.*
5. *$F \subseteq Q$ is the set of accepting states.*

---

[5] http://codeforces.com/.

The words that are read along a communicating program are a symbolic representation of the program behaviors. We refer to such a word as a *trace*. Each such trace induces *executions* of the program, which are formed by concrete assignments to the program variables in a way that conforms to the actions along the word. We think of the program automaton as the generator of the behaviors of the program – a word in the language of the automaton is a program run, which induces a set of executions.

More formally, a *run* r in a program automaton M is a finite sequence of states and actions starting with the initial state and following δ. The *induced trace* t of r is the sequence of the actions in r. If r reaches an accepting state, then t is an *accepted trace* of M. An *execution* p of t is a sequence of valuations of X that respects the semantics of the alphabet. That is, the valuation of a variable x can only change by a read action through a communication channel, e.g. $g?x$, or through an assignment $x := e$. In addition, the valuations must satisfy the constraints along t. That is, if $\beta(\bar{x})$ is a valuation in p at location i, and t_i is a constraint at i, then $\beta(\bar{x}) \models t_i$. We say that t is *feasible* if there exists an execution of t.

Example 2. The trace $(x := 2 \cdot y,\ g?x,\ y := y+1,\ g!y)$ is feasible, as it has an execution $(x = 1, y = 3), (x = 6, y = 3), (x = 20, y = 3), (x = 20, y = 4), (x = 20, y = 4)$. The trace $(g?x,\ x := x^2, x < 0)$ is not feasible since no valuation can satisfy the constraint $x < 0$ if $x := x^2$ is executed beforehand.

The *symbolic language* of M, denoted $\mathcal{T}(M)$, is the set of all *accepted* traces induced by runs of M. The *concrete language* of M is the set of all executions of accepted traces in $\mathcal{T}(M)$.

Parallel Composition. We now describe the parallel composition of two communicating programs, and the way in which they communicate.

In *parallel composition*, the two components synchronize on their communication interface only when one component writes data through a channel, and the other reads it through the same channel. The two components cannot synchronize if both are trying to read or both are trying to write. We distinguish between communication of the two components with each other (on their common channels), and their communication with their environment. In the former case, the components must "wait" for each other in order to progress together. In the latter case, the communication actions of the two components interleave asynchronously.

Let M_1 and M_2 be two programs, where $M_i = \langle Q_i, X_i, \alpha_i, \delta_i, {q_0}^i, F_i \rangle$ for $i = 1, 2$. Let G_1, G_2 be the sets of communication channels occurring in actions of M_1, M_2, respectively. We assume that $X_1 \cap X_2 = \emptyset$. The *interface alphabet* αI of M_1 and M_2 consists of all communication actions on channels that are common to both components. That is, $\alpha I = \{\,g?x,\ g!x\ :\ g \in G_1 \cap G_2,\ x \in X_1 \cup X_2\,\}$.
Formally, the parallel composition of M_1 and M_2, denoted $M_1 \| M_2$, is the program $M = \langle Q, X, \alpha, \delta, q_0, F \rangle$, defined as follows.

1. $Q = (Q_1 \times Q_2) \cup (Q_1' \times Q_2')$, where Q_1' and Q_2' are new copies of Q_1 and Q_2, respectively. The initial state is $q_0 = (q_0^1, q_0^2)$; $X = X_1 \cup X_2$; $F = F_1 \times F_2$.

2. $\alpha = \{ (g?x_1, g!x_2), (g!x_1, g?x_2) : g * x_1 \in (\alpha_1 \cap \alpha I)$ and $g * x_2 \in (\alpha_2 \cap \alpha I) \} \cup ((\alpha_1 \cup \alpha_2) \setminus \alpha I)$. That is, the alphabet includes pairs of read-write communication actions on channels that are common to M_1 and M_2. It also includes individual actions of M_1 and M_2, which are not communications on common channels.
3. δ is defined as follows.
   (a) For $(g * x_1, g * x_2) \in \alpha^6$:
       i. $\delta((q_1, q_2), (g * x_1, g * x_2)) = (q_1', q_2')$.
       ii. $\delta((q_1', q_2'), x_1 = x_2) = (\delta_1(q_1, g * x_1), \delta_2(q_2, g * x_2))$.
       That is, when a communication is performed synchronously in both components, the data is transformed through the channel from the writing component to the reading component. As a result, the values of x_1 and x_2 equalize. This is enforced in M by adding a transition labeled by the constraint $x_1 = x_2$ that immediately follows the synchronous communication.
   (b) For $a \in \alpha_1 \setminus \alpha I$ we define $\delta((q_1, q_2), a) = (\delta_1(q_1, a), q_2)$. Similarly, for $a \in \alpha_2 \setminus \alpha I$ we define $\delta((q_1, q_2), a) = (q_1, \delta_2(q_2, a))$. That is, on actions that are not in the interface alphabet, the two components interleave.

Figure 6 demonstrates the parallel composition of components M_1 and M_2. The program $M = M_1 || M_2$ reads a password from the environment through channel *pass*. The two components synchronize on channel *verify*. This synchronization is represented by the constraint $x = y$, which describes the result of the synchronization. Assignments to x are interleaved with reading the value of y from the environment.

3.2 Regular Properties and Their Satisfaction

We now describe the syntax and semantics of the properties that we consider. These can be represented as finite automata, hence the name *regular properties*. However, the alphabet of these automata includes communication actions and first-order constraints over program variables. Thus, such automata are suitable for specifying the desired (and undesired) behaviors of communicating programs over time.

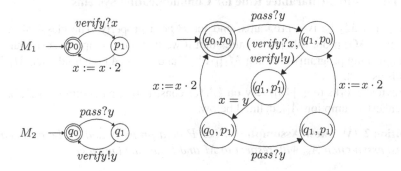

Fig. 6. Components M_1 and M_2 and their parallel composition $M_1 || M_2$.

---

[6] According to item 2., one of the actions must be a read and the other must be a write action.

We require our properties to be deterministic and complete. Since we consider symbolic representation of systems, we require also *semantic* determinism and completeness. That is, if $\langle q, c_1, q' \rangle$ and $\langle q, c_2, q'' \rangle$ are in δ for constraints $c_1, c_2 \in \mathcal{C}$ such that $c_1 \neq c_2$ and $q' \neq q''$, then $c_1 \wedge c_2 \equiv false$; and let C_q be the set of all constraints on transitions leaving q. Then $(\bigvee_{c \in C_q} c) \equiv true$.

A *property* is a deterministic and complete program with no assignment actions, whose language defines the set of allowed behaviors over the alphabet αP.

A trace is accepted by a property P if it reaches a state in F, the set of accepting states of P. Otherwise, it reaches a state in $Q \setminus F$, and is rejected by P.

Next, we define the satisfaction relation $\vDash$ between a program and a property. Intuitively, a program M satisfies a property P (denoted $M \vDash P$) if all executions induced by accepted traces of M reach an accepting state in P. Thus, the accepted behaviors of M are also accepted by P.

Conjunctive Composition. In order to capture the satisfaction relation between M and P, we define a *conjunctive composition* between M and P, denoted $M \times P$. Unlike parallel composition, in conjunctive composition the two components synchronize on their common communication actions when both read or both write through the same communication channel. In addition, if M is the result of a parallel compositions, then they might synchronize on alphabet of the type $(g * x, g * y)$. They interleave on constraints and on actions of αM that are not in αP. The set of accepting states of $M \times P$ is $F = F_M \times (Q_P \setminus F_P)$. As a result, accepted traces in $M \times P$ are those that are *accepted* in M and *rejected* in P. Such traces are called *error traces* and their corresponding executions are called *error executions*. Intuitively, an error execution is an execution along M which violates the properties modeled by P. Such an execution either fails to synchronize on the communication actions, or reaches a point in the computation in which its assignments violate some constraint described by P. Since a feasible error trace in $M \times P$ is an evidence to $M \nvDash P$, we define $M \vDash P$ iff $M \times P$ contains no feasible accepted traces.

3.3 The Assume-Guarantee Rule for Communicating Systems

Let M_1 and M_2 be two programs, and let P be a property. The classical Assume-Guarantee (AG) proof rule [46] assures that if we find an assumption A (in our case, a communicating program) such that $M_1 || A \vDash P$ and $M_2 \vDash A$ both hold, then $M_1 || M_2 \vDash P$ holds as well.

Previous works (e.g. [13]) rely on $\mathbf{L}^*$ for constructing an assumption A, based on the weakest assumption A_w, defined below.

Definition 2 (Weakest Assumption). *Let P be a property and M be a system. The weakest assumption A_w with respect to M and P has the language*

$$\mathcal{L}(A_w) = \{w : M || w \vDash P\}.$$

That is, $\mathcal{L}(A_w)$ is the set of all words that together with M satisfy P.

A crucial point of a learning-based AG method is that A_w is *regular* [24], and so can be learned by $\mathbf{L}^*$. However, this is not always the case in our setting, as the next example shows.

Example 3. Over the alphabet $\{x := 0, \; y := 0, \; x := x + 1, \; y := y + 1\}$ we can construct a system for which the weakest assumption requires an equal number of actions of the form $x := x + 1$ and $y := y + 1$, which is not a regular property.

To cope with this difficulty, we change the focus of learning. Instead of learning the (possibly) non-regular language of A_w, we learn $\mathcal{T}(M_2)$, the set of accepted traces of M_2. This language is guaranteed to be regular, as it is represented by the automaton M_2. As a result, our AG rule is sound and complete, as stated in the theorem below.

Theorem 1. *Our AG rule for communicating programs is sound and complete.*

3.4   The Assume-Guarantee-Repair (AGR) Framework

In this section we discuss our Assume-Guarantee-Repair (AGR) framework for communicating programs. The framework consists of a learning-based Assume-Guarantee algorithm, called $AG_{\mathbf{L}^*}$, and a REPAIR procedure, which are tightly joined.

Recall that the goal of $\mathbf{L}^*$ in our case is to learn $\mathcal{T}(M_2)$. The nature of $AG_{\mathbf{L}^*}$ is such that the assumptions it learns before it reaches M_2 may contain traces of M_2 and more, but still be represented by a smaller automaton. Therefore, similarly to [13], $AG_{\mathbf{L}^*}$ often terminates with an assumption A that is much smaller than M_2. Indeed, our tool often produces very small assumptions (see Fig. 8).

When $M_1 \| M_2 \nvDash P$, the $AG_{\mathbf{L}^*}$ algorithm returns an error trace t as a witness to the violation. In this case, we initiate the REPAIR procedure, which eliminates t from M_2, resulting in M_2'.

We then return to $AG_{\mathbf{L}^*}$ with a new goal, M_2', to search for a new assumption A' that allows to verify $M_1 \| M_2' \vDash P$. As we have mentioned, $AG_{\mathbf{L}^*}$ is incremental: when learning an assumption A' for M_2' we can use the membership answers we obtained for M_2, since these have not changed. The difference between the languages of M_2 and M_2' lies in words (traces) whose membership has not yet been queried on M_2. Learning M_2' can then start from the point where learning M_2 has left off, resulting in a more efficient algorithm.

As opposed to the case where $M_1 \| M_2 \vDash P$, we cannot guarantee the termination of the repair process in case that $M_1 \| M_2 \nvDash P$. This is because we are only guaranteed to remove one (bad) trace and add one (infeasible) trace in every iteration (although in practice, every iteration may remove a larger set of traces). Thus, we may never converge to a repaired system. Nevertheless, in case of violation, our algorithm always finds an error trace, thus a progress towards a "less erroneous" program is guaranteed.

It should be noted that the $AG_{\mathbf{L}^*}$ part of our AGR algorithm deviates from the AG-rule of [13] in two important ways. First, since our learning goal is M_2 rather than A_w, our membership queries are different in type and order. Second, in order to identify real error traces and send them to REPAIR as early as possible, we add queries to the membership phase that reveal such traces. We then send them to REPAIR without ever

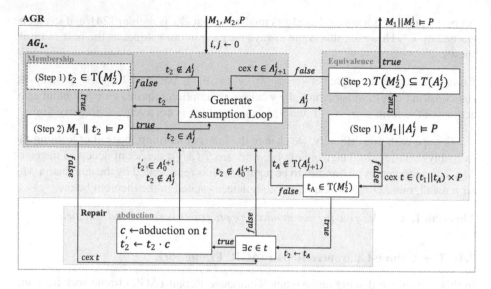

Fig. 7. The flow of AGR

passing through equivalence queries, which improves the overall efficiency. Indeed, our experiments include several cases in which all repairs were invoked from the membership phase. In these cases, AGR ran an equivalence query only when it has already successfully repaired M_2, and terminated.

The Assume-Guarantee-Repair (AGR) Algorithm. We now present an overview of our AGR algorithm. For a detailed description, see [21,22]. Figure 7 describes the flow of the algorithm.

AGR comprises two main parts, namely AG_{L^*} and REPAIR. The input to AGR are the components M_1 and M_2, and the property P. While M_1 and P stay unchanged during AGR, M_2 is repeatedly updated as long as it needs repair. In every iteration of AGR an updated M_2^i is calculated. Initially, $M_2^0 = M_2$. An iteration starts with the membership phase, and ends either when AG_{L^*} successfully terminates, or when REPAIR is called. When constructing M_2^i (based, as noted, on the construction of M_2^{i-1}), the new iteration is given new trace(s) that have been added or removed from M_2^{i-1}.

AG_{L^*} consists of two phases: membership, and equivalence. The membership phase is a loop in which the learner constructs the next assumption A_j^i according to answers it gets from the teacher on a sequence of membership queries on various traces. These queries are answered in accordance with traces we allow in A_j^i. These are the traces in M_2^i that in parallel with M_1 satisfy P. If a trace t in M_2^i in parallel with M_1 does not satisfy P, then t is a bad behavior of M_2^i. Therefore, if such t is found during the membership phase, REPAIR is invoked.

Once the learner reaches a stable assumption A_j^i, it passes it to the equivalence phase. A_j^i is a suitable assumption if both $M_1||A_j^i \models P$ and $\mathcal{T}(M_2^i) \subseteq \mathcal{T}(A_j^i)$ hold. AGR then terminates and returns M_2^i as a successful repair of M_2. In case $M_1||A_j^i \not\models P$, a counterexample t is returned, that is composed of bad traces in M_1, A_j^i, and P. If the bad trace t_2, the restriction of t to the alphabet of A_j^i, is also in M_2^i, then t_2 is a bad behavior of M_2^i, and REPAIR is invoked. Otherwise, AGR returns to the membership phase with t_2 as a trace that should not be in A_j^i, and continues to learn A_j^i.

Next we describe in more detail how repair is applied. We distinguish between semantic and syntactic repairs, which are solved differently.

Semantic Repair by Abduction. In case the error trace t contains constraints, we *semantically* repair M_2^i by inferring a new constraint that makes t infeasible. The new constraint is then added to the alphabet of M_2^i and may eliminate additional error traces.

The process of inferring new constraints from known facts about the program is called *abduction* [17]. Given a trace t, let φ_t be the first-order formula (a conjunction of constraints), which constitutes the SSA representation of t [3]. In order to make t infeasible, we look for a formula ψ such that $\psi \wedge \varphi_t \rightarrow false$.[7]

Note that $t \in T(M_1 \| M_2^i) \times P$, and so it includes variables both from X_1, the variables of M_1, and from X_2, the variables of M_2^i. Since we wish to repair M_2^i, the learned ψ is only over X_2. The formula $\psi \wedge \varphi_t \rightarrow false$ is equivalent to $\psi \rightarrow (\varphi_t \rightarrow false)$. Then, $\psi = \forall x \in X_1 : (\varphi_t \rightarrow false) = \forall x \in X_1(\neg \varphi_t)$, is such a desired constraint: ψ makes t infeasible and is only over X_2. We now use quantifier elimination [54] to produce a quantifier-free formula over X_2. Computing ψ is similar to the abduction suggested in [17], but the focus here is on finding a formula over X_2 rather than over any minimal set of variables as in [17]; further, [17] looks for ψ such that $\varphi_t \wedge \psi$ is not a contradiction, while we specifically look for ψ that blocks φ_t. We use Z3 [15] to apply quantifier elimination and to generate the new constraint. After generating $\psi(X_2)$, we add it to the alphabet of M_2^i. We also produce a new trace $t_2' = t_2 \cdot \psi(X_2)$, which is returned as the output of the abduction. AGR now returns to AG_{L_*} in order to learn an assumption for the repaired component M_2^{i+1}, which now includes t_2' but not t_2.

Syntactic Removal of Error Traces. In case that the error trace t does not contain constrains, we can remove t from M_2 by constructing a system whose language is $T(M_2) \setminus \{t\}$. We call this the *exact* method for repair. However, removing a single trace at a time may lead to slow convergence, and exponentially blows-up the repaired systems. Moreover, in some cases there are infinitely many such traces, in which case AGR may never terminate.

For faster convergence, we have implemented two additional heuristics, namely *approximate* and *aggressive*. These heuristics may remove more than a single trace at a time, while keeping the size of the systems small. While "good" traces may be removed as well, the correctness of the repair is maintained, since no bad traces are added. Moreover, an error trace is likely to be in an erroneous part of the system, and in these cases our heuristics manage removing a set of error traces in a single step.

All three methods modify the structure of the underlying automaton. In the *approximate* method we add an intermediate state on the way to an accepting state, to which

---

[7] Usually, in abduction, we look for ψ such that $\psi \wedge \varphi_t$ is not a contradiction. However, since φ_t is a violation of the specification, we want to infer a formula that makes φ_t unsatisfiable.

the error trace, and potentially more erroneous behaviours, are diverted. The *aggressive* method simply makes the state that M_2 reaches upon reading t, non-accepting. In case that every accepting state is reached by some error trace, this might result in an empty language, creating a trivial repair. However, our experiments show that in most cases, this method quickly leads to a non-trivial repair.

For further details of syntactic and semantic repair, see [21,22].

3.5 Experimental Results

We implemented our AGR framework in Java, integrating $\mathbf{L}^*$ implementation from the LTSA tool [35]. We used Z3 [15] as the teacher for the satisfaction queries in $AG_{\mathbf{L}^*}$, and for abduction in REPAIR. Figure 8 demonstrates the effectiveness of our approach on several examples (the x-axis indicates their indices). The examples are based on simple examples from [24] adapted to our setting. Note that the assumption sizes are mostly shown to be much smaller than the original components. The syntactic repair method presented in Fig. 8 is the approximate repair, however the same holds also for the other repair methods. Additional results are available in [21], and the full examples are available on [1].

3.6 Correctness and Termination

We assume a sound and complete teacher who can answer the membership and equivalence queries in $AG_{\mathbf{L}^*}$. We use Z3 [15] in order to answer satisfiability queries issued in the learning process. Our examples were over the theory of linear arithmetic, for which Z3 is indeed sound and complete.

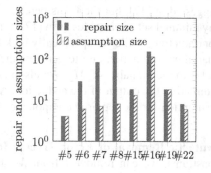

Fig. 8. Repair vs. assumption size (log. scale).

As noted, AGR may not terminate, and there are cases in which REPAIR is called infinitely many times. However, in case that no repair is needed, or if a repaired system is eventually obtained, then AGR is guaranteed to terminate correctly.

To see why, consider a repaired system M_2^i for which $M_1||M_2^i \vDash P$. Since the goal of $AG_{\mathbf{L}^*}$ is to syntactically learn M_2^i, which is regular, this stage will terminate at the latest when $AG_{\mathbf{L}^*}$ learns exactly M_2^i (it may terminate sooner if a smaller appropriate assumption is found). Notice that, in particular, if $M_1||M_2 \vDash P$, then AGR terminates with a correct answer in the first iteration of the verify-repair loop.

REPAIR is only invoked when a (real) error trace t is found in M_2^i, in which case a new system M_2^{i+1}, that does not include t, is produced by REPAIR. If $M_1||M_2^i \nvDash P$, then an error trace is guaranteed to be found by $AG_{\mathbf{L}^*}$ either in the membership or equivalence phase. Therefore, also in case that M_2^i violates P, the iteration is guaranteed to terminate. In particular, since every iteration of AGR finds and removes an error trace t, and no new erroneous traces are introduced in the updated system, then in case that M_2 has finitely many error traces, AGR is guaranteed to terminate with a repaired system, which is correct with respect to P.

4   Conclusions and Discussion

We presented two approaches for automated program repair, using formal methods techniques. Both approaches aim to verify infinite state C-like programs and handle both the syntax and the semantics of the program. Both approaches are incremental in the sense of reusing information from previous iterations in order to verify the current program.

Despite the common grounds, each approach handles the verification and repair differently. The mutation-based approach handles sequential imperative programs with assertions in the code. It relies on a reduction to the problem of finding unsatisfiable sets of constraints and uses SAT and SMT solvers to realize a generate-and-validate loop. Efficiency is achieved through incremental solving and efficient pruning.

The AGR approach is based on automata learning and offers a verify-repair algorithm that takes the advantages of the automata representation in order to apply automata learning. It modifies the components both syntactically by eliminating error traces, and semantically by adding constraints using abduction.

We have implemented both algorithms and our experimental results demonstrate the effectiveness of our approaches for program repair.

Acknowledgement. This work was partially supported by the Israel Science Foundation (ISF), Grant No. 979/11.

References

1. https://github.com/hadarlh/AGR
2. Albarghouthi, A., Dillig, I., Gurfinkel, A.: Maximal specification synthesis. In: POPL **51**(1), 789-801(2016)
3. Alpern, B., Wegman, M.N., Zadeck, F.K.: Detecting equality of variables in programs. In: POPL (1988)
4. Angluin, D.: Learning regular sets from queries and counterexamples. Inf. Comput. **75**(2), 87-106 (1987)
5. Assiri, F.Y., Bieman, J.M.: MUT-APR: mutation-based automated program repair research tool. In: Arai, K., Kapoor, S., Bhatia, R. (eds.) FICC 2018. AISC, vol. 887, pp. 256-270. Springer, Cham (2019). https://doi.org/10.1007/978-3-030-03405-4_17
6. Attie, P.C., Dak, K., Bab, A.L., Sakr, M.: Model and program repair via SAT solving. ACM Trans. Embed. Comput. Syst. **17**(2), 1-25 (2017)
7. Bloem, R., Drechsler, R., Fey, G., Finder, A., Hofferek, G., Könighofer, R., Raik, J., Repinski, U., Sülflow, A.: FoREnSiC– an automatic debugging environment for C programs. In: Biere, A., Nahir, A., Vos, T. (eds.) HVC 2012. LNCS, vol. 7857, pp. 260-265. Springer, Heidelberg (2013). https://doi.org/10.1007/978-3-642-39611-3_24
8. Chaki, S., Strichman, O.: Optimized L*-based assume-guarantee reasoning. In: Grumberg, O., Huth, M. (eds.) TACAS 2007. LNCS, vol. 4424, pp. 276-291. Springer, Heidelberg (2007). https://doi.org/10.1007/978-3-540-71209-1_22

9. Chen, Y.-F., Clarke, E.M., Farzan, A., Tsai, M.-H., Tsay, Y.-K., Wang, B.-Y.: Automated assume-guarantee reasoning through implicit learning. In: Touili, T., Cook, B., Jackson, P. (eds.) CAV 2010. LNCS, vol. 6174, pp. 511–526. Springer, Heidelberg (2010). https://doi.org/10.1007/978-3-642-14295-6_44

10. Chen, Y.-F., Farzan, A., Clarke, E.M., Tsay, Y.-K., Wang, B.-Y.: Learning minimal separating DFA's for compositional verification. In: Kowalewski, S., Philippou, A. (eds.) TACAS 2009. LNCS, vol. 5505, pp. 31–45. Springer, Heidelberg (2009). https://doi.org/10.1007/978-3-642-00768-2_3

11. Clarke, E., Kroening, D., Lerda, F.: A tool for checking ANSI-C programs. In: Jensen, K., Podelski, A. (eds.) TACAS 2004. LNCS, vol. 2988, pp. 168–176. Springer, Heidelberg (2004). https://doi.org/10.1007/978-3-540-24730-2_15

12. Clarke, E., Kroening, D., Yorav, K.: Behavioral consistency of C and verilog programs using bounded model checking. In: Design Automation Conference, 2003. Proceedings, pp. 368–371 IEEE (2003)

13. Cobleigh, J.M., Giannakopoulou, D., Păsăreanu, C.S.: Learning assumptions for compositional verification. In: Garavel, H., Hatcliff, J. (eds.) TACAS 2003. LNCS, vol. 2619, pp. 331–346. Springer, Heidelberg (2003). https://doi.org/10.1007/3-540-36577-X_24

14. D'Antoni, L., Samanta, R., Singh, R.: QLOSE: program repair with quantitative objectives. In: Chaudhuri, S., Farzan, A. (eds.) CAV 2016. LNCS, vol. 9780, pp. 383–401. Springer, Cham (2016). https://doi.org/10.1007/978-3-319-41540-6_21

15. de Moura, L., Bjørner, N.: Z3: an efficient SMT solver. In: Ramakrishnan, C.R., Rehof, J. (eds.) TACAS 2008. LNCS, vol. 4963, pp. 337–340. Springer, Heidelberg (2008). https://doi.org/10.1007/978-3-540-78800-3_24

16. Debroy, V., Wong, W.E.: Using mutation to automatically suggest fixes for faulty programs. In: 2010 Third International Conference on Software Testing, Verification and Validation (ICST), pp. 65–74. IEEE (2010)

17. Dillig, I., Dillig, T.: EXPLAIN: a tool for performing abductive inference. In: Sharygina, N., Veith, H. (eds.) CAV 2013. LNCS, vol. 8044, pp. 684–689. Springer, Heidelberg (2013). https://doi.org/10.1007/978-3-642-39799-8_46

18. Do, H., Elbaum, S., Rothermel, G.: Supporting controlled experimentation with testing techniques: an infrastructure and its potential impact. Empir. Softw. Eng. 10(4), 405–435 (2005)

19. Elkader, K.A., Grumberg, O., Păsăreanu, C.S., Shoham, S.: Automated circular assume-guarantee reasoning. In: Bjørner, N., de Boer, F. (eds.) FM 2015. LNCS, vol. 9109, pp. 23–39. Springer, Cham (2015). https://doi.org/10.1007/978-3-319-19249-9_3

20. Abd Elkader, K., Grumberg, O., Păsăreanu, C.S., Shoham, S.: Automated circular assume-guarantee reasoning with N-way decomposition and alphabet refinement. In: Chaudhuri, S., Farzan, A. (eds.) CAV 2016. LNCS, vol. 9779, pp. 329–351. Springer, Cham (2016). https://doi.org/10.1007/978-3-319-41528-4_18

21. Frenkel, H.: Automata over infinite data domains: learnability and applications in program verification and repair, Ph. D thesis (2021)

22. Frenkel, H., Grumberg, O., Păsăreanu, C., Sheinvald, S.: Assume, guarantee or repair. In: TACAS 2020. LNCS, vol. 12078, pp. 211–227. Springer, Cham (2020). https://doi.org/10.1007/978-3-030-45190-5_12

23. Gheorghiu, M., Giannakopoulou, D., Păsăreanu, C.S.: Refining interface alphabets for compositional verification. In: Grumberg, O., Huth, M. (eds.) TACAS 2007. LNCS, vol. 4424, pp. 292–307. Springer, Heidelberg (2007). https://doi.org/10.1007/978-3-540-71209-1_23

24. Giannakopoulou, D., Păsăreanu, C.S., Barringer, H.: Assumption Generation for Software Component Verification. In: IEEE Computer Society. ASE (2002)

25. Giannakopoulou, D., Păsăreanu, C.S., Barringer, H.: Component verification with automatically generated assumptions. Autom. Softw. Eng. 12(3), 297–320 (2005)

26. Gupta, A., McMillan, K.L., Fu, Z.: Automated assumption generation for compositional verification. Formal Methods Syst. Des. **32**(3), 285–301 (2008)
27. Jobstmann, B., Griesmayer, A., Bloem, R.: Program repair as a game. In: Etessami, K., Rajamani, S.K. (eds.) CAV 2005. LNCS, vol. 3576, pp. 226–238. Springer, Heidelberg (2005). https://doi.org/10.1007/11513988_23
28. Kneuss, E., Koukoutos, M., Kuncak, V.: Deductive program repair. In: Kroening, D., Păsăreanu, C.S. (eds.) CAV 2015. LNCS, vol. 9207, pp. 217–233. Springer, Cham (2015). https://doi.org/10.1007/978-3-319-21668-3_13
29. Könighofer, R., Bloem, R.: Automated error localization and correction for imperative programs. In: Formal Methods in Computer-Aided Design (FMCAD), pp. 91–100. IEEE (2011)
30. Könighofer, R., Bloem, R.: Repair with on-the-fly program analysis. In: Biere, A., Nahir, A., Vos, T. (eds.) HVC 2012. LNCS, vol. 7857, pp. 56–71. Springer, Heidelberg (2013). https://doi.org/10.1007/978-3-642-39611-3_11
31. Le Goues, C., Nguyen, T., Forrest, S., Weimer, W.: GenProg: a generic method for automatic software repair. Softw. Eng. IEEE Trans. **38**(1), 54–72 (2012)
32. Li, B., Dillig, I., Dillig, T., McMillan, K., Sagiv, M.: Synthesis of circular compositional program proofs via abduction. In: Piterman, N., Smolka, S.A. (eds.) TACAS 2013. LNCS, vol. 7795, pp. 370–384. Springer, Heidelberg (2013). https://doi.org/10.1007/978-3-642-36742-7_26
33. Lin, S.-W., Hsiung, P.-A.: Compositional synthesis of concurrent systems through causal model checking and learning. In: Jones, C., Pihlajasaari, P., Sun, J. (eds.) FM 2014. LNCS, vol. 8442, pp. 416–431. Springer, Cham (2014). https://doi.org/10.1007/978-3-319-06410-9_29
34. Liu, K., Koyuncu, A., Bissyande, T.F., Kim, D., Klein, J., Le Traon, Y.: You cannot fix what you cannot find! an investigation of fault localization bias in benchmarking automated program repair systems. In: ICST, pp. 102–113 (2019)
35. Magee, J., Kramer, J.: Concurrency - State Models and Java Programs. Wiley (1999)
36. McMillan, K.L.: Circular compositional reasoning about liveness. In: Pierre, L., Kropf, T. (eds.) CHARME 1999. LNCS, vol. 1703, pp. 342–346. Springer, Heidelberg (1999). https://doi.org/10.1007/3-540-48153-2_30
37. Mechtaev, S., Nguyen, M.-D., Noller, Y., Grunske, L., Roychoudhury, A.: Semantic program repair using a reference implementation. In: ICSE, pp. 129–139 (2018)
38. Mechtaev, S., Yi, J., Roychoudhury, A.: Angelix: scalable multiline program patch synthesis via symbolic analysis. In: ICSE, ICSE (2016)
39. Misra, J., Chandy, K.M.: Proofs of networks of processes. IEEE Trans. Software Eng. **7**(4), 417–426 (1981)
40. Namjoshi, K.S., Trefler, R.J.: On the completeness of compositional reasoning. In: Emerson, E.A., Sistla, A.P. (eds.) CAV 2000. LNCS, vol. 1855, pp. 139–153. Springer, Heidelberg (2000). https://doi.org/10.1007/10722167_14
41. Nguyen, H.D.T., Qi, D., Roychoudhury, A., Chandra, S.: SemFix: program repair via semantic analysis. In: Proceedings of the 2013 International Conference on Software Engineering, pp. 772–781. IEEE Press (2013)
42. Nguyen, T.V., Weimer, W., Kapur, D., Forrest, S.: Connecting Program Synthesis and Reachability: Automatic Program Repair Using Test-Input Generation. In: Legay, A., Margaria, T. (eds.) TACAS 2017. LNCS, vol. 10205, pp. 301–318. Springer, Heidelberg (2017). https://doi.org/10.1007/978-3-662-54577-5_17
43. Nguyen, T.-T., Ta, Q.-T., Chin, W.-N.: Automatic program repair using formal verification and expression templates. In: Enea, C., Piskac, R. (eds.) VMCAI 2019. LNCS, vol. 11388, pp. 70–91. Springer, Cham (2019). https://doi.org/10.1007/978-3-030-11245-5_4

44. Păsăreanu, C.S., Giannakopoulou, D., Bobaru, M.G., Cobleigh, J.M., Barringer, H.: Learning to divide and conquer: applying the L* algorithm to automate assume-guarantee reasoning. Form. Methods Syst. Des. **32**, 175–205 (2008). https://doi.org/10.1007/s10703-008-0049-6

45. Peirce, C., Hartshorne, C.: Collected papers of charles sanders peirce. Belknap Press (1932)

46. Pnueli, A.: In transition from global to modular temporal reasoning about programs. In: Logics and Models of Concurrent Systems, NATO ASI Series (1985)

47. Repinski, U., Hantson, H., Jenihhin, M., Raik, J., Ubar, R., Guglielmo, G.D., Pravadelli, G., Fummi, F.: Combining dynamic slicing and mutation operators for ESL correction. In: Test Symposium (ETS), 2012 17th IEEE European, pp. 1–6. IEEE (2012)

48. Rothenberg, B.-C.: Formal automated program repair, Ph. D. thesis (2020)

49. Rothenberg, B.-C., Grumberg, O.: Sound and complete mutation-based program repair. In: Fitzgerald, J., Heitmeyer, C., Gnesi, S., Philippou, A. (eds.) FM 2016. LNCS, vol. 9995, pp. 593–611. Springer, Cham (2016). https://doi.org/10.1007/978-3-319-48989-6_36

50. Rothenberg, B.-C., Grumberg, O.: Must fault localization for program repair. In: Lahiri, S.K., Wang, C. (eds.) CAV 2020. LNCS, vol. 12225, pp. 658–680. Springer, Cham (2020). https://doi.org/10.1007/978-3-030-53291-8_33

51. Singh, R., Giannakopoulou, D., Păsăreanu, C.: Learning component interfaces with may and must abstractions. In: Touili, T., Cook, B., Jackson, P. (eds.) CAV 2010. LNCS, vol. 6174, pp. 527–542. Springer, Heidelberg (2010). https://doi.org/10.1007/978-3-642-14295-6_45

52. Tan, S. H., Yi, J., Yulis, Mechtaev, S., Roychoudhury, A.: Codeflaws: a programming competition benchmark for evaluating automated program repair tools. In: Proceedings - 2017 IEEE/ACM 39th International Conference on Software Engineering Companion, ICSE-C 2017, pp. 180–182 (2017)

53. von Essen, C., Jobstmann, B.: Program repair without regret. Formal Methods Syst. Des. **47**(1), 26–50 (2015). https://doi.org/10.1007/s10703-015-0223-6

54. Weispfenning, V.: Quantifier elimination and decision procedures for valued fields. In: Müller, G.H., Richter, M.M. (eds.) Models and Sets. LNM, vol. 1103, pp. 419–472. Springer, Heidelberg (1984). https://doi.org/10.1007/BFb0099397

Embedded Domain Specific Verifiers

Ranjit Jhala[✉]

University of California San Diego, San Diego, USA
jhala@cs.ucsd.edu

Abstract. Refinement types allow for automatic, SMT-based compositional specification and verification of program properties by liberating assertions from control locations. Recent work has shown how to increase the expressiveness of specifications by allowing arbitrary user-defined functions within assertions, while still preserving decidable verification. In this paper we illustrate the benefits of this expressiveness by showing how to embed a verified Floyd-Hoare style verifier *within* the refinement type checker LIQUIDHASKELL, *i.e.,* we show how to implement a library function verify p c q that only automatically type checks only when the Floyd-Hoare triple {p} c {q} is legitimate.

1 Introduction

Refinement types are a generalization of Floyd-Hoare style contracts where *logical assertions* are liberated from *control* elements (*e.g.,* function or loop entries) and instead associated directly the *data* on which the code operates. For example, the refinement type {v:Int|0 < v} denotes the basic type Int refined with a logical assertion that restricts the underlying values to be positive. Similarly, the (dependent) function type x :{Int|0 < x} →{v:Int|v < x} describes functions that take a positive argument x and return outputs exceeding x.

Refinements allow the programmer to specify complex properties by *composing* quantifier-free predicates with type constructors, *e.g.,* writing List {v:Int|0 < v} to describe a list of positive integers. Dually, they allow the machine to automatically verify those properties by *decomposing* the corresponding subsumption checks, *e.g.,* to verify that the List {v:Int|a ≤v} is subsumed by the list of positives when a is positive, by asking an SMT solver to validate the formula $0 < a \Rightarrow a \leq v \Rightarrow 0 < v$.

Earlier work focused on relatively simpler properties like array bounds checking [24,33], data structure invariants [9] or security policies [4] by restricting the language of assertions to linear arithmetic and uninterpreted functions which yield SMT-decidable validity queries. However, recent work has unearthed several ways to encode sophisticated specifications within the contracts, *e.g.,* using Horn clauses [28] or user-defined functions, thereby permitting "computation" within the assertions [1,30]. This added expressiveness makes it possible to encode a variety of *domain-specific* constraints within the type system, effectively implementing new kinds of code verification simply as type-checking with a suitably refined interface. For example, [23] shows how to encode Information Flow Control using refinements, and [19] shows how to then encode the semantics of SQL operators within refinement types in order to precisely and automatically track security policies across web applications.

© Springer Nature Switzerland AG 2022
J.-F. Raskin and K. Chatterjee (Eds.): Principles of Systems Design, LNCS 13660, pp. 535–553, 2022.
https://doi.org/10.1007/978-3-031-22337-2_26

In this paper we illustrate this method of *embedded domain specific verification* by using the refinement type based verifier LIQUIDHASKELL [29], to implement a verified Floyd-Hoare style verifier [10, 13] for a small imperative language IMP. Crucially, the verification of IMP code itself is carried out via LIQUIDHASKELL's automatic refinement type checking. That is, we show how to implement a (library) function `verify` such that `verify p c q` only type checks for legitimate Floyd-Hoare triples {p} c {q}. We develop `verify` via the following concrete steps.

1. Programs and Operational Semantics. First, in Sect. 3, we show how to represent the syntax of IMP *programs* via plain datatypes, and illustrate how to represent their "big-step" semantics via refined datatypes that represent valid executions.

2. Axiomatic Semantics. Second, in Sect. 4, we recall the elements of Floyd-Hoare *logic* and show how proofs in the program logic can also be reified as refined data. We use this data to formally verify the soundness of the program logic by writing a function that uses the structure reifying each proof to demonstrate the legitimacy of the triple.

3. Verification Conditions. Third, in Sect. 5, we show how to turn the deductive Floyd-Hoare proof system into an *algorithm* via a function `vc p c q` that converts each triple into a *verification condition*: a logical formula whose validity implies the legitimacy of the triple. We establish the soundness of vc generation by using the validity of `vc p c q` to construct a Floyd-Hoare derivation for the triple {p} c {q}.

4. An Embedded Verifier. Finally, in Sect. 5.2 we use vc to implement `verify` as a function whose precondition requires that `vc p c q` be valid. That is, expressions `verify p c q` are well typed only when the corresponding VC is valid, and further the refinement typing reduces exactly to checking the validity of the computed VC. We conclude by showing how to use our embedded verifier to check some IMP programs via refinement typing.[1]

2 Refinement Types

Lets begin with a brisk introduction to refinement types that illustrates how they can be used to formally specify and verify properties of programs.

2.1 Refinements

A *refinement type* a plain type like `Int` or `Bool` decorated by a logical predicate which restricts the *set of values*. For example, the refinement type `Nat` defined as

```
type Nat = {v:Int|0 ≤ v}
```

denotes the set of non-negative `Integer` values.

Specification. Consider the function `sum n` which computes $1 + \ldots + n$

```
sum :: n:Nat → {v:Int|n ≤ v}
sum n = if n == 0 then 0 else n + sum (n - 1)
```

---

[1] This entire paper is written as a program verified by LIQUIDHASKELL that the interested reader may find at https://github.com/liquidhaskell/floyd-hoare.

The signature for sum is a refined *function* type that specifies: (1) A *pre-condition* that sum only be called with non-negative inputs n, (as otherwise it diverges), and (2) A *post-condition* that states that the output produced by the function is no smaller than n.

Under classical *strict* or *call-by-value* evaluation semantics (where a function's arguments must be evaluated before the call proceeds) refinement types represent *safety* properties, *i.e.,* they correspond to the classic notion of *partial correctness*. That is, the output type only specifies that *if* a value is returned, it will exceed the input n. *Lazy* evaluation muddies the waters introducing an unexpected intertwining of safety and termination [29]. For simplicity, we will assume that the underlying language follows the usual strict semantics, and not concern ourselves with termination.

Verification. Refinement type checking algorithmically verifies the implementation of sum meets its specification by (1) computing a logical formula called a *verification condition* (VC) (2) and then using an SMT solver to check the *validity* of the VC [14]. For sum the VC is the formula that combines the assumption $0 \leq n$ from the precondition to establish that the returned values $v = 0$ and $v = n + sum(n - 1)$ in each branch are indeed greater than n. In the latter case, the assumption $n - 1 \leq sum(n - 1)$ is established by "inductively" assuming the post-condition of sum for the recursive call.

$$\forall n, v.\ 0 \leq n \Rightarrow n = 0 \Rightarrow v = 0 \Rightarrow n \leq v \ \wedge$$
$$n \neq 0 \Rightarrow n - 1 \leq sum\ (n - 1) \Rightarrow v = n + sum(n - 1) \Rightarrow n \leq v$$

Assertions. We can encode *assertions* as function calls by defining a function that requires its input be a Bool that is True

```
assert :: {b:Bool|b} → ()
assert b = ()
```

Subsequent refinement type checking then statically verifies classical assertions

```
checkSum1 = assert (1 ≤ sum 1)
```

2.2 Reflection

Refinement type checking is *modular*, which means that at call-sites, the only information known about a function is *shallow*, namely that which is stated in its type specification. Consequently, the following assertion fails to verify

```
checkSum2 = assert (3 ≤ sum 2)
```

The only information about the call sum 2 is that encoded in its type specification: that the output exceeds 2, and so checkSum2 fails to verify due the *invalid* VC

$$2 \leq sum(2) \Rightarrow 3 \leq sum(2)$$

Reflecting Implementations into Specifications. To prove *deeper* properties about sum we can reflect the implementation (*i.e.,* definition) of the function into its specification. To do so, the programmer writes {- @ reflect sum @-} which *strengthens* the specification of sum to n:Nat $\rightarrow \{v:n \leq v \wedge \phi_{sum}(n, v)\}$ where

$$\phi_{sum}(n, v) \doteq (v = sum(n)) \wedge (n = 0 \Rightarrow v = 0) \wedge (n \neq 0 \Rightarrow v = n + sum(n-1))$$

Logical Evaluation. To ensure that validity checking remains *decidable*, sum is *uninterpreted* in the refinement logic. This means, that the new VC for checkSum

$$\forall b.\ 2 \leq sum(2) \wedge \phi_{sum}(2, sum(2)) \Rightarrow b \Leftrightarrow (3 \leq sum(2)) \Rightarrow b$$

is still *invalid* as there is no information about $sum(1)$. Fortunately, the method of *Proof by Logical Evaluation* (PLE) [30] lets the SMT solver strengthen the hypotheses by *unfolding the definition* of sum to yield the following valid VC that verifies checkSum2.

$$\phi_{sum}(0, sum(0)) \wedge \phi_{sum}(1, sum(1)) \wedge 2 \leq sum(2) \wedge \phi_{sum}(2, sum(2)) \Rightarrow 3 \leq sum(2)$$

Proofs by Induction. Reflection and logical evaluation let us specify and verify more interesting properties about sum. For example, consider the following *tail-recursive* version which can be compiled into an efficient loop

```
reflect sumTR'
sumTR' :: Nat → Int → Int
sumTR' n a = if n == 0 then a else sumTR' (n-1) (a+n)

reflect sumTR
sumTR :: Nat → Int
sumTR n = sumTR' n 0
```

We can now specify that sumTR is *equivalent* to sum by first establishing that

$$\forall n, a.\ 0 \leq n \ \Rightarrow\ \mathsf{sumTR'}(n, a) = a + \mathsf{sum}(n) \tag{1}$$

and then using the lemma to prove that

$$\forall n.\ 0 \leq n \ \Rightarrow\ \mathsf{sumTR}(n) = \mathsf{sum}(n) \tag{2}$$

Proofs as Programs. Our approach uses the Curry-Howard correspondence [32] to encode logical *propositions* as refinement types, and provide *proofs* of the propositions by writing functions of the appropriate type. Briefly, Curry-Howard shows how universally quantified propositions $\forall x : \mathtt{Int}.\ P(x)$ correspond to the function type x:Int →{ P(x)}, and that code implementing the above type is a constructive proof of the original proposition. For example, the proposition Eq. (1) is specified and verified by

```
lem_sumTR :: n:Nat → acc:Int → {sumTR' n acc = acc + sum n}
lem_sumTR 0 _   = ()
lem_sumTR n acc = lem_sumTR (n - 1) (acc + n)
```

At a high-level, the method of logical evaluation is able to verify the above code by using the post-condition from the recursive invocation of lem_sumTR (that "adds" the induction hypothesis as an antecedent of the VC) and automatically unfolding the definitions of sumTR' and sum. Similarly, we translate Eq. (2) and prove that it is a corollary of Eq. (1) by "calling" the lemma (function) with the appropriate arguments.

```
thm_sumTR :: n:Nat → { sumTR n == sum n }
thm_sumTR n = lem_sumTR n 0
```

2.3   Reification

Some proofs require the ability to *introspect on the evidence* that establishes why some proposition holds. As a textbook example, let us recall the notion of the *reachability* in a graph. Let V and $E \subset V \times V$ denote the set of *vertices* and *directed edges* of a directed graph. We say that a vertex u *reaches* v if either (a) $u = v$ or (b) $(u, v) \in E$ and v reaches w. Suppose that we wish to prove that the notion of reachability is *transitive*, *i.e.*, if u reaches v and v reaches w then u reaches w. To prove the above property, it is not enough to know *that* u reaches v and v reaches w. Instead, we need additional evidence: a "path" that describes *how* the evidence was established.

Our third key piece of machinery is a way to *reify* such evidence using data types that can be introspected and manipulated to provide evidence that establishes new properties. This machinery corresponds to the notion of *inductive* propositions or predicates used by proof assistants like Coq or Isabelle [5, 22]. As an example, lets see how to formalize the notion of reachability. Suppose that we represent the directed edge relation as a predicate over vertices v

```
type Edge v = v → v → Bool
```

Step 1: Propositions as Data. We encode reachability as a relation $x \longrightarrow^*_e y$ that says x reaches y following the edges e. We can represent this relation as proposition: a *value* Reach e u v that denotes that u reaches v following the edges e.

Step 2: Evidence as Data. We can specify reachability via two rules

$$\frac{}{x \longrightarrow^*_e x}[\text{SELF}] \qquad \frac{(x, y) \in e \qquad y \longrightarrow^*_e z}{x \longrightarrow^*_e z}[\text{STEP}]$$

We can formally represent the *evidence* of reachability as a refined datatype whose constructors correspond to the informal rules.

```
data ReachEv a where
     Self :: e:Edge a → x:a →
             Reach e x x
     Step :: e:Edge a → x:a → y:{a|e x y} → z:a →
             Reach e y z →
             Reach e x z
```

Following the Curry-Howard correspondence, (1) the universally quantified variables of the rules become input *parameters* for the constructor, (2) the antecedents of each rule are translated to *preconditions* for the corresponding constructor, and (3) the consequent of each rule is translated into the *postcondition* for the constructor. The above datatype says there are exactly two ways to *construct* evidence of reachability: (1) Self e x is evidence that a vertex x can reach *itself* following the edge-relation e; (2) Step e x y z yz uses the fact that (a) x has an edge to y (established by the precondition e x y) and (b) y reaches z (established by yz which is evidence that Reach e y z) to construct evidence that x reaches z. Note that the above are the *only* ways to provide evidence of reachability (*i.e.*, to construct values that demonstrate the proposition Reach e x y).

Step 3: Consuming and Producing Evidence. Finally, we can prove properties about reachability, simply by writing functions that consume and produce evidence. For example, here is a proof that reachability is transitive.

```
reachTrans :: e:Edge a → x:a → y:a → z:a →
              Reach e x y → Reach e y z →
              Reach e x z
reachTrans e x y z (Self _ _) yz             = yz
reachTrans e x y z (Step _ _ x1 _ x1y) yz = Step e x x1 z x1z
   where x1z = reachTrans e x1 y z x1y yz
```

The *specification* of reachTrans represents the proposition that reachability is transitive: for any edge relation e and vertices x,y,z if we have evidence that x reaches y and that y reaches z then we can construct evidence that x reaches z. The *implementation* of reachTrans demonstrates the claim via code that explicitly constructs the evidence via recursion, *i.e.*, by induction on the path from x to y. In the base case, that path is empty as x equals y, in which case the evidence yz that shows y reaches z *also* shows x reaches z. In the inductive case, the path from x to y goes via the edge from x to x1 followed by a path x1y from x1 to y. (As when proving thm_sumTR we *apply* the induction hypothesis by recursively "calling" reachTrans on the sub-paths x1y and yz to obtain evidence that x1 reaches z, and then link that evidence the edge from x to x1 (*i.e.*, Step e x x1) to construct the path from x to z. (The termination checker automatically verifies that the recursion in reachTrans, and hence the induction, is well-founded [30].)

3 Programs

Next, lets spell out the syntax and semantics of IMP, that language that we wish to build a verifier for. We will define a datatype to represent the *syntax* of IMP programs and then formalize their *semantics* by defining evaluation functions and transition rules.

3.1 Syntax

IMP is a standard imperative language with integer valued variables, arithmetic expressions, boolean conditions, assignments, branches and loops.

Variables and Expressions. IMP has (integer valued) identifiers Id and arithmetic expressions AExp, represented by the datatypes

```
type Val = Int
type Id = String

data AExp
  = N Val            --  ^ 0,1,2...
  | V Id             --  ^ x,y,z...
  | Plus  AExp AExp  --  ^ e1 + e2
  | Minus AExp AExp  --  ^ e1 - e2
  | Times AExp AExp  --  ^ e1 * e2
```

We can define infix operators

```
b1 .+. b2 = Plus  b1 b2
b1 .-. b2 = Minus b1 b2
b1 .*. b2 = Times b1 b2
```

For example, we can represent the expression $x + 2 * y$ as

```
e0 = V "x" .+. (N 2 .*. V "y")
```

Conditions. We use relations on integer expressions to build *conditions* which can be further combined using boolean operators

```
data BExp
  = Bc   Bool        -- ^ True, False
  | Not BExp         -- ^ not b
  | And BExp BExp    -- ^ b1 && b2
  | Leq AExp AExp    -- ^ a1 ≤ a2
  | Eql AExp AExp    -- ^ a1 == a2
```

We can define other relations and boolean operations using the above.

```
e1 .==. e2 = Eql e1 e2
e1 .!=. e2 = Not (e1 .==. e2)
b1 .≤.  b2 = Leq b1 b2
b1 .<.  b2 = (b1 .≤. b2) .&&. (b1 .!=. b2)
b1 .&&. b2 = And b1 b2
b1 .||. b2 = Not (Not b1 .&&. Not b2)
b1 .=>. b2 = (Not b1) .||. b2
```

Commands. We can use AExp and BExp to define the syntax of *commands* Com

```
data Com
  = Skip                          -- skip
  | Assign Id   AExp              -- x ← a
  | Seq    Com  Com               -- c1; c2
  | If     BExp Com  Com          -- if b then c1 else c2
  | While  BExp BExp Com          -- while {inv} b c
```

We can introduce some helper functions to improve readability, *e.g.,*

```
(←) :: Id → AExp → Com
x ← e = Assign x e
```

The following IMP program sums up the integers from 1 to n with the result stored in r

```
com_sum inv =
  ("i" ← N 0) @@                          -- i ← 0;
  ("r" ← N 0) @@                          -- r ← 0;
  While inv (V "i" .!=. V "n")            -- WHILE (i != n)
    ("r" ← V "r" .+. V "i") @@            -- r ← r + i;
    ("i" ← V "i" .+. N 1)                 -- i ← i + 1
```

3.2   Semantics

Next, we the semantics of programs via *states*, *valuations* and *transitions*. A *state* is map from Identifiers to (integer) Values

```
type State = Map Id Val
```

where a Map k v is a sequence of key-value pairs, with a Default value for missing keys

```
data Map k v = Def v | Set k v (Map k v)
```

We can set the value of a variable and get the value of a variable in a state, via

```
get :: (Eq k) => Map k v → k → v
get (Def v)       _  = v
get (Key k v s) k' = if k == k' then v else get s k'

set :: Map k v → k → v → Map k v
set s k v = Set k v s
```

For example, suppose that s0 is the State

```
s0 = set "y" 30 (set "x" 20 (set "y" 10 (def 0)))
```

Then get"x" s0 and get "y" s0 respectively evaluate to 20 and 30 and get z s0 evaluates to 0 for any other identifer z.

Evaluating Expressions and Conditions. We can lift the notion of valuations from states to arithmetic expressions via the function aval

```
aval                  :: AExp → State → Val
aval (N n) _          = n
aval (V x) s          = get s x
aval (Plus  e1 e2) s = aval e1 s + aval e2 s
aval (Minus e1 e2) s = aval e1 s - aval e2 s
aval (Times e1 e2) s = aval e1 s * aval e2 s
```

For example aval e0 s0 evaluates to 80 where s0 is the state where "x" and "y" were respectively "20" and "30" and e0 is the expression representing $x + 2 \times y$.

Evaluating Conditions. Similarly, we extend the notion of valuations to boolean conditions via the function bval

```
bval :: BExp → State → Bool
bval (Bc   b)     _ = b
bval (Not  b)     s = not (bval b s)
bval (And  b1 b2) s = bval b1 s && bval b2 s
bval (Leq  a1 a2) s = aval a1 s ≤ aval a2 s
bval (Eql  a1 a2) s = aval a1 s == aval a2 s
```

For example, is x_lt_y = V "x".<. V "y" then bval x_lt_y s0 is True.

Transitions. The execution of a Command c from a state s *transitions* the system to some successor state s'. The direct route would be to formalize transitions as a function that takes as input a command and input state s and returns the successor s' as output.

Big-Step Transition $\boxed{\langle c, s \rangle \Downarrow s'}$

$$\frac{}{\langle \text{Skip}, s \rangle \Downarrow s}\,[\text{B-SKIP}] \qquad\qquad \frac{}{\langle x \leftarrow e, s \rangle \Downarrow \text{set } x \text{ aval } e\ s}\,[\text{B-ASSIGN}]$$

$$\frac{\langle c_1, s \rangle \Downarrow s' \qquad \langle c_2, s' \rangle \Downarrow s''}{\langle \text{Seq } c_1\ c_2, s \rangle \Downarrow s''}\,[\text{B-SEQ}] \qquad \frac{\text{bval } b\ s \qquad \langle c_1, s \rangle \Downarrow s'}{\langle \text{If } b\ c_1\ c_2, s \rangle \Downarrow s'}\,[\text{B-IF-T}]$$

$$\frac{\neg\text{bval } b\ s \qquad \langle c_2, s \rangle \Downarrow s'}{\langle \text{If } b\ c_1\ c_2, s \rangle \Downarrow s'}\,[\text{B-IF-F}] \qquad \frac{\neg\text{bval } b\ s}{\langle \text{While}_I\ b\ c, s \rangle \Downarrow s}\,[\text{B-WHILE-F}]$$

$$\frac{\text{bval } b\ s \qquad \langle c, s \rangle \Downarrow s' \qquad \langle \text{While}_I\ b\ c, s' \rangle \Downarrow s''}{\langle \text{While}_I\ b\ c, s \rangle \Downarrow s''}\,[\text{B-WHILE-T}]$$

Fig. 1. Big-step transitions for IMP commands.

Unfortunately, this path is blocked by two hurdles. First, the function is *partial* as for certain starting states s, certain commands c may be *non-terminating*. Second, more importantly, our Floyd-Hoare soundness proof will require a form of induction on the execution traces that provide evidence of *how* s transitioned to s'.

Big-Step Semantics. Thus, we represent the transitions via the classical *big-step* (or *natural*) style where $\langle c, s \rangle \Downarrow s'$ indicates that the execution of command c transitions the machine from a state s to s'. The rules in Fig. 1 characterize the transitions in terms of sub-commands of c. [B-SKIP] states that Skip leaves the state unchanged (*i.e.,* yields a transition from s to s). [B-ASSIGN] says that the command Assign x e transitions the system from s to a new state where the of x has been set to aval $e\ s$: the valuation of e in se [B-SEQ] says that Seq $c_1\ c_2$ transitions the system from s to s'' if c_1 transitions s to some s' and c_2 transitions s' to s''. The rules for sequencing branches [B-IF-T, B-IF-F] and loops [B-WHL-T, B-WHL-F] similarly describe how the execution of the sub-commands yield transitions from the respective input states to their outputs, using bval to select the appropriate sub-command for conditionals.

Reifying Transitions as a Refined Datatype. We represent the big-step transition relation $\langle c, s \rangle \Downarrow s'$ as a *proposition* BStep c s s', and reify the *evidence* that establishes the transitions via the refined datatype in Fig. 2. Each rule in Fig. 1 is formalized by a data constructor of the corresponding name, whose *input* preconditions mirror the hypotheses of the rule, and whose *output* establishes the postcondition. For example the BSeq constructor takes as input the sub-commands c1 and c2, states s, s' and s'', and evidence BStep c1 s s' and BStep c2 s' s'' (that c1 and c2 respectively transition s to s' and s' to s'') to output evidence that Seq c1 c2 transitions s to s''.

This reification addresses both the hurdles that block a direct encoding via a transition function. First, the evidence route sidesteps the problem of non-termination by letting us work with *derivation trees* that correspond exactly to terminating executions. Second, the trees provide a concrete object that describes *how* a state s transitioned to s' and now we can do inductive proofs over traces, via recursive functions on the derivation trees.

```
data BStep where
    BSkip ::
        s:_ → BStep Skip s s

    BAsgn ::
        x:_ → a:_ → s:_ →
        BStep (Assign x a) s (asgn x a s)

    BSeq  ::
        c1:_ → c2:_ → s:_ → s':_ → s'':_ →
        BStep c1 s s' → BStep c2 s' s'' →
        BStep (Seq c1 c2) s s''

    BIfT  ::
        b:_ → c1:_ → c2:_ → s:{bval b s} → s':_ →
        BStep c1 s s' →
        BStep (If b c1 c2) s s'

    BIfF  ::
        b:_ → c1:_ → c2:_ → s:{not (bval b s)} → s':_ →
        BStep c2 s s' →
        BStep (If b c1 c2) s s'

    BWhlF ::
        i:_ → b:_ → c:_ → s:{not (bval b s)} →
        BStep (While i b c) s s

    BWhlT ::
        i:_ → b:_ → c:_ → s:{bval b s} → s':_ → s'':_ →
        BStep c s s' → BStep (While i b c) s' s'' →
        BStep (While i b c) s s''
```

Fig. 2. Reifying the derivation of $\langle c, s \rangle \Downarrow s'$ with the refined datatype BStep c s s'.

4 Deductive Verification

Next, let us build (and verify!) a *deductive* verifier for IMP using the classical method of Floyd-Hoare (FH) logic [10,13] and show how to prove it sound.

4.1 Floyd-Hoare Triples

Assertions. An *assertion* is a boolean condition over the program identifiers.

```
type Assertion = BExp
```

An assertion p *holds* at a state s if bval p s is True, *i.e.,* the assertion evaluates to True at the state. For example, the assertion b0 = V "x".<. V "y" holds at s0 where get s0 "x" and get s0 "y" were respectively 20 and 30.

Validity. An assertion p is *valid* if it holds *for all* states, *i.e.*, $\forall s.\text{bval p } s = \text{True}$. Following the Curry-Howard correspondence, we can formalize validity as

```
type Valid P = s:State → {bval P s}
```

Logical evalation [30] makes it easy to check validity simply by refinement typing. For example, we can establish the assertion

```
cond_x_10_5 = (N 10 .≤. V "x") .=>. (N 5 .≤. V "x")
```

is valid, simply by writing

```
pf_valid :: Valid cond_x_10_5
pf_valid = \_ → ()
```

Logical evaluation discharges the typing obligation via the SMT validated VC

$$\forall s.\ 10 \leq \text{get ``}x\text{''} s \Rightarrow 5 \leq \text{get ``}x\text{''} s$$

Floyd-Hoare Triples. A *Floyd-Hoare triple* $\{p\}\ c\ \{q\}$ comprising a *precondition p*, command *c* and *post-condition q*. The triple states that if the command *c* transitions the system *from* a state *s* where the precondition *p* holds, *to* a state *s'*, then the postcondition *q* holds on *s'*.

Legitimacy of Triples. We say a triple is *legitimate*, written $\models \{p\}\ c\ \{q\}$ if

$$\models \{p\}\ c\ \{q\} \ \dot{=}\ \forall s, s'.\ \text{bval } p\ s \Rightarrow \langle c, s \rangle \Downarrow s' \Rightarrow \text{bval } q\ s'$$

We can use the Curry-Howard correspondence to formalize the above notion as:

```
type Legit P C Q =
      s:{bval P s} → s':_ → BStep C s s' → {bval Q s'}
```

We can specify and verify the triple $\{0 \leq x\}\ y \leftarrow x + 1\ \{1 \leq y\}$ as

```
y_x_1 :: Com
y_x_1 = ("y" ← V "x" .+. N 1)

leg_y_x_1 :: Legit (N 0 .≤. V {"x"}) y_x_1 (N 1 .≤. V {"y"})
leg_y_x_1 :: Legit
leg_y_x_1 s s' BAsgn {} = ()
```

Note that evidence for the big-step transition tells us that the final state s' is obtained by setting the value of y to 1 + the value of x in the initial state s. Thus, refinement typing verifies legitimacy by generating the following VC for leg_y_x_1 (simplified after logical evaluation unfolds the definition of bval for the pre- and post-conditions)

$$\forall s, s'.\ 0 \leq \text{get ``}x\text{''} s \Rightarrow s' = \text{set ``}y\text{''} 1 + \text{get ``}x\text{''} s\ s \Rightarrow 1 \leq \text{get ``}y\text{''} s'$$

PLE then further unfolds the definition of set to allow the SMT solver to automatically verify the VC and hence, check legitimacy.

As a second example, let x20_y30 be a command that sequentially assigns x and y to 20 and 30 respectively:

```
bsub :: Id → AExp → BExp → BExp
bsub x a (Bc   b)     = Bc  b
bsub x a (Not  b)     = Not (bsub x a b)
bsub x a (And b1 b2) = And (bsub x a b1) (bsub x a b2)
bsub x a (Leq a1 a2) = Leq (sub  x a a1) (sub   x a a2)
bsub x a (Eql a1 a2) = Eql (sub  x a a1) (sub   x a a2)

sub :: Id → AExp → AExp → AExp
sub x e (Plus   a1 a2)  = Plus  (sub x e a1) (sub x e a2)
sub x e (Minus a1 a2)  = Minus (sub x e a1) (sub x e a2)
sub x e (Times a1 a2)  = Times (sub x e a1) (sub x e a2)
sub x e (V y) | x == y = e
sub _ _ a              = a
```

Fig. 3. Substituting a variable x with an expression e.

```
x20_y30 = ("x" ← N 20) @@ ("y" ← N 30)
```

We can verify that $\models \{true\}$ x20_y30 $\{x \leq y\}$ as

```
legXY :: Legit bTrue x20_y30 (V {"x"} .≤. V {"y"})
legXY s s'' (BSeq _ _ _ _ _ (BAsgn {}) (BAsgn {})) = ()
```

Here, the "pattern-matching" on the refined BStep evidence establishes that the final state s'' = set"y"30,s' where the intermediate state s' = set "x"20,s. Thus, refinement typing for legXY proceeds by generating the VC

$$\forall s, s', s''.s' = \text{set } “x” \ 20 \ s \Rightarrow s'' = \text{set } “y” \ 30 \ s' \Rightarrow \text{get } “x” \ s'' \leq \text{get } “y” \ s''$$

which is readily validated by the SMT solver.

4.2   Floyd-Hoare Logic

The above examples show that while establishing the legitimacy of triples *explicitly* from the big-step semantics is possible, it quickly gets tedious for complex code. The ingenuity of Floyd and Hoare lay in their design of a recipe to derive triples based on *symbolically* transforming the assertions in a *syntax* directed fashion.

Substitutions. The key transformation is a means to *substitute* all occurrences of an identifier x with an expression e in a boolean assertion, as formalized respectively by sub and bsub in Fig. 3.

Derivation Rules. We write $\vdash \{p\} \ c \ \{q\}$ to say there exists a tree whose root is the triple denoted by p, c and q, using the syntax-directed rules in Fig. 4. As with the big-step semantics we can reify the evidence corresponding to a Floyd-Hoare derivation via the refined datatype FH p c q specified in Fig. 5. Note that the constructors for the datatype mirror the corresponding derivation rules in Fig. 4, and that we have split the classic rule of *consequence* into separate rules for strengthening preconditions ([FH-PRE]) and weakening postconditions ([FH-POST]).

Floyd-Hoare Logic $\boxed{\vdash \{p\}\, c\, \{q\}}$

$$\frac{}{\vdash \{\mathsf{Skip}\}\, q\, \{q\}}\text{[FH-SKIP]} \qquad\qquad \frac{}{\vdash \{\mathsf{bsub}\, x\, e\, q\}\, x \leftarrow e\, \{q\}}\text{[FH-ASGN]}$$

$$\frac{\vdash \{p\}\, c_1\, \{q\} \qquad \vdash \{q\}\, c_2\, \{r\}}{\vdash \{p\}\, \mathsf{Seq}\, c_1\, c_2\, \{r\}}\text{[FH-SEQ]}$$

$$\frac{\vdash \{p \wedge b\}\, c_1\, \{q\} \qquad \vdash \{p \wedge \neg b\}\, c_2\, \{q\}}{\vdash \{p\}\, \mathsf{If}\, b\, c_1\, c_2\, \{q\}}\text{[FH-IF]}$$

$$\frac{\vdash \{inv \wedge b\}\, c\, \{inv\}}{\vdash \{inv\}\, \mathsf{While}\, b\, c\, \{inv \wedge \neg b\}}\text{[FH-WHL]} \qquad \frac{\mathtt{Valid}(p' \Rightarrow p) \qquad \vdash \{p\}\, c\, \{q\}}{\vdash \{p'\}\, c\, \{q\}}\text{[FH-PRE]}$$

$$\frac{\vdash \{p\}\, c\, \{q\} \qquad \mathtt{Valid}(q \Rightarrow q')}{\vdash \{p\}\, c\, \{q'\}}\text{[FH-POST]}$$

Fig. 4. Syntax-driven derivation rules for Floyd-Hoare logic

4.3   Soundness

Next, let us verify that the Floyd-Hoare derivation rules are *sound, i.e.,* that $\vdash \{p\}\, c\, \{q\}$ implies $\models \{p\}\, c\, \{q\}$. To do so, we will prove *legitimacy* lemmas that verify that if the antecedents of each derivation rule describe legitimate triples, then the consequent is also legitimate.

Legitimacy for Assignments. For assignments we prove, by induction on the structure of the assertion q, a lemma that connects state-update with substitution

```
lemBsub :: x:_ → a:_ → q:_ → s:_ →
    {bval (bsub x a q) s = bval q (set x (aval a s) s) }
```

after which we use the big-step definition to verify

```
lemAsgn :: x:_ → a:_ → q:_ →
    Legit (bsub x a q) (Assign x a) q
```

Legitimacy for Branches and Loops. Similarly, for branches and loops we use the big-step derivations to respectively prove that

```
lemIf :: b:_ → c1:_ → c2:_ → p:_ → q:_ →
    Legit (p .&&. b) c1 q → Legit (p .&&. Not b) c2 q →
    Legit p (If b c1 c2) q
```

The proof (*i.e.,* implementation of lem_if) proceeds by splitting cases on the big-step derivation used for the branch and applying the legitimacy function for the appropriate branch to prove the postcondition q holds in the output.

```
lemIf b c1 c2 p q l1 l2 =
    \s s' bs → case bs of
        BIfT _ _ _ _ _ c1_s_s' →    -- then branch
```

```
data FH where
    FHSkip :: q:_ →
             FH q Skip q

    FHAsgn :: q:_ → x:_ → a:_ →
             FH (bsub x a q) (Assign x a) q

    FHSeq  :: p:_ → c1:_ → q:_ → c2:_ → r:_ →
             FH p c1 q → FH q c2 r →
             FH p (Seq c1 c2) r

    FHIf :: p:_ → q:_ → b:_ → c1:_ → c2:_ →
            FH (p .&&. b) c1 q → FH (p .&&. Not b) c2 q →
            FH p (If b c1 c2) q

    FHWhl :: inv:_ → b:_ → c:_ →
             FH (inv .&&. b) c inv →
             FH inv (While inv b c) (inv .&&. Not b)

    FHPre  :: p':_ → p:_ → q:_ → c:_ →
              Valid (p' .=>. p) → FH p c q →
              FH p' c q

    FHPost :: p:_ → q:_ → q':_ → c:_ →
              FH p c q → Valid (q .=>. q') →
              FH p c q'
```

Fig. 5. Reifying Floyd-Hoare proofs as a refined datatype

```
    l1 s s' c1_s_s'              -- ... post-cond via l1
  BIfF _ _ _ _ _ c2_s_s' →     -- else branch
    l2 s s' c2_s_s'             -- ... post-cond via l2
```

The legitimacy lemma for loops is similar.

```
lemWhile :: b:_ → c:_ → inv:_ →
  Legit (inv .&&. b) c inv →
  Legit inv (While b c) (inv .&&. Not b)
```

Soundness of Floyd-Hoare Logic. We use the above lemmas to establish the soundness of Floyd-Hoare logic as:

```
thmFHLegit :: p:_ → c:_ → q:_ → FH p c q → Legit p c q
```

The implementation of thm_fh_legit is an induction (*i.e.*, recursion) over the *structure* of the evidence FH p c q, recursively invoking the theorem to inductively assume soundness for the sub-commands, and then using *legitimacy lemmas* that establish legitimacy for that case via the big-step semantics.

5 Algorithmic Verification

The Floyd-Hoare proof rules provide a *methodology* to determine whether a triple is legitimate. However, to do so, we must still construct a valid derivation, which requires us some manual effort to (1) determine where to use the *consequence* rules, and (2) check that various *side conditions* hold for loop invariants.

5.1 Verification Condition Generation

Next, we show how to automate verification by computing a single *verification condition* whose validity demonstrates the legitimacy of a triple.

Weakest Preconditions. In the first step, we *assume* the side conditions hold to check if the given pre-condition establishes the desired post-condition, thereby automating the application of consequence. We will do so via Dijkstra's *predicate transformers* [8]: a function pre which given a command c and a postcondition q computes an assertion p corresponding to the *weakest* (*i.e.,* most general) condition under which the c is guaranteed to transition to a state at which q holds.

```
pre :: Com → Assertion → Assertion
pre Skip           q = q
pre (Assign x a)   q = bsub x a q
pre (Seq c1 c2)    q = pre c1 (pre c2 q)
pre (If b c1 c2)   q = bIte b (pre c1 q) (pre c2 q)
pre (While i _ _) _ = i
```

In the above, bIte p q r = (p .=> q).&&. (Not p .=> r) and the substitution bsub x a q replaces occurrences of x in q with a.

We can verify a triple $\{p\}$ c $\{q\}$ by checking the validity of the assertion p .=>. (pre c q). For example to check the triple $\{10 \leq x\}$ x ← x + 1 $\{10 \leq x\}$ we would compute the weakest precondition $10 \leq (x + 1)$, and then check the validity of $10 \leq x \Rightarrow 10 \leq (x + 1)$.

Invariant Side Conditions. The definition of pre blithely *trusts* the invariants annotations for each While-loop are "correct", *i.e.,* are preserved by the loop body and suffice to establish the post-condition. To make the verifier sound, in the second step we must guarantee that the annotations are indeed invariants, by checking them via *invariant side-conditions* computed by the function ic

```
ic :: Com → Assertion → Assertion
ic Skip           _ = bTrue
ic (Assign {})    _ = bTrue
ic (Seq c1 c2)    q = ic c1 (pre c2 q) .&&. ic c2 q
ic (If _ c1 c2)   q = ic c1 q .&&. ic c2 q
ic (While i b c)  q = ((i .&&. b)     .=>. pre c i) .&&.
                      ((i .&&. Not b) .=>. q        ) .&&.
                      ic c i
```

In essence, ic traverses the entire command to find additional constraints that enforce that, at each loop While i b c the annotation i is indeed an invariant that can be used to find a valid Floyd-Hoare proof for c, as made precise by the following lemma

```
lemIC :: c:_ → q:_ → Valid (ic c q) → FH (pre c q) c q
```

That is, we can prove by induction on the structure of c that whenever the side-condition holds, executing command c from a state pre c q establishes the postcondition q.

Verification Conditions. We combine the weakest preconditions and invariant side conditions into a single *verification condition* vc whose validity checks the correctness of a Floyd-Hoare triple

```
vc :: Assertion → Com → Assertion → Assertion
vc p c q = (p .=>. pre c q) .&&. ic c q
```

We combine lem_ic with the rule of consequence FHPre to establish that the validity of the vc establishes the existence of a Floyd-Hoare proof

```
lemVC :: p:_ → c:_ → q:_ → Valid (vc p c q) → FH p c q
```

We combine the above with the soundness of Floyd-Hoare derivations thm_fh_legit to show that verification conditions demonstrate the legitimacy of triples

```
thmVC :: p:_ → c:_ → q:_ → Valid (vc p c q) → Legit p c q
```

5.2 Embedded Verification

Finally we *embed* the vc generation within a typed API, turning the type checker into a domain-specific verify function

```
verify :: p:_ → c:_ → q:_ → Valid (vc p c q) → ()
verify :: Assertion → Com → Assertion → Valid → ()
verify _ _ _ _ = ()
```

Only the type signature for verify is interesting: it says that verify p c q ok type-checks *only* if ok demonstrates the *validity* of vc p c q, which can be done, simply via the term _ → () as shown in pf_valid (in Sect. 4). Lets put our embedded verifier to work, by using it to check some simple IMP programs

Example: Absolute Value. As a first example, lets write a small branching program that assigns r to the *absolute value* of x.

```
ex_abs = verify p c q (\_ → ())
  where
    p = bTrue

    c = If (N 0 .≤. V "x")
           ("r" ← V "x")
           ("r" ← N 0 .-. V "x")

    q = (N 0 .≤. V "r") .&&. (V "x" .≤. V "r")
```

Example: Swap. Here's a second example that *swaps* the values held inside x and y via a sequence of arithmetic operations

```
ex_swap = verify p c q (\_ → ())
  where
    p = (V "x" .==. V "a") .&&. (V "y" .==. V "b")

    c = ("x" ← (V "x" .+. V "y")) @@
        ("y" ← (V "x" .-. V "y")) @@
        ("x" ← (V "x" .-. V "y"))

    q = (V "x" .==. V "b") .&&. (V "y" .==. V "a")
```

Example: Sum. Let us conclude with an example mirroring the one we started with in Sect. 2 – a loop that sums up the numbers from 0 to n. Here, we supply the loop invariant that relates the intermediate values of r with the loop index i to establish the post condition that states the result holds the (closed-form value of the) summation.

```
ex_sum _ = verify p c q (\_ → ())
  where
    p   = N 0 .≤. V "n"

    c   = ("i" ← N 0) @@
          ("r" ← N 0) @@
          While inv (V "i" .!=. V "n") (
            ("r" ← (V "r" .+. V "i")) @@
            ("i" ← (V "i" .+. N 1))
          )

    q   = N 2 .*. V "r" .==. (V "n" .*. (V "n" .-. N 1))

    inv = p .&&.
          ((N 2 .*. V "r") .==. ((V "i" .-. N 1) .*. V "i"))
```

6   Related Work

Refinement Types. Over the past two decades, several groups have designed refinement based verifiers for several languages, starting with the ML family [4,9,17,24,27, 33], to Racket [16], Scala [12], C [25], JavaScript [6,31] and Ruby [15]. We refer the interested reader to [14] for more details on how refinement types.

Specifications over User-Defined Functions. Refinements are a particular instance of the more general method of *auto-active* (as opposed to interactive) verifiers which, following the early work Floyd [10] and Hoare [13], work by a combination of VC generation and SMT solving [21]. Other prominent SMT-based verifiers like DAFNY and F* support specifications over user defined functions by encoding their semantics with universally-quantified *axioms* that are instantiated via *triggers* [7]. DAFNY and F* use a notion of *fuel* [1] to limit triggering to some fixed depth. This style of unfolding can be shown to be complete for *sufficiently surjective* recursive catamorphisms over algebraic datatypes, *e.g.*, which compute the length of a list or height of a tree [26].

Embedded Verifiers. The notion of embedding verifiers has been explored in several pieces of closely related work. The LMS-VERIFY system [2] uses Scala's lightweight-modular staging feature to compile high-level contracts and code into low-level systems code which can then be automatically verified via an external SMT-based C verifier [3]. The ARMADA system [20] shows how to embed a custom verification framework for concurrent programs with support for *reduction* based refinement proofs [18] within the DAFNY verifier. Finally, the VALE system [11] shows how to build an embedded verifier for a subset of assembly within F^* by writing a verified VC generator in F^* and then reducing assembly verification to type checking in the host language by using F^*'s support for type-level normalization (computation).

Acknowledgements. Many thanks to the reviewers for feedback on early drafts of this work. This work was supported by the NSF grants CCF-1514435, CCF-2120642, CCF-1918573, CCF-1911213, and CCF-1917854, and generous gifts from Microsoft Research.

References

1. Amin, N., Leino, K.R.M., Rompf, T.: Computing with an SMT solver. In: Seidl, M., Tillmann, N. (eds.) TAP 2014. LNCS, vol. 8570, pp. 20–35. Springer, Cham (2014). https://doi.org/10.1007/978-3-319-09099-3_2
2. Amin, N., Rompf. T.: LMS-verify: abstraction without regret for verified systems programming. In: Castagna, G., Gordon, A.D. (eds.) Proceedings of the 44th ACM SIGPLAN Symposium on Principles of Programming Languages, POPL 2017, Paris, France, 18–20 January 2017, pp. 859–873. ACM (2017)
3. Baudin, P., et al.: The dogged pursuit of bug-free C programs: the Frama-c software analysis platform. Commun. ACM **64**(8), 56–68 (2021)
4. Bengtson, J., Bhargavan, K., Fournet, C., Gordon, A.D., Maffeis, S.: Refinement types for secure implementations. ACM Trans. Program. Lang. Syst. **33** (2011)
5. Bertot, Y., Castéran, P.: Coq'Art: The Calculus of Inductive Constructions. Springer Verlag, Heidelberg (2004). https://doi.org/10.1007/978-3-662-07964-5
6. Chugh, R., Herman, D., Jhala, R.: Dependent types for javascript. In: OOPLSA (2012)
7. Detlefs, D., Nelson, G., Saxe, J.B.: Simplify: a theorem prover for program checking. J. ACM **52**(3), 365–473 (2005)
8. Dijkstra, E.W.: Guarded commands, nondeterminacy, and formal derivation of programs. Commun. ACM **18**(8), 453–457 (1975)
9. Dunfield. J.: Refined typechecking with stardust. In: PLPV (2007)
10. Floyd, R.W.: Assigning meanings to programs. In: Mathematical Aspects of Computer Science. Springer, Cham (1967). https://doi.org/10.1007/978-3-319-72453-9
11. Fromherz, A., Giannarakis, N., Hawblitzel, C., Parno, B., Rastogi, A., Swamy, N.: A verified, efficient embedding of a verifiable assembly language. In: Proceedings of the ACM on Programming Languages (PACMPL) , vol. 3, pp. 63:1–63:30 (2019)
12. Hamza, J., Voirol, N., Kuncak, V.: System FR: formalized foundations for the stainless verifier. In: Proceedings of the ACM on Programming Languages (PACMPL), vol. 3, pp. 166:1–166:30 (2019)
13. Hoare, C.A.R.: An axiomatic basis for computer programming. Commun. ACM **12**, 576–580 (1969)
14. Jhala, R., Vazou, N.: Refinement types: a tutorial. Found. Trends Program. Lang. **6**(3–4), 159–317 (2021)

15. Kazerounian, M., Vazou, N., Bourgerie, A., Foster, J.S., Torlak, E.: Refinement types for ruby. CoRR, abs/1711.09281 (2017)
16. Kent, A.M., Kempe, D., Tobin-Hochstadt, S.: Occurrence typing modulo theories. In: PLDI (2016)
17. Knowles, K.W., Flanagan, C.: Hybrid type checking. ACM Trans. Program. Lang. Syst. **32** (2010)
18. Kragl, B., Qadeer, S., Henzinger, T.A.: Refinement for structured concurrent programs. In: Lahiri, S.K., Wang, C. (eds.) CAV 2020. LNCS, vol. 12224, pp. 275–298. Springer, Cham (2020). https://doi.org/10.1007/978-3-030-53288-8_14
19. Lehmann, N., et al.: STORM: refinement types for secure web applications. In: Brown, A.D., Lorch, J.R. (eds.). 15th USENIX Symposium on Operating Systems Design and Implementation, OSDI 2021, 14–16 July 2021, pp. 441–459. USENIX Association (2021)
20. Lorch, J.R.,et al.: Armada: low-effort verification of high-performance concurrent programs. In: Donaldson, A.F., Torlak, E. (eds.) Proceedings of the 41st ACM SIGPLAN International Conference on Programming Language Design and Implementation, PLDI 2020, London, UK, 15–20 June 2020, pp. 197–210. ACM (2020)
21. Nelson, C.G.: Techniques for program verification. Ph.D. thesis, Stanford University (1980)
22. Nipkow, T., Paulson, L.C., Wenzel. M.: Isabelle/HOL – a proof assistant for higher-order logic. Lecture Notes in Computer Science, Springer, Heidelberg (2002). https://doi.org/10.1007/3-540-45949-9
23. Polikarpova, N., Stefan, D., Yang, J., Itzhaky, S., Hance, T., Solar-Lezama, A.: Liquid information flow control. Proc. ACM Program. Lang. 4(ICFP), 105:1–105:30 (2020)
24. Rondon, P., Kawaguchi, M., Jhala, R.: Liquid types. In: PLDI (2008)
25. Rondon, P., Kawaguchi, M., Jhala, R.: Low-level liquid types. In: POPL (2010)
26. Suter, P., Sinan Köksal, A., Kuncak, V.: Satisfiability modulo recursive programs. In: SAS (2011)
27. Swamy, N., et al.: Dependent types and multi-monadic effects in F*. In: Principles of Programming Languages (POPL) (2016)
28. Vazou, N., Bakst, A., Jhala, R.: Bounded refinement types. In: ICFP (2015)
29. Vazou, N., Seidel, E.L., Jhala, R., Vytiniotis, D., Peyton-Jones, S.L.: Refinement types for haskell. In: ICFP (2014)
30. Vazou, N., et al.: Refinement reflection: complete verification with SMT. In: Proceedings of ACM Programming Languages (POPL), vol. 2, pp. :53:1–53:31 (2018)
31. Vekris, P., Cosman, B., Jhala, R.: Refinement types for typescript. In: PLDI (2016)
32. Wadler, P.: Propositions as types. In: Commun. ACM **58**(12), 75–84 (2015)
33. Xi, H., Pfenning, E.: Eliminating array bound checking through dependent types. In: PLDI (1998)

Software Model Checking: 20 Years and Beyond

Dirk Beyer[1]([✉])[iD] and Andreas Podelski[2][iD]

[1] LMU Munich, Munich, Germany
Dirk.Beyer@sosy-lab.org
[2] University of Freiburg, Freiburg im Breisgau, Germany

Abstract. We give an overview of the development of software model checking, a general approach to algorithmic program verification that integrates static analysis, model checking, and deduction. We start with a look backwards and briefly cover some of the important steps in the past decades. The general approach has become a research topic on its own, with a wide range of tools that are based on the approach. Therefore, we discuss the maturity of the research area of software model checking in terms of looking at competitions, at citations, and most importantly, at the tools that were build in this area: we count 76 verification systems for software written in C or Java. We conclude that software model checking has quickly grown to a significant field of research with a high impact on current research directions and tools in software verification.

Keywords: History · Software Verification · Programming · Formal Methods · Program Correctness · Automatic Verification · Verification Tools · Provers

1 Introduction

This paper is meant as a journey through the development of a technology that started as a completely intractable endeavor and now plays a key role in the success of various commercial projects (e.g., [10, 14, 51, 69, 125]).

We contribute this report to the Festschrift for Tom Henzinger, who has influenced the development in several ways. In particular, he led the BLAST project with Ranjit Jhala and Rupak Majumdar, and he pushed for the convergence of data-flow analysis, model checking, and software testing.

Dirk came to UC Berkeley as a young postdoc to join Tom's group. Dirk thought that he would work on topics such as timed and hybrid systems, but Tom had asked him whether he would have a problem with working on software model checking instead. He became immediately infected with the charm of the BLAST project and since then he has never stopped working in this area, instantiating some of the joint ideas in the CPACHECKER project and in the competition on software verification.

Andreas would discuss possible approaches with Tom in an earlier period of time, when software model checking did not exist yet but many people thought about it. Andreas distinctly remembers one discussion in front of the coffee machine at the Max Planck Institute for Computer Science in Saarbrücken,

J.-F. Raskin and K. Chatterjee (Eds.): Principles of Systems Design, LNCS 13660, pp. 554–582, 2022.
https://doi.org/10.1007/978-3-031-22337-2_27

when he and Tom concluded that abstracting a program to a finite-state system seemed a bad idea (Tom, matter-of-factly: "a loser right from the start"). How inspiring a bad idea can be.

2 Timeline of Formal Verification of Software

This section outlines a few milestones in the area of software verification which we think were instrumental to the success and led to the breakthrough in technology.

2.1 Before 1962

First Insights (1880–1940). Mathematicians were concerned with the verification of consistency of arithmetic axioms since a long time. Giuseppe Peano described an arithmetic system of axioms [158], and David Hilbert was interested to know whether a contradiction can be generated after finitely many proof steps [113, 2nd problem]. The dream of a machine that can generate all truth ended after only a few decades, when Kurt Gödel showed that there are certain theorems that cannot be proven [101], and Alonzo Church and Alan Turing showed that our abilities to prove the correctness of programs are limited [62,191]. Despite these initial 'bad' news, software verification can solve many interesting and practical problems. One of the approaches is to restrict the proof system to a decidable theory, for which Presburger arithmetics [167] is a prominent example, which is still often-used today.

Computing Machinery (1940s). Z3, the first working digital, automatic, and programmable computer, was constructed by Konrad Zuse and was ready to be used in 1941. It was a binary computer, built using relays. The second computer, ENIAC, was completed in 1944, based on vacuum tubes. Leibniz and Babbage also constructed computers, but they were not digital, automatic, and programmable. The unavailability of good hardware foundations had hindered the development of computers for a long time. Not only the hardware foundations were missing as an enabling technology: The enabling theories in logics were also not yet sufficiently developed. Predicate logic was needed to prove that the halting problem of Turing machines is undecidable [191]. In parallel, Shannon showed how to implement Boolean algebra using electric circuits [185], which is still how computers are built today (just using transistors instead of relays and somewhat smaller).

Assertions, Proof Decomposition, and Abstraction. As early as 1949, Alan Turing published a method —based on *assertions*— to prove the correctness of computer programs [192]. He wrote: *"In order that the man who checks may not have too difficult a task the programmer should make a number of definite assertions which can be checked individually, and from which the correctness of the whole program easily follows."* Assertions are nowadays one of the most common notations to write invariants in software development.

Abstraction was considered the key for proving correctness, and assertions are abstracting the states at a certain location in the program. Konrad Zuse understood that programming requires abstract languages, and developed the first high-level programming language designed for a computer (Plankalkül [180]).

Craig Interpolation (1950s). But how to automatically compute abstractions? William Craig defined interpolation for logic formulas in 1957 [75]. Given two formulas ϕ_1 and ϕ_2 such that ϕ_1 implies ϕ_2, an interpolant for ϕ_1 and ϕ_2 is a formula ψ that is implied by ϕ_1 and that implies ϕ_2, and contains only symbols that occur in both ϕ_1 and ϕ_2. Applied to program verification, if ϕ_1 represents a program path and ϕ_2 represents a safety property, then the interpolant ψ is an abstraction of the program path ϕ_1 that (1) can be automatically constructed and (2) makes it potentially easier to prove that the property ϕ_2 holds.

2.2   After 1962

Decision Procedures (1960s). The advent of programmable computers and continuous advancements of the theory made it possible to implement automatic theorem proving [79,80,95,166,170]. The algorithm of Davis, Putnam, Logemann, and Loveland is still used today and led to the notion of *decision procedures*. Such decision procedures where further extended to combinations with other theories [153,154] and led to the theorem prover SIMPLIFY [81], which was used as backend in the Extended Static Checkers ESC/Java [88] and ESC/Modula-3 [139].

Program Correctness. In the 1960s, the availability of computers led to an enormous growth of software production. At the same time, the fundamental principles of programming and engineering of large software systems were not yet sufficiently studied. The term *software engineering* was established and a conference held: the first NATO Software-Engineering Conference took place 1968 in Garmisch, Germany. One of the solutions was to support the software development by *formal methods* [82,83,89,114,143,200], which were establishing mathematically precise foundations of computer programming.

Data-Flow Analysis and Abstract States (1970s). In his famous POPL 1973 paper "A Unified Approach to Global Program Optimization" [126], Gary Kildall provided many of the technical ingredients of data-flow analysis that we still use today (fixed-point iteration, lattice operations, ...). The mathematical foundation for more general forms of program analysis was then given by Patrick and Radhia Cousot [74]. The general idea is to define an abstract domain via a lattice and then compute a fixed point in order to construct an overapproximation of the behavior of the program (see also [155]).

LTL and Model Checking (1980s). Zohar Manna, Amir Pnueli, Ed Clarke, Allen Emerson, and Joseph Sifakis contributed theoretical and conceptional foundations to the verification of systems (not only software systems), leading to the notion of *model checking* [68,169]. Manna and Pnueli developed LTL as a specification language and used it to formally specify the behavior of a system using temporal logic [142]. Tools based on model checking became more and more important. Binary decision diagrams [3,137] were extended to their shared and reduced versions by Randy Bryant [47], and he introduced BDDs as a data structure with a wide applicability in formal methods. For many years, the article by Randy Bryant was the most cited article in computer science. We refer to the Handbook of Model Checking [67] for overviews on specific topics on model checking, specifically temporal logic [160] and binary decision diagrams [48].

Symbolic Model Checking (1990s). While the 80s produced many of the theoretical foundations, the 90s brought verification algorithms to practice. Ken McMillan introduced BDDs as the data structure for symbolic model checking [50,144]. BDDs and other symbolic state-space representations became an enabling technology to verify large systems.

Predicate Abstraction. In 1997, as a step towards connecting model checking with program verification, Susanne Graf and Hassen Saïdi developed a deduction-based method to partition the state space of a program according to an equivalence relation defined by a given finite set of state predicates [96]. We obtain a finite abstract system if we associate each block in the partition with an abstract state. The abstract system contains a transition between two blocks if the program has a transition between a state from one block to a state from the other block. If the state predicates and the program's transition relation are represented by logical formulas, then the existence of such states in each of the two blocks reduces to the satisifiability of a logical formula (and this is how deduction comes in).

2.3   Software Model Checking

Tools for Software Model Checking (2000s). The time was ripe for software model checking. In summer 2000, Tom Ball and Sriram Rajamani, with help from others, notably Rupak Majumdar and Todd Millstein, developed SLAM [10,11,14], a tool that performs an *abstraction-refinement loop*. In each iteration of the loop, the tool, using a first-order logic theorem prover, abstracts the given C program (with procedures, possibly recursive) for a given set of predicates. If an error path is found, it checks the feasibility of the sequence of transitions that corresponds to the error path in the abstract system by checking satisifiability. If the error path is infeasible, it uses the proof of unsatisfiability to derive new predicates for the refined abstraction in the next iteration of the loop. The notion of **counterexample-guided abstraction refinement (CEGAR)** was born, developed around the same time in the context of software programs [13] and in the context of finite-state systems [65,66]. In fall 2000, Tom Henzinger, Ranjit Jhala, Rupak Majumdar, and Grégoire Sutre, with help from others, developed BLAST [32,111,112], a tool that implements a similar abstraction refinement but circumvents the abstraction of the whole C program by *lazily* constructing an abstract reachability tree.

These early developments received a lot of attention, and software model checking became a research topic on its own. The SLAM project paved the road for the success of software model checking in industrial software development. The success of SLAM is witnessed by the Static Driver Verifier project[1], which is based

---

[1] https://www.microsoft.com/en-us/research/project/slam

on SLAM and was used as part of Microsoft's Windows Driver Development Kit in daily software production. The BLAST project showed the effects of applying Craig interpolation to the abstraction-refinement process in program analysis [111], first using McMillan's original FOCI library [146] and later the independently developed SMT solver CSIsAT [40]. Later versions of BLAST, which was by that time maintained by a different group [188], received gold medals in the category *Device Drivers* of the competition on software verification[2] in 2012, 2014, and 2015. Both projects were highly influencial in the research community: the PLDI '01 paper on SLAM [11] received a PLDI test-of-time award in 2011[3], and the POPL '04 paper on BLAST [111] received a POPL test-of-time award in 2014[4].

Also, as a sign of maturity, survey papers appeared, on software verification [85], on software model checking [121], and on deductive verification [19]. A recent survey addresses the current status of formal methods [92], and competition reports give an overview over the status of tools for software verification [30].

Satisfiability Modulo Theory. In the early 2000s, there was an enormous progress in research on satisfiability (SAT), with the appearance of efficient implementations of algorithms for SAT solving, most notably CHAFF [149]. Theory combinations led to the notion of *satisfiability modulo theories* (SMT), an integration of SAT with theories like linear arithmetics, bitvectors, and arrays. The SMTLIB format for input formulas [16] facilitated the use of SMT tools. Some SMT solvers support interpolation; examples are CSIsAT [40], MATH-SAT [46], and SMTINTERPOL [61].

Boolean and Cartesian Abstraction. At the beginning, when predicate abstraction was first used for the abstraction of C programs (by SLAM and BLAST), it was implemented by Cartesian abstraction [12]. At that time, disjunctions were not efficiently supported by automatic solvers such as SIMPLIFY [81]. Only later, interpolating SMT solvers such as CSIsAT [40] and MATHSAT [46] could handle disjunctions efficiently. Cartesian predicate abstraction seemed suitable as long as only simple program paths were encoded in path formulas. In connection with *large-block encoding* [31,36], however, when it was possible to delegate large amounts of work (i.e., large formulas) to the SMT solvers, it became feasible to use Boolean abstraction [129] to implement predicate abstraction, as done in CPACHECKER [35].

Verification with Interpolants. Ken McMillan published how to use Craig interpolation [75] for finding abstract descriptions of the behavior of transition systems [145]. Later, Craig interpolation was also applied to program paths, in order to automatically learn abstractions for the verification of computer programs [111]. For every program path we can construct a formula such that the program path is infeasible (there is no execution of all statements along the path) if and only if the formula is unsatisfiable. Assume that we have split a given infeasible program path at a certain program location, and the path prefix and the path suffix correspond to the path formulas ϕ^{pre} and ϕ^{post}, respectively. Then ϕ^{pre} implies the

---

[2] https://sv-comp.sosy-lab.org
[3] https://www.sigplan.org/Awards/PLDI
[4] https://www.sigplan.org/Awards/POPL

negation of ϕ^{post}. The interpolant $\psi = itp(\phi^{pre}, \neg\phi^{post})$ represents an abstraction; i.e., it describes what we need to know about the states after executing the path prefix in order to derive that continuing the execution of the path suffix is not possible. Ken McMillan also developed the first tool for automatically computing interpolants [146]. An overview on the use of interpolation for verification is given in a chapter in the Handbook on Model Checking [147].

Trace Abstraction. As an alternative to constructing a sequence of (more and more refined) abstractions (abstract systems or abstract reachability graphs), the approach of trace abstraction [108] is to construct a sequence of programs until all paths of the input program are covered. Each program in the sequence is constructed from the proof of the infeasibility of a (spurious) counterexample. The covering check can be reduced to automata inclusion.

Termination. After a series of breakthroughs in making safety analysis of large software systems practically relevant, also liveness properties were investigated. Algorithmic approaches for constructing ranking functions [161] made it possible to perform termination analysis. Since termination of functions in the operating system are a major concern, e.g., for Microsoft, tool support for termination analysis [70, 162] became important.

Competition on Software Verification (2010s). In order to make progress explicit and show that there are many good tools for software verification available, a competition on software verification (SV-COMP) was developed 2010–2011, with the first results published in 2012 [20]. Such competitions create awareness of tools and the available technology, provide comparative evaluations, and establish standards (e.g., input formats, results formats, comparability, reproducibility). The most recent instance of the competition evaluated 47 verification tools.

Property-Directed Reachability. Property-directed reachability (PDR) is a SAT/SMT-based reachability algorithm that incrementally constructs inductive invariants. After it was successfully applied to hardware model checking [43, 44], several adaptations to software model checking have been proposed [42, 63, 64, 130, 131].

Interpolation-Based Model Checking. While interpolation became a key ingredient in many verification approaches for software, the original algorithm from 2003 [145] was adopted to the verification of software only recently [37].

Approaches Used in Tools. Current tools usually combine a set of approaches. We report in Table 4 which approaches are used by tools for software verification.

2.4   Current Developments (2022)

While the focus of the past decades was on contributing tools that implement verification approaches in order to make the research results practically usable, we today observe a move from a *lack* of tools to an *abundance* of tools (see Sect. 3.3).

A new research question arises in this context: How can we integrate existing verification systems in order to maximally benefit from their respective strengths. To enable cooperation between verification tools, we need standardized interfaces that make it possible to pass artifacts with valuable information from one tool to another. Such verification artifacts include, besides the programs and their specifications, also transformed or reduced programs, error paths, invariants, witnesses, and partial verification results in general [39,41].

3   Maturity of the Research Area

The area of software model checking is 22 years old at the time of writing, and several aspects indicate that software model checking is a mature research area. We outline a few such indicators in the following.

3.1   Competitions

It is well understood that competitions are an important scientific method. Competitions provide regular comparative evaluations. In the area of formal methods, there are plenty of competitions [17], most of them being concerned with comparisons of tools that solve a certain kind of problem, most prominently, SAT and SMT solving. Five competitions are concerned with the verification of software: RERS, SV-COMP, Test-Comp, VerifyThis, and TermComp (Table 1).

Table 1. Competitions in the area of software verification

Competition	Where	What	How	Reference
RERS	off-site	tools	open	[118]
SV-COMP	off-site	automatic tools	controlled	[20]
Test-Comp	off-site	automatic tools	controlled	[27]
VerifyThis	on-site	teams and tools	interactive	[119]
TermComp	off-site	automatic tools	controlled	[94]

The Competition on Software Verification (SV-COMP) provides annually a comparative evaluation of automatic tools for software verification. The first results were published in 2012 [20]. The objectives of the competition include:

- create awareness of tools,
- provide yearly comparative evaluations,
- create and maintain a benchmark collection (SV-BENCHMARKS repository),
- establish standards (input, exchange, comparability, reproducibility),
- conserve tools at a central place and make them available, and
- educate PhD students and postdocs on benchmarking and reproducibility.

The competition was a success, in that all of the above-mentioned objectives were achieved. Over the last ten years, more and more verification tools participated, and the last edition was comparing 47 verification tools.

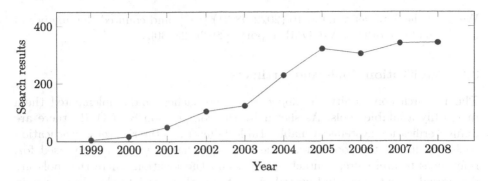

Fig. 1. Number y of search results found by Google Scholar for "software model checking" per year x; illustrates growing interest in the topic in the first 10 years

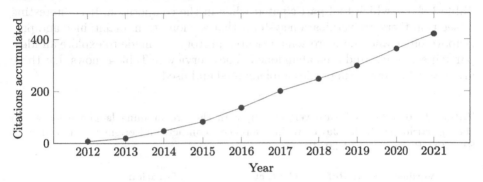

Fig. 2. Number y of citations up to year x of SV-COMP reports according to the COCI CSV data set [157]; illustrates constant interest in verifier competitions

3.2   Publication Venues and Research Activity

Software model checking is a research field at the intersection of programming languages, software engineering, and theory of computation. Thus, the research results are mainly published in outlets in the area of programming languages, such as POPL, PLDI, and OOPSLA, of software engineering, such as ICSE, ESEC/FSE, ASE, and ISSTA, and of formal methods, such as CAV, TACAS, and ATVA.

Figure 1 illustrates the development of the research area. We created a mapping from each year in the range 1999–2008 to the number of search results of Google Scholar for the search term "software model checking" in its first 10 years. The graph drawn in Fig. 1 illustrates how the interest in software model checking was growing in the early 2000s s years, and how it stabilized afterwards.

As mentioned above, the competition SV-COMP serves as a platform for creation and maintenance of benchmark sets and community standards. To illustrate the continuous interest in the topics of the competition, we counted the number y of citations up to year x and draw the function in Fig. 2. We used COCI [106], an open citation index that is regularly extended by OpenCitations.

We used the data set version 16 (2022-08-31) [157], and counted the number of citations of any of the SV-COMP reports [20–26, 28–30].

3.3 Verification Tools and Artifacts

The research community developed new approaches, and implemented them in readily available tools. As shown by the competition SV-COMP, there are many verification systems available. Table 2 illustrates the rich set of verification tools, by listing the tool names, the language that they are mainly used for, references to literature, contact persons, and the location where the tools are developed, maintained, and hosted. All listed tools participated at least once in the competition on software verification SV-COMP. This is also a sign of maturity: Researchers develop tool implementations and hand them in for evaluation. Table 3 shows which tool participated when in the competition. It is interesting to see that there are verification systems that are long-term maintained and participate often, and there are some research prototypes, made to explore an idea, participated once, and then abandoned. The overview in Table 4 shows that there are many different technologies implemented and used.

Table 2. Tools for software verification, with the progamming language for which they participated (J for Java), main references, contact, and origin (assembled from SV-COMP reports 2012–2022)

Verifier	L. Ref.	Contact	Location
2LS	C [45, 141]	Viktor Malík	Brno, Czechia
APROVE	C [110, 189]	Jera Hensel	Aachen, Germany
BEAGLE	C	Dexi Wang	Beijing, China
BLAST	C [32, 188]	Vadim Mutilin	Moscow, Russia
BRICK	C [49]	Lei Bu	Nanjing, China
CASCADE	C [198]	Wei Wang	New York, USA
CBMC	C [127]	Michael Tautschnig	London, UK
CEAGLE	C	Guang Chen	Beijing, China
CIVL	C [203]	Stephen Siegel	Newark, USA
COASTAL	J [194]	Willem Visser	Stellenbosch, South Africa
CONSEQUENCE	C	Anand Yeolekar	Pune, India
COVERITEAM	C [33, 34]	Sudeep Kanav	Munich, Germany
CPACHECKER	C [35, 77]	Thomas Bunk	Munich, Germany
CPA-BAM	C [6, 197]	Vadim Mutilin	Moscow, Russia
CPALIEN	C [152]	Petr Muller	Brno, Czechia
CPALOCKATOR	C [7, 8]	Pavel Andrianov	Moscow, Russia
CPAREC	C [59]	Ming-Hsien Tsai	Teipei, Taiwan
CRUX	C [84, 183]	Ryan Scott	Portland, USA
CSEQ	C [73, 120]	Omar Inverso	L'Aquila, Italy
DARTAGNAN	C [93, 163]	Hernán Ponce de León	Munich, Germany

(continues on next page)

Table 2. Tools for software verification (*continued*)

Verifier	L. Ref.	Contact	Location
DEAGLE	C [105]	Fei He	Bejing, China
DEPTHK	C [177, 179]	Omar Alhawi	Manchester, UK
DIVINE	C [15, 132]	Henrich Lauko	Brno, Czechia
EBF	C	Fatimah Aljaafari	Manchester, UK
ESBMC	C [90, 91]	Rafael Sá Menezes	Manchester, UK
FOREST	C [5]	Pablo Sanchez	Santander, Spain
FORESTER	C [115]	Martin Hruska	Brno, Czechia
FRAMA-C-SV	C [38, 76]	Martin Spiessl	Munich, Germany
FRANKENBIT	C [99]	Arie Gurfinkel	Pittsburgh, USA
FSHELL	C [117]	Helmut Veith	Vienna, Austria
FUNCTION	C [193]	Caterina Urban	Paris, France
GACAL	C [171]	Benjamin Quiring	Boston, USA
GAZER-THETA	C [1, 103]	Ákos Hajdu	Budapest, Hungary
GDART	J [151]	Falk Howar	Dortmund, Germany
GOBLINT	C [181, 196]	Simmo Saan	Tartu, Estonia
GRAVES-CPA	C [138]	Will Leeson	Charlottesville, USA
HIPREC	C [135]	Quang Loc Le	Singapore, Singapore
HIPTNT+	C [136]	Ton Chanh Le	Singapore, Singapore
HSF(C)	C [97]	Andrey Rybalchenko	Munich, Germany
IMPARA	C	Björn Wachter	Oxford, UK
INFER	C [52, 124]	Thomas Lemberger	Munich, Germany
INTERPCHECKER	C	Zhao Duan	Xi'an, China
JAVA-RANGER	J [186, 187]	Soha Hussein	Minnesota, USA
JAYHORN	J [122, 184]	Ali Shamakhi	Tehran, Iran
JBMC	J [71, 72]	Peter Schrammel	Sussex, UK
JDART	J [140, 150]	Falk Howar	Dortmund, Germany
JPF	J [9, 195]	Cyrille Artho	Stockholm, Sweden
KORN	C [86]	Gidon Ernst	Munich, Germany
LART	C [133, 134]	Henrich Lauko	Brno, Czechia
LCTD	C [182]	Keijo Heljanko	Espoo, Finland
LLBMC	C [87]	Stephan Falke	Karlsruhe, Germany
LOCKSMITH	C [165]	Vesal Vojdani	Tartu, Estonia
LPI	C [123]	George Karpenkov	Grenoble, France
MAP2CHECK	C [176, 178]	Herbert Rocha	Boa Vista, Brazil
PAC-MAN	C [58]	Ming-Hsien Tsai	Taipei, Taiwan
PERENTIE	C [53]	Franck Cassez	Sydney, Australia
PESCO	C [174, 175]	Cedric Richter	Oldenburg, Germany
PINAKA	C [57]	Saurabh Joshi	Hyderabad, India
PREDATOR	C [116, 159]	Veronika Šoková	Brno, Czechia
SATABS	C [18]	Michael Tautschnig	Oxford, UK
SEAHORN	C [100]	Jorge Navas	Mountain View, USA
SESL	C	Xie Li	Beijing, China

(*continues on next page*)

Table 2. Tools for software verification (*continued*)

Verifier	L. Ref.	Contact	Location
SKINK	C [54]	Franck Cassez	Sydney, Australia
SMACK	C [104, 173]	Zvonimir Rakamaric	Salt Lake City, USA
SPF	J [156, 168]	Willem Visser	New York, USA
SYMBIOTIC	C [55, 56]	Marek Chalupa	Brno, Czechia
THETA	C [190, 204]	Vince Molnár	Budapest, Hungary
THREADER	C [164]	Corneliu Popeea	Munich, Germany
UFO	C [4, 98]	Aws Albarghouthi	Toronto, Canada
ULTIMATE	C [107, 109]	Matthias Heizmann	Freiburg, Germany
VERIABS	C [2, 78]	Priyanka Darke	Pune, India
VERIFUZZ	C [60, 148]	Raveendra Kumar M.	Pune, India
VIAP	C [172]	Pritom Rajkhowa	Hong Kong, China
VVT	C [102]	Alfons Laarman	Vienna, Austria
WOLVERINE	C [128, 199]	Georg Weissenbacher	Vienna, Austria
YOGARCBMC	C [201, 202]	Liangze Yin	Bejing, China

Table 3. Participation in SV-COMP evaluations 2012–2022

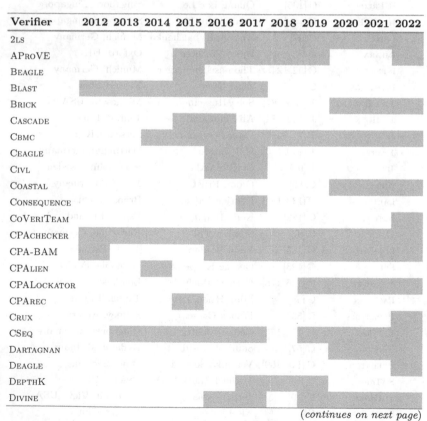

Verifier	2012	2013	2014	2015	2016	2017	2018	2019	2020	2021	2022
2LS											
APROVE											
BEAGLE											
BLAST											
BRICK											
CASCADE											
CBMC											
CEAGLE											
CIVL											
COASTAL											
CONSEQUENCE											
COVERITEAM											
CPACHECKER											
CPA-BAM											
CPALIEN											
CPALOCKATOR											
CPAREC											
CRUX											
CSEQ											
DARTAGNAN											
DEAGLE											
DEPTHK											
DIVINE											

(*continues on next page*)

Table 3. Participation in SV-COMP evaluations 2012–2022 (*continued*)

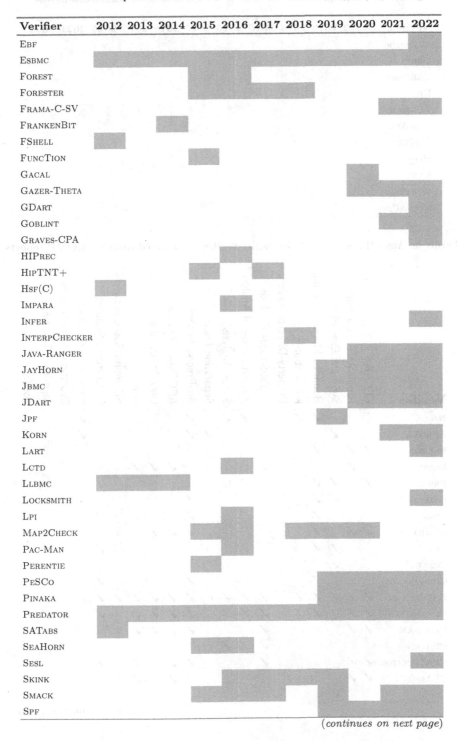

Verifier	2012	2013	2014	2015	2016	2017	2018	2019	2020	2021	2022
EBF											
ESBMC											
FOREST											
FORESTER											
FRAMA-C-SV											
FRANKENBIT											
FSHELL											
FUNCTION											
GACAL											
GAZER-THETA											
GDART											
GOBLINT											
GRAVES-CPA											
HIPREC											
HIPTNT+											
HSF(C)											
IMPARA											
INFER											
INTERPCHECKER											
JAVA-RANGER											
JAYHORN											
JBMC											
JDART											
JPF											
KORN											
LART											
LCTD											
LLBMC											
LOCKSMITH											
LPI											
MAP2CHECK											
PAC-MAN											
PERENTIE											
PESCO											
PINAKA											
PREDATOR											
SATABS											
SEAHORN											
SESL											
SKINK											
SMACK											
SPF											

(*continues on next page*)

Table 3. Participation in SV-COMP evaluations 2012–2022 (*continued*)

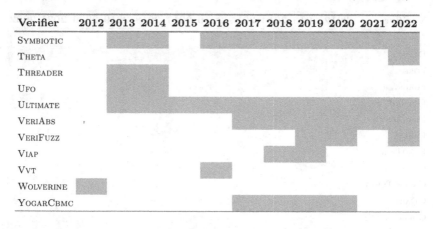

Verifier	2012	2013	2014	2015	2016	2017	2018	2019	2020	2021	2022
SYMBIOTIC											
THETA											
THREADER											
UFO											
ULTIMATE											
VERIABS											
VERIFUZZ											
VIAP											
VVT											
WOLVERINE											
YOGARCBMC											

Table 4. Algorithms and techniques, by verifier (assembled from SV-COMP reports)

Verifier	CEGAR	Predicate Abstraction	Symbolic Execution	Bounded Model Checking	k-Induction	Property-Directed Reach.	Explicit-Value Analysis	Numeric. Interval Analysis	Shape Analysis	Separation Logic	Bit-Precise Analysis	ARG-Based Analysis	Lazy Abstraction	Interpolation	Automata-Based Analysis	Concurrency Support	Ranking Functions	Evolutionary Algorithms	Algorithm Selection	Portfolio
2LS				✓	✓		✓	✓			✓						✓			
APROVE			✓				✓	✓			✓	✓					✓			
BEAGLE	✓	✓		✓																
BLAST	✓	✓					✓					✓	✓	✓						
BRICK	✓		✓	✓			✓									✓				
CASCADE			✓	✓							✓									
CBMC			✓								✓					✓				
CEAGLE	✓	✓		✓							✓	✓	✓							
CIVL			✓	✓				✓								✓				
COASTAL			✓																	
CONSEQUENCE			✓								✓					✓				
COVERITEAM	✓	✓	✓	✓	✓		✓	✓	✓		✓	✓	✓	✓	✓	✓	✓		✓	✓
CPACHECKER	✓	✓	✓	✓	✓		✓	✓	✓		✓	✓	✓	✓		✓	✓		✓	✓
CPA-BAM	✓	✓					✓				✓	✓	✓	✓						
CPALIEN							✓		✓											
CPALOCKATOR	✓	✓					✓				✓	✓	✓	✓		✓				
CPAREC	✓	✓										✓	✓	✓						
CRUX			✓																	

(*continues on next page*)

Table 4. Algorithms and techniques (*continued*)

Verifier	CEGAR	Predicate Abstraction	Symbolic Execution	Bounded Model Checking	k-Induction	Property-Directed Reach.	Explicit-Value Analysis	Numeric. Interval Analysis	Shape Analysis	Separation Logic	Bit-Precise Analysis	ARG-Based Analysis	Lazy Abstraction	Interpolation	Automata-Based Analysis	Concurrency Support	Ranking Functions	Evolutionary Algorithms	Algorithm Selection	Portfolio
CSEQ				✓							✓					✓				
DARTAGNAN				✓							✓					✓				
DEAGLE																				
DEPTHK				✓	✓						✓					✓				
DIVINE			✓				✓				✓					✓			✓	✓
EBF				✓																
ESBMC				✓	✓			✓			✓					✓				
FOREST			✓	✓							✓									
FORESTER	✓								✓						✓					
FRAMA-C-SV							✓													
FRANKENBIT				✓							✓			✓						
FSHELL				✓																
FUNCTION								✓									✓			
GACAL																				
GAZER-THETA	✓	✓		✓			✓				✓	✓	✓	✓						✓
GDART			✓								✓									✓
GOBLINT								✓								✓				
GRAVES-CPA	✓	✓		✓	✓		✓	✓	✓		✓	✓	✓	✓		✓	✓		✓	✓
HIPREC									✓	✓										
HIPTNT+									✓	✓							✓			
HSF(C)	✓	✓											✓	✓	✓					
IMPARA				✓			✓	✓			✓	✓	✓	✓	✓					
INFER								✓	✓	✓										✓
INTERPCHECKER																				
JAVA-RANGER				✓							✓									
JAYHORN	✓	✓				✓			✓			✓	✓							
JBMC				✓							✓					✓				
JDART			✓								✓									✓
JPF				✓			✓	✓			✓					✓				
KORN			✓	✓			✓													✓
LART			✓				✓				✓									✓
LCTD	✓		✓	✓							✓									
LLBMC				✓																
LOCKSMITH																✓				
LPI	✓				✓			✓				✓	✓							

(*continues on next page*)

Table 4. Algorithms and techniques (*continued*)

Verifier	CEGAR	Predicate Abstraction	Symbolic Execution	Bounded Model Checking	k-Induction	Property-Directed Reach.	Explicit-Value Analysis	Numeric. Interval Analysis	Shape Analysis	Separation Logic	Bit-Precise Analysis	ARG-Based Analysis	Lazy Abstraction	Interpolation	Automata-Based Analysis	Concurrency Support	Ranking Functions	Evolutionary Algorithms	Algorithm Selection	Portfolio
Map2Check				✓							✓									
Pac-Man			✓													✓				
Perentie	✓		✓				✓							✓	✓					
PeSCo	✓	✓		✓	✓		✓	✓	✓		✓	✓	✓	✓		✓	✓		✓	✓
Pinaka			✓	✓							✓									
Predator									✓											
SATabs	✓	✓													✓					
SeaHorn				✓	✓		✓					✓	✓	✓			✓			
Sesl			✓							✓										
Skink	✓						✓							✓	✓					
Smack				✓							✓		✓		✓					
SPF			✓						✓						✓					
Symbiotic			✓		✓			✓	✓		✓				✓					✓
Theta	✓	✓					✓				✓	✓	✓		✓				✓	✓
Threader	✓	✓										✓	✓		✓					
Ufo	✓	✓		✓			✓					✓	✓	✓						
Ultimate	✓	✓					✓	✓			✓		✓	✓	✓	✓	✓		✓	✓
VeriAbs	✓			✓	✓		✓	✓										✓	✓	✓
VeriFuzz				✓			✓											✓		
Viap																				
Vvt	✓	✓		✓		✓	✓							✓		✓				
Wolverine	✓											✓	✓	✓						
YogarCbmc	✓			✓							✓		✓			✓				

4   Conclusion

We have given an overview over several mile stones in the history and the development of software verification, and have illustrated the maturity of the research area. This report also show-cases the research area by providing a comprehensive collection of competition-evaluated verification systems for the programming languages C and Java. We will not speculate about the future of software verification, but current trends are concerned with, for example, verification witnesses, concurrent programs, unbounded parallelism, termination, cooperative verification, machine-learning-based invariant generation, hyper-properties, and quantum programs.

Funding Information. This project was funded in part by the Deutsche Forschungs-gemeinschaft (DFG) – 378803395 (ConVeY).

Data Availability Statement. The search results in Fig. 1 were manually looked up from Google Scholar on 2022-04-30. The citation counts in Fig. 2 were calculated from the COCI CSV data set [157]. The data to assemble Tables 2, 3 and 4 were looked up from SV-COMP reports [20–26, 28–30] and the SV-COMP web site at https://sv-comp.sosy-lab.org.

References

1. Ádám, Zs., Sallai, Gy., Hajdu, Á.: GAZER-THETA: LLVM-based verifier portfolio with BMC/CEGAR (competition contribution). In: Proc. TACAS (2). pp. 433–437. LNCS 12652, Springer (2021). https://doi.org/10.1007/978-3-030-72013-1_27

2. Afzal, M., Asia, A., Chauhan, A., Chimdyalwar, B., Darke, P., Datar, A., Kumar, S., Venkatesh, R.: VERIABS: Verification by abstraction and test generation. In: Proc. ASE. pp. 1138–1141 (2019). https://doi.org/10.1109/ASE.2019.00121

3. Akers, S.B.: Binary decision diagrams. IEEE Trans. Computers **27**(6), 509–516 (1978). https://doi.org/10.1109/TC.1978.1675141

4. Albarghouthi, A., Li, Y., Gurfinkel, A., Chechik, M.: UFO: A framework for abstraction- and interpolation-based software verification. In: Proc. CAV, pp. 672–678. LNCS 7358, Springer (2012). https://doi.org/10.1007/978-3-642-31424-7_48

5. de Aledo, P.G., Sanchez, P.: Framework for embedded system verification (competition contribution). In: Proc. TACAS. pp. 429–431. LNCS 9035, Springer (2015). https://doi.org/10.1007/978-3-662-46681-0_36

6. Andrianov, P., Friedberger, K., Mandrykin, M.U., Mutilin, V.S., Volkov, A.: CPA-BAM-BNB: Block-abstraction memoization and region-based memory models for predicate abstractions (competition contribution). In: Proc. TACAS. pp. 355–359. LNCS 10206, Springer (2017). https://doi.org/10.1007/978-3-662-54580-5_22

7. Andrianov, P., Mutilin, V., Khoroshilov, A.: CPALOCKATOR: Thread-modular approach with projections (competition contribution). In: Proc. TACAS (2). pp. 423–427. LNCS 12652, Springer (2021). https://doi.org/10.1007/978-3-030-72013-1_25

8. Andrianov, P.S.: Analysis of correct synchronization of operating system components. Program. Comput. Softw. **46**, 712–730 (2020). https://doi.org/10.1134/S0361768820080022

9. Artho, C., Visser, W.: JAVA PATHFINDER at SV-COMP 2019 (competition contribution). In: Proc. TACAS (3). pp. 224–228. LNCS 11429, Springer (2019). https://doi.org/10.1007/978-3-030-17502-3_18

10. Ball, T., Levin, V., Rajamani, S.K.: A decade of software model checking with Slam. Commun. ACM **54**(7), 68–76 (2011). https://doi.org/10.1145/1965724.1965743

11. Ball, T., Majumdar, R., Millstein, T., Rajamani, S.K.: Automatic predicate abstraction of C programs. In: Proc. PLDI. pp. 203–213. ACM (2001). https://doi.org/10.1145/378795.378846

12. Ball, T., Podelski, A., Rajamani, S.K.: Boolean and Cartesian abstraction for model checking C programs. In: Proc. TACAS. pp. 268–283. LNCS 2031, Springer (2001). https://doi.org/10.1007/3-540-45319-9_19
13. Ball, T., Rajamani, S.K.: Boolean programs: A model and process for software analysis. Tech. Rep. MSR Tech. Rep. 2000-14, Microsoft Research (2000). https://www.microsoft.com/en-us/research/wp-content/uploads/2016/02/tr-2000-14.pdf
14. Ball, T., Rajamani, S.K.: The SLAM project: Debugging system software via static analysis. In: Proc. POPL. pp. 1–3. ACM (2002). https://doi.org/10.1145/503272.503274
15. Baranová, Z., Barnat, J., Kejstová, K., Kučera, T., Lauko, H., Mrázek, J., Ročkai, P., Štill, V.: Model checking of C and C++ with DIVINE 4. In: Proc. ATVA. pp. 201–207. LNCS 10482, Springer (2017). https://doi.org/10.1007/978-3-319-68167-2_14
16. Barrett, C., Fontaine, P., Tinelli, C.: The SMT-LIB Standard: Version 2.5. Tech. rep., University of Iowa (2015), available at https://smtlib.cs.uiowa.edu/
17. Bartocci, E., Beyer, D., Black, P.E., Fedyukovich, G., Garavel, H., Hartmanns, A., Huisman, M., Kordon, F., Nagele, J., Sighireanu, M., Steffen, B., Suda, M., Sutcliffe, G., Weber, T., Yamada, A.: TOOLympics 2019: An overview of competitions in formal methods. In: Proc. TACAS (3). pp. 3–24. LNCS 11429, Springer (2019). https://doi.org/10.1007/978-3-030-17502-3_1
18. Basler, G., Donaldson, A.F., Kaiser, A., Kröning, D., Tautschnig, M., Wahl, T.: SATABS: A bit-precise verifier for C programs (competition contribution). In: Proc. TACAS. pp. 552–555. LNCS 7214, Springer (2012). https://doi.org/10.1007/978-3-642-28756-5_47
19. Beckert, B., Hähnle, R.: Reasoning and verification: State of the art and current trends. IEEE Intelligent Systems **29**(1), 20–29 (2014). https://doi.org/10.1109/MIS.2014.3
20. Beyer, D.: Competition on software verification (SV-COMP). In: Proc. TACAS. pp. 504–524. LNCS 7214, Springer (2012). https://doi.org/10.1007/978-3-642-28756-5_38
21. Beyer, D.: Second competition on software verification (Summary of SV-COMP 2013). In: Proc. TACAS. pp. 594–609. LNCS 7795, Springer (2013). https://doi.org/10.1007/978-3-642-36742-7_43
22. Beyer, D.: Status report on software verification (Competition summary SV-COMP 2014). In: Proc. TACAS. pp. 373–388. LNCS 8413, Springer (2014). https://doi.org/10.1007/978-3-642-54862-8_25
23. Beyer, D.: Software verification and verifiable witnesses (Report on SV-COMP 2015). In: Proc. TACAS. pp. 401–416. LNCS 9035, Springer (2015). https://doi.org/10.1007/978-3-662-46681-0_31
24. Beyer, D.: Reliable and reproducible competition results with BENCHEXEC and witnesses (Report on SV-COMP 2016). In: Proc. TACAS. pp. 887–904. LNCS 9636, Springer (2016). https://doi.org/10.1007/978-3-662-49674-9_55
25. Beyer, D.: Software verification with validation of results (Report on SV-COMP 2017). In: Proc. TACAS. pp. 331–349. LNCS 10206, Springer (2017). https://doi.org/10.1007/978-3-662-54580-5_20
26. Beyer, D.: Automatic verification of C and Java programs: SV-COMP 2019. In: Proc. TACAS (3). pp. 133–155. LNCS 11429, Springer (2019). https://doi.org/10.1007/978-3-030-17502-3_9
27. Beyer, D.: Competition on software testing (Test-Comp). In: Proc. TACAS (3). pp. 167–175. LNCS 11429, Springer (2019). https://doi.org/10.1007/978-3-030-17502-3_11

28. Beyer, D.: Advances in automatic software verification: SV-COMP 2020. In: Proc. TACAS (2). pp. 347–367. LNCS 12079, Springer (2020). https://doi.org/10.1007/978-3-030-45237-7_21

29. Beyer, D.: Software verification: 10th comparative evaluation (SV-COMP 2021). In: Proc. TACAS (2). pp. 401–422. LNCS 12652, Springer (2021). https://doi.org/10.1007/978-3-030-72013-1_24

30. Beyer, D.: Progress on software verification: SV-COMP 2022. In: Proc. TACAS (2). pp. 375–402. LNCS 13244, Springer (2022). https://doi.org/10.1007/978-3-030-99527-0_20

31. Beyer, D., Cimatti, A., Griggio, A., Keremoglu, M.E., Sebastiani, R.: Software model checking via large-block encoding. In: Proc. FMCAD. pp. 25–32. IEEE (2009). https://doi.org/10.1109/FMCAD.2009.5351147

32. Beyer, D., Henzinger, T.A., Jhala, R., Majumdar, R.: The software model checker BLAST. Int. J. Softw. Tools Technol. Transfer 9(5-6), 505–525 (2007). https://doi.org/10.1007/s10009-007-0044-z

33. Beyer, D., Kanav, S.: COVERITEAM: On-demand composition of cooperative verification systems. In: Proc. TACAS. pp. 561–579. LNCS 13243, Springer (2022). https://doi.org/10.1007/978-3-030-99524-9_31

34. Beyer, D., Kanav, S., Richter, C.: Construction of Verifier Combinations Based on Off-the-Shelf Verifiers. In: Proc. FASE. pp. 49–70. Springer (2022). https://doi.org/10.1007/978-3-030-99429-7_3

35. Beyer, D., Keremoglu, M.E.: CPACHECKER: A tool for configurable software verification. In: Proc. CAV. pp. 184–190. LNCS 6806, Springer (2011). https://doi.org/10.1007/978-3-642-22110-1_16

36. Beyer, D., Keremoglu, M.E., Wendler, P.: Predicate abstraction with adjustable-block encoding. In: Proc. FMCAD. pp. 189–197. FMCAD (2010), https://www.sosy-lab.org/research/pub/2010-FMCAD.Predicate_Abstraction_with_Adjustable-Block_Encoding.pdf

37. Beyer, D., Lee, N.Z., Wendler, P.: Interpolation and SAT-based model checking revisited: Adoption to software verification. arXiv/CoRR 2208(05046) (July 2022). https://doi.org/10.48550/arXiv.2208.05046

38. Beyer, D., Spiessl, M.: The static analyzer FRAMA-C in SV-COMP (competition contribution). In: Proc. TACAS (2). pp. 429–434. LNCS 13244, Springer (2022). https://doi.org/10.1007/978-3-030-99527-0_26

39. Beyer, D., Wehrheim, H.: Verification artifacts in cooperative verification: Survey and unifying component framework. In: Proc. ISoLA (1). pp. 143–167. LNCS 12476, Springer (2020). https://doi.org/10.1007/978-3-030-61362-4_8

40. Beyer, D., Zufferey, D., Majumdar, R.: CSIsat: Interpolation for LA+EUF. In: Proc. CAV. pp. 304–308. LNCS 5123, Springer (2008). https://doi.org/10.1007/978-3-540-70545-1_29

41. Beyer, D.: Cooperative verification: Towards reliable safety-critical systems (invited talk). In: Proc. FTSCS. pp. 1–2. ACM (2022). https://doi.org/10.1145/3563822.3572548

42. Birgmeier, J., Bradley, A.R., Weissenbacher, G.: Counterexample to induction-guided abstraction-refinement (CTIGAR). In: Proc. CAV. pp. 831–848. LNCS 8559, Springer (2014). https://doi.org/10.1007/978-3-319-08867-9_55

43. Bradley, A.R.: SAT-based model checking without unrolling. In: Proc. VMCAI. pp. 70–87. LNCS 6538, Springer (2011). https://doi.org/10.1007/978-3-642-18275-4_7

44. Bradley, A.R., Manna, Z.: Property-directed incremental invariant generation. Formal Asp. Comput. **20**(4–5), 379–405 (2008). https://doi.org/10.1007/s00165-008-0080-9
45. Brain, M., Joshi, S., Kröning, D., Schrammel, P.: Safety verification and refutation by k-invariants and k-induction. In: Proc. SAS. pp. 145–161. LNCS 9291, Springer (2015). https://doi.org/10.1007/978-3-662-48288-9_9
46. Bruttomesso, R., Cimatti, A., Franzén, A., Griggio, A., Sebastiani, R.: The MATH-SAT 4 SMT solver. In: Proc. CAV. pp. 299–303. LNCS 5123, Springer (2008). https://doi.org/10.1007/978-3-540-70545-1_28
47. Bryant, R.E.: Graph-based algorithms for boolean function manipulation. IEEE Trans. Computers **35**(8), 677–691 (1986). https://doi.org/10.1109/TC.1986.1676819
48. Bryant, R.E.: Binary decision diagrams. In: Handbook of Model Checking, pp. 191–217. Springer (2018). https://doi.org/10.1007/978-3-319-10575-8_7
49. Bu, L., Xie, Z., Lyu, L., Li, Y., Guo, X., Zhao, J., Li, X.: BRICK: Path enumeration-based bounded reachability checking of C programs (competition contribution). In: Proc. TACAS (2). pp. 408–412. LNCS 13244, Springer (2022). https://doi.org/10.1007/978-3-030-99527-0_22
50. Burch, J.R., Clarke, E.M., McMillan, K.L., Dill, D.L., Hwang, L.J.: Symbolic model checking: 10^{20} states and beyond. In: Proc. LICS. pp. 428–439. IEEE (1990). https://doi.org/10.1109/LICS.1990.113767
51. Calcagno, C., Distefano, D., Dubreil, J., Gabi, D., Hooimeijer, P., Luca, M., O'Hearn, P.W., Papakonstantinou, I., Purbrick, J., Rodriguez, D.: Moving fast with software verification. In: Proc. NFM. pp. 3–11. LNCS 9058, Springer (2015). https://doi.org/10.1007/978-3-319-17524-9_1
52. Calcagno, C., Distefano, D., O'Hearn, P.W., Yang, H.: Compositional shape analysis by means of bi-abduction. ACM **58**(6), 26:1–26:66 (2011). https://doi.org/10.1145/2049697.2049700
53. Cassez, F., Matsuoka, T., Pierzchalski, E., Smyth, N.: PERENTIE: Modular trace refinement and selective value tracking (competition contribution). In: Proc. TACAS. pp. 439–442. LNCS 9035, Springer (2015). https://doi.org/10.1007/978-3-662-46681-0_39
54. Cassez, F., Sloane, A.M., Roberts, M., Pigram, M., Suvanpong, P., de Aledo Marugán, P.G.: SKINK: Static analysis of programs in LLVM intermediate representation (competition contribution). In: Proc. TACAS. pp. 380–384. LNCS 10206, Springer (2017). https://doi.org/10.1007/978-3-662-54580-5_27
55. Chalupa, M., Strejček, J., Vitovská, M.: Joint forces for memory safety checking. In: Proc. SPIN. pp. 115–132. Springer (2018). https://doi.org/10.1007/978-3-319-94111-0_7
56. Chalupa, M., Řechtáčková, A., Mihalkovič, V., Zaoral, L., Strejček, J.: SYMBIOTIC 9: String analysis and backward symbolic execution with loop folding (competition contribution). In: Proc. TACAS (2). pp. 462–467. LNCS 13244, Springer (2022). https://doi.org/10.1007/978-3-030-99527-0_32
57. Chaudhary, E., Joshi, S.: PINAKA: Symbolic execution meets incremental solving (competition contribution). In: Proc. TACAS (3). pp. 234–238. LNCS 11429, Springer (2019). https://doi.org/10.1007/978-3-030-17502-3_20
58. Chen, Y.F., Hsieh, C., Lengál, O., Lii, T.J., Tsai, M.H., Wang, B.Y., Wang, F.: PAC learning-based verification and model synthesis. In: Proc. ICSE. pp. 714–724. ACM (2016). https://doi.org/10.1145/2884781.2884860

59. Chen, Y.F., Hsieh, C., Tsai, M.H., Wang, B.Y., Wang, F.: CPAREC: Verifying recursive programs via source-to-source program transformation (competition contribution). In: Proc. TACAS. pp. 426–428. LNCS 9035, Springer (2015). https://doi.org/10.1007/978-3-662-46681-0_35

60. Chowdhury, A.B., Medicherla, R.K., Venkatesh, R.: VERIFUZZ: Program-aware fuzzing (competition contribution). In: Proc. TACAS (3). pp. 244–249. LNCS 11429, Springer (2019). https://doi.org/10.1007/978-3-030-17502-3_22

61. Christ, J., Hoenicke, J., Nutz, A.: SMTINTERPOL: An interpolating SMT solver. In: Proc. SPIN. pp. 248–254. LNCS 7385, Springer (2012). https://doi.org/10.1007/978-3-642-31759-0_19

62. Church, A.: A note on the Entscheidungsproblem. Journal of Symbolic Logic $\mathbf{1}(1)$, 40–41 (1936). https://doi.org/10.2307/2269326

63. Cimatti, A., Griggio, A.: Software model checking via IC3. In: Proc. CAV. pp. 277–293. LNCS 7358, Springer (2012). https://doi.org/10.1007/978-3-642-31424-7_23

64. Cimatti, A., Griggio, A., Mover, S., Tonetta, S.: Infinite-state invariant checking with IC3 and predicate abstraction. Formal Methods in System Design $\mathbf{49}(3)$, 190–218 (2016). https://doi.org/10.1007/s10703-016-0257-4

65. Clarke, E.M., Grumberg, O., Jha, S., Lu, Y., Veith, H.: Counterexample-guided abstraction refinement. In: Proc. CAV. pp. 154–169. LNCS 1855, Springer (2000). https://doi.org/10.1007/10722167_15

66. Clarke, E.M., Grumberg, O., Jha, S., Lu, Y., Veith, H.: Counterexample-guided abstraction refinement for symbolic model checking. J. ACM $\mathbf{50}(5)$, 752–794 (2003). https://doi.org/10.1145/876638.876643

67. Clarke, E.M., Henzinger, T.A., Veith, H., Bloem, R.: Handbook of Model Checking. Springer (2018). https://doi.org/10.1007/978-3-319-10575-8

68. Clarke, E.M., Emerson, E.A.: Design and synthesis of synchronization skeletons using branching-time temporal logic. In: Proc. Logic of Programs 1981. pp. 52–71. LNCS 131, Springer (1982). https://doi.org/10.1007/BFb0025774

69. Cook, B.: Formal reasoning about the security of Amazon web services. In: Proc. CAV (2). pp. 38–47. LNCS 10981, Springer (2018). https://doi.org/10.1007/978-3-319-96145-3_3

70. Cook, B., Podelski, A., Rybalchenko, A.: TERMINATOR: Beyond safety. In: Proc. CAV. pp. 415–418. LNCS 4144, Springer (2006). https://doi.org/10.1007/11817963_37

71. Cordeiro, L.C., Kesseli, P., Kröning, D., Schrammel, P., Trtík, M.: JBMC: A bounded model checking tool for verifying Java bytecode. In: Proc. CAV. pp. 183–190. LNCS 10981, Springer (2018). https://doi.org/10.1007/978-3-319-96145-3_10

72. Cordeiro, L.C., Kröning, D., Schrammel, P.: JBMC: Bounded model checking for Java bytecode (competition contribution). In: Proc. TACAS (3). pp. 219–223. LNCS 11429, Springer (2019). https://doi.org/10.1007/978-3-030-17502-3_17

73. Coto, A., Inverso, O., Sales, E., Tuosto, E.: A prototype for data race detection in CSEQ 3 (competition contribution). In: Proc. TACAS (2). pp. 413–417. LNCS 13244, Springer (2022). https://doi.org/10.1007/978-3-030-99527-0_23

74. Cousot, P., Cousot, R.: Systematic design of program-analysis frameworks. In: Proc. POPL. pp. 269–282. ACM (1979). https://doi.org/10.1145/567752.567778

75. Craig, W.: Linear reasoning. A new form of the Herbrand-Gentzen theorem. J. Symb. Log. $\mathbf{22}(3)$, 250–268 (1957). https://doi.org/10.2307/2963593

76. Cuoq, P., Kirchner, F., Kosmatov, N., Prevosto, V., Signoles, J., Yakobowski, B.: Frama-C. In: Proc. SEFM. pp. 233–247. Springer (2012). https://doi.org/10.1007/978-3-642-33826-7_16

77. Dangl, M., Löwe, S., Wendler, P.: CPACHECKER with support for recursive programs and floating-point arithmetic (competition contribution). In: Proc. TACAS. pp. 423–425. LNCS 9035, Springer (2015). https://doi.org/10.1007/978-3-662-46681-0_34

78. Darke, P., Agrawal, S., Venkatesh, R.: VERIABS: A tool for scalable verification by abstraction (competition contribution). In: Proc. TACAS (2). pp. 458–462. LNCS 12652, Springer (2021). https://doi.org/10.1007/978-3-030-72013-1_32

79. Davis, M., Logemann, G., Loveland, D.: A machine program for theorem proving. Commun. ACM 5(7), 394–397 (1962). https://doi.org/10.1145/368273.368557

80. Davis, M., Putnam, H.: A computing procedure for quantification theory. J. ACM 7(3), 201–215 (1960). https://doi.org/10.1145/321033.321034

81. Detlefs, D., Nelson, G., Saxe, J.B.: SIMPLIFY: A theorem prover for program checking. J. ACM 52(3), 365–473 (2005). https://doi.org/10.1145/1066100.1066102

82. Dijkstra, E.W.: A constructive approach to the problem of program correctness. BIT Numerical Mathematics 8, 174–186 (1968). https://doi.org/10.1007/BF01933419

83. Dijkstra, E.W.: Guarded commands, nondeterminacy, and formal derivation of programs. Comm. ACM 18(8), 453–457 (1975). https://doi.org/10.1145/360933.360975

84. Dockins, R., Foltzer, A., Hendrix, J., Huffman, B., McNamee, D., Tomb, A.: Constructing semantic models of programs with the software analysis workbench. In: Proc. VSTTE. pp. 56–72. LNCS 9971, Springer (2016). https://doi.org/10.1007/978-3-319-48869-1_5

85. D'Silva, V., Kröning, D., Weissenbacher, G.: A survey of automated techniques for formal software verification. IEEE Trans. on CAD of Integrated Circuits and Systems 27(7), 1165–1178 (2008). https://doi.org/10.1109/TCAD.2008.923410

86. Ernst, G.: A complete approach to loop verification with invariants and summaries. Tech. Rep. arXiv:2010.05812v2, arXiv (January 2020). https://doi.org/10.48550/arXiv.2010.05812

87. Falke, S., Merz, F., Sinz, C.: LLBMC: Improved bounded model checking of C programs using LLVM (competition contribution). In: Proc. TACAS. pp. 623–626. LNCS 7795, Springer (2013). https://doi.org/10.1007/978-3-642-36742-7_48

88. Flanagan, C., Leino, K.R.M., Lillibridge, M., Nelson, G., Saxe, J.B., Stata, R.: Extended static checking for Java. In: Proc. PLDI. pp. 234–245. ACM (2002). https://doi.org/10.1145/512529.512558

89. Floyd, R.W.: Assigning meanings to programs. Mathematical Aspects of Computer Science, Proc. Symposia in Applied Mathematics 19, 19–32 (1967), Republished: https://doi.org/10.1007/978-94-011-1793-7_4

90. Gadelha, M.Y.R., Monteiro, F.R., Cordeiro, L.C., Nicole, D.A.: ESBMC v6.0: Verifying C programs using k-induction and invariant inference (competition contribution). In: Proc. TACAS (3). pp. 209–213. LNCS 11429, Springer (2019). https://doi.org/10.1007/978-3-030-17502-3_15

91. Gadelha, M.Y.R., Ismail, H.I., Cordeiro, L.C.: Handling loops in bounded model checking of C programs via k-induction. Int. J. Softw. Tools Technol. Transf. 19(1), 97–114 (2015). https://doi.org/10.1007/s10009-015-0407-9

92. Garavel, H., ter Beek, M.H., van de Pol, J.: The 2020 expert survey on formal methods. In: Proc. FMICS. pp. 3–69. LNCS 12327, Springer (2020). https://doi.org/10.1007/978-3-030-58298-2_1

93. Gavrilenko, N., Ponce de León, H., Furbach, F., Heljanko, K., Meyer, R.: BMC for weak memory models: Relation analysis for compact SMT encodings. In: Proc. CAV. pp. 355–365. LNCS 11561, Springer (2019). https://doi.org/10.1007/978-3-030-25540-4_19

94. Giesl, J., Mesnard, F., Rubio, A., Thiemann, R., Waldmann, J.: Termination competition (termCOMP 2015). In: Proc. CADE. pp. 105–108. LNCS 9195, Springer (2015). https://doi.org/10.1007/978-3-319-21401-6_6

95. Gilmore, P.C.: A proof method for quantification theory: Its justification and realization. IBM J. Res. Dev. 4(1), 28–35 (1960). https://doi.org/10.1147/rd.41.0028

96. Graf, S., Saïdi, H.: Construction of abstract state graphs with Pvs. In: Proc. CAV. pp. 72–83. LNCS 1254, Springer (1997). https://doi.org/10.1007/3-540-63166-6_10

97. Grebenshchikov, S., Gupta, A., Lopes, N.P., Popeea, C., Rybalchenko, A.: Hsf(c): A software verifier based on Horn clauses (competition contribution). In: Proc. TACAS. pp. 549–551. LNCS 7214, Springer (2012). https://doi.org/10.1007/978-3-642-28756-5_46

98. Gurfinkel, A., Albarghouthi, A., Chaki, S., Li, Y., Chechik, M.: UFO: Verification with interpolants and abstract interpretation (competition contribution). In: Proc. TACAS. pp. 637–640. LNCS 7795, Springer (2013). https://doi.org/10.1007/978-3-642-36742-7_52

99. Gurfinkel, A., Belov, A.: FRANKENBIT: Bit-precise verification with many bits (competition contribution). In: Proc. TACAS. pp. 408–411. LNCS 8413, Springer (2014). https://doi.org/10.1007/978-3-642-54862-8_32

100. Gurfinkel, A., Kahsai, T., Navas, J.A.: SEAHORN: A framework for verifying C programs (competition contribution). In: Proc. TACAS. pp. 447–450. LNCS 9035, Springer (2015). https://doi.org/10.1007/978-3-662-46681-0_41

101. Gödel, K.: Über formal unentscheidbare sätze der principia mathematica und verwandter systeme i. Monatsh. f. Mathematik und Physik 38(1), 173–198 (1931). https://doi.org/10.1007/BF01700692

102. Günther, H., Laarman, A., Weissenbacher, G.: Vienna Verification Tool: IC3 for parallel software (competition contribution). In: Proc. TACAS. pp. 954–957. LNCS 9636, Springer (2016). https://doi.org/10.1007/978-3-662-49674-9_69

103. Hajdu, Á., Micskei, Z.: Efficient strategies for CEGAR-based model checking. J. Autom. Reasoning 64(6), 1051–1091 (2019). https://doi.org/10.1007/s10817-019-09535-x

104. Haran, A., Carter, M., Emmi, M., Lal, A., Qadeer, S., Rakamarić, Z.: SMACK+CORRAL: A modular verifier (competition contribution). In: Proc. TACAS. pp. 451–454. LNCS 9035, Springer (2015). https://doi.org/10.1007/978-3-662-46681-0_42

105. He, F., Sun, Z., Fan, H.: DEAGLE: An SMT-based verifier for multi-threaded programs (competition contribution). In: Proc. TACAS (2). pp. 424–428. LNCS 13244, Springer (2022). https://doi.org/10.1007/978-3-030-99527-0_25

106. Heibi, I., Peroni, S., Shotton, D.: Software review: COCI, the OpenCitations Index of Crossref open DOI-to-DOI citations. Scientometrics 121(2), 1213–1228 (11 2019). https://doi.org/10.1007/s11192-019-03217-6

107. Heizmann, M., Chen, Y.F., Dietsch, D., Greitschus, M., Hoenicke, J., Li, Y., Nutz, A., Musa, B., Schilling, C., Schindler, T., Podelski, A.: ULTIMATE AUTOMIZER and the search for perfect interpolants (competition contribution). In: Proc. TACAS (2). pp. 447–451. LNCS 10806, Springer (2018). https://doi.org/10.1007/978-3-319-89963-3_30

108. Heizmann, M., Hoenicke, J., Podelski, A.: Refinement of trace abstraction. In: Proc. SAS. pp. 69–85. LNCS 5673, Springer (2009). https://doi.org/10.1007/978-3-642-03237-0_7

109. Heizmann, M., Hoenicke, J., Podelski, A.: Software model checking for people who love automata. In: Proc. CAV. pp. 36–52. LNCS 8044, Springer (2013). https://doi.org/10.1007/978-3-642-39799-8_2

110. Hensel, J., Mensendiek, C., Giesl, J.: AProVE: Non-termination witnesses for C programs (competition contribution). In: Proc. TACAS (2). pp. 403–407. LNCS 13244, Springer (2022). https://doi.org/10.1007/978-3-030-99527-0_21

111. Henzinger, T.A., Jhala, R., Majumdar, R., McMillan, K.L.: Abstractions from proofs. In: Proc. POPL. pp. 232–244. ACM (2004). https://doi.org/10.1145/964001.964021

112. Henzinger, T.A., Jhala, R., Majumdar, R., Sutre, G.: Lazy abstraction. In: Proc. POPL. pp. 58–70. ACM (2002). https://doi.org/10.1145/503272.503279

113. Hilbert, D.: Mathematische Probleme. Vortrag, gehalten auf dem internationalen Mathematiker-Kongreß zu Paris 1900. Nachrichten von der Königl. Gesellschaft der Wissenschaften zu Göttingen. Mathematisch-Physikalische Klasse. **1900**(3), 253–297 (1900), https://www.deutschestextarchiv.de/book/show/hilbert_mathematische_1900

114. Hoare, C.A.R.: An axiomatic basis for computer programming. Commun. ACM **12**(10), 576–580 (1969). https://doi.org/10.1145/363235.363259

115. Holík, L., Hruška, M., Lengál, O., Rogalewicz, A., Simácek, J., Vojnar, T.: Forester: From heap shapes to automata predicates (competition contribution). In: Proc. TACAS. pp. 365–369. LNCS 10206, Springer (2017). https://doi.org/10.1007/978-3-662-54580-5_24

116. Holík, L., Kotoun, M., Peringer, P., Šoková, V., Trtík, M., Vojnar, T.: Predator shape analysis tool suite. In: Hardware and Software: Verification and Testing. pp. 202–209. LNCS 10028, Springer (2016). https://doi.org/10.1007/978-3-319-49052-6

117. Holzer, A., Kröning, D., Schallhart, C., Tautschnig, M., Veith, H.: Proving reachability using FShell (competition contribution). In: Proc. TACAS. pp. 538–541. LNCS 7214, Springer (2012). https://doi.org/10.1007/978-3-642-28756-5_43

118. Howar, F., Isberner, M., Merten, M., Steffen, B., Beyer, D.: The RERS grey-box challenge 2012: Analysis of event-condition-action systems. In: Proc. ISoLA. pp. 608–614. LNCS 7609, Springer (2012). https://doi.org/10.1007/978-3-642-34026-0_45

119. Huisman, M., Klebanov, V., Monahan, R.: VerifyThis 2012: A program verification competition. STTT **17**(6), 647–657 (2015). https://doi.org/10.1007/s10009-015-0396-8

120. Inverso, O., Trubiani, C.: Parallel and distributed bounded model checking of multi-threaded programs. In: Proc. PPoPP. pp. 202–216. ACM (2020). https://doi.org/10.1145/3332466.3374529

121. Jhala, R., Majumdar, R.: Software model checking. ACM Computing Surveys **41**(4) (2009). https://doi.org/10.1145/1592434.1592438

122. Kahsai, T., Rümmer, P., Sanchez, H., Schäf, M.: JayHorn: A framework for verifying Java programs. In: Proc. CAV. pp. 352–358. LNCS 9779, Springer (2016). https://doi.org/10.1007/978-3-319-41528-4_19

123. Karpenkov, E.G., Monniaux, D., Wendler, P.: Program analysis with local policy iteration. In: Proc. VMCAI. pp. 127–146. LNCS 9583, Springer (2016). https://doi.org/10.1007/978-3-662-49122-5_6

124. Kettl, M., Lemberger, T.: The static analyzer INFER in SV-COMP (competition contribution). In: Proc. TACAS (2). pp. 451–456. LNCS 13244, Springer (2022). https://doi.org/10.1007/978-3-030-99527-0_30

125. Khoroshilov, A.V., Mutilin, V.S., Petrenko, A.K., Zakharov, V.: Establishing Linux driver verification process. In: Proc. Ershov Memorial Conference. pp. 165–176. LNCS 5947, Springer (2009). https://doi.org/10.1007/978-3-642-11486-1_14

126. Kildall, G.A.: A unified approach to global program optimization. In: Proc. POPL. pp. 194–206. ACM (1973). https://doi.org/10.1145/512927.512945

127. Kröning, D., Tautschnig, M.: CBMC: C bounded model checker (competition contribution). In: Proc. TACAS. pp. 389–391. LNCS 8413, Springer (2014). https://doi.org/10.1007/978-3-642-54862-8_26

128. Kröning, D., Weissenbacher, G.: Interpolation-based software verification with Wolverine. In: Proc. CAV. pp. 573–578. LNCS 6806, Springer (2011). https://doi.org/10.1007/978-3-642-22110-1_45

129. Lahiri, S.K., Nieuwenhuis, R., Oliveras, A.: SMT techniques for fast predicate abstraction. In: Proc. CAV. pp. 424–437. LNCS 4144, Springer (2006). https://doi.org/10.1007/11817963_39

130. Lange, T., Prinz, F., Neuhäußer, M.R., Noll, T., Katoen, J.: Improving generalization in software IC3. In: Proc. SPIN'18. pp. 85–102. LNCS 10869, Springer (2018). https://doi.org/10.1007/978-3-319-94111-0_5

131. Lange, T., Neuhäußer, M.R., Noll, T.: IC3 software model checking on control flow automata. In: Proc. FMCAD. pp. 97–104 (2015)

132. Lauko, H., Ročkai, P., Barnat, J.: Symbolic computation via program transformation. In: Proc. ICTAC. pp. 313–332. Springer (2018). https://doi.org/10.1007/978-3-030-02508-3_17

133. Lauko, H., Ročkai, P.: LART: Compiled abstract execution (competition contribution). In: Proc. TACAS (2). pp. 457–461. LNCS 13244, Springer (2022). https://doi.org/10.1007/978-3-030-99527-0_31

134. Lauko, H., Ročkai, P., Barnat, J.: Symbolic computation via program transformation. In: Proc. ICTAC. pp. 313–332. LNCS 11187, Springer (2018). https://doi.org/10.1007/978-3-030-02508-3_17

135. Le, Q.L., Tran, M., Chin, W.N.: HIPrec: Verifying recursive programs with a satisfiability solver (2016), https://loc.bitbucket.io/papers/hiprec.pdf

136. Le, T.C., Ta, Q.T., Chin, W.N.: HIPTNT+: A termination and non-termination analyzer by second-order abduction (competition contribution). In: Proc. TACAS. pp. 370–374. LNCS 10206, Springer (2017). https://doi.org/10.1007/978-3-662-54580-5_25

137. Lee, C.Y.: Representation of switching circuits by binary-decision programs. Bell Syst. Tech. J. **38**(4), 985–999 (1959). https://doi.org/10.1002/j.1538-7305.1959.tb01585.x

138. Leeson, W., Dwyer, M.: GRAVES-CPA: A graph-attention verifier selector (competition contribution). In: Proc. TACAS (2). pp. 440–445. LNCS 13244, Springer (2022). https://doi.org/10.1007/978-3-030-99527-0_28

139. Leino, K.R.M., Nelson, G.: An extended static checker for Modula-3. In: Proc. CC. pp. 302–305. LNCS 1383, Springer (1998). https://doi.org/10.1007/BFb0026441

140. Luckow, K.S., Dimjasevic, M., Giannakopoulou, D., Howar, F., Isberner, M., Kahsai, T., Rakamaric, Z., Raman, V.: JDART: A dynamic symbolic analysis framework. In: Proc. TACAS. pp. 442–459. LNCSS 9636, Springer (2016). https://doi.org/10.1007/978-3-662-49674-9_26

141. Malík, V., Schrammel, P., Vojnar, T.: 2LS: Heap analysis and memory safety (competition contribution). In: Proc. TACAS (2). pp. 368–372. LNCS 12079, Springer (2020). https://doi.org/10.1007/978-3-030-45237-7_22

142. Manna, Z., Pnueli, A.: Temporal verification of reactive systems: Safety. Springer (1995). https://doi.org/10.1007/978-1-4612-4222-2

143. McCarthy, J.: Towards a mathematical science of computation. In: Information Processing, Proc. DFIP Congress. pp. 21–28. North-Holland (1962), Republished: https://doi.org/10.1007/978-94-011-1793-7_2

144. McMillan, K.L.: Symbolic Model Checking. Springer (1993). https://doi.org/10.1007/978-1-4615-3190-6

145. McMillan, K.L.: Interpolation and SAT-based model checking. In: Proc. CAV. pp. 1–13. LNCS 2725, Springer (2003). https://doi.org/10.1007/978-3-540-45069-6_1

146. McMillan, K.L.: An interpolating theorem prover. Theor. Comput. Sci. **345**(1), 101–121 (2005). https://doi.org/10.1016/j.tcs.2005.07.003

147. McMillan, K.L.: Interpolation and model checking. In: Handbook of Model Checking, pp. 421–446. Springer (2018). https://doi.org/10.1007/978-3-319-10575-8_14

148. Metta, R., Medicherla, R.K., Chakraborty, S.: BMC+Fuzz: Efficient and effective test generation. In: Proc. DATE. pp. 1419–1424. IEEE (2022). https://doi.org/10.23919/DATE54114.2022.9774672

149. Moskewicz, M.W., Madigan, C.F., Zhao, Y., Zhang, L., Malik, S.: Chaff: Engineering an efficient SAT solver. In: Proc. DAC. pp. 530–535. ACM (2001). https://doi.org/10.1145/378239.379017

150. Mues, M., Howar, F.: JDART: Portfolio solving, breadth-first search and SMT-Lib strings (competition contribution). In: Proc. TACAS (2). pp. 448–452. LNCS 12652, Springer (2021). https://doi.org/10.1007/978-3-030-72013-1_30

151. Mues, M., Howar, F.: GDart (competition contribution). In: Proc. TACAS (2). pp. 435–439. LNCS 13244, Springer (2022). https://doi.org/10.1007/978-3-030-99527-0_27

152. Müller, P., Vojnar, T.: CPALIEN: Shape analyzer for CPACHECKER (competition contribution). In: Proc. TACAS. pp. 395–397. LNCS 8413, Springer (2014). https://doi.org/10.1007/978-3-642-54862-8_28

153. Nelson, G., Oppen, D.C.: Simplification by cooperating decision procedures. ACM Trans. Program. Lang. Syst. **1**(2), 245–257 (1979). https://doi.org/10.1145/357073.357079

154. Nelson, G., Oppen, D.C.: Fast decision procedures based on congruence closure. J. ACM **27**(2), 356–364 (1980). https://doi.org/10.1145/322186.322198

155. Nielson, F., Nielson, H.R., Hankin, C.: Principles of Program Analysis. Springer (1999). https://doi.org/10.1007/978-3-662-03811-6

156. Noller, Y., Păsăreanu, C.S., Le, X.B.D., Visser, W., Fromherz, A.: Symbolic PATHFINDER for SV-COMP (competition contribution). In: Proc. TACAS (3). pp. 239–243. LNCS 11429, Springer (2019). https://doi.org/10.1007/978-3-030-17502-3_21

157. OpenCitations: COCI CSV dataset of all the citation data, version 16 (2022). https://doi.org/10.6084/m9.figshare.6741422.v16

158. Peano, G.: Arithmetices Principia: Nova Methodo Exposita. Fratres Bocca (1889), https://n2t.net/ark:/13960/t0xp7g625

159. Peringer, P., Šoková, V., Vojnar, T.: PREDATORHP revamped (not only) for interval-sized memory regions and memory reallocation (competition contribution). In: Proc. TACAS (2). pp. 408–412. LNCS 12079, Springer (2020). https://doi.org/10.1007/978-3-030-45237-7_30

160. Piterman, N., Pnueli, A.: Temporal logic and fair discrete systems. In: Handbook of Model Checking, pp. 27–73. Springer (2018). https://doi.org/10.1007/978-3-319-10575-8_2

161. Podelski, A., Rybalchenko, A.: A complete method for the synthesis of linear ranking functions. In: Proc. VMCAI. pp. 239–251. LNCS 2937, Springer (2004). https://doi.org/10.1007/978-3-540-24622-0_20

162. Podelski, A., Rybalchenko, A.: Transition predicate abstraction and fair termination. In: Proc. POPL. pp. 132–144. ACM (2005). https://doi.org/10.1145/1040305.1040317

163. Ponce-De-Leon, H., Haas, T., Meyer, R.: DARTAGNAN: Leveraging compiler optimizations and the price of precision (competition contribution). In: Proc. TACAS (2). pp. 428–432. LNCS 12652, Springer (2021). https://doi.org/10.1007/978-3-030-72013-1_26

164. Popeea, C., Rybalchenko, A.: THREADER: A verifier for multi-threaded programs (competition contribution). In: Proc. TACAS. pp. 633–636. LNCS 7795, Springer (2013). https://doi.org/10.1007/978-3-642-36742-7_51

165. Pratikakis, P., Foster, J.S., Hicks, M.: LOCKSMITH: Practical static race detection for C. ACM Trans. Program. Lang. Syst. **33**(1) (January 2011). https://doi.org/10.1145/1889997.1890000

166. Prawitz, D.: An improved proof procedure. Theoria **26**(2), 102–139 (1960). https://doi.org/10.1111/j.1755-2567.1960.tb00558.x

167. Presburger, M.: Über die Vollständigkeit eines gewissen Systems der Arithmetik ganzer Zahlen, in welchem die Addition als einzige Operation hervortritt. Comptes Rendus du I Congrès de Mathématiciens des Pays Slaves, Warszawa pp. 92–101 (1929)

168. Păsăreanu, C.S., Visser, W., Bushnell, D.H., Geldenhuys, J., Mehlitz, P.C., Rungta, N.: Symbolic PathFinder: integrating symbolic execution with model checking for Java bytecode analysis. Autom. Software Eng. **20**(3), 391–425 (2013). https://doi.org/10.1007/s10515-013-0122-2

169. Queille, J.P., Sifakis, J.: Specification and verification of concurrent systems in CESAR. In: Proc. Symposium on Programming. pp. 337–351. LNCS 137, Springer (1982). https://doi.org/10.1007/3-540-11494-7_22

170. Quine, W.V.: A proof procedure for quantification theory. J. Symbolic Logic **20**(2), 141–149 (1955). https://doi.org/10.2307/2266900

171. Quiring, B., Manolios, P.: GACAL: Conjecture-based verification (competition contribution). In: Proc. TACAS (2). pp. 388–392. LNCS 12079, Springer (2020). https://doi.org/10.1007/978-3-030-45237-7_26

172. Rajkhowa, P., Lin, F.: VIAP 1.1 (competition contribution). In: Proc. TACAS (3). pp. 250–255. LNCS 11429, Springer (2019). https://doi.org/10.1007/978-3-030-17502-3_23

173. Rakamarić, Z., Emmi, M.: SMACK: Decoupling source language details from verifier implementations. In: Proc. CAV. pp. 106–113. LNCS 8559, Springer (2014). https://doi.org/10.1007/978-3-319-08867-9_7

174. Richter, C., Hüllermeier, E., Jakobs, M.C., Wehrheim, H.: Algorithm selection for software validation based on graph kernels. Autom. Softw. Eng. **27**(1), 153–186 (2020). https://doi.org/10.1007/s10515-020-00270-x

175. Richter, C., Wehrheim, H.: PESCo: Predicting sequential combinations of verifiers (competition contribution). In: Proc. TACAS (3). pp. 229–233. LNCS 11429, Springer (2019). https://doi.org/10.1007/978-3-030-17502-3_19

176. Rocha, H.O., Barreto, R.S., Cordeiro, L.C.: Memory management test-case generation of C programs using bounded model checking. In: Proc. SEFM. pp. 251–267. LNCS 9276, Springer (2015). https://doi.org/10.1007/978-3-319-22969-0_18

177. Rocha, H.O., Ismail, H., Cordeiro, L.C., Barreto, R.S.: Model checking embedded C software using k-induction and invariants. In: Proc. SBESC. pp. 90–95. IEEE (2015). https://doi.org/10.1109/SBESC.2015.24

178. Rocha, H.O., Menezes, R., Cordeiro, L., Barreto, R.: MAP2CHECK: Using symbolic execution and fuzzing (competition contribution). In: Proc. TACAS (2). pp. 403–407. LNCS 12079, Springer (2020). https://doi.org/10.1007/978-3-030-45237-7_29

179. Rocha, W., Rocha, H.O., Ismail, H., Cordeiro, L.C., Fischer, B.: DEPTHK: A k-induction verifier based on invariant inference for C programs (competition contribution). In: Proc. TACAS. pp. 360–364. LNCS 10206, Springer (2017). https://doi.org/10.1007/978-3-662-54580-5_23

180. Rojas, R., Göktekin, C., Friedland, G., Krüger, M., Scharf, L., Kuniß, D., Langmack, O.: Konrad Zuses Plankalkül – Seine Genese und eine moderne Implementierung, pp. 215–235. Springer (2004). https://doi.org/10.1007/978-3-642-18631-8_9

181. Saan, S., Schwarz, M., Apinis, K., Erhard, J., Seidl, H., Vogler, R., Vojdani, V.: Goblint: Thread-modular abstract interpretation using side-effecting constraints (competition contribution). In: Proc. TACAS (2). pp. 438–442. LNCS 12652, Springer (2021). https://doi.org/10.1007/978-3-030-72013-1_28

182. Saarikivi, O., Heljanko, K.: LCTD: Tests-guided proofs for C programs on LLVM (competition contribution). In: Proc. TACAS. pp. 927–929. LNCS 9636, Springer (2016). https://doi.org/10.1007/978-3-662-49674-9_62

183. Scott, R., Dockins, R., Ravitch, T., Tomb, A.: CRUX: Symbolic execution meets SMT-based verification (competition contribution). Zenodo (February 2022). https://doi.org/10.5281/zenodo.6147218

184. Shamakhi, A., Hojjat, H., Rümmer, P.: Towards string support in JayHorn (competition contribution). In: Proc. TACAS (2). pp. 443–447. LNCS 12652, Springer (2021). https://doi.org/10.1007/978-3-030-72013-1_29

185. Shannon, C.E.: A symbolic analysis of relay and switching circuits. Transactions of the American Institute of Electrical Engineers **57**, 713–723 (1938). https://doi.org/10.1109/T-AIEE.1938.5057767

186. Sharma, V., Hussein, S., Whalen, M.W., McCamant, S.A., Visser, W.: Java Ranger at SV-COMP 2020 (competition contribution). In: Proc. TACAS (2). pp. 393–397. LNCS 12079, Springer (2020). https://doi.org/10.1007/978-3-030-45237-7_27

187. Sharma, V., Hussein, S., Whalen, M.W., McCamant, S.A., Visser, W.: JAVA RANGER: Statically summarizing regions for efficient symbolic execution of Java. In: Proc. ESEC/FSE. pp. 123–134. ACM (2020). https://doi.org/10.1145/3368089.3409734

188. Shved, P., Mandrykin, M.U., Mutilin, V.S.: Predicate analysis with BLAST 2.7 (competition contribution). In: Proc. TACAS. pp. 525–527. LNCS 7214, Springer (2012). https://doi.org/10.1007/978-3-642-28756-5_39

189. Ströder, T., Giesl, J., Brockschmidt, M., Frohn, F., Fuhs, C., Hensel, J., Schneider-Kamp, P., Aschermann, C.: Automatically Proving Termination and Memory Safety for Programs with Pointer Arithmetic. J. Autom. Reasoning **58**(1), 33–65 (2016). https://doi.org/10.1007/s10817-016-9389-x

190. Tóth, T., Hajdu, A., Vörös, A., Micskei, Z., Majzik, I.: THETA: A framework for abstraction refinement-based model checking. In: Proc. FMCAD. pp. 176–179 (2017). https://doi.org/10.23919/FMCAD.2017.8102257

191. Turing, A.: On computable numbers, with an application to the Entscheidungsproblem. In: Proc. LMS. vol. s2-42, pp. 230–265. London Mathematical Society (1937). https://doi.org/10.1112/plms/s2-42.1.230

192. Turing, A.: Checking a large routine. In: Report on a Conference on High Speed Automatic Calculating Machines. pp. 67–69. Cambridge Univ. Math. Lab. (1949), https://turingarchive.kings.cam.ac.uk/publications-lectures-and-talks-amtb/amt-b-8

193. Urban, C.: FUNCTION: An abstract domain functor for termination (competition contribution). In: Proc. TACAS. pp. 464–466. LNCS 9035, Springer (2015). https://doi.org/10.1007/978-3-662-46681-0_46

194. Visser, W., Geldenhuys, J.: COASTAL: Combining concolic and fuzzing for Java (competition contribution). In: Proc. TACAS (2). pp. 373–377. LNCS 12079, Springer (2020). https://doi.org/10.1007/978-3-030-45237-7_23

195. Visser, W., Havelund, K., Brat, G.P., Park, S., Lerda, F.: Model checking programs. Autom. Softw. Eng. **10**(2), 203–232 (2003). https://doi.org/10.1023/A:1022920129859

196. Vojdani, V., Apinis, K., Rõtov, V., Seidl, H., Vene, V., Vogler, R.: Static race detection for device drivers: The Goblint approach. In: Proc. ASE. pp. 391–402. ACM (2016). https://doi.org/10.1145/2970276.2970337

197. Volkov, A.R., Mandrykin, M.U.: Predicate abstractions memory modeling method with separation into disjoint regions. Proceedings of the Institute for System Programming (ISPRAS) **29**, 203–216 (2017). https://doi.org/10.15514/ISPRAS-2017-29(4)-13

198. Wang, W., Barrett, C.: CASCADE (competition contribution). In: Proc. TACAS. pp. 420–422. LNCS 9035, Springer (2015). https://doi.org/10.1007/978-3-662-46681-0_33

199. Weissenbacher, G., Kröning, D., Malik, S.: WOLVERINE: Battling bugs with interpolants (competition contribution). In: Proc. TACAS. pp. 556–558. LNCS 7214, Springer (2012). https://doi.org/10.1007/978-3-642-28756-5_48

200. Wirth, N.: Program development by stepwise refinement. Commun. ACM **14**(4), 221–227 (1971). https://doi.org/10.1145/362575.362577

201. Yin, L., Dong, W., Liu, W., Li, Y., Wang, J.: YOGAR-CBMC: CBMC with scheduling constraint based abstraction refinement (competition contribution). In: Proc. TACAS. pp. 422–426. LNCS 10806, Springer (2018). https://doi.org/10.1007/978-3-319-89963-3_25

202. Yin, L., Dong, W., Liu, W., Wang, J.: On scheduling constraint abstraction for multi-threaded program verification. IEEE Trans. Softw. Eng. (2018). https://doi.org/10.1109/TSE.2018.2864122

203. Zheng, M., Edenhofner, J.G., Luo, Z., Gerrard, M.J., Dwyer, M.B., Siegel, S.F.: CIVL: Applying a general concurrency verification framework to C/Pthreads programs (competition contribution). In: Proc. TACAS. pp. 908–911. LNCS 9636, Springer (2016). https://doi.org/10.1007/978-3-662-49674-9_57

204. Ádám, Z., Bajczi, L., Dobos-Kovács, M., Hajdu, A., Molnár, V.: THETA: Portfolio of cegar-based analyses with dynamic algorithm selection (competition contribution). In: Proc. TACAS (2). pp. 474–478. LNCS 13244, Springer (2022). https://doi.org/10.1007/978-3-030-99527-0_34

Artificial Intelligence and Machine Learning

T4V: Exploring Neural Network Architectures that Improve the Scalability of Neural Network Verification

Vivian Lin[1(✉)], Radoslav Ivanov[2], James Weimer[1], Oleg Sokolsky[1],
and Insup Lee[1]

[1] PRECISE Center, University of Pennsylvania, Philadelphia, PA 19104, USA
{vilin,weimerj,sokolsky,lee}@seas.upenn.edu
[2] Computer Science Department, Rensselaer Polytechnic Institute,
Troy, NY 12180, USA
ivanor@rpi.edu

Abstract. This paper focuses on improving the scalability of NN verification through exploring which NN architectures lead to more scalable verification. We propose a general framework for incorporating verification scalability in the training process by identifying NN properties that improve verification and incentivizing these properties through a verification loss. One natural application of our method is robustness verification, especially using tools based on interval analysis, which have shown great promise in recent years. Specifically, we show that we can greatly reduce the approximation error of interval analysis by forcing all (or most) NNs to have the same sign. Finally, we provide an extensive evaluation on the MNIST and CIFAR-10 datasets in order to illustrate the benefit of training for verification.

1 Introduction

In the past several years, deep learning has shown great promise in traditionally challenging learning tasks such as image classification [38], natural language processing [5] and reinforcement learning [30]. Due to this impressive performance, neural networks (NNs) are also increasingly being used in safety-critical systems such as autonomous vehicles [2] and air traffic collision avoidance systems [21]. At the same time, however, researchers have discovered numerous robustness issues with NNs, e.g., adversarial examples where small input perturbations may lead to drastic changes in the NN outputs [37]. Since such issues might compromise the safety of NN-based systems, it is essential to verify the safety of NN components at design time, before these systems are deployed at large.

There has been a significant amount of work in the last few years on analyzing the safety of NNs [7,9–11,15,22,41–43,47]. However, although these methods employ a variety of techniques, scalability remains a major obstacle to applying any such method to realistic systems. For example, verifying even simple

---

R. Ivanov—Work was done while Radoslav was a postdoc fellow at the University of Pennsylvania.

© Springer Nature Switzerland AG 2022
J.-F. Raskin and K. Chatterjee (Eds.): Principles of Systems Design, LNCS 13660, pp. 585–603, 2022.
https://doi.org/10.1007/978-3-031-22337-2_28

input-output properties such as interval constraints on the inputs and outputs of fully-connected NNs with rectified linear units (ReLUs) is known to be NP-complete (exponential both in the number of inputs and the number of neurons in the NN) [22,34]. To get around this challenge, researchers have developed a number of useful heuristics such as combining interval analysis with linear programming [42] in order to make use of optimized solvers such as Gurobi [32].

As researchers continue to propose better tools through effective heuristics and implementations, an orthogonal approach to alleviating the scalability challenge is through exploring the properties of NN architectures that result in more scalable verification by existing tools and their corresponding heuristics [16,18]. However, there exists no formal general procedure of incorporating such properties into the training process and explicitly analyzing the trade-offs between verifiability (i.e., verification scalability) and the original property that the NN was trained for (e.g., classification accuracy).

In this paper, we propose to incorporate verifiability into the training process, through a method called *training for verification* (T4V). Such an approach can in principle be added to any training task. The high-level idea is as follows: suppose the original training loss, L_o, is designed to achieve a desired property, ϕ_o, such as classification accuracy and robustness; the goal is to identify an NN architecture property ϕ_v that results in more scalable verification and a corresponding loss L_v that can be added to L_o during training. Thus, by assigning different weights to L_o and L_v, one can explore the trade-off between verifiability and the original property and choose a desired setting.

To illustrate the process of T4V, we note that the verifiability property ϕ_v depends greatly on the specific verification approach. For example, as mentioned above, having a small Lipschitz constant is desirable for sampling-based methods [16]. In this work, we focus on approaches based on interval analysis since those tools have shown promising results in both open-loop [39,42,47] and closed-loop settings [18]. We have identified an important verifiability property related to interval analysis, namely that all (or most) NN weights in any layer should have the same sign. We show theoretically and through examples that if this property does not hold, then interval analysis can result in drastic overapproximation error. Finally, we propose a corresponding loss function, L_v, that promotes same-sign weights through penalizing negative weights and that is added to the original loss, L_o, through a weighted average.

We evaluate the proposed method by training a number of NN architectures on the MNIST [24] and CIFAR-10 [23] datasets where the goal is to verify robustness properties of the trained NN using the interval-analysis-based tool Fast-and-Complete [47]. We show that in all cases one might achieve significant improvements in verifiability at a small cost in robustness and accuracy. Eventually, an inflection point is reached after which the gains in verifiability are offset by prohibitive loss in robustness and accuracy. Although we perform this evaluation on robustness verification, our proposed T4V framework can also be used for verifying properties other than robustness. Some examples of these other applications can be found in Sect. 4.

In summary, this paper has three contributions: 1) a general framework for T4V that explicitly incorporates verifiability in the training process; 2) an illustration of the framework on the robustness verification problem; 3) extensive evaluation on the MNIST and CIFAR-10 datasets.

2   Related Work

A number of directions have been studied by existing work on the NN safety problem. One type of approach is to train NNs so that they are guaranteed to satisfy some safety property. For example, robustness certification techniques [13,29,33,44,45] aim to compute an upper bound on the robustness of a NN, then minimize this bound during training by incorporating it into the loss function. However, these works do not provide guarantees on unseen data. A related method [8] proposes predictor-verifier training (PVT), in which a predictor NN learns a task and a verifier network learns a robustness bound on the predictor NN. Although this approach empirically improves NN robustness to adversarial examples, the learned robustness bound only provides an approximation of the true bound. Finally, another area of interest has been in training NNs that are correct by construction [25,28]. However, these methods only provide guarantees for global properties and are unable to provide local robustness guarantees during training.

Due to the challenges in training provably robust NNs, the formal verification of NNs after training is an important alternate approach to solving the NN safety problem. Several techniques exist to analyze the input-output properties of NNs: 1) casting the problem as a satisfiability modulo theory (SMT) program [15,22] or a mixed-integer linear program (MILP) [7,39,42,47]; 2) computing reachable sets for the NN outputs using various abstractions such as polyhedra [35], zonotopes [11], or star sets [41]; 3) estimating the NN Lipschitz constant [10] or the distance to the classification boundary for a given image [43] through relaxed linear or convex optimization programs. Furthermore, approaches have been developed for verifying the safety of closed-loop systems with NN controllers [6,16–20,36,40] by combining some of the above ideas with classical hybrid system reachability methods [4,14]. Despite this impressive progress, existing verification tools struggle to scale to the large size of NNs typical in real-world problems [22,34].

In response to the scalability issues of existing verification tools, a third type of approach to the NN safety problem has emerged. Specifically, many papers leverage various heuristics to make the formal verification of large NNs more attainable. For example, the verification tool Neurify [42] combines interval analysis with linear programming, which can be efficiently solved by existing optimization tools (e.g., Gurobi [32]). Other prior work is motivated by the observation that certain NN architectures are easier to verify by their proposed tools [16,18], e.g., NNs with smaller Lipschitz constants are better for sampling-based methods [16]. These techniques, which are perhaps the most relevant predecessors to T4V, train NNs to adopt properties that make them more amenable to verification by existing tools. One paper [46] identifies a heuristic, namely that NNs with ReLU activations are easier to verify when their ReLUs are stable for all possible perturbations of an input, and encodes it into the loss function during training. Another method [31] penalizes an interval bound on the output of the NN in the loss function, which (although originally intended to improve training stability in interval bound propagation [13]) inherently reduces the overapproximation error of interval analysis verification tools. Despite these advances, our T4V framework is the first formal general procedure for training NNs to adopt these properties and explicitly analyzing the trade-offs that result.

3   Preliminaries and Problem Statement

This section first introduces the standard approach to NN training and verification, with a focus on robustness verification tools. Finally, we state the T4V problem.

3.1   Standard NN Training

The standard classification setting can be summarized as follows: given a training dataset, $\mathcal{Z} = \{(x_0, y_0), \ldots, (x_N, y_N)\}$, of N examples $\{(x_0, \ldots, x_N\}$ (e.g., images) and corresponding labels $\{y_0, \ldots, y_N\}$, an NN f is selected from a family of NN architectures $\mathcal{F}$ so as to minimize some loss, $L_o : \mathcal{F} \times \mathcal{Z} \to \mathbb{R}$, such as negative log likelihood or least squares [12]. Typically, the family $\mathcal{F}$ is a parameterized set of NN architectures such that selecting f amounts to choosing the NN parameters, θ, that minimize L_o:

$$\min_{\theta} \sum_{i=1}^{N} L_o(f_\theta, (x_i, y_i)). \tag{1}$$

A large number of NN architectures have been proposed in the last several years, including fully-connected, convolutional, residual, etc. To simplify the presentation, in this paper we consider standard feedforward NNs, which includes fully-connected and convolutional NNs. Formally, a feedforward NN f can be represented as a composition of its M layers:

$$f(x) = f_M \circ f_{M-1} \circ \cdots \circ f_1(x), \tag{2}$$

where each layer $f_i(x) = \sigma_i(W_i x + b_i)$ performs a linear function with weight matrix W_i and biases b_i, followed by a non-linear activation σ_i, such as the ReLU: $\sigma_i(x) = \max(0, x)$. Note that the NN parameters $\theta := \{W_0, b_0, \ldots, W_M, b_M\}$ are identified during training as illustrated in (1). A classifier $f_c(x)$ can then be constructed from the neural network $f(x)$ by taking the argmax of its last layer:

$$f_c(x) = \text{argmax}_i \; f_i(x), \tag{3}$$

where $f_i(x)$ is the ith component of $f(x)$.

3.2   NN Verification

As discussed in the introduction, a number of formal verification methods have been developed recently to analyze various properties of trained NNs. The vast majority of these techniques were proposed for robustness analysis, as motivated by the discovery of adversarial examples [37]. In this work, we also focus on robustness verification as the main property of interest, though our proposed T4V method can be applied to any other property as well.

Robustness Property. Intuitively, an NN is robust if perturbing its inputs by a small amount leads to a correspondingly small change in the output. Since it is not feasible to compute robustness bounds for all inputs, existing methods focus on verifying robustness around a given example. Specifically, given an example x and a perturbation bound ϵ, the robustness verification problem is to establish whether there exists an ϵ-bounded perturbation of x that leads to a change in the label predicted by f_c Formally, given f_c, x, and ϵ, the robustness property is stated as follows:

$$\forall x' \in \mathcal{B}_\epsilon(x), f_c(x') = f_c(x), \tag{4}$$

where $\mathcal{B}_\epsilon(x) = \{x' \mid \|x' - x\|_\infty \leq \epsilon\}$ is an L_∞ ball around x.[1] Thus, the bigger the ϵ for which (4) holds, the more robust f_c is.

Verification Methods. As noted in the introduction, verifying (4) is NP-complete for fully-connected NNs with ReLU activations, exponential both in the number of inputs (i.e., the dimension of x) and in the number of neurons in f [22,34]. To circumvent this limitation, a variety of heuristics have been proposed, ranging from casting the problem as a MILP [7] to performing reachability analysis [41]. In this work, we focus on methods based on interval analysis [39,42,47] since they have shown great promise in the last couple of years [1].

We now provide a high-level overview of the tools Neurify [42] and Fast-and-Complete (FAC) [47], which employ similar approaches in terms of combining interval analysis with linear programming. Intuitively, the ultimate goal of these methods is to cast (4) as a relaxed LP and use an optimized solver such as Gurobi. Since ReLUs are non-linear, one needs to obtain a linear relaxation of each ReLU neuron. Such a linear relaxation can be obtained by computing bounds on the inputs to each ReLU (using interval analysis) and then approximating the ReLU with a linear function over those bounds [42].

Once a linear relaxation of each ReLU is obtained, the entire LP is solved using Gurobi. If no counterexample is found, then the property is true. If a counterexample is found, one needs to check if it is a true or false positive: if it is a true positive, then the property is false; if the counterexample is a false positive, then the LP needs to be refined by splitting an overapproximated ReLU into its individual components and solving both resulting LPs (thus potentially leading to an exponential number of splits). Please consult prior work [42,47]

---

[1] We use L_∞ in the interest of clarity, though other norms can be used as well.

about various improvements in terms of which ReLUs to split first and how to obtain the tightest bounds $[l, u]$ for the input to each ReLU.

As noted above, this procedure has an exponential complexity in the worst case due to the possibility of having to split each ReLU in the NN. Thus, the run-time of such an approach can be greatly improved by tightening the bounds obtained using interval analysis, which is the goal of T4V.

3.3   Problem Statement

We now state the T4V problem, both in its general version as well as the specific instantiation related to robustness verification.

Problem 1 (Training for Verification). Suppose some base loss function L_o has been selected to achieve some property ϕ_o, e.g., classification accuracy, of an NN during training. Suppose also that a verification algorithm $\mathcal{A}$ is used to verify a given property ψ. The training for verification (T4V) problem is 1) to identify an NN property ϕ_v that results in more scalable verification of ψ by $\mathcal{A}$ and 2) incorporate ϕ_v into the NN during the training process using a corresponding loss function L_v.

Problem 2 (Training for Robustness Verification). The training for robustness verification problem is an instantiation of the T4V problem, where $\mathcal{A}$ is an interval-analysis-based verification algorithm [42, 47] and ψ is a robustness property.

4   Training for Verification: High-Level Approach

This section provides our high-level approach to T4V. This method can in principle be applied to any training approach and any desired verification algorithm, although the specifics may vary as discussed below.

In a standard training setting, the NN parameters are selected so as to minimize some loss L_o, as discussed in Sect. 3. In classification problems, this loss is usually negative loss likelihood or cross entropy. If robustness is considered in addition to classification accuracy, then one can also add an additional term such as adversarial robustness [27] or interval bound propagation [13]. None of these methods consider verification during the training phase, however, since verification is usually performed post-hoc.

In this paper, we propose introducing verification considerations to the training process. Since NNs are usually highly overparameterized, there exist multiple NNs within the same family that achieve a similar loss L_o. Thus, it makes sense to choose an NN that not only achieves a low L_o but is also easy to verify. In order to do so, one needs to identify an NN property ϕ_v that leads to more scalable verification. The property ϕ_v is likely to be specific to the verification task and the tool being used, since different tools use different heuristics to tackle the scalability challenge.

Assuming for now that such a property ϕ_v is identified (examples are provided at the end of the section), the next task is to choose a corresponding loss function, L_v, that incentivizes this property during training. Given L_v, one can now modify the training loss by combining L_o and L_v, for example in a convex combination:

$$L = \alpha L_o + (1 - \alpha) L_v, \tag{5}$$

where $\alpha \in (0, 1)$. Thus, by varying α and observing the corresponding effect on L_o, the user can select the appropriate trade-off between verifiability and the original property. Note that in some cases, the loss L_v might even improve the original property, e.g., regularization is known to improve generalizability in classification tasks, especially with overparameterized models such as NNs [12]. We now provide two example properties ϕ_v and corresponding losses L_v.

Example 1 (Sampling-based Reachability Analysis). Reachability analysis is a useful technique in closed-loop verification, e.g., when NNs are used as controllers [16,18]. In this setting, the task is to compute the reachable set of outputs of the NN given a set of inputs. One way of approximating the reachable set is by constructing a polynomial approximation of the NN over the input set using polynomial regression [16]. In order to bound the error of the approximating polynomial, one could use a sampling-based method by making use of the NN's Lipschitz constant. Thus, NNs with lower Lipschitz constants would improve the scalability of the above method since fewer points would need to be sampled.

In the context of the proposed T4V method, the desired verifiability property ϕ_v is that the NN has a low Lipschitz constant. One way to incentivize this property is to introduce an L_2 regularizer on the NN weights W, i.e., $L_v = W^T W$. While prior work [16] has made the observation that lower Lipschitz constants improve verification scalability, we believe our proposed framework can make explicit the relationship between NN verifiability and performance as a controller. For example, for an NN used as an agent in a deep reinforcement learning problem, our framework can help understand the trade-off between NN verifiability and rewards earned by the NN agent.

Example 2 (Taylor-model-based Reachability Analysis). An alternative method to reachability analysis is to construct a polynomial approximation with error bounds (i.e., a Taylor model) for each neuron in the NN [19,20]. This method makes use of interval analysis to propagate the error bounds through the NN. Thus, the error bounds can grow quickly, especially in large NNs. One way to reduce the error growth, as discussed also in Sect. 5 in the context of robustness verification, is to ensure that all weights in a given layer have the same sign.

Thus, the property ϕ_v is that all weights are positive, without loss of generality. One way of promoting this property is through introducing a higher penalty on negative weights, explained further in Sect. 5.

The remainder of this paper considers in more detail another example of T4V, namely for the case of robustness verification using interval analysis.

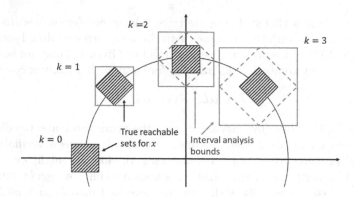

Fig. 1. Illustration of the growth of the approximation error incurred by interval analysis on the harmonic oscillator system.

5 Training for Robustness Verification

This section presents an illustration of the proposed T4V method, for the case of robustness verification using interval-analysis-based tools. We first identify a property ϕ_v that results in smaller approximation error due to interval analysis. We then introduce the corresponding verifiability loss, L_v, and show how to combine it with the original loss, L_o.

5.1 On the Benefit of Same-Sign Weights for Interval Analysis

As discussed in Sect. 3, interval analysis is a major component of state-of-the-art robustness verification tools. At the same time, interval analysis can introduce significant approximation error, especially in high-dimensional settings. Prior work [26] has discussed multiple reasons for the error growth, such as rotations, ill-conditioned matrices, etc.

To illustrate one such case of approximation error growth, consider the harmonic oscillator dynamical system [26]:

$$x_{k+1} = \begin{bmatrix} \cos\phi & \sin\phi \\ -\sin\phi & \cos\phi \end{bmatrix} x_k, \tag{6}$$

where $\phi = 45°$, and $x_0 \in [-1-\epsilon, -1+\epsilon] \times [-\epsilon, \epsilon]$. In this example, the initial set for x_0 is a box with size 2ϵ (ϵ can take on any positive value). With each step $k = 1, 2, 3, \ldots$, the reachable set for x_k is rotated by $45°$. If one were to use interval analysis to approximate the reachable set, the approximation error would grow quickly over time, as shown in Fig. 1, due to the rotation present in the harmonic oscillator system.

The harmonic oscillator example is instructive because an NN can be considered a dynamical system, where the neurons at layer k are x_k. Thus, for the purposes of analyzing error growth, we can view the NN description in (2) as a linear system of the sort:[2]

$$x_{k+1} = W_{k+1}x_k, \qquad (7)$$

where $k = 0, \ldots, M$, x_0 is the input to the NN, and W_k are the individual layer weights. Note that we ignore the bias terms b_k because they do not affect the shape of the sets.

With this intuition in mind, we can choose a property for each W_k and enforce it during training. Unfortunately, most properties that result in lower approximation error [26] are difficult to enforce as they would significantly constrain the NN architecture: e.g., eliminating rotations would mean that we a priori fix the directions of all rows of each W_k and only train their magnitudes. Hence, we have identified a new property that can be more easily incentivized during training as a soft constraint. Namely, interval analysis approximation error is reduced when all (or most) entries of each W_k have the same sign. The benefit of this property is illustrated in the following theorem.

Before stating the theorem, we introduce some notation relevant to interval analysis. Let $x \in [l, u]$, i.e., x lies in the (potentially multidimensional) interval $[l, u]$. When clear from context, we use the shorthand notation $[x] := [l, u]$. We say a matrix $A \in \mathbb{R}^{m \times n}$ is a *same-sign matrix* if all entries of A have the same sign. As a reminder, for a scalar constant $a \geq 0$, $a \times [l, u] = [al, au]$; when $a < 0$, $a \times [l, u] = [au, al]$. Finally, when $A \in \mathbb{R}^{m \times n}$ with rows $a_1, \ldots a_m$ and $x \in \mathbb{R}^n$, we use the shorthand notation $A[x]$ to mean the interval vector $[y]$ where the first component is the interval $[l_1, u_1] = a_1^T[x]$, and so on.

Theorem 1. *Let $x \in [x]$ and let $A = A_M \ldots A_1$ be the product of M matrices with compatible dimensions. If all A_i are same-sign matrices, then the set $A[x]$ is the same as the set $A_M \ldots [A_1[x]]$.*

Proof. We prove the claim by induction on the number of matrices M. The claim is trivially true for $M = 1$.

Suppose that the claim is true for k, i.e., $A[x] = A_k \ldots [A_1[x]]$. Now consider A_{k+1}. We need to show that $A_{k+1}[A[x]] = (A_{k+1}A)[x]$.

Let $[x] = [a, b]$, with a and b vectors. Note that all entries of each A and A_{k+1} must have the same sign, so we can write $A = \text{sign}(A)|A|$ and $A_{k+1} = \text{sign}(A_{k+1})|A_{k+1}|$, where $|A|$ denotes the element-wise absolute value of A.

Note that since $|A|$ has non-negative values, $[|A|[x]] = [|A|a, |A|b]$, which implies $A_{k+1}[A[x]] = \text{sign}(A)\text{sign}(A_{k+1})|A_{k+1}|[|A|a, |A|b]$. Similarly, since $|A_{k+1}|$ has non-negative values, $|A_{k+1}|[|A|a, |A|b] = [|A_{k+1}| \cdot |A|a, |A_{k+1}| \cdot |A|b]$.

Conversely, since $A_{k+1}A = \text{sign}(A_{k+1})\text{sign}(A)|A_{k+1}| \cdot |A|$, then $(|A_{k+1}| \cdot |A|)[x] = [|A_{k+1}| \cdot |A|a, |A_{k+1}| \cdot |A|b]$, which proves the claim. ∎

Theorem 1 means that if we have a sequence of same-sign matrices $A_1, \ldots, A_M$ applied to an interval vector $[x]$, using interval approximation after each multiplication is the same as premultiplying the matrices and using interval

---

[2] Note that the ReLU activations may sometimes reduce the approximation error since all negative values are mapped to 0. However, they do not add any further error, so analyzing only the linear parts of the NN is an important first step.

analysis only once. This is important because in an NN we cannot premultiply all layer weights due to the presence of activations. Thus, Theorem 1 means that if all weights have the same sign, then applying interval analysis at each layer does not result in drastic approximation error growth. Note that if the conditions of Theorem 1 do not hold, the error could grow substantially, as shown in the following example.

Example 3. Let $x \in [[-0.01, 0.01], [-0.01, 0.01]]^{\top}$. Let $v_1 = [1, 1]^{\top}, v_2 = [3, 3]^{\top}$, $v_3 = [5, -3]^{\top}$. Suppose we want to compute $v_3^{\top}[v_1 \ v_2]^{\top}[x]$.

Note that $(v_3^{\top}[v_1 \ v_2]^{\top})[x] = [-4 \ -4][x] = [-0.08, 0.08]$. On the other hand, if we apply interval analysis sequentially, we get $v_3^{\top}[[v_1 \ v_2]^{\top}[x]] = v_3^{\top}[[-0.02, 0.02], [-0.06, 0.06]]^{\top} = [-0.28, 0.28]$, which is a significantly larger interval.

5.2   Incentivizing Same-Sign Weights During Training

There are multiple ways to achieve the same-sign property during the training process. One approach would be to use constrained optimization and train the NN under the constraint that all weights in a layer have the same sign. However, such a constraint might be too limiting and might significantly affect training performance. Thus, we choose instead to relax these constraints using mechanisms inspired by the common Lagrangian relaxations from optimization [3]. Specifically, we incorporate our same-sign weights constraint directly in the loss through a larger penalty on negative weights. While it may be possible to achieve better training results using a scheme where some layers have only negative weights and others have only positive weights, we leave this analysis for future work. Specifically, the verification loss has the form:

$$L_v = \sum_{i=1}^{M} \gamma \|W_i^n\| + (1 - \gamma)\|W_i^p\|, \tag{8}$$

where $W_i^n = \min(0, W_i), W_i^p = \max(0, W_i)$, $\| \cdot \|$ denotes the Frobenius norm, and $\gamma \in [0, 1]$ is a hyperparameter that determines how big the penalty on negative weights should be. Note that computing W_i^p and W_i^n requires a max and min function, similar to the ReLU implementation. We also emphasize that our verification loss L_v, when incorporated with the original L_o loss via (5), is reminiscent of the standard weight norm penalizations used in machine learning. Such regularization techniques have been shown to improve generalizability [12], and although we have repurposed them to achieve an imbalance of weight distribution (weighted more heavily towards negative weights or positive weights), our loss L_v is likely to improve generalization over a non-regularized NN. This is also observed in our experiments.

The choice of γ in (8) depends on the specific training task. Since NNs are overparameterized for many benchmarks such as MNIST and CIFAR-10, NNs can be well trained even with a γ that is close to 1. However, as the complexity of the training task increases, it is possible that even small deviations of γ past

0.5 may significantly hurt training performance. In our experiments, we chose $\gamma = 0.9$ since we were able to train NNs with very small negative weights while maintaining high accuracy.

Finally, note that a more effective strategy may be to also assign different weights to different layers, so as to recognize their relative importance. In particular, larger layers, both in terms of the number of inputs and number of neurons, result in larger approximation error when using interval analysis (interval analysis does not maintain relationships between variables, which accrues additional error in higher dimensions). Hence, it is natural to introduce a larger penalty for larger layers. Furthermore, earlier layers are more important in terms of error growth since the error is magnified as the analysis progresses through the following layers. Since a formal analysis of these factors is not straightforward, we assign the same weight to all layers and leave this investigation for future work.

6   Experiments

This section provides an evaluation of the proposed T4V method on the MNIST [24] and CIFAR-10 datasets [23]. MNIST is a dataset of 28×28 grayscale images of handwritten digits, and CIFAR-10 is a dataset of $3 \times 32 \times 32$ color images of 10 classes of objects such as airplane, automobile, etc. We use the FAC tool [47] in the verification evaluation, which is described at a high level in Sect. 3.[3]

6.1   Experimental Setup

We illustrate the benefit of our approach in two different scenarios, one in which the original loss is purely classification-oriented, and one in which the original loss promotes both classification accuracy and robustness. For each scenario, we evaluate the effect of T4V on NN verifiability. We also evaluate NN robustness, as the T4V process could improve verifiability by reducing robustness (a non-robust network can be trivially proven unsafe via counterexample). Our results alleviate such concerns. We show that in both scenarios, adding the verification loss L_v improves verifiability, often at little or no cost in accuracy and robustness.

Scenario 1: Classification Accuracy. In the first scenario, the original loss is cross-entropy loss, denoted by L_{CE}, which is a standard loss in classification tasks [12]. In the interest of space, we omit the formal definition of cross-entropy; intuitively, for each example x, L_{CE} tries to minimize the difference between the NN's output label "distribution" (e.g., a softmax layer) and the true label's distribution (given as a one-hot encoding, for example). Thus, the final T4V loss in this case is:

$$L := \alpha L_{CE} + (1 - \alpha)L_v. \tag{9}$$

---

[3] All code used to produce the experiments can be found at https://github.com/vwlin/T4V.

Scenario 2: Classification Accuracy and Robustness. In the second scenario, the original loss enforces not only classification accuracy but also robustness. This scenario illustrates two points: 1) the proposed method is general and can be used for a variety of original losses; 2) since the proposed L_v loss naturally improves robustness over a non-regularized network (as discussed in Sect. 5), we show that it can improve verifiability even in settings where the NN is already quite robust.

There are a number of existing methods that are aimed at improving NN robustness such as adversarial training [27] and interval bound propagation (IBP) [13]. In this work, we use IBP since it performs fairly well on the MNIST and CIFAR-10 datasets; we leave the evaluation over other robustness losses for future work. At a high level, IBP works as follows: for a given batch of B training examples $x_1, \ldots, x_B$, an interval of size $2\epsilon_{IBP}$ is created around each point; then we propagate the intervals $[x_1 - \epsilon_{IBP}, x_1 + \epsilon_{IBP}], \ldots, [x_B - \epsilon_{IBP}, x_B + \epsilon_{IBP}]$ through the NN using interval analysis; the size of the output interval is used as the IBP loss, L_{IBP}. Note that, in addition to improved robustness, IBP also alleviates the approximation error of interval analysis. Thus, the final loss becomes

$$L := \alpha(\beta L_{CE} + (1 - \beta)L_{IBP}) + (1 - \alpha)L_v, \qquad (10)$$

where β is a hyperparameter regulating the relative weight of L_{IBP}.

6.2   Implementation Details

For our evaluation on MNIST, we train three different fully-connected NN architectures of increasing size in order to illustrate the benefit of our approach: 1) an NN with 2 hidden layers and 50 neurons per hidden layer; 2) an NN with 2 hidden layers and 200 neurons per hidden layer; and 3) an NN with 5 hidden layers and 200 neurons per hidden layer. Without regularization, these NNs achieve classification accuracy of 95.6%, 95.8%, and 97.5%, respectively (as averaged over 3 trials with different random seeds).

To train the NNs for Scenario 2 on MNIST, for each NN we used values of β and ϵ_{IBP} that do not greatly affect the original L_{CE} loss; the specific values are $\epsilon_{IBP} = 0.04$ (normalized from the pixel range $[0, 255]$ to $[0, 1]$), and $\beta = 0.84, \beta = 0.96, \beta = 0.97$ for the three NNs, respectively. Note that bigger values of β are needed for larger NNs since interval analysis can result in large output intervals, as discussed in Sect. 5.

For our evaluation on CIFAR-10, we note that CIFAR-10 is a significantly harder dataset than MNIST, both due to the number of dimensions and to the richness of the images. In addition, since FAC does not support regularization such as dropout and batch normalization, it is challenging to train NNs with very high accuracy that can be encoded in the tool. Thus, we use the following architecture (as inspired by the CIFAR-Base model in the original FAC paper [47]): 1) a convolutional layer of 8 filters (with a kernel size of 4 and stride of 1); 2) a convolutional layer of 16 filters (with a kernel size of 4 and stride of 1); and 3) a fully-connected layer of 128 neurons. Note that when expanded, the convolutional layers have 6728 and 10816 neurons, respectively, which is significantly larger than the NNs used for MNIST. Without regularization, this NN achieves an average (over 3 trials) classification accuracy of 73.38%.

For both scenarios and datasets, to evaluate verification scalability, we randomly select 200 images from the test set and run the FAC tool with a selected perturbation size ϵ on each NN for each correctly classified image. An image is said to be verified if the verification completed within a timeout of 60s for the MNIST dataset and 120s for the CIFAR-10 dataset. We define verifiability to be the fraction of images that were verified by FAC. We evaluate robustness with respect to the same safety property that we verify with FAC (i.e., that an ϵ perturbation will not cause a change in classifier decision). We first ϵ-perturb 1000 randomly selected images from the test set (a superset of the 200 images used to evaluate verifiability) using the PGD attack [27]. We then measure robustness as the fraction of images for which the classification decision of the NN did not change after the attack. Note that this robustness measure is an overestimate of the NN's true robustness, as the PGD attack is not guaranteed to find the optimal adversarial perturbation for each image. Thus, for a closer estimate of robustness, we use 1000 images rather than 200 images. Finally, to obtain informative evaluations of verifiability and robustness, we select the perturbation ϵ (the same ϵ is used for both evaluations) so that the robustness verification task is neither overly trivial (ϵ too small) nor insurmountably difficult (ϵ too large) for the FAC tool to complete on each NN.

6.3   Distribution of Weights

For a subset of the NNs trained on MNIST for Scenarios 1 and 2, the distribution of learned weights are shown in Fig. 2. We find that without our verification loss L_v (i.e., when $\alpha = 1.00$), the weights roughly follow a bell shaped distribution centered at 0. In contrast, after training with L_v (i.e., when $\alpha < 1$), all negative weights are of nearly zero magnitude. For our NNs trained on CIFAR-10 for Scenarios 1 and 2, we show the distribution of learned weights in Fig. 3. Just as with the NNs trained on MNIST, the addition of our verification loss L_v greatly reduces the magnitude of negative weights.

6.4   MNIST Evaluation

The MNIST evaluation on Scenario 1 is shown in Fig. 4.[4] We observe that, as we decrease α (i.e., we assign more weight to L_v) verifiability increases significantly for each setup, reaching as high as 90% for the two-layer NNs. Also note that the increase in verifiability usually comes at the expense of some drop in accuracy (more pronounced in the five-layer NN). At the same time, for values of α very close to 1, one can obtain significant benefits in verifiability at only minor costs in accuracy. Finally, the proposed L_v also naturally improves robustness. However, the improvements in robustness and verifiability are not always correlated, as discussed next.

---

[4] For assessing the magnitude of ϵ, note that image pixels can only take discrete values between 0 and 255.

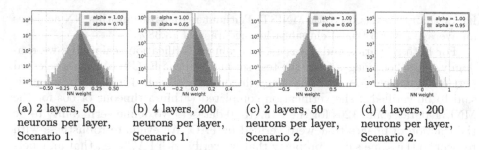

(a) 2 layers, 50 neurons per layer, Scenario 1.

(b) 4 layers, 200 neurons per layer, Scenario 1.

(c) 2 layers, 50 neurons per layer, Scenario 2.

(d) 4 layers, 200 neurons per layer, Scenario 2.

Fig. 2. MNIST weight distributions on Scenarios 1 and 2. Each histogram is over a single trial. The vertical axes are on a log scale.

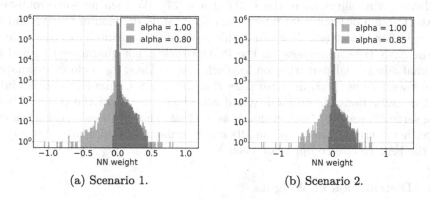

(a) Scenario 1.

(b) Scenario 2.

Fig. 3. CIFAR-10 weight distributions on Scenarios 1 and 2. Each histogram is over a single trial. The vertical axes are on a log scale.

The evaluation on Scenario 2 is shown in Fig. 5. Once again, the verifiability improves significantly as we decrease α. Note that, due to the addition of L_{IBP}, these NNs are much more robust (for larger ϵ) to input perturbations. In this case, the increase in verifiability comes at some cost in both accuracy and robustness, with the degree of this trade-off tunable by the hyperparameter α just as in Scenario 1. However, for the five-layer NN, the suitable range of α is much narrower than for the smaller networks. Due to the larger size of the five-layer NN, it is increasingly difficult as α decreases to balance the competing objectives of accuracy, low IBP loss, and low verification loss. The result of this complex loss is great variance across seeds when α is reduced beyond a certain threshold (analyzing the reasons for this variance, e.g., the importance of layer weighting in L_v, is left for future work).

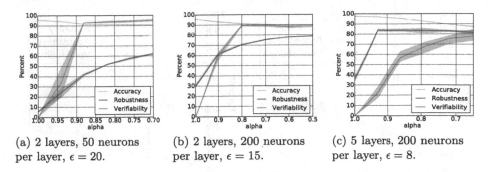

(a) 2 layers, 50 neurons per layer, $\epsilon = 20$.

(b) 2 layers, 200 neurons per layer, $\epsilon = 15$.

(c) 5 layers, 200 neurons per layer, $\epsilon = 8$.

Fig. 4. MNIST evaluation on Scenario 1. All curves are averaged over 3 trials. Shaded regions indicate min/max outcomes for each setup.

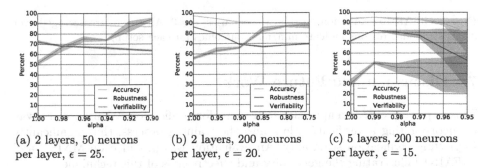

(a) 2 layers, 50 neurons per layer, $\epsilon = 25$.

(b) 2 layers, 200 neurons per layer, $\epsilon = 20$.

(c) 5 layers, 200 neurons per layer, $\epsilon = 15$.

Fig. 5. MNIST evaluation on Scenario 2. All curves are averaged over 3 trials. Shaded regions indicate min/max outcomes for each setup.

6.5 CIFAR-10 Evaluation

The CIFAR-10 evaluation is shown in Fig. 6, where the verifiability definition is the same as in the case of MNIST (with a timeout per image of 120s). We observe the same overall trends as in the MNIST case – adding the L_v loss improves verifiability significantly, at some cost in accuracy (though robustness is improved in both scenarios). Note that there is more variance across seeds in the CIFAR-10 evaluation, most likely due to the challenging dataset and the larger size of the NNs. Finally, note that the robustness benefits of L_{IBP} are less pronounced than in the MNIST case – this is consistent with prior work where achieving robustness has been shown to be significantly harder for color images such as those in CIFAR-10 [27]. As part of future work, we will explore whether using other robustness losses leads to a better robustness/verifiability combination on CIFAR-10.

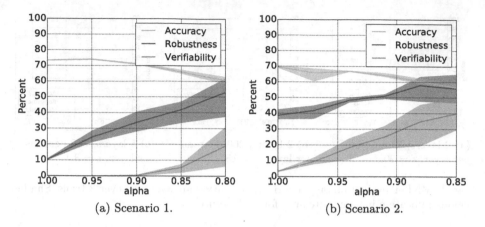

(a) Scenario 1.   (b) Scenario 2.

Fig. 6. CIFAR-10 evaluation on the two scenarios, $\epsilon = 3$. All curves are averaged over 3 trials. Shaded regions indicate min/max outcomes for each setup.

7   Discussion and Future Work

This paper presented an approach to training for verification. We proposed a way of incorporating a verification loss into the training process, thus significantly improving verification scalability. An evaluation was provided on MNIST and CIFAR-10 illustrating the generality and effectiveness of this technique.

Since T4V is a new area, there are a number of interesting directions for future work. As shown in Sect. 6, the proposed method introduces greater variance during the training process for larger NNs, so an important question is whether verifiability is fundamentally at odds with accuracy or whether it is simply a matter of finding the right local optimum during training. As a first step, we intend to investigate the effect on the training process of assigning different values of the γ hyperparameter at each layer.

Another interesting direction is to apply this technique in closed-loop settings. Since in closed-loop verification one needs to perform reasoning over multiple time steps, an extra challenge in this problem is that if the NN controller is not robust, verification is likely to fail even if the NN itself is "verifiable". Finally, we intend to apply the proposed method to other losses and verification tasks (e.g., semantic robustness) in order to investigate its benefits and limitations.

Acknowledgements. This work was supported in part by DARPA/AFRL FA87 50-18-C-0090 and ARO W911NF-20-1-0080. Any opinions, findings and conclusions or recommendations expressed in this material are those of the authors and do not necessarily reflect the views of the Air Force Research Laboratory (AFRL), the Army Research Office (ARO), the Defense Advanced Research Projects Agency (DARPA), the Department of Defense, or the United States Government.

References

1. Bak, S., Liu, C., Johnson, T.: The second international verification of neural networks competition (VNN-COMP 2021): summary and results. arXiv preprint arXiv:2109.00498 (2021)
2. Bojarski, M., et al.: End to end learning for self-driving cars. arXiv preprint arXiv:1604.07316 (2016)
3. Boyd, S., Boyd, S.P., Vandenberghe, L.: Convex Optimization. Cambridge University Press, Cambridge (2004)
4. Chen, X., Abraham, E., Sankaranarayanan, S.: Taylor model flowpipe construction for non-linear hybrid systems. In: 2012 IEEE 33rd Real-Time Systems Symposium (RTSS), pp. 183–192. IEEE (2012)
5. Collobert, R., Weston, J., Bottou, L., Karlen, M., Kavukcuoglu, K., Kuksa, P.: Natural language processing (almost) from scratch. J. Mach. Learn. Res. **12**, 2493–2537 (2011)
6. Dutta, S., Chen, X., Sankaranarayanan, S.: Reachability analysis for neural feedback systems using regressive polynomial rule inference. In: 22nd International Conference on Hybrid Systems: Computation and Control, pp. 157–168 (2019)
7. Dutta, S., Jha, S., Sankaranarayanan, S., Tiwari, A.: Output range analysis for deep feedforward neural networks. In: Dutle, A., Muñoz, C., Narkawicz, A. (eds.) NFM 2018. LNCS, vol. 10811, pp. 121–138. Springer, Cham (2018). https://doi.org/10.1007/978-3-319-77935-5_9
8. Dvijotham, K., et al.: Training verified learners with learned verifiers. arXiv preprint arXiv:1805.10265 (2018)
9. Ehlers, R.: Formal verification of piece-wise linear feed-forward neural networks. In: D'Souza, D., Narayan Kumar, K. (eds.) ATVA 2017. LNCS, vol. 10482, pp. 269–286. Springer, Cham (2017). https://doi.org/10.1007/978-3-319-68167-2_19
10. Fazlyab, M., Robey, A., Hassani, H., Morari, M., Pappas, G.: Efficient and accurate estimation of lipschitz constants for deep neural networks. In: Advances in Neural Information Processing Systems, vol. 32 (2019)
11. Gehr, T., Mirman, M., Drachsler-Cohen, D., Tsankov, P., Chaudhuri, S., Vechev, M.: AI2: safety and robustness certification of neural networks with abstract interpretation. In: 2018 IEEE Symposium on Security and Privacy (SP) (2018)
12. Goodfellow, I., Bengio, Y., Courville, A.: Deep Learning. MIT Press, Cambridge (2016)
13. Gowal, S., et al.: Scalable verified training for provably robust image classification. In: Proceedings of the IEEE/CVF International Conference on Computer Vision, pp. 4842–4851 (2019)
14. Henzinger, T.A.: The theory of hybrid automata. In: Inan, M.K., Kurshan, R.P. (eds.) Verification of Digital and Hybrid Systems, pp. 265–292. Springer, Heidelberg (2000). https://doi.org/10.1007/978-3-642-59615-5_13
15. Henzinger, T.A., Lechner, M., Zikelic, D.: Scalable verification of quantized neural networks. In: Proceedings of the AAAI Conference on Artificial Intelligence, vol. 35 (2021)
16. Huang, C., Fan, J., Li, W., Chen, X., Zhu, Q.: Reachnn: reachability analysis of neural-network controlled systems. ACM Trans. Embed. Comput. Syst. (TECS) **18**(5s), 1–22 (2019)
17. Ivanov, R., Carpenter, T., Weimer, J., Alur, R., Pappas, G.J., Lee, I.: Case study: verifying the safety of an autonomous racing car with a neural network controller. In: International Conference on Hybrid Systems: Computation and Control (2020)

18. Ivanov, R., Weimer, J., Alur, R., Pappas, G.J., Lee, I.: Verisig: verifying safety properties of hybrid systems with neural network controllers. In: 22nd ACM International Conference on Hybrid Systems: Computation and Control (2019)

19. Ivanov, R., Carpenter, T., Weimer, J., Alur, R., Pappas, G., Lee, I.: Verisig 2.0: verification of neural network controllers using taylor model preconditioning. In: Silva, A., Leino, K.R.M. (eds.) CAV 2021. LNCS, vol. 12759, pp. 249–262. Springer, Cham (2021). https://doi.org/10.1007/978-3-030-81685-8_11

20. Ivanov, R., Carpenter, T.J., Weimer, J., Alur, R., Pappas, G.J., Lee, I.: Verifying the safety of autonomous systems with neural network controllers. ACM Trans. Embed. Comput. Syst. **20**(1), 1–26 (2020). https://doi.org/10.1145/3419742

21. Julian, K.D., Lopez, J., Brush, J.S., Owen, M.P., Kochenderfer, M.J.: Policy compression for aircraft collision avoidance systems. In: 2016 IEEE/AIAA 35th Digital Avionics Systems Conference (DASC), pp. 1–10. IEEE (2016)

22. Katz, G., Barrett, C., Dill, D.L., Julian, K., Kochenderfer, M.J.: Reluplex: an efficient SMT solver for verifying deep neural networks. In: Majumdar, R., Kunčak, V. (eds.) CAV 2017. LNCS, vol. 10426, pp. 97–117. Springer, Cham (2017). https://doi.org/10.1007/978-3-319-63387-9_5

23. Krizhevsky, A., Hinton, G., et al.: Learning multiple layers of features from tiny images. Master's thesis, University of Toronto (2009)

24. LeCun, Y., Bottou, L., Bengio, Y., Haffner, P.: Gradient-based learning applied to document recognition. Proc. IEEE **86**(11), 2278–2324 (1998)

25. Lin, X., Zhu, H., Samanta, R., Jagannathan, S.: Art: abstraction refinement-guided training for provably correct neural networks. In: Formal Methods in Computer-Aided Design (2020)

26. Lohner, R.J.: On the ubiquity of the wrapping effect in the computation of error bounds. In: Kulisch, U., Lohner, R., Facius, A. (eds.) Perspectives on Enclosure Methods, pp. 201–216. Springer, Vienna (2001). https://doi.org/10.1007/978-3-7091-6282-8_12

27. Madry, A., Makelov, A., Schmidt, L., Tsipras, D., Vladu, A.: Towards deep learning models resistant to adversarial attacks. In: International Conference on Learning Representations (2018)

28. Mell, S., Brown, O., Goodwin, J., Son, S.H.: Safe predictors for enforcing input-output specifications. arXiv preprint arXiv:2001.11062 (2020)

29. Mirman, M., Gehr, T., Vechev, M.: Differentiable abstract interpretation for provably robust neural networks. In: International Conference on Machine Learning, pp. 3578–3586. PMLR (2018)

30. Mnih, V., et al.: Human-level control through deep reinforcement learning. Nature **518**(7540), 529 (2015)

31. Morawiecki, P., Spurek, P., Śmieja, M., Tabor, J.: Fast and stable interval bounds propagation for training verifiably robust models. In: European Symposium on Artificial Neural Networks (2020)

32. GUROBI Optimization: Gurobi optimizer. https://gurobi.com

33. Raghunathan, A., Steinhardt, J., Liang, P.: Certified defenses against adversarial examples. In: International Conference on Learning Representations (2018)

34. Sälzer, M., Lange, M.: Reachability is NP-complete even for the simplest neural networks. In: Bell, P.C., Totzke, P., Potapov, I. (eds.) RP 2021. LNCS, vol. 13035, pp. 149–164. Springer, Cham (2021). https://doi.org/10.1007/978-3-030-89716-1_10

35. Singh, G., Gehr, T., Püschel, M., Vechev, M.: An abstract domain for certifying neural networks. Proc. ACM Program. Lang. **3**(POPL), 1–30 (2019)

36. Sun, X., Khedr, H., Shoukry, Y.: Formal verification of neural network controlled autonomous systems. In: Proceedings of the 22nd ACM International Conference on Hybrid Systems: Computation and Control, pp. 147–156. ACM (2019)
37. Szegedy, C., Zaremba, W., Sutskever, I., Bruna, J., Erhan, D., Goodfellow, I., Fergus, R.: Intriguing properties of neural networks. In: International Conference on Learning Representations (2014)
38. Taigman, Y., Yang, M., Ranzato, M., Wolf, L.: Deepface: closing the gap to human-level performance in face verification. In: Proceedings of the IEEE Conference on Computer Vision and Pattern Recognition, pp. 1701–1708 (2014)
39. Tjeng, V., Xiao, K., Tedrake, R.: Evaluating robustness of neural networks with mixed integer programming. In: International Conference on Learning Representations (2019)
40. Tran, H., Cai, F., Lopez, D.M., Musau, P., Johnson, T.T., Koutsoukos, X.: Safety verification of cyber-physical systems with reinforcement learning control. ACM Trans. Embed. Comput. Syst. **18**(5s), 105 (2019)
41. Tran, H.-D., et al.: NNV: the neural network verification tool for deep neural networks and learning-enabled cyber-physical systems. In: Lahiri, S.K., Wang, C. (eds.) CAV 2020. LNCS, vol. 12224, pp. 3–17. Springer, Cham (2020). https://doi.org/10.1007/978-3-030-53288-8_1
42. Wang, S., Pei, K., Whitehouse, J., Yang, J., Jana, S.: Efficient formal safety analysis of neural networks. In: Advances in Neural Information Processing Systems, pp. 6367–6377 (2018)
43. Weng, T., et al.: Towards fast computation of certified robustness for relu networks. In: International Conference on Machine Learning, pp. 5273–5282 (2018)
44. Wong, E., Kolter, Z.: Provable defenses against adversarial examples via the convex outer adversarial polytope. In: International Conference on Machine Learning, pp. 5286–5295. PMLR (2018)
45. Wong, E., Schmidt, F., Metzen, J.H., Kolter, J.Z.: Scaling provable adversarial defenses. In: Advances in Neural Information Processing Systems, vol. 31 (2018)
46. Xiao, K.Y., Tjeng, V., Shafiullah, N.M., Madry, A.: Training for faster adversarial robustness verification via inducing relu stability. In: International Conference on Learning Representations (2019)
47. Xu, K., et al.: Fast and complete: enabling complete neural network verification with rapid and massively parallel incomplete verifiers. In: International Conference on Learning Representations (2020)

A Framework for Transforming Specifications in Reinforcement Learning

Rajeev Alur, Suguman Bansal, Osbert Bastani, and Kishor Jothimurugan[✉]

University of Pennsylvania, Philadelphia, USA
kishor@seas.upenn.edu

Abstract. Reactive synthesis algorithms allow automatic construction of policies to control an environment modeled as a Markov Decision Process (MDP) that are optimal with respect to high-level temporal logic specifications. However, they assume that the MDP model is known a priori. Reinforcement Learning (RL) algorithms, in contrast, are designed to learn an optimal policy when the transition probabilities of the MDP are unknown, but require the user to associate local rewards with transitions. The appeal of high-level temporal logic specifications has motivated research to develop RL algorithms for synthesis of policies from specifications. To understand the techniques, and nuanced variations in their theoretical guarantees, in the growing body of resulting literature, we develop a formal framework for defining transformations among RL tasks with different forms of objectives. We define the notion of a sampling-based reduction to transform a given MDP into another one which can be simulated even when the transition probabilities of the original MDP are unknown. We formalize the notions of preservation of optimal policies, convergence, and robustness of such reductions. We then use our framework to restate known results, establish new results to fill in some gaps, and identify open problems. In particular, we show that certain kinds of reductions from LTL specifications to reward-based ones do not exist, and prove the non-existence of RL algorithms with PAC-MDP guarantees for safety specifications.

Keywords: Reinforcement learning · Reactive synthesis · Temporal logic

1 Introduction

In reactive synthesis for probabilistic systems, the system is typically modeled as a (finite-state) Markov Decision Process (MDP), and the desired behavior of the system is given as a logical specification. For example, in robot motion planning, the model captures the physical environment in which the robot is operating and how the robot updates its position in response to the available control commands; and the logical requirement can specify that the robot should always avoid obstacles and eventually reach all of the specified targets. The synthesis algorithm then needs to compute a control policy that maximizes the

© Springer Nature Switzerland AG 2022
J.-F. Raskin and K. Chatterjee (Eds.): Principles of Systems Design, LNCS 13660, pp. 604–624, 2022.
https://doi.org/10.1007/978-3-031-22337-2_29

probability that an infinite execution of the system under the policy satisfies the logical specification. There is a well developed theory of reactive synthesis for MDPs with respect to temporal logic specifications, accompanied by tools optimized with heuristics for improving scalability and practical applications (for instance, see [6] for a survey).

Reactive synthesis algorithms assume that the transition probabilities in the MDP modeling the environment are known a priori. In many practical settings, these probabilities are not known, and the model needs to be learnt by exploration. Reinforcement learning (RL) has emerged to be an effective paradigm for synthesis of control policies in this scenario. The optimization criterion for policy synthesis using RL is typically specified by associating a local reward with each transition and aggregating the sequence of local rewards along an infinite execution using discounted-sum or limit-average operators. Since an RL algorithm is learning from samples, it is expected to compute a sequence of approximations to the optimal policy with guaranteed convergence. Furthermore, ideally, the algorithm should have a PAC (Probably Approximately Correct) guarantee regarding the number of samples needed to ensure that the value of the policy it computes is within a specified bound of that of an optimal policy with a probability greater than a specified threshold. RL algorithms with convergence and efficient PAC guarantees are known for discounted-sum rewards [32,33].

A key shortcoming of RL algorithms is that the user must manually encode the desired behavior by associating rewards with system transitions. An appealing alternative is to instead have the user provide a high-level logical specification encoding the task. First, it is more natural to specify the desired properties of the global behavior, such as "always avoid obstacles and reach targets in this specified order", in a logical formalism such as temporal logic. Second, logical specifications facilitate testing and verifiability since it can be checked independently whether the synthesized policy satisfies the logical requirement. Finally, we can assume that the learning algorithm knows the logical specification in advance, unlike the local rewards learnt during model exploration, thereby opening up the possibility of design of specification-aware learning algorithms. For example, the structure of a temporal-logic formula can be exploited for hierarchical and compositional learning to reduce sample complexity in practice [20,23].

This has motivated many researchers to design RL algorithms for logical specifications [3,8,11,13,17–19,21,24,27,28,34,36]. The natural approach is to (1) translate the logical specification to an automaton that accepts executions that satisfy the specification, (2) define an MDP that is the product of the MDP being controlled and the specification automaton, (3) associate rewards with the transitions of the product MDP so that either discounted-sum or limit-average aggregation (roughly) captures acceptance by the automaton, and (4) apply an off-the-shelf RL algorithm such as Q-learning to synthesize the optimal policy. While this approach is typical to most papers in this rapidly growing body of research, and many of the proposed techniques have been shown to work well empirically, there are many nuanced variations in terms of their theoretical guarantees. Instead of attempting to systematically survey the literature, we classify it in following broad categories: some only consider finite executions with a known time horizon [3]; some provide convergence guarantees only when the optimal policy satisfies the specification almost surely; some provide PAC guarantees only when certain properties regarding the transition probabilities of the MDP are known [5, 10, 12]; some include a parameterized reduction [7, 13]— the parameter being the discount factor, for instance, establishing correctness for some value of the parameter without specifying how to compute it. The bottom line is that there are no known RL algorithms with convergence and/or PAC guarantees to synthesize a policy to maximize the satisfaction of a temporal logic specification (or an impossibility result that such algorithms cannot exist).

In this paper, we propose a formal framework for defining transformations among RL tasks. We define an RL task to consist of an MDP $\mathcal{M}$ together with a specification ϕ for the desired policy. The MDP is given by its states, actions, a function to reset the state to its initial state, and a step-function that allows sampling of its transitions. Possible forms of specifications include transition-based rewards to be aggregated as discounted-sum or limit-average, reward machines [19], safety, reachability, and linear temporal logic formulas. We then define *sampling-based reduction* to formalize transforming one RL task $(\mathcal{M}, \phi)$ to another $(\bar{\mathcal{M}}, \phi')$. While the relationship between the transformed model $\bar{\mathcal{M}}$ and the original model $\mathcal{M}$ is inspired by the classical definitions of simulation maps over (probabilistic) transition systems, the main challenge is that the transition probabilities of $\bar{\mathcal{M}}$ cannot be directly defined in terms of the unknown transition probabilities of $\mathcal{M}$. Intuitively, the step-function to sample transitions of $\bar{\mathcal{M}}$ should be definable in terms of the step-function of $\mathcal{M}$ used as a black-box, and our formalization allows this.

The notion of reduction among RL tasks naturally leads to formalization of preservation of optimal policies, convergence, and robustness (that is, policies close to optimal in one get mapped to ones close to optimal in the other). We use this framework to revisit existing results, fill in some gaps, and identify open problems.

We begin with preliminaries in Sect. 2 followed by a discussion of various kinds of specifications in Sect. 3. In Sect. 4, we show that it is not possible to reduce all LTL specifications to (discounted-sum) reward machines (which are reward functions with an internal state) when the underlying MDP $\mathcal{M}$ is kept fixed. We then define the notion of sampling-based reduction and restate existing results using our framework. In Sect. 5, we introduce the notions of robust specifications and robust reductions, and show that robust sampling-based reductions do not exit for transforming safety (as well as reachability) specifications to discounted rewards. Finally, we present our result on non-existence of RL algorithms with PAC-MDP guarantees for safety (and reachability) specifications in Sect. 6. Some proofs are omitted and can be found in the full version [4].

Related Work

In Sect. 4.3, we discuss some existing work on reducing LTL specifications to rewards. There is work on similar reductions for more complex lexicographic ω-regular objectives [16] as well as in the context of stochastic games [15]. We discuss existing PAC learning results for logical specifications in Sect. 6.1. Concurrent to our work, the authors of [35] show that PAC-MDP algorithms do not exist for any *non-finitary* LTL objective.

Closely related to this work is the work on expressivity of discounted rewards [1] which studies whether certain kinds of tasks can be encoded using discounted rewards. There are a couple of key differences to our work. First, they do not consider reductions that involve modifying the underlying MDP $\mathcal{M}$. Second, the tasks considered are based on explicit orderings among policies or trajectories rather than succinct formal specifications.

2   Preliminaries

Markov Decision Process. A Markov Decision Process (MDP) is a tuple $\mathcal{M} = (S, A, s_0, P)$, where S is a finite set of states, s_0 is the initial state,[1] A is a finite set of actions, and $P : S \times A \times S \rightarrow [0, 1]$ is the transition probability function, with $\sum_{s' \in S} P(s, a, s') = 1$ for all $s \in S$ and $a \in A$.

An *infinite run* $\zeta \in (S \times A)^\omega$ is a sequence $\zeta = s_0 a_0 s_1 a_1 \ldots$, where $s_i \in S$ and $a_i \in A$ for all $i \in \mathbb{N}$. Similarly, a *finite run* $\zeta \in (S \times A)^* \times S$ is a finite sequence $\zeta = s_0 a_0 s_1 a_1 \ldots a_{t-1} s_t$. For any run ζ of length at least j and any $i \leq j$, we let $\zeta_{i:j}$ denote the subsequence $s_i a_i s_{i+1} a_{i+1} \ldots a_{j-1} s_j$. We use $\mathtt{Runs}(S, A) = (S \times A)^\omega$ and $\mathtt{Runs}_f(S, A) = (S \times A)^* \times S$ to denote the set of infinite and finite runs, respectively.

Let $\mathcal{D}(A) = \{\Delta : A \rightarrow [0, 1] \mid \sum_{a \in A} \Delta(a) = 1\}$ denote the set of all distributions over actions. A policy $\pi : \mathtt{Runs}_f(S, A) \rightarrow \mathcal{D}(A)$ maps a finite run $\zeta \in \mathtt{Runs}_f(S, A)$ to a distribution $\pi(\zeta)$ over actions. We denote by $\Pi(S, A)$ the set of all such policies. A policy π is *positional* if $\pi(\zeta) = \pi(\zeta')$ for all $\zeta, \zeta' \in \mathtt{Runs}_f(S, A)$ with $\mathtt{last}(\zeta) = \mathtt{last}(\zeta')$ where $\mathtt{last}(\zeta)$ denotes the last state in the run ζ. A policy π is deterministic if, for all finite runs $\zeta \in \mathtt{Runs}_f(S, A)$, there is an action $a \in A$ with $\pi(\zeta)(a) = 1$.

Given a finite run $\zeta = s_0 a_0 \ldots a_{t-1} s_t$, the *cylinder* of ζ, denoted by $\mathtt{Cyl}(\zeta)$, is the set of all infinite runs starting with prefix ζ. Given an MDP $\mathcal{M}$ and a policy $\pi \in \Pi(S, A)$, we define the probability of the cylinder set by $\mathcal{D}_\pi^\mathcal{M}(\mathtt{Cyl}(\zeta)) = \prod_{i=0}^{t-1} \pi(\zeta_{0:i})(a_i) P(s_i, a_i, s_{i+1})$. It is known that $\mathcal{D}_\pi^\mathcal{M}$ can be uniquely extended to a probability measure over the σ-algebra generated by all cylinder sets.

Simulator. In reinforcement learning, the standard assumption is that the set of states S, the set of actions A, and the initial state s_0 are known but the transition probability function P is unknown. The learning algorithm has access to a simulator $\mathbb{S}$ which can be used to sample runs of the system $\zeta \sim \mathcal{D}_\pi^\mathcal{M}$ using any policy π. The simulator can also be the real system, such as a robot, that $\mathcal{M}$ represents. Internally, the simulator stores the current state of the MDP which is denoted by $\mathbb{S}.\mathtt{state}$. It makes the following functions available to the learning algorithm.

---

[1] A distribution η over initial states can be modeled by adding a new state s_0 from which taking any action leads to a state sampled from η.

S.reset(): This function sets S.state to the initial state s_0.

S.step(a): Given as input an action a, this function samples a state $s' \in S$ according to the transition probability function P—i.e., the probability that a state s' is sampled is $P(s, a, s')$ where $s = $ S.state. It then updates S.state to the newly sampled state s' and returns s'.

Simulation models without the reset() function have also been studied [26,32]. In this paper, we allow resets, however, we believe that our results also apply to settings in which resets are not allowed.

3   Task Specification

In this section, we present many different ways in which one can specify the objective of the learning algorithm. We define a *reinforcement learning task* to be a pair $(\mathcal{M}, \phi)$ where $\mathcal{M}$ is an MDP and ϕ is a specification for $\mathcal{M}$. In general, a specification ϕ for $\mathcal{M} = (S, A, s_0, P)$ defines a function $J_\phi^{\mathcal{M}} :$ $\Pi(S, A) \to \mathbb{R}$ and the reinforcement learning objective is to compute a policy π that maximizes $J_\phi^{\mathcal{M}}(\pi)$. Let $\mathcal{J}^*(\mathcal{M}, \phi) = \sup_\pi J_\phi^{\mathcal{M}}(\pi)$ denote the maximum value of $J_\phi^{\mathcal{M}}$. We let $\Pi_{\text{opt}}(\mathcal{M}, \phi)$ denote the set of all optimal policies in $\mathcal{M}$ w.r.t. ϕ—i.e., $\Pi_{\text{opt}}(\mathcal{M}, \phi) = \{\pi \mid J_\phi^{\mathcal{M}}(\pi) = \mathcal{J}^*(\mathcal{M}, \phi)\}$. In many cases, it is sufficient to compute an ε-optimal policy $\tilde{\pi}$ with $J_\phi^{\mathcal{M}}(\tilde{\pi}) \geq \mathcal{J}^*(\mathcal{M}, \phi) - \varepsilon$; we let $\Pi_{\text{opt}}^\varepsilon(\mathcal{M}, \phi)$ denote the set of all ε-optimal policies in $\mathcal{M}$ w.r.t. ϕ.

3.1   Rewards

The most common kind of specifications used in reinforcement learning is reward functions that map transitions in $\mathcal{M}$ to real values. We first define the more general *reward machines* and then define standard transition-based reward functions as a special case.

Reward Machines. Reward Machines [19] extend simple transition-based reward functions to history-dependent ones by using an automaton model. Formally, a reward machine for an MDP $\mathcal{M} = (S, A, s_0, P)$ is a tuple $\mathcal{R} = (U, u_0, \delta_u, \delta_r)$, where U is a finite set of states, u_0 is the initial state, $\delta_u : U \times S \to U$ is the state transition function, and $\delta_r : U \to [S \times A \times S \to \mathbb{R}]$ is the reward function. Given an infinite run $\zeta = s_0 a_0 s_1 a_1 \ldots$, we can construct an infinite sequence of reward machine states $\rho_{\mathcal{R}}(\zeta) = u_0 u_1, \ldots$ defined by $u_{i+1} = \delta_u(u_i, s_{i+1})$. Then, we can assign either a discounted-sum or a limit-average reward to ζ:

– *Discounted Sum.* Given a discount factor $\gamma \in]0, 1[$, the full specification is $\phi = (\mathcal{R}, \gamma)$ and we have

$$\mathcal{R}_\gamma(\zeta) = \sum_{i=0}^{\infty} \gamma^i \delta_r(u_i)(s_i, a_i, s_{i+1}).$$

Though less standard, one can use different discount factors in different states of $\mathcal{M}$, in which case we have $\gamma : S \to]0,1[$ and

$$\mathcal{R}_\gamma(\zeta) = \sum_{i=0}^{\infty} \Big(\prod_{j=0}^{i-1} \gamma(s_j) \Big) \delta_r(u_i)(s_i, a_i, s_{i+1}).$$

The value of a policy π is $J_\phi^\mathcal{M}(\pi) = \mathbb{E}_{\zeta \sim \mathcal{D}_\pi^\mathcal{M}}[\mathcal{R}_\gamma(\zeta)]$.

– *Limit Average.* The specification is just a reward machine $\phi = \mathcal{R}$. The t-step average reward of the run ζ is

$$\mathcal{R}_{\mathrm{avg}}^t(\zeta) = \frac{1}{t} \sum_{i=0}^{t-1} \delta_r(u_i)(s_i, a_i, s_{i+1}).$$

The value of a policy π is $J_\phi^\mathcal{M}(\pi) = \liminf_{t \to \infty} \mathbb{E}_{\zeta \sim \mathcal{D}_\pi^\mathcal{M}}[\mathcal{R}_{\mathrm{avg}}^t(\zeta)]$.

A standard transition-based reward function R is simply a reward machine $\mathcal{R}$ with a single state u_0; in this case, we use $R(s, a, s')$ to denote $\delta_r(u_0)(s, a, s')$.

3.2   Abstract Specifications

The above specifications are defined w.r.t. a given set of states S and actions A, and can only be interpreted over MDPs with the same state and action spaces. In this section, we look at *abstract specifications*, which are defined independently of S and A. To achieve this, a common assumption is that there is a fixed set of propositions $\mathcal{P}$, and the simulator provides access to a labeling function $L : S \to 2^\mathcal{P}$ denoting which propositions are true in any given state. Given a run $\zeta = s_0 a_0 s_1 a_1 \ldots$, we let $L(\zeta)$ denote the corresponding sequence of labels $L(\zeta) = L(s_0)L(s_1)\ldots$. A *labeled MDP* is a tuple $\mathcal{M} = (S, A, s_0, P, L)$. WLOG, we only consider labeled MDPs in the rest of the paper.

Abstract Reward Machines. Reward machines can be adapted to the abstract setting quite naturally. An *abstract reward machine* (ARM) is similar to a reward machine except δ_u and δ_r are independent of S and A—i.e., $\delta_u : U \times 2^\mathcal{P} \to U$ and $\delta_r : U \to [2^\mathcal{P} \to \mathbb{R}]$. Given current ARM state u_i and next MDP state s_{i+1}, the next ARM state is given by $u_{i+1} = \delta_u(u_i, L(s_{i+1}))$, and the reward is given by $\delta_r(u_i)(L(s_{i+1}))$.

Languages. Formal languages can be used to specify qualitative properties about runs of the system. A language specification $\phi = \mathcal{L} \subseteq (2^\mathcal{P})^\omega$ is a set of "desirable" sequences of labels. The value of a policy π is the probability of generating a sequence in $\mathcal{L}$—i.e.,

$$J_\phi^\mathcal{M}(\pi) = \mathcal{D}_\pi^\mathcal{M}(\{\zeta \in \mathrm{Runs}(S, A) \mid L(\zeta) \in \mathcal{L}\}).$$

Some common ways to define languages are as follows.

- *Reachability.* Given an accepting set of propositions $X \in 2^{\mathcal{P}}$, we have $\mathcal{L}_{\text{reach}}(X) = \{w \in (2^{\mathcal{P}})^{\omega} \mid \exists i.\ w_i \cap X \neq \emptyset\}$.
- *Safety.* Given a safe set of propositions $X \in 2^{\mathcal{P}}$, we have $\mathcal{L}_{\text{safe}}(X) = \{w \in (2^{\mathcal{P}})^{\omega} \mid \forall i.\ w_i \subseteq X\}$.
- *Linear Temporal Logic.* Linear Temporal Logic [30] over propositions $\mathcal{P}$ is defined by the grammar

$$\varphi := b \in \mathcal{P} \mid \varphi \vee \varphi \mid \neg\varphi \mid \bigcirc \varphi \mid \varphi \, \mathcal{U} \, \varphi$$

where $\bigcirc$ denotes the "Next" operator and $\mathcal{U}$ denotes the "Until" operator. We refer the reader to [31] for more details on the semantics of LTL specifications. We use $\Diamond$ and $\Box$ to denote the derived "Eventually" and "Always" operators, respectively. Given an LTL specification φ over propositions $\mathcal{P}$, we have $\mathcal{L}_{\text{LTL}}(\varphi) = \{w \in (2^{\mathcal{P}})^{\omega} \mid w \models \varphi\}$.

3.3 Learning Algorithms

A learning algorithm $\mathcal{A}$ is an iterative process that in each iteration (i) either resets the simulator or takes a step in $\mathcal{M}$, and (ii) outputs its current estimate of an optimal policy π. A learning algorithm $\mathcal{A}$ induces a random sequence of output policies $\{\pi_n\}_{n=1}^{\infty}$ where π_n is the policy output in the nth iteration. We consider two common kinds of learning algorithms. First, we consider algorithms that converge in the limit almost surely.

Definition 1. *A learning algorithm $\mathcal{A}$ is said to converge in the limit for a class of specifications $\mathbb{C}$ if, for any RL task $(\mathcal{M}, \phi)$ with $\phi \in \mathbb{C}$,*

$$J_{\phi}^{\mathcal{M}}(\pi_n) \to \mathcal{J}^*(\mathcal{M}, \phi) \ \text{as } n \to \infty \quad \text{almost surely.}$$

Q-learning [33] is an example of a learning algorithm that converges in the limit for discounted-sum rewards. There are variants of Q-learning for limit-average rewards [2] which have been shown to converge in the limit under some assumptions on the MDP $\mathcal{M}$. The second kind of algorithms is *Probably Approximately Correct* (PAC-MDP) [25] algorithms which are defined as follows.

Definition 2. *A learning algorithm $\mathcal{A}$ is said to be PAC-MDP for a class of specifications $\mathbb{C}$ if, there is a function h such that for any $p > 0$, $\varepsilon > 0$, and any RL task $(\mathcal{M}, \phi)$ with $\mathcal{M} = (S, A, s_0, P)$ and $\phi \in \mathbb{C}$, taking $N = h(|S|, |A|, |\phi|, \frac{1}{p}, \frac{1}{\varepsilon})$, with probability at least $1 - p$, we have*

$$\left| \left\{ n \mid \pi_n \notin \Pi_{opt}^{\varepsilon}(\mathcal{M}, \phi) \right\} \right| \leq N.$$

We say a PAC-MDP algorithm is *efficient* if the *sample complexity* function h is polynomial in $|S|, |A|, \frac{1}{p}$ and $\frac{1}{\varepsilon}$. There are efficient PAC-MDP algorithms for discounted-sum rewards [26,32].

4   Reductions

There has been a lot of research on RL algorithms for reward-based specifications. The most common approach for language-based specifications is to transform the given specification into a reward function and apply algorithms that maximize the expected reward. In such cases, it is important to ensure that maximizing the expected reward corresponds to maximizing the probability of satisfying the specification. In this section, we study such reductions and formalize a general notion of *sampling-based reductions* in the RL setting—i.e., the transition probabilities are unknown and only a simulator of $\mathcal{M}$ is available.

4.1   Specification Translations

We first consider the simplest form of reduction, which involves translating the given specification into another one. Given a specification ϕ for MDP $\mathcal{M} = (S, A, s_0, P, L)$ we want to construct another specification ϕ' such that for any $\pi \in \Pi_{opt}(\mathcal{M}, \phi')$, we also have $\pi \in \Pi_{opt}(\mathcal{M}, \phi)$. This ensures that ϕ' can be used to compute a policy that maximizes the objective of ϕ. Note that since the transition probabilities P are not known, the translation has to be independent of P and furthermore the above *optimality preservation* criterion must hold for all P.

Definition 3. *An optimality preserving specification translation is a computable function $\mathcal{F}$ that maps the tuple (S, A, s_0, L, ϕ) to a specification ϕ' such that for all transition probability functions P, letting $\mathcal{M} = (S, A, s_0, P, L)$, we have $\Pi_{opt}(\mathcal{M}, \phi') \subseteq \Pi_{opt}(\mathcal{M}, \phi)$.*

A first attempt at a reinforcement learning algorithm for language-based specifications is to translate the given specification to a reward machine (either discounted-sum or limit-average). However there are some limitations to this approach. First, we show that it is not possible to reduce reachability and safety objectives to reward machines with discounted rewards.

Theorem 1. *Let $\mathcal{P} = \{b\}$ and $\phi = \mathcal{L}_{reach}(\{b\})$. There exists S, A, s_0, L such that for any discounted-sum reward machine specification $\phi' = (\mathcal{R}, \gamma)$, there is a transition probability function P such that for $\mathcal{M} = (S, A, s_0, P, L)$, we have $\Pi_{opt}(\mathcal{M}, \phi') \not\subseteq \Pi_{opt}(\mathcal{M}, \phi)$.*

The main idea behind the proof (see full version [4]) is that one can make the transition probabilities small enough so that the expected time taken to reach the goal is large while maintaining an optimal probability of 1 for eventually reaching the goal. Using this idea, it is possible to define transition probabilities such that the expected reward w.r.t. an optimal policy is smaller than the expected reward obtained by a suboptimal policy.

We do not use the fact that the reward machine is finite state in our proof; therefore, the above result applies to general non-Markovian reward functions of the form $R : \text{Runs}_f(S, A) \to [0, 1]$ with γ-discounted reward defined by $R_\gamma(\zeta) =$

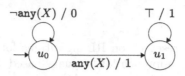

Fig. 1. ARM for $\phi = \mathcal{L}_{\texttt{reach}}(X)$.

$\sum_{i=0}^{\infty} \gamma^i R(\zeta_{0:i})$. The proof can be easily modified to show the result for safety specifications as well.

The main challenge in translating to discounted-sum rewards is the fact that the rewards vanish over time and the overall reward depends primarily on the first few steps. This issue can be partly overcome by using limit-average rewards. In fact, we have the following theorem.

Theorem 2. *There exists an optimality preserving specification translation from reachability and safety specifications to abstract reward machines (with limit-average aggregation).*

Proof. An abstract reward machine for the specification $\phi = \mathcal{L}_{\texttt{reach}}(X)$ is shown in Fig. 1. Each transition is labeled by a Boolean formula over $\mathcal{P}$ followed by the reward. We use $\texttt{any}(X)$ to denote $\bigvee_{b \in X} b$. It is easy to see that for any MDP $\mathcal{M}$ and any policy π of $\mathcal{M}$, we have $J_{\mathcal{R}}^{\mathcal{M}}(\pi) = J_{\phi}^{\mathcal{M}}(\pi)$. An ARM for $\phi = \mathcal{L}_{\texttt{safe}}(\mathcal{P} \setminus X)$ is obtained by replacing the reward value r by $1 - r$ on all transitions. $\square$

However, we can show that there does not exist an ARM for the specification $\phi = \mathcal{L}_{\text{LTL}}(\Box\Diamond b)$, which requires the proposition b to be true infinitely often. Intuitively, the result follows from the fact that, given any ARM, we can construct an infinite word $w \in (2^{\mathcal{P}})^{\omega}$ in which b holds true rarely but infinitely often such that w achieves a lower limit-average reward than another word w' in which b holds true more frequently. A complete proof can be found in [4].

Theorem 3. *Let $\mathcal{P} = \{b\}$ and $\phi = \mathcal{L}_{\text{LTL}}(\Box\Diamond b)$. For any ARM specification $\phi' = \mathcal{R}$ with limit-average rewards, there exists an MDP $\mathcal{M} = (S, A, s_0, P, L)$ such that $\Pi_{opt}(\mathcal{M}, \phi') \not\subseteq \Pi_{opt}(\mathcal{M}, \phi)$.*

Note that the above theorem claims only the non-existence of *abstract* reward machines for the LTL specification $\Box\Diamond b$, whereas Theorem 1 holds for arbitrary reward machines and history dependent reward functions. We do not rule out the possibility of a specification translation that constructs different ARMs (with limit-average rewards) for the same LTL objective depending on S, A, s_0 and L. This leads to the following natural question.

Open Problem 1. *Does there exist an optimality preserving specification translation from LTL specifications to reward machines with limit-average rewards?*

4.2   Sampling-Based Reduction

The previous section suggests that keeping the MDP $\mathcal{M}$ fixed might be insufficient for reducing LTL specifications to reward-based ones. In this section, we formalize the notion of a *sampling-based reduction* where we are allowed to modify the MDP $\mathcal{M}$ in a way that makes it possible to simulate the modified MDP $\bar{\mathcal{M}}$ using a simulator for $\mathcal{M}$ without the knowledge of the transition probabilities of $\mathcal{M}$.

Given an RL task $(\mathcal{M}, \phi)$ we want to construct another RL task $(\bar{\mathcal{M}}, \phi')$ and a function f that maps policies in $\bar{\mathcal{M}}$ to policies in $\mathcal{M}$ such that for any policy $\bar{\pi} \in \Pi_{\mathrm{opt}}(\bar{\mathcal{M}}, \phi')$, we have $f(\bar{\pi}) \in \Pi_{\mathrm{opt}}(\mathcal{M}, \phi)$. Since it should be possible to simulate $\bar{\mathcal{M}}$ without the knowledge of the transition probability function P of $\mathcal{M}$, we impose several constraints on $\bar{\mathcal{M}}$.

Let $\mathcal{M} = (S, A, s_0, P, L)$ and $\bar{\mathcal{M}} = (\bar{S}, \bar{A}, \bar{s}_0, \bar{P}, \bar{L})$. First, it must be the case that $\bar{S}$, $\bar{A}$, $\bar{s}_0$, $\bar{L}$ and f are independent of P. Second, since the simulator of $\bar{\mathcal{M}}$ uses the simulator of $\mathcal{M}$ we can assume that at any time, the state of the simulator of $\bar{\mathcal{M}}$ includes the state of the simulator of $\mathcal{M}$. Formally, there is a map $\beta : \bar{S} \to S$ such that for any $\bar{s}$, $\beta(\bar{s})$ is the state of $\mathcal{M}$ stored in $\bar{s}$. Since it is only possible to simulate $\mathcal{M}$ starting from s_0 we must have $\beta(\bar{s}_0) = s_0$. Next, when taking a step in $\bar{\mathcal{M}}$, a step in $\mathcal{M}$ may or may not occur, but the probability that a transition is sampled from $\mathcal{M}$ should be independent of P. Given these desired properties, we are ready to define a step-wise sampling-based reduction.

Definition 4. *A step-wise sampling-based reduction is a computable function $\mathcal{F}$ that maps the tuple (S, A, s_0, L, ϕ) to a tuple $(\bar{S}, \bar{A}, \bar{s}_0, \bar{L}, f, \beta, \alpha, q_1, q_2, \phi')$ where $f : \Pi(\bar{S}, \bar{A}) \to \Pi(S, A)$, $\beta : \bar{S} \to S$, $\alpha : \bar{S} \times \bar{A} \to \mathcal{D}(A)$, $q_1 : \bar{S} \times \bar{A} \times \bar{S} \to [0, 1]$, $q_2 : \bar{S} \times \bar{A} \times A \times \bar{S} \to [0, 1]$ and ϕ' is a specification such that*

- *$\beta(\bar{s}_0) = s_0$,*
- *$q_1(\bar{s}, \bar{a}, \bar{s}') = 0$ if $\beta(\bar{s}) \neq \beta(\bar{s}')$ and,*
- *for any $\bar{s} \in \bar{S}$, $\bar{a} \in \bar{A}$, $a \in A$, and $s' \in S$ we have*

$$\sum_{\bar{s}' \in \beta^{-1}(s')} q_2(\bar{s}, \bar{a}, a, \bar{s}') = 1 - \sum_{\bar{s}' \in \bar{S}} q_1(\bar{s}, \bar{a}, \bar{s}'). \tag{1}$$

For any transition probability function $P : S \times A \times S \to [0, 1]$, the new transition probability function $\bar{P} : \bar{S} \times \bar{A} \times \bar{S} \to [0, 1]$ is defined by

$$\bar{P}(\bar{s}, \bar{a}, \bar{s}') = q_1(\bar{s}, \bar{a}, \bar{s}') + \mathbb{E}_{a \sim \alpha(\bar{s}, \bar{a})}[q_2(\bar{s}, \bar{a}, a, \bar{s}') P(\beta(\bar{s}), a, \beta(\bar{s}'))]. \tag{2}$$

In Eq. 2, $q_1(\bar{s}, \bar{a}, \bar{s}')$ denotes the probability with which $\bar{\mathcal{M}}$ steps to $\bar{s}'$ without sampling a transition from $\mathcal{M}$. In the event that a step in $\mathcal{M}$ does occur, $\alpha(\bar{s}, \bar{a})(a)$ gives the probability of the action a taken in $\mathcal{M}$ and $q_2(\bar{s}, \bar{a}, a, \bar{s}')$ is the (unnormalized) probability with which $\bar{\mathcal{M}}$ transitions to $\bar{s}'$ given that action a in $\mathcal{M}$ caused a transition to $\beta(\bar{s}')$. It is easy to see that, for any P, $\bar{P}$ defined in Eq. 2 is a valid transition probability function.

Algorithm 1. Step function of the simulator $\bar{\mathbb{S}}$ of $\bar{\mathcal{M}}$ given β, α, q_1, q_2 and a simulator $\mathbb{S}$ of $\mathcal{M}$.

---

function $\bar{\mathbb{S}}.\mathtt{step}(\bar{a})$
  $\bar{s} \leftarrow \bar{\mathbb{S}}.\mathtt{state}$
  $p \leftarrow \sum_{\bar{s}'} q_1(\bar{s}, \bar{a}, \bar{s}')$
  $x \sim \mathtt{Uniform}(0, 1)$
  if $x \leq p$ **then**
    $\bar{\mathbb{S}}.\mathtt{state} \leftarrow \bar{s}' \sim \dfrac{q_1(\bar{s}, \bar{a}, \bar{s}')}{p}$
  else
    $a \sim \alpha(\bar{s}, \bar{a})$
    $s' \leftarrow \mathbb{S}.\mathtt{step}(a)$
    $\bar{\mathbb{S}}.\mathtt{state} \leftarrow \bar{s}' \sim \dfrac{q_2(\bar{s}, \bar{a}, a, \bar{s}')\mathbb{1}(\beta(\bar{s}') = s')}{1 - p}$ {Ensures $\beta(\bar{s}') = s'$}
  return $\bar{\mathbb{S}}.\mathtt{state}$

Lemma 1. *Given a step-wise sampling-based reduction $\mathcal{F}$, for any MDP $\mathcal{M} = (S, A, s_0, P, L)$ and specification ϕ, the function $\bar{P}$ defined by $\mathcal{F}$ is a valid transition probability function.*

Example 1. A simple example of a step-wise sampling-based reduction is the product construction used to translate reward machines to regular reward functions [19]. Let $\mathcal{R} = (U, u_0, \delta_u, \delta_r)$. Then, we have $\bar{S} = S \times U$, $\bar{A} = A$, $\bar{s}_0 = (s_0, u_0)$, $\bar{L}(s, u) = L(s)$, $\beta(s, u) = s$, $\alpha(a)(a') = \mathbb{1}(a' = a)$, $q_1 = 0$, and $q_2((s, u), a, a', (s', u')) = \mathbb{1}(u' = \delta_u(u, s'))$. The specification ϕ' is a reward function given by $R((s, u), a, (s', u')) = \delta_r(u)(s, a, s')$, and $f(\bar{\pi})$ is a policy that keeps track of the reward machine state and acts according to $\bar{\pi}$.

Given an MDP $\mathcal{M} = (S, A, s_0, P, L)$ and a specification ϕ, the reduction $\mathcal{F}$ defines a unique triplet $(\bar{\mathcal{M}}, \phi', f)$ with $\bar{\mathcal{M}} = (\bar{S}, \bar{A}, \bar{s}_0, \bar{P}, \bar{L})$, where $\bar{S}, \bar{A}, \bar{s}_0, \bar{L}, f$ and ϕ' are obtained by applying $\mathcal{F}$ to (S, A, s_0, L, ϕ) and $\bar{P}$ is defined by Eq. 2. We let $\mathcal{F}(\mathcal{M}, \phi)$ denote the triplet $(\bar{\mathcal{M}}, \phi', f)$. Given a simulator $\mathbb{S}$ of $\mathcal{M}$, we can construct a simulator $\bar{\mathbb{S}}$ of $\bar{\mathcal{M}}$ as follows.

$\bar{\mathbb{S}}.\mathtt{reset}()$: This function internally sets the current state of the MDP to $\bar{s}_0$ and calls the reset function of $\mathcal{M}$.

$\bar{\mathbb{S}}.\mathtt{step}(\bar{a})$: This function is outlined in Algorithm 1. We use $\bar{s}' \sim \Delta(\bar{s}')$ to denote that $\bar{s}'$ is sampled from the distribution defined by Δ. It takes a step without calling $\mathbb{S}.\mathtt{step}$ with probability p. Otherwise, it samples an action a according to $\alpha(\bar{s}, \bar{a})$, calls $\mathbb{S}.\mathtt{step}(a)$ to get next state s' of $\mathcal{M}$ and then samples an $\bar{s}'$ satisfying $\beta(\bar{s}') = s'$ based on q_2. Equation 1 ensures that $\frac{q_2}{1-p}$ defines a valid distribution over $\beta^{-1}(s')$.

We call the reduction step-wise since at most one transition of $\mathcal{M}$ can occur during a transition of $\bar{\mathcal{M}}$. Under this assumption, we justify the general form of $\bar{P}$. Let $\bar{s}$ and $\bar{a}$ be fixed. Let $X_{\bar{S}}$ be a random variable denoting the next state in $\bar{\mathcal{M}}$ and X_A be a random variable denoting the action taking in $\mathcal{M}$ (it takes a dummy value $\perp \notin A$ when no step in $\mathcal{M}$ is taken). Then, for any $\bar{s}' \in \bar{S}$, we have

$$\Pr[X_{\bar{S}} = \bar{s}'] = \Pr[X_{\bar{S}} = \bar{s}' \wedge X_A = \perp] + \sum_{a \in A} \Pr[X_{\bar{S}} = \bar{s}' \wedge X_A = a].$$

Now, we have

$$\Pr[X_{\bar{S}} = \bar{s}' \wedge X_A = a]$$
$$= \Pr[X_A = a] \Pr[X_{\bar{S}} = \bar{s}' \mid X_A = a]$$
$$= \Pr[X_A = a] \Pr[\beta(X_{\bar{S}}) = \beta(\bar{s}') \mid X_A = a] \Pr[X_{\bar{S}} = \bar{s}' \mid X_A = a, \beta(X_{\bar{S}}) = \beta(\bar{s}')]$$
$$= P(\beta(\bar{s}), a, \beta(\bar{s}')) \cdot \Pr[X_A = a] \Pr[X_{\bar{S}} = \bar{s}' \mid X_A = a, \beta(X_{\bar{S}}) = \beta(\bar{s}')].$$

Taking $q_1(\bar{s}, \bar{a}, \bar{s}') = \Pr[X_{\bar{S}} = \bar{s}' \wedge X_A = \perp]$, $\alpha(\bar{s}, \bar{a})(a) = \Pr[X_A = a]/\Pr[X_A \neq \perp]$, and $q_2(\bar{s}, \bar{a}, a, \bar{s}') = \Pr[X_{\bar{S}} = \bar{s}' \mid X_A = a, \beta(X_{\bar{S}}) = \beta(\bar{s}')] \cdot \Pr[X_A \neq \perp]$, we obtain the form of $\bar{P}$ in Definition 4. Note that Eq. 1 holds since both sides evaluate to $\Pr[X_A \neq \perp]$.

To be precise, it is also possible to reset the MDP $\mathcal{M}$ to s_0 in the middle of a run of $\bar{\mathcal{M}}$. This can be modeled by taking $\alpha(\bar{s}, \bar{a})$ to be a distribution over $A \times \{0, 1\}$, where $(a, 0)$ represents taking action a in the current state $\beta(\bar{s})$ and $(a, 1)$ represents taking action a in s_0 after a reset. We would also have $q_2 : \bar{S} \times \bar{A} \times A \times \{0, 1\} \times \bar{S} \to [0, 1]$ and furthermore $q_1(\bar{s}, \bar{a}, \bar{s}')$ can be nonzero if $\beta(\bar{s}') = s_0$. For simplicity, we use Definition 4 without considering resets in $\mathcal{M}$ during a step of $\bar{\mathcal{M}}$. However, the discussions in the rest of the paper apply to the general case as well. Now we define the *optimality preservation* criterion for sampling-based reductions.

Definition 5. *A step-wise sampling-based reduction $\mathcal{F}$ is optimality preserving if for any RL task $(\mathcal{M}, \phi)$ letting $(\bar{\mathcal{M}}, \phi', f) = \mathcal{F}(\mathcal{M}, \phi)$ we have $f(\Pi_{opt}(\bar{\mathcal{M}}, \phi')) \subseteq \Pi_{opt}(\mathcal{M}, \phi)$ where $f(\Pi) = \{f(\pi) \mid \pi \in \Pi\}$ for a set of policies Π.*

It is easy to see that the reduction in Example 1 is optimality preserving for both discounted-sum and limit-average rewards since $J_{\phi'}^{\bar{\mathcal{M}}}(\bar{\pi}) = J_{\phi}^{\mathcal{M}}(f(\bar{\pi}))$ for any policy $\bar{\pi} \in \Pi(\bar{S}, \bar{A})$. Another interesting observation is that we can reduce discounted-sum rewards with multiple discount factors $\gamma : S \to]0, 1[$ to the usual case with a single discount factor (proof in full version [4]).

Theorem 4. *There is an optimality preserving step-wise sampling-based reduction $\mathcal{F}$ such that for any $\mathcal{M} = (S, A, s_0, P)$ and $\phi = (R, \gamma)$, where $R : S \times A \times S \to \mathbb{R}$ and $\gamma : S \to]0, 1[$, we have $f(\mathcal{M}, \phi) = (\bar{\mathcal{M}}, \phi', f)$, where $\phi' = (R', \gamma')$, with $R' : \bar{S} \times \bar{A} \times \bar{S} \to \mathbb{R}$ and $\gamma' \in]0, 1[$.*

4.3 Reductions from Temporal Logic Specifications

A number of strategies have been recently proposed for learning policies from temporal specifications by reducing them to reward-based specifications. For instance, [3] proposes a reduction from Signal Temporal Logic (STL) specifications to rewards in the finite horizon setting—i.e., the specification φ is evaluated over a fixed T_φ-length prefix of the rollout ζ.

The authors of [17,18] propose a reduction from LTL specifications to discounted rewards which proceeds by first constructing a product of the MDP $\mathcal{M}$ with a Limit Deterministic Büchi automaton (LDBA) $\mathcal{A}_\varphi$ derived from the LTL formula φ and then generates transition-based rewards in the product MDP. The strategy is to assign a fixed positive reward of r when an accepting state in $\mathcal{A}_\varphi$ is reached and 0 otherwise. As shown in [13], this strategy does not always preserve optimality if the discount factor γ is required to be strictly less that one. Similar approaches are proposed in [9,22,36], though they do not provide optimality preservation guarantees.

A recent paper [13] presents a step-wise sampling-based reduction from LTL specifications to limit-average rewards. It first constructs an LDBA $\mathcal{A}_\varphi$ from the LTL formula φ and then considers a product $\mathcal{M} \otimes \mathcal{A}_\varphi$ of the MDP $\mathcal{M}$ with $\mathcal{A}_\varphi$ in which the nondeterminism of $\mathcal{A}_\varphi$ is handled by adding additional actions that represent the choice of possible transitions in $\mathcal{A}_\varphi$ that can be taken. Now, the reduced MDP $\bar{\mathcal{M}}$ is obtained by adding an additional sink state $\bar{s}_\perp$ with the property that whenever an accepting state of $\mathcal{A}_\varphi$ is reached in $\bar{\mathcal{M}}$, there is a $(1-\lambda)$ probability of transitioning to $\bar{s}_\perp$ during the next transition in $\bar{\mathcal{M}}$. They show that for a large enough value of λ, any policy maximizing the probability of reaching $\bar{s}_\perp$ in $\bar{\mathcal{M}}$ can be used to construct a policy that maximizes $J^\mathcal{M}_{\mathcal{L}_{\mathrm{LTL}}(\varphi)}$. As shown before, this reachability property in $\bar{\mathcal{M}}$ can be translated to limit-average rewards. The main drawback of this approach is that the lower bound on λ for preserving optimality depends on the transition probability function P; hence, it is not possible to correctly pick the value of λ without the knowledge of P. A heuristic used in practice is to assign a default large value to λ. Their result can be summarized as follows.

Theorem 5 ([13]). *There is a family of step-wise sampling-based reductions* $\{\mathcal{F}_\lambda\}_{\lambda \in]0,1[}$ *such that for any MDP $\mathcal{M}$ and LTL specification $\phi = \mathcal{L}_{\mathrm{LTL}}(\varphi)$, there exists a $\lambda_{\mathcal{M},\phi} \in]0,1[$ such that for all $\lambda \geq \lambda_{\mathcal{M},\phi}$, letting $(\bar{\mathcal{M}}_\lambda, \phi'_\lambda, f_\lambda) = \mathcal{F}_\lambda(\mathcal{M}, \phi)$, we have $f_\lambda(\Pi_{opt}(\bar{\mathcal{M}}_\lambda, \phi'_\lambda)) \subseteq \Pi_{opt}(\mathcal{M}, \phi)$ and $\phi'_\lambda = R_\lambda : S \times A \times S \to \mathbb{R}$ is a limit-average reward specification.*

The authors of [14] show that the above approach can be modified to get less sparse rewards with similar guarantees using two discount factors $\gamma_1 < 1$ and $\gamma_2 = 1$ (where $\gamma_2 = 1$ is only used in steps at which the reward is zero).

Another approach [7] with an optimality preservation guarantee reduces LTL specifications to discounted rewards with two discount factors $\gamma_1 < \gamma_2 < 1$ which are applied in different states. This approach uses the product $\mathcal{M} \times \mathcal{A}_\varphi$ as $\bar{\mathcal{M}}$ and assigns a reward of $1 - \gamma_1$ to the accepting states (where discount factor γ_1 is applied) and 0 to the remaining states (where discount factor γ_2 is applied). Applying Theorem 4 we get the following result as a corollary of the optimality preservation guarantee of this approach.

Theorem 6 ([7]). *There is a family of step-wise sampling-based reductions* $\{\mathcal{F}_\gamma\}_{\gamma \in]0,1[}$ *such that for any MDP* $\mathcal{M}$ *and LTL specification* $\phi = \mathcal{L}_{\mathrm{LTL}}(\varphi)$, *there exists* $\gamma_{\mathcal{M},\phi} \in]0,1[$ *such that for all* $\gamma \geq \gamma_{\mathcal{M},\phi}$, *letting* $(\bar{\mathcal{M}}_\gamma, \phi'_\gamma, f_\gamma) = \mathcal{F}_\gamma(\mathcal{M}, \phi)$, *we have* $f_\gamma(\Pi_{opt}(\bar{\mathcal{M}}_\gamma, \phi'_\gamma)) \subseteq \Pi_{opt}(\mathcal{M}, \phi)$ *and* $\phi'_\gamma = (R_\gamma, \gamma)$ *is a discounted-sum reward specification.*

Similar to [13], the optimality preservation guarantee only applies to large enough γ, and the lower bound on γ depends on the transition probability function P.

To the best of our knowledge, it is unknown if there exists an optimality preserving step-wise sampling-based reduction from LTL specifications to reward-based specifications that is completely independent of P.

Open Problem 2. *Does there exist an optimality preserving step-wise sampling-based reduction* $\mathcal{F}$ *such that for any RL task* $(\mathcal{M}, \phi)$ *where* ϕ *is an LTL specification, letting* $(\bar{\mathcal{M}}, \phi', f) = \mathcal{F}(\mathcal{M}, \phi)$, *we have that* ϕ' *is a reward-based specification (either limit-average or discounted-sum)?*

5 Robustness

A key property of discounted reward specifications that is exploited by RL algorithms is *robustness*. In this section, we discuss the concept of robustness for specifications as well as reductions. We show that robust reductions from LTL specifications to discounted rewards are not possible due to the fact that LTL specifications are not robust.

5.1 Robust Specifications

A specification ϕ is said to be *robust* [29] if an optimal policy for ϕ in an estimate $\mathcal{M}'$ of the MDP $\mathcal{M}$ achieves close to optimal performance in $\mathcal{M}$. Formally, an MDP $\mathcal{M} = (S, A, s_0, P, L)$ is said to be δ-*close* to another MDP $\mathcal{M}' = (S, A, s_0, P', L)$ if their states, actions, initial states, and labeling functions are identical and their transition probabilities differ by at most a δ amount—i.e.,

$$|P(s, a, s') - P'(s, a, s')| \leq \delta$$

for all $s, s' \in S$ and $a \in A$.

Definition 6. *A specification* ϕ *is robust if for any MDP* $\mathcal{M}$ *for which* ϕ *is a valid specification and* $\varepsilon > 0$, *there exists a* $\delta_{\mathcal{M},\varepsilon} > 0$ *such that if MDP* $\mathcal{M}'$ *is* $\delta_{\mathcal{M},\varepsilon}$-*close to* $\mathcal{M}$, *then an optimal policy in* $\mathcal{M}'$ *is an* ε-*optimal policy in* $\mathcal{M}$—*i.e.,* $\Pi_{opt}(\mathcal{M}', \phi) \subseteq \Pi_{opt}^\varepsilon(\mathcal{M}, \phi)$.

The simulation lemma in [26] proves that discounted-sum rewards are robust. On the other hand, [29] shows that language-based specifications, even safety specifications, are not robust. Here, we give a slightly modified example to show that the specification $\phi = \mathcal{L}_{\mathtt{safe}}(\{b\})$ is not robust which also shows that limit-average rewards are not robust.

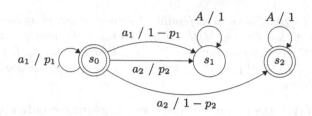

Fig. 2. Example showing non-robustness of $\mathcal{L}_{\texttt{safe}}(\{b\})$.

Theorem 7 (*[29]*). *There exists an MDP $\mathcal{M}$ and a safety specification ϕ such that, for any $\delta > 0$, there is an MDP $\mathcal{M}_\delta$ that is δ-close to $\mathcal{M}$ which satisfies $\Pi_{opt}(\mathcal{M}_\delta, \phi) \cap \Pi_{opt}^\varepsilon(\mathcal{M}, \phi) = \emptyset$ for all $\varepsilon < 1$.*

Proof. Consider the MDP $\mathcal{M}$ in Fig. 2 with $p_1 = p_2 = 1$; the double circles denote states where b holds. Then, an optimal policy for $\phi = \mathcal{L}_{\texttt{safe}}(\{b\})$ always selects action a_1 and achieves a satisfaction probability of 1. Now let $\mathcal{M}_\delta$ denote the same MDP with $p_1 = p_2 = 1 - \delta$. Then, any optimal policy for ϕ in $\mathcal{M}_\delta$ must select a_2 almost surely, which is not optimal for $\mathcal{M}$. In fact, such a policy achieves a satisfaction probability of 0 in $\mathcal{M}$. Therefore, we have $\Pi_{\text{opt}}(\mathcal{M}_\delta, \phi) \cap \Pi_{\text{opt}}^\varepsilon(\mathcal{M}, \phi) = \emptyset$ for any $\delta > 0$ and any $\varepsilon < 1$. □

5.2 Robust Reductions

In our discussion of reductions, we were interested in optimality preserving sampling-based reductions mapping an RL task $(\mathcal{M}, \phi)$ to another task $(\bar{\mathcal{M}}, \phi')$. However, in the learning setting, if we use a PAC-MDP algorithm to compute a policy $\bar{\pi}$ for $(\bar{\mathcal{M}}, \phi')$, it might be the case that $\bar{\pi} \notin \Pi_{\text{opt}}(\bar{\mathcal{M}}, \phi')$. Therefore, we cannot conclude anything useful about the optimality of the corresponding policy $f(\bar{\pi})$ in $\mathcal{M}$ w.r.t. ϕ. Ideally, we would like to ensure that for any $\varepsilon > 0$ there is a $\varepsilon' > 0$ such that an ε'-optimal policy for $(\bar{\mathcal{M}}, \phi')$ corresponds to an ε-optimal policy for $(\mathcal{M}, \phi)$.

Definition 7. *A step-wise sampling-based reduction $\mathcal{F}$ is robust if for any RL task $(\mathcal{M}, \phi)$ with $(\bar{\mathcal{M}}, \phi', f) = \mathcal{F}(\mathcal{M}, \phi)$ and any $\varepsilon > 0$, there is an $\varepsilon' > 0$ such that $f(\Pi_{opt}^{\varepsilon'}(\bar{\mathcal{M}}, \phi')) \subseteq \Pi_{opt}^\varepsilon(\mathcal{M}, \phi)$.*

Observe that for any optimal policy $\bar{\pi} \in \Pi_{\text{opt}}(\bar{\mathcal{M}}, \phi')$ for $\bar{\mathcal{M}}$ and ϕ', we have $f(\bar{\pi}) \in \bigcap_{\varepsilon > 0} \Pi_{\text{opt}}^\varepsilon(\mathcal{M}, \phi) = \Pi_{\text{opt}}(\mathcal{M}, \phi)$; hence, a robust reduction is also optimality preserving. Although a robust reduction is preferred when translating LTL specifications to discounted-sum rewards, the following theorem shows that such a reduction is not possible. This is primarily due to the fact that LTL specifications are not robust whereas discounted-sum rewards are (proof in [4]).

Theorem 8. *Let $\mathcal{P} = \{b\}$ and $\phi = \mathcal{L}_{safe}(\{b\})$. Then, there does not exist a robust step-wise sampling-based reduction $\mathcal{F}$ with the property that for any given $\mathcal{M}$, if $(\bar{\mathcal{M}}, \phi', f) = \mathcal{F}(\mathcal{M}, \phi)$, then ϕ' is a robust specification and $\Pi_{opt}(\bar{\mathcal{M}}, \phi') \neq \emptyset$.*

We observe that the above result holds when the reduction is only allowed to take at most one step in $\mathcal{M}$ during a step in $\bar{\mathcal{M}}$ (and can be generalized to a bounded number of steps). This leads to the following open problem.

Open Problem 3. *Does there exist a robust sampling-based reduction $\mathcal{F}$ such that for any RL task $(\mathcal{M}, \phi)$, where ϕ is an LTL specification, letting $(\bar{\mathcal{M}}, \phi', f) = \mathcal{F}(\mathcal{M}, \phi)$, we have that ϕ' is a discounted reward specification (allowing $\bar{\mathcal{M}}$ to take unbounded number of steps in $\mathcal{M}$ per transition)?*

Note that even if such a reduction is possible, simulating $\bar{\mathcal{M}}$ would computationally hard since there might be no bound on the time it takes for a step in $\bar{\mathcal{M}}$ to occur.

6   Reinforcement Learning from LTL Specifications

We formalized a notion of sampling-based reductions for MDPs with unknown transition probabilities. Although reducing LTL specifications to discounted rewards is a natural approach towards obtaining learning algorithms for LTL specifications, we showed that step-wise sampling-based reductions are insufficient to obtain learning algorithms with guarantees. This leads us to the natural question of whether it is possible to design learning algorithms for LTL specifications with guarantees. Unfortunately, it turns out that it is not possible to obtain PAC-MDP algorithms for safety specifications.

Theorem 9. *There does not exist a PAC-MDP algorithm for the class of safety specifications.*

Theorem 8 shows that it is not possible to obtain a PAC-MDP algorithm for safety specifications by simply applying a step-wise sampling-based reduction followed by a PAC-MDP algorithm for discounted reward specifications. Also, Theorem 8 does not follow from Theorem 9 because, the definition of a robust reduction allows the maximum value of ε' that satisfies $f(\Pi_{\text{opt}}^{\varepsilon'}(\bar{\mathcal{M}}, \phi')) \subseteq \Pi_{\text{opt}}^{\varepsilon}(\bar{\mathcal{M}}, \phi)$ to depend on the transition probability function P of $\mathcal{M}$. However the sample complexity function h of a PAC-MDP algorithm (Definition 2) should be independent of P.

Intuitively, Theorem 9 follows from that fact that, when learning from simulation, it is highly likely that the learning algorithm will encounter identical transitions when the underlying MDP is modified slightly. This makes it impossible to infer an ε-optimal policy using a number of samples that is independent of the transition probabilities since safety specifications are not robust.

Proof. Suppose there is a PAC-MDP algorithm $\mathcal{A}$ for the class of safety specifications. Consider $\mathcal{P} = \{b\}$ and the family of MDPs shown in Fig. 3 where double circles denote states at which b holds. Let $\phi = \mathcal{L}_{\text{safe}}(\{b\})$ and $0 < \varepsilon < \frac{1}{2}$. For any $\delta > 0$, we use $\mathcal{M}_\delta^1$ to denote the MDP with $p_1 = 1$ and $p_2 = 1 - \delta$, and $\mathcal{M}_\delta^2$ to denote the MDP with $p_1 = 1 - \delta$ and $p_2 = 1$. Finally, let $\mathcal{M}$ denote the MDP with $p_1 = p_2 = 1$. Now we have the following lemma (proof in full version [4]).

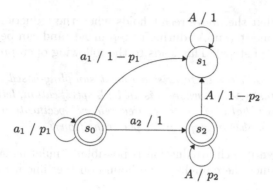

Fig. 3. A class of MDPs for showing no PAC-MDP algorithm exists for safety specifications.

Lemma 2. *For any $\delta \in]0,1[$, we have $\Pi_{opt}^{\varepsilon}(\mathcal{M}_{\delta}^1, \phi) \cap \Pi_{opt}^{\varepsilon}(\mathcal{M}_{\delta}^2, \phi) = \emptyset$.*

Now let h be the sample complexity function of $\mathcal{A}$ as in Definition 2. We let
$p = 0.1$ and $N = h(|S|, |A|, |\phi|, \frac{1}{p}, \frac{1}{\varepsilon})$. We let $K = 2N + 1$ and choose $\delta \in]0,1[$
such that $(1 - \delta)^K \geq 0.9$. Let $\{\pi_n\}_{n=1}^{\infty}$ denote the sequence of output policies of
$\mathcal{A}$ when run on $\mathcal{M}$ with the precision $\varepsilon < \frac{1}{2}$ and $p = 0.1$. For $j \in \{1, 2\}$, let E_j
denote the event that at most N out of the first K policies $\{\pi_n\}_{n=1}^K$ are *not* ε-
optimal for $\mathcal{M}_{\delta}^j$ (when $\mathcal{A}$ is run on $\mathcal{M}$). Then we have $\mathrm{Pr}_{\mathcal{A}}^{\mathcal{M}}(E_1) + \mathrm{Pr}_{\mathcal{A}}^{\mathcal{M}}(E_2) \leq 1$
because E_1 and E_2 are disjoint events (due to Lemma 2).

For $j \in \{1, 2\}$, we let $\{\pi_n^j\}_{n=1}^{\infty}$ be the sequence of output policies of $\mathcal{A}$ when
run on $\mathcal{M}_{\delta}^j$ with the same precision ε and $p = 0.1$. Let F_j denote the event that
at most N out of the first K policies $\{\pi_n^j\}_{n=1}^K$ are *not* ε-optimal for $\mathcal{M}_{\delta}^j$ (when
$\mathcal{A}$ is run on $\mathcal{M}_{\delta}^j$). Then PAC-MDP guarantee of $\mathcal{A}$ gives us that $\mathrm{Pr}_{\mathcal{A}}^{\mathcal{M}_{\delta}^j}(F_j) \geq 0.9$
for $j \in \{1, 2\}$. Now let G_j denote the event that the the first K samples from $\mathcal{M}_{\delta}^j$
correspond to the deterministic transitions in $\mathcal{M}$—i.e., taking a_1 in s_0 leads to s_0
and taking any action in s_2 leads to s_2. We have that $\mathrm{Pr}_{\mathcal{A}}^{\mathcal{M}_{\delta}^j}(G_j) \geq (1-\delta)^K \geq 0.9$
for $j \in \{1, 2\}$.

Applying union bound, we get that $\mathrm{Pr}_{\mathcal{A}}^{\mathcal{M}_{\delta}^j}(F_j \wedge G_j) \geq 0.8$ for $j \in \{1, 2\}$. The
probability of any execution (sequence of output policies, actions taken, resets
performed and transitions observed) of $\mathcal{A}$ on $\mathcal{M}_{\delta}^j$ that satisfies the conditions
of F_j and G_j is less than or equal to the probability of obtaining the same
execution when $\mathcal{A}$ is run on $\mathcal{M}$ and furthermore such an execution also satisfies
the conditions of E_j. Therefore, we have $\mathrm{Pr}_{\mathcal{A}}^{\mathcal{M}}(E_j) \geq \mathrm{Pr}_{\mathcal{A}}^{\mathcal{M}_{\delta}^j}(F_j \wedge G_j) \geq 0.8$ for
$j \in \{1, 2\}$. But this contradicts the fact that $\mathrm{Pr}_{\mathcal{A}}^{\mathcal{M}}(E_1) + \mathrm{Pr}_{\mathcal{A}}^{\mathcal{M}}(E_2) \leq 1$. $\square$

We can also conclude that PAC-MDP algorithms do not exist for limit-
average rewards since safety specifications can be encoded using limit-average
rewards. Our proof of Theorem 9 can be modified to show the result for reachability as well.

A concurrent work [35] characterizes the class of LTL specifications for which PAC-MDP algorithms exist. An LTL formula φ is *finitary* if there exists a horizon H such that infinite length words sharing the same prefix of length H are either all accepted or all rejected by φ. Then, their result can be summarized as follows.

Theorem 10 (*[35]***).** *There exists a PAC-MDP algorithm for an LTL specification $\phi = \mathcal{L}_{LTL}(\varphi)$ if and only if φ is finitary.*

Next, to the best of our knowledge, it is unknown if there is a learning algorithm that converges in the limit for the class of LTL specifications.

Open Problem 4. *Does there exist a learning algorithm that converges in the limit for the class of LTL specifications?*

Observe that algorithms that converge in the limit do not necessarily have a bound on the number of samples needed to learn an ε-optimal policy; instead, they only guarantee that the values of the policies $\{J_\phi^{\mathcal{M}}(\pi_n)\}_{n=1}^{\infty}$ converge to the optimal value $\mathcal{J}^*(\mathcal{M}, \phi)$ almost surely. Therefore, the rate of convergence can be arbitrarily small and can depend on the transition probability function P.

6.1 Exisiting PAC Results

It has been shown that one can obtain PAC algorithms for learning from logical specifications under some additional assumptions. For instance, some stochastic model checking (SMC) algorithms [5,10] have PAC guarantees with the sample complexity function h depending on the smallest positive probability $p_{\min}$ of $\mathcal{M}$. A recent paper [12] proposes a PAC algorithm for LTL specifications under the assumption that the structure of the MDP $\mathcal{M}$ (transitions with non-zero probability) is known.

7 Concluding Remarks

We have established a formal framework for sampling-based reductions of RL tasks. Given an RL task (an MDP and a specification), the goal is to generate another RL task such that the transformation preserves optimal solutions and is (optionally) robust. A key challenge is that the transformation must be defined without the knowledge of the transition probabilities.

Our framework offers a unified view of the literature on RL from logical specifications, in which an RL task with a logical specification is transformed to one with a reward-based specification. We define optimality preserving as well as robust sampling-based reductions for RL tasks. Specification translations are special forms of sampling-based reductions in which the underlying MDP is not altered. We show that specification translations from LTL to reward machines with discounted-sum objectives do not preserve optimal solutions. This motivates the need for transformations in which the underlying MDP may be altered. By revisiting such transformations from existing literature within our framework, we expose the nuances in their theoretical guarantees about optimality preservation. Specifically, known transformations from LTL specifications to rewards are not strictly optimality preserving sampling-based reductions since they depend on parameters which are not available in the RL setting such as some information about the transition probabilities of the MDP. We show that LTL specifications, which are non-robust, cannot be robustly transformed to robust specifications, such as discounted-sum rewards. We wrap up by proving that there are LTL specifications that do not admit PAC-MDP learning algorithms.

Finally, we are left with multiple open problems. Notably, it is unknown whether there exists a learning algorithm for LTL that converges in the limit and does not depend on any unavailable information about the MDP. However, existing algorithms for learning from LTL specifications have been demonstrated to be effective in practice, even for continuous state MDPs. This shows that there is a gap between the theory and practice suggesting that we need better measures for theoretical analysis of such algorithms; for instance, realistic MDPs may have additional structure that makes learning possible.

Acknowledgements. We would like to thank Michael Littman, Sheila McIlraith, Ufuk Topcu, Ashutosh Trivedi and the anonymous reviewers for their feedback on an early version of this paper. This work was supported in part by CRA/NSF Computing Innovations Fellow Award, DARPA Assured Autonomy project under Contract No. FA8750–18–C–0090, NSF Awards CCF–1910769 and CCF–1917852, ARO Award W911NF–20–1–0080 and ONR award N00014–20–1–2115.

References

1. Abel, D., et al.: On the expressivity of Markov reward. In: Advances in Neural Information Processing Systems 34 (2021)
2. Abounadi, J., Bertsekas, D., Borkar, V.S.: Learning algorithms for Markov decision processes with average cost. SIAM J. Control. Optim. **40**(3), 681–698 (2001)
3. Aksaray, D., Jones, A., Kong, Z., Schwager, M., Belta, C.: Q-learning for robust satisfaction of signal temporal logic specifications. In: Conference on Decision and Control (CDC), pp. 6565–6570. IEEE (2016)
4. Alur, R., Bansal, S., Bastani, O., Jothimurugan, K.: A framework for transforming specifications in reinforcement learning. https://arxiv.org/abs/2111.00272 (2021)
5. Ashok, P., Křetínský, J., Weininger, M.: PAC statistical model checking for Markov decision processes and stochastic games. In: Dillig, I., Tasiran, S. (eds.) CAV 2019. LNCS, vol. 11561, pp. 497–519. Springer, Cham (2019). https://doi.org/10.1007/978-3-030-25540-4_29
6. Baier, C., de Alfaro, L., Forejt, V., Kwiatkowska, M.: Model checking probabilistic systems. In: Handbook of Model Checking, pp. 963–999. Springer, Cham (2018). https://doi.org/10.1007/978-3-319-10575-8_28
7. Bozkurt, A.K., Wang, Y., Zavlanos, M.M., Pajic, M.: Control synthesis from linear temporal logic specifications using model-free reinforcement learning. In: 2020 IEEE International Conference on Robotics and Automation (ICRA), pp. 10349–10355. IEEE (2020)
8. Brafman, R., De Giacomo, G., Patrizi, F.: LTLf/LDLf non-Markovian rewards. In: Proceedings of the AAAI Conference on Artificial Intelligence, vol. 32 (2018)

9. Camacho, A., Toro Icarte, R., Klassen, T.Q., Valenzano, R., McIlraith, S.A.: LTL and beyond: formal languages for reward function specification in reinforcement learning. In: International Joint Conference on Artificial Intelligence, pp. 6065–6073 (2019)
10. Daca, P., Henzinger, T.A., Křetínský, J., Petrov, T.: Faster statistical model checking for unbounded temporal properties. ACM Trans. Comput. Logic (TOCL) **18**(2), 1–25 (2017)
11. De Giacomo, G., Iocchi, L., Favorito, M., Patrizi, F.: Foundations for restraining bolts: Reinforcement learning with LTLf/LDLf restraining specifications. In: Proceedings of the International Conference on Automated Planning and Scheduling, vol. 29, pp. 128–136 (2019)
12. Fu, J., Topcu, U.: Probably approximately correct MDP learning and control with temporal logic constraints. In: Robotics: Science and Systems (2014)
13. Hahn, E.M., Perez, M., Schewe, S., Somenzi, F., Trivedi, A., Wojtczak, D.: Omega-regular objectives in model-free reinforcement learning. In: Tools and Algorithms for the Construction and Analysis of Systems, pp. 395–412 (2019)
14. Hahn, E.M., Perez, M., Schewe, S., Somenzi, F., Trivedi, A., Wojtczak, D.: Faithful and effective reward schemes for model-free reinforcement learning of omega-regular objectives. In: Hung, D.V., Sokolsky, O. (eds.) ATVA 2020. LNCS, vol. 12302, pp. 108–124. Springer, Cham (2020). https://doi.org/10.1007/978-3-030-59152-6_6
15. Hahn, E.M., Perez, M., Schewe, S., Somenzi, F., Trivedi, A., Wojtczak, D.: Model-free reinforcement learning for stochastic parity games. In: 31st International Conference on Concurrency Theory (CONCUR 2020). Schloss Dagstuhl-Leibniz-Zentrum für Informatik (2020)
16. Hahn, E.M., Perez, M., Schewe, S., Somenzi, F., Trivedi, A., Wojtczak, D.: Model-free reinforcement learning for lexicographic omega-regular objectives. In: Huisman, M., Păsăreanu, C., Zhan, N. (eds.) FM 2021. LNCS, vol. 13047, pp. 142–159. Springer, Cham (2021). https://doi.org/10.1007/978-3-030-90870-6_8
17. Hasanbeig, M., Kantaros, Y., Abate, A., Kroening, D., Pappas, G.J., Lee, I.: Reinforcement learning for temporal logic control synthesis with probabilistic satisfaction guarantees. In: Conference on Decision and Control (CDC), pp. 5338–5343 (2019)
18. Hasanbeig, M., Abate, A., Kroening, D.: Logically-constrained reinforcement learning. arXiv preprint arXiv:1801.08099 (2018)
19. Icarte, R.T., Klassen, T., Valenzano, R., McIlraith, S.: Using reward machines for high-level task specification and decomposition in reinforcement learning. In: International Conference on Machine Learning, pp. 2107–2116. PMLR (2018)
20. Icarte, R.T., Klassen, T.Q., Valenzano, R., McIlraith, S.A.: Reward machines: exploiting reward function structure in reinforcement learning. arXiv preprint arXiv:2010.03950 (2020)
21. Jiang, Y., Bharadwaj, S., Wu, B., Shah, R., Topcu, U., Stone, P.: Temporal-logic-based reward shaping for continuing learning tasks (2020)
22. Jothimurugan, K., Alur, R., Bastani, O.: A composable specification language for reinforcement learning tasks. In: Advances in Neural Information Processing Systems, vol. 32, pp. 13041–13051 (2019)
23. Jothimurugan, K., Bansal, S., Bastani, O., Alur, R.: Compositional reinforcement learning from logical specifications. In: Advances in Neural Information Processing Systems (2021)
24. Jothimurugan, K., Bansal, S., Bastani, O., Alur, R.: Specification-guided learning of Nash equilibria with high social welfare (2022)

25. Kakade, S.M.: On the sample complexity of reinforcement learning. University of London, University College London (United Kingdom) (2003)
26. Kearns, M., Singh, S.: Near-optimal reinforcement learning in polynomial time. Mach. Learn. **49**(2), 209–232 (2002)
27. Li, X., Vasile, C.I., Belta, C.: Reinforcement learning with temporal logic rewards. In: IEEE/RSJ International Conference on Intelligent Robots and Systems (IROS), pp. 3834–3839. IEEE (2017)
28. Littman, M.L., Topcu, U., Fu, J., Isbell, C., Wen, M., MacGlashan, J.: Environment-independent task specifications via GLTL (2017)
29. Littman, M.L., Topcu, U., Fu, J., Isbell, C., Wen, M., MacGlashan, J.: Environment-independent task specifications via GLTL. arXiv preprint arXiv:1704.04341 (2017)
30. Pnueli, A.: The temporal logic of programs. In: 18th Annual Symposium on Foundations of Computer Science, pp. 46–57. IEEE (1977)
31. Sistla, A.P., Clarke, E.M.: The complexity of propositional linear temporal logics. J. ACM (JACM) **32**(3), 733–749 (1985)
32. Strehl, A.L., Li, L., Wiewiora, E., Langford, J., Littman, M.L.: PAC model-free reinforcement learning. In: Proceedings of the 23rd International Conference on Machine Learning, pp. 881–888 (2006)
33. Watkins, C.J., Dayan, P.: Q-learning. Mach. Learn. **8**(3–4), 279–292 (1992)
34. Xu, Z., Topcu, U.: Transfer of temporal logic formulas in reinforcement learning. In: International Joint Conference on Artificial Intelligence, pp. 4010–4018 (2019)
35. Yang, C., Littman, M., Carbin, M.: Reinforcement learning for general LTL objectives is intractable. arXiv preprint arXiv:2111.12679 (2021)
36. Yuan, L.Z., Hasanbeig, M., Abate, A., Kroening, D.: Modular deep reinforcement learning with temporal logic specifications. arXiv preprint arXiv:1909.11591 (2019)

Robustness Analysis of Continuous-Depth Models with Lagrangian Techniques

Sophie A. Neubauer$^{(\boxtimes)}$ and Radu Grosu

Technische Universität Wien (TU Wien), Vienna, Austria
`sophie.neubauer@tuwien.ac.at`

Abstract. This paper presents, in a unified fashion, deterministic as well as statistical Lagrangian-verification techniques. They formally quantify the behavioral robustness of any time-continuous process, formulated as a continuous-depth model. To this end, we review LRT-NG, SLR, and GoTube, algorithms for constructing a tight reachtube, that is, an over-approximation of the set of states reachable within a given time-horizon, and provide guarantees for the reachtube bounds. We compare the usage of the variational equations, associated to the system equations, the mean value theorem, and the Lipschitz constants, in achieving deterministic and statistical guarantees. In LRT-NG, the Lipschitz constant is used as a bloating factor of the initial perturbation, to compute the radius of an ellipsoid in an optimal metric, which over-approximates the set of reachable states. In SLR and GoTube, we get statistical guarantees, by using the Lipschitz constants to compute local balls around samples. These are needed to calculate the probability of having found an upper bound, of the true maximum perturbation at every timestep. Our experiments demonstrate the superior performance of Lagrangian techniques, when compared to LRT, Flow*, and CAPD, and illustrate their use in the robustness analysis of various continuous-depth models.

Keywords: Verification · Machine learning · Continuous-depth models

1 Introduction

Due to the revival of neural ordinary differential equations (Neural ODEs) [9], modern cyber-physical systems (CPS) increasingly use deep-learning systems powered by continuous-depth models, where the dynamics of the hidden states are defined by an ordinary differential equation (ODE) and the output is a function of the solution of the ODE at a given time. They are used within the cyber part of the CPS responsible for state-estimation, planning, and (adaptive) optimal control, of the physical part of the CPS. As the use of continuous-depth models on real-world applications increases [20, 25, 37, 48, 49], so does the importance of ensuring their safety through the use of verification techniques.

Code: https://github.com/DatenVorsprung/GoTube.

© Springer Nature Switzerland AG 2022
J.-F. Raskin and K. Chatterjee (Eds.): Principles of Systems Design, LNCS 13660, pp. 625–649, 2022.
https://doi.org/10.1007/978-3-031-22337-2_30

Since all these networks represent nonlinear systems of ordinary differential equations, it is impossible, that is, undecidable, to exactly predict their behavior, as they do not have a closed-form solution. This is very problematic because safety is an important concern in many of such systems, as for example, smart mobility, industry 4.0, or smart health-care. Fortunately, it is possible to approximate this behavior. Robustness analysis of continuous-depth models, can be seen as a special case of reachability analysis of nonlinear ordinary differential equations (ODEs), as it measures the ability to resist change in the input values.

In this case, the problem is how to over-approximate the system dynamics, and thus the behaviour of the system, in as tight a way as possible, so that one can rely upon and use the huge potential of these continuous-depth models even in safety-critical systems, when it comes to difficult tasks. To avoid false positives when looking for intersections of the systems with unsafe regions, it is crucial to have as-tight-as-possible reachtubes. Otherwise it would e.g. predict that a car driven by a controller would cause a crash even if the neural network controller is behaving perfectly and never causes a crash. Such wide reachtubes are thus not useful for actually putting continuous depth-models into operation.

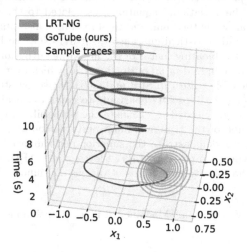

Fig. 1. Reachtubes of LRT-NG [31] and GoTube [33] for a CT-RNN controlling Cart-Pole-v1 environment. LRT [11], CAPD [45], and Flow* [10] failed on this benchmark.

In this work, we focus on the importance of the variational equation used in our tools. We review our conservative, set-based reachability tool LRT-NG [31], our non-conservative, stochastic theory SLR [32], and scalable statistical tool GoTube [33]. The stochasticity of SLR is only introduced through the algorithm, we are not looking at stochastic dynamical systems. Deterministic verification approaches ensure conservative bounds [6,10,29,45,56], but often sacrifice speed and accuracy [18], especially due to the wrapping effect caused by interval arithmetic, and thus scalability; see CAPD, Flow*, LRT, and LRT-NG in Figs. 1 and 5. Statistical methods, on the other hand, only ensure a weaker notion of conservativeness in the form of confidence intervals (statistical bounds). This,

Table 1. Related work on the reachability analysis of continuous-time systems. Determ. is the abbreviation for deterministic, and no indicates a statistical method. The table content presented here is partially reproduced from [32].

Technique	Determ.	Parallel	Wrapping effect	Arbitrary time-horizon
LRT [11] (Ours) with Infinitesimal strain theory	Yes	No	Yes	No
CAPD [45] implements Lohner algorithm	Yes	No	Yes	No
Flow-star [10] with Taylor models	Yes	No	Yes	No
δ-reachability [27] with approximate satisfiability	Yes	No	Yes	No
C2E2 [17] with discrepancy functions	Yes	No	Yes	No
LDFM [22] by simulation, matrix measures	Yes	Yes	No	No
TIRA [55] with second-order sensitivity	Yes	Yes	No	No
Isabelle/HOL [44] with proof-assistant	Yes	No	Yes	No
Breach [15,16] by simulation	Yes	Yes	No	No
PIRK [14] with contraction bounds	Yes	Yes	No	No
HR [51] with hybridization	Yes	No	Yes	No
ProbReach [63] with δ-reachability	No	No	Yes	No
VSPODE [19] using p-boxes	No	No	Yes	No
Gaussian process (GP) [5]	No	No	No	No
LRT-NG [31] (**Ours**)	Yes	No	Yes	No
Stochastic Lagrangian reachability SLR [32] (**Ours**)	No	Yes	No	No
GoTube [33] (**Ours**)	No	Yes	No	**Yes**

however, allows them to achieve much more accurate and faster verification algorithms that scale up to much larger dynamical systems [5,64].

We compared LRT-NG and GoTube with LRT, Flow*, and CAPD, on a comprehensive set of benchmarks, including continuous-depth models. Our results show that LRT-NG is very competitive with both Flow* and CAPD. Moreover, it is the only conservative tool able to handle the continuous-depth models. GoTube substantially outperforms all state-of-the-art verification tools, in terms of the size of the initial ball, time-horizon, task completion, and scalability.

2   Related Work

Global Optimization. Efficient local optimization methods such as gradient descent cannot be used for global optimization since optimization problems related to robustness analysis are typically non-convex. Thus, many advanced verification algorithms tend to use global optimization schemes [6,8]. Depending on the properties of the objective function, e.g., smoothness, various types of global optimization techniques exist. For instance, interval-based branch-and-bound (BaB) algorithms [35,59] work well on differentiable objectives up to a certain scale, which has recently been improved [13]. There are also Lipschitz-global optimization methods for satisfying Lipschitz conditions [47,54]. For example, a method for computing the Lipschitz constant of deep neural networks to assist with their robustness and verification analysis was recently proposed in [24] and [4]. Additionally, there are evolutionary strategies for global optimization using the covariance matrix computation [36,43]. In our approach, for global optimization, we use random sampling and compute neighborhoods (Lipschitz caps) of the samples, where we have probabilistic knowledge about the values, such that we are able to correspondingly estimate the statistical global optimum with high confidence. [72].

Verification of Neural Networks. A large body of work tried to enhance the robustness of neural networks against adversarial examples [28]. There are efforts that show how to break the many defense mechanisms proposed [2,50], until the arrival of methods for formally verifying robustness to adversarial attacks around neighborhoods of data [40]. The majority of these complete verification algorithms for neural networks work on piece-wise linear structures of small-to-medium-size feedforward networks [62]. For instance, [7] has recently introduced a BaB method that outperforms state-of-the-art verification methods [46,67]. A more scalable approach for rectified linear unit (ReLU) networks [57] was recently proposed based on Lagrangian decomposition; this approach significantly improves the speed and tightness of the bounds [13]. The proposed approach not only improves the tightness of the bounds but also performs a novel branching that matches the performance of the learning-based methods [53] and outperforms state-of-the-art methods [3,39,65,71]. While these verification approaches work well for feedforward networks, they are not suitable for recurrent and continuous neural network instances, which we address.

Verification of Continuous-Time Systems. Reachability analysis is a verification approach that provides safety guarantees for a given continuous dynamical system [34,68]. Most dynamical systems in safety-critical applications are highly nonlinear and uncertain in nature [49]. The uncertainty can be in the system's parameters [19,64,70], or their initial state [19,42]. This is often handled by considering balls of a certain radius around them. Nonlinearity might be inherent in the system dynamics or due to discrete mode-jumps [26]. We provide a summary of methods developed for the reachability analysis of continuous-time ODEs in Table 1. A fundamental shortcoming of the majority of the methods described in Table 1 is their lack of scalability while providing conservative bounds. In this paper, we show that our algorithms establish the state-of-the-art for the verification of ODE-based systems in terms of speed, time-horizon, task completion, and scalability on a large set of experiments.

3 Background

3.1 Reachability Analysis of ODEs

For linear ordinary differential equations (ODEs) there exists a general closed-form solution, describing the behavior of the solution-traces over time, for every initial state. For nonlinear ODEs, there is no closed-form solution any more. One is able to calculate the solution for different initial states, but one does not know what happens in between of these already calculated traces.

The main goal in the reachability analysis of nonlinear ODEs, is to over-approximate the reachable states of the ODEs, starting from a set of initial states, such as, an interval, a ball, or an ellipsoid, in a way that one can guarantee that all traces are inside the over-approximation. We call such an over-approximation a *reachtube*. Let us now define this mathematically:

Definition 1 (Initial value problem (IVP)). *We have a time-invariant ordinary differential equation $\partial_t x = f(x), f : \mathbb{R}^n \to \mathbb{R}^n$, a set of initial values defined by a ball $\mathcal{B}_0 = B(x_0, \delta_x)$ with center $x_0 \in \mathbb{R}^n$ and radius $\delta_0 \in \mathbb{R}$, the initial condition $x(t_0) \in \mathcal{B}_0$ and a sequence of k timesteps $\{t_j : j \in [1, \dots, k] \wedge (t_0 < t_1 < \cdots < t_k)\}$. For every t_j, we want to know the solution $x(t_j)$ of*

$$\partial_t x = f(x), \quad x(t_0) \in \mathcal{B}_0 = B(x_0, \delta_x). \tag{1}$$

The definition can be generalized to time-variant ODEs, as time can be just seen as an additional variable x_{n+1} with $\partial_t x_{n+1} = 1$. Let $\chi(t_j, x_0) = x(t_j)$ be the solution of Eq. (1) at time t_j, for $x(t_0) = x_0$. In reachability analysis, the goal is to find for every time step t_j an overapproximation $\mathcal{B}_j \supseteq \{\chi(t_j, x) : x \in \mathcal{B}_0\}$, such that the set of these over-approximations build up a reachtube, containing the reachable states.

Definition 2 (Reachtube). *Given a set of initial values $\mathcal{B}_0 \in \mathbb{R}^{n \times n}$, a nonlinear ODE as in Eq. (1), the pointwise solution function $\chi(t_j, \cdot) : \mathbb{R}^n \to \mathbb{R}^n$ and over-approximations $\mathcal{B}_j \supseteq \{\chi(t_j, x) : x \in \mathcal{B}_0\}$. The Reachtube for a sequence of k timesteps $\{t_j : j \in [1, \dots, k] \wedge t_0 < t_1 < \cdots < t_k)\}$ is defined as*

$$\mathcal{R} = \{\mathcal{B}_0, \mathcal{B}_1, \dots, \mathcal{B}_k\}. \tag{2}$$

As we are going to use balls and ellipsoids, we call $\mathcal{B}_j$, *bounding balls*. For every ellipsoid there is a metric such that the ellipsoid equals a ball in that metric. Let $M_j \in \mathbb{R}^{n \times n}$ be a positive definite matrix $(M_j \succ 0)$, then there exists a decomposition: $A_j \in \mathbb{R}^{n \times n}$ with $A_j^\top A_j = M_j$. Every ellipsoid can be defined as $B_{M_j}(x_j, \delta_j) = \{x : \|x - x_j\|_{M_j} = \delta_j\}$ with center x_j, weighted radius δ_j and norm $\|x\|_{M_j} = \sqrt{x^\top M_j x} = \|A_j x\|_2$. If M_j is the identity matrix, then $\mathcal{B}_j$ is a ball in the Euclidean metric, so we will omit the subscript and use $B(x_j, \delta_j)$.

When using reachability analysis to check for intersections with bad states, it is crucial to compute as tight as possible reachtubes.

3.2 Interval Arithmetic and Lohner Method

There are different ways to define conservative regions by set representations: intervals, balls, ellipsoids, polytopes and more. In the papers [30,31] we relied on interval arithmetic, so we want to shortly review the benefits and problems with that method. The set of intervals on the real numbers is defined as ([58]):

$$\mathbb{IR} = \{[a] = [\underline{a}, \overline{a}] : \underline{a}, \overline{a} \in \mathbb{R}, \underline{a} \leq \overline{a}\}, \tag{3}$$

whereas an *interval vector* $[x] \in \mathbb{IR}^n$ is a vector with interval components and an *interval matrix* $[A] \in \mathbb{IR}^{n \times m}$ is a matrix with interval components. The biggest problem in interval arithmetic is the wrapping effect, which happens if we apply concatenated functions on intervals (see Fig. 2).

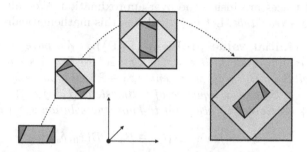

Fig. 2. *Wrapping effect.* Symbolic illustration for wrapping of a parallelogram (green) when applying a consecutive rotation of 45° to it with interval boxes (grey) and with interval boxes in adapted coordinated systems using Lohner's QR method (yellow). (Color figure online)

In the Lagrangian Reachability algorithms [30,31] an improved version of Lohner's QR method [52,58] is used to directly address the wrapping effect caused by interval arithmetic. Intuitively, the rotational part Q of a function evaluation is extracted, which is subsequently used as a new coordinate system. For a more detailed discussion of the steps mentioned above, please refer to [30].

3.3   Lipschitz Constant and the Variational Equation

The Lipschitz constant defines a relation between the domain and the range of a function, more precisely it bounds the distance in the range by a multiple of the distance in the domain.

Definition 3 (Local Lipschitz constant). *Let $\chi : A \to \mathbb{R}^m$ ($A \subseteq \mathbb{R}^n$) be a function, $M_A, M_B \succ 0$ be respectively metrics on the domain and the range, $S \subseteq A$ be a subset of the domain and*

$$\exists \lambda_S : \|\chi(x) - \chi(y)\|_{M_B} \leq \lambda_S \|x - y\|_{M_A}, \quad \forall x, y \in S, \tag{4}$$

then the smallest such λ_S is called the Local Lipschitz constant of χ on set S.

An upper bound of the Lipschitz constant can be computed using the mean value theorem from calculus with the statement either for scalar or for vector valued functions:

Theorem 1 (Mean value theorem (generalized Rolle's Theorem)). *Let $M_1, M_2 \succ 0$ be respectively metrics on the domain and the range with $M_1 = A_1^\top A_1, M_2 = A_2^\top A_2$ and norm $\|x\|_{M_{1,2}} = \|A_2 x A_1^{-1}\|_2$. Considering the change* *of metric [11, Lemma 2] and the well-known mean value theorems, we are able to make the following statements:*

1. *Let $d : A \to \mathbb{R}$ ($A \subseteq \mathbb{R}^n$) be a scalar function. Then it holds $\forall x, y \in A$:*

$$\exists h \in [0,1] : \|d(x) - d(y)\|_{M_2} \leq \|\partial_x d(x + h \cdot (y - x))\|_{M_{1,2}} \cdot \|x - y\|_{M_1} \quad (5)$$

2. *Let $\chi : A \to \mathbb{R}^n$ ($A \subseteq \mathbb{R}^n$) be a vector-valued function and the norm of the Jacobian matrix of χ be bounded by some constant $\Lambda_{1,2} \geq \|\partial_x \chi(x + h \cdot (y - x))\|_{M_{1,2}}$ for all $h \in [0,1]$ and all $x, y \in A$. Then it holds:*

$$\|\chi(x) - \chi(y)\|_{M_2} \leq \Lambda_{1,2} \cdot \|x - y\|_{M_1} \quad \forall x, y \in A, \quad (6)$$

and thus $\Lambda_{1,2}$ is an upper bound of the Lipschitz Constant λ_S of Definition 3.

The mean value theorem can be used to find an upper bound of the local Lipschitz constant. We will need such an upper bound for the deterministic as well as for the statistical guarantees. In both cases we will need to compute the jacobian matrix for the solution function $\chi(t_j, \cdot)$ of Eq. (1), so the question is how to compute the jacobian matrix for the solution of a differential equation, for which we do not even have a closed form solution? For this purpose, we introduce $F_x : \mathbb{R} \to \mathbb{R}^{n \times n}$ with $F_x(t) = \partial_x \chi(t, x)$ called the *deformation gradient* in [1,66], and the *sensitivity analysis* in [15,16]. $F_x(t)$ describes how much a small perturbation in the initial value x changes the solution to the IVP at time t.

Definition 4 (Variational equation). *Let f be the system equations of the initial value problem defined in Eq. (1) and $\chi(t, x_0)$ be the solution at time t for $x(t_0) = x_0$, then the following equation is called the variational equation:*

$$\partial_t F(t) = (\partial_x f)(\chi(t, x))F(t), \quad F(t_0) = I, \quad (7)$$

with $I \in \mathbb{R}^{n \times n}$ being the identity matrix.

Intuitively, Definition 4 describes how an initial perturbation in the initial value evolves over time. In [31] it was shown that F_x is a solution of the *variational equations* associated to the system equations in Eq. (1).

3.4 Continuous-Depth Models

ODE's are used to describe the dynamics of the hidden states of continuous-depth neural models [9]. The output is a function of the solution of the ODE at a given time. So the derivative of the unknown states x is described by a parameterized vector-valued function $f_\theta : \mathbb{R}^n \to \mathbb{R}^n$, which is assumed to be Lipschitz-continuous and forward-complete:

$$\partial_t x = f_\theta(x), \quad x(t_0) \in \mathcal{B}_0 \quad (8)$$

By adding time as an additional variable x_{n+1} with $\partial_t x_{n+1} = 1$, a continuous-depth model can be seen as a special case of Eq. (1).

Algorithm 1. LRT-NG

Require: initial ball $\mathcal{B}_0 = B(x_0, \delta_0)$, initial metric M_0, initial metric decomposition A_0 ($M_0 = A_0^\top A_0$), time horizon T, sequence of timesteps t_j ($t_0 < \cdots < t_k = T$), system dynamics f

1: **set** $[\mathcal{F}] \leftarrow \{I\}, [\mathcal{X}] \leftarrow$ overapproximation of $\mathcal{B}_0$
2: **for** $(j = 1; j \leq k; j = j + 1)$ **do**
3:     $x_j \leftarrow solveIVP(f, x_{j-1}, [t_{j-1}, t_j])$
4:     $[\mathcal{F}] \leftarrow F_{[\mathcal{X}_0]}(t_j) = rungeKuttaVariational((\partial_x f)([\mathcal{X}]), [\mathcal{F}], [t_{j-1}, t_j]))$
5:     $M_j \leftarrow computeOptimalMetric(F_{x_j}(t_j), A_0)$
6:     **for all** $M \in \{M_j, I\}$ **do**
7:         **compute** $\Lambda \geq \|[\mathcal{F}]\|_M$ (stretching factor)
8:     **end for**
9:     $\mathcal{B}_j \leftarrow B_{M_j}(x_j, \delta_{M_j})$
10:     $\mathcal{B}_j^{circle} \leftarrow B(x_j, \delta_I)$
11:     $[\mathcal{X}] \leftarrow intersectionBox(\mathcal{B}_j, \mathcal{B}_j^{circle})$
12: **end for**
13: **return** $(\mathcal{B}_1, \ldots, \mathcal{B}_k), (\mathcal{B}_1^{circle}, \ldots, \mathcal{B}_k^{circle})$

---

4 Deterministic Guarantees (LRT-NG)

The most straightforward way to compute a conservative reachtube as defined in Definition 2, would be to use an interval enclosure $[\mathcal{X}_0] \supseteq \mathcal{B}_0$ of the initial values and just use interval-arithmetic evaluations of an integration method, for example, the Runge-Kutta method, to propagate them from timestep to timestep.

Due to the infamous wrapping effect (as shown in Fig. 2), this would lead very soon to a blow-up in space. As already mentioned in the related work in Sect. 2, there are different approaches on how to avoid that blow-up in space and create as tight as possible reachtubes.

Lagrangian Reachability is a bloating based technique: starting with an initial ball $\mathcal{B}_0 = B(x_0, \delta_0)$, at a sequence of k timesteps $\{t_j : j \in [1, \ldots, k] \wedge (t_0 < t_1 < \cdots < t_k)\}$, it propagates the center of the ball and computes the new radius δ_j, by multiplying δ_0 with a stretching factor Λ_j. Using Theorem 1 it holds that:

$$\max_{x \in \mathcal{B}_0} \|\chi(t_j, x) - \chi(t_j, x_0)\|_{M_j} \leq \max_{x \in \mathcal{B}_0} \|F_x(t_j)\|_{M_j} \max_{x \in \mathcal{B}_0} \|x - x_0\|_{M_0} \qquad (9)$$

We compute $\max_{x \in \mathcal{B}_0} \|F_x(t_j)\|_{M_j}$ by using interval arithmetic to propagate all possible deformation gradients as an interval $[\mathcal{F}_j] \supseteq \{F_x(t) : x \in \mathcal{B}_0\}$ with an interval arithmetic version of the variational equation Eq. (7):

$$\partial_t[\mathcal{F}] = (\partial_x f)([\mathcal{X}_t])[\mathcal{F}], \qquad (10)$$

where $[\mathcal{X}_{t_j}]$ is an as-tight-as-possible interval overapproximation of $\mathcal{B}_j$. Thus the challenge is to bound the norm of the interval deformation gradients:

$$\|[\mathcal{F}_j]\|_{M_j} \leq \Lambda_j \Rightarrow \delta_j = \Lambda_j \delta_0. \qquad (11)$$

We call Λ_j - the upper bound of the Lipschitz constant of $\chi(t_j, \cdot)$ - the *stretching factor (SF)* associated to the interval gradient tensor, as it shows by how much the initial ball $\mathcal{B}_0$ has to be stretched, such that it encloses the set of all reachable states. Having the interval gradient $[\mathcal{F}_j]$ at time t_j we solve Eq. (11) using algorithms from [41, 60, 61], and choosing the tightest result available. The correctness of Lagrangian Reachability is rooted in [11, Theorem 1].

As the tightness of the bounding balls $\mathcal{B}_j$ depends on the previous values, for example $\mathcal{B}_{j-1}, [\mathcal{X}_j]$ or $[\mathcal{F}_j]$, the wrapping deficiencies accumulate in time, as shown in Fig. 2. This is why the theoretical advances of LRT-NG concentrate on minimizing the volume of the bounding balls and their enclosure, and thus on creating tighter and longer reachtubes.

4.1 Lagrangian Reachtubes: The Next Generation

This section presents the theoretical advances of LRT-NG in [31]. In particular, we first state the optimization problem to be solved in order to get the optimal metric, and thus the bounding ball with minimal volume. We first describe an analytic solution of an optimal metric minimizing the volume of the ellipsoid and prove that it solves the optimization. Finally, we focus on the new reachset box $[\mathcal{X}_j]$ computation, the interval overapproximation of the ellipsoid-ball-intersection.

As shown in Algorithm 1, LRT-NG iterates over the sequence of k timesteps, until it reaches the given time horizon T. After propagating the center point, it computes the interval deformation gradient by integrating Eq. (10) in line 4. After computing the optimal metric M_j, it bounds the maximum singular value of $[\mathcal{F}]$ in the Euclidean norm, as well as in M_j norm, such that LRT-NG constructs an ellipsoid $\mathcal{B}_j$ and Euclidean bounding ball $\mathcal{B}_j^{circle}$. This enables us to define an as-tight-as-possible interval box $[\mathcal{X}]$, over the intersection of the ellipsoid and the ball. This intersection-based approach considerably reduces the wrapping effect of the next integration of the interval variational equation.

Computation of the Metric. To obtain an as-tight-as-possible over-approximation, we wish to minimize the volume of the n-dimensional ball $\mathcal{B}_j$, that is, of $B_{M_j}(x_j, \delta_j)$. Hence, the optimization problem is given by:

$$\underset{M_j \succ 0}{\arg \min} \operatorname{Vol}(B_{M_j}(x_j, \delta_j)), \tag{12}$$

where $\delta_j = \Lambda_j(M_j) \cdot \delta_0$. Let us further define $\hat{F}_{j-1,j} = \partial_x \chi_{t_{j-1}}^{t_j}(x)|_{x=x_{j-1}}$ as the deformation gradient from time t_{j-1} to t_j at the center of the ball. Using the chain rule it holds that $F_j = \prod_{m=1}^{j} \hat{F}_{m-1,m}$, where F_j is defined as the deformation gradient at x_0. The following theorem defines a metric $\hat{M}_j$ and shows that this metric minimizes the ellipsoid volume, and it is therefore optimal.

Theorem 2 (Thm. 1 in [31]). *Let the gradient-of-the-flow matrices F_j and $\hat{F}_{j-1,j} \in \mathbb{R}^{n \times n}$ be full rank, and the coordinate-system matrix of the last*

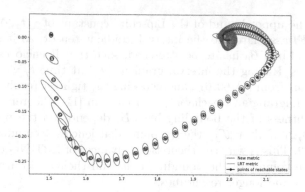

Fig. 3. Reachtube for the Robotarm model, obtained with the LRT (in blue) and LRT-NG metric (in purple), respectively. The time is bounded to the interval $t \in [0,5]$, and it evolves starting at the top left corner of the figure, and going to the right. (Color figure online)

time-step $A_{j-1} \in \mathbb{R}^{n \times n}$ be full-rank and $A_{j-1} \succ 0$. Define metric $\hat{M}_j(F_j) = \hat{A}_j(F_j)^{\top} \hat{A}_j(F_j)$:

$$\hat{A}_j(F_j) = A_{j-1}\hat{F}_{j-1,j}^{-1} = A_0 F_j^{-1} \tag{13}$$

When F_j is known, we simply abbreviate $\hat{A}_j(F_j)$ with $\hat{A}_j$, and $\hat{M}_j(F_j)$ with $\hat{M}_j$. Let $\Lambda_{0,j}(M_j)$ be given by (with M_0 fixed):

$$\Lambda_{0,j}(M_j) = \sqrt{\lambda_{\max}\left((A_0^{\top})^{-1}F_j^{\top}M_jF_jA_0^{-1}\right)}.$$

Then, it holds that $\mathrm{Vol}\left(B_{\hat{M}_j}(\chi_{t_0}^{t_j}(x_0), \Lambda_{0,j}(\hat{M}_j)\,\delta_0)\right)$ is equal to:

$$\min_{M_j \succ 0} \mathrm{Vol}\left(B_{M_j}(\chi_{t_0}^{t_j}(x_0), \Lambda_{0,j}(M_j)\,\delta_0)\right).$$

In other words, the symmetric matrix $\hat{M}_j \succ 0$ minimizes the volume of the ellipsoid $B_{M_j}(\chi_{t_0}^{t_j}(x_0), \Lambda_{0,j}(M_j)\,\delta_0)$ as a function of M_j.

Thus, Theorem 2 gives us an analytic solution for the optimal metric, releasing us from either solving an optimization problem with semi-definite programming in every time-step like in [11,22], or risking false-positive consequences of using a suboptimal metric as in LRT [12,30].

A comparison of the reachsets obtained with LRT metric $\tilde{M}_j$ [12, Definition 1] and the one obtained with LRT-NG metric $\hat{M}_j$ is illustrated in Fig. 3. It shows that the LRT metric is by far not an optimal choice, and it also shows how well our new analytically computed metric $\hat{M}_j$ follows the shape of the set of reachable states.

Intersection of the Bounding Balls. Another novelty in LRT-NG, is that the next reachset is the intersection of an ellipsoid computed in the optimal metric and an Euclidean ball. This considerably reduces the volume and therefore enables LRT-NG to work also for continuous-depth models.

An effective way of getting a much tighter conservative bound $[\mathcal{X}_j]$ is taking the intersection of the ellipsoid in the optimal metric $\hat{M}_j$, and the ball in Euclidean metric. As small errors accumulate in interval arithmetic, taking the intersection leads to a considerable improvement especially as the time horizon increases. That new approach is conservative is shown in Lemma 1 of [31], which allows us to dramatically reduce the volume of the reachtube and combat the wrapping effect in a way that has not been considered before by bloating-based techniques [11, 12, 21–23, 30].

5   Statistical Guarantees (SLR and GoTube)

To avoid state explosion as in the conservative methods, we developed a statistical version of Lagrangian reachability and provided convergence guarantees for computing the upper bound of the confidence interval for the maximum perturbation at time t_j with confidence level $1 - \gamma$ and tube tightness μ.

We review first SLR, a purely theoretical statistical version of Lagrangian reachability framework [32], and then GoTube, a practical statistical verification algorithm for continuous-time models [33], where we achieved technical solutions for fundamental issues in applying SLR.

In this work, we describe *reachability as an optimization problem* and solve that problem for every timestep such that the size of the bounding ball $\mathcal{B}_j$ at time t_j does not depend the previous values $\mathcal{B}_{j-1}, [\mathcal{X}_j]$ or $[\mathcal{F}_j]$ like in LRT-NG. To compute a bounding tube, we have to compute at every time step t_j, the maximum perturbation δ_j in metric M_j for $x \in \mathcal{B}_0$, which is defined as a solution of the optimization problem:

$$\delta_j \geq \max_{x \in \mathcal{B}_0} \|\chi(t_j, x) - \chi(t_j, x_0)\|_{M_j} = \max_{x \in \mathcal{B}_0} d(\chi(t_j, x)) = m^*, \qquad (14)$$

where $d_j(x) = d(\chi(t_j, x))$ denotes the *distance* at time t_j, if the initial center x_0 and metric M_j is known from the context.

As we require Lipschitz-continuity and forward-completeness of the continuous-depth model in Eq. (8), the map $x \mapsto \chi(t_j, x)$ is a homeomorphism and commutes with closure and interior operators. In particular, the image of the boundary of the set $\mathcal{B}_0$ is equal to the boundary of the image $\chi(t_j, \mathcal{B}_0)$. Thus, Eq. (14) has its optimum on the surface of the initial ball $\mathcal{B}_0^S = \text{surface}(\mathcal{B}_0)$, and we will only consider points on the surface.

In order to be able to optimize this problem, we describe the points on the surface with (n-dimensional) polar coordinates such that every point $x \in \mathcal{B}_0^S$ is represented by a tuple (δ_0, φ), with angles $\varphi = (\varphi_1, \ldots, \varphi_{n-1})$ and center x_0, having a conversion function $x((\delta_0, \varphi), x_0)$ from polar to Cartesian coordinates. Whenever the center x_0 and the radius δ_0 of the initial ball $\mathcal{B}_0$ are known from the context, we will use the following notation: $x(\varphi)$ for the conversion from polar to Cartesian coordinates, and just x if we do not want to mention the polar coordinates explicitly (Fig. 4).

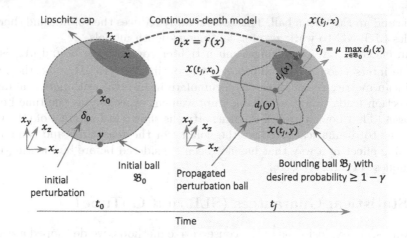

Fig. 4. Statistical Guarantees in a nutshell. The center x_0 of ball $\mathcal{B}_0 = B(x_0, \delta_0)$, with δ_0 the initial perturbation, and samples x drawn uniformly from $\mathcal{B}_0$'s surface, are numerically integrated in time to $\chi(t_j, x_0)$ and $\chi(t_j, x)$, respectively. The Lipschitz constant of $\chi(t_j, x)$ and their distance $d_j(x)$ to $\chi(t_j, x_0)$ are then used to compute Lipschitz caps around samples x, and the radius δ_j of bounding ball $\mathcal{B}_j$ depending on the chosen tightness factor μ. The ratio between the caps' surfaces and $\mathcal{B}_0$'s surface are correlated to the desired confidence $1 - \gamma$.

Forward-Mode Use of Adjoint-Sensitivity Method. For both algorithms, we will need F_x for several sample points. The integral of Eq. (7) has the same form as the auxiliary ODE used for reverse-mode automatic differentiation of Neural ODEs, when optimized by the adjoint sensitivity method [9] with one exception: our F_x defines the differential of the solution by the initial value and their equivalent function a defines the differential of the loss function by the initial value. Their approach computes gradients by solving a second, augmented ODE backwards in time. In our case, solving the variational Eq. (7) until target time t_j, already gives us the required gradient F_x, but requires knowledge of $\chi(t, x)$ for all $t \in [t_0, t_j]$. This is why in our forward-mode adjoint sensitivity method, we propagate for all samples x using Eq. (1) and $F_x(t)$ using Eq. (7) forwards in time together until t_j, starting from its augmented (combined) initial state (x, I) and using its augmented dynamical system $(f(x), (\partial_x f)(\chi(t, x))F(t))$.

5.1 Theoretical Statistical Verification Framework

In this section, we review *stochastic Lagrangian reachability* (SLR) from [32], where we solve each optimization problem globally, via uniform sampling, and locally, through gradient descent, whereas gradient descent is avoided in spherical-caps around the start/end states of previous searches. The cap radius is derived from its local Lipschitz constant, computed via interval arithmetic.

Algorithm 2. Stochastic Lagrangian Reachability (SLR)

Require: initial ball $\mathcal{B}_0 = B(x_0, \delta_0)$, time horizon T, sequence of timesteps t_j ($t_0 \leq$ $t_1 \leq \cdots \leq t_k = T$), tolerance $\mu > 1$, confidence level $\gamma \in (0, 1)$, distance function d_j, gradient of loss $\nabla_\varphi L$

1: **for** $(j = 1; j \leq k; j = j + 1)$ **do**
2:      $\mathcal{V}, \mathcal{U} \leftarrow \{\}$ (list of visited and random points)
3:      $x_j \leftarrow solveIVP(f, x_{j-1}, [t_{j-1}, t_j])$
4:      $[\mathcal{F}] \leftarrow F_{[\mathcal{X}_0]}(t_j) = rungeKuttaVariational((\partial_x f)([\mathcal{X}]), [\mathcal{F}], [t_{j-1}, t_j]))$
5:      **compute** $\Lambda \geq \|[\mathcal{F}]\|$ (interval arithmetic Lipschitz constant)
6:      $\bar{p} \leftarrow 0$
7:      **while** $\bar{p} < 1 - \gamma$ **do**
8:          sample $x \in \mathcal{B}_0$ and add sample to $\mathcal{V}$ and $\mathcal{U}$
9:          $\chi(t_j, x), F_x(t_j) \leftarrow forwardModeAdjointSensitivity(x, I, [t_0, t_j])$
10:         **if** $x \notin \mathcal{S}$ **then** $findLocalMinimum(x, \nabla_\varphi L, F_x(t_j))$ and add x to $\mathcal{V}$
11:         $\bar{m} \leftarrow \max_{x \in \mathcal{V}} d_j(x)$
12:         $r_x \leftarrow computeSafetyRegionRadius(d_j(x), \bar{m}, \Lambda)$ $\forall x \in \mathcal{V}$
13:         $\mathcal{S} \leftarrow \bigcup_{x \in \mathcal{V}} B(x, r_x)$
14:         $\bar{p} \leftarrow \Pr(\mu \cdot \bar{m} \leq m^\star)$
15:     **end while**
16:     $\mathcal{B}_j \leftarrow B(x_j, \mu \cdot \bar{m})$
17: **end for**
18: **return** $(\mathcal{B}_1, \ldots, \mathcal{B}_k)$

Gradient Computation. The SLR algorithm uses gradient descent locally, when solving the global optimization problem of Eq. (14). In [32] the *loss function* $L(\varphi) = -d_j \circ x(\varphi)$ is introduced in polar coordinates at time t_j to be able to do gradient descent on the surface in order to find the optimum. Note that L also depends on the initial radius δ_0 and initial center x_0; as these are fixed inputs, we do not consider them in the notation. Gradient descent is started from uniformly sampled points, which are not contained in already constructed safety regions.

In [32], we introduced a new framework to compute the loss's gradient which is needed to find the local minimum ain a unified fashionnd improved the optimization runtime by 50%, compared to the optimization scheme used in [9]: we save half of the time because we do not have to go backward to compute the loss.

Safety-Region Computation. In contrast to [32], we will switch back to talking about a global maximum of $d_j(x)$ for points $x \in \mathcal{B}_0$ instead of the equivalent problem of finding a global minimum of $L(\varphi)$ for points $\varphi \in \mathbb{R}^{n-1}$. With our global search strategy, we are covering the feasible region $\mathcal{B}_0^S$ with already visited points $\mathcal{V}$. Consequently, we have access to the current maximum in $\mathcal{V}$:

$$\bar{m}_{j,\mathcal{V}} = \max_{x \in \mathcal{V}} d_j(x) \tag{15}$$

with $\bar{m} \leq m^\star$, where $m^\star$ is the global maximum of Eq. (14). We now identify safety regions for a continuous-depth model flow and describe how this is incorporated in the SLR algorithm.

Definition 5 (Safety Region). *Let $x_i \in \mathcal{V} \subseteq \mathcal{B}_0$ be an already-visited point. A safety-radius $r_{x_i} = r(x_i)$ defines a safe spherical-cap $B(x_i, r_{x_i})^S = B(x_i, r_{x_i}) \cap \mathcal{B}_0^S$, if it holds that $d_j(y) \leq \mu \cdot \bar{m}$ for all $y \in B(x_i, r_x)^S$.*

In the following theorem, we use Theorem 1 to bound the local Lipschitz constant (Definition 3) and to define the radius r_x of the safety region $B(x, r_x)^S$ around an already-visited point $x \in \mathcal{V}$.

Theorem 3 (Radius of Safety Region ([32], Thm. 1)). *At target time t_j, let $\bar{m}$ be the current global maximum, as in Eq. (15). Let $x \in \mathcal{V}$ be an already-visited point with value $d_j(x)$, and let r_x and $B(x, r_x)^S$ be defined as follows:*

$$r_x = \lambda_{\Sigma_x}^{-1} \left(\mu \cdot \bar{m} - d_j(x) \right) \tag{16}$$

with $\mu > 1$, $\lambda_{\Sigma_x} = \max_{y \in \Sigma_x} \|F_y(t_j)\|_{M_{0,j}}$ and $\Sigma_x \supseteq B(x, r_x)^S$, then it holds that:

$$d_j(y) \leq \mu \cdot \bar{m} \quad \forall y \in B(x, r_x)^S \tag{17}$$

We can now use the safety regions around the samples to compute the probability needed in Line 14 of Algorithm 2:

$$\Pr(\mu \cdot \bar{m} \geq m^\star) \geq \Pr(\exists x \in \mathcal{U} : S_x \ni x^\star) = 1 - \prod_{x \in \mathcal{U}} (1 - \Pr(S_x)), \tag{18}$$

with $S_x = B(x, r_x)^S$ being the safety region around x. In [32], we provide a convergence guarantee as well as a convergence rate for the probability $\Pr(S_x) = \text{Area}(S_x) / \text{Area}(\mathcal{B}_0)$. Theorem 2 of [32] shows that in the limit of the number of samples, the constructed reachset converges with probability 1 to the smallest ellipsoid that encloses the true reachable set using tightness bound μ.

5.2   Scalable Statistical Verification

As we implemented the SLR algorithm, we observed that even after resolving the first-occurring inefficient sampling and their vanishing gradient problems, the algorithm still blew up in time, even for low-dimensional benchmarks such as the Dubins Car. Our GoTube algorithm and its associated theory solve fundamental scalability problems of related works (see Table 1) by replacing the interval arithmetic used to compute deterministic caps, with statistical Lipschitz caps. This enables us to verify continuous-depth models up to an arbitrary time-horizon, a capability beyond what was achievable before.

GoTube starts by sampling a batch (tensor) $x^B \in \mathcal{B}_0^S$ and if needed, it adds new samples to that tensor in Line 14 and computes every step in a tensorized manner, for all samples at the same time. In each iteration, it integrates the center and the already available samples from their previous time step, and the possibly new batches from their initial state (for simplicity, the pseudocode does not make this distinction explicit). GoTube then computes the maximum distance from the integrated samples to the integrated center, their local Lipschitz

---

Algorithm 3. GoTube

Require: initial ball $\mathcal{B}_0 = B(x_0, \delta_0)$, time horizon T, sequence of timesteps t_j ($t_0 <$ $\cdots < t_k = T$), error tolerance $\mu > 1$, confidence level $\gamma \in (0, 1)$, batch size b, distance function d

1: $\mathcal{V} \leftarrow \{\}$ (list of visited random points)
2: **sample batch** $x^B \in \mathcal{B}_0^S$
3: **for** ($j = 1; j \leq k; j = j + 1$) **do**
4:    $\bar{p} \leftarrow 0$
5:    **while** $\bar{p} < 1 - \gamma$ **do**
6:       $\mathcal{V} \leftarrow \mathcal{V} \cup \{x^B\}$
7:       $x_j \leftarrow solveIVP(f, x_{j-1}, [t_{j-1}, t_j])$
8:       $\bar{m}_{j,\mathcal{V}} \leftarrow \max_{x \in \mathcal{V}} d(t_j, x)$
9:       $x, F_x(t_j) \leftarrow forwardModeAdjointSensitivity(x, I, [t_0, t_j])$ $\forall x \in \mathcal{V}$
10:      **compute** local Lipschitz constants $\lambda_x = \|F_x\|$ for $x \in \mathcal{V}$
11:      **compute** statistical quantile $\Delta\lambda_{\mathcal{V}}$
12:      **compute** cap radii $r_x(\lambda_x, \Delta\lambda_{\mathcal{V}})$ (Thm. 4) for $x \in \mathcal{V}$
13:      $\bar{p} \leftarrow computeProb(\gamma, \{r_x : x \in \mathcal{V}\}, n, \delta_0)$
14:      **sample batch** $x^B \in \mathcal{B}_0$
15:   **end while**
16:   $\mathcal{B}_j \leftarrow B(x_j, \mu \cdot \bar{m}_{j,\mathcal{V}})$
17: **end for**
18: **return** $(\mathcal{B}_1, \ldots, \mathcal{B}_k)$

---

constant according to the variational Eq. (7) using the forward-mode adjoint sensitivity method. Unlike SLR, F_x is not used with gradient descent to find local optima, but to compute local Lipschitz constants for all samples.

Based on this information GoTube then computes a statistical upper bound for Lipschitz constants and the cap radii accordingly. The total surface of the caps is then employed to compute and update the achieved confidence (that is, probability). Once the desired confidence is achieved, GoTube exits the inner loop, and computes the bounding ball in terms of its center and radius, which is given by tightness factor μ times the maximum distance $\bar{m}_{j,\mathcal{V}}$. After exiting the outer loop, GoTube returns the bounding tube.

Definition 6 (Lipschitz Cap). *Let $\mathcal{V}$ be the set of all sampled points, $x \in \mathcal{V}$ be a sample point on the surface of the initial ball, $\bar{m}_{j,\mathcal{V}} = \max_{x \in \mathcal{V}} d_j(x)$ be the sample maximum, and $B(x, r_x)^S = B(x, r_x) \cap \mathcal{B}_0^S$ be a spherical cap around that point. We call the cap $B(x, r_x)^S$ a γ, t_j-Lipschitz cap if it holds that $\Pr(d_j(y) \leq \mu \cdot \bar{m}_{j,\mathcal{V}}) \geq 1 - \gamma$ for all $y \in B(x, r_x)^S$.*

Lipschitz caps around the samples, are a statistical version of the safety regions around samples, commonly used to cover a state space. Intuitively, the points within a cap do not have to be explored. The difference with Lipschitz caps is that we statistically bound the values inside that space, and develop a theory enabling us to calculate a probability of having found an upper bound of the true maximum $m_j^\star = d_j(x_j^\star) = \max_{\{x_1, \ldots, x_m\} \subset \mathcal{B}_0} d_j(x)$ for any m-dimensional set of the optimization problem in Eq. (14).

Our objective is to avoid the usage of interval arithmetic, for computing the Lipschitz constant - as done in SLR - as it impedes scaling up to continuous depth models. Instead, we define statistical bounds on the Lipschitz constant, to set the radius r_x of the Lipschitz caps, such that $\mu \cdot \bar{m}_{j,\mathcal{V}}$ is a γ-statistical upper bound for all distances $d_j(y)$ at time t_j, from values inside the ball $B(x, r_x)^S$.

Theorem 4 (Radius of Statistical Lipschitz Caps ([33], Thm. 1)). *Given a continuous-depth model f from Eq. (1), $\gamma \in (0,1)$, $\mu > 1$, target time t_j, the set of all sampled points $\mathcal{V}$, the number of sampled points $N = |\mathcal{V}|$, the sample maximum $\bar{m}_{j,\mathcal{V}} = \max_{x \in \mathcal{V}} d_j(x)$, the IVP solutions $\chi(t_j, x)$, and the corresponding stretching factors $\lambda_x = \|\partial_x \chi(t_j, x)\|$ for all $x \in \mathcal{V}$, then: let $\nu_x = |\lambda_x - \lambda_X| / \|x - X\|$, for $x \in \mathcal{V}$, be a new random variable, where $X \in \mathcal{B}_0^S$ is the random variable which is thrown by random sampling on the surface of the initial ball. Let the upper bound $\Delta\lambda_{\mathcal{V}}$ of the confidence interval of $\mathbb{E}\nu_x$ be defined as follows:*

$$\Delta\lambda_{\mathcal{V}}(\gamma) = \overline{\nu_x} + t^*_{\gamma/2}(N-2)\frac{s(\nu_x)}{\sqrt{N-1}}, \tag{19}$$

with $\overline{\nu_x}$ and $s(\nu_x)$ being the sample mean and sample standard deviation of ν_x, and t^* being the Student's t-distribution. Let r_x be defined as:

$$r_x = \frac{\left(-\lambda_x + \sqrt{\lambda_x^2 + 4 \cdot \Delta\lambda_{\mathcal{V}} \cdot (\mu \cdot \bar{m}_{j,\mathcal{V}} - d_j(x))}\right)}{2 \cdot \Delta\lambda_{\mathcal{V}}}, \tag{20}$$

then it holds that:

$$\Pr\left(d_j(y) \leq \mu \cdot \bar{m}_{j,\mathcal{V}}\right) \geq 1 - \gamma \quad \forall y \in B(x, r_x)^S, \tag{21}$$

and thus that $B(x, r_x)^S$ is a γ, t_j-Lipschitz cap.

Using conditional probabilities, we are able to state that the convergence guarantee holds for the GoTube algorithm, thus ensuring that the algorithm terminates in finite time, even using statistical Lipschitz caps around the samples, instead of deterministic local balls [33][Thm. 2].

6   Experimental Evaluation

We performed a rich set of experiments with LRT-NG and GoTube, evaluating their performance and identifying their characteristics and limits in verifying continuous-time systems with increasing complexity. We ran our experiments on a standard hardware setup (12 vCPUs, 64 GB memory) equipped with a single GPU with a per-run timeout of 1 h (except for runtimes reported in Fig. 7).

6.1   On the Volume of the Bounding Balls

Our first experimental evaluation concerns the overapproximation errors of the constructed bounding tubes. An ideal reachability tool should be able to output

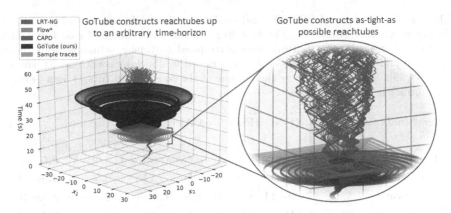

Fig. 5. Visualization of the reachtubes constructed for the Dubin's car model with various reachability methods. While the tubes computed by existing methods (LRT-NG, Flow* and CAPD) explode at $t \approx 20\,$s (this moment is shown on the right side of the figure, where GoTube's reachtube is still very close to the sample traces) due to the accumulation of overapproximation errors (the infamous wrapping effect), GoTube can keep tight bounds beyond $t > 40\,$s for a 99% confidence level (using 20000 samples, $\mu = 1.1$ and runtime of one hour). Note also the chaotic nature of 100 executions.

an as tight as possible tube that encloses the system's executions. Consequently, as our comparison metric, we will report the average volume of the bounding balls, where less volume is better. We use the benchmarks and settings of [31] (same radii, time horizons, and models) as the basis of our evaluation. In particular, we compare GoTube to the deterministic, state-of-the-art reachability tools LRT-NG, Flow*, CAPD, and LRT. We measure the volume of GoTube's balls at the confidence levels of 90% and 99%, using $\mu = 1.1$ as the tightness factor (in the third experiment we will talk in more detail about the trade-off between tightness and runtime).

The results are shown in Table 2, and exemplary in Fig. 6. For the first five benchmarks, which are classical dynamical systems, we use the small time horizons T and small initial radii δ_0, which the other tools could handle.

LRT-NG is the only conservative tool able to handle the continuous-depth models. GoTube, with 99% confidence, achieves a competitive performance to the other tools, coming out on top in 3 out of 5 benchmarks - using $\mu = 1.1$ as the tightness bound. Intuitively this means, we are confident that the overapproximation includes all executions with a confidence level $1 - \lambda$, but this overapproximation might not be as tight as desired.

GoTube is able to achieve any desired tightness by reducing μ and increasing the runtime. The specific reachtubes and the chaotic nature of hundred executions of Dubin's car are shown in Fig. 5. As one can see, the GoTube reachtube extends to a much longer time horizon, which we fixed at 40 s. All other tools blew up before 20 s. For the two problems involving neural networks, GoTube produces significantly tighter reachtubes.

Table 2. Comparison of LRT-NG and GoTube (using tightness bound $\mu = 1.1$) to existing reachability methods. The first five benchmarks concern classical dynamical systems, whereas the two bottom rows correspond to time-continuous RNN models (LTC = liquid time-constant networks) in a closed feedback loop with an RL environment [38,69]. The numbers show the volume of the constructed tube. Lower is better; best number in given in boldface.

Benchmark	LRT-NG	Flow*	CAPD	LRT	GoTube (90%)	(99%)
Brusselator	1.5e−4	9.8e−5	3.6e−4	6.1e−4	8.6e−5	**8.6e−5**
Van Der Pol	4.2e−4	**3.5e−4**	1.5e−3	3.5e−4	3.5e−4	**3.5e−4**
Robotarm	**7.9e−11**	8.7e−10	1.1e−9	Fail	2.5e−10	2.5e−10
Dubins Car	0.131	4.5e−2	0.1181	385	2.5e−2	**2.6e−2**
Cardiac Cell	**3.7e−9**	1.5e−8	4.4e−8	3.2e−8	4.2e−8	4.3e−8
CartPole-v1+LTC	4.49e−33	Fail	Fail	Fail	2.6e−37	**4.9e−37**
CartPole-v1+CTRNN	3.9e−27	Fail	Fail	Fail	9.9e−34	**1.2e−33**

6.2   GoTube Provides Safety Bounds Up an Arbitrary Time Horizon

In our second experiment, we evaluate for how long LRT-NG, GoTube and existing methods, can construct a reachtube before exploding due to overapproximation errors. To do so, we extend the benchmark setup by increasing the time horizon for which the tube should be constructed, use tightness bound $\mu = 1.1$ and set a 95% confidence level, that is, probability that $\max_{\{x_1,...,x_m\} \subset \mathcal{B}_0} d_j(x)$ is for any m-dimensional set and any time t_j smaller than the bounding ball's radius.

The results in Table 3 demonstrate that LRT-NG is the only conservative tool able to run on continuous-depth models and that GoTube produces significantly longer reachtubes than all considered state-of-the-art approaches, without suffering from severe overapproximation errors. Figure 1 visualizes the difference to the existing methods and gives over-approximation margins, for two example dimensions of the CartPole-v1 environment and its CT-RNN controller.

Table 3. Results of the extended benchmark by longer time horizons. The numbers show the volume of the constructed tube, "Blowup" indicates that the method produced `Inf` or `NaN` values due to a blowup. Lower is better; the best method is shown in bold.

Benchmark	CartPole-v1+CTRNN		CartPole-v1+LTC	
Time horizon	1 s	10 s	0.35 s	10 s
LRT	Blowup	Blowup	Blowup	Blowup
CAPD	Blowup	Blowup	Blowup	Blowup
Flow*	Blowup	Blowup	Blowup	Blowup
LRT-NG	3.9e−27	Blowup	4.5e−33	Blowup
GoTube (ours)	**8.8e−34**	**1.1e−19**	**4.9e−37**	**8.7e−21**

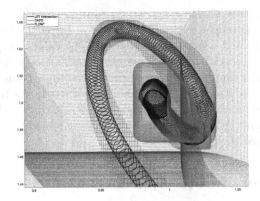

Fig. 6. Comparison of the conservative reachtubes computed by the Flow* (in green), CAPD (in orange), and LRT-NG (in violet). Flow* blows up already before time $t = 10$, while CAPD works up to $t = 19.1$ and LRT-NG up to $t = 22.6$. As clearly shown in this figure of the reachtube until time $t = 14$, LRT-NG is superior to both Flow* and CAPD on this Brusselator model. (Color figure online)

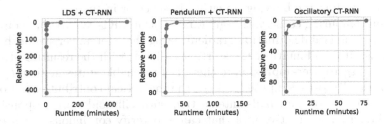

Fig. 7. GoTube's runtime (x-axis) and volume size (y-axis) as a function of the tightness factor μ. The volume was normalized by the volume obtained with the lowest μ (4.3e−13, 2.4e−12, and 2.1e−38 in particular).

6.3 GoTube Can Trade Runtime for Reachtube Tightness

In our last experiment in [33], we introduced a new set of benchmark models entirely based on continuous-time recurrent neural networks. The first model is an unstable linear dynamical system of the form $\dot{x} = Ax + Bu$ that is stabilized by a CT-RNN policy via actions u. The second model corresponds to the inverted pendulum environment, which is similar to the CartPole environment but differs in that the control actions are applied via a torque vector on the pendulum directly, instead of moving a cart. The CT-RNN policies for these two environments were trained using deep RL. Our third new benchmark model concerns the analysis of the learned dynamics of a CT-RNN trained on supervised data. In particular, by using the reachability frameworks, we aim to assess if the learned network expressed oscillatory behavior. The CT-RNN state vector consists of 16 dimensions, which is twice as much as existing reachability benchmarks [31].

Here, we study how GoTube can trade runtime for the volume of the constructed reachtube through its tightness factor μ. In particular, we run GoTube on our newly proposed benchmark with various values of μ. We then plot GoTube's runtime (x-axis) and volume size (y-axis) as a function of μ. The resulting curves show the Pareto-front of runtime-volume trade-off with GoTube.

Figure 7 shows the results for a time horizon of 10 s in the first two examples, and of 2 s in the last example. Our results demonstrate that GoTube can adapt to different runtime and tightness constraints and set a new benchmark for future methods to compare with.

7 Comparison of Both Approaches

A common aspect of LRT, LRT-NG, SLR, and GoTube, is that they all make use of the variational Eq. (7), together with the mean value Theorem 1. They allow our algorithms to have tighter bounds, less wrapping effect, and to be more efficient than other tools, as shown in the experimental evaluation. It is nevertheless important to know that for each tool, we had to develop new theoretical methods, avoiding the blowing up either in space or in time.

When computing conservative guarantees, as in LRT-NG [31], we employ the propagated interval deformation gradient, using the interval version of the variational Eqs. (10), and multiply the starting radius δ_0 with the resulting stretching factor $\|\mathcal{F}_j\|_{M_j}$ to over-approximate the set of reachable states at time t_j. As we need to use $[\mathcal{X}_{j-1}]$ to compute $\|\mathcal{F}_j\|_{M_j}$, the theoretical contributions of optimal metric computation and balls intersection with ellipsoids, are responsible for being the only conservative tool that can also verify continuous-depth models, by avoiding the accumulation of small errors (wrapping effect).

For the theoretical stochastic version of Lagrangian Reachability (SLR [32]), we use the variational equations even in two different ways: 1) To propagate the deformation gradient for several samples - using the forward mode adjoint sensitivity method - to calculate the gradient of loss needed to find local minima. 2) To propagate the interval variational equations and use Theorem 1 to compute an upper bound of the Lipschitz constants for the distance function $d_j(x)$. This upper bound is used to compute the safety region radiuses.

In our scalable statistical robustness analysis tool GoTube, we completely avoid the use of interval arithmetic, as the interval Lipschitz constant in SLR leads to a blow-up in time. In Algorithm 3, the variational equation is used to compute $F_x(t)$ via the forward mode adjoint sensitivity method for a tensorized batch of samples. Using Theorem 1, we compute local Lipschitz constants λ_x for the samples, which we use to compute the cap radiuses and thus the probability.

Instead of using Lipschitz constants as a bloating factor for the ball's radius as in LRT-NG, we use it to define regions (caps) around already visited points on the surface, and to compute an upper bound for the values inside that caps - either deterministic safety regions (SLR) or statistical Lipschitz caps (GoTube). This knowledge allows us to compute the probability of having an upper bound for the global maximum of Eq. (14). The bigger the Lipschitz constant, the smaller the safety region radius and thus the probability. So a huge difference between the conservative and the statistical method is that a too large upper bound of the Lipschitz constant results in a state explosion for LRT-NG but in a time explosion for SLR and GoTube.

Another difference is that LRT-NG always computes as-tight-as-possible reachtubes, given the dynamical system. In contrast, SLR and GoTube allow to trade between time and accuracy, by using the tightness bound parameter μ. Thus, after finishing our global search strategy for timestep t_j, we have the statistical guarantee that the functional values of every $x \in \mathcal{B}_0$ are less or equal to $\mu \cdot \bar{m}$. This implies that we should initiate the search with a relatively large $\mu = \mu_1$, obtaining for every x a relatively large value of r_{x,μ_1} and therefore obtain a faster coverage of the search space. Subsequently, we can investigate whether the reachset $\mathcal{B}_j$ with radius $\delta_j = \mu_1 \cdot \bar{m}$ intersects with a region of bad (unsafe) states. If this is not the case, we can proceed to the next timestep t_{j+1}. Otherwise, we reduce μ to $\mu_2 < \mu_1$. Accordingly, we can find a first radius for $\mathcal{B}_j$ faster and refine it as long as $\mathcal{B}_j$ intersects with the region of bad states.

8   Conclusions and Future Work

In this work, we considered the robustness analysis of continuous-depth models to ensure safety of closed-loop cyber-physical systems with a neural network controller. We showed how to achieve tight reachtubes with deterministic (LRT-NG) or with statistical (SLR and GoTube) guarantees. We also compared the methods theoretically, by showing their common grounds in mathematical theory, and their distinct usage of that basis. As our experiments show, LRT-NG is superior to LRT, CAPD, and Flow*. Moreover, GoTube is stable and sets the state-of-the-art in terms of its ability to scale to time horizons well beyond what has been previously possible. Lastly, LRT-NG's and GoTube's scalability enables them to readily handle the verification of advanced continuous-depth neural models, a setting where state-of-the-art deterministic approaches fail.

Our current algorithms and methods require the availability of an ODE model of the environment. However, this is often not the case in complex applications, such as in autonomous driving, or in individual artificial pace makers. The ultimate goal is to scale up to high dimensional continuous-depth models and complex tasks, without knowing the model of the environment in advance.

References

1. Abeyaratne, R.: Continuum Mechanics. Lecture Notes on The Mechanics of Elastic Solids (1998)
2. Athalye, A., Carlini, N., Wagner, D.: Obfuscated gradients give a false sense of security: Circumventing defenses to adversarial examples. In: ICML, pp. 274–283. PMLR (2018)
3. Bak, S., Tran, H.-D., Hobbs, K., Johnson, T.T.: Improved geometric path enumeration for verifying ReLU neural networks. In: Lahiri, S.K., Wang, C. (eds.) CAV 2020. LNCS, vol. 12224, pp. 66–96. Springer, Cham (2020). https://doi.org/10.1007/978-3-030-53288-8_4

4. Bhowmick, A., D'Souza, M., Raghavan, G.S.: LipBaB: Computing exact Lipschitz constant of ReLU networks. arXiv preprint arXiv:2105.05495 (2021)

5. Bortolussi, L., Sanguinetti, G.: A statistical approach for computing reachability of non-linear and stochastic dynamical systems. In: Norman, G., Sanders, W. (eds.) QEST 2014. LNCS, vol. 8657, pp. 41–56. Springer, Cham (2014). https://doi.org/10.1007/978-3-319-10696-0_5

6. Bunel, R., et al.: Lagrangian decomposition for neural network verification. In: UAI, pp. 370–379. PMLR (2020)

7. Bunel, R., Mudigonda, P., Turkaslan, I., Torr, P., Lu, J., Kohli, P.: Branch and bound for piecewise linear neural network verification. JMLR **21**(2020), 1–39 (2020)

8. Bunel, R.R., Turkaslan, I., Torr, P., Kohli, P., Mudigonda, P.K.: A unified view of piecewise linear neural network verification. In: Bengio, S., Wallach, H., Larochelle, H., Grauman, K., Cesa-Bianchi, N., Garnett, R. (eds.) NeurIPS. vol. 31. Curran Associates, Inc. (2018). https://proceedings.neurips.cc/paper/2018/file/be53d253d6bc3258a8160556dda3e9b2-Paper.pdf

9. Chen, T.Q., Rubanova, Y., Bettencourt, J., Duvenaud, D.K.: Neural ordinary differential equations. In: Bengio, S., Wallach, H., Larochelle, H., Grauman, K., Cesa-Bianchi, N., Garnett, R. (eds.) NeurIPS 31, pp. 6571–6583. Curran Associates, Inc. (2018)

10. Chen, X., Ábrahám, E., Sankaranarayanan, S.: Flow*: an analyzer for non-linear hybrid systems. In: Sharygina, N., Veith, H. (eds.) CAV 2013. LNCS, vol. 8044, pp. 258–263. Springer, Heidelberg (2013). https://doi.org/10.1007/978-3-642-39799-8_18

11. Cyranka, J., Islam, M.A., Byrne, G., Jones, P., Smolka, S.A., Grosu, R.: Lagrangian reachabililty. In: Majumdar, R., Kunčak, V. (eds.) CAV 2017. LNCS, vol. 10426, pp. 379–400. Springer, Cham (2017). https://doi.org/10.1007/978-3-319-63387-9_19

12. Cyranka, J., Islam, M.A., Smolka, S.A., Gao, S., Grosu, R.: Tight continuous-time reachtubes for Lagrangian reachability. In: CDC, pp. 6854–6861. IEEE (2018)

13. De Palma, A., et al.: Improved branch and bound for neural network verification via Lagrangian decomposition. arXiv preprint arXiv:2104.06718 (2021)

14. Devonport, A., Khaled, M., Arcak, M., Zamani, M.: PIRK: scalable interval reachability analysis for high-dimensional nonlinear systems. In: Lahiri, S.K., Wang, C. (eds.) CAV 2020. LNCS, vol. 12224, pp. 556–568. Springer, Cham (2020). https://doi.org/10.1007/978-3-030-53288-8_27

15. Donzé, A.: Breach, a toolbox for verification and parameter synthesis of hybrid systems. In: Touili, T., Cook, B., Jackson, P. (eds.) CAV 2010. LNCS, vol. 6174, pp. 167–170. Springer, Heidelberg (2010). https://doi.org/10.1007/978-3-642-14295-6_17

16. Donzé, A., Maler, O.: Systematic simulation using sensitivity analysis. In: Bemporad, A., Bicchi, A., Buttazzo, G. (eds.) HSCC 2007. LNCS, vol. 4416, pp. 174–189. Springer, Heidelberg (2007). https://doi.org/10.1007/978-3-540-71493-4_16

17. Duggirala, P.S., Mitra, S., Viswanathan, M., Potok, M.: C2E2: a verification tool for stateflow models. In: Baier, C., Tinelli, C. (eds.) TACAS 2015. LNCS, vol. 9035, pp. 68–82. Springer, Heidelberg (2015). https://doi.org/10.1007/978-3-662-46681-0_5

18. Ehlers, R.: Formal verification of piece-wise linear feed-forward neural networks. In: D'Souza, D., Narayan Kumar, K. (eds.) ATVA 2017. LNCS, vol. 10482, pp. 269–286. Springer, Cham (2017). https://doi.org/10.1007/978-3-319-68167-2_19

19. Enszer, J.A., Stadtherr, M.A.: Verified solution and propagation of uncertainty in physiological models. Reliab. Comput. **15**(3), 168–178 (2011). http://interval. louisiana.edu/reliable-computing-journal/volume-15/no-3/reliable-computing-15-pp-168-178.pdf

20. Erichson, N.B., Azencot, O., Queiruga, A., Mahoney, M.W.: Lipschitz recurrent neural networks. arXiv preprint arXiv:2006.12070 (2020)

21. Fan, C., Kapinski, J., Jin, X., Mitra, S.: Locally optimal reach set over-approximation for nonlinear systems. In: ICES, EMSOFT 2016, pp. 6:1–6:10. ACM, New York (2016)

22. Fan, C., Kapinski, J., Jin, X., Mitra, S.: Simulation-driven reachability using matrix measures. ACM Trans. Embed. Comput. Syst. **17**(1), 1–28 (2017)

23. Fan, C., Mitra, S.: Bounded verification with on-the-fly discrepancy computation. In: Finkbeiner, B., Pu, G., Zhang, L. (eds.) ATVA 2015. LNCS, vol. 9364, pp. 446–463. Springer, Cham (2015). https://doi.org/10.1007/978-3-319-24953-7_32

24. Fazlyab, M., Robey, A., Hassani, H., Morari, M., Pappas, G.: Efficient and accurate estimation of Lipschitz constants for deep neural networks. In: Wallach, H., Larochelle, H., Beygelzimer, A., d' Alché-Buc, F., Fox, E., Garnett, R. (eds.) NeurIPS. vol. 32. Curran Associates, Inc. (2019). https://proceedings.neurips.cc/paper/2019/file/95e1533eb1b20a97777749fb94fdb944-Paper.pdf

25. Finlay, C., Jacobsen, J.H., Nurbekyan, L., Oberman, A.: How to train your neural ODE: the world of Jacobian and kinetic regularization. In: ICML, pp. 3154–3164. PMLR (2020)

26. Fränzle, M., Hahn, E., Hermanns, H., Wolovick, N., Zhang, L.: Measurability and safety verification for stochastic hybrid systems. In: HSCC, pp. 43–52 (2011)

27. Gao, S., Kong, S., Clarke, E.M.: Satisfiability modulo odes. In: 2013 Formal Methods in Computer-Aided Design, pp. 105–112 (2013)

28. Goodfellow, I.J., Shlens, J., Szegedy, C.: Explaining and harnessing adversarial examples. arXiv preprint arXiv:1412.6572 (2014)

29. Gowal, S., et al.: On the effectiveness of interval bound propagation for training verifiably robust models. arXiv preprint arXiv:1810.12715 (2018)

30. Gruenbacher, S., Cyranka, J., Islam, M.A., Tschaikowski, M., Smolka, S., Grosu, R.: Under the Hood of a Stand-Alone Lagrangian Reachability Tool. EPiC Series in Computing, vol. 61 (2019)

31. Gruenbacher, S., Cyranka, J., Lechner, M., Islam, M.A., Smolka, S.A., Grosu, R.: Lagrangian reachtubes: the next generation. In: CDC, pp. 1556–1563 (2020)

32. Gruenbacher, S., Hasani, R., Lechner, M., Cyranka, J., Smolka, S.A., Grosu, R.: On the verification of neural odes with stochastic guarantees. In: AAAI 35(13), pp. 11525–11535 (2021)

33. Gruenbacher, S., et al.: GoTube: scalable stochastic verification of continuous-depth models. CoRR abs/2107.08467 (2021). https://arxiv.org/abs/2107.08467

34. Gurung, A., Ray, R., Bartocci, E., Bogomolov, S., Grosu, R.: Parallel reachability analysis of hybrid systems in XSpeed. Int. J. Softw. Tools Technol. Transf. **21**(4), 401–423 (2019)

35. Hansen, E., Walster, G.W.: Global Optimization Using Interval Analysis: Revised and Expanded, vol. 264. CRC Press, Boca Raton (2003)

36. Hansen, N., Ostermeier, A.: Completely derandomized self-adaptation in evolution strategies. Evol. Comput. **9**(2), 159–195 (2001)

37. Hasani, R., Lechner, M., Amini, A., Rus, D., Grosu, R.: The natural lottery ticket winner: reinforcement learning with ordinary neural circuits. In: ICML. JMLR.org (2020)

38. Hasani, R., Lechner, M., Amini, A., Rus, D., Grosu, R.: Liquid time-constant networks. In: AAAI 35(9) (2021)
39. Henriksen, P., Lomuscio, A.: Efficient neural network verification via adaptive refinement and adversarial search. In: ECAI 2020, pp. 2513–2520. IOS Press (2020)
40. Henzinger, T.A., Lechner, M., Zikelic, D.: Scalable verification of quantized neural networks. In: AAAI, vol. 35, pp. 3787–3795 (2021)
41. Hladik, M., Daney, D., Tsigaridas, E.: Bounds on real eigenvalues and singular values of interval matrices. SIAM J. Matrix Anal. Appl. **31**(4), 2116–2129 (2010)
42. Huang, C., Chen, X., Lin, W., Yang, Z., Li, X.: Probabilistic safety verification of stochastic hybrid systems using barrier certificates. ACM Trans. Embed. Comput. Syst. **16**(5s), 1–19 (2017)
43. Igel, C., Hansen, N., Roth, S.: Covariance matrix adaptation for multi-objective optimization. Evol. Comput. **15**(1), 1–28 (2007)
44. Immler, F.: Verified reachability analysis of continuous systems. In: Baier, C., Tinelli, C. (eds.) TACAS 2015. LNCS, vol. 9035, pp. 37–51. Springer, Heidelberg (2015). https://doi.org/10.1007/978-3-662-46681-0_3
45. Kapela, T., Mrozek, M., Wilczak, D., Zgliczynski, P.: CAPD::DynSys: a flexible C++ toolbox for rigorous numerical analysis of dynamical systems. Pre-Print (2020). ww2.ii.uj.edu.pl
46. Katz, G., Barrett, C., Dill, D.L., Julian, K., Kochenderfer, M.J.: Reluplex: an efficient SMT solver for verifying deep neural networks. In: Majumdar, R., Kunčak, V. (eds.) CAV 2017. LNCS, vol. 10426, pp. 97–117. Springer, Cham (2017). https://doi.org/10.1007/978-3-319-63387-9_5
47. Kvasov, D.E., Sergeyev, Y.D.: Lipschitz global optimization methods in control problems. Autom. Remote Control **74**(9), 1435–1448 (2013). https://doi.org/10.1134/S0005117913090014
48. Lechner, M., Hasani, R.: Learning long-term dependencies in irregularly-sampled time series. arXiv preprint arXiv:2006.04418 (2020)
49. Lechner, M., Hasani, R., Amini, A., Henzinger, T.A., Rus, D., Grosu, R.: Neural circuit policies enabling auditable autonomy. Nat. MI **2**(10), 642–652 (2020)
50. Lechner, M., Hasani, R., Grosu, R., Rus, D., Henzinger, T.A.: Adversarial training is not ready for robot learning. arXiv preprint arXiv:2103.08187 (2021)
51. Li, D., Bak, S., Bogomolov, S.: Reachability analysis of nonlinear systems using hybridization and dynamics scaling. In: Bertrand, N., Jansen, N. (eds.) FORMATS 2020. LNCS, vol. 12288, pp. 265–282. Springer, Cham (2020). https://doi.org/10.1007/978-3-030-57628-8_16
52. Lohner, R.: Computation of guaranteed enclosures for the solutions of ordinary initial and boundary value problems. In: Computational Ordinary Differential Equations. Clarendon Press, Oxford (1992)
53. Lu, J., Mudigonda, P.: Nueral network branching for nueral network verification. In: ICLR 2020. Open Review (2020)
54. Malherbe, C., Vayatis, N.: Global optimization of Lipschitz functions. In: Proceedings of the 34th ICML, ICML 2017, vol. 70, pp. 2314–2323. JMLR.org (2017)
55. Meyer, P.J., Devonport, A., Arcak, M.: TIRA: toolbox for interval reachability analysis. In: HSCC 2019, pp. 224–229. Association for Computing Machinery, New York (2019)
56. Mirman, M., Gehr, T., Vechev, M.: Differentiable abstract interpretation for provably robust neural networks. In: ICML, pp. 3578–3586. PMLR (2018)
57. Nair, V., Hinton, G.E.: Rectified linear units improve restricted Boltzmann machines. In: ICML, pp. 807–814 (2010)

58. Nedialkov, N., Jackson, K., Corliss, G.: Validated solutions of initial value problems for ordinary differential equations. Appl. Math. Comput. **105**(1), 21–68 (1999)
59. Neumaier, A.: Complete search in continuous global optimization and constraint satisfaction. Acta Numerica **13**, 271–369 (2004)
60. Rohn, J.: Bounds on eigenvalues of interval matrices. ZAMMZ. Angew. Math. Mech. **78**, 1049–1050 (1998)
61. Rump, S.M.: Computational error bounds for multiple or nearly multiple eigenvalues. Linear Algebra Appl. **324**(1), 209–226 (2001)
62. Salman, H., Yang, G., Zhang, H., Hsieh, C.J., Zhang, P.: A convex relaxation barrier to tight robustness verification of neural networks. In: Wallach, H., Larochelle, H., Beygelzimer, A., d'Alché-Buc, F., Fox, E., Garnett, R. (eds.) NeurIPS. vol. 32. Curran Associates, Inc. (2019). https://proceedings.neurips.cc/paper/2019/file/246a3c5544feb054f3ea718f61adfa16-Paper.pdf
63. Shmarov, F., Zuliani, P.: ProbReach: a tool for guaranteed reachability analysis of stochastic hybrid systems. In: Bogomolov, S., Tiwari, A. (eds.) SNR-CAV, vol. 37, pp. 40–48 (2015)
64. Shmarov, F., Zuliani, P.: ProbReach: verified probabilistic delta-reachability for stochastic hybrid systems. In: HSCC, pp. 134–139. ACM (2015)
65. Singh, G., et al.: Eth robustness analyzer for neural networks (ERAN) (2020). https://github.com/eth-sri/eran
66. Slaughter, W.: The Linearized Theory of Elasticity. Springer, Boston (2002). https://doi.org/10.1007/978-1-4612-0093-2
67. Tjandraatmadja, C., Anderson, R., Huchette, J., Ma, W., Patel, K.K., Vielma, J.P.: The convex relaxation barrier, revisited: Tightened single-neuron relaxations for neural network verification. In: Larochelle, H., Ranzato, M., Hadsell, R., Balcan, M.F., Lin, H. (eds.) NeurIPS. vol. 33, pp. 21675–21686. Curran Associates, Inc. (2020). https://proceedings.neurips.cc/paper/2020/file/f6c2a0c4b566bc99d596e58638e342b0-Paper.pdf
68. Vinod, A.P., Oishi, M.M.: Stochastic reachability of a target tube. Automatica **125**, 109458 (2021)
69. Vorbach, C., Hasani, R., Amini, A., Lechner, M., Rus, D.: Causal navigation by continuous-time neural networks. arXiv preprint arXiv:2106.08314 (2021)
70. Wang, Q., Zuliani, P., Kong, S., Gao, S., Clarke, E.M.: SReach: a probabilistic bounded delta-reachability analyzer for stochastic hybrid systems. In: Roux, O., Bourdon, J. (eds.) CMSB 2015. LNCS, vol. 9308, pp. 15–27. Springer, Cham (2015). https://doi.org/10.1007/978-3-319-23401-4_3
71. Zhang, H., Weng, T.W., Chen, P.Y., Hsieh, C.J., Daniel, L.: Efficient neural network robustness certification with general activation functions. In: Bengio, S., Wallach, H., Larochelle, H., Grauman, K., Cesa-Bianchi, N., Garnett, R. (eds.) NeurIPS. vol. 31. Curran Associates, Inc. (2018). https://proceedings.neurips.cc/paper/2018/file/d04863f100d59b3eb688a11f95b0ae60-Paper.pdf
72. Zhigljavsky, A., Zilinskas, A.: Stochastic Global Optimization. Springer Optimization and Its Applications, vol. 9. Springer, New York (2008). https://doi.org/10.1007/978-0-387-74740-8

Correct-by-Construction Runtime Enforcement in AI – A Survey

Bettina Könighofer[1]([✉]), Roderick Bloem[1], Rüdiger Ehlers[2], and Christian Pek[3]

[1] Institute IAIK, Graz University of Technology, Graz, Austria
{bettina.koenighofer,roderick.bloem}@iaik.tugraz.at
[2] Clausthal University of Technology, Clausthal-Zellerfeld, Germany
ruediger.ehlers@tu-clausthal.de
[3] KTH Royal Institute of Technology, Stockholm, Sweden
pek2@kth.se

Abstract. Runtime enforcement refers to the theories, techniques, and tools for enforcing correct behavior with respect to a formal specification of systems at runtime. In this paper, we are interested in techniques for constructing runtime enforcers for the concrete application domain of enforcing safety in AI. We discuss how safety is traditionally handled in the field of AI and how more formal guarantees on the safety of a self-learning agent can be given by integrating a runtime enforcer. We survey a selection of work on such enforcers, where we distinguish between approaches for discrete and continuous action spaces. The purpose of this paper is to foster a better understanding of advantages and limitations of different enforcement techniques, focusing on the specific challenges that arise due to their application in AI. Finally, we present some open challenges and avenues for future work.

Keywords: Formal methods · Runtime enforcement · Shielding · Safety in AI · Reinforcement learning

1 Introduction

Safety of learning-based or learned controllers is a major concern when using them in physical systems and in the proximity of humans. Particularly during the exploration phase of learning, when an agent chooses random actions to examine its surroundings, it is important to avoid actions that may cause unsafe outcomes.

Formal runtime enforcement techniques aim at guaranteeing safe execution of learning-enabled systems. Due to their applicability to AI-based agents, they gain more and more attention. Such an enforcer not only detects unsafe choices by an agent, but also corrects them, so that the learning process can continue without interruption.

Which approaches are suitable for enforcing safety depends on the environment in which the learner operates and the challenges induced by the environment. First, it is often the case that a learner interacts with a physical system,

© Springer Nature Switzerland AG 2022
J.-F. Raskin and K. Chatterjee (Eds.): Principles of Systems Design, LNCS 13660, pp. 650–663, 2022.
https://doi.org/10.1007/978-3-031-22337-2_31

which induces the need to detect the unsafe behavior *early enough to prevent it*. For dynamical systems, doing so involves planning ahead for a sufficient time span, whose length may not even be known. As a second challenge, many runtime enforcers must be *real-time capable*. In particular, when analysing the safety of an agent's actions, a runtime enforcer cannot halt the environment, but rather must immediately decide whether the action issued by the agent should be executed in the environment or replaced by a safe one. A third challenge for runtime enforcement is that the dynamics of the *environment may be partially unknown* before the learning process starts. This makes guarding the system's behavior against unsafe behavior difficult, as it is then unknown exactly which actions by an agent are unsafe. Thus, runtime enforcement may have to base on data-driven model identification.

In this paper, we give an overview of state-of-the-art correct-by-construction runtime enforcement techniques that address the challenges that arise from the application of runtime enforcement to AI.

We start by discussing a diverse set of techniques developed in the field of AI addressing uncertainty in learning to increase the chance of the learning system to behave safely. These techniques tend to address the safety problem from a learning perspective aiming to increase the observed probability of safe system behavior. We discuss such approaches in Sect. 2.

To keep systems safe with provable guarantees, more formal approaches are necessary. Since a learning system's behavior is not known in advance (and often randomized), the learner's safety cannot be verified upfront even if it were safe. Rather, the concept of *runtime monitoring* is used to observe a learner's behavior, coupled with correcting the learner's choices whenever needed. How to monitor systems is studied in the field of *runtime verification* [4], which transfers concepts from the field of formal verification to testing a system's correctness at runtime. Classical runtime verification approaches can often deal with complex temporal specifications and are applied whenever a system is too complex to be analyzed upfront or when errors induced by the employed hardware are to be detected as well.

The majority of approaches from runtime verification are purely *trace-based* and do not take the interaction between environment and system to be monitored into account to decide on when an error has been reached. This makes sense for most applications – the possibility for the environment to force the system to violate its specification is often irrelevant as the environment itself only exhibits certain behaviors, for which the system may work correctly. This trace-based view is also present in the *runtime enforcement literature* [14,53,54] for non-AI-based systems, where the behavior of a system is only modified once the trace observed would start to violate the specification. When monitoring self-learning systems, this may however be too late to guarantee safety. This problem is addressed in some more recent works that employ a game-based perspective on monitoring [12] and enforcement [56], which is suitable for settings with known environment capabilities. Approaches for runtime enforcement of AI-based agents base on such ideas, can be broadly distinguished by whether they address *discrete* or *continuous state spaces*, and are addressed in Sect. 3 and Sect. 4 respectively.

In Sect. 3, we discuss approaches for *discrete agent-environment systems*. The state space of the environment and the action space of the agent are modelled to be discrete and finite, sometimes with stochastic transitions. In this context, runtime enforcement techniques can be further distinguished by whether unsafe actions are blocked by the learner or are used for reward shaping. Differentiating aspects of approaches for runtime enforcement in discrete agent-environment systems are the different interference and communication techniques of the runtime enforcer with the agent, the used formal specification language, the used runtime enforcer synthesis techniques, and whether the safety analysis of actions is computed offline or online. We discuss several recent works for discrete agent-environment systems with a focus on advantages, limitations, and potential in their application to AI.

In Sect. 4, we discuss runtime enforcement techniques for *continuous and hybrid agent-environment systems*. These systems pose additional challenges since they operate in continuous time, the state/action spaces are continuous, and the system dynamics are usually more complex, e.g., by having non-linearities or jumps between different modes of the hybrid system. These challenges increase the effort to monitor such systems and to provide an accurate safety analysis (i.e., such that safety is guaranteed while the enforcer is comparably permissive towards the agent). Such systems are even more susceptible to the curse of dimensionality (i.e., the state space of the system becomes unwieldy large) than discrete agent-environment systems. Hence determining proper abstractions and approximations of the system is even more important, particularly if the safety analysis is to be performed in real time. For the surveyed approaches that base on the automatic computation of such abstractions or approximations, we discuss how they address this challenge.

After giving an overview of a good number approaches for runtime environment in AI-based systems, we then summarize some observations in Sect. 5, followed by the identification of future research directions.

2   Safety in Data-Driven AI Methods

Increasing the safety of AI approaches gains more and more attention within the AI community [51,59]. Besides classical approaches, such as improving training data, removing biases, improving architectures and (hyper-)parameters, they aim to address safety from a system-level perspective. We can roughly categorize recent state-of-the-art approaches into three clusters: 1) understanding the capabilities and limitations of the AI system; 2) detecting and rejecting out-of-distribution/outlier inputs to the AI system; and 3) increasing the robustness of the AI system against unseen inputs and making decisions/actions of the system interpretable. In the following paragraphs, we briefly review existing approaches in each of the categories.

Understanding the AI System: The training data of an AI system consists of a set of examples (pairs of inputs and outputs) that solve the desired task. Ideally, these examples are informative enough so that the system can generally solve the task, i.e., correctly mapping any input data to desired output data. Yet, real-world training data may be far from being *perfect*, resulting in approximation errors and uncertain mapping results of the system [25,50,67]. To estimate the residual uncertainty or prediction variance in the AI system, popular approaches use Bayesian methods [34,35,62], apply Monte Carlo dropout [17,21], or utilize Deep Ensembles [25,37]. Yet, these uncertainty estimates are still not reliable, since perfect estimates can only be done given an infinite amount of data samples.

Outlier Detection: Uncertainties within an AI system can also be due to a distributional shift in which the data distributions are different in the training and operation domain [45]. For instance, the training dataset may lack corner cases that the system will encounter. Moreover, learned features, such as the shape or color of objects, may look different in the operating domain of the AI system. In general, these out-of-distribution (OOD) inputs may be detectable as outputs with a large prediction variance, but they can also be undetectable by having a low prediction variance. Thus, it is important to already detect OOD inputs before feeding them to the system or explicitly consider them within the system. The detection can be done, e.g., by including prediction-confidences in the network architecture [9], employing classifiers [68] and outlier detectors [30], monitoring neuron activity outside the training data ranges [31], using self-supervised representation learning [22], active monitoring with human input [41], incorporating temperature scaling [38] or by incorporating generative adversarial networks [49]. OOD detection is very powerful, but often requires additional data or domain knowledge, rendering OOD detection infeasible for some applications.

Robust and Interpretable AI: Yet another way to increase the safety of the AI system is to enhance its robustness and resiliency against unseen/OOD inputs, perturbations or corner cases [23]. The overall aim is to improve the system's generalization capabilities. These improvements can be made through transfer learning [29], regularization of the network [70], verifying the networks robustness [41], data augmentation [10], generative models [18,44,48], or removing non-robust features from the training dataset [32]. Generalization improves robustness, yet there are no automated approaches to make a system more general or to check whether a system is general enough to not cause unsafe outputs. Interpretability approaches aim at making the output generation traceable [8,39]. For instance, by illustrating and explaining how the system derived a decision [3,43,57,60,61]. As a result, (non-)experts are able to check whether the system can actually justify its decision.

Although the presented approaches increase the safety of AI systems and help to get a better understanding of the systems' limitations, these approaches cannot provide strict safety guarantees or even soft probabilistic guarantees [63]. Moreover, similar to testing-based validation, these approaches can often only reveal the presence of failures but not their absence. Formal runtime enforcement approaches aim specifically at providing strict safety guarantees by leveraging formal analysis techniques.

3   Runtime Enforcement in Discrete Domains

In *reinforcement learning* (RL) [66], an agent aims to compute an optimal policy that maximizes the expected total amount of reward received from the environment. RL algorithms can be mainly divided into two categories: *model-based RL* and *model-free RL*. In the model-based approach, the learning agent constructs a model of its environment in form of a Markov decision process (MDP). By learning the model and applying planning approaches on the model, model-based RL can quickly obtain optimal policies, but the approach becomes impractical as the state space and action space grows. In contrast, model-free RL does not try to understand the environment and aims to learn a task through trial-and-error via interactions with the environment. Model-free RL is very scalable and has successfully been applied in solving various complex tasks, from playing video games to robotic tasks, but requires many samples for good performance. Therefore, safety is an especially challenging problem for model-free RL, since the learning agent needs to explore many unsafe behaviour in order to learn that it is unsafe. As a consequence, most formal runtime-enforcement techniques focus on ensuring safety in model-free RL, either during training or after training, or for both.

In most work, safety properties are formulated in linear temporal logic (LTL). Several works consider only simple *invariant safety properties* like "two robots should never collide" [19], other works consider the full safety fragment of LTL, which allows to formulate temporal safety properties like "whenever the first signal rises, the second signal has to rise within the next 5 time steps".

There are two popular directions of research for runtime enforcement for model-free RL: (1) using the safety property to compute a maximally permissive enforcer, often called a shield, or (2) using the safety property for reward shaping.

Safety via Shielding. Shields have been used in model-free RL to enforce safe operation of an agent during training and after training (safety is guaranteed as long as the shield is used). A shield [5] can automatically be computed from a given safety LTL specification and a model that captures all safety-relevant dynamics of the environment. The synthesis approach constructs a *safety game* from the safety specification and the environmental model. The *maximally permissive winning strategy* of the safety game allows all actions that will not cause a safety violation on the *infinite horizon* and is implemented in the shield. Shields have been categorized in post-shields and pre-shield [2]. Post-shields monitor the actions selected by the agent and overwrite any unsafe action by a safe one. Pre-shields are implemented before the agent and block, at every time step, unsafe actions from the agent (also referred to as action masking). At every time step, the agent can only choose from the set of safe actions.

Jansen et al. [33] considered shielding in scenarios that incorporate uncertainty and therefore safety cannot be guaranteed. They introduce the concept of a probabilistic shield that enables RL decision-making to adhere to safety constraints with high probability. Probabilistic model checking techniques are used to compute the probabilities of all states and actions of the MDP to satisfy a safety LTL property, called the safety value of an action. A shield blocks an action if its safety value is smaller than some absolute threshold or relative threshold. Considering safety as quantitative measure allows risk taking and to tune the trade-off between safety and performance. Giacobbe et al. [19] applied the same technique on Atari 2600 games and specified 43 safety properties for 31 games. The authors computed shields using a bounded horizon for all properties. Applying these shields resulted in the safest RL agents for Atari games currently available.

ElSayed-Aly et al. [13] considered shielding for multi-agent reinforcement learning (MARL) and proposed to either synthesize a single centralized shield that monitors and corrects all agents' joint actions, or to synthesize multiple shields where each shield is only responsible for a subset of agents at each step. Furthermore, the authors introduced a minimal interference criteria for the MARL setting: a shield should change the actions of as few agents as possible when correcting an unsafe joint action.

To compute a shield upfront, the safety of all actions for all reachable states has to be analyzed and stored. For large environments, this results in long offline computation times and huge shielding data bases, rendering shielding not tractable, and for dynamic or partially unknown environment, the offline computation is not possible. To tackle this issue, Könighofer et al. [36] perform the safety analysis of the actions *online*. Using the time between two successive decisions of an agent, their approach builds an MDP quotient that captures the behaviour of the environment in the next n steps and analyzes the actions for the next decision states on the fly. However, the approach does not provide any worst-case guarantee on the computation time of the safety analysis. Therefore, the approach is suited for settings in which the agent does not have to make a decision in every time step and if needed, halting the agent to wait for a decision of the shield does not cause any harm.

Achiam et al. [1] encoded safety in terms of constraints, leading to the line of research on *constrained policy optimization*. Constrained Markov decision processes (CMDPs) are used to decouple safety from reward, where an independent signal models the safety aspects. An optimal policy balances the trade-off between safety and performance, but there are no safety guarantees during learning. Therefore, this line of work was extended by Simão et al. [64] by using a factored MDP that represents only the safety aspects of the full CMDP. The factored MDP is used to restrict the exploration of the learner and thereby allowing the RL agent to learn an optimal policy for the CMDP without violating the constraints.

Safety via Reward Shaping. Several recent works [26,27] use safety properties expressed in LTL for reward shaping and are often referred to as *logically-constrained RL*. Approaches based on reward shaping will result in agent that will minimize the risk of safety violations after training. To ensure safety during training, such approaches need to be extended by restricting the exploration during training [28].

In logically-constrained RL, a formula expressing some desired properties is first converted to an automaton, which is then translated into a state-adaptive reward structure. Any RL-agent trained with this reward structure results in policies that maximise the probability of satisfying the given formula. In the context of safe RL, the formula expresses a safety property and the trained agent will minimize the risk of violating the property.

Most works mentioned in this section discuss the impact of enforcing safety on the learning performance and provide requirements that the enforcement mechanism needs to satisfy to preserve the convergence guarantees of the learner [2,64]. Several papers show empirically that enforcing safety during learning has the potential to increase the agent's performance if the safety and the performance properties are aligned.

4   Runtime Enforcement in Hybrid/Continuous Domains

Ensuring the correct behavior of a system is particularly important for *safety-critical* systems. These operate in the physical world, which means that quantities of space and time become continuous. This complicates the enforcement of properties of such systems – as many verification problems for hybrid systems are undecidable, maximally permissive enforcement is undecidable in the general case, too. At the same time, many optimization problems for system behavior are equally undecidable in such environments and the aspects of the environment dynamics that are relevant for optimizing the system behavior can be unknown a-priori, which makes reinforcement learning attractive to allow an agent to adapt to the environment dynamics.

Multiple streams of research have emerged that circumvent the undecidabilty of maximally permissive enforcement in various ways, such as focusing on simpler system dynamics and restricting the system's behavior in ways that are not maximally permissive.

A good example of the first stream of research is the work by Goorden et al. [24], in which a maximally permissive controller is computed from a model in which the discrete behavior of the system may only depend on clock variables, so that controller synthesis algorithms from the area of timed automata can be used. This maximally permissive controller is then used as a system behavior constraint in a reinforcement learning process.

Another example is a safe learning approach by Perkins and Barto [52], in which they propose restricting a safe learning process to letting an agent learn how to switch between different Lyapunov-stable control laws that are known to be safe even when switching between them in an arbitrary manner.

To handle also complex learner's behavior in complex environments, the learners can be restricted to safe behavior in a way that is not maximally permissive. For instance, Fisac et al. [15] present an approach to compute controlled invariant sets for known system dynamics that is based on a closed-form characterization of this set, which encodes the least-restrictive control law, which is subsequently approximated numerically (in the case of complex system dynamics).

Another approach is to synthesize control barrier functions for known system dynamics, as done by Cheng et al. [7]. These lead to guaranteed safety of the learner when restricting it so that the learner never uses an action not allowed by the control barrier. The drawback of their approach is that the computed control barrier functions have to be affine, so that in order for them to be safe, they have to be computed in a way that makes them overly conservative. On the plus side, affine control barrier functions are easy to compute and completely continuous.

Fulton and Platzer [16] provide an approach called *Justified Speculative Control* that operates by using a provably correct runtime monitor to filter the unsafe actions of a system and enforce that the learner only takes safe actions. Their approach builds on a provably correct non-deterministic backup strategy, for which the learner has to select actions allowed by a boundary strategy until it (possibly) becomes apparent that the environment of the learner does not behave in the way assumed for the formal safety proof of the boundary strategy (in which case the learner can also potentially choose unsafe actions). Their approach has the interesting property that it can also be applied if the backup strategy is only defined and verified for a part of the environment's state. In this case, by integrating a distance metric to the modeled states into the learning process, the learner can be guided back to the safe states, which reduces the probability of unsafe behavior even for partially unknown environments.

Nageshrao et al. [47] discuss an approach to integrate so-called "short horizon safety checks" into a reinforcement learning approach. Learner actions that are unsafe according to these checks are altered. They also record whenever this happens so that the unsafe situation can be replayed to the learner to speed up the convergence of the learner's policy to a safe one.

Since self-learning systems are particularly interesting for unknown system dynamics, there is also a rich body of works dealing with the question of how to enforce the safety of a learner in this case. The starting point is usually that the environment dynamics are only *partially known*, as if they are fully unknown, it is not even possible to guarantee the safety of the learner with the first step of the system's execution.

For instance, Gillulga and Tomlin [20] define an approach in which a self-learning controller is embedded into a safety controller that enforces the safety of a controlled physical system. In the approach, reachability analysis for the physical system is used in tandem with observing the disturbances observed at runtime, so that the safety wrapper becomes neither too conservative nor too permissive.

Then, the safety enforcement approach by Fisac et al. [15] mentioned above also includes a means to identify the magnitude of disturbances at runtime to adapt the enforcer at runtime to avoid being unnecessarily conversative. Of course, this means that if disturbances perform a sudden increase, this leads to temporarily unsafe behavior. Learning the unknown aspects of the environment dynamics is also present in other work.

Cheng et al. [7] provide an approach for safe reinforcement learning that bases on the use of control barrier functions to detect unsafe actions by a learner as well as to guide the behavior of the learner. Such control barrier functions can be used under uncertain system dynamics, but the authors also include a process to learn a more precise model of the system dynamics over time, which enables a refinement of the control barrier functions to become less conservative when more information on the environment dynamics becomes available.

5   Discussion on Runtime Enforcement in AI

5.1   Observations from the State of the Art

In a variety of applications, AI systems will only unfold their full potential if such systems are safe during their operation. In our overview, we observed that the formal methods and AI communities often address safety from different perspectives. Formal runtime verification approaches aim at providing formal or probabilistic guarantees at all times, whereas AI-based safety approaches focus on improving safety as much as possible while not decreasing the system's performance, e.g., by detecting out-of-distribution data or enhancing the system's overall robustness. Formal methods usually regard the AI system as a black box whose actions might be adversarial. To detect (potentially) unsafe actions while lowering computational efforts, runtime verification approaches usually make use of abstractions or simplified models of the AI system (as, e.g., in [2]). However, such simplifications might result in more conservative behavior of the system [6] or be even incorrect for complex applications. AI-based approaches, on the other hand, commonly strive for model-free solutions so that the system is as free as possible to learn the desired task.

Specifically for formal methods approaches, we saw that significant advances have been made in recent years, from introducing new theory to applying runtime verification to highly complex AI systems. Yet, we also observed that the conducted experiments are hard to compare with each other. In contrast to machine learning, the formal methods community has only first traces of a standard benchmark set [40] that allows one to compare the results of published approaches with each other. This lack of a big standardized benchmark set possibly hinders the community to advance theory but also to provide significant practical contributions.

This problem is caused by different problem domains, various challenges within each application, as well as differing technical foundations in the runtime verification approaches. For instance, techniques based on reachability checking are hard to compare against barrier function-based approaches.

Moreover, the common metrics to assess the performance of runtime verification approaches (e.g., runtime overhead in runtime monitoring or the expressivity of the specification language, [58]) are not appropriate when an unavoidable degree of conservativeness is used in monitoring (black-box) AI systems. Hence, in order to establish a common comparison, new metrics are needed. However, we see that more and more research groups are investigating these challenges and contributing towards enforcing safety in AI-based systems.

5.2 Future Directions and Conclusions

Our communities need to overcome several challenges to make AI systems safe to use. Most AI approaches aim for being free of any model; yet, most formal methods approaches require a model. Model identification for large systems is still a challenging task and for certain applications, e.g., a robot that needs to make contact with a human, it is even difficult to design neural networks that approximate the dynamics or to mathematically define safety [42,69]. We need to explore new techniques to analyze AI systems and to automatically generate models or abstractions of them. Moreover, many AI systems will be deployed in uncertain and partially observable environments, such as in autonomous driving. In such environments, it is even more challenging to verify safety, since the environment might be unknown and needs to be explored online, the behavior of agents may be unknown, and information on the system may be partial and even incorrect. We need more research in analyzing and exploring the environment and system on-the-fly during its operation. To make our research more comparable, our communities need to come up with challenging benchmarks that help us to measure the performance of our algorithms as well as to advance theory. In robotics and AI, the availability of benchmarks have led to new research that drastically improves the performance of algorithms [11,46,65]. Even though environments such as the OpenAI safety gym [55] exist, they are made from the perspective of the AI community and do not reflect the requirements for runtime enforcement. Finally, both the AI and formal methods communities need to closely work together and foster synergies. In this way, we can increase safety, performance, and interpretability of AI-based systems together.

References

1. Achiam, J., Held, D., Tamar, A., Abbeel, P.: Constrained policy optimization. In: Proceedings of the 34th International Conference on Machine Learning, ICML 2017, Sydney, NSW, Australia, 6–11 August 2017. Proceedings of Machine Learning Research, vol. 70, pp. 22–31. PMLR (2017)
2. Alshiekh, M., Bloem, R., Ehlers, R., Könighofer, B., Niekum, B., Topcu, U.: Safe reinforcement learning via shielding. In Proceedings of the 32nd International Conference on Artificial Intelligence, AAAI 2018, New Orleans, Louisiana, USA, 2–7 February 2018, vol. 32, pp. 2669–2678. AAAI Press (2018)
3. Amir, D., Amir, O.: Highlights: summarizing agent behavior to people. In Proceedings of the 17th International Conference on Autonomous Agents and MultiAgent Systems, pp. 1168–1176 (2018)
4. Bartocci, E., Falcone, Y. (eds.): Lectures on Runtime Verification - Introductory and Advanced Topics. LNCS, vol. 10457. Springer, Cham (2018). https://doi.org/10.1007/978-3-319-75632-5

5. Bloem, R., Könighofer, B., Könighofer, R., Wang, C.: Shield synthesis: runtime enforcement for reactive systems. In: Baier, C., Tinelli, C. (eds.) TACAS 2015. LNCS, vol. 9035, pp. 533–548. Springer, Heidelberg (2015). https://doi.org/10.1007/978-3-662-46681-0_51

6. Brunke, L., et al.: Safe learning in robotics: from learning-based control to safe reinforcement learning. arXiv preprint arXiv:2108.06266 (2021)

7. Cheng, R., Orosz, G., Murray, R.M., Burdick. J.W.: End-to-end safe reinforcement learning through barrier functions for safety-critical continuous control tasks. In: Proceedings of the 33rd International Conference on Artificial Intelligence, AAAI 2019, Honolulu, Hawaii, USA, 27 January– 1 February 2019, pp. 3387–3395 (2019)

8. de Carvalho, D V., Pereira, E.M., Cardoso, J.S.: Machine learning interpretability: a survey on methods and metrics. Electron. (Sect. Artif. Intell.) **8**, 832 (2019)

9. DeVries, T. , Taylor, G.W.: Learning confidence for out-of-distribution detection in neural networks. arXiv preprint arXiv:1802.04865 (2018)

10. Dreossi, T., Ghosh, S., Yue, X., Keutzer, K., Sangiovanni-Vincentelli, A., Seshia, S.A.: Counterexample-guided data augmentation. arXiv preprint arXiv:1805.06962 (2018)

11. Duan, Y., Chen, X., Houthooft, R., Schulman, J., Abbeel, P.: Benchmarking deep reinforcement learning for continuous control. In Proceedings of the 33nd International Conference on Machine Learning, ICML 2016, New York City, NY, USA, 19–24 June 2016, vol. 48, pp. 1329–1338. JMLR.org (2016)

12. Ehlers, R., Finkbeiner, B.: Monitoring realizability. In: Khurshid, S., Sen, K. (eds.) RV 2011. LNCS, vol. 7186, pp. 427–441. Springer, Heidelberg (2012). https://doi.org/10.1007/978-3-642-29860-8_34

13. Elsayed-Aly, I., Bharadwaj, S., Amato, C., Ehlers, R., Topcu, U., Feng, L.: Safe multi-agent reinforcement learning via shielding. In: Proceedings of the 20th International Conference on Autonomous Agents and Multiagent Systems, AAMAS 2021, Virtual Event, UK, 3–7 May 2021, pp. 483–491. ACM (2021)

14. Falcone, Y., Mounier, L., Fernandez, J., Richier, J.: Runtime enforcement monitors: composition, synthesis, and enforcement abilities. Formal Methods Syst. Des. **38**(3), 223–262 (2011)

15. Fisac, J.F., Akametalu, A.K., Zeilinger, M.N., Kaynama, S., Gillula, J.H., Tomlin, C.J.: A general safety framework for learning-based control in uncertain robotic systems. IEEE Trans. Autom. Control **64**(7), 2737–2752 (2019)

16. Fulton, N., Platzer, A.: Safe reinforcement learning via formal methods: toward safe control through proof and learning. In: McIlraith, S.A., Weinberger, K.Q. (eds.) Proceedings of the 32nd International Conference on Artificial Intelligence, AAAI 2018, New Orleans, Louisiana, USA, 2–7 February 2018, pp. 6485–6492. AAAI Press (2018)

17. Gal, Y., Ghahramani, Z.: Dropout as a Bayesian approximation: representing model uncertainty in deep learning. In: Proceedings of the 33nd International Conference on Machine Learning, ICML 2016, New York City, NY, USA, 19–24 June 2016, vol. 48, pp. 1050–1059. JMLR.org (2016)

18. Ghadirzadeh, A., Poklukar, P., Kyrki, V., Kragic, D., Björkman, M.: Data-efficient visuomotor policy training using reinforcement learning and generative models. arXiv preprint arXiv:2007.13134 (2020)

19. Giacobbe, M., Hasanbeig, M., Kroening, D., Wijk, H.: Shielding Atari games with bounded prescience. In: Proceedings of the 20th International Conference on Autonomous Agents and Multiagent Systems, AAMAS 2021, Virtual Event, UK, 3–7 May 2021, pp. 1507–1509. ACM (2021)

20. Gillula, J.H., Tomlin, C.J.: Reducing conservativeness in safety guarantees by learning disturbances online: iterated guaranteed safe online learning. In: Robotics: Science and Systems VIII, University of Sydney, Sydney, NSW, Australia, 9–13 July 2012 (2012)
21. Globerson, A., Roweis, S.T.: Nightmare at test time: robust learning by feature deletion. In: Proceedings of the 23th International Conference of Machine Learning, ICML 2006, Pittsburgh, Pennsylvania, USA, 25–29 June 2006, vol. 148, pp. 353–360. ACM (2006)
22. Golan, I., El-Yaniv, R.: Deep anomaly detection using geometric transformations. arXiv preprint arXiv:1805.10917 (2018)
23. Goodfellow, I.J., Bengio, Y., Courville, A.C.: Deep Learning. MIT Press, Cambridge (2016)
24. Goorden, M.A., Larsen, K.G., Nielsen, J.E., Nielsen, T.D., Rasmussen, M.R., Srba, J.: Learning safe and optimal control strategies for storm water detention ponds. In: Proceedings of the 7th International Conference on Analysis and Design of Hybrid Systems, ADHS 2021, Brussels, Belgium, 7–9 July 2021, pp. 13–18 (2021)
25. Guo, C., Pleiss, G., Sun, Y., Weinberger, K.Q.: On calibration of modern neural networks. In: Proceedings of the 34th International Conference on Machine Learning, ICML 2017, Sydney, NSW, Australia, 6–11 August 2017, vol. 70, pp. 1321–1330. PMLR (2017)
26. Hahn, E.M., Perez, M., Schewe, S., Somenzi, F., Trivedi, A., Wojtczak, D.: Faithful and effective reward schemes for model-free reinforcement learning of omega-regular objectives. In: Hung, D.V., Sokolsky, O. (eds.) ATVA 2020. LNCS, vol. 12302, pp. 108–124. Springer, Cham (2020). https://doi.org/10.1007/978-3-030-59152-6_6
27. Hasanbeig, M., Abate, A., Kroening, D.: Certified reinforcement learning with logic guidance. CoRR, abs/1902.00778 (2019)
28. Hasanbeig, M., Abate, A., Kroening, D.: Cautious reinforcement learning with logical constraints. In: Proceedings of the 19th International Conference on Autonomous Agents and Multiagent Systems, AAMAS 2020, Auckland, New Zealand, 9–13 May 2020, pp. 483–491. International Foundation for Autonomous Agents and Multiagent Systems (2020)
29. Hendrycks, D., Lee, K., Mazeika, M.: Using pre-training can improve model robustness and uncertainty. In: Proceedings of the 36th International Conference on Machine Learning, ICML 2019, Long Beach, California, USA, 9–15 June 2019, vol. 97, pp. 2712–2721. PMLR (2019)
30. Hendrycks, D., Mazeika, M., Dietterich, T.: Deep anomaly detection with outlier exposure. arXiv preprint arXiv:1812.04606 (2018)
31. Henzinger, T.A., Lukina, A., Schilling, C.: Outside the box: abstraction-based monitoring of neural networks. arXiv preprint arXiv:1911.09032 (2019)
32. Ilyas, A., Santurkar, S., Tsipras, D., Engstrom, L., Tran, B., Madry, A.: Adversarial examples are not bugs, they are features. In: Proceedings of the 32th International Conference on Neural Information Processing Systems, NeurIPS 2019, Vancouver, BC, Canada, 8–14 December 2019, pp. 125–136 (2019)
33. Jansen, N., Könighofer, B., Junges, S., Serban, A., Bloem, R.: Safe reinforcement learning using probabilistic shields (invited paper). In: Proceedings of the 31st International Conference on Concurrency Theory, CONCUR 2020 (Virtual Conference), Vienna, Austria, 1–4 September 2020. LIPIcs, vol. 171, pp. 3:1–3:16. Schloss Dagstuhl - Leibniz-Zentrum für Informatik (2020)
34. Jensen, F.V., et al.: An introduction to Bayesian networks, vol. 210. UCL Press, London (1996)

35. Kendall, A., Gal, Y.: What uncertainties do we need in Bayesian deep learning for computer vision? arXiv preprint arXiv:1703.04977 (2017)

36. Könighofer, B., Rudolf, J., Palmisano, A., Tappler, M., Bloem, R.: Online shielding for stochastic systems. In: Dutle, A., Moscato, M.M., Titolo, L., Muñoz, C.A., Perez, I. (eds.) NFM 2021. LNCS, vol. 12673, pp. 231–248. Springer, Cham (2021). https://doi.org/10.1007/978-3-030-76384-8_15

37. Lakshminarayanan, B., Pritzel, A., Blundell, C.: Simple and scalable predictive uncertainty estimation using deep ensembles. arXiv preprint arXiv:1612.01474 (2016)

38. Liang, S., Li, Y., Srikant, R.: Enhancing the reliability of out-of-distribution image detection in neural networks. arXiv preprint arXiv:1706.02690 (2017)

39. Linardatos, P., Papastefanopoulos, V., Kotsiantis, S.: Explainable AI: a review of machine learning interpretability methods. Entropy **23**(1), 18 (2021)

40. Livingston, S.C., Raman, V.: Benchmarks and competitions on formal methods for robotics (2017). Archived version https://web.archive.org/web/20210228031948/https://fmrchallenge.org

41. Lukina, A., Schilling, C., Henzinger, T.A.: Into the unknown: active monitoring of neural networks. In: Feng, L., Fisman, D. (eds.) RV 2021. LNCS, vol. 12974, pp. 42–61. Springer, Cham (2021). https://doi.org/10.1007/978-3-030-88494-9_3

42. Mitsioni, I., Karayiannidis, Y., Stork, J.A., Kragic, D.: Data-driven model predictive control for the contact-rich task of food cutting. In: Proceedings of the 19th International Conference on Humanoid Robots, Humanoids 2019, Toronto, ON, Canada, 15–17 October 2019, pp. 244–250. IEEE (2019)

43. I. Mitsioni, J. Mänttäri, Y. Karayiannidis, J. Folkesson, and D. Kragic. Interpretability in contact-rich manipulation via kinodynamic images. arXiv preprint arXiv:2102.11825, 2021

44. Mohamed, S., Lakshminarayanan, B.: Learning in implicit generative models. arXiv preprint arXiv:1610.03483 (2016)

45. Mohseni, S., Pitale, M., Singh, V., Wang, Z.: Practical solutions for machine learning safety in autonomous vehicles. arXiv preprint arXiv:1912.09630 (2019)

46. Moll, M., Sucan, I.A., Kavraki, L.E.: Benchmarking motion planning algorithms: an extensible infrastructure for analysis and visualization. IEEE Robot. Autom. Mag. **22**(3), 96–102 (2015)

47. Nageshrao, S., Tseng, H.E., Filev, D.P.: Autonomous highway driving using deep reinforcement learning. In: Proceedings of the International Conference on Systems, Man and Cybernetics, SMC 2019, Bari, Italy, 6–9 October 2019, pp. 2326–2331. IEEE (2019)

48. Nalisnick, E., Matsukawa, A., Teh, Y.W., Gorur, D., Lakshminarayanan, B.: Do deep generative models know what they don't know? arXiv preprint arXiv:1810.09136 (2018)

49. Nitsch, J., et al.: Out-of-distribution detection for automotive perception. arXiv preprint arXiv:2011.01413 (2020)

50. Papadopoulos, G., Edwards, P.J., Murray, A.F.: Confidence estimation methods for neural networks: a practical comparison. IEEE Trans. Neural Netw. **12**(6), 1278–1287 (2001)

51. Pereira, A., Thomas, C.: Challenges of machine learning applied to safety-critical cyber-physical systems. Machine Learning and Knowledge Extraction **2**(4), 579–602 (2020)

52. Perkins, T.J., Barto, A.G.: Lyapunov design for safe reinforcement learning. J. Mach. Learn. Res. **3**, 803–832 (2002)

53. Pinisetty, S., Preoteasa, V., Tripakis, S., Jéron, T., Falcone, Y., Marchand, H.: Predictive runtime enforcement. Formal Methods Syst. Des. **51**(1), 154–199 (2017). https://doi.org/10.1007/s10703-017-0271-1

54. Pinisetty, S., Roop, P.S., Smyth, S., Allen, N., Tripakis, S., von Hanxleden, R.: Runtime enforcement of cyber-physical systems. ACM Trans. Embed. Comput. Syst. **16**(5s), 178:1–178:25 (2017)

55. Ray, A., Achiam, J., Amodei, D.: Benchmarking safe exploration in deep reinforcement learning. arXiv preprint arXiv:1910.01708, 7 (2019)

56. Renard, M., Rollet, A., Falcone, Y.: Runtime enforcement of timed properties using games. Formal Asp. Comput. **32**(2–3), 315–360 (2020)

57. Ribeiro, M.T., Singh, S., Guestrin. C.: "Why should I trust you?" Explaining the predictions of any classifier. In: Proceedings of the 22nd ACM SIGKDD International Conference on Knowledge Discovery and Data Mining, pp. 1135–1144 (2016)

58. Sánchez, C., et al.: A survey of challenges for runtime verification from advanced application domains (beyond software). Formal Methods Syst. Des. (1), 1–57 (2019). https://doi.org/10.1007/s10703-019-00337-w

59. Schwalbe, G., Schels, M.: A survey on methods for the safety assurance of machine learning based systems. In: 10th European Congress on Embedded Real Time Software and Systems (ERTS 2020) (2020)

60. Selvaraju, R.R., Cogswell, M., Das, A., Vedantam, R., Parikh, D., Batra, D.: Grad-CAM: visual explanations from deep networks via gradient-based localization. Int. J. Comput. Vis. **128**(2), 336–359 (2020)

61. Selvaraju, R.R., Das, A., Vedantam, R., Cogswell, M., Parikh, D., Batra, D.: Grad-CAM: why did you say that? arXiv preprint arXiv:1611.07450 (2016)

62. Sensoy, M., Kaplan, L., Kandemir, M.: Evidential deep learning to quantify classification uncertainty. arXiv preprint arXiv:1806.01768 (2018)

63. Seshia, S.A., Sadigh, D., Sastry, S.S.: Towards verified artificial intelligence. arXiv preprint arXiv:1606.08514 (2016)

64. Simão, T.D., Jansen, N., Spaan, M.T.J.: AlwaysSafe: reinforcement learning without safety constraint violations during training. In: Proceedings of the 20th International Conference on Autonomous Agents and Multiagent Systems, AAMAS 2021, Virtual Event, UK, 3–7 May 2021, pp. 1226–1235. ACM (2021)

65. Sucan, I.A., Moll, M., Kavraki, L.E.: The open motion planning library. IEEE Robot. Autom. Mag. **19**(4), 72–82 (2012)

66. Sutton, R.S., Barto, A.G.: Reinforcement Learning: An Introduction. MIT Press, Cambridge (1998)

67. Toubeh, M., Tokekar, P.: Risk-aware planning by confidence estimation using deep learning-based perception. arXiv preprint arXiv:1910.00101 (2019)

68. Vyas, A., Jammalamadaka, N., Zhu, X., Das, D., Kaul, B., Willke, T.L.: Out-of-distribution detection using an ensemble of self supervised leave-out classifiers. In: Ferrari, V., Hebert, M., Sminchisescu, C., Weiss, Y. (eds.) ECCV 2018. LNCS, vol. 11212, pp. 560–574. Springer, Cham (2018). https://doi.org/10.1007/978-3-030-01237-3_34

69. Zhang, D., Wei, B.: A review on model reference adaptive control of robotic manipulators. Annu. Rev. Control **43**, 188–198 (2017)

70. Zhang, X., LeCun, Y.: Universum prescription: regularization using unlabeled data. In: Proceedings of the 31st Conference on Artificial Intelligence, AAAI 2017, San Francisco, California, USA, 4–9 February 2017, pp. 2907–2913. AAAI Press (2017)

Author Index

Printed in the United States
by Baker & Taylor Publisher Services

Printed in the United States
by Baker & Taylor Publisher Services